ATTLEE

ATTLEE

Kenneth Harris

Weidenfeld and Nicolson
London

First published in Great Britain by
George Weidenfeld and Nicolson Ltd
91 Clapham High Street London SW4

Designed by Myles Dacre

ISBN 0 297 77993 1

Printed by Butler & Tanner Ltd
Frome and London

Contents

Illustrations

Henry Attlee
With his brothers Laurence and Tom
In his first term at Northaw Place
At Haileybury, aged 16 (*BBC Hulton Picture Library*)
In his first term at University College, Oxford (*BBC Hulton Picture Library*)
With members of the Haileybury Boys' Club, Stepney
    (*BBC Hulton Picture Library*)
With the staff of Toynbee Hall, Whitechapel
Captain Attlee in 1915
Mayor Attlee of Stepney walking to Downing Street in 1920
    (*BBC Hulton Picture Library*)
Attlee announces his engagement to Violet Millar (*Barratt's Photo Press*)
Under-Secretary of State for War, 1924
With the other members of the Simon Commission, 1928
Addressing a Labour Party rally in Hyde Park (*BBC Hulton Picture Library*)
Attlee's brother Tom
Vi
The annual family holiday in North Wales, 1938 (*Fox Photos*)
At home with the family, 1940 (*BBC Hulton Picture Library*)
At the Labour Party Conference, 1945 (*BBC Hulton Picture Library*)
The Leader of the Opposition sets out for the Potsdam conference
    (*BBC Hulton Picture Library*)
Victory in the 1945 General Election (*BBC Hulton Picture Library*)
With Ernest Bevin, en route for Potsdam (*BBC Hulton Picture Library*)
Attlee and his Cabinet in 1945 (*Barratt's Photo Press*)
Attlee and Sir Stafford Cripps (*Keystone Press; Labour Party Photograph Library,*
Attlee and Hugh Dalton (*Labour Party Photograph Library*)
The Cabinet Room, 10 Downing Street
Attlee visits his constituency during the 1950 General Election
A warm greeting from President Truman (*Labour Party Photograph Library*)
Aneurin Bevan, 1952 (*Labour Party Photograph Library*)
Sam Watson and Hugh Gaitskell, 1955 (*Labour Party Photograph Library*)
Earl Attlee with his daughter, Lady Felicity Harwood
    (*BBC Hulton Picture Library*)
The Attlees with one of their grandchildren
Attlee and Churchill in conversation
    (*Camera Press; Labour Party Photograph Library*)
Attlee in 1966, the year before he died (*photo by Jorge Lewinski*)

Acknowledgements

I owe an outstanding debt of gratitude to my friend Oliver Coburn, who helped me to find material for this book, advised me how to use much of it, but, alas, did not live to see its completion.

I must thank Lord Weidenfeld for his patience in waiting for this book to be delivered. His editorial colleagues Robert Baldock and Benjamin Buchan have been most helpful. I am also indebted to John Turner, Lecturer in History at Bedford College, University of London, for his assistance in editing down the lengthy original MS. Heather Adlam and Gloria May helped with research and the organization of the documents.

My considerable debt to the authors of books relating to Attlee or to the period is recorded in *Sources* at the back of the book.

1
Youth,
1883–1905

I

In 1883, the most destructive of the critics of capitalist society died and the most constructive of its critics was born. Marx died in March, Keynes was born in June. On 3 January of the same year, in Putney, at 'Westcott', 18 Portinscale Road, the first British Labour prime minister to form a majority government came into the world: Clement Attlee. No bells rang, no portents blazed across the sky. There was no great excitement in Portinscale Road in a household which had already seen six babies into the world – this undersized little boy, the fourth son, would be the seventh child out of eight. Life at 'Westcott' went on much as usual that day, except for the mother, Ellen Attlee. The father, Henry Attlee, arrived at his solicitor's office in the City to begin his day's work at his accustomed hour.

The Attlee family had lived in Surrey for many generations, the name occurring in English medieval records in the twelfth, thirteenth, four-teenth and fifteenth centuries. Since genealogy was a family hobby we know a good deal about them. Bernard, an elder brother, the family's amateur archivist, prepared table after table, tree after tree, so that the family papers are a forest of them. Clem took a hand in later life – in his seventies he carefully penned a set of trees on the back of a First World War officer's map which ran into five hundred items. The derivation of the name is probably 'At the Lee', becoming 'Att-Lee' – 'lee' or 'lea', an Anglo-Saxon term, meaning a clearing or a meadow. There is a Great Lee Wood at Effingham, a small village near Dorking, Surrey, in pretty rolling wooded countryside just off the main road running southwest from London to Portsmouth, twenty miles as the crow flies from the Houses of Parliament. This was the original Attlee country. The Attlees believed they took their name from this wood, and that the family home was Lee House of the Manor of La Lee or La Leigh, just outside the village.

I

By 1722, when John Attlee, 'churchwarden', man of property and repute, was born, the Attlees had migrated every bit of four miles, southeast across the wooded hills from Effingham, and were well established as millers, merchants and farmers at Rose Hill, now on the southwestern perimeter of the town of Dorking.

Clement Attlee's grandfather, Richard, born in 1795, was a very able man. If he had inherited a good start in life, which is not at all certain, he certainly made the most of it. There were ten children. Richard took two of the seven boys into the family corn mill, set up two as brewers, allowed the fifth to follow his bent and become a clergyman, and articled Henry, the future prime minister's father, to a firm of solicitors in the City of London called Druce's, with offices at 10 Billiter Square, EC3. Henry, born in 1841, found himself at sixteen able to embark at his father's expense on a career which, if unexciting, combined the maximum of expectation with the minimum of risk. From then on he was expected to stand on his own two feet and prosper, and so he did. He became senior partner of his firm, he educated eight children and made them all financially independent at the age of twenty-one, and he rose to the top of his profession, becoming President of the Law Society in 1906. He earned every penny he spent, and died worth £70,000 in 1908.

Henry Attlee was a hard worker. As they grew older his children felt he worked *too* hard. Every night after dinner he retired to his study and worked. His holiday was limited as though by statute to a fortnight in the year. The day he died at his desk of a heart attack, he had travelled up to London from Putney as he had travelled day in day out for just over half a century, slogging away with that amalgam of Christian sense of duty and respect for material success which was the ethos of the Victorian middle class. At his memorial service they sang his favourite hymn, 'Fight the Good Fight'.

Henry was of middle height, very upright, with light-blue eyes that had fire in them. As a young man he was handsome, lean, with a fine head, strong chin with a slightly protruding lower jaw, Byronic brown hair, and a beard. In later life, as his hair thinned and his beard grew, he resembled a composite of Lord Salisbury and William Morris. His temperament was interesting, if only because Attlee inherited some of it. He was never cross – the children never saw him show ill temper – but this was much more due to self-control than natural equanimity. In a letter to his son Bernard, Henry says: 'You inherited from me a baddish temper but it seems to me you have quite conquered it.' Henry could never put his work aside for long, and he took it very seriously. When the children went up to bed they would hear him behind the closed door of his study arguing aloud with himself the brief he was to submit the following day.

There was anxiety in his personality – he fussed when there was a train to be caught – and he was self-critical.

Henry Attlee was distinctly – some of his friends and relatives thought embarrassingly – interested in politics. Though his parents and family were loyal Conservatives, Henry Attlee was a committed Liberal. Gladstone was his idol. He was a Home-Ruler and a pro-Boer. Considering his times and his background, his views were radical. He did not proselytize, but he did not dissimulate. In his earlier years he canvassed for his old friend Bryce, later ambassador to Washington. Indeed, a moment came when Henry's friends thought he would stand for Parliament. His senior partner, old Druce, dissuaded him, by arguments of which we have no record. Thereafter Henry withdrew from the front line of the Liberal Party's battle, without ceasing to be active in support. His friend Haldane, later lord chancellor, interested him in education. Henry joined the governing bodies of several schools, including Haileybury, where he later sent his sons.

In 1870 Henry Attlee, then lodging in London, married Ellen Bravery Watson, the niece of a miller who was one of his father's Dorking friends. They were married at her family's church, St Anne's in Wandsworth, when he was twenty-eight and she was twenty-three.

Ellen was an attractive woman. She was not beautiful but her face was strikingly warm and sensitive, with brown eyes which Clem inherited. Like Henry she had good carriage, and was a vigorous walker. She adored her husband, lived for her children, and was a most affectionate and perceptive mother. Like Henry she believed in discipline for children, but discipline inculcated through the desire to imitate good examples. Both were Christians by religion and philanthropists on principle. Whereas Henry was a Liberal, Ellen was a Conservative. There was never any political discussion between Ellen and her husband, at any rate not in front of the children. She knew all about his controversial views, opinions different from those of nearly everybody they knew. She seemed to think it best to keep the conversation off these matters. When subjects like Home Rule for Ireland came up in Attlee's infancy, he remembered well, his mother changed the subject very quickly.

Ellen had inherited a love of the arts and literature from her father. Thomas Watson had been born in Soho, where his father had a very successful medical practice. After tutoring for various prosperous families he took advantage of his private income to become secretary of the Art Union of London, which published reproductions of good pictures at moderate prices. His wife died in her thirties. Ellen was the eldest child, and the burden of bringing up the other five children fell on her. They lived at the Gables, on Wandsworth Common, a mile from Putney – a power-house stands on the site today. Her father was a most lovable man.

Photographs of him show youthful dark eyes gleaming benevolently from under a fine white-haired brow. Watson was particularly interested in the 'modern' paintings of his time, and Ellen was reared a disciple of the Pre-Raphaelites. It was to give pleasure to Ellen that Henry Attlee bought so many paintings; to please himself he bought books, only a few of which he had time to read.

When they married, Henry and Ellen decided to live somewhere near grandfather Watson. Putney was attractive, had easy access by train to London, and was less than a mile from Wandsworth. Only six miles from the centre of London, Putney was then almost a village, with few roads built up apart from the High Street, leading to the new stone bridge which spanned the Thames *en route* for London. There were market gardens between Putney and Wandsworth, which, though bigger than Putney, was also still a small country town, the green fields stretching almost up to the High Street. They made their first home there in Keswick Road, in a house which Henry renamed 'Westcott', after the name of the village in which the family mills were located. Later they moved to 18 Portinscale Road, off Keswick Road, only a few yards away. Henry also named this house 'Westcott'. The Attlees were very conscious of the family's associations. When Clement Attlee built his own house at Prestwood, near Great Missenden, he called it 'Westcott'.

Henry's 'Westcott' was a large, ugly, comfortable house with a front gate and a short drive wide enough to admit 'carriages'. On the ground floor was a dining room, a drawing room, a study and a full-size billiard room. Upstairs there was a bathroom, a lavatory, a day nursery, used also as a schoolroom, a night nursery for the three small children, large bedrooms for the mother and father, for the two elder boys and for the two elder girls, a small bedroom and a spare room and a box room. Henry put down a tennis court. Apart from this he did little to add to the amenities of life as his fortunes progressed, nor was he inclined to spend money to increase his social status. He needed servants, and employed a cook, a housemaid and a parlour maid full time; the gardener and the governess came in daily. Throughout his life he never kept a carriage. When the weather was tolerable he walked to the station. When it was wet he hired a cab.

Clem always gave the impression that his childhood was very happy, and very much spent in the bosom of the family. This was true of all his brothers and his sisters, but particularly of him. For some reason he was not allowed to go to school until he was nine. His other brothers began at private schools in Putney when they were much younger. Clem got his first lessons from his mother. He could have done much worse. She spoke French, some Italian, was extremely well read, played the piano and sang agreeably, painted watercolours, and knew a great deal about design. Adoring her, Clem lapped up her culture with delight, and spent several childhood years being educated at home with his sisters. Henry Attlee did not care for boarding schools for girls, though when they got older he sent them all to finishing schools on the Continent.

Attlee may have been kept at home because he had a lengthy illness, of which he had a shadowy recollection, chicken pox perhaps, from which he took a long time to recover. According to his younger brother Laurence, he was taught at home so long because he was undersized or because he was so painfully shy. As a boy, he was very conscious of his small physique, especially when Laurence, eighteen months younger, overtook him in height and weight. It was a rare case – the older brother wore the younger one's cast-off clothing. The little Clement grew up as something of a solitary in this brood of happy extroverts. When the rest of them were climbing trees or scaling walls he would lie reading on the lawn or indoors on a sofa. Though shy in varying degrees, none of the other brothers or sisters was so afflicted as Attlee. In later life, he felt that their shyness was his beloved mother's fault. 'She was too essentially a family woman and had, I think, a certain jealousy of the family showing independence and seeking friends outside the circle. This attitude tended to make us self-conscious and shy.' The others certainly did not suffer from what his sister Mary recorded as his 'violent fits of temper'. These were so serious that his mother had to train him out of them. 'She was so successful that, if he saw her coming, he would bury his head in a chair. This was known as "Clem 'penting", or in ordinary language, "Clem repenting". I have never seen my brother in a temper in his adult life. He is an extraordinarily quiet and controlled person and very, very discreet.' The remarkable Ellen seems to have developed one of the most effective assets of the prime minister to be, and to have provided most useful early training for a future leader of the Labour Party.

The family day was regular. They rose at seven; family prayers with the servants present at 7.30: the Lord's Prayer, a short lesson from the Bible lasting for five to ten minutes, a short prayer. Grace at the breakfast table, then unfettered chatter. Henry would not say a great deal – much of the time his face would be behind *The Times*. If it were a fine morning Clem might walk down to Putney station with him, Henry wearing frock coat and top hat, to catch the nine o'clock train to Fenchurch Street station. Lessons would begin after breakfast, starting with a session with the Bible. 'Ours was a deeply religious home,' recorded Mary; 'we all knew the Gospels and the Acts by heart.' This was not regarded as formal study but extracurricular, a labour of love. They did the Gospels and the Acts in term time, the Psalms in the holidays. Each child had his or her own Bible, and would take it in turns to read a verse until the reading was complete.

5

After the Bible readings, the secular education of the future prime minister began. His mother's greatest love was poetry, and Clem followed her into *Idylls of the King* as a duckling its mother into water. For him poetry became a natural element. He learned it easily and recited it without inhibition. At five years old, he could spout short poems by Wordsworth and chunks of Tennyson. The lines 'My strength is as the strength of ten Because my heart is pure' were, when he was eighty-four, the earliest he could remember learning. When he was a little older, he took lessons with his sisters' governesses. One of them was French. From her he learned to recite the *Fables* of La Fontaine with an admirable French accent, which, 'with other nonsense, was speedily knocked out of me when I went to school'. Another Attlee governess, Miss Hutchinson, had formerly been employed by Lord Randolph Churchill to instruct the young Winston. She had made it clear to the Attlees that educating Winston had had its problems. On one occasion at the Churchill home a maid had gone into a room to answer the bell, to be informed by the infant Winston: 'I rang. Take away Miss Hutchinson. She is very cross.'

In the holidays, or on Saturdays, there was a Bible reading after breakfast, but no lessons. The children then went off to the garden to play cricket, to swing, to walk in the fields, or play hide-and-seek. In summer, there was hay-making in the fields behind the house. Their mother would have lunch with them, and afterwards, if it was fine, they would go for a walk, over to Kew perhaps – for strawberry teas – or across to Wandsworth, to grandfather Watson's. If it was wet Clem might take out his stamp collection. If he tired of stamps he went back to his books. The children would reassemble for the evening meal. Henry would be there; he would take a single glass of claret and encourage the children to talk. Then he would retire to the study. Afterwards the children would play draughts, make up verses, play paper games like 'consequences', all organized and supervised by the ever-present mother. Bedtime was 9.30, a liberal hour in those days for children under ten. It was indeed, considering the period, a very tolerant, permissive home; the little Attlees had more freedom than most children of Victorian families. They also had more self-discipline. Their neighbours said: 'The Attlee family was brought up not to waste a minute.' Boys and girls were taught to be careful of their clothes. The servants did not do any mending. Mother and girls mended the boys' clothes and darned their socks. They made their brothers' shirts for them when they went away to school, and their pyjamas for them when they went to Oxford. Though they sewed and stitched, the girls were not encouraged to think of themselves as seamstresses: Henry set them essays on subjects like 'How to Govern an Island'. They were expected to be as knowledgeable as their brothers and to be able to run a home as well.

6

Attlee's brother Laurence has admitted wryly that the childhood of the Attlees is a story almost too good to be true. None of the children got into scrapes. They did not fight. They did not steal the farmer's apples. The father and mother were never tense with one another. A cross word between them would have struck the children as inconceivable. They were as considerate to the servants as to their children. They did not gossip, they did not criticize their neighbours. They were a very self-sufficient family, an inward-looking group of outward-looking individuals. They rarely went out, because to be at home was more amusing. The tone was set by the ambition of the two elder boys, which was to grow up to be like their father, and of the three younger boys, which was to be like their elder brothers. Yet the home of these paragons was always full of laughter. There was no sabbatical silence on the walk across the common to Hinkson Vale Church on a Sunday morning.

Only Clem seems to have had difficulty in adjusting himself to the Anglican ambience which pervaded 18 Portinscale Road. In his childhood it was not so much the Christianity but the church services that put him off. He could not, at his age, refuse to attend without upsetting the other members of the family. So, not in spirit, but in the flesh, he was always on church parade. Sitting bored in church, unable, under the eyes of the congregation, to use pencil or paper, he would survey the big west window, and in his mind disassemble and then reconstruct the patterns of its many-coloured glass, or plan routes by which he might climb from the floor to the roof.

In the summer of 1892 Clement, at nine years of age, still undersized and now much smaller than his younger brother, was judged big enough to go away to school. Tom, his elder brother, was at Northaw Place, a preparatory school for thirty-five boys at Potters Bar, Hertfordshire, run by the Reverend F. J. Hall, an old friend of the Attlee family. Hall ran the school with an assistant, another clergyman, the Reverend F. Poland. Academically Northaw left something to be desired. Hall and Poland had two great interests: a moderate one in the Bible, and a fanatical one in cricket. To his own subject, mathematics, Hall attached very little importance, and even less to Latin and Greek. Like many boys who had been at Northaw Place, Attlee left with a great knowledge of cricket statistics and a vast accumulation of names, dates and places to be found in the books of the Old Testament. He knew so much about the Old Testament at this time that he was assumed by those who knew no better to be 'religious-minded'. In an examination set by the bishop he passed top of the diocese, and there was talk of him possibly 'having a vocation'.

The teaching may have been bad at Northaw, but the boys were extremely well looked after and all were very happy. Clem settled down well. Though he was still light and small for his age, he got his rugger

7

colours early. He was never much good at cricket – he described himself as 'a good field, nothing of a bowler and a most uncertain bat' – but provided a boy turned out for the game and subscribed to the doctrine of the straight bat, the Head and his assistant were not censorious about the number of runs he failed to score. Since nobody bothered him with Latin and Greek he could go on reading poetry and history. He thought in later life that he must have seemed a bit of a prig to other boys, but they gave no sign of thinking so. He blushed a good deal in those days, but nobody mocked at this, dismissing it lightly with: 'Now you've made him smoke.' Elder boys were encouraged to protect the younger ones. Sitting alone at tea on his first day, looking rather sorry for himself, he was observed by an older boy, Hilton Young, later Lord Kennet, and a Labour minister of health, who, seeing that Attlee had no jam for his bread, gave him some from his own pot. New boys were officially assigned to older boys who were to act as guardians to them. Attlee's first charge, at the age of thirteen, was a new boy aged nine, called William Jowitt, 'nice, bright, clever little chap. Never gave me any trouble.' Fifty years later Jowitt became lord chancellor in the first postwar Labour government.

In the beginning of the spring term of 1896, when he was thirteen, Attlee left Northaw and went to Haileybury College, founded by the East India Company to educate men for service to the Empire. Many old Haileyburians had done well in the Civil Service, but on the whole it had not been a particularly successful school, and at the time he went there it was short of pupils. The headmaster, Edward Lyttelton, later to become headmaster of Eton, dealt with the problem partly by reducing the fees, and partly by slowing down the rate at which boys passed through the school, with the result that the lower forms included a large proportion of sixteen- and seventeen-year-olds. Henry Attlee sent his sons to Haileybury partly because its fees were low, partly because Hall, the master of Northaw, had earlier on taught mathematics at Haileybury, and recommended it to him. Conditions there were spartan. Attlee wrote in his autobiographical notes:

There were only two baths for eight boys, the rest using zinc 'toe pans'. Our sanitary needs were supplied by three rows of earth closets. ... Many of the form rooms opened straight on to the quadrangle. In winter one was either frozen or roasted according to one's geographical position between the fire and the door. Forks and spoons were washed by being thrown in a large tub of hot water and stirred with a brush. ... The general arrangements were very rough. Lower boys had to pig it in the form rooms or class rooms where there was no privacy and a good deal of opportunity for bullying. The food was extremely bad at first but improved later. It was disgustingly served. I can clearly remember thinking often that one of the blessings of leaving would be decent food properly served. ... The teaching was on the

8

whole bad ... no one was considered anything unless he was good at games
... Lyttelton, a great man in his way, was a hopeless headmaster.

Lyttelton was in many ways a very liberal man. In the late nineties his
school reflected the general climate of opinion in Britain, which was
imperialistic and very anti-Boer. Lyttelton, however, was pro-Boer, and
on this and other issues stood against the currents of emotion in his own
school. In 1900, when the news of the relief of Ladysmith came through,
the school expected a half-holiday. To its disgust, Lyttelton – pro-Boer
– refused to grant it. The boys mutinied, cut their classes, and marched
in procession through the nearby towns of Hertford and Ware. Though
no devotee of corporal punishment, in an age when it was regarded as an
integral part of the public school education, Lyttelton decided on this
occasion to administer it. To cane the small boys he felt would be unfair
– they had been misled by their seniors. To cane the upper school, on the
other hand, with its large complement of prefects, might undermine the
school's internal discipline. To ask masters to punish transgressions at
which he suspected they had connived would be equally invidious. So
the Canon took his coat off and thrashed the middle third of the school
himself: seventy-two boys. 'A fine physical feat' was Attlee's judgement.
'And without doubt the proper thing to do.' An enthusiastic anti-Boer
and imperialist, he was one of the seventy-two, 'but the Canon was tiring
when he got to me. ... It was just as well – he had a lovely wrist.'

Attlee kept all his school reports. The last of them, written when he
was eighteen, was the best. His housemaster's assessment of him was: 'He
thinks about things and forms opinions – a very good thing. ... I believe
him a sound character and think he will do well in life. His chief fault is
that he is very self-opinionated, so much so that he gives very scant
consideration to the views of other people.' There was nothing spectacular about his schooldays. He got no house colours, he won no prizes.
Haileybury did not bring him out. Games worship was at its height there
in those days, and being still small in body, and not good at games, his
'inability to excel increased a natural diffidence'.

His time at Haileybury 'was enjoyable on the whole though there were
periods of black misery'. There was bullying, and being small he suffered
his share of it; but it was his incapacity, through size and shyness, to make
a mark that made him feel frustrated. The one exception to his failures
was the cadet corps. He was an outstandingly good cadet, and enjoyed it
very much: the drill and discipline put his deficiencies at a discount, and
like many lightweights he found the military routine an opportunity to
equalize with bigger-bodied men. He left the school intellectually im-
mature and underdeveloped. Though he was generally well read, he had
not thought about what he had imbibed. He knew little of the social or

economic side of history, and of science he was completely ignorant. On the bottom of the Haileybury report were five divisions – *Good*, *Moderate*, *No Complaint*, *Indifferent* and *Bad*, with a space in each division for the headmaster to sign. For the whole time he was at Haileybury Attlee scored only 'No Complaint', except for the last term's report, in 1901, when he rose to a 'Moderate'.

Attlee's only original thinking at Haileybury was about religion. He came to the conclusion that he did not believe in God. He fully shared his parents' sense of moral and social responsibility, with its emphasis on a high standard of duty towards the poor and sick; this feeling became, as it did for other Attlee children, the basis of his future socialism. But he could not share their fundamentalist belief that to question faith was a sin. He did not in consequence feel any sense of revolt; the subject simply bored him. He pondered the matter when the time came to be confirmed, and decided that: 'So far as I was concerned it was mumbo-jumbo. It worked for many of those I most liked and admired, so it was nothing to laugh at or asperse. But it meant nothing to me one way or the other.' At sixteen, long before he knew what the word meant, he became an agnostic. For the rest of his life his closest friends were Christians, and a large number of them were Anglican clergymen. But Attlee himself 'could not take it'. He had no wish to disturb his parents, and to other people, he assumed, his opinion did not matter. So characteristically he went through the motions of being confirmed, and thenceforward did not give God or the Life Everlasting very much thought.

At home by now he was regarded as much the most studious of the Attlee brothers. Laurence was impressed by the amount of voluntary reading he did at school – 'at least four books a week, good books, not thrillers or adventure stories' – and the enthusiasm with which he maintained this rate at home during the holidays. 'It wasn't so much the amount he read but the amount he could remember.' But Laurence's most significant recollection of him at the time was of his interest in politics. In spite of Ellen's resolution to prevent political arguments breaking out, there was much talk of politics in the Attlee household. The talk was of parliamentary politics rather than of major social and economic problems which might raise questions about the basis of society. The Attlee parents accepted society basically as they found it. They revered men like Wilberforce and Shaftesbury, were prepared for reforms, accepted the need for change, but trusted much in the inevitability of human progress. As Attlee put it: 'The capitalist system was as unquestioned as the social system. It was just there. It was not known under that name because one does not give a name to something of which one is unconscious.' Nor did the duty of succouring the poor entail liking, let alone admiring, the working classes. One of Attlee's earliest memories was of walking with brothers and sisters on the rocks in the Isle of Wight. 'Look at those little kids walking on the rocks,' somebody shouted in a cockney accent, to which Bernard replied: 'Essence of vulgarity'; which, Attlee noted, 'we thought a very fine retort.' Patriotism was taken for granted. Even some of the pro-Boers were more concerned about England letting down her own standards than about what was being suffered by the Boers. At home, at Haileybury and at Oxford, Attlee breathed the same welcome air of loyalty to, and pride in, Queen and Country. It was in his lungs, from the days of his first memory of the outside world – going out of the house on to the porch to hang up flags to celebrate the Queen's birthday.

Henry Attlee was not averse to encouraging his children in political discussion, provided it took place within this unquestioned framework; so much so that, according to Mary, 'Our friends used to say that when the little Attlees went to a party, their first words were "Are you Oxford or Cambridge, Liberal or Conservative?"', the first question referring to the Boat Race, its juxtaposition with the second being some indication of the depth at which politics were being discussed. Clem's political education at this time consisted of the political cartoons in the family's collection of bound volumes of *Punch*. 'He would lie on a sofa and pore over it for hours while the rest of us were on bicycles or playing family cricket.'

Laurence's other main recollection is of Clem's readiness to argue – 'not merely to give you his own views but to take yours to pieces. He was really quite an argumentative boy, and most of all he liked to argue about politics. Not so much about policies, but about the personalities. He could be very cutting about them, and very funny.' Arguing about politics was his way of self-expression. 'It struck us all – it made him quite a character. And though he was shy and tongue-tied with outsiders, he wasn't backward in coming forward within the family, the study and in class.' Perhaps he was finding a field in which his small size and shyness did not prevent him from excelling, and perhaps a sense of physical inadequacy gave a sharpness to his view and an edge to his tongue. Nevertheless, his shyness persisted. If he and Laurence went out together, on a walking tour or a trip to the Hook, it was Laurence the junior brother who did the talking, took the tickets and booked the rooms. 'When we went into our hotel, and I went up to the desk to register, Clem hung back.'

When the time came for him to go up to University College Oxford, in October 1901, he had a stroke of luck which so much enabled him to cope with his shyness that he looked back on his three years there as among the happiest of his life. He spent his first year sharing 'digs' in

'The High', a few yards from the college, with 'Char' Bailey and another old Haileyburian, George Way. Charles Bailey had been his best friend at school, and it was because Char went to 'Univ' that Attlee decided to go there. He had plenty of other company. His elder brother Tom was in his third year at Corpus Christi College, and Bernard, who had recently been up at Merton, was now the vicar of Wolvercote, a mile or so away. The eldest brother, Robert, now in the family law firm, had left many friends at Oriel, with invitations to 'drop in on Clem'. Life was very enjoyable. His total bill for tuition, food and board came to about £100 a year, but his father had given him a comfortable allowance of £200 a year.

In his second year he was moved into college. His rooms were in the right-hand corner of the first quadrangle, on the first floor of the staircase nearest to the Shelley memorial. Bailey had rooms immediately below him. 'I rather took advantage of Clem's good nature,' Bailey recorded.

> I wasn't very well off. If I had people coming to lunch I used to send my scout up to pinch Clement's silver. He never minded. He breathed out loving kindness. He may have learned from me to be a little less shy. I thought him insignificant until I got to know him – terribly shy – when a blood came into the room he'd twitch with nervousness. But when you got to know him you realized his selflessness; and others came to know it, showed it, and Clem became less shy.

In his second year, Char was elected a member of Vincent's, a club for outstanding undergraduates, with a strong contingent of sportsmen. He went up to give the news to Clem: 'I didn't know I was so popular.' Replied Clem: 'I always knew you were a "blood".' The friendship of this attractive, successful and much respected 'blood' might well have given Attlee confidence.

His second year at Oxford was 'the happiest and most carefree of my life'. He lost some of his shyness. He found that 'athletic excellence was not necessary to becoming accepted' and that he now 'played games well enough to get exercise and amusement'. Nor was it necessary to be a brain. 'Excluding a few outsiders, everybody knew everybody.' No cliques, no rowing set or football set, or barriers between intellectuals and athletes – the categories overlapped. 'I knew practically everybody in college, most of them very well.' He was proud of being a member of Univ during a golden age. In Clem's first year, two out of the three presidents of the Union were Univ men, the college was Head of the River, and housed the captains of the university rugger and soccer teams. Its corporate spirit was high. His happy college life was lived in a most agreeable university setting. Oxford itself was then 'unspoilt'; the town, dominated by the university, existed to serve the university's needs.

Beerbohm's *Zuleika Dobson*, published in 1911, gives some impression, for all its fantasy, of how the undergraduates were treated, and behaved, as a class apart.

Though he assumed in a desultory kind of way that he would follow his father and become a lawyer, he decided to read History. While, as Attlee says in his autobiography, he 'did not read for schools with any great assiduity', according to Charles Bailey he 'worked pretty hard', and 'would have got a first if he had not done so much miscellaneous reading'. He went on with his poetry and read widely in English literature. As his special period he took Italian History 1495-1512, for which he learned Italian. Only one of his tutors made any impact on him – Ernest Barker. 'He made his history live because he cared about the people in it.' It was not Barker's Liberal views that impressed him but his attractions as a teacher. He liked his north-country accent, his good looks and his enthusiasm for his calling.

Attlee showed little sign of political interests at this time. He was very easygoing, 'quite prepared to take life comfortably and as it came'. He reacted emotionally only when 'those damned radicals' were praised. 'I remember being quite surprised when an East End person said what a good chap Will Crooks was, while I was quite shocked at an educated man expressing admiration for Keir Hardie.' He may have exaggerated when he said in his autobiography that at Oxford he adopted 'a common pose of cynicism', but spoke the truth when he said he 'gave no real thought to social problems'. Some of his friends at Oxford were already interested in settlements in the East End of London sponsored by the university. Alec Paterson, the future prison reformer, then a close Univ friend, held meetings for undergraduates. Clem went to several, listened politely but doodled sketches of other undergraduates, and worked out ways of climbing the chapel roof. His views on party politics if vague were right-wing Tory. The Liberals he regarded with contempt – 'waffling, unrealistic have-nots who did not understand the basic facts of life'. Only the Tories were fit to govern. They understood men, they understood power.

Power had come to fascinate him, largely through his study of the Renaissance. The Italian princes of the fifteenth century thrilled him. He was intrigued by their unsentimental view of human nature. Perhaps he also enjoyed their contrast with his father's political opinions, which he thought dangerously radical – when a North Welsh quarry-owner imposed a lockout in the course of a dispute on wages, and Henry subscribed to a fund established to support the locked-out workers, young Attlee 'was shocked'. In fact, he 'had fallen under the spell of the Renaissance. I admired strong, ruthless rulers. I professed ultra-Tory opinions.' This did not incline him to join the University Conservative Club any more than to join any of the religious or do-gooding societies, some of which even the 'blood' Bailey patronized. Though he read a great deal in the Union he rarely went to hear debates; the thought of having to make a speech on the paper would have cost him a week's sleep. He did make one speech in a debate while up at Oxford, in the intimate, informal atmosphere of the college's debating society, controlling his shyness sufficiently to defend Protection against Free Trade. He found the Shakespeare Reading Society, which he helped to form, much more congenial.

For the most part, Attlee's Oxford was a social interlude rather than an intellectual adventure. Tennis on the Univ or Corpus courts. Playing hockey for the college. Squash. Watching rugger or soccer, hands in pockets on the touchlines. Sitting back in a deckchair, watching cricket, hands clasped at the back of his neck, straw hat tilted forward on his brow, the brim almost resting on the bowl of his pipe, eyes half closed in the Oxford sun. Walks along the river to Wolvercote with brother Tom to see Bernard, back through Long Meadow. Games of billiards – 'the only game I was proficient at – I was brought up at the billiard table'. He got his half-blue for billiards, and when Univ beat BNC in the university championship, Clem won his only prize at school or Oxford – a billiard cue. Sailing on the river in winter, or punting up the Cherwell in the spring; rambling excursions to surrounding villages on Sunday afternoons. Tea with dons and local vicars. Books.

In his last two terms he worked very hard indeed – eight hours a day he reckoned. As his final examinations approached in the June of 1904, Ernest Barker told him he might get a first. He got a second. 'I was quite content.' If he had got a first, he would have stayed up, and tried to become a Fellow of some college. 'I've no regrets, but in fact it's been the second-best thing,' he said in his old age. 'If I could have chosen to be anything in those days I'd have become a Fellow of Univ'. Now that it had come to choosing a career, 'my general idea was to find some way of earning my living which would enable me to follow the kind of literary and historical subjects which interested me.' He chose the Bar. Towards the end of his time at Oxford he had become interested in politics, not as a process so much as a spectacle, as theatre rather than the struggle for power. If somehow he could acclimatize himself to speaking in public, the Bar would give him argumentation to his heart's content, and once established at the Bar, he says in his autobiography, 'there was a possibility of entering politics, for which I had a sneaking affection'. If he had had one eye on emulating Ernest Barker, he now had half an eye on F.E. Smith.

So, the future prime minister came down from Oxford not very different from the schoolboy who had gone up three years before. He came down with much the same interests as those with which he had gone up, more knowledge, a half-blue at billiards, a passion for pipe-smoking, and many friends. He had discovered what scholarship and the life of the mind was about. He had met a number of men who he believed were 'good'. He left Oxford 'with an abiding love for the city and the University and especially for my own College'. The small circle of the Oxford men who knew him would have endorsed the report of his Haileybury form master – 'A sound character and should do well in life.' Pressed, they might have doubted if he would do as well in life as his father. Outside that small circle nobody had noticed him. One of his tutors, Johnson of All Souls, wrote a brief general reference for him: 'He is a level-headed, industrious, dependable man with no brilliance of style or literary gifts but with excellent sound judgement.'

II

In the autumn of 1904, at the age of twenty-one, Attlee entered the Lincoln's Inn chambers of Sir Philip Gregory, one of the leading conveyancing counsel of the day, with a high reputation as a teacher. Gregory made his pupils work. He was soon pleased with Attlee. He found him 'very intelligent and industrious ... promise of considerable ability'. Attlee was not so pleased with Gregory – 'Task master – drove you to death'. Gregory, a master of the art of drafting documents, believed in putting his pupils mercilessly through this particular mill. In after life Attlee was grateful to him for this mental discipline, a corrective after the discursive treatment he had found encouraged by the Oxford History School. The skill in reading and drafting quickly which Gregory taught him 'came in very useful later'. At the time, he responded gamely to the pressure and passed his Bar examinations well by the following summer.

His father, pleased with this beginning, took him into the family business, now Druces and Attlee, to 'derive from a spell in our firm a comprehensive knowledge of what happens at the solicitor's end of the Bar'. Henry so far succeeded that his son made up his mind after four months with Druces and Attlee that the solicitor's end of the Bar was not for him. What conservatism there was in Henry's temperament expressed itself in the appearance and organization of his office. There were files, but no filing system: when documents were required, it was the function of the clerk, the ingenious but much harassed Mr Powell, to produce them, relying on his powers of recollection to decide where the papers had last been seen. There were no typewriters: Henry thought they corrupted good handwriting. There was a telephone, but it was to be used only for the making of appointments, or in case of fire. The rooms were dingy, dark and dusty. Young Attlee's assignment was to sit at a small table and take notes while the partners interviewed their clients. This made him 'feel self-conscious and foolish. And terribly bored. I spent much of the time doodling – mostly dragons, breathing fire and smoke.'

At the beginning of 1906, he 'transferred at my own request' and was sent as a pupil to Theobald Mathew. Mathew, a friend of Attlee's father, was a remarkable man, already an outstandingly good barrister and an authority on the Commercial Court. He kept his legal work within carefully chosen limits; he never took silk, and arranged his affairs so that he had time to wine, dine, write and become one of the great wits of his generation. Attlee found Mathew's chambers most congenial. He was very taken with Mathew's wit, which mocked the pompous and de-bunked the great, but was utterly free of malice.

In March 1906 he was called to the Bar. His career thereat lasted less than three years. He had appeared in court on only four occasions, once at Maidstone and three times in London. He had earned about fifty pounds. When he came down from Oxford in 1904, he continued to receive the annual allowance his father made him when he was at Univ: £200 a year. Like the eldest son, Robert, now a solicitor in the family business, and Tom, studying to be an architect, he lived at his parents' home. The tedium of the Bar apart, he seemed to find post-Oxford life comparatively agreeable. 'When my brother came down from Oxford,' recorded Mary, 'he became something of a man about town. He was passably good-looking, paid attention to his clothes, and enjoyed theatres and town life.' He lived the life of a gentleman, and a gentleman, in his view, was what he was and should continue to be. He took his claret glass to his lips the long way, and set it down the shortest, and always spared a second or two to appreciate the bouquet. Sometimes he whiled away part of the morning by going some way to the City on foot. Sometimes, in the spring and early summer, he walked the whole seven miles from Portinscale Road to Billiter Square. Occasionally on a warm day in high summer he travelled to his briefless chambers by pleasure steamer from Putney to the Temple.

There were congenial outlets for unused mental energy. On Wednes-days there would be a jolly lunch with a group of Tom's friends from Corpus, who had formed a discussion club which met at the Cottage Tea Rooms in the Strand. There was the Hazlitt Essay Club which invited poets and writers on the way to fame to read and talk about their work. In the evenings there were institutions like the Crosskeys, a literary club at Putney, which met for discussions, readings and debates. There were frequent trips to the continent with his parents or his parents' friends. Now and again he would go on a walking tour with one or another of his brothers. For several weekends he took out the expensive gun which his father had bought him and went down to the shoot which Henry shared with friends in Sussex, until he found that shooting bored him. He learned to ride a horse – he came to ride quite well – and was on the point of buying a hack when he discovered that riding bored him too. Billiards fascinated him. When he returned home early from an empty day in chambers, he went straight to the billiard room, and potted patiently on his own, steadily improving at 'the only game in which I have shown any proficiency'.

In October 1905, a year after leaving Oxford, 'an event occurred which was destined to alter the whole course of my life'. His brother Laurence decided to pay a visit to the Haileybury Club in Stepney, and asked Clem to go with him. He decided he would go. He owed the club a visit – indeed he should have visited it before. He owed to his family and his Alma Mater, if not a genuflection, a respectful nod in that direction. Their mother was now a district visitor in one of the worst slums in London. An aunt was managing a club for factory girls in Wandsworth. Robert was working two nights a week at a mission in Hornsey. Tom was helping at a working men's hostel in Hoxton. Attlee decided he would go and look the place over and see, as he drily put it fifty years later, 'if the angels were wasting our parents' hard-earned money'.

Stepney, in dockland, was reputed to be the roughest and least law-abiding borough in London. The Haileybury Club was in Durham Road. Whereas some of the East End clubs had been established on a religious basis, Haileybury House, in spite of its physical proximity to Stepney Church, and the Christian convictions of most of its Haileyburian helpers, was a secular institution. In essence, it was for the poor boys what the public school's Officer Training Corps was for the rich. Notwithstanding the avowed military character of its organization, the club's objects were social and educational. It, and similar clubs founded by other schools, aimed to give London boys that side of school life which education by the state did not provide. The motto of the Club was the Haileybury motto: *Sursum Corda*.

The Haileybury Club was 'D' Company of the 1st Cadet Battalion of the Queen's (Royal West Surrey) Regiment. Membership of the club, for London working boys of from fourteen to eighteen years of age, was on condition of joining this junior section of the Territorial Army; the adults running the club took Volunteer Commissions in the TA, and acted as company officers. There was always a waiting list; very few boys left until they were forced to do so by the age limit. The club was open five nights a week. Wearing uniform gave these ragged boys a pride in their appearance which they had never previously been able to enjoy. The discipline braced them, the team work gave them a sense of belonging. It was the dread of having to give this up through the ultimate sanction of expulsion which was the basis of the club's discipline. Boxing, gymnastics, shooting, single-stick, swimming, the week's camp in the summer at the seaside improved their health. Many boys left the club to join the Regular Army.

The manager of the club, Cecil Nussey, a fine scholar and outstanding athlete, made his mark with Attlee, who left that night in a thoughtful mood. He liked the look of the lively but earnest lads whose lives, according to Nussey, were being transformed by the fellowship of the club. 'Good show, that,' he said. 'Might look in from time to time.' From then he went every week. Five months later he took a commission as an officer of 'D' Company – second lieutenant. He was now committed to a share in the responsibility of running the club, and to be on parade at least once a week. What began as duty became a pleasure. 'I had always been painfully shy,' he wrote, 'and it took me some time to settle down, but East London boys are very friendly.'

He enjoyed the club's activities: the drilling on spring evenings in the gardens of the rector of Stepney, going into barracks at Kingston for a few days at Easter and Whitsun – and marching down there over Wimbledon Common singing lustily; summer Saturday nights in bell tents, in a field lent by the rector of Chislehurst; the August camp at Rottingdean. It gave him the security in which he could unbend. His daily work had not been giving him satisfaction, had been diminishing his small stock of self-confidence. Now he had a sense of purpose. He began to sense that the boys liked and respected him. He was complimented on his efficiency. His parents were pleased that their son was doing something voluntary and useful. He felt a filial satisfaction in moving in the family tradition of social service.

Eighteen months after Attlee became an officer of the club, Nussey asked Attlee if he would take over as manager. Attlee felt apprehensive, but when Nussey insisted on the difficulty the club would be in if Attlee refused, he agreed to carry on until somebody else could be found. This meant living on the club premises. He and his family assumed that he would stay there for a year or so at the most, and, having done a stint of duty long enough to be consistent with the social obligation of an Old Haileyburian and a young Attlee, resign and return. In fact, he left home for good, to live seven years at the club, for fourteen years in the East End.

The Haileybury Club manager drew a salary of fifty pounds a year. He was a Stepney resident: he encountered not only the boys who came to the club, but the boys who did not. He met their parents, visited their homes, saw how the poor lived. The effect on the erstwhile young Tory Imperialist was profound. In his first year, the inexperienced Attlee had to cope virtually single-handed, since there was a shortage of Old Haileyburian help. Attlee, however, was already displaying his gift for establishing discipline. In his first annual report he noted briskly: 'There has been a marked improvement, a few expulsions having a salutary effect.' But his reports are more interesting for what they record of his first vision of how poor, uneducated, uncultured boys, given half a chance, would give, not take, in fellowship:

> A word of praise is due to those boys who give up their time to helping the smaller ones; it is no small sacrifice for a boy who has worked from six in the morning to six at night to hurry his tea and come to the Club to look after and instruct small boys ... [and] there is no doubt that the small boy, though very amusing, is also exceedingly irritating. ... I have been particularly struck by the many instances of unselfishness shown by the [elder] boys; for instance, a corporal of the Band, which at that time contained so many seniors that promotion was blocked, offered to resign his much-coveted stripes in order to give another boy who had been working well a chance of promotion ...
>
> I remember taking the Club's football team by local train to play an 'away' match. Young Ben had come straight from work with his week's money – a half-sovereign – and somehow he had lost the gold coin. There was no hesitation amongst the boys. Jack said, 'Look, a tanner each all round will make 'alf of it.' They readily agreed, yet probably that 'tanner' was all that most of them would have retained for themselves from their wages.

As it turned out, there was no need for their sacrifice. Attlee assured them that if they searched the railway compartment thoroughly they would find the lost half-sovereign. They searched, and found it: he had slipped it behind a cushion when none of them was looking. Such opinions about loyalty, unselfishness and a sense of duty within a group influenced his conduct in his later life. As party leader he expected politicians to behave at least as well as the lads of the Haileybury Club; and if they did not he believed in 'a few expulsions having a salutary effect'.

His annual reports on the activities of the club are curious reading. At times he makes the club sound more like a TA Headquarters than a YMCA. True, there is always a brief commendation of the loyal Miss Elliott who 'has continued to hold her voluntary class in the elements of religion on Monday nights'. But the tone of the reports is essentially military:

> The New Year brings with it several changes of personnel: HTH Bond has been appointed Adjutant to the Battalion, and his new duties will necessarily prevent his assisting in the work of the Company and the Club. Three years ago we were able to get a Haileyburian to take on a Company that was in danger of dissolution, and now, once more, it is a Haileyburian that helps the Battalion in its time of need.

The most interesting feature of his annual reports, however, is the light they throw on his progress towards socialism. Some of his predecessors were content to try to alleviate effects rather than come to grips with causes. But Attlee, his natural impatience and realism mobilized against the *laissez-faire* and sentimentality of his father's generation, wanted not relief but reform. In his first report he analysed the particular social evil which faced the managers of East End boys' clubs – 'The abuse of boy labour and the consequent waste of good material, that is always going on in our great cities.' It was not enough for the managers of the club to point out the evils. As 'keepers of the School's conscience [they] should try to point out the underlying causes and possible preventions ...' He begins with a description of the abuses of casual labour similar to one by Nussey three years earlier, but whereas Nussey had simply described the evils, Attlee went much further, and took to task a committee, of which Nussey had been a member, for publishing a report which 'revealed an extraordinary failure to realize that anything beyond sympathy was necessary to cope with these problems':

> Now it is very easy to be sentimental over hard cases, and it is possible to do something to assist individuals, but it appears to me that we want a great deal more than sentiment and individual charity: we want know-ledge and we want thought. There is plenty of excellent feeling on such subjects as boy labour, sweating and infant mortality; but as there is far too little consideration as to the causes of, and the connection between, these phenomena ...

Within a few months of taking up residence, he had seen the light: 'From this it was only a step to examining the whole basis of our social and economic system. I soon began to realize the curse of casual labour. I got to know what slum landlords, and sweating, meant. I understood why the Poor Law was so hated. I learned also why there were rebels.' The slums, the suffering, the poverty were not the necessary consequence of the character of the poor. Given opportunities even remotely compar-able to those of the boys who went to Haileybury, the Limehouse lads responded. Most of the poor were poor because they were being exploited by the rich. The message for the well-to-do should not be just 'help the poor who are always with us' but 'get off the people's backs'.

By the time Attlee had written that report for the Haileybury Council he had become a socialist.

2
The Making of a Socialist, 1906–18

At the weekends Attlee went home to Putney. So did Tom, his favourite brother and mentor, now also living five nights a week in the East End. Tom was a deeply convinced Christian, and he had been strongly influenced by the social and political ideas of the Reverend F. D. Maurice, the Christian Socialist. Tom worked at the Maurice Hostel in Hoxton. At these weekends during his first few months as manager of the Haileybury Club, Attlee spent much time with Tom, the talk in the early weeks being not about political ideology but on mundane matters, such as drains. Attlee was anxious to do well at the club, but was very conscious of his lack of practical knowledge. Tom, on the other hand, was very practical. He knew all about bricks and mortar, roofs, windows and rising damp. When Attlee decided that Haileybury House needed more fresh air, Tom drew up the plans for a new ventilation system and superintended its installation. Talk moved from how to repair the club-house to the question of how to reform society. By this time Tom had become a great reader of Ruskin and Morris, finding in them an amalgam of those artistic, religious and political ideas which were germinating in his own mind. What he found he imparted to his brother. Hours of Sunday talk on the banks of the Thames at Putney, and frequent late-night discussion over their pipes under the sooty eaves of Hoxton, made another convert. Attlee started to read. Soon 'I too admired those great men, and came to understand their social gospel.'

The conversion of Attlee from a middle-class, rather unreflecting Conservative into a dedicated socialist politician owed much to his brother Tom and the books to which Tom introduced him, and later, much to the Stepney branch of the Independent Labour Party.

The F. D. Maurice who had so much inspired Tom advocated radical social change based on the application of Christian principles to secular life, accepting the term 'Christian Socialism' as necessary 'to commit us to the conflict which we must engage in sooner or later with the un-social Christians and the un-Christian socialists'. He rejected secular socialism and state collectivism, and made his starting point the responsibility of the individual. Rather than aiming to introduce new forms of social organization he called on employer and public, as individual Christian believers, to transform the status and treatment of the worker. To understand Attlee's socialism, however, one must begin with Carlyle. His study of *Chartism* published in 1839 thundered out the warning that 'if something be not done, something will *do* itself one day, and in a fashion that will please nobody.' England's disgrace was the unbearable life of the poor: 'The sum of their wretchedness merited and unmerited welters, huge, dark and baleful, like a sunken Hell, visible there in the statistics of Gin.' Carlyle offered little by way of a practical programme, but Attlee responded readily to his call that men should rise to their responsibilities, *act*, and not speculate, do, and not talk. He was struck by the directness with which Carlyle addressed himself to the middle class, implying that only an enlightened, dynamic middle-class minority could make the first bold swerve off the headlong path which led to the abyss. Above all, Attlee responded to Carlyle's indignation, what Chesterton called his 'divine disgust'.

But it was Ruskin, through *Unto This Last*, who did more than anyone to lay the foundations of Attlee's socialism: 'it was through this gate I entered the Socialist fold.' Ruskin had achieved a vast influence as an art critic when, then in his early forties, he published in 1853 in the second volume of his *Stones of Venice* a chapter entitled 'On the Nature of Gothic Architecture; and herein one of the true functions of the workman is art'. In this he extolled those architectural styles which were most compatible with the welfare of the workman, praising the Gothic and condemning the art of the Renaissance. If this was odd as architectural criticism, it was nevertheless an intoxicating social commentary. Ruskin insisted that society must be rescued from the economic ideas of the commercial middle classes, so that the lot of the working classes could be improved: 'Government and co-operation are in all things the Laws of Life; anarchy and competition the Laws of Death.'

Ruskin venerated Carlyle as his master, but improved on his master's work by offering at least something of a practical programme. In the preface to *Unto This Last*, published in 1862, he made four proposals. There should be 'training schools for youth established, at Government cost, and under Government discipline'. There should be 'also entirely under Government regulation, manufactures and workshops for the production and sale of every necessary of life, and for the exercise of every useful art. And that, interfering no whit with private enterprise, nor setting any restraints of tax on private trade, but leaving both to do their best, and beat the Government if they could.' Thirdly, 'those who fell out of employment should be re-trained at the nearest Government school, and if unemployable ... be looked after at the State's expense.' Ruskin's fourth proposal was that 'for the old and the destitute, comfort and home should be provided. ... It ought to be quite as natural and straightforward a matter for a labourer to take his pension from his parish, because he has deserved well of his parish, as for a man in higher rank to take his pension from his country, because he has deserved well of his country.' Ruskin foresaw not a socialist but a welfare state.

Ruskin's disciple, William Morris, was the third formative influence on Attlee's socialism. Morris's contribution was to see that the social problem – poverty – and the aesthetic problem – desiccation – had been created by the same force, the Industrial Revolution. This had released forces of greed, cruelty and selfishness which had rendered society ugly in aspect and materialistic in outlook. Art, being an expression of everyday life, was creative only where everyday life was creative, and everyday life could not be creative for the community when many of the people who lived in it had not enough to eat. The first step therefore was to re-humanize everyday life, warped and corrupted by the Industrial Revolution, and restore it to health in a reconstructed society. In his analysis of the consequences of industrialization, Morris had much in common with Marx; and in the early 1880s, when he reached his conclusions, he saw the Social Democratic Federation, a league of London working men's clubs with a distinct Marxist tendency, as the best instrument of great social change. He joined the Federation in 1883, but left it the next year to help found the Socialist League, whose journal, *Commonweal*, he founded, financed and managed. He preached revolution, and was arrested in 1885 at a revolutionary meeting in the East End, though in later life he preferred to believe that the road to socialism lay not through revolt but through the education of public opinion.

It is not easy to reconcile the aesthetic and the Marxist sides of Morris's socialism. Attlee studied enthusiastically *How We Live and Might Live*, *A Factory as it Might Be*, and *Useful Work and Useless Toil*; but in later life he remembered the Utopian studies *News From Nowhere* and *A Dream of John Ball* as his favourite books. *News From Nowhere* expresses Morris's yearnings for a life that was simple, clean and colourful. For many of the chapters the Narrator sculls leisurely for miles along the sunny upper reaches of the Thames, accompanied by the beautiful Ellen, 'light-haired and grey-eyed, but with her face and hands and bare feet turned quite brown with the sun'. There are salmon in the Thames. Flowers abound.

There is no sound of engines, no smell of oil, no dust. It is a land of 'work which is pleasure and pleasure which is work'.

So read, and re-read, Attlee. And as he raised his eyes and looked out of his little bedroom in the Haileybury Club on to the sooty slates of the slums of Stepney, he pondered the message in Ellen's sad last parting look toward the dreamer as he turned back into the past:

> Go back and be happier for having seen us, for having added a little hope to your struggle. Go on living while you may, striving, with whatever pain and labour needs must be, to build up little by little the new day of fellowship, and rest, and happiness.

His favourite passage, though, came from *A Dream of John Ball*:

> Forsooth, brothers. Fellowship is heaven and lack of fellowship is hell: fellowship is life, and lack of it is death: and the deeds ye do upon the earth, it is for fellowship's sake that ye do them.

Morris was above all an artist. He saw life in aesthetic terms, of beauty and ugliness. Mankind should seek what was beautiful, in art, in nature and in human relationships. The ideal society was one in which everything that was made was 'a joy to the maker and the user' and in which all men could enjoy life at work as well as at leisure. A society in which ill-fed, ill-housed men joylessly manufactured ill-conceived, ill-designed commodities, to be sold to indiscriminating consumers for the profit of some tasteless tycoon, was a society at death's door. The aestheticism and fellowship which Morris preached were essential to Attlee's conversion to socialism.

II

Within a year of starting work at Haileybury House the Attlee brothers had come to the conclusion that individual action was not enough. They must act politically. Which was the party to join? Certainly not the Conservative Party: it was the Conservatives who owned the Stepney slums and exploited its casual labour. It was the Tories who brewed the beer which drugged and demoralized the working man and perpetuated the system which dragged him down. The Liberal Party was equally repugnant. It stood for the *laissez-faire* of the landlords, industrialists and businessmen, against whom Carlyle, Ruskin and Morris had inveighed. This left the Labour Party, which had been formed in 1900 as the Labour Representation Committee, a coalition of groups to get 'Labour' representatives elected to Parliament. To join it, one had to become a member of one of the participating organizations: a trade union, the Fabian Society, or the Independent Labour Party. The Attlees were not members of a trade union and did not consider themselves eligible for membership;

they knew little about the ILP, which they thought was the preserve of the working class; they knew the Fabian Society was middle class like themselves. So in early October 1907 they went to the Fabian Society headquarters in the Strand, and applied to join.

They attended their first Fabian meeting a few days later. 'The platform seemed to be full of bearded men. Aylmer Maude, William Saunders, Sidney Webb and Bernard Shaw. I said to my brother, "Have we got to grow a beard to join this show?" ' The Fabians were not all bearded. H. G. Wells was there, 'speaking with a little piping voice, he was very unimpressive'. Shaw and Webb got higher marks; the former 'confident and deadly in argument; Webb, lucidly explanatory'. He was not quite sure what to make of them. 'My impression was a blurred one of many bearded men talking and roaring with laughter.' But he was now committed. 'In two years the rather cynical Conservative had been converted into an unashamed enthusiast for the cause of Socialism.'

The Fabians provided Attlee with the bridge by which he crossed to socialism. No sooner was he on the other side than he began to feel uncomfortable. It was not that the Fabians had taken him too far but because they would not take him far enough. The society had been founded in 1884 by Beatrice and Sidney Webb, Graham Wallas, Bernard Shaw and other young middle-class intellectuals. Its original intention was not to create a new politicial party but to permeate the Tory and the Liberal parties and persuade them to carry out reforms which would lead to the evolution of a socialist state whose main feature would be the collective control of the economic forces of society, 'in accordance with the highest moral possibilities'. Attlee had been drawn to it by the Webbs' explicit sympathy with the aesthetic origins of socialism, and by the Fabians' emphasis on practical measures of improvement, 'gas and water socialism'. But once a Fabian, he found that though his new colleagues wanted to give the working man a society fit to live in, they did not consider that he could provide the leadership to produce it. This patronizing attitude offended him. Life in Stepney had already convinced him that given the chance the working class would be fit to govern, and moreover that it had virtues and values which were in some respects superior to those of the middle-class Fabians.

The alternative for a non-trade unionist in the Labour Party was the Independent Labour Party. This body had been founded in 1893 in Bradford, extending its influence rapidly in industrial centres. Its leading figure was Keir Hardie, a Scottish collier who had taken a prominent place in the 'new unionism' of the 1880s which for the first time enlisted unskilled workers in trade unions in large numbers. A Liberal until 1887, Hardie had decided that in the interests of the working class the trade unions must break from the Liberals and put into Parliament Labour representatives to bring about the emancipation of the worker by a socialist programme, beginning with the nationalization of the railways and the banks.

The ILP was distinctive in the coalition known as the Labour Party. Unlike the majority of trade unions, it was avowedly socialist; unlike the Fabians, it was boldly committed to the moral leadership of the working class. Early in January 1908 Attlee was discussing the shortcomings of the Charity Organization Society with an East End wharf-keeper, Tommy Williams, who had described how the COS had refused to help the parents of a boy in the Haileybury Club. 'They believe in charity,' said Williams, 'but I am a Socialist.' 'I don't believe in the COS either,' Attlee replied. 'I am a Socialist.' 'If you're a Socialist, join the ILP,' said Williams. Attlee went to the next meeting of the Stepney ILP and joined. Sitting round a stove in a small, grim East London church hall, with a dozen working men, he suddenly, and for the first time, felt in his element. 'I knew at once this was the right show for me.'

Attlee did not become a martyr when he joined the ILP, but he 'occasioned a certain amount of comment' among family and friends. To become a Fabian was one thing: to join the party of the militant working class was another. His mother heard the news with good-natured resignation. Henry outwardly remained his tolerant self, but, he confided in Laurence, 'I wish I were a younger man. I'd argue it out with him, and knock all that nonsense out of his head.' Attlee was acutely aware of his parents' real feelings. Years later, in *The Labour Party in Perspective*, he wrote: 'Anyone who has been brought up in a conventional home will know the difficult adjustment necessary for the member of the family who chooses another faith.'

Attlee joined the Stepney branch of the ILP because he felt morally obliged to associate himself openly with the only men who had organized to bring about the order of society he himself had come to believe in. He did not see himself as a political activist, but this was what he immediately became. In January 1908 the Stepney branch of the ILP numbered sixteen. All were members of a trade union, so he immediately joined the only one for which he was eligible, the National Union of Clerks. At the time he joined the Stepney ILP he was the only member of it who was not fully employed, who had enough spare time for political activities during the day. Within a few weeks, somewhat to his embarrassment, he was asked to act as its branch secretary. This meant not only organizing branch meetings, and keeping the minutes, but also standing in for speakers who failed to turn up to proselytize on street corners. The idea of mounting the soapbox to indict the leaders of his own class did not appeal to him, and the thought of speaking in public he found alarming. But, again, he felt he must show the courage of his convictions.

Attlee made a reluctant début in Barnes Street on a wild night in March 1908. His five comrades took up their positions under a gaslamp. Attlee mounted a chair borrowed from the nearby home of a sympathizer. The hissing and gulping of the gaslamp in the wind rendered him almost inaudible, but when a dozen or so passers-by had paused to listen and did not immediately go away, he felt a sense of achievement. He finished his speech, and was asked questions. In answering, he displayed the argumentativeness which his family had well noted. On the way home his five comrades congratulated him. From now on, they said, he must be permanent meeting-opener, since, being his own master, he alone could be relied on to be on time. He made his first fully-fledged political speech the following Sunday morning at the corner of Salmon Lane. Tom, now sporting a beard in spite of his misgivings about the Fabians' hirsute chins, was in the audience. Attlee's message was not a feat of rhetoric: he demanded only that the Stepney Public Health Committee should ensure a supply of cheap milk to the women and children of the borough. 'Comrade Attlee was no orator at the time,' reported a colleague, 'but he put up a good case.' His self-confidence was boosted.

The tightly-knit personal loyalties of the ILP, the stronger because they were a small minority with much to lose and little to gain, inspired a camaraderie which Attlee needed, and which, since he came down from Oxford, he had missed. He was accepted in the Stepney ILP and he felt it. His new colleagues found him reserved, a little nervous, and laconic, but they felt he was one of them. They liked him.

The greatest problem facing the ILP in 1908 was how to get closer to the trade unions. The ILP men had ideas, but the union members had votes. To establish contact with trade union leaders was not always easy, but to make it with trade union rank and file was harder still. There was a certain incompatibility between the ILPer and the trade union member which was partly political and partly personal. Local ILP branches up and down the country usually held their weekly business meetings in a church or chapel hall: and frequently opened and closed proceedings with a hymn. Many ILP men were teetotallers. The trade union branch usually met in a pub. The ILP minority contained earnest, restless men who sought the kingdom of heaven here on earth; the purpose of the trade union movement, on the other hand, was fulfilled when its members were in work, decently clothed and housed, their old age provided for. In spite of a century of oppression and suffering, bitterly fought strikes and lockouts, passionate loyalties and generous self-sacrifice, the general temper of the British trade unionist had remained individualistic.

One of Attlee's tasks as Stepney ILP branch secretary was to try and convert trade unionists to socialism. Accompanied by one other member, for the temper of East End trade unionists rendered it more prudent to visit them in couples than in dozens, he would call in on the Boiler Makers' Association, at the 'Cape of Good Hope', in the Commercial Road; on the Canal, River and Dock Watermen's Society at the 'Railway Tavern', further along; then go north to the Bricklayers' meeting, in the 'Hayfield Tavern' in the Mile End Road; on to the Plumbers' Association at the 'Silver Tavern', Burdett Street. He would report to the ILP meeting at the end of the week: 'At some of these places we were able to get a hearing, and may have made some progress.' He never had any illusions about the difficulty of making working men into socialists. In this respect he had learned a lesson from the club. In spite of their poverty the boys who came to Haileybury House had no inclination to join the ILP. With rare exceptions they were Conservatives. One member, 'a clever boy', did join the Stepney ILP. But he did well for himself, rose to be secretary of the Master Butchers' Federation, and when Attlee saw him next, some decades later, he was 'lobbying in the House in top hat and tails'.

By the middle of 1908 it was clear to Attlee that he had no future at the Bar. Hence a dilemma: he did not wish to go on being dependent on his father's income, but he did not wish to hurt Henry's feelings by leaving the family profession and taking a job. The dilemma was soon resolved. Henry Attlee died suddenly of a heart attack on 19 October 1908. It was ironic that a man who eight months earlier had wished for a new lease of life so that he might argue his son out of his socialism, by his death made it easier for his son to practise it. With his share of Henry's estate, Attlee's yearly income now rose to £400. He could now afford to look for a job which, though it would 'bring in some income', would also fit in with work for the ILP and Haileybury House. Now that his father was dead he need not be concerned about continuing in the legal profession. This was the point of no return. From being a voluntary do-gooder, a barrister – albeit briefless – who 'did social work' in his spare time, he became a committed party worker, virtually a professional – though unpaid – politician.

In the first year of his new way of life Attlee took on a number of varied assignments. He assisted J. J. Mallon, then secretary of the National League to Establish a Minimum Wage, who was focusing public attention on the plight of the workers in the sweated industries in a campaign to get Parliament to protect them by legislation. Attlee contributed to a survey of labour in the East End, and helped Mallon with the organization of the *Daily News* 'Sweated Industries' exhibition. Mallon's campaign was successful: the Trades Board Act of 1909 established boards composed of employers, workers and nominated members, to investigate industrial conditions and fix minimum rates of pay.

Meanwhile Attlee had been put up as an ILP candidate for the Stepney Borough Council. He polled only sixty-nine votes. In the street the morning after the election an ILP colleague greeted him with the rhetorical question 'Are we down-hearted?' Attlee did not believe in rhetoric. 'Of course we are,' he snapped. For the next three months he stood in temporarily as secretary of the School Care Committee at Ben Jonson School, his main contribution being to organize voluntary workers in the supervision of school meals in neighbouring church halls – there were no facilities at the schools. Drawing on his Haileybury House experience, he solved the supervision problem by organizing a kind of lunchtime prefectorial system. He bribed the elder children to keep order by taking them out on occasional evening and Saturday morning trips around London. Mary wrote that he asked her to come over from Putney and teach them to sing Grace. 'He himself bought teaspoons and small forks for the younger children because he considered those supplied too large for them, and he also trained the elder girls to cut up the meat of the little ones and to look after them.'

In June 1909 he undertook the task of organizing propaganda for the Webbs, now pressing for the reform of the Poor Law. Earlier that year the Royal Commission on the Poor Law had produced two memorable reports: the Majority Report and the Report of the Dissenting Minority, the former mildly progressive, the latter radical. The Majority Report found, predictably, that the concept of the Poor Law of 1834 was now out of date, and that the poor should no longer be supervised by local 'guardians' elected for the purpose, working through 'poor law officers', but should be looked after under local government, working through expert officials. The minority group, which included George Lansbury and Beatrice Webb, went much further, arguing that responsibility for the care of the poor must be assumed by the state, and that the state must give itself the powers to discharge that responsibility. The Webbs saw the Minority Report on Poor Law reform as a classic Fabian cause, and decided to finance a series of lectures to make its proposals known to the general public. They hired Attlee, now known to some of the Fabians as a result of his attendance at several East London Labour conferences, to provide and assign the lecturers.

When Beatrice Webb wrote to thank him for his work she added some advice:

> What I think you need to make you a *first rate organiser* is rather more of the quality of 'Push' and the habit of a rapid transaction of business. You should always keep before you the attitude of the first rate Chairman of a Committee of pushing forward to 'the next business'.... I only mention it by way of a counsel of perfection from an elderly observer of men and affairs.

In September 1909 he was offered his first full-time job: secretary at Toynbee Hall, the oldest and best-known of the East End university settlements. The prospect sounded most attractive. Arnold Toynbee had specialized at Oxford in the teaching of economic history as the key to the improvement of the moral and material condition of the masses. Toynbee Hall was established by his friends and admirers to develop relationships between the universities and the working classes. Attlee gave up his post as manager of the Haileybury Club and his room on the top floor. The move turned out to be a great mistake. He found the atmosphere at Toynbee Hall 'out of date', by which he meant good-natured, ameliorative, charitable, bourgeois, lacking the positive approach to the East End's problem which socialism provided. Although he 'made many good friends' there, he did not care for Toynbee Hall. Nor did Toynbee Hall care for him. His colleagues may have found him 'a bit of a bolshie', he later conceded. No tears were shed on either side when a year later a thoughtful reorganization of duties at Toynbee Hall eliminated the post of secretary, and Attlee was made redundant.

The year of 1910, with its two tumultuous general elections, gave a great impetus to Attlee's activities as a political propagandist. The issue that dominated the two elections was the power of the House of Lords. In 1909, to pay for pensions and the naval arms race, Lloyd George, Chancellor of the Exchequer, introduced a budget which the House of Lords refused to pass. Two elections were held in the same year, the dust settling only with the passing of the Parliament Act of 1911, which took away the power of the Lords to amend or reject a money bill, and ensured that a bill passed in three successive sessions by the Commons would automatically become law.

The Stepney ILP meanwhile increased its membership from sixteen to seventy-two and expanded its activities. Attlee spoke at fifty-three public meetings, twenty-nine of them in May and June. He met the up-and-coming men in the London Labour Movement. 'Herbert Morrison in West Ham and Alf Barnes in East Ham ... young lads of promise'. His staple subjects were 'Socialism and Tariff Reform', 'Boy Labour' and 'Trade Boards', but 'I kept a lecture up my sleeve which I could adapt to anything, which I called "The Crisis".' He kept records of all his meetings. He was meticulous to the point of being obsessional in recording meetings and functions. His private papers abound with detailed statistics: records of memberships of local government councils for the prewar years, menus and programmes of club, civic or political dinners; all annotated in his neat but crabbed and frequently barely legible handwriting.

The termination of his job at Toynbee Hall at the end of 1910 meant that he had to look for somewhere to live. He and Tom decided to share an LCC flat in Brightlingsea Buildings, Narrow Street, alongside the river in Limehouse. Narrow Street was inhabited mainly by dock labourers. The Attlees rented four good rooms for 8s 6d a week; there were friendly neighbours who offered to do their washing and mending for nothing. In 1911, Attlee was, 'to use the admirable phrase by Sir William Beveridge – "a man of discontinuous employment"'. He had applied without success for a variety of jobs, including an inspectorship of industrial schools, under the Home Office, and as an organizer of trade schools for boys under the LCC, for both of which he was recommended by Sidney Webb and the warden of Toynbee. In March he went up to Oxford to give a series of lectures on trade unionism at Ruskin College. The summer he spent as an 'official explainer' of the Lloyd George National Insurance Act of 1911, which prescribed compulsory insurance against unemployment in a limited number of trades. The government enrolled a staff of temporary civil servants to tour the country and explain the Act in detail to the public.

Attlee was not enthusiastic about the Act, because though it did something to alleviate unemployment it did nothing to prevent it. He bought a bicycle and a set of ordnance survey maps, and, pipe between his teeth, pedalled earnestly around the small towns and villages of Somerset. On a fine day, in between one village and another, he would get off his bicycle, eat his sandwiches sitting beside the road, and ruminate on the injustice, the poverty, the ugliness and the misery from which the people back in Stepney were suffering. He wrote a parody of Kipling's 'Sussex':

> God gave all men our earth to use
> But since our island's small,
> And landlords make what laws they choose
> We own no land at all;
> And as He watched Creation's birth
> So they see, well content,
> Our work create out of the earth
> Their economic rent.
>
> Some men live in Marylebone,
> Others in Rottingdean,
> One has a house at Leytonstone,
> And one in Bethnal Green;
> We have no choice; I'll not rejoice
> The lot has fallen to me
> In a vile place – a vile place –
> In Stepney, London E.

That he did not have a regular daily occupation continued to irk him, and he was very pleased when the following year, 1912, he was appointed tutor in the newly established Social Service Department at the London School of Economics. The LSE had been founded in 1890 as a college of the University of London, and owed its initial success to Sidney Webb. In 1912, assisted by funds which the Webbs provided, the LSE took over and reorganized a small school of sociology which had previously been run by the Charity Organization Society, and appointed Professor Urwick to run it. The school was to award a diploma in social studies. A lecturer and tutor to work under Urwick was now required. There were two candidates for the job: Attlee and a young barrister called Hugh Dalton. Webb was chairman of the selection committee. Attlee got the job, his qualifications, according to Webb, being his first-hand experience of local government, social work and living conditions in the East End, and his ability to lecture.

Just before Christmas, Tom came home to the flat and announced that he would be getting married. 'I knew something had happened – he'd got rid of his beard.' As well as working at the Maurice Hostel at Hoxton, Tom had put in some time on the youth service organized by the Wandsworth Labour Exchange. The secretary of this organization was an attractive and energetic young woman called Katherine Medley. Attlee went back to live in Haileybury House.

No period of Attlee's life was as varied and full as his seven prewar years in Stepney. As well as the temporary jobs and part-time assignments, there were all the 'emergencies'. He cut up loaves to feed dockers' children during the dock strike of 1911. He stood at the dock gates holding a collecting box during the Irish Transport and General Workers' strike in 1913. He attended Labour demonstrations – 'I know what it is to carry a banner from Mile End Waste across Central London to Hyde Park.' He led parties from Stepney to gatherings of international socialists – 'I remember hearing Jean Jaurès, the French Socialist leader, speak, and seeing Anatole France kiss Bernard Shaw.' He worked for the suffragettes. In the evenings he climbed on to a borrowed chair at East End street corners, and talked to the empty street till a handful of a crowd appeared.

He was always the servant. He never set the pace himself, never emerged as the natural 'leader', who by oratory or agitation caused other men to follow. 'I had no idea of anything more than working as a member of the rank-and-file and perhaps getting on to a local council.' He answered all calls. He went to court to plead mitigation when a half-starving boy had been caught thieving. He led marches of protest to the Board of Guardians and the mayor. When the local ILP set up its own headquarters above a funeral parlour in Galt Street Attlee provided the furniture and part of the rent. The fact that he did more, and talked less, than any other socialist in Stepney was widely observed.

These were the years in which he learned his basic lessons in politics. He and his colleagues sat up late after meetings discussing the idealism and self-sacrifice and inexhaustible energy of the few and the apathy of the many. They discussed the pros and cons of revolutionary and reformist tactics, industrial, as opposed to political, action. Would a general strike be necessary if a socialist society was to be established? Would it be the twentieth-century equivalent of 1789? Did the road to the socialist society lie in syndicalism, in a state run by the worker-leaders of individual industries – by a union of unions? Was nationalization enough? Should nationalized industries be run by the workers or by the politicians? They argued about the relevance of the struggle with the House of Lords to the Labour Movement, the place in Labour strategy of the controversy over Home Rule for Ireland, and what Labour should do about the militant suffragettes.

These seven years in Stepney led Attlee to two conclusions which were to remain with him for the rest of his life and to colour his attitude to people and politics. He discovered the kind of people he admired: 'those who did the tedious jobs, collecting our exiguous subscriptions, trying to sell literature, and carrying the improvised platform from one street to another. They got no glamour. They did not expect to live to see victory, but, uncomplainingly, they worked to try and help on the cause.' These were the real leaders of the Labour Movement. Orators and dialecticians came and went, but the stuff of the resistance to poverty and privilege was the rank-and-file party worker. The first prerequisite of the Labour leader was that he should have fought the street-corner battle. His other conclusion was that national politics should be regarded as an extension of local politics: it was what happened on the street corner which determined whether Parliament burned with zeal or merely smouldered. Politics should reflect a man's compassion and concern for his neighbour, not merely his interest in broad national issues. Politics was not a career but a charge.

When, much later on, after the First World War, the Labour Party looked with mixed feelings – and some suspicion – on middle-class intellectuals who wished to make a career of Labour politics, Attlee had been long established in their minds as the man who had lived among the East End poor and had tried to help without thought of personal gain. The reputation he earned in Stepney was to stand him in good stead in the years to come.

Yet, in spite of the challenge, the satisfaction, the sublimation, of his social and political work, he was still the romantic part-solitary, part-lonely and sensitive creature he had been even in the bosom of his secure and affectionate family. It was a point of honour with him never to communicate his depression or yearnings to anybody else, most of all those who he felt had to bear burdens of poverty, pain and heartbreak from which money, friends and family had fortunately protected him. But he was lonely, and he longed for love. One of his sonnets may have expressed his feelings at this time:

> My life is passing like a lonely stream
> Winding through meadows flecked with white and gold
> That farseen distant castled hills enfold
> Yearnings and visions, memories of a dream
> Like tributary brooks my friendships seem
> Into the volume of the river rolled
> So in my heart their added wealth I hold
> But still my life is lonely like the stream.
> Sudden a change in this calm life I see
> The cataracts and shoals of Love are near
> Life is a torrent and within my heart
> The calling of another stream I hear
> This is the waters meet, never to part
> Love let us flow together to the Sea.

III

When war was declared, on 4 August 1914, Attlee was on holiday in Devon with Tom and his wife Katherine. Like the great majority of members of the Labour Party, the Attlee brothers had not given much thought to what they or the party should do in the event of war. Until the war broke out the big issues had been domestic issues, and the Labour Movement had never tackled the problem of what it should do in the event of international hostilities. As an affiliated member of the Socialist International, British Labour supported the line laid down at the Stuttgart Conference of 1907. In the event of war, Labour parties should try to bring it to an end, and use the crisis 'to rouse the populace from its slumbers and to hasten the fall of capitalist domination'. The tenet was that war could be prevented – or stopped if it began – by 'the international solidarity of the workers'; though how this theory would be translated into practice had never been worked out.

When war broke out, British Labour MPs passed a resolution demanding that Britain stay out. When Britain announced that she would go to the defence of Belgium, the Labour Party decided to support the war, Ramsay MacDonald consequently resigning the leadership of the party, to be succeeded by Henderson. The Labour Movement as a whole, with the trade unions, backed Henderson and the government.

Down in Seaton, Tom decided that as a Christian he must become a conscientious objector. Attlee thought it was his duty to fight. He told Tom that 'some measures of police' were sometimes necessary and it was now necessary to take them against Germany. Tom's principles, he said, would logically carry him 'as far as the Jains who can hardly act in their lives for fear of killing a living creature'. Two days after war was declared he returned to London to enlist. He was nettled when friends in the Stepney ILP reproached him for ignoring Tom's example: he was later to say of one of them: 'If I come back without an arm at least Jack Lawder won't have to shake hands with me.' At thirty-one he was twelve months too old to get into the Army. As an indirect route to a commission he joined the Inns of Court Officer Training Corps as an instructor, but this seemed to bring him no nearer the fighting. Finally, early in September, he was gazetted as lieutenant to the 6th Battalion of the South Lancashire Regiment, through the good offices of a former pupil at the LSE, a young woman whose brother-in-law commanded the battalion.

The 6th South Lancashires consisted mainly of raw lads from Wigan, Warrington and Liverpool – 'excellent material'. Because of his age, and his experience with the cadets, Attlee was given command of a company – seven officers and 850 men. He was the only non-regular company commander in the battalion. They were kept hard at work at platoon training; a route march before breakfast, then drill, musketry instruction and, in the afternoon, physical training. There were night operations several times a week, and one half holiday, devoted to football. In February 1915 they left Tidworth, famous for its mud, and moved to Winchester for battalion training. He became a captain. Winchester was very comfortable – billets – but in March they went into huts at Black Down, where life was hard, uncomfortable and monotonous, consisting mainly of learning how to dig trenches and of excessively heavy route-marching. In June, the South Lancs sailed from Avonmouth on the *Ausonia*, bound for Gallipoli.

The Gallipoli campaign had been launched four months previously, in February. It had been strongly urged on the Cabinet by Lloyd George and Churchill, who believed that such a landing in southeastern Europe would not only take Turkish pressure off the Russians but would create a diversion from the deadlocked Western Front, counter Turkey's threat to the Suez Canal, and shorten the war by several years. The chiefs of staff, on the other hand, were reluctant to send any of their troops elsewhere than to France. From the beginning the Gallipoli operation was tragically muddled. The Army and the Navy did not see eye to eye. The landing was accomplished, but only after a delay which doomed the object of the enterprise from the start. When Attlee and the 6th South Lancashires arrived on the scene in June, they found the British and

Australian infantry pinned down in trenches, as uselessly employed as the troops in Flanders.

Attlee wrote a detailed account of his Gallipoli experiences during a spell in hospital. His battalion came into Mudros – on the island of Lemnos, forty miles east of Gallipoli peninsula – towards the end of June. Lemnos delighted him. But he preferred Stepney:

Lemnos 1915

Many a time I've longed these ways to go,
To wander where each little rugged isle
Lifts from the blue Aegean's sparkling smile
Its golden rocks or peaks of silent snow.
The land of magic tales of long ago,
Ulysses' wanderings and Circe's wile,
Achilles and his armour, Helen's smile,
Dear-won delight that set tall Troy aglow.

Happy the traveller whose eye may range
O'er Lemnos, Samothrace and Helles' strait,
Who smells the sweet thyme-scented breezes. Nay,
How willingly all these I would exchange
To see the buses throng by Mile End Gate
And smell the fried fish shops down Limehouse way.

They bivouacked at Mudros for two nights, in a vineyard in heavy rain – 'a first hint of what we afterwards called 13th Div weather'. On the third day they went up on destroyers to the peninsula. In the small hours they disembarked and after trudging up and down corkscrew ravines for several miles in full kit, most men carrying extra ammunition and supplies, resting for two days in dugouts along the way, they reached the firing line. Came four weeks of heat and stench. Flies, well-directed rifle fire from snipers, water tasting of sand, shells landing frequently on their dugouts, put a strain on these still raw troops. Since a major Turkish attack was expected at any time, the South Lancs were required to stand to at 8 pm and 4 am. 'The Turks used to have a morning and evening hate with much vain firing.' Keeping awake was the main problem; Attlee used to try and beat it by reciting poetry to himself, and, when occasionally he was moved back a trench or two, by composing verses in his head:

Stand to. The huddled sheeted figures creep
From step and dugout, yawning from their dreams
Of home and England . . . .

The South Lancs were soon smitten with dysentery. Attlee held up for another month, collapsed, was sent down to the beach on a stretcher, rested for three days, started to walk back up to the line, collapsed again, and, unconscious, was put on the hospital ship, the *Devanha*, bound for England. When he woke up next day, he protested at having been evacuated without his consent, and demanded to be put off the ship at Malta. He was 'swung out of the ship on a stretcher by a derrick – a most unpleasant sensation', and taken by ambulance to Hamrun Hospital. Dysentery probably saved his life. Two weeks after he had been evacuated, his company went into the assault, and two-thirds of them were killed. Early in November he rejoined his battalion at Suvla. He went straight up to the firing line, in which he remained until the evacuation about two months later. The terrible weather harassed them more than the snipers. His men stood in water to their knees. Then came snow, and after it a freezing wind: dysentery was followed by frostbite. Men were drowned; some died of exposure. Casualties in Attlee's company were the lowest in the division, mainly, according to Private F. A. Green (formerly of Black Down Camp), because 'the Captain bullied us'. Attlee recorded: 'I got our men who would stand shivering under the trees to run about, chasing them round and we had frequent issues of rum. . . . I also collected a lot of old tins and issued fuel and some petrol and got braziers going. I then had foot inspection and made all men with sodden feet rub them with snow.'

By now the government adjudged the Gallipoli campaign a failure. Orders were given for the evacuation. Attlee's company was to hold the perimeter line around the point from which the last British troops would be taken off – 'the final lines'. All went well. He left the beach just before midnight on 20 December. General Maude was the last man to leave the beach; Attlee was the last but one. The South Lancashire officers speculated that Attlee would at least get a mention in dispatches. He did not, though the brother officer who carried out a much less exacting evacuation at Helles two weeks later received a decoration.

After the war the Gallipoli campaign met with general condemnation, and Churchill's reputation as a military strategist was vilified. Attlee defended Churchill then, and years later. In 1964 he wrote: 'How near we were to a great success which might have shortened the war and saved tens of thousands of lives . . . [only] incredible blunders marred Churchill's fine strategic conception.' He concludes:

One who had the privilege of serving in the wartime cabinet of the Second World War thinks of what might have been if Sir Winston, rather than the collection of civilians without any knowledge of war, had had control and if, instead of the unco-ordinated services dominated by Kitchener, there had been the Chiefs of Staff of 25 years later.

The South Lancs were now redirected to the campaign in Mesopotamia, which was intended to protect the Suez Canal and the Persian oil wells. After a spell in Alexandria he made the long sea voyage down the Red Sea and into the Persian Gulf. At Basra they changed into paddle-steamers and moved up the Tigris, disembarking eventually at Sheikh Said. From here, it was explained to them by the divisional commander, the much admired General Maude, they would be required to launch a major attack on the Turks at El Hannah. It rained in torrents. 'I found war in the middle east suprisingly wet.' For the first time the South Lancashires were to go over the top; the 'show' was expected to involve severe hand-to-hand fighting.

Attlee went over the top ahead of the centre of his line, carrying the large red flag which was a warning to the supporting artillery to lift the barrage so as not to endanger their own troops. As he ran Attlee saw that the Turks had withdrawn from their first line trenches, but that the British artillery barrage was still landing on where the Turks had been, and that the advancing British troops would be caught in it. He must get forward himself and plant his flag. Shouting to his subalterns to slow the adjoining companies down, he ran forward towards the Turkish trenches, reached them, and as he planted his flag was knocked down from behind by shrapnel. The next day he was on a hospital ship bound for Bombay. He told Tom:

> I expect you have heard from Rob that I got one bullet through the left thigh and a large piece of shell-case tore a considerable hole in my right buttock and I have also a small one in the fork, together with sundry burns from the fumes. . . .
>
> By the way it may interest the comrades to know I was hit while carrying the red flag to victory. . . . I pointed out to the CO that I thought the colour was a delicate compliment to my political persuasions.

As soon as he could hobble he was sent back to England, and spent the next four months in various depots contriving his return to the fighting. Being wounded as well as over-age this was extremely difficult, but the terrible rate of casualties and his own persistence assisted him. On a snowy night in December 1916 Attlee arrived at Wool, near Lulworth in Dorset, for three months 'training in tank warfare without any tanks'. When the battalion went over to France, though promoted Major, he was left behind. 'Absolutely sickening,' he told Tom, going on to give his views on events in Russia after the 1917 Revolution. Lenin and Trotsky, he said, reminded him of 'the wilder types of the Social Democratic Party. . . . I can imagine the state of the country run by the Whitechapel branch of the SDP.' In June 1917, after several months of disappointments but continuous hard retraining, his perseverance was rewarded. He was 'invited' back to his beloved South Lancs, this time not to the 6th but to the 5th battalion – a territorial battalion – which had just taken part in the much praised defence of the Givenchy–Festubert sector by the 55th Division under General Jeudwine. The fighting was heavy, but he found it much less of a strain than the trench warfare in Gallipoli. Troops spent less time in the front line, and the combat cycle was more regular – four days in the front line, four in support, four in reserve, and then four days' rest.

Among the incidents he recorded, with an indifference to punctuation which remained with him all his life, was his threat to shoot an officer:

> Our line was not continuous. There was a detached post called Cailloux Keep at the corner where our line bent back eastwards. I had sent orders to a subaltern whose name I forget [to move forward with his platoon]. I went to the line to see them set out and the corporal met me saying this officer said he would not go and was weeping and upsetting the morale of the men. [Attlee went up and found this officer, who] said his nerve had gone and he would not go. I said, you bloody well will go, and drew my revolver. He went, but when I came back to see what had happened I found he had fainted. I had to report him to the CO who wanted to have him shot, but I said, you can't do that because he said he'd go. So we sent him down to the transport. The spirit was willing but the flesh was weak.

If the officer had refused to go, would Attlee have shot him? 'Probably. So many men standing around – their lives at stake. Can't be sure, looking back. But my duty was clear.'

Sometimes in the desperate conditions of the front-line trenches he applied the techniques he had learned at Haileybury House. A soldier was brought up to him in handcuffs:

> He had accumulated sentences of twelve years' imprisonment which would await him at the end of the war. I told him that he must now set to work to get remission and that we would help him. Our lads, too, were all determined to help. As one lad of nineteen said, 'I reckon that poor lad has never had a chance. He's been dragged up.' I think myself that he was not entirely sane. However, we all set out to help him. He volunteered for every patrol. He lay out between the lines sniping and in a few weeks I got about six years of his sentence remitted. A little later I recommended the remission of the rest. Next evening, I found him and his sergeant outside my dugout. The sergeant said that he refused to go back to the line. On my questioning him, he talked wildly about being fed up and so on. I was much annoyed that all our trouble should go for nothing, so I adopted a method that I found useful with disobedient boys. I took out my watch and said, 'You've got one minute to return to duty,' and then counted slowly. At forty-five seconds he sloped arms and returned to the trench. I suppose it was irregular, but I did not put him on a charge, and when I left the unit he was still doing well.

In August 1918, during the successful Entente offensive which finished the war, the 5th South Lancs were ordered to go in with a major attack on their sector of the front before Lille. 'A' and 'B' Companies were to go first. They went over the top and captured the German trenches opposite according to plan, but with casualties, and their commander was wounded. Attlee was ordered to take his place. Attlee had just reached the next German trench when a shell landed in it and he was felled by a blow on the back from falling timber. Within a few days he was in hospital in Wandsworth, where Tom, as a conscientious objector, 'was in prison almost next door'. He was still there two months later when the armistice was announced.

3
A Rising Politician,
1919–22

I

On the morning of 16 January 1919, Major C. R. Attlee was officially discharged from His Majesty's forces at Wandsworth Hospital. He made for the nearest tube station and took the underground to Stepney East, and within an hour he was limping northwards up White Horse Road to Haileybury House. He proposed to live in the club, try to get back his job at the London School of Economics, and go back to work for the Stepney ILP.

When he reached the church at the top of Stepney High Street he saw that the upstairs windows of the club had been boarded over. The grass patch at the back was discoloured and overgrown. The door was locked up; nobody answered the bell. Hearing him knocking, an old couple living in one of the little houses in Ben Jonson Road took him in and gave him a cup of tea. They told him that the young officers of the club had, one after another, gone off to the war. He discovered that the club was still carrying on a couple of nights a week but the residential side had been shut down, so he walked west to Toynbee Hall, and arranged to take up residence there again the following week.

From Toynbee Hall he went to the London School of Economics, where Professor Urwick welcomed him with warmth. Attlee could not have arrived at a more opportune moment. Professor Urwick's social science department was required to provide a part-time lecturer for two dozen or so students who wished to qualify for the LSE's Social Welfare Certificate. Many ex-servicemen, their social consciences sharpened by their wartime experience, had enrolled. They were potential converts to socialism. Leadership for these promising troops, Urwick said, was available in the persons of men like Hugh Dalton, Harold Laski and R. H. Tawney. Attlee took the job.

The socialist proselytizer went back to Putney that night to the comfortable home of his Conservative mother. Next morning he packed a suitcase and returned to Stepney, making for a tiny chemist's shop in Harford Street, off the Mile End Road, the home of Oscar Tobin, then the East End of London's most influential political 'boss'. By birth a Romanian Jew, Tobin had been sent to Britain by his parents at the age of eighteen so that he could escape the Bucharest persecutions. He soon earned enough to enable him to study for a chemist's diploma, to which later he added a medical degree. He was a socialist, as were many of the Jews who lived in Mile End. He had entered East End politics just before the war as secretary of the local branch of the National Union of Shop Assistants, and his ambition was to fuse trade union members and the ILP with Labour Party supporters in a broad-based socialist movement which could get control of the Stepney borough council, and win its three parliamentary seats, Limehouse, Mile End and Whitechapel. Tobin's aims, especially the last, had been made much more viable in the short term by the introduction in 1918 of a new constitution for the Labour Party. This made possible the formation of Labour parties in every parliamentary constituency, which could be joined by individual Labour supporters who could not, or would not, join an affiliated organization – for instance a trade union.

Tobin had a powerful ally in the Limehouse Irishman, Matt Aylward, a Roman Catholic radical trade unionist, much respected by his fellow Irish who formed a large and politically conscious element in Stepney. In 1918 Aylward, a scientific-instrument-maker by profession, and leader of the United Irish League in Limehouse, founded the Limehouse Labour Party a few weeks before Tobin founded the Mile End Labour Party. Matt Aylward led the Limehouse Irish into the Stepney borough Labour Party which Tobin formed in 1918, and under Tobin's generalship made them a unique power in Stepney politics. The Irish came into the Stepney Labour Party not as socialists but as reformers. In 1919, therefore, Tobin was the leader of a new and potentially powerful Labour Party grouping in a part of London which he declared had recently been 'the most reactionary borough in London'.

Twenty-four hours after he had been demobilized, Attlee was taken through the room at the back of the shop where Tobin kept his stock, and up to the room on the first floor in which the politically ambitious chemist held his cabinets. While Attlee smoked his pipe Tobin described with pride the new composition of Stepney Labour, and with enthusiasm the prospect of power in the East End. The success which the Limehouse Labour Party had registered in the recent elections to the Board of Guardians had shown that Jewish socialists and Irish radicals, who had been at loggerheads in the past, were now working together. The outlook for local power was consequently transformed: a majority on the borough council was in sight. After that, the capture of the constituency. Tobin proposed that Attlee should stand for one of the two Mile End seats at the next London County Council elections in two months' time. Tobin was sure he could get Attlee the nomination: he was neither Irish nor Jewish, but respected by both; he was ILP but not a pacifist; he had an excellent war record, an East End record of social service, and a private income which would give him leisure for political activities. Attlee took out his pipe, and said: 'Think it over.' Tobin said: 'I already thought it over.' '*I'll* think it over,' said Attlee, and took his leave.

That night Attlee consulted Aylward, who advised him to run for the council not for Mile End but for Limehouse, where he had lived for several years and had a strong local reputation. Attlee took his advice. He ran for the second Limehouse seat; Con Bryan, a well-known Roman Catholic trade unionist, ran for the other. Attlee was presented as a middle-class philanthropist who had sacrificed the prospect of a remunerative but unspecified career in the great world outside in order to devote himself to the East End poor, interrupting this altruistic calling only to serve his country, voluntarily, in war. Bryan won his seat, Attlee lost, but by only eighty votes. He was beaten by a Liberal, a local baker called Marks. But the best opinion in Limehouse was that if the Conservative candidate had not been a local parson Attlee must have won – he would have picked up the vital eighty middle-class-reformist 'be-good-to-the-poor' and the 'King and Country' votes. Attlee's conduct during the campaign made a favourable impression on Aylward, who immediately proposed him as parliamentary candidate at the next general election.

There was opposition. The ILP admired Attlee personally, but several were pacifists who thought that by volunteering to fight Attlee had shown himself a 'deviationist'. Some of the trade unionists on the constituency committee, representing comparatively well-to-do workers of conservative outlook, did not care for Attlee's socialist principles, suggested he might be an 'intellectual' and doubted the wisdom of nominating a man who spoke with an 'Oxford accent'. Because Tobin was known to favour Attlee, some of the Irish opposed him. They wanted Con Bryan as the candidate. Aylward argued that as a political representative Attlee was more 'trustworthy' than the middle-class socialist doctrinaires now soliciting working-class constituencies for parliamentary nominations. Attlee was a gentleman. Con Bryan's tongue had made many enemies; Attlee had none. He had used his private income to help the socialist cause in the East End; he was able to give more time to public work than the rest of them could afford; he had promised to contribute his war service gratuity to the campaign fund for the coming general election. He would be immune to the temptations of the perks of office. He did not drink, or drab or damn. Finally, he was working on a book, *The Social Worker*, to be published in the next few months, which could establish him as a man of intellectual stature.

Aylward got his way. Attlee was invited to stand as prospective parliamentary candidate for the Limehouse division of the borough of Stepney. Limehouse was expected to go Labour at the next parliamentary election. Attlee was delighted. At the age of thirty-six, for the first time in his life, he had a goal clear enough to be explicable to his family and friends.

Once he had been nominated he looked around for a home and headquarters in his constituency. He selected 'Norway House', a large, empty, dilapidated 'barracks of a place' a few yards off Commercial Road in a cul-de-sac behind the old Limehouse Free Library, where the children's library stands today. The railway ran almost below the back-bedroom window, and fifty yards away, beyond the coal wharfs, was the river. The house had once belonged to a well-to-do merchant. He had sold the lease cheaply to the local Tories and at one time the premises had been used as a Conservative club. Attlee took the lease. He handed over the use of the ground floor to the Limehouse Labour Party for their headquarters, complete with canteen, table tennis, card tables, and a three-quarter-size billiard table. He converted the first floor into a flat for himself, and made another flat on the second floor.

Behind the house was a small garden and two stables. One of these he let to a local Limehouse Labour Party costermonger at a rock-bottom price, the other to a Tory butcher, at the top of the market. The bedroom had a good view on to the Thames, though on warm summer days, when he wanted to open his windows, dust floated in from the coal wharfs. The noise of the engines and the shunting of trucks did not disturb him – 'too busy by day, too tired by night'. He paid a local builder to repair the roof and make the structural alterations; the minor jobs he did himself. His sitting room was 'quite jolly – brown paper with white paint and an Adam fireplace'. Watched by his devoted housekeeper 'Griff', Charlie Griffiths, a former member of the Haileybury Club, he spent hours kneeling on the hearth, late at night, pipe firmly clenched between his teeth, chipping patiently away at the paint put on by the previous occupants. 'Fine fireplace, Griff! Trust the Tories to put paint on it.'

The day was a full one. Griff called him at seven, ran his bath and gave him his breakfast, a boiled egg, marmalade and toast, and tea. He would scan the newspapers, growl imprecations against further evidence of the incompetence of the Conservatives and the duplicity of the Liberals, and then, with 'I'm off, Griff', clatter down the uncarpeted stairs. Some days he would come in about 5.30 pm, other days Griff would not see him again until midnight, but at whatever hour he came in he seemed as fresh as when he left the house, ascending the stairs three steps at a time, 'except when he had dysentery'. During the first two years, he had several attacks, usually lasting for four or five days – 'a few times he was lying there like death', Griff recalled, 'and once I thought he was a goner and ran round for the doctor':

> When they knew he was back in the house, people would get in to see him, with their troubles. Women about the rent. 'Pull up the fire, mother. Pot of tea, Griff. Now, stop crying, mother.' Often as not it would be the same story: father out of work, mother behind with the rent, one of the kids ill, a daughter pregnant, perhaps, son pinched by the police for nicking coal. . . . If he had a bit of time to spare after his tea, he'd light his pipe, and say 'hundred up, Griff?' and we'd go down to the billiard table. He was very hot. He didn't like to lose. He'd have given you the shirt off his back, but when he played billiards, he played to win. He was a cunning devil; he'd never leave a thing.
>
> They all knew about him. You could be in a Limehouse pub and run down the Tories, and you could run down the Labour Party, but if you ran down the Major, somebody might come up and give you the old one-two.

It would be interesting to know what his Fabian colleagues, living comfortably in Bloomsbury, made of this rentier living in a 'barracks of a place' backing on to a coal wharf, and what some of his Limehouse supporters thought of an ILP agitator who went to his mother's bourgeois home in Putney at the weekend and had his morning bath run by his manservant.

In November 1919, Attlee came to greater prominence as campaign manager for the Stepney Labour Party in its bid to win power in the borough elections – Aylward had vetoed a move by Tobin to make him a candidate, on the grounds that his duty was to nurse the parliamentary constituency. Labour, which had never before held a seat on the Stepney council, took forty-three seats out of sixty. In Limehouse, Attlee's own ground, Labour won fifteen seats out of fifteen. The East London land-slide may have owed more to the nationwide swing towards Labour than it did to the zeal or ingenuity of Tobin and Aylward, or to the hearty invectives of Attlee's manifesto. But Attlee had his share of glory. The coup in Stepney, and in particular in the Limehouse parliamentary constituency, was noticed everywhere in the Labour Party. In London Labour circles, where a strong force of socialist MPs in the national Parliament was regarded as the next objective, Attlee was seen as one of the prototypes of the desirable candidate: well-to-do middle-class intellectual, committed socialist, but neither Marxist nor pacifist, involved but disinterested, sober, respectable, trusted. This was the kind of standard-bearer that would enable the up-and-coming Labour Party to replace the Liberals as the alternative to the Tories.

The first business of the new Stepney borough council was to appoint a mayor. Attlee was again the beneficiary of a situation in which there was a need for compromise. Labour leaders in each of the three divisions of Stepney had equal claims to influence the choice. In Whitechapel, the biggest division, with thirty seats out of sixty on the council, the power of the Labour contingent was divided between immigrant Irish Catholics, working in various trades, members of a variety of unions, dominating about two-thirds of the seats; and Protestant members of the Transport and General Workers' Union, mainly dockers and drivers, who dominated the remainder. In Mile End, Tobin's citadel, with fifteen seats, the power was with the Jewish garment workers. In Limehouse, Attlee's ground, which had won fifteen seats out of fifteen at the election, the ILP minority had now established an excellent working relationship with the Irish.

The ILP leaders in Limehouse were a sober lot, most of them Christians and all of them 'decent'; they got on well with the Irish Roman Catholics. Of the three Labour blocs in Stepney, Limehouse was the most cohesive and consequently the strongest. In a tussle with the Labour parties of the other two divisions it could usually get its way. Attlee had served the borough well in recent elections and they pushed his claims. Aylward argued that, besides his other qualifications, Attlee would stand a better chance of getting the Tory minority on his side. He got his way. Attlee, at the age of thirty-six, was appointed the first Labour mayor of Stepney, while also prospective Labour candidate for Limehouse. A Labour Party aspirant to national politics could not have wished for a better start.

Aylward was quite right when he predicted that Attlee as mayor would get at least some of the Tories on his side. An anonymous former London mayor, a Conservative, was quoted in the *East London Observer* as saying: 'Now the one thing I do admire them for is their choice of leader ... they couldn't have found a better man. He's a thorough gentleman, you see, and that's what goes in the East End.'

As a school for a future Labour leader, destined later to preside over a coalition of often conflicting attitudes and interests, the mayoralty of Stepney could not have been bettered. The main cause of the troubles was the friction between the Irish and the Jews, mainly about the allocation of borough funds. In Whitechapel some streets were largely Jewish, and others were filled with Irish; discussions about, for instance, which street was to be the first beneficiary of better lighting or paving was frequently sectarian. Racial feeling was involved: the Irish were not antisemitic, but they were religious; most of the Jews on the council were agnostic. The Irish were trade unionists whose attitude to politics was empirical; they thought of themselves as 'Labour'. The Jews were individualistic workers, sometimes owning their own small shops; yet they were more doctrinaire in their politics; they thought of themselves as 'Socialist'. The ILP men, largely English, thought the Irish too conservative and the Jews too doctrinaire. So: 'The year that followed was one of very hard work and gave me a great deal of useful experience ... some diplomacy was needed to get harmonious working.'

Feuding notwithstanding, the Stepney borough council threw itself into its work with vigour. Its legal powers were limited, but it appointed many more sanitary inspectors, made a complete survey of the borough, served over 40,000 legal notices on house-owners to repair their property, and followed up to see that these were enforced. Infant mortality had been high: the council instituted health visitors and antenatal clinics, and brought the death-rate down – in eighteen months it was one of the lowest in London. They set up advice bureaux for tenants on their rights under the Rent Restriction Acts and so 'got many thousands of pounds out of the clutches of slum landlords'. During 1920, when the five-yearly valuation of property in the borough came due, the Valuation Committee, of which Attlee was chairman, called in professional valuers and added over £200,000 to the borough's rateable value without increasing the assessment of residential property. Building programmes and street improvement schemes created work for the growing numbers of unemployed in Stepney. The rates went up to over twenty shillings in the pound, but the horrified protests of the landlords and businessmen did not disturb the sleep of Stepney's mayor.

It was the unemployment problem, caused by the collapse of the postwar boom, which gave the young mayor of Stepney his first, quite modest ration of national publicity. Herbert Morrison, the young Hackney Labour leader who was secretary of the London Labour Party, had formed an Association of London Labour Mayors. As a result of the borough council election of November 1919, fifteen of London's twenty-eight metropolitan councils had Labour mayors. The new mayor of Stepney was asked to become chairman. He was also invited on to the executive committee of the London Labour Party, an elevation which immediately raised his status within the national party, and multiplied his contacts with Labour MPs all over the country. Taking advantage of this, and encouraged and guided by the veteran Lansbury, Attlee called a National Conference of Mayors and Provosts to be held in London at Shoreditch Town Hall. Resolutions by Lansbury and others were discussed and carried.

The Lord Mayor of London now invited the twenty-eight metropolitan mayors to the Mansion House, and outlined what Attlee considered 'some mild measures' to deal with the unemployment problem – his concern, like that of the Conservative and Liberal mayors, being less in creating work than in reducing the burden of relief measures on rates.

Traditionally when the Lord Mayor had made a speech there was an exchange of compliments and everybody went home. On this occasion Attlee broke the precedents and 'made a forcible appeal for more vigorous measures'. His fifteen fellow Labour mayors also asked leave to speak, each of them holding forth on similar lines, this mayoral sit-in being 'rather to the consternation of the City Fathers'.

The only other occasion on which Mayor Attlee of Stepney received some notice outside London was as leader of a deputation of London mayors to press the needs of the unemployed upon the Prime Minister at Number Ten.

This encounter with the Prime Minister – 'one of the most exciting events of my mayoral year' – was spectacular. The unemployed of London, largely ex-servicemen, were assembled by their mayors and led, borough by borough, to converge upon the Embankment, where the battalions were to be stationed while their commanders went on to Downing Street. Attlee, having led the Stepney contingent in from Mile End Waste, led the posse of mayors to Downing Street, looking most soldierly with his erect bearing, heavy moustache, and infantry officer's walking stick. What happened to the men on the Embankment after their mayors had disappeared into Number Ten is not clear, but when the disgruntled mayors re-emerged – Lloyd George 'had very little to offer' – they found that some of the marchers had broken ranks and had appeared in Whitehall, and that mounted police were trying to control an angry crowd, which included 'rough elements determined to provoke a riot'. George Lansbury tried to make a speech, explaining what the demonstration was about, but Attlee hurried to the Embankment: 'I found the Stepney contingent marching down Bridge Street in perfect order with a police sergeant at its head, about to be led into the scrimmage. I ordered the column to halt and turn about, and led them back to Stepney, thus saving some broken heads.'

His book, *The Social Worker*, was published towards the conclusion of his mayoral year. Readable, pithy, workmanlike, based on his own experiences and supported by personal anecodotes rather than case studies, it was intended to be read by people coming into social work from a middle-class background, and was not political. In the early pages of the book he attacks the Victorian conception of 'charity' as the panacea for the problems of poverty. He does so not only on practical but on spiritual grounds. Conventional religious 'charity' applied itself to effects and ignored causes. It was concerned more with the effect of good works on the souls of those who gave than on what happened to those who received. There was 'a hellish corruption' in this notion of 'charity': the rich, with the means of giving, *needed* the poor to receive, in order to ease their sense of guilt. Far from presenting a Marxist interpretation of the evils of contemporary society, the book has a moral approach to the problem which might have come straight out of St Paul, and an aesthetic one which could have come out of Ruskin.

In the same year Attlee sat on an informal committee which aimed to get advanced 'workers control' into the ILP manifesto. This marked the beginning, and apparently the end, of Attlee's interest in Guild Socialism, a programme devised by the young Oxford don G. D. H. Cole to circumvent the daunting obstacles to the parliamentary achievement of socialism by direct, but gradual, action in industry. Unions or other organizations of workers would take over the functions of employers piecemeal, acquire the ownership of industry and thereafter control of the state. Guild socialism represented an attempt to strike a balance between William Morris's utopian socialism of the workshop and the more drastic systematic syndicalism advocated in France before the First World War by Georges Sorel, who urged the working class to destroy the capitalist state by the political use of the general strike. Even this compromise made little headway in the Labour Party: leading trade unionists like Bevin preferred to bargain within the capitalist system as it was, while the leaders of the PLP identified guild socialism with syndicalism and revolution. The more militant guild socialists joined the British Communist Party when it was formed in the summer of 1920, and the movement dissolved. There seems to be no evidence that Attlee maintained an interest in the industrial route to socialism, and in later years he maintained rigorously that Parliament must be the unchallenged authority in a democratic state.

His mayoral year ended in November 1920. 'Very full – went like lightning. Rather tiring.' The importance of the year for Attlee was the first-hand knowledge it gave him of the day-to-day workings of municipal government and the direct personal contact with the men and women who lived in Stepney's back streets. He gained this as chairman of the Valuation Committee; council representative on three Whitley councils; on the Electricity Board and on the Metropolitan Boroughs Standing Joint Committee; vice chairman of the London and Home Counties Conference of Local Authorities; Justice of the Peace; and member of the Board of Guardians, of three hospital committees, and of the governing bodies of four schools.

Just before his mayoral year ended, Attlee had a stroke of luck which transformed him from a respected spokesman into something of a political boss in his own right. He became an alderman. The aldermen were elected by the borough councillors. They held office for five years. Their prestige, their long tenure of office, and the fact that they were elected not by popular vote but by the wheeling and dealing of sixty politicians, gave them a very firm base, from which they could exert influence and dispense patronage. They stood a very good chance of being re-elected for another five years. When he ceased to be mayor, Attlee might well have become an admired, respected and affectionately remembered bird of passage, especially since he was known to be on his way to a precarious seat in the House of Commons, and since – though this was not yet known – he was going to move his residence from the East End to marry a woman who did not want to live there. Alderman Brennan died a week or two before the mayoral term came to an end; Attlee was elected to the vacant seat. It could not have come at a more useful moment: it gave him a secure long-term base in the power structure of the London Labour Party, by far the most important socialist concentration in the country.

The mayoral year had brought about other, more personal, changes in his life. He had been exposed to a degree of publicity he had never experienced. He had to come to grips with the attitudes of old friends, neighbours and wartime comrades. He knew he was spoken about as a traitor to his class. 'What upset some of them was not so much that I marched with the workers but that I preferred their company.' In May, his mother died of cancer. Her death hit him hard. He had always gone home to Putney at weekends when he was not speaking or campaigning, and even when under pressure would try and get down for lunch or tea on Sundays. The old home at Putney was broken up. The house was sold. His breaks from the strenuous life in Stepney, walking on the banks of the Thames, came to an end.

In the midst of the bustle of his public life he began to feel very lonely. His friend Jack Lawder, sitting with him in the flat at Norway House one night, asked: 'Why don't you get married?' Attlee looked into his Adam fireplace, puffed at his pipe and said nothing. Lawder thought: 'Perhaps he's not the marrying sort.' The loneliness had been there before; with his mother's death it deepened. He was ready for his one and only romance. He was as lucky in his personal life as he had been in his political career. What he needed came just at the right time.

II

The strenuous year as mayor, followed by the death of his mother, left Attlee feeling tired. He decided that he would take a holiday, his first since coming out of the Army three years previously. When Tom mentioned that Cedric Millar wanted to go to Italy again, Attlee said he would like to join him. When Cedric told him he was bringing his mother and his youngest sister Violet, he did not demur. He had met Mrs Millar several times, and liked her. He had seen Violet only once, just after the war, when Cedric asked some of the Attlees to tea. When he greeted Vi on the platform of Victoria Station in the late summer of 1921, therefore, she was almost a stranger to him: a very attractive one; large blue eyes, radiant smile, slim, bright, a little shy, and agreeably deferential. He was thirty-seven; she was twenty-four.

Violet Millar was born in Hampstead in 1896. She and her twin sister Olive were the youngest children of a family of eleven. Henry Millar was a well-to-do export and import merchant with a comfortable house on Hampstead Heath overlooking the Vale of Health. The children were as strictly brought up as the Attlees, and like the Attlees they had enjoyed a happy, large-family childhood; cheerful, comfortable winters in the warm home on the heath and long summer holidays at Nevin, on the Caernarvonshire coast. Unlike the Attlees, the Millars were not brought up in a tradition of social work. They produced gifted civil servants rather than welfare workers.

As a child Vi had felt overshadowed by her twin sister Olive, who had been 'much taller than I was, and about two years older mentally and physically'. She found her situation disturbing and sometimes rebelled against it. 'As I couldn't shine, I suppose I got the limelight by being naughty. I remember once when I was young and had been very tiresome, my mother, instead of being cross with me, held out her arms and said: "Come into the drawing-room with me." I remember still the gratitude which filled my heart, and think this memory helped me when dealing with my own children when they were troublesome.' Her health was not robust. Good at games, she relied for her success on nervous energy, not physical. She got tired quickly, often felt out of sorts, 'not able to cope'. There were occasions when she woke up in the middle of the night, screaming from nightmares, and once or twice she walked in her sleep. In her adolescence she suffered from bouts of sudden fatigue. She grew up a 'good' girl, but not altogether a happy one. When she left school before the First World War, she decided to 'stay at home and be with mother'. Her twin went to Newnham College Cambridge, was an academic and a social success, and at the age of twenty married a most eligible young naval officer, later Admiral of the Fleet Sir Algernon Willis. While Olive dazzled in Cambridge, Vi worked as a wartime nurse in a convalescent hospital in Hampstead.

When Cedric Millar was contemplating the Italian tour, Vi was living at home, looking after her mother, who had been ill for some months: it was for Mrs Millar's benefit that Cedric had planned the expedition. The holiday lasted five weeks. It had been assumed that the two women would spend most of their time sitting in the shade admiring the vistas, while the two men would walk around the galleries. In the event, it was Vi and Attlee who did the walking, and Cedric who sat in the shade with Mrs Millar, Vi observing demurely: 'I knew no Italian history, and history was Clem's subject, so he and I were frequently together.' They travelled mainly in Tuscany and Umbria, with a detour via Rimini, recommended by Attlee, so that he could take Vi to see Dante's tomb.

In the train from Rimini that night, he and Vi sat opposite each other. Mrs Millar and Cedric were soon asleep. Attlee and Vi talked long into the night about Dante, then Vi also went to sleep. Attlee read the newspapers. The train rattled on towards the Lakes. In the small hours Vi woke up, and through lidded eyes looked across at Attlee. Thinking she was still asleep, he was gazing at her. 'That was when I thought he might be in love with me,' she told her daughter Felicity, thirty years later. 'Of course, *I* was in love with *him* already.' He was indeed in love with her by then. He thought she was divine. She was not only very pretty; now that she was no longer shy with him, she was vivacious. But she was also serious. She listened to everything he had to say with a naïve respect which he found relaxing. He was flattered to feel that this lovely girl might reciprocate his feelings.

The idea of marriage appealed to him strongly. Not only had he felt lonely living in Norway House, but when he was mayor he had many times thought that his public life would be much more agreeable if he were married. Vi knew nothing of public life or politics. No matter: wives with political views could be a nuisance. But Vi's family background was Conservative. Before his relationship with her could progress, he must be sure that she knew what being a Socialist meant. 'I was just a street-corner agitator. I had thought it only fair that she should see me orating from a platform on Hampstead Heath before I proposed, so that she might know the worst.' So in his first letter to her, written two days after they returned from Italy, he told her that he would be speaking at an open-air meeting on the Heath the following Sunday; if she cared to go up to the Heath and listen to him she would be very welcome.

Vi accepted. Her new admirer's socialism was far indeed from her experience. Attlee was at this moment deeply involved in the attack on the government's new contributory insurance scheme. It was no more than a palliative for unemployment, and the method of financing it threw burdens on the working-class boroughs of the East End. The scheme imposed a time limit for the drawing of benefits, after which the responsibility for relief was to go back to the local guardians under the Poor Law, which meant further increases in the rates. The metropolitan rating system threw a disproportionate share of the costs of unemployment relief on the highly populated poor boroughs of the East, while the rich boroughs of the West got off very lightly. This anomaly pressed down hardest on the reforming socialist mayors, since budgets for housing, health and educational programmes had to be cut back to release funds for the increasing cost of unemployment benefit.

Under the scheme, the unemployment relief fund was administered not by the boroughs separately but by the London County Council as a whole. In Poplar, Lansbury and his council announced that they would not pay the borough's contributions to the LCC's unemployment fund. The LCC brought an action against the borough of Poplar, and won. Lansbury and the members of his council were sent to prison. They were soon released, and in due course the rate burden in London was more fairly distributed, 'Poplarism' thenceforward becoming a term for local defiance of central 'tyranny'. Attlee supported Lansbury, and voted on Stepney council in favour of following his lead. To the *Daily Herald* on 26 September 1921 he wrote: 'I have always been a constitutionalist but the time has come when it is necessary to kick.' The theme of his speeches was defiance of an unjust law, and this was probably his subject when Vi heard him speak in Hampstead.

But Attlee the agitator did not put her off Attlee the aesthete. Her next letter to him, on 4 October, begins: 'My dear Clement, Please don't go to prison.' It is not an intimate letter, and the most personal sentiment it contains is: 'I'm sorry your weekends are lonely, but you can always come up here, can't you?' It is signed 'Yours, Vi' and the next letter, two days later, reverts to 'Yours ever, Vi Millar'. A few days later he asked her to go and watch a rugby match. She went. The ground was too hard for play, so they went for a walk in Richmond Park. The next letter begins 'My dear Clem,' and ends 'All my love – your sweetheart, Vi.' He had proposed to her, and had been accepted. A short swift courtship: Attlee style.

Whatever Vi thought of him as a politician, as husband-to-be she thought him perfect:

> I feel I must just write a line to you as I haven't seen you all day. . . . I have longed to have you with me for just a minute or two, and to have that lovely comforting feeling that I always have when I am in your arms – I am going to bed early tonight especially to have a nice long time to think of you. . . . Goodnight my own dear love. . . . I just long for tomorrow to see you and walk by your side and watch that adorable mouth of yours . . .

She adored him for the rest of her life. He was a lover, a cuddly dog and a father figure all in one. 'Sex problems?' she asked, incredulously, when talking to her daughter about the problems of the marital state, thirty years later. 'Clem and I didn't have any sex problems. Everything was marvellous from the start.' The record of Attlee's view of Vi, his engagement, and the marriage is confined to a letter dated 12 October written to Bernard asking him to officiate at the marriage, now arranged for the following January:

> I had only seen Vi twice before Italy – once just after the war and once a week before we went, but five weeks together is worth more than two years

of dances and weekend calls. I am sure you will both be fond of Vi but it's not much good attempting a description now. A photograph will be circulated in due course, but she does not take very well.

This letter is an amazingly sober and coherent effort for a person in my position but affords no index as to my sanity or insanity. Actually, I am as mad as a march hare with joy.

Attlee thought he should also break the news to the Limehouse Labour Party. After sitting for an hour or two in Matt Aylward's house one night, discussing the prospect of getting Tobin accepted as candidate for mayor, he suddenly said: 'By the way, I'm getting married.' Matt congratulated him. 'Local girl?' 'No. Met her on holiday.' The betrothal was noticed by several national newspapers. A caption to a photograph of him arm-in-arm with Vi read: 'An influential Labour leader in the East End, where he lives at the top of a deserted house.' The marriage took place at Christ Church, Hampstead, on 10 January 1922, the service being conducted by the family clerics, Bernard Attlee and Basil Millar. Brother Rob was best man. The honeymoon was modest: golf and walking at Abbotsbury in Dorset. They returned to 17 Monkham's Avenue, which Laurence and Letty found for them in a street adjoining their own, a semi-detached house about two hundred yards from Woodford Green Station. The door was opened by their new servant, 'dear old Mrs Gledhill', who had looked after Attlee at the Haileybury Club before the war. There began what was to become as happy a husband and wife relationship as British politics can record.

A general election was in the offing. Attlee was well placed to fight it. He was a well-established parliamentary candidate with a strong power base in his own constituency. He was making his first bid for a seat in the Commons at a time when the Labour Party had a thrilling sense of the imminence of parliamentary power. The 1918 Representation of the People Act had for the first time brought 8.5 million women on to the register, and had increased the voting roll from 7 to more than 20 million. The Liberal Party was badly weakened by the split between Lloyd George and Asquith. The choice for the new voters and for many former Liberal voters lay between Conservative and Labour, and Labour was an attractive choice not only for working-class electors but also for some of the middle class. Labour's appeal for middle- and upper-class voters had been enhanced by the foundation of the British Communist Party, which had drawn most of the revolutionaries out of the Labour Movement. Labour had become respectable.

The Lloyd George coalition collapsed in October 1922. So many of the election promises of 1918 had been dishonoured that his downfall had seemed only a matter of time. The scandal of the sale of honours, especially in the Birthday Honours List of 1922, which King George v called 'an insult to the Crown and to the House of Lords', had shocked public opinion. On the home front there was high unemployment and industrial unrest; abroad, there were continual conferences but no significant results. In August Lloyd George made a final and fatal attempt to restore his wartime prestige by siding with the Greeks against Turkey's new dictator, Kemal Ataturk. Disregarding the advice of his generals and of most members of his Cabinet, he brought Britain to the brink of war with Turkey. Hostilities were averted, but the crisis created a mood in which national excitement, euphoria and desperation were curiously mingled. Lloyd George's decision to call a general election released the pent-up dissatisfaction of the Conservative backbenchers. At the Carlton Club meeting on 19 October they voted by 187 to 87 to withdraw from the coalition. Lloyd George resigned, Bonar Law undertook to form a Conservative government, and the general election was set for the following month, 15 November 1922.

Attlee's opponent, the sitting member for Limehouse, was still the well-liked and respected local businessman Sir William Pearce, who had held the seat as a Liberal since 1906. It was a sign of the times that Pearce now stood for Limehouse with the official support of the Conservative Party. Attlee's election address was terse:

> The coalition is dead, and with its passing comes the opportunity for the electors to pass judgement on those who have betrayed their trust. The Tories and the Liberals ... have parted company in order to deceive you once more ... the real contest is between Capital and Labour. Like many of you I took part in the Great War in the hope of securing lasting peace and a better life for all. We were promised that wars should end, that ... the men who fought in the War would be cared for, and that unemployment, slums and poverty would be abolished. I stand for *life against wealth*. I claim the right of every man, woman and child in the land to have the best life that can be provided. Instead of the exploitation of the mass of the people in the interests of a small rich class, I demand the organisation of the country in the interests of all as a co-operative commonwealth in which land and capital will be owned by the nation and used for the benefit of the community.

He attacked the late government vigorously for its record on unemployment, housing ('a disgrace to a Christian country'), foreign affairs ('the Peace Treaties must be scrapped'), and the redistribution of wealth ('a levy on capital will relieve the taxpayer and lower prices'). Finally, 'I demand for the people of Limehouse the right to live.' The result was:

Attlee, Major C. R. (Lab) 9,688
Pearce, Sir W. (NL)   7,789

Labour Majority   1,899

To dispossess the popular Sir William of the seat which he had held for sixteen years was a noteworthy achievement, even though Labour had done well all over London. The Labour candidate – Charlie Mathew – had won in Whitechapel, and in Mile End, the other Stepney divison, the Labour candidate, John Scurr, lost by only 800 votes. In the country as a whole the Labour Party had won 142 seats. The Conservatives had 345 seats, a majority of 77 over other parties combined.

This was Vi's first experience of campaigning. Before meeting Attlee she had shown little interest in public affairs. 'She plays tennis and golf, we hear,' observed Laurence Attlee, 'and is not political.' Before the announcement of the general election, for which her lover was longing, she had asked, as though inquiring about the prospect of bad weather for her January wedding: 'Do you think the general election will come soon? I do hope it will keep off until after January.' Nevertheless she had entered his political life from the first days of the marriage. Her political views were the same on election night in Limehouse as they were on the day of her death. Socialism she thought about only to the extent that she vaguely disapproved of it. She had never met a socialist until she fell in love with Attlee, and she could never understand why it was necessary for him to be labelled as one. Reforms were necessary to remedy poverty and injustice, and she saw no reason why reasonable Conservatives could not support people like her husband who were trying to effect them.

'Most of our friends are Conservatives,' Vi said to the author once in the late 1950s. 'Clem was never really a socialist, were you, darling?' Attlee, sitting next to her reading *The Times*, pipe in mouth, made a mildly dissenting noise. 'Well, not a rabid one,' she said. And that, she obviously thought, was that. In the Labour Party her shyness protected her, and the warmth behind it made her friends. She had two great natural gifts which were evident immediately: she loved children, especially babies, with a spontaneous affection entirely free from sentimentality; and, possibly because of her illnesses in her youth, she showed great compassion for the sick. She soon had a reputation in her own right.

Vi's first election campaign came too soon for her health. Longing to support her husband, and anxious to impress his friends, she stood on wet street corners, sat in draughty halls, pounded the pavements, knocked on doors, canvassed housewives, and overtaxed herself. She was now six months pregnant. When, after the result was declared, a horse and cart came to the town hall to bear the victorious major through the streets, Vi's doctor forbade her to accompany him. She was loaded with flowers, taken home in a taxi, and put to bed. From then on she had an uncomfortable time until Janet was born three months later.

4
The New Member,
1922-4

I

On the morning of his first day in the House of Commons, Attlee wrote to his brother Rob:

> We are very pleased with the results, which have given us a fine fighting force. We shall have the best intellects of the party in the House now, MacDonald, Trevelyan, Webb, Snowden, Buxton, etc. . . .

There had been a marked change in the class structure of the Parliamentary Labour Party as a result of the general election. In the previous Parliament nearly all the Labour MPs were of working-class origin, and all but three were trade unionists. In the new House of Commons the trade unionists numbered only 80 out of 142, and upper-class as well as middle-class MPs sat on the Labour benches for the first time. Most of the new Labour members were almost as new to the party as to the House. They had joined the Labour Party after the war, in protest against the policy of the coalition government, especially against Lloyd George's conduct of foreign affairs. A number of them had formerly been Liberals. They had joined the Labour Party not in support of the socialists but in opposition to the Conservatives. Among the 1922 middle-class Labour MPs, therefore, Attlee was in a sense a veteran.

In the new House, Labour was led by Ramsay MacDonald, who narrowly defeated J. R. Clynes in the leadership election. Attlee voted for MacDonald. He was still an ardent ILP man, and MacDonald was the ILP idol. MacDonald's pacifism did not deter him; after all, his brother had been sent to gaol for the same offence. He admired the courage MacDonald had shown in openly opposing the war when the official leadership of the party under Henderson had supported it and had joined the government to help wage it. In 1922, to disillusioned ex-servicemen like Attlee, it was MacDonald who seemed to have been right

57

about Labour and the war: that year Attlee was himself publicly renouncing war as an instrument of policy and calling on Labour to refuse
to 'put arms into the hands of the capitalists'.

Aware of Attlee's standing with the ILP on one hand, and with the
middle-class and trade union contingent on the other, MacDonald appointed him one of his two parliamentary private secretaries. The other
was the Durham miner, Jack Lawson. This was the beginning of a long
personal friendship between Attlee and Lawson, which became the basis
of an important long-term political relationship. It led to an association
between the Durham miners and Attlee which in years to come gave him
an additional power base. It continued into Attlee's last days as leader of
the party through Lawson's protégé Sam Watson, who was later to become
General Secretary of the Durham miners and in the fifties the most
powerful trade unionist on the Labour Party's National Executive. Attlee
was devoted to Lawson. Jack Lawson, Arthur Jenkins and Arthur Moyle,
he said in his old age, were the most unselfish men he had ever met in
politics.

The newly elected Parliament met on 20 November, five days after the
election. It was an obstreperous House, its tone set by working-class
socialists in the ILP like David Kirkwood, who had shouted to the crowd
who thronged to see him off at Glasgow Central Station: 'When we come
back, this station, this railway, will belong to the people.' This style
embarrassed MacDonald, who wished the Labour Party to look like an
alternative government, and it annoyed many Labour backbenchers.
During the debate on the Gracious Speech, Kirkwood and his Clydeside
colleagues monopolized the discussion, plugging unemployment in Scotland. The Speaker, realizing that the House was getting restive, decided
he must change the bowling. Some other representatives of the Labour
Party must speak, with different accents and on other subjects. He in-
timated this to Charles Ammon, the London Labour MPs' Whip, who saw
Attlee enter the Chamber at that moment. Attlee agreed to be called next.

This was a remarkable opportunity for a new member who might have
waited weeks to make his maiden speech. Ammon had told him that the
suffering and injustice of unemployment had already been described by
a succession of Clydesiders, and the government backbenchers, having
had enough, were shouting back noisily, more from boredom than hostility. Attlee, therefore, instantly decided to make a speech which he
thought might appeal to public-spirited Conservatives:

> There is one particular waste that is never mentioned, and that is the waste
> of the man-power of this nation. When I throw my mind back to the war
> period, I remember how we were told that every man in this country was
> valuable, how we were told that every man was wanted either in munitions
> or in the trenches – men of every character, men of every capability. ...

The only time when unemployment was practically non-existent was the time of the war; and despite all the rationing, despite all the food substitutes, on the whole the living conditions of our people were actually better during the war period.

Unlike the Clydesiders, he did not attack; he simply asked for the sympathy and understanding of the enlightened members opposite, referring in particular to Nancy Astor, the first woman MP, with whom ever after he had a friendly relationship. Lady Astor, he said, had properly stressed:

.... the intimate way in which housing is bound up with morality. We know it very well down our way. We know, too, the results of the census, which showed that in our area alone there are 600,000 persons who are living in one-room tenements. You are not going to get a moral nation under those conditions.

But his mildness had the steel of socialism in it:

Why was it that in the war we were able to find employment for everyone? It was simply that the Government controlled the purchasing power of the nation. They said what things should be produced; they said, 'We must have munitions of war. We must have rifles; we must have machine-guns; we must have saddles.' They took, by means of taxation and by methods of loan, control of the purchasing power into making those things that were necessary for winning the war.

That is what we are demanding shall be done in time of peace. As the nation was organised for war and death, so it can be organised for peace and life if we have the will for it.

The speech went down well with the Labour Party, especially with the Clydesiders, because it was about unemployment, and it was well received by the Conservatives. It did not go down so well with the long-suffering Speaker, who had wanted one of the new Labour MPs to talk about something else.

Attlee began his personal association with MacDonald in the 1922 Parliament with high hopes and no doubts. He saw MacDonald as a giant of the Labour Movement, as a prophet and statesman, a combination of William Morris and Keir Hardie. Decades after he had been disillusioned about MacDonald as a political leader, he reminisced about his magnificent voice, the grace and richness of his language, his noble presence. It never occurred to him that the brave pacifist might not be a bold radical.

It was not long before MacDonald's faithful began to have their doubts. MacDonald believed he had two missions to carry out and that unless he succeeded quickly the socialist cause would be lost. One was to persuade his party that social progress could best be achieved through Parliament. The other was to persuade the country that Labour was fit to govern. Meanwhile the Clydesiders on the back benches, ignoring their leader's aspirations, ranted revolution and roared out personal insults across the floor of the House. MacDonald winced, fumed, and inwardly disowned them. He began to confide to his friends, especially middle-class members like Attlee, his fears that many of his colleagues, lieutenants as well as rank and file, had neither the ability nor the character to win the respect of the electorate. Attlee did not relish hearing MacDonald's strictures about the manners of the working class. Disloyalty was a high crime in Attlee's book. Next to it came disparagement. Writing many years after, he recorded: 'He had no idea of treating his colleagues properly. He used to recall to me the contempt he had for his colleagues. I thought it was quite wrong. I was only his PPS.' At this time Attlee saw all this only as a blemish in a man for whom otherwise he retained profound respect. He did not suspect that a day would come when he would speak of MacDonald as a traitor to the cause.

For Attlee personally 1923 was a busy year. Halfway through he had to resign his post at the LSE. As a parliamentary private secretary his main job was to find out what the members of the party were thinking and communicate this to his master. MacDonald did not listen much to what the party thought of him, but he spoke very freely about what he thought of the party. Attlee's first year in the House, therefore, was a rare course of instruction in the internal politics of the Parliamentary Labour Party. His contribution to his party's fortunes was hardly noticeable. He stood with the left wing of the ILP on disarmament. At its annual conference in June, a resolution was tabled to the effect that the Labour Party in Parliament should, as a continuing policy, vote against all military and naval estimates. Henderson and most senior leaders of the ILP denounced the resolution; Attlee spoke uncompromisingly in favour. He said he realized a small army would meantime have to be retained – cries of 'Oh, oh', according to *The Times* – but there was a difference between a temporary arrangement while they were engaged in the task of abolishing armaments, and supporting arms for a government to whose policy the Labour Party was opposed – a view which was to become a much impugned feature of Labour Party policy in the thirties. In 1923, however, it found little favour: the resolution was easily defeated.

Home life began to impose some unfamiliar burdens on him. Janet was delivered successfully and punctually in February 1923, but Vi took a long time to get over the birth, and then became quite ill. The doctors said she should not have any more children. She became tense and tearful. One doctor suggested that she was over-anxious to be of help to her husband; she should take things more easily. In the spring she went to a clinic at Kings Langley, where, she recorded later, she was 'taught to relax'. In the autumn she was herself again, but did not adjust easily to marriage and motherhood. Attlee's first three years of home life, coinciding with his first three years in the House – and three general elections – were not easy.

Within six months of the election of 1922 the stage was being set for the election of 1923. In May Baldwin became Prime Minister in place of Bonar Law, now a sick man. Baldwin typified a feeling in party and country that 'tranquillity and economy', sought by decent, solid men, was preferable to the adventures of men like Lloyd George, who might have genius but also might lack character. Attlee had no regard for Lloyd George because he thought him untrustworthy. Bonar Law he did not have the chance of assessing. Baldwin he admired for his humane attitude to industrial relations, and his considerate manner to Labour members of Parliament. Baldwin believed profoundly that a spirit of reconciliation and cooperation could and should dispel class conflict. If his approach was paternalistic it did not seem the worse for that to the former manager of the Haileybury Boys' Club. Above all Baldwin wanted to persuade the country to accept the idea of partnership as the basis of the employer-worker relationship. He held, to the annoyance of some of his colleagues, that a party based on Labour had as much claim to govern as a party based on ownership. These beliefs he exemplified in the House by the courtesy with which he treated the Opposition. To Attlee 'he always seemed more at home with our people, particularly the older trade union people, than with his own lot.'

The outstanding problem was unemployment, standing in 1923 at the unprecedented level of 1,300,000. Baldwin offered a solution which took the country – and most of his party – by surprise. Consulting with only a few of his colleagues he came to the conclusion that unemployment could be dealt with only by the introduction of tariffs to protect the home manufacturer. This sudden reversion to the policy which had so grievously weakened the Tories at elections before 1914 astonished many of his followers. In December 1923 he called a general election; whether to anticipate Lloyd George, who was rumoured to have been converted to protection, or to restore the historic unity of his party even at the cost of an election defeat, is not certain. Free Trade was the dominant issue in the election, and the two Free Trade parties, Labour and Liberal, each made gains. Labour, polling 4.4 million votes, held all but 16 of the seats won in 1922, and gained 63 new seats, bringing their total to 191. The Liberals, polling 4.3 million votes, won 159 seats. With 5.5 million votes the Conservatives held 258 seats, a minority in the House of Commons.

In Limehouse the Liberals did not put up a candidate, so Attlee's only opponent was a Conservative called Miller Jones, 'a pleasant man' (as Attlee recalls in his autobiography) but without 'much platform ability'. A feature of the campaign was an agreement by both party managers that their candidates would from the same platform address an assembly of those men and women in the constituency who were out of work. Miller Jones created an uproar at this meeting by getting up and beginning his speech with: 'I know nothing of politics or economics.' His admission reverberated around the constituency. Attlee won impressively. His majority, 1,899 in November 1922, rose to 6,185 in December 1923. Labour also won the other two Stepney seats. The number of Labour MPs for the Greater London area rose from 16 to 37.

This was the first time that Parliament was divided so inconclusively between three parties. No constitutional precedent for such a situation existed. It was the strength of the Labour Party in so divided a House of Commons that most disturbed its critics. It was clear that the Labour Party might be asked to form a government, either on its own or in association with the Liberals. The *Daily Mail*, the City, and many prominent politicians clamoured for an anti-socialist alliance. Winston Churchill, who had stood as a Liberal at West Leicester and had been defeated, declared: 'The enthronement in office of a Socialist Government will be a serious national misfortune such as has usually befallen great states only on the morrow of defeat in war.' By contrast, most responsible Conservative and Liberal leaders expressed far more realistic views. Neville Chamberlain thought that an anti-socialist alliance would only strengthen the Labour Party: it should be given office because it would be 'too weak to do much harm, but not too weak to get discredited' – a prognosis which he could later claim was justified by events. Asquith told the Parliamentary Liberal Party a fortnight after the election: 'Whoever may be for the time being the incumbents of office, it is we, if we understand our business, who really control the situation. ... If a Labour Government is ever to be tried in this country, as it will be sooner or later, it could hardly be tried under safer conditions.'

As the largest of the two parties which had defeated the Conservatives, Labour was entitled to form the next government. Would the Labour leaders be willing to take office under these conditions? Their success had come as a complete surprise to them. The idea of a coalition with the Liberals was considered, but was quickly discarded. Several prominent Labour men were against taking office whether with or without the support of the Liberals. MacDonald, Snowden, Clynes, Thomas, Henderson and Webb met for dinner at the Webbs to consider what they should do. As a result MacDonald decided to form a government, and the party supported his decision. Attlee thought then, and continued to think, that MacDonald was right: 'The electors at the time needed to see a Labour Government in being, if they were to appreciate that Labour was now the alternative to a Conservative administration. Refusal on our part to accept responsibility might have given a new lease of life to the Liberal Party.' MacDonald and his senior colleagues also decided that, in Snowden's words, they 'should not adopt an extreme policy but should confine our legislative proposals to measures that we were likely to be able to carry. . . . We must show the country that we are not under the domination of the wild men.' A radical socialist programme was therefore rejected even before MacDonald was asked to form an administration.

Once the Labour leadership had announced that it would take office if asked, there was no doubt that it would be called to do so. Labour held a big victory demonstration on 8 January 1924, the day Parliament reassembled. Baldwin had decided to carry on his government until formally defeated by a vote in the House. On 21 January the Labour Party moved a vote of censure, the Liberals supported it and the government was defeated. Baldwin resigned next day, and the King immediately sent for MacDonald.

II

The character of the first Labour government became evident very soon. After his initial meeting with MacDonald, King George v wrote in his diary: 'I had an hour's talk with him . . . he impressed me very much; he wishes to do the right thing.' Appointed to the Colonial Office, J. H. Thomas was said to have introduced himself to his departmental heads with the statement: 'I'm here to see there is no mucking about with the British Empire.' MacDonald's first decision, as first Prime Minister of the first Labour government, involved him in turning his back on one of his party's most cherished objectives – a Cabinet whose membership would be determined not personally by the leader but by a consensus. He spent a few days in retreat at Lossiemouth and planned his Cabinet without consulting the party Executive.

Unlike some of MacDonald's followers, Attlee defended MacDonald's behaviour at the time, and when a proposal to have the Cabinet elected by the National Executive or the Parliamentary Party was put forward at the next party conference he urged its rejection. A fundamental fallacy, he said, underlay such proposals – 'that it is possible by the elaboration of machinery to escape the necessity of trusting one's fellow human beings.'

Having been MacDonald's PPS in Opposition, Attlee was a certainty for a job in the new administration. He became Under-Secretary to the War Office, under Stephen Walsh, MP for the Ince division of Lancashire, an ex-miner, who had supported the Lloyd George coalition during the war. When consulted about an under-secretary Walsh asked for Attlee, a gallant ex-serviceman who was known to admire much in the military life and was always still referred to as 'Major Attlee'. This was one of the few of MacDonald's appointments which was welcomed by the *Morning Post*. 'For the War Office, Major Attlee has the recommendation of excellent war service. He was not ... a conscientious objector.' Attlee's erstwhile colleague as PPS to MacDonald, Jack Lawson, was given the junior post of Financial Secretary at the War Office. They were amused to find themselves in control of generals under whom only a few years previously they had served. 'Jack Lawson and I got on excellently with all the soldiers and they frankly told us that it was pleasant to work with men who were keen on their jobs in contrast to our Conservative prede- cessors, who were, they said, idle fellows.'

The experience of a government department's inner workings was useful, but neither Attlee nor the department had much to do. The most burdensome task was to help the party continue in power. 'We had a very interesting time at the War Office, but a strenuous time in the House, as, with no real majority, we always had to be in attendance.' As an under-secretary he learned very little of what went on in the Cabinet. Looking back on it he did not write with enthusiasm about life as a junior minister.

At the beginning of the 1924 government Lawson observed that Attlee was 'something new to us, unknown, and apparently would remain un- known, for he said very little'. There was little, indeed, that Attlee could say, having accepted his ministerial post. Only a few months previously he had said in the House of Commons: 'Personally I think the time has come when we ought to do away with all armies and all wars.' Amplifi- cation of this observation would hardly have gone down well with the generals. To enthuse about his job, on the other hand, even if he had cared to, would not have been agreeable to his friends in the ILP. To accept it meant having to carry out the broad lines of an Army policy laid down by the Conservative government before a snap election which had given Labour no time to propose alternatives. When, in the debates on the Defence Estimates in March 1924, Labour backbenchers de- nounced not only war but the War Office, Attlee must have been glad that as a junior minister it was incumbent upon him to be silent. Jack Lawson's reservations about his new friend Attlee were not shared by observers outside the party. In April the weekly *Time and Tide* went out of its way to say: 'At some future date, if public confidence in the Labour Party continues to grow, Attlee should make an excellent Home Secre- tary.' By the end of the year Jack Lawson seems to have raised his original rating of him. 'He worked hard and had his facts at his finger ends when necessary. He was a master of detail, which means much in a department. Patient, then caustic, he fitted the Department. ... There was steel in him.'

From the moment it took office, the Labour Party had to face the problem of reconciling its pre-election propaganda with the need to govern, promises with responsibility. There is no evidence that Attlee had doubts about this fundamental issue. His equanimity was based on two principles already embryonic in his mind. The first was that in opposition Labour must speak for itself, whereas in government it must act for the country. The second was that socialists should not necessarily eschew powers which they should try to deny to capitalists. In later years the first principle influenced his view on the relationship between Labour Party, Labour Executive and Labour government; the second, his views on rearmament in the later 1930s.

Meanwhile, in 1924, Attlee said 'very little'. What he found most to criticize in the 1924 Labour government was what he later called 'a fatal lack of clarity as to the order in which domestic reforms were to be attempted'. The high hopes Labour had raised before the election that they would be 'different' from the Tories in office only made things more difficult for them when they came into office with such limited power. It was not only that they failed to act soon enough, but that when they acted they did not do enough: they offered palliatives not cures, a course of action of which Attlee had complained so bitterly in the past.

This was most noticeable in the field in which they had most enthusiastically promised resolute state action – unemployment. They brought in improvements in unemployment benefits, but this was a superficial treatment of the problem, and one which either of the other parties would have soon applied. MacDonald was soon being taunted by Tories and Liberals with failure to carry out his electoral promises to bring the unemployment figures down. It was not till July that Snowden announced government support for a public works programme, and it was not only the Liberals and the Tories who wanted to know why, if this were the remedy, it had not been applied before.

The one big positive achievement of the first Labour government in the domestic field was Wheatley's Housing Act, which became law in August: by greatly increasing the state subsidy and by negotiations with the building trade, Wheatley produced 'the basis of a vast expansion in municipal house-building'. But there was nothing socialist about the Act, which did no more than expand the basis laid down by Neville Chamberlain in the previous government. Attlee was soon unhappy about the absence of a socialist approach to the problems of the day, and began to wonder if this might be due as much to a weakness of will as to the need 'to go steady to stay in power'.

He was somewhat happier with overseas policy. Thomas at the Colonial Office was conservative to a fault, but MacDonald, acting as his own Foreign Secretary, supported the League of Nations and promoted Germany's acceptance into it. In February 1924 MacDonald announced Britain's recognition of the Soviet regime, and invited its representatives to a conference in London. During the conference the Soviet government attacked MacDonald; and Trotsky talked of foreign loans, which the British were offering, as an aid to 'the inevitable bitter struggle' with capitalism. The Tories denounced MacDonald for negotiating with revolutionaries. Attlee contemplated his leader's efforts with mixed feelings. Many years later he observed to the author that Labour governments:

> catch it all ways when they deal with the Soviet Union. British Socialists expect them to get closer to the Russians, and, if at the time it suits them so does the Foreign Office; public opinion wants them to keep their distance, and any move they make will be capital for the Tory opposition. As for the Russians, they're the most difficult of the lot. They see the British Labour Party as International Capitalism's stalking horse. They'll pat it, or kick it in the shins, as it suits them.

In 1924 he thought again of Russia under Lenin and Trotsky as being 'run by the Whitechapel branch of the SDP'. He did not like the Russians, and he did not trust them. Yet MacDonald was patiently and courageously living up to the highest standards of internationalism in which socialists by definition must believe. He defended MacDonald's policy towards Russia with vigour and conviction.

The Labour government left office, as it had entered it, abruptly and unexpectedly. In August Labour MPs protested at the Attorney General's decision to prosecute J.R. Campbell, acting editor of the Communist *Workers' Weekly*, on a charge of incitement to mutiny. When the Attorney General changed his mind, the Conservatives moved a vote of censure and the Liberals demanded a committee of inquiry. MacDonald made these motions a matter of confidence, stumbled into untruth when explaining himself to the House of Commons, and lost on a division by 364 votes to 198. The eighteen-day election which followed was dominated by a Red Scare. Five days before polling, the 'Zinoviev Letter' was published by the Foreign Office to forestall its use by the *Daily Mail*. Giving the impression that the Third International was urging the British Communist Party to revolution, the letter, almost beyond doubt a forgery perpetrated specially for this purpose, provoked an anti-Bolshevik hysteria which gravely damaged the Labour Party.

In Limehouse, however, the hysteria arising from the 'Red Letter' was little in evidence. Whereas meetings in 1923 had often been noisy, this time they were quiet. Indeed, wrote *The Times*: 'There are parts of the East End of London which may be condemned to a silent campaign.'

This report followed the publication in *The Times* of a letter from Attlee complaining about allegations in a previous report that 'the Unionist candidate in Limehouse cannot hold meetings'. Attlee pointed out that he had offered Miller Jones a series of 'joint meetings to guarantee him a fair hearing'. There were no more complaints. A Captain King, late RN, Attlee told Bernard in a letter, arrived to speak for Miller Jones, but on learning of Attlee's relationship with Bernard, and that he had served at Gallipoli, 'gave me a personal testimony as being your brother'. In a three-cornered contest, with a larger overall poll, Attlee's vote went up by 240 (to 11,713), his majority down by 164 over Miller Jones the Conservative (who won some 500 more votes – 5,692); the Liberal decline was reflected by the poll of only 2,869 for Marks, the baker – 'the excellent man ... with a strong local following' – who had beaten Attlee in 1919 in the election for the London County Council.

All over the country the great majority of Labour supporters remained loyal: in fact the Labour vote went up by a million, while the Liberal vote was reduced by a million and a quarter. Although the Labour government had few striking achievements to its credit, many Labour supporters felt it had made a good start and were ready to excuse it for not having moved faster and further on the grounds that it had been a minority government. Despite their increased vote, however, Labour lost 40 seats, giving them a total of 151 seats in the House. The Liberals were reduced to a rump of 40. The Conservatives gained 155. With 413 seats in the House they were twice as many as Labour and Liberals put together. Opinion had been polarized for the first time between two different big parties, one tied to property and business interests, the other to organized labour. The middle ground left for the Liberals was much reduced; Labour could console itself for loss of office with the hope that they had now permanently replaced the Liberals as the party of opposition.

Asked many years later what lessons he thought the Labour Party learned from their first experience of government, Attlee replied: 'None. Different people interpreted the results differently.' Some were confirmed in their view that Labour should never have taken office as a minority government. Others did not regret the experiment but were now convinced that in future a majority was essential: Ernest Bevin moved a resolution at the 1925 party conference at Liverpool on the inadvisability of the party accepting office again while in a minority in the House of Commons. The motion was heavily defeated. Snowden and others blamed the defeat of the party on incompetent leadership, and there was an attempt to replace MacDonald by Henderson – ineffective, since Henderson refused to participate. Many Labour supporters recognized with misgiving that for such immediate practical problems as unemployment a Labour government seemed to have no answer; for others the main lesson was that a Labour government which put forward moderate policies and deliberately muted its manifestos would never acquire the popular backing which would enable it to make the basic changes in society which socialism was all about.

The other problem revealed in Labour's few months of power was the relationship between a Labour government and the trade unions. A confrontation was only just averted in February 1924, when the port employers backed down in face of a dockers' strike called by Bevin in defiance of the Cabinet's known wishes. In March Bevin called out the London tramway workers in a dispute which had begun long before Labour came to power. When the railway unions proposed to take sympathetic action, MacDonald invoked the Emergency Powers Act, well hated by the Labour Movement when Lloyd George introduced it in 1920. Again a clash was avoided, but only by the hasty introduction of a London Transport Bill. The strike ended after ten days, but the scars remained.

Bevin proclaimed the unions' right to defend their members' interests whatever party was in power: 'We must not lose sight of the fact that governments may come and governments may go, but the workers' fight for betterment of conditions must go on all the time.' If the political leaders continued to excuse themselves, claiming that they could not have enacted socialist legislation because they had been dependent on Liberal votes, then let them now promise never to accept office until they had a majority in the House. In these circumstances Bevin moved his resolution at the party conference, seeking to prevent the party from forming or participating in a minority government, and supported a move to remove MacDonald from the leadership. If Bevin and like-minded union leaders began to distrust a Labour government's attitude to the unions, the Labour leaders began to worry about the union leaders' attitude to government. That Bevin had made no move to call off his strike was bad enough; even worse was the arrogance of his response to their pleas, and his offensive remarks about 'the politicians'. MacDonald thought him 'disloyal and irresponsible', pursuing a sectional interest when Labour had pledged itself to serve the national good.

Attlee was on MacDonald's side in 1924. He thought he had been right to take office and eschew a radical programme. But now his reservations about MacDonald mounted. He disapproved of Bevin's uncooperativeness when Labour was in office, and he disapproved even more of his insulting words about politicians. But as the MP for a dockers' constituency with high unemployment and bad housing, he shared Bevin's anxieties. He had seen, too, MacDonald's inept handling of the Zinoviev Letter, and he had been shocked by his evasiveness in the Commons about the Campbell case. 'I was still for MacDonald, but I had some food for thought.'

5
Out of Office,
1925–30

I

Between 1925 and 1927 Attlee's home life was the most leisurely he was able to enjoy until he resigned the leadership of the party nearly thirty years later. In the first three years of their married life the Attlees saw three elections, and then the party's tumultuous first year in office. Vi had not found it easy to adapt herself to her husband's long absences and late hours in the House. She had recovered from her illness after Janet's birth, but she continued to be over-anxious about her responsibilities as the wife of a public man. After the fall of the government he was able to spend more time at home. In this period she gained confidence enough to ignore her doctor's advice that she should not have another child. Felicity was born in August 1924, and there was no postnatal depression.

The House used to sit until 11 pm, so from Monday to Thursday inclusive Vi did not expect him home before midnight. If she were tired she would go to bed. He had a gas ring in his study, and would make himself a mug of cocoa before he went to sleep. The weekends he tried to devote to her and the children. Sometimes he had speaking engagements and she would have to stay at home, partly to look after the children, partly because they could not afford the expense of her going with him. But what time he had at weekends he shared with her. He would get home early for supper on Friday, and spend an hour reading to her: on Saturday and Sunday they would play golf or tennis, or walk. Most Sundays Vi would go to the eight o'clock communion service: he would go to his odd-job room – he had one in every house they lived in – and put a new seat on a chair or re-cover an ironing-board (many years later he once did this for a WREN at Chequers). In season they would work together in the garden, she directing, he dutifully but unenthusiastically doing the weeding. He never wanted to go off and do anything on his own.

They spent their holidays by the sea, often sharing a house with other Attlees or Millars because they could not afford hotels. Vi loved swimming and games with the children on the beach. Clem would take books on holiday; while the rest of the family were in the sea, he would read detective stories; when Vi was with him, he would read Jane Austen or the Brontës to her.

When the new House assembled in November 1924, Attlee as an ex-junior minister took his seat on the Opposition front bench, and was appointed one of the temporary chairmen of committees of the whole House. He had mixed feelings about the appointment. Since he would now preside periodically at these committees, he would have a chance to study parliamentary procedure in detail, a useful preparation for what might lie ahead. On the other hand: 'The position of an ex-Junior Minister does not give one much opportunity of speaking in the House except when the Estimates of one's previous Department are under consideration. I spoke regularly on the Army Estimates, but had it not been that the Government introduced two measures on which I could speak with some authority I should have been rather a silent Member.'

In fact he spoke far more often than he had before. He had made fourteen speeches during the 1922–3 Parliament, only five while in office in the Parliament of 1923–4. In 1924–5 he made forty-eight, and forty in 1925–6, occupying eighty-four and eighty-six and a half columns of Hansard respectively, and dealing with topics which varied from armed forces recruitment to the molasses subsidy. He urged employers to encourage their employees who were members of the Territorial Army, a change of attitude since the days when as mayor of Stepney he had campaigned against recruitment. He also spoke on the motoring offences clauses of the Criminal Justice Bill, contending that the reckless motorist was 'generally the wealthy motorist who owned a high powered car'. (Opposition cheers, and ministerial cries of 'No'.)

In 1924–6 his speeches were mostly on the two measures on which he could speak with authority, Neville Chamberlain's Rating Bill (1925) and the Electricity Bill (1926). Both had much Labour support, and to the Rating Bill the opposition came mainly from Chamberlain's own party. The bill was intended to consolidate rating power in the hands of local councils, removing outdated Poor Law machinery. The Labour spokesman on rates was the fiery Colonel Josiah Wedgwood. He knew the subject well, but he took a fancy to Attlee, made great use of his knowledge gained in Stepney, and gave him plenty to do. Since most of the ILP members were still stronger on revolution than on rates, Attlee had plenty of opportunity to impress the House.

On the Electricity Bill, Attlee was regarded as an expert, since he had been a member of the Stepney Borough Council Electricity Committee since 1919, and for some years its chairman. The fundamental question was whether electricity should become a public service or a private monopoly. The 1926 Bill transferred the wholesale distribution of electricity to a national body, the Central Electricity Board, which was to establish a National Grid. By putting a business enterprise under a public board appointed by the Minister of Transport, the bill created a model for later measures of nationalization. Attlee was originally cast in the somewhat nominal role of a member of the committee on the bill, but when three front-bench Labour men, who were not authorities on the subject, quickly dropped out, he was made the party's spokesman. Most of the opposition came from the many Conservative members on the committee who had interests in the private companies. The Labour members, about a quarter of the committee, held the balance of power, and accepted Attlee's guidance throughout. The Conservative ministers in charge of the bill soon became so dependent on his approval or disapproval that they would wait to discover how he felt before they accepted amendments, and at the Report Stage 'a Conservative objected to the undue deference shown to my views'.

When the bill became law he was asked to serve on the Joint Industrial Council of the industry, representing the employers. This put him in an interestingly equivocal position when strikes were threatened; in Stepney, when the employees wanted to hold a meeting to discuss strike action, they would ask for the use of a room in the Labour Club on Attlee's premises, and get it. He saw to it that as well as hearing the pros and cons from their union leaders they would hear the views of some of his Conservative Stepney councillors. As a result of this diplomacy no stoppage took place in Stepney until the General Strike of 1926. This stoppage, and the action which Attlee took to deal with it, very nearly produced an interruption in his political career which might have proved a considerable handicap.

II

The General Strike was the result of the miners' union rejecting, after several weeks of negotiation, the demand of the coal-owners for longer hours and reduced wages, a demand made in consequence of a falling-off in coal exports due to the rise in price caused by the return to the Gold Standard in 1925. The miners appealed unavailingly to the government to put pressure on the coal-owners. The TUC called a General Strike in the belief that the threat would induce the government to change its mind and intervene. Baldwin called their bluff, and before the TUC had realized what they had let themselves in for the General Strike was on. It began on 4 May 1926 and lasted nine days; the TUC then threw in its hand. The miners remained on strike for five months, then drifted back to work, feeling they had been trampled underfoot by government and employers, and betrayed by the leaders of the TUC.

In the weeks before the strike, Attlee hoped that it could be averted. Unlike some Labour MPs and many more trade unionists, he did not believe that it could give the miners what they wanted, and he feared that even if well managed by the TUC it would end at best in a stalemate which would only postpone a reasonable settlement. But as a parliamentarian he could do little. The miners, led by A. J. Cook, took for granted the support of the Labour Party, to a degree which annoyed many Labour MPs. In the Commons, MacDonald supported the miners while becoming more anxious in private about their intentions, and despaired of influencing the outcome. Attlee, like most Labour MPs, shared this view. The representatives of the mining constituencies took on the employers and the government, while the rest of the Parliamentary Party looked on, and supported as and where it could.

When the General Strike began, Attlee was most deeply involved, not as an M P but as chairman of the Stepney Borough Electricity Committee. The National Electrical Workers' Union, following the instructions of the TUC issued to the unions as a whole, had instructed its members to stop work at midnight on the first day of the strike. Nearly all the Stepney electrical workers would have been called out, so that the borough would have had no heat or light unless the Electricity Committee of the Stepney borough were willing to call on the government to man the plant with troops. Such a course of action was not acceptable to a borough committee with a Labour majority, but if the strike was carried out to the letter, and troops were not allowed to man the plant, essential services – for example, the hospital – would be cut off.

In his capacity as chairman of the Borough Electricity Committee, Attlee called an emergency meeting of the committee and obtained authority to contact the T U C General Council to seek a compromise. The T U C agreed that the Stepney men could continue to supply light for the borough, but *power* for hospitals only. If consumers other than hospitals were supplied with *power*, the agreement would be made void. Attlee accepted the arrangement. There was now another problem. Light and power were mostly supplied by the same mains, and the would-be strikers at the plant wanted to know how abuse of the agreement was to be prevented. Attlee undertook that if any consumer other than a hospital was seen by the workers at the generating plant to be using power, the workers were entitled to pull the fuses and shut off the current. This satisfied the workers at the generating plant and they remained at work. The Borough Committee, which included several Conservatives, regarded this as a feather in Attlee's cap.

One firm, Scammels, defied the committee's warning and used current for power. Its fuses were pulled at once. Scammels immediately took out a civil action for conspiracy against Attlee and the Stepney committee's other Labour members – the Conservative members were disregarded despite their agreement to the decision. After a long delay, the jury found against the committee on grounds of malice, and Attlee was personally ordered to pay about £300 in damages. He appealed, but it was only in the summer of 1928, while he was in India with the Simon Commission, that the appeal was upheld.

The ending of the strike by what was virtually the collapse of the TUC was a victory for the government. They had prepared for a struggle in advance, politically and administratively; the TUC had not. The union leaders had thought that the threat of a strike would suffice to cause the government to intervene in the dispute, and when their bluff was called, the fact that they had never thought out how they would conduct a long strike, and what the political implications of a 'victory' against the government would be, inhibited their leaders from the start. Though once again the miners were the worst victims of the failure of industrial action – the owners had got everything they asked for – the strike was disastrous for British trade and industry as a whole. On the other hand, the experience increased the aversion in the unions to militant industrial action and led them further into tentative moves for regular cooperation with the employers. Bevin, though he had been by far the most determined of the TUC leaders once the strike had been declared, and had been the strong man of the TUC's Strike Organization Committee, had learned his lesson: whatever the shortcomings of the Labour politicians, to ignore them and rely on industrial action simply would not pay. Meanwhile, Labour's political leaders felt confirmed in their view that the workers' salvation lay in Parliament alone. The outcome of the strike improved Labour's long-term prospects of coming to political power. It toughened Labour's supporters, and it made friends for the Labour Party among many floating voters who felt the miners had been treated harshly and unjustly.

Attlee had mixed feelings about the strike. Remembering Liberal passive resistance to the Balfour Education Act of 1902, and Conservative obstruction of the 1911 National Insurance Act, he condemned as hypocrisy any criticism from those quarters of the TUC's resort to 'extra-parliamentary action'. On the other hand, he felt that the TUC had so bungled the affair that they should never be allowed to control the policy of the Labour Party. He was angry with the government and furious with the leaders of business: 'their behaviour, and their general attitude, confirmed what I had come to believe about capitalists when I saw what they did when I lived in Stepney.' He retained a special sympathy for the miners for the rest of his life. He concluded that Baldwin was a good, humane and far-sighted man who could modulate Conservative policy without ever being able to change it: Baldwin's acceptance of the return to gold had set the scene for the coal strike, he had been conciliatory during the General Strike, but in the aftermath he had not prevented the Trade Disputes Act of 1927, which had banned sympathetic strikes and reduced the Labour Party's income by requiring trade unionists to 'contract in' instead of 'contracting out' of the political levy. Most important, Attlee was relieved to see the end of the General Strike as a political weapon:

> I'd heard a general strike discussed for 15 years: when it came, it collapsed, because nobody knew what to do with it, and most of them discovered they didn't really want it. It had to come some day, and it had to go. A good thing to get it out of the way. The Labour movement got back on the political track.

In the August of the year of the General Strike, Attlee went with Bernard and Laurence on an organized pilgrimage to the scenes of the Gallipoli fighting. Most of the party – about 250 – were relatives of the dead, with a sprinkling of survivors. He described the journey for his brother Tom in a long letter which he wrote, some weeks after he got back, from Weymouth where he was on holiday with Vi and the children.

After crossing the Channel they went overland to Marseilles, where they took an Italian boat, 'well found and comfortable', to Constantinople. He described Constantinople in great detail, especially the architecture, which he thought would interest his brother. He was enthusiastic about the Palace of Topkapi:

> ... some glorious sculptures. In particular a very delicate boy in a cloak. The pick of the collection was a sarcophagus of a King of Lydia of Alexander the Great's time ornamented with reliefs of hunting [scenes]. You know the impression one got from the Singing Gallery sculptures at Florence. Well, this simply left them out of the running.

In the party, 'one respectable looking paterfamilias whom I took at first to be a typical bourgeois turned out to be an original and continuing member of the central Branch of the SDF, a pal of old Hyndman's and quite a good sort'; there was also 'a young Haileybury master ... a very good type'. From Constantinople they went to the Dardanelles.

> Landed at Helles where B[ernard] had the joy of preaching at the commemorative service. I lectured the previous evening on the campaign. We drove in cars over execrable tracks right up to [a village] under Achi Babar and then after investigating the old front line I wandered all down the Gully now very wild and overgrown and met a wolf or jackal, I think the

former, at the northern end. Next day ... I decided to climb straight up the heights to Sari Bair – a pretty stiff climb up gullies choked with brushwood ... a hot job at 11 o'clock.... From the top a great view. It was interesting to me to trace out on the spot the doings of my old comrades. I experienced before I got back to the ship the old Gallipoli thirst.

While Attlee was still in Gallipoli, Vi took the two children on holiday to Weymouth, where Attlee joined them on his return to England. She was accompanied by the family's great acquisition, a seventeen-year-old nannie, Nellie Evans. When Vi had interviewed her for the job, back in 1925, Nellie had thought 'she was lovely'. Vi concluded: 'I think you should meet my husband before you make up your mind.' Attlee came in, shook hands, sat down, murmured agreeable observations and sucked his pipe. When Nellie rose to go, Attlee 'jumped up and hurried to open the door for me'. Nellie said to herself as she passed through it: '*She*'s charming. I don't like *him* – he's too polite. I'm not coming.' Before she had reached the garden gate she had changed her mind. She stayed, and became a friend of the family for life.

From Weymouth Vi wrote to Attlee in Gallipoli giving him advice about how to make the transition from Asia Minor to Weymouth via Woodford Green:

> Your two suits have gone off to be cleaned and will be back for you. If you have time and think of it you might pay the bill.... Janet said yesterday, 'Daddy is coming down to the seaside. It will be nice to see him – I shall be so exciting!!' She said it so sweetly.... I bought her an emerald green bathing dress in case she needed it.... Nannie has ordered *The Times* for every day.... How lovely it will be when you join us ... I was certainly never meant to be a widow!

III

In November 1927, the Secretary of State for India, Lord Birkenhead, formerly F.E. Smith, announced the appointment of a Statutory Commission to examine developments in India since the Government of India Act of 1919. Attlee's appointment as one of the Labour members of the commission launched him, against his will, on a preoccupation with India that lasted the rest of his political life.

The Act of 1919 had provided that within ten years a commission was to be set up to inquire how the Act was working, and, in Baldwin's words, 'to consider the desirability of establishing, extending or restricting the degree of responsible government existing there'. The Act assumed that the objective of British rule in India was to guide what was then a colony towards responsible self-government within the Empire. It created a 'dyarchical' system. In the provinces, certain powers were transferred to elected legislative councils, powers over justice, police and finance being reserved to the governors. For the country as a whole it established in Delhi a bicameral legislature, largely elective, but with powers severely limited by the functions reserved to the Viceroy and his Executive Council, on which Indian members were in a minority.

To the British in 1919 the reforms embodied in the Act had seemed generous; the Indians found them insignificant. In 1920 Gandhi launched his non-violent civil disobedience campaign for independence – 'Swaraj', Home Rule. In 1922, horrified by the violence which it had unleashed, he called the campaign off, but he was nevertheless arrested, and sentenced to six years' imprisonment. During this period India was relatively calm, though outbreaks of violence continued, especially between the Hindu and Muslim communities, and frequent strikes kept the political temperature high. Progressive Indians distrusted the British. Hindus feared the Muslims. The princes of the independent states were opposed to any reduction in their power. The Statutory Commission was not due until 1929. The decision to bring it forward by two years was made by the Secretary of State. Birkenhead thought it was 'frankly inconceivable that India will ever be fit for Dominion self-government'. He feared that if a commission did not act until 1929 a Labour government might then be in power, and would send out a commission which would come back and make a report which would precipitate Dominion status; MacDonald was already promising it in public.

Birkenhead pressed, therefore, for an early commission which a Conservative government could control in the hope of obtaining a cautious report. The choice of Simon, the Liberal 'elder statesman', as chairman was calculated to this end. The selection of a 'Liberal' sounded encouraging to those progressive Indians and British who were not aware that Simon had denounced the General Strike as illegal, and since then had moved further and further to the right. He was known by Birkenhead and Baldwin to have returned from a visit to India with the view that Indian reform should proceed very slowly indeed. The other six commissioners were chosen with the object of getting a 'sober' report. Four of them were Conservatives. Lord Burnham, a diehard Tory, was the owner of the *Daily Telegraph*. Lord Strathcona was a close friend of Baldwin. George Lane Fox was a fox-hunting Tory MP with a background similar in some respects to that of his fellow Yorkshireman and brother-in-law, the Viceroy – Lord Irwin, later Lord Halifax. Edward Cadogan was much esteemed for his public work, especially by Attlee, because of his work for discharged Borstal boys. The two Labour members named were Attlee and Stephen Walsh. Soon after his appointment Walsh withdrew on grounds of ill health; his place was taken by Vernon Hartshorn, according to Attlee 'the ablest of the South Wales miners in the House'.

For Labour representation on the commission, Birkenhead had consulted MacDonald. Walsh and Hartshorn were both safely orthodox figures. Why MacDonald chose Attlee is not clear. By the end of 1927 Attlee had established a reputation in the House as hardworking and well informed, but he had no Indian experience; his expertise was 'gas-and-water' socialism in Britain. Attlee had no wish to leave Vi for several months when she had two small babies to look after, and another child on the way. He did not think the job would benefit his political career, and went to some trouble to ascertain from MacDonald that his absence from Britain would not affect his chances of office in the next Labour government. MacDonald may have chosen Attlee because he knew that Birkenhead wanted the kind of report which was bound to be unpopular with the Labour Party, and he did not wish a shadow minister of the first rank to be associated with it. Nor would MacDonald have wanted a Labour man on the Statutory Commission who would come home and provide ammunition with which the extremists of the party would try to commit the leadership to immediate Home Rule. Attlee would have fitted these requirements admirably.

By becoming a member of the commission, Attlee became a suspect in the eyes of many Labour Party backbenchers, who soon divined why a commission was going out to India two years before constitutionally necessary. Labour Party doubts were fed by such newspaper comments as: 'Mr Stephen Walsh and Major Attlee are both such good Englishmen that we often wonder how they contrive to remain in the Labour Party.'

The commission was to make two visits, the first a reconnaissance, the second, a few months later, a detailed inquiry. The members left London on the first expedition on 19 January 1928. They arrived in Bombay two weeks later. Their reception was mixed. Large crowds met them, carrying banners bearing the words 'Simon Go Back', though there were also smaller parties carrying leaves and flowers. The former regarded the Statutory Commission as the latest expression of Britain's determination to maintain its Raj. For the latter, the arrival of the commission heralded the next advance towards self-government. Heavy rain dampened the effects of the demonstration, and the commissioners were not able to appreciate the predominant Indian reaction until they got to Delhi. Here it was made quite clear to them from the moment they entered their hotel. They had been led to expect that they would be able to rub shoulders and hobnob with Indian politicians and prominent citizens. In fact they were either greeted with reserve, or cut dead.

It was clear to Attlee that the prospect of being able to make important political recommendations was bleak, since the Congress Party and the Muslim League had boycotted the commission on the grounds that it had no Indian representatives. But he was not despondent. The reception

77

given to the commission did not disturb him: he did not think the attitude of the Indians towards it was as hostile as some of the British newspapers made it out to be. And he learned much. He wrote to Tom with some sharp sidelights on Indian problems:

> I gather in this province that politically the peasant proprietor is going to get into power. [He has] the usual defects of the peasant. I hear the village councils are grossly oppressed. I should like to make G.K. Chesterton [come out] and see how he found his ideal peasantry work out in practice.

The commissioners came back to Britain in April 1928. They returned to India the following October. This was a much longer visit, covering every province, including Burma. The commissioners heard oral evidence in all the provincial capitals. Again, the Congress Party refused to co-operate; its members continued to greet the commission with black-flag processions and demonstrations.

On this second visit the commissioners were allowed to take their wives. For Vi it was 'the chance of a lifetime'. Friends and relations took it in turns to live in the Woodford house and look after the children, so that she was able to be in India for three months. They disembarked at Bombay on 12 October. Two days later, on arrival at Poona, 'she was profusely garlanded'. In Delhi the commissioners and their wives were entertained by the Viceroy. 'Vi's dinner partner was old Lord Airedale – very deaf so that she had to speak into his ear trumpet. He amused her by asking how her father (me) was enjoying India. She had a pleasant chat with the Viceroy who was as usual perfectly charming.' There was a big dinner for the Nizam of Hyderabad, 'a dreadful person and a confirmed miser'. Vi 'went in' with a minor prince, 'rather a pleasant fellow'. The following night, 'there was a huge dinner given by Victor Sassoon ... dancing afterwards. I was bored to distraction and managed to get away by 12 o'clock. Vi enjoyed herself hugely and danced till 2 o'clock. She has another dance tonight, to which, thank goodness, I'm not going.... The trip has done Vi a great deal of good and I imagine she will never be shy of functions of any sort again.'

For the journey Attlee had been provided with 'an excellent bearer who speaks many languages.... He insists on dressing one, but I rather bar not tucking in my own shirt.' Attlee formed a friendship with this bearer which lasted for the rest of his life. His name was A.N.A. Aseervatham; Attlee called him 'Philip', and addressed him as such from then on. They exchanged letters and birthday presents. 'Philip' clearly regarded Attlee as a patron saint. When he fell on hard times in the 1950s, he appealed to Attlee and obtained through references from him a licence to open a bar in Bangalore. He became prosperous. In 1956, when Attlee was the guest of the government of India, 'Philip' wrote to

Nehru and got himself attached to Attlee as guide-cum-valet for the whole of the tour. Ever after they exchanged photographs and greeting cards. Mr Aseervatham pays for an annual Requiem Mass at St Francis Xavier Cathedral in Bangalore to be said on Attlee's birthday.

Early in the Statutory Commission's second visit, Attlee formed an impression of the way ahead for India. He wrote to Tom:

> This problem is very difficult. . . . I think myself at present that the only line is l'audace, toujours l'audace. I don't think one can devise effective safeguards. The real trouble is that India's disabilities are social and economic and we have to deal with political change.

For him the wisdom was in Cromwell's words:

> 'It is not the manner of settling these constitutional things or the manner of one set of men or another doing it. There remains always the general question after that. The general question lies in the acceptance of it by those who are concerned to yield it and accept it.'
>
> OC, as usual, hits the nail on the head. The failure of dyarchy lies in its own non-acceptance. I am now trying to set down on paper some of the leading conclusions to which I have come. I fear it will be difficult to make people at home understand that we are not dealing with a *tabula rasa*, but a paper that has been much scribbled over. Our people, like many out here, British and Indian, are apt to make a ready-made government for India, often on some model used elsewhere, without trying to see how far it will fit and how far it will be suitable to work in.

Vi had returned to England from Calcutta on 24 January 1929, when the commission was about to leave Bengal for the fourteen-day visit to Burma. Her three months in India was, and remained, incomparably the most exciting and successful episode of her life. She had played tennis and golf, as never before, and in uninterruptedly good weather – it rained only at Poona, for an hour or two. She had danced if not all night at least for several hours at a time. She had seen many of the most fascinating places in India. She knew that she had received the VIP treatment, and had not encountered much of the India of Gandhi or Nehru – 'I didn't, I suppose, see the real India, as we travelled round in our train and were given hospitality wherever we went.' But that was not her fault, and she made the most of the India that she was given.

IV

The commission embarked at Bombay on 13 April 1929. By then Baldwin had announced a general election, and on his return to London Attlee was immediately thrown into the campaign. The 1929 election provided no stunts or excitements. There was no Red Letter. Baldwin's slogan was 'Safety First' – a campaign for safety on the roads had just been launched – and Baldwin was in no mood to initiate or innovate. The Conservatives felt on the defensive: by-elections showed signs of a swing towards Liberals and Labour. Unemployment remained high; progress towards disarmament was slow. MacDonald, too, was careful: he had managed to avoid both Bevin's and the TUC's demand for a programme of immediate objectives when Labour came to power, and the ILP's pressure for full-blooded socialism. He did not want the public to think that either the unions or the ILP could tell the Labour Party what to do. His platform was *Labour and the Nation*, a document agreed at the last party conference which Attlee described as 'a declaration of faith and aspirations rather than a political programme'.

In Limehouse Attlee faced a four-cornered contest – a Communist ran against him. The main issues were unemployment, then housing. Attlee complained of Conservative failure to promote disarmament. He made little mention of India. At 13,872 votes, his total was 2,000 more than in 1924, and more than double that of the Conservative runner-up. The national result, in terms of votes, was unexpectedly close. The Conservatives led, with 8,664,000; Labour's poll rose by nearly three million to 8,365,000. The Liberals polled 5,301,000, an increase of more than two million. Labour won 287 seats, the Conservatives 261, and the Liberals only 59. For the first time, Labour, though still without an overall majority, were the largest party in the House. Now, at last, Attlee told Tom, they could do something positive, in Bevin's words, 'deliver the goods'.

In his autobiography Attlee records that, in response to a direct question, MacDonald had assured him that membership of the Simon Commission would not affect his chances of office if Labour were to win the next election. Hartshorn was told the same. In the event, 'neither of us was included, and it was characteristic of MacDonald that he did not take the trouble to inform us of his decision.'

It was MacDonald's behaviour in not telling him in advance that he would not have a post that annoyed Attlee. He knew that the writing of the commission's report would take up too much time to allow him to carry out departmental responsibilities as well, and the following year, when he had finished work on the report, a job was forthcoming. But he resented MacDonald leaving him to find out that he was jobless only by reading the newspapers. He raised the matter with MacDonald immediately. Two days after becoming prime minister, MacDonald wrote to him in his own hand, saying only:

> I am in a fix about this Indian affair. Obviously we cannot put members on it into the Ministry. It is a terrible concern for me, but I shall not forget you. There must be changes before very long in some of the offices and both Vernon and you must be amongst my cares. I shall send a notice to the press so that you will not suffer.

This letter did not mollify Attlee's feelings, and the observation that 'obviously' members of the commission could not be given ministerial posts he found particularly irritating. This was precisely the issue he had raised when MacDonald had asked him to join the commission. He had a second grievance, which he describes in his autobiography:

> The Indian Commission had not yet reported, but it might be supposed that its members had acquired some useful information. MacDonald proposed to deal with the Indian question himself, but neither then nor subsequently did he give even five minutes to ascertain the views of his emissaries.

The fact that events in India, and a consequent change of British policy, made the Simon Report out of date months before it was published did not, in Attlee's view, excuse him. Attlee attributed MacDonald's behaviour to what he thought one of his greatest weaknesses: he could not admit to ignorance.

For the first year of the new Labour government, therefore, Attlee was 'free' to help write the Commission's Report. It was published in June 1930. In brief it recommended responsible government in the provinces, and negotiations between the British government, the Indian government and the princes on the structure of the central government. By then, however, the report had been not merely superseded but invalidated. The Viceroy, observing the rising tide of Indian hostility, had decided in the summer of 1929, after Labour had come to power, and after he had visited Britain to confer with the new government, that something must be done for India to demonstrate Britain's understanding and goodwill. First, he proposed the calling of a 'round table' conference of British *and* Indians. Secondly, though he had criticized MacDonald for making such a promise in public the year before, he now proposed that the government should publicly pledge itself to Dominion status 'as the natural issue of India's constitutional progress'. MacDonald was only too ready to support the Viceroy: as far back as May 1928 he had said: 'I hope that within a period of months rather than years there will be a new Dominion added to the Commonwealth of our nation, a Dominion which will find self-respect as an equal within the Commonwealth. I refer to India.' This, while Attlee was a member of a commission which was known to be coming to the conclusion that Dominion status was a goal many years ahead.

The announcement of the 'round table' conference and the declaration of Dominion status were made on 31 October 1929. The news was greeted with enthusiasm in India. In Britain there were outbursts of anger. Some people were annoyed and bewildered that the Simon Commission's Report had been made a dead letter before the commissioners had finished writing it. Birkenhead and a former Viceroy, Lord Reading, attacked the declaration of Dominion status with fury. The Conservative shadow Cabinet sent a telegram of protest. Labour attempts to argue that the October announcements were meant to create an atmosphere in India in which the Simon Report would be acceptable were dismissed. Simon himself, though he had been the first to suggest a round table conference, was not pleased by the relegation of his report to minor status, and spoke of resigning without presenting his report. It particularly irked him to learn that the Viceroy would announce that the agenda of the promised conference would not be tied to the Simon Report. The other commissioners were equally unhappy.

Attlee's feelings were ruffled. He was aware that many of his Labour colleagues regarded his agreement to serve on the commission as a readiness to associate himself with a 'right-wing' policy towards India. He had spent several months away from his family, his constituency, and from Parliament, had been passed over by MacDonald when the jobs were given out, and was now left standing on the verge of a road along which the Labour Party had swept past to a new stage of thinking about India which made him and his fellow commissioners look not only out of date but reactionary. This was hard luck on a man who had privately concluded that the answer to India's problems was '*l'audace, et toujours l'audace*'. He continued to think that the commissioners knew better how to deal with India than the backbenchers of the Labour Party. This was the first occasion on which he made up his mind that a Labour government could be in danger of subjecting political realism and responsibility to propaganda at home and clamour abroad.

Attlee made large contributions to the second volume of the report, which gave the commissioners' conclusions. They recommended 'a very great advance' on self-government for the provinces, but advised caution in moving towards self-government at the centre for three reasons: communal tensions between Muslim and Hindu, the rights of the independent princes, and the difficulty of finding Indians to officer the armed forces. Attlee's work on the commission had brought him face to face with the fundamental problem of India:

> The real difficulty in dealing with the Central Government is that there is no feasible territorial stage between a government responsible to Great Britain and a government responsible to the Indian people.

The conclusion throws much light on his decision during the postwar Labour government to 'throw the reins on the horse's neck'.

The report, though well received by *The Times* as 'the most hopeful advance of our generation towards the solution of the problem of India', did not appeal to the Indian nationalists, who wanted Dominion status or independence. They refused to take part in any round table negotiations and called for a boycott of the central and provincial governments and for the launching of a civil disobedience campaign. In nine months 54,000 people were convicted of offences of civil disobedience. The Simon Report was less relevant than ever, and less likely to be judged on its merits.

The Simon Commission, doomed from lack of Indian goodwill, brought Attlee a wide knowledge of India which was to be of immense use to him as a leader of the Labour Party in the 1930s and as premier after the war. It was what his experience on the commission taught him of his own ignorance that impressed him most. In a debate on India, 2 December 1931, soon after the national government had come into power and the Labour Party was back in opposition, he said: 'There are various stages of knowledge of India. I have only reached the second stage, when one knows how little one knows.' The main lesson he learned was the prerequisite of self-determination. In the same speech he declared with great prescience:

> I believe that India is suffering from a variety of economic and social ills that will require a giant's hand to remove them, and I am certain that that hand cannot be an alien hand. It can only be done by the people of India themselves. Every national or nationalist movement ... is almost always based on economic ills which, either justly or unjustly, are attributed to the lack of the power of self-determination.

Everything he said in debate in the 1930s stressed the need for gradual advance to Dominion status, which was all that seemed practical politics at the time to him and most other British observers. His cast of mind was not prophetic or visionary; but when he became premier, he was quicker than most to recognize the realities of the situation and to see that India had to be given immediate independence.

Looking back, forty years later, on what membership of the Simon Commission had taught him about India, Attlee told the author: 'You've got to go to a place, see it and smell it, before you can say what's got to be done about it. Especially India – so many different races, dozens of minorities, all frightened of each other, and all wanting special representation. There was no one real India. India was a British invention – if we hadn't gone there it would have remained a conglomeration of groups.' The most important discovery he made was that the popular democratic movement at the time, though highly articulate, was comparatively small. At least ninety million Indians lived under the princes, and liked it, and Britain was committed to support these native rulers by treaties. Secondly, his experience on the Simon Commission educated him in the realities of India's defence. India was vulnerable, inside and out, and her protection came from the Indian Army, composed of Indians largely under British officers and from British forces posted to India. Before Britain could hand over to an Indian government, therefore, competent Indian officer material would have to be found and trained. He also learned how embarrassing the behaviour of an uncooperative opposition – an opposition within an opposition, for the Conservative Party as a whole were 'sound' on India – could be to a government trying to carry out a well-informed and acceptable policy. He thought that Churchill and his 'diehard' supporters 'hadn't a leg to stand on, and knew it – extremely irresponsible'. He was charitable enough to feel at the time that Churchill would have behaved more responsibly if he had been given more information, confidentially, by the government of the day. But, as we shall see, in this view he was wrong.

6

Minister of the Crown, 1930–1

For almost the whole of the Labour government's first year in office, Attlee spent most of his time working on the Simon Report. He appeared in the chamber only to vote in the division lobbies. In the eleven months between the assembling of the new Parliament and his appointment to office he made only two speeches in the House. Even allowing for his preoccupation with the report, this meagre record is surprising. Dissatisfaction with the government's performance in home affairs, particularly with unemployment, had been growing rapidly within the Labour Party. Attlee had made his maiden speech on the subject, and in the next seven years it had been the theme of most of his major speeches. Yet he took little part in the debates about the problem inside the party. In several letters to Tom in 1929 and the first six months of 1930 the great majority of his political references are to India. There is no mention of unemployment or of economic affairs.

In his first speech to the new Parliament, MacDonald set the tone for his second government: 'I wonder how far it is possible,' he said, 'without in any way abandoning any of our Party positions ... to consider ourselves more as a Council of State and less as arrayed regiments facing each other in battle ... so that by putting our ideas into a common pool we can bring out ... legislation and administration that will be of substantial benefit to the country as a whole.' Attlee thought later, as many on the left of the party thought at the time, that having accepted office the party should introduce a full socialist programme, even if it were defeated at once and another general election had to be held. 'It would have been a good fighting policy,' he wrote in 1937, 'and in view of the economic trend of the period, the wisest policy.' But in 1929 he subordinated his opinion to his confidence in MacDonald's judgement.

In choosing his Cabinet, MacDonald, recalling the attempts to remove him from the leadership in 1924, took care to consult his four chief colleagues, Snowden, Henderson, Clynes and Thomas. Without argument, Snowden returned to the Exchequer and Clynes took the Home Office. MacDonald wanted the Foreign Office for himself or for Thomas, whom he could control; but Henderson threatened to resign if he could not have it, and the job went to him. His vigorous and largely effective foreign policy diverted the attention of many loyal Labour men from the inadequacy of Labour's attack on unemployment. Responsibility for industry and employment, which MacDonald had wanted Henderson to take, went to Thomas as Lord Privy Seal, assisted by Thomas Johnston, Under-Secretary for Scotland, Sir Oswald Mosley as Chancellor of the Duchy of Lancaster, and by Lansbury. The only prominent left-winger in the Cabinet, Lansbury had been given the Office of Works where, Snowden thought, he could 'do a good many small things' without having the opportunity of 'squandering money'.

After the Wall Street Crash in October 1929, world trade, already weak, began to falter, and unemployment in Britain rose ominously from $1\frac{1}{2}$ million in January 1930 to $2\frac{1}{2}$ million in December. Thomas and his unemployment team were divided among themselves. In vain Johnston urged national relief schemes; Lansbury advocated retirement pensions and raising the school-leaving age; Mosley proposed planned foreign trade and the control of credit to promote industrial expansion. Thomas merely deferred to the rigid and cantankerous financial orthodoxy of the Chancellor of the Exchequer, and in Cabinet Lansbury lacked the expertise to argue his case.

In the spring of 1930 Lansbury decided in consultation with Mosley and Johnston to put into one document all the suggestions upon which the unemployment quartet were agreed. The document, drafted by Mosley and afterwards known as the Mosley Memorandum, proposed public control of banking; the use of credit to revive home purchasing power; control of imports by direct limitation and by bulk purchase from the Dominions; development of the social services; retirement pensions; re-equipment and reorganization of industry, to increase production rapidly both for home and foreign markets; and active development of home agriculture. Snowden rejected it as repugnant to all his economic beliefs; most Labour MPs rejected it, some because it was too extreme, some because they could not understand it; and the Cabinet rejected it as a political impossibility. Mosley resigned. Under heavy Opposition pressure, the PLP closed ranks against him, and threw out by 202 votes to 29 a resolution put by him, condemning the government's failure to deal with unemployment. MacDonald moved Thomas to the Dominions Office, substituting Hartshorn, and replaced Mosley by Attlee, taking over responsibility for unemployment himself, thus downgrading the

86

posts of Lord Privy Seal and Chancellor of the Duchy of Lancaster. The two Labour men on the Simon Commission, hitherto neglected, now held office.

In modern times the ancient office of Chancellor of the Duchy of Lancaster is a sinecure to which a minister can be appointed, free of departmental responsibility, to help in an advisory capacity with important problems. MacDonald's choice of Attlee to succeed the troublesome Mosley indicated his view that Attlee was 'safe'. Nevertheless, the appointment was most fortunate for Attlee. It widened his range of experience; it relieved him of the burden of having seemed 'reactionary' on India; and it enabled him to be identified with those who, as a result of the crisis of 1931 would later break with 'the traitors', MacDonald, J.H. Thomas and Philip Snowden.

His immediate task was to assist MacDonald with the Imperial Conference of 1930. This brought useful contact with Commonwealth problems. Canada and Australia, he later wrote, 'gave no trouble on political matters, were very difficult over economic questions, whereas South Africa and Eire were all sweetness in the latter field but very awkward on Commonwealth political relations.' The economic questions were mainly on imperial preference, the political ones mainly on constitutional independence. Agreement reached on the latter led to the passing of the Statute of Westminster in 1931, which in Attlee's view 'really gave statutory effect to what was already accepted in practice, the equality of all the Dominions'. Attlee also worked with Addison, the former Liberal minister who became Minister of Agriculture in 1930. Attlee helped him to prepare a number of bills, including the measure which established the Milk and Potato Marketing Boards. Addison became his model for how ministers should behave, and also gave Attlee his first lesson about the failings of the Labour government: 'In his [Addison's] fight for getting through his policy, not least of the obstacles to be overcome was the inertia of MacDonald and the negative attitude of Snowden.'

Attlee himself was soon to be victim of his leaders' passivity in the face of economic challenge. As Chancellor of the Duchy he was a member of the Economic Advisory Council, created by MacDonald in January 1930 to keep the government in touch with current economic problems and ideas. It included Keynes, Tawney, G.D.H. Cole, Bevin, Citrine and several businessmen, with an expert staff of five. It met infrequently and rarely agreed, but it gave Attlee new insights on Britain's economic problems. In its search for a policy on industrial reorganization, the Cabinet invited the new Chancellor of the Duchy 'to make an intensive study of what is wrong with British industry and what steps ought to be taken to provide a remedy'. Attlee's efforts, submitted on 30 July under the title 'The Problems of British Industry', reflected ideas then current in 'progressive' economic circles, and perhaps owed much to his secretary, Colin Clark, who had previously assisted Mosley. There was no mention of socialism or nationalization. Britain's economic ills were identified as labour immobility and lack of innovation, and the cure was to be 'rationalization' of industry, a term then used to describe the process of mergers, closure of uneconomic factories, and investment of the resources thus freed in more efficient and profitable productions.

Attlee pointed out that this would require the 'Deliberate Direction of the Economic Life of the Nation'. A ministry of industry was needed, 'an executive arm, which . . . will express policy in action. The country is face to face with an emergency like that of war.' An industrial development board, of 'industrial administrators, representatives of organized labour, and a minority of bankers' with the minister of industry as chairman, should have considerable powers of financing and directing industrial development, over public works, bank credit and labour. The most interesting – and characteristic – feature of the Attlee Memorandum is the insistence on *action*. He was trying to succeed where Oswald Mosley had failed, and he was taking political risks with his superiors in so doing. By the way in which they had treated Mosley's Memorandum, MacDonald and Snowden had shown they did not *wish* to act. The price of action was too high. But, wrote Attlee: 'the essential thing is the translation of ideas into action'.

The Attlee Memorandum, given in full as Appendix I to this book, sank without trace. The Treasury prepared a vitriolic attack on it which was never used, because though prepared as a Cabinet Paper the memorandum never came to Cabinet for discussion. Attlee and Hartshorn, who had written a brief supporting paper, were loyal to their leaders, but did not suffer entirely in silence. 'Several times the Cabinet asked us to wind up debates on unemployment, but we both replied that until we saw signs of a more vigorous policy we would not speak.' In any case Attlee's impatience was tempered by the lingering hope that sooner or later his scheme would be accepted. At the party conference at Llandudno in October 1930, Mosley's renewed attack on the government's inactivity was greeted with considerable support; but Attlee, like Lansbury, spoke in defence of MacDonald despite his private reservations. In November he wrote to his brother Tom that his proposals, though 'hung up', were 'now more or less accepted in principle. The actual working of [the proposals] depends on who is put in charge. It seems rather likely to be me.'

Attlee did not become minister of industry. Instead, the direction of his career was changed by a minor squall within the government, presaging the storm which would eventually destroy it. In February 1931 Mosley left the Labour Party to found the New Party, later the British

Union of Fascists. In the same month, Snowden accepted a Liberal amendment to a Conservative censure motion, and agreed to the establishment of an independent committee to review government expenditure. He had determined to balance the budget by the end of the year, and hoped that the committee, under Sir George May, would help educate the public in the necessity for harsh measures. His Labour critics were appalled by his uncompromising defence of financial orthodoxy and his opposition to expenditure on public works or industrial investment. Soon afterwards Sir Charles Trevelyan, President of the Board of Education, resigned because the Lords threw out a bill to raise the school-leaving age to fifteen, and decided to make his resignation a protest against MacDonald's leadership. The PLP heard him in silence and rallied to MacDonald's call for loyalty. Attlee, who complained privately to his brother about 'the timidity and conservatism of some ministers', was among the many who continued to insist in public that 'we have not a majority for full Socialist measures in this House'. On Trevelyan's resignation, H.B. Lees Smith went to the Board of Education, and Attlee took over from Lees Smith as Postmaster-General. He was now in a departmental post which did not involve him in the main problem of the day. When the government failed to solve it, and collapsed, Attlee would not be blamed. It was a lucky break.

II

The next five months provided Attlee with the first and virtually the only experience of being a departmental minister before he became prime minister in 1945. Among twentieth-century British premiers only Mac-Donald, Bonar Law and Heath have had such slight departmental experience, though the other three did not have five years as deputy prime minister as a preparation for their job. Until he became Postmaster-General, Attlee's experience of administration had been confined to the Haileybury Club and a wartime infantry company. He was very conscious of this, and consequently he asked Clement Davies, the Liberal MP, then legal consultant to ICI, if he would arrange a few weeks' crash course for him at the company's headquarters.

Attlee took up his new post with relief at being removed from a position in which he felt he could do nothing. He enjoyed his short period as Postmaster-General. 'We had a great time at the Post Office.' One of the first jobs he tackled was the development of the GPO's public relations, a field in which the department had not previously shone. He formed a publicity committee, set up a public relations department, and called in outside advertising experts. Hearing from one, unnamed, newspaper magnate 'that there was a very close link between the advertising and editorial management of his newspapers, and that anything given to the first had an immediate effect on the second', he began to advertise the Post Office in the press with great success: 'I found that he was quite right, a small expenditure yielding good results.' The Post Office was particularly keen to increase the use of the telephone. Attlee launched a campaign to sell more telephones. It was a great success, and received much publicity. 'Not a very easy task considering the industrial depression.'

The Permanent Under-Secretary in charge of the Post Office was Sir Evelyn Murray. Very tall, handsome, with great presence, he was, said Attlee, 'the complete aristocrat'. He had occupied the post for seventeen years, and was accustomed to getting his own way. When Baldwin congratulated Attlee on his appointment he added: 'You'll find your real difficulty will be Murray.' Attlee decided that instead of discussing how the GPO should be run only in private conversation with Sir Evelyn, he would hold meetings which would be attended by all heads of departments. For the first of these 'council meetings' Murray arrived very late, sat down, and ostentatiously immersed himself in various documents he had brought in with him, taking no part in the discussion. Attlee decided that Murray must at once be cut down to size. 'I sent for him and said: "You were bored with the meeting, weren't you?" He said: "Yes." I said: "You showed it. That mustn't happen again." I had no more trouble with him.'

Attlee soon became convinced that the structure of the department was in need of considerable change, and that Murray was not the man to effect it. He therefore called in an industrial consultant, who concluded that Murray's regime had led to over-centralization and recommended the establishment of a council of officers under the chairmanship of the postmaster-general, which would deal with policy matters. Attlee was out of office before anything could be done, but these suggestions were taken up by his successor, Kingsley Wood.

In his brief tenure, Attlee had time to come to some general conclusions about the Post Office which influenced his views on methods of public ownership. He formed the view that the office of postmaster-general should not continue to be a political one. He found that ministers tended to regard it as a stepping-stone to higher posts, and were inclined to hurry any steps they might take to reorganize its structure of administration. As a result of this, too many changes occurred too fast, and the department was never able to settle down to a steady level of efficiency. He concluded that general responsibility for the Post Office should be assigned to the ministry of transport, which would maintain parliamentary control and answer for GPO policy in an occasional general debate, but should appoint either a non-political administrator or a board to direct its day-to-day running. He criticized the way chancellors of the exchequer were inclined to drain off Post Office profits in order to balance their budgets. Their terms of office often being short, they failed to appreciate schemes of improvement which did not produce quick increases in revenue.

In his last official note to MacDonald, Attlee told the Prime Minister he was 'engaged in a close examination of the financial relation of the Post Office with the Treasury, and shall submit a scheme for the consideration of the Chancellor in due course'. He was out of office before he could do so, but he outlined his ideas in a newspaper article written a few months later: 'The Chancellor is in the position of a shareholder in a company who is not out for a long-term investment, but wants the biggest return on his money before he clears out. . . . The position of the Post Office as the milch cow of the Exchequer [is] intolerable.' The GPO should pay to the Treasury a sum calculated on a number of measurable factors, such as, for instance, interest on invested capital and the monopoly value of the authority. Its responsibility, and subjection, to the Treasury should end there. The Post Office had 'two sides to its balance sheet', and the Treasury official, trained to deal with one side only, tried to exercise a control 'wholly incompatible with the flexibility necessary in the conduct of a business concern'.

As prime minister, Attlee was to take the view that if an undertaking were nationalized it should not be subjected to the degree of supervision which he had found to be plaguing the Post Office in 1931. He therefore supported Morrison's view that nationalized industries should be administered by public boards.

Attlee's enjoyment of his work at the Post Office was marred by anxieties about Vi's health. Their fourth, and last, child, Alison, had been born in April 1930, shortly before he took office as Chancellor of the Duchy of Lancaster. During the summer there were evening engagements in London in connection with the Imperial Conference – 'a lot of junketing went with the job', Attlee told Tom – and wives were frequently invited. Later in the year there was the Round Table Conference on India, with many dinners and receptions in the evening. Vi looked after the three elder children's suppers, bathed and fed Alison, then went into London for the evening's engagement.

After one of these official dinners she caught a cold. The following Sunday, when she walked to church, she was unsteady on her feet. That night she had an acute headache. In the morning she felt too giddy to get out of bed to nurse Alison, so she asked Attlee to bring the baby to her bed. Over the next few days she found it difficult to concentrate. When she moved uncertainly across the room, Nellie had to walk behind her. She was sent to hospital for a fortnight's rest, then convalesced at Torquay for two weeks. She came home no better, and was taken to the Westminster Hospital, where what Attlee called sleepy sickness, but what was probably *encephalitis lethargica*, was diagnosed. She was in hospital for several weeks. When she came out she stayed with her mother at Bushey Heath. A few months later she had another spell in Westminster Hospital. More fluid was taken from the spine, and there was another course of injections. Slowly she made progress, but when she was discharged she had to learn to walk again. She had several falls. A nurse lived in the house for several months. It was a long and very worrying year.

Vi began to feel normal about twelve months after the illness had begun. Attlee, said Nellie Evans, bore it stoically. 'There was just the one day when he was sharp with the children: they were noisy; "Be quiet," he said. "Your mother is resting." Sometimes he looked tired. . . . When he was in the house he was never away from her.' He never spoke of her illness to the children, and only the eldest, Janet, realized that something was seriously wrong with her mother's health.

Vi's illness led to the move from Woodford Green to Stanmore. With four children they were already finding 17 Monkham's Avenue small; a move was desirable and, since there was now Vi's health to consider, they thought it would be best to move in the direction of Vi's family. While staying with her mother at Bushey Heath, Vi looked around for a house. She found 'Heywood', a few hundred yards out of Stanmore, a solid detached house, standing in its own grounds, thirty yards back from the main road. One they had decided to buy it, she moved into it without ever going back to live in Monkham's Avenue. She was glad to get away from it. Her first home as a married woman, it was associated with a new way of life, bringing many problems of personal and political responsibilities; looking after four small children; a husband who spent most of his hours away from the house, and several long periods away from the country. Heywood, Stanmore, promised a new and easier existence. When, followed by the van carrying the rest of the furniture, Attlee drove the children over to Stanmore from Woodford, Vi was waiting on the steps of Heywood to welcome them.

The decision to move to Heywood in October 1931 was taken in July. October then 'seemed a safe time when nothing much was doing', Attlee recorded. In fact the move took place in the middle of the election campaign that had followed a time of crisis. His remark shows how little presentiment of crisis there had been in the summer of 1931. In early August, at the end of the parliamentary session, Attlee went off to Frinton with the children and Nellie Evans for the family's annual seaside holiday. Vi joined them a few days later. It was from Frinton, three weeks later, that Attlee was recalled to London by the Prime Minister, not, as he supposed, to discuss how Post Office policy might be affected by the economic crisis, but to be told that MacDonald, in view of the economic crisis, had decided to form a national government.

7

Labour Divides,
1931-3

Just before he left Frinton, Attlee wrote to his brother Tom:

> The political scene is full of alarms and excursions and what will be the
> upshot God knows. I have been summoned to see the PM tomorrow, but
> whether on certain GPO matters or on the general situation I know not.
> *The Times* is giving prominence to letters from some of the biggest fools
> going, both MPs and other.

Like most MPs, Attlee had taken his family holiday unsuspectingly
during the first stages of the greatest crisis in the Labour Party's history.
Its origins lay in the collapse of the German banking system following
the failure of an Austrian bank in May. With their German assets frozen,
large investors in search of liquidity withdrew their sterling from London.
To meet the run on the pound which had developed by July, Snowden
was convinced that he had to restore foreign confidence by balancing the
budget with stringent measures. The report of Sir George May's committee, published on the last day of July, gave him the ammunition he
needed. To meet a predicted deficit of £120,000,000 by the next April,
the committee recommended cuts in public service salaries, reductions in
public works programmes, a 20 per cent reduction in unemployment
benefit, and the imposition of a 'means test' on applicants for transitional
benefits. The attack on unemployment benefits, above all else, infused
Labour's recollections of the crisis of August 1931 with a bitterness which
remains to this day.

The immediate effect of the publication of the May Report was to
accelerate the run on the pound. By 11 August the acting governor of the
Bank of England, Sir Ernest Harvey (the Governor, Sir Montagu Norman, was ill), informed Snowden that there was practically no foreign
currency left. Snowden asked MacDonald to break off his holiday and

return to London to meet the Bank of England's representatives. They made it clear that if the government wished to remain on the gold standard, a large American loan would have to be raised within a few days. To get it the government would have to show the Americans in advance that it would balance its budget by means of immediate cuts in public expenditure, which would have to include a reduction in unemployment benefits, and also present the Americans with the approval of its measures by the leaders of the other two parties. There then followed a series of meetings of the Cabinet and of the Cabinet Economy Committee, a sub-committee set up by MacDonald to consider the May Report, consisting of MacDonald, Henderson, Snowden, Thomas and Graham, the President of the Board of Trade. MacDonald himself had frequent meetings with the Bank of England and with Opposition leaders. The Cabinet was deeply divided, especially over the cuts in unemployment benefit. Henderson, knowing that he was backed by Bevin and the TUC, called for a revenue tariff and other expansionist measures which were now being urged by Keynes. Snowden demurred: substantial cuts were essential to please the American bankers.

Henderson and his Cabinet supporters reluctantly agreed to discuss further cuts. On 22 August 1931 the Cabinet decided that MacDonald should discover from Opposition leaders whether they would support the government if it proposed a programme of cuts, including a reduction of 10 per cent in unemployment benefit. MacDonald was later to claim that this decision – to discuss cuts with the Opposition – represented an implicit acceptance of the cuts by Henderson and his colleagues; Henderson, on the other hand, maintained that he had not committed himself to the cuts, and that he had only taken part in a 'preliminary examination' of the proposals, though the acting Cabinet secretary's notes show no trace of any such reservation on his part. (Malcolm MacDonald told the author Henderson may have changed his mind under pressure from Ernest Bevin.) After the meeting MacDonald went to Baldwin and Samuel, who agreed to support his government provided the programme he outlined was acceptable to the American bankers. The next day MacDonald saw the King, and explained that several Cabinet ministers would resign if the economies were put through, and that this would mean the fall of the government and his own resignation. The King said he would consult Baldwin and Samuel; MacDonald approved, but it is not known whether he actually proposed such a meeting. When consulted, separately, later that day, both Opposition leaders suggested that only a Labour prime minister could carry out unpopular measures which would chiefly affect the working classes. Both said they would serve in a national government under MacDonald.

Meanwhile MacDonald had asked the Cabinet to give formal approval to the economy measures to which, he averred, they had already agreed and which the Bank and the Opposition leaders had accepted. Eleven accepted; nine refused. Henderson and his supporters maintained that the government should resign rather than accept the cuts. MacDonald accordingly went to the Palace and tendered his resignation to the King; in what terms and with what force, we do not know. It was not accepted. MacDonald returned to his waiting Cabinet and, without telling them that the King thought him the only man who could lead the country through a crisis, reported that he was meeting the leaders of the Opposition parties the next morning.

Apparently none of the Cabinet objected to his doing so; but then, they said afterwards, they did not know what MacDonald was going to say to the Opposition leaders. On the Monday morning (24 August) the King saw MacDonald with Baldwin and Samuel, and said he wanted MacDonald to stay on as Prime Minister, and Baldwin and Samuel to serve under him. All three agreed. It was implicit that the arrangement was to last only for the emergency, and the Opposition leaders stipulated that there should be a general election as soon as the financial crisis was over. After discussing details of the new administration, MacDonald drove to Downing Street and informed his Cabinet that he had been asked, and had agreed, to form a national government.

Most of the Cabinet, including several of the eleven who had earlier supported the cuts, denounced the decision. There is no evidence that MacDonald had consulted anyone, even Snowden, before agreeing to form a national government; and it seems unlikely that he asked anyone at that meeting to join him in a 'Cabinet of Individuals', as was later alleged. Instead he waited until after the meeting to ask Snowden, Thomas and Lord Sankey (the Attorney General) to join the new government. At 4.10 that afternoon MacDonald formally tendered the Labour Cabinet's resignation to the King. The establishment of the national government was announced at 9.15 that night, Monday 24 August 1931. The Cabinet was to include, besides MacDonald and the three Labour men, four Conservatives, Baldwin (as Lord President), Chamberlain, Hoare, Cunliffe-Lister, and two Liberals, Samuel and Lord Reading.

Attlee arrived in London on the morning of 24 August and lunched with Hugh Dalton, who recorded that: 'He [Attlee] is hot against JRM for his indecision and his inferiority complex, especially in all economic questions, and hotter still against Snowden who, he says, has blocked every positive proposal for the past two years.' There are several accounts of MacDonald's meeting with the junior ministers. On the main issues these agree. Attlee recorded:

> The Prime Minister told us that he had hoped merely to tell us that our salaries were to be cut, but now he must ask for our resignation. He made

us a long and insincere speech in which he begged us to remain with the Party out of regard for our careers, but really because he had all the appointments fixed up and any adhesions would have gravely embarrassed him. Except for a question by Dalton and one by me, we received his speech in silence and left without a word.

Attlee's question was about what he called 'the rentier': what sacrifice was being demanded of the recipients of unearned income? MacDonald replied that he could not answer that question: to do so would be to anticipate a budget statement. This answer did not please Attlee. What angered him most was MacDonald's remark that the political crisis was the result of members of the Labour Cabinet going back on commitments which they had previously agreed to and which, if they had adhered to them, would have secured the loan. Like most of those present, Attlee believed that from the beginning the defenders of the masses, led by Henderson and Graham, had refused to agree that cuts in unemployment benefit were necessary or acceptable. In his autobiography, Attlee recalled that MacDonald assured them the coalition government was only a temporary measure:

> He did not wish any of us to join and said there would certainly not be a 'coupon' General Election. He would soon be back with us. These remarks were received with scepticism by those who knew him best. Having already distributed the offices in the new Government, he would have been embarrassed if any Labour Ministers had wished to join, though this did not prevent him in the future from denouncing them for deserting him. Probably he had counted on more members following him than the handful who did so.

Attlee's statement that MacDonald would have been embarrassed if any Labour ministers had wished to join should not be accepted as it stands. MacDonald may have by then 'distributed the offices in the new Government' so far as the senior posts were concerned but there were many junior positions to be filled. If he had found any supporters, he would doubtless have tried to make places for some of them. He certainly approached Shinwell and Cripps, who declined directly, and Morrison, who had accepted the unemployment cuts and hesitated before finally refusing. But the story of MacDonald's determination to abandon the Labour Party was soon firmly established. Three months previously, Fenner Brockway had published an article warning the Labour Party that MacDonald was secretly discussing with representatives of the two other parties a plan 'to scuttle the Labour Government and to form a National Government'. Many who had not taken this article seriously when it appeared now changed their minds. Attlee was one. He now recalled that he had heard MacDonald, when talking about his difficulties, murmur now and then: 'We must have a *national* government.' Attlee had not attached much importance to such remarks at the time. He did so now. He came to the conclusion that MacDonald 'had for some years been more and more attracted by the social environment of the well-to-do classes. He had got more and more out of touch with the rank and file of the Party, while the adulation which is almost inseparable from the necessary publicity given to the leader of the great movement had gone to his head and increased his natural vanity.'

Attlee's opinion of MacDonald's behaviour at this time never changed. In his autobiography he was scathing:

> The unpopular line which he took during the First World War seemed to mark him as a man of character. Despite his mishandling of the Red Letter episode, I had not appreciated his defects until he took office a second time. I then realised his reluctance to take positive action and noted with dismay his increasing vanity and snobbery, while his habit of telling me, a junior Minister, the poor opinion he had of all his Cabinet colleagues made an unpleasant impression.
>
> I had not, however, expected that he would perpetrate the greatest betrayal in the political history of this country.

These bitter words, written a quarter of a century later, are not in character. Attlee could occasionally be biting in personal encounters and in private correspondence; and he could be surgically frank, as we shall see, in dismissing ministers who had failed, in his view, to meet their responsibilities. But he did not publicly condemn men in the uncompromising terms he used about MacDonald, and particularly when the men were dead he found good things to say of them, or said nothing. There may be more than one reason for his vehemence about MacDonald. His feelings at the time may have been exasperated by a sense of guilt about his own behaviour – that he had been too 'loyal' to MacDonald for too long, that earlier he should have 'spoken out'. During his nine months as chancellor of the duchy of Lancaster, Attlee saw what was happening clearly. Yet – as was later pointed out by Snowden – Attlee supported the appointment of the May Economy Committee, which he was afterwards to denounce, although, he admits, he knew 'the result might have been anticipated', and that 'the proposals [of the Committee] were directed to cutting the social services and particularly unemployment benefit.'

Whether or not an element of guilt was an ingredient in Attlee's denunciation of MacDonald's 'betrayal' of the Labour Party and the British working class in 1931, we know that he meant what he said. By laying hands on the relief of the unemployed MacDonald had outraged the feelings of compassion and sense of social justice which had brought Attlee into politics in the first place, and had remained his first concern ever since. Moreover, MacDonald had revealed himself as fundamentally untrustworthy. He had misled Attlee when he told him that going to

India would not mean exclusion from office if Labour came to power. Attlee now concluded that MacDonald's style of leadership must never again be tolerated in a leader of the Labour Party. MacDonald had put himself on a pedestal, and led the party from above. This was not only undemocratic; it had now proved to be dangerous. This kind of leadership must never be permitted again. The party must be led as though by a chairman of a committee. MacDonaldism, as well as MacDonald, must be denounced in the interests of the future of the party, which henceforth must be led in a different kind of way.

After the 'farewell' from MacDonald, the ex-ministers walked across to Transport House for an emergency meeting of the Parliamentary Labour Party. Henderson was elected the new leader. Writing afterwards, and having given the names of the ministers who were 'going National', Attlee added: 'There were about ten other rats in the Commons.' After the PLP meeting Attlee went to St Martin's-Le-Grand to clear up his departmental work at the Post Office and say goodbye to his chief permanent officials. 'We have heard the crack of the master's whip, and we have got to go,' he told them. 'He is filling our places with other men.' Nine days after the formation of the national government, Attlee wrote to Tom:

> Things are pretty damnable – I fear we are in for a regime of false economy and a general attack on the workers' standard of life. . . . The real trouble to my mind has been the failure of Snowden all through to face the financial situation. He has always rather slavishly followed City opinion while JRM has been far too prone to take his views from bankers and big business.

At first Snowden's policy seemed to succeed. The American loan was received, and with an increase in taxation he was able to balance the budget. But the cuts in service pay caused a mutiny in the fleet at Invergordon which, though soon ended, caused a further run on the pound. There was no choice left but to go off the gold standard. Snowden did so on 21 September, less than a fortnight after he had presented the budget which was designed to prevent just that. It was a terrible humiliation for Snowden and it compounded his bitterness. Contrary to his predictions the heavens did *not* fall as a result of Britain's going off gold. What the TUC had told him a month previously, proved correct. Meanwhile the long-term economic problems remained. Many Conservatives wanted a protective tariff, which was repugnant to Snowden. On 5 October 1931 MacDonald resolved a Cabinet deadlock about the tariff by introducing a formula according to which each party would draft its own manifesto, but the government would go united to the country to seek a 'doctor's' mandate.

MacDonald had not wanted an election, which was inconsistent with his promises to Labour leaders in August. One factor which had helped change his mind, as well as convincing Snowden of the need for an election, was that on 28 September both had been expelled from the Labour Party at its annual conference at Scarborough. All other members of the party who had associated themselves with the national government received the same treatment. This made it clear to MacDonald that feelers towards reconciliation which Henderson was said to be putting out would not be countenanced by the Labour Party as a whole.

Snowden had already indicated in Parliament his relish at the imminent destruction of the Labour Party. He received notice of his expulsion on 2 October, the day on which he made his last speech in the House of Commons, winding up on the third reading of the Finance Bill. His speech ruined any chance of a bridge being built across the gulf between MacDonald and the Labour Party. Attlee was Labour's official spokesman in the debate. What Attlee said to Snowden, and what Snowden said to Attlee, established the mood in which Labour fought the 1931 election, and in consequence influenced the Labour Party's state of mind for the rest of the 1930s; it has retained some impress upon Labour Party thinking up to this day.

With Dalton, Addison, Alexander, Cripps and other former junior ministers, Attlee was now a member of a Labour Party policy committee. Most of his colleagues were up at Scarborough, Attlee being left to hold the fort in Westminster, a fact with which Snowden was to make a lot of play. In the debate, Attlee launched an attack on Snowden's economic policy. The Chancellor, he said, had broken all parliamentary records. He had not merely produced two budgets in one session; he had produced one on behalf of the Labour Party and the other on behalf of 'the united capitalist parties'. The budgets were based on entirely different social philosophies. 'The first one still retains, to some extent at all events, the social philosophy which the right honourable gentleman has preached with such extreme success for the last thirty or forty years; and the second one is based on a wholly different outlook.' Both, however, were 'quite inadequate to deal with the position of the national finances of the day'. Snowden had started the scare by his speech in February, 'but took no action to meet it, except of course to appoint committees. . . . Instead of facing the urgent economy that he said was needed when he spoke in February, he entrusted that to the May Committee.' A Conservative MP interrupted to ask: 'Did not you support that?' Attlee answered: 'No, I do not support the May Committee.' This interrogator countered with: 'But you voted for the setting up of the May Committee.'

Attlee went on with his assault on Snowden's two 'failed' budgets. The September 'emergency' budget had been devised to keep us on the gold standard. Now we were off the gold standard. He then attacked the inequality of the sacrifices the Chancellor had imposed. He denounced the reduction in family allowances. The Chancellor was taking the luxuries of the poor, but not of the rich. The country was carrying an inflated rentier class, which it could not afford. He opposed entirely 'the idea that this country is to be run in such a way as to establish the utmost confidence among capitalists'. He rejected not only the budget but the philosophy on which it was based:

> On all constructive measures [Snowden] has been sterile and obstructive.... At one time he was prepared to deal in a broad statesmanlike way with the problem of society, but ... he has gradually slipped back and back to a more *laissez-faire* individualism.... He has brought forward this Bill, as the result of a total misconception of the financial conditions of the world, and it is an example of that deflationist policy which has done so much to bring the world to its present situation; and we deplore that the right honourable gentleman should have closed his career with the production of this Budget.

Snowden began his reply with a sneer at Attlee's speech:

> His speech reminded me of a saying of Disraeli's describing an amateur debating society – in which the honourable member has evidently graduated – that the speeches contained a superabundance of intended sarcasm. The honourable member paid me the compliment of saying that I was a master of invective, but I must say that his attempt to imitate my invective was a lamentable failure.

Snowden reiterated the charge that Attlee had supported the appointment of the May Committee, insisted that a minority government could never have carried out the required economies, and went on to attack in bitter language not only Labour's arguments in the debate, but the party's general conduct. In his autobiography Snowden claimed that he had not planned this attack. Until the event he had 'ignored the offensiveness of a section of the Labour Party'; then, its official spokesman 'made a speech which gave me the opportunity to say frankly what I thought about their attitude and their action in running away from their duty to deal with the financial situation ... their hypocritical conduct in disowning proposals to which the majority of them agreed as members of the late Government.'

As official spokesman, Attlee acquitted himself with credit. It was a cogent speech, and, considering that most of his supporters were absent from the House because they were at the party conference, a brave one. It was not one of the memorable attacks on an established leader which presages the arrival of a future statesman, but he did an impressive job of exploiting the strongest points in a far from powerful case. Labour's case was vulnerable. So was Attlee's personal record. Snowden pounded both. If he had not sneered as well, Attlee might have been in trouble.

II

It was a fierce election. Snowden, making effective use of the new medium of radio, condemned the Labour Party's manifesto, *Labour's Call to Action*, as 'Bolshevism run mad'. On the hustings MacDonald waved German banknotes from the great inflation of the early twenties. A National Liberal, with Snowden's support, prophesied that Labour would confiscate deposits in the Post Office Savings Bank. The *Manchester Guardian* pronounced it 'the most fraudulent election campaign of modern times'. Though the feelings of political activists ran high, the mood of the country during the election campaign was grim rather than bitter. In Limehouse 'the campaign pursued its usual quiet course, and it did not appear that anything unusual was in the wind.'

Attlee was opposed by a young Conservative, Richard Girouard, a stockbroker, and by a 'Mosleyite' taxi-driver, H. L. Hodge. For Girouard, the main issues were the need for national unity in the face of economic crisis, protection, Empire free trade, and the maintenance of the independence of local Catholic schools. Girouard was only twenty-six years of age, and he was an overt admirer, and supporter, of Attlee's public work in the East End, but he fought a formidable campaign against him. He mobilized a number of nationally known Tories to come and speak for him, including Beaverbrook. Addressing one meeting, Beaverbrook declared that Empire free trade would bring down the price of silk stockings. 'Down here we don't wear silk stockings!' Beaverbrook replied: 'Madam: vote for Dick Girouard and you will.' Attlee scraped through with a majority of only 551. Noting the attention that was focused on Vi during the campaign, Girouard still thinks that if his wife had been with him on the hustings he would have won. Lady Blanche Girouard was an able and attractive young woman, well known and liked in the East End because she had done a great deal of voluntary work there. She took no part in the campaign because she was about to give birth to a son. If Girouard's wife had not been pregnant in the autumn of 1931, perhaps some chapters of our history would have read differently.

The votes were counted in Limehouse the day after the poll. Many other results, however, were announced on the night of polling day. Attlee, returning to the new house at Stanmore, was greeted at the station with the news that Labour had lost St Helens, a safe seat, by a large majority. Until then he had high hopes of Labour's prospects in the election. The news of St Helens shattered him. 'It was clearly a landslide. I decided to sleep on it, and in the morning I discovered the extent of the rout.' What was going to happen to him? He went back to Limehouse with far less confidence than he had come away with the night before, and heard the result declared with profound relief. The figures were:

Attlee   11,354
Girouard   10,803
Hodge   307

The Labour members for the other two Stepney divisions were both defeated, though narrowly. East London was, with South Wales and the Yorkshire mining areas, one of the three parts of the country where Labour held its own; fifteen Labour MPs, almost a third of Labour's contingent in the new Parliament, were Welsh. Overall the government won 556 seats. There were only forty-six MPs from the official Labour Party who, with six independent Labour and four Lloyd George Liberals, made up an opposition of fifty-six.

All the 'non-National' former Cabinet ministers except George Lansbury lost their seats: Henderson, Clynes, Graham, Johnston, Dalton, Greenwood, Addison, Alexander, Pethick Lawrence, Shinwell, Lees Smith and Herbert Morrison. Their loss was Attlee's gain. Had they been re-elected to Parliament, several of these would have had a far better prospect than Lansbury of being chosen leader of the Parliamentary Labour Party. Any of them would have been selected as deputy leader in preference to Attlee. Neither Lansbury nor Attlee had been a member of the Labour Party's National Executive, nor of the Executive of the PLP. With the exception of Morrison, all of the others were members of the NEC. But the giants were not re-elected; Lansbury and Attlee were, and the outcome was a foregone conclusion, Cripps being a comparative newcomer to the party who had spent only a year in the House. At the first meeting of the fifty-two members of the Parliamentary Labour Party after the election, therefore, Lansbury was elected leader and Attlee his deputy. The ill wind for Labour had blown Attlee nothing but good.

III

The forty-six Labour MPs faced a stiff task. They had to keep up a fight against a government whose seats outnumbered them by twelve to one. About a third of them were elderly trade union members holding safe seats in the mining areas, who, as limited by experience and training as by age, could vote in a division, but contribute little else. Only a few of the forty-six were able to share the strain of long hours of committee and debate. Aneurin Bevan made speech after speech on the plight of the depressed areas; Tom Williams spoke on agriculture with a growing authority which soon earned the respect of the Conservatives; and Jimmy Maxton, supported by a handful of ILP members, for several years acquitted himself well on domestic affairs. But the weight of work came down on the shoulders of the front-bench triumvirate, and because Lansbury was old, and Cripps was inexperienced, the bulk of it fell on Attlee's.

The first two years after the débâcle of 1931, therefore – in terms of hours worked, speeches made in and out of the House, committees attended – were the busiest of Attlee's parliamentary experience. One of the triumvirate was always on the front bench, and since Attlee's portfolio had the widest range, he was the most frequently on duty. He had to deal with many major subjects he had not previously much studied, including foreign affairs and finance. He frequently spoke three or four times a week. In 1932 he filled more space in Hansard than any other member. Some of his colleagues said that he seemed always in a hurry. He was. One job done, he was up and off to the next, and to be late was an unforgivable sin. His gait became a little faster, his shoulders stooped a little. Lansbury's daughter, who worked as his secretary in the Opposition leader's office, called him 'The White Rabbit'.

Led by a triumvirate which worked well and happily together, the tiny Parliamentary Labour Party put up a surprisingly stout opposition. Their policies and programme did not much impress the House but their spirit and their organization did. Small in numbers, the morale of the Parliamentary Labour Party was high. The lack of consultation between the leader and the led had been a continuing cause for complaint under MacDonald. Lansbury decided to remedy this: the PLP would meet at least once a week, and the PLP Executive Committee would assemble every day before Question Time to decide on tactics. The forty-six soon became a fighting force.

As leader, Lansbury was in many ways ideal, in others quite unsatisfactory. He was the only one of the veteran Labour leaders who had survived the carnage of 1931. He had been the wartime pacifist idol of the ILP. He had been the prophet of 'Poplarism'. He had built up the *Daily Herald* and had founded *Lansbury's Weekly*. In the 1931 crisis, nobody had more strenuously resisted the cuts in unemployment pay than he had. More than any living Labour leader, Lansbury represented socialist idealism – under no other leader could the little band of forty-six have marched into the voting lobby singing 'The Red Flag'. His followers loved him, and trusted him. They knew that in no circumstances would any duchess want to kiss him.

Towards the other member of the triumvirate, Stafford Cripps, Attlee's feelings at this time were a mixture of admiration and affection. Between 1931 and 1933 he and Vi stayed several times with the Crippses at their house in the Cotswolds. 'The only people in the Labour Party I know at all well,' said Vi. 'Lady Cripps was most kind to me, passing on her daughter's outgrown clothes.' Attlee thought highly of Cripps's intellect, integrity and debating skill. He suspected Cripps's practical judgement and was well aware of his lack of knowledge of the Labour Movement, but because of his own class background he appreciated Cripps's idealistic attachment to the objectives of the party. Moreover, in 1931 Cripps was valuable not only for his mind but for his money. He was rich, and he was generous. All the long-distance speaking assignments went to him: he could pay the travelling expenses.

Whatever its courage and capability, and the quality of its leadership, the 46-member Labour Opposition could not have much dinted a government commanding 556 seats out of 635. It had little support from public opinion. Even some Labour sympathizers outside the House believed with Snowden that the Parliamentary Labour Party had run away from its responsibilities in 1931, that far from having been betrayed *by* MacDonald Labour had betrayed *him*. Though it came to be respected inside the House, therefore, outside it the Opposition was regarded even by many of its previous supporters as ineffective, unrealistic and puny. The government was able to do what it pleased, and choose its time for doing it.

Coming to power in November 1931, committed to Protection, in February the government introduced the one legislative measure which it hoped would bring about economic recovery and therefore in time a solution to the unemployment problem – the Import Duties Bill. A general tariff of 10 per cent was imposed in March. This done, the government relied on hope and a belief in the healing powers of nature. Neville Chamberlain's budget in April 1932 introduced few changes except to make economies – expenditures on arms fell to their lowest level between the wars. Attlee was the party's spokesman in the budget debate. He spoke well, but confided to Tom that 'it was quite an ordeal as I have never previously taken part in debates on financial matters ... foreign exchange, gold standard, etc. Today I shall probably have to take part in discussing exchange stabilisation – rather a technical matter.' At the end of the session, in July, Attlee wrote to Tom: 'It has been pretty strenuous. I find that I have delivered 93 speeches in this House, being second only to Cripps.' He had become, by necessity, a parliamentary economic expert, making speeches attacking not only the government's economy measures but the whole of its international economic policy.

In August 1932 the ILP decided to withdraw from the Labour Party. They thought the party had been corrupted as a result of the gradualism with which MacDonald had infected it between 1924 and 1931. Attlee's feelings were mixed. It was the ILP which had first made him feel at home in the socialist movement. He shared their distrust of MacDonald, and he now believed, as they did, that to dilute socialist programmes in order to win power would frustrate the use of that power when it had been obtained. On the other hand:

> I see that the ILP have determined to go their own way and I fancy that they will lose a very big proportion of their membership. The trouble is that they have no real ideas on which to work. They talk revolution, but Brockway has the phrases, and Maxton the appearance, of revolutionaries, but nothing more. We anticipate an accession of strength to SSIP.

The SSIP – the Society for Socialist Information and Propaganda – had been founded a year previously to reinject the Labour Party with the ideas and objectives supplied by the Fabians a quarter of a century before, and to educate its leaders in what to do with parliamentary power when the day came and they acquired it. Ernest Bevin was its chairman. Attlee did not foresee the direction in which this 'accession of strength to SSIP' would take the party in the short term.

The annual Labour Party conference at Leicester in October 1932 was one of the most important in the party's history. It showed how strong was the movement to the left, and it saw the beginnings of the blueprints for a socialist state, which, elaborated throughout the thirties, became the basis of the postwar Labour government's policies. Attlee had referred to these blueprints several times in letters to Tom: 'We are hard at work on defining policy; my idea is a plan of action to be agreed on, so that when we win next time we shall know exactly what to do, how to do it ... a definite programme [being discussed with] GL, Stafford and I, with sundry pundits such as Cole, Laski, Lloyd, Dalton.'

The 1932 conference met in a militant and confident mood. Within less than a year, the position which MacDonald and Snowden, supported by the Conservative and Liberal leaders, had taken against the rest of the Labour Party had totally disintegrated: Britain was off gold; the budget was not balanced; free trade had been abandoned. The 10 per cent tariff, which Keynes and the Labour leaders had proposed and Snowden had rejected, had now been applied as the master-remedy. The national government had been wrong about everything. The Labour Party, to its own satisfaction, had been proved right. Moreover, the collapse of Labour in 1931 could now be rationalized. Because MacDonald had no socialist solution to the financial crisis, it was held, he turned to the bankers. Next time Labour came to power, it must have a clear programme for immediate implementation; otherwise the City would move in again. The atmosphere of the conference, therefore, was one of resentment against betrayal, hostility to capitalism, and enthusiasm for 'a definite programme' seen not only as an electoral manifesto, but as shield and buckler when in power.

The rapidly growing strength of the movement to the left was manifested at Leicester by the foundation of the Socialist League. When the
ILP broke away, some of its members decided to remain as a group in the
party and try from within to convert it to 'real' socialism. This was the
origin of the 'League'. Its most eloquent spokesman was Stafford Cripps.
He had begun his rapid journey to the left. A great many SSIP members joined the League at once. One of the consequences was the removal of Bevin from the SSIP chairmanship – the League thought him
'reactionary'.

The mood of the conference was almost as militant as that of the
League. The emphasis was on getting the party as a whole to make as
irrevocable a break with MacDonaldism and Snowdenism as the ILP had
made at Bradford. Sir Charles Trevelyan struck the keynote by moving
from the floor a resolution which called on the next Labour government,
whether it had a majority in Parliament or not, to put into effect a
practical socialist programme immediately on entering office and to
stand or fall by it. Henderson urged the conference not to tie Labour's
hands in advance, but Trevelyan's resolution was carried without a card
vote. By this time men like Henderson, who a year before at the time of
the split with MacDonald had been regarded as 'left', were now being
regarded as dangerously like him, and on the 'right'. Attlee supported
Trevelyan and opposed Henderson:

> We are in duty bound to those whom we represent to tell them quite clearly
> that they cannot get Socialism without tears, that whenever we try to do
> anything we will be opposed by every vested interest, financial, political,
> social; and I think we have got to face the fact that even if we are returned
> with a majority, we shall have to fight all the way, that we shall have
> another crisis at once, and that we have got to have a thought-out plan to
> deal with that crisis ...

The main business at Leicester was to discuss the 'definite programme'
put forward by the policy committee of the NEC which had been set up in
December 1931 to draft a better manifesto than *Labour and the New Social
Order* or *Labour and the Nation*. Dalton presented a report recommending
public ownership of the Bank of England, a national investment board,
and price stabilization as a substitute for the gold standard. Morrison
presented reports on the national planning of transport and electricity,
and the conference also received a report on agriculture. Despite the
general shift to the left, two sharp differences of opinion emerged at
Leicester. A motion to nationalize the joint stock banks was carried only
by a narrow majority, with Cripps's support, and Morrison and Bevin
differed strongly about the composition of the boards of nationalized
industries, Morrison opposing the automatic appointment of trade union

representatives, Bevin favouring it. Both arguments were pregnant with consequences for the future.

Nevertheless the Leicester conference put the party in good heart. Lansbury's prestige was at its peak. He was now, as well as leader of the Parliamentary Labour Party, leader of the party as a whole. Throughout the winter he went from strength to strength. He was the symbol of the rescue and redemption of the Labour Movement. Attlee wrote to Tom on 7 February 1933: 'We had a most wonderful demonstration in Hyde Park on Sunday.... George had a great reception all along the route. We tell him he is almost a Gandhi.... George, Stafford and I endeavour to give them the pure milk of the word and no blooming gradualism and palliatives.' He wrote about MacDonald with an insight which later proved to have been remarkably accurate:

> It is difficult to get at MacDonald's mind at any time. It is, I think, mainly fog now. I think that while at the back of his mind he realises his own incompetence for the job which he has in hand, he sees himself in a series of images in the mirror, images which constantly fade and melt into each other. Now he is the Weary Titan, or the good man struggling with adversity; anon he is the handsome and gallant leader of the nation, or the cultured and travelled patron of art and letters. Whatever he does, he is the central figure keeping things going. Despite this, however, there is some leaven of shame, hence his irritation at the existence of GL, which is a standing reproach to him. What I think annoys him is that GL has taken his place entirely with the masses of the people and is also obviously popular with a House of Commons which is entirely indifferent to *him*. He cannot stand the cold blast of criticism. Ceremony and respect due to his position are for him a necessity now, a shell for adulation.

Attlee's disapproval of MacDonald was not confined to his letters. As the months went by some of the Labour MPs who had denounced Mac-Donald in 1931 became more charitable in their personal behaviour towards him. Not Attlee. About this time, Malcolm MacDonald was walking slowly with his father in the House of Commons along the corridor outside the Prime Minister's room. In the distance – there was nobody else in the corridor – they saw Attlee approaching them. As he came near, Malcolm MacDonald told the author, the Prime Minister smiled at Attlee and addressed him. 'Attlee cut him dead and hurried on.'

The party was now committed to socialist programmes, and to putting them into effect. Attlee put everything he could into broadcasting the seed. He would go anywhere, do anything, any time. Nothing was too much trouble. He never said No. He was 'available', 'useful', and 're-liable', three qualities indispensable to the ascent of the party politician. He wrote to Tom:

Thanks very much for your letter of the 19th and for the notes on self determination. I should have replied before but last week was somewhat hectic. I had to speak three times in the House. Then on Tuesday afternoon a lad, Frank Owen, formerly, at a tender age, Lib MP for Hereford, came in to say that Aneurin Bevan had flu and could not debate with Tom Mosley at the Cambridge Union. I agreed to take his place. He drove me up in an open car through a succession of snow storms and we got there just in time for dinner. Mosley talked pretty fair rot to a crowded house. I laughed him to scorn pretty effectively and got a good majority. I had to frame my speech from what he said. He has not any coherent ideas. It is really Mosley and nothing more. As if this was not enough, on Wednesday, when I had to open a new telephone exchange in Mile End at 2.15, and speak in the House on India about 4.15, I was rung up and asked to broadcast instead of Megan Lloyd George, who was ill, so I had hurriedly to compose a 'Week in Westminster' for Thursday morning.

He was still thinking in terms of rescuing the Labour Party from the curse of compromise and gradualism. In August 1933 he wrote to Tom:

I think you are quite right as to the need for our emphasizing that we come not to destroy but to fulfil, but the need at the moment in the older official quarters of the Labour Party is to emphasize that we mean to act and not to sit still and just carry on. There is a lot more hard thinking needed.

As a result of 'hard thinking', the party had by now produced two more special reports, one on housing, the other on colonial development, and another, wider in scope, *Socialism and the Condition of the People*. This third report, mainly about employment and the standard of living, dealt with one problem which had been left unsolved at Leicester the previous year, notably the question of what was to be done about the joint stock banks. It proposed that they should be amalgamated in a publicly owned and controlled banking corporation, which in turn would act under a nationalized Bank of England. This report also set out plans for the public 'ownership or control' of steel and other essential industries not dealt with by previous reports.

These reports were presented to the annual Labour Party conference at Hastings in October 1933. At this conference Cripps set a socialist pace which many Labour leaders, particularly those on the TUC General Council, found disturbing. In April he had written an article in the *Daily Herald* intimating that because of the need to meet the resistance of 'those who at present hold the economic power' a new Labour government must have 'a machinery of government which is capable of rapid action'. He was immediately accused of suggesting a socialist dictatorship – Bevin and Citrine conceded that this was a reasonable interpretation of his article. At the Hastings conference Cripps called on the next Labour government to abolish the House of Lords and then pass an 'Emergency

Powers Act', which would 'take over or regulate the financial machine, and put into force any measure that the situation may require for the immediate control or socialisation of industry and for safeguarding the supply of food and other necessaries'. This was stiff left-wing stuff for the leadership of the party to take, even though it had a year previously turned its back on MacDonald's gradualism.

Many resolutions went further. There were demands that the next Labour government should frame their legislative policy according to the resolutions of the annual conference, and should write the King's speech accordingly. Another required that if Labour took office its policy should be based on conference resolutions and the party's election manifesto. A Labour prime minister must be governed by majority decisions in the Cabinet. Anxious to avoid a showdown on these proposals, the Executive played for time, and accepted them – without enthusiasm.

The profound and lasting controversies over domestic policies which began in these years had an important, if indirect, effect on Attlee's career. They made great inroads on the standing of the men who were then in the running for the succession to the leadership. Because he insisted on the public commitment to the nationalization of the banking system, Cripps was now at odds with Dalton. He was also at odds with Morrison because he advocated extreme left-wing measures which Morrison thought would antagonize moderate middle-class Labour supporters. Bevin, already the most influential of the trade union leaders, was at odds with Cripps, Morrison and, to some extent, Dalton, because he believed that their doctrinaire approach would not lead to effective government if Labour came to power.

Though the chances of these men becoming leader of the party were much discussed, nobody thought much of Attlee's chances of coming up between the front runners. Few people thought much about Attlee at all. Lansbury thought his successor would be Cripps. He had a high opinion of Attlee, but 'no more than anyone else . . . foresaw a great future for this rather diffident committee man'. In a year in which Attlee, making 125 speeches, filled more columns of Hansard than any other member, Citrine, discussing who could succeed Lansbury, mentioned several names, but not Attlee's. Tawney talked of Morrison and Cripps, and did not notice Attlee. Bernard Shaw, writing to Fenner Brockway, refers to the leadership of the Labour Party in the House as though it consisted only of Lansbury and Cripps. Though the Labour Party had made up its mind that charismatic individualistic leadership of the party as practised by MacDonald was never to be permitted again, it looked around for 'big' men. Attlee was left out of account as a potential leader by the Labour Party's pundits precisely because *he* behaved in practice as in principle they thought a leader of the party should. He had long accepted, and acted upon, the 'spokesman' conception of leadership, as his last letter to Tom in 1933 indicates:

> I shall have rather a difficult task tomorrow, having to wind up for us when all the big guns have been firing. It is difficult to anticipate the course of the debate. There is further the fact that the movement is not, I think, quite clear on the question.

A few days after Attlee wrote that letter, Lansbury began to sicken, and by December 1933 he was so ill that Attlee, as deputy, was asked to take over the leadership of the Parliamentary Labour Party. He was to be in charge for nine months, months which proved the making of him as the future leader of the party.

At this time, for family and financial reasons, Attlee was seriously considering withdrawing from politics. The acting leadership would only make matters more difficult by reducing the time available for freelance work. He had considered writing socialist film scripts to buttress his income. At the end of 1933 he wrote to Cripps that he could not afford to carry on as leader until Lansbury was fit – probably four months. 'I think that the only thing for me to do is to resign my position as temporary leader and for you to take over.' Cripps, born rich, was earning large fees at the Bar. He immediately wrote a letter to Attlee urging him to stay, and undertaking to give the party 'a special donation of £500 [the sum which Attlee had calculated as his shortfall for the year] to be used as salary for the Deputy Leader until the Leader is fit to resume his duties,' adding gracefully, 'I shall of course easily earn this sum by non-attendance at Executive meetings, etc.'

A few months later Attlee repaid the family firm, Druces and Attlee, a loan of £487. Though in the next few years he found Cripps's left-wing extremism maddening, the personal bond between them never diminished. And without this timely help it is unlikely that he would have become prime minister.

8

To the Leadership, 1933-5

I

In the nine months in which Attlee deputized for Lansbury, fate might have been planning events to make him the permanent leader. The rise of Hitler and Mussolini required rethinking, directed mainly by Bevin, about the PLP's policy on rearmament, and since Lansbury was a pacifist his position as leader raised doubts in many minds. Henderson was not expected to make a comeback. Cripps, choosing the beginning of 1934 to accelerate his movement to the left, antagonized the right and centre of the party. Morrison was criticized for paying too much attention to the London County Council, and not enough to the Labour Party. Dalton, sharing with Morrison the disadvantage of not having a seat in the House of Commons, was involved in the controversies about the party's policy reports. Arthur Greenwood was thought to be slow and ineffective.

Moreover, the issues of the day favoured Attlee. The rank and file were still concerned about unemployment, and this was of all subjects the nearest to his heart. In this period India was a major problem: on India he was by now clearly established as his party's chief spokesman. Attlee had the good luck to be leading the party when it completed two years of thinking out its 'practical programme' at the party conference at Southport in 1934. Without being involved in the collisions between Morrison and Bevin over workers' control of industry, between Dalton and Cripps over the nationalization of the banks, he was associated with the party's sense of satisfaction when its programme for the next socialist government was completed. Finally, he was acting leader in the period in which the influence of the left was obviously diminishing. The complexion of the conference at Southport in 1934 was quite different from that at Leicester in 1932. Attlee was the leader associated in the minds of the rank and file with the reduction of the influence of the doctrinaires and idealists.

In 1934, unemployment, though decreasing, was still the issue of the day. The Labour Party exploited the slow rate of decline, and pointed out that the statistics for the country as a whole concealed the plight of the depressed areas. Attlee left no stone unthrown, but his main theme was that the government had produced no general policy for dealing with the workless. The government had reduced the unemployed to the breadline by the cuts in benefit in 1931, and had roused class feeling by the Means Test. In February 1933 he had started a speech by congratulating the Minister of Health and the Chancellor of Exchequer on the clarity with which they had put the government case: 'Their lucidity has revealed the nakedness of the land, as far as Government policy is concerned, nakedness ... more or less hidden by the cloudy rhetoric of the Prime Minister.'

In a powerful speech in November 1933 he had attacked the government for refusing to face the economic facts of the problem. They refused to develop the country's resources in material and manpower. Their slum clearance proposals were hopelessly inadequate. 'I lived for many years in, and I represent now, a slum area, where the houses are utterly worn out. The Minister of Health reminds me of a lady who came some years ago to our district, whose object was to help the poor by showing them how to make a baby's cradle out of an old banana crate.' Part of the government's failure to deal with unemployment was due to their reliance on the cushion of unemployment insurance, when their objective should be the fundamental one of eliminating unemployment. Labour's solution was large schemes for public works.

Nineteen thirty-four saw the establishment of the Unemployment Assistance Board – an autonomous 'non-political' body, outside existing government departments, administering unemployment benefit from London through a network of local representatives direct to the recipients. The object was to supersede the local public assistance committees, whose administration of the Means Test was especially resented by the long-term unemployed. Attlee dismissed it as a 'centralized Poor Law'. Because the Act preserved the Means Test it did not take the curse of 'class' off government policy. Then, in December, it became clear that the new national rates to be introduced in January 1935 would, for some people in some areas, be lower than the rates paid by the public assistance committees. The 'Hunger Marchers' took to the road again, and Labour continued the attack in Parliament, winning much public support. The government agreed that despite the new board's 'immunity' from politics it would be told not to reduce the previous rates. Labour's victory on this issue brought laurels to Attlee, who had made most of the running in Parliament.

He was also fortunate that developments in India since 1930 came to a head while he was acting leader of the party. The round table conference of British and Indian leaders had opened in London in November 1930, the Prime Minister presiding in person. Neither Simon nor Attlee was asked to attend. They could have been left out only because Mac-Donald judged they had been compromised, with Labour backbenchers as well as with the Indians, by their membership of the Simon Commission. The conference was the first of three to be held over the next two years. The Congress boycotted the first conference, but progress was made towards a solution of one of the three outstanding problems on which Attlee had laid great emphasis: the Indian princes were represented, and agreed to enter a future all-India federation, the condition which he had envisaged as the prerequisite for Dominion status. The conference was adjourned a few weeks later. Thanks to wise speeches by Baldwin, Lord President of the Council, and the strength behind MacDonald, co-opera-tion between the two front benches was established, which Churchill did his best to disrupt. Meanwhile tension in India was mounting. The Viceroy released Gandhi from prison unconditionally and then started negotiations with him as an equal – a 'nauseating and humiliating spectacle', thundered Churchill. The initiative succeeded. Gandhi called off civil disobedience, and in September 1931 he and a Congress dele-gation came to London for the second round table conference, just after the national government had been formed. Gandhi demanded Dominion status, with immediate control of foreign policy and defence. He also claimed to speak for all India, including the Muslims. The conference ended without making any headway.

Gandhi returned to India to organize another civil disobedience cam-paign. This was crushed by the new Viceroy, Lord Willingdon, making full use of the most drastic emergency powers. Even so, MacDonald, with Sir Samuel Hoare at the India Office, still tried to get agreement, and in August 1932 he produced his own 'Communal Award', which he repre-sented as a step towards Dominion status. It was bitterly attacked by Hindus and Muslims in India and by the Tory diehards in the British Parliament, led by Churchill.

'Winston made an awful bloomer in the House last week,' Attlee wrote to Tom on 19 May, 'and was severely castigated by Ll G. He takes these things very badly. I thought at one moment that he was going to burst out into oaths. His stock is much down just now.' A third session of the round table conference was held at the end of the year. It lasted only five weeks. Gandhi's chair was empty. The upshot was a White Paper con-taining the conference proposals, and a joint select committee of both Houses to review those proposals and make recommendations.

Attlee was a member of the committee, which sat for eighteen months and presented its report to Parliament in November 1934. This became the basis of the Government of India Act of August 1935, which provided for an all-India federation (so long as half the princely states agreed to join); the central government remained under the Viceroy with considerable reserved powers, though there was some devolution to the provinces. Burma was to have its own government. In the Commons it was a great victory for Baldwin, who had supported the ideas behind the Act for four years and had become Prime Minister two months before the Act passed into law, and a notable defeat for Churchill.

In a broadcast on India in January 1935 Attlee criticized the extent to which the Indian problem was being treated 'as a continuation of the debate at the Conservative Conference', so that the country's attention was diverted from the real issues. The essential question was: 'Will these reforms be accepted and worked by Indian politicians and will they make for the happiness of the Indian people?' The Labour Party accepted the claim of Indians to govern themselves, yet it was not simply a matter of replacing a white oligarchy by a brown one but of insuring, as far as possible, that Indian self-government would not mean handing over the poor to be exploited by the rich. The committee had rightly provided for All-Indian Federation, but they had failed to satisfy the Indians' sense of self-respect by including a definite recognition of India's equal status in the British Commonwealth of Nations. Indeed, there was 'evidence of distrust of the nationalist forces'. There should be a promise of Dominion status as demanded by the Indians – unlike MacDonald in 1929 he still avoided a promise of Dominion status *now* – and the new constitution should show the path by which this could be achieved. All functions except defence, Attlee said, should have been transferred to popular control. Foreign affairs and finance should have been handed over completely, and the few powers reserved to the governor-general regarded as transitional, and gradually allowed to become inoperative. Nevertheless he granted that the reforms now recommended 'constituted a very big advance over the present system of Government'. In the eleven provinces Indians would now control nine-tenths of what concerned the ordinary citizen, and they would have powers of self-government comparable to those enjoyed by the citizens of most democratic states. At the centre, an All-India Federation, the prerequisite to full self-government, was constituted and the principle of responsibility was conceded.

It would indeed have been strange if Attlee had not supported the general principles of the bill. He always maintained that it was in general an implementation of the Simon Commission Report. This attitude did not endear him to many of his Labour colleagues, who continued to believe that he was 'reactionary' on India.

II

In his nine months as acting leader, Attlee also learned, on his own behalf and on behalf of the Labour Party, some important lessons about foreign affairs. Like most of his colleagues Attlee believed in the early 1930s in disarmament, the League of Nations, and the need to restore to Germany the territories unjustly stripped away by the Treaty of Versailles. Before Hitler's rise to power in January 1933, Labour's attack on the national government's foreign policy had centred on the charge that the British government, by conniving at Japanese aggression in Manchuria, was sabotaging the League of Nations. As principal spokesman for the Labour Party, Attlee attacked Sir John Simon, who as Foreign Secretary had the unenviable task of reconciling the two irreconcilable ideas of the function of the League, coercing the aggressor and reaching a compromise between the combatants. 'Simon was a lawyer – justify anything, believed in nothing,' he was to remark many years later.

Attlee made the most of Simon as a target. 'The Foreign Secretary said he would not take sides,' said Attlee. He would inquire into who had a right to what. 'While my house was being overrun and my family were being ill-treated, an inquiry about title deeds would have been cold comfort to me.' He lampooned Simon in a satire preserved among his papers entitled *Chapters from the Life of the Bullion Family*, the surname indicating Attlee's continuing view that the deficiencies of Conservative policy at home and abroad were due to the machinations of the bankers. The Bullions:

> put their boy Simon on the Vigilance Committee. He was by no means simple. The first time he was on his beat he heard an awful noise in the house of Mr Tael. He looked in and saw that Mr Yen had got Mr Tael by the throat with one hand and was going through his pockets with the other. Simple Simon said, 'I wonder who is wrong', and went to consult the rest of the residents. After some time they decided that Mr Yen was in the wrong. Simple Simon went back and found Mr Tael sitting on the floor half dazed. Mr Yen had got his watch and valuables and was making himself comfortable in the front room. 'It looks to me,' said Simple Simon, 'that they are coming to an agreement.'

Attlee also voiced Labour's complaint that Simon was dragging his feet at the Disarmament Conference, which opened in February 1932.

Attlee reacted more slowly than some of his colleagues, above all Bevin, to the need to reconsider the party's foreign policy in the light of the rise of Hitler. Though, like Bevin, he made frequent trips abroad to meet foreign socialists, it was not until an international socialist conference in 1933, where he met 'some very tough-looking Nazis', that he came to share his colleague's view of the threat to European democracy. In speeches on Germany he began to distinguish between a fair share of security for Germans and an increase in German armaments, between justice for Germany and support for the Nazis. The rise of Hitler and Mussolini constituted a threat, and the threat must be recognized and met. 'I think this country ought to say that we will not countenance for a moment the yielding to Hitler and force what was denied to Stresemann and reason.' Just before Hitler's elevation to power in January 1933, Attlee wrote to Tom of his aspirations for 'a real long range policy which will envisage the abolition of the conception of the individual sovereign state'. A mere three months later he was deeply pessimistic:

> The situation on the Continent is terribly serious. There is so much loose powder lying about and one cannot tell where the match will be applied. I fear Social democracy in Germany is down and out for a generation and Austria is likely to be crushed. Thus all Europe, with the possible exception of Czecho Slovakia, that lies east of the Rhine and south of the Baltic is lost to democracy.
>
> It raises most difficult problems of policy for our movement. How are we to frame a world plan for socialism with these conditions on the Continent? I expect that the movement will be driven underground abroad and hence become more communist. The result may well be a war against Russia by the Fascist powers.
>
> I rather anticipate a period during which Socialism will be increasingly national ie economic forces will make for a transformation of society on collectivist but national lines. The crux will be whether this development will result in another war between socialistically organised but national states or whether the nationalism will pass away and give way to a federation of socialist states.

Though some of these observations show remarkable prescience, in hindsight it looks as though, particularly compared with Bevin, Attlee was slow to realize that British rearmament to deal with the dictators, not a plan for world government, was the urgent need of the day. This was not so clear at the time. Conservatives as well as socialists failed to see the short-term danger. Throughout this whole year the tide of British opinion was still running for disarmament. In February 1933 the Oxford Union passed (275 votes to 153) the famous motion: that 'this House will in no circumstances fight for its King and Country'. Attlee never saw this as a vote for pacifism. 'It was a vote for internationalism against nationalism,' he commented to Tom. 'A vote *for* the League.'

The debate on defence and disarmament at the party conference at Hastings in October 1933 centred on a document entitled *Democracy versus Dictatorship*. After Hitler had come to power in January, the Communists with ILP support had renewed their demand for a united front of all socialists against Fascism. The Labour Party declined to co-operate with the Communists and the ILP, and issued *Democracy versus Dictatorship*, in which it denounced dictatorships in Berlin *and* Moscow. The Hastings conference supported the manifesto, and rejected by show of hands a proposal for a united front. But the party also declared that it would not support any national war, even in self-defence, except at the bidding of the League of Nations.

Attlee repeated this view the following month during a House of Commons debate on disarmament: 'You have got to make the League a real League, and you have to put loyalty to the League above loyalty to your country.' This was the main theme of his speeches on foreign affairs as acting leader throughout 1934. He continued to oppose the government's plans for rearmament: 'We deny the need for increased armaments. We deny the proposition that an increased British Air Force will make for the peace of the world.' But a letter to Tom shows that he was fully aware of the ambiguities in the party's position: Labour 'has not really made up its mind as to whether it wants to take up an extreme disarmament and isolationist attitude or whether it will take the risks of standing for the enforcement of the decisions of a world organisation against individual aggressor states.'

The party's position was clarified at the 1934 conference at Southport. This was an acrid affair which turned out well for Attlee. A number of special policy reports on housing, rent control, education, nationalization, water supply, a state health service, and parliamentary procedure were passed with little amendment. A more general document, *For Socialism and Peace*, precipitated bitter clashes between left and right, for it included a fervent reassurance that the Labour Party believed in parliamentary democracy. Members of the Socialist League, already smarting under a number of attacks on Cripps, mostly engineered by Bevin, took offence at this apparent condemnation of extra-parliamentary action and put down seventy-five amendments to the draft. Their move failed: but a critical press made much of the degree of 'socialism' contained in the document, and even more of the number of delegates who complained at the amount of 'socialism' which had been left out.

On foreign affairs a draft document, *War and Peace*, accepted 'the duty unflinchingly to support our Government in all the risks and consequences of fulfilling its duty to take part in collective action against a peace-breaker'. The League of Nations, and the collective security it alone could provide, were still the basis of Labour's policy, but the declaration was now made 'that there might be circumstances under which the Government of Great Britain might have to use its military and naval forces in support of the League in restraining an aggressor nation'. Led by Cripps, the Socialist League set out to demolish *War and Peace*. Cripps denounced the League as an organization of capitalist states. The British Labour Party should leave the League, and form constructive relationships with the Soviet Union and with all other countries with socialist governments. If Britain were to be led into war by its present government the Labour Party should resist such a war 'by every means in its power, including a general strike'.

Attlee rose to expound Labour's official policy, and defend it against Cripps's attack. He said bluntly that he himself had once supported unilateral disarmament, but in the light of what was now happening he did not think such a course was practical or responsible. 'We cannot wash our hands of responsibility for [the fate of] Socialist workers and comrades in other countries.' *War and Peace* did not mean a reversion to nationalism: it meant a more international outlook. 'We are for sanctions in the hands of the League. I shall be told, "You will have a Capitalist League using that Capitalist force." I do not believe this is likely or possible.' The Labour Party had the greatest chance ever of showing the world the way out of war. 'That way is only on the lines laid down here – of collective security and a world commonwealth.' The Socialist League's attack on *War and Peace*, inadequately disguised as an amendment, was defeated by 1,519,000 votes to 673,000.

III

Though Lansbury's return to the leadership relegated Attlee to his former position as deputy leader of the Parliamentary Party, the 1934 conference marked a rise in his authority in the party as a whole. In the fights between right and left the major figures had made new enemies as well as new friends, while Attlee had adopted what seemed a generally acceptable neutrality. He was elected to the National Executive for the first time, and sat on the Policy Committee as a full Executive member. In 1935 he became a Privy Councillor. During that year he was increasingly prominent as Labour's chief spokesman on defence, maintaining the party's case that the national government intended to ditch the League and make deals with other capitalist powers. He spoke against the Defence White Paper of March 1935. In May, at a meeting of the PLP, the National Executive, and the TUC General Council, he spoke against a proposal that the PLP should drop its practice of voting against the defence estimates. Labour opinion outside Parliament was hardening against the practice, and the proposal had been supported by Bevin and the TUC General Secretary, Walter Citrine. Dalton, who had also supported it, recorded Attlee's argument that 'we must relate our armaments, not competitively with any one country, but to the forces available to support Collective Security.'

The debate over collective security, both in the party and in the country, was sharpened in the summer of 1935 by the Abyssinian crisis, and by the publication in June of the results of the Peace Ballot, which showed strong public support for sanctions against aggressors. In September, Hoare, now Foreign Secretary, pledged the British government before the Assembly of the League in Geneva to 'steady and collective resistance to all acts of unprovoked aggression', though he made the significant proviso that Britain would be 'second to none in its intention to fulfil, within the measure of its capacity', its League obligations. Attlee now made several speeches claiming that the Foreign Secretary had been converted to the policies of the Labour Party. The TUC conference in early September had passed by three million votes to 177,000 a resolution that the Italian aggression against Abyssinia must be stopped, if necessary by force, whereupon Cripps resigned from the NEC and Lansbury expressed public disagreement. Bevin and Citrine were infuriated by what they saw as the irresponsibility and treachery of the 'intellectuals' who led the PLP, and prepared for a showdown at the Labour Party conference which opened at Brighton on 1 October.

Mussolini invaded Abyssinia two days after the conference opened. The resolution, calling for sanctions against Italy, and on the government to use 'all necessary measures provided by the Covenant', was put on 5 October. Cripps opposed it. The League, he said, had become nothing but the tool of the 'satiated' powers, the 'Haves against the Have-nots'. It was 'the International Burglars' Union'. Every war entered upon by a capitalist government, he concluded, 'is and must be an imperialist and capitalist war'. Attlee was the only one of the three leaders of the Parliamentary Party to support the resolution. 'We are against the use of force for imperialists and capitalist ends, but we are in favour of the proper use of force for ensuring the rule of law.... Non-resistance is not a political attitude, it is a personal attitude. I do not believe it is a possible policy for people with responsibility.'

Lansbury then made a highly emotional speech restating his Christian pacifist attitude. With what mixture of motives it is hard to say, the delegates gave him as great an ovation as a Labour Party conference has ever recorded. Perhaps it was the warmth of that reception which inspired Bevin to get up and make a speech which was less a contribution to debate than a personal attack – and a brutal one – on Lansbury. He castigated his leader not so much for his pacifism as his disloyalty – he had supported sanctions in September and now, in October, he was against them. 'I hope this conference will not be influenced by either sentiment or personal attachment,' said Bevin. He then looked up directly at Lansbury and said: 'It is placing the Executive and the Labour Movement in an absolutely wrong position to be taking your conscience round from body to body asking to be told what to do with it.' The speech antagonized many delegates who did not share Lansbury's views. As Morrison recorded: 'The impact of Bevin's attack, with all the prestige of half-a-million votes in his pocket, made the result even more a foregone conclusion.' The resolution was carried by a majority of more than two millions: 2,168,000 voted for it; 102,000 against.

Attlee was critical about the proceedings at the conference. He thought that the Labour Party had spent too much time quarrelling and had not capitalized on its opportunities of hammering its enemies. For example, they had not made enough of the fact that the Foreign Secretary was now expounding a view which Labour had been expressing for several years. With a general election in the offing, the conference could have turned this 'conversion' to great effect. Attlee, like Bevin, was annoyed that Lansbury and Cripps had behaved in a way that exaggerated the impression of a party divided; though unlike Bevin he would have also put some blame for this on the 'bellicose' speeches made by some of the TUC leaders. He kept his criticism of the behaviour of his colleagues to himself. The overriding need, as he saw it – typically – was to keep the party together in face of the general election which was, correctly, presumed to be only a few weeks ahead.

When the House of Commons reassembled on 8 October 1935, Lansbury tendered his resignation to the PLP. Fifteen days later, for a number of reasons including Labour's disarray, Baldwin announced that a general election would be held on 14 November. Who was to lead Labour in the campaign? There was no real resistance to the motion moved by David Grenfell and seconded by Tom Williams in favour of Attlee carrying on. Williams and Grenfell were prominent among the miner MPs, who made up the largest section of the Parliamentary Labour Party. It was a section with a strong feeling for the ILP and for the Christian inheritance of the Labour Party. Neither Morrison's middle-class interpretation of Labour politics nor Cripps's near-Communism appealed to them. They were for Attlee to a man, and Attlee never forgot it. Attlee himself saw his election as a holding action until the majority of the Labour Party leaders, still seatless since the débâcle of 1931, would shortly be returned to the House. It was not an expression of modesty. He – and the seatless leaders – thought it was common sense.

There was no hope that the national government would lose the general election. On foreign policy there seemed little difference between Labour and the government. Both supported the League of Nations, and sanctions against Italy. On the sanctions issue Attlee had put Labour in a difficult position by his speech at the party conference. He had made the point that Hoare, in his September speech supporting the League and the use of sanctions, had shown himself 'a convert' to the Labour Party's views. This had identified Labour's policy with that of the government. Attlee later tried to make a distinction by saying that Hoare should have announced his 'conversion' earlier in the year, when Mussolini could still have been stopped and Abyssinia could have been saved. To Baldwin's assertion that Labour supported the League, but not the necessary armaments, he could only reply that Labour was 'prepared to support such arms in this country as are necessary to fulfil our obligations and responsibilities towards the League'; on another occasion, though, he 'gathered that the election campaign was for the purpose of piling up armaments'.

It was not a powerful case, but in the event the government's position was so strong that it hardly mattered. A slow improvement in the unemployment figures, highlighted by new measures announced during the campaign, weakened Labour's arguments. Above all, Labour fought the election with Attlee as a caretaker leader whom some of his colleagues described in public as a stopgap. Labour looked no alternative government, and the election was essentially about confidence in Baldwin. Labour polled 8,326,000, as against 6,649,000 in 1931, and won 154 seats. The Conservatives, with a poll of just under twelve million, took 432 seats. There were twenty Opposition Liberals in the new House, led by Sir Archibald Sinclair since Samuel had lost his seat. In his constituency, Attlee's vote was the highest so far, 14,600 against 7,355 for his only opponent, a Conservative.

As anticipated, the 1935 election brought back the senior Labour parliamentarians: Morrison, Dalton and Clynes. Who now would take over from Attlee? Morrison was the favourite, but Bevin used his influence against him because at the party conference in October he had muted his criticisms of Lansbury and the left, supposedly to win their votes for the leadership. Under Bevin's pressure, the trade unions were for Greenwood. The PLP, who saw more of Greenwood than did the union leaders, reckoned either that he was 'past it' or that he drank too much. Dalton had put himself out of the running by offering to serve as foreign secretary or chancellor of the exchequer under Morrison, and Cripps, leader of the opposition within the Opposition, was out of the question. The choice was therefore between Morrison (supported by Dalton), Greenwood (supported by Bevin) and Attlee.

The PLP met to elect their new leader on Tuesday 26 November. On the first ballot Attlee, proposed once again by Grenfell of the miners, led with fifty-eight votes to forty-four for Morrison and thirty-three for Greenwood. On the second ballot Attlee took most of the Greenwood vote, winning eighty-eight to Morrison's forty-eight. Attlee's clear victory is largely explained by the loyalty of the forty-six MPs, mostly trade unionists – the miners in the majority – who had sat in the 1931-5 Parliament. Dalton thought that the Greenwood votes which clinched

Attlee's victory in the second ballot had been organized by the group of Labour MPs who were Freemasons. Morrison was suspected of being too unsympathetic to the left and too sympathetic to MacDonald, and it was feared that he was too much interested in the leadership of the LCC and not enough in the PLP. Morrison favoured control of nationalized industries by public boards; Bevin wanted worker control: Morrison's views worried those Labour MPs who depended on union sponsorship. Attlee's own view was that the party did not want another charismatic leader who might 'do another MacDonald'. They wanted a leader who would lead as a good chairman leads a committee.

Attlee's position was further strengthened by Morrison's decision not to run for the deputy leadership – he told the PLP he was too busy with the LCC. Greenwood became deputy leader, and nobody was likely to want to put him in Attlee's place. Dalton greeted the PLP's vote for Attlee as 'a wretched disheartening result! And a little mouse shall lead them.' His disciples, up-and-coming young Labour intellectuals like Gaitskell, Douglas Jay and Evan Durbin, shared his disappointment. Others comforted themselves in the belief that the PLP had voted for Attlee because they thought he could be removed at any time. 'So the leader of the Socialist Opposition is to be Major Attlee,' wrote a *Daily Mail* columnist. 'I am afraid he will not be so for long, but he deserves the success that is his momentarily.' The writer went on:

> He is not very tall, and is rather bald, his head being shaped like Lenin's, but he is far from being a revolutionary. Courteous and hard-working, he perhaps can never be an out-and-out extremist; when he speaks you feel that however much you disagree with him, it is what he thinks, and thinks sincerely, about the subject.
>
> He is the type of man badly wanted by the Socialist Party. One, in fact, who is as sincere and enthusiastic a Labour man as anyone, yet has not graduated through the trade union machine. His speeches are rather long, rather tied to notes, rather lacking in spontaneity, but well thought out. The House of Commons likes him, and if the House of Commons likes a man, it is praise indeed; however much one may abuse the Commons of England, the members have a sense for finding out (from the point of view of character) what is good and what is not.

9
Taking Charge,
1935–7

I

In the new Parliament, Attlee led Labour's attack on the national government with a condemnation of its Abyssinian policy. It was the now familiar charge that the government supported the League in words but in practice conducted a 'balance of power' policy in negotiations with France and Italy: 'You would hardly think there was an Abyssinian point of view.' By the end of December 1935 a large part of Abyssinia was in Mussolini's hands. British public opinion, influenced by newspaper reports of tribesmen armed only with spears being mown down by tanks, swung round in favour of the application of economic sanctions against Italy, particularly by cutting off oil supplies.

Hoare, the Foreign Secretary, was nevertheless anxious to have Italy as an ally against Germany, and in early December initialled an agreement with Laval, the French Foreign Minister, which would have given half of Abyssinia to Italy as the price of ending the war. When this was leaked by the French there was an uproar in Britain and Hoare was forced to resign. Moving Labour's vote of censure after Hoare's resignation speech, on 19 December, Attlee also voiced the feelings of a large number of Conservatives. The Hoare–Laval agreement was 'the surrender to an aggressor of half an Empire in exchange for a corridor for camels'. Britain had seemed to be standing firm for a new system in international affairs, but:

> if you turn and run away from the aggressor, you kill the League, and you do worse than that, or as bad as that; you kill all faith in the honour of the country. ... If ... the Prime Minister won an election on one policy and immediately after the election was prepared to carry out another, it has an extremely ugly look; and ... this is not being said by political opponents of the Prime Minister only.

As a parliamentary intervention this was perhaps ill-judged: the attack on Baldwin's personal integrity probably induced doubtful Conservatives to support the government. Nevertheless the Hoare–Laval affair marked the beginning of a rapid movement towards realism in the foreign policy attitudes of the Labour Party. With Eden now at the Foreign Office, Baldwin's government fudged the policy of oil sanctions, and by May 1936, when the Emperor Haile Selassie at last fled his country and Mussolini proclaimed a new Roman Empire in Africa, oil sanctions had not been applied.

A few weeks after the Hoare–Laval crisis a temporary truce between the two parties was called as a result of the death of King George v on 20 January 1936. Baldwin might have been born to pay tributes to dead good kings. Attlee followed him, nervously – 'I always feel anxious when making speeches of this kind. It is so easy to sound a false note' – but with almost an equal mastery of the art of obituary. He had only met the King a few times, but Attlee judged on impressions. He discriminated between character and political views. Prejudices and ignorance did not deter him. Honesty, courage and dedication he put above political sophistication. So he was able to eulogize the dead King.

> King George showed an incomparable understanding of what is required of a King in the modern world. It has been a great piece of good fortune, I think, for our generation that we should have had on the throne a man who so well understood how to speak to his people, a man who set before the nation ideals of peace, justice and service. We have seen the end of a noble life, a life devoted to the welfare of humanity. In the long roll of British Sovereigns none will, I think, take a higher place than King George.

In March 1936, Hitler had remilitarized the Rhineland, in breach of the Versailles Treaty and the more recent Locarno agreement; Eden and the British government diverted the French from any form of resistance, with the aid of Hitler, who offered a non-aggression pact. Now was the opportunity for Labour to take an attractive position, distinct from that of the government. Attlee roundly condemned the Rhineland occupation. 'No sympathy for the injustices inflicted on the German people by the Versailles Treaty,' he told a Scottish audience, 'should blind us to the true nature of the act of the German Government.' In proposing an alternative policy he was still painfully limited by the Labour Party's resistance to rearmament, soon to be shown again in a vote against the estimates, but he set out to change Labour's attitudes to defence by establishing a Labour Party Defence Committee. He wrote in his autobiography:

As soon as the new 1935 Parliament met, I determined to take steps to create a better knowledge of defence problems in the Party. There were now back in the House a number of men who had experience in the Service ministries: Alexander and Ammon in the Admiralty: Lawson, Shinwell and myself in the War Office; and Montagu in the Air Ministry. There were also those who, like Dalton, had served in the First World War. I accordingly formed a [Labour Party] Defence Committee which met regularly and discussed defence problems. We got able officers to address us on various points. We made a very careful study of air warfare and we employed a very able man to engage in research into this vital question. At a later stage we presented our conclusions to Chamberlain and held a number of meetings with Sir Kingsley Wood, the Secretary of State for Air, at which we were able to put a number of searching questions. Some of us were acquainted with high-ranking officers in the three Services. The result was seen in the far more informed contribution which Labour men were able to make in Service debates.

Thirty years later came a comment on this speech from Arthur Moyle, Attlee's parliamentary private secretary in the postwar Labour government and thereafter one of his very few confidants. Moyle's letter is dated 6 May 1965:

Just a note to say that I have unearthed your speech on Defence which you made on Sir Murray Sueter's Bill. The date of it is 14 February 1936. Leo Amery followed it with an admirable tribute to your speech. I have read it now and think it excellent. Most of your speeches in this period on Defence repeatedly dealt with the need for a ministry of Defence and I do not think that you have been given credit for your foresight in this field. I am not guilty of this, for I have always said that in the inter-war years no one in the Party but yourself, ever gave any thought really to the question, let alone the reorganisation, of Defence. Why? Because we were too fearful of criticism from our own Movement. Apart from yourself most of us were cowards in this field. I except Dalton and Bevin from this charge.

As a result of the impression made by the realism and unexpected expertise of the February speech, Attlee was invited to address the Imperial Defence College, the Naval Staff College and other service gatherings. He was very pleased to be able to record in his memoirs that the Ministry of Defence Bill which he introduced into the House of Commons in 1946, 'though slightly modified by experience gained in the Second World War, was, in essence, the same proposal that I had adumbrated ten years before'.

II

In August, at the invitation of Maisky, the Soviet Ambassador, with whom he had been friendly for some years, Attlee made his first visit to Russia. He wrote to Tom from Moscow on 12 August 1936:

I have been most of the day at the Park of Rest and Culture which was full of people as it was a holiday. I had every chance of seeing people as they were – its sum total in itself justifies the revolution. You can have no idea of what such a great number of quiet happy and well mannered people mean until you see it.... The children were simply delightful. The people were all quiet happy and well behaved. No silly ragging, but just reasonable amusement. Family parties were frequent, fathers with small children a prominent feature. The Russian father is very devoted to babies.

Litvinov, the Foreign Minister, invited Attlee to his country villa.

I came into an almost English atmosphere. Madame Litvinov told me that her husband and Maisky were walking round the farm with the dogs and I found them feeding the ducks. After lunch, I played billiards with the children. [I also] visited a small town and a village, but I think that they were really showplaces and not in the least typical. The biggest impression made on me was the cult of Stalin, his picture being shown everywhere. This was amusingly exemplified in the War Museum, where great pains had been taken to eliminate every reference to Trotsky. Our guides were anxious to explain that every success had been due to Stalin – every failure to Trotsky.

From my observations I should judge that the ordinary citizen supports the existing rulers because he believes they are carrying out a programme which is for his good and which he himself desires.... There is a great deal of skilful propaganda which is directed to connecting every success with the personality of Stalin and other Commissars; but this could not be done unless there were successes.

Attlee did not meet Stalin, but he talked to several other notables besides Litvinov, including Kaganovich, Minister of Transport, Bulganin, President of the Moscow Soviet, and Marshal Tukhachevsky. The Marshal explained the position of the commissars in the Army, and their function in promoting morale. 'They are like Army chaplains,' said Attlee. On the contrary, said Tukhachevsky, the priests were the most despised men in the Tsarist Army. Attlee retorted: 'I did not mean *your* priests. I mean men like Cromwell's chaplains with the root of the matter in them.' Attlee admired much of what he saw in Russia, especially the attitude of the people, who seemed to him conscious that they were building up their own society, not working for landlords or capitalists: 'Their work was for the good of all and was worth doing.' His greatest reservation sprang from the realization that he had seen mostly what he was meant to see.

III

When Attlee returned from Moscow in late August 1936 the Spanish Civil War, which began in July, had polarized Europe. In Britain the

Labour Party was united in support of the Republican government against Franco's 'Nationalist' insurgents; but it was divided over the question of whether to call for arms to be sent to Spain. From the first, Franco had been receiving arms and planes from Germany and Italy, and the Republicans soon formed an International Brigade of foreign volunteers. German and Italian personnel arrived in Spain in September. In reply the French 'Popular Front' government under Léon Blum had wished to support the Republicans but, fearing the reaction of French right-wingers to such a move, proposed an international Non-Intervention agreement, which was signed at the end of August. Germany and Italy gladly accepted Non-Intervention, which enabled them openly to blockade the Republicans and covertly to supply the Nationalists.

The Spanish Civil War increased the pressure on the Labour Party to reconsider the PLP's practice of voting against the arms estimates. At the party conference in Edinburgh in October 1936, it was the dominant issue. Dalton and Morrison, speaking for the NEC in support of a resolution condemning the government for having 'betrayed the League of Nations and Abyssinia', conceded that a Labour government would have to rearm against Germany, but did not suggest any change in its practice in opposition. In response, Bevin went to the heart of the matter: 'Which is the first institution that victorious Fascism wipes out? It is the trade union movement.' He called for a clear departure from the PLP's policy on rearmament. As leader, Attlee had to wind up the debate. He supported arms, and the use of arms in the hands of a government loyal to the League, but:

> We are not prepared to support a Government that has betrayed the League, that is not, I believe, in earnest, and that has not related its arms policy to any intelligible foreign policy. Their armaments policy is entirely unintelligible, and we shall therefore continue to oppose this government on its foreign policy and its arms policy, and endeavour to get rid of it at the earliest possible moment.

Attlee took this position because he judged that a formal change in party policy at this time would be premature: the party would tear itself apart, without having any effect on the government's policy, or on opinion outside Britain. He preferred to leave the policy as it was, even though this meant leaving Labour Party policy as contradictory – and as vulnerable to criticism – as it had been before. So, in an ambiguous speech, he made only one thing clear: the Parliamentary Labour Party should be left to decide 'how we shall vote on any particular issue'. The resolution condemning the government's League policy was carried by a majority of nearly three to one. All it did, as Bevin said, was to 'pass the buck' to the Parliamentary Party. The latter did not resist. They feared

the conference not when it passed the buck to them but when it claimed
the right to tell them what to do. As for the party as a whole, it was
accustomed to vague or ambiguous resolutions being passed by solid
majorities after bitter debates.

Attlee's concern to hold the party together cannot absolve him from
the charge that he still thought it was *right* to oppose the government's
rearmament programme. He described his view in a letter to Tom:

> Edinburgh was pretty rotten though it ended up better than it started.
> There is a good deal of scare feeling over Hitler which is not without
> justification, but makes some people want to support Government policy
> over armaments, which is stupid. The Government have no clear foreign
> policy and their armaments programme is futile and wasteful.... I see little
> signs of improvement in the foreign situation. It is possible that there may
> be some sort of lead from Roosevelt after the elections.

The debate on Spain at Edinburgh was passionate. Greenwood moved
the official resolution advocating non-intervention, which reflected
French Socialist views. With little animation, Greenwood argued that a
policy of open intervention would favour Franco. Led by Aneurin Bevan,
delegates attacked the resolution while Bevin forcefully defended it.
Attlee wound up for the Executive and 'as his gift is', recorded Dalton,
'lowered the temperature'. He stressed the risk of bringing down the
Socialist government in France, and warned that: 'The danger of a
European war [if Britain were openly to supply arms to the Republicans]
is not to be lightly brushed aside.' The resolution against 'Arms for Spain'
was carried by 1,836,000 to 519,000. But this was not the end of the
matter. Next day, the NEC reluctantly allowed Isabel de Palencia, who
had come over from Spain, to address the conference. Speaking excellent
English, she evoked such a response that the conference decided forthwith
that Attlee and Greenwood should go to Downing Street at once and ask
the Prime Minister to investigate allegations that non-intervention was
being breached wholesale in Franco's favour. On their return, Attlee
moved a new resolution demanding that Britain and France should
restore to the Spanish government its right to buy arms. It was passed
unanimously. Labour could no longer support non-intervention; the
Republicans must be allowed to buy arms where they could. This did
much to hold the party together, but the reversal of policy in the space of
forty-eight hours exposed its leaders to some bitter criticism.

Meanwhile Franco was rapidly gaining ground. Only three weeks
after arguing for non-intervention at Edinburgh, Attlee said in Parliament that the policy of non-intervention had failed and should be ended.
In November 1936, however, a French Popular Front delegation came
to London to seek British support for the French government if it denounced non-intervention. The delegation found that Labour leaders

would not support a policy which they thought would increase the risk of war, and returned home baffled by the contradictions and equivocations in Labour policy. To the fury of Labour's left, the party never issued a statement of its Spanish policy. Though Attlee had condemned 'the device of non-intervention' in November 1936, Bevin was still urging support for non-intervention in March 1937. Some of Attlee's statements on Spain can be forgiven him: he had to keep his party together, and he had to oppose the government. But there is no evidence that he was any clearer in his mind about what should be done than most of those whose policy he assailed.

IV

Attlee's ability to lead the Labour Party was based not only on his hard work in Parliament and his capacity to 'lower the temperature', if necessary by ambiguous compromises over policy, but also on his expositions of the Socialist viewpoint, which were written in terms and language very acceptable to the party worker. Even before the 1935 election, in *The Will and the Way to Socialism*, he had roundly equated capitalism with Fascism, and had hammered away at the ailing Ramsay MacDonald. In contrast to the compromises of Liberal, Conservative and National Labour, he insisted: 'The Labour Party exists to challenge the whole basis of society ... not by violent revolution, but by a series of legislative and administrative measures.' There was now widespread agreement, he said, that:

> ... it is necessary to plan the economic life of the community.... Conservative politicians like Mr Macmillan and businessmen like Sir Basil Blackett and Lord Melchett would subscribe to the general idea. I would put the difference between the Conservatives and the Socialist Plans in this way. Conservatives would plan this country on the model of the old English village. There would be a large house for the squire, a few of fair size for the parson, the gentry and the farmers, and a row of cottages for the workers. The squire would rule. In the Socialists' plan there would be no little cottages and no large private houses. All would be reasonably well housed, while the only large buildings would be those owned and used by the community, in one of which the villagers would meet to settle their common affairs.

To the standard exposition of Labour policies, Attlee added his own touch:

> Society is a garden, where are to be found a great variety, every one of which must have soil, air and space enough to allow it to grow to perfection. In this garden there must be some pruning, lest the coarser growths take all the light and air from the more delicate. The gardener wants variety. The

garden, seen from a distance, reveals a general plan and harmony, but viewed closely, every plant is unique. This general harmony is not fixed like a mosaic pattern. It is always changing. Each plant and the garden itself is in a state of becoming. The gardener's work is never done.

In the autumn of 1936 he accepted an invitation from Victor Gollancz to write a book for the Left Book Club, setting out Labour's general position. *The Labour Party in Perspective* was published the following year. Its 65,000 words have a brisk authority which might have come as a surprise to people who had not worked closely with Attlee. Its tone is that of a statement of faith:

> Some thirty years ago, when I was a young barrister just down from Oxford, I engaged in various forms of social work in East London. The conditions of the people in that area as I saw them at close quarters led me to study their causes and to reconsider the assumptions of the social class to which I belonged. I became an enthusiastic convert to Socialism. . . . Circumstances have called me to occupy a position of high responsibility in the movement. Throughout these years I have never wavered in my faith in the cause of Socialism. I have never lost my early enthusiasm. I have never doubted that the Labour Party, whatever faults or failings it may have, is the only practical instrument in this country for the attainment of a new order of society.

He portrayed the Labour Party as 'an expression of the Socialist movement adapted to British conditions', but contrasted its development with that of socialism in other countries. Robert Owen and the early pioneers were not influenced by Marx, but they were profoundly influenced by the Bible, so 'full of revolutionary teaching'.

> I think that probably the majority of those who have built up the Socialist movement in this country have been adherents of the Christian religion – and not merely adherents, but enthusiastic members of some religious bodies. Not only the adherents of dissenting bodies . . . but also many clergy and laymen of the Established Church, found that the Capitalist system was incompatible with Christianity. . . . In no other country has Christianity been converted to Socialism to such an extent as in Britain.

Socialism in Britain 'is not the creation of a theorist. It does not propagate some theory produced in another country. It is seeking to show the people of Britain that Socialism which it preaches is what the country requires in order in modern conditions to realise to the full the genius of this nation.'

To allay public doubts about the internal divisions of the party, he insisted that: 'In a Party of the Left there should always be room for differences of opinion and emphasis'; but he was harsh in his criticism of Mosley, the 'self-righteous isolation' of the ILP, and the Fascist fallacy of

MacDonaldism, which was that 'there was really no need for the existence of separate parties', when in fact 'more than ever today there stands out the difference between the two systems, Socialism and Capitalism'. On the role of the trade unions in the party, even then a source of controversy, he observed that: 'The truth about the relationship between the political and industrial sides is really very simple. There is no attempt by either side to "boss" the other. There is a recognition of their partnership in action on behalf of the workers, and of their freedom of action in their respective spheres.' The party's final authority was the party conference, which 'lays down the policy of the Party, and issues instructions which must be carried out by the National Executive, the affiliated organisations, and its representatives in Parliament and on local authorities.... [It] is in fact a parliament of the movement. It is more; it is a constituent assembly, because it has the power of altering its own constitution.'

The statement that the party conference is the party's 'final authority' and that its 'instructions ... must be carried out by ... its representatives in Parliament' must be read alongside another passage a few pages later:

> Action in the House is a matter for the Parliamentary Party, the members of which decide on the application of Party Policy. The Labour Party Executive is the body to initiate policy between Conferences, but in its own sphere the Parliamentary Party is supreme.

The irreconcilability of the two statements, giving 'final' or 'supreme' authority to two different bodies within the movement, was not the product of imprecise thinking or careless drafting. He wanted to leave the question unresolved in principle so as to be able to resolve it suitably when it arose in practice. More than twenty years later, a few days after Gaitskell's failure at the party conference of 1959 to persuade the party to rescind Clause IV of the Constitution, which prescribes across-the-board public ownership, Attlee observed to the author: 'The Party's passion for definition must always be resisted. Gaitskell stimulated it. He should have sedated it.'

Attlee set out to relieve his public of any fear that Britain could not be converted into a socialist state except by a revolution. The Labour Party believed, wrote Attlee, that 'when it has obtained the support of a majority of the electors for its policy', most of its opponents would acquiesce in the changes. British socialists 'have not generally adopted the class war as a theory of society', and in Attlee's view 'a violent struggle in this country would be extremely dangerous to civilisation, whichever side ultimately conquered'. On the other hand, in one of the most forthright passages in the whole book he rejected the idea of Labour running a capitalist economy. They would not want it: they could not do it. A socialist party could not 'hope to make a success of administering the Capitalist system because it does not believe in it.... Socialists cannot make Capitalism work. The 1929 experiment demonstrated this. No really effective steps could be taken to deal with the economic crisis, because any attempt to deal with the fundamentals brought opposition from the Liberals.'

Reviews of the book were as favourable as he could have hoped for. The very Conservative *Morning Post* wrote scathingly about 'the proponents of Socialism' who 'flounder in grandiloquent phrases and nebulous aspirations, Mr Attlee no less than his predecessors'. But *The Times* said there was 'a pleasant modesty about Mr Attlee's book.... Promotion of good understanding governs the whole treatment.'

V

At the beginning of the parliamentary session, in October 1936, Attlee was re-elected leader of the PLP, unopposed but without acclamation. The *Morning Post* predicted that he would be replaced, probably by Dalton, after the coronation of Edward VIII in the summer. By November the scene had changed, to the benefit both of party unity and Attlee's personal position. Unemployment came into prominence again, and Attlee spoke on 8 November to a hunger march demonstration in Hyde Park, sharing a platform with Aneurin Bevan and the Communist organizer of the National Unemployed Workers' Movement, Wal Hannington. The weakness of Labour's foreign policy was partly masked by the poor standing of the government: Baldwin admitted, to his discredit, that he had not campaigned for rearmament in 1933 because nothing 'would have made the loss of the [East Fulham] election from my point of view more certain'. As a result, the PLP's ambiguous position on rearmament seemed less vulnerable, even though its leaders stayed away from a major rally on 3 December in favour of the League and rearmament, attended by Churchill, Citrine, and the new Liberal leader, Sir Archibald Sinclair.

Suddenly the Abdication crisis swept into the centre of the political stage. The new King's wish to marry the twice-married Mrs Wallis Simpson became public knowledge in Britain on 3 December. Attlee had been forewarned in confidence by Baldwin a few weeks earlier. The King's outspoken concern for the unemployed had embarrassed Baldwin in the past, and he feared that Labour would make political capital out of the crisis. Attlee had met the King on several occasions and had been 'struck by his genuine solicitude for the unemployed', but he was in no doubt about what he should say to Baldwin. 'The talk was absolutely private – I could not consult my colleagues. I had to take it on myself. I told him that I thought our people would not mind him marrying an American, but Mrs Simpson was out of the question. And I was sure the Commonwealth would take the same view.'

Before he went to his most important meeting with the King, 25

November, Baldwin asked Attlee, Sinclair and Churchill to confer with him. He asked Attlee what he would do if the King insisted on marrying Mrs Simpson *and* remaining on the throne, and the government therefore decided to resign. Attlee replied flatly that he would refuse to form an alternative government. So did Sinclair, though what the Liberals might have chosen to do in such a situation was considerably less important. Churchill said that he would support the government, but he avoided saying what he would do if the government had to resign. Baldwin found Churchill far less direct than Attlee, and the following week Churchill much embarrassed the government by stating in public that Baldwin had obtained promises from the Opposition leaders that they would not form governments in the event of his resignation. Attlee came to Baldwin's rescue by making a public statement that the Prime Minister had *not* sought any promise or undertaking from him to provide a means of coercing the King.

Attlee's support was invaluable to Baldwin. It was public knowledge that many Labour Party members wished to exploit the Abdication crisis. By refusing to support Baldwin against the King, and advocating a morganatic marriage, they reasoned, they might force his resignation. They would then refuse to join an alternative government, precipitating a general election in which Labour would play up the King's concern for the unemployed and attack the government on Abyssinia and Spain. Dalton, who had at first taken this view, changed his mind: the consequences for Labour of an election turning on Mrs Simpson and the King would have been disastrous, since the 'most formidable and pervasive Puritanism in the electorate' would have ensured a victory for Baldwin. But neither sentiment nor calculations of political advantage seem to have influenced Attlee's decision. He was a constitutionalist who believed in parliamentary government, and he abhorred the thought of an election fought about whether the King's will or Parliament's should prevail. In the debate on the Abdication Bill, 10 December 1936, he urged the country to regard the crisis as over:

> We are not to be diverted into abstract discussions about monarchy and republicanism.... The one essential is that the will of the people should prevail in a democratic country. Further, we want the mind of the nation to return as soon as possible to the urgent problems of the condition of the people, the state of the world and the great issue of peace.

He also helped Baldwin by ensuring that the *Daily Herald* supported the Prime Minister's constitutional line. Bevin, who dominated the trade union leaders controlling the paper, wrote to him on 7 December:

> We cannot forget that old Baldwin 'did' us over the Trade Unions Act, over Abyssinia, over rearmament, and over Peace at the last general election....

> The risk of personal government is great, on the other hand so is the risk of backing the Government without the facts.

Attlee met him privately and gave him 'the facts'. As a result Bevin was convinced, for the first time, that Attlee was a man to be trusted; and the *Herald*, alone among the popular newspapers, backed up Baldwin.

Looking back on the crisis in old age, Attlee had three things to say to the author. First, that there was no foundation to the charges that Baldwin had behaved improperly in consulting the Commonwealth prime ministers when this was the prerogative of the Monarch. 'Nonsense. He did nothing which the King didn't know about. Constitutionally he never put a foot wrong. He was firm and fair. He loved the young man.' Second, he had been astonished by the line taken by Churchill, and by Beaverbrook in his newspapers, that Abdication would weaken the Commonwealth. On the contrary, Attlee believed, it was marriage – any kind of marriage or continued relationship between the King and Mrs Simpson – which would have undermined it. Third, he had strong reservations about the King. 'He was compassionate, but he was unstable. He would start things, and not see them through. He didn't know good information from bad information, right people from wrong 'uns. He meant very well – *very* well – but he'd have got us into trouble. I don't think he would have made a good king.'

VI

The Abdication crisis restored much of Baldwin's authority and pushed Churchill further into the wilderness. It did nothing for Attlee. The country had taken little notice of his behaviour, and the Labour left was furious with him. Aneurin Bevan, writing anonymously in the first issue of *Tribune*, condemned the missed opportunity:

> Against the cant and hypocrisy of the Court scandals, the Parliamentary Labour Party should have limned its own message.... It has shown that when it likes it can put the workers at the centre of the parliamentary stage. But from beginning to end of the monarchical crisis it revealed one grave defect. *The Labour Party* has too much reverence.

The appearance of *Tribune* marked a new phase in the struggles between right and left in the party. The demand for a 'Popular Front' had been renewed at the Edinburgh conference. In resisting this, and the affiliation of Communists to the Labour Party, the Executive pulled no punches, accusing the Communists of being subsidized by Russia to produce 'one long stream of invective and vilification of the British Labour movement'. Attlee made a carefully argued speech against the 'Front'. French Communists, he said, did not vilify Léon Blum in the way that British Communists denounced British Labour leaders. The Communists' application for affiliation, and the motion for a United Front, were overwhelmingly defeated.

Undeterred, in January 1937 the Socialist League, the Communist Party and the ILP issued a joint 'Unity Manifesto', calling for 'unity of all sections of the working class' and 'the adoption of a fighting programme of mass struggle, through the democratisation of the Labour Party and the Trade Union Movement'. It condemned 'class-collaboration', citing Attlee's cooperation with Baldwin over Abdication as an example. Among the Labour signatories of the 'Unity Manifesto' were the *Tribune* backers and writers, Cripps, Bevan, Harold Laski and John Strachey. A crowded meeting in the Free Trade Hall, Manchester, 24 January, gave the campaign a spectacular start. Cripps called it 'the most remarkable experience of my short political career'. Three days after the meeting, the NEC voted to expel the Socialist League from the Labour Party. 'You talk about driving Cripps out,' Bevin wrote to G.D.H. Cole: 'Cripps is driving himself out. The Annual Conference came to certain decisions. If I did not accept the decisions of the Conference of my union I know jolly well what the members would do with me.'

The NEC also banned association with the Communist Party, and association with organizations working for a United or Popular Front. Faced with this, in the following March the Socialist League dissolved itself, under protest, declaring that its former members would go on *individually* supporting the Unity Manifesto. It had been a thorn in the side of the Labour leadership since its foundation in 1932, advocating rapid nationalization, cooperation with Communists both domestically and internationally, and a cavalier attitude to Parliament and the ballot box. Its virtually forced dissolution in March 1937 represented not only a defeat for the left over the 'Popular Front', but a blow against the advocacy of extreme socialist views within the party.

In March the NEC policy committee under Dalton produced *Labour's Immediate Programme*. This reflected Attlee's own prescription for dealing with dissent – 'avoid debates, and get them working on something they all agree with'. A reprise of the Edinburgh conference decisions, it did nothing to unite right and left, and in May the NEC found it necessary to forbid organized movements within the party in support of a Popular Front: members of the party were advised to 'concentrate on Labour's constructive proposals' as set out in *Labour's Immediate Programme*.

Acrimony between right and left did nothing to resolve the contradictions in Labour's defence and foreign policies. *Labour's Immediate Programme* said nothing about Spain. Bevin supported non-intervention, while Attlee said it had failed. In April 1937 British merchant ships bound for Bilbao were attacked by Italian submarines. Attlee's attack on the government in the subsequent censure debate was masterly, but he did not suggest that he would have been prepared to go to war to break Franco's blockade, which was what his left-wingers wanted him to do. On rearmament, Attlee continued to steer an unconvincing course between Bevin, who claimed in May 1937 that British rearmament had already fortified the 'liberty-loving nations of the world', and Bevan, who claimed that Labour support of rearmament 'put a sword in the hands of our enemies that may be used to cut off our own heads'.

Until July Attlee stuck obstinately to the line that Labour opposed rearmament and supported collective security through the League of Nations. At its July meeting the NEC, besides ordering a further restriction on Popular Front activities, decided at last that the policy of voting against the arms estimates was wrong: and Attlee put this view forcefully and successfully to a meeting of the PLP. The resolution was carried by forty-five votes to thirty-nine. Dalton records that after the vote some of the South Wales miners, led by Jim Griffiths and Arthur Jenkins, 'rushed about trying to convene a special miners' meeting and to commit it to a block vote against the majority decision. . . . Others of the minority rushed round to Attlee demanding that another Party meeting should be held on Monday to reconsider the question. Attlee very wisely discouraged this idea.' Once decisions were taken, Attlee did not permit post-mortems. Only eleven members of the Parliamentary Labour Party voted against the service estimates. Those who shared the *Daily Express* view that after such a fundamental change in policy Attlee would have to resign the leadership ignored Attlee's views on leadership as stated in *The Labour Party in Perspective*: 'Unless acquiescence in the views of the majority conflicts with my conscience, I shall fall into line ... at no time have I opposed armaments on a point of conscience.'

The scene was now set for the 1937 Labour Party conference, to be held at Bournemouth in October. Attlee told Tom he had 'fears of another Edinburgh'. Following the victory in the PLP for Labour's rearmers – 'a patent breach of Conference decisions,' thundered Aneurin Bevan – the National Council of Labour issued a statement written by Dalton entitled *International Policy and Defence*. This blamed the British government for the present ineffectiveness of the League of Nations, recorded Labour's abandonment of non-intervention, and called for a conference at which Hitler and Mussolini should be invited to discuss their grievances. A Labour government should be returned at once, 'strongly equipped to defend this country, to play its full part in Collective Security, and to meet any intimidation by the Fascist Powers'. This statement was opposed at the conference by Lansbury as a Christian pacifist and by Aneurin Bevan as a party 'constitutionalist'. Bevan demanded that the party should revert to its former policy, and vote against the annual arms estimates. The Lansbury–Bevan combination was ineffective. *International Policy and Defence* was accepted by a majority of nearly ten to one, and this vote was interpreted as the Labour Party's endorsement of a policy of active rearmament.

The quarrel between the leaders of the now dissolved Socialist League and the NEC came to a head at the conference. Cripps challenged the authority by which the NEC had declared that members of the Labour Party must not cooperate with the Communist Party. Cripps failed. By a large majority the conference refused to restore recognition of the Socialist League if it re-established itself, and rejected a United Front. On the other hand, the conference strengthened the position of the left *vis-à-vis* the trade unions by increasing the representation of constituency parties on the NEC from five to seven, and ruling that the unions could no longer participate in the election of constituency representatives. In another move to reduce the influence of the trade unions, the date of the annual conference was shifted from October to June so that it should not follow too closely the TUC meeting in September.

The Bournemouth conference also ratified *Labour's Immediate Programme* as a manifesto for the next election. On foreign policy, ignoring Spain and the Soviet Union, it promised to revive the League of Nations and slow down the arms race, but 'unhesitatingly maintain such armed forces as are necessary to defend our country and to fulfil our obligations as a member of the British Commonwealth and League of Nations'. Domestically it offered a remarkably precise programme which needed little updating when the election finally came in 1945. It assumed that four 'levers' controlled the economic machine – finance, land, transport, and coal and power. The next Labour government would manage credit in the interests of trade and employment, by taking control of the Bank of England. A National Investment Board would be set up. The land 'should belong to the people' and a bill enabling compulsory purchase would be introduced. Coal, electricity and gas would be nationalized, and a National Transport Board set up to run the railways 'and such other transport services as are suitable' for nationalization, and to coordinate all other transport. The social services would be extended, and the school-leaving age raised; 'drastic and immediate' action would be taken about the distressed areas. *Labour's Immediate Programme* was already a bestseller, and it offered a striking alternative to the woolly nostrums of the national government.

Attlee was able to tell Tom that the Bournemouth conference was 'remarkably successful'. The delegates had spoken kindly of *The Labour Party in Perspective*, and his leadership was manifestly secure. A *Sunday Dispatch* report that Bevin would shortly enter Parliament and take over the leadership was angrily squashed by Bevin himself, who feared not so much its effect on Attlee as the impression it might make on his fellow trade union leaders. Even on Spain the unity of the party was growing. After the Bournemouth conference the NEC organized a series of mass demonstrations in favour of the Republicans; and in December 1937 it dispatched to Spain a fraternal delegation including Attlee, Ellen Wilkinson, Philip Noel-Baker and John Dugdale.

In Barcelona the delegates stayed with Dr Negrín, the Socialist Prime Minister – whose greatest problem, Attlee learned, was Communist intrigue. They flew from Barcelona to Valencia in Negrín's private plane – 'we went up to 10,000 feet, which makes one's ears crackle' – and then on to Madrid, staying there at the Palace Hotel, where only one floor was available for visitors, the others being used as hospital wards. The following morning they lunched with General Miaja, commander-in-chief of the government forces defending Madrid. The front was only four miles away. That night they were taken to the theatre. Attlee was given a great welcome, and the orchestra struck up 'God Save the King'. Next day they started a round of visits. They began with a school, 'children of the working class, keen as needles, but so thin', recorded Ellen Wilkinson; 'every day they had to come through falling shells or casual bullets to a school only $2\frac{1}{2}$ miles from the trenches'. She asked a young teacher how she could stand it. ' "It's all right if we can keep the children fed. That keeps up their nerves and it is wonderful then what they can resist." Attlee smiled, but his eyes were wet as we passed on through the school.' They spent an hour walking in the front-line trenches. Attlee addressed one company, and gave permission for it to be called the 'Major Attlee Company'.

It was an exacting tour. A few hours' sleep in the small hours; by day, walks over rough ground, often under artillery fire. Flying back to Barcelona in Negrín's plane, very low over the sea, close to the shore, they were followed by Franco planes, but fortunately, Attlee recorded, 'the Fascist aircraft were just too late'. Back in Barcelona they experienced an air-raid by three Franco planes, 'a very mild prelude', he comments, 'to what was to come a few years later'. They left Barcelona for France, and returned to England, immediately producing an eight-page broadsheet, with excellent photographs, entitled *We Saw in Spain*. Attlee's contribution was headlined 'Spain Fights for Democracy'. He described the strength and optimism of the people, their hatred of war, but their even greater hatred of tyranny, and their courage. He denounced the policy of non-intervention which so much threatened them:

> Throughout, the Republic has been greatly hampered by the denial of its right to obtain arms for its defence.
> In my view the policy of non-intervention is responsible to a great extent

for the food difficulty, and the acquiescence in the activities of the Fascist powers in their efforts to starve the people of Spain.

There has been a great deal of propaganda designed to represent the Spanish contest as one between rival ideologies, Fascism and Communism. I believe that is entirely false.

The Government of Spain is composed of various political and religious views, including fervent Catholics, such as the Minister of Justice. There are hundreds of thousands of good Catholics supporting the Republic. The real contest in Spain is between liberty and tyranny...

Continued acquiescence in a one-sided non-intervention has made the British Government an accessory to the attempt to murder democracy in Spain.

When he returned to Britain he found that for the first time the left wing of the Labour Party were pleased with him. Various British newspapers had criticized him for having given the clenched fist sign in reply to the Spanish forces' salute; they alleged that by doing so he was signifying approval of Communism. 'This story,' he remarked in his autobiography, 'constantly meets me on the public platform. In fact, at that time the salute was commonly used by all supporters of the Republic whether they were Liberals, Socialists, Communists or anarchists.' He made himself even more agreeable to the left when he counter-attacked his critics in the columns of *Tribune*. He pressed his point at a rally in the Albert Hall on 19 December, and two days later in the House of Commons. He wrote to Tom:

We went on to the Albert Hall which was a tremendous success both for numbers and enthusiasm. I, on account of the furore over the Spanish visit, had a tremendous reception. The visit has done a lot for the movement and has also had a good effect internationally. I followed it up with a speech last week, which enthused our side, and curiously enough was approved by a great many on the other, so that the Session closed very happily for us.

10
Attlee At Home

By the mid-1930s Vi's health, though not always good, was very much better than before 1931. Though she saw little of her husband except at the weekends she became too busy to be lonely. The minutes she spent with him were treasured. The children knew their father loved them, but they understood that with him their mother came first. They knew too that, much as she loved them, the centre of her life was 'Pa'. Ten years of marriage, long absences, chores, illnesses and the care of four children had done nothing to diminish Vi's still awed devotion to her husband. He was still the most glamorous as well as the most loving man a woman could wish for. Though she saw even less of him in the thirties than she had in the twenties, he dominated her life more and more: besides being a husband and a member of Parliament, he was now a statesman as well.

Vi's main problem was to deal with her own perfectionism, at a time when they were financially in their most difficult period. She could not afford the number of servants to run 'Heywood' up to the standards to which the Millars and Attlees had been accustomed. Sometimes, after the children had been put to bed, she would take an anxious look at the state of the house, grab an apron and a pair of gloves, and begin to scrub the kitchen floor as if her life depended on it. When Attlee came upon the scene, though, it was always: 'Don't worry. It'll all get done.' She would take off her gloves, take off her apron, and he would pick up her bucket and empty it into the sink. Then he would go into the sitting room, and sit in his chair by the fire. She would follow him in, and sit at his feet. He would bend down and kiss her. Sometimes they would just sit there. Sometimes he would talk a little. Sometimes he would read to her.

After the midday meal with the children on Sundays, he would go to his chair by the fire in the sitting room. Vi would follow him and sit on the floor at his feet. The elder children would troop in and Nellie would go in and sit with the baby on her lap. Attlee would read aloud from a book. As he read Vi would look up at him. Sometimes he would stop for a moment, in mid-sentence, bend down and kiss her. One Sunday Felicity, then four years old, asked Nellie: 'If I look up like Mummy does, would Daddy kiss *me*?' Though Vi loved babies, other people's as well as her own, childbirth was always a trial for her, and the after-effects were a burden and a risk. When Alison was on her way, Vi, for the first time, confessed to Nellie that she was apprehensive. She did not look forward to Alison's coming. 'You *love* babies,' said Nellie. 'I do,' said Vi, 'but you can have too many.' Alison was the last. After having had four children, Vi was still as girlish-looking as ever. On the tennis court, swimming in the sea, playing cricket on the beach, she was as lithe, straight and as quick of movement as a sixteen-year-old, as feminine as ever.

Attlee was her comfort and support. If one of the children proposed to do something which Vi did not favour she would say: 'If you do that I shall have to tell your father.' If one of them *did* misbehave she would say: 'I shall have to tell Daddy.' This announcement had a twofold effect. Not only would the culprit not want father to know, but, since father was almost certainly not in the house, and might not be due back for some days, the prospect of him being told would hang for an age above the wrongdoer's head. Sometimes nerve would go, and there would be an earnest 'Please don't tell Daddy: I'll be good from now on.'

On the rare occasions Daddy was in fact 'told' he was never cross. He would explain what was undesirable about what had been done and point out how difficult such peccadilloes made life for an already busy mother. He never made them feel guilty: he made them feel 'unhelpful'. He would ask them to be better not on moral but on social grounds. Janet was once reported to Daddy for losing her temper. He described the losing of temper not as a moral but a mental problem, which might be solved not by moral but mental effort, and told her the story of the lorry going up hill: 'I think I can do it. . . . I *think* – I – can – do it.'

One of the advantages of his returning home late was that he could sometimes deal with night-time fears. Felicity – now known as 'Flip' – had a spell of being fearful of cows: they might come out of the meadow, enter the garden, and walk up the stairs and into the bedrooms. Her father explained to her that the shape of a cow's legs, the narrowness of the stairs and the preference cows showed for staying in the fields made visits by cows to bedrooms totally impossible. He was very good at dealing with the occasional nightmare, and was nearly always working at a speech or an article in his study within easy reach of the sufferer at the times when visitations might take place. One of his most important roles was to enable Vi to maintain her regime yet sometimes relax her restrictions. She had what she called her 'Rules'. If sometimes the children pressed her and she wished to bend a 'Rule' she would say: 'Go and ask your father.' Attlee, recognizing the cue, would always say Yes. The children got their way, and Vi's Rules remained intact.

He was an excellent reader aloud. There was as much expression in his voice as was necessary, and his timing was good; but what the family liked most was his knack of reading quickly and lightly so that he took his listeners along with the pace of the prose and the plot. For poetry the single volume, *Lyra Heroica*, was his standby. Jane Austen was his favourite author, Meredith his favourite poet. He read contemporary novels. He liked Priestley. He read them *The Good Companions* and *Angel Pavement*. John Buchan was another favourite. He read them all of Kipling. When the children were older they took it in turns to read. He did not share Vi's love of music, but with her gramophone and radio she indulged that in the many hours when he was away. She, on the other hand, came to share his zest for billiards. She played billiards with him most evenings at Monkham's Avenue, and frequently beat him.

The billiard table was in the 'Ullage Room'. There was always an 'Ullage Room' in an Attlee house, if big enough. Nobody is sure why it had the name: according to the Oxford dictionary 'ullage' means 'what a cask etc wants of being full. . . dregs and by extension, waste, refuse or rubbish'. The 'Ullage Room' at Monkham's Avenue had a large, green-covered set of lamps above the billiard table that could be lowered or raised, and on the wall a large relief map of Europe modelled in Plasticine which Vi and he had manufactured a few weekends before Janet was born. There was no billiards room at Heywood; he decided not to take the table with them because there would be no time to play; the 'Ullage Room' at Heywood was his workshop. They were fond of rummy: Attlee liked to play it on Sunday evenings, and as he played he chewed butterscotch made by Nellie. Vi and Nellie knitted a great deal. Sometimes Vi got the wool into inextricable tangles; she always left the mess for Attlee to unravel. He was undefeatable, and enjoyed the challenge. A gleam would come into his eye as he took up what he called 'the spaghetti'. He would light his pipe and start to puff. 'Nice to have *one* problem with a solution,' he used to say. Sometimes they would go to bed and leave him working on it. In the morning they would find the mess had become a neat round ball.

Vi used to worry about money. She was very conscious of the fact that Attlee had decided to move from Woodford Green to Stanmore on her account, and that largely because of her he had elected to buy a house larger and more attractive than he might otherwise have contemplated. The contract had only just been completed when out of the blue in the autumn of 1931 had come the political crisis, entailing Attlee's relegation from ministerial rank to the back benches and a substantial reduction in his income. They had hardly finished arranging the furniture in Heywood before the anxious Vi was driving around the district looking at smaller houses. These explorations soon petered out, but the sense of money being short remained with the children. Vi would get very upset if a plate or a cup were broken. For a few years there was no going away for summer holidays. Clothes were passed down. On the other hand there was a car, the lawn was just big enough to make a rough tennis court, and there were occasional games of golf.

Many relatives came to the house, but hardly ever any other visitors. Aunt Mary stayed with them on holidays from her mission in South Africa, and Uncle Rob, unmarried, was often there for lunch on Sundays. Neighbours never came, nor political friends: whether this was because the neighbours were Tories and the political friends had too far to come, or because the family was so large that it did not need company, the children never discovered. In any case, Attlee at home at weekends was too precious to be shared with visitors. The children seemed as happy as children could be. They loved their parents; their parents loved them; and their parents patently loved each other. The children were not aware that there was anything remarkable about the relationship between their parents. Janet told the author:

> We simply didn't *register* the fact that they loved each other so much. Or that this was at all unusual in married life. We assumed that that was how all fathers and mothers behaved to each other. They never talked about it. As a matter of fact they never *told* us how to behave about anything. I never learned anything from them about human values by being *told*. For instance, they never told us how we should behave to relatives, when they visited us, or when we went to see them. We just did what they did; and thought it would be all right.

He never told them what to do about careers. When, later, during the war, Janet decided on her own initiative to join the services, and was asked by a newspaper reporter what her father thought about her having done so, she could only say that she didn't know. He never asked the children how they were doing at school. If they had bad reports he did not mention the matter. If one of them did well he would say: 'Good report, Janet.' No blame, rare praise, was the principle.

Attlee never introduced talk about politics into the home, but if any of the children asked questions about politics he would always answer them. When Janet was eleven years old she asked him why he had become a member of Parliament. He told her what he had seen in the East End when he worked at the Haileybury Club, and she remembers in particular the story recorded in his autobiography about the little boy who was going home not to tea, but to see if there *was* any tea. If the children asked about politicians he would talk about them as though he were talking to adults. He never gossiped about his colleagues or his opponents. His assessments were critical, but never personal. Loyalty was obviously the supreme political virtue. Not until he became leader of the Opposition in 1935, and feature writers and photographers came to the house, did the children have any feeling of being members of a 'political' family. The children at school, almost without exception from Tory families, would sometimes refer to Attlee's politics – 'Your father won't get in *this* time' – but these remarks made no impression on them.

The focus of the Attlees' family life was the weekend, or, rather, the weekends at which Attlee was at home. Frequently he would get back to Heywood for tea by 5.30 on a Friday. They all knew that father being at home was a special occasion in the week: tea on Friday would be 'special', with extra things to eat. After tea he would play games with the younger children, and read some stories to the older ones or tell them a few he had made up, an art in which he was proficient.

> When he played games he really played. He gave his whole attention to it. If the baby had a doll, Daddy would listen to what she was saying very seriously. If he played cards with us he always played to win. It was the same with tennis. I used to play bezique with him. He never babied me. If he found that playing a particular game with us was boring, he'd invent a more complicated set of rules for himself – for instance, when we played 'Lexicon', we played our rules and he'd play his, more complicated.

If he could not get home for tea on Friday, he would have a late supper alone with Vi. He would talk about everything that had happened during the week except politics; politics came into his report to Vi only if something dramatic or amusing had occurred. She would sit rapt, the cares of the week forgotten. He would light his pipe. Then they would sit in front of the fire, she knitting and he reading to her, until it was time for bed.

The children had the feeling when he was there that whatever went wrong he could put right, in an instant. After breakfast one Sunday, outside the back door, playing with Janet, Felicity jammed her finger in the hood of her doll's pram and started to scream. When he heard her, Attlee was still at the breakfast table, reading the paper. Instead of coming through the door to the rescue, he jumped through the open ground-floor window, and released her finger in a second. In emergencies he seemed to the children to act with incredible speed and authority. One Sunday morning the spirit lamp, keeping the bacon warm, blazed up. The children were appalled. 'Run to the kitchen and get a cloth,' he rapped out to Janet. Janet ran out of the room, bumped her head on the brass keyhole of the kitchen door, felt the blood run down her face, panicked, and ran back to her father, screaming. 'Go back and get that cloth,' he snapped. Janet forgot her bleeding forehead, ran to the kitchen and got the cloth. He doused the spirit lamp, quietened the younger children, then plastered Janet's forehead. 'First things first, *always*,' he said.

Saturday began with odd jobs, which he usually performed surrounded by the children, breaking off the repair of a nursery table or the fitting of a new chair leg to deal with a demand for a rabbit hutch or to provide a battered rag doll with a new arm stuffed with sawdust produced by his own carpentry. While he put new hinges on the garage doors or fitted new catches to the window the children stood around, and he told them about what the streets of London were like, with horse-drawn-buses, when he was a little boy. They came and went to his carpentry room as and when they pleased. He made plate-racks, bookshelves and cupboards for their bedrooms. He could re-upholster chairs and put new eyes into a stuffed rabbit. They thought he was a magician.

Their first car was a Morris with a dicky seat. He designed and made an extension so that both Nellie and Janet could sit in it as well as all the others. When after several attempts a local architect failed to produce a suitable plan for enlarging the house at Monkham's Avenue to include a garage, Attlee drew up the plans himself and got it built. At Christmas time he met the seasonal demand for swords, magic wands and furniture for dolls' houses. There was a pond in the garden for which he made sailing boats, making sails out of old bed-sheets, which he sewed very neatly. He was adept at reconstructing china with the use of seccotine, and he was a good French polisher. He built swings, and when the rope frayed near the seats, and the children complained, he would put down *The Times* or *Hansard* and come out into the garden and make the rope good.

He was so versatile and so good-tempered that the children seemed to think he could make or mend anything for them. He never seemed to say 'No', or 'Wait till later.' If he were pressed he would explain the priorities. In autumn the leaves must be swept up. He would sweep up the leaves, push the wheelbarrow, and the children would march solemnly along behind to light the bonfire. In summer the lawn must be cut. The children would follow him as he pushed the mower. He was very clever at involving them. He gave them jobs to keep them quiet, but he took the trouble to organize significant jobs which would make them feel useful. There was never any noise, tears or friction when Attlee was with the children; he always contrived to get them so preoccupied that he was free to get on with his job. It was a gift he displayed in a different milieu when he became prime minister.

None of them remembers him ever looking worried, downcast or preoccupied. Nor did he ever seem exhilarated or elated. He showed no emotion, except for this steady affection to the children and devotion to their mother. Otherwise he always seemed the same. He took no great pleasure in food – small portions of everything; his only obvious indulgence was his cup of tea. He wore plus-fours sometimes at the weekends, and a very old pair of slacks for gardening or carpentry. Clothes were just something to wear. Mainly for economy he bought his suits off the peg. Each suit he bought seemed exactly like its predecessor. His one luxury was his pipe.

There was plenty to do in the garden, though part of it behind the house was mainly occupied by the tennis court. There were trees and shrubs and flowerbeds. Vi was a good gardener. He was not. Just as, in spite of his admiration for her, and appreciation of her femininity, he never observed what she was wearing and had to be told if she were wearing a new hat, he seemed not to observe what was growing in the garden. He left all that to Vi and the part-time gardener. He would mow the tennis court, mark the lines, point and re-roof the potting shed, but he would neither plant nor prune. While Vi used a trowel she would hear the sound of his typewriter from his study as with one finger he knocked out another newspaper article or parliamentary speech. But he would weed, very assiduously and thoroughly, often lying down on his stomach. 'I'm a good rough weeder. Good training for democracy. Count the plants, and pull out the majority. They'll be the weeds.'

Saturday afternoons were mainly for Vi. In summer they would play tennis. They kept up the custom formed at Woodford Green of going over to Buckhurst Hill to play with the Crossmans. They would come back to be with the children in good time before supper. Unless they went out to a political engagement or, very rarely, to a party, they would stay at home, partly for economy, partly because they had so little time together.

Sunday was the big day of the week. Vi would go to Communion at 8 am accompanied when they were old enough by the children. In the mornings Attlee would do more odd jobs in the garden or in his carpentry room. Vi and the children would go to church at eleven. The Sunday midday meal was the peak hour of the week. The children sat down, and Attlee carved. He carved with his tongue out, and 'the knife used to go the same way as his tongue'. They were not allowed to talk to him while they were waiting to be served, nor were they allowed to chatter while waiting for their food – 'We shall be pleased to listen to you when we are *all* sitting,' he used to say in a half-comic, half-serious tone.

Once every child had been served, lunch was a great time for talk, especially in the pursuit of 'General Knowledge'. This took the form of father putting questions to the rest, including to Vi. He had a number of different 'programmes', but he conducted them in the same way: very simple questions for the youngest child, more difficult for the next youngest. Years afterwards the children discovered that these games were constructed partly for the unobtrusive education of Vi: the more difficult questions about foreign statesmen, British politicians and items in the news were thrown in so that she could tactfully be briefed.

On all points of information he was regarded as an oracle. This was Vi's doing. She spoke of him in his absence as though there was no question which he could not answer. When silk stockings first came into fashion, Nellie asked Vi: 'Where do these things come from?' Vi replied: 'I don't know. I'll ask Clem. He'll know.' He frequently exploited this credulity at Sunday lunches, and gave out ludicrous misinformation until stopped with a plaintive: 'Now, Clem, are you pulling our legs?' 'Why *shouldn't* I pull your legs? If you're all silly enough to believe it, why should I worry?' and he would look slowly round the table with an expression of supercilious indifference on his face from one dubious little face to another until one of them started to laugh. Then he would tell them how important it was not to believe everything one was told but to ask questions to get at the truth. He told them how to use dictionaries, encyclopaedias and reference books so that they could check what they were told, and find out things for themselves.

After lunch he would take the children for a walk. At Woodford Green Martin was too small to walk far, but since he always clamoured to be taken, his father used to take the pram. There were several stiles on the route, and Attlee had to lift the pram over them. The two older children found this very irritating, but their father patiently explained that they should put up with it, 'so that Martin could come with us'. Attlee would talk to them all the way. These Sunday walks reminded him of family walks in his boyhood days at Putney, and he would recount various stories of the doings and idiosyncrasies of the Attlee and the Bravery tribes. Janet used to ask him about the war, and he would tell them of the battles that had to be fought by brave 'Tommies' because the generals were so stupid. He talked about the heroism and comradeship of the troops, and sang them marching songs, folk songs or historical ballads, like his favourite, 'Lillibullero'. They would ask him questions about what they saw on the route – a water-pump, a plough or an oddly shaped barn. He would explain things to them with great thoroughness, always talking to them as if they were adults. They would talk about trains. Janet travelled with him to London one day and he told her about Stephenson and the Rocket and how a locomotive worked. He drew sketches of pistons and boilers on the back of an envelope.

Sometimes they would all go out in the car – first a bull-nosed Morris, later a red Fiat. Attlee never cared for driving, and was never very good.

When he backed the car out of the garage to the front of the house for Vi to take over, it would buck like a rabbit. If the children found him at the wheel when they ran out of the house to pile into the back, Janet would shout: 'Hold tight everybody: *Daddy's* driving!' He was not a good judge of when to begin to apply his brakes, and when he changed gear the car lurched forward, as Vi once said, 'like a wounded animal'. But in the first year at Stanmore, while Vi was recovering her health, he drove the children two miles to their grandmother at Bushey every morning, from where they were taken on to school, and then caught his train to Westminster.

Until the late thirties holidays were governed by the need to economize. For parts of the Christmas and Easter holidays the children would go off to stay with relatives, and in the summer the whole family would stay with some of the Millars in North Wales. There was golf at Nevin. Hotels or houses to let were too expensive, but Vi and he would have a few days on their own in a boarding house or in rooms at somewhere like Weymouth or Seaton, where they would read, talk and play golf. All members of the family would swim except Attlee. He did not care for the water; he preferred to sit on the sands with his pipe and a book, and watch. He didn't like swimming and didn't like dancing, though Vi enjoyed both.

It was fortunate for Vi that she loved being a mother and loved helping other people, and that she found her beloved husband's personality so congenial, for she had to spend a great deal of time on her own. She did not enjoy housework, but any kind of looking after the children was a pleasure. Whether they were well or ill she poured out her affection on them. Bathing and drying them, dabbing bruises, bandaging cuts – this was not so much a maternal duty as an expression of personality. She loved them all, and understood them all. For Nellie, Martin, came first. He was forgiven everything, the naughty boy, even when aged six he pushed a playmate into the pond. Whereas Attlee behaved to the children as though they were as old as he was, Vi behaved to the children as if she were their age. She played cricket on the beach, or snakes and ladders in the house, with the unselfconsciousness of a child; and she shared their affectionate, half reverent, half leg-pulling attitude to their father.

In spite of the strains put upon it, which are common to those of most men in political life, it was a happy marriage and it produced a happy home life for the children. Laurence Attlee said just after Vi had died: 'She would not have been the right wife for everybody, but she was the right wife for Clem.' Felicity said: 'She enjoyed a clever man not dominating her, but loving her, so she surrendered completely to him.' His lovely young wife, his happy children and his undemanding home gave Attlee an emotional support which he never mentioned but continually felt.

11
The Approach of War, 1937-9

I

When Parliament reassembled in October 1937, Labour's criticism of the government once more was concentrated on foreign policy. Attlee denounced Britain's failure to take strong measures against Japan, and refuted the government's charge that Labour was warmongering. 'If we suggest that any steps be taken against aggression,' he said on 21 October, 'the Government will say we want war.' In this he was not entirely objective. He himself believed that Labour demands for military action were irresponsible. After visiting his old colleague Charles Trevelyan at the end of November he wrote to Tom: 'I find CT rather bellicose. He contemplates war with far more equanimity than I can compass. I distrust his judgment.' But while more aware of the risks than most members of his party, he pressed hard for the rapid development of a defence policy of which war in the imminent future was a consequent risk.

Labour's chances of forcing the government to abandon appeasement seemed for a while to be improved by the clash between Chamberlain and Eden. They had differed for some months about what Eden tactfully defined as their 'assessment of how to handle the dictators'; and Eden's ambition to succeed Chamberlain as Conservative leader – understandable if not laudable in the circumstances – made him look for a convenient opportunity to resign. Disagreement over the proper response to a proposal from President Roosevelt for an international conference, which Chamberlain spurned, and over negotiations with Italy, in which Chamberlain was in Eden's view over-anxious to recruit Italy as an ally against Germany, led to Eden's resignation on 20 February 1938.

In the debate on the resignation, Attlee supported Eden. Though he had been told nothing about the Roosevelt initiative, or about the angry exchanges which had taken place between Eden and Chamberlain in private, Attlee got to the heart of the matter. Instead of trying to deal with the cause of war, the government had always been trying in a feeble way to play off one dictator against another. 'That is a policy which sooner or later leads to war.' Eden's resignation, he said, would be 'hailed everywhere as a great victory for Mussolini', which had come just when Mussolini's weakness might have been exposed, with Abyssinia still unconquered and the Spanish War another drain on his resources. Attlee's later analysis of Eden's behaviour was rather less flattering:

> He did nothing at all. He could have joined forces with Churchill, but he kept his distance from him. His silence strengthened Chamberlain's position. He did not want to antagonize the Conservative Party. Might have been loyalty: Eden was a gentleman. Might have thought that if he kept quiet he would have become leader of the Conservative Party when the time came to turn Chamberlain out. Might have been lack of resolution.

In March 1938 Hitler's troops entered Austria. Mussolini, to Chamberlain's surprise and regret, did nothing. Attlee responded vigorously, emphasizing that there was now only one place where resistance to the dictators was physically practical: Spain. In this, 'the speech of his life' according to Aneurin Bevan, he denounced Chamberlain's policy and ranged himself with Churchill and Eden. 'Having followed [the Prime Minister's] speech very closely,' said Attlee, 'I could not discern anything in it in the nature of a policy which made for peace.... I found the Prime Minister stating very strongly the principle that the rule of force should give way to the rule of law, but in actual fact he yields to force all the time.' Eden, said Attlee, with 'far more experience of foreign affairs and of Signor Mussolini', had 'recited in this House, in the memory of all of us, the number of occasions on which he had received pledge after pledge and these pledges had been broken'. What evidence had Chamberlain, beyond Mussolini's assurance, that Italy was not actively intervening in Spain? 'Of course he is.' Attlee quoted several instances. 'Oh yes, the Prime Minister's loyalty to his friend is so great that he is for the moment more Roman than the Romans – his Government denies the actions in which Il Duce glories.'

Attlee had no time for Chamberlain's efforts, which Eden opposed, to separate Mussolini from Hitler. The talks between Britain and Italy, to which Eden had refused to agree unless Mussolini had first begun to withdraw his troops from Spain, had now culminated in an Anglo-Italian agreement. By this Mussolini promised to evacuate Italian 'volunteers' from Spain, and Chamberlain promised to raise the *de jure* recognition of Italy's conquest of Abyssinia at the League of Nations. Attlee declared this to be another step towards a war which the government did not want but, since it had neither the courage nor imagination to reorientate its foreign policy, could not avoid. At the end of April he wrote to Tom:

This government is leading the country into war. The Italian agreement is not really a move for peace but an endeavour to get Italy to line up against Germany. The conversations with France which are now on are directed to the same end. We are really back in 1914. The Government will, I think, continue to allow the smaller democratic states to be swallowed up by Germany, not from a pacifist aversion to war, but because they want time to develop armaments. There is really no peace policy at all. Chamberlain is just an imperialist of the old school but without much knowledge of foreign affairs or appreciation of the forces at work. It is a pretty gloomy outlook

When the Italian agreement came up in the House he said: 'The gravamen of our attack is that this Treaty does not bring peace but a sword.' The government regarded a settlement of the Spanish question as a prerequisite of the entry into force of the agreement, yet: 'Signor Mussolini never pretends that he is not [also] engaged in aggression in Abyssinia. He puts Spain and Abyssinia on exactly the same level.'

With the reversal of its policy on the arms estimates, the PLP at last had some recommendations to make about defence. In April 1938 Attlee asked Dalton 'to be responsible for accumulating material on our air defences, both constructive and critical', which was used on 11 and 12 May when the Commons debated air defence. There were three separate motions, each demanding an immediate inquiry: one, moved by Churchill, was backed by twenty-six Conservatives, the others were moved by Sinclair for the Liberals and by Attlee for Labour. As a result Lord Swinton, the Air Minister, was replaced by Sir Kingsley Wood. Soon after the debate, Attlee, Greenwood and Dalton went to Downing Street and presented Chamberlain with a detailed document on air defence. This was one of the most substantial results of the Labour Party Defence Committee which Attlee had set up the previous year. Chamberlain received them with characteristic coldness: 'I assume that you have come to see me from patriotic, and not from party political motives.' But Kingsley Wood, to whom Chamberlain had referred them, was reasonable and continued to have useful talks with Dalton.

During the spring and summer of 1938, the Labour leaders also assailed the government on domestic issues. During a debate on unemployment assistance in July, Attlee deplored the fact that there were still 1,800,000 unemployed; a 'huge poverty problem at a time when we are supposed to be enjoying real prosperity in the richest country in the world after seven years of a government with all the talents'. In the autumn of 1938 the Opposition, to the despair of Bevan and some other Labour backbenchers, abstained on the government's measure to prolong its Special Areas legislation, on the grounds that to resist would expose them to the charge of voting against more money for more jobs. No great feeling was displayed in the House: attention was now all the more firmly fixed on foreign policy.

II

In June, Attlee went to Denmark. The trip was arranged and paid for by the Workers' Travel Association, an organization created by Ernest Bevin; he thought Attlee deserved a holiday. Attlee chose to go to Denmark because at that time a Danish girl was living at 'Heywood', helping to look after the children, and because of talk with her and her friends he decided to inspect Denmark's social services. Vi went too. They were greeted at the airport by Alsing Andersen, a member of the Danish government, whom Attlee had met at various international conferences. They had 'a splendid time'. Asked in his eighties which country he would have chosen to be born in if he had not been born in Britain, he replied without hesitation: 'Denmark.'

The last four weeks of the session passed very quickly. His major speeches were on the Special Areas, housing and the international situation. He attended several meetings to discuss the disaffection with the NEC's line on the Popular Front which had once more become an issue. There were many consultations on air defence. He spent a weekend at Cripps's house in Gloucestershire to discuss India with Nehru, and it was here, he recorded later, that the basis of his policy for India when he became prime minister was laid down. Becoming more and more interested in American policy towards the dictators, he had several meetings with the American ambassador. He met Lloyd George a few times to discuss the situation in Europe. He gave tea on the terrace to the Aga Khan. One event gave him immense pleasure – a dinner for Don Bradman, the Australian cricketer. In mid-August he joined the family for their summer holiday at Tyr Pwll dairy farm at Nevin.

In September 1938 Hitler demanded that the Czechoslovak government should grant local autonomy to the German-speaking communities in the Sudetenland. Until that moment Attlee, relying on Bevin's information, had thought there was a fair chance that a show of firmness would deter the German leader. Fearing that if the Czechs rejected these demands Hitler would resort to force and involve Britain in a European war, Chamberlain sent Lord Runciman to put pressure on Beneš, the Czech Prime Minister. No sooner had Beneš agreed than Hitler, to Chamberlain's embarrassment, increased his demands.

Attlee immediately called on the government to make a firm stand. Except for the small pacifist minority, the Labour Party was united. Because of the change in date arranged the previous year, no party conference was scheduled for 1938, but the Joint National Council decided at once to meet at Blackpool, where the Trades Union Congress was in session, and on 8 September it issued the 'Blackpool Declaration' which called on the government to condemn Hitler's new demands and face the consequent risk of war:

> The British Government must leave no doubt in the mind of the German Government that they will unite with the French and Soviet Governments to resist any attack upon Czechoslovakia.... The British Labour Movement demands the immediate summoning of Parliament.... Whatever the risks involved, Britain must make its stand against aggression.... Labour cannot acquiesce in the destruction of the rule of law by savage aggression.

The 'Blackpool Declaration' made no impression on Chamberlain. He now depended heavily on his special adviser, Sir Horace Wilson, whose expertise was industrial matters, and of whose abilities Attlee once said – the simile being drawn from the names of the BBC radio channels of the day – 'Not National, only Midland Regional.' Chamberlain had no intention of 'uniting with the Soviet Government to resist any attack on Czechoslovakia', since he believed that Russia not Germany was the real enemy of the West. He decided to make a personal visit to Hitler. Before he left he asked Attlee to come and see him, and told him that if he saw Hitler 'there was a chance of doing something'. The meeting was very brief. Attlee said that nobody could stand in the way of an attempt to prevent a war, but 'we mustn't give way to threats, we had a duty to the Czechs, and principles which all parties in Britain now adhered to must not be compromised. I reminded him of the Blackpool Declaration. He had very little to say: nothing really.'

Chamberlain flew to Berchtesgaden on 15 September 1938 accompanied only by Sir Horace Wilson and a Foreign Office adviser, William Strang. On his return he recommended in the Cabinet that the Czechs should make even more sweeping concessions than those which had been previously publicized. Alarmed by what they heard, the Labour leaders asked Chamberlain to receive a three-man delegation from the Joint National Council of Labour. The delegation, consisting of Citrine, Morrison and Dalton, urged Chamberlain not to betray the Czechs and to warn Hitler that aggression would be met by force. Chamberlain responded only with an account of the uncompromising attitude displayed by Hitler, and a description of Czechoslovakia's unpreparedness. Dalton reported back to Attlee, who concluded: 'Chamberlain was out of his depth. Hitler bullied him, and then buttered him up. He had lost his grip.'

The following day the National Council of Labour issued a public statement reaffirming the Blackpool Declaration. Churchill immediately telephoned Attlee to say that the statement had 'done honour to the British nation', for which Attlee thanked him. Dalton was later vexed that Attlee had missed the cue for investigating ground for common action. Many members of the PLP still abhorred the use of force, and they would have been dubious, as even Eden was, about a public alignment with Churchill. It was safer for the Labour Party for the time being to continue to operate on its own.

On 21 September Attlee and Greenwood had a disagreeable interview with the Prime Minister. Defensive and irritable, Chamberlain evaded Attlee's questions about the contents of the Anglo-French plan which had been presented to the Czechs. Years later Attlee remembered feeling personally angry during the exchanges. All his suspicions of Chamberlain, and of the 'old gang' on whom successive Conservative prime ministers had leaned, were mobilized and concentrated at this bitter meeting. He accused the prime minister of 'simply giving way to Hitler', and told him that Britain would naturally be blamed if Eastern Europe was overrun by Hitler.

The following day a Labour Party deputation went to Paris to meet leading French socialists and discuss means of bringing pressure on the two governments to take further steps to save Czechoslovakia. Blum, embarrassed and apologetic, gave them a daunting account of the defeatism of the French Socialist movement. Meanwhile Chamberlain had flown to Godesberg to meet Hitler, who demanded further concessions from the Czechs. Chamberlain returned to London without committing himself. The Czechs rejected the demands 'absolutely and unconditionally'. Attlee set out to stiffen Chamberlain by writing him a letter, for publication, restating the essence of the Blackpool Declaration; and on 26 September, with other Labour leaders, he went to a huge rally at Earls Court calling on Britain to 'stand by the Czechs'.

Still striving to avert the use of force which would lead to war, Chamberlain sent Sir Horace Wilson to Berlin with the promise that Hitler could have the Sudetenland, provided the terms of transfer were settled by discussion not force. Hitler brushed the offer aside and threatened to occupy the whole territory by the first day of October unless his demands were met before that date. Chamberlain sanctioned the mobilization of the fleet. The news was announced next day. British and French ministers were summoned to London. The PLP met and, after submitting Attlee to a thoroughgoing interrogation, passed, with only about half a dozen pacifists dissenting, a resolution approving everything done by Attlee and the PLP Executive during the previous weeks. On the evening of 27 September Chamberlain addressed the nation on the BBC, making the famous statement: 'How horrible, fantastic, incredible, it is that we should be digging trenches and trying on gas-masks here because of a quarrel in a far-away country between people of whom we know nothing.'

On 27 September, after an exchange of messages between Chamberlain, Hitler, Mussolini and Daladier, the French Prime Minister, a four-power conference on Czechoslovakia was arranged – without Czech representatives. On 28 September Chamberlain announced in the Commons that Hitler had invited the other leaders to Munich. The great majority of Conservatives were jubilant.

According to the account of Duff Cooper, then in the government as First Lord of the Admiralty: 'The Opposition sat glum and silent. And then when Attlee gave the plan his blessing our side all rose again and cheered *him*, cheers in which the Opposition had to join, though looking a little foolish.' Attlee gave the plan his blessing on the assumption that: 'I am sure every member of this House is desirous of neglecting no chance of preserving the peace without sacrificing principles.' He either did not recognize, or did not realize, that the decision to sacrifice principles, and the Czechs, had already been made. When Chamberlain returned from Munich bearing his piece of paper, Attlee led the Labour Party in a denunciation of what Chamberlain had in any case intended to do.

> In the mind of every thoughtful person in the country when he heard that this settlement had been arrived at there was a conflict. On the one hand there was enormous relief that war had been averted, at all events for the time being; on the other, there was a sense of humiliation and foreboding for the future. If I may compare my feelings at that time, they were akin to those I felt on the night that we evacuated the Gallipoli Peninsula. There was sorrow for sacrifice. There was sorrow over the great chance of ending the war earlier that had passed away. There was, perhaps, some feeling of satisfaction that for a short time one was getting away from the firing line, but there was the certain and sure knowledge that before very long we should be in it again.
>
> The events of these last few days constitute one of the greatest diplomatic defeats that this country and France have ever sustained.... It is a tremendous victory for Herr Hitler. Without firing a shot, by the mere display of military force, he has achieved a dominating position in Europe which Germany failed to win after four years of war..... He has destroyed the last fortress of democracy in Eastern Europe which stood in the way of his ambitions.

There had been no contact with the Czech government, which stood out as a model of civilized behaviour in Eastern Europe. Attlee attacked the government for trusting Hitler and spurning Russian help. The Prime Minister, he said, should not have assumed that he knew how Hitler's mind worked. 'I have five pages of statements made by Herr Hitler, from every one of which he has receded.'

The motion approving Chamberlain's policy was carried by 366 votes to 144. Churchill abstained. He had been one of the prominent Conservatives who had spoken against the government, but these 'thirty or more dissident Conservatives,' he wrote later, 'could do no more than register their disapproval by abstention ...'

Most Conservatives were delighted and relieved by the Munich settlement. So were most of the British people. Gallup polls – introduced in October – showed that public opinion on the whole supported Chamberlain. and continued to do so even after war broke out ten months later.

III

Attlee's reward for his behaviour over Munich was an attempt by Cripps to remove him from the leadership. Cripps was now more anxious than ever to drive out Chamberlain, but had come to the conclusion that this could only be done if Labour could get the support of the anti-Chamberlain Tories. Immediately after the Munich debate in the House he approached Dalton. Britain, he said, was now in 'a new and desperate situation'. The Labour Party could never turn Chamberlain out on its own. The older idea of a Popular Front no longer applied. Labour, said Cripps, should now make common cause with the anti-Chamberlain Tories including Churchill, Eden and Amery. These Tories should be offered a programme which would preserve democratic liberties, rebuild collective security, maintain national control of the country's economic life, and – an indication of how anxious Cripps was to woo the dissident Tories – put socialism for the present on one side. The Liberals also should be approached. Attlee should be replaced as leader by Herbert Morrison.

Dalton told Cripps that to replace Attlee would be extremely difficult, especially if Morrison were the alternative, with his reputation for spending too much time at County Hall and not enough in the House of Commons. Dalton himself had become disenchanted with Morrison: he had shown no understanding of foreign affairs, and had been wobbly when Dalton had been fighting for rearmament. Attlee, on the other hand, had done nothing wrong over Munich, and though he inspired little enthusiasm, he had presented the party's case with vigour and clarity. But Dalton favoured approaches to the anti-Chamberlain Tories, and undertook to consult Attlee and Morrison.

Attlee was in favour, Morrison less so, possibly because he thought that he was more acceptable to the Tories than Attlee, and that therefore the alignment should be negotiated on the assumption that he would be the new leader. Dalton, who may well have calculated that he himself might become the leader if an alignment were formed, then conferred with Harold Macmillan, one of the leading Tory dissidents, who was agreeable to the Labour Party because of his efforts to stir the government to action in the Distressed Areas. Macmillan listened readily, but pointed out that the dissident Tories not only disagreed with Chamberlain but to some extent disagreed with each other. After further talks with Dalton, in which Attlee joined, he got as far as agreeing on a four-pronged plan of attack to be pursued by a Labour–Tory–Liberal alignment in the House. The alliance would play up the element of humbug in Chamberlain's talk of guarantees to the Czechs; press for specific pledges on future foreign policy; criticize deficiencies in the armament and air-raid defence programmes; and, to appeal to British businessmen, protest at the loss of East European trade through 'economic appeasement'.

The plan came to nothing. Macmillan found that Duff Cooper would not move unless Eden did, and Eden would not move at all. Only Churchill was ready to risk it. The arrangement was called off, but when eighteen months later Chamberlain had to be replaced by another Conservative, Attlee remembered that Churchill had been ready to stand openly with the Labour Party against Chamberlain when other Tories had not.

Attlee spent a quiet family Christmas. He wrote to Bernard on Boxing Day:

> Thanks very much for the excellent pipe with the cunning arrangements for drainage. I was discussing methods of pipe construction with the King when we met at dinner the other day. He had a most ingenious one which scraped the bowl every time so that it always kept the same size.
>
> I was pleased to see that Powell of Univ has been made a bishop. That makes two from my year, and five from the men of my time. When you add Professors Dodd and Grensted we had a pretty good theological output . . . .
>
> I had a long talk with Liddell Hart last week. He was very interesting on Army reforms. I doubt if Hore Belisha has really done what is necessary: I met one of my old lads the other day. He asked me if I remembered him and I said Yes, I posted you with a Lewis Gun in Serpent Trench in the last push. He was much bucked at my remembering him . . .
>
> We had a very good Xmas following our usual ritual. The Bushey folk, less Granny, who found it too cold, came over to tea and we supped there taking J and F with us. . . . . I think Janet is now taller than Vi. Felicity produced a ribald verse which was new to me:
>
>> Hark the herald angels sing
>> Mrs Simpson's pinched our King.

IV

Chamberlain still hoped to draw Mussolini away from Hitler. The Anglo-Italian Agreement, declared to be in effect from 2 November, had stipulated that Italian troops were to be withdrawn at once from Spain: not a man had been moved, but Chamberlain lived in hopes. Early in

January 1939, he told a press conference that he was 'astonished at the pessimism which seems to possess some of our critics'. Later that month, he and Halifax went to Rome and at a state banquet joined in a toast to King Victor Emmanuel as Emperor of Ethiopia. In a debate on 31 January, Attlee asked him why he had not discussed Spain with Mussolini at the meeting in Rome. Italy was increasing her pressure in Spain to win the war for Franco. Feeling was growing in Britain that the government wanted Franco to win. Attlee demanded that Britain should 'cease the hypocritical farce of non-intervention', and restore to the Spanish government their rights as the government of a sovereign state. The speech which Chamberlain made in reply is probably the one of which Ciano wrote in his diary: 'The British Ambassador has submitted for our approval the outlines of the speech that Chamberlain will make in the House of Commons in order that we may suggest changes if necessary.' A month later, Chamberlain recognized Franco's regime as the government of Spain. Attlee's censure motion was defeated by 344 votes to 137. Eden was among those who spoke for recognition. Chamberlain seemed invincible.

His strength led to a new clamour for a Popular Front. Cripps, who three months previously had declared the idea was dead, now wrote to the leaders of the Labour Party advocating an alliance of all parties and individuals to bring down the Chamberlain government, not only because it was incompetent but because it was Fascist. Cripps made clear that in order to defeat Chamberlain at the next general election he was willing in the short term to surrender a great deal of the socialist programme in which he believed. The Executive turned down Cripps's proposals by seventeen votes to three. He immediately sent out a circular appealing for public support for his 'Alliance'. The Executive threatened to expel him unless he reaffirmed his loyalty to the party and its official policy, and issued a second circular withdrawing his mass appeal for support. Cripps refused, and the Executive expelled him on 25 January. At a packed public meeting that night, Aneurin Bevan shouted amid tumultuous cheers: 'If Sir Stafford Cripps is expelled for wanting to unite the forces of freedom and democracy, they can go on expelling others. They can expel *me*.' They did, a month later.

Unabashed, Cripps set up a national organization with a central office in London and several branches up and down the country to 'launch a nationwide petition' demanding a Popular Front. It was 'a petition to save Spain, to save China, to save democracy, to save civilisation itself. It is a petition to save our own people from Fascism, war, poverty and unemployment.' Attlee's position was quite clear. Throughout his career he was emotionally, and in principle, disinclined to expel people from the party. It was one thing to keep undesirables out; another to 'chuck people out once they were in'. But he attacked Cripps in public. Putting the 'Case against the Popular Front' in the *Daily Herald*, 22 February, he expressed – for the first time – personal criticism of Cripps:

> The swing over by a man of great ability in a few months from the advocacy of a rigid and exclusive unity of the working classes to a demand for an alliance with capitalists, and from insistence on the need for a Government carrying out a Socialist policy to an appeal to put Socialism in cold storage for the duration of the international crisis, is a remarkable phenomenon. Such instability gives me little trust in Cripps's judgement. In a few months he may ask us all to change again . . . .
>
> Any alliance with the Communists would be electorally disastrous. . . . I ask all our members not to be diverted by constant new departures, but to remain faithful to the spirit of Keir Hardie. I ask all those who value freedom and democracy to support the only party which can turn out the Chamberlain Government.

The next day he wrote to Tom:

> We are having a lot of trouble over this Popular Front business. . . . I don't know if you noticed [some] regrettably scurrilous verses in the DH on the People's Flag in palest Pink. They came from my pen. I don't much like direction from those who have entered our movement from the top. It is a great pity about Stafford, but like all the Potter family he is so absolutely convinced that the policy which he puts forward for the time being is absolutely right that he will listen to no arguments.

The parody he referred to began:

> The people's flag is palest pink,
> It is not red blood but only ink.
> It is supported now by Douglas Cole
> Who plays each year a different role.
> Now raise our Palace standard high,
> Wash out each trace of purple dye,
> Let Liberals join and Tories too,
> And Socialists of every hue.

On 10 March Chamberlain told the press that 'Europe was settling down to a period of tranquillity'. A week later Hitler, having twenty-four hours earlier incited the Slovaks to declare their independence of the Czechs, forced the Czech president to sign an agreement recognizing the dismemberment of his country. Nazi forces then occupied Prague, and took over almost the whole of Czechoslovakia. Chamberlain, in the tone of a man who had been personally insulted, denounced Hitler's breach of faith, but bewildered his own party by telling the House that the guarantees given to the Czechs by Britain at the time of Munich would not now apply, because 'the position has altered since the Slovak Diet yesterday declared the independence of Slovakia under German protection'.

He rejected Russian proposals for a conference of the British, French, Russian, Polish, Romanian and Turkish governments to concert means of resisting aggression, but he proposed a declaration by Britain, France, Russia and Poland that they would act together against aggression.

The Poles were too suspicious of Russia to agree to this; but when, on 21 March, Hitler seized the Lithuanian port of Memel, the Polish government, feeling themselves the next target, appealed to Britain for help. On 31 March Chamberlain announced a guarantee to Poland of assistance in the event of any aggression, a guarantee in which France joined. 'In principle at any rate,' said Attlee, 'that marked the end of appeasement.' The question of whether the guarantee could be of practical use to Poland was not officially discussed – the answer would have given little satisfaction. The Poles were still almost as hostile to Russia as they were to Germany, and without the cooperation of the Russians the British guarantee was valueless. But the guarantee was of great significance, and Greenwood, deputizing for Attlee, absent with flu, welcomed it in the House. The government, with no enthusiasm, began talks with the Russians to discover what the Soviet Union would do to enable the Anglo-French guarantee to Poland to be put into practical effect if Hitler attempted another coup.

Attlee's flu was a precursor of the illness that was to keep him out of politics during the summer and autumn. He stayed at home, read the papers, caught up with his documents, read a few books, and wrote to Tom:

> I was interested to see Teddy Hall go head of the river. How different from our day. Do you remember the Latin verses on the toggers my first year?

> > Mille passuum distans
> > Teddes remigavit trans.

This was the first time since his spells of dysentery in Limehouse after the war – apart from his bout in India – that he had been laid low enough to be ordered to bed. He was there for a week, but the effects persisted.

On Good Friday, 7 April 1939, Mussolini's troops invaded Albania. It seemed as if the whole of southeast Europe might now fall to the Axis powers. The same day, Spain joined Germany, Italy and Japan in the anti-Comintern Pact. Attlee was fit enough to go to the House and speak in the foreign affairs debate. His speech followed the lines of the position he took after Munich. The emphasis was on the shamefulness of appeasement, and on the disasters which the policy now had brought about. The dictators had deceived the Prime Minister, and broke their word whenever it suited them.

Chamberlain now proposed to extend the Polish guarantee to Greece, and perhaps to Romania. Attlee and Dalton met the Prime Minister on

13 April, before he went into Cabinet. For fifteen minutes they pressed the need to announce a guarantee to Romania that day. Attlee emphasized the need for the government to draw the Soviet Union into such guarantees. Chamberlain replied that the Poles and Romanians did not want to risk the Russians entering their countries to defend them, since, once in, the Russians might never get out. That afternoon he announced in the House that Britain and France would guarantee Romania as well as Greece. He did not refer to Russia until, under pressure from the Labour benches, he was forced into making some vague remarks expressing goodwill towards the Soviet Union. The barracking upset him; to judge by his diary, he believed that because he had told Attlee about the problem of association with Russia privately that morning, Attlee would wish, and be able, to prevent Labour backbenchers from harassing him in the debate, and when he found that they did not, he blamed Attlee. He wrote in his dairy: 'Attlee behaved like the cowardly cur he is. . . . I have done with confidences to the Labour Party.'

The Soviet Union welcomed the new guarantees, and a few days later proposed a triple alliance of Britain, France and Russia to guarantee all the smaller states from the Baltic to the Black Sea. Chamberlain sat on the offer for nearly three weeks. His reply on 9 May was a repetition of weaker proposals made to Russia a week or so previously, just before Litvinov, the Soviet Foreign Minister friendly to the Western powers, had been replaced by the hostile Molotov. The talks with the Soviet Union, in Eden's words, 'dragged on through this unhappy month of May', now entering a phase characterized by what seemed a lack of urgency on the part of the British and of suspicion on the part of the Russians.

Attlee repeatedly pressed the Prime Minister to explain the delay in coming to those arrangements with the Soviet Union which circumstances demanded and the Russians offered. He put down several questions throughout May. There was little or no reaction from Chamberlain. The talks were obviously unproductive. The British government was represented only by a Foreign Office official, even though Eden warned Chamberlain that Stalin would expect comparable treatment to Hitler, personal meetings with British leaders. The Anglo-Soviet discussions petered out. Stalin, concluding that he could get more from Hitler, signed the Nazi–Soviet pact at the end of August.

At the end of April the government had brought in a bill to introduce military conscription. Men aged twenty were to be called up for six months. The bill created difficulties for the Labour Party. Only a few weeks before, the government had given assurances that there would be *no* conscription. On the strength of these assurances the Labour Party and the trade unions had agreed with some reluctance to support a scheme for *voluntary* military service. Now, the government had broken its pledges. Labour had special reasons for objecting to compulsory national service. Ernest Bevin feared that military conscription would open the way to industrial conscription, a danger magnified in the unions' sight by the general assumption that since any future war would be highly mechanized, industrial war-workers would vastly outnumber servicemen.

Liddell Hart, regarded as the leading military commentator, pronounced conscription to be useless. Voluntary service would bring in adequate numbers, and in any case for some time to come there would not be enough guns and uniforms to go around. 'Don't enlist men before there is adequate equipment to train them,' he wrote to *The Times*. In consequence, the National Council of Labour had reaffirmed 'its uncompromising opposition to Conscription'. When the National Service Bill was announced on 26 April, Attlee told the House that it would weaken and divide the country, and that Labour would oppose it. He protested at the government's failure until the last moment to consult with trade union leaders: in line with Bevin he complained that military conscription might well be followed by industrial conscription. He pointed out that the government's appeal for *voluntary* service had met with a magnificent response. Conscription in peacetime was a reversal of all British traditions.

The Labour leaders continued to oppose conscription. The charge of advocating resistance to Hitler and yet refusing to will the means was now renewed at a time when public opinion had been coming round to the idea that Labour, not the Tories, were the patriots. Dissident Conservatives, notably Eden, who had been impressed by the growing alignment of Labour's position with their own, felt disturbed and discouraged. In his last years Attlee told the author that the line he took against conscription in 1939 was a mistake. There were, he pointed out, various rational objections to conscription at the time, but the real motive for resisting the idea was distrust of Chamberlain. The Labour Movement, divided about the pros and cons of conscription, was united in suspicion of a prime minister who, having given assurances to the Labour Party that conscription would not be introduced in return for their support for the government's scheme for voluntary recruitment, then demanded conscription. Attlee admitted that at the time the Labour Party did not realize the extent to which its stand on conscription would be misinterpreted, just as a few years before they had not realized how their policy of voting against the service estimates would be misunderstood.

V

The 1939 Labour Party conference at Southport, the first for eighteen months, began on 29 May. Attlee was present, but because of his state of health was almost a passenger. He had been warned that his prostate trouble required an operation, but he had hoped to postpone it 'until the international sky was clearer'. He arrived at Southport in pain, and could not attend the opening session. Deputizing for him, Dalton presented a lengthy report, issued subsequently as a pamphlet, entitled *Labour and Defence*. It restated the Labour Party's opposition to conscription in times of peace – 'the voluntary system has not failed' – but also put forward two far broader propositions. The first urged the democratization of the armed forces by improvements in pay and conditions, assimilation of the rights of soldiers to those of civilians, and changes in the systems of recruitment and promotion of officers and other ranks. This part of Labour's policy came to be widely discussed in the forces during the war, and some credited it with the unexpectedly large number of servicemen's votes cast for Labour in 1945. The second important proposal in *Labour and Defence* dealt with the need for a ministry of supply, with industrial functions and considerable powers.

An official resolution calling for support of *Labour and Defence* was moved by Herbert Morrison. On the subject of conscription the resolution protested 'that the voluntary system has not failed', and called 'for every effort to ensure its increasing success'. As a result Labour continued to suffer from the charge of willing the end but opposing the means, and Attlee's remark, 'It is very dangerous to give generals all they want', though it drew a very telling lesson from the carnage of the First World War, was considered lame. However, though Labour MPs from time to time railed at the Military Service Act, the Labour Movement as a whole made no attempt to oppose its operation. The conference defeated a resolution calling for a Popular Front and listened with little sympathy to Cripps's defence – though still expelled, he was allowed to speak – of his conduct the previous January. An era for the left had come to an end.

In the closing hours of the conference, Attlee, still in pain, appeared on the platform and made a noticeably short speech. It was impossible, he said, to have a policy for foreign affairs run on one set of principles, and a policy for home affairs run on another. 'I want us to devote ourselves to making people realize that if they want peace abroad they must have social justice at home.' A general election was quite likely in the near future. The Labour Party, alone and independent, could be successful. Labour had a team that could beat the government every time. Giving Cripps and the United Front rebels a final shove into the wings, he urged 'our people to have nothing to do with defeatism, to have confidence in themselves, and to go forward now as a united body to the victory which I am quite certain we can win.' On his return to London he wrote to Tom:

> You are right in surmising that it is the family trouble. I had been wanting to get it dealt with for some time but could not find a quiet period. I had arranged to go into a clinic this week anyway, but a spot of trouble at Southport precipitated matters – I got a chill on the bladder which induced a temperature and considerable pain in the JT.
>
> Southport went off very well – an excellent tone. I was just able to look in on it before returning to town.

Though Southport registered 'an excellent tone', the proceedings renewed doubts about Attlee's leadership. The following Sunday a newspaper article by Ellen Wilkinson, Herbert Morrison's friend and admirer, posed the question of how Neville Chamberlain would feel if he found himself confonted across the dispatch box by Herbert Morrison as leader of the Opposition, flanked by Dalton, Greenwood and Cripps. Within the week Wilkinson pointed out, in *Time and Tide*, that Attlee's almost total absence from the conference 'made not the slightest difference.... At Southport most people felt Morrison was the dominating figure.' She again praised Dalton and Cripps, but pointedly ignored Greenwood. In the same week Francis Williams wrote a piece for the *Daily Herald*, of which he was editor, lauding Herbert Morrison and praising Dalton and Cripps. He, too, did not mention Attlee or Greenwood.

Greenwood – Attlee was still *hors de combat* – decided to act. At a meeting of the NEC the following week, he reported from the chair that the Parliamentary Party's Executive officially deplored the appearance of three newspaper articles which cast doubts on the capacity of the leader, particularly when he was known to be ill, and when times were so critical. He invited Ellen Wilkinson to defend herself. Frequently fiery, on this occasion she made a poor show, and was lucky to escape the NEC's formal censure. Morrison intervened, very briefly, and somewhat lamely, to say that he had had nothing to do with the article, and that if he had seen it beforehand, he would have opposed its publication. If the NEC tabled a resolution of confidence in Attlee he would vote for it. 'He was heard silently,' records Dalton, 'but I was conscious of some hostility in the atmosphere while he was speaking.'

The result of the meeting was a unanimous vote of sympathy with Attlee in his illness, plus a vote of personal confidence in him, Ellen Wilkinson abstaining. If there had been a real move on Morrison's part to get rid of Attlee it got ludicrously little support. Attlee was aware of it: years later he told the author: 'Dalton wouldn't have backed Morrison, Morrison wouldn't have backed Cripps, and Cripps wouldn't have backed Dalton. The PLP wouldn't have let Greenwood go, and Greenwood was loyal to me.' Did he think that Morrison had instigated or encouraged these moves to unseat him? 'Probably not. He talked a lot about how well he could do things, and younger people sometimes thought he talked that way because he was encouraging them to try and make him leader. But he talked that way because he was vain. He liked the sound of his own voice.'

A long convalescence was needed. He spent the whole of August with the family at Nevin. Greenwood kept in close touch with him. He was told all about Dalton's unsuccessful attempts to persuade Chamberlain and Halifax to conclude a pact with Russia, of the rumours that Russia was going to sign a pact with Germany, and that the Poles were now convinced that Hitler, in spite of his protestations to Britain, would soon take over Poland. In late August, sitting on the sands, watching Vi and the children in the sea, listening to a portable radio, he heard the news of Stalin's pact with Hitler. A week later, sitting on the same spot, he heard that Hitler had invaded Poland. Two days later, on 3 September 1939, he heard Chamberlain announcing that Britain was at war. What were Attlee's thoughts when sitting on the sands at Nevin he heard that Britain was at war with Germany again? 'Some of us have been here before. We beat them last time: we'll beat them again. But Chamberlain will have to go.'

12

Patriotic Opposition, 1939–40

When Hitler's troops marched into Poland, Chamberlain asked Greenwood as acting leader of the Opposition if Labour would be prepared to join a re-formed administration. Before consulting the PLP Executive, Greenwood referred Chamberlain's inquiry to Attlee up at Nevin. Attlee's response was a brusque rejection. He advised Greenwood to have as little discussion as possible with his colleagues so that there would be no impression of hesitation. Chamberlain should be told that Labour thought it could best help the government from outside, though, Attlee said again, the real reason for refusing to join a Chamberlain administration, however reconstituted, was that Labour did not trust Chamberlain, and was sure he would soon have to go. 'Put all pressure you can on the PM,' Attlee ended. 'We've got to fight.'

On Saturday evening 2 September, forty-eight hours after Hitler had begun to bomb Poland, Chamberlain made a statement in the House which fell so far short of honouring Britain's pledges to the Poles that many of his own party were shocked. 'The House was aghast,' recorded Amery. 'For two whole days the wretched Poles had been bombed and massacred, and we were still considering within what time limit Hitler should be invited to tell us whether he felt like relinquishing his prey!' When, in Attlee's absence, Greenwood rose to reply, the hostility in the atmosphere flowed not from front bench to front bench but from both sides of the House towards Chamberlain. As Greenwood rose, Amery called out to him: 'Speak for England!' His cry was taken up on the Tory benches, with supporting shouts from the Labour benches of 'Speak for Britain!' and 'Speak for the Workers!' Greenwood pledged the Labour Party to support the government in honouring our obligation to stand by the Poles. After the debate, records Amery: 'Greenwood followed the Prime Minister to his room and told him that, unless the inevitable decision for war was taken before we met next day, it would be impossible to hold the House.' 'Greenwood,' said Attlee later, 'rose finely to the occasion.'

At 9 am the next day, Sunday, the British Ambassador in Berlin delivered an ultimatum to the German Foreign Minister. The ultimatum expired two hours later. Chamberlain announced a state of war in the House, and immediately broadened his government by bringing in Churchill as First Lord of the Admiralty (and member of the War Cabinet) and Eden as Dominions Secretary. Four days later, the Germans overran Pomerania and Silesia, and by 10 September they were in control of the whole of Western Poland. Seven days later they had reached Brest-Litovsk. That day, 17 September, the Russians invaded Poland from the east. Attlee wrote to Tom:

> The whole position is pretty damnable and we are I think in for a bad time. I was not greatly surprised at the Russian defection though this could and should have been avoided if the Govt had played straight the last few years. I recall without satisfaction that more than a year ago I warned them that they are leading us straight to a war in which we should be left to face the music with only France to help us.

Attlee returned to take over the leadership of the party on 20 September. By this time there was considerable discussion in the party, not out of intrigue, but from a genuine doubt about his health, as to whether he was fit enough to carry on. He had been out of the saddle for three months. As a result of his conduct immediately before and after the outbreak of war, Greenwood's stock had risen with the party and the country. He alone was talked of as the alternative, and his appointment would not have aroused the old animosities between Bevin, Cripps, Morrison and Dalton.

Attlee made his first speech from the front bench on 20 October replying to Chamberlain's report on the war situation. By now he had learned how unprepared the government was for the administrative and organizational problems presented by the war. He therefore appealed for a smaller Cabinet, whose members were to be free of departmental responsibilities; for immediate economic reorganization to meet the burden of war; and for the release of all possible information to the civilian population. His next major speech followed within the fortnight. Russia had joined Germany in carving up Poland, bringing the fighting on that front to an end within three weeks. It was consequently expected that Hitler might offer peace proposals to the Western powers. The possibility was debated in the House. Attlee came out strongly against any proposals being considered which would allow Hitler to keep what he had conquered. It was a good speech, but he was obviously still not fit. He spoke again in the next few weeks, but it was noticed that he announced that he would not resume all his official duties as leader until the end of October.

A speech on 8 November marked his full return to active politics; it so impressed the PLP that it was immediately circulated as a pamphlet defining Labour's 'War Aims'. He called for a new and strong League of Nations, a new international authority, with wide economic as well as political powers and with a strong armed force of its own, which could deter potential aggressors, or, if necessary, go to war and defeat an actual aggressor. This new international authority should be 'democratic', by which he meant that it would give voice and power to the small nations. It must not be controlled by the Great Powers, and become 'merely an Imperialism in commission'. As for Germany, 'we have no desire to humiliate, to crush, or to divide the German nation.... We wish the German people to know that they can even now secure, if they will, an honourable peace.' But the German people must first produce 'a Government which can be trusted, a Government which has abandoned Hitlerism and is prepared to enter into negotiations for peace on the basis of the repudiation of a policy of aggression'. Though the Labour Party would support any move to end the war on terms consistent with the principles on which Britain had entered it, 'anyone who urges that the war should be ended at any price is no real friend of peace.' Restitution would have to be made to the Czechs, Poles, Austrians and other victims of Nazi aggression.

Attlee took care not to stipulate that the pre-Nazi frontiers of the European states should be restored: a new settlement was needed, under the auspices of the new international authority. 'Europe must federate or perish' – a remarkably forward-looking opinion for that time. Attlee was against the idea that a defeated Germany should at the end of the war be placed under military occupation by the Allies: 'an administration and forces drawn from neutral states' should occupy territories in dispute till there was a final settlement. He repudiated a 'dictated peace', and took his stand on the 'rule of law' in international affairs. These statements became the basis of the party's official declaration in February 1940, *Labour, the War and the Peace*.

His friends were delighted by the success of this speech in the House, and its effects on opinion in the country. The Parliamentary Party met to elect the leader the following week. For the first time in four years he was opposed: Greenwood, Morrison and Dalton were nominated. When the meeting opened, Attlee was asked what he thought about his leadership being challenged. He replied that he would never resent, or regard as 'disloyal', the nomination of any colleague to replace him: 'the Labour Party is a democratic Party.' Again Greenwood rose to the occasion. He declared in impressively unequivocal terms that he would not stand against Attlee, and that a contest for the leadership at this time would serve only to encourage Hitler. Morrison rose next and said that he would not accept nomination this year while Attlee was still unwell, though he would reconsider this decision if some other nominee decided to force an election. Dalton spoke last: he said that he had made it known the day before the meeting that he would not accept nomination. All three nominations having been withdrawn in one way or another by the candidates themselves, Attlee was re-elected unopposed.

In early January Attlee made a much-praised live broadcast on the BBC, to explain why after years of criticizing Chamberlain the Labour Party was now supporting the government. His theme was that the Labour Party saw the war in the context of the beliefs of British socialists, and that the basis of these beliefs was a moral one: Nazism, he said, was the outstanding menace to civilization. Its leaders did not accept as valuable the virtues which in Britain were accepted as desirable by all, 'even by those who honour them with very little in their actions'. At home and abroad, brutal cruelty was the mark of the Nazi regime.

> But there is something more than these outward expressions of the return to barbarism in the Nazi regime. There is a denial of the value of the individual. Christianity affirms the value of each individual soul. Nazism denies it. The individual is sacrificed to the idol of the German Leader, German State or the German race.... The ordinary citizen is allowed to hear and think only as the rulers decree. The basic idea of democracy is thereby rejected. The Labour Party owes its inspiration not to some economic doctrine or to some theory of class domination. It has always based its propaganda on ethical principles. We believe that every individual should be afforded the fullest opportunity for developing his or her personality. The founder of our Party, Keir Hardie, always made his appeal on moral grounds. He believed that the evils of our society were due to the failure to put into practice the principles of the brotherhood of man.

Attlee went out of his way to assert that the Labour Party was not only supporting the government of the day in the cause of security and justice but was in the war to fight for its own existence and its own vision of what society should be. After reminding the listeners of the 'materialist system of society' which Labour had fought at home in Britain, he explained why Labour must now fight against the Nazis:

> But all this achievement of the workers is threatened by the Nazis. The German workers who had built up a great structure of trade unionism, cooperation and social services have seen it destroyed. They have lost all their democratic rights. Wherever Nazism is, there is cruelty, tyranny and the rule of the secret police. The Labour Party, therefore, has taken its stand with the rest of the country to stop this evil thing spreading although we have our own quarrel with the present system of society. The victory of Nazism would destroy all our hopes for many years to come.

He did not encourage his listeners to assume that the British people had a record of spiritual strength and purpose, a natural moral superiority, which would make victory inevitable and ensure an unexceptional peace. On the contrary, he emphasized the moral self-control and criticism during war and peace which real success would require. In language which disturbed many members of the Conservative Party he said:

> I think that the majority of people in this country have now abandoned the old boastful imperialism, but it was not so long ago in my own lifetime when our Press used to be filled with the same kind of arrogant boasting which one hears from Hitler. We did pursue a policy of what was called expansion and brought under our sway great tracts of territory. I think that we have now realised the falsity of such ideals, but we still continue to retain the fruits of that policy....
>
> We must be prepared to bring all our colonial territories under the mandatory principle and to extend and widen the scope of international control. We must rid ourselves of any taint of imperialism. Only so can we put ourselves into a position to ask for a world organised on the democratic principle.

The broadcast inspired Labour and, as an important side-effect, impressed President Roosevelt, always critical of British imperialism.

The Labour Party's decision to support the war effort wholeheartedly did not mean that they would refrain from criticizing the government's conduct of affairs. An electoral truce was agreed, and arrangements made for leading members of the Executive to keep in touch with leading ministers, but none of this was to inhibit Labour. During the winter and spring of 1940, while manfully supporting the Chamberlain government in general, Attlee censured the tactless way in which the government had declared India at war without consulting Indian opinion; inadequacies of the Ministry of Information; unsatisfactory evacuation measures; the plight of old-age pensioners ('an immediate improvement is needed'); other failures in the social services; poor pay and conditions in the armed forces; hardships connected with the call-up; inefficiency in controlling prices, in sharing fairly the burdens of war, in mobilizing the country's economic resources, and in making the best use of its manpower. In March he wanted to know why after six months of war there were still 1,400,000 unemployed, why so many pits, ships and ports were still idle. He returned to one of the themes of his major speech in the previous November: there should be proper machinery for economic coordination under an Economic General Staff, and the War Cabinet should be smaller, so that it could be an instrument of decision, which it could not be if it continued to be burdened by departmental duties.

In the first week of January 1940, Attlee was invited to France by the British Commander-in-Chief, Lord Gort. Gort discussed the situation with him in detail. He made a three-day tour of the lines. The Commander-in-Chief listened to him with more than polite attention, and asked him pointedly if he would repeat his observations to the General Staff in London. Attlee did. He reported that he had found the BEF troops very keen, but that he had come back worried about the general strategy. British plans, he had found, were dominated by the French High Command, in which he had little confidence. 'Our reserves to meet a breakthrough seemed quite inadequate.' Having reported, he found that the General Staff, under Ironside, 'were not much interested in the view of an ex-major and politician'.

In February, Attlee and Dalton went to see Blum in Paris. It was 'a most depressing meeting. . . . Most of those whom we met were either pacifist or defeatist. Léon Blum and Grumbach were the outstanding exceptions.' There was a full day of discussion, divided into two parts. In the morning the French Socialists told the British about opinion in France: in the afternoon the British did the reverse. Apart from their own defeatism, the French Socialists were handicapped by sixty or so Communist MPs, most of whom were now denouncing France and Britain for fighting an imperialist war. Blum's courage, however, stood out like a beacon. He 'was for helping the Finns to the utmost and at all costs, even though this led to war with Russia'. Blum's combination of courage, realism, socialist idealism and style left a lasting impression on Attlee: he seems to have admired Blum more than any other man he ever met.

Chamberlain's position was now weakening. When the Finns capitulated to Russia on 12 March, the French government fell. Daladier was succeeded by Reynaud, who was more disposed to a concerted initiative with Britain. He supported Churchill's plan to mine Norwegian waters, which, though neutral, were extensively used by German ships transporting iron ore from Narvik. The British War Cabinet agreed to the Churchill plan on 8 April. Chamberlain still appeared to be confident that the war was going his way. In a speech to a Conservative meeting on 4 March he claimed that Hitler had 'missed the bus'. He could not have chosen a worse moment to say so. Four days later Hitler reacted to the mining of Norwegian waters by invading Norway and Denmark. Within two days the Germans had occupied all Norwegian ports. On 14 April British troops landed in Norway at Narvik. Two more landings, north and south of Trondheim, were made a few days later. The expedition was a complete failure. Short of weapons and supplies, British forces were evacuated on 2 May.

By mid-April there was so much talk of Chamberlain's imminent departure that the Labour Party had to consider its attitude. If a political crisis came, the Labour leaders would have to act quickly. Greenwood suggested that the party conference, to be held at Whitsun, four weeks ahead, should be asked to empower the Executive to use its own discretion as to whether to join a new government. Dalton and others feared that such a move would create suspicion at the conference. Attlee suggested that the Executive should take its decision, then summon a special conference to approve its action.

By now, the failure of the Norway expedition being the last straw, the Liberals, and many Conservatives, were resolved that Chamberlain must go. Clement Davies, 'the other Clem', a leading Liberal, came to Attlee as intermediary from a group of prominent Conservatives, headed by Lord Salisbury. Was there sufficient possibility of agreement for a joint move to replace Chamberlain? Several confidential meetings took place. Attlee wanted to be sure this time whether or not the Tory rebels could be relied upon to vote against the government if the issue were joined. In the past, when a parliamentary showdown seemed in sight, they had hung back. Churchill's position was a difficulty. Until the outbreak of war he had been Chamberlain's leading critic, but he had joined Chamberlain's government, as First Lord of the Admiralty, and as such he had instigated the Norway landings. Since the patent failure of this expedition was the occasion for trying to get Chamberlain out, Churchill was in no position to resume his role as leader of the dissident Tories.

Attlee now demanded a two-day debate on the failure of the Norway expedition, to open on 7 May. He resisted Clement Davies's urgings to present it as an issue of confidence, lest the dissident Tories should rally round their harassed leader. Attlee launched the attack himself. He assailed the government, not only on the failure in Norway but on the whole conduct of the war. Planning and intelligence had been inadequate. The War Cabinet was an inefficient instrument. Organization of food supplies and manpower was being criticized by all who knew the facts. The general lack of leadership was undermining national morale. The outcry about the failure in Norway was merely the culmination of many other discontents. 'People are saying that those mainly responsible for the conduct of affairs are men who have had an almost uninterrupted career of failure.' There was a widespread feeling in this country, he concluded, that 'to win the war we want different people at the helm from those who have led us into it'.

Attlee's strategy was successful. He had set the scene for action without risk of antagonizing the Tory dissidents by trying to drag them into it. The debate continued with a speech from Admiral Sir Roger Keyes, in full uniform, denouncing the government for not ordering a major naval attack on Trondheim; and with Amery's memorable citation of Cromwell: 'Depart, I say, and let us have done with you. For God's sake go.' The first day's debate revealed, Attlee recorded, 'that discontent had gone far deeper than we thought, and I was assured that if a division were called we should get a lot of support from the Conservatives, especially from the serving soldiers, sailors and airmen.' He now knew what he had wanted to know. When the Parliamentary Labour Party met the following morning – before the second day of the debate – he recommended that the Opposition demand that the motion be treated as one of censure. If the government fell, Labour would be ready to help replace it.

The credit for this decision to divide the House was later claimed by Morrison. In fact it was Attlee who put the proposal at the meeting of the PLP, and a few years before he died he said that Morrison was not happy with the idea. Why was Morrison originally against it? Possibly because he still thought that Labour should join Chamberlain in a coalition, and calculated that Chamberlain regarded him, Morrison, as a more acceptable Labour leader than Attlee. At the PLP meeting, however, Morrison supported Attlee. The majority voted in favour of demanding a division. The minority included Dalton, who feared that a vote would consolidate the Conservatives behind Chamberlain and give him another lease of life. It might have done so if Chamberlain had not let his emotions get the better of him. When he heard the announcement that the Opposition would force a vote, he rose, unnecessarily, and in Dalton's words 'showing his teeth like a rat in a corner', cried, 'I accept the challenge. I ask my friends, and I still have some friends in the House, to support the Government tonight in the lobby.'

When the vote was taken, Attlee to his delight – and somewhat to his surprise – saw 'Conservative MP after Conservative MP crowding with Labour and Liberal members into the same lobby'. Forty-three Conservatives voted with the Labour Party. Another seventy abstained. The government, which normally had a majority of about 250, carried the day by 281 to 200. This was a crippling and spectacular reverse. Chamberlain was still not ready to resign, but there was general agreement that night in all three parties that he would soon be replaced by Halifax or Churchill.

Subject to certain conditions, Labour was willing to join a coalition under either. Various accounts have appeared of Attlee's personal preference. Amery claimed that Attlee dined with Brendan Bracken and told him that Labour would never serve under Churchill, because they could never forgive him for sending troops to Tonypandy in South Wales during a mining dispute in 1912, and that therefore they would enter a coalition only under Halifax. Informed of this account, Attlee said he had never in his life dined with Bracken alone, and had never had any such conversation with him or with anybody else. It is unlikely that Attlee would have talked in this way to any Tory, so early in the crisis, and least of all to Brendan Bracken. Attlee in fact preferred Churchill.

He knew the Labour Party remembered Churchill and Tonypandy, but he personally remembered Gallipoli. He did not feel that the Labour Party's longstanding distrust of Churchill, mainly because of his behaviour during the General Strike, was a bar to serving under him in a wartime coalition.

The fact that Attlee preferred Churchill did not mean that he would get him. Labour's objective was not to get a new man in, but to get Chamberlain out. Chamberlain might make way for Halifax, but not necessarily for Churchill; moreover, Churchill might not have the Conservative support that Halifax could certainly command. There was talk of a new government led by Halifax, with Churchill as minister of defence and Attlee as leader of the House of Commons. Chamberlain, preferring Halifax himself, might well cite the supposed hostility of Labour to Churchill to persuade his party that if he had to go, he should be replaced by Halifax. It was essential for Labour, therefore, to keep its choices open if it wanted to get Chamberlain out without jeopardizing the chances of getting a new government which would be strong enough to start to wage a vigorous war.

Chamberlain still hung on. He tried to propitiate the Tory rebels, offering a post to Amery, who refused because Chamberlain was unwilling to include Labour and the Liberals in government. On 9 May Chamberlain invited Attlee and Greenwood to 10 Downing Street. Churchill and Halifax were there. 'He seemed to have no idea that he was finished,' Attlee told the author.

> He seemed to think he could carry on. He said that it was now necessary to have a national government and he asked us if we would serve in it under him as leader. It was incredible. When he finished, Winston spoke up and said we should come in under Chamberlain. That was understandable; in any case Winston had Norway on his back. And he cared more about getting a government that could win the war than about who was to be prime minister. Was quite sincere. Halifax said nothing.

Attlee decided that it was necessary to bring Chamberlain back to reality. He told the Prime Minister that no Labour leader would serve under him, and that the Labour Party would not support a government led by him. 'Our Party won't have you and I think the country won't have you either.' Chamberlain was silent, seeming to accept for the first time that he would have to resign. 'Until that moment he thought he could hang on.' Chamberlain then asked if Labour would serve under a Conservative leader other than himself. Attlee said that he believed so, but he would have to consult his colleagues. The NEC was to meet at Bournemouth the following day in preparation for the party conference opening the next Monday. Attlee undertook to put two questions to his NEC colleagues, and report the answers immediately to Downing Street:

'Are you prepared to join a government led by Chamberlain?' and 'Would you be prepared to serve under somebody else?'

That night, Thursday 9 May, German forces invaded Holland, Belgium, Luxemburg and France. Attlee, Greenwood and Dalton met to discuss their next steps. Rather than remain in London to ask for the recall of Parliament, they decided to go to Bournemouth where their colleagues were on hand for consultation. If they stayed in London, Chamberlain might try to have further conversations with them on his home ground. If Parliament were recalled, Chamberlainite Tories might launch a counter-attack that would keep Chamberlain in power. This was a real danger: the Liberals were wobbling, and Sinclair had suggested to Attlee that in view of the invasion of France Chamberlain should be left to carry on a little longer. Chamberlain asked Attlee for a public statement that in this crisis of the war the Labour Party reaffirmed its support of the present government, but was disappointed by what they gave him, which read: 'The Labour Party, in view of the latest series of abominable aggressions by Hitler, while firmly convinced that drastic reconstruction of the Government is vital and urgent in order to win the war, reaffirms its determination to do its utmost to achieve victory. It calls on all its members to devote all their energies to this end.'

Attlee, Greenwood and Dalton then went to Bournemouth. The atmosphere can be imagined: while they sat with the NEC, a (false) report came that the Germans were bombing Canterbury. The party's view on Chamberlain's questions was already known: Labour would not serve under Chamberlain, but might serve under another Tory. A resolution was passed stating that Labour should take its 'share of responsibility, as a full partner, in a new Government, which, under a new Prime Minister, commands the confidence of the nation'. The Executive agreed that this was a *decision* to be put not for discussion, but for approval, to the conference when it assembled on the following Monday. They also decided that Attlee and Greenwood should return immediately to London to negotiate the membership of the new government.

As he was about to leave the hotel for the station, Attlee received a telephone call from the Prime Minister's secretary: was Mr Attlee yet in a position to give Mr Chamberlain a reply to the two questions? Attlee went to the phone and said: 'The answer to the first question is, No. To the second, Yes.' He read out the NEC's resolution at dictation speed. Accompanied by Greenwood, and instructing Dalton to remain at Bournemouth as their link with the Executive, he narrowly managed to catch the 5.15 for Waterloo.

The Conservative leaders had anticipated Labour's vote. Shortly before the fateful telephone call, Chamberlain, Halifax, Churchill and the Chief Whip, Margesson, had met at Downing Street. Chamberlain raised the question that Churchill might not win Labour support; Margesson reported that some Conservatives preferred Halifax. There was a prolonged silence which sealed the fate both of Chamberlain and his favoured candidate, Halifax. Realizing that Churchill would not offer to serve under him, Halifax conceded on the grounds that he could not lead a government from the Lords. With this point settled, Attlee was consulted. Hearing his news, Chamberlain went to Buckingham Palace and offered his resignation to the King, who immediately summoned Churchill.

Attlee and Greenwood reached Waterloo at 9 pm, to be met by an emissary of Churchill's who informed them that the new Prime Minister was anxious to see Mr Attlee as soon as possible. Attlee went straight to the Admiralty, where Churchill formally stated that he had been asked to form a government, and he now invited Attlee and his colleagues to join. One thought was now uppermost in Attlee's mind: 'I remembered how at a critical stage in the Dardanelles campaign ... vital decisions were delayed because of the long-drawn-out bargainings over the formation of Asquith's Coalition in 1915. I was resolved that I would not, by haggling, be responsible for any failure to act promptly.' All he demurred about was Winston's suggestion of the role for Chamberlain:

> Winston proposed that we should have rather more than a third of the places in the Government, seven Ministers, I think, and some Under-Secretaries, and that there should be a small War Cabinet of five or six, something I'd always urged, in which we should have two seats. I at once accepted. We then discussed names. He mentioned Bevin, Morrison, Dalton and A.V. Alexander as among those he would like, in addition to Greenwood and myself. I said I thought there should be no difficulty, although I must of course speak to them and have a talk with Ernie, who was not in the House. He also asked me to let him have a list of suggested offices and we discussed the general composition of the Government. Winston said he had asked Chamberlain to lead the House. I said I was absolutely opposed to that. I didn't think the House would stand for it and certainly our people wouldn't. So it was dropped. Otherwise there was no disagreement.... We talked for some time, and then I telephoned and told the people in Bournemouth what had happened and went home to bed.

In fact the meeting lasted well into the night. Next day he and Churchill agreed to a War Cabinet consisting of themselves, Chamberlain, Greenwood and Halifax; to the composition of the Defence Committee; and to the allocation of several other offices. The new administration, constructed in a few hours, lasted until the end of the war in Europe, though there were several changes. Only Churchill and Attlee remained in the War Cabinet for the entire period.

At 11 am Saturday 11 May Attlee rang Ernest Bevin at Transport House, where he had come to collect his papers before going down to the party conference. Bevin had taken no part, even by telephone, in the discussions at Bournemouth. Attlee first asked what he thought of Labour joining a coalition. Bevin answered: 'You helped to bring the other fellow down; if the Party did not take its share of responsibility, they would say we were not great citizens but cowards.' Attlee then asked him if he would be willing to join the government. Bevin asked for time to think it over. At 3 pm he met Attlee at the House of Commons. He said he could only serve if it was clear that he had the support of the General Council of the TUC and of the Labour Party Executive. He asked which office he would be expected to take. Attlee said: 'Ministry of Labour,' adding that Churchill had particularly asked for Bevin in this post. Bevin persuaded the TUC leaders, some of whom thought he should be in a different office, that the appointment gave him 'the chance to lay down the conditions under which we shall start again' after the war. Bevin's reasons for joining the coalition reflect the thrust of Attlee's January broadcast: 'Labour must do all it could to save Britain and the world for Democracy; but it must deploy in war to prepare a Socialist peace.'

At 5.30 on the Saturday afternoon Attlee telephoned to Dalton at Bournemouth asking for the Executive's authority to accept for the party two seats out of five in the new War Cabinet, to be filled by Greenwood and himself; one of the three service departments (Alexander at the Admiralty; the other two were Eden at the War Office and Sinclair as Air Minister); a fair share of other offices; and Chamberlain as a member of the War Cabinet but with no department. Attlee urged Dalton to ask the Executive to accept these terms at once. Dalton should tell them that to resist Chamberlain's inclusion would be a mistake. To get him out altogether was impossible, and even if it could be done it would create such ill-feeling among his many friends in the Conservative Party that the position of the new government would be jeopardized from the outset. Labour's resentments towards the 'old gang' would be mollified by the translation of Simon to the House of Lords, as Chancellor – 'There,' said Attlee, 'he will be quite innocuous' – and by Hoare being left out altogether.

Dalton recorded in his diary afterwards that 'some of the Executive boggled a bit at some of this, and Morrison was rather awkward.' Later, Morrison made it clear that he did not relish the offer made to him of the Ministry of Supply; he would have preferred to be in the War Cabinet without a department. He told friends he was inclined to stay out, but had decided to accept in the national interest.

The NEC agreed to all Attlee's requests. The following morning, Attlee and Greenwood returned to Bournemouth by car. Attlee gave the NEC and also the TUC General Council an account of the downfall of Chamberlain and the formation of the Churchill coalition. Greenwood also spoke, and in the same matter-of-fact tone. Laski observed to Dalton: 'I felt as though the cook and the kitchen maid were telling us how they had sacked the butler.'

On Monday 13 May the party conference began. Attlee had to leave early, so as to reach London in time to be present in the House of Commons when Churchill appeared for the first time as Prime Minister. Since he had to be able to inform the new Prime Minister of the conference's official confirmation of the Executive's accepting the terms for Labour participation in the new government, so that Churchill could announce them that afternoon, the conference debate, and the vote, had to be resolved by lunchtime. Attlee emphasized to the conference that he and his colleagues were entering the government as representatives of the Labour Movement, that he had told Churchill: 'We come in only provided we have the support or our movement. . . . We go in . . . as partners, and not as hostages.' He warned the party bluntly that in the new government: 'We shall none of us get all that you want. What Trade Unionist had ever got exactly what he wanted? . . . there must be included in the Government perhaps some people we do not like. Yes, but there are some of us *they* do not like.' To tremendous applause, he ended with these words:

> Friends, we are standing here today to take a decision not only on behalf of our own movement but on behalf of Labour all over the world. We have to stand today for the souls in prison in Czechoslovakia, in Poland, yes, and in Germany. . . . I have no doubt at all as to what the feelings of our people are. . . . Life without liberty is not worth living. Let us go forward and win that liberty and establish that liberty for ever on the sure foundation of social justice.

In the subsequent debate, pacifists, Communists, fellow-travellers and ILP were given plenty of chance to speak. A number of left-wingers urged that Labour should cooperate only if it dominated the coalition. But the resolution endorsing the terms of the Executive's decision was carried by an overwhelming 2,413,000 votes to 170,000.

Attlee did not know the result of the debate until he arrived in London. When he entered the House of Commons, many Tories came up to him, delighted by the size of the majority at Bournemouth, congratulating him on the role he had personally played in the last few days, and praising his speech. When the new Prime Minister entered the Chamber he was warmly cheered by the Labour members, but not enthusiastically by the bulk of the Conservative Party. When Chamberlain entered, the Tory majority rose cheering to their feet. Only Labour cheered when Churchill offered 'nothing . . . but blood, toil, tears and sweat'.

13
Member of the War Cabinet,
1940-2

I

For the five years between the formation of the coalition and the end of the war in Europe, Attlee alone of Churchill's colleagues remained continuously a member of the War Cabinet. His principal task was to keep the coalition together: to make political sense of Churchill's dictum: 'Everything for the war, whether controversial or not, and nothing controversial that is not *bona fide* needed for the war.' He had to conciliate Conservative backbenchers, reassure Labour, mediate between Labour and Conservative ministers and even between quarrelling Labour ministers, and manage Churchill's political and personal idiosyncrasies. These were enormous burdens, borne largely in private; in the public eye he was overshadowed by Churchill, Morrison (as Home Secretary) and Bevin (Minister of Labour).

The overall conduct of the war was in the hands of three interconnected committees: the War Cabinet, the Defence Committee, and the Lord President's Committee which ran the civil side of the war. Only Attlee was a member of all three, and, more important, he was Churchill's deputy on the first two and the chairman of the third. The coalition's first War Cabinet consisted of Churchill, Attlee, Chamberlain, Halifax and Greenwood, and the three service ministers, Eden (War), Sinclair (Air) and Alexander (Navy). The Defence Committee, of which Churchill as Minister of Defence was chairman, included Attlee as vice-chairman, the three service ministers and their chiefs of staff, and later, when he returned to the Foreign Office in 1941, Eden. The Lord President's Committee included five, sometimes six, senior home front ministers. Churchill did not sit on it. When Churchill made Chamberlain Lord President of the Council, he envisaged that he would run home affairs through the Lord President's Committee, much as Churchill intended to conduct the war through the Defence Committee. When Chamberlain's illness compelled him to resign in October, Churchill appointed as his successor Sir John Anderson, the former civil servant, whom Chamberlain had brought in to the Cabinet direct from Whitehall in 1938 as Lord Privy Seal.

Attlee made the Lord President's Committee the engine of government on the home front. On entering the War Cabinet he conducted a review of Cabinet machinery, and cut down the number of ministerial and official committees, in the process getting rid of Chamberlain's trusted adviser, Sir Horace Wilson. ('He had a hand in everything, ran everything. We got rid of him at once. It was essential.') To save even more of the Cabinet's time, he suggested the institution of the Lord President's Committee. As the committee's influence grew over the course of the war, Attlee's presence on it acquired a critical importance. Anderson had remarkable administrative ability but no political standing; Attlee could win support for the committee's policies in the trade union movement and the House of Commons. When Anderson became Chancellor of the Exchequer in 1943, Attlee succeeded him as Lord President and chairman of the committee. His determination to use Labour's power in war to reconstruct society for peace was given full rein in a committee whose leading members were his Labour colleagues Morrison and Bevin.

To keep the parliamentary process going in the circumstances of a coalition with an overwhelming majority, it was necessary to have an official leader of the Opposition. 'The problem was solved,' wrote Attlee in his autobiography, 'with that practical illogicality which is one of the virtues of the British character.' On 21 May the PLP Executive decided to recommend H.B. Lees-Smith as leader of the Labour Party in the House. He was, in Dalton's words, 'very calm, sensible, loyal, experienced and, no disadvantage in his proposed new duties, a little slow'. The next day Attlee recommended the arrangement to the PLP, which accepted it despite the opposition of Shinwell, who called for an official Opposition from which the Labour ministers would be excluded. Henceforth Attlee acted, though without formally taking the title, as leader of the House, arranging for the conduct of ordinary business, answering many of the questions put down for the Prime Minister, and reporting on the war situation. Churchill, who found the House uncongenial in the early months of his premiership, rarely attended, and it fell to Attlee to introduce the most important of the coalition's early legislation.

When he entered the government Attlee went into premises in Richmond Street, but because it was thought these would not stand up to bombs or blast, he was moved to 11 Downing Street, where he slept as well as worked. His office looked out on to the Prime Minister's garden, with, he told Tom, 'just a desk, a large conference table, chairs and war maps on the walls, a bathroom and a bedroom upstairs.' He told Tom he could sleep through the heaviest gunfire, and the noise of bombs exploding woke him only if they were very near. His Whitehall day was full and regular. Normally he got up at 7.30 and walked across St James's Park to breakfast at the Oxford and Cambridge Club, if he had time strolling in the park before he went to his office. He spent most mornings reading memoranda and attending Cabinet committees. He usually lunched at the House of Commons and sat on the Front Bench throughout the afternoon, in the evening further Cabinet committees and meetings with ministers. More often than not he dined at the Oxford and Cambridge, then more talk with ministerial colleagues or Labour MPs, followed by another session with Cabinet papers. He hoped that his day would end with the midnight news. When he went to bed he was asleep in a few minutes.

Whatever the pressure of work and the noise of the Blitz, he kept up his correspondence with Tom:

I saw Rowse the other day at Oxford. He is maturing a bit, but should certainly stick to history. [A.L. Rowse, the Oxford don, had earlier sought a political career.]

We had very much an OH evening at the Guildhall last week as I proposed the toast of Chatham House and Lionel Curtis responded while the Chairman's health was proposed by Clement Jones...

Vi and I were at Chequers last weekend. Its a wonderful place and I was very glad to see it. I slept in a magnificent Elizabethan four-poster.... I have recently read a work I commend to you called *Fame is the Spur* [by Howard Spring] founded more or less on J R M's career [MacDonald] very well done.

He visited the blitzed cities.

Everywhere was the same fine spirit. I think that the bombing did more than anything else to break down class barriers. I always remember a shelter made by a West End businessman at his own cost. He attended there every night, serving a canteen. He was a strong Conservative politically, but his chief helper was a man whom I had last seen in Spain, where he had been fighting for the Republic in the Foreign Legion.

In the *Daily Herald* (17 February 1940) Ritchie Calder wrote:

Mr Attlee's speeches have had an outstanding theme during a weekend tour of hundreds of miles through South Wales – that never again shall such a vital area be allowed to go derelict. He emphasised it once more when the biggest hall in the Rhondda Valley was packed out and hundreds were turned away. It was the climax of his tour and he made one of the greatest speeches of his career.

Calder quoted a number of passages. 'The differences of opinion which separate us in this country, whether political or religious, are like little ditches compared with the great gulf which separates us from Hitler and

Mussolini,' said Attlee; then he went on, as Churchill and the Tories would not, indeed could not, to promise a planned society which would abolish unemployment and poverty and promote social justice and equality. Churchill thought of visits to blitzed cities only as morale boosters. Attlee emphasized, as he invariably did, and as Churchill could not, the amount of common ground between the national parties. Unlike Churchill he combined uplift with political commitment: 'Never again are we going to put up with the bad housing, with poverty and with the unemployment scandal. Our failures in the past have been lack of grasp of opportunity, lack of an active social conscience.' One of his audiences numbered more than 2,000 workers. Calder concluded: 'He has certainly in this week-end proved the value of members of the War Cabinet getting as close to the actual conditions in the country as possible.' Attlee was also proving the value of Labour leaders taking the opportunity to shape the British workers' ideas of what kind of Britain should emerge after the war.

II

On his second day as acting leader of the House, 22 May 1940, Attlee rose to introduce the Emergency Powers Bill, which passed through all its stages the same day.

It gave the government the power to direct any person to perform any services that might be required of him or her in the national interest, to take control over any property, and to take over any industrial establishment and direct its operation. The same night, speaking for the government, Attlee broadcast a message to the nation. 'A great battle is proceeding in the North of France. We cannot tell yet what will be the issue. . . . Today, on your behalf, Parliament has given to the Government full power to control all persons and property. . . . The direction of persons to perform services will be under the Minister of Labour, Mr Ernest Bevin.' He concluded: 'Above all, don't get rattled. There is no justification for it. With brave hearts and cool heads we will come through.' Two days later, Ernest Bevin addressed a special conference of 2,000 trade union executives, representing 150 unions, at the Albert Hall:

> I have to ask you virtually to place yourselves at the disposal of the State. We are Socialists and this is the test of our Socialism . . . if our Movement and our class rise with all their energy now and save the people of this country from disaster, the Country will always turn with confidence to the people who saved them.

To reconcile the trade union movement to the new powers of the state was the greatest political task facing Attlee and Bevin in 1940. Attlee addressed the Trades Union Congress in October 1940, conveying the 'fraternal greetings' of the Labour Party, but more importantly explaining the role of the Labour Movement in wartime government. Close consultation between organized Labour and the government, he said, was absolutely essential to success. 'All of us are in the fighting line.... The airman who shoots down an enemy raider wins a victory. The worker who carries on under danger in the factory wins a victory.' He reminded the delegates that Britain was not only fighting for her own liberty, but to restore that of trade unionists and socialists throughout conquered Europe. 'In one sense Britain stands alone today in Europe. In another sense we are not alone at all; we stand as the strong representative of the great Trade Union and Labour movement.... Those great movements we used to meet in friendly conference have been crushed, but they are with us, we are fighting their battle.'

The government's first task was to defeat the enemy, said Attlee. The second was to keep Britain united. The third task was to preserve freedom. Britain eschewed 'the strength that comes from giving orders to blind, dumb slaves forced to do the behest of a ruler'. This was a welcome assurance to the delegates, who feared that Bevin might feel obliged to introduce conscription of industrial labour; but Attlee already knew that the Ministry of Labour was uncovering problems which could only be solved by extensive controls which would be unwelcome to the trade union movement. The working man who joined the Army and went off to fight the Germans could leave his legacy of industrial strife behind him with his civilian clothes. The working man who remained at home on war production had the task of adapting himself psychologically to regarding the state and his employer as his allies.

III

The TUC's enthusiastic reception of Attlee was occasioned not only by his reassurances about the use of state powers, and his rousing determination that 'the principles of the Labour movement, freedom, democracy, a collective security and social justice, will enable us to build a new world and establish peace on firm foundations', but also by his news of the war. By October 1940 he could justifiably claim that the new coalition had lived through a major military crisis, and that Hitler's plans for the invasion of Britain had failed.

Attlee had first attended a War Cabinet on 13 May 1940. The next month saw a major crisis of the war, the withdrawal of the British expeditionary force through Dunkirk. He was concerned that the evacuation plans were inadquate. 'Aren't we in danger of falling between two stools ... neither the plan agreed with General Weygand will be carried out, nor will we use our forces to best advantage in retaining our hold on the

Channel Ports,' he told the Cabinet. Attlee later recollected that his Gallipoli experience inclined him to optimism, while the chiefs of staff did not expect a successful evacuation. Churchill was persuaded by Attlee's view.

A few days later, Attlee intervened in a more fateful question. In late May, when the German invasion of France was patently unstoppable, the French premier, Reynaud, proposed that the Allies should offer concessions to Mussolini in return for his good offices to persuade Hitler to negotiate a general peace. Halifax and Chamberlain were in favour, Churchill at first equivocal. Attlee from the first opposed any kind of dealings with Mussolini. When the War Cabinet met he argued that it was essential not to let up on Hitler for a moment. Greenwood supported him, and, sustained by the two Labour leaders, Churchill declared that 'whatever happens at Dunkirk, we shall fight on'. Halifax considered resignation. What would have happened if a few days earlier Halifax, not Churchill, had become prime minister and had supported the Reynaud proposal? Would Attlee have agreed to it? 'No,' he said, years later, 'We'd rather have left the government.'

The government's immediate war objective was to try and persuade the demoralized French government to fight on. Churchill involved Attlee in this, not only because of his position in the government but because of his influence with the French left, whose leaders were much readier to continue to fight against Fascism than the French government as a whole. At the Bournemouth conference Blum, having flown over from Paris for the purpose, had spoken to the delegates of the determination of the French to fight alongside Britain to the end. Receiving private reports from Attlee of declining morale in Paris, Blum flew back to Paris at once. There was little he could do. Attlee continued to encourage him in his efforts to rally his compatriots. On 31 May Attlee accompanied Churchill to Paris with Ismay, Churchill's military aide, and Dill, the new CIGS. Attlee described the French leaders in his autobiographical notes:

> They were pretty much at the end of their tether. They had decided they would rather lie down than fight. It was a terrible thing. They had no one to take hold of them this time, no Clemenceau, and the country was infested with Communism and riddled with Fascists and a lot of defeatists. Weygand looked like a little rat caught in a trap: a Staff Officer put in command who didn't know what to do. Pétain looked like a great old image, past everything. Darlan was trying to show that he was a bluff sailor. Paul Reynaud – a little man doing his best but no one to depend on. And the rest of the politicians snatching at anything. The only man you felt meant anything was de Gaulle, glowering at the back. I thought they were a hopeless lot. For twenty-four hours Winston put a bit of heart into them and then it wore off.

Afterwards I drove round Paris with Spears. One felt an atmosphere of utter hopelessness.

On 3 June 1940 Dunkirk was successfully evacuated, as Attlee had predicted. On 11 June, for the first time, he deputized in the House for Churchill, who was once more in Paris to buttress the French. His statement on the situation was grim: it dealt with the last stage of the withdrawal from Norway, the loss of the aircraft carrier *Glorious*, and Italy's entry into the war the previous day. On 13 June, deputizing for Churchill in Cabinet, he urged that a statement be made, in dramatic terms, to hearten the French people. De Gaulle and Jean Monnet, then on the French Economic Mission, together with Halifax and Vansittart produced a plan for the 'indissoluble union' of the British and French peoples. Churchill was lukewarm. Attlee, with Blum's speech at Bournemouth still ringing in his ears, warmly supported the 'union' scheme. The draft came and was unanimously approved by the War Cabinet on 16 June. The document was handed at once to de Gaulle to deliver personally to Reynaud. The British Ambassador, Sir Ronald Campbell, was instructed to inform Reynaud that the proposal was on its way, and that Churchill and Attlee, accompanied by Sinclair as leader of the Liberals and by the chiefs of staff, would leave that night for Southampton in a cruiser and be in Brittany by noon next day for a meeting with the French Cabinet.

Churchill and Attlee got only as far as the railway behind Addison Road, between Paddington and Shepherd's Bush, where a special train was waiting to take them to Southampton. There they heard that there had been a Cabinet crisis in Paris, and that no member of the French government was prepared to meet the British delegation. 'Reynaud had lost. We got out of the train and drove back to Downing Street and went back to work.' Reynaud resigned, Pétain sued for peace. From 18 June Britain was going it alone.

On 19 July Hitler directed his 'peace offer' at Britain. The only question that it raised for the War Cabinet was how most effectively to reject it. Churchill, ever the showman, wanted motions of rejection put down in the House of Commons and the House of Lords, so that the full weight of Parliament could be mobilized behind a contemptuous rejoinder. Attlee argued that this would invest Hitler's offer with undue importance. The statement of rejection, therefore, was made by the Foreign Secretary, not to Hitler but to the British people. The precious May Churchill had declared Britain's war aims: total victory, or Germany's request for an armistice, with a promise to hand back the territories which she had occupied by force. Now, on 3 August, he further demanded 'effective guarantees by deeds not words' to restore the free and independent life of all the injured or invaded countries, 'as well as the effectual security of Great Britain and the British Empire in a general peace'. This brief statement, made in the context of Hitler's peace offer, was generally thought acceptable, but many found it 'negative'. After the collapse of Hitler's air offensive against Britain in September, and the consequent abandonment of his invasion plans, the demand grew for a more positive statement of Britain's war aims.

IV

The resignation of Chamberlain on 1 October 1940 – he died two months later – gave Churchill the opportunity to reshape his administration. Anderson moved from the Home Office to replace Chamberlain as Lord President of the Council. Sir Kingsley Wood became Chancellor of the Exchequer, Herbert Morrison became Home Secretary, and Bevin, remaining Minister of Labour, moved into the War Cabinet. In December, when Halifax became Ambassador to the United States, Eden became Foreign Secretary. Beaverbrook, as Minister of Aircraft Production, was also in the War Cabinet – at the end of 1940 it numbered eight. At Attlee's suggestion Greenwood was given special responsibilities for problems of postwar reconstruction. Churchill, to the annoyance of many members of the Labour Party, accepted the position of leader of the Conservative Party.

Attlee was now to bear the brunt of demands for a restatement of war aims, which the extreme left accompanied with pressure for a quick end to the war. On 5 December a number of ILP members tabled a motion calling for a negotiated peace. Attlee responded with a personal but good-tempered dissertation on the traits of his old colleague Maxton: 'His irresponsibility is part of his charm. He throws his amiable smoke-clouds of sentiment about, but he has not taken responsibility yet.' He went on more seriously:

> A conference means that the other side must come in. Why does he [Maxton] not go to Herr Hitler and ask him to come in? Our old friend George Lansbury ... went round to plead with Herr Hitler and Signor Mussolini, but he got nothing from them. ... There is something worse than killing the body, and that is killing the soul. ... It is no good suggesting that *all* the German people are the simple kindly people we used to know. A great many are being corrupted, and used as an instrument, by this abominable tyranny of Hitler's. That is the greatest crime of all. Recognising it as a crime, we must also recognise that Herr Hitler has that grip.

The debate which Maxton had begun, Attlee observed, 'is one which no other country in the war would tolerate at all'.

186

The Cabinet was already concerned about the weakness of British morale. In early autumn Churchill had declared in Cabinet that the *Sunday Pictorial* and the *Daily Mirror*, by criticizing certain politicians and generals for the botched attempt to seize the West African port of Dakar from the Vichy government, were preparing public opinion for 'surrender and peace'. Morrison, Attlee and Beaverbrook argued that the criticism, however misconceived, was intended to be constructive rather than subversive. Attlee and Beaverbrook were deputed to talk informally to the Newspaper Publishers' Association. Summoned to Attlee's office, and advised that 'irresponsible' criticism would lead to compulsory censorship, the NPA representatives warned that if censorship were introduced the government would fall. Attlee was unmoved. He interviewed representatives of the offending newspapers, and reported to the Cabinet that there was nothing sinister behind the articles; 'at the end of the interview they had both appeared somewhat chastened and had undertaken to exercise care in the future'.

The same leniency was not extended to the *Daily Worker*, which since the Russo-German pact of August 1939 had supported 'revolutionary defeatism'. Morrison suppressed it in January 1941 for carrying advertising for a 'People's Convention' to lobby support for a negotiated peace.

Since Churchill's rejection of Hitler's peace offer in July 1940, Attlee had been concerned that the government's 'purely negative' attitude would encourage such agitation for an early peace. He thus pressed for 'a positive and revolutionary aim admitting that the old order has collapsed and asking people to fight for the new order'. In August he was appointed chairman of a Cabinet Committee on War Aims, but when it reported in January 1941 Churchill refused to make a public statement on the grounds that 'precise aims would be compromising, whereas vague principles would disappoint'. Even with the help of Eden, who had succeeded Halifax as Foreign Secretary in December 1940, Attlee was unable to make any impression on Churchill, and he was unwilling to put extreme pressure on him so long as the Prime Minister's parliamentary position was insecure. Accordingly, in February 1941, he told the House that: 'Writing down peace aims is a thing that cannot be done in a moment. . . . When you make a statement of peace aims, it is on record and therefore requires great consideration.'

No further progress was made until August 1941, when at Roosevelt's suggestion the British and American governments both subscribed to the seven broad principles of the Atlantic Charter. As Attlee observed in the House, these were appropriately vague: 'In a general statement made by the heads of two great States you cannot expect to get more than general principles. The application has to be worked out later on, and it is impossible to elaborate at the present time a detailed plan for the future of the world.' If it was not the 'positive and revolutionary' document for which Attlee had called in 1940, the Charter, incorporating Ernest Bevin's call for 'improved labour standards, economic advancement, and social security', did at least commit Britain to progressive war aims.

V

A mutual suspicion between Labour and Conservatives over war aims in early 1941 was merely a prelude to more serious difficulties for the governing coalition. On 7 May 1941 Attlee opened for the government in a major debate about the conduct of the war, in which he fought off an attack from Hore-Belisha, formerly Chamberlain's secretary for war, about the shortage of tanks and the government's military strategy in general. It was a solid speech and the House finally gave Churchill a vote of confidence by 477 to 3; but this did not reflect the misgivings widely felt in and out of Parliament. Attlee's defence of Churchill and affirmation of national unity did not please all members of the Labour Party, especially since it came just before the party conference in June. On the eve of the conference Aneurin Bevan made an attempt to jolt the party out of the role Attlee had accepted in the coalition government. 'The Labour leadership,' he complained, 'insists upon regarding itself as a junior partner in the Government when in fact it is alone the custodian of those inspirations and policies through which victory can be achieved.'

Attlee's speech to the conference in defence of Labour's role in the coalition was welcomed by a large majority, but there was an uncomfortable measure of truth in Bevan's accusation. Attlee had, for example, tried without success to persuade Churchill to repeal the 1927 Trade Disputes and Trade Union Act. Though in a long and cogent letter he argued to Churchill that the Act 'was imposed on the Unions as a kind of Brest-Litovsk Peace and the memory rankles', the Prime Minister would not budge, and Attlee could not realize his hope of announcing its repeal at the party conference. Hitler's invasion of Russia on 22 June 1941 reduced left-wing pressure for a negotiated peace, but substituted for it a sustained demand for 'Arms for Russia' which was no less embarrassing.

In July, writing in *Tribune*, Bevan described Churchill as 'completely illiterate in all matters connected with industry'; the Prime Minister was 'running a one-man government'; and by talking only of an imminent invasion of Great Britain rather than a sustained industrial effort to help Russia's battle on the Eastern Front was 'infinitely defeatist'. Implicit in this was an attack on Attlee and the Labour ministers: had Churchill 'been subject to proper pressures and guidance from his colleagues, he could never have made the appointments which brought upon him the furtive derision' of the House of Commons.

It was therefore in defence of his own position as Labour leader, as well as of Churchill, that Attlee dwelt in his public statements of late 1941 on the degree of Britain's help to the Soviet Union. There would be no 'stand-easy in Britain' while Russia was fighting Hitler. On 9 September he counter-attacked. 'There is nothing more stupid than to make a futile and dangerous gesture for fear someone should think you are not doing your best. . . . We shall give all we can to Russia, but remember, it has to come out of our production, which is not yet adequate for our own needs.' Members of the government, he said, fully shared the public anxiety that everything possible should be done to help Russia; 'Britain does not regard the Russo-German fight in the east and the fight in the west as separate wars; they are part of a single fight against a common adversary.'

At the Trades Union Congress at Edinburgh in September, Attlee pulled out all the stops on the political organ. Reminding his audience of the social and economic promises of the Atlantic Charter, he went on: 'It is not too much to say that the principles for which the Trade Unions have fought throughout their history have now been recognised as something fundamental to civilisation.' It was not possible yet to produce detailed programmes or commitments, or to know when this would be possible. For the time being, uniting to win the war came first. 'We cannot yet know the time or place where we shall make harbour [but] we are making plans to be carried out on our arrival; Arthur Greenwood is in charge of these [as chairman of the Reconstruction Committee] but meanwhile he and I and all the rest of us are heavily engaged in seeing that the ship weathers the storm.'

The unity of the Labour Movement, no less than national unity, was now at the head of Attlee's political concerns. Just after his Edinburgh speech he had to resolve a fierce public row between Bevin as Minister of Labour and the TUC General Secretary, Citrine. Citrine had criticized Bevin for the extent to which skilled men were being conscripted into the Army, there to do unskilled jobs. Bevin accused the *Daily Herald*, which endorsed Citrine's position, of conducting a 'Quisling' policy. 'In the end,' recorded Citrine:

> Attlee stepped in as peacemaker and wrote in his own hand to both Bevin and myself. Without touching on the basic issue, with his customary clear-headedness he pointed out that friction between us was gravely detrimental to the war effort. I replied at once. . . . I fancy that Attlee informed Bevin of this letter, as a reply came to me next day from Bevin, denying that he had ever used the word 'Quisling' with reference to the *Daily Herald*. . . . So ended a distasteful public controversy. . . . We never referred to it on any subsequent occasion.

A different kind of problem developed as a result of the disinclination of some Tory ministers to cooperate with their Labour colleagues. The tension between Brendan Bracken and Dalton gave Attlee a great deal of trouble for most of 1941. When Dalton became Minister for Economic Warfare in May 1940, Churchill gave him responsibility for the Special Operations Executive, the purpose of which was to coordinate subversion and sabotage against the enemy overseas. In early 1941 Dalton complained to Attlee that Brendan Bracken and 'other conspirators' at Number Ten 'are constantly trying to poison the wells, not only against me and you but against Labour Ministers in general. Bracken, in particular, is still violently anti-Labour and takes the view that, though we were necessary last May in order to bring about a change in Government, we are not really necessary any longer and should be gradually pushed out of the picture.' With this letter, Dalton sent Attlee a detailed account submitted to him by a senior member of his staff of remarks made to him by Brendan Bracken, who had 'particularly criticised Dr Dalton and the organisation under him [SOE] as being entirely incapable of this kind of warfare.... He [Bracken] criticised Dr Dalton personally and said that nobody would work with him, neither the Chiefs of Staff nor any of the Ministries.' Attlee was well aware of Dalton's own capacity for intrigue, but he also knew Bracken's. He took the matter up privately with Churchill, and Dalton's situation, and temper, much improved.

Trouble recurred later in the year. Dalton became alarmed that the new Political Warfare Executive was being built up at the expense of his SOE, and that his own position was being undermined. It was being put about, he told Attlee, 'that, whereas Eden and Bracken had the ear of the Prime Minister, I had not'. This time Attlee decided he would make an issue of the matter with the Prime Minister and with this in mind he told Dalton to make a considered statement in writing. Consequently, in a long and detailed letter to Attlee in September, written 'as I promised, to confirm and elaborate earlier conversations', Dalton referred to his complaints about Bracken early in the year, set out his new complaints, and ended his lengthy letter:

> I am sure, and I do not think you disagree with this, that there is a set being made in certain influential quarters, some political and some official, against Labour Ministers. The game is to discredit some of us by whispering campaigns and to reduce to a minimum our influence upon the conduct of the war. I believe that I am only one of several who are now the objects of such a campaign. If this goes on, the time must come when each of us must seriously reconsider his position. The Labour Party, as has been said more than once, are not in this Government as poor relations of the Tories. Nor will our Party in Parliament or in this country tolerate our being so treated.
>
> I have written to you thus frankly and without reserve, both as my friend and as the Leader of the Labour Party in the Government. Not since I joined this Government 16 months ago, have I felt so deeply dissatisfied both with the conduct of affairs and with my personal ambition.

Attlee discussed the situation with Churchill – privately. From then on there were no more complaints from Dalton. The following year the nature of his duties changed when he became President of the Board of Trade.

VI

Not long after the Edinburgh TUC conference Attlee visited the United States and Canada, primarily to attend the conference of the International Labour Organization in New York. His party left on 21 October 1941, on a flying boat, travelling via Lisbon, the Azores and Bermuda.

> Lisbon is rather charming with a pleasant Southern architecture and one magnificent church very lofty with a huge span supported by slender columns. The City, of course, full of spies. It was curious to see Germans walking about the town and a German plane on the aerodrome.

In the United States he met many prominent citizens, and 'all the members of the Cabinet separately'. He had several talks with Miss Frances Perkins, the Secretary of Labour, and took part in a broadcast with her, 'a pleasant soul rather in the style of Maggie Bondfield'. At the ILO meeting he spoke of the 'determination to win the peace as well as the war, determination that economic questions and questions of universal improvements of standards of living shall not be neglected as they were after the last war owing to preoccupation with political problems'. From New York he went to Washington and stayed with the Ambassador. There was 'a very jolly trip down the Potomac on the President's yacht. FDR is excellent company.' He formed a disagreeable impression of American trade unionism. It seemed to him 'to suffer from a lack of the idealist spirit that adherence to the Socialist creed brings with it. The general outlook at that time appeared to me to be materialist, differing little from that of other acquisitive groups.'

At Washington he had his first experience of an American-style press conference. 'I was bombarded with questions; some were handed in, others were put straight from the floor. House of Commons experience enabled me to deal with them at great speed without difficulty, and this seemed to surprise some of the audience. I gather that I did not drop any bricks or tread on any corns.' Apparently not. The *Manchester Guardian* reported that the leader of the Labour Party was 'as spry as ever' on his return to London, and commented that 'the first question asked here, as over there, was about American strikes. He evaded it as nimbly as he must have done in New York' – pointing out that collective bargaining over there was only in its early stages, and that difficulties were inevitable. From Washington he went to Ottawa by train, staying as guest of the

Governor General, the Earl of Athlone, and his wife Princess Alice, 'pleasant simple people' he calls them in his letter to Tom. 'The Princess had interesting stories about her childhood and grandmamma and Gladstone etc.' He addressed the Canadian House of Commons and several meetings, and was entertained by Mackenzie King, the Prime Minister, and members of his government. This started a friendship between Attlee and King which lasted till King's death in 1950.

The party flew home by Clipper on the long roundabout route by which they had come, landing at Bristol. They then had another half-hour's flight to Hendon, where Vi met Attlee and drove him home for a cup of tea and a nap at 'Heywood'. By early evening he was at his desk in the Cabinet offices, signed some papers, and then reported on his impressions of the tour. He confirmed Churchill's own feeling that Roosevelt would get into the war as soon as he could. Neither of them could have imagined that this would come about within a month.

When writing to Tom to sum up his impressions of his tour, he also dealt with Tom's request for some observations he might make about Churchill in a talk he proposed to give. Attlee made two comments:

> In talking of Winston you might make one point which I made when addressing some 300 Pressmen after lunch off the record, that is his extreme sensitiveness to suffering. I remember some years ago his eyes filling with tears when he talked of the suffering of the Jews in Germany while I recall the tone in which looking at Blitzed houses he said, 'poor poor little homes'. This is a side of his character not always appreciated. Another is his intense realisation of history. He sees all events taking their place in the procession of past events as seen by the historian of the future: the gallantry of Greece, the heroism of our people, the breakdown of the French are always seen in perspective.

VII

On 7 December 1941 the Japanese bombed the American fleet in Pearl Harbor. Fulfilling Churchill's promise a month earlier, Britain immediately declared war on Japan. Hitler followed suit by declaring war on the United States. On 13 December Churchill and the British chiefs of staff went to Washington for 'Arcadia', the first conference at which they met as allies. Eden had left for a meeting with Stalin in Moscow on 7 December, and was concerned about prime minister and foreign secretary being out of the country simultaneously. He raised the matter with Attlee, who remonstrated with Churchill, this time to no avail. So Attlee was left in charge, though still without official status as his deputy. 'As you can imagine,' he wrote to Tom on the twenty-seventh, 'I am pretty busy carrying the baby while the PM is away in America. The secret is not too badly kept on the whole.'

Attlee carried the baby for four weeks. Churchill's reputation was low, and his Labour colleagues' stock had sunk with his. In the December issue of *World Review* its proprietor, Edward Hulton, printed a scathing attack on them headed 'Attlee, Greenwood and Halifax must go': 'This is the war of wars, the struggle of struggles. In the inner Cabinet of Ministers whom do we find? Attlee and Greenwood. It is enough to make one turn one's face to the wall and give up the ghost. Can you tell me that no better men can be found than these?'

Attlee's qualities in government could not be shown to full advantage. Sir Alan Brooke, who took over as CIGS a fortnight before Attlee was left in charge, found that he ran Cabinet and Defence Committee meetings 'very efficiently and quickly' compared with the Prime Minister. Brooke had already formed a good impression of Attlee's calming influence over Churchill, and Attlee reciprocated his admiration. On 8 January 1941 it was Attlee's duty to tell the House that the Japanese, who had taken Hong Kong on Christmas Day, were now preparing to invade the Dutch East Indies and Burma. The House wanted Churchill there and, resenting his absence, took it out on Attlee. 'We have missed the Prime Minister,' said Sir Percy Harris. 'The remaining members of the War Cabinet are all excellent in their own way, but none of them has the potentialities of a War Minister to fill the Prime Minister's place. Is the Premiership in commission; or is the Lord Privy Seal [Attlee] Acting Prime Minister; or have important decisions to be referred to the Prime Minister by cable or telegram?' Eden said Yes, Attlee acted as prime minister in Churchill's absence. The Conservative backbenchers displayed no satisfaction with the Foreign Secretary's reply.

VIII

Soon after his return from the United States, Churchill was forced to make the first major Cabinet reconstruction since Chamberlain's resignation in October 1940. By mid-February war news was very bad. The Japanese had invaded Burma, Borneo was occupied, the *Prince of Wales* and the *Repulse* had been sunk, and most of Malaya was overrun. In North Africa Rommel had launched a new offensive in the Western Desert, and the Eighth Army had evacuated Derna. On 15 February came the terrible news that Singapore, which Churchill had insisted 'must be converted into a citadel and defended to the death', had fallen. At home, Conservative backbenchers were calling him a 'dictator' and criticizing him for trying to perform three roles – prime minister, minister of defence, and leader of the House of Commons. Moreover, he was troubled by sharp personal disagreements among his ministerial colleagues. Attlee had taken a hand in smoothing over difficulties between Dalton – Minister for Economic Warfare – and Churchill's protégé Brendan Bracken; but the conflict between Bevin and Beaverbrook could not be handled by private courtesies.

On 4 February Beaverbrook had been appointed Minister of Production, a post which was intended by Churchill to make him overlord of the whole economic front: production, supply and – most important politically – manpower. Bevin made up his mind that such an appointment would be made only over his dead body: he distrusted and disliked Beaverbrook, and he was utterly opposed in principle to the transfer of responsibility for manpower and labour from the Ministry of Labour – one of the conditions on which Labour had joined the coalition was that manpower should be in the hands of a trade union leader. Faced with this dispute, Churchill consulted Attlee, who advised that the Ministry of Labour's present powers must remain untouched, and be seen to be so: otherwise there would be trouble with the party as well as with Bevin. In any case, handing over manpower to Beaverbrook was unthinkable because the trade unions distrusted him, and had done so for decades. Churchill responded that if Beaverbrook did not get manpower he would resign the new job. Attlee said that if he *did* get manpower Bevin would resign, and that would precipitate a political crisis at a time when all the war news was bad. Churchill gave in. Beaverbrook resigned his new post. Lyttelton was appointed Minister of Production. He was not to be in charge of manpower – in such matters, 'the Minister of Production and the Minister of Labour will work together'.

Beaverbrook's removal was the most contentious element in the reshuffle: moreover, it crystallized the mutual suspicion between Beaverbrook and Attlee, whom Beaverbrook blamed for his dismissal. Beaverbrook thought Attlee a 'miserable little man'; and in 1959, when asked to write an appreciation of Beaverbrook to be published after his death, Attlee said mildly: 'No. He was the only evil man I ever met. I could find nothing good to say about him.' Beaverbrook, he believed, had had a corrupting influence on young men which he maintained by entertaining them lavishly, or by hiring them professionally at extravagant rates.

On 18 February 1942, Churchill, Eden, Attlee and Stuart, the Conservative Chief Whip, met to settle the Cabinet changes. Churchill, remaining Minister of Defence, gave up the leadership of the House, which he had delegated so often to Attlee, and passed it to Cripps, who became Lord Privy Seal. Attlee now became Deputy Prime Minister officially, and also Dominions Secretary. Bevin, Eden and Anderson kept their positions, and Kingsley Wood remained Chancellor of the Exchequer, but without a seat in the War Cabinet. Greenwood resigned.

According to Eden, it was expected that Attlee 'would struggle to prevent' Greenwood's removal, but there is no record of him doing so: Attlee knew that Greenwood, who had attracted little attention as minister in charge of postwar planning, was not up to his job; and the introduction of Cripps – and Beaverbrook's fate – more than compensated for Greenwood's demotion. Greenwood took over the leadership of the Labour Party in the House, and his position on Labour's National Executive remained secure.

Though Attlee was convinced that it was in the national interest that Greenwood should go, he was unhappy about it. 'These questions [of loyalty] are the very devil,' he told Tom. Beaverbrook, meeting Citrine, 'was resentful that Attlee had – as he asserted – deliberately sacrificed Arthur Greenwood as a member of the War Cabinet and bargained for his own position as Deputy Prime Minister in return.' Considering Greenwood's record, and Attlee's character, it is highly improbable that Attlee could have saved him by any kind of bargaining, and Greenwood's role as leader of the Opposition enabled him to make a much greater contribution to the war effort than by sitting in the War Cabinet.

Churchill could reasonably hope that the new Cabinet would be more popular in the House and in the country. Attlee's problems, of reconciling the Labour Movement in and out of Parliament with a government led by a Conservative, did not change.

14
Deputy Prime Minister, 1942

I

In his first few months as Deputy Prime Minister Attlee had a rough passage. Morale at home was low, and the Cabinet received disquieting reports of morale in the forces abroad. At the beginning of March, Lyttelton, recently back from North Africa, reported to the Defence Committee that the troops had lost faith in their equipment, mainly the tanks. For Auchinleck to launch an offensive at this time would be out of the question. Attlee wanted to know why Rommel had been able to return to the offensive with such speed after having so recently been defeated. Unless we could return to the attack, he said, 'our whole strategy would be upset'. After a long and outspoken discussion, Attlee was asked to inquire into the matter. The gist of his long report, which he produced in June, was that the Crusader tanks had been brought into production prematurely.

It was perhaps his disquiet with the progress of the campaign in Libya that led Attlee to make an ill-judged, and ill-received, statement on the war situation on 19 May 1942. In one passage he appeared to blame the men in the line rather than the politicians who authorized the strategy. He made no friends by loyally defending Churchill against the charge of interfering with the generals, when many MPs suspected, quite rightly, that Churchill was putting pressure on Auchinleck to take the initiative in Libya.

Within a week of this statement, it fell to Attlee to announce in the House the Anglo-Russian Treaty, which many MPs took to mean that a second front would soon be established. His part in the making of this treaty and its implementation had been controversial. On 24 June 1941, two days after Russia was invaded by Germany, he made a broadcast promising that Britain would assist the Soviet Union, but also stressing the irreconcilability of Labour Party views with Communism. In the first few weeks of 1942, when Stalin was pressing hard for a second front, with much support in Britain headed in the Government by Beaverbrook, Churchill became much exercised about the need to improve Anglo-Soviet relations. Stalin wanted the treaty to include agreement to a postwar settlement which would give Russia security in Europe. Eden, recently returned from Moscow, told the War Cabinet that, in view of Stalin's expostulations about the vulnerability of Poland, he would insist on the frontiers to which Russia had advanced being made the permanent Polish–Soviet border. Pointing out that in the event of the Allies winning the war Russian troops would almost certainly be further west in Europe than ever before, Eden recommended that the Americans be urged to face these potential Russian claims forthwith. Beaverbrook, still in the Government at this time, and at the height of his enthusiasm for close cooperation with Stalin, advocated that Stalin's claims should be accepted at once.

Attlee opposed Beaverbrook vigorously. To enter such an arrangement, he said, would be inconsistent with the principles for which the war was being fought. Such deals about frontiers would create the problems which had bedevilled the settlement after the First World War. Attlee talked of resigning if Russia's 1941 frontiers were recognized; Beaverbrook threatened to resign if they were not. Though not all Labour leaders shared his view – Morrison and Dalton were ready for cooperation with Russia – Attlee was able to prevent the Cabinet from recommending to Roosevelt that Stalin's conditions should be accepted. By the time Molotov arrived in England in May 1942 to negotiate the Anglo-Soviet Treaty, Stalin was far more interested in a second front than in postwar frontiers. The treaty was signed; but it did not include recognition of the frontiers for which Stalin had asked. A lunch was given to mark the signing. Beaverbrook – now out of the government – refused to attend.

II

The signing of the Anglo-Russian Treaty gave Attlee some help in dealing with the dissidents at the party conference from 25 to 28 May at Central Hall, Westminster. His task was to reunite the Labour Party and rally it behind the government at a time when the news from all fronts was bad. It was an uphill struggle. In March 1942, for the first time, a government candidate had been defeated in a by-election by an Independent. A month later two more seats went the same way. Much concerned, Attlee had recommended to his Labour colleagues that, not only to fortify the government but to protect the party, Labour should abstain from putting up their own candidates in by-elections and support all government candidates. He pointed out that: 'Irresponsible freak candidates were now coming forward, perhaps with some support from less responsible organs of the press.' He quoted the example of Sir James Grigg, an entirely non-party man, standing for the government in Cardiff, being opposed by Fenner Brockway, who, though a Socialist, was a pacifist. In such a case, said Attlee, it was clearly the duty of Labour voters to support the government candidate. The conference resolution to this effect was strongly opposed. The miners', engineers', and railwaymen's unions voted against it, and the resolution passed only narrowly – 1,275,000 to 1,209,000 on a card vote.

Dissatisfaction with the government in general and with the Prime Minister in particular reached its highest point when Tobruk surrendered to Rommel on 21 June 1942. Attlee had to bear the immediate brunt of national dismay. Since Churchill was still in America, it fell to him to make the statement to the House on the fall of Tobruk. All he could say was that it was only one reverse in a long battle. This carried little conviction: the whole British position in the Middle East now seemed likely to disintegrate. The situation still looked desperate at the end of June when Churchill returned from America. In a by-election at Maldon, Essex, a Conservative majority of eight thousand had been overturned by Tom Driberg, a socialist standing as an Independent, who won by a majority of six thousand. Sir John Wardlaw-Milne, one of the most influential Conservative backbenchers, with support from members of all three parties, tabled a motion of censure on 25 June: 'That this House, while paying tribute to the heroism and endurance of the Armed Forces of the Crown ... has no confidence in the central direction of the war.' The stage seemed set for a showdown whose consequences could not be assessed.

Attlee did not speak in the debate, but he played an important part in the series of events, of which the debate was only one, whereby Churchill was vindicated and his critics routed. At the last minute, Wardlaw-Milne, recoiling from the hornet's nest he had stirred up at such a time, suggested to the Cabinet that the debate on his motion should be deferred, giving as his grounds for making the suggestion the fact that a major battle – the first battle of El Alamein – had begun in Libya. But Attlee refused to agree. He had been in close touch with the House during Churchill's absence, and he believed that if the government accepted Wardlaw-Milne's challenge they would be given an overwhelmingly large vote of support.

Attlee also thought that a debate on the Wardlaw-Milne motion would enable the War Cabinet to neutralize the influence of Beaverbrook. In public Beaverbrook advocated a second front, to which he knew the War Cabinet was opposed, and in private he complained about Churchill's direction of the war. He maintained that Tobruk had been lost because of a shortage of munitions; his employee, Driberg, had produced a pamphlet saying the same thing, and many people credited his victory at the Maldon by-election to it. About ten days before the Wardlaw-Milne debate, Beaverbrook had tried to draw Bevin into a discussion of how the government should be reconstituted. Bevin reported this to Churchill, who affected not to believe him, and to Attlee, who certainly did believe him, and resolved that the government should take on its critics inside the House, and Beaverbrook outside it.

Attlee then proceeded to smooth the way for a strong government majority in the debate by taking a firm line with the Parliamentary Labour Party, whose meeting on 30 June had resolved to put down an amendment demanding an inquiry into the loss of Tobruk and the deficiencies of the Eighth Army's equipment. He pointed out that it was he, the leader of their party, who at the time of the fall of Tobruk, with Churchill out of the country, had been in charge of running the war. Bevin supported him to the hilt. By the time the debate opened, therefore, powerful forces were ranged on Churchill's side. In the debate the critics, ranging along the political spectrum from Aneurin Bevan on the left to Sir Roger Keyes on the right, got in each other's way. Churchill, winding up the debate, was at his best. The government was victorious by 475 to 25. Bevan and seven other Labour MPs voted for the motion. Attlee carpeted them. Characteristically he reproved them not because they had voted against the government but because they had defied the party line. They had offended not against Churchill but against the Labour Party.

III

In the following weeks Attlee stoutly defended Churchill's leadership in public speeches in different parts of the country. In private he was anxious about the progress of the war. In July he sent Eden a long memorandum on British military failures, given in full as Appendix II to this book. He identified mobility and adaptability as the keys of Japanese and German successes. In every theatre the Germans had used air transport or air attack to force home their offensives. British efforts were hampered by the British military mind:

> We think in categories. Our unit is the Division, a huge mass of men (40,000) cumbrous to a degree, provided with an immense litter of ancillary services which almost swallow up the fighting men. The provision of a mass of mechanised transport in order to make it mobile has immobilised it. The elaboration of staffs hampers effective staff work.
>
> It has grown on the foundation of the Division of the last war in the tradition of static warfare. Have its establishments ever been overhauled by young fighting soldiers who have experienced modern war?

The Air Ministry regarded the use of aircraft with troops as 'an illegitimate filching away of their own resources', yet the assumption that the war could be won by big bombers had never been critically examined. Attlee feared that the preparations for an invasion of Europe might be dominated by the amassing of guns and shells which might never be used.

The government record on the home front, as well as its conduct of the war, had fallen under increasing criticism in the spring and early summer of 1942. The first sign of an inter-party dispute on prewar issues appeared in April, when Dalton, now at the Board of Trade, published a coal-rationing scheme which had been prepared by Beveridge. Conservative backbenchers decided to oppose it, for a variety of reasons – irritation with the miners, lobbying from the owners, general dissatisfaction with the conduct of the war, and, according to one Tory MP, 'because they felt that the Labour Party in the Government was getting too much of its own way'. Many had heard that Bevin had recently told a gathering of coal-owners: 'In this war you are not employers any more; you are agents of the State.'

Meanwhile, the miners were discontented because the Essential Works Order tied them to the pits and government regulations limited their wages. The National Council of Labour produced a Coal Plan which was unanimously accepted by the Labour Party conference on 25 May: the mines should be requisitioned for the duration of the war, and be run by a National Board on which owners, workers and government would be represented. A government White Paper on 3 June merely prescribed requisitioning and evaded the question of ownership. The Parliamentary Labour Party fought the White Paper but eventually swallowed it. The miners' unions, disappointed to have to give up nationalization, were sweetened for the time being by an immediate wage increase. Only eight MPs went into the lobbies against the government over the White Paper recommendations, but many members of the Labour Party regarded this as yet another sellout to the Tories by their leaders in the Cabinet.

Conservatives, too, harboured political grievances about the coal question which were to erupt later against the coalition. They suspected Dalton of using the Board of Trade, as they said he had used the Ministry of Economic Warfare, to further the interests of socialists; in this instance by recruiting Hugh Gaitskell, Harold Wilson and Douglas Jay as temporary civil servants. Dalton consulted Attlee about his problems with the Conservatives over coal as he had about his problems with them over SOE. Attlee talked to Churchill, with good results, as Dalton recorded: 'The Prime Minister became disturbed, but I found him friendly. "Don't let them all form up on you," he said, and offered to make a broadcast on the need for coal economy, and, if it failed, to introduce a rationing scheme.' Attlee took a special interest in the coal problem: the miners' leaders and their MPs had been his rock of support in the rough days of the early thirties.

Such discontent and suspicion plagued relations between the Labour ministers and the PLP. An angry confrontation between leaders and backbenchers in July caused Ernest Bevin to take a step along the road which eight months later almost led him out of the PLP. The government had announced its proposal to increase old age pensions by 2s 6d a week. Attlee tried to persuade his backbenchers to accept this on the grounds that it was only an interim proposal pending the Beveridge Report, expected in only a few months' time, which would make proper provision for pensioners. This attempt to pour oil on troubled waters failed: the malcontents claimed that the Labour leaders in the Cabinet were continually surrendering socialist principles to the Tories. The PLP decided to table an amendment. In the debate in the Commons, 29 July, Sidney Silverman demanded to know whether Bevin would dare stand up 'and assure this Party and the people that the Government would have collapsed if he had insisted that the increase in the pension should be 5s instead of 2s 6d.' Until now Attlee might have been able to pacify the party; but Bevin began to counter-attack. Tempers rose, and Labour backbenchers pressed the amendment to a division. Sixty-three voted against the government, the biggest vote against Churchill since he became Prime Minister.

IV

Besides making him Deputy Prime Minister in name and in fact, the Cabinet reshuffle of February 1942 had given Attlee a departmental responsibility as Secretary of State for the Dominions. This brought him once again face to face with the problem of governing India; his first duty was to take the chair of the Cabinet's India Committee. Attlee was now regarded at home and among Indian leaders as an expert on India. The *News of the World* had spoken of him becoming the next Viceroy. It was his own view that 'my principal service during the years between the Simon Report and the coming in of the third Labour Government was in educating the Labour Party into a greater sense of reality on the problem, and bringing them to realise that there were other views than those of Hindu congressmen which deserved their attention.' The mutual respect between Attlee and his colleagues on the committee – Anderson, Amery, Cripps, Simon and Grigg – smoothed the path of business; the major obstacle was Churchill, whom Attlee found 'both obstinate and ignorant' about Indian problems. 'This was the time when he said he had not become Prime Minister to preside over the dissolution of the British Empire – I had a good many stiff contests with him', he recorded in his autobiographical notes. The committee's discussions gave Attlee the opportunity to make his mark on Indian policy and, correspondingly, led to his embroiling himself still further with the Labour left.

The Cabinet India Committee was set up in February 1942 to devise a response to the attempt by Jinnah, the leader of the Indian Muslims, to force the government into declaring in favour of an independent Muslim state. At the beginning of the war the Congress Party, representing the Hindus, had withdrawn from all provincial governments in protest at the Viceroy's decision to declare India at war without consultation. Their abstention from government increased the influence of the Muslim League, and in March 1940 Jinnah proclaimed at Lahore the idea of a Muslim state within a state – Pakistan. In August 1940 the British government offered a representative assembly to be held after the war, at which Indians themselves would take primary responsibility for framing their constitution. Unsatisfied, Gandhi led the Congress Party in a civil disobedience campaign. In a parliamentary debate on India in September 1940 Attlee had condemned Gandhi's behaviour and supported the government's proposals to such an extent that the Viceroy recorded: 'Both Gandhi and Nehru were known to be annoyed by the comparative steadiness of the Labour leadership in contrast with some of its rank and file who swallowed Congress's propaganda.'

At the end of 1941 Japan's entry into the war made it more urgent to reach a *modus vivendi* which would insulate India from subversion organized by the Japanese. In January 1942 a prominent Indian leader, Sir Tej Sapru Bahadur, appealed for another British initiative. Churchill, from Washington, demurred, but with the War Cabinet's support Attlee insisted: 'No one is more alive than I am to the complexities of the problem, but I do not think that we can safely ignore its existence which the extension of the war zone makes more acute.' On Churchill's return the War Cabinet decided to defer any reply to Sapru. Attlee urged that a representative be sent to India with full powers to negotiate with the Indian leaders, but this was also deferred: Amery, the India Secretary, argued that it was not the time for interior constitutional advances. When Jinnah took his campaign to the British Parliament, the War Cabinet, which was also under pressure from Roosevelt to accommodate Indian aspirations, changed its mind and set up the India Committee.

Attlee took a firm line with Amery and with Linlithgow, the Viceroy, who both agreed with Churchill that Indian leaders were so hostile to the Empire that it was worthless to try to conciliate them. They were quite wrong, he said.

If it were true it would form the greatest possible condemnation of our rule in India ... educated Indians *do* accept British principles of justice and liberty.... It is precisely this acceptance ... which puts us in the position of being able to appeal to them to take part with us in the common struggle; but the success of this appeal and India's response does put upon us the obligation of seeing that we, as far as we may, make them sharers in the things for which we and they are fighting.

The India Committee rapidly prepared a draft declaration, setting out plans for progress towards self-government at the end of the war, and, albeit only in general terms offering the Indians participation in the government of India at once, subject to the British government through the Viceroy retaining control of defence. Jinnah's demand for a separate state of Pakistan was dealt with by conceding the right of individual provinces to independence outside the new Indian state, a provision which extended also to the states governed by the princes.

Though much of the new draft only restated what had been offered in August 1940, its provisions held out more to India than had ever been offered before. Nehru's reaction, however, was hostile. Promise of reforms at the end of the war was 'mere quibbling': he demanded a provisional national government, responsible to the Indian people, to be set up at once.

Cripps then offered to visit India and discuss the situation with the leaders of the main Indian parties. Attlee urged Churchill to accept the offer. Cripps flew to India on 22 March 1942, with high expectations on the British side: it was thought that he if anyone could square the circle of insoluble conflict between Congress and the Muslim League. But Gandhi refused to accept 'post-dated cheques upon a bankrupt Empire', talks broke down on 10 April, and Cripps returned to Britain with his prestige much reduced both in the Labour Party and the country generally. If the Indians *had* accepted Cripps's proposals the government would have been in difficulty. He had offered the Indians more than he had been authorized to, and on the day that his proposals were rejected had begun an argument with the Cabinet which did not look as if it could be resolved. As for Attlee's view of the mission we have his own words on it:

It was a great surprise when he [Churchill] embraced the idea of the Cripps Mission. The lines on which Cripps was empowered to go went far beyond anything previously conceived by the Government. It embodied in fact some of the main ideas discussed by Cripps, Nehru and myself one weekend at Filkins [Cripps's home in Gloucestershire, in June 1938]. It was a great pity that eventually the Indians turned this down, as full self-government might have been ante-dated by some years.

The failure of the mission meant that there would be no acrimony in the ranks of the Conservative Party about the terms of settlement.

Officially Labour was glad an attempt had been made to achieve a solution. It gave the credit for the attempt not to Cripps – Labour leaders, like Churchill, eyed Cripps's new stardom with misgivings – but to Attlee: at the party conference in May, Morrison observed that perhaps the outstanding man who played a part in those discussions was the leader of the Labour Party, Mr Attlee. 'He bore his full share of the burden, and he ought to have his full share of credit for the advance.'

Attlee's 'share of the burden' was to increase. So far as India was concerned, the failure of the mission had made the situation worse. Gandhi undertook a mass civil disobedience movement. While Churchill was on a visit to the Middle East and Moscow, it fell to Attlee to chair the Cabinet which in August approved the detention of the Congress leaders. Gandhi threatened that he would fast to death. Labour MPs were worried. When Churchill, back from his travels, announced in Parliament the imprisonment of the Congress leaders, and suggested that their activities might have been aided by 'Japanese fifth-column work on a widely extended scale', Aneurin Bevan interrupted to ask whether Attlee and Cripps had approved his statement. When Churchill answered that Attlee and he had drafted the statement the night before, Bevan shouted: 'Then they ought to be ashamed of themselves. They do not represent us.' Even Arthur Greenwood, as leader of the Opposition, condemned the government's policy.

In subsequent debates, in October 1942 and March 1943, Attlee wound up for the government, defending its policies and censuring the irresponsibility of Congress politicians in attacking them. His emphasis was always on the difficulty of devising a constitutional solution which Indians would accept. 'Running through all political life in India there is a desire for self-government ... with which we all sympathise. The trouble is, they do not all desire to be governed by the same people,' he observed in October. In March 1943 he insisted that:

> The responsibility is theirs [the Indians']. Our first offer was made to them in the dark days. It may have been suggested that it was made because the days were dark, but we have reaffirmed that offer when our position is vastly improved, and I suggest that it still holds the field as the only practical proposal ... put up whereby all sections of Indian opinion will be able to act together and frame their own Constitution.

From now on the situation in India remained much the same until the end of the war. When Attlee next made an attempt to deal with it he was prime minister.

V

In late September, with Parliament in recess, Attlee decided, as Dominions Secretary, to visit Newfoundland, where the constitution had been suspended owing to financial difficulties and the island was being run by a commission. He concluded that the question of restoring self-government must be held over until the end of the war. On his return to England he found himself under attack from several quarters. Aneurin Bevan, in a *Tribune* leader, delivered a devastating attack on Attlee's opposition to a second front and his incapacity to represent, let alone to lead, the Labour Party.

If Mr Attlee has gained some of the toughness which comes with high position in politics, it has been reserved for the members and policies of his own Party.

His record as spokesman of the Labour Party in Cabinet is somewhat arid on the positive side. His initial act conscripting men and property has remained largely confined to men; he failed to carry Labour's views in forcing a miserable increase in Old Age Pensions; he failed to stand up to Lyttelton and the 1922 Committee in their opposition to fuel rationing and a thoroughgoing nationalisation of the coal industry; he left the financial structure of the railways untouched, and now in the name of Labour and Socialism has underwritten one of the blackest documents that imperialist bigotry has yet devised – Mr Churchill's India effusion.

Were merely Mr Attlee's reputation at stake we would find it worthy of comment as the passing of yet another Socialist into the limbo of collaboration. But ... of more profound concern is that Mr Attlee is involving the entire Labour Party in the disrepute which his actions – and even more, lack of actions – have earned.

This was bad enough, but attacks made on Attlee by Harold Laski were in many respects worse. Laski sat on the NEC as a representative of the constituency parties. Before the war he had been on good personal terms with Attlee, and until the spring of 1941 he gave Attlee much confidential information and advice. As the war went on he became increasingly impatient with Attlee's leadership. In late 1941 he drew up a reconstruction plan for the Labour Party, entitled 'Great Britain, Russia and the Labour Party', which he wanted published as a Labour Party pamphlet. He presciently told his friend Felix Frankfurter that the critical stage would come when 'the Labour ministers try to water it down so as to maintain their happy subordination to Winston. That, Bevin always partly excepted, seems to be the only role they really enjoy. The real tragedy is that they are satisfied with their position.' His theme was that the postwar settlement could and should be dominated by Russia and Britain working closely together.

By now Attlee had concluded that Laski's judgement had proved itself to be unsound in general and on some issues dangerous. On 27 December 1941 he wrote a brisk critique – 'while danger of US and Britain insisting on ideological conditions is stressed, USSR credited [by Laski] with tolerance it has never yet displayed. Yet danger of enforcement of Communist ideology is as great as the other' – and nothing more was heard of Laski's draft.

In March 1942, while Beaverbrook was sounding Bevin about the removal of Churchill, Laski was sounding Bevin, with no more success, about the removal of Attlee. 'It is a time for a fighting leader and you are the right person for that place,' he wrote to Bevin on 9 March, after Attlee had snubbed him at an NEC meeting. Bevin ignored him. Attlee told Tom that Laski was talking about the birth of a new world. 'My comment was that in the matter of birth, sometimes, if it was very difficult, people demanded a Caesarean.' Laski's biting and widely disseminated private criticisms of Attlee's leadership gravely upset the NEC, which on 12 October held what Dalton described as 'a long inquest into the misdemeanours of Laski'. Laski did not deny that he had lost confidence in Attlee or that he had approached Bevin about Attlee's removal. He declared that, besides Bevin, there was another suitable candidate for the leadership; Dalton thought this might have been Morrison or possibly Dalton himself. 'Attlee sits through all this, but says nothing,' recorded Dalton. There was no disciplinary action, but Laski's machinations were for the moment foiled.

Meanwhile Attlee had to deal with a more dramatic challenge from Cripps – still outside the Labour Party. In January 1942 Cripps had returned after eleven months as ambassador to Russia, and immediately made himself a popular hero by his advocacy of closer Anglo-Soviet relations. The following month he had been made Lord Privy Seal, with a place in the War Cabinet, in the hope of buying off his opposition to Churchill's leadership. In April 1942 a public opinion poll revealed that if anything happened to Churchill 37 per cent of respondents would have chosen Eden to succeed him, 34 per cent would have liked Cripps, and only 2 per cent would have preferred Attlee.

Attlee regularly stood at the bottom of such polls, usually trailing behind Bevin and standing level with Morrison. But Bevin and Morrison implicitly accepted Attlee's leadership of the Labour Party, his key part in the Churchill coalition, and they shared his view that Churchill's leadership was essential to the war effort. Cripps disagreed on all three counts, especially the last. With a clear intention of replacing Churchill as prime minister, he pressed for a new military planning agency which would take strategy out of the Prime Minister's hands. On 1 October Cripps told Eden that he was prepared to resign over the issue. Over the next two days Eden and Attlee cooperated to defuse the crisis. With the grudging agreement of Churchill, who would have much preferred a fight, they persuaded Cripps to take the Ministry of Aircraft Production without a seat in the War Cabinet. Attlee told Cripps in private that he 'would never be forgiven' if he provoked a crisis on the eve of the Anglo-American landings in North Africa. Cripps offered a major hostage to fortune by writing to Churchill that he would have resigned over the conduct of the war if circumstances had not been so critical. At the end of October, when he finally moved to the Ministry of Aircraft Production, the military situation was improving, and the success of the North African landings in early November entrenched Churchill's political position. Cripps had failed.

The rise and fall of Cripps was a warning to Attlee. Though Churchill was now politically impregnable, Attlee was somewhat vulnerable to the political threat which Cripps represented. After the confidence debate in July 1942 a Labour backbencher asserted that 'the bulk of the Labour Party would prefer Cripps to Attlee' even though Cripps's stock with the left had fallen since he had taken office. What the Labour Party wanted was a vigorous and visible criticism of Churchill's running of the war, and clear progress towards social reconstruction after the war. Even after Cripps failed in his attempt to provide such leadership, Attlee's shortcomings seemed obvious. On 4 December 1942, after Attlee had hit back in the House at ILP criticisms of postwar planning, R.H. Tawney, already regarded as an elder statesman of the party, wrote to Beatrice Webb: 'As far as I can see the Labour Party has temporarily ceased not only to count but to believe in itself. . . . The only man who, in my opinion, might stop the rot is Bevin.'

15
Deputy Prime Minister, 1943-4

I

From the beginning of 1943 Attlee's position in the war administration steadily grew in importance, giving meaning to the idea of 'deputy prime ministership'. Both in foreign affairs and on the home front he came to occupy a position of real power, distinct from the places held by Churchill, the charismatic natural leader, or by Labour's other leading lights in the coalition, Bevin, Morrison and Cripps. After the victories in North Africa had turned the tide, Churchill was frequently out of the country for meetings and conferences. In consequence of the Prime Minister's absences Attlee made more speeches in the House, acted more often as chairman of the Cabinet and of the Defence Committee. Churchill, abroad, conceived many initiatives, but, punctilious about the constitutional position, he invariably referred them back to the Cabinet – not for advice but for approval. This added to Attlee's – and to Eden's – burdens. A closer personal, as well as working, relationship developed between the Deputy Prime Minister and the Foreign Secretary. Within the Cabinet a kind of Attlee–Eden axis came about, whose object was to 'put a brake on Winston's wild ideas'.

At the Casablanca Conference in January the question arose of whether the British and American governments should continue to insist on 'unconditional surrender as an essential condition of an armistice with Italy'. To encourage Italian forces to lay down their arms, Churchill wanted to announce that 'unconditional surrender' would not be forced on Italy. He cabled the Cabinet for their support. Attlee cabled back that they were against it: to start making exceptions might create uncertainties and misunderstandings in Eastern Europe. There must be one line for all the Axis countries and their allies. Churchill gave way at once.

Attlee then made a statement in the House. Against considerable opposition he justified the demand for unconditional surrender and supported Stalin's view that the whole German people shared the guilt of the war. For long into the war a distinction had been preserved between the Hitlerian state and the German people. Hitler's invasion of Russia and news of German atrocities in occupied countries began to erode it, and it began to make no practical sense when the bombing of German cities assumed its terrible mid-war scale. Nevertheless, news of the resumption of the demand for unconditional surrender from Casablanca worried many people on both sides of the House. In May Richard Stokes, a Labour rebel at this time, launched another campaign on behalf of the 'ever-growing volume of opinion in this country which considers the indiscriminate bombing of civilian centres both morally wrong and strategic lunacy'. Attlee replied flatly – and against the evidence: 'There is no indiscriminate bombing.' Reginald Sorensen, another Labour critic, asked whether the government would consider representations made by the Christian churches on this matter. Attlee said: 'We have not received any, we must wait until we do.' Privately, he recorded later, he had doubts about the strategy of 'Bomber' Harris.

This question and the answer echoed through the proceedings for the rest of the year, indeed up to D-Day in June 1944. We find Attlee regularly declaring that it was 'still Government policy to reinforce and accelerate to the maximum the bombing effort against German production'. When Rhys Davies asked the Prime Minister whether he was aware of the recent International Red Cross appeal to all belligerents to refrain from indiscriminate bombing affecting lives and property devoid of military importance, and what was the government's attitude, Attlee refused to admit indiscriminate bombing. His suggestion that the questioner 'might turn his attention to those who began it' went down very badly.

Having had to make statements on the war situation in singularly gloomy circumstances in 1942, he had the duty in 1943 of making far more cheerful communications. It was he who announced the spring series of great victories in North Africa, culminating on 11 May with the surrender of the German Army in Tunisia. Attlee told Tom:

> I have had rather a strenuous bout of speech making lately with the crowding of events in North Africa which allowed but scant time for preparation. It is not easy to sub for the PM. It is obviously futile to try to put on Saul's armour, but I seek in a more pedestrian style to preserve a mean between dignity and dullness. I have too in rendering thanks to be careful to avoid sins of omission.

At the end of July 1943 Attlee took the chair for a Cabinet committee to consider the structure of postwar Europe. Italy's collapse meant that Germany's defeat seemed now in sight, and that measures not only to deal with a disarmed Germany but with the victorious Russian armies who would be on German soil must be considered. As chairman of this committee Attlee was in a strong position. Churchill and Eden were frequently out of Britain. The three resident Conservative members of the committee, Anderson, Lyttelton, and later Woolton, had far less political strength than Bevin, Morrison and himself.

Attlee's views on Germany and Russia were firm. No member of the government, with the possible exception of Dalton, was as determined as he was to see that the Germans could never make war again, and nobody spoke so uncompromisingly of the German people's responsibility for the policies of their leaders. His attitude to the Soviet Union has been described in earlier chapters. Attlee read his Foreign Office papers assiduously; everything he read stiffened his resolve to be as tough in assessing Soviet motives as people like Laski had in his view been soft. As the events of 1943 unfolded Attlee became more and more pessimistic about Stalin's postwar intentions. According to Dalton, who still favoured cooperation with Russia – in order to ensure that after the war the Germans could be contained – Attlee had formed the view that Stalin intended to absorb all the East European states.

In the summer of 1943 many papers began to circulate between London and Washington about the future of Germany. In June the Cabinet studied two memoranda, one from Eden, the other from Cripps. Eden proposed that occupied Germany would be divided into three zones, a British, a Russian and an American, with forces from the other allies to make the occupation a United Nations undertaking. Cripps argued that dividing Germany into three zones would lead to the pursuit of spheres of influence, and advocated a 'mixed' unitary UN occupation throughout all Germany, a proposal not dissimilar to one which Roosevelt favoured.

The following month Attlee submitted two memoranda of his own to the Cabinet. In the first he put his view on Germany. He was not so much concerned with the organization of the occupation as with what the occupation must do. After the First World War the Allies had failed to deal with the real German problem, 'the real aggressive elements', by which he meant the Junkers and the industrialists. 'Very positive action will have to be taken by the victorious powers if there is to be a new orientation of the German nation.' He wanted much more than the eradication of Nazism; he wanted social and political change, which could not be left to German officials.

In his second memorandum Attlee set out how his policy for Germany should fit into the broad views about the postwar occupation and settlement which Churchill was now advocating – and with which Attlee agreed. The treatment he recommended for the Germans, he conceded, would so weaken the German state that the danger might arise that the Russians would be able to dominate Western Europe. There was only one way to prevent this, and that was for Britain to involve herself in Europe as she never had before. If she tried to shoulder this burden on her own, she would have no strength to deploy in the rest of the world, and the Americans would become the power in areas now parts or dependents of the British Empire. The dilemma therefore was this: if, Germany being neutralized, Britain did not involve herself in Europe, the Russians would dominate there. If Britain did so involve herself, the Americans would dominate the Empire. The solution, said Attlee, was to persuade the Americans to take over a large share of the burden in Europe: then Europe could be made secure against Russian domination, and Britain could still preserve her Empire.

There were now so many ideas in circulation about the occupation of Germany and the structure of postwar Europe – the short-term and the long-term problem – that three Cabinet sub-committees were set up to coordinate them. Attlee was appointed chairman of all three. His most important contribution to the formulation of foreign policy during the rest of 1943 was as chairman of the Armistice Terms and Civil Administration Committee. Much work was done for it by the chiefs of staff, and in November their terms of reference were extended as a result of a recommendation to the War Cabinet by Attlee. In December they submitted a report to the committee on the structure of the occupation. Its most important recommendations were in line with Attlee's fundamentalist thinking about Germany: the occupation should be total – essential if Germany was to be disarmed and 'its military spirit broken'; the arms industries must be destroyed; there should be three zones of occupation – Berlin to be a tripartite zone – and, most important of all, Britain should occupy the northwestern zone, where nearly all the heavy industry was located. These recommendations formed the basis of Britain's policy, which was subsequently accepted almost completely by the Allies.

Attlee's Armistice Terms and Civil Administration Committee met several times in 1944, usually about Germany. Its minutes show Attlee to have been a strong chairman who expressed his own views in trenchant language. He was opposed to an occupied Germany being policed by Germans – law and order should be left to the occupation forces. He was opposed to giving the German armed forces, when at the end of the war they had been disarmed or had surrendered, status as prisoners of war: if they were given that status they could claim the protection of the Geneva Convention, which would put enormous pressure on food supplies. He was opposed to the Germans being given anything but the minimum humanitarian treatment: 'they had brought the war on themselves'.

In April 1944 the responsibilities of the committee were extended, and it was renamed 'the Armistice and Post-War Committee'. Known as the

APW it became the forum and clearing house for all decisions affecting Germany in particular and the postwar European settlement in general. It did not make decisions on policy – the War Cabinet did that – but since it formulated the issues and provided the information with which the War Cabinet was supplied, its influence in the making of decisions was immeasurable. Attlee remained in the chair. Churchill was not a member of it, Bevin was – 'it was on this all-important committee', says Bullock, 'that Bevin learned about foreign policy.' Though seven ministers were entitled to be invited to the committee, their participation varied. Attlee frequently went over their heads to the War Cabinet. In June he asked for the list of war criminals drawn up by Eden to be expanded: as well as Nazis, he said, generals who had ordered atrocities should be put on trial. But Attlee's main theme on the committee at this time was the need to ensure that the occupation terms would not be confined to disarming the Germans and then restoring 'normal life'. The occupation must root out Nazi influence and destroy the historic power of the Prussian Junkers and the Ruhr industrialists which were the props of German militarism, and had made Germany a menace to Europe in the 'normal period' before the Nazis were heard of. Those views brought him into conflict with Eden. Attlee complained that to judge by the papers being submitted to his committee, the Foreign Office was in favour of the occupation restoring 'normalcy'.

Bevin now made the radical suggestion that instead of working through the central governmental system of Germany as established by the Nazis, the occupying powers should administer the country through the individual states of Germany as these had been demarcated in Bismarck's day. Attlee was ready to agree. Central government was a Nazi creation, devised and structured to preserve and breed Nazism. He was all for any scheme which involved dismantling it.

These suggestions caused some rethinking in the Foreign Office, which by now was proceeding on the assumption that the existing German governmental systems would be maintained and that the occupation would be administered through three zones. The difference between the views now being canvassed by Attlee and those which the Foreign Office was working on raised the whole question of the 'dismemberment' of Germany, which Stalin was pressing for. Eden did not oppose this in principle, provided it was not imposed by force, and was sought by the Germans themselves. He was dubious, however, about any scheme which in the short term meant abolishing the central government, because without it, he believed, the tripartite control arrangement could not work. Attlee did not agree, and asked Eden to substantiate his view.

Before the matter was resolved Churchill and Eden met Roosevelt for the Quebec Conference in early September and Churchill had discussed the plan for the 'pastoralization' of Germany devised by Henry Morgenthau, the US Secretary of the Treasury, and strongly supported by Lord Cherwell. Attlee personally was strongly against the Morgenthau plan. He was prepared to see the Germans suffer, but not forced into economic ruin. Churchill, on the other hand, favoured the plan, and even though Attlee cabled to him at the Casablanca Conference stating the War Cabinet's objections he initialled the proposal. The following week Attlee took the matter up with his committee. They agreed that the proposals in the plan were impracticable, and called for a detailed official report on them. This appeared some weeks later, and was very critical. Then the plan was put quietly away.

Though he played his part in steering Churchill away from the Morgenthau plan, Attlee did not modify his view that Britain should be tough towards Germany and realistic towards Russia. In the autumn the British chiefs of staff began to consider carefully what plans should be made to deal with the postwar situation in Central Europe in the event of the Russians being uncooperative. What they feared most was that Russia might draw Germany into her orbit and thus dominate all Europe. British occupation of the northwest section of a zonally *divided* Germany, they argued, was therefore essential. Their views, naturally, were entirely acceptable to Attlee but not to Eden. The Foreign Office view was that Britain should *not* advocate any 'dismemberment' of Germany, and that the view that a part of Germany could be used 'against' Russia was irresponsible. Eden warned that if Stalin learned of such a ploy, and concluded that the British were organizing Germany against Russia, the very hostility which the chiefs of staff now only hypothesized would become a reality and the Anglo-Soviet Alliance, which was the linchpin of Anglo-Soviet relations, would be imperilled.

The issue between Attlee and the chiefs of staff on one side and Eden on the other did not come to a head, and later developments overtook it. But Attlee's committee, and the views he recorded as its chairman, continued to set the pace for the formulation of Britain's policy for postwar Germany. At the APW's committee meeting on the eve of the Yalta Conference in February 1945, Dalton pressed so hard for taking raw material and equipment from Germany for British use – and avowedly to emasculate Germany's industrial strength – that Lyttelton accused him of applying to Germany a modified kind of Morgenthau plan. By the time of the conference the British government had not worked out a comprehensive long-term policy for Germany. But its short-term policy was very much what Attlee had been advocating as a suitable long-term plan.

In the middle of 1944 Attlee began to advocate the creation of a Western European bloc. Churchill and Bevin took the view that the security of Western Europe could only be maintained by a world organization sustained and directed from within by a concert of Britain, Russia and the United States. The concept of the bloc apppealed to Attlee largely because he was concerned about the potential of the flying bombs now being launched by Germany into London from bases in the Low Countries. Britain's frontiers now lay in the Low Countries, Attlee argued, and in a Cabinet memorandum on 'Foreign Policy and the Flying Bomb' he insisted that as well as disarming Germany, and ensuring that she remained disarmed, Britain must impose some arrangement which would prevent a potential enemy from using Norway, Denmark, Holland and France as bases for the new form of air attack. 'We can only do this by bringing into the closest association with ourselves the countries which hold the keys of our fortress.' Within a general system of security as advocated by Bevin and Churchill 'there should be a close military alliance between Britain and the States above mentioned'.

Attlee's proposals for a Western European bloc were not accepted. Yet they proved to be more relevant to what was to happen in the late forties, when cooperation with the Soviet Union proved impossible, than the view of Churchill and Bevin that the security of Western Europe could be maintained by the concert of the three great powers. NATO was much more a relative of Attlee's brainchild in 1944 than of Churchill's – or Bevin's – thinking at that time.

II

Attlee's position as Churchill's deputy gave him considerable influence over war policy, especially towards France, as well as over discussions of postwar conditions. While Churchill was in Washington in May 1943, Anglo-American divisions about policy towards France came to another crisis, in which Attlee had to intervene to support Eden against Churchill and the Americans. De Gaulle was determined to set up a single Committee of National Liberation to take over the administration of France as the fighting line moved forward. The Americans, who like Churchill found de Gaulle prickly and self-willed, feared that he would refuse to cooperate with other French leaders or with Britain and America; they consequently preferred to set up Free French regimes in each locality as it was liberated. Churchill was in any case disposed as a matter of principle to agree with any of Roosevelt's proposals, and in late May he telephoned from Washington 'suggesting that his colleagues should urgently consider whether de Gaulle should not now be eliminated as a political force'.

The precipitating occasion had been the difficulty the Americans had experienced in bringing together de Gaulle and General Giraud, commander of the Free French in North Africa. On 23 May Attlee presided over a Cabinet which rejected Churchill's proposal. On this occasion the Attlee–Eden axis won: Churchill agreed to take no action until the two French generals had met. When they did so, they agreed to form a Committee of National Liberation on which both were represented.

Preparations in early 1944 for the invasion of France produced more differences of opinion between Churchill and Eden, and Attlee was drawn into them. On 30 March, the chiefs of staff had put up to the Prime Minister a request from Eisenhower for freedom to bomb railway targets in France by day and night in advance of D-Day, bombings which could involve high civilian casualties. Eden discussed the risks with Attlee, who agreed that Eisenhower's request should be refused. The chiefs of staff were told that the existing restrictions must be upheld. The Americans repeated their request. Attlee and Eden opposed the extension of bombing not only on humanitarian grounds but as a matter of policy: if the French people were antagonized by high civilian casualties they would be less disposed to cooperate with the Allies. Attlee felt strongly that the Americans should be restrained, with the full authority of the War Cabinet. To precipitate a decision he asked Eden on 27 April to give the Defence Committee an assessment of the political consequences this might have for British policy. The matter went to the War Cabinet, which decided to restrict targets to those where the estimated casualties were few.

Eisenhower suspended bombing on one third of his targets for ten days. From then on the Americans could not be restrained, but as a result of the pressure from Eden and Attlee they had re-estimated the amount of bombing they would need to do. When Eden sent a paper to him complaining about American policy, and to some extent supporting de Gaulle, Churchill became furious. 'Again soon after midnight W rang up in a rage because Bevin and Attlee had taken my view,' recorded Eden. 'He said that ... de Gaulle must go ... FDR and he [Churchill] would fight the world.' At the War Cabinet meeting the next day Attlee handled Churchill with great tact. He argued that since the Resistance groups represented on the French National Committee were influential among the French people, the more the allies could do to build up the prestige and authority of the committee the better. In this conflict Britain and America should try to avoid upsetting de Gaulle personally, difficult though he was. There was always the risk that if they did so they would give him a grievance, the result of which would be that they would consolidate his position in France and elsewhere, since the true facts of the situation could not of course be known.

Churchill agreed, and relations with de Gaulle got back on to an even keel. However, the sea was still stormy, and de Gaulle continued to complain about the dependence of British policies on those of the Americans. After the first landings had been made, he asked to be allowed to visit France at once. The Americans and the British finally agreed. Eden gave a dinner for him at the Foreign Office the night before he was to leave, and asked Attlee to attend. During the dinner Eden received a written message from the Prime Minister: Churchill now wanted to cancel de Gaulle's visit. Eden records: 'But the others present, and especially Attlee, supported me in maintaining the original decision.' De Gaulle went to France.

In a letter to Tom dated 8 June 1944 Attlee gives his own response to the invasion of Europe:

> We have been having exciting days lately. I was up in the small hours on the day of the landing at the Admiralty War Room, hearing of the progress of the Armada and then woke up at five to hear the sound of mighty wings continually beating overhead as the air force went in. I see that the Huguenots scattered old William the Conqueror's bones at Caen so he could not turn in his grave at time's revenges. Do you remember our walk in Normandy – Bayeux, Caen, Pont l'Eveque, Pont au de Mer to Quillebœuf?

In August he made his first visit to France after the invasion.

> The spirit of the French people was very good, the tricolour flying everywhere over the ruins while family groups of père et mère et bébé with the family bedding on a cart and small children leading the cows were to be seen on the roads returning to their homes and waving cheerfully to us as we passed.

III

Despite his interest in and influence over foreign policy, Attlee's main activity as Deputy Prime Minister lay with domestic policy. In 1943 he faced the opportunity, and the challenge, of bringing Labour's ideas to bear on postwar reconstruction: of facing Britain's future, and Labour's place in it. The vast increase of state intervention in the First World War owed more to German submarines than to Keir Hardie; when the blockade began to throttle Britain's food supplies even Churchill told the House of Commons he preferred 'War Socialism' to a negotiated peace. It was much the same in the Second World War, and national planning and national ownership, which in the period 1945–51 seemed the result of a Labour government putting socialist principles into effect, were to a great degree the legacy of a state which had been organized to fight a total war.

Owing to the number and influence of active socialists in the government or in the upper ranks of the temporary civil service, and to the strong socialist commitment of the trade union leaders in some of the basic industries, the solution to the nation's wartime planning problems was frequently coloured, if not fashioned, by socialist attitudes or objectives. Yet many of the wartime currents which flowed in the direction of a welfare state came from Liberal, Conservative and non-political sources, and emanated much less from theories about social organization than from a feeling that the poverty, ill health and injustice of the twenties and thirties could, and should, be eliminated, if not during the war, at least after the war was over.

Many emotional currents mingled with the rational to produce the great broad steady wave that bore Britain towards the welfare state far more effectively than any government of any complexion could have managed. Affection for Russia had for millions temporarily taken the curse off socialism, and admiration for the Russians' military success had given the lie to the claim that socialism was inherently inefficient. Rationing, the sharing of limited transport, common hardship, common suffering had created an atmosphere of communal spirit and egalitarianism, which though unselfconscious was none the less real. Even if they had not made any effort to profit by this, the Labour Party would have done much better than the Conservatives. When the Tories talked about the war, although they usually gave the impression that they were ready to die for their country, it was for *their* country, as it was, and as *they* had made it; whereas Labour men – and Attlee's speeches, already quoted, serve as an example – spoke of a new and better Britain to be created when the war was won.

Churchill's attitude to politics in the Second World War, compared with his attitude in the First, was blinkered. In the first war he faced the social implications of the military effort; in the second he regarded the military effort as a warrior only. Admitted that since he had to *run* the second war, and for more than two years faced nothing but military stalemate or defeat, his attitude was bound to be restricted, he took little interest in social policy and discouraged it in others. Of the Army Bureau of Current Affairs, which was intended to educate the forces in what the war was about, he observed that it seemed likely at best to take their minds off the fighting and at worst to fill them full of 'socialist' ideas and expectations. 'I hope you will wind up this business as quickly and decently as possible ...' Fed on report and gossip by Brendan Bracken, Churchill believed that socialists in high places were losing no opportunity of using the war to build a socialist Britain. He tried to counter this by instructing his personal assistants to supervise the activities of the 'home' committees and, as Attlee put it: 'Whatever they are doing, tell them to stop.'

Whenever Churchill got wind that a report or a memorandum on something outside his ken was coming up,' said Attlee, 'he would get somebody to spy out the land so that he could counter our machinations. He used to call this "getting a second, highly qualified and objective opinion on the issue". In fact what he wanted was a hatchet job.' In an essay on Churchill he wrote:

> First there was Old Man River – Cherwell. I got fed up with this. One day I said to Winston, 'if Cherwell is going to come in on these things let's have him on the Committee, and then he can scotch anything you want scotched at the start.' Winston thought this was an admirable idea, so Cherwell came on to the Committee. As soon as Cherwell was having full access to the facts he began to agree with us. Winston was quite incensed. So then he got another character whom he could use as a hatchet-man – old Beaverbrook ... but now the War was practically won, and it didn't matter.

Taking all this into account it is not hard to understand Attlee's surprise when in February 1942 Churchill told the Cabinet that he proposed to appoint as the next Archbishop of Canterbury William Temple, well known as a supporter of the Labour Party. After the Cabinet meeting Attlee accompanied Churchill to a lunch. On the way he asked why Churchill had appointed 'a Socialist' to the post. 'Because', said Churchill, 'he was the only half-a-crown article in a sixpenny bazaar.'

Attlee's attitude to the war and socialism was not Churchill's, but it was not as progressive as some of his Labour colleagues would have liked. In April 1942, discussing with the National Executive another of Laski's demands for progress towards socialist objectives, Attlee said that 'with his colleagues in the government he held the view that the Labour Party should not try to get socialist measures implemented under the guise of winning the war'. If the Labour ministers in the Cabinet behaved as Laski wished they would risk bringing the government down. 'What would be the effect on the Party if, in fact, it left the Government?' The general opinion would be 'that the Party had slipped out of responsibility when things looked black'. Attlee's views were so well received that the NEC did not put them to a vote. On the other hand, the Labour Party should recognize that the war would require reorganization, and make sure that such reorganization, where it was in line with socialist objectives, remained a permanent part of national life. His position on war and socialism is epitomized in an instruction for an insertion in the draft of a statement on Labour's Home Policy being prepared in early 1940. His covering note reads: 'For insertion in "Labour's Home Policy". Without this [the] document is purely futuristic. I want it linked with the present':

> Supreme interests of a nation at war compel the adoption of socialistic measures by a Government which does not accept the need for socialism. Planning and control needed for war should be undertaken with full realisation that there can be no return to old order as after last war. Take

occasion to lay foundations of planned economic system. Transport system and mining should be made national services now.

On 1 December 1942 the Beveridge Report appeared. Nominally it was the product of the Social Insurance Committee set up by the Ministry of Health in May 1941; in fact it was the work, almost unaided, of William Beveridge, the former director of the LSE and writer on unemployment, who had been put at the head of the committee because Bevin could not get on with him at the Ministry of Labour. Beveridge gave systematic shape to ideas about social security which had been current in the 1930s. Social insurance would be reorganized to provide a national minimum income. His proposals for it depended on three assumptions: a national health service, family allowances, and full, or nearly full, employment, for the level of which the state would take responsibility. His assumptions had far broader implications for the structure of society than the insurance scheme, taking the subject beyond the administrative context of the civil servants who sat with him on the committee, so he was told to sign the report himself as a personal document. Meanwhile the Treasury was discussing plans for the maintenance of peacetime employment which would eventually blossom in the Employment White Paper of 1944.

As Minister for Reconstruction, Greenwood had taken a keen interest in Beveridge's work and encouraged favourable publicity for the committee's early inquiries. Thus when the report appeared, it was the greatest non-war event of the war. Brendan Bracken, then Minister of Information, fearing the 'socialism' of the report, first tried to muffle it and then almost overnight changed his mind and exploited it as propaganda. Its publication coincided with the culmination of a series of victories – 'Torch', El Alamein, Stalingrad and Guadalcanal. The country had suddenly begun to think about the prospects of peace, and of what postwar Britain would be like.

The Beveridge Report appeared at the perfect moment. Its arrival, however, was not welcomed by Churchill. It would be unfair to say that he was opposed to all its contents, but he was suspicious of what it might lead to. Just as he had not become the King's First Minister in order to preside over the dissolution of the British Empire, he had not taken his seals of office to make Britain into a socialist state. While he did not swallow everything Brendan Bracken told him about the alleged socialist plotting of Dalton and his colleagues at the Ministry of Economic Warfare, he knew that Attlee believed that much of the planning and control which it was necessary to produce in war must be made permanent in the interests of making Britain into a socialist state.

Attlee had already made it clear that he saw the Beveridge proposals in this context. While Churchill had been away in Casablanca meeting

Roosevelt, Attlee had given a newspaper interview in which he said that far from social security being an alternative to socialism, 'Socialism does not admit an alternative, Social Security to us can only mean Socialism.' He went on to describe a sweeping social programme of which social security would only be a part. It included the redistribution of industry and the development of new communities, 'a better and brighter Britain ... a spring-cleaning to sweep away not only drab industrial areas and deceptive rural slums but scour the very air itself'. There must, Attlee said, be security against ill health, unemployment and old age, an adequate and steadily rising standard of living, a decent and well equipped house in healthy surroundings for every family, full and equal education, and complete medical care throughout life.

Bracken's original move to delay publication of the Beveridge Report and clamp down on official publicity immediately aroused suspicions that the report was to be pigeon-holed. Greenwood, now leader of the Labour backbenchers, called for a debate which was arranged for 16 February 1943. In preparation for this, Churchill circulated a memorandum which, though expressing no hostility to the report, rejected any attempt to implement it during the war or even make firm promises. He pleaded the constitutional impropriety of making such changes without an election. He spoke of the uncertainty about the country's economic position at the end of the war, which might mean a choice 'between social insurance and other urgent claims on limited resources', a line based on the Chancellor of the Exchequer's and Lord Cherwell's positions. Attlee knew that such an attitude would be intolerable to the Labour Party, and could provoke a revolt which might bring the government down. And he suspected that Churchill intended to keep the Beveridge plan in reserve until after the war had ended, and then present it to the voters as part of a Tory Party programme. He responded swiftly in a counter-memorandum to the Prime Minister:

> ... I doubt whether in your inevitable and proper preoccupation with military problems you are fully cognisant of the extent to which decisions must be taken and implemented in the field of post war reconstruction *before* the end of the war. It is not that persons of particular political views are seeking to make vast changes. These changes have already taken place. The changes from peacetime to wartime industry, the concentration of industry, the alterations in trade relations with foreign countries and with the Empire, to mention only a few factors, necessitate great readjustments and new departures in the economic and industrial life of the nation. When you speak of men returning to their jobs as one of the first essentials at the end of the war I agree, but without planning there won't be the jobs ...
>
> ... the doctrines set out in your note to me would destroy all hope of this country playing an effective part in carrying the world through the difficult period of transition.
>
> I am certain that unless the Government is prepared to be as courageous

in planning for peace as it has been in carrying on the war, there is extreme danger of disaster when the war ends. I doubt if any of our colleagues who have been giving attention to post war problems would be content with the mere preparation of paper schemes.

I do not think the people of this country especially the fighting men would forgive us if we failed to take decisions to implement them because of some constitutional inhibition. I am not concerned at the moment with the Beveridge Report and its merits or demerits, but with the general principle ...

My contention is that if, as I think is generally agreed, it is not possible at the present time to have a general election the Government and the present House of Commons must be prepared to take responsibility not only for winning the war but for taking the legislative and administrative action which is thought necessary for the post war situation.

The night before the debate the Cabinet met and Churchill made concessions to Attlee. It was agreed that though the government must not be *committed* to introducing legislation to reform the social services during the war, there was to be no commitment *against* such legislation being introduced during the life of the present government, and negotiations with various organizations and associations concerned could go ahead.

The debate on the Beveridge Report on 16 February was opened for the government by Anderson as Lord President of the Council. He failed to convey to the House that the government accepted most of the report in principle, and created a disastrously negative impression of the government's intentions. This was heightened on the following day by the Chancellor of the Exchequer's speech. The government could not make promises for postwar schemes, said Kingsley Wood, until it knew what money there would be in the till. The Labour rebels' amendment urging early implementation of the report was better received than had been anticipated. Shinwell asked whether, since 'the country as a whole has quite plainly made up its mind' that the report's recommendations 'ought to be implemented forthwith, will it not be desirable at once to start on this task?' The coalition now faced a crisis far more grave than the Wardlaw-Milne motion at the time of the fall of Tobruk eight months before. More than forty Tories, mostly of the Tory Reform Committee, led by Quintin Hogg and Hinchingbrooke, were rumoured to be ready to vote against the government. If they did, and if the Labour rebels voted with them, the government would be in serious trouble.

In a stormy meeting of the Parliamentary Labour Party Attlee and Morrison tried to persuade, Bevin bullied, but all three voiced the same theme: backbenchers must not vote against the government. In the debate Morrison, the most enthusiastic supporter of the Beveridge Report in the Cabinet, heroically wound up, defending a policy he had fought in Cabinet to improve. Bevin angered Labour backbenchers by his aggressive tone and language, and by threats that he would resign if Labour went into the lobby against the government. Attlee made one of his finest parliamentary performances – but to no avail. Though Conservatives and Liberals withdrew their amendments, the Labour backbenchers insisted on theirs being left on the table, and though it was defeated by 335 to 119 they registered the biggest parliamentary revolt of the war. Only twenty-three Labour MPs supported the government, and twenty-two of these were ministers; ninety-seven voted against it, and another thirty or so abstained. Attlee told Tom, in his first letter for nearly four months:

> The Beveridge debate was not a good show though Morrison was first class. On these questions so many of our fellows good men not mischief makers tend to use their hearts to the exclusion of their heads. There was also a certain desire to vote against the Government as an answer to the vote on the Catering Wages Bill. But also I fear our people cannot ever understand when they've won. In fact they really prefer 'a glorious defeat' in the lobbies to victory. However no doubt it will all blow over.

Yet Attlee could not ignore the fact that the bulk of the Labour Party in the House had voted not only against the government but against its own leaders. Some formal action was required; the situation required at least discussion of whether disciplinary action should be taken, though for a handful of leaders to attempt to discipline a large majority whose disobedience had been expressed within proper party procedure would obviously present great difficulties.

The most intractable problem was Ernest Bevin's attitude. Bevin as a trade union leader worked on the principle that once his union had made an agreement with an employer that agreement must be honoured. In his view the Labour Party had made such an agreement when it supported the entry of its leaders into the coalition government. Those Labour MPs who had rebelled against the Labour leaders in the Beveridge debate were therefore traitors. He demanded their heads, and when Attlee pointed out that they could not be delivered Bevin became irate. On the Monday after the debate Attlee called a meeting of all Labour ministers to discuss what should be said when the Parliamentary Party met later in the week to discuss the implications of the Beveridge vote. Bevin, in a belligerent mood, said that in voting for the government against the PLP's decision to oppose it he had contravened the Labour Party's Standing Orders: therefore the PLP must either expel him or publicly acquit him. He then stalked out of the meeting. His twenty colleagues were nonplussed. If the PLP expelled Bevin it would have to expel the other twenty. If it 'acquitted' Bevin it would have to 'acquit' twenty others. Either course would be farcical.

Fortunately the situation was resolved the next day by the Parliamentary Party's Administrative Committee, which decided to defend its decision to go into the lobby against the government on only two grounds: first, that it had only behaved like the Tories who had voted against Bevin's Catering Wages Bill less than a fortnight before; secondly, that the offending amendment was not meant as a vote of censure, but only to assist the Labour ministers by creating pressure from outside. This explanation was acceptable to all except Bevin. The National Council of Labour, the Parliamentary Party and the National Executive of the Labour Party all met, and decided to take no disciplinary action. All they did was reaffirm support for the Beveridge Report. But from now almost to the last year of the war Bevin, who could not tolerate accusations of disloyalty, suspended relations with the Labour Party, though his relationship with Attlee was unaffected.

There was one more revolt linked with the Beveridge Report before in Michael Foot's words 'the Parliamentary Party relapsed into acquiescence'. In May 1943, on the eve of the annual party conference, forty Labour MPs, led by Aneurin Bevan, put down a motion condemning a government pensions bill on the grounds that it offered no increase. Their leaders pleaded with them that piecemeal increases granted now would jeopardize the chances of pensions being comprehensively examined and improved in the light of the report. Bevan and his supporters refused to withdraw, and fifty-nine of them voted against the government: they were duly rebuked at the party meeting. In the midsummer Gallup polls, after Churchill had made an unconvincing broadcast about the coalition's attitude to postwar reconstruction, Labour registered an 11 per cent lead over the Conservatives.

The 1943 Labour Party conference opened on 14 June at Central Hall, Westminster. At the time there was much rejoicing in the country – the German Army in Tunisia had surrendered and Germany was now being bombed on an unprecedented scale – but the atmosphere at the conference was one of frustration and anxiety. The fate of the Beveridge Report had deepened suspicions that so long as the coalition lasted the Labour Party would not be able to exploit the movement of public opinion towards reform and reconstruction which the polls had been recording for months, and the general improvement of the Allies' military situation gave rise to feelings that Labour could now afford to pull out. Aneurin Bevan and his supporters complained bitterly about the Labour leaders' attitude on many domestic issues – coal, old age pensions, the Beveridge Report, town and country planning, and other questions of postwar reconstruction. On foreign policy, the future of Europe and the world, they protested, Churchill and Eden did all the talking: Attlee said nothing.

In reply to this attack, moving acceptance of the Executive's report on 'The Labour Party and the Future', Attlee was able to describe the great changes which had taken place, in the war and on the home front, since the Bournemouth conference three years before. 'How welcome then would have been the knowledge that we should have received the surrender of 250,000 of our enemies; that Africa had been cleared of our enemies, that it is now the turn of our enemies to talk fearfully of invasion.' Labour's leaders had participated in the government which had brought these changes about, and the British people would remember them for it:

> I doubt if we recognise sufficiently the progress our ideas have made. The British never know when they are beaten, and British socialists seldom know when they have won.

He went on to make a statement of which not much notice was taken at the time – it was flatly contradicted by Bevan and the left – but which was to be proved prophetic two years later:

> The people of this country will not forget that some of the most onerous posts in Government have been held by Labour men who have shown great ability, ability to administer and courage to take unpopular decisions.... We have a body of men and women who are experienced in administration and have proved themselves fit to govern. Had we remained merely a body of critics who left others to do the work, the Party would not have gained the respect and confidence of the country which I know it has today.

Morrison wound up for the Executive. By now he was very popular in the country; for eight months he had been making stirring speeches about postwar reconstruction. His support of the war effort in Cabinet had appealed to Churchill. Beaverbrook wrote to him: 'Churchill apart, you are today by far the biggest figure in the country.' He now moved to strengthen his position in the Labour Party, resigning from the Constituency section of the NEC to run for the post of party treasurer.

This time it was Ernest Bevin who cooked his goose. Bevin's personal hostility towards Morrison had become more marked since Morrison had been brought into the War Cabinet eight months previously. The two men sat on either side of Eden, facing Churchill and Attlee on the other side of the oval table. Eden told the author that he was frequently embarrassed by the audible comments, some in very poor taste, which Bevin made while Morrison was addressing his colleagues. Morrison was meant to hear them, did, was obviously hurt, but never said anything in reply. What he resented most, and deserved least, were Bevin's innuendoes that Morrison was espousing the cause of postwar reconstruction in order to displace Attlee as leader of the party. Bevin was not at the party conference but he controlled the Transport and General Workers' vote. He used it to ensure that Morrison was defeated by Arthur Greenwood, and Morrison, now off the Executive altogether, was laid low. Bevin also used his influence with trade union leaders to secure a solid vote in favour of continuing the electoral truce; and the Executive's position on the Beveridge Report was upheld, though without a great majority.

At the end of the conference Attlee and his Labour colleagues in government could feel that their authority, which was much shaken at the time of the Beveridge debate, was to a great extent restored. Attlee's own position was much stronger: Bevin was on very bad terms with the party, Morrison, without an Executive seat, had no position, and Cripps, a comet only a few months previously, was now scarcely visible.

IV

In September 1943 Kingsley Wood, the Chancellor of the Exchequer, died and was succeeded by Sir John Anderson. Attlee took over as Lord President of the Council. He now occupied the key position on the home front.

Pressure on the government to announce specific policies for the postwar period was rapidly mounting on both sides of the House. In Cabinet, on 14 October, Attlee warned his colleagues that decisions about postwar planning should not be postponed on the grounds that conditions at the end of the war could not currently be foreseen: decisions should be taken on the basis of the best assumptions that could be made about those conditions. There would probably, he said, be a large measure of agreement on many questions between ministers of different political parties. The government must shortly make statements to demonstrate that problems of postwar planning were being faced.

Churchill was somewhat put out. Attlee's predecessor, Anderson, had never talked like this, and what Attlee said was strongly endorsed by Morrison and Bevin. Churchill's ability to resist them was much reduced, since he no longer had Kingsley Wood to support his objections to postwar projects with the financial authority of the Chancellor of the Exchequer and the political authority of a leading Conservative. In any case he felt his overriding responsibility was to harmonize policies between the Americans and the Russians. More and more of his time was being taken up with conferences overseas. He realized that he would have to some extent to give Attlee what he wanted. Initially he went only so far as to promise that he would consider any matter which Attlee brought up where it could be shown that necessary preparations for dealing with postwar problems were being held up for lack of decisions by the War Cabinet. This was not enough for Attlee. A large number of non-partisan questions affecting trade and industry, he told Churchill, not party issues, urgently required action now; he was not going 'to wait for them to be held up' before he was allowed to bring them to Churchill's attention. Churchill felt bound to yield more ground. He asked for a list of four or five major projects on which progress could be made at once.

Attlee provided this. As a result, though he made it clear that he was anxious to avoid specific promises about policy in the postwar period, Churchill circulated a memorandum on 19 October 1943 entitled 'War – Transition – Peace', listing five urgent postwar tasks: a demobilization scheme; food; export trade; conversion of industry from war to peace; 'And above all the provision, during a transition period, of employment ... especially for ex-Servicemen'. In view of what had happened in Cabinet on 14 October, one paragraph of Churchill's memorandum was particularly significant: he accepted that, on food and employment, measures 'must be taken now, whether they involved legislation and whether they are controversial or not'.

Churchill, at the beginning of November, pledging himself to the provision of 'food, work and homes for all', reluctantly appointed a Minister of Reconstruction with a seat in the Cabinet, and agreed to set up a new Cabinet Committee on Reconstruction, of which the new minister would take the chair. By now he was anxious not to appear opposed to measures for postwar reconstruction, but wanting as little action as possible he proposed Beaverbrook for the post. Attlee pointed out that such an appointment would 'have to be made over Bevin's dead body'. The appointment went to Lord Woolton. A businessman without a political record, he had been brought into the government as Minister of Food, and had been a great success. According to his memoirs, Churchill persuaded him on the grounds that he had the great advantage of being regarded as independent and yet known to be strongly anti-socialist. Attlee had known Woolton since as young men they had been welfare workers. Beaverbrook was one kind of anti-socialist, Woolton quite another, and Attlee welcomed the appointment.

To persuade Churchill to set up the new Reconstruction Committee, and to appoint Woolton instead of Beaverbrook as Minister for Reconstruction, was a great achievement for Attlee. That this was so was well attested by Churchill himself in a note which he prepared for Attlee but which he did not apparently send:

> A solid mass of four socialist politicians of the highest quality and authority, three of whom are in the War Cabinet, all working together as a team, very much dominates this Committee.... I feel very much the domination of these Committees by the force and power of your representatives when those members who come out of the Conservative quota are largely non-Party or have little political experience or Party views.

The members of the Reconstruction Committee knew that they had to work within the field of agreement which was possible between the parties, indeed which was known to exist between the majorities of the parties. Attlee was opposed to attempting ambitious strides forward which might either split the committee or result in vague compromises which both sides would find it hard to defend to their parties in the House.

The model of what the committee achieved, though the project had been in train before the committee was formed, was the Education Act of 1944. Reasonably known as the Butler Act, since R.A. Butler, as Minister of Education, urged the bill on Churchill in 1941, it was the fruit of the cooperation of Butler for the Conservatives and his under-secretary Chuter Ede for Labour, and of the care they took to make its contents palatable to each other's parties in the House, the main features of the Act having been worked out by civil servants in the Ministry of Education long before Butler became their head. 'Its provisions', Butler writes, 'were broadly acceptable to moderate and progressive Conservative opinion and consistently supported by Labour men. . . . *The Times* noted that in a two-day debate on the White Paper "not a single voice was raised in favour of holding up or whittling down any of the proposals for educational advance".'

Going through the committee stages before it became law, the bill, however, ran into heated controversy, and at the end of March 1944 the government was defeated by one vote (117 to 116) on an amendment by Mrs Cazalet-Keir proposing equal pay for women teachers. In the Cabinet Attlee shared Churchill's indignation at a situation which he said was 'a culmination of a course of irresponsible conduct pursued by certain members of the House'. He asked for the matter to be treated as a major issue of confidence. It was, and on a vote of confidence a few hours later the earlier result was reversed and the offending amendment was withdrawn.

V

If he had received Churchill's note complaining of the socialists in the Reconstruction Committee 'all working together as a team', Attlee might have permitted himself a wry smile. Conflicts between his colleagues did not diminish as Labour got more of a grip on planning reconstruction. On the contrary, as the prospect of carrying out socialist policies in the postwar period came nearer, socialist ministers became more concerned to get to the centre of power. Among his papers is a letter from Dalton, 22 October 1943. Dalton was much 'bucked by yesterday's Cabinet. . . . I enclose a short note, as promised, on what I have been doing, in relation to Cherwell's agenda. *I . . . bluntly press that I should sit on any Committee which has to deal with those Transition problems* – and they are a *substantial number* – *which concern the Board of Trade.* (I don't ask to be in on "Beveridge").'

Meanwhile Bevin's animosity towards Morrison, always simmering and never concealed, boiled up in November 1943, a week or two after Morrison had announced that Sir Oswald Mosley, who had been interned under the Defence Regulations, was being released on the grounds of ill health. As foreseen, the decision excited controversy. The Labour Party Executive passed a resolution expressing regret; the National Council of Labour and the TUC General Council dissociated themselves from Morrison's action. Bevin threatened in Cabinet to resign if Mosley was not reinterned. Attlee joined Anderson in supporting Morrison. Bevin's outburst was not backed by any of the Cabinet, and when he had calmed down he changed his mind and voted with other ministers on 1 December for Mosley's release. Attlee's personal view was clearly put in a letter to Tom:

We are fighting for the British idea of the supremacy of law and against the conception that an Executive can keep anyone in quod whom they don't like. How often have not you and I heard old Blimps talk about damned Labour agitators causing strikes and how they would like to imprison or shoot the swine. Its quite natural and it happens on the Continent but not here. The real test of one's belief in the doctrine of Habeas Corpus is not when one demands its application on behalf of one's friends but of one's enemies.

In the first half of 1944 the government suffered a number of by-election defeats. On 9 January Shipton, a Conservative seat, fell to the Commonwealth Party, a radical group founded by Sir Richard Acland in 1942, which had won many middle-class converts and appealed to Labour supporters who did not care for reactionary local Tories thrust upon them as 'government' candidates and, under the electoral pact, officially supported by the Labour Party. A month later, the Conservative majority at Brighton was reduced from 40,000 to 2,000 by an Independent. Two weeks later the Duke of Devonshire's son lost West Derbyshire, the family seat. The national mood was one of impatience and disappointment. The previous year had been a year of victories, but these now seemed not to have led to the 'sunlit uplands' which Churchill had pointed to at the time.

If the nation was dissatisfied with the government, the Labour Party was dissatisfied with its leadership. Attlee hit back hard against his critics. Speaking at West Hartlepool on 30 January he observed that:

If you were to write down all the social advances that have taken place in the last three years and nine months and then travel back in time to 1937, and come down to Hartlepool and make a speech demanding all these things, it would have been considered a pretty big demand, and if someone had told you you were going to get them, you would have been very pleased.

In a series of speeches over the next four months he emphasized both the opportunities and the responsibilities which Labour had won by entering the government, and appealed to Labour supporters to stand firm behind their leaders. 'Those who belong to a great Party such as ours, which aspires to power so that we may bring about great changes, cannot tread the primrose path of independence.'

At this stage the Labour Party was shaken by another major clash between Bevin and Bevan. During the winter of 1943-4 negotiations for a new minimum wage in the coalfields had culminated in widespread miners' strikes, which reached their peak in March. Bevin, by a combination of negotiation and public threats, got the miners back to work by mid-April 1944 and signed a new wage agreement on 20 April. He remained convinced that such strikes, however just the cause, were 'worse than if Hitler had bombed Sheffield'; and accordingly he drafted an amendment to the Defence Regulations which gave the government additional powers to deal with incitement to strike in the essential services. Aneurin Bevan fulminated against Bevin for acting on a matter of individual liberty without first bringing it before the House of Commons. The government agreed to a debate. Attlee did his best to prevent another split in Labour's ranks. This was no time for another internecine clash like the one over the Beveridge Report. Attlee persuaded Bevin to attend a PLP meeting on the eve of the debate – it was the first time he had come to one since he had walked out of the discussion about the Beveridge Report, sixteen months previously.

The attempt to sweeten the critics did not succeed. Next day, in the House, Bevan went for Bevin tooth and nail: the Minister of Labour had been unjust to the miners and he had undermined the sovereignty of Parliament. He had behaved as though all that was necessary to govern the country was to square the union leaders and the employers. When the time came for the vote, his 'prayer' was defeated by 314 to 23 (16 of the 23 being Labour votes), but only 56 Labour MPs out of 165 voted for the Regulations. 'Bevin knows,' Bevan claimed afterwards, 'that my 23 represent more trade unionists in the country than his 314.' This clash was to influence future events within the Labour Party. Bevin and the union leaders never forgave Bevan for accusing them of betraying the miners and undermining the constitution.

Attlee decided that disciplinary action was required. He talked to Greenwood, still leader of the official Opposition. A special meeting was called to discuss Bevan's expulsion. The attendance was the highest since the heyday of the second Labour government in 1929. Attlee made it clear that he endorsed the recommendation for expulsion. Once he had declared himself, he did not press. Greenwood behaved in the same way. Shinwell then introduced an amendment; the question of expulsion should be shelved pending discussion between the PLP and the NEC. This was carried by 71 to 60. By no means all of the Parliamentary Party wanted to vindicate Bevin against Bevan: some of them had suffered in their time from Bevin's bullying and, in attacking him, Aneurin Bevan was in a sense revenging them.

Following the joint meeting, the National Executive passed a resolution 'deploring the action of Mr Aneurin Bevan in deliberately flouting decisions of the Parliamentary Party and thereby causing disunity within its ranks', and permitted him to remain in the party only on condition that within a week he would promise that in future he would obey the party's Standing Orders. Bevan complied, stating publicly, however, that he chose to remain in the Labour Party only because there were 'elements in the Party which wish to continue association with the Tories when the war is over [and] I refuse to allow myself to be manœuvred out of the party and thus leave them with a clear field in which to accomplish the ruin of the Labour Movement.'

VI

In the Reconstruction Committee, ministers were now dealing with the White Paper on employment policy. The Labour ministers wanted the government to make an uncompromising commitment to full employment. Bevin, with Dalton's support, threw all his weight into securing two objectives – built-in Keynesian proposals to deal with recessions by maintaining or increasing government expenditure, and state power over the location and development of industry. Attlee's views on both had been formed, as we have seen, as far back in time as his period as chancellor of the duchy of Lancaster in 1930.

The White Paper had taken some time to materialize and its ideas were of mixed parentage. Beveridge had made full (or nearly full) employment one of the three assumptions on which his social insurance scheme was based, and had therefore taken a great interest in its preparation. After the publication of the Beveridge Report, the temporary civil servants in the economic section of the War Cabinet had started work on a Keynesian approach to the problem, and their findings came before the new Reconstruction Committee in January 1944. The arguments between the Keynesians in the economic section of the Cabinet and the Hendersonians in the Treasury (who thought that structure not finance was the key to high employment) was reflected by arguments between Labour and Tory leaders in the Reconstruction Committee.

The White Paper on employment was not a plan, or even a set of proposals; it was a point of view for the long and short term, but one which committed the government to action on Keynesian lines if large-scale unemployment threatened. It postulated the manpower shortage which would have to be faced in the first years of the postwar period, in which industry would have to be converted from war to peace, and the need therefore to retain some of the major wartime controls over the movement of labour and the location of industry. There was enough 'socialism' in its recommendations to antagonize most Tories, and enough provision for the priming of the private enterprise pump to annoy the Labour rank and file. 'Sham' was an epithet used by both back benches and, unlike the Beveridge Report, the White Paper on employment did not excite the popular imagination.

Bevin moved its adoption in the House of Commons a week after D-Day. If he had expected that on this occasion at least he would receive a sympathetic cheer from the Labour benches he was to be disappointed. On the contrary, it was his own backbenchers who led the attack. They told him that he had sold out to the capitalists. Where was the White Paper's socialism? Where was the New Order which Labour had been demanding for fifty years? In one of his most devastating parliamentary speeches, Aneurin Bevan accused Bevin of rejecting the solutions to which socialists had been committed for years. Bevin was proposing an empirical approach to the problems of unemployment; but socialists believed in the intervention of the state in the organization of industry as a matter of principle. If the panaceas described in the White Paper would work, Bevan said, there was no reason for the existence of the Labour Party: 'There is no longer any justification for this Party existing at all.' Nearly every other Labour speaker in the debate took Bevan's line: capitalism and unemployment were symbiotic. Unemployment could only be cured by socialism. Tory backbenchers added fuel to the fire by congratulating Bevin for having come to terms with private enterprise.

Attlee's position was the same in relation to the White Paper as it was to progress on all sections of the domestic front at all times. His own tactic was to preach Labour Party *general* objectives in public, but never to be so specific as to offend his Tory colleagues in the Cabinet: in Cabinet he pressed as hard as he could for measures which would build the apparatus of a socialist state without attaching socialist labels to them which would incite his Tory colleagues to oppose them as a matter of political principle. His temperament enabled him to carry out this strategy, Ernest Bevin's did not. After working hard and long on a social or economic problem with a pragmatic approach similar to Attlee's, a jibe in the House could sting Bevin to a furious attack on socialist doctrinaires which upset his own party, or to expostulations that nobody was doing more for socialism than he was, which upset the Tories. He frequently antagonized both parties in the same debate. Such occasions created special problems for Attlee. The debate on employment was one of them.

He did not think that Bevan was taking the right public line on the White Papers, but he had misgivings about Bevin's also. To the public it seemed that Bevin was putting pressure on Bevan, Bevin on Bevan. In fact, Attlee, as was so often the case, was under pressure from both.

Holding the party together, never an easy task, was now becoming much more difficult. The frustrations of three years of 'artificial' opposition, combined with years of expectation that the war would soon be over, created a demand for Labour to leave the government and go it alone. Feeling was rapidly mounting in the PLP that Labour could make no progress until there was a general election. As speculation about Labour leaving the coalition mounted, so did the discussion of who would lead it best in a fight for possession of 'the commanding heights'. Many Labour MPs thought that Attlee lacked that appeal to the electors without which nobody could hope to beat Churchill. There is something of that implication in the otherwise very favourable profile of him in *The Observer* on 5 May 1944.

> At Cabinet meetings the Deputy Prime Minister always sits on the edge of his chair. The trick is typical of the man. It is the sign of a diffidence, a lack of confidence, perhaps better, a modesty, that must be almost unique in high politics.
>
> Yet this is the man who, on merit, is wartime Number 2 to Mr Churchill of all people. The debt owed to loyal Clem Attlee by the Prime Minister, the country, and the Labour Party is big. The post of Deputy Prime Minister was literally made for him and he for it; he fills it without envy.
>
> Outside the Councils of State, too, Mr Attlee is true to type. He is almost anonymous. Slight in figure, he does not stand out in a crowd. Thin in voice, he is at a disadvantage in this Broadcasting Age. He is the forgotten Minister who four years ago brought in the forgotten Bill to put all persons and all property at the nation's disposal.
>
> How is it that he can be called the 'brace' of the Cabinet? Back in the Cabinet room, or at Party meetings, the answer is plainer. Puffing at his pipe, he puts sound points well and simply. He is no colourful figure or champion of stirring causes; he is the impeccable Chairman – at a time when both Cabinet and Party, ill-sorted and on edge, much need a Chairman. Clem Attlee is the honest broker, the good man who came to the aid of his Party. The fact is, the Labour Party distrusts leadership. The case of Ramsay MacDonald frightened it. Nor does anyone, inside or outside the Party, know where it wishes to be led. All that is certain is that the motley group has somehow to be held together. Clem Attlee is neither bigot, doctrinaire, Labour boss, nor careerist. He puts the whole before the parts. He is a Party man, not a partisan. So he keeps the caravan in line. Can he go on doing so now the crack of the whip by Ernest Bevin is resented.
>
> There, in Downing Street, is indeed a Leader. Mr Churchill needs a Chairman for the humdrum essential work of government. The Deputy Prime Minister is also Lord President of the Council, Chairman of the

Ministerial Committee that sits on home affairs. He is, in these offices, the first-class captain of a first-class cricket side who is not himself a headliner. He makes men work together. He is a political catalyst.

Historians will give Clem Attlee his due, even under the shadow of Churchill, for he, too, in his own way, is equally an English worthy, though not a Great one. But they will also show how his worth to us in our tangled counsels of these days is a reflection of today's discontents and frustrations. Beneath the surface of politics there is a deep surge towards progressive ways. But there is no channel to take it. The head men are too busy shoring up the banks of the old ones. While Churchill wages war, his Chairman keeps the peace behind the lines. The one, co-ordinating much more than creative, is at least as much a man of his times as the other, the captain general.

Indeed the committee men and the collective bargainers, Sir John Anderson, Clem Attlee and Ernest Bevin, typify our state more even than the fighting Winston Churchill – road menders – not road-builders, conservatives in the true sense of the word. The fire has not gone from the people; it has from the politicians. Clem Attlee is a Fabian; it is an infinite progress to the Brave New World he believes in. But his faith is at least real; he is a man of character.

'I am glad you liked the *Observer* Profile,' he wrote to Tom. 'I don't know who did the text, but a man came round to do the sketch.'

16

The End of the Coalition, 1944-5

During August and September 1944, pressures mounted on the Labour Party leadership to leave the coalition. It was generally expected that the war would be won by Christmas: the Normandy expedition had broken out of the bridgehead, Paris was liberated, there were landings in the South of France, and the Soviet Army had driven the Germans out of Russia and back into Romania and Poland. The clamour for Labour to free its hand for a general election rose as never before. Tory back-benchers were also restive; where Labour members feared that social legislation agreed by coalition leaders was not going far enough, Tories thought it was going too far.

Back-bench reaction to the Uthwatt Report on Town and Country Planning and the bill introduced in June 1944 well illustrates the difficulty. The party conference was committed to the Uthwatt Report, which advocated the control of building and the nationalization of development rights in underdeveloped land, and which was to become the basis of Labour's 1947 Town and Country Planning Act. The 1944 bill postponed until after the war all large questions, concentrating on the rehabilitation of blitzed areas. Particularly because it did not face the issue of nationalization, the left wing of the Labour Party condemned it roundly. 'Soon', said Aneurin Bevan, 'there will be no escape from the grim alternatives looming up before the Labour Party. It will have to abandon either its principles or its leaders.' Substitute 'Conservative Party' for 'Labour Party', and many Tories would have said the same. The corollary of such discontent on both sides of the House was the end of the coalition and a general election.

Concern about the coalition consensus was not confined to the Labour Party dissidents. Some of its leaders were worried. Cripps wrote to Attlee on 27 September 1944 that he was 'very concerned' about a paper on

'Economic Controls in the Transition' which was to be discussed at a meeting of the Reconstruction Committee which Cripps could not attend. The paper implied, Cripps said, the '"return to normalcy" which wrecked the situation after the last war'. Cripps believed that 'Controls should be regarded ... as an essential fact of the permanent full employment policy and the transition period should be used for adapting our wartime controls – based on shortage of manpower – to a form suitable for peace time when we contemplate the likelihood of an excess of manpower.'

Comparable exchanges were being conducted between Beaverbrook and Bracken on the one hand, and Anderson and Butler on the other. In view of these pressures and of speculation and misleading reports in the press, Churchill and Attlee decided that they should make an agreed public statement on the duration of the coalition. Churchill suggested it should last six months; Attlee argued for a longer period, on the grounds that a short lease would be likely to excite party feeling, and encourage the public to expect a quicker end to the war than seemed likely on the basis of the present state of knowledge. On 27 September the Cabinet consequently decided to prolong Parliament for a year as from 28 November 1944.

In the three weeks which preceded the Cabinet of 27 September, Attlee moved with a dispatch and decisiveness which subjected him to the criticism of some of his senior colleagues, especially Ernest Bevin. He personally drafted the declaration of the pros and cons of Labour remaining in the coalition, of which he later wrote so proudly to his brother: 'For a wonder it was accepted practically unaltered. It has the merit of brevity, a virtue not often found in the drafts of Transport House.' It was indeed 'a wonder' that the document was accepted. Each of the two contending factions within the party could have claimed from the document that they had won: Attlee's draft discussed how Labour could get out while insisting that Labour should stay in. Without first showing it to Bevin, Morrison or Cripps, he submitted it to the National Executive of the Labour Party, which adopted it immediately and decided to publish it at once in order to ensure that when the Cabinet met to decide on a prolongation period Attlee would have the full authority of the Labour Party behind him. On 9 September, the day of publication, he sent it to Bevin and Morrison:

> I should be glad if you would glance through the enclosed and let me know by bearer whether you have any major objection.
> The position is that we had not wished to make any statement now about the future but there have been so many mischievous statements in the Press that our hands have been forced. I drafted the enclosed in anticipation and it has received the general approval of the National Executive subject to

the consideration of detail by a small Committee. I said that you and Herbert ought to be consulted and this was agreed to. As you cannot attend the Committee I thought it right to give you a chance of seeing it as it is to go out tonight. I think that it fairly covers the situation.

Bevin's response, written in longhand with a fist apparently shaking with anger, was swift:

This seems to me an amazing Procedure, all your Government colleagues except two or three of us left entirely in the Dark until they read it in the Press, a strange method to maintain loyalty. I do not like the draft of the Document at all. You have tried to state two Problems in one document upon which we shall be torn to pieces. I have had only five minutes to study it. I did not even know such a publication was contemplated, frankly I don't like it.

For all Bevin's displeasure, Attlee's behaviour was perfectly proper: the NEC had decided to put Labour into the coalition in 1940, and it was for the NEC to decide whether, and on what terms, it should now get out.

Attlee continued to exhibit pride in the government's record. Two important developments in late September gave him an opportunity of adding to his praise of Labour's contributions. Two White Papers had been published setting out the government's plans for implementing Beveridge: the first on social insurance, published on the twenty-sixth; the second on industrial injury insurance the following day. In a speech, on 8 October, to a Labour conference at Millom in Cumberland, he said:

These proposals, the most far-reaching and comprehensive ever submitted by a responsible Government, have had in all quarters a very good reception. ... This scheme has been worked out by a Government of all Parties. I doubt whether having regard to the magnitude of the work, it could have been done by any one Party with any hope of getting general acceptance. All Parties have collaborated. The initiating of the scheme and the setting Sir William Beveridge to work on it were due to Arthur Greenwood ... for the acceptance of the underlying conception of the scheme, the nation is mainly indebted to the Labour Movement.

Attlee and Bevin were now agreed that it was desirable to finish the war before Labour left the coalition and a general election was held, and that prior to such an election Labour should not press for major changes in policy or legislation which would involve a showdown with their Conservative colleagues. Morrison, on the other hand, was beginning to change his mind about meeting the need for 'socialist' legislation in the interests of preserving harmony in the coalition – much to the disgust of Bevin, who interpreted Morrison's new line as preparation for another bid for the party leadership. In October Morrison produced a memorandum outlining 'a great national plan of capital re-equipment and technical reorganisation' which involved a major extension of public control in the reorganization of the principal industries, to which Bevin reacted with what was almost a snub: 'When the Leader puts a policy before all of us we shall have to give it our serious consideration.'

Whatever Bevin thought, the party rank and file wanted progress, and the party conference was to take place in December. So in November 1944 Attlee produced a memorandum of his own, containing proposals covering the same ground as Morrison's, which he discussed at 11 Downing Street on the 22nd with Morrison, Bevin and Dalton.

Bevin did not like these proposals either: tactically, because they would expose the extent of disagreement in the Cabinet, strategically, because to set up the sort of organization suggested would prejudice the whole of the plans for the socialization of industry. 'I myself am being forced to the conclusion that a country run by a series of London Transport Boards would be almost intolerable' – a dig at Morrison, who as Minister of Transport (1929-31) had produced a bill to set up the LTB. 'The only real way', Bevin wrote to Attlee the same day, 'to bring these big basic industries to serve the public is not to apologise for the State but to come right out for state ownership. ... This is not the time and this is not the Cabinet to take that course. We must have the general public behind us and a clear idea of what we are going to do if we are to face the most formidable opposition we shall undoubtedly meet.' Dalton shared this view. Though unrepentant, Morrison could do little against the opposition of his senior colleagues, and after the conference he wrote on 20 December to Attlee withdrawing the suggestion that his ideas should be put before the Cabinet. The letter, which starts 'My dear Clem', ends: 'I am sending copies of this letter to Bevin and Dalton.' (No Christian names for them.) 'Yours sincerely, Herbert Morrison.'

The episode of Morrison's memorandum left Attlee in a strong position. He had shown Morrison that he was willing to submit a major proposal for industrial reorganization to the Cabinet, even going so far as to prepare a draft himself, based on Morrison's proposals. He had then submitted the draft to his senior colleagues in the Labour Party, and, saying very little himself, had watched them, as he knew they would, rapidly decide that no action should be taken. His own position, therefore, remained uncompromised. What happened to Morrison's memorandum was typical of what was to happen many times again. It was part of Attlee's formula for managing the strong men in his postwar Cabinet.

Meanwhile, the government had to face the debate on the Address, and the Labour ministers had to face the annual conference a few days later. In Cabinet on 30 November, where Attlee offered Churchill the Cabinet's seventieth birthday congratulations, agreement was reached on the line to be taken in the debate: the government intended to make as much progress as possible with the legislative programme, including reconstruction, but the extent of progress would depend on matters outside the government's control.

The debate opened on 5 December. For the Parliamentary Labour Party James Griffiths made a reasoned and eloquent criticism of the government for the delays in introducing new legislation, and pressed for more and speedier action. He restated the need to end the coalition as soon as possible, but accepted that this was not immediately feasible. In that case, he said, there was all the more need for speedy action on the legislation which the government had already agreed to:

> I have been in this House of Commons in one day's sitting in which forty measures were passed, because there was the sense of urgency. Are we going to send a message to the people of this country that we are only going to tackle business quickly when there is a war, that this instrument of Parliament cannot work quickly for peace ... that when it is a question of peace we dawdle and waste opportunities?

Answering this and other critical speeches, Attlee said that large and complicated measures could not be 'thrown' through the House as could measures which were immediately necessary for the war. Members should be very careful not to create the impression on the public that 'only a kind of Government cussedness' prevented or delayed the necessary action. Griffiths was right to point out the danger of not fulfilling promises. On reflection he would see it was impossible to give a timetable. As for the wider programme, Griffiths had urged three priorities – jobs, houses and security – but Attlee did not think it was possible for the government to decide at this time on the order of priority of legislation. Once again the line he took strengthened his position with Churchill on the one hand, and his Labour colleagues in the government on the other: he had loyally and cogently delivered the government line in the House. Having done that, capitalizing on the feelings expressed in the debate, he submitted a memorandum to the Cabinet the following week urging the three priorities, jobs, houses and social security, which, he had told Jim Griffiths, could not then be determined.

The party conference in December did not produce the challenges to the Executive which might have been expected. The manifesto issued in October on 'Labour and the General Election' passed intact. It did so partly because it was presented as a reply to Churchill's proposal earlier in the year for a postwar coalition to work on a four-year reconstruction programme, and partly because Greenwood, on behalf of the Executive, quietened feelings of distrust when he stressed that it must be for the party conference, not the Executive, to decide how long the coalition should last. Attlee moved the International Post-War Settlement section of the Executive's report. He promised full support for the United

Nations war effort. The next priority was the building of peace on firm foundations:

> The First World War shook European civilisation to its foundations, and showed the power and destructiveness of modern weapons. We thought that the world and Europe in particular would have learnt its lesson. We said never again must we allow such a catastrophe, but despite all our efforts war came. The lesson had not been learnt. Now, for more than five years, a worse war has been raging. Will the lesson be learnt this time? If it is not, I do not believe that our civilisation can endure. ... A new world organisation must be created. Rather it is already being created. The nucleus is the close and intimate co-operation of the British Commonwealth of Nations, the USA and the USSR ...

He warned the delegates that in order to make such an organization effective 'some cession of sovereignty would be needed'. But the most important need was to look to the future with a new vision and perspective.

> I believe that our own boys and girls when they come back from the fighting services or from war work will be little interested in the past. They will not want to hear stories of why the war came. They will ask, and rightly ask: 'How are you going to prevent our children going through what we and our fathers have endured? How are you going to secure a lasting peace?' I ask you by voting for this resolution to give them their answer.

The resolution was carried by an overwhelming majority.

The only major dispute at the conference was over the presence of British troops in Greece, who were supporting the Greek monarchy against the Resistance movement. On 8 December, on a motion of censure, only twenty-three Labour members supported the government: twenty-four voted against and the rest abstained. To avoid a vote against the government at the Labour Party conference, it was arranged that Greenwood would introduce a resolution calling for an armistice in Greece, while Bevin, whose stock with the left was for the time being high because of his demobilization proposals, would defend the government's policy. Attlee, who had suggested in Cabinet that British troops should be sent to Greece ostensibly for relief purposes, did not speak in the debate. According to Bevin's biographer he was 'too shrewd a politician to involve himself in a head-on collision with the Party Conference: he left the job to Bevin.'

In their hearts and minds the delegates may have been with Aneurin Bevan and his declaration that 'we cannot be carried very much farther along this road', but their votes went to Ernest Bevin, by 2,455,000 to 137,000. Attlee's declaration on Greece was reserved for a later occasion. Labour's left kept up the attack in the House, and used the debate on the war situation, 18 January 1945, to assail Churchill for establishing a reactionary regime in Greece. Attlee made a short intervention. It was 'entirely wrong' that the new Greek government was of the right. Almost all of its members had been against the dictatorship, many were in exile or prison.

> They consist of Socialists, Liberals, followers of Venizelos. ... There is always a danger in people who want to be very Left shifting the application of Right until it includes a great many people more Left than some who profess to be Left. ... I would ask honourable Members to get away from that typically British habit of dealing with the Balkans by falling in love with one party or one nationality. I would say that on the record of this Government and on the known opinions of this Government, we have the right to be trusted to carry out the principles in which we believe.

At this there was a cry from Aneurin Bevan of 'No!' Attlee retorted: 'I have stuck a great deal more closely to carrying out the principles in which I believe, and in working with my Party, than has the honourable Member opposite.' This time, Bevan was silenced. The storm over Greece died down.

One of the reasons why delegates left the 1944 conference much less acrimoniously than might have been expected was that the National Executive had accepted a resolution from the floor which pledged it to the nationalization of coal, steel and transport. The NEC had not intended to commit itself to the nationalization of any particular industry: its document *Economic Controls, Public Ownership and Full Employment*, much influenced by Dalton, spoke of 'the transfer to the State of power to direct the policy of our main industries' and specified only the intention to take over the Bank of England. But when Ian Mikardo moved a resolution calling for 'the transfer to public ownership of the land, large-scale building, heavy industry, and all forms of banking, transport and fuel and power', it was carried in spite of the NEC's resistance. What has been recorded already about the views of Attlee, Bevin and Dalton makes it clear that some of these industries were going to be nationalized in any case when Labour came to power. But the Mikardo resolution was important because, when a few months later Morrison came to draft the 1945 election manifesto, he found to his annoyance that as a result of the 1944 party conference he *had* to include a pledge to nationalize iron and steel as soon as Labour came to power.

Another important result of the conference was the re-election of Morrison to the Executive. He accordingly resumed his place on various sub-committees, and became chairman of the Policy Committee, and, in consequence of that, also of the Special Campaign Committee which was established in January, and on which he was able to exert considerable influence over preparations for the election. This five-man committee consisted of Morrison, Attlee, Dalton, Greenwood and Morgan Phillips (the new party secretary, elected to succeed Middleton). According to

Dalton, the other four 'gave Morrison plenty of elbow room'. Ellen Wilkinson became chairman of the National Executive Committee, an important post in an election year. We have met her as Morrison's devoted admirer, doing her best to get him in as party leader, and Attlee out. She had not changed her mind in the intervening years, and was very ready to 'promote' Morrison in her new position.

At the end of the conference Attlee made a presentation to Middleton, the retiring party secretary. Middleton remarked when responding: 'I share one trait with Clem Attlee – neither of us is given to seeking limelight and publicity.' To those present, this may have seemed a doubtful virtue for a man who might lead the Labour Party into the election campaign which was expected to take place very soon.

II

At the beginning of 1945 there was no particular dissatisfaction with Attlee's leadership but no great enthusiasm for it either. Bevin, Morrison, Cripps and Dalton all seemed to have done things during the war; Attlee seemed only to sit on committees or deputize for Churchill. When many years later Attlee's autobiography *As It Happened* appeared, Aneurin Bevan observed: 'It's a good title. Things happened to him. He never did anything.' In early 1945 the majority of the party would probably have agreed.

They would have been surprised if they had known what went on behind the closed doors. When he decided it was necessary to manage or manœuvre his colleagues, Labour or Tory, Attlee did so with confidence, however quietly. When he thought it was necessary to speak he spoke, and in clear and cogent words. He was ready to stand up to any of his colleagues, Labour or Conservative, when he thought they were going wrong. He is the only man to have rebuked the Prime Minister for his conduct of the Cabinet, and this at the height of Churchill's reputation. He wrote Churchill the following letter on 19 January 1945:

Prime Minister

I have for some time had it in mind to write to you on the method or rather lack of method of dealing with matters requiring Cabinet decisions. The proceedings last night (Wednesday) at the Cabinet have brought matters to a head. I consider the present position inimical to the successful perform- ance of the tasks imposed upon us as a Government and injurious to the war effort. I am stating the views I hold bluntly and frankly as I consider that it is my duty to do so. I am sure you will not resent plain speaking. My complaint relates mainly but not wholly to the method of dealing with civil affairs. I quite understand that, occupied so heavily as you are with the military conduct of the war, it is not possible for you to give as much attention as you would wish to civil affairs. But, that being so, I should have thought that you would have reposed some confidence in your Cabinet colleagues, but on the contrary you exhibit a very scanty respect for their views.

You have set up a number of committees over some of which I have the honour to preside to deal with various aspects of our affairs. They have been framed by you to give a fair representation of political opinion and to bring to bear on particular subjects the minds of Ministers of experience. Other ministers when matters concerning their departments are concerned are summoned to attend.

I doubt if you realise the length of time and the amount of work entailed on busy ministers not only by attendance at these committees, but by reading the relevant papers and by seeking advice from persons of know-ledge. No one grudges the time and labour, provided that the work done bears fruit, but it must be recognised that the strain of a long war inevitably begins to tell on Ministers. If to this is added exasperation and a sense of frustration, the tension becomes great. At these committees we endeavour and I claim with marked success to reach agreement and to subordinate party views to the general interest. It is quite exceptional for Party issues to arise. The conclusions of the Committees are brought to the Cabinet in memoranda which we try to keep as short as possible in an attempt to save members the trouble of reading long disquisitions.

What happens then?

Frequently a long delay before they can be considered. When they do come before the Cabinet it is very exceptional for you to have read them. More and more often you have not read even the note prepared for your guidance. Often half an hour and more is wasted in explaining what could have been grasped by two or three minutes reading of the document. Not infrequently a phrase catches your eye which gives rise to a disquisition on an interesting point only slightly connected with the subject matter. The result is long delays and unnecessarily long Cabinets imposed on Ministers who have already done a full day's work and who will have more to deal with before they get to bed.

I will give two recent instances.

Instead of assuming that agreement having been reached, there is a prima facie case for the proposal, it is assumed that it is due to the malevolent intrigues of socialist Ministers who have beguiled their weak Conservative colleagues. This suggestion is unjust and insulting to Ministers of both Parties and is simply absurd when applied to such proposals as those of the Minister of Health in the discussion of which in Committee no point of political difference ever arose.

But there is something worse than this. The conclusions agreed upon by a Committee on which have sat five or six members of the Cabinet and other experienced Ministers are then submitted with great deference to the Lord Privy Seal and the Minister of Information, two Ministers without Cabinet responsibility neither of whom has given any serious attention to the subject. When they state their views it is obvious that they know nothing about it. Nevertheless an hour is consumed in listening to their opinions. Time and again important matters are delayed or passed in accordance with the decision of the Lord Privy Seal. The excuse is given that in him you have the mind of the Conservative Party. With some knowledge of opinion in the Conservative Party in the House as expressed to me on the retirement from and reentry into the Government of Lord Beaverbrook I suggest that this view would be indignantly repudiated by the vast majority. There is a serious constitutional issue here. In the eyes of the country and under our constitution the eight members of the War Cabinet take responsibility for decisions. I have myself assured members of both Parties who have been disturbed by the influence of the Lord Privy Seal that this was so. But if the present practice continues I shall not be able to do so in the future. It is quite wrong that there should be a feeling among ministers and civil servants that it is more important to have the support of the Lord Privy Seal and the Minister of Information than of Cabinet Ministers, but I cannot doubt that that is a growing impression.

I have spoken very frankly on these discontents. I have written on my own account, but I am well aware that I am expressing much that is in the minds of many colleagues in the Government whether Conservative, Labour, Liberal or independent.

We are now in a period when difficulties are likely to increase and when the strain of the war is at its greatest. I do not think that you can complain of any lack of loyalty on my part, but I think that your Cabinet colleagues have the right to ask that in matters to which you cannot give your personal attention you should put confidence in them.

In conclusion I would ask you to put yourself in the position of your colleagues and would ask yourself whether in the days when you were a Minister you would have been as patient as we have been.

According to Sir John Colville, then Churchill's private secretary, the Prime Minister was thunderstruck by this letter. Talking to the author many years later Sir John said that Churchill first telephoned Bracken. Bracken said: 'Attlee's quite right.' He then rang Lord Beaverbrook, who also supported Attlee. Churchill, in bed with a cold at the time, then dictated a furious, eloquent but far from convincing reply. Later that afternoon, while Colville was sitting beside his bed, 'feeding' him with work, Mrs Churchill came into the room. Churchill's rage returned – 'Darling, a most disgusting thing has happened' – and he told her of the contents of Attlee's letter, and of his blistering reply. According to Colville, Mrs Churchill said without a second's hesitation: 'I admire Mr Attlee for having the courage to say what everyone is thinking.' Churchill glowered at Colville, who averted his gaze, and mentioned that as it happened the dispatch of the letter had been inadvertently delayed, and that if the Prime Minister *did* wish to reconsider it, it could be recovered. It was. Churchill then dictated the following letter:

My dear Lord President

I have to thank you for your Private and Personal letter of January 19. You may be sure I shall always endeavour to profit by your counsels.

Yours sincerely,

Winston Churchill.

After signing his letter, Churchill said: 'Now let us think no more of Hitlee or Attler. Let us go to the Movies.' But Colville took care to dispatch the letter first. It was never referred to again. Churchill's high regard for Attlee was not in the least diminished by the exchange. After the war one quip which went the rounds of Westminster was attributed to Churchill himself. 'An empty taxi arrived at 10 Downing Street, and when the door was opened Attlee got out.' When Colville repeated this, and its attribution, to Churchill he obviously did not like it. His face set hard, and 'after an awful pause' he said: 'Mr Attlee is an honourable and gallant gentleman, and a faithful colleague who served his country well at the time of her greatest need. I should be obliged if you would make it clear whenever an occasion arises that I would never make such a remark about him, and that I strongly disapprove of anybody who does.' Yet Churchill did not find Attlee personally congenial. Colville once suggested to him that he might elect him to 'The Other Club', an extremely exclusive small dining society, of which Churchill and Birkenhead had been the founding members. 'I think not,' said Churchill. 'He is an admirable character, but not a man with whom it is agreeable to dine.'

III

Attlee continued to bear heavy responsibilities as Deputy Prime Minister. He presided over the War Cabinet when Churchill attended the Yalta Conference in February 1945, and in March toured France, Belgium and Holland to investigate the shortage of food in the liberated areas. At the end of February it was announced that he would be a member of the British delegation to the founding conference of the United Nations at San Francisco. His decision to go met with criticism from the Labour Party. For Aneurin Bevan, who had complained about Attlee's 'pitiful failure to represent the Socialist view in the Cabinet on Greece, Italy and the future of Germany', this was Attlee's 'crowning blunder': the Tories wanted him as a cover to identify Labour as closely as possible with the coalition government's foreign policy. Bevan was even more incensed when it was announced that Attlee had agreed to be second to Eden in the delegation. *Tribune* thundered:

We did not expect that he would affront his own followers and demean the status of the whole Labour movement by agreeing to serve as lieutenant to

Anthony Eden. Much more is involved in this than a mere question of personal merits. We are not prepared to argue which of the two men is the abler. That the question should ever arise is due to the way Mr Attlee has consistently underplayed his position and opportunities. He seems determined to make a trumpet sound like a tin whistle. . . . He brings to the fierce struggle of politics the tepid enthusiasm of a lazy summer afternoon at a cricket match.

Bevin also thought it was wrong for the leader of the Labour Party to act as junior to a Conservative foreign secretary. Among Attlee's papers there is an unfinished letter to Eden, presumably a first draft, unmistakably typed out by himself:

> 11 Downing Street
> Whitehall, SW
>
> 2 March 1945
>
> My dear Anthony
>
> With regard to the San Francisco delegation I find that Bevin is a bit upset at the decision of the PM that I should be subordinate to you and I have received a similar suggestion from another quarter. Bevin's point is that when the PM goes with you, he takes the lead, but that the Deputy PM does not. He says Labour is always treated as a poor relation.
>
> As you know I am the last person to raise this kind of point. I have said that it is natural that on a matter of Foreign Affairs the Foreign Secretary takes the lead, but Bevin remains unconvinced.
>
> I am certain that you and I will work in harmony and that in practice no difficulty will arise, but you know how parties feel on points of this kind. I was wondering whether it was necessary to make any specific statement as to priority. If we were just the principal delegates the matter would not arise as in practice we should agree on what part each should play whatever was the formal position.

Attlee's suggestion was not accepted: it was stated that Eden would *lead* the British delegation to San Francisco. Several Labour members protested when the formal announcement came up in the House on 22 March. There were also protests inside the Labour Party. There were complaints that as leader Attlee had been altogether too modest throughout the war, had kept out of the limelight too much and that he might soon become an electoral liability. Attlee himself considered the protest 'silly'. The storm in a teacup soon subsided. The general view was that the arrangements made good sense.

On 1 March there was a wide-ranging debate in the House on the Yalta Conference. Attlee spoke, supporting the concessions which Churchill had made to Stalin, which had virtually the effect of moving Poland bodily from east to west. Poland was to receive compensating territory on the west from Germany, so that the Russians would feel more secure.

If it is necessary to take some German soil, to make it up to the entirely innocent Dutch people who have seen their land destroyed, I shall not complain; nor if it is found necessary to take certain areas in order to enable the Polish people to lead a free, full life. I do not think the Germans have a right to complain. I shall judge all these changes not by whether they fit into past history or whether they are performing an act of revenge, but entirely as to whether they will make for a peaceful Europe in future.

After warning the House not to listen to talk of masses of Germans trying to 'get back to democracy', and reminding members that the 'younger generation of Germans had been perverted by the Nazis', he turned to the coming conference in San Francisco:

I hope to go to San Francisco as an idealist, but not as what I believe is called a 'starry-eyed idealist', because I believe that international co-operation for the prevention of war, the provision of means of preventing aggression and the acceptance of obligations imposed by the implementing of this policy, is not 'starry-eyed idealism', but cold common sense.

Between the Yalta debate and his departure for San Francisco, Attlee made a number of speeches which were virtually a call for a non-partisan, or bipartisan foreign policy. On 17 April he defended the constitution of the new United Nations:

One of the League's great weaknesses was the absence of the USA and the USSR. Today they are with Great Britain and China responsible for the present proposals. The outstanding feature of the plan now before us is that the Security Council should have such overwhelming strength as not merely to defeat an aggressor but to prevent aggression. Power and responsibility must be commensurate, which they were not in the League.

Bevan: It is like the Holy Alliance.

Attlee: You may have an alliance and it may be holy or unholy. There is no need to qualify everything with an adjective. But power must not be arbitrary. The Holy Alliance had unholy principles. I hope we are going to build an organisation or at least principles that we can all approve.

To the extreme annoyance of Bevan and the left, who continued to demand 'a socialist foreign policy', Attlee supported the line being taken by the coalition government, and urged the pursuit so far as possible of a British foreign policy in a cooperative atmosphere: 'Nothing is easier than for a debate on foreign affairs to become an arena in which members of various parties form up for battle fully armed with the missiles of their opponents' past mistakes.'

The British delegation to the San Francisco Conference, besides Eden and Attlee, included Lord Salisbury, Lord Halifax as British Ambassador in Washington, and junior ministers from all three parties. The other Labour delegates were George Tomlinson, Ellen Wilkinson, and John

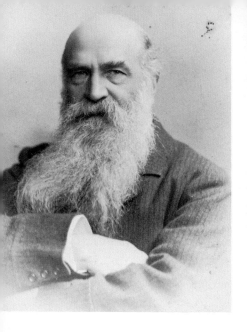

Above. Attlee's father, Henry.

Above right. Attlee, aged 4, with two of his brothers. Laurence, 2, is in the middle; Tom, 6, is on the right.

Right. 1892: Attlee in his first term at his preparatory school, Northaw Place, at Potters Bar, Hertfordshire.

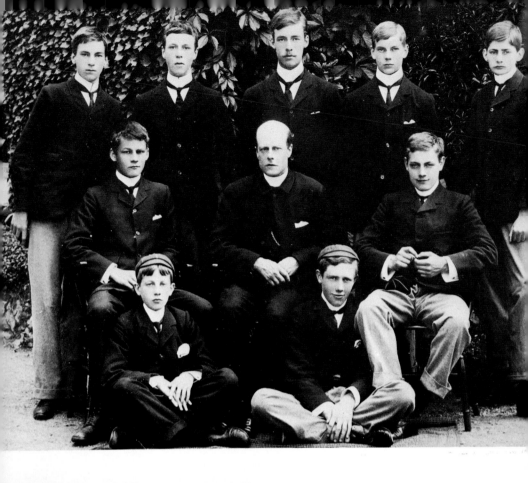

Attlee, aged 16, at Haileybury. He is on the left of the back row.

Attlee in his first term as an undergraduate of University College, Oxford in 1901.

1912: Attlee, aged 29, with members of the Haileybury Boys' Club, Stepney. He was live-in manager from 1907 to 1909, but after he left he continued to help run the club until the 1914 war broke out.

Attlee in 1910 with the staff of Toynbee Hall, Whitechapel, where he served as secretary for a year. He is standing on the left end of the back row.

Captain Attlee, aged 32, commanding
'B' company of the 6th South Lancashire
Regiment, photographed in 1915 just
before going out to Gallipoli.

Below. Mayor Attlee of Stepney – his first
public office – accompanied by other
East End mayors, walking to 10
Downing Street in 1920 to protest to the
Prime Minister, Lloyd George, about the
government's failure to deal with the
unemployment problem.

October 1921: Attlee, aged 38, announces his engagement to Miss Violet Millar. They were married in January 1922.

1924: Attlee is given his first ministerial job: Under-Secretary of State for War in the first Labour Government, which fell in less than a year.

Attlee addressing a Labour Party rally in Hyde Park in 1936.

Members of the Simon Commission in 1928 – Sir John Simon sits centre front – which went to India in 1927 and 1928 to make recommendations on progress to Indian self-government. Attlee is second right, middle row.

Attlee's elder brother Tom.

Vi

Left. 1938: on the annual family holiday at Nevin, North Wales. Janet is on Vi's right, Felicity on her left.

Below left. 1940: at home for the weekend just after he had led the Labour Party into the wartime coalition government. From left to right, Janet, Martin, Vi and Alison.

Right. Mid-July 1945: Attlee, no longer Deputy Prime Minister of the wartime coalition government but now leader of the Opposition, sets out for the Potsdam conference at the invitation of the Prime Minister, Winston Churchill. The General Election has been held, but the results are not yet known.

Below. At the Labour Party conference in May 1945: listening, and planning for power.

26 July 1945: the Labour Party has won the General Election. Attlee and Vi at headquarters, Transport House.

Two days after the General Election victory, Attlee as Prime Minister and Ernest Bevin as Foreign Secretary set out for Potsdam to resume the British government's role at the conference.

The Prime Minister and his Cabinet in 1945 in the gardens of 10 Downing Street. *Left to right, front row:* Lord Addison, Lord Jowitt, Sir Stafford Cripps, Arthur Greenwood, Ernest Bevin, C. R. Attlee, Herbert Morrison, Hugh Dalton, A. V. Alexander, Chuter Ede and Helen Wilkinson. *Standing behind:* Aneurin Bevan, George Isaacs, Lord Stansgate, George Hall, Lord Pethwick Lawrence, J. J. Lawson, Joseph Westwood, Emmanuel Shinwell, T. E. Williams and Tom Williams.

1945: Attlee and Sir Stafford Cripps, then President of the Board of Trade.

The Cabinet Room in 10 Downing Street. When he was prime minister, Attlee liked to do most of his work here.

1945: Attlee and Hugh Dalton, then Chancellor of the Exchequer.

Attlee being greeted by President Truman in Washington on 4 December 1950. He had flown over at a few days' notice after rumours that the atomic bomb might be used in Korea.

During the General Election campaign of February 1950 Attlee visits his constituency, West Walthamstow, with Vi.

1952: Aneurin Bevan speaking at the annual
Labour Party conference at Morecambe,
described by Michael Foot as 'rowdy,
convulsive, vulgar, splenetic' and
culminating in a great victory for the
Bevanites and the ousting of Morrison and
Dalton from the National Executive
Committee.

Sam Watson, leader of the Durham Miners
and member of the Labour Party's National
Executive Committee, talking to Hugh
Gaitskell in 1955. Attlee considered making
Sam Watson foreign secretary after Ernest
Bevin resigned.

1956, the year after his retirement: Earl Attlee, aged 73, with
his daughter Lady Felicity ('Flip') – married to Keith Harwood.

The Attlees at the christening of Jo, the Harwoods' daughter, in 1958.

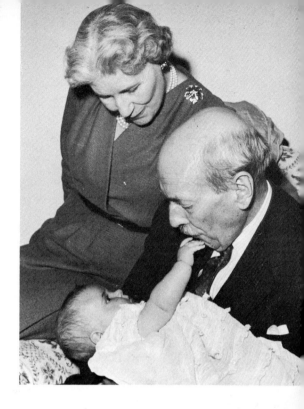

Two ex-prime ministers in conversation.

January 1966: in his rooms in King's Bench Walk, Temple, the year before he died.

Dugdale, formerly Attlee's private secretary, now an MP who had taken over from Arthur Jenkins as his parliamentary private secretary. This was his first visit to California, 'amazingly beautiful country – something like Devonshire,' he wrote to Tom. He spent a little time sightseeing, and visited a former member of Stepney ILP who had emigrated in 1912 and now lived in a middle-class suburb, 'the general aspect [of which] was that of a very well kept garden suburb inhabited by the intelligentsia'. At the conference:

> We proceed slowly owing to the need for every nation to produce its principles at great length through the mouth of its delegate in Plenary Session ...
>
> I held a Press Conference on arrival for some 400 pressmen. It is held to have been a great success. One Australian journalist told me yesterday that he was with a bunch of American newspapermen. After my preliminary statement and before questions began, one said 'now you'll see a sucker torn to pieces by the lions.' At the end another said 'I guess this sucker eats lions.'

He was still in San Francisco when the news came that the war with Germany was over:

> While we were at the conference the news came through that the war against the Nazis had ended. We gathered to celebrate the event in a room at the top of a skyscraper. In San Francisco the Japanese War was nearer and of greater concern to the citizens than the European contest and we were sorry not to be at home for the celebrations.

The San Francisco Conference gave institutional shape to the ideas on international organization which had been current since 1943. In his autobiography Attlee recorded:

> The biggest issue at the conference was the question of the Veto in the Security Council. We agreed with the Americans and the Russians that the Veto was necessary, but many delegates of the smaller Powers, especially Peter Fraser of New Zealand, opposed it strongly. It was clear to me that the Veto was essential, but the assumption was that it would be used very sparingly. Its subsequent misuse by the Russians was quite contrary to the spirit with which it was accepted. Another matter of some controversy was that of Trusteeship, in which Powers with Colonial possessions found themselves at variance with those whose views were based on admirable sentiments but great lack of practical knowledge of actual conditions.

President Roosevelt died shortly before the conference opened. Before leaving the United States, Attlee flew to Washington to meet Harry Truman, the new President. They hit it off with each other immediately. It had taken some time for Truman to adjust to Churchill's rhetoric. Acheson told the author that the President 'recognized Attlee as somebody like himself, a man with his feet on the ground, who spoke in simple, direct terms, and as briefly as possible, and whose thinking about politics was inspired not by admiration of heroes but by identification with "the common man".' Attlee, never averse to forming first impressions, thought Truman was straight, strong, unassuming and warm-hearted. 'Of course when I met him world affairs were new to him – he didn't know much about them. But he had good instincts and his judgement was sound. It was a great blow when Roosevelt went, but when I met Truman I felt fate had been good to us. We talked the same language. We became friends.'

IV

When Attlee returned from San Francisco, electioneering was already in the air. In January the draft Labour Party manifesto had been submitted to the NEC. In late February the political temperature had begun to rise, partly as a result of a speech by Attlee in which he had referred in public to Conservative ministers' objections to Morrison's plan to set up a public corporation to manage the electricity generating industry. He was accused of taking the issue out of the Cabinet Committee and on to the hustings. In the same speech he had foreshadowed both the continuance of wartime economic controls and the inevitability of a mixed economy in the postwar period.

Encouraged by Beaverbrook, who had been running a press campaign against controls for several weeks, Churchill now decided to denounce them root and branch at the Conservative Party conference held in the middle of March. The chief item of the party's election programme was to be the abolition of controls and the restoration of private enterprise. In a powerful speech Churchill inveighed against controls, whether those who imposed them intended it or not, as the beginning of totalitarian government:

> Controls under the pretext of war or its aftermath, which are in fact designed to favour the accomplishment of totalitarian systems, however innocently designed, whatever guise they take, whatever liveries they wear, whatever slogans they mouth, are a fraud which should be mercilessly exposed to the British public.

He went on to attack the Labour Party for adopting a programme of nationalization which would destroy 'the whole of our existing system of society' and establish 'another system ... borrowed from foreign lands and alien minds'. Churchill added that this 'alien' programme had been adopted by the Labour Party 'much to the disgust of some of their leaders'. This apparent attempt to sow dissension in the Labour Party leadership infuriated the Labour rank and file.

Ernest Bevin, conscious that it was he whom most Labour members had in mind when they heard Churchill speak of 'the disgust of some of their leaders' with the party's nationalization programme, now took a hand. He knew there were murmurings that he wished to prolong the coalition, rumours that if Labour decided to withdraw from it he would remain in it under Churchill, and 'do another Ramsay MacDonald'. In a pounding speech at Leeds in April he attacked the years of Tory misrule before the war and scorned the idea that if Labour left the coalition he would stay in it. He made it clear that he trusted Churchill as a war leader, but not as leader of the Conservative Party. The speech received immense publicity and to a large degree restored the unity of the Labour Movement.

Attlee *may* have had all this in mind when, during a Cabinet meeting just before he left for San Francisco, he passed a note across the table to Bevin, which read: 'I am telling the PM to look to you for guidance in my absence. It would be well for you to keep in touch with Herbert if there are any questions of elections coming up, as he is on the National Executive.' The subsequent announcement, that in Attlee's absence Bevin would act as liaison between the Cabinet and the Parliamentary Labour Party, did not mean, as some thought, that Attlee now regarded Bevin, not Morrison, as the man most likely to succeed him, but it threw some light on what would be Attlee's relationship with each of the two men when Labour came to power. There was one specific reason why Attlee wanted Bevin to have direct access to Churchill when an election was discussed: he knew that Morrison wanted to end the coalition, whereas he knew that Bevin shared his own view that if possible the coalition should be prolonged at least until the end of the war against Japan, generally expected to last at least another year.

At the end of the first week of May 1945, the Germans surrendered. Some Conservative leaders, notably Beaverbrook and Bracken, now wanted to exploit Churchill's personality and record to win a snap election. Churchill, who wanted to postpone the election at least until the defeat of Japan, agreed reluctantly to make a decision before the Labour Party conference, which was to take place on 18 May. Since Attlee was still in San Francisco, Bevin and Morrison went to see Churchill on 11 May. They had consulted the National Executive first. Morrison, with Bevin's support, put a strong case in the national interest that October was the proper time: the arrangements for taking the armed forces vote would be properly organized by then, and an accurate new register would have been completed. He made it clear, however, that Labour was ready to take on the Tories immediately. Churchill then raised the question of continuing the coalition until after the defeat of Japan. Bevin said he was not averse, but Morrison said he could not agree.

When the two men left Churchill, therefore, the proposition before the Prime Minister was the current official NEC position: Labour would not remain in the government after the end of the current session of Parliament; when the next session began in November it would be with a new government. Morrison cabled an account of the meeting to Attlee in San Francisco. Attlee approved, but he still hoped that the Labour Party might accept a new formula which would enable the coalition to be maintained until Japan had been defeated.

Attlee arrived in London four days later. After talks with Bevin and Morrison he had a long and friendly talk with Churchill about the timing of the election. Both men knew exactly what their parties wanted: the Conservatives an immediate election, the Labour Party an election at the end of this Parliament's life in October. But both wished to preserve the coalition until the end of the war with Japan. Both expected the war to last for several months. Attlee, unlike Churchill, did not know that the atomic bomb was now in existence, and even Churchill did not know that it would be such a cataclysmic success. Churchill formed the impression that Attlee 'would do his best to keep us together', and produced a draft letter which he proposed to send formally to Attlee, offering the choice of an immediate election or the extension of the coalition until the end of the war with Japan. After consulting Bevin, Attlee added a rider, to which Churchill agreed without demur, that if the life of the coalition was extended, the government would do its utmost to implement the proposals for security and full employment already laid before Parliament. He told Churchill that this sentence would give him a better chance of persuading the Labour Party conference to stay in the coalition until the war with Japan was over.

Four days later the Labour Party conference opened at Blackpool. The National Executive met the day before to discuss the Churchill letter before it was put before the delegates. Attlee, as chairman, confined himself to a statement of the pros and cons: his preference for remaining in the coalition was well known. Bevin and Dalton strongly advocated staying in the coalition. Morrison, speaking with the authority of the chairman of the Campaign Committee, contended that the mood of the party would not brook continued participation in the coalition government. The Chief Whip, William Whiteley, said that this was also the feeling among the members of the Parliamentary Party. Three other members of the NEC stood with Attlee, Bevin and Dalton. Bevan, for once, supported Morrison. Morrison carried the day. Attlee immediately wrote to Churchill saying that the party wanted an election in October and would remain in the coalition only until then. The die was cast. While the Labour conference was still in session, Churchill went to the King and submitted his resignation.

Churchill thought Attlee had let him down. Nevertheless, according to Colville the first draft of his letter accepting Attlee's decision contained a warm tribute to their association during the war – a tribute which Beaverbrook successfully urged him to leave out. Eden recorded in his diary: 'Winston rang up in morning ... had strong impression from Attlee twice that he would recommend acceptance, but I think this was only Attlee's timidity in the interview.' The simple fact was that Attlee had promised to *recommend* acceptance to his party but had not guaranteed to get it. It is difficult, however, to understand why Churchill should have felt so incensed when there was so little difference between what he was proposing and what the Labour Party was willing to accept. He wanted the coalition to continue until the end of the war with Japan, which he thought would be in six months' time. The Labour Party were willing to stay in the coalition until October, which was in five months' time.

At Blackpool the news that the coalition was over was greeted with applause. 'Never before', claimed Ellen Wilkinson, the party chairman, 'was Labour so united or in such fighting fettle.' Morrison was given a big ovation. The burden of his speech was that the only solution was to socialize industry in order to get a firm economic base for social reform. The *Daily Express* spoke of 'a remarkable scene of enthusiasm ... delegates cheered for minutes on end.' Morrison was 'the present idol of delegates and the undoubted leader of the Party today'. During the conference, Dalton records: 'Ellen Wilkinson approached me, and no doubt others ... and earnestly pressed upon me the idea that Attlee should now step aside before the election campaign began, and let Morrison become leader of the Party.' Dalton was discouraging, suggesting in any case that many MPs would prefer Bevin.

On the third day of the conference, Attlee introduced the international section of the Executive's Report. 'Though overshadowed by his colleagues he coordinates the Party,' conceded *Picture Post*. Morrison had dealt with domestic policy. Attlee dealt with the war, the San Francisco Conference, India, the treatment of Germany, the peace settlement, the need for world economic planning, and the need for Britain, the United States and the Soviet Union to continue to work in peace as they had in war. It was a general survey, contrasting in content as well as in delivery with the stirring commitments to specific action which Morrison had thundered out. But it was an effective speech, which according to Dalton won a 'fine ovation'. Many of its points were taken up by Bevin in a speech on foreign affairs which Dalton thought won the 'loudest and longest' ovation of the conference.

The coalition's funeral obsequies took place the following Monday, 28 May. A farewell party was held in the Cabinet Room. About forty ex-ministers were also invited to attend. Lord Chandos wrote in his memoirs:

The departing Labour members looked rather gloomy and sheepish and I could not help remembering all that we had been through together. Clem Attlee adopted a very correct but rather chilly attitude. He did not allow his humour off the chain that afternoon. Ernest Bevin looked shaken and anxious, Morrison expectant, and Albert Alexander made some remarks about 'my Navy', which raised a smile. It was at this meeting that Churchill said that when he went to meet Stalin and Truman at Potsdam, he wanted to take with him 'my good friend, Clem Attlee'. He was deeply moved throughout.... We had all come together as a united band of friends in a very trying time. History would recognise this. 'The light of history will shine on all your helmets.' Attlee and Sinclair made very brief replies.

Attlee was made a Companion of Honour. Bevin, offered the same distinction, declined.

The day after the coalition ended, the new party chairman, Harold Laski, wrote a long letter to Attlee about the widespread feeling in the party 'that the continuance of your leadership is a grave handicap to our hopes of victory in the coming election'. Attlee should 'draw the inference that your resignation of the leadership would now be a great service to the Party. Just as Mr Churchill changed Auchinleck for Montgomery before El Alamein, so, I suggest, you owe it to the Party to give it the chance to make a comparable change on the eve of this greatest of our battles.' Attlee replied:

Dear Laski

Thank you for your letter, contents of which have been noted.

C. R. Attlee

V

Attlee had played a vital role in the success of the coalition. In the House, he was an admirable partner for Churchill. His personality, his style, his manner, his use of language were so unobtrusive that the deputy was the perfect foil for the colourful and charismatic leader. More important, Attlee's way of dealing with the House minimized the risk of the Labour members resisting government policy. There were still suspicions of a Conservative Party in which those who had inspired the 'Bankers' Ramp' and the Means Test were well represented. Misgivings about Churchill's capacity to run 'a people's war' were always present. To keep down the Labour Party's temperature in the House was as important as it was difficult. The burden of so doing fell more heavily on the Deputy Prime Minister than on any other Labour minister: not only because of his official role but because he had to speak, or answer questions, so much more often – and perform not only in the House but at meetings of the PLP.

His ability to calm the House was due not only to avoidance of rousing language but to cultivation of a laconic idiom which neutralized attempts to heighten feeling or make political capital. His terse replies to questions in parliament were much quoted and enjoyed. Asked in 1943 why only two out of twenty-seven dispatches received from the commanders-in-chief of the war theatres had been published, Attlee replied: 'Because they would give information of value to the enemy.' His questioner then observed: 'In the last war all dispatches of Army chiefs were published within a few months of their receipt by HMG.' Attlee: 'I have responsibility only for this war. I cannot say why the same course was not adopted in the last war.' Shinwell, always ready to make trouble, asked Attlee a question. Attlee rose and said he would deal with the matter 'immediately'. Shinwell did not wait for Attlee to go on speaking, but rose, and demanded: 'What does my Right Hon friend mean by immediately?' Attlee: 'As soon as my Hon friend sits down.' Occasionally he showed a lighter touch. Announcing a debate on Welsh affairs for the following week, he was asked what he proposed the English and Scottish members should do that day. He replied gravely: 'It will be an opportunity for them to listen to the eloquence of their colleagues from Wales.'

In Cabinet his cool, efficient performance contrasted with the florid style of Churchill's leadership. Eden later observed to the author: 'whenever he spoke in the War Cabinet or the Defence Committee – and it was really the Defence Committee that ran the war – I agreed with what he said. I often wished he had opened his mouth more often.... I don't know whether it was shyness or modesty, but he was more reticent than he need have been.' Moreover, Eden thought him objective: 'I can't remember him ever making a point which I felt came from him as leader of the Labour Party. Though his concern about postwar policy was evident it never affected his general conduct.'

He concentrated on winning the war. This was precisely the charge that Labour's left made against him. Attlee, they argued, failed to use his Cabinet position to advance the policies to which as leader of the Labour Party he should have been dedicated. He entered the War Cabinet not as a conqueror but as a prisoner. Attlee's reply to this charge, made often but never better than in a long letter to Laski in 1944, may serve as a concluding comment on his membership of Churchill's government:

> As I see it, your argument amounted to this, that unless our socialist principles had been by the end of the war put into force, then obviously all of us in the party who support the maintenance of this government in power in order to win the war are making ourselves responsible with our eyes open to bringing the world to disaster. The logic of that position would be that we should at once break the coalition and seek for a general election now in the hope of getting a Socialist majority . . .

Whether the postwar government is Conservative or Labour it will inevitably have to work in a mixed economy. If it is a Labour government it will be a mixed economy developing towards socialism. If a Conservative government it will be an economy seeking to retain as much as possible of private enterprise. But both governments will have to work with the world and the country as it exists. There are limits to the extent to which the clock can be put forward or back.

At the present time I am engaged for a good many hours a day on postwar problems which cover a very wide range from detailed matters of our internal economy to the widest matters of international and political and economic import. I discuss these with my colleagues and endeavour naturally to get as much as possible of our policy accepted, and I find on many matters more agreement than you would perhaps expect, but on other matters I may have to accept a compromise. Why? Because for better or worse this country has got to play a big part in shaping the post-war settlement, and geographically and also ideologically we are situated between the USSR and the USA. I believe that it is of primary importance for the peace of the world that these three great powers should work in harmony. It is, therefore, necessary that we should discuss with them both the immediate and longer-distance problems of the peace, and we cannot do that if we cannot come to some understanding among ourselves.

On home affairs there are a vast number of matters which do not involve party politics but which are nonetheless important. There are other matters on which some agreement can be come to. There are others in which party differences are so great that they must await a decision by the country. We have to work today with the House of Commons which we have got . . .

What then should be our tactics? I have never suggested that we should drop our principles and programme, but it is, I suggest, better to argue from what has been done to what may be done rather than to suggest that very little has been accomplished. For myself I should on the practical side argue for our programme on the basis that the acceptance of the doctrines of abundance, of full employment, and of social security require the transfer to public ownership of certain major economic forces and the planned control in the public interest of many other economic activities. I should further argue that our planning must now be based on a far greater economic equality than obtained in the prewar period and that we have demonstrated in this war that this can be obtained . . .

I am sorry that you suggest that I am verging towards MacDonaldism. As you have so well pointed out, I have neither the personality nor the distinction to tempt me to think that I should have any value apart from the party which I serve. I hope you will also believe that because I am face to face every day with the practical problems of government I am nonetheless firm in my Socialist faith and that I have not the slightest desire to depart from it.

17
Into Power,
1945

I

Once the Labour and Liberal contingents had departed from the coalition, Churchill formed his 'Caretaker Government' and announced that Parliament would be dissolved on 5 June 1945 and a general election would be held on 5 July.

At first the exchanges between the leaders of the two major parties were in keeping with their relationship as colleagues in government for a period of five years. Announcing plans for demobilization, Churchill paid a tribute to Bevin: 'The broad and properly considered lines of the demobilisation proposals which Mr Bevin has elaborated with much wisdom will be adhered to.' Bevin was invited to the opening of the West End office of the Resettlement Advice Service, and was given the place of honour. Attlee wrote to Eden, who was ill, early in June, and Eden replied in his own hand:

6 June

My dear Clem,

It was really kind of you to think of sending me that note and I was much touched by it.

It is a bore to have to break off just now with FO things at rather a crucial phase and de Gaulle on an even higher horse than usual. But it couldn't be helped. My doctor could not have been firmer, so that I lie in bed reading Gibbon and old Prof Webster's history books! A pleasant change I must admit so far as literature goes.

Again, thank you so much for this and many personal acts of friendship during our five years together which I shall never forget.

Yours ever
Anthony.

There came a dramatic change in the political atmosphere when, on 4 June Churchill made the famous election campaign broadcast in which

255

he virtually said that the Labour Party coming to government would mean the introduction of the Gestapo. 'Socialism', he warned his listeners, 'is inseparably woven with totalitarianism and the abject worship of the state.' If a Labour government committed itself to carrying out its socialist programme, it would have to fall back on some form of Gestapo, 'no doubt very humanely directed in the first instance'. Socialists found a free parliament 'odious'. He even resorted to the savings scare which MacDonald had used against his erstwhile colleagues in the general election of 1931. 'There is no man or woman in this country who has, by thrift or toil, accumulated a nest-egg, however small, who will not run the risk of seeing it shrivel before his eyes.' Beaverbrook has often been blamed for the ideas expressed in this broadcast, but it seems in fact that they were Churchill's own. Whoever conceived it, the broadcast was a great mistake. Twenty-five years later, Lord Butler recorded that it had been 'by common consent a strategic blunder'.

Churchill rendered Attlee a service. Attlee's broadcast reply ('The voice we heard last night was that of Mr Churchill, but the mind was that of Lord Beaverbrook') not only established the right line for dealing with Churchill's irresponsible rhetoric, but immediately made an immense impact, which gave him some of the popularity and prestige he had so long lacked by comparison with other Labour leaders.

> When I listened to the Prime Minister's speech last night, in which he gave such a travesty of the policy of the Labour Party, I realised at once what was his object. He wanted the electors to understand how great was the difference between Winston Churchill the great leader in war of a united nation and Mr Churchill, the Party Leader of the Conservatives. He feared lest those who had accepted his leadership in war might be tempted out of gratitude to follow him further. I thank him for having disillusioned them so thoroughly.

Before 'turning to the issues that divide the Parties', Attlee went out of his way to pay a tribute to his colleagues of all parties in the coalition government. In the most generous terms he expressed gratitude for 'the privilege of serving under a great leader in war, the Prime Minister', adding that

> No political differences will efface the memory of our comradeship in this tremendous adventure, of the anxieties shared, of the tasks undertaken together and of the spirit of friendly co-operation in a great cause which prevailed. I know well the contributions made by one and all to the achievement of victory.

He reproached Churchill for 'painting to you a lurid picture of what would happen under a Labour Government in pursuit of what he called a Continental conception'. The Prime Minister's memory was at fault.

'He has forgotten that socialist theory was developed in Britain long before Karl Marx by Robert Owen.'

He followed with an attack on the Conservatives' blind faith in private enterprise inspired by the motive of private profit, 'a pathetic faith resting on no foundation of experience', and described how many people, and industries, had suffered in the past from the Tory myth. He mentioned the controls and the state interventions which had been introduced with the agreement of the Conservatives because they were necessary to the conduct of the war. It had been necessary to plan the location of industry. It had not been possible to leave the management of industries, like the coal industry, in private hands. Such controls would be needed to deal with the now pressing problems of peace. He mentioned the need to control, in particular, rents and prices, and reminded his listeners of what had happened after the First World War, under 'a huge reactionary majority [elected] at the instance of the War Leader, Lloyd George'. A Labour government would nationalize selectively. 'No one supposes that all the industries of this country can or should be socialised forthwith, but there are certain great basic industries which from their nature are ripe for conversion into public services.' He went on to deal with the question of political parties and class:

> Forty years ago the Labour Party might with some justice have been called a class Party, representing almost exclusively the wage earners. It is still based on organised labour but has steadily become more and more inclusive ...
>
> The Conservative Party remains as always a class Party. In twenty years in the House of Commons I cannot recall more than half a dozen from the ranks of the wage earners. It represents today, as in the past, the forces of property and privilege. The Labour Party is, in fact, the one Party which most nearly reflects in its representation and composition all the main streams which flow into the great river of our national life.

Without Churchill's grand rhetoric, but in words which less anachronistically combined patriotism, public spirit, pride in the achievement of the past and a sense of adventure for the future, he ended with a peroration which stressed the need for an altruistic attitude to public affairs:

> Our appeal to you, therefore, is not narrow or sectional. We are proud of the fact that our country in the hours of its greatest danger stood firm and united, setting an example to the world of how a great democratic people rose to the height of the occasion and saved democracy and liberty. We are proud of the self sacrifice and devotion displayed by men and women in every walk of life in this great adventure.
>
> We call you to another great adventure which will demand the same high qualities as those shown in the war; the adventure of civilisation ...
>
> We have to plan the broad lines of our national life so that all may have the duty and the opportunity of rendering service to the nation, everyone

in his or her sphere, and that all may help to create and share in an increasing material prosperity free from the fear of want.

We have to preserve and enhance the beauty of our country to make it a place where men and women may live finely and happily, free to worship God in their own way, free to speak their minds, free citizens of a great country.

The next day he began a personal campaign which became very strenuous. His own constituency of Limehouse had been devastated by bombing, and evacuation had reduced the number of voters to about sixteen thousand. His agent was confident about the outcome in Limehouse, so Attlee spent most of the campaign speaking up and down the country. Vi drove him everywhere in their own small car. This method of travel contrasted with Churchill's: the Prime Minister was driven in a cavalcade and was accompanied by a massive entourage. The difference in style was given a great deal of publicity.

Attlee's election tour was a success. Huge crowds did not line the route to get a glimpse of him as they did when Churchill's cavalcade went by, but his meetings were packed, and his audiences listened intently. His speeches were well reported, but not so extensively as those of Bevin, who was given more publicity than any other Labour leader. Foreign policy played very little part in the election, except in so far as the Conservatives claimed that Churchill's experience of it made him indispensable. On domestic issues Labour attacked the Tories as the party responsible for what had gone wrong between the wars, particularly for mass poverty and unemployment, a party which because of its vested interests in finance and property could not be trusted to plan in the public interest, no more to be trusted to provide adequate housing in 1945 than it had been in 1918. The Tories dismissed the Labour Party as inexperienced, inept and doctrinaire.

Social justice and security, Beveridge and a better life – these were the issues, not socialism. Taking the achievements of the wartime coalition into account, the programme which Labour offered was comparatively conservative. On the eve of the poll, Attlee wrote to Tom:

Thank you for your letter. We are getting near the end of this election now. I can't find that my opponent is getting any support. I had a good four days in Northants last week. Vi drove me round to packed and enthusiastic meetings with large crowds listening to the Mike outside. These little towns like Kettering and Wellingborough are very pleasant.

Winston keeps slogging away at this silly Laski business, but I don't think he gets the better of the exchanges with me.

The 'silly Laski business', the major political scandal of the campaign, was precipitated by Churchill's announcement that he proposed to invite Attlee to accompany him to the coming peace conference at Potsdam.

'In the last few years we have always thought alike on the foreign situation, and there will be an opportunity for saying that although governments may change and parties may quarrel, we stand together on some of the main aspects of foreign policy.' Attlee, after consulting his colleagues, accepted. Harold Laski, now chairman of the party, immediately made a lengthy statement which the *Daily Herald* published the following morning, the main point being:

> It is therefore essential that, though Mr Attlee should attend the three-power talks, Labour and he should not accept responsibility for agreements which on the British side will have been conducted by Mr Churchill as Prime Minister. It is essential also that Mr Churchill, Marshal Stalin, and President Truman should be fully aware of the position.

Laski's intervention incurred so much disapproval, within the Labour Party as well as outside it, that he felt it necessary to defend his action in a memorandum to the National Executive. The matter seemed to be resolved almost as soon as it had been made known by an amicable public exchange of letters between Churchill and Attlee on 16 June, Laski immediately commenting that the exchange of these letters had made the position 'entirely satisfactory'. There the matter would have ended, but for Beaverbrook. The following day the *Daily Express* carried headlines: SOCIALISTS SPLIT: ATTLEE REPUDIATES LASKI ORDER. A photograph of Laski accompanied a quotation from his *Labour Party and the Constitution* arguing that monarchy and social democracy 'are not, in the long run, easily compatible'. A leader attacked Laski and 'the rule of the secret party caucus'. Laski meanwhile was making electioneering speeches in various parts of the country. According to a report in the *Newark Advertiser* he had publicly advocated the use of force to bring about a socialist state. The *Express* followed this up. 'Laski Unleashes Another General Election Broadside: Socialism Even If It Means Violence'. Laski issued a writ against both newspapers.

Beaverbrook seems to have decided, in spite of the recoil of Churchill's 'Gestapo' speech, that in Laski's two effusions he had the ingredients of another 'Red Letter' scare. Many Conservatives, including several parliamentary candidates, followed his lead. The 'Gauleiter' Laski became their bogey. Attlee was a puppet, Laski pulled the strings. If Labour were returned, Britain's prime minister would be manipulated by the chairman of the Labour Party, who was not an elected member of Parliament, was a left-wing totalitarian, and advocated violence to obtain power. There would be a 'secret Socialist foreign policy', hatched behind closed doors. The sovereignty of Parliament would be no more, and Britain would be governed by the National Executive Committee of the Labour Party.

Attlee's path was not made smooth by Laski's public statements, but he decided to make as little of them as possible. A greater problem was to cope with Churchill's strenuous attempt to make capital out of Laski's interventions. Churchill wrote him a series of public letters, designed in Attlee's words 'to show that I was a mere tool in the hands of a non-Parliamentary body, the National Executive of the Labour Party'. On 30 June, in Churchill's last broadcast (he chose to deliver four out of the ten allotted to the Conservatives), he returned to the 'meagre hare' (as Attlee called it in one of his speeches), talking of the dictatorship of the Labour caucus and even suggesting that under a Labour government state secrets might have to be communicated to the NEC, 'this committee of 27 members, very few of whom are Privy Councillors'. Attlee at once issued an indignant statement:

> I must deal with the Prime Minister's disgraceful suggestion that Cabinet and military secrets would be divulged by Labour Ministers to the Labour Party Executive. He must know perfectly well that there is no foundation whatever for this allegation. He knows and I know that during the last five years he has never suggested this and no such thing has occurred. He must indeed be badly rattled to stoop to making such charges against colleagues who served with him so loyally.

The public exchange of letters between Attlee and Churchill took place just before polling day. Much of it was concerned with the long-standing question of the extent to which decisions of the National Executive and the party conference could influence the policy of a Labour government. Attlee's first letter had been a patient explanation of the constitution of the Labour Party, intimating that this was something of which Churchill was evidently in need, and ending drily: 'I am sorry that you have been so distressed owing to your lack of acquaintance with the procedure of democratic parties in general and of the Labour Party in particular.' Churchill replied:

> Thank you for your letter. While I welcome the assurances contained in it, I regret that I cannot accept your explanation as satisfactory because it leaves a number of very important points unanswered.
>
> Under your Party's constitution it is provided that 'The work of the Party shall be under the direction and control of the Party Conference....' and the Executive Committee shall, 'subject to the control and directions of the Party Conference, be the Administrative Authority of the Party.'
>
> It is further laid down, as you say in your letter, that the Executive may call a Conference of the Parliamentary Labour Party at any time on any matters relating to the work of the Party.
>
> What is the real interpretation of these provisions? It is clear that the Conference, working through its Executive Committee, is the controlling body so far as the work and policy of the Labour Party is concerned,

whether in office or not. Moreover, the Executive Committee has the power at any time to call a conference to challenge the actions and conduct of the Parliamentary Leaders. If the Labour Party is in office the Committee has the power to summon Ministers to ad hoc Conferences in order to try and force them to reverse policies which have been presented to the House of Commons by the Government of the day after full consideration of all the facts and circumstances which only a Government can possess. I am informed that this has actually happened in the past.

By way of illustration, the constitution would apparently enable the Executive Committee to call upon a Labour Prime Minister to appear before them and criticise his conduct of the Peace negotiations. How he could defend his actions without the disclosure of confidential information I fail to see.

Personally, I do not believe that the controversy on these very important issues can be satisfactorily cleared up until the public has a statement signed jointly by yourself and the Chairman of the Executive Committee regarding the use of these powers in the future.

Attlee replied:

Your messenger with your letter only arrived at my house shortly before 11.30 pm when it had already been sent to the Press. I must, therefore, apologise to you for sending my reply to the Press before my letter will have actually reached you.

I am surprised that you, who are apparently becoming acquainted with the Constitution of the Labour Party for the first time, should on the authority of an unnamed informant seek to attach to its provisions meanings other than those accepted by myself and others who have spent years in the service of the Labour Party.

Much of your trouble is due to your not understanding the distinction between the Labour Party and the Parliamentary Party. This leads you to confuse the organisational work of the Party with the actions of the Parliamentary Labour Party.

Despite my very clear statement you proceed to exercise your imagination by importing into a right to be consulted a power to challenge actions and conduct.

It was ironic that so lengthy a controversy was precipitated by Churchill's invitation to Attlee to accompany him to Potsdam. According to Sir John Colville, then private secretary to the Prime Minister, Churchill invited Attlee to go as an act of courtesy – 'he did not dream that he would lose the election'.

Attlee flew out to Berlin on 15 July 1945, with Churchill and Eden. The opening session of the three-power conference was to be held two days later. 'We landed at the aerodrome near Potsdam and drove to a villa near a lake where we were to stay,' he recorded. 'It had been the property of a German engineer whose library consisted of German technical and

Fascist books but included, oddly enough, Miss Mitford's *Our Village.*'
The Russians thought it odd that the leader of the Opposition was
included in the British delegation. 'At first,' Eden records in his *Memoirs*,
'I thought they suspected us of contriving to secure extra representation
at the Conference, but Mr Attlee was so subdued and terse a figure that
this hardly seemed possible.'

They flew back to London on 25 July. Churchill went to see the King
that evening and told him that he expected a Conservative majority of
between thirty and eighty. Attlee arrived at Stanmore on the eve of the
count. Vi drove him to Stepney with Janet and Felicity, to be present
when the boxes were opened. Attlee's vote was 6,789 out of 10,006; he
had polled more than five times as many votes as his Conservative
opponent. Vi then drove to Waterloo Station, picked up Alison, who was
returning from school, and went on to Transport House. There they
found that there were indications of a landslide in favour of Labour. The
first portent came at 10.25: Harold Macmillan had been defeated at
Stockton-on-Tees. A quarter of an hour later came news of a great swing
to Labour in Birmingham. The following day brought the news that five
members of the caretaker Cabinet and eight senior ministers had lost
their seats, and that a great many Liberals had forfeited their deposits.
By lunchtime Labour had gained 106 seats. Now the country results,
usually favourable to the Conservatives, began to come in, and confirmed
the trend to Labour. By the middle of the afternoon it was clear that
Labour had won a great victory.

The number of votes cast showed that though there had been a
landslide in seats the Labour Party had not won an overall majority in
the country. They had polled nearly 12 million, against nearly 10 million
for the Conservatives and their allies, $2\frac{1}{4}$ million for the Liberals and over
three-quarters of a million for other candidates. Labour's share of the
vote was 47.8 per cent. The seats were as follows: Labour 393, with 6
more on the left; Conservatives and allies just under 220; Liberals 12.
The government's overall majority was nearly 150. Later in the afternoon
Churchill sent a message to Attlee conceding defeat, and offering congratulations. He went to the Palace at 7 pm, tendered his resignation,
and advised the King to ask Attlee to form a government.

The message from Churchill was the beginning of a brief drama in
which a small cast of Labour leaders played a part, the scene being
Transport House. Attlee had gone there that afternoon when the result
of the election was clear to confer informally with Morrison, Bevin and
Morgan Phillips. They sat in Bevin's room; Laski and other members of
the Executive were in Phillips's room still listening to the results coming
in on the radio. The day before the general election Morrison had warned
Attlee that whatever the result he would, if returned himself, run against

Attlee for the leadership of the party. When Attlee read out Churchill's message, Morrison said that Attlee should not accept an invitation from the King to form a government before the Parliamentary Labour Party had met and had elected its leader. The clear implication was that after such an election the leader might not be Attlee. Since May, Morrison had been aligned with Laski, Ellen Wilkinson, and Maurice Webb, who was later to be chairman of the PLP, in a campaign to press for a free vote of the PLP to determine the leadership. Because Morrison had not until the last minute declared himself a candidate, Laski had also approached Bevin, without success. Morrison now told his colleagues that he could not offer to serve under Attlee there and then, implying that if Attlee decided to go and see the King before a leadership election were held, Attlee was not free to tell the King that Morrison would serve in the new Cabinet.

Attlee and Bevin protested that it was out of the question for the leader of the party, who had led the party into wartime coalition and then to victory at a general election, and had now been asked by the King to form a government, to submit to a leadership election within the party. For him to do so was not required by the constitution of the party, and would be contrary to the constitution of the country. Morrison continued to argue. The telephone rang in the adjoining room. It was a call for Morrison from Cripps. On returning to Bevin's room Morrison announced that he had Cripps's support. While he was out of the room, Bevin asked Morgan Phillips: 'If I stood against Clem, should I win?' Morgan Phillips replied: 'On a split vote I think you would.' Bevin turned to Attlee and said: 'Clem, you go to the Palace straight away.' When Morrison was back in the room Attlee said no more about waiting for a meeting of the PLP. In consequence Morrison did not know that Attlee had been to see the King until later that night. In the meantime he made remarks to his friends suggesting that he believed there would be a leadership election and that he would win.

Attlee's mind had been made up at Transport House before any of them had spoken. The matter was not political but constitutional: 'If the King asks you to form a government you say Yes or No, not "I'll let you know later." If you are asked, you try to form a government, and if you can't you go to the King and tell him so, and advise him to ask somebody else.' Attlee went to the Palace at 7.30 that evening. Vi drove him there and waited outside in the car. 'The King pulled my leg a bit. He told me I looked more surprised by the result than he felt.' After receiving the King's commission to form a government, Attlee drove with Vi to the party's great victory rally at Central Hall. Here he joined a throng only just become aware of the extent of its success. What he most vividly remembered twenty years later was joining in the singing of 'England

Arise': he had sung the song many and many a time in Stepney when there were only half a dozen there to sing it. After the rally, he went home to bed: 'It had been quite an exciting day.'

Attlee now turned his attention to Cabinet-making. It was commonly suggested that it was at the King's suggestion – made when Attlee was summoned to the Palace to be asked to form a government – that Bevin became Foreign Secretary, rather than Dalton; in later years Attlee did not recollect any such intervention on the King's part. The essential point, as Attlee wrote for *The Observer* in 1959, was that: 'Ernie and Herbert did not get on together ... if you'd put both on the home front there might have been trouble, therefore it was better that Ernie should operate mainly in foreign affairs.' On the day after the audience with the King, Attlee had become aware that the bad personal relations between Morrison and Bevin had suddenly worsened. Bevin had been incensed by Morrison's behaviour on the leadership question the previous afternoon at Transport House. Next day he learned that even after Attlee was publicly known to have accepted the King's commission to form a government, Morrison was pressing for a leadership election while simultaneously asking Attlee to make him foreign secretary. Bevin became so angry about Morrison's behaviour, according to Dalton, that he telephoned Morrison and told him angrily: 'If you go on mucking about like this, you won't be in the bloody government at all.'

Meanwhile Attlee was coming to his conclusion about the disposition of the two main offices. The key to it was whether Morrison would swallow his pride, give up his hopes of becoming foreign secretary, and accept the Lord Presidency. If he did so, Bevin must become foreign secretary so that there would be no conflict of personalities on the home front. By four o'clock he had told Dalton that he might have to go to the Treasury.

In spite of Bevin's explosive telephone call Morrison had not given up his attempt to become leader of the party. He had stirred up the issue at the party's victory rally the previous night, before he had realized that Attlee had already gone to the King and had agreed to form a government. According to Morrison's biographers, he and his friends were 'canvassing Labour MPs at the Rally and urging them to demand that the Parliamentary Labour Party should have a chance for a free vote on the leadership.... [Morrison] approached John Parker entering the Gents and said "We cannot have this man [Attlee] as our leader."' Morrison also sent for George Isaacs, president of his union, and asked him to write to Attlee urging him to wait to go to the Palace till after the next day's parliamentary meeting. It was at this moment that Attlee arrived at the rally from the Palace to announce from the platform that he had accepted the King's invitation to form a government. There was a great and prolonged outburst of cheering. This did not deter Morrison and his friends from carrying on their campaign.

At 3 pm, Friday 27 July, there was a meeting of the former Administrative Committee of the Parliamentary Party, consisting of elected members of the Parliamentary Election Committee, plus the party officers. This committee had been set up in 1940 to provide liaison between backbenchers and Labour ministers in the coalition government. Attlee was in the chair. He made an opening statement in which he stressed the urgency of establishing a 'skeleton' government to conduct the administration while he and the Foreign Secretary were at Potsdam. To the surprise of most of those present, Morrison raised the question of the leadership. Taking his stand on the party's decisions at the Hastings conference in 1933, he pointed out that certain formalities were necessary for the forming of a Labour government. The committee, however, took the view that the 1933 decisions were intended primarily to prevent the leader of the party from agreeing to form a government without consultation with the party as MacDonald had done in 1931, and that there was no need of these safeguards in 1945: here, after all, was Attlee sitting in consultation with the Administrative Committee. This settled the issue. Attlee was at once authorized to go ahead and form a Labour administration. The meeting was over in thirty minutes.

Morrison came out of this very badly. Apart from the egotism which he was generally thought to have displayed, he did not have a case for querying Attlee's right to be premier. The 1933 rules did not state, as Morrison had implied they did, that after a general election the leader must be elected by the PLP before he was entitled to accept a commission from the King to form a government. His contention was even less consistent with common sense than it was with party procedures. To suggest that a leader who had led the party in a general election, had won it, and had got the majority of the electorate to vote for it, should then stand down and make way for somebody else to become prime minister whom the electorate had not visualized in that capacity was, as Attlee told the author, 'cockeyed'.

The skeleton government was announced next day, 28 July. Though Dalton was not displeased to be given the Exchequer, Bevin was disappointed to be given the Foreign Office. Morrison was disappointed too. If he could not be prime minister he wanted to be foreign secretary. Attlee had some difficulty in persuading him to become Lord President of the Council, leader of the House *and* unofficially deputy prime minister. 'He asked to be number two, which I readily accepted,' Attlee recorded in his biographical notes. As well as Bevin, Dalton and Morrison, the Cabinet included Cripps as President of the Board of Trade, Jowitt as Lord Chancellor, Greenwood as Lord Privy Seal.

That morning 392 Labour MPs gathered at the Beaver Hall in the City, in jubilant and expectant mood. The new ministers came there directly from Buckingham Palace. As soon as they were seated, Whiteley, the Chief Whip, rose and said: 'The Foreign Secretary.' Bevin moved a vote of confidence in the new Prime Minister. Attlee was given an ovation which lasted for several minutes. Everybody present knew something about Morrison's efforts to oust him during the previous forty-eight hours. Attlee's response was brief. He must return to Potsdam. He handed the meeting over to Morrison, and left the hall. In a few hours he and Bevin were in an aircraft bound for Berlin.

II

Eden and Churchill declined an invitation to return to Potsdam with Attlee, and Bevin went as Foreign Secretary, but otherwise there was not a single change in the personnel of the thirty-five-member delegation. This much surprised the Americans and the Russians. The new leader of the British delegation was accompanied by the same principal private secretary who had attended Attlee's predecessor, and even by the same valet – hearing at the last minute that Attlee was going without a manservant, Churchill arranged for his own man to accompany him. The fact that the Attlee delegation to Potsdam was identical with Churchill's compounded the mystification which the Russians already felt as a result of the unexpected outcome of the elections. On his first visit to Potsdam, Attlee, when asked to predict the result by Molotov, had replied that it would be 'a close thing'. When Attlee returned to Potsdam after the result had been announced, he found that Molotov was very suspicious:

> Molotov kept saying, 'But you said the Election would be a close thing, and now you have a big majority.' I said, 'Yes, we could not tell what would be the result.' But he kept repeating the phrase. He could not understand why we did not know the result. I am sure he thought Churchill would have 'fixed' the election.

The reappearance of Churchill's valet, reported to Molotov by the Russian secret police, completed their bewilderment.

So far as continuity of policy was concerned, James Byrnes, then American Secretary of State, noted that 'Britain's stand before the Potsdam Conference was not altered in the slightest, so far as we could discern' by the replacements. Indeed, Bevin's manner towards the Russians was 'so aggressive' that 'both the President and I wondered how we would get along with this new Foreign Minister'. Though Churchill in his memoirs alleged that the new administration, through inadequate briefing, had failed to carry out the plans he had prepared before the election, 'namely to have a "showdown" at the end of the Conference, and, if necessary, to have a public break rather than allow anything beyond the Oder and the Eastern Neisse to be ceded to Poland', neither Eden nor subsequent commentators have held that Bevin and Attlee could have done more.

Attlee and Bevin arrived in Berlin by air late in the evening, 28 July. They drove out to their quarters in Babelsburg, a suburb of Berlin which before the war had been the German Hollywood. After a call on Truman, they went to the Cecilienhof, a mock-Tudor palace – 'Stock Exchange Gothic', Attlee called it – standing in wooded parkland on the banks of a lake. There was to be a late session that same night. Stalin was not glad to see them. He had expected Churchill to be returned; when the next day the Marshal took a day off saying that he felt unwell, Truman thought that he was 'not so sick but disappointed over the English elections'. Attlee was unperturbed by Soviet coolness towards a Labour minister. He had formed his impressions of Stalin in the earlier part of the conference. He was a tyrant. 'Reminded me of the Renaissance despots – no principles, any methods, but no flowery language – always Yes or No, though you could only count on him if it was No.' Attlee's earlier visit to Potsdam had taught him that the Russians would put forward their claims to compensation for all that their people had suffered and promise little in return. Listening to exchanges between Stalin and Churchill he had soon concluded that there was no possibility of real Anglo-Soviet cooperation.

Before proceeding with the agenda on that first night, Stalin announced that the Japanese government had asked the Soviet Union to mediate to end the war. Stalin said he proposed to reject the request, Truman thanked him and nothing more was said about Japan, although it was only eight days before the first atomic bomb was dropped. At the pre-election session at Potsdam, Truman had informed Churchill, and later Attlee, of a successful test of the bomb at Los Alamos. He did not tell Stalin until a week later, just before Churchill and Attlee returned to England. Stalin had made no comment. At the time Attlee thought that his silence concealed the fact that the disclosure had come to him as a shock; in fact Stalin had already been informed by the British and American spies Fuchs and Greenglass that the test was about to be made. After the test had been made Stalin probably knew more about the bomb's capabilities than Attlee did.

What Attlee had been told by Truman led him to understand only that the bomb had much greater explosive force than a conventional bomb and would have greater effects, which were not specified: he was told nothing of possible genetic effects, or the likely extent of fall-out.

The idea that Attlee and Truman could have used their knowledge of the power balance which the atomic bomb would give the West to threaten the Russians with a 'showdown' at Potsdam is hindsight. Nor could Attlee, if he had known what the bomb could do, have prevented Truman from using it: that the Americans were free to use it had already been agreed by Churchill in a secret meeting with Truman on 21 July, a meeting which will be referred to later.

There has been general agreement that the atmosphere of the Potsdam Conference when Churchill and Eden were there was far more stimulating than that of the Attlee–Bevin period. It was not only a matter of personalities; the major political commitments had already been argued out, and many of them had been made. When he arrived Bevin made some impression with his remark to Ismay, 'I'm not going to have Britain barged about', but in fact Britain's role had already been revealed to be minor compared to the parts the other two powers were playing, and there was little to be done about it. Attlee personally made no impact at the conference. The highest compliment he got was Truman's recollection: 'Attlee had a deep understanding of the world's problems, and I knew there would be no interruption in our common efforts.' On the first night of the second session, Churchill might have signalled his return with a big dinner party: Attlee dined with two relatively junior members of the British delegation because, it was said, they were the only two he knew at all well.

Cadogan, Permanent Under-Secretary for Foreign Affairs, recorded in his diary that the Prime Minister was overshadowed by Bevin who 'effaces Attlee and ... does all the talking while Attlee nods his head convulsively and smokes his pipe.' Attlee would not have been worried by this observation. He knew that 'Ernie' grasped the fundamentals of foreign policy, and believed that a prime minister should rarely intervene in departmental policy-making. 'You don't keep a dog and bark yourself; and Ernie was a very good dog.' As for the position in which the British government found itself at Potsdam, he knew that the time for a 'showdown' with Russia was long past.

Much was discussed at the conference; little of it was reassuring. The main agreements can easily be summarized. The principal decision was that the supreme authority in Germany should be left in the hands of the Allied Control Council, which was to proceed to disarm and demilitarize Germany and eliminate or control her war industries. The reparation claims of the Allies, especially of Russia and Poland, were to be met as soon as possible, and the boundaries of Poland were provisionally demarcated. A Five-Power Council of the foreign secretaries of Britain, the United States, Russia, France and China should be set up to meet nominally in London to draw up peace treaties with Italy and Germany's former satellites. Spain was to be excluded from the United Nations organization.

The wartime friendship formed between Eden and Attlee lasted through the years of Conservative opposition, and Eden's attacks on Attlee and the government were as a rule much less scathing than Churchill's. Several times Attlee praised Eden's speeches. Bevin, too, was well treated by Eden, who recorded in *Full Circle*: 'I would have publicly agreed with him more, if I had not been anxious to embarrass him less.' This mutual respect contributed greatly to the continuity of foreign policy in the immediate postwar period, its tone being registered publicly in the debate on the Address, on 16 August 1945. When Churchill spoke of the disappointments and anxieties and the divergences of view which had been revealed especially about affairs in Eastern and Middle Europe, he did not blame the government, nor did he when, commenting on events in Poland and Czechoslovakia, he said it was not impossible that 'tragedy on a prodigious scale was unfolding itself behind the iron curtain which at the moment divides Europe in two'. In the debate Attlee echoed Churchill's sombre views on Potsdam. Bevin followed in more detail, 20 August, concluding that: 'The basis of the Government's policy is in keeping with that marked out by the Coalition Government.' Eden congratulated Bevin 'warmly' on his speech and expressed agreement with him 'on practically every point'. The Opposition made it clear that they accepted foreign policy as bipartisan. There was no mention of Professor Laski.

III

Japan surrendered on 14 August. At ten next morning Attlee appeared on the balcony of the Ministry of Health building in Whitehall, followed by Bevin and then Morrison, acknowledging the crowd's chant of 'We want Clem.' He used the occasion to sound an early note of warning. 'It is right for a short time that we should relax and celebrate the victory. But I want to remind you that after we have had this short holiday we have to work hard to win the peace as we have won the war.' Soon afterwards the three Labour leaders left the balcony. The crowd remained, calling repeatedly, but in vain, for Churchill. Later that day the King opened his first peacetime Parliament since 1938. At 4.05 pm Attlee, addressing the House, said, with another excursion into Christian terminology: 'One feeling, I am sure, is predominant in all our hearts, the feeling of gratitude to Almighty God for this great mercy.' During the debate on the Address the following day Attlee paid an eloquent, and generous, tribute to Churchill:

The surrender of Japan has brought to an end the greatest war in history, and a General Election, which was not of his seeking, has resulted in the Right Honourable Member for Woodford being on the opposition benches at a time when the fruits of his long leadership of the nation were being garnered.

I think it is fitting that today I should pay a tribute to one of the greatest architects of our victory. However we may be divided politically in this House, I believe I shall be expressing the views of the whole House in making acknowledgement here of the transcendent services rendered by the Right Honourable Gentleman to this country, to the Commonwealth and Empire, and to the world during his tenure of office as Prime Minister.

In the rest of his speech he outlined, simply, briefly and predictably, the problems which confronted the new government, and its special approach to them: there were shortages of coal, transport, food and raw materials, and each of these aggravated the others. 'We are still cut to the bone at home.' The government was resolved to have no inflation, and there would be a minimum of unemployment. 'We must keep the financial and economic controls which served us so well during the war.' A very heavy programme was being laid before Parliament, 'but we are living in a time when great changes are due.' He outlined the government's public ownership programme, and referred specifically to the bills for the nationalization of the Bank of England and the nationalization of the coalmines, and to the repeal of the Trade Disputes Act and the Trade Union Act.

This temper of the Labour Party and the mood of the Conservatives combined to produce an atmosphere in Parliament that was unique. Neither party had expected that such a huge majority would be returned. The Labour members were intoxicated, the Tories were stunned. It was not the best time for cool judgement. Temper sometimes was high. The fight was on, but the feeling immediately engendered was the reaction to the victory and defeat in the election, rather than the product of the clash over policies.

Labour came to power with a profound sense of mission and of vindication. This was something the party had not experienced since 1929. At this vital moment in British history, it was Labour that Britain had chosen to put in charge. That Labour had polled less than 50 per cent of the vote did not vitiate the Party's sense of mandate. Even Churchill's wartime record had not been enough to keep Labour out. In Labour ranks, therefore, was a feeling not only of exhilaration but of destiny. The Tories, on the other hand, could not make out what had gone wrong. If Churchill had not been able to win, who or what could?

Seven days after the war with Japan was over, on 21 August 1945,

President Truman signed a document which had been put in front of him by Mr Leo Crowley, the head of the Foreign Economic Administration, and at the stroke of his pen, the Lend–Lease agreement was at an end. From that moment on, Britain would have to pay for everything the United States supplied. This shattering news came only a few days after the Board of Trade had issued figures showing that since 1938 the value of *non-military* imports into Britain had increased more than five-fold. Britain's postwar economic battle had begun. Mr Crowley was not an enemy of Britain. He simply reported to the President that, according to the law, Lend–Lease must be terminated, and Mr Truman acted on his advice.

Britain, in Dalton's words, was now in 'an almost desperate plight'. The country did not have the resources to pay the bills which would be necessary to meet her obligations, to feed the people and bring the troops back home. In 1945 external aid would have enabled her to overspend her income by more than £2,000 million a year. This facility was now abruptly terminated. Even if some use were made of the gold and dollar reserves, and if £200 million were borrowed from the sterling area, at least £1,250 million, or 5 billion dollars, would have to be raised over the next three years if Britain were to be able to carry out her essential programmes.

Mr Truman's action in ending Lend–Lease totally without warning or discussion was one of the greatest and least defensible mistakes made by a president of the United States in the twentieth century. Apart from its immediate economic consequences, Truman's precipitate action aroused European fears of an American return to isolationism. The Russians, deprived at a moment's notice of valuable supplies of food, clothing and raw materials, believed themselves betrayed. The feeling of being let down by the American government on a question of money renewed in the Labour Party memories of the 'Bankers' Ramp' allegedly organized by Wall Street in 1931, and planted in British public opinion those seeds of anti-Americanism which in spite of the Marshall Plan and the Berlin Airlift bore unwelcome fruit during the Korean War. It influenced the left because it reduced the chances of giving the nation the 'socialist' amenities which had been promised during the campaign, and antagonized the general public because it put an end to hopes of a speedy improvement in living conditions. The urgent need for increased manpower for industrial production put an unforeseen strain on the demobilization scheme. The precipitate ending of Lend–Lease taught Britain a bitter lesson which had a part in Attlee's decision that Britain should possess her own atomic bomb.

It says much for Truman's success as a statesman in other respects that his sudden breaking-off of Lend–Lease has not weighed too heavily in the balance against him. The law was clear: the Lend–Lease arrangement ended with the cessation of hostilities. But Truman could have found the means to extend economic support to Britain and Europe if he had fully understood the need to do so. Later, Mr Truman wrote in his memoirs: 'Crowley ... taught me this lesson early in my administration – that I must always know what is in the documents I sign.'

Attlee was shocked. It was one of the few occasions on which a severe reverse left him with a sense of personal disappointment. He had formed a high opinion of Truman's character, and set great store by the relationship which seemed to have developed between them. In public he was tactful. On 24 August, with his usual restraint of manner, he said in the House that the ending of Lend–Lease placed Great Britain 'in a very serious financial position'; there was no alternative but to seek further help from the United States. He naturally did not express any misgivings about Truman's action at a time when a British delegation was preparing to go cap-in-hand to Washington. More interesting is that he was so forbearing on the subject when writing several years later: 'I doubt if the American administration realised how serious was the blow which they struck.'

The government's problems were compounded by the muddle the Americans themselves were in. At the moment when the telegram arrived, two key American officials were in London discussing United Nations business with British experts. The first they heard of it was a bulletin on the BBC news. Lord Halifax, the British Ambassador, also on a brief visit to London, was taken by surprise. The Americans – Clayton of the State Department and Collado of the Treasury Department – obtained agreement that payment for goods in the pipeline could be regarded as still negotiable; but were told that the decision to stop Lend–Lease as a whole, having already been published, could not be reversed. It was their task now to convey to the British government the full implications of the irrevocable decision which President Truman had so ill-informedly taken.

Attlee acted quickly. R.H. Brand, representing the Treasury in Washington, was ordered to return to London at once. When he arrived, Attlee summoned him, Keynes and Halifax to a meeting of ministers at 10 Downing Street. Brand told them that even if the administration were prepared to provide some kind of economic assistance, Congress might very well not agree to pass the necessary legislation. Keynes more optimistically pointed out that Britain had an overwhelming case for requesting financial aid from the Americans. Her economic difficulties were entirely due to her war effort, which had been as much in America's interest as her own. He believed that he could probably get a free gift or grant in aid of £1,500 million (6 billion dollars). Keynes 'was almost starry-eyed', recorded Dalton. 'When I listen to Keynes talking, I seem to hear those coins jingling in my pocket,' said Bevin; adding shrewdly: 'But I'm not so sure that they are really there.'

They were not. Keynes and his negotiating team left for Washington in early September 1945. As soon as he arrived Keynes found that the atmosphere he had known in the war had changed. The Americans, though personally friendly, made it clear that the war was over, and now, domestically, America had its problems too. It was soon obvious that a gift or grant or interest-free loan was out of the question. Eventually, Keynes got the loan, but he did not get as much as he had expected. American public opinion, which Congress, not the State Department, represented, was not interested in the British claim that per head of population they had sacrificed more to win the war than the United States. There was a widespread feeling that American free enterprise was being asked to finance British Socialism, a feeling aggravated by articles and statements from Laski very critical of American capitalism.

Apart from its cost, the Americans feared that a loan could be the beginning of a permanent peacetime involvement in European affairs. The argument that without economic assistance America's European allies might have difficulty in keeping the Russians out of Western Europe cut little ice: at this period the American people still regarded the Russians as allies, and believed that they could work with the Russians if the British did not interfere. There were few signs of that understanding of the world situation which two years later was to produce the Marshall Plan. Keynes had thought that the loan, or grant, could be arranged between two old wartime comrades in a matter of days. In fact the transaction took several months, and turned out to be a hard bargain, ending in a loan agreement that created no joy for the British government.

The Cabinet followed Keynes's negotiations in Washington on tenterhooks. If a loan was not forthcoming, Britain would have to face a period of austerity far more severe than anything it had borne during the war. The reconstruction programme, as it had been promised to the voters, would have to be reduced. The rate of demobilization would be drastically slowed down – there would be no jobs for the homecoming heroes. Though Britain had no alternative but to accept what the Americans finally offered, there were occasions when the Cabinet considered breaking off the negotiations, with Bevan and Shinwell particularly critical of the Americans, and Bevin, Cripps and Dalton taking the opposite view.

The Cabinet had to face the fact that even on the disagreeable terms which would have to be accepted, the loan might never be granted. When he went to meet Truman in Washington in November to discuss atomic energy questions, Attlee tried to woo the support of American public opinion for financial aid. The American negotiators impressed on Keynes that they were preparing stiff terms only because Congress would have to authorize the loan, and Congress would be chary of lending money to a foreign country governed by a political party committed to the abolition of private enterprise.

At the beginning of December the question of 'convertibility' threatened to break up the negotiations. The American negotiators demanded that within one year of the loan coming into effect the British should make sterling exchangeable for dollars on demand. Although Keynes was personally in favour of convertibility – he believed that it was essential to the re-establishment of a healthy international economy – to impose it at such short notice he thought irrational, since it would risk running the reserves down to a level that would render Britain economically impotent. But Keynes was anxious to conclude the negotiations for the American loan before the end of December, so that the Bretton Woods agreement of 1944 could be ratified. Bretton Woods, to which Keynes had contributed ideas and enthusiasm, had set up the International Monetary Fund and the World Bank. The Americans had stipulated that they would not adhere to it unless the other signatories had formally adhered to it by December 1945. Keynes believed that it was in Britain's interest that Bretton Woods should become effective at the appointed time, and he knew that the Americans would not accept any bilateral agreement which was not consistent with the Bretton Woods principles of liberalized international trade. Convertibility was one such principle: all the more reason to conclude a loan agreement on American terms.

Since Keynes seemed to have come to the end of his tether, Sir Edward Bridges, Permanent Head of the Treasury and Secretary to the Cabinet, was sent out to Washington. He obtained some slight concessions, which the Cabinet reluctantly accepted. In Dalton's judgement no one could have achieved better terms than Keynes had managed to get: a loan of 3,750 million dollars, repayable at 2 per cent over fifty years beginning in December 1951; the interest rate to be waived any years Britain did not earn enough foreign exchange: wartime costs of Lend–Lease to be written off, Britain receiving an extra credit of 650 million dollars on the same terms to pay for the postwar delivery of goods in the pipeline on vj Day.

The government could not admit to its disappointment in public. On the contrary, it chose to mislead the country about what had happened. In the House, Dalton said of the agreement: 'I value this settlement very highly. Lend–Lease, a great scheme greatly begun by the late President Roosevelt – that most unsordid act in history as Mr Churchill aptly called it – has had a fine clean end, which we should welcome.' By the

274

terms of the loan agreement, Britain undertook to promote international commercial cooperation, reduce tariffs and eliminate discrimination, and to accept the Bretton Woods plan. For better or worse she had tied her economic future to that of the Americans.

Attlee announced the conclusion of the agreement in the Commons on 7 December 1945. The newspapers reported the terms of the loan the following day. There was an outcry, since the public had clung to the notion that their wartime comrades would come through with a generous loan to set them on their postwar way. In the Commons a two-day debate started on 12 December. The Conservative Party was even more divided about accepting the loan than the Labour Party. Churchill was personally for approval of the loan, but so many Tory MPs said they would oppose it that Churchill finally recommended abstention. The Bretton Woods Agreement went through the House of Commons on 14 December.

Fifteen years later, talking to the author, Attlee remained convinced that there was no alternative to accepting the terms of the loan. Britain, he said, had been in no position to bargain. Her needs were 'desperate'; she had nothing to offer in return. The Americans were ignorant, and consequently they thought the British had exaggerated their difficulties and were resisting conditions out of self-interest. 'Nearly all of them thought we wanted to get what we could and preserve our freedom of action.' All the government could do ultimately was to concede what the Americans insisted on. 'We had to have the loan. We knew how much we risked when we accepted convertibility, but Keynes urged us to take the risk – you see, he believed profoundly in Free Trade.' There was no time for arguing – 'our reserves were running out fast, we were as tough as we dared.' Britain had to have her loan, and in a matter of weeks. And from the end of the war on, Attlee was always aware of the risk that the Americans might decide to pull out of Europe as they had done after the First World War. 'So far as possible nothing should be done to make them feel we were not grateful to them. They had to be humoured.'

It is not clear how far Attlee threw his weight in Cabinet behind the agreement. The 'Inner Cabinet' of Attlee, Morrison, Bevin, Dalton and Cripps were obviously kept in very close touch with the negotiations throughout, but Dalton on two occasions speaks of the 'firm coalition' between Bevin, Cripps and himself; from which it might seem that Attlee exercised here his usual chairman's practice of listening hard to all the participants in a discussion, saying little himself and summing up at the end with a decision in favour of the strongest case. There is no evidence that Attlee took the lead in accepting the inevitable.

The problems which arose with the end of Lend–Lease included an immediate demand for an increase in manpower, and consequently a large and swift acceleration in the rate of demobilization. This put Attlee in another dilemma. In the debate on the Address, Attlee had warned the House that the call-up for young men up to thirty must continue; but in response to the clamour for faster demobilization he gave a public pledge, 3 September, that the government would do its utmost to get men and women out of the armed services and back to civilian life as soon as possible. Knowing the edginess of public opinion on this issue, he stressed the government's interest in speedy demobilization. 'We want you out just as much as you want to come and we want you back as quickly as possible.' He said that the number of men needed to restore employment in civilian industries to the prewar level was at least five million above the figure to which it had fallen by the end of the war. But the export trade had to be greatly expanded beyond the prewar level, and there was a desperate shortage of workers for the housing and reconstruction programme. He again gave warning, however, that while conditions remained unsettled in Europe, Britain must continue to find large forces for the occupation of Germany, and that there were other exacting commitments in Europe, the Mediterranean, the Middle East and the Far East.

The Opposition – and many Labour MPs – continued to complain that the pace of demobilization was far too slow, especially when compared with that of the Americans. A more ominous degree of dissatisfaction was displayed in mid-September by the Trades Union Congress in Blackpool. An emergency resolution, calling for a re-examination of the Bevin scheme for demobilization, was introduced not from the floor but by the General Council, and was carried by acclamation. The following day, Attlee made a speech to the Congress – the first time a prime minister had addressed the TUC. He spoke in general terms, and left it to George Isaacs, the Minister of Labour, who was to speak the following day, to defend the government's plans. But he promised that the government would take another look at military manpower requirements. Attlee stuck to his guns: Bevin's plans were as fair as they could be; British armed forces must not be run down to the point of endangering European security – especially as American forces had been transferred in large numbers to the Far East.

Nevertheless, he now gave instructions that everything possible must be done to increase the rate of demobilization that was permitted by the plan, and, to do so, put strong pressure on Truman to release British ships which were being used to transport American troops home from Japan. A firmness and acerbity crept into his relations with Truman which occasionally recurred. Just as Attlee fearlessly took on Churchill, his chief political competitor at home, he was never afraid to speak directly and firmly to the man who led the greatest power on earth.

The impact on the British economy of the end of Lend–Lease showed how important the Anglo-American connection would be to Attlee's government, and how much strain would be put on the personal relations between the two leaders. The Anglo-American dispute over the exchange of atomic energy information, the other great foreign policy problem of the first months of Attlee's prime ministership, put a further strain on the friendship between Truman and Attlee. More significantly, perhaps, it challenged Attlee to show what he could do to lead Britain, once a first-rate power but now critically weakened, into a significant role in the postwar world.

One of the first major diplomatic events with which the new government had to deal was the end of the war with Japan, and the repercussions of the dropping of the atom bomb. Churchill had insisted that knowledge of the bomb and of the plans for its use must be kept to the smallest possible circle. Even the chiefs of staff were given only the barest outline of what was to come. All Attlee knew before the Potsdam Conference was that the Americans were working on a new, different and bigger kind of bomb, and he had deliberately refrained from trying to find out what progress was being made with it. On 21 July 1945 Truman and Churchill had agreed that an atomic bomb must be dropped on Japan if she did not accept an ultimatum calling for unconditional surrender. On 1 August, the day before the Potsdam Conference ended, Truman told Attlee by letter that the Americans were ready to drop the bomb, and Attlee did not demur. His information was that the Japanese would fight for at least another six months, at great cost of life to the Allies, and that victory over Japan could only be achieved by shifting American troops from Europe and thus further prejudicing the European balance of power in favour of Russia. If the bomb would end the war in six weeks rather than six months, Attlee was for it.

As soon as he heard of the cataclysmic effects of the Hiroshima bomb dropped on 6 August, Attlee sent a telegram to President Truman proposing a joint declaration on the control of use of this unprecedentedly powerful weapon:

> The attack on Hiroshima has now demonstrated to the world that a new factor pregnant with immense possibilities for good and evil has come into existence. . . . There is widespread anxiety as to whether the new power will be used to serve or to destroy civilisation. . . . I consider, therefore, that you and I, as heads of the Governments which have control of this great force, should without delay make a joint declaration of our intentions to utilise the existence of this great power, not for our own ends, but as trustees for humanity in the interests of all peoples in order to promote peace and

justice in the world. .... I believe that a declaration of intentions made now
will have great value.

Three days later, the Americans dropped a second atomic bomb, on
Nagasaki. Five days later Japan surrendered. After an exchange of telegrams, Truman and Attlee agreed to postpone a statement until the full
implications for international relations could be worked out. Attlee made
a public statement from Downing Street to reassure the British public,
and Lord Halifax in Washington and Bevin at the Foreign Office were
asked to press the State Department to urge an early conference between
the two countries.

A few days later, 21 August, Attlee announced the setting up of the
'Advisory Committee on questions involved in the use of atomic energy'.
The chairman of the new committee was Sir John Anderson, then shadow
chancellor of the exchequer, still nominally an Independent, though
sitting with the Tories on the front bench, and constantly denouncing
the iniquities of the Labour government. As far back as 1941, when he
was lord president of the council, Anderson had been put in charge of the
British atomic energy programme. When he ceased to be lord president,
and became chancellor of the exchequer, he was left to continue his role
in respect of atomic energy. By the end of the war he knew far more about
the subject than any other politician. It was he who in June that year
had put up the paper to Churchill, then prime minister, which had
recommended the establishment of the Advisory Committee.

Attlee had taken over the policy programme and set-up which Anderson had recommended to Churchill. His first thought was to give responsibility for atomic energy development to the chiefs of staff, but he
was warned that this might create problems in dealing with the industrial
potential of atomic energy, so he left Anderson in charge. Though it
seemed irregular for a leading Tory front bencher to be in charge of a
highly important Labour government committee, and to have access to
more secret information than the Prime Minister ever obtained for himself, there was much to be said for the arrangement. Anderson was not
only trusted by Attlee: he was trusted by the Americans. It was essential
for there to be continuity of policy between Conservative and Labour
governments on such an important matter. This was achieved, and
Anderson had much to do with it.

On 25 September, Attlee sent Truman a long private letter, analysing
the new situation which had been created by the bomb. His broad
conclusion was: 'We have, it seems to me, if we are to rid ourselves of this
menace, to make very far-reaching changes in the relationship between
States.' The letter struck an urgent note: it emphasized the fact that since
America and Britain had moved so rapidly in the field of atomic energy
there was no reason to suppose that other nations would not also have a

bomb in the near future. There might only be a short time left in which America and Britain could use their lead in the field 'to lend our utmost energies to secure that better ordering of human affairs which so great a revolution at once renders necessary and should make possible'. He proposed a meeting between him and Truman as soon as it could be arranged. Truman agreed. Eight days later he told Congress that discussions would shortly take place, 'First with our associates in this discovery, Great Britain and Canada, and then with other nations, in an effort to effect agreement on the conditions under which co-operation might replace rivalry in the field of economic power.' The meeting was to take place on 8 November, in Washington.

Truman's public statements about the bomb were now becoming an embarrassment to Attlee's policy. On 21 September there had been a dispute in Truman's Cabinet over the proposal by the Secretary of State for War, Colonel Stimson, that basic scientific data about the bomb should be shared with Russia. The suggestion, leaked in a garbled form to the press, caused an uproar in Congress. To stay American fears that he was about to 'share the bomb with Russia', Truman declared at a press conference that though *scientific* knowledge relating to atomic energy would be available to all scientists, the United States would not divulge *technical* information about atomic energy, either about the making of weapons or about the harnessing of it for industrial purposes. Truman had in mind the denial of information to the Russians, though some of his officials were also anxious to prevent an exchange of information with France's Communist scientists.

Attlee's new concern was to ensure that Truman's statement did not mean that considerations of American security were going to undermine Britain's rights under the Quebec Agreement of 1943, under which Britain had handed over technical information about atomic energy for the Americans to use in developing a bomb, on the understanding that Britain would share the information gained by the Americans in their work. Attlee was anxious to make certain that the embargo on atomic information would not guarantee a permanent monopoly for the three countries which already had the secrets of the bomb. He wanted agreement that such information would be passed on to the United Nations as soon as such a course seemed safe, and to have all this established publicly. One particular obstacle bedevilled discussions: very few American officials knew of the Quebec Agreement, and those who did, with President Truman's knowledge, kept the 'exchange' clauses in the greatest of secrecy, fearing that if Congressional leaders got to hear of them the consequent outcry would be hysterical.

Attlee flew to Washington, accompanied by Sir John Anderson, on 9 November 1945, after telling a Mansion House luncheon that he was going to discuss world affairs with Truman and the Canadian Prime Minister, Mackenzie King, 'in the light, the terrible light, of the discovery of atomic energy'. During the flight Attlee talked about cricket, recommended Wisden as always good reading for settling the mind, and expounded on the similarities between selecting a cricket side and choosing a Cabinet. In Washington, a motorcycle escort conveyed him through the streets of the city with sirens at full blast, an experience which he found 'rather comical'. The talks with Truman and Mackenzie King began at once. There was a state dinner that evening, the next day Attlee attended Armistice Day celebrations with Truman, and the conference continued in the afternoon on the Potomac River on board the yacht of James Forrestal, Secretary to the Navy – 'convenient for evading the attentions of the Press'.

Although for the content of the atomic energy discussions Attlee wanted as little publicity as possible, for the stated purpose of his visit he wanted as much as he could get. As well as dealing with the bomb he wanted to use his visit to allay the suspicions of the American people about the character and objectives of a British socialist government. The American loan to Britain was still being negotiated, and relations between the two teams of experts were at their most strained. The American negotiators' estimate of their people's distrust of 'Socialist Britain' was a factor in their determination to make the terms of the loan as tough as possible. This was indeed a suitable time for Attlee to try and, as he put it, 'assist in removing some misapprehensions'. It was with this phrase that he began the last section of what the *New York Times* called 'a momentous speech', made to a joint session of Congress, 13 November. After eulogizing Churchill and Roosevelt and praising Truman, he gave a dissertation on how Britain had learned that 'we cannot make a heaven in our own country and leave a hell outside'. This was meant to be a tactful warning to the Americans that they could not afford to turn back to isolationism.

He devoted the remainder of his speech to a very necessary description of the nature and philosophy of the British Labour Party. The Americans had been stunned by the defeat of Churchill in the general election, and alarmed by the sweeping victory of the Labour Party. They had been antagonized by the immediate announcement which followed that victory of a programme of nationalization which seemed to many of them more to resemble Communism in Russia than Free Enterprise in America.

Of British Socialism and the British Labour Party Attlee said:

> I come before you as the Prime Minister of Great Britain, but, in accordance with our constitutional practice, I am also a party leader – the leader of a majority recently returned to power in the House of Commons. ... You

have heard that we are Socialists, but I wonder just what that means to you.

I think that some people over here imagine that the Socialists are out to destroy freedom, freedom of the individual, freedom of speech, freedom of religion, and the freedom of the Press. They are wrong; the Labour Party is in the tradition of freedom-loving movements which have always existed in our country, but freedom has to be striven for in every generation, and those who threaten it are not always the same. . . . We in the Labour Party declare that we are in line with those who fought for Magna Carta and *habeas corpus*, with the Pilgrim Fathers, and with the signatories of the Declaration of Independence.

There is, and always will be, scope for enterprise; but when big business gets too powerful, so that it becomes monopolistic, we hold it is not safe to leave it in private hands. Further, in the world today we believe, as do most people in Britain, that one must plan the economic activities of the country if we are to assure the common man a fair deal. One further word: you may think that the Labour Party consists solely of wage-earners. It is our pride that we draw the majority of our members from the ranks of wage-earners, and many of our Ministers have spent long years working with their hands in the coal mines, the factory, or in transportation. But our party today is drawn from all classes of society – professional men, business men, and what are sometimes called the privileged classes . . .

In our internal policies each country will follow the course decided by the people's will. You will see us embarking on projects of nationalisation, on wide all-embracing schemes of social insurance designed to give security to the common man. We shall be working out a planned economy. You, it may be, will continue in your more individualistic methods. It is important that we should understand each other and other nations whose institutions differ from our own. It is essential, if we are to build up a peaceful world, that we should have the widest toleration, recognising that our aim is not uniformity, but unity in diversity. It would be a dull world if we were all alike . . .

Man's material discoveries have outpaced his moral progress. The greatest task that faces us today is to bring home to all people before it is too late that our civilisation can only survive by the acceptance and practice in international relations and in our national life of the Christian principle that we are members of one another.

Exercised as the Americans were about the possibility of Britain's 'going red', public opinion was much more concerned about the bomb. The leaked misinformation about the Stimson memorandum was another ingredient in an atmosphere already volatile. The original feeling of guilt induced by the dropping of the bomb had soon been heightened by the series of reports about the genetic effects. At the same time fears aroused by the Russians in Eastern Europe were hardening the view in Congress that no information about atomic energy whatsoever should pass outside the United States, even to the most trusted of friends. The McMahon

Bill then under discussion aimed at preventing the American government from exchanging atomic energy information with foreign governments. Truman did not like the McMahon Bill, but he knew he would have to accept it as the price Congress would exact for leaving atomic energy under civilian, not military, control. The outlook for the success of Attlee's twin missions was not good. He wanted, first, to get the United States to declare its readiness to give up its monopoly of the bomb, and make over control of it to the UN as soon as the development of international confidence permitted; secondly, to prevent American security measures from denying Britain her rights under the Quebec Agreement.

The Quebec Agreement, concluded between Churchill, Roosevelt and Mackenzie King in 1943, had set up a Combined Policy Committee through which American scientists would divulge information to the British and the Canadians. The participants at Quebec also agreed never to use the bomb against each other, and that they would not use it against anybody else without each other's consent – nothing was said about consultation. They also agreed that they would not pass on any information about atomic energy in general to any third country without the agreement of the other two. The most important clauses were the fourth and fifth: issues arising out of the postwar industrial development of atomic energy should be settled by the president of the United States; and there should be full cooperation between the countries in the sharing of materials and information.

By the time Attlee went to Washington in November 1945, it had become clear that the American officials were not interpreting clauses four and five in the spirit which Britain had expected, and in the letter were dishonouring them. The American members of the Combined Policy Committee were divulging neither military nor industrial information to the British. The clauses in the Quebec Agreement relating to atomic energy information, they said, had been in the nature of an executive agreement, not a binding treaty. Attlee contested this.

Truman was much influenced by General Groves, then in charge of American military developments in the atomic field, who was unwilling to accept the implications of the Quebec Agreement as Britain interpreted them, and unwilling to agree to new specific undertakings to exchange information. Truman, while sympathetic to Attlee's arguments, supported Groves. He also explained to Attlee that because the exchange clauses were secret, it would be politically impossible to divulge them and announce new commitments to replace them. It should suffice for the British government to know that information about atomic energy would in fact be exchanged, but that the public announcement of 'co-operation' in the field would be put in general terms.

Attlee agreed, believing that what would not be made public would be honoured. Taking into account the circumstances, Attlee's visit to Truman was more productive than might have been anticipated, and his success looked greater than it was. A joint communiqué – the 'Agreed Declaration' – was issued on 15 November, proposing the establishment of a United Nations Commission on Atomic Energy. A memorandum was drawn up which promised 'full and effective co-operation in the field of atomic energy'. Though this was a very general statement, it was to be read, Attlee and Anderson assumed, in conjunction with the minutes of the talks, and they therefore believed when they left Washington that the United States government had now agreed that the ban on the exchange of atomic energy information did not apply to the UK and Canada. Attlee was questioned about this at a press conference, some newspapermen present having got wind of the attitude taken by Groves, and of the failure to get a public statement of the clauses in the Quebec Agreement. It was understood, he was told, that the conditions for sharing atomic energy 'secrets' could not be met. Attlee said: 'That is the wrong interpretation, since the joint statement clearly indicated that the intention was to proceed by steady stages to set up such safeguards as would make possible reciprocal sharing of this and other scientific discoveries.'

Attlee and Anderson returned to London via Ottawa, believing that they were bringing back 'a satisfactory agreement'. On 22 November Attlee gave the House a general account of his visit, though he was unable to divulge the most important element, the substance of his private conversations with Truman. In the debate Eden proposed, to cheers from the Labour benches and silence from his own, that the only way to make the world safe from the atomic bomb was for all nations to modify their ideas of national sovereignty. Another suggestion widely canvassed was to set up an international commission to eliminate atomic weapons. Attlee could not support this proposal:

I do not believe that in a warring world, except to a very limited extent, there can be a set of Queensberry Rules. I think an attempt on these lines is as futile as the attempt of the knightly combatants at the close of the Middle Ages to ban that unsporting method, gunpowder. If the world lapses again into large-scale war, every weapon including the atomic will be used. The only complete protection for the civilized world from the destructive use of scientific knowledge lies in the prevention of war. We – the three countries concerned in discovering and developing atomic energy – have already made available to the world the scientific information essential to its development for peaceful purposes. [A large claim, whose implications could not all be substantiated.] I would like to end with the words I used in addressing the Canadian Parliament: Unless we apply to the solution of those problems a moral enthusiasm as great as that which scientists bring to their research work, then our civilization, built up over so many centuries, will surely perish.

Within two months it was clear that Attlee had failed to get what he thought he had got from the American government. As Truman had anticipated, in order to secure *civilian* control for atomic energy development he was being urged to accept clauses in the McMahon Bill which would transfer domestic control of atomic energy from the War Department to a five-man civilian Atomic Energy Commission, but which would also forbid the transmission of atomic information, industrial as well as military, to any other country. At a meeting of the Combined Policy Committee in February 1946 the American representatives, briefed by General Groves, refused a British request for a new agreement on the exchange of information.

Meanwhile the pressures in Washington for a tough McMahon Bill were mounting. Attlee understood Truman's difficulties, but he felt he had been let down. There was still time to act. He began a campaign of correspondence with Truman which lasted for nearly three months, ending with the President's silence. His first move was to warn the American Ambassador in London, Averell Harriman, that if the McMahon Bill became law Britain would build atomic plants for military as well as civil production of atomic energy, news which he knew would not please the Americans. His second move was to ask the British Ambassador in Washington formally to exercise Britain's rights under the Quebec Agreement and the Washington Agreement of the previous November and request the Combined Policy Committee at its next meeting to supply data necessary for the construction of atomic plant in Britain.

The committee met in April; Britain's request was refused. Within a few hours Attlee cabled to the President personally. Again referring to the Quebec Agreement and the November memorandum, he said: 'I am gravely disturbed . . . "full and effective co-operation in the field of atomic energy between the United States, the United Kingdom and Canada" [the words of the November Agreement] cannot mean less than full interchange of information and a fair division of material.' The two agreements had only enshrined what was Britain's right. 'The war-time arrangements under which the major share of the development work and the construction and operation of full-scale plants were carried out in the United States have naturally meant that technological and engineering information has accumulated in your hands. . . . It seems essential that this information should be shared.' The Combined Policy Committee, therefore, should make a further attempt to work out a satisfactory basis for cooperation. In the last resort, the three heads of government should *order* the interchange of information, which the President was entitled to do under that part of the Quebec Agreement which stipulated that issues arising out of the use of atomic energy would be resolved by him personally.

In reply, Truman claimed that the Quebec Agreement did not bind the United States to supply to the UK 'in the post-war period the designs and assistance in construction and operation of plants necessary to the building of a plant'. The undertaking in the Washington Agreement of November 1945, 'full and effective co-operation', was 'very general' and did not alter the situation. For America to supply atomic information to Britain for the construction of atomic plants would be contrary to the Washington Declaration. Truman ended by saying that if Britain were to construct another atomic energy plant after agreeing in Washington to the establishment of an international commission, this would have a most damaging effect on the development of the United Nations Organization.

Attlee's reply, a last effort to resolve the issue amicably, took several weeks to prepare and ran to 2,000 words. He restated the history of Britain's development of nuclear technology until 1941, by which time the strain on Britain's resources was immense. In October 1941 Roosevelt had suggested a coordinated effort on the part of Britain and the United States, and British assistance was given 'in the confident belief that the experience and knowledge gained in America would be made freely available to us, just as we made freely available to you the results of research in other fields such as radar and jet propulsion. . . . I must repeat that, but for that system, we should have been forced to adopt a different distribution of our resources in this country, which would not have been so advantageous to the common interest.' This understanding was embodied in the Quebec Agreement of 1943. Whenever Britain had been tempted to resume atomic energy work on her own, 'we came back to the principle of the Quebec Agreement – that the earliest possible realization of the project must come first, and before any separate national advantage, and that while our scientists could still contribute anything to the work in the United States, they should not be withdrawn.' Attlee went on to argue that the Washington Agreement of November 1945 confirmed the principle of the Quebec Agreement. He rejected Truman's arguments against helping Britain build her own atomic plant: the Washington Declaration was 'certainly not intended to stifle all further developments in other countries, any more than it was suggested that the development which has already taken place in the United States should be abandoned'. What the refusal of the United States to provide information amounted to was a dissolution of their partnership with Britain and with Canada.

Truman did not reply; in his memoirs he said that he could not do so before Congress had acted on the McMahon Bill. When passed, in August, the McMahon Act forbade the administration to pass atomic information to any other government. Then, as Attlee recorded, 'we had to go ahead on our own.'

Attlee had now been let down twice by Truman. The precipitate termination of the Lend–Lease agreement could be dismissed as short-sightedness; the American attitude to the exchange of atomic information smacked of duplicity. Attlee knew that Truman had to pay a price to keep the ultimate control of atomic energy out of the hands of the generals, and his verdict was: 'It wasn't Truman's fault. Congress was to blame.' Nobody knew better than Attlee that leadership was limited by the hopes and fears of the led, and that if 'his people wouldn't have it', even the President must pretend in public that a declaration had a meaning different from that which had induced another government to sign it.

V

The first months of Attlee's prime ministership contained the seeds of the main problems which would face him as he led the country into the postwar world. Britain's economy was almost fatally weakened, and she was therefore dependent on the generosity and good sense of the United States not only for the maintenance of her standard of life, but also for her capacity to act as a Great Power. Attlee saw it as his task to hold on to as much independence as possible in these unpromising conditions. It was essential, as never before, to govern the country with administrative efficiency and with drive and imagination. As leader of a socialist party, and a capable administrator, Attlee was ready for both those challenges. But he needed as well the political courage to make demands on the United States, not to be overawed by Truman, not to be discouraged by the huge disparity in power and resources between the two allies. In later years he was to be accused, especially by the left wing of his own party, of an excessive deference to American policy. The two episodes of the end of Lend–Lease and the atomic energy dispute show that he had few illusions about American policy even in 1945. In later years the essence of his leadership was to make the best of an impossible situation.

These events were the beginnings of the road which led Attlee to decide in January 1947 that Britain should manufacture her own nuclear bomb, a decision for which he has since been profoundly criticized. Though many felt that as the years went on Attlee's usual open-mindedness seemed to desert him where atomic energy was concerned, others cite his atomic energy policy as an example of his readiness to act quickly and vigorously when the occasion required. His 'success', both in manipulating the Estimates to conceal £100 million of expenditure from Parliament and in perpetrating what some have pronounced an egregious blunder, has since been subjected to thorough scrutiny in the work of Professor Margaret Gowing and Lorna Arnold.

So far as possible, from earliest days in the war until the early fifties, the Cabinet was kept in the dark about atomic energy and the bomb. When major atomic decisions had to be taken at Cabinet level, as much of the information as could be was deliberately obscured or made highly secret. After 1945, the principle was that so far as possible atomic energy and the bomb should be left to the personal surveillance of Attlee, guided by the Advisory Committee of service officials, civil servants and scientists which he had set up under the chairmanship of Sir John Anderson. There was thus no official or political link between the highly important committee and the rest of the ministers in the Cabinet.

Anderson was in a sense a deputy prime minister for atomic energy, until in August 1946 his committee was in effect replaced by another committee, the 'Atomic Energy Official Committee', which consisted of representatives of the Chiefs of Staff Secretariat, the Foreign Office, the Treasury, the Dominions Office, and the Ministry of Supply. It continued to practise the highest possible secrecy. The Anderson committee disappeared the following year. When the Ministry of Defence was set up in 1946, a Defence Research Policy Committee was also set up to advise it. But this committee was unable to give the Defence Ministry advice about atomic weapons because it was not informed about what was being done, and therefore its reports to the chiefs of staff on research and development were so inadequate as to be nonsensical. The arrangements seemed strange enough in the days when only the military uses of atomic energy were being determined: when peacetime developments came up a little later they seemed bizarre – for example, the Minister of Supply, who was to pay for development and use the product, not only had no say in what was going on but knew very little about it.

The secrecy, and the consequent muddle, went on for the rest of the Attlee government's life. The last phase was the oddest. By that time the Ministry of Supply had so far been let into the secret that it had been given responsibility for the production of atomic energy and had been allowed to set up a research establishment. Lord Portal, the first Controller of Atomic Energy, belonged to the Ministry of Supply, but again he reported directly to the Prime Minister, and in the discussions of whether Britain should make its own bombs or not thought it was his duty to withhold, as far as possible, all information about developments from his ministerial chief. When Portal resigned in 1951 he was replaced as Controller by a soldier, General Sir Frederick Morgan, who had commanded a parachute brigade during the war. The story in Whitehall was that Sir Frederick's appointment was a mistake: Attlee had got him confused with Sir William Morgan, who he thought had done a good job in Washington as the representative of the chiefs of staff.

The most important decision Attlee made in relation to atomic energy was that Britain should produce her own bomb. He did so on the advice of the chiefs of staff. The Defence Research Policy Committee was not consulted. The head of the committee, Sir Henry Tizard, did not know about the fateful decision until six months later, and if he had known about it he would have opposed it. The die was cast in January 1947 (the House of Commons was not informed until May 1948) by an *ad hoc* committee which consisted of Attlee, Morrison, Bevin, Christopher Addison (Commonwealth Relations), A.V. Alexander (Defence) and John Wilmot (Supply). Attlee has been much criticized for coming to that decision: it is said that he should have foreseen that the 'independent deterrent' would be impossibly expensive and would never be independent, since it could never be used unless the Americans agreed to its use. In the late 1950s its existence threatened to split the Labour Party, brought about the leftwing-led Campaign for Nuclear Disarmament, and precipitated the demonstrations and protests for unilateral nuclear disarmament which caused much turbulence in Anglo-American relations.

A judgement on Attlee for giving the word for Britain to manufacture her own atomic bomb should take into account the circumstances in which he had to make the decision. In the first days of 1947 the Russians were strongly entrenched in Europe. The 'Truman Doctrine' of containment of the Russians was in its infancy. There was a possibility that the presidential election of the following year would result in the election of an isolationist Republican who would withdraw the American presence from Europe, leaving Britain to resist further expansion of the Russians to the west. Britain could not have resisted the Russian advance with conventional weapons. It is therefore not surprising that the chiefs of staff asked for the British bomb. A prime minister would have taken a great risk if he had decided to refuse their request.

Attlee had no doubts about it:

> If we had decided not to have it, we would have put ourselves entirely in the hands of the Americans. That would have been a risk a British government should not take. It's all very well to look back, and to say otherwise, but at that time nobody could be sure that the Americans would not revert to isolationism – many Americans wanted that, many Americans feared it. There was no NATO then. For a power of our size and with our responsibilities to turn its back on the Bomb did not make sense.

This was the general consensus. Professor Gowing concludes:

> The British decision to make an atomic bomb had 'emerged' from a body of general assumptions. It had not been a response to an immediate military threat but rather something fundamentalist and almost instinctive – a feeling that Britain must possess so climacteric a weapon in order to deter an atomically armed enemy, a feeling that Britain as a great power must

acquire all major new weapons, a feeling that atomic weapons were a manifestation of the scientific and technological superiority on which Britain's strength, so deficient if measured in sheer numbers of men, must depend.

Though Attlee had made up his mind that Britain must have her own bomb, and though he had been disappointed by Truman's failure to re-establish a special Anglo-American relationship in the field of atomic energy, he continued to hope for a new era of collaboration. The outlook for real cooperation between the two countries in the atomic energy field brightened in January 1947, when General Marshall, Britain's wartime friend and comrade in arms, succeeded Byrnes as Secretary of State. Marshall was an internationalist, a statesman, and an Anglophile, and he was revered by Truman. His appointment inaugurated a period of much closer Anglo-American relations, beginning with the Marshall Plan, and following through to the signature of the NATO alliance in 1949. Attlee lost no time in trying to take advantage of what seemed to be the dawning of a new era, and at once sought to re-establish the Anglo-American partnership in the field of atomic energy.

As it happened, talks on atomic energy had already been proposed by the Americans, with the undisclosed motive of acquiring access to Britain's large reserves of uranium (from the Congo) which had been stockpiled in the United Kingdom. The talks concluded in an agreement which gave the US the whole of the Belgian Congo raw materials until the end of 1949, and, if this supply was inadequate, the right to draw on Britain's reserves. The British government acquired very little and conceded a great deal, giving up the right to veto the use of the bomb by the Americans which had been enshrined in the Quebec Agreement, and also the right even to be asked to 'consent'. The British were not gulled; they accepted this unsatisfactory *modus vivendi* because they thought, and were advised, that if they made trouble for the administration with a presidential election due that year, they would do themselves no good, whereas if they settled for what was possible now, those American officials who were friendly to Britain would seize the first opportunity to improve the arrangement. The power of veto was not recovered until October 1951.

In January 1949 Marshall resigned as Secretary of State, and was succeeded by Dean Acheson, who had always felt guilty about the way Britain had been treated over atomic energy. The Americans were still anxious to obtain more ore, and the period of the *modus vivendi* was running out. Britain had developed a great deal of technical knowhow and was well on the way to producing her own bomb. Her bargaining position, as Acheson pointed out to the President, was month by month becoming stronger. Acheson's task was lightened by the news in

September that the Russians had exploded an atomic bomb. With the device, wrote Acheson, the Russians also exploded 'a good deal of senatorial nonsense about our priceless secret heritage'. For the rest of the year the talks were 'jogging along comfortably'. By the end of the year British objectives had changed in a way which made them more acceptable to the Americans. Now that the Russians were known to possess the bomb, the British had to face the fact that they did not have the lead they thought they had – the first British test was not expected for another three years. The British government's main objective therefore switched to getting a supply of American bombs on to British soil, rather than continuing to press for information to hasten the manufacture of her own. To obtain these the British government was prepared to subordinate their strategic planning to that of the Americans – 'integration' rather than 'independence'.

But it was not to be. In February 1950 the British atomic scientist Klaus Fuchs, who had worked in the US during the war, was arrested in London and charged with giving information to the Russians. In the same month Senator McCarthy began his series of attacks on the State Department, alleging that it harboured crypto-Communists and Russian sympathizers. 'The talks with the British and Canadians returned to square one, where there was a deep freezer from which they did not emerge in my time,' recorded Acheson ('my time' ending in 1952). Britain did not get her bombs from America, and instead tested her own in 1952. Not until the middle fifties, well after the Labour government had fallen, did Anglo-American cooperation in the atomic field reach a level even comparable with that which had developed in almost all other areas of the special relationship.

Whether or not Attlee did right to provide Britain with an independent deterrent, his handling of his atomic energy problems is vulnerable on other grounds. From the beginning he pursued a line of maximum secrecy and minimum publicity which made a sensible policy difficult to obtain. Whereas in the United States an Atomic Energy Commission was set up, with a Congressional Committee to overlook it and the press encouraged to discuss it, Attlee and his advisers did their best to discourage and avoid press and parliamentary inquiries. During the whole of the Labour government of 1945–50 there was not a single House of Commons debate on atomic energy. Questions about the subject and references to it were squelched. After the first Russian bomb test in 1949, thirty-four MPs put down a motion asking the Prime Minister to take the initiative and call for an international conference of heads of state to break through the barrier on the exchange of atomic information. Attlee told them he thought it would be fruitless and dangerous to discuss the motion, largely because it might give the impression of 'appeasement politics'. Bevin minuted in a Foreign Office file: 'Keep it off' [the order paper]. The government used every means it could to prevent the newspapers from mentioning the subject.

Any prime minister in his position might have done the same, but Attlee, in his readiness to shroud in secrecy what Britain was doing about her bomb, connived at arrangements which were constitutionally dubious. Nearly all his Cabinet ministers were systematically kept ignorant about a most expensive, and possibly hazardous, national commitment. The Defence Committee never discussed it, and the main committee responsible for atomic energy had only limited facilities for discovering, let alone determining, what was being done. The only politician who knew enough about what was going on to make an effective contribution to government policy was Anderson, a prominent member of the Opposition.

Perhaps Attlee sought to suppress discussions of atomic energy because he did not want to risk trouble with the left wing of his party; perhaps he was afraid that Churchill knew more about the subject than the Labour government did, and might embarrass the present government in parliamentary debates by arousing public apprehension. Attlee was certainly aware of one good reason for not having atomic energy publicly debated: the risk of arousing anti-Americanism. There were fears that the Americans might use the bomb unilaterally. They were known to be unwilling to exchange information for the peacetime use of atomic energy. Anxiety and resentment in Britain at this time could poison Anglo-American relations in general, and in particular reduce the chance of the resumption of Anglo-American cooperation in the atomic energy field.

The last word might well be left with Professor Gowing:

> If it had not been for the extraordinary competence of three men at the working level – John Cockcroft, Christopher Hinton and William Penney – the Attlee Government's atomic energy project might have been an expensive fiasco. Instead it was to prove in the period of the Labour Government, within the objectives set for it, one of the most successfully executed programmes in British scientific and technological history.

18
Cold Warrior,
1945-9

I

So much has been said in praise of Ernest Bevin's period as foreign secretary in the postwar Labour government that it is easy to forget that, until he unexpectedly took the post instead of becoming chancellor of the exchequer, the repository of the Labour Party's expertise on British foreign policy had been Attlee. Though he delegated an unprecedented amount of planning and decision-making to his Foreign Secretary there was no question that all responsibility was his, and he made a number of interventions in the execution of policy. In Cabinet Bevin presented the topics, and usually suggested the course to be followed. But Attlee's view is always clear – more often so than in some discussions of domestic problems – and there is no instance of his view failing to prevail.

The general situation which faced the Attlee government was complex, and confused. The main problem was Russia. It was clear that there was a conflict of interest between the Soviet Union and Britain, but it was not so clear how deep this went, and how far Russian demands would go. Russian armies, in vast strength, were now stationed far into Eastern Europe. In dealing with Stalin Attlee had to take into account the immense strength of the armed Russian presence in Europe; the pro-Russian, anti-capitalist sympathies, very articulate, of the left wing of the Labour Party – and by no means confined to that section; the incompetence of an American foreign policy which in the last months of the war had suffered from Roosevelt's belief that if he could sufficiently dissociate himself from Britain's long-term foreign policy commitments, and muzzle Churchill, he could do business on a basis of trust with Stalin; and, in the first few months of the Truman regime, a Secretary of State, James Byrnes, who thought that Roosevelt had been right and Churchill had been wrong, and that the Americans could handle Europe's problems far better than the British could.

The problem of what to make of the intentions of the Russians in the first few months of the Labour government was compounded by the question of what to make of the Americans. Attlee and Truman got on very well together personally, but it was evident to Bevin and his Foreign Office advisers that Byrnes, for the US, was willing to concede far more to the Soviet Union than the British thought just or safe. Bevin left Potsdam annoyed and disturbed by Byrnes's 'inconsistency'. He talked to Attlee about it. He was worried about things the Americans did, or did not do, which indicated a general lack of judgement. Those sins of commission or omission were best exemplified by the decision the Americans had taken a few weeks before, in May 1945, not to allow American forces to occupy Prague. A few weeks earlier the British government had urged the Americans to order Eisenhower to occupy Berlin. The US government replied that it would leave the decision to Eisenhower, who took the view that military policy should not be influenced by political considerations. He said he preferred not to drive forward to Berlin, and took it on himself to communicate his decision direct to Stalin. He thereby enabled the Russians to occupy the capital at their leisure – a tragic naïveté.

These and other comparable decisions diminished the confidence of the coalition government in the judgement of their American allies, and Labour inherited this lack of confidence. Further decisions raised similar doubts. Truman's decision to end Lend–Lease, and American positions in regard to the loan and to sharing information about atomic energy, were all alarming. Once the war was over, American attitudes towards Britain seemed to become cool if not clinical. Britain was at the same time under suspicion for being too reactionary and too radical. Hostility to British imperialism was coupled with the conviction that Britain was too weak to be any longer a factor in world politics. Harry Hopkins, whom Truman had sent to Moscow before the Potsdam Conference, came back and reported to him that whereas Britain's interests could bring her into conflict with those of the United States, those of Russia would not. If the British government had doubts about the wisdom of the Americans, the Americans had doubts about Britain's health and strength. Admiral Leahy, Truman's military adviser at Potsdam, informed him that Britain was 'prostrate economically' and 'relatively impotent militarily'. And as well as the problems of assessing and adapting to the policies of her two allies, Britain in the early postwar period was faced by the special difficulty of operating in a world not only shattered by war but now plagued by food shortages.

Attlee's internationalism, like Bevin's, was never in doubt, and like Bevin's it was as much the product of his pragmatic approach to world affairs as of his commitment to international socialism. The United

Nations was to be the basis of Britain's foreign policy. His speech in the House on 22 August 1945 on the ratification of the UN Charter was a classic expression of this. The basic provisions of the Charter corresponded to the realities of world power. 'The success of the new organization will not depend so much on the exact provisions as on the spirit in which they are worked. If a Great Power resolves not to carry out the principles, laid down in the Charter, no paper provisions will restrain it.' After the atomic bomb, 'I am quite certain that all of us in this House realise that we are now faced with a naked choice between world co-operation and world destruction.' He struck the same note in this address to the Trades Union Congress on 12 September 1945. In October there was an all-party demonstration for the United Nations Association at the Albert Hall, at which Attlee said: 'As Prime Minister, I wish to say quite simply that it is the firm intention of His Majesty's Government to make the success of the United Nations the primary object of their foreign policy.'

Attlee did not think that diplomats or Foreign Office officials had special gifts or knowledge which others could not understand or share. Nor did he think that 'great men' could suddenly produce solutions which their subordinates had failed to find. British foreign policy may have been mistaken in the period 1945-50 but it was integrated. It suffered very little from such tensions as had existed between Churchill and Eden in the period from 1940-4, and not at all from the fundamental contradictions which bedevilled it in the days of Eden and Chamberlain. Attlee and Bevin were friends, and on all broad issues they agreed. Attlee never asked himself whether Bevin had had enough experience of foreign affairs to make a successful foreign secretary. In a review for *The Observer* of the first volume of Bullock's massive life of Bevin, Attlee wrote: 'Years before he went to the Foreign Office, he had a vast knowledge of industrial, financial and social conditions in many different countries.'

There was a bond of affection between them. 'My relationship with Ernest Bevin was the deepest of my political life. I was very fond of him and I understand he was very fond of me.' Above all Attlee admired Bevin's loyalty. 'Loyalty is a great virtue in private life and an even greater one in the stormy seas of politics – second only to courage, with which indeed it goes hand in hand. Ernest was the living symbol of loyalty ... once he gave his trust to you he was like a rock.' Bevin talked a great deal to Attlee. No differences seem to have arisen between them. When major issues came up, Bevin, according to Lord Franks, Ambassador to Washington 1948-52, 'would not move until he knew he had Attlee with him'.

It is generally agreed that Attlee's strength as Prime Minister owed much to loyal support from Bevin based on his standing with the trade unions, the industrial wing of the Labour Movement. It is not so generally acknowledged that Bevin's strength as Foreign Secretary owed much to Attlee's capacity for controlling the political wing of the Labour Movement. Bevin abhorred his left-wing parliamentary critics. They were 'irresponsible'. In Attlee's words, 'there was no place for the rebel in Ernest's organization. He was a majorities man and was impatient with minorities, in which respect he ran counter to one of the most important traditions in the Labour Party.' At no time did this attitude more threaten trouble for Bevin than in the first few months of the postwar period, when there was a strong demand in the party for a distinctive 'socialist' foreign policy in general, and for 'friendship with Russia' in particular. The minorities had to be dealt with. Bevin would have tried to hammer them.

Attlee had his own way of dealing with minorities. In September 1945 Fenner Brockway, Attlee's old syndicalist friend of the twenties, wrote expressing concern about reports from Annam and Java that British policy was being used to suppress independent movements. Attlee replied: 'You may be certain that the Government is carrying out the principles for which it always stood.'

> There is always a tendency on the part of some people in the Labour Party to over-simplify foreign affairs. It's partly due to a certain woolly idealism; seeing everything black and white when in fact there are all sorts of shades of grey. They mean well but they don't like looking at unpleasant facts. Some of them thought we ought to concentrate all our efforts on building up a Third Force in Europe. Very nice, no doubt. But there wasn't either a material or a spiritual basis for it at that time. What remained of Europe wasn't strong enough to stand up to Russia by itself. You had to have a world force because you were up against a world force .... Without the stopping power of the Americans, the Russians might easily have tried sweeping right forward. I don't know whether they would, but it wasn't a possibility you could just ignore. It's no good thinking that moral sentiments have any sway with the Russians, there's a good deal of old-fashioned imperialism in their make-up, you know. Their foreign policy has been carried on in much the same way from the days of Queen Catherine the Great. Some of our friends wouldn't see that.

In February 1946, Konni Zilliacus, now regarded as on the extreme left of the Party, sent Attlee a lengthy memoradum on foreign policy, reminding him how 'we worked together for so many years before the war, particularly between 1931 and 1935'. Attlee replied:

> My dear Zilly,
> Thank you for sending me your memorandum which seems to me to be based on an astonishing lack of understanding of the facts.
> Yours ever,
> Clem.

The continuity of British foreign policy over the period of the change of government has already been described. The personal regard of Churchill, Eden, Attlee and Bevin for each other contributed to it. This incipient bipartisanship on major issues was another problem for the Labour government. The left wing of the party deplored it; the fact that leading Tories supported what Bevin was doing was another reason for opposing his foreign policy. A political price had to be paid for Bevin's success as Foreign Secretary; and the largest subscription had to come from his Prime Minister.

II

Attlee would always intervene on specific issues when asked; Bevin would always consult him without any loss of *amour propre*. In April 1946 Churchill wrote to Bevin urging him to intercede with Tito to save the life of Mihailovich, Tito's rival for the leadership of Yugoslav Resistance in the early years of the war, later his opponent in the Yugoslav civil war. Bevin referred the matter to Attlee, who had already made up his mind. A personal minute to Bevin reads: 'I do not see that we are called upon to intervene. Mihailovich did nothing against the Germans for a long time. He then was a party to attacks on Tito's forces.' Mihailovich was tried, found guilty, and was executed in July.

From time to time, Attlee made his own contribution to the conduct of foreign affairs, as exemplified by his minutes as Prime Minister reproduced in Appendix IV below. The first occasion was the result of the original meeting of the Council of Foreign Ministers in London on 11 September 1945. It had been agreed at Potsdam that there would be frequent meetings, normally in London, of the five foreign ministers of Britain, America, Russia, France and China. The 'immediate and important task' of the council was the preparation and drafting for submission to the UN of peace treaties with Italy, Bulgaria, Finland, Hungary and Romania – a treaty with Germany would follow. France, never having entered the war against the hastily formed Italian government which had surrendered to Britain and the United States, was not legally entitled to participate in discussions of the Italian peace treaty, much less China; but 'in a spirit of cordiality and co-operation' the Big Three at Potsdam formally ruled that France 'shall be regarded as a signatory to the terms of surrender for Italy', and China was invited to attend.

By the time of the first meeting of the council, the 'spirit of cordiality and co-operation' had given way to some mutual suspicion. The dropping of the atomic bomb and the swift defeat of Japan had established the dominance of the United States in the Far East, and the Russians were alarmed. They in turn had disturbed the Allies by flouting in

Bulgaria and Romania that section of the Yalta Agreement which obliged the victorious powers to establish democractic regimes in all liberated countries. In London, anticipating that the French and the Chinese would consistently line up with the British and the Americans against them in all discussion of treaties with Bulgaria and Romania, the Russians contended that it had been decided at Potsdam that France could discuss only treaties affecting *Western* Europe, and that China could not discuss European matters at all. Bevin and the US Secretary of State, James Byrnes, resisted this vigorously and prevailed: Molotov gave in.

This concession was most promising, but cooperation did not last. The Soviet Union asked to be given trusteeship over the Italian colony of Tripolitania. This was refused. The Cabinet Papers reveal how determined Attlee and Bevin were to prevent Russia getting a foothold in the Mediterranean. On the other side Britain and the US refused to recognize the Russian-sponsored regimes in Romania and Bulgaria until these had promised to hold free elections to determine the long-term basis of government in these countries. On 22 September, only eleven days after agreeing to seat France and China, Molotov demanded the scrapping of that agreement, and reverted to his view that neither France nor China would be able to join in discussion of any of the treaties with the satellites. Bevin and Byrnes conceded that France and China would be excluded from *voting* on the treaties, but claimed that they were to participate in *discussing* them. Byrnes asked Truman to appeal to Stalin. Stalin replied, endorsing Molotov's position. The council was now deadlocked. It broke up a few days later, 2 October.

Attlee also got in touch with Stalin, sending a long telegram to Moscow on 23 September. He summarized Bevin's arguments and supported them. He pointed out that Molotov himself had shared the view, and had agreed to act on it on the first day of the London conference.

> I should view with great misgiving the institution of a precedent for calling in question decisions so taken and seeking to reverse them and therefore rejecting the conclusion arrived at by the British Foreign Minister acting in concert with other Ministers and introducing an element of confusion into their proceedings. Indeed I doubt whether it would be possible to gain unanimous consent of the Council to reversal of its earlier decision and any attempt to do so would clearly cause great offence to France and China and would be completely misunderstood here by the public and Parliament, to whom we reported in good faith that the Council would act as a Council of Five, a statement which was received with a sense of relief in this country.... Therefore I earnestly hope that you will agree to authorise your delegation to adhere to the decision taken on September 11. After all it is peace we are endeavouring to establish, which is more important than procedure.

When the Council of Foreign Ministers next met, in Paris, the following

May, Molotov made no attempt to pursue his campaign to exclude France and China.

If Churchill's speech at Fulton, Missouri, 5 March 1946, did not mark the beginning of the Cold War, the support which the US accorded to his references to the Iron Curtain showed that the Americans had now abandoned the Rooseveltian dream of cooperation with Stalin. Attlee had been consulted about Churchill's visit and had raised no objection. He was always ready to be helpful to Churchill, permitting him to use government aircraft to travel on holidays, and never putting protocol between him and meetings with leading political figures abroad. From his point of view, Churchill's conduct in America was exemplary, though left-wing backbenchers complained that his visit should never have been allowed.

Far from creating trouble for the Attlee government by references to an 'Iron Curtain', Churchill had given it some assistance. Sir Ben Smith, Minister of Food, who was in Washington at the time, reported in a personal telegram to Attlee three days later that he had been present at the lunch which the National Press Club had given to Churchill. Sir Ben praised Churchill's behaviour. Under strenuous cross-examination Churchill had 'vigorously repudiated the suggestion that the loan would merely be a subsidy to socialism and stressed the fundamental solidarity of the British people. ... Altogether he gave us helpful support and his statements should go a good way to offset the effects here of the attitude of the Opposition to the loan agreement.' Attlee telegraphed to Churchill the following day:

> I have just heard from Ben Smith of the very helpful remarks which you made at the National Press Club luncheon about the American loan, and I should like to send you my warm thanks and appreciation for the friendly line you took.
>
> Thank you also for the long and interesting telegram which you sent Bevin and me on March 7 – I hope we may have a talk on your return. I have shown the telegram to Eden.
>
> I trust that the remainder of your stay will be pleasant, and that you are keeping well. Best wishes to Mrs Churchill and yourself.

Stalin's reaction to the Fulton speech was to denounce Churchill as a warmonger. The left wing of the British Labour Party were disturbed by it. Bevin found it necessary to try to calm their fears by emphasizing that the government were not in any way a party to the speech and by reiterating his willingness to extend the wartime alliance with Russia. In view of this, Attlee could not express approval of the speech in public; in private he was delighted with it, and with the impact it had made on the Americans, whom he still considered to be naïve in their attitude to Stalin.

III

One of the most important factors in Britain's foreign policy was the shortage of dollars.

In the first Cabinet meeting of 1946, Bevin reported his recent conversations with Stalin in Moscow. Stalin had expressed the hope that Britain would remain a power in the Middle East, that she would not withdraw from Egypt. Bevin was sceptical about these sentiments. Attlee shared his doubts, but did not reject Stalin's statements out of hand. The coat must be cut according to the cloth, but what was the pattern to be? How his mind worked in the early months of 1946 is illustrated by two extracts from Dalton's diary. The first is dated 18 February. Dalton had spent the weekend at Chequers, talking at length to Attlee,

> ... getting him more and more aware of the seriousness of the overseas deficit. .... Attlee is fresh-minded on Defence. It was no good, he thought, pretending any more that we could keep open the Mediterranean route in time of war. That meant we could pull troops out of Egypt and the rest of the Middle East, as well as Greece. Nor could we hope, he thought, to defend Turkey, Iraq or Persia against a steady pressure of the Russian land masses. And if India 'goes her own way' before long, as she must, there will be still less sense in thinking of lines of Imperial communications through the Suez Canal. We should be prepared to work round the Cape to Australia and New Zealand. If, however, the USA were to become seriously interested in Middle Eastern oil, the whole thing would look different. Meanwhile, the USA seem to be repeating their post-last-war experience. Little men were nominally in charge, but the whole political machine was out of control.

Immediately after the Fulton speech, Dalton recorded on 9 March 1946:

> Attlee is pressing on the Chiefs of Staff and the Defence Committee a large view of his own, aiming at considerable disengagement from areas where there is a risk of clashing with the Russians. We should pull out, he thinks, from all the Middle East including Egypt and Greece, make a line of defence across Africa from Lagos to Kenya, and concentrate a large part of our forces in the latter. In view of India's uncertain attitude in future, we should put a large part of Commonwealth Defence, including many industries, into Australia. We should put a wide glacis of desert and Arabs between ourselves and the Russians. This is a very fresh and interesting approach, which appeals to me.

Attlee toned down his hopes of disengagement as a result of Russian behaviour at the meeting of the foreign ministers in Paris in April. The ministers met to agree on drafts of five treaties to be submitted to the peace conference scheduled to assemble, also in Paris, the following month. When the foreign ministers met, belatedly, on 25 April, two things were clear: that there was no hope of them getting drafts of treaties ready for the scheduled date of the peace conference, 1 May, and that Byrnes, the American Secretary of State, had abandoned hope of appeasing Russia. On the eve of the conference Bevin had been taken ill, and Attlee had to go out at the last minute to replace him. The British delegation did not impress at least one observer, Harold Nicolson:

> Attlee, so small, so chétif; A. V. Alexander, sturdy but scrubby; Hector McNeil, Scotch and dour; Glenvil Hall, a secondary school teacher. How insignificant they look there in their red plush stalls! How different from Lloyd George and Balfour, how terribly different from Winston.

The conference did not manage to conclude the treaties: further sessions of the conference and the Council of Foreign Ministers were necessary before they were signed early the following year. Moreover, its proceedings confirmed that Stalin would take every chance that presented itself of expanding his position in the Mediterranean and Eastern Europe, and that what he had told Bevin to the contrary in Moscow seven months previously was totally misleading.

IV

During 1946 more and more rumblings of discontent about foreign policy came from Labour backbenchers, not only from the 'fellow-travellers' but from many who saw Britain 'ganging up' with the United States against Russia, and disapproved. At the annual party conference in June 1946, Laski referred to Russian suspicions of Great Britain, and had said that a socialist government required as the central principle of its policy in the United Nations Organization the fullest understanding with Russia. Bevin had to defend himself against several resolutions criticizing the government's foreign policy.

In September the American Secretary of Commerce, Wallace, made a speech opposing what he described as an Anglo-American policy of 'get tough with Russia'. His theme was not so much in praise of Russian policies as in condemnation of Britain's: 'We must not let British balance-of-power manipulation determine whether and when the USA gets into war.' Wallace was sacked. The speech and the sacking had a pronounced effect on the British left. Wallace was the nearest thing to a socialist in the American government. That he should be removed for proclaiming what they themselves feared alarmed them. They made speeches similar to his except that instead of speaking of British 'balance-of-power manipulation' they spoke of 'American'. Whereas in March 1946 only six members of the PLP dissented from a motion completely endorsing the government's foreign policy, in October twenty-one of them signed a private letter to Attlee calling on the government to abandon Bevin's foreign policy and to follow a distinctly socialist line.

Bevin came back from the Paris Peace Conference on 22 October and made a report on its proceedings to date in the House, criticizing behaviour of the Soviet Union. Two days later Attlee attended the annual TUC conference at Brighton. A resolution before Congress strongly condemned various aspects of the government's foreign policy, and in particular complained that Britain tended to side with America against Russia. Attlee referred to the resolution in his speech:

> Democracy is becoming a much-abused word. It is often used by those who have never understood or practised democratic principles to mean the achievement of power – by hook and, more often, by crook – by the Communist party, while freedom means the denial of liberty to all those who refuse to accept the Communist philosophy. Everyone who does not take orders from the Communists is described as a fascist. The criterion by which these people judge their actions is a simple one. If in any part of the world the Communist party, by no matter what means, is in power, that is democracy. If anywhere the Communists fail, then, however fair the conditions, it is Fascism. Thus an election in Greece, supervised internationally, which results in an anti-Communist majority, is at once denounced. On the other hand, a plebiscite taken where the Communist party is in power is regarded as the sacred voice of the people. We as democrats are not concerned to decide for others how they should vote; we are concerned to see that the method of arriving at the conclusion should be just and fair. I notice on your agenda that the only resolution on foreign affairs is one which seems to me to be filled with the kind of misrepresentation to which we have become accustomed from the members of the Communist party, their dupes, and fellow-travellers.

The resolution was rejected by $3\frac{1}{2}$ to $2\frac{1}{2}$ million votes. The full weight of the big unions had to be thrown in to secure its defeat. The applause went to the speeches made in favour of it.

Attlee now had considerable trouble on his hands. Just as during the war, as deputy prime minister, he had so often to take the lightning for Churchill, absent on conferences overseas, now he had to take it for his Foreign Secretary, who, as Dalton put it, was 'much abroad and out of touch with Parliamentary opinion'. If Bevin was conducting foreign policy, it was Attlee who most of the time had to defend it in the House of Commons. The Conservatives did not embarrass him. Attlee's problem was the feeling in his own party. When Parliament began its second session, on 12 November 1946, critics on his own side of the House decided to concert their forces and table an amendment to the Address, calling on the government to 'provide a democratic and constructive socialist alternative to an otherwise inevitable conflict between American capitalism and Soviet Communism'. There were fifty-seven signatures.

This was a formidable challenge to Attlee's claim that his government represented a country united on foreign policy. The following day at a meeting of the Parliamentary Labour Party he rebuked those who had tabled the amendment and asked for it to be withdrawn. The PLP carried a motion to withdraw the amendment by a majority of four to one, but the 'rebels' insisted that the amendment would be moved, and there was so much feeling that the number of signatures increased to nearly a hundred. Nevertheless, Attlee's call for discipline had steadied the malcontents in their tracks. They had talked of forcing a division on the amendment: on that they now hung back.

The amendment was moved five days later by Dick Crossman. The Labour Party, he claimed, had fought the general election on a claim that only a Labour government could prevent the division of the Western world into two blocs, the American and the Russian. The Labour government had now created the impression that British foreign policy was governed by 'an exclusive Anglo-American tie-up between the two front benches'. He challenged Attlee to disavow the proposals for an Anglo-American alliance which Churchill had made 'in his notorious speech at Fulton'. Much of what the government was doing was justifiable only on the assumption that 'it was necessary to deal with Soviet Russia as Nazi Germany had been dealt with'.

Bevin was at the conference of foreign ministers in New York. It was for Attlee to reply to Crossman. It was one of his best speeches, a point-by-point refutation of Crossman's charges. He began with a counter-attack on those who were assailing Bevin personally, and on those who described cooperation with the Americans as 'ganging up' against the Soviet Union:

> I resent the attacks made on the Foreign Secretary, made often by people whose services in the cause of Labour and Socialism are as dust in the balance compared to his. . . . I am in very close touch with him, and I know how hard he has striven to get both our great Allies to work together. He has never been one for 'ganging up' in one way or the other.

It was remarkable, he said, that Crossman had 'managed to get through a speech on foreign affairs without once mentioning the United Nations'.

> Let me state emphatically that the Government does not believe in the forming of groups and opposes groups East, West or centre. We stand for the United Nations. There are two other feelings which find expression in the Amendment: that it is disconcerting to find that British foreign policy secures support among members of other parties and therefore it must be wrong; and that there is a difference of approach of His Majesty's Government to home and to foreign affairs. It is suggested that at home we pursue a Socialist policy while abroad we do not.

The difference is that in home affairs a Government commanding a majority can as a rule – if they are all right with another place – carry out a theoretical programme subject only to the limit of the conditions obtaining at any given time. But in foreign affairs, however perfect our policy, it can be carried out only in conjunction with other nations. ... We have to work with them, and sooner or later, with whatever particular policy we go into foreign affairs, we find that we are up against this: 'Shall I compromise on this point, or shall I refuse co-operation and break?' ...

Take San Francisco. A great many representatives disliked the veto; we did not like it ourselves. The question facing us was not 'what is the ideally best constitution for the United Nations?' but 'will you have a United Nations with this disadvantage, or will you have a United Nations without Soviet Russia?'

The House was impressed. Crossman asked leave to withdraw the amendment. Attlee had won, but not outright. The two ILP members, McGovern and Stephen, called for a division. Nobody voted for the amendment, but about a hundred Labour members abstained.

This was the first major crisis within the party which Attlee had to face, and the beginning of the process which culminated the following year in the formation of a consistently critical group on the left mainly identifiable by its anti-Americanism – the 'Keep Left' group. After the debate feelings ran high for several days. At a meeting of the PLP on 28 November, the majority demanded disciplinary action against the rebels. Morrison handled the situation well, moving a motion deploring the action of organized minorities against party policy, but also urging that standing orders remain suspended – if they had been restored such action as the 'rebels' had taken could render them liable to disciplinary action. The temperature was lowered. But it had been a trying time for Attlee. The *Daily Worker* had alleged that Dalton, Bevan and Morrison had been encouraging the rebels behind the scenes. Bevan had done so; as early as the previous January, after listening to Bevin's report on his talks with Stalin, he had told the Cabinet that 'we must not allow Russian intransigence to drive us into an untenable position in foreign policy', by which he meant 'ganging up' with the United States. Dalton and Morrison had not, but they were known to be sympathetic to some of the complaints. Morrison was not averse to hearing criticism of Bevin. It was Attlee, therefore, who had to meet the attack on the government's foreign policy and on the Foreign Secretary who was carrying it out.

V

In the opening weeks of 1947 Attlee decided that the time had come to tackle Britain's overseas commitments. More and more backbenchers were criticizing on political grounds commitments abroad which the government could not afford to sustain on economic grounds. The unusually severe winter had added to the burden of feeding the people of Europe, and had heightened the risk that if they were not fed their regimes would collapse under political pressures from the Russians. The government dared not satisfy the Keep Left group on the one hand, the Treasury on the other, by a policy of withdrawal which would open the door to Russian expansion. For a solution Attlee turned to those ideas about disengagement which Dalton had recorded a year previously. But he now thought that Britain should disengage only in areas into which the Americans could be persuaded to come and take her place. The two parts of the world to which this thinking most immediately might apply were Greece and Turkey, both expensive pensioners since 1944. On Friday 21 February the British Ambassador in Washington rang the State Department to arrange a visit to present two Notes. These would announce the decision of the British government to take its troops out of Greece and Turkey and to terminate its economic assistance to both countries.

By now the conduct of American foreign policy was in different hands. Byrnes had been succeeded as Secretary of State by General Marshall. Dean Acheson remained as Under-Secretary of State. Acheson had long been an internationalist, believing not only that the United States should not turn away from Europe when the war had ended, but that a degree of American involvement in Europe was necessary to American security. Marshall was a newcomer to the State Department, who had spent the previous twelve months in China as special ambassador, and was consequently out of touch with the situation in Europe. He relied heavily on Acheson for advice.

Acheson was not surprised when he heard that Britain wished to withdraw from Greece and Turkey: but he was alarmed by the information the Notes provided about the situations in the two countries, and by the speed with which the British government proposed to withdraw from them. Within a week he was putting the case to congressional leaders for massive and immediate economic and military aid to Greece and Turkey. This programme was soon to become known as 'the Truman Doctrine'. The essence of it, as the President put it to Congress, was that the United States must 'support free people who are resisting subjugation by armed minorities or outside pressures ... primarily through economic and financial aid.' On 12 March, the President asked for a vote of 400 million dollars for assistance to Greece and Turkey. Meanwhile Acheson persuaded the British government to postpone the date of withdrawal from Greece, and conveyed to them that they should not set such 'short and arbitrary deadlines, especially for the withdrawal of their troops'. By now 'short and arbitrary deadlines' had become a feature of Attlee's style of government. He did not create the Truman Doctrine, but the speed with which he announced Britain's withdrawal from Greece precipitated it. The Truman Doctrine paved the way for the Marshall Plan.

Britain's withdrawal from Greece and Turkey forced Acheson and others in the State Department to think about the short-term problems of Europe as a whole. They realized now that they had overestimated Europe's capacity to recuperate from the war. Economic recovery would take far longer than they had assumed. Before it had been achieved the Russians might have moved into Western Europe. Communist penetration might have undermined Europe even if Russian forces had not taken it over.

At the foreign secretaries' meeting in Moscow which began on 10 March 1947, Marshall and Bevin found the Russians even more uncooperative than before. The solution of the German problem was obviously not imminent. To wait for four-power assent about the rehabilitation of Europe was to stand by and wait for Europe to be controlled by the Soviet Union. When Bevin, writing from Moscow to Attlee, reported the Russian attitude, Attlee's reaction was that Bevin should impress on Marshall that it was unrealistic to expect the Russians to cooperate in the rehabilitation of Europe, and that accepting this view entailed an extension of American aid to Europe. Marshall returned to Washington in late April 'absolutely convinced' that the Soviet Union was set on a policy of exploiting a divided Germany and a helpless Europe to extend not only Communist influence but also a Russian presence. This, he thought, required some rethinking of American policy, a conclusion which was welcomed by Acheson.

On 8 May, at Truman's request, Acheson delivered a speech in Cleveland, Mississippi, suggesting that the United States should embark on economic aid to Europe on a long-term basis. Only if the 'stricken countries' could be made 'self-supporting' could their freedom and the security of Western democracies be made safe. General Marshall made his famous speech at Harvard University on 5 June, offering economic assistance to all countries which were 'willing to assist in the task of recovery'. He sought to accommodate those critics who had thought that the Truman Doctrine had laid too much stress on confrontation with the Soviet Union by saying that: 'Any government that is willing to assist in the task of recovery will find full co-operation, I am sure, from the United States Government. ... Our policy is directed not against any country or doctrine but against hunger, poverty, desperation, and chaos.' Marshall made it clear that if European countries were interested in receiving American aid they should volunteer to make the arrangements for distributing it. 'It would be neither fitting nor efficacious for this government to undertake to draw up unilaterally a programme designed to place Europe on its feet economically. This is the business of Europeans. The initiative must come from Europe.'

When Marshall made this speech Ernest Bevin was not in a sanguine state of mind. He had come back from the Moscow Conference convinced that the Russians were determined to keep Germany divided, and intended not to remedy but to protract the sufferings of an invalid Europe. He feared that in spite of their decision to replace the British presence in Greece and Turkey, the Americans would not take up such responsibilities in Western Europe. The economic life of Western Europe would therefore continue to decline until it reached a nadir at which it would be easy prey to the Russians. When, at 10.30 pm on 5 June, Bevin heard a broadcast about Marshall's speech by the BBC's Washington correspondent, Leonard Miall, he immediately grasped the main point which Miall, who had been briefed by Acheson, was determined to convey: that whether Europe got what Marshall was offering depended on whether Europe would respond to the Harvard speech *immediately*, and with a plan.

This was the cardinal point. The next morning Bevin telephoned Bidault, the French Foreign Secretary, to arrange a meeting. They met on 17 June, and then invited Molotov to join them. He arrived ten days later, only to denounce the Marshall Plan as 'an imperialist plot for the enslavement of Europe'. Bevin and Bidault invited twenty-two countries to a conference to be held in Paris the following month. The Organization for European Economic Cooperation (OEEC) came into being the following April. This was the reaction which Acheson had wanted. It also ensured that the Cold War was now on in earnest. In October, the Cominform was established, to conduct the offensive against 'bourgeois democracy'. When the three foreign ministers met in London on 25 November, Molotov delivered a series of diatribes against Marshall and Bevin, denouncing them for trying to impose an 'imperialist peace' on the German people, and refusing to cooperate with any of the proposals they put forward. By the time the conference ended, late in December 1947, it was clear that a point of no return had been passed, signalized by Bevin's outburst to his advisers after one of Molotov's vituperations: 'Now 'e's gone too bloody far.'

VI

After the debate on American policy in November 1946, in which a hundred Labour MPs had declined to support the government, criticism of Bevin had become acute. In April 1947 the famous 'Keep Left' pamphlet appeared. Though its main target was the government's domestic policy, it also assailed Bevin's 'anti-Russian and pro-American' foreign policy. The 'Keep Left' Group were a particular embarrassment to Attlee since there were marked resemblances between the criticisms they expressed and the views being put to him by members of his own Cabinet, notably Dalton and Bevan. The fact that many members of the Labour Party believed that these views were being leaked to the group from the Cabinet – there is no evidence that this was so – added to Attlee's difficulties. The 'Keep Left' Group were not so much pro-Russian as anti-American. The Marshall Plan exacerbated their suspicions. Crossman had seen Roosevelt's New Deal as American capitalism forced onto the defensive. He now saw the Marshall Plan as a counter-offensive by American capitalism to prevent the development of a socialist Europe. He and his friends believed that the real menace was the likelihood of American capitalism becoming an American type of Fascism and imposing this character upon the countries of Europe. If there were no Marshall Plan, Britain would be forced to adopt the socialist measures which her predicament, as well as her longer-term interest, required. If Britain turned to the Marshall Plan for her salvation, British socialism was doomed, and Britain would be the front line of America's offensive in the third world war.

In the weeks before the 1947 party conference, held at Whitsun in Margate, the 'Keep Left' Group kept up a successful anti-American propaganda campaign. Attlee had great difficulty in dealing with this. If he spoke publicly of America moving in to shoulder Britain's responsibilities in Greece and Turkey, he would antagonize the American Congress – who had so far not voted a dollar for the project. On the other hand, if he could not silence the left, the Americans might conclude that it was the left which spoke for Britain, and decide that an American presence in Europe was unwelcome. An attempt to deal with this problem was made by the publication before the party conference of a pamphlet entitled *Cards on the Table – An Interpretation of Labour's Foreign Policy*, drafted by Denis Healey, then in charge of foreign policy research at Transport House.

Looking back on what had happened in 1945, Healey concluded that it had been 'a major tragedy of socialist history that the advent to power of a pro-Soviet Labour Government in Britain coincided with the opening of a sustained and violent offensive against Britain by her Russian ally.' While emphasizing that the Labour government's policy was consistent with some of the Keep Lefters' insistence that Britain should be, or form part of, a third force, the pamphlet made no bones about criticizing the Russians. However, the policy of the Soviet Union had failed for two reasons:

The Labour government of Britain stood patiently firm against Russian encroachment, and where necessary answered Russian accusations with the facts. Secondly the immoderate ineptitude with which the programme was pursued swung American public opinion into support of Britain.... The most dramatic example so far was the Truman declaration on Greece and Turkey in March 1947.... The world situation is now clarified and the cards are clearly on the table.

The pamphlet returned to the theme that America could make it more, not less, possible for Britain to be a third force. 'Moreover if, as it appears, the USA is about to take the weight of Russian expansion off British shoulders, Britain will be freer to pursue a constructive initiative for improving Big Three Relations.'

The pamphlet went on to promise that there was no question of the Labour government advocating 'an exclusive Anglo-American alliance directed against Soviet Russia'. As for receiving American aid: 'We can only be gratfeul if America is prepared in any way to make it easier for us to defend our security. So the gibe that America provides the money while we provide the men is simply answered – for that suits us better than providing both the men and the money!'

Cards on the Table was vigorously attacked at the party conference. Zilliacus condemned it as 'crypto-Fulton–Winston', a betrayal of the party's promise at the 1945 general election that its foreign policy would be based on support of the United Nations. Crossman best expressed the Keep Left line, supported by many who were not in that group but wanted a reduction in the armed forces and further running down of commitments.

At the time of the censure debate in the previous November Ernest Bevin had been absent. This time he was on hand. Before he made his speech he had a talk with Attlee. Attlee told him that this was a time for 'letting them have it'. Bevin took him at his word. His speech contained more hammer-blows than arguments, but the arguments were sound. Michael Foot wrote that Bevin 'sank without trace all the disputes about demobilization and defence expenditure with a broadside against those who had "stabbed him in the back" during the previous October. The critics were not converted, but the rank and file rallied.'

VII

When Attlee delivered the Prime Minister's New Year broadcast on his sixty-fifth birthday, 3 January 1948, his warnings made it clear that 1948, unlike 1947, would be a year in which foreign rather than domestic policy would dominate the political scene. The background was the intransigence which the Russians had displayed at the foreign ministers' conference in London which had broken down three weeks before. In his broadcast Attlee drew a sad contrast between 1848 and 1948. A hundred years ago, he said: 'Europe revolted against absolute governments which suppressed all opposition, but today the absolutists who suppress opposition masquerade under the name of upholders of liberty.' Although in this broadcast he talked of Britain's potential as a third force between 'downright capitalism and tyrannical communism', he said that Britain and the United States – the Palestine problem apart – were being drawn closer and closer together by the continued and increasing aggressiveness of Russian policy, especially over Germany.

His broadcast paved the way for the initiative which Bevin was to launch two weeks later in the parliamentary debate on foreign affairs. Bevin had concluded that enough was enough. Russia, he said, intended to dominate the whole of Europe. The Marshall Plan had caused the Soviet Union to show its hand. The Russians wished to take Europe over, not to cooperate in its rebuilding. So, 'I believe the time is ripe for a consolidation of Western Europe.' He advocated the drawing together of the Western democracies which two months later he embodied in the Brussels Pact. Attlee wound up the debate on 23 January. He called Russian communism 'an economic doctrine wedded to the policy of a backward state, which has but very slight appeal to those who have experience of Western civilisation but makes a strong appeal to backward people who have never known anything better. ... It is rather like the attitude of the early adherents of Islam. Everyone outside is an infidel.' A few days later, addressing the Oxford University Labour Club, he said: 'This great fight is on and we are all enlisted in it.' British socialism was rooted in the historical experience of the British people, 'in European civilisation, in humanism, in Christianity', whereas in Russia, Communism had turned out to be 'inverted Czarism'.

In February the Communists seized power in Czechoslovakia. The following day, Britain, France and the United States protested that the so-called 'change of government' was in fact 'the establishment of a disguised dictatorship of a single party under the cloak of a Government of National Union'. On 17 March Attlee interrupted a debate in Parliament to announce the signing of the Treaty of Brussels. Britain, France and the Benelux countries, Belgium, Holland and Luxemburg bound themselves in a fifty-year pact of mutual aid and defence against any aggressor, with permanent consultative machinery, and to continuous economic, social and cultural as well as military cooperation. Montgomery, the CIGS, would be chairman of a military committee of the five powers.

Montgomery's behaviour in this new role brought to a climax the mutual distrust between the CIGS and A. V. Alexander, the Minister of

Defence. In 1947 Alexander had complained of Montgomery's propensity to make 'political speeches' – on that occasion about Palestine – and in April 1948 Montgomery took it upon himself to inspect the French Army, without permission from Alexander. In the subsequent, rather acrid, exchange of correspondence, Montgomery appeared to be blaming ministers for condoning the poor state of the French and Belgian armies, and, as Alexander complained to Attlee, to be 'insinuating that we are running our country into danger by disregarding his views'. Attlee admired Montgomery for his spirit and his willingness to lead by example rather than exhortation. Ten years later, reviewing Montgomery's *Memoirs*, he wrote:

> Field-marshal Montgomery was a great soldier: great, in my opinion, not only by the standards of his generation but in the eye of history. He is – as I am – an admirer of Oliver Cromwell. To my mind he is not unworthy of comparison with Cromwell ... both of them not only were inspired and made dynamic by profound religious belief, but relied on expressing this, day in, day out, for their moral authority over their men ...
>
> Some of the difficulties he gave his colleagues and superiors were due not so much to a profound intellectual disagreement with their views as, I think, to the fact that occasionally he could, and did, behave almost as a child ... even at 70 he is still something of a naughty boy.
>
> As Prime Minister I had to give him more than one tick-off, and once I had to give him a really good raspberry. But he took it well, and takes it well looking back on it.

It was the episode of the visit to France which occasioned the 'really good raspberry'. Montgomery bore no rancour. A few weeks later he wrote to Attlee: 'Will you sign a photograph of me in a car driving past the Royal Stand at the Victory Parade with King, Queen, you, Churchill and Smuts? All rest have signed.' Attlee said, 'Yes.' Montgomery also asked: 'Can I give the address to the Bradford Textile Society on "Leadership"?' Attlee said, 'No.' In 1958, a few days after Attlee's review of the *Memoirs* had appeared, they found themselves next to each other in the Robing Room of the Lords on the day of the Queen's Speech. 'You got me right,' said Montgomery, 'and nobody else ever has' (Attlee to the author).

Attlee's 'crusade' against Communism abroad, of which the Brussels Treaty was the major element, antagonized many members of the Labour Party. They were even more critical of the views he expressed about Communism at home when, on 15 March 1948, he announced that Communists and Fascists (the lumping together of the two infuriated the left) would no longer be employed on any kind of work in which state security was involved – 'membership of, and other forms of continuing association with, the Communist Party may involve the acceptance by the individual of a loyalty which in certain circumstances can be inimical to the State'. When Communists attacked him for making such a statement he replied: 'The Workers of the country are well aware now, from events abroad and events here, what the Communist Party stands for.' Forty Labour members signed a motion declaring such a policy a 'departure from the principles of democracy and civil liberty'.

The vigour and speed with which Attlee condemned the Communists in Czechoslovakia now involved him in difficulties with the Labour Party over the Communists in Italy, difficulties which were doubly embarrassing since they raised again the question of the Labour Party Executive's authority over members of Parliament. In Italy, where a general election was pending, the Italian socialists, led by Nenni, were cooperating with the Communist Party in the campaign. After the Prague coup, Labour's NEC had issued a statement which as well as condemning the Communists had given a stern warning to socialist parties to refrain from cooperating with Communists. The government coup in Prague had depended for its success on the support of the Social Democrats. Notwithstanding this pronouncement, a message of good wishes was sent to Nenni in the name of a number of Labour MPs. A sub-committee of the Executive, with Attlee present, decided to expel John Platts-Mills, MP for Finsbury, from the party. Several of the thirty-eight signatories stated that their names had been affixed to the telegram without their consent. The twenty-one members who did not deny signing the telegram were asked to give assurances that they would not do such a thing again; if they did they faced expulsion. They complied. Meanwhile the Opposition had made capital out of these events. Conservative MPs raised the question of the power of the Labour Party Executive over members of Parliament.

The publicity for the 'Nenni' situation, unfortunate as it was for the government, was compounded when the NEC wrote to forty Labour MPs who had announced that they would attend the Hague Conference on European Union (over which Churchill was to preside) deprecating their intention, on the grounds that the concept of European unity 'might be corrupted in the hands of reaction'. This again raised a question of whether the National Executive of the Labour Party, which had no mandate from the electorate, should interfere with the action of forty Labour MPs, who had. All these troubles had blown over by the time the Hague Conference took place, but the strains they caused in the early spring weakened the Labour government at home and abroad.

VIII

Attlee was now faced with the Russian blockade of Berlin. This was the culmination of mounting pressure on the position of the Western Allies in

Berlin, exerted steadily by the Russians ever since January 1948, when the British and the Americans had submitted proposals for a reform of the Bi-zonal Economic Council in Frankfurt. The Russians alleged that the effect of these reforms would be to establish a separate German government and state. They rejected them. When the British and the Americans proposed a reform of the German currency, the Russians reacted swiftly by attempting to interfere with westward-bound military trains. In April they imposed new controls on all road and rail traffic into and out of Berlin. That month a Soviet fighter collided with a British airliner at Berlin's Gatow Airport and fourteen British passengers were killed. In May the Allies went ahead with the reform of the Bi-zonal Council at Frankfurt; in June they established a separate West German currency. The Russians banned it from the Soviet zone, announced a currency reform of their own for Eastern Germany, and stopped all rail and road traffic into Berlin. On 1 July they withdrew from the Allied *Kommandatura*, and four-power rule in Berlin came to an end. When they stopped barge traffic, on 10 July, the blockade of Berlin was complete.

There was only one way in which the Western Allies could maintain communication with, and supply food to, West Berlin, and they took it: the Berlin Airlift. According to Morrison the idea came from Philip Noel-Baker, Secretary of State for Commonwealth Relations. Though at first his Cabinet colleagues were sceptical, they came round to the conclusion that they should recommend it to the Americans. Attlee did not doubt that an airlift would be practicable, but he hesitated before he urged it upon Truman because he thought that if it succeeded it might anger the Russians and lead to reprisals from them. 'But there was no real choice. Either we did it, or West Berlin was lost to us. We were fairly sure that the Russians didn't want a show-down at that time, not sufficiently recovered from the war, but you can never be sure about that kind of thing, and we certainly weren't at the time.' For 323 days the million people living in West Berlin were supplied with food by air. Then the Russians opened up road and rail again.

The most profound consequence of the Berlin Airlift was the North Atlantic Treaty, which was was first discussed just before the blockade was put fully into effect. The idea was originally suggested by the Canadian Prime Minister, St Laurent, on 28 April 1948, and taken up first by Bevin and then by the Senate Foreign Relations Committee under Senator Vandenberg. Negotiations between Canada, the US and the signatories of the Brussels Pact followed in July. This profound and unprecedented development in American foreign policy – which converted it from isolationism to involvement – was in foreign affairs the outstanding achievement of the Attlee government. It owed much to timing: throughout early 1948 the Russians decided to put on pressure in

Europe; had the alliance of the Western democracies not been mooted then, and negotiated with all speed, it might never have been effected. In 1949, with Britain's recognition of Communist China, and in 1950, with deep division about the conduct of the Korean War, the strain on America's relations with Britain might well have prevented President Truman from taking America into such a binding permanent commitment to long-term involvement in Europe.

The successful negotiations in 1948 owed much to Attlee's firm anti-Soviet stance, which put yet more strain on his relations with Labour's left. The annual party conference was held in May at Scarborough. It was clear that because of Attlee's anti-Communist speeches, and his strictures against the signatories of the Nenni telegram, he was in for trouble from the left. Undeterred, he used a Labour rally at Plymouth two weeks before the conference to deliver another indictment of the Soviet Union:

> Russia was always in my young days the supreme example of the police state – the land of fear and suppression, the land where free speech, free thought and freedom of the Press were banned. It is the same today as it was then, only with a different set of rulers. It has yet to overtake several centuries of progress which have left their mark on Western civilisation.
>
> It was also the supreme example of imperialism stretching out across Asia and ever seeking to extend. It still is today. Its imperialism is ideological. It employs different methods, but in effect the countries of Eastern Europe have been brought within its imperialist sway.

The Plymouth speech was the more heinous in the eyes of the left because it was explicitly a response to the 'Nenni-goats'. Part of it was a castigation of the 'active instigators of the Nenni telegram' who 'wanted to sabotage the foreign policy of the Government they were returned to support'. At the party conference, Attlee continued to berate the rebels, characteristically indicting them not for their views but for their disloyalty, always the cardinal sin in his book.

Defensive in intention though the North Atlantic Treaty was, and though the preliminaries may have persuaded the Russians to lift the Berlin blockade, the moves had the effect of further polarizing East and West. International tension relaxed after the lifting of the blockade, but the climate hardened again when, on 23 September 1949, it was announced that the Russians had exploded an atomic bomb. At a foreign ministers' conference in New York, Bevin, reporting the Russian attitude to Attlee at the end of September, found the American State Department stiff and unconciliatory even on quite unimportant points. 'The general feelings regarding Russia all combine to make settlement appear very difficult.'

Bevin was still hoping to act as mediator between Americans and

Russians. His assessment of Russian attitudes was not so realistic as Attlee's. Britain was now so dependent on American economic aid that the Russians could hardly regard her as a neutral go-between. The Russians were becoming suspicious of what they thought was a move on the part of the British government to become part of an American-inspired United States of Europe. Had they known what Attlee's real attitude to Europe was, their apprehension would have been reduced. In November 1948 a strong British delegation led by Dalton went to a conference in Paris which the Brussels Treaty powers had convened to consider the next steps towards 'a closer union'. At the end of January 1949 these powers approved a constitution for a 'Council of Europe'; in May they invited Italy, Norway, Sweden, Denmark, Iceland, Eire, Greece and Turkey to join; there was to be a Council of Members and a Consultative Assembly, with a delegation from each member state chosen by its government; but delegation members would vote individually, not in national blocs.

The division of opinion between the 'federalist' and the 'functionalist' approach to European unity, with Attlee and most of the Labour leaders firmly in favour of the latter, made progress towards European union hard to achieve. Although this anticipates part of the story, Attlee's views in *As It Happened* are worth quoting at length in this context, because he never changed them: as always he was preoccupied, perhaps excessively, with 'the art of the possible':

> The Brussels Treaty and the Atlantic Pact were both designed to strengthen and to unify the Western democracies. They were a recognition of the fact of the changed balance of power in the world. It is hard for those whose memories go back to the nineteenth century to realise that Western Europe, so long the dominant factor in the world, is today a collection of disunited elements lying between two great continental Powers, the USA and the USSR. ... A realisation of this has created a demand for some form of federation, but there is a general recognition that without Britain such a grouping would not be strong enough to hold its own. On the other hand, Britain has never regarded itself as just a European power. Her interests are world-wide. She is the heart of a great Commonwealth and tends to look outwards from Europe, though maintaining a close interest in all that goes on in that Continent.
>
> As a general proposition it is obvious that a closer association of the Western European States is desirable; indeed I am on record as having said 'Europe must federate or perish', but to bring such ideas into the region of the practical is a very difficult proposition. Every state has its old traditions and its special ideological set-up. Some of our American friends did not always realise this. They did not appreciate the difference between European federation of old-established communities and the federation of the thirteen American colonies.
>
> As a Government, we favoured every effort to effect greater European

314

integration, such as the Benelux agreement and the setting up of the Coal and Steel Organisation under the Schuman Plan, but we could not enter engagements to the full extent possible to the Continental Powers.

Attlee did not wish to stand too close to Churchill on the question of Britain's relationship with a European union. He believed that Churchill's public statements about Europe had led the Americans to expect that if the Conservatives won the next election he would put his shoulder to the European wheel – and that their expectations would be disappointed. Attlee was right, as events were to prove. He felt, too, as did nearly all the leading members of the Labour Party, that it was still possible that in the immediate future Europe would be dominated by reactionary governments, and that for Britain to move too far into European arrangements would be imprudent. A third inhibition was his hopes for the emergence of some kind of world government, from which broad avenue a close European union might prove a time-wasting detour. Finally, there was his personal attitude to Europe. He was not a Little Englander, but in old age he would frequently, half in earnest, half in jest, make such remarks as 'Can't trust the Europeans – they don't play cricket.' He admired and liked Frenchmen, Germans and Italians, admired their cultures, but did not approve of the way they ran their countries. What would have happened to his thinking about Europe if he had lived and died ten years later is a matter for speculation.

The North Atlantic Treaty was finally signed on 4 April 1949. Anticipating Labour Party resistance to the signing of the pact, Attlee decided to use a party rally in Glasgow to make a speech on relations with Britain's allies and the Soviet Union. An audience of nearly 3,000 gave him an enthusiastic reception.

Our Foreign Secretary last week signed the North Atlantic Treaty which in my view will be an immense support to the cause of peace ...

We still believe the United Nations can be made a great instrument for enduring peace. We still hold that what we need is an effective world organisation, but I have to recognize hard facts. If we cannot get an effective all-in collective security we must get what we can. ... The Atlantic Pact is in full harmony with the principles and purposes of the United Nations. ... It is not aggressive, it is purely defensive.

We should have welcomed the co-operation in the Marshall Plan of the countries of Eastern Europe because we have no wish for a divided world. The responsibility of dividing the world ... rests squarely on the shoulders of the rulers of the Kremlin. We do not give up hope of uniting the world, but it can be done only if the Communists give up their ideological imperialism, their attempt to bring the whole world into one line, to confine every single person in the strait-jacket of Marx-Leninism.

Some people still believe the Communists are on the Left Wing of the Socialist movement. They are not. ... From the point of view of freedom the Communists are on the extreme right, more reactionary than some of the old tyrants we fought against in the past.

No clearer statement could be wanted of the principles of Attlee's foreign policy at the height of his power.

19
Home Affairs, 1945-6

I

Almost from the start of the Labour government, problems of foreign policy hung about it like dark clouds. On the home front, for twelve months or so the government seemed impressively successful. The two great objectives of policy were nationalization of basic industries – 'not an end in itself but an essential element in achieving the ends which we sought' – and the establishment of the welfare state. Though the direction in which they were moving did not give universal pleasure, the Labour Party leaders seemed to know where they were going.

Attlee's personal stock was rising. The success of his visit to Washington in November 1945 had enhanced his standing with the Parliamentary Party, and when, immediately on his return to Westminster, he made a brief appearance at one of its meetings, all present stood and cheered him for several minutes. In the debate on the nationalization of the Bank of England in October, he did extremely well. 'In this debate,' in the view of James Callaghan, 'Attlee began to demonstrate his supremacy over his party and a growing mastery over the House.' The nationalization of the Bank of England, of great symbolic importance to the Labour Party, was achieved with far less trouble than had been anticipated. The decision to make it the main feature of Labour's legislative programme was vindicated. That decision was Attlee's: the Prime Minister alone was responsible for the determination of legislative priorities.

This was a good start. Attlee consolidated his position by an outstanding parliamentary performance eight weeks later. The occasion was the second day of the debate on the Vote of Censure, 5 and 6 December, which had been demanded by Churchill, after mutterings that he and his front bench had been too passive in the debate on the Bank of England. The debate opened on 5 December. The Conservatives assailed the government tooth and nail, and their intention of doing so, much publicized in advance, invested the debate with an importance and excitement which no exchange in the House had registered since the Labour government had come to power. Winding up that debate, Callaghan recalled, 'Attlee not only showed us he could stand up to Churchill at his best; he showed that he could cut Churchill down to size.'

Churchill's theme had been that the government's policies were creating strife at a time when to cause division was to put the nation in danger:

> If I had obtained a substantial majority at the last Election, my first thought would have been to seek the co-operation of the minority, and gather together the widest and strongest measure of agreement over the largest possible area. . . . I charge the Government with deliberately trying to exalt their partisan interests at the cost not only of the national unity but of our recovery and our vital interest. There is the foundation and the gravamen of this Motion of Censure. For my part, I believe profoundly that the attempt to turn Great Britain into a socialist State will, as it develops, produce widespread political strife, misery and ruin at home and that, if this attempt involves nationalisation of all the means of production, distribution and exchange – to quote the orthodox phrase which I understand was reaffirmed at the Labour Party meeting in May – then this island will not be able to support above three-quarters of the population which now inhabits it . . .

Attlee resented the speech. He thought it irresponsible. Though it contained several arguable criticisms of specific government policies, especially demobilization, its object was, as Churchill freely said, to make out that the government was putting sectional political interest before the national interest. It was delivered at a time when the British delegation in Washington was struggling to secure reasonable terms for the American loan. Attlee thought that Churchill's speech would provide an excuse for American congressmen either to reject the loan when it came before them, or to try to impose conditions on how the money should be spent – and how it should not. It was Churchill's behaviour, not the government's, in Attlee's view, that deserved the criticism of being 'unpatriotic'. So when he rose to speak, for the first time since the general election, he decide to 'let the old boy have it'.

He began by meeting Churchill's charge head-on. His first words were:

> The Right Hon Gentleman the Leader of the Opposition opened today on a quiet note of injured innocence. We were the people, according to him, who had driven this public-spirited opposition into putting down a Motion of Censure, we were the people who had driven a wedge between the parties in the State. I have not forgotten the Right Hon Gentleman's broadcast at the beginning of the Election, nor have the people of this country.

At this there was a tremendous roar of approval from the Labour benches – their majority was so vast, and interest in the debate was so high, that several of them could not seat themselves in the Chamber: they stood or sat in the gangways, or occupied the galleries. It was the Tories, said Attlee, not Labour, who had sought to create national strife. Churchill had announced that he proposed to do so in his speech at the Conservative Central Council four weeks previously. As for his Commons speech:

> The burden of the Right Hon Gentleman's speech is this: Why, when you were elected to carry out a Socialist programme, did you not carry out a Conservative programme? To the Right Hon Gentleman everything that is Conservative is normal, anything that sees a changing world, and wishes to change it, must be wrong.... We were not returned for that purpose.

Attlee went on to praise Churchill as the great war leader of a united nation. But today, he said Churchill had spoken as a partisan. The former prime minister should not pretend that he was still speaking for the nation. He criticized Churchill for introducing to the Vote of Censure a number of topics which could have been more appropriately dealt with over the previous weeks – for instance, in debates on finance, trade and industry, denationalization and, indeed, on the first Labour budget. 'Why could not these points have been made then?' It was a telling blow. Churchill's frequent absences from the House had been much commented on by members of his own party. There was gossip, to which Attlee did not refer, that Churchill had elected to make his attack on the government only to re-establish his authority as leader of the party.

Attlee then dealt with Churchill's criticisms one by one, with a cool, clinical dialectic which, now that he had rattled Churchill and roused the House, was the ideal weapon for the occasion. Churchill became restless when Attlee demonstrated that his attack on the demobilization scheme was inconsistent with his previous utterances; and the Labour backbenchers laughed at him as they had never laughed before. Showing more courage than acumen, Churchill continued to interrupt Attlee's speech. These interruptions were not effective, and some seemed to rebound against him, as in the following exchange during Attlee's contention that public ownership had sometimes been undertaken by Conservative governments:

> *Attlee*: Electricity – that was half done by a Conservative Government. I very well remember the Bill going through; there were no cries about 'wicked Socialist Measure'.

> *Mr Churchill*: I was Chancellor.

Attlee: I know. It was introduced by the chairman of the Anti-Socialist Union. I may say he got it through with the help of a Socialist who was leading the Labour side of the Committee and myself.

There was no brilliance about Attlee's repartee, but his swift, waspish retorts, delivered with almost contemptuous self-confidence, so obviously stung – and discomposed – Churchill that the Labour Party were delighted. Attlee was able also to capitalize on the peculiarity of Churchill's position as leader of the Conservative Party. Churchill could hardly be regarded as a traditional Tory.

Only a few years back the Right Hon Gentleman was telling us that [when] the Conservative Party was running the country, he was himself called to the Premiership not by the Tory Party, by whom he was despised and rejected, but by the action, and with the support, of the doctrinaire Socialists.

Attlee ended his speech with a severe headmasterly rebuke. Churchill was behaving like 'a spoiled prima donna'. He had insulted the British electorate by making out that because the voters had not returned him to office they had let the country down. Quoting Churchill's description of the vote at the general election as 'one of the greatest disasters which have smitten this country', Attlee ended his speech:

That was because the electors did not accept the Right Hon Gentleman. Because the alternative to Labour and a Socialist programme was the Right Hon Gentleman. Throughout the Election he had the spotlight. All those able and experienced Front-Benchers, and those who have fallen by the wayside, were, after all, mere chorus girls: the prima donna held the stage. The very candidates, Hon Gentlemen opposite, were commended to the electors not on their individual merits, but as the chosen supporters of the Right Hon Gentleman.

The Conservatives smarted. There were many among them who believed that Churchill had personally lost them the election. The outcome was a victory for the government and a triumph for Attlee. That the Motion of Censure could be defeated by an irresistible majority was a foregone conclusion. What had not been anticipated was the psychological value of the debate. The very thing which in tabling the Vote of Censure the Opposition had hoped to do for Churchill, they in fact had done for Attlee. He had spoken to Churchill as Churchill had never before been spoken to in the House. He had indeed, in Callaghan's words, 'cut Churchill down to size'.

II

Civil aviation was nationalized on 24 January 1946; the coal nationalization bill had its second reading on 30 January, its third on 20 May.

Cable and wireless communications, road and rail transport, electricity and gas were all nationalized during the 1945/46 sessions of Parliament. As Attlee commented in his autobiography, except for iron and steel there was 'not much real opposition to our nationalization policy'; and as he also noted, much of the social reform programme was widely supported by all parties. The National Health Service Bill, published on 22 March, was to prove more controversial. But the National Insurance Bill was an example of such bipartisan support. In his speech at the second reading, 7 February, Attlee said that the bill was part of the policy of full employment. To afford it, 'we need a high level of national production', but this must be achieved, for the bill was an immense advance in its contribution to human happiness, freedom from worry and insecurity. 'This and the National Health Service will stop deterioration in the human capital of this country. So it is a true economy and addition to the national wealth in the long term.... Experience has shown that unmerited misfortune is not a spur to effort.'

At the end of February 1946, in a debate on economics and manpower, Attlee appealed for national unity in the face of shortages, and on 3 March he broadcast an appeal to the nation for a new and sustained effort in what he described as the 'war against want'. Acknowledging the shortages in food, fuel, clothes and other necessaries, he made a brief survey of the problem of overseas supplies and then addressed himself in turn to the women and older workers, to trade unionists and employers. 'I ask my fellow trade unionists,' he said, 'to look carefully to see whether there are not customs and rules established for the protection of the workers before the days of full employment which are today unnecessary and hampering to full production.' He asked employers to seek the speedy redress of grievances and to make the fullest use of the labour available. Greater production, he said, was the only way to get more goods into the shops and the only way to bring about a reduction of high taxation.

It was not a speech meant to extol the doctrines of the Labour Party, but a non-partisan appeal to the nation. It reiterated his old theme, that if arrangements could be made to win a war, arrangements could be made to solve the problems of the peace:

> The enormous task of demobilisation has proceeded smoothly. The process of reconverting industry from war to peace is being accomplished with great credit to all concerned. The flow of goods into the shops is steadily increasing and will increase week by week. Our export trade is growing month by month. A great work has been done in repairing war-damaged houses, and as the year proceeds and fine weather comes the erection of new houses will get under way.
>
> We have in this country great resources in factories, machinery and plant of every kind, a fertile soil, above all, a people second to none in energy, skill,

adaptability, and resolution, a people always at their greatest when difficulties have to be faced.

I have not the slightest doubt that we shall come triumphantly through this testing time of 1946 just as we came through 1940. We shall come through now just as we did then by the team spirit of our people and by the close co-operation between the Government and the nation.

The 'enormous task of demobilisation' which he mentioned in his speech had indeed proceeded smoothly. The Minister of Labour, George Isaacs, was able to announce on 2 October 1945 that the review of the military requirements of manpower which Attlee had promised in his speech to the TUC the previous month had been completed, and that the rate of release could now be increased. By June 1946, Isaacs said, the government hoped to have three million out of uniform, instead of the 1,400,000 Attlee had quoted to the TUC in September.

Demobilization, however, remained a major problem for the Labour leaders. In January 1946 there were minor mutinies in India and the Middle East. The Conservatives made the rate of demobilization a central issue in their attacks on the government's economic policy in general. Protest focused on the principle which Bevin had insisted on when drawing up the demobilization scheme for the coalition government: the men who happened to be stationed in Britain or Europe when the war ended should not be demobilized before the men from the Far East had got back to Britain. This was naturally more agreeable to men in Burma than to men in Aldershot, and it was unwelcome too to industrialists needing labour urgently to get their factories back into production.

In order to get as many men as possible demobilized in the shortest possible time, Bevin, as wartime minister of labour, had stipulated that in order to replace them in the forces, men between the ages of eighteen and thirty would continue to be called up. This, too, was unacceptable to industrialists and to public opinion generally. In the middle of November Attlee was faced with a minor crisis on this account. The leading members of his Manpower Committee wanted Bevin to revoke his promise: Bevin, writing to Attlee on 15 November, said that 'if there is any violation of the pledge ... I should have great difficulty in being associated with an administration that would go back on its word to those men who have done so much for us.' Bevin also complained that, because of the lack of planning, labour shortages were quite as bad as in wartime despite the high rate of demobilization. Attlee supported Bevin. The pledge was kept. The planning of labour resources went ahead – later the government took powers for the direction of labour.

Meanwhile the problem of how to provide manpower for defence commitments in the long term had to be faced. At a Cabinet meeting on 24 October 1946 Attlee had to tell his colleagues that if Britain were to carry out her responsibilities in the next few years, and at the same time provide for the needs of industry, permanent conscription would have to be considered. Bevin backed him. A revised form of National Service, to operate from January 1949, was then discussed, and the Cabinet agreed that in the welfare state there was an obligation on all citizens to undertake National Service.

To go back to the problem of manpower and demobilization that Attlee had to face in early 1946: at the end of February there was a manpower debate in the House. Lyttelton once again complained that there was an excessive number of men in the forces or producing munitions, and that of the remainder far too many were providing goods for export. Attlee said: 'I think we have to face what I have never concealed – nor have any of my colleagues – the immediate difficulties of the post-war period. . . . I never suggested in 50 or 60 speeches that immediately after the war there was going to be a wonderful paradise. . . . The country is paying economically as well as humanly for our victory very dearly, particularly in the loss of our foreign investment income.' The rate of demobilization was good, and compared favourably with that of any other country.

Reactions to his speech were mixed. Even some Conservatives praised the policy it stated. Thorneycroft thought he had prepared 'a kind of manpower budget with some skill'. The criticism came from those who believed that there was public discontent with both demobilization of troops and distribution of labour, and that Attlee's speech had failed to deal with that discontent. Some Labour members would have agreed with a Tory backbencher, Colonel Erroll, who remarked that: 'The Prime Minister reminded me very much of an elderly science master turning the wheels of a Wimhurst machine, and producing a pale spark of high voltage but no power whatever. It is a disappointing statement when we had expected so much.'

In 1946 Attlee had more time for public appearances outside the House. In February he was guest of the Foreign Press Association at their first postwar dinner, at the Savoy. There was a cartoon of him on the menu, with the caption, 'No suspension of diplomatic relations between the British Government and the Foreign Press Association'. He was the guest at the Jubilee Congress of the Free Church Federal Council. He went to Merthyr Tydfil, to receive his first 'freedom'. He had a very good time – 'great crowds in the street,' he wrote to Tom, 'and [received] a very handsome casket in white stone'. At the end of April, speaking to a North Regional Party Rally, he said: 'I remember some of our opponents saying to me before the election, "Don't you hope you won't get in?" or "Any Government that has to deal with the post-war situation will have a hard time." And I replied: "I know that, but I believe these difficulties can be met and surmounted by the application of the principles in which we of the Labour Party believe." ' Opening the sixth Imperial Press Conference at Grosvenor House early in June, he declared that no freedom was more important than that of the press. Sometimes newspapers' appetite for facts were an embarrassment to politicians. 'Sometimes, seeing political correspondents awaiting them in the House of Commons, they are tempted to mutter in the words of Duncan in *Macbeth*: "What bloody man is this? He can report ..." '

The first postwar party conference opened at Bournemouth on 10 June 1946. He was able to be there for only one day. He wrote to Tom: 'It went very well.' The Prime Minister was to present the Parliamentary Report. Laski, the outgoing chairman, seemed to forgive him everything:

> I'm sure it is the wish of every delegate present that I should say to Mr Attlee, on your behalf as well as my own, that the last ten months in particular have won for him from us a deep regard, an affectionate regard, for the quiet integrity and the consolidated efficiency with which he has conducted the Government of this country. Everyone is proud of his achievement.

'I recall very well,' Attlee opened his report, 'meeting the new Parliamentary Labour Party in the Beaver Hall in the City of London, and I stated then that our intention was to carry out our full programme.' His success in dealing with Churchill in the debate on the Motion of Censure six months before had not been forgotten, and Attlee returned to the theme with which he had then routed the Opposition:

> This vigorous and forceful action rather upset our opponents, for some of them seemed to be rather scandalised that having gone to the country with a clear and definite programme we should proceed to carry it out. It was always their pretence that programmes of nationalisation were theoretical, ideological fads, drawing the Government's attention from its proper duties. Indeed they went so far as to embody that view in a vote of censure which was well and truly defeated. The fact is, these measures of ours are not theoretical trimmings. They are the essential part of a planned economy that we are introducing into this country ... vital to the efficient working of the industrial and political machinery of this country, the embodiment of our Socialist principle of placing the welfare of the nation before that of any section.

The nationalization of the Bank of England, he said, had gone through with scarcely a ripple on the surface of either House. On coal nationalization the Opposition had been critical in detail, but it was quite clear that in general they had no alternative. The Cable and Wireless Bill was in committee, so was the Civil Aviation Bill. 'You mustn't overload the political machine.' Since the Labour Party had come to office, fewer than twelve months previously, seventy-three bills had been introduced, and fifty-five had already received the Royal Assent. 'There are a lot of fish in the basket, and they are not just minnows. There are pretty big salmon among them.' He made much of the Labour Government's repeal of the hated 1927 Trade Disputes Act. Much remained to be done, but the Parliamentary Labour Party was ready and able to do it. 'Much as I love and admire my colleagues of the past, I think that we now have in the House certainly the ablest and youngest, as well as the largest, Parliamentary Labour Party we have ever had.'

III

It remained to be seen how efficiently the nationalized industries and services would work. Shinwell, in what was to prove a very vulnerable ministry (of fuel and power), complained that the party had been talking about nationalizing the mines for over fifty years, but had omitted to prepare any plans for actually doing it. Harold Neal, secretary of the Miners' Parliamentary Group, wrote to Attlee that the miners were 'annoyed' that a miners' MP had not been selected for the job of parliamentary secretary to the Ministry of Fuel and Power, especially with the Coal Nationalization Bill before the House. Attlee, who had chosen Hugh Gaitskell for the job, much to Shinwell's annoyance, replied:

> I must consider a suitable individual for the work of the Ministry. Electricity, gas and oil will become more important for the Ministry, while the new Coal Board will take over much of the Ministry's former work. No group or interest can have a prescriptive right to a particular office – or I would be bound to put a doctor in the Health Ministry, a regular soldier in the War Office and an ex-service man in the Ministry of Pensions in place of the able miners' representatives who fill these positions so well.

The left wing complained that the Nationalization Bill was too generous to mine-owners and would saddle the nationalized industries with a heavy burden of debt. They also complained that the government's nationalization proposals in general were not so much intended to 'socialize' the industries concerned, as to make them more efficient. The management of these industries would remain in the hands of the same men who would have been employed to run them by the owners. Where were the measures to introduce workers' control? In October 1946 Cripps replied that 'there is not yet a very large number of workers in Britain capable of taking over large enterprises. Until there has been more experience by the workers of the managerial side of business, I think it would be almost impossible to have worker-controlled industry in Britain, even if it were on the whole desirable.'

Attlee agreed with Cripps, and particularly with his rider, 'even if it were on the whole desirable'. Not only were there obstacles to the imposition of a full socialist programme; the imposition of such a programme was not desirable in principle. His experiences at the Haileybury Club and in the Army had developed Attlee's sense of social justice but had not led him to assume that all men were capable of running all things at all times. His view was that the Labour government was trying to introduce a mixed economy, and make it work in a transition period; no estimate of the duration of that period was ever given. In November 1946 he told the National Union of Manufacturers that in a mixed economy both sectors of industry should be healthy. 'Industry constantly asks the help of the Government, and it is entitled to that help, but in return the Government is entitled to rely on the help of industry. In our view, the relation between Government and industry should be flexible, with co-operation between workers, management and government.' On the whole, Attlee found industrial leaders helpful and cooperative. As for the employment in the top jobs in nationalized industries of the workers' representatives, he always claimed that the Labour government used as many trade unionists as it could – 'subject to our decision that nationalised boards should represent the public, not particular interests. Morrison was right about that.' The supply was limited: 'Not all trade union men were capable of becoming managers and some of those that were didn't like the idea of becoming bosses' men.' Bevin's idea that the workers should be represented on the nationalized boards was not acceptable. Nor was the suggestion that nationalized industries should be directly, and in detail, accountable to Parliament: they were to be public corporations.

For involving and educating the worker in the management of the industry which employed him, Attlee had looked to joint consultation. Through that, Attlee thought, empirically, the worker might come to participate in some kind of control of industry. But as the years went by he found the response of the workers to joint consultation disappointing. He told the author: 'They had been against the boss for so long they found it difficult to start co-operating with him. And some of them didn't want to. Didn't want the responsibility or couldn't get used to the feeling of it – some thought it was wrong to share in management. "Us and them" problems, you know.' His view that a great many of the former leaders of private industry would work hard and constructively as members of nationalized boards turned out to be correct. 'They put their backs into it.'

His greatest disappointment was the failure, generally speaking, of the workers to respond to the philosophy of public ownership. 'It didn't seem to make much difference to them, of course work is work whether it's for the nation or the boss.' In some industries workers, though supporters of the Labour Party, were against nationalization. 'On the Railways, for example. Chaps who worked for the Great Western or the LMS didn't like being lumped in with all the other companies in BR.' The miners were a great exception. 'Nationalisation meant a great deal to them. They felt the private owners had exploited them, and there were a lot of idealistic socialists among them. They made sacrifices to make nationalisation work – longer hours, and so on.'

IV

In the spring of 1946 the world shortage of grain brought a food crisis in Britain which caused the first serious division in the Cabinet. The government still had the responsibility for helping to feed India and the British zone in Germany. Attlee supervised the food problem in person. He took the view that the burden on Britain had again become disproportionate: there was no food rationing in America; so the Americans must be asked to increase their supplies to Europe. In the British zone of Germany grain stocks declined to enough for a fortnight only. In May, he sent Morrison to Washington. After tough negotiations the US government agreed to treat the American and British zones as a joint responsibility, and to treat India also as a special famine case. In return, however, Morrison had to promise (having cabled the Cabinet for approval and obtained it) that Britain would give up 200,000 tons of the wheat supplies due to her the following September. This made it virtually certain that bread rationing would have to be imposed in Britain.

Several members of the Cabinet became restive; but Attlee had already made up his mind that bread rationing would be necessary. Morrison's account of the promise he had made in Washington led to a stormy debate in the House. The government was greatly embarrassed when the Americans claimed that what Morrison had announced as an American commitment had in fact been only an American intent. Just before the debate Sir Ben Smith, the Minister of Food, resigned, having predicted 'widespread disaffection and discontent, and possibly even in some places, bread riots' unless rationing were introduced. He had been piqued at Attlee's decision to send Morrison to Washington instead of himself, but he gave up office on grounds of 'overwork' – he was sixty-six. Morrison and Dalton had been complaining of Smith's incapacity for several months, and Attlee had made up his mind that Smith 'would soon have to go'. (His relations with Smith remained friendly: in his papers there is a letter from Smith, 6 July 1950, which begins: 'My dear Clem, how in the midst of all your troubles you could find time to write to me during my illness, I frankly don't know.')

The Conservatives made much of Smith's resignation, and were very critical of Morrison, complaining that the shortage had been obvious the previous February and that action to deal with it should have been taken then. Even the government's spokesman, the Minister of Agriculture, recognized that Britain was in 'a grim and melancholy situation'.

The new Food Minister was John Strachey, formerly the under-secretary of state for air. Strachey and his officials at the Food Ministry maintained Smith's advocacy of bread rationing. Strachey told Attlee that as Food Minister he should be made a member of the Cabinet: it was important that he should be able to argue his case there, and not merely obey orders from Morrison. On the eve of his departure for Washington, Morrison had publicly said of the food crisis: 'This is above a departmental matter.... I am going on Prime Minister's level and I don't expect to have to consult the Cabinet much.'

Attlee told Strachey to 'just get on with the job'. Strachey remained outside the Cabinet, and got on with the job. On 27 June he had the painful task of announcing in the House that bread rationing would be introduced the following month. The Tories cited the announcement as evidence of the failure of socialist policies. At the Bexley by-election – 'the bread-rationing by-election' – Edward Heath, the Tory candidate, reduced the Labour majority from about 11,000 to 1,000. Strachey was bitterly attacked in the press. The National Association of Master Bakers announced that they would defy the law and continue to supply bread until a more practicable system was introduced. Strachey again raised the matter of his inclusion in the Cabinet, writing to Attlee on 5 July 1946:

> The food position is greatly affected by almost every major policy decision. It is asking too much of one man to give him responsibility for securing adequate food supply without a voice in the Government.
>
> I know I am a junior member of your party, but then someone else should have been made Minister of Food. I'm sure you must see that point, so if you can't include me in Cabinet, do find someone else whom you feel you *can* include in Cabinet.

Attlee still had no intention of bringing Strachey into the Cabinet, but soon found that Morrison was alarmed at the danger of leaving him out. A note from Morrison to Attlee on 5 July reads: 'This resignation on this point will be an awful nuisance.... Can you and Bevin persuade him off? Or can Cab. press him?' Attlee had a word with Strachey: he would be asked to attend all Cabinet meetings in which food or related matters would be discussed. Strachey obtained his 'voice in the Government', but no encouragement for his political ambitions.

Morrison was not only anxious to prevent Strachey from resigning: he was opposed to bread rationing. The party manager in him recoiled from the electoral consequences. Bexley was a terrible portent. He knew also that when the election came he, as the man who had gone to Washington to do the deal in wheat in May, would be associated with ration cards coming back in July. He therefore decided on a bold course. Two days before rationing was to be introduced, Attlee, Dalton, Law, Whiteley and Bevan went up to Durham for the Miners' Gala. Dalton travelled up later, taking with him a Cabinet Paper from Strachey, who, he recorded in his diary, was 'trying at the last moment to run away from bread rationing' because of the prospects for the Canadian wheat crop. When he got to Durham Attlee informed him that Morrison had sent a message to say that he proposed to call a Cabinet meeting the following morning in order, as Dalton recorded, 'to discuss the case for another scuttle'.

Attlee had already acted. He was annoyed with Morrison. 'I soon had him on the scrambler.' He told Morrison that he was wrong to oppose bread rationing and wrong to consider calling a Cabinet when so many senior ministers were unable to attend it. 'Morrison had not realised how bad the position was: a dock strike and Britain would have starved.' Attlee followed up his telephone call with a prime ministerial minute to Morrison dictated over the scrambler:

> I have here Dalton, Lawson, Bevan, the Chief Whip and myself. We have considered the situation, and are all strongly of the opinion that it would be a grave mistake to alter our decision. I think it a mistake to have called a Cabinet; there are 6 Cabinet Ministers at least up here, and I do not think your meeting tomorrow could be at all representative.

Attlee then repeated the views which had led him to make the original decision, views shared by the ministers at Durham.

> I will have my Cabinet colleagues present here at 10 a.m. and we can give you our views on the scrambler, and hear yours, but I am not prepared to take a decision to reverse our previous attitude without a full Cabinet; if necessary that will have to be held on Saturday if the view you take is strongly supported.
> The members of the Cabinet up here consider it would be a grave mistake if any announcement were made by wireless or in the press or in the House of Commons.

Morrison called off his 'Cabinet meeting' at once. A meeting was arranged for the Sunday, Attlee and the other ministers travelling back to London overnight. After some altercation it was decided to go ahead with bread rationing. 'The order authorising bread rationing continued in force from July 21 1946 to July 25 1948,' recorded Dalton. 'That we should have to do such an unpopular thing illustrates vividly the urgent shortages of the early post-war years, and the inescapable reasons for our gradual loss of backing in the country.'

Morrison's behaviour in calling a Cabinet while the Prime Minister and the Chancellor of the Exchequer were up in Durham, with the object of reversing a major political decision which had virtually been arrived at, was extraordinary to the point of aberration. Perhaps the strain of office, which was to lay him low the following winter, was already telling upon him. It was certainly affecting some of his colleagues. Bevin collapsed on the eve of the peace conference in Paris, and Attlee had to go instead of him. Cripps, after returning from the Cabinet mission to India, had to go to a sanatorium in Zürich for treatment of the illness which was eventually to kill him.

After a year of strain, albeit of success, the time was clearly right for a reshuffle, and in any case Attlee wanted to introduce his long-standing scheme for the integration of the three armed forces under a single minister of defence. As usual when moves were imminent, Attlee played his cards very close to his chest. Dalton thought Bevin might know what moves were intended, but found that Bevin was as much in the dark as he was. 'I can't ever get Clem to say anything. Can you?' Dalton also sounded out Morrison. It was the same with him. Dalton concluded: 'NEITHER Morrison nor Bevin nor I got any change out of this talk on junior personnel.' Attlee's changes included a successor to the War Minister, Jack Lawson, his oldest friend in the government, who resigned on health grounds. Attlee kept a letter from Lawson among his private papers. It begins:

> You are a friend in very truth to be writing me such a letter when you have gone through some eight years of work that would kill the average man. And I thought I was tough.

As well as the reshuffle there was a major change in the government structure. Attlee carried out the scheme which he had conceived when a junior minister at the War Office in the first Labour government: he brought the three services under a minister of defence. In mid-September he sent a long letter to the King describing the changes he proposed to make and giving his reasons for making them. The prime minister would be 'chiefly' responsible for defence. He would be the chairman of a new defence committee, which would be a development of the old Committee of Imperial Defence, and be responsible to the Cabinet both for current strategy and for the coordination of departmental action in preparation for war. The deputy chairman, the effective head of the committee, would be the new minister of defence. The three service ministers would not be members of the Cabinet, though they would attend Cabinets when summoned. Attlee reminded the King that 'I have long advocated this', and that though the reorganization, 'a break with the past', was advocated in the interests of obtaining the best possible national defence organization, and was 'based on experience of the last war', the 'reduction in the size of the Cabinet was desirable in itself'.

He also outlined for the King the changes he intended to make in the distribution of ministries. Since this was the first reshuffle since Labour came to power and since he proposed to bring in several younger men, he wrote to the King in some detail. He explained why he had not been able to make these changes before – Stansgate, for instance, was seventy, but he had been in the middle of negotiations with Egypt, George Hall had been involved with Palestine, and so on. A.V. Alexander was 'the obvious choice' for the new defence ministry. With his copy of the letter to the King there are notes in Attlee's own hand of the six outstanding backbenchers he hoped now to be able to promote: John Freeman, Evan Durbin, L.J. Edwards, James Callaghan, Kenneth Younger and George Brown. Attlee had made several changes in order to remove dead wood and give the young men a chance.

When the names were announced there were many long faces and much criticism. Dalton noted in his diary:

Recent changes in the Government have, no doubt, caused a good deal of jealousy among our many talented MPs not promoted. One of our MPs whom I asked what was the general feeling, said that it seemed that, to get on in this Government, you must have been at Eton, or Haileybury, or in the Guards, or in the Railway Clerks Association.... I keep on prodding the PM to promote more of our bright young men and push out some of the older ones. He says that people don't realise that there are already twenty-two members of the Government who were elected for the first time at the last general election. I agree that this is pretty good, but we must not weary in well-doing.

20

Year of Crisis, 1947

I

In the first few days of 1947, Attlee's supporters could claim that the government had moved a long way towards its two main objectives – the conclusion of the programme of social legislation to which the Labour Party had committed itself in 1945, and a solution of the balance of payments problem by means of a long-term export drive. In spite of difficulties, ministers could afford in the early days of January to talk in optimistic tones: on 7 January, for instance, Marquand, the Secretary for Overseas Trade, reported that whereas the government's export target for 1946 had been £750 million, goods worth £900 million had been sold abroad, and the days lost in industrial disputes had been only one seventeenth of those for the corresponding year after the First World War.

No sooner had he spoken than the troubles began. The first of them was a wave of strikes. An unofficial strike of road haulage workers at Stratford, in the East End, caused the meat rations to be reduced in the London area, and porters at Billingsgate and Smithfield struck in sympathy when the government put in troops to move food supplies. A few days later 50,000 Glasgow shipyard and engineering workers struck, and a general dock strike was threatened. A coal shortage loomed. But for Attlee the most immediate problem was to contain dissension in the Cabinet about manpower requirements for defence.

On 16 January 1947 the Cabinet met to discuss the shortage of manpower in British industry. The Ministerial Committee on Economic Planning – Morrison, Cripps, Isaacs (Minister of Labour) and Dalton – had made proposals to deal with the gap in the 'manpower budget', including reductions in the armed forces. 'A very bad and rowdy Cabinet,' Dalton recorded, 'in which a substantial group ganged up against Cripps and myself.' Morrison and Bevin were away ill. Most of the others, according to Dalton, displayed 'easy-going, muddle-headed irresponsibility'.

Dalton was impatient with Attlee: 'the PM says that the gap is only two and a half per cent of the total labour force and should easily be able to be removed by "greater productivity".' The Cabinet minutes show that Attlee had argued that experience after the 1914-18 war 'showed the disastrous effect on British foreign policy of allowing the Armed Forces to be unduly weakened'; he had also urged that a solution to the manpower gap should be sought in higher productivity, though the minutes do not suggest the optimism which Dalton criticized. Dalton contemplated resignation, and on 20 January wrote Attlee a 'Note on a Difference of Opinion' – it ran to several hundred words – in which he complained of 'a bad failure to face unpleasant facts' on the part of the Cabinet.

Attlee reacted by asking the Defence Minister, A.V. Alexander, to make a small concession, and on 27 January in Cabinet the Defence Estimates were cut by 5 per cent – £40 million. 'And so, for the moment, it ended,' recorded Dalton, 'leaving a faint trail of antagonism, I fear, between me and the Prime Minister.' Dalton was right to scent antagonism: Attlee disapproved strongly of a passage in Dalton's covering letter to the 'Note on a Difference' in which the Chancellor had observed that: 'At least I have gone on record against future possibilities.' In Attlee's view 'going on the record', even in private, showed a wish to be absolved from responsibility and a concern for political self-preservation, as well as vanity. These were high crimes in his political book.

This was the first time in the Attlee government that the division of opinion in the Cabinet about how to reconcile the needs of the economy with the cost of defence reached a point of crisis. The division of opinion in early 1947 was not resolved. Dalton's warnings exonerate him from the charge that the financial crisis of the following August was due to his complacency. Attlee has been blamed for a failure to see the signals at this time, or, if he saw them, for failure to take action. He was probably still too influenced by Bevin's views of what was necessary for defence, and for good relations with the Americans, which he understood, than by Dalton's views on finance, which he did not.

Political circumstances did not encourage Attlee to do any more than temporize. Only a few weeks earlier he had had to deal with Crossman and the Keep Left amendment. Dalton was known to have sympathies with Crossman and his group. With Bevin so much absent, and Morrison ill, Attlee could not afford to have a showdown with Dalton on this issue at this time. As well as precipitating a domestic crisis, it would give an impression of national disunity which would disturb the Americans. On the other hand, if Attlee had given Dalton all he wanted – withdrawal from overseas commitments on a major scale – the Americans would have been even more alarmed. So Attlee, with Alexander's help, made the maximum concessions to Dalton which were consistent with minimum damage to the main objectives – to avoid political upset, and to keep on the closest possible terms with the Americans, with a view to them replacing British military strength abroad and paying more British bills at home.

The Dalton crisis was soon followed by the Shinwell Cabinet crisis. The shortage of coal was precipitated by the exceptionally cold weather in the last weeks of 1946, the demands of the factories producing goods for export, and, as more and more men were demobilized from the forces, a general increase in consumption. 'We are coming right up against the gap of two to five million tons of coal of which Mr Shinwell has repeatedly warned the country,' said the Parliamentary Secretary to the Ministry of Fuel and Power, Hugh Gaitskell, loyally giving his chief credit which he did not deserve. Shinwell, the Minister of Fuel and Power, had been telling Cabinet and country that no crisis was in sight. Though the unusually bad weather had aggravated the effects of the coal shortage, a fuel crisis – in spite of Shinwell's reports – had been foreseen several months previously.

Well briefed by Douglas Jay, Attlee had been active on the fuel front as early as June the previous year. The Cabinet Papers for 1946 contain several minutes from him to ministers concerned (samples of which can be seen in Appendix IV below). He wrote to the Minister of Labour in June, urging an increase in the labour force. A few days later he called for monthly progress reports on coal production and asked for a survey of the possibilities of substituting fuel oil for coal. In July 1946 he wrote to the Chancellor: 'I have no doubt that coal is now the most urgent economic problem which confronts the government and that a disastrous failure can be averted only if it is most boldly and resolutely tackled.' Long before the bad weather began, Attlee was worried about coal supplies: 'Coal prospects are disturbing,' he minuted to the Chancellor at the end of October. 'It looks as though we may just get through if it is a mild winter; but I fear that in any case it will be touch and go. And we shall be starting the new year with deplorably low stocks.' But though he saw the danger that was looming, Attlee left the handling of the coal shortage to Shinwell, who gambled on the winter weather being average and made no plans to deal with extreme weather.

In early January Cripps was put in charge of emergency measures to deal with the rapidly developing coal crisis. On 13 January he announced what came to be known as the 'Cripps Plan' – absolute priority for coal for the power stations, half the normal quota of solid fuels for industry in general, supplementary supplies for those providing essential goods. The 'Cripps Plan' had been based on Shinwell's estimate of the situation. As far back as the previous November, his civil servants were apprehensive about how supply could be made to match demand. Their figures were submitted to the Cabinet, but Shinwell insisted that his personal relationship with the miners was such that production would be far higher than the officials predicted. In the Cabinet office, Douglas Jay, briefed by Gaitskell, warned Attlee that the civil servants were right and that Shinwell was wrong.

In the last week of January 1947 there was heavy snow, followed by a blizzard on 30 January, and then 'the great freeze', introducing the worst four weeks of winter weather since 1881. There were eight days of continuous frost. London's temperature was below freezing point for a week. Villages were cut off. Factories were closed. The effect on fuel supplies, which were already critically low, was catastrophic: even where coal was available, the icy condition of the roads frequently prevented supplies being moved to where they were required.

A debate was arranged for 6 February. The day before the debate, Dalton wrote a note to Attlee, saying that he and Cripps feared that Shinwell would make another 'of his sloppy sunshine talks, and that we shall, once more, be discredited by events'. Attlee saw Shinwell privately and ordered him to tell the House the facts. In the course of the debate, Shinwell staggered the House by announcing that electricity for industry in various parts of the country, including London, could no longer be supplied, that current for domestic use would now be rationed to certain hours of the day, and that some power stations would be closed so that the limited supplies of coal could be concentrated on others. 'A complete thunderclap,' recorded Dalton. As a result of Shinwell's orders for the control of the use of coal, 1,800,000 people were put out of work. Ten days later $15\frac{1}{2}$ per cent of the labour force, more than $2\frac{1}{4}$ million, were unemployed. The crisis lasted three weeks. The weather then improved, restrictions were lifted, coal was moved, and by 12 March unemployment had gone down to $\frac{3}{4}$ million.

The government faced a political as well as a fuel crisis. The National Coal Board flag had been hoisted above Lansdowne House on the first day of the year. The blizzards of January and February hit nationalization as well as coal supplies. The Opposition blamed socialism for the coal shortages; Shinwell unconvincingly blamed the shortages on the myopia of the former capitalist proprietors. Throughout February the government was under heavy attack. Attlee and his colleagues would have been spared much of this if they had attributed the fuel shortage to the misjudgements of the past and had exhorted the nation to grin and bear it until the return of normal weather. But Cripps had presented his plan as a panacea which would effectively solve the short-term fuel problem before the bad weather had hit the country. Shinwell might well tell the country that the 'realistic' Cripps plan never had a chance because of the unprecedented weather, but the country was in no mood to listen. It had been 'Starve with Strachey'; now it was 'Freeze with Shinwell'. The crisis, said Lord Swinton, was due not to 'an act of God, but the inactivity of Emmanuel'.

The Cripps plan hung around the government's neck like an albatross. The Opposition castigated another, only too palpable, failure for social-ism, and the Liberal Party demanded a Council of State. The government's decision to suspend the supplies of newsprint to the periodicals in order to save power was represented by the Opposition, and by most newspapers, as an interference with the right of free discussion. Dalton was furious with Shinwell. So was Cripps: his much publicized 'plan' was now revealed to have been inadequate from the start. In drawing it up he had used Shinwell's discredited statistics. Almost everything the government had said about the fuel situation in the critical weeks had been immediately negated by events. Both men called for Shinwell's dismissal.

Attlee decided to assume that Shinwell had not personally been at fault. He told Dalton and Cripps that if any major change in the conduct of policy were to be made, it would be to hand over the fuel crisis to Morrison as overlord of the domestic front, a suggestion which so horrified both critics that it silenced them at once. Though he was very critical to Shinwell within the Cabinet – he is said to have reduced him to tears at one meeting – he defended him outside it. Shinwell, no showerer of compliments, recorded in his autobiography that during this most daunt-ing period Attlee never ceased to defend him publicly and 'in no uncertain terms'. Attlee concluded that Shinwell was 'more concerned with politics than with the job', but he retained him in the Cabinet until the autumn reshuffle. He knew that if he sacked Shinwell the miners would be upset, but that he must do something which showed the government was responding to the crisis. Accordingly he set up an emergency Fuel and Power Committee of the Cabinet under his own chairmanship, and it was Attlee's Fuel Committee, not Shinwell's Fuel Ministry, which dealt with the crisis:

> To Ministry of Transport: As I mentioned to you last night, it is essential that the most vigorous action shall be taken by the railways to ensure the maximum movement of coal traffic and the supply of emergency waggons needed to enable the collieries to continue production. I should like a high official to be placed in charge on each railway to see that this priority is effected. When necessary passenger services must be withdrawn.

On the night of 10 February, three days after Shinwell had astonished Parliament (and flabbergasted his own party) with his frank – for the first time – description of the fuel shortage and of the measures necessary to deal with it, Attlee made a broadcast on the BBC. The broadcast reads well enough, but this was one of the occasions when Attlee's kind of language and delivery did not inspire the nation. It was an extremely miserable February; Attlee's plea to his countrymen to pull together did not arouse the spirit of Dunkirk. With Labour voters, his matter-of-fact statement of the situation went down well. When he told a party rally in Manchester that the nation's economic position was 'like that of a man severely wounded in war who pulls through thanks to a strong constitution, courage and the will to live', they cheered. A few days later, speaking at Hanley, Staffordshire, he was greeted by a heavily overcoated and bescarfed audience of 2,500 with 'For he's a jolly good fellow'. On this occasion he scoffed at newspaper editorials which claimed that only a new coalition government could solve the country's problems. Talk about a coalition was 'utter nonsense.... We have no intention whatever of having a coalition, and I don't think the other side would want it.' (They didn't.)

With hindsight it may seem that there was bad overall planning of the economy in general and of fuel and power in particular; on the other hand the unprecedented spell of bad weather offers substantial extenuating circumstances, and once the emergency was declared the government acted firmly and energetically enough. If Attlee is to be blamed it could be said that he had been overworked. He had been giving great attention to India; his momentous decisions, dealt with in another chapter, to send out Mountbatten as the last Viceroy, with a firm date for the withdrawal of the Raj, and the declaration of Indian independence were announced to the House of Commons on 20 February, while the country was still shivering and demoralized. Dalton recorded: 'This has not been the end of the world.... But it was certainly the first really heavy blow to confidence in the Government and in our post-war plans. This soon began to show itself in many different and unwelcome ways. Never glad, confident morning again.'

A few days later, on 10 March, the House debated the Economic Survey for 1947. It was one of the most important debates in the history of the postwar Labour government. The survey presented a programme of 'universal' and 'democratic' planning. This impressive manifesto had to be debated against the background of the recent fuel crisis. Cripps, deputizing for Morrison, who was ill, spoke for two hours. Britain now faced immense and unprecedented economic problems. These could be met only by long-term planning, requiring the voluntary cooperation of both sides of industry. Full-time planning units would be established in all government departments, coordinated by a small joint central planning board.

Cripps's analysis of Britain's problems predicated a long period of austerity ahead. The government, if anything, had been too easygoing. Major long-term changes in the economy must be made. Exports must be greatly increased; imports, if not reduced, must be purchased, so far as possible, in soft currency markets. The bigger industries must be reorganized. A wages policy was necessary. Profits and dividends must be limited. There could be no wage increases without higher productivity. This indeed was the key. Cripps's powerful speech marked the end of the period in which austerity had been thought of as the short-term aftermath of war, and the beginning of the period in which it had to be accepted as a long-term condition of the peace.

Attlee wound up on the third day in good form and relaxed, confident fashion. To the delight of his backbenchers, who at this time needed all the encouragement they could get, and knew it, he gave Churchill a ribbing:

> He always amuses me a little because he gets up with such an air of injured innocence.... His complaint is always this, 'Why cannot you follow a Conservative Party policy, and then we will support you?'

It required courage to attack the great war leader in personal and specific terms, and it also required judgement; this was no time for Attlee to antagonize public opinion, and he therefore balanced his criticisms of Churchill's competence with kind words about his character:

> He has an intense sympathy with suffering, and I am perfectly certain that if he went over to any country for which we were responsible, and saw people suffering from lack of food, he would come back and demand that we should help them. I do not think he knows what the conditions were like in the mining villages, in the depressed areas or in the East End of London, or he would never have suggested that people were better fed before the war than they are now.

Having dealt with Churchill, he turned to the major theme of his speech, democratic planning:

> ... in a world such as we are living in today, even if we have the money, or we can borrow the money, we cannot get the goods. We are living in a world of shortages. It is in these shortages that we have to plan.... What we require are not plans conceived by a Government in isolation, implemented by a Government by compulsion, but plans worked out in consultation with both sides of industry and willingly carried out under the general guidance of the Government. We are not blind to the difficulties of planning, but this is – and we recognize it – a great experiment. This is democratic planning.

He emphasized, tellingly – for most members of the Conservative front bench privately agreed with him – that there was far more agreement

338

between the parties on the need for planning than anybody would deduce from listening to Churchill, and that in spite of Churchill's contentions to the contrary, nationalization was not an end in itself but a means to the end of 'a fine standard of life for all people, and putting the interests of the community before that of certain private property interests'. He came out strongly for the mixed economy to a degree that annoyed his own left wing:

> Private interest and public interest should be mingled, and in our planning we are not suggesting that the profit motive should not operate at all. On the contrary, we have today two great sectors of industry. One sector is nationalised, the other is in private hands.

Attlee's difficulties were now compounded by the National Service Bill. It had become clear that, though cuts were being made, the level of military manpower necessary to carry out the country's commitments would not be met by voluntary enlistment. A new National Service Bill, which would introduce peacetime conscription, had been foreshadowed in a White Paper in February. There was great opposition. In the Labour Party, socialist pacifists, anti-imperialists and those who objected to the financial strain of Britain's military commitments combined to form a formidable potential revolt. The Liberals called it an interference with the liberty of the individual. The vote for the bill, on 1 April 1947, was high, 386 against 85, but this was due to the support of the Conservatives: Labour MPs voted against it, and many of the Labour MPs who had voted for it had done so under protest. There were widespread abstentions.

Feelings in the Labour Party continued to run so high that two days after the debate the Minister of Defence announced that the period of National Service would be reduced from eighteen to twelve months. Churchill called this change 'ridiculous and deplorable': the country had been told that after consultation with the chiefs of staff the government had decided that eighteen months was the proper period. Two days later the government was telling the country that twelve months would suffice. The government had capitulated to 'seventy or eighty pacifists, or "cryptos", or that breed of degenerate intellectuals who must have done so much harm'. Churchill's charge was not without foundation. Attlee had indeed given way to the pressures within the Labour Party.

The winter went on and on: thirty-foot snowdrifts and widespread flooding did not provide a propitious background for the announcement that the miners' working week would be reduced to five days on the first Monday of May, and for Attlee to state that it might be necessary to import coal. But spring was coming. The Cripps Plan, with its allocation to industry, would soon be given a chance to work. The government decided to spend £400,000 to publicize the economic situation and mobilize public opinion to meet it; posters – 'We're up against it. We Work or Want' – appeared. The most intractable problem the government had to face were the export figures: these showed that even if the fuel crisis had not occurred production would have been lower in February than it had been the previous November. The weather had not been entirely to blame. Attlee could look forward to great discontent at the party conference scheduled for Whitsun.

This prospect did not perturb him. At the end of April, addressing the Scottish TUC at St Andrews, he delivered a slashing attack on Churchill, 'the most disastrous Chancellor of the century', who 'brought us back on to the gold standard, which led to a crisis in credit from which we are suffering today'. Churchill had never understood economics. 'He inflicted untold misery on the people of this country . . . by accepting the advice of the Bank of England – a sin of ignorance.' He told Tom on 2 May: 'My speech seems to have been well received as it was generally felt that Winston had asked for a bit of correction. He is singularly inept as an opposition Leader and there is much discontent in Tory ranks.' On the eve of the conference he wrote again to Tom, indulging his keen interest in ecclesiastical appointments, and with reference to Father Groser, a distinguished radical priest in the East End of London:

> I know Groser and have considered him. But I am inclined to think him a bit of an advertiser and not quite the quality for a Bp. There seems today to be a dearth of really able Socialist parsons such as we knew in our younger days . . .
> Oswald Birley has just done a very good portrait of me for Univ. . . . We're all delighted with it. DCL robes made a pleasing bit of colour. . . .

The annual party conference opened on 27 May at Margate. The trouble awaiting Attlee on the foreign front has already been described. This was to be compounded with the protests about the high level of defence commitments and the resentment against the National Service Bill. The Keep Left Group, rebels on these issues, also led the party in criticism of domestic policy. On the whole the conference gave the leadership less trouble than had been anticipated. Even Laski had praise for Attlee, observing on the subject of conscription: 'Mr Attlee has many qualities, no doubt Mr Attlee has some defects, but he has a glorious obstinacy of purpose when he has made up his mind.' Introducing the parliamentary report, Attlee's theme was that the government was carrying out two great historical tasks, the transition from war to peace, and the movement from a capitalist to a socialist economy. These would be achieved because the government had its socialist faith, a clear programme, and 'a fine majority'. The tide was behind the Labour Party. 'We have a young and eager Parliament and a nation demanding great things.... Today there is no coherent alternative policy to Labour's in this country. Our opponents are bankrupt of ideas.' Two days after the conference he wrote to Tom:

> The Margate Conference was a great success and the newspapers have been hard put to it to invent splits and dissensions ...
>
> I have the King coming to dinner here tomorrow to meet some Cabinet colleagues. It is an all-men affair in the small dining room.

Attlee's account of the conference is euphoric. If he really believed what he said he must have been unusually unperceptive at that time. Shinwell had collided with Morrison on a fundamental issue. At the conference, speaking of the Labour Party, he said: 'We represent the workers by hand and brain. As for the rest they don't matter two hoots.' This conflicted with many public statements made by Attlee, Cripps and Morrison, aimed at reducing class consciousness and promoting a sense of national unity. The conference also produced a difference of opinion between trade union leaders about the attitude which the government should adopt towards wage claims, after Cripps had stressed the need for relating wage claims to increases in productivity. Though the Executive was defeated only twice – the conference voted for the abolition of tied cottages and for equal pay for women – there was a general sense of strain, eloquently expressed by the Keep Left Group. Attlee's remark that 'the newspapers have been hard put to it to invent splits and dissensions' might have been forgivable as public propaganda, but not as a private assessment for Tom. He must have been feeling rather cross.

II

As mid-1947 approached, the state of the party became unsettled. The divided vote on the Conscription Bill, the mounting opposition to foreign policy, the activities of the Keep Left Group and the shock of the fuel crisis had damaged backbench morale. The leaders were unhappy. Dalton looked forward with apprehension to the day – 15 July – when convertibility was due to be restored. Cripps was worried about trade union demands for wage increases. Morrison had returned from convalescence in late April, but was taking time to get back into his stride. Attlee's stock with all three of these colleagues was low. 'Some doubted whether Attlee had the personality, or the strength of popular appeal to be the Leader in those increasingly critical months,' recorded Dalton. Cripps wanted to bring Bevin from the Foreign Office to run the home front. Morrison was critical of Attlee's reshuffle in the spring. Attlee, he told Dalton, 'likes moving all these people round like pieces on a chess board, when he should get rid of some of them altogether.' Meanwhile suspicion was spreading through Labour's rank and file that its leaders might not have the skill and resolution to face the political and economic problems that lay ahead. The combination of the disturbances over the steel industry and the dollar involved the party in its stormiest passage in the whole of the 1945–50 period, and Attlee came nearer to losing the leadership than at any other time.

Though for the left, and for many others in the Labour Party, the nationalization of steel was contemplated with almost mystical fervour, the party had no detailed blueprint for bringing steel into public ownership; it had been low on the list of priorities of Morrison's Future Legislation Committee in 1945. He had tried, unsuccessfully, to keep the commitment out of the 1945 election manifesto, and had included it only because of pressure on the NEC. In March 1946 Wilmot, the Supply Minister, had submitted plans for full nationalization. Morrison argued that nationalization would antagonize public opinion and interfere with production at a time critical for the economy. Attlee was undecided. Bevin, Dalton, Bevan and Cripps were for nationalization. It was agreed that no action would be taken for the time being. Throughout the rest of 1946 there was firm resistance from the steel industry. But at a Cabinet meeting in April 1947 it was decided to include the nationalization of steel in the 1947–8 legislative programme.

While Morrison was ill during the early spring of 1947, Sir Andrew Duncan and Ellis Hunter, leaders of the steel industry, at their own request discussed the question with Attlee. When Morrison returned to duty he found that Attlee now shared his view that for the time being they should leave steel alone. According to Dalton, Morrison received 'an agitated approach by the Prime Minister ... saying that he was quite sure he had made a mistake'. In any case, some ministers, like Shinwell, wanted to nationalize gas first. As a result of these considerations Attlee authorized Morrison to investigate the possibility of some kind of compromise about the party's undertaking to nationalize steel. By July Morrison had produced a scheme, at first sight acceptable to Attlee, Wilmot and the steelmasters, which would leave the industry un-nationalized but bring it under public supervision.

When the Cabinet discussed the Morrison plan on 31 July, Bevan threatened to resign if it were accepted. By now the return to convertibility on 15 July had precipitated a financial crisis; leading bankers were advising the Chancellor privately that an announcement that the government was not going to nationalize steel would help to restore confidence. The Cabinet ignored Bevan's threat and decided not to proceed with nationalization in the 1947–8 session. News of the decision leaked, and disturbed the PLP, where it was known that Dalton, Cripps and Bevan were in favour of nationalization 'now'. On 7 August the Cabinet changed its mind: it rejected the Morrison scheme, confirmed that steel would be nationalized, but confirmed also that nationalization should not be introduced until the 1948–9 session.

Four days later, in what Dalton described as a 'very hysterical and steamed up' Parliamentary Party meeting, Bevin and Attlee spoke on the economic situation. After they had finished, Morrison dealt with a resolution from the floor refusing to accept the recent Cabinet decision that it could not promise to nationalize steel in the next session. A majority of the party seemed in favour of this resolution, but a clear expression of opinion was prevented by a procedural technicality. Officially the resolution was deemed to have been defeated 81 to 77. Notwithstanding the defeat of the resolution – a narrow one – it was obvious that the party was deeply divided. The government was saved by the bell.

The steel crisis shook Attlee's hold over the rank and file of the PLP. At the same time it severely injured the reputation of Morrison, who was condemned for the compromise plan which he had devised. Attlee said very little in the discussion in Cabinet, later telling Morrison's biographers that he did not support the compromise plan in Cabinet because it 'was not my job to do so'. This is another example of Attlee's conception of the party leadership. If the compromise plan for steel, after being clearly outlined to the party, was not acceptable to it, that was that. If Morrison did not accept that party feelings – and those of the Cabinet – were strongly opposed to his plan, he, Attlee, did. In his philosophy, the party leaders were obligated to try and carry out what the party was publicly committed to if they could not persuade the party that the implementation of the commitment should be deferred. If an ad hoc meeting of Labour MPs asked for action on some matter which had arisen contingently, that was another matter: in that case the Labour government must act not as the executives of Labour Party aspirations but as the government of the country – as for instance in the case of emergent problems in the field of defence, notably that of the atomic bomb.

As was so often the case, once he was sure how the party felt, and knowing that this was just a party matter, Attlee moved swiftly. Steel nationalization would come back on to the menu. Morrison's reputation suffered a setback. Wilmot was sacked a few weeks later, and never got another job. Much of the trouble over steel throughout the summer of 1947, in Attlee's view, had been due to Wilmot's failure to resolve the division of opinion among his civil servants, and to stand up to the steelmasters. 'And all the argument about nationalisation diminished his standing in the Party. He had to go.' Dalton and Cripps pressed Attlee to bring Bevan, the strongest advocate of full steel nationalization, to the Ministry of Supply in Wilmot's stead. Disregarding strong objections from Morrison, who thought that Bevan had deliberately used the steel issue to advance his position in the party, Attlee made the offer to Bevan. The offer was refused – Bevan was busy with large schemes at the Ministry of Health – and Attlee instead accepted George Strauss, Morrison's nominee. The steel issue did not increase Morrison's regard for Attlee, and aggravated the dissatisfaction with his leader which had been growing since the previous spring.

Attlee's difficulties over steel cannot be appreciated unless they are seen against the background of the major economic crisis of the late summer of 1947. From the moment sterling became convertible into dollars, on 15 July 1947, there was a run on the pound such as had not been seen since 1931 – was this 'another American Bankers' Ramp'? For the Labour Party, this evoked the fear that a half-constructed socialist state might now be reduced to ruins, with no chance of it being put together again.

That there would be difficulties when sterling was made convertible had been obvious, though the Treasury had advised the Chancellor that Britain would take the strain. Countries holding sterling were now free to exchange it for dollars to buy the American raw materials and goods for which they had so long been waiting. In the months preceding the return to convertibility the Treasury and the Bank of England had taken various measures in the attempt to distribute the impact of the demand for dollars over several months. Official forecasts, however, had underestimated the damage that would ensue, largely because they had assumed that higher levels of exports, and of domestic coal and steel production, would have been attained. These expectations were not met, partly because of the terrible winter, and partly because of the underlying problem, the shortage of labour – Britain was still more than half a million short of the manpower level required. Dalton had done his best to persuade his colleagues to release more men from the services – he had complained of meeting a 'blank wall' from Attlee and the service ministers – but he had not succeeded in organizing the Treasury to meet a catastrophic run on the pound when convertibility came into effect.

Failure to respond quickly enough to the crisis was partly due to disagreements between Morrison, as economic overlord, and the Treasury about the functions of the new National Planning Board. Morrison's illness had also weakened his grasp of the economic situation. When he marked his return as economic overlord, 8 July, by opening the big economic debate, his account of the state of the nation's economic situation, not well presented, was impressive only for its pessimism.

The crisis lasted nearly five weeks, ending with the return to convertibility on 17 August. Coinciding with the rising tide of disaffection over steel nationalization, the run on sterling hit the Cabinet broadside-on.

The atmosphere of crisis developed within a week. On 23 July, fourteen backbenchers called for a statement of the government's plans to meet the economic crisis, to inspire confidence among the Parliamentary Party and in the country. They called for cuts in imports, cuts in foreign commitments, cuts in the armed forces, and measures to expand production. On 30 July the senior five ministers met to prepare for the next day's Cabinet meeting – which had to deal with the problem of steel, as well as the economic crisis. Dalton outlined measures similar to those put forward by the fourteen backbenchers. According to Dalton, Bevin had had too much to drink – his 'drunken monologue' causing Morrison to walk out of the meeting in disgust – and Attlee showed 'no power of gripping and guiding the talk'. Next day, Dalton and Cripps told Attlee they would resign unless Dalton's measures were approved. When the Cabinet assembled, Attlee was able to meet everybody's wishes, and accommodate their temper, by calling on Morrison, who proposed the so-called Supplies and Services Transitional Bill, the essence of which was to give the government emergency powers. It was agreed that there would be a debate on 'the State of the Nation' the following week.

On 6 August Attlee rose in the House to introduce the Transitional Powers Bill. 'His speech had much substance in it,' Dalton recorded, 'but how painfully it had to be built up from a multitude of confused, ambiguous and imprecise Cabinet decisions.' It was clear by now that only Attlee carried enough guns to make a frontal attack on Churchill, and he used them effectively to divide Churchill from the Conservative front bench; but the burden of his speech was a forthright explanation of the country's difficulties and a call to the nation to recognize 'the difference between gravity and panic'. He was able to announce a number of specific measures, longer hours in the pits, an expansion of steel production, the restriction of some imports, and the release of 80,000 men from the forces. Dalton and Cripps developed his points in the subsequent debate.

The new measures evoked predictable obloquy. Conservatives objected to the inadequacy of the drive for productivity; nineteen Labour MPs, writing to the *Daily Herald*, demanded more socialism, including a capital levy and the nationalization of steel. Churchill described the bill as a 'blank cheque for totalitarian government'. The bill was finally passed after an all-night sitting. Sir Wilfred Eady of the Treasury, armed with the government's proposals for cuts and new powers – an Order had been drafted which in effect restored the wartime Order for the Control of Labour – flew to Washington to ask the Americans for a new lease of life.

Having put the government's emergency measures to Parliament, Attlee put them to the people in a BBC broadcast on 10 August:

I have no easy words for you tonight, nor, as you may have read in the Press, must you expect high phrases or eloquence, but I want to hold your interest and stir your imagination, and this is best done by simple and straightforward words. Listen with me to the end, and think and talk over what I have said afterwards. I have a heavy responsibility upon me, but you have too.

The parliamentary session – and his broadcast – over, Attlee went off on holiday to North Wales. Dalton went to Sussex, Bevin to Dorset. Morrison, still economic overlord, and Deputy Prime Minister, stayed in London.

Within a few days Morrison was on the telephone to summon them back to London. The pace of the dollar drain had accelerated – the effect of overseas holders of sterling converting pounds into dollars was now having its impact. An emergency Cabinet was summoned for Sunday 17 August. Eady had returned from Washington, and reported the view of the American government. After a three-hour deliberation Attlee decided to suspend convertibility. Bevin, Dalton, Cripps and Alexander would stay in London with Morrison, who would preside over the consequences of the change of policy. The suspension of convertibility was formally announced by Dalton three days later, on 20 August 1947. The short-term crisis had been dealt with.

Morrison and his colleagues turned to the longer term, with plans for increased exports, restrictions on consumer spending and cuts in public expenditure. On 21 August Dalton wrote to Attlee in Wales:

We are running out of foreign exchange, and if this goes on much longer, *we shall not be able to go on buying anything*. We must reduce the tremendous import stream. I can't continue responsibility for our financial affairs if my colleagues can't see this very simple point, and *act on it*. We must reduce the armed forces. . . . There is nothing more inflationary than having all these non-productive people absorbing supplies of all kinds.

What was Attlee's share of responsibility for the crisis? As we have seen, Dalton had repeatedly argued from the beginning of the year for the reduction of the armed services, which would have gone a long way towards remedying the manpower shortage, which was, at any rate in the first six months of the year, at the heart of the economic problem. Bevin, as Foreign Secretary, and Alexander, as Minister for Defence, had opposed these reductions, and Attlee had backed them up. On the other hand, Dalton, advised by his Treasury officials, had underestimated the impact which convertibility would have on the reserves, and Attlee could be blamed for not questioning Dalton's views on that point. Morrison blamed the crisis on the faulty administration at the Treasury, and their failure to cooperate with his Planning Board. Cripps blamed events on Attlee's 'lack of grip'. Dalton agreed with him.

346

Could Attlee have done more? He had the problems of India, Palestine and steel nationalization on his hands. He had had to deal with the fuel crisis, the agitation in the party over foreign policy, and the argument about the pace of socialist change. The people of Britain were still expecting a relaxation of the demands made by war, not a new call to austerity. A Labour prime minister with a better grasp of foreign policy, a more dynamic conception of party leadership, and a more charismatic personality might have done better than Attlee seemed to have done by the end of the convertibility crisis of 1947, but it is far from certain. Nonetheless, the dissatisfaction with his conduct on the part of his four senior colleagues in the government had led two of them, Dalton and Cripps, to decide that 'Clem must go'. As we shall see, it was Dalton who 'went', and with only himself to blame.

III

The first hint of Cabinet manœuvres against Attlee's leadership came in April 1947, when Cripps suggested to Dalton that Bevin should take over the supervision of domestic policy from Morrison. Dalton raised this with Attlee, who demurred; at this news, Cripps observed that 'unless we can get our planning done right, we shall be sunk'. Two months later the principal witness to these plots, Dalton, heard from his PPS, George Brown, that backbenchers were muttering at the lack of leadership, and suggesting that Bevin take Attlee's place. Returning from the Durham Miners' Gala on 26 July, Bevin and Dalton had an inconclusive conversation during which Dalton urged on his colleague that 'it was natural that many should think of him as our predestined leader'. Bevin was later to say indignantly that Dalton 'had tempted him into being disloyal to Attlee'. Now Cripps took over the running, soliciting Bevan's support in early August, without success. Despite Bevan's reluctance, Cripps and Dalton took the opportunity presented by the convertibility crisis to urge Bevin to take Attlee's place. 'What's Clem ever done to me?' replied Bevin, or in another version: 'Who do you think I am? Lloyd George?'

Undaunted, Cripps took up the matter again in September, proposing to Dalton 'that he and I and Morrison should go together to Attlee and tell him that he ought to resign in favour of Bevin. Attlee would then have to agree, and, at a Party meeting, Morrison could move and I could second Bevin, and that would settle it.' Cripps, obtuse or foolishly optimistic, had chosen to ignore Morrison's ill will towards Bevin, which had become even more heartily reciprocated. In any case, Morrison wanted to be prime minister himself, 'simply because he felt he could do the job better than anybody else could'. Dalton, receiving this confidence, 'thought this was rather engaging' and described Morrison with characteristic patrician condescension as 'a strange mixture of genius and stupidity'.

In spite of Morrison's refusal, Cripps persisted, explaining to Dalton on 8 September that he did so because he was increasingly concerned at the failure of the Cabinet to make crucial economic policy decisions. 'They were whittled away, or referred to further official committees. There was no drive at the centre. With Bevin in charge, it would be quite different. He would send for individual Ministers, and settle things there and then, and everyone would much prefer it.' Cripps told Dalton that he had replanned the Cabinet: Dalton would be foreign secretary, Attlee would be chancellor of the exchequer, Morrison would be deputy prime minister and leader of the House. Bevan would be made minister of supply, to nationalize iron and steel. Dalton's recollections continue:

> He intended, therefore, the following evening after dinner, to see Attlee and tell him that he thought he should give way, as Prime Minister, to Bevin. If Attlee took this reasonably well, and said that the suggestion was so important that he must consult his colleagues, Cripps would be willing to wait ... for a few days. If Attlee was 'tempery' and brushed it aside, Cripps would say that he must resign. If he resigned – in addition to the usual exchange of letters, in which he would speak, in general terms, of the need for 'a major reconstruction of the Government' – he would hold a Press Conference, or address a meeting, and say that he thought Bevin should be Prime Minister. This would start a great commotion in the country, in the Press and in the Party. A Party meeting would probably have to be summoned at once. There was a danger that Bevin wouldn't stand, unless he felt sure of winning. On the other hand, he might be greatly encouraged to stand by a good Press. If Morrison won at the Party meeting, Cripps doubted whether he would be able to form a Government. Neither Bevin nor he would serve under Morrison. If Attlee was maintained as Leader by the Party meeting, the Government would stagger on for a few months longer and then collapse. He would tell Bevin and Morrison, before he saw Attlee, what he was going to say to him. He would tell me afterwards, before any formal resignation, what had passed.

Clearly Cripps had no doubt that he could handle Attlee. Dalton did not share his confidence, and Morrison carefully sent Cripps a hedging letter, affirming: 'I cannot be a party to the proposed arrangement.' As a result, Cripps went to see Attlee on 9 September, after dinner, in circumstances very different from those he had envisaged. Attlee had just got back from his holiday. Cripps had hoped to go round to Number Ten as leader of a powerful delegation which would be able to depose Attlee on the spot. Instead he was alone. Nevertheless he bravely suggested that Attlee should make way for Bevin. He explained to his old friend Attlee that only Bevin could lead that great assault on Britain's economic problems which would finally resolve them in the cause of worldwide socialism. There is a well circulated story that when Cripps had finished speaking, Attlee picked up the scrambler and asked for Bevin. When Bevin came on the phone, the story goes, Attlee said: 'Ernie, Stafford's here. He says you want my job.' Bevin said, No, he didn't. 'Thought not,' said Attlee. Having replaced the phone, he told Stafford that he agreed that a great and coordinated assault must be launched on the economic front forthwith, and that Morrison was no longer up to it. A new man must take his place as economic overlord: would Stafford like to have the job? Cripps, with that 'egotism of the altruist' which Attlee had known so well since the early thirties, had no qualms about saying Yes. He went into Number Ten a rebel and, a few minutes later, came out the leader's right-hand man.

Attlee's own version of the story of the telephone call to Bevin differs, but only slightly. He telephoned Bevin, but did not ask if it was true that 'you want my job'. (Such a question, if it had been put, could not be squared with his claim that he 'knew nothing of any plots'.) What he said to Bevin was: 'Stafford's here: he says you want to change your job.' Bevin replied that he had no intention of leaving the Foreign Office. Attlee replaced the phone, reaffirmed to Cripps that Bevin should not be moved from the Foreign Office, agreed with him that *somebody* should take over the economic front, and said it would be best for him to replace Morrison. In his diary Dalton recorded: 'Attlee once more reigned without challenge.... Within the Government, the movement, begun by Cripps with my support, to put Bevin in Attlee's place, has now turned into a movement to put Cripps in Morrison's place, or at least the most important part of it.'

And so it was. While Morrison was on holiday in Jersey in September, Attlee addressed to him a long, detailed, and comradely letter about the changes he thought it necessary to make in the composition of the administration. A number of junior ministers were not up to the job, he said. The government needed strengthening in the House of Lords. A number of junior ministers, including Strauss, Gaitskell and Wilson, deserved promotion. The Cabinet's committee structure needed to be overhauled and simplified to reduce the burden on senior ministers. The letter, as Morrison's biographers observe, was 'strikingly authoritative in tone':

I propose to have now a single Economic Committee over which I should preside.... With regard to your own work, you have a very heavy task on the Home Front and with A. G. [Greenwood] retiring there is too much for one man, however efficient, especially when he is the second man in the Cabinet who, like the PM, must have time to think of matters of major policy.

Attlee then went on to point out how many responsibilities Morrison had been carrying out, and would have to continue to shoulder, including the management of the Labour Party. Then he delivered the real message:

> This is clearly too great a charge and I think that we require to separate off the co-ordination of the Economic Front from these other important functions. I propose, therefore, to make a Minister for Economic Affairs, whose job would be to co-ordinate our economic efforts at home and abroad and to see to the carrying out of the economic plan under the general direction of the Committee detailed above. I propose that Cripps should fill this office.

The letter showed consideration for Morrison's feelings. Its sound sense alone made it possible for Morrison to agree without loss of face. Morrison's reply accepted the changes in personnel, but he had views of his own to put. He repeated his view that nationalization of the steel industry should not be brought forward in the next session, and objected strongly to the suggestion that Aneurin Bevan should become minister of supply: 'If you put the colleague you mention there *and* his policy it will be a smack in the eye for you, me and the TUC who have been helpful and would have been more helpful if my hands in advocacy had not been tied.' As to the appointment of Cripps, he asked only that the press announcement should make it clear that he (Morrison) had been consulted, that he remained Deputy Prime Minister, and that the change had nothing to do with his health.

The 1947 'plot' was over. Attlee did not refer to it in letters, autobiography, or in his autobiographical notes. He did not bother about intrigue. He was always ready to go if the party wanted him to go, and he knew that the party knew it, but he never had any intention of giving way to ambitious colleagues. His well-chosen PPS, Arthur Moyle, was always ready to make this clear, and did so frequently. This message about Attlee was one of the very few to which the rest of the party were treated. The plot did not affect Attlee's relations with the plotters. He was as fond of Cripps as ever, and was no more distrustful of Dalton and Morrison than he had ever been. As for Attlee's own position, Dalton's words are worth repeating: 'Attlee once more reigned without challenge.' So are Ernest Bevin's. 'What a man,' he said to Moyle. 'He plucked victory from disaster. I love the little man. He is our Campbell-Bannerman.'

IV

When October came food rations had been reduced, there were fewer unrationed foods, and coupons issued for purchase of clothing had been restricted. The butter, bacon and meat rations had been cut. Finance for travel overseas was no longer available without official sanction. The basic petrol ration had been abolished. A few weeks later potatoes were rationed for the first time. Churchill talked of 'setting the people free'. George Isaacs, the Minister of Labour, complained of 'spivs and drones'.

In the King's Speech, on 21 October 1947, the government put forward sixteen measures for the new session. It proposed to nationalize the gas industry, 'in completion of the plan for the co-ordination of the fuel and power industries', and, much more controversial, to introduce 'a Bill to amend the Parliament Act', so as to reduce the power of the House of Lords to veto bills from two years to one. Winding up in the debate on the Address, when Attlee described the proposal to limit the powers of the Lords as 'a wise precautionary measure', he was interrupted by Churchill, who called out: 'A deliberate act of socialist aggression!' Attlee retorted that Churchill 'must be in a reminiscent mood ... thinking of the things said to *him* when he stood at this Box in 1911' (Laughter in the House). Attlee went on to observe: 'If, as I hope, the Members of another place are not inclined ever again to exercise those menacing powers in order to render nugatory the decisions of the elected chamber, then our proposals will do them no harm and we should be taking away a weapon they have no intention of using.'

The debate on the Parliament Bill took place three weeks later. Morrison moved the second reading to 10 November in an able speech which did more to suggest that he was back to normal health than could anything he had wished Attlee to say at the time of the reshuffle. The bill, he said, was 'the rational act of a rational Government', which believed that parliaments were elected 'to do things' and could not accept the existing power of the Lords to hold up legislation. Churchill spoke the following day, with great feeling. He believed, he said, in government based on public opinion. The socialists had a different conception of democracy – once they had got their majority they believed in doing what they liked. Attlee wound up for the government. He said that for the thirty-six years since the Parliament Act of 1911 there had always been a majority in the Lords of a Conservative complexion, and that the government had been 'carrying on for two years under the protection of the Parliament Act ... a very limited protection'. This situation must be dealt with, and the new bill was the way to do so.

In spite of Churchill's vehemence in the Commons and criticism in the press, there was far less excitement in Westminster than might have been expected. One reason was that it became known that the King had raised no difficulty. Attlee had explained to him that nothing had been done about the Lords for thirty-six years, and that apart from a quantitative reduction in the power of the Lords to 'delay' legislation necessary in the period of the war, the functions of the Second Chamber would be left intact. This was the practical kind of argument which the King appreciated, and he had already come to trust Attlee as a bulwark against demagogic change. At the time of the debate on the emergency powers legislation in August, for instance, the King, alarmed by Churchill's denunciation of it as 'a blank cheque for totalitarian government', had written to Attlee asking for reassurance.

> I need not say that I know very well that, so long as you are at the head of any Government, due regard will be given to the rights of Parliament itself, and that Parliament will be offered the opportunity of exercising its proper functions.... I know that your attitude towards this supremely important matter is the same as my own.

And Attlee had had no difficulty in reassuring him: 'I can, of course, assure Your Majesty that no question of evading Parliamentary control would arise.... May I add my sincere hope that Your Majesty and the Royal Family are enjoying a restful time in Scotland?' They were getting on splendidly, reassuring each other. In the battle over the House of Lords, therefore, as in many other battles at this time, the Conservative guns, though not muzzled, fired with powder a little damp. Attlee had more trouble from his own left, some of whom wanted to abolish the Lords, than he experienced from the Opposition. The bill was rejected by the House of Lords in June and September 1948, but was reintroduced in July 1949, and passed over the heads of the peers. The reduction in powers was important; the Lords were sure to resist the controversial plans to nationalize steel.

In the course of the debate on the Address at the end of October, Cripps announced the measures proposed by the government to deal with the short-term economic problem. To meet the anticipated dollar deficit, exports would be increased, while imports of raw materials and tobacco, and expenditure on the armed forces abroad, would be reduced. New houses would not be started in 1948. New factories would be built only if they contributed to exports or essential home production. There would be cuts in food imports. There was a battle ahead, said Cripps. It was a battle for economic solvency, and for democracy. It was a battle which could only be won in the spirit. Only Christian faith would see the people through. Though this speech by Cripps did the government a power of good, it was not enough to prevent the standing of the Attlee government sinking to its nadir in the first few days of November. In the municipal elections the Conservatives won 636 seats, losing only 18. The Labour Party lost 687, winning only 43. Labour supporters called it 'a food and basic petrol election'. Churchill called it 'a nation-wide protest against Socialist mis-management'. The result of the Gravesend by-election – Labour held the seat, occupied by a Conservative for twenty-one years previous to 1945 – was a consolation.

By now Dalton's much publicized air of booming confidence was coming in for criticism. It was attacked by the Liberals as 'lazy'; for the Tories, Oliver Stanley talked of Dalton's 'opportunities having been wasted in jaunty optimism'. As the time came for him to present his budget, 12 November, fewer and fewer MPs, including those on his own side of the House, expected a clarion call. His budget had the simple aim: 'To strengthen ... our budgetary defences against inflation.' As it turned out, Dalton's career as Chancellor was to come to an unforeseen end as a result of an off-the-cuff reference to the contents of his budget which he made to a lobby correspondent on his way into the chamber. Francis Williams, then Attlee's personal press adviser, called it 'one of the silliest indiscretions in recent political history'. That night, several hours after the budget speech had been made in the House, Williams was recalled urgently to Downing Street. When he arrived in the small hours he found the Prime Minister engaged, but a private secretary showed him the budget story in *The Star* and informed him that all Fleet Street knew that the disclosed information had come from the Chancellor. He was summoned into the Cabinet Room to talk to the Prime Minister. Attlee was fully aware that something in the budget had 'got out', but did not know how. 'What's all this about?' demanded Attlee. Williams, without enthusiasm, but now knowing all the facts, said: 'It seems that the Chancellor talked to the Press.' Attlee was clearly astounded. 'Talked to the Press?' he said in a tone raised with incredulity. 'Why on earth did he want to talk to the *Press*?'

Attlee was astounded, said Williams many years afterwards, not so much because a chancellor had been indiscreet, 'but because anybody in his senses had chosen to talk to a *journalist*'. Williams may have exaggerated, but he had not invented: Attlee found Dalton's indiscretion totally incomprehensible. Asked in a Granada TV interview what he felt about Dalton and the budget indiscretion, Attlee said: 'Perfect ass. His trouble was he *would* talk. He always liked to have a secret to confide to somebody else to please him. He did it once too often.'

Q: 'If he hadn't resigned, would you have fired him?'

A: 'I would have had to. There was never any trouble over that. He realized.'

After the Cabinet meeting the next day, there was a meeting between Attlee, Dalton, Morrison, Cripps and the Chief Whip. Dalton offered his resignation. Attlee did not accept it at that stage. In the afternoon, in answer to the expected question in Parliament, Dalton admitted 'a grave indiscretion on my part, for which I offer my deep apologies to the House'. He went to see Attlee again and for a second time offered his resignation. Attlee, he recorded, 'replied that he felt he must [accept it] but I was moved to see that he was much more deeply moved than I was at this moment. He said he hated – hated – he repeated this word several times – hated to lose me.' They then prepared and cleared an official exchange of letters which appeared in the press next day. Attlee's letter was warm and helpful: 'I realize that this indiscretion in itself did not result in any action detrimental to the State, but the principle of the inviolability of the Chancellor of the Exchequer, who necessarily receives many confidential communications, must be beyond question ... our friendship remains.'

Attlee had no doubt about who should succeed Dalton. It could only be Cripps. It was a change of men, not measures, of personalities, not policies, but it was important. Cripps symbolized spiritual faith and physical self-discipline. If austerity could be made charismatic he was the man to do it. He lifted the government and, to some extent, the nation out of a rut, on to a level where there was a sense of purpose and a hope for the future. Before the year ended, 18 December, after the unfreezing of the balance of the American loan, Cripps was able to give the House of Commons a relatively cheerful account of how the country had improved its position since the August crisis and the imposition of the economic measures designed to deal with it. In November the Coal Board had been able to say that the coal production target for the year, which had seemed unattainable two months previously, was now 'within sight'. In December the Coal Board was given permission to *export* coal. Steel production in the autumn was up by a third compared with the figure for the year before the war. More food was coming in from Eire. A great new supply of wheat would arrive from Australia, and there was to be a great credit made available by Canada. Harold Wilson, now President of the Board of Trade, had negotiated an agreement for the import of animal feeding stuffs from the Soviet Union.

As the year ended, therefore, Cripps, with a combination of encouraging reports and stirring calls to national pride and sense of Christian mission, was able to impart some reassurance to the population. If he brought about a degree of confidence, it was at the price of a clear exposition of unwelcome facts. The British people now faced the truth that the battle of the dollar gap was real and that austerity had come to stay. Cripps was now the epic figure on the domestic scene. On the foreign front Bevin, now symbol as well as architect of resistance to the Soviet Union, was an equally dominant presence. Between these two towering characters in the dramas at home and abroad, the Prime Minister seemed to many to play a small and inconsequential role.

Yet 1947 had been the year of the government's most conspicuous achievement: the granting of independence to India. And this achievement, the high point of the Labour government's colonial policy, had been virtually Attlee's own.

21
The End of Empire:
India

The British Empire was one of the major casualties of the Second World War. The economic damage caused by six years of fighting made it impossible for Britain to consider paying for the armed forces which would be needed to protect a far-flung scatter of dependent countries. In the same years, political turmoil in many colonies forced Britain to face the fact that she was not wanted; and the cost of staying, unwanted, was beyond her means. American pressure, overt and covert, was directed to reducing Britain's influence outside Europe. Attlee's government had to arrange for an orderly withdrawal from Empire, in circumstances which were often unfavourable to a peaceful transfer of power and in the face of a British public opinion which was often unsympathetic or uncomprehending. The biggest problem was India, which Attlee took in hand himself. His great success was to choose Mountbatten, whose work in Burma he had admired, to become Viceroy for the handover of power. The other major overseas territory to be abandoned was Palestine, where Attlee's intervention was less direct, but nonetheless influential. On Palestine and India the government's record, and Attlee's own, stand to be judged: but neither is comprehensible without reference to the withdrawal from Burma, which was Attlee's first effort in decolonization.

I

Attlee's policy in Burma was important not only for its effect on Burma but because it became a model for policies elsewhere, including India. Burma was the first former colony to be liberated from the Japanese, and the first to be given its independence. In the process Attlee learned lessons – including those from his mistakes – which he applied in other countries. In particular, he came to prefer Mountbatten's judgement about Asian

355

nationalism, and his ability to manage it, to that of the Colonial Office experts. The path along which Mountbatten advanced to become Viceroy of India in 1947 began in Rangoon two years previously. Within a few weeks of becoming Prime Minister, Attlee made a major departure from the policy of the wartime coalition, and gave Mountbatten, Supreme Allied Commander, South-East Asia, a freedom of action on military grounds which Mountbatten, with Attlee's support, used to bring about political consequences of the most fundamental kind.

Burma had been separated from India in 1935, as recommended by the Simon Commission. A separate Burma Office was set up under the secretary of state for India; in Burma, except for certain reserved powers such as defence, the governor was to act on the advice of a responsible ministry. There was considerable friction between Burma's political parties, and it was soon clear that political stability would take some time to achieve. The two years before the war saw labour strikes, students' strikes, and religious rioting between Burmese and Indian Muslims. In February 1939 the government of Ba Maw, the first Prime Minister, fell. After further troubles the 'Patriots' Party' formed a government under U Saw. Meanwhile the student leader Aung Sang had risen to the leadership of the Thakin Party, a nationalist revolutionary organization holding only a handful of parliamentary seats.

When the war broke out, the Thakins, Ba Maw and U Saw all formed private armies. U Saw announced that he would fight with the British if they promised Burma dominion status at the end of the war. Dr Ba Maw and the Thakins discussed joint action against the British and the U Saw government. The Governor and the Prime Minister took no chances, and arrested as many leaders of the 'disloyal' parties as they could. U Saw journeyed to London to try to obtain a guarantee of Dominion status. Churchill would have none of it, and U Saw started back to Burma an embittered man. On his way, in Lisbon, he made contact with the Japanese ambassador. The British heard of this, arrested him for treason, and interned him for the duration.

To avoid arrest, Aung Sang had fled from Burma and, since they promised Burmese independence, joined the Japanese. When the Japanese invaded Burma after Pearl Harbor, Aung Sang accompanied them wearing Japanese uniform, and commanding a contingent of Burmese reorganized by the Japanese as the Burma Independence Army, later known as the Burma National Army. He soon grew suspicious of Japanese intentions, and in 1942 approached the British, offering to lead an underground movement against Japan. The offer was accepted. In March 1945, on Mountbatten's instructions, Aung Sang launched a rebellion against the puppet regime of Ba Maw. His political group also came into the open – the Anti-Fascist Organization (AFO), later the

Anti-Fascist People's Freedom League (AFPFL), consisting of several parties, including the Communist Party, the People's Revolutionary Party, and the Thakin Party, all of which had been suppressed by the British government before the war as 'illegal organizations'.

The British government had made no *political* commitment to Aung Sang, and regarded his followers with suspicion. Their record was bad: they were anti-British originally; they were Communist; they had collaborated with the Japanese; and they were extremists in the cause of Burmese independence. Moreover, Aung Sang was not acceptable to those Burmese who had remained loyal to the British regime and suffered much at the hands of the Japanese and the Burmese 'traitors' who had re-entered Burma at their side. Even if Aung Sang had been acceptable, his demand for Burmese independence 'now' would have conflicted with the policy of the War Cabinet, which was to withhold self-government in South-East Asia until re-established British colonial regimes had restored political and economic stability. So, though as the Japanese retreated Aung Sang was able to set up local provisional administration under his control, the British government refused to give him political recognition and instructed Mountbatten to avoid discussing it with him.

Mountbatten was in some difficulty as a result of these instructions. In the early spring of 1945, though the Japanese were in retreat, it was far from clear that their complete defeat in Burma was at hand. The assistance of the Burmese resistance movement under Aung Sang was a military imperative. Even when the Japanese had been expelled from Burma, Mountbatten would require all the help he could get to fight them outside Burma's frontiers. Nobody could have foreseen how quickly the Japanese would capitulate: nothing was known of the atomic bomb. Mountbatten, therefore, wanted to exploit Aung Sang to the full. While respecting the War Cabinet's directive that military considerations must not involve political commitments, Mountbatten made it clear that to maximize military cooperation with Aung Sang, political involvement with him to some extent was desirable and indeed inevitable. His position was strengthened by the appointment of Brigadier Rance as his chief military adviser on civilian affairs. Rance, a signals officer, arrived in Burma early in 1945. Within a few weeks he had come to the conclusion that there must be full cooperation with Aung Sang, even if this meant political commitments to him. Holding these views Rance and Mountbatten were soon in conflict with the Governor, Sir Reginald Dorman-Smith, who adhered, in his enforced exile in India, to the letter of the War Cabinet's policy.

The British government's official position at this time was conveyed in a telegram to Mountbatten sent through Attlee's India Committee in March 1945, authorizing the Supreme Commander to give all military support to Aung Sang and accept all help in return. In accepting Aung Sang's help, Mountbatten was to remind him that, in view of the assistance his forces had given the Japanese invader in 1945, he had 'a lot of leeway to make up, in our eyes as well as those of their compatriots who have suffered at the hands of the enemy'. He was to discourage Burmese resistance groups from imagining that they would be able 'to use the comparatively trifling aid given by them to us as an argument for the grant of a predominant position in the government and perhaps constitutional advances which the home government would not feel ready to consider'.

By May 1945 the British had liberated Burma. Mountbatten was most anxious to get Aung Sang to maximize his military effort against the Japanese outside Burma. Moreover, now that he had seen the political state of affairs in Burma for himself, he believed that the Governor and the War Cabinet were out of date. Self-government would have to come much sooner than was currently envisaged, and would be dominated by the nationalists led by Aung Sang. They should therefore be converted into friends from the very beginning. On 16 May 1945, Mountbatten proposed that the Governor should announce that when he was able to restore civil government in Burma he would include members of Aung Sang's AFPFL in the new Advisory Council. Dorman-Smith and the War Cabinet rejected this as an intolerable departure from the British government's policy.

Worse was to come. On 17 May the coalition government published a White Paper on Burma. The government repeated its intention to assist the political development of Burma towards Dominion status, but stated firmly that the conditions for democratic government in Burma were lacking, and that for the moment Burma would be ruled by the Governor and an executive council of officials directly responsible to Westminster. Elections would take place, it was hoped, soon after December 1948. No date was given for Burmese independence. The White Paper was supported by the Labour Party. For the Burmese nationalists it put the clock back to before 1937. Aung Sang responded by publicly inviting all nationalists to join his AFPFL, turn it into a national congress and strive for Burmese independence. He received widespread support. Rance immediately appointed some AFPFL representatives to his own military advisory council. Meanwhile Mountbatten pressed ahead with the incorporation of Aung Sang's guerrillas in the British Army.

The Japanese capitulated on 14 August 1945. Dorman-Smith lost no time in pressing the Secretary of State for the handover of Burma to the civil government. He was concerned that unless this was done at the earliest possible moment the political situation would deteriorate and the extremists would be in charge. Mountbatten did not share his anxieties

– his attitude to the extremists was in any case different – but reluctantly agreed to an early handover. Civil government was restored to most of Burma in October 1945. Dorman-Smith, ignoring the advice of Mountbatten and Rance, now proceeded to put into effect the policy laid down by the wartime coalition government the previous May. He proposed to appoint an executive council of nine Burmese and a European deputy chairman to help him govern the country pending a general election and the return to government by a council of ministers responsible to an elected legislature. Making some concession to the advice of Mountbatten and Rance, he invited Aung Sang and the AFPFL to participate, but made it clear that he, not Aung Sang, would choose the AFPFL representatives. Aung Sang replied that he would accept only if the AFPFL were allotted seats in ratio to the political strength he claimed for it, a quota which would have given it almost all the seats on the council, and if he were free to choose the AFPFL representatives himself. The Governor refused. Aung Sang refused to participate in the government.

When full responsibility for the whole government of Burma was transferred from Mountbatten to Dorman-Smith on 1 January 1946, Aung Sang demanded a fundamental change in the policy outlined in the 1945 White Paper: independence forthwith, and recognition of the AFPFL as the national governing party of Burma. Dorman-Smith refused. Aung Sang denounced the government. The Governor threatened to arrest him. This antagonized Burmese nationalists outside the AFPFL. Meanwhile social and economic conditions heightened the frustration of the nationalists, and carried public opinion on to their side. There were no goods in the shops; dacoity (robbing by organized bands) frightened the workers in the rice fields. The production of rice was held up, with grave effects on exports to India and Europe.

Dorman-Smith's appreciation of the situation, and his handling of the government, now began to raise grave doubts in Attlee's mind. The day-to-day handling of Burma had been the responsibility of Pethick-Lawrence, the Secretary of State. When he left for India on the Cabinet mission in March 1946, his job was taken over for the time being by Attlee personally. Attlee had already begun to have misgivings about policy in Burma. 'As soon as I began to read Pethick's papers I realised we would have to change our line.'

The new policy could be described as following Mountbatten instead of Dorman-Smith. Instead of keeping Aung Sang out of the government unless he would come in on British terms, he must be brought in as soon as possible. Dorman-Smith must be removed. Attlee wrote to Pethick-Lawrence on 10 May: 'The Burma situation is difficult. I have decided to hold my hand for the time being as there is no one on the spot to take over from Dorman-Smith, but I am convinced that we must have a

359

change there.' A few days later, U Saw, now leading the influential Myochit Party, threatened to withdraw his representative from the Executive Council and join a united front of all parties. Dorman-Smith took no action; the Myochit men left the council. This was a great blow to Dorman-Smith's credibility. Aung Sang began to speak of 'a full-scale battle for freedom . . . civil disobedience or a parallel government'. Burma was on the boil.

Mountbatten retired as Supreme Commander in May. Attlee telephoned him in London, discussed the worsening situation and asked what he should do. 'Consult Rance,' said Mountbatten. Rance, now Chief Civil Affairs Officer in Mountbatten's military administration, was summoned to Downing Street. After an hour's talk with Attlee he left Number Ten – to his great surprise – as the new Governor-General of Burma. Mountbatten was staggered by the speed of the decision. Rance immediately allotted six of the nine Executive Council seats for Aung Sang to fill from the AFPFL. Aung Sang himself became Minister of Defence and External Affairs, and deputy chairman of the council (the chairman was Rance). A substantial step forward to Burmese independence had been taken.

The prescient and capable Rance replaced Dorman-Smith too late in the day. The frustrations of the previous nine months proved too much for the nationalists, and precipitated hostility between the major parties. A rift developed within the AFPFL, and Aung Sang, once the leader of the far left, found himself in a central position, vilified from either side. Attlee had now made up his mind that Aung Sang was the man to back, and that all speed must be made to full independence for Burma. In December he invited a delegation of nationalist leaders to London, with Aung Sang among them. By this time Aung Sang, to preserve his position, had committed his colleagues to a demand for independence outside the Commonwealth. 'This is going to be a strenuous week,' Attlee told Tom. 'We have to talk with their leader Aung Sang. He is very impressive, quite young, very straight, honest and broadminded.'

Attlee's statement to the House on 20 December 1946, that Aung Sang had been invited to London for discussions which would 'expedite' Burmese independence, drew from Churchill one of his most famous and quoted diatribes, and the first use of the pejorative term 'scuttle':

> It was said in the days of the great administrator, Lord Chatham, that you had to get up very early in the morning not to miss some great acquisition of territory which was then characteristic of our fortunes. The not less memorable administration of Mr Attlee is distinguished for the opposite set of experiences. The British Empire seems to be running off almost as fast as the American loan. The steady and remorseless process of divesting ourselves of what has been gained by so many generations of toil, admini-

stration, and sacrifice continues. In the case of Burma, it is hardly a year since by the superb exertions of the 14th Army and the enormous sacrifices of British and Indian blood, the Japanese were forced to surrender or were destroyed and driven out, and the country liberated. Yet there is this extraordinary haste, although barely a year has passed, in order that we should take the necessary measures to get out of Burma finally and for ever.... This haste is appalling. 'Scuttle' is the only word that can be applied.

An agreement was signed in London by the British and Burmese national leaders on 27 January 1947. Elections would be held within four months, and the Burmese people would be free to decide the future position of Burma. Aung Sang's Council would meantime be the interim government of Burma, its powers being on a par with those of any Dominion Cabinet. The British government would make loans, help with the reconstruction of Burma, and support its application for membership of the UN. Writing to Tom a few days after the agreement was signed, Attlee said: 'Our Burmese talks passed off well and if Aung Sang can control his wild men, we may make a success there. Winston was the only objector in the House, to the unconcealed distaste of his party.'

Churchill had indeed excelled himself in denunciation of Attlee's Burma policy. The announcement of the impending talks in December had brought forth the diatribe on Labour's policy of 'scuttle'. After the agreement he condemned this settlement with a former traitor:

> I certainly did not expect to see U Aung Sang, whose hands were dyed with British blood and loyal Burmese blood, marching up the steps of Buckingham Palace as the plenipotentiary of the Burmese Government.

But blood and treachery seemed to be the stuff of Burmese politics. U Saw, who had only leaned to treachery after Churchill snubbed him in the early days of the war, made a desperate bid for power on the eve of Burma's independence. Three of his men, armed with machine-guns, burst into Aung Sang's Cabinet room on 19 July 1947, killing the prime minister and all his ministers. Despite these assassinations, Attlee, supported and guided by Rance, persisted with his programme. U Nu, a leading member of Aung Sang's Thakin Party, was appointed Prime Minister. Independence was granted formally to Burma on 17 October, and in January 1948 she withdrew from the Commonwealth to become a sovereign republic.

Attlee's only regrets about Burma were that he had not realized early enough that Aung Sang was the man to back, and that Aung Sang did not live long enough to do for Burma what Burma then required:

> Had we been in touch with U Aung Sang from the start I think Burma would have stayed in the Commonwealth; but they had committed themselves to independence. I think too that if U Aung Sang had lived they

might have stayed in, but the murder removed the one man who might have done it and ridden the storm.

II

More than any of the other great achievements of the postwar Labour government, the granting of independence to India will be linked with the name of Attlee. It was his own most important contribution to the history of his times, and the role he played in bringing it about surpassed that of any of his colleagues. He knew more about India than any member of his Cabinet, Cripps possibly excepted, and he intended to ensure that his government's India policy would be his own. He dominated the conduct of policy in the two years leading up to India's independence. It is significant that he appointed to the office of Secretary of State for India a member of the House of Lords who could not deal with Indian policy in the House of Commons. Attlee was in fact his own secretary of state for India. The crucial decisions made in the last few months of the Raj bore the unmistakable impress of his character and methods.

In spite of his expertise on India, built up steadily through the eighteen years since his first visit in 1927, Attlee had much to learn between 1945 and 1947. His most important discovery was that many errors in official thinking in London were the result of the failure to grasp the strength and obduracy of Muslim nationalism, and the pace at which it was carrying the Muslim League toward a demand for *two* independent Indias, one of which would contain a Muslim majority under Muslim rule – a Pakistan. This was an objective totally incompatible with the insistence of the Congress Party on *one* India, in which Congress would be the majority party and dominate the all-India government. The second most important lesson Attlee had to learn was that, in spite of earnest and categorical statements made by successive British governments, the Indians believed almost to the last minute that the British did not want, and did not intend, to leave; that the Raj would continue for years to come. When the Labour government began to talk about the possibility of a multi-state India, the Congress at first interpreted this as another application of the principle of *divide et imperare*, aimed at perpetuating British rule. As Attlee frequently said in later years, had these aspects of the Indian situation been fully understood in 1945, an independent India might have been brought about much sooner.

To see the problem of India as Attlee saw it when Labour came to power in 1945 it is necessary to recall the main events of Britain's relations with India over the previous decade. The Government of India Act of 1935 had established elective government in the eleven British India provinces, but not at the centre. The Act looked to the setting up of an all-India federated government in Delhi, incorporating a representative parliamentary system; but this could not be established, since too few Princely States acceded to the proposal. At the centre, therefore, India continued to be governed by the Viceroy and his appointed twelve-man Executive Council – eight Indians, four Europeans – the Viceroy holding the vital portfolios of defence and foreign affairs.

In eight of the eleven British India provinces, the first elections, held in 1937, had provided the Congress Party with impressive majorities. When these Congress administrations refused to include Muslims in their Cabinets, they created the belief that whenever the Congress Party had a majority the Muslim minority would have no part in government. Muslims, therefore, concluded that they must demand independent states in which *they* would be in the majority. The Congress continued to insist that India was *one* country, of *one* people, and that no political divisions need, or should, be made on the basis of race or religion.

When war broke out, the Viceroy, Lord Linlithgow, declared India at war with Germany, without first consulting Indian leaders. Gandhi, Nehru and the leaders of the Congress Party, though sympathizing with Britain's resistance to Nazism, objected to Linlithgow's action and refused to support the war effort. They complained that they had not been given a statement of Britain's war aims, particularly in relation to India, and asked for one. Dissatisfied with the Viceroy's response, the eight congressional provincial administrations resigned *en bloc*.

The leader of the Muslim League, Jinnah, quickly exploited this turn of events. All Muslim ministers in the provinces were instructed to remain at their posts and offer the British government all assistance. The Sikh leaders took a similar course. This had a lasting effect on how Muslims and Sikhs were regarded in Westminster and Whitehall, and profoundly influenced official British thinking on policy towards India over the next eight years. Meanwhile, in March 1940, Jinnah announced the 'Lahore Resolution' calling for a separate independent India – a Pakistan for areas in which Muslims were in a majority. In August 1940, the Viceroy made what came to be known as the 'August offer'. This renewed the pledge of Dominion status for India after the war was over, provided there was agreement on this between Hindu and Muslim, and promised that a representative Indian body would be set up to work out a new constitution. What was new in the 'offer' was the emphasis on the commitment that the framing of the new constitution should be primarily the responsibility of the Indians. Demanding complete independence, Congress rejected the 'August offer'. The Muslim League used the occasion to give fresh publicity to the 'Lahore Resolution'. Both parties interpreted the emphasis on the need for Hindu and Muslim to get together to plan a united India as a British ploy to use the division between the two communities as an excuse for putting off the day when the Raj would end.

In March 1942, to meet the threat to India newly posed by Japan's entry into the war, the Cabinet India Committee, recently set up under Attlee, sent Stafford Cripps to India bearing the 'Cripps Plan'. The plan offered an elected assembly after the war to frame a constitution, and the further involvement of Indians in wartime government. The Congress Party rejected the plan, mainly because the wartime 'national' government which Cripps proposed would not be a Cabinet government with full executive power. Cripps said that the Congress was demanding a constitutional change which could not possibly be made in a time of war; and he returned home empty-handed. Though the plan was rejected, one of its provisions had important consequences. Against the advice of the Viceroy it stated 'the right of any Province that was not prepared to accept the new constitution to retain its existing constitutional position'. The Muslim League used this statement to justify its demand for one or more independent Muslim-dominated states.

In July 1942 Congress issued a demand that Britain 'quit India' at once. The following month Gandhi called on the British to 'get out and leave India in God's hands'. On the grounds that Gandhi's utterances were an incitement to violence, the Viceroy declared the Indian National Congress an illegal association, and ordered the internment of the working committee of the Congress Party for the duration of the war. Attlee, defending the Viceroy's action in the House, said: 'We are not prepared to negotiate with people who are in rebellion.' For the rest of the war British policy towards India was based on military not political requirements. When the Viceroy retired in 1943, he was replaced by the former Governor-General, Wavell, whose main brief was to fight the Japanese and keep order in India for the duration.

In March 1945 Wavell came to London for talks on the military and political situation in India. He was not particularly welcome. The Japanese were no longer at the gates of India, and Churchill considered he now had more pressing problems on his mind. The Labour leaders in the coalition government were more interested in the coming general election and Britain's postwar domestic problems than in discussing a new constitution for India. Wavell's main proposal was a new executive council, appointed, not elected, but all Indian, apart from the Viceroy and the Commander-in-Chief. Churchill did not approve of this, nor, for different reasons, did Attlee, still chairman of the Cabinet's powerful India Committee.

Attlee, according to Wavell, 'inveighed against my proposals as undemocratic'. Attlee was in favour of a new executive council dominated by Indians, but he wanted its members to be selected from a panel chosen by the provincial and central legislatures. Nevertheless, Wavell received enough support to enable him on his return to Delhi in June to make the first important announcement about their future which the Indians had heard for nearly three years. Congress leaders who had been interned since August 1942 would be released forthwith. A new executive council would be appointed, which would include Muslims and Hindus, in equal proportion, and, apart from the Viceroy and the Commander-in-Chief, all its members would be Indians. To select the members of the council a conference of twenty-one all-India political leaders, including Gandhi and Jinnah, would be held – at Simla. The most urgent task of the new council when formed, Wavell was able to declare, would be to prepare the way for India's independence.

The Simla Conference assembled, but broke down after three weeks. The breaking point was Jinnah's insistence that the five seats to be held by Muslims on the new council must be held by members of his Muslim League. Faced by Jinnah's demand, Wavell withdrew his scheme. What happened to the Simla Conference was typical of what was to happen again and again for the next two years: proposals made from Delhi or London came to nothing because Congress and the Muslim League refused to cooperate with each other in a new government on any terms but their own, each putting forward terms unacceptable to the other. A fortnight after the failure of the Simla Conference, on 26 July, Labour came to power.

Attlee believed that the Simla Conference had failed because the Viceroy had not been empowered by Churchill's 'caretaker' government to offer enough to the Indians. His selection of Lord Pethick-Lawrence as Secretary of State for India was intended to be a clear signal that he meant business. It was not that Pethick-Lawrence had great ability or drive, but 'Pethick' had great standing in India, and was trusted by all Indian nationalists. This was the front for Attlee's advance. Behind it, he 're-formed the India Committee, the nucleus of which was Cripps, myself and Pethick-Lawrence'. Wavell was asked to come to London as soon as possible and to announce immediately that elections to the central and provincial assemblies of India would be held in the autumn.

Just as Wavell had found Churchill too slow to move forward on India, he found Attlee too fast. From the beginning, he distrusted Attlee's judgement. Attlee, on the other hand, began to feel that the Viceroy was unimaginative if not negative, displaying the same deficiencies of which Churchill had complained when Wavell was commander-in-chief in North Africa. Wavell opposed any renewal of the Cripps proposals. Attlee had already made up his mind that a modification of them was the inevitable next step. Wavell was also convinced, as he explained to

Pethick-Lawrence, that 'we had to face the Pakistan issue and bring its real implications into the light before we could get any further.' Attlee had still to learn this lesson. He was still, as he years after told the author, underestimating Jinnah and the League. Wavell's protests were therefore not congenial. On 4 September, Wavell had an hour's talk with Attlee. He recorded that Attlee:

> made it clear, without intending to do so, that the Cabinet was thinking more of placating opinion in their own party and in the USA than of the real good of India.... They are obviously bent on handing over India to their Congress friends as soon as possible.... I may have to decide whether to refuse to be a party to their plans to quit India, or to go back and try to keep them out of disaster as much as possible.

In spite of these reservations Wavell publicly associated himself with the government's policy. Two weeks later, on 16 September, he and Attlee made broadcasts simultaneously from New Delhi and Downing Street. They announced that as soon as possible after the elections to the central and provincial legislatures in the autumn, a constitution-making body would be convened. Indian leaders would be asked if the Cripps Plan of 1942 was acceptable with modifications to be negotiated – this part of the announcement was intended to humour Muslims pressing for a Pakistan. A new reconstituted executive council would be set up, based on the support of the major Indian political parties. Attlee appealed to the Indians to sink their differences and 'join together in a united effort to work out a constitution which majority and minority communities will accept as just and fair'. The proposals were immediately rejected by Congress as 'vague and inadequate', the same reason they gave for rejecting the Cripps Plan in 1942. The Muslim League declined to participate in the establishment of a constitution-making assembly until the British government had given a commitment to the establishment of Pakistan.

Congress, with Nehru prominent, now began to whip up anti-British feeling. The threat of widespread violence became so acute that Attlee decided that he must do something quickly to reduce the tension. In early December he announced that the setting up of a constitution-making body was regarded as urgent; to enable progress towards self-government to be accelerated, a parliamentary delegation of eight MPs and two peers would leave London for India four weeks later. This 'goodwill' mission left London on the last day of 1945 and, dividing into groups, visited many parts of the sub-continent and met leaders of all parties. The mission did something to lower the political temperature in India, but on its return its members pressed on Attlee the urgent need for action, and confirmed the view that the Indians would not accept a rehash of the 1942 Cripps Plan.

Yet Attlee was still convinced that the 1942 Plan had got so near to being accepted that something similar must be tried. 'It was clear to me,' he wrote in his autobiography, 'that the problem could not be handled by a Secretary of State and a Viceroy, however able they might be.' He now decided to go ahead at once with a new Cripps mission, which would not attempt to get agreement to the 1942 Plan, but would try to find out how its provisions could be developed, modified and made acceptable. The India 'Cabinet' mission was announced on 19 February 1946. Cripps, then President of the Board of Trade, would be accompanied by Pethick-Lawrence and by A. V. Alexander, First Lord of the Admiralty, a party stalwart whom Attlee trusted. The mission's brief was to try to find agreement on principles and procedures which could lead to the setting up of the machinery by which the Indians *themselves* could establish the constitution of an independent India. The mission would leave at the end of March.

Later, Attlee observed in the House that 'we cannot allow a minority to place their veto on the advance of the majority'. This so antagonized the Muslim League that on his arrival in India Pethick-Lawrence was instructed by Attlee to 'clarify' the situation, which he did by remarking that: 'while the Congress are representative of large numbers, it would not be right to regard the Muslim League as merely a minority party; they are in fact majority representatives of the great Muslim community.' Attlee also stated: 'We must recognize that we cannot make Indians responsible for governing themselves and at the same time retain over here the responsibility for the treatment of minorities and the power to intervene on their behalf.' In retrospect it is clear that the combined effect of these two statements was virtually to ensure that there must be two Indias. Congress quoted the first as a promise that Muslim League demands for guarantees should not hold up progress toward independence; and the Muslim League quoted the second as promising that Muslims should not be subjected anywhere to an all-India Congress-dominated central government but should have an independent India of their own.

By the time the Cabinet mission arrived in India at the end of March 1946, the results of the elections had been declared. More than ever it was clear that Indian politics consisted solely of the Congress Party versus the Muslim League. In spite of this unambiguous message, Attlee continued to canvass the view that an all-India central government was possible, and that the Congress would be able to provide terms for the Muslim League which would enable Jinnah to relinquish his demand for a Pakistan.

The Cabinet mission remained in India for seven weeks. From the beginning its work was bedevilled by the tactics of the Indian parties. Muslim League and Congress leaders bargained with the mission over the terms of their participation in the new executive council to improve their position for bargaining about representation in the future constituent assembly. When the commission agreed terms which satisfied the Muslim League, they found that these terms were unacceptable to the Congress. When they agreed terms which satisfied the Congress, the Muslim League reneged on the terms they had previously agreed to and negotiations had to start all over again. Within a fortnight Attlee had accepted the fact that if the deadlock was to be broken the mission would have to put forward proposals of its own.

A new scheme for Indian independence was issued on 16 May. In part it was a reissue of the Cripps Plan of 1942, but important additions were included. An independent Pakistan was rejected, but the two Muslim areas were to have autonomy in everything but foreign policy, defence and communications. In the long term, the scheme proposed what became known as the 'three-tier' plan. The central government would control foreign policy, defence and communications, with an executive and legislative body constituted from British India and the Princely States. The eleven provincial governments would deal with everything else. Between the provincial government and the centre, those provinces which wished to could form themselves into groups for 'selected subjects' or 'selected purposes in common'. There were to be three permitted groups: Group 'A' consisted of the Punjab, the North-West Frontier Province, Baluchistan and Sind; 'B' Group of Bengal and Assam; 'C' the rest of British India. The point of the 'tier-group' system was that it could bring about an independent India with a non-communalist central government in control of defence and foreign policy, but which would be an India over whose domestic affairs Muslims would exercise control in the two 'groups' in which they were in a majority.

The Cabinet mission's *short-term* plan was for an 'Interim Government' which apart from the Viceroy and the Commander-in-Chief would consist only of Indians – five Congress Party nominees, five Muslim League nominees, and four representatives of other parties. This would be much more representative of Indian opinion than the existing Executive Council, and in line with what Attlee had proposed to Wavell when the Viceroy had appeared before the coalition government in the spring of 1945.

The exchange of dispatches between Attlee and the Cabinet mission indicates quite clearly that it was he who was in charge of Indian policy. It was essential for constitutional as well as political and personal reasons for the mission to get the Prime Minister's assent to the proposals, but before he gave his permission Attlee sent back so many amendments that, according to Wavell: 'Cripps and the Secretary of State became quite bellicose about it and even began to talk of resignation.'

A conference of Indian leaders with the mission and the Viceroy was held at Simla the following month. The Muslim League accepted short-term and long-term plans, but the Congress made difficulties over both. Negotiations were suspended and the mission returned to England on 29 June. To carry on government, Wavell set up a 'caretaker' council of officials which included Hindus and Muslims.

In his diary Wavell deplored the mission's obsequiousness to the Congress, and attributed it with some justification to guidance coming from Attlee. But Attlee's attitude, unlike that of Cripps, was not the result of a predilection for the Congress point of view. What Wavell failed to realize was that uppermost in Attlee's mind were two anxieties: that an independent Pakistan was not economically viable, and that the north-western part of the potential Pakistan was very close to Russian territory. In Attlee's view an independent India, controlled by Congress, was still the most desirable solution, and he knew that the American government concurred.

The failure of the Cabinet mission taught Attlee three lessons which formed a turning point in his policy towards India: first, that in spite of their close relations with the Labour Party, the Congress would not yield an inch to produce an agreement on India which fell short of their maximum terms; secondly, that the Muslim League was determined to obtain an independent Pakistan; thirdly, that Wavell's continued presence was an obstacle to further negotiations. Cripps and Pethick-Lawrence complained to Attlee that Wavell was out of touch with the thinking and feeling of both Hindu and Muslim leaders, and confirmed what Attlee had believed for many months: Wavell, appointed by the coalition government to hold the fort in India, was now another Dorman-Smith. 'I agree very much with what you say,' he wrote back to Pethick-Lawrence on 10 May, 'with regard to the need for providing the Viceroy with first-class advisers. I will turn this over in my mind and discuss it with you on your return.' Three weeks after the mission got back to London, Wavell recorded in his diary:

> This morning I had a letter from the PM pressing on me again Maurice Gwyer as Political Adviser. He had obviously been told that I receive nothing but official [Indian civil service] advice and that my political judgement is therefore unsound, ie not sufficiently pro-Congress. . . . I think my judgement is better than HMG's and shall say so, and tell him that if HMG don't like it, their duty is to find another Viceroy, as I will not be a figurehead.

Soon after the Cabinet mission left, Wavell sent letters to Nehru and Jinnah reopening negotiations with a view to forming an interim government. Nehru responded with what 'practically amounted to an ultimatum . . . the Viceroy was to be a complete cipher in the Government'.

The Muslim League revoked its decision of 6 June to accept the mission's long-term proposal for the establishment of the constituent assembly, Jinnah claiming that the Viceroy had betrayed him by 'concocting a dishonest interpretation' of the terms on which the League had agreed to accept the mission's short-term proposals for the construction of the new interim government. When the League met in Bombay, on 29 July, it issued the 'Bombay resolutions', reasserting that it would settle for nothing less than an independent Pakistan, and would immediately start to achieve this by a 'direct action' campaign. On the League's 'Direct Action Day' on 16 August 1946, there were communal clashes in many cities: it was estimated that 5,000 died in Calcutta alone.

Wavell was convinced that unless the Congress and the League could be persuaded to resume negotiations, violence on a similar scale would break out all over India. He dismissed his 'caretaker' government of officials, and announced an Executive Council of fourteen members. When Jinnah refused to take up his quota of five seats, the Viceroy appointed five Muslims to the council; these were proposed by the Congress, and were *not* members of the Muslim League. Wavell was convinced that this interim government by one party would not last long 'without serious trouble arising', and he informed the British government that he must try again to bring the two sides together. Characteristically he also considered the problem which would face him if he failed. In the first week of September 1946, he sent to the Secretary of State his controversial 'Breakdown Plan', a scheme for a phased withdrawal of the British Raj from India in the event of India becoming ungovernable.

Wavell had decided that if it proved impossible to get Congress and the League to join an interim government leading to participation in a constituent assembly, the Raj should hand over to a government dominated by the Congress Party those provinces in which the Congress had a majority, while the Viceroy would continue to administer the Muslim-majority provinces out of which Jinnah wanted to create Pakistan. This would mean that the two areas of outstanding importance for the security of the sub-continent's frontiers would remain under British control. Wavell recommended that the Viceroy should also continue to control the two *Hindu*-majority provinces in the northwest, a retention of power, he thought, which would disabuse both Hindu and Muslim of the notion that the plan for Viceregal control in this area encouraged or envisaged the creation of Pakistan. He also introduced a time schedule with two deadlines: first, that 'Breakdown' was to be published and set in motion by 31 March 1947 at the latest; second, there would be complete withdrawal from the whole of India by 31 March 1948.

Attlee found the 'Breakdown' plan utterly repugnant. Years later he described it as 'an extraordinary plan'. It was the 'combined thinking of

Wavell and his ICS advisers. They were going to move all the British out of India, up the line of the Ganges, and put them on ships in Bombay. Winston would have been right to call it "operation scuttle". Out of the question. Indians would have assumed the Raj was on the run.' The 'Breakdown' plan confirmed Attlee's view that under pressure Wavell would always substitute for the political problem, in which he was out of his depth, the law and order problem, with which he was more at home. He informed Wavell that 'Breakdown', especially with the emphasis on its contents being published, was unacceptable. Withdrawal from India might eventually become a necessity, Attlee said, but if so, *all* India would be vacated, at the same time, not bit by bit, and as quickly as possible. Giving early notice of such a prolonged withdrawal at this time would do more harm than good. A *military* plan for the protection and evacuation of Europeans in the event of crisis was desirable – but such a plan already existed. He instructed Wavell to continue his efforts to get a *political* agreement.

Wavell complied with these instructions, and seemed soon to have some success: Jinnah announced on 25 October that the Muslim League had decided to end its boycott of cooperation with the Raj and take up its quota of seats in an interim government. But Wavell was still despondent: 'These political negotiations are entirely foreign to my military training, and there seems no firm ground in political matters and no one whom one can trust.' He informed the government that in spite of the Muslim League coming in, the new interim government was not a real coalition – there was no inclination to compromise, the spirit of cooperation was lacking.

Wavell, becoming more and more unhappy, now wrote to Attlee asking for a 'definite policy'. In July and August there had been a fruitless exchange of letters in which Attlee had urged the Viceroy to accept a political adviser, and the Viceroy had diplomatically declined:

> I think India's troubles at present are due mainly to the fact that her leaders view politics purely from the Party angle; and that what is really required is a great deal more commonsense, good administration and firm guidance.

In response for this new request for a policy, Attlee merely replied:

> I shall discuss it with my colleagues in order that you may have a reply to the specific questions which you ask. You may be sure that we are very conscious of your anxieties and of the potential danger of the situation.

In the late autumn, communal hatred in the provinces erupted in protracted rioting. In November Pethick-Lawrence had to inform the House that nearly 7,000 were known to have died in the two months since the interim government had taken office in September, a figure regarded as an extremely conservative estimate. At the end of the month, Wavell was asked to come to London bringing with him two representatives of Congress and two of the League. The two League leaders, Jinnah and Liaquat Ali Khan, accepted at once. Nehru refused. Attlee cabled to him personally, and Nehru came, accompanied by Singh, the Sikh Defence Minister. Four days of intensive talks produced no results. The Indians flew home. The Viceroy remained in London.

The Cabinet Minutes for 10 December 1946 gave a clear picture of how Attlee's mind was working; of how the Cabinet was responding to his assessment of the situation, and in particular to his rejection for once and for all of the Wavell 'Breakdown' plan. Reporting to the Cabinet on behalf of the India Committee: 'The Prime Minister said it was impossible to be confident that the main political parties had any real will to reach agreement between themselves.'

After a discussion of his report:

> Some ministers felt that in the event our only course might prove to be to evacuate India and leave the Indians to find, after a period no doubt of chaos, their own solution to their own problems.

On the subject of Wavell's 'Breakdown' plan, Attlee told the Cabinet:

> Even if such evacuation were practicable as a military operation – and it would not be an easy operation to carry out – it was not politically realistic to suppose that we should be able to adopt that course. Would it be acceptable to parliament and to public opinion that we should leave India in chaos, having obtained no guarantee for fair treatment for the Muslims or for the other minorities? That would indeed be an inglorious end to our long association with India. World opinion would regard it as a policy of scuttle unworthy of a great power.

Two days after the conference with the Indian leaders in London ended, Attlee had a talk with the King, who recorded in his diary:

> I told [Attlee], I was very worried over the breakdown of the Indian leaders' talks, and that I could see no alternative to Civil War between Hindus and Muslims for which we should be held responsible. ... The PM agreed. ... Nehru's present policy seemed to be to secure complete domination by Congress throughout the Government of India. The Muslims would never stand for it and would probably fight for Pakistan which the Hindus dislike so much. ... We have plans to evacuate India, but we cannot do so without leaving India with a workable Constitution. The Indian leaders have got to learn that the responsibility is theirs and that they must learn how to govern.

Wavell, still in London, continued to press 'Breakdown' on Attlee, recording in his diary that: 'In the end no one had really shaken my plan and the PM seemed prepared to accept it ... on the whole I felt I had got

HMG down to realities at last.' The Viceroy was mistaken. Attlee visited the King, who recorded the Prime Minister as saying that: 'Lord Wavell's plan for our leaving India savours too much of military retreat and that he does not realise it is a political problem and not a military one. Wavell has done very good work up to now, but Attlee doubts whether he has the finesse to negotiate the next steps when we must keep the two Indian parties friendly to us all the time.'

Attlee said that he was prepared to stake a great deal on the personality of the new Viceroy: he proposed Mountbatten, and, in response to the King's hope that the new Viceroy should have 'concrete orders', assured him that his task would be to bring British rule to an end as soon as possible. Two days later, on 19 December, Wavell had what he described in his journal as a 'disastrous' meeting at Downing Street:

> Two hours of desultory discussion resulted in no progress at all, with the PM now definitely hostile to the Breakdown Plan. They are all frightened of anything which involves Parliamentary legislation, and therefore try to make out that the Plan is either unnecessary or misguided. It is all very disheartening, once again they have run out.

III

By now Attlee had made up his mind to replace Wavell with Mountbatten if Mountbatten would accept the appointment. There is no record of the date on which he took this decision. Attlee later wrote:

> It was my own thought entirely to choose Mountbatten to negotiate India's independence. I knew his record in the war, and I decided he was the man to get good personal relations with the Indians, which he did. He and I agreed entirely. I told him I wanted a man to end the British Raj. He wanted a definite date to bring the Indians up to scratch of decision.

Discussing this later with the author Attlee said:

> We weren't getting anywhere. The only thing that was clear was that if we let the Congress have their way, the Muslims would start a war to get their Pakistan. Apart from that, nothing was in sight. Both parties were asking for everything and blaming us for not getting anything when they should have been blaming themselves. I decided there was only one thing to do – give them a deadline, and tell them 'on that date we go out. So you'd better get together right away.' It was the only thing that would bring them together. Next thing was to find the right man to carry out the new policy. Dickie Mountbatten stood out a mile. Burma showed it. The so-called experts had been wrong about Aung Sang, and Dickie had been right.

In one sense there was indeed a 'new policy', in another there was not. Mountbatten was to go out and try once again to get Muslim and Hindu

373

to agree that there should be one, unified, independent India. What was 'new' was Attlee's decision that there must be an announced deadline for withdrawal, not for the safety of the British in India, but in order to intimidate the two parties into agreeing on a constitution. The idea of a withdrawal as though from a hostile territory was repugnant to him. He saw 'no reason why we could not leave without both parties in India regarding us as their friend'. Also in the 'new policy' was his growing feeling that it would not be possible to achieve an India both independent *and* united: and that this would have to be conveyed to the Congress Party, with the corollary that they would have to come to terms with the Muslims for a separate Pakistan. Finally, the two Indian parties must be convinced that the British really meant to get out of India at the earliest possible moment – there must be no lingering suspicion that the Indian parties were being played off against each other so that the British could prolong their stay.

As a result of some statements he made in later years, Mountbatten created the impression, possibly inadvertently, that the idea of a deadline was his. What happened as seen in Whitehall was for many years neglected. Redressing the balance when the Cabinet papers became available in 1978, Lord Listowel, Secretary of State for India in 1947, wrote:

> I do not think that anyone who has tried to follow the accounts published in this country of the transfer of power could fail to be struck by the fact that they have almost all emanated from authors who had either served in the Government of India, or in the entourage of Lord Mountbatten, or had derived their information from his writings and recollections.

Although Mountbatten and Attlee corresponded extensively about a withdrawal date during December and January, the minutes of the Cabinet India Committee show that the need for such a date had been discussed for several days before Mountbatten was offered the viceroyalty on 18 December 1946. When Attlee offered him the post, Mountbatten would have been told by Attlee that a deadline for withdrawal was essential. If Mountbatten had insisted on a withdrawal date, he would have been knocking on an open door.

On 20 December, the India Committee considered a suggestion by Cripps that Parliament should be asked 'to hand over power in India not later than 31 March 1948', a day three months earlier than the one asked for at a later date by Mountbatten. The Cabinet minutes make it clear that this particular date was influenced by Wavell's view that 'we cannot in fact continue longer', though the committee once again made it clear that determining a deadline, and announcing it, was not conceived as being conditioned by military calculations, but by the need to make both Indian parties realize that the British were on their way out, and that the

Indians must therefore come to terms with each other. On 24 December Attlee wrote a memorandum on behalf of the India Committee to the Cabinet. The committee, he reported, had had a series of meetings with Wavell before he had returned to India. There seemed no hope that the Muslims would cooperate in a constituent assembly which might produce a united India. He reported that: 'Viceroy says we shan't be able to hold India beyond March 1948, and possibly not for so long.' Attlee then outlined Wavell's recommendations: 'There are therefore in his view only two alternatives, either withdrawal by phased process over about 12 months, or reasserting our authority. He considers this not totally impossible but that it can only be done if we declare our intention to govern India for a further 15 years at least.' The India Committee recommended neither course, but: 'The Committee were impressed with the possibility that an early announcement of our intention to withdraw was the most hopeful means of inducing the Congress and the Muslim League to come to an agreement.'

The India Committee gave the Cabinet its view that the Muslim League would finally decide not to join the constituent assembly and that this would become clear by the end of January. Once that became clear, the India Committee recommended, it should be stated in Parliament that: 'It is HMG's intention to recommend Parliament to hand over power in India by 31 March 1948.' The draft of the India Committee's proposals to the Cabinet was heavily amended by Attlee in his own hand. In particular, he changed '31 March 1948' to 'an appointed day which will not be later than the first half of 1948'.

The Cabinet discussed India a week later, on 31 December, without mentioning Mountbatten's appointment or his ideas or his conditions. Attlee told his colleagues:

> Our main objective now was to bring the principal communities in India to cooperate so that there should be a properly representative authority to whom we could hand over power.
>
> If the Viceroy was correct in his estimate that we should in any case be unable to continue effectively to rule India beyond the early part of 1948, and if the announcement of our intention to leave India by a specified date might have the effect of bringing the communities together, then it would be well to derive whatever advantage we could from the early announcement of the action which would, in fact, be inevitable.

Cripps objected to the early announcement of a withdrawal date on the grounds that it might prejudice the creation of a united India; evidently he did not share Attlee's view that Jinnah was determined to get an independent Pakistan. Bevin objected to an early withdrawal because it would create unrest in Egypt; the Egyptians had been told that British troops could not be withdrawn until 1949. Accordingly the decision on the timing of the announcement was deferred; but as a result of the discussions in Cabinet and the India Committee, the decision to 'effect a transference of power in India by a date not later than the middle of 1948' was confirmed.

Division of opinion within the Cabinet continued to present Attlee with problems. Cripps and Pethick-Lawrence felt that the Muslims were bound to exploit the announcement of a deadline so as to antagonize Congress; Alexander thought that the announcement of a deadline date would give an unfair advantage to Congress. Bevin, writing privately to Attlee on 1 January 1947, roundly denounced the policy which he saw Attlee adopting towards India. Among his objections were: 'The defeatist attitude adopted both by the Cabinet and by Field Marshal Wavell is just completely letting us down. . . . I would strongly recommend that he be recalled.' Cripps was too much pro-Congress, Alexander pro-Muslim. Bevin once more declared against announcing a date:

> I am against fixing a date . . . you cannot read the telegrams from Egypt and the Middle East nowadays without realising that not only is India going, but Malaya, Ceylon, and the Middle East is going with it, with a tremendous repercussion on the African territories. . . . Why cannot we use the United States to put pressure on Nehru and Jinnah? We appear to be trying nothing but to scuttle out of it . . . and I am convinced that if you do that our Party . . . will lose and lose irrevocably when the public becomes aware of the policy of the Cabinet at this moment.

Attlee replied patiently:

> I agree with you that Wavell has a defeatist mind and I am contemplating replacing him, but in fairness to him, I must say he has the support of the most experienced civil servants in India. I am not defeatist but realist.
>
> You suggest that we are knuckling under at the first blow [a quote from Bevin's letter] but this entirely ignores the history of the past 25 years . . .
>
> I do not understand your paragraph 4. The declaration that we are determined to hand over as a going concern is precisely what we are making clear to the Indians, and we are placing responsibility on their shoulders. [Bevin had said that this must be made clear.]
>
> The American representative in Delhi has tried his hand but without success.
>
> If you disagree with what is proposed, you must offer a practical alternative. I fail to find one in your letter.

On 8 January 1947, Attlee told a Cabinet meeting that 'since the Muslim League were still considering whether they would collaborate in the work of the Constituent Assembly, there was no occasion for issuing the withdrawal statement for the purpose of making the two Parties get together.' He then went on to bring out the fundamental agreement and the fundamental *dis*agreement between the government and Wavell, and what should be done about it. Both agreed that it was important to fix a date for withdrawal, but the Cabinet wished to do so to bring about a political solution, while Wavell wanted to bring about a military withdrawal from hostile territory.

> The difference between ministers and the Viceroy was fundamentally one of approach; and it seemed unlikely that the Viceroy's attitude could be changed by means of constructions conveyed by telegram. It would be preferable that he should be asked to return to London for further personal talks with ministers.

Attlee therefore wrote Wavell a letter which the Viceroy described in his diary as 'cold, ungracious and indefinite, the letter of a small man'. Wavell replied on 17 January 1947:

> I am very sorry that the Cabinet have not been able to give me a more definite policy. .... All I can do at present is to draw up plans against the possibility of an emergency withdrawal. .... I do not think there would be any advantage in my coming home again in the near future. .... I suggest, therefore, that I might return in March or April for further discussions.

If Wavell intended to invite Attlee to ask for his resignation he could not have written a more suitable letter. Cripps wanted him both to be dismissed and rebuked for his refusal to come home immediately, but Attlee simply wrote plainly on 31 January:

> In view of all these circumstances and of the fact that it is specially necessary that the Viceroy should be in full agreement with the policy of His Majesty's government I think that you may agree that the time has come to make a change in the Viceroyalty.

By this time Attlee and Mountbatten had been in correspondence for six weeks about the conditions on which Mountbatten would accept the viceroyalty. Mountbatten had on 20 December asked that his appointment should be at 'the open invitation of the Indian parties'. Attlee thought this impractical. Instead, at a meeting on 1 January 1947, he suggested to Mountbatten that Cripps would inform the leading Indian politicians personally, shortly before the appointment was announced, that Mountbatten wanted their support. This Mountbatten accepted by letter on 3 January, adding:

> It makes all the difference to me to know that you propose to make a statement in the House, terminating the British 'Raj' on a definite and specified date; or earlier than this date, if the Indian Parties can agree a constitution and form a Government, before this. I feel very strongly that I could not have gone out there with confidence, if it had been possible to

construe my arrival as a perpetuation, at this moment, of the viceregal system, or of our imposing our nominee to arbitrate in their affairs.

Mountbatten's account of these transactions in his 1949 'Report on the Last Viceroyalty' submitted to the Cabinet states that:

> I saw the Prime Minister again on 1 January. At this interview he explained that my suggestion, that an open invitation should be secured from the Indian Party leaders, was not practicable: and I fully accept this. He suggested as an alternative that a statement should be made in Parliament signifying the intention to terminate British rule in India on a definite and specified date.

These passages suggest very strongly that although the Cabinet was wavering about the announcement of a withdrawal date, Attlee was personally convinced that it was necessary. As early as 19 December Mountbatten told his aide, Alan Campbell-Johnson, that 'it was clear to him that there would have to be the earliest time limit for the transfer of power if his mission was not to be hopelessly compromised with Indian opinion from the outset'. Campbell-Johnson does not record Mountbatten as saying that it was he who had suggested the time limit. Nevertheless, because Mountbatten wanted a time limit, and the Cabinet could not agree about announcing it, there were still difficulties to be overcome before Mountbatten would accept the appointment.

At the meeting on 1 January Mountbatten made a bid for complete freedom of action in India. Recollecting the meeting in 1979 he stated:

> I said I could not negotiate in India with Whitehall ministers breathing down my neck. I must be allowed to make my own decisions in India and the Secretary of State would have to accept and support these.
>
> Mr Attlee consulted Sir Stafford Cripps and even after twenty-two years I can remember his next words: 'You are asking for plenipotentiary powers above His Majesty's Government. No one has been given such powers in this century.' There was silence for quite a while, then he went on 'surely you can't mean this?' 'Escape at last' I thought as I firmly replied that I did indeed mean just that and would quite understand if as a result the appointment was withdrawn. But Cripps nodded his head and Attlee replied 'All right, you've got the powers, and the job.'

Mountbatten wrote to the King that 'they offered me "carte blanche".' It was clearly a political risk, and Attlee took a further risk by making his offer without consulting the whole Cabinet. Lord Listowel, who became secretary of state for India four months later, approved when writing in 1978 of the decision not to inform the Cabinet, but regretted that Attlee did not confide in him when he was appointed to the India Office. But Attlee never gambled, and the risks he took were well considered. He knew his man, and he knew how he would behave. Mountbatten, he judged, though brave, enterprising and daring, was too concerned about his reputation and his future career to commit the government to a hazardous step without consultation.

As to the fixing of a date for withdrawal, Attlee wrote to Mountbatten on 9 January: 'As at present advised we think it inadvisable to be too precise as to an actual date, but I will bear the point in mind in case at a later stage we think it well to name a day.' Although Campbell-Johnson recorded on 15 January that 'Mountbatten's acceptance of the Viceroy-alty is at last firm,' this hesitation over an exact date disturbed the Viceroy-to-be and he continued to press the point. On 8 February Attlee wrote to him, enclosing the Cabinet's draft directive on the policy he should pursue in India. Attlee made it clear that it was still 'the definite objective of HMG to obtain if possible a unitary government for all India ... in accordance with the Cabinet Mission's plan, and you should do the utmost in your power to persuade all parties to work to this end. ... You should aim at June 1 as the effective date for the transfer of power.' Mountbatten, who had earlier asked for and received assurances that the public statement should contain no 'escape clauses', was dissatisfied with the draft statement which Attlee enclosed:

> The draft of the proposed statement, however, contains the phrase 'the middle of 1948'; a term which I still consider so wide as not to be in keeping with your declaration that any form of escape clause must be avoided. And the vagueness of this term is underlined by certain points which could easily be misinterpreted. ...
>
> I hope you will not think I am pulling the document to pieces in a spirit of carping. But I am disappointed on reading it, because in doing so I can recapture little of the enthusiasm which I felt when you told me of HM Government's proposal.

Attlee was inclined to take his advice and make a public announcement of the deadline. At a Cabinet meeting on 13 February, the Prime Minister reminded his colleagues that five days earlier they had agreed to defer the issue of a proposed statement about the date for the transfer of power. But, he said, 'the time had now come to make a final effort, by the issue of this statement, to compel the two political parties in India to face the realities of the situation and collaborate in framing a new Constitution'. He therefore recommended that 'the statement should be issued in the course of the following week'. Pethick-Lawrence still demurred. But now a new crisis suddenly appeared: Wavell had a change of mind about the idea of a date for withdrawal, and urgently cabled Attlee to stay his hand. Attlee told the Cabinet on 18 February that there could be no question of accepting Wavell's advice. The Cabinet agreed, and it was decided to make a definite announcement in the House on 20 February.

It was accepted, with regret by some, that this decision meant in practice abandoning the hope of transferring power to a unitary India.

The announcement of the deadline in the House on 20 February 1947 surprised and shocked the Conservatives. It was 'an unjustifiable gamble'. But no uproar ensued. The Liberals were ready to support the new policy. Clement Davies pronounced the appointment of Mountbatten a stroke of genius. 'It was Attlee alone who had thought of Mountbatten and offered him the appointment,' he told Campbell-Johnson. 'Attlee was handling the situation with tact and firmness ... his move was wise and courageous ... removing all misconceptions and suspicions.' Mountbatten was to fly out to Delhi on 20 March. A House of Commons debate on India was arranged for 6 March, to be preceded by a debate in the Lords on 25 and 26 February. For the Lords, what was virtually a motion of censure on the government was put down by Lord Templewood, formerly Sir Samuel Hoare, who as secretary of state for India had steered the India Act of 1935 through the Commons against Churchill's opposition. He was supported by Lord Simon. For a large part of the debate it looked as if the government would be defeated. The tide was turned by a Conservative, Lord Halifax, the only ex-Viceroy taking part, who observed that:

> ... the conclusion I reach – with all that can be said against it – is that I am not prepared to condemn what His Majesty's Government are doing unless I can honestly and confidently recommend a better solution. ... I should be sorry if the only message from the House to India at this moment was one of condemnation, based on what I must fully recognise as very natural feelings of failure, frustration and foreboding.

Many Conservative peers changed their minds after this speech, and Templewood, while remaining critical, withdrew his motion. What happened in the Lords was to have an important effect in the Commons two weeks later.

The debate in the Commons was opened by Cripps. He made a lucid and cogent speech, delivering it with the emotion of a man who had been deeply and passionately involved in the future of India for thirty years. He did not refer at all to Wavell, and the omission gave the Opposition an opening of which Churchill took full advantage the following day. He held no brief for Wavell, Churchill said, since he had been 'the willing or unwilling agent of the Government in all the errors and mistakes into which they had been led', but why had the Viceroy been cast aside at this juncture? Would he be allowed to make a statement? Attlee indicated assent. As for the new Viceroy, Churchill went on:

> Is he to make a new effort to restore the situation, or is it merely Operation Scuttle on which he and other distinguished officers have been dispatched?

I am bound to say the whole thing wears the aspect of an attempt by the Government to make use of brilliant war figures to cover up a melancholy and disastrous transaction whose consequences will darken, aye, redden the coming years.

Attlee wound up the debate. By all accounts it was one of his greatest speeches. Campbell-Johnson recorded in his diary that night:

Although I have often listened to Attlee on various themes, this is the first time I have heard him on India, which is undoubtedly his special subject. ... This man burns with a hidden fire and is sustained by a certain spiritual integrity which enables him to scale the heights when the great occasion demands. Churchill was raked with delicate irony.

Attlee dealt with the replacement of Wavell. He could not say in public that Wavell was tired out, irresolute, and deeply distrusted by the Indians, so he took the line that there was no occasion for Wavell to be *required* to make a personal statement on his return. 'To put it colloquially, if a change of bowling is desired it is not always necessary that there should be an elaborate explanation.' He then dealt politely with Conservative speeches, and firmly with Churchill:

In approaching this subject, we all have to recognise how little we know about India, and how soon what knowledge we have gets out of date. I quite recognize that I am out of date. I ended my time on the Simon Commission nearly 18 years ago. I therefore hesitate to be dogmatic or prophetic about what may happen in India. In this, I admit, I differ from the leader of the Opposition. I think his practical acquaintance with India ended some fifty years ago. He formed some strong opinions – I might almost say prejudices – then. They have remained with him ever since.

Though Attlee refrained from any kind of recrimination he made reference to the past in order to dispose of Churchill's charge that for the British government to leave India before *all* her problems were solved was to 'betray her trust'. Churchill had attacked the policy of admitting Indian politicians into the government, and wanted to keep the caretaker administration going:

but the essence of the Indian problem is to get Indian statesmen to understand what are the real problems they have to face. ... A very grave fault of the reforms we have carried out over the years is that we have taught irresponsibility. All Indian politicians were permanently in opposition, and, speaking with long experience, it is not always good to be in opposition.

He concluded:

We cannot wait. I would have liked a message to go from this House ... without a dissentient voice saying: 'It is our earnest will that the Indians should grasp now this great opportunity of showing that all of them, without distinction of creed, place the good of India's millions before the interests of any section whatever'; and that today we should have said in this House: 'We have placed this responsibility squarely on you, and we believe you can carry it.' I close by saying that whatever the differences there may be between us in the House on these matters, I am sure that the whole House will wish 'God speed' to the new Viceroy in his great mission. It is a mission, not, as has been suggested, of betrayal on our part. It is a mission of fulfilment. Anyone who has read the lives of the great men who have built up our rule in India and who did so much to make India united will know that all these great men looked to the fulfilment of our mission in India, and the placing of responsibility for their own lives in Indian hands.

Despite a division on strict party lines, Campbell-Johnson recorded: 'one could not help coming away from this historic Debate with the sense that the gulf between Government and Opposition was far narrower than some of Mr Churchill's more sombre polemics might suggest.'

IV

Mountbatten arrived in India on 20 March 1947. Within a few days he had reported to the government:

> The only conclusion that I have been able to come to is that unless I act quickly I may well find the real beginnings of a civil war on my hands. . . . I am convinced that a fairly quick decision would be the only way to convert the Indian minds from their present emotionalism to stark realism and to counter the disastrous spread of strife.

By 19 April, after extensive negotiations with Indian political leaders and Indian and British officials, he was preparing a plan of partition. He intended to try once more to get the Indian leaders to accept a united India, and if it were rejected, as he knew it almost certainly would be, to 'fire my last shot in the shape of our announcement of partition'. The Cabinet received the Partition Plan at the beginning of May; it was approved by the India Committee, with minor amendments, on 8 May, and Attlee expected to put it to the Cabinet on 13 May. On 10 May Mountbatten privately showed the approved plan to Nehru. It was as well that he did, especially for his reputation. To his consternation Nehru objected that the plan 'would lead to the Balkanization of India'. Mountbatten immediately reported this dramatic change in the situation to London. 'A difficult moment,' said Attlee, many years later, 'but of course we had to press on.'

Mountbatten flew to London on 14 May, by which time he had a 'Revised Plan' which Nehru and Jinnah had approved. Nehru had objected that the original plan would have permitted the provinces to vote for their own independence, either for themselves or in groups, the

Princely States probably following this lead. The Revised Plan would deal with Nehru's objection by restricting the provinces to a vote to join India or a vote to join Pakistan. The plan would avoid actually stating what the earlier version had said – namely that power would be transferred to more than one authority – and make it clear that the procedure envisaged by the plan was intended to find out whether such a step would prove to be necessary. This would be determined by the will of the people, voting in their various assemblies. If it turned out that Partition did not prove necessary, the united India would have Dominion status. If two Indias were to prove necessary, *both* would have Dominion status.

'Mr Attlee was splendid in ensuring quick Cabinet approval to the new plan,' recorded Mountbatten. 'We could hardly do less than agree without a murmur to a scheme that had the blessing of both the Viceroy and the two communities,' concluded Listowel. 'Mr Attlee,' recorded Campbell-Johnson on 22 May, 'who throughout has assumed full personal control of the Government's India policy and any action arising from it, has successfully injected a sense of the utmost urgency into his colleagues.' On 27 May, after discussions in the India Committee, Attlee told the Cabinet that Mountbatten was convinced that only the announcement of a very early transfer of power, in the autumn of the year, could bring about a settlement and stem communal violence. Mountbatten was to return to India, make a last formal effort to preserve a united India, then announce that power would be transferred to more than one authority.

Mountbatten met the Indian leaders formally on 2 June and told them that he had concluded that there was no possibility of agreement on the Cabinet mission plan. He then gave them copies of the British government's statement, incorporating the Revised Plan. The next day the Indian leaders returned to signify their acceptance of the plan; and later that day Attlee rose in the House of Commons to make his prepared announcement. Churchill stated that the Opposition would not oppose the passage of the necessary legislation, and paid a compliment to Attlee:

> The Prime Minister said that credit was due to the Viceroy. There are matters about which it is extremely difficult to form decided opinions now, but if the hopes that are contained in this declaration are borne out, great credit will indeed be due to the Viceroy and not only to the Viceroy, but to the Prime Minister who advised the British government to appoint him.

That night Mountbatten broadcast to the people of India, being followed by Nehru and Jinnah. At a press conference the next day, in answer to a question, he remarked that: 'I think the transfer could be about 15 August.' His announcement of such an early date caused consternation, some among his own staff, but more in London. The

Secretary of State prepared a draft cable on the subject at once, and submitted it to Attlee. Before it reached the Prime Minister, his principal private secretary, Leslie Rowan, noted on it: 'If we had trouble in Parliament it might not be feasible to fix appointed day as 15 August.' Attlee was imperturbable. His instruction, written in his own hand, was: 'Accept Viceroy's proposal.'

The question now arose of what role should be performed by Mountbatten when on the transfer of power he ceased to be Viceroy. Nehru had proposed that he should become either joint governor-general of both new dominions, or governor-general of India alone. Up to mid-May, Jinnah had appeared to agree that Mountbatten should become joint governor-general, but by early July he made it clear that he intended to become governor-general of Pakistan himself. Mountbatten therefore hesitated to accept Nehru's invitation to become governor-general of India. When consulted, Attlee said without hesitation that he should. Asked many years after what were the main reasons for him coming to that conclusion, Attlee said:

> For him to accept an invitation to be the first Governor-General of an independent India was a great boost for Britain, and for the Commonwealth. I thought it would do more than anything to keep India in the Commonwealth. If he had refused the job it would have worsened relations between India and Pakistan – Nehru would have said Jinnah's *volte-face* had driven Mountbatten out of India. It was essential for him to stay. Both countries trusted him. If Mountbatten *had* left India, it would have looked like a victory for that twister, Jinnah.

The legislative feat required to put the Indian Independence Act on the statute book in time for the transfer of power on 15 August was prodigious. No comparable piece of British legislation was drafted, debated and passed into law in so short a time. The second reading took place on 10 July, a week after the first. Attlee made another powerful speech. Harold Macmillan congratulated him 'on the lucidity, moderation and dignity with which he has performed his formidable task'. The House of Lords gave the same approval to the bill. Halifax among other Conservative peers paid tributes to Attlee as well as to Mountbatten. For the Liberals Lord Samuel declared: 'This Bill is a moral to all future generations; it is a Treaty of Peace without a war.' The bill had its third reading unopposed on 14 July. Attlee said: 'In parting with this Bill from this House, I do it not with a feeling of elation, but with a feeling of responsibility, some feelings of anxiety, but also with an unquenchable hope that these things will work out for the good of all the people of India.'

The bill received the Royal Assent on 18 July and became effective on

15 August 1947 – six months after the February declaration instead of the fourteen months which the original deadline allowed. Mountbatten wrote personally to Attlee, and sent over his private secretary, Sir George Abell, to report to the Prime Minister 'the extraordinary scenes at the handing over'. Attlee wrote to Tom after seeing him:

> Mountbatten was surrounded by about a quarter of a million Indians all violently enthusiastic for him. He has certainly captured the Indian imagination. I doubt if things will go awfully easily now as the Indian leaders know little of administration, but at least we have come out with honour instead, as at one time seemed likely, of being pushed out ignominiously with the whole country in a state of confusion.

'The man who made it possible,' Mountbatten concluded in a letter to Attlee, 'was you yourself. Without your original guidance and your unwavering support nothing could have been accomplished out here.'

VI

Much of what Attlee's government did between 1945 and 1951 at home and abroad would have been done by a Conservative government headed by Winston Churchill. The Conservatives would have developed an American–European alliance at least akin to NATO, and they would have introduced, though in different form, some of the most important provisions of the welfare state. But in many fields the Labour government did things which the Conservative Party, at any rate under Churchill, would not have done. The grant of independence to India within two years of the Second World War coming to an end was certainly one of these, and given the importance of that historic decision, and of its immediate and long-term consequences, its Indian policy must weigh very heavily in an assessment of the Labour government's record. It must have even greater weight in an assessment of Attlee as prime minister. Though some of those who might have led the government in his stead – Morrison, Cripps or Dalton, for instance, though probably not Ernest Bevin – would have pressed for the granting of India's independence as soon as they thought practicable, Indian policy, as we have seen, was very much Attlee's own. The man, the method, the speed with which he decided to bring it about, were mainly of his conceiving and his execution. He was the party's long-term expert in this field, and the conduct of policy bore the stamp of his mind. For what happened in India in 1947 and in the aftermath he must take the praise or bear the blame.

At the time, opinion in Britain was on the whole opposed to Attlee's solution of the India problem. A majority perhaps was in favour of Indian independence, but Partition was regarded as an undesirable price to pay for it, and as one which could have been avoided. The early post-independence experience of the Punjab, where possibly as many as half a million people died in intercommunal violence between August and November 1947, seemed to confirm this view of Attlee's policy; and many then thought that Pakistan was not viable, politically or economically, as an independent state. But the chances of securing a united India had decreased steadily since 1935. The rise of the Muslim League, the inertia of British wartime policy and the negativism of the Congress Party combined to make Partition the only realistic policy by the time Mountbatten went out to India.

Even if it is granted that Partition was inevitable, Attlee can be criticized for the haste with which it was carried out. There were those who argued that the speed of British departure contributed to the bloodshed, to the failure to protect minorities, and to the unfair treatment accorded by independent India to the Princely States. But it is difficult to see how things would have been better had Attlee moved more slowly. Even though there was great bloodshed, much more than had been bargained for, it is hard to say what plans could have been laid in advance to lessen it, or to argue that delaying the transfer could have prevented or even reduced it. It would have been extremely difficult for the British government to give independence to India and Pakistan, and at the same time to prescribe how the two new independent states should treat sections of their inhabitants.

The best that could have been done even at leisure was in fact done notwithstanding the haste. When Britain handed over power in India and Pakistan she also handed over all her commitments to the protection of the minorities. There was no way in which the Raj could have ensured that these commitments would be observed to the letter by the two new governments without interfering with their independence. Nor could the Raj have given independence to India and Pakistan, and then continued to supervise their relations with the Princes. 'It was one thing or the other,' said Attlee years later. 'We gave the Princes fair warning that they must make their own arrangements with the two new states. They were very slow to set about it – they couldn't blame us for that.'

Attlee's policy for India between 1945 and 1947 shows him at his best and most characteristic, and entitles him to rank not only as a great prime minister but as a statesman. From start to finish he moved steadily and unshakably, coolly and adroitly, according to his plan, stepping up the pace towards the end with fine judgement. His first great task was to show the Congress and the Muslim League that Britain meant to quit, and to quit soon; he was not helped in this by the unfortunate impression which Wavell continued to create. His first achievement in the process of winning Indian confidence was the sending of the Cabinet mission. He faced the fact that the mission had failed. At that point all Attlee's authority and skill were needed to keep his Cabinet together.

His decisions to recall Wavell, to devise a new approach, to appoint the controversial Mountbatten, to give him 'plenipotentiary' powers, and to nominate a deadline, were bold and risk-laden. He did not flinch when Mountbatten pressed for withdrawal to be dramatically accelerated. He had the self-confidence to give up the hope of a united India, and accept Partition. He succeeded in his prime objective: to ensure that when Britain left India, she did so on the friendliest possible terms with both the new Dominions. As a result of his handling of the negotiations leading to their independence, both chose to remain in the Commonwealth, the Congress freely abandoning its long-established intention to declare India 'a sovereign independent republic'. Above all, Attlee could claim that the Indians, as he had promised they should, had settled their destiny for themselves.

22

The End of Empire: Palestine

Britain left India with the good will and respect of the main communities in conflict; she left Palestine her name anathema to Jews and Arabs, her relations with the United States embittered, and her reputation in the rest of the world diminished. Whereas in India she handed over to two independent governments by agreement with them, in Palestine she left only anarchy. The sequel to her abdication in that part of the Middle East was not an agreed Partition of the 'twice promised land', but war between Jews and Arabs, which brought about a Partition by force, carved out the new state of Israel, left huge conglomerations of Arab refugees, and established a recurrent threat to world peace. While India was the postwar Labour government's great success in external affairs, Palestine was its greatest failure. If Attlee could have devoted himself to the problem of Palestine as he did to the problems of India, he might have had more success. As it was he delegated Palestine to his Foreign Secretary. Bevin misunderstood, and consequently mishandled, the problem from the start. For the discreditable consequences of Bevin's policy Attlee must take the blame.

He and Bevin inherited a muddled policy from previous British governments and an unintegrated alternative policy from the Labour Party. Since Britain had made its commitment to the 'establishment in Palestine of a national home for the Jewish people' in the 1917 Balfour Declaration, and had undertaken the League of Nations Mandate for Palestine in 1920, her dilemma was to resolve the conflicting aspirations of Arabs and Jews. When Hitler began to persecute the Jews in Germany in the early thirties, the rate of Jewish immigration into Palestine increased. So did the resistance of the Arabs, rising to a level of violence with which Britain, dependent on Arab support for oil and her strategic position on the Suez Canal, found it difficult to deal. In 1936, a commission chaired by Lord

388

Peel reported that Jews and Arabs could not be expected to live together in the same country, that the British government had committed itself to two incompatible policies in the same country, and that the only solution was Partition.

Jews and Arabs had both expected to become sovereign in Palestine, and the Peel recommendations led to serious violence which was met with repression. In 1938, under the shadow of a European war, the British government most feared the loss of oil and the breakdown of strategic routes if Arabs in the Middle East were antagonized. Britain therefore retreated from a commitment to Partition and from any other commitment which might increase disaffection among the Arabs. After Munich, with the threat lifted, the government became less anxious for the wholesale appeasement of Arabs in Palestine, and convened a conference in London of Jewish and Arab representatives. When the conference failed, the Colonial Secretary, Malcolm MacDonald, produced the British government's last initiative before the war: the White Paper of 1939, which limited Jewish immigration to 75,000 over a five-year period, providing for a review at the end of that time. Arab consent would be required for any immigration beyond that period. Other clauses limited the purchase of land by Jews – a second focus for Arab suspicion.

The White Paper angered the Arabs, but its effect on the Jews was profound: they concluded that the future of the Jewish community in Palestine could no longer be entrusted to the British government. The Jews in Palestine began a campaign of violence and destruction which was suspended only because the European war broke out within three months. With Britain now fighting Hitler, the Jews, in the words of the historian Martin Gilbert, decided 'they would fight the war as if there were no White Paper, but at the same time continue to fight the White Paper as if there was no war.' For the duration of the war, British official policy remained that of the 1939 White Paper.

As well as inheriting a government policy when he became Prime Minister in 1945, Attlee was the legatee of a Labour Party policy which differed from that of the prewar Conservative government and the war-time coalition in many significant respects. Labour's attitude to Palestine was partly a reflection of the Zionism of the many Jewish MPs and supporters of the party, and partly due to the feeling of solidarity between British Labour and Zionists in America and in Palestine. When the White Paper appeared in 1939, Herbert Morrison, the Labour spokesman on Palestine, described it as 'this breach of faith which we regret, this breach of British honour'. Attlee was entirely behind Morrison, but agreed that nothing could be done at the time to reverse or modify the government's policy. During the war Laski, Bevan, Strauss and Dalton did their best to ensure that when the war ended the Labour Party could be committed to support of a Jewish homeland, which an increasing number of Jews could enter, and which would eventually become a self-governing state; they gained almost unopposed acceptance of a resolution in this sense at their annual party conference in 1944.

The problem of Palestine as Attlee saw it immediately on becoming Prime Minister might be summarized as follows. The murder of six million Jews by the Nazi government had aroused guilt and shame in the Western world which manifested itself in a desire to rescue ill, aged and distraught Jews from displaced persons' camps, and find a refuge for them. American Jews were anxious to ease the lot of European Jews, and American Jews were a powerful political force which no American politician, especially the leader of the Democratic Party, could ignore. Britain had no troops to spare to police the Middle East. On the other hand, Britain's main interests in the Middle East predicated support for the Arabs. Oil was vital; so was the security of the routes to Egypt and India. There was a threat of Russian expansion, which had to be contained. To support Zionist aspirations would achieve comparatively little for British or for Western interests but would risk immense loss. If war broke out between Jews and Arabs, the Foreign Office and the British Chief of Staff reported categorically, the Arabs would throw the Jews into the sea. The American State Department, like the British Foreign Office, was in favour of humouring the Arabs and of giving very little to the Jews. But President Truman was at heart a Zionist, and politically was ready to fashion his Palestinian policy to provide the Democratic Party with Zionist votes and Zionist funds. Finally, if the many pro-Jewish American congressmen became too critical of British policy in Palestine, Britain might not receive the all-important American loan.

Bevin went to the Foreign Office expecting to reach a negotiated settlement of the Palestine problem. Dalton, who would have taken a markedly different line, observed that: 'He suffered, however, from an inhibition due to his belief, which I heard him more than once express, that "the Jews are a religion, not a race or a nation." And I heard Attlee several times express the same opinion.' In this attitude, Bevin and Attlee were a long way from the traditional sentiments of the Labour Party. However, the Foreign Office's line on the Middle East told its own tale. There were many British ambassadors in Arab countries, and many Arab desks in the Foreign Office: the Jews had none. Within a few days of being at the Foreign Office, Bevin went to Attlee and said: 'Clem, about Palestine. According to my lads in the office we've got it wrong. We've got to think again.' So in spite of the Labour Party having denounced it in 1939, the White Paper became for the time being the Palestinian policy of the Labour government.

When Attlee entered 10 Downing Street as Prime Minister on 27 July

1945, he found a letter written by President Truman to Winston Churchill just before the result of the British general election had been announced – an election which Truman confidently expected Churchill to
win. Truman knew that Churchill was a strong Zionist: hence some of
the wording of the letter. Truman was also a Zionist, who, unlike Attlee,
regarded Zionism not as a matter of religion but of race. Attlee and Bevin
did not know of Truman's ardent Zionism when they took over the
Palestine problem, and they were inclined to regard it only as a response
to political pressure. In this they were probably wrong – Dean Acheson
writes of Truman's Zionism as 'a deep conviction, in large part implanted
by his close friend and former partner, Eddie Jacobson, a passionate
Zionist' – but it is evident that Truman was also interested in Palestine
for political reasons. As he explained to a gathering of Arab ambassadors:
'I have to answer to hundreds of thousands who are anxious for the
success of Zionism. I do not have hundreds of thousands of Arabs among
my constituents.'

Truman's letter expressed 'the hope that the British Government may
find it possible without delay to take steps to lift the restrictions of the
White Paper on Jewish immigration into Palestine', and asked Churchill
to 'arrange at your early convenience to let me have your ideas on the
settlement of the Palestine problem, so that we can at a later but not too
distant date, discuss the problem in concrete terms'. Attlee replied from
Potsdam on 31 July with a brief acknowledgement, promising 'early and
careful consideration' of Truman's letter. Meanwhile the Foreign Office
was advising Bevin that the American State Department was counselling
Truman to resist domestic pressure to support unlimited Jewish immigration into Palestine. On 31 August 1945 Truman sent Attlee a further
letter which upset Anglo-American relations, spoiled the chances of a
joint Anglo-American policy on Palestine, and put a strain on the personal relationship between himself and Attlee which nearly broke their
friendship. Citing a report on Jewish refugees in Europe which he had
commissioned, he urged Attlee to grant an additional 100,000 immigration certificates.

Attlee replied at length, not in a personal letter, but in a telegraphed
message. He pointed out first that the Jews were not in fact using all the
certificates already available to them, and that there were some vacancies
to be taken up. Secondly, the Arab case had an equal right to be
considered. Arab consent had to be obtained for any future immigration
scheme. Thirdly, the Muslims of India had to be taken into consideration
– they could be easily aroused by inconsiderate treatment of the Arabs.
Fourthly, the Jews in camps in Europe should not be regarded as a special
case. Other nationals had suffered in concentration camps: there was no
reason why the Jews should be put 'at the head of the queue', and in

their own interests every reason why they should not be treated as 'a special racial category'.

Meanwhile Bevin was working out a policy for the Middle East, which was predicated as British political hegemony and economic primacy: he advised the Cabinet that nothing should be done which would 'assist American commercial penetration into a region which for generations has been an established British market'. At the same time, the Cabinet's Palestine Committee concluded that Britain's strategic interests demanded a policy which would not antagonize the Arabs.

To deal with the political difficulty posed by Truman, Attlee proposed an Anglo-American court of inquiry. The purpose, as Acheson noted in his memoirs, was 'to move us from our position of private exhorter to a publicly responsible partner in Palestine affairs'. The Court of Inquiry had first been suggested by Bevin, who saw it in terms of the bodies which by arbitration frequently brought about settlements in industrial disputes. The Cabinet supported him, and even Dalton, who with hindsight believed that it would have been right to grant Truman's request for 100,000 certificates simply to improve Anglo-American relations, wished 'to give Bevin's method, of the negotiator's approach, a fair chance'. The proposal to Truman was accompanied by a stiff memorandum in which Attlee, on behalf of the Cabinet, declined to depart from the current immigration policy. Despite Zionist pressure to persist in the demand for 100,000 certificates, Truman accepted the Court of Inquiry, which was set up on 15 November 1945.

The Anglo-American Committee's report appeared on 1 May 1946. Outstanding among its recommendations were the immediate grant of 100,000 immigration certificates and an end to the land purchase restrictions of the 1939 White Paper. Most of its other recommendations were not nearly so favourable to the Jews. The report expressly disapproved of the view that Palestine had in some way been ceded or granted to the Jews of the world: it recommended the continuation of the British Mandate; it laid down the principle that 'Jew shall not dominate Arab and Arab shall not dominate Jew in Palestine', and that Palestine should be 'neither a Jewish state nor an Arab state'. It ruled out as impracticable any early attempt to establish an independent state or states in Palestine; and it called on the Jewish Agency to cooperate in suppressing terrorism and illegal immigration.

President Truman was pleased by the recommendation for 100,000 immigration certificates; 'he latched on to one of the recommendations of this report,' recorded Acheson; Attlee's response was that the admission of more immigrants would have to be conditional on the disbandment and disarmament of the illegal Jewish forces. To let in 100,000 immigrants would risk antagonizing the Arabs beyond control. Here was another contretemps in Truman's relations with Attlee. Acheson, in charge at the State Department at the time, recorded: 'Mr Attlee was annoyed by Mr Truman's taking the plum out of the pudding, and President Truman by what some of his advisers thought was Mr Attlee's stalling on the central issue of immigration.' To improve relations between the two leaders, Acheson persuaded Truman to propose to Attlee that within two weeks there should be consultations with the Jews and Arabs about the military and financial implications of the report.

At this point Attlee and Bevin were engaged in the delicate business of renegotiating the Egyptian treaty of 1936, which covered such matters as Britain's rights in the Suez Canal Zone, Britain's position in the Sudan, and Britain's right to a military presence in Egypt, all of the highest strategical importance. In November 1945 there had been anti-Zionist riots in Cairo and Alexandria, and the Egyptian Cabinet had fallen in February 1946. This was no time for the British to incense the Arabs by making concessions to the Jews. Attlee therefore replied to Truman's proposal by agreeing to consultations with Jews and Arabs but asking, 'in view of the delicate negotiations which we are at present conducting in Egypt', for a postponement for at least three weeks. He also suggested Anglo-American consultations on the financial and military implications of the report, which would precede conversations with Jews and Arabs.

Truman interpreted this request for a postponement as an attempt to stall on the immigration issue, a view shared by many British MPs. Without warning Attlee or waiting for the views of his own experts, he announced publicly that he endorsed the Court of Inquiry's recommendation that 100,000 Jews be admitted to Palestine at once. It was an irresponsible act, justifiable only if Truman believed that Attlee was deceiving him. Attlee responded immediately. The terms of his message – which he deliberately chose to deliver in Parliament – did not conceal his anger. He made two things very clear. First the US government would be asked to share any military and financial responsibilities that arose from the acceptance of the Anglo-American Committee's report; secondly, large-scale immigration would not begin until illegal Jewish armed units had been eliminated.

Truman declared this response 'unsympathetic', but admitted that opinion in the United States, though keen on immigration, 'was neither disposed nor prepared to assume risks and obligations that might require us to use military force'. Attlee took advantage of this admission to press home his case: if the Americans wanted to call the shots in Palestine they must say so in public and help face the consequences. He cabled Truman on 26 May, setting out in forty-five points the agenda for the experts' discussion. Truman, sobered by Attlee's firm contention that if the Americans wanted to make policy they must be prepared to share the bill, conceded that before action was taken which might later be regretted the experts should meet. On 12 June, at the annual Labour Party conference, Bevin publicly rejected the granting of 100,000 extra certificates, but tactlessly added that the Americans wanted Jews to go to Palestine only because they did not want 'to have too many of them in New York'.

In Palestine, violence mounted. In the British Parliament the crisis had created deep divisions in the ranks of the Labour Party. Many MPs, while emotionally and traditionally pro-Jewish, were revolted by the activities of the Irgun and the Stern Gang, which the more moderate Haganah and Jewish Agency seemed if not to condone, at least not to condemn. Feelings were raised to greater heights by reports of pogroms against the Jews in Poland, Czechoslovakia and along the Danube. When Parliament debated the Palestine situation on 2 July, Attlee declared that the government could no longer tolerate a direct challenge to its authority; illegal organizations would be broken up; no government could act otherwise in face of terrorism. Again Attlee insisted that there was no question of favouring the establishment of a Jewish state in Palestine. 'One would almost have thought from Mr Silverman's speech that we were in Palestine as partners with the Jewish Agency for the creation of a Jewish State.' The Anglo-American report, Attlee said, was:

> a very good basis for discussion, but if asked here and now if I accept that Report, I cannot accept it because we have not fully discussed it, and the implications are very far-reaching and need very wide and careful examination. . . . It is really no good suggesting that we have not an obligation to the Arabs as well as the Jews. . . . We should like to get our troops out of this difficult position, but unfortunately we have this position and our troops are there. While they are there, they must carry out the primary duty of a Government.

At the same time Attlee was pressing Truman to make some public statement condemning the violence in Palestine, which reached a climax on 22 July 1946 with the destruction by the Irgun of the King David Hotel in Jerusalem. The British Cabinet met on 23 July under great pressure. The High Commissioner in Palestine wanted to make a wide-ranging search for arms. For the chiefs of staff, Tedder said that this would lead to all-out fighting with the Jews, but that British forces could manage this. Attlee poured cold water. He was against 'any severe action'. The Cabinet should initiate as little as possible, while doing all that should be done to meet the situation. The important thing was to strengthen the moderate Jewish leaders. He defended the Haganah: 'It has been implicated in some of the earlier acts of violence,' he said, but it 'would be a mistake to rush in to a widespread search for arms. . . . Such action would have the effect of alienating all sections of Jewish opinion in

Palestine.' A few days later in Cabinet, Attlee strongly rejected a suggestion that the government should make a show of strength and stop
immigration altogether for the time being. This, he said, would be a
punitive measure, which 'would cause hardship to innocent and suffering
people'.

Attlee's voice in these Cabinet meetings at a time of great tension was
the voice of sympathy and moderation – much more than Bevin's. And
Attlee got his way, though he agreed to one measure about which he had
doubts – that refugees caught trying to enter Palestine illegally should be
directed to Cyprus. The Anglo-American experts, representing the State
Department and the Foreign Office, and the Treasury and Defence
departments, reported in July that in the short term 100,000 refugees
could be admitted only with Arab agreement and help. For the long term
they prepared a federal system of two semi-autonomous provinces, one
Jewish, and one Arab, with a strong central trustee government which
could supervise immigration and control the religious centres of Bethlehem and Jerusalem. This became known as the Morrison–Grady plan,
Morrison being chairman of the Cabinet's Palestine Committee, Grady
the American representative on the expert committee. Attlee, Bevin and
the majority of the Cabinet thought that, with the support of the American President, the Morrison–Grady plan might work. This hope was
thwarted when the scheme was leaked to the American newspapers on
25 July.

After a month of sustained pressure from American Zionists, Truman,
realizing that in Acheson's words, 'Attlee had deftly exchanged the
United States for Britain as the most disliked power in the Middle East,'
rejected the Morrison–Grady plan on the very day that Jewish and Arab
representatives were meeting in London to discuss it. As an alternative
he put to Attlee a scheme for the Partition of Palestine which had been
provided for him by the Jewish Agency. It was now clear that Truman
was personally directing American Palestine policy, that the officials of
the State Department had little weight with him, that his views were
governed by his Zionist partisanship, and his political calculations. Attlee
cabled back, expressing his disappointment, and the conference went
ahead.

This was bad enough, but on Yom Kipper, 4 October, a month before
polling day in the mid-term congressional elections, Truman announced
that he would continue to press for the admission of 100,000 Jews into
Palestine and that the United States would support a plan for Partition.
Attlee was warned the previous day, not by the President, and was
appalled. Bevin was in the middle of talks with Zionist leaders and was
hopeful that they might yield some results: if the Yom Kippur statement
were released, his efforts would be wasted. Attlee immediately tele-

graphed to Truman, asking him to postpone his statement for long enough only to enable him 'to consult with Mr Bevin'. The President ignored the request. Attlee cabled indignantly to the President:

> I have received with great regret your letter refusing even a few hours grace to the Prime Minister of the country which has the actual responsibility for the government of Palestine, in order that he may acquaint you with the actual situation and the probable result of your action. These may well include the frustration of our patient efforts to achieve a settlement and the loss of still more lives in Palestine. I shall await with interest to learn what were the imperative reasons which compelled this precipitancy.

This was the lowest point ever reached in the personal relationship between Attlee and Truman. It was paralleled by one of the lowest points in Anglo-American relations. American citizens were bitterly angry about the alleged conduct of British forces in Palestine. New York newspapers recorded 'British atrocities'. Ben Hecht's anti-British play, *A Flag Is Born*, was playing to packed houses on Broadway. In November, Bevin, visiting the United States, was pelted with eggs. He talked to Byrnes, the Secretary of State, and to the President, and came back to London convinced that no support could be expected from the Americans, and that it was time for Britain to surrender the Mandate.

The last phase of the Attlee government's attempt to provide a British solution to the Palestinian problem began with the London Conference of January 1947. By now Attlee had replaced the Colonial Secretary, Hall, with Creech Jones, a known Zionist sympathizer, committed to Partition. This made little difference. The Jews, rendered intractable by Truman's support, refused to sit at the negotiating table. The Arabs were equally intransigent. Attlee and Bevin were very sensitive to the Foreign Office warning that whatever happened they must not incur Arab wrath. The CIGS, Montgomery, warned that it was essential to have troops in Palestine to defend the Suez Canal, while Tedder, Chief of the Air Staff, argued that 'our whole military position in the Middle East depends on the co-operation of the Arab states'. Bevin urged the importance of oil supplies. Meanwhile Bevan, Dalton, Creech Jones and Shinwell urged support for a Jewish state.

In the view of the Foreign Office there were now only three possible solutions to the Palestine problem: first, Partition; second, negotiations with the Arabs for an independent unitary state, with special rights for the Jewish minority, who would live in self-governing cantons; third, the surrender of the Mandate. After spending some days seeing the two delegations in separate meetings, Bevin came to the following conclusions: Partition, which the Jews had now come to accept as their official line, would evoke such resistance from the Arabs that British influence might be wiped out 'in the vast Muslim area between Greece and India'. Negotiations with the Arabs for an independent unitary state, with special rights for the Jewish minority living in cantons, would precipitate an immediate Jewish insurrection. Lastly, to surrender the Mandate would be interpreted by the Arabs as a withdrawal from the Arab world altogether, with the result that the Arabs would make their own arrangements about how to deal with the Palestine problem, with the likelihood of terrible consequences for the Jews and critical danger to British interests. Attlee told the Cabinet that it might be necessary 'to impose a solution in Palestine which will be actively resisted by one or both of the two communities there'. But Britain no longer had the military strength to impose any positive solution. There seemed to be no way ahead. Bevin told Attlee: 'I am at the end of my tether.'

So Attlee had to face the collapse of Bevin's policy. On 14 February the Cabinet accepted a recommendation made jointly by Bevin and Creech Jones that Britain should submit the Palestine problem to the United Nations. The question came up: should there in the meantime be an increase in permitted Jewish immigration? There was considerable support for this in the Cabinet, but Attlee firmly said No. In submitting the problem of Palestine to the United Nations, Britain had a duty to preserve the problem in its present dimensions. Four days later, on 18 February 1947, Bevin announced in the House of Commons that he was not prepared to sacrifice any more British lives in trying to sustain what had been made an impossible burden. The problem of Palestine would be taken to the UN. Britain would give notice that when the Mandate expired on 15 May 1948 she would withdraw.

Arabs and Jews now pleaded their case before the United Nations. The result was the setting up of the United Nations Special Committee on Palestine – UNSCOP – on 15 May. Unrest and suffering continued. UNSCOP produced its findings in September 1947. A majority report advocated Partition – a Jewish state. Bevin told the Cabinet on 18 September that Britain could not possibly accept Partition – it was manifestly unjust to the Arabs: a Jewish government, pushed by a swelling population and nationalistic politicians, would not accept the new frontiers; it would expand them; 'the existence of a Jewish State might prove a constant factor of unrest in the Middle East'. A depressed Cabinet met on 20 September and heard Attlee announce that Britain would abandon the Mandate, and withdraw from Palestine, on 1 August 1948. In his view there was 'a close parallel' between the position in Palestine and the situation which had recently existed in India, and he hoped that the announcement of the deadline would cause Jews and Arabs to come to a compromise.

The UNSCOP Report came to the vote at the UN on 29 November. A majority in the General Assembly voted for Partition, among them the United States and the USSR. Britain abstained. The British delegate declared that Britain would not undertake the task of imposing a policy by force of arms: the Mandate would end on 15 May 1948, and until then she would not share it with any other body. The United Nations, in recommending Partition, also voted to appoint a five-nation commission to take over the administration of Palestine when the British Mandate came to an end, and prepare for the transfer of power to the two provisional governments.

There followed six months of unofficial war. As the day of the end of British rule approached, Jews and Arabs increased their efforts to strengthen their hand for what lay ahead. Arab troops attacked the village of Kfar Etzion, near Bethlehem, and killed a hundred Jews, leaving only four survivors. Jewish forces occupied towns like Tiberias, Haifa and Acre. The armies of Egypt, Transjordon, Syria and Lebanon took up position on the borders. Britain, responsible for law and order in Palestine, adopted a policy which Abba Eban, a subsequent Israeli foreign minister and ambassador to the UN, described as 'sympathetic neutrality [which] enabled the Arabs to operate with ease, while it hindered the Jews'.

On the day after the end of the Mandate, 16 May, the Jews proclaimed the existence of the state of Israel, which was officially recognized a quarter of an hour later by the United States. More than thirty other members of the United Nations, including Russia, followed suit. Britain delayed recognition for several months. On 17 May Egyptian planes bombed Tel Aviv. The armies of Lebanon, Syria, Jordon, Iraq and Egypt crossed the borders into Palestine. The Security Council ordered a ceasefire, and appointed a mediator, but fighting went on, with two major intervals, until January 1949. Twenty months after the British had quit Palestine, the new state of Israel had won a tremendous victory. It was clear that Attlee's government had been totally wrong in predicting that if war broke out, the Arabs would hurl the Jews into the sea.

Winding up a debate on 26 January 1949, Attlee defended his policy. Churchill had said we could have imposed a settlement: then why hadn't Churchill done so immediately after the war in Europe? The United States had only accepted one recommendation in the Anglo-American Committee's report (the admission of 100,000 refugees). President Truman had been ill-advised to rush into recognition of Israel. The government were trying to act with the United Nations. There had been 'meticulous care taken in handing over to local authorities throughout Palestine ... and the handing over went extremely smoothly in the Jewish areas' (the last claim in particular has been much disputed). Viewed from one aspect, Attlee's policy of withdrawal from Palestine could be considered a success. He maintained Britain's resistance to the foundation of a Jewish state to the very end – he could say that the Arabs had not been betrayed, or driven into insurrection, by an act of Britain's, and that not to antagonize the Arabs *deliberately* was Britain's first priority.

By surrendering the Mandate and vacating Palestine, Britain relieved herself of her commitments to Zionism, in the form of a hopelessly ambiguous and conflicting pair of promises going back to the First World War, and avoided being identified by the Arabs as begetter of the Jewish state. For many years thereafter, Britain was able to preserve a good deal of her historic influence throughout the Middle East. She controlled the Suez Canal for another nine years, bases in Iraq for ten, and could maintain troops around the Gulf until the early 1970s. On the other hand, the British record in Palestine between 1945 and 1947 had many critics, especially in the United States. The behaviour of British troops towards the Jews was generally regarded as far below the standard which Britain had herself led people to expect. Finally, there was no disputing the fact that Britain had left Palestine for no principle, and out of no wisdom, but simply because the government believed that there was nothing else to do. Attlee's handling of the Palestine problem was the first clear signal that Britain no longer possessed the strength and resources of an imperial power; the message was not lost on the nationalists in her colonies and dependencies.

Attlee's failure to produce a solution to the Palestine problem is the worst entry on his record. Could he have done better? Certainly he did not realize until too late that the passion of the Israeli Jew to have a country of his own was out of all proportion to his numbers and his weapons. While not in the least antisemitic, Attlee was pro-Arab, in the sense that while he was fully aware of the need for Arab oil, he believed that Britain had a duty to promote the welfare of the millions of Arab peasants, protect them from their extortionate Arab rulers, and lead them on to independent democratic regimes, securely based on progressive economies. His eye was on the problem of the Middle East as a whole, of which Palestine, he continued to believe, was only a peculiar part.

The fact that he delegated Palestine to his Foreign Minister, Bevin, more than he delegated any other problem of foreign and colonial policy, and was misled by the Foreign Office appreciation of the situation, does not excuse Attlee from having made judgements which experience was to prove unsound. His greatest failure was to understand Truman's attitude to the Palestine problem. He did not realize until it was too late that American policy would be governed not by the State Department but by the President's personal Zionism and his political concern to get the Jewish vote. Given the excellent personal relationship between the two men, Attle should have discovered this long before he did. Since his first objective, in spite of misgivings, was to maintain the Anglo-American special relationship, and his personal relationship with Truman, he should have stood back early in the unhappy two-year history of events and decided to work with Truman first, and the British Foreign Office second. It came to that in the end: Attlee should have brought it there before.

23

A Man and a Leader, 1945-51

Attlee was the only prime minister of this century to come to Downing Street with a well-considered view of the nature of the job, the demands of Cabinet government and the best method of running an administration. His only contribution to Labour Party thinking before the war had been a long memorandum on the reorganization of government, written in 1932. (This is given in full as Appendix III below.) His main point was that Cabinet ministers were so overburdened with departmental administration that they lacked the time to arrive at sound decisions on broad policy. His solution was the grouping of departmental ministers under a small body of upper echelon ministers without departmental responsibility. Such organization was necessary for any government; for a Labour government it was essential, since Labour would have 'a definite programme' which must be transmitted into action at once, and govern the activities of all departments. Writing of this memorandum in June 1948, he observed: 'This Memorandum was written by me some time in the thirties before I had had any active experience of Cabinet government. It is not without interest in view of modern developments.' He elaborated the idea to some extent in *The Labour Party in Perspective*, and on joining Churchill's War Cabinet urged upon the prime minister some use of 'overlords' in civil administration.

His own Cabinet only partly incarnated these ideas. He reduced the Cabinet's size, partly by putting the three service ministers under a minister of defence who alone had Cabinet rank. He toyed with the idea of an inner ring of 'overlords' – Morrison, Dalton, Bevin, Cripps and Greenwood – but eventually gave Dalton, Bevin and Cripps departments to run. He maintained the principle of using committees of departmental ministers to make decisions under the chairmanship of a senior non-departmental minister. 'It is important,' he recorded in his autobiographical notes, 'not to multiply committees which tend to waste Ministers, and it is important not to blur the departmental responsibilities of Ministers. On the other hand committees help to bring non-Cabinet Ministers and Under-Secretaries into contact with general policy even though some time may be wasted.' He was particularly proud of introducing committees of junior ministers. It was the coordination that was essential, the system need not be formal. There was, for instance, a committee which dealt with the social services, presided over by Arthur Greenwood, and a committee for the coordination of economic affairs, first under Morrison, later under Cripps.

There was no committee for foreign or commonwealth affairs, but Bevin was always in close contact with him and the rest of the Cabinet. There was, however, a Defence Committee, a special arrangement which Attlee introduced himself. So long as the war with Japan had continued he remained Defence Minister, and when it was over, though he had appointed first Alexander and then Shinwell to the post, he continued to preside at all the more important meetings himself. Unlike the Cabinet committees which met when circumstances seemed to require it, the Defence Committee was a new, continuing piece of government machinery. A new Economic Committee also broke fresh ground: its existence meant that the Treasury was no longer the sole voice on economic policy, and that the economic front was no longer studied in terms only of finance. The Economic Committee introduced the Economic Survey, and finance was seen as part of the general planning of the economy.

By his own standards, Attlee started with a Cabinet that was too big: he favoured 'sixteen at most', but his first Cabinet numbered twenty. However, he carefully observed his own principle of making selections in terms, first, of which would be the key posts, secondly the fitness of the individual for his post, and thirdly his status in the party. Chuter Ede had very much wanted to be minister of education, and was eminently qualified, but was made home secretary: the job was more demanding, and he was the best equipped to do it. Attlee decided on who should and should not be included in the Cabinet less in relation to status within the party than in relation to the current importance of the department and the nature of the task in hand. He would not normally have included the minister of fuel and power in the Cabinet, but since mines, electricity and gas were to be nationalized, Shinwell was included. Purely administrative jobs, like the postmaster general's, should not usually be included in the Cabinet – though exceptions might be made since sometimes the minister's personality would outweigh the secondary importance of the job. It was important, he thought, to arrange responsibilities so that some members of the Cabinet were underemployed: 'You must have a certain number with leisure to look around and think. It's a mistake to have just a collection of hardworking Departmental Ministers.'

II

Attlee's conduct of Cabinet meetings, like all his administrative work, was crisp, and authoritative and to the point. His Cabinet meetings were on average shorter than those held by any prime minister since the First World War; and his object, visible from the opening of business, was to get the meeting over as soon as possible. He sat with Bevin on one side of him, Morrison on the other. 'Extremely businesslike,' recalls George Strauss, who as minister of supply sometimes attended Cabinet meetings. 'He could be formidable. As a subject came up he would introduce it with a sentence or two, and immediately ask for views. When he had got them, he would simply say, "The general view seems to be ..." and nearly always he would express it in terms of what should be done next. And that would be that.' On major issues, when all the senior members were present, he would ask for Morrison's opinion first, and work around the table to end with Bevin's. Attlee's Cabinets were relatively easy to minute and act on, largely because of the concise and concrete terms in which he had delivered his summing-up. His own views on Cabinet method were clear:

> A Prime Minister has to know when to ask for an opinion. He can't always stop some Ministers offering theirs – you always have some people who'll talk on everything. But he can make sure to extract the opinions of those he wants when he needs them. The job of the Prime Minister is to get the general feeling – collect the voices. And then, when everything reasonable has been said, to get on with the job and say, 'Well, I think the decision of the Cabinet is this, that or the other. Any objections?' Usually there aren't. I didn't often find my Cabinet disagreeing with me.... To go through the agenda you must stop people talking – unnecessary talk, unnecessary approval of things already agreed, pleasant byways that may be interesting but not strictly relevant. And you shouldn't talk too much yourself however good you are at it.

Dalton recorded that he could 'name two, perhaps three, Ministers in the Attlee government who lost their jobs, at least for a while, because they talked too much in Cabinet'.

Since Attlee liked to do as much work as he could in the Cabinet Room, and not in the Prime Minister's study, he would almost invariably be in his chair when the ministers assembled outside the door. He hardly ever kept them waiting, was extremely punctual, and a minister who arrived late would be reprimanded. Much of his authority came from the knowledge that he, unlike some of those present, had always read his documents in advance, and had assimilated the information. He would address searching questions to the ministers concerned, and if it was clear that they knew less about their briefs than he did he would say so. He once reduced Shinwell, of whom he was very fond, almost to tears by telling him to come back to the Cabinet only after he had studied his facts, though behind this remark was the more serious charge that figures which Shinwell was quoting to justify his handling of the coal crisis had been found to be false by the Prime Minister's personal staff.

Nobody was permitted to read out his departmental paper in Cabinet; Attlee assumed – and made it clear that he assumed – that everybody present had already read all the departmental papers, and that the discussion therefore would be a stage ahead of what was already known. Attlee exemplified the view he had recorded in the 1930s: 'the Cabinet is there primarily to act'. For some weeks after the decision to nationalize the railways had been taken, one minister continued to send papers to Attlee advocating that the Cabinet reconsider its 'proposals'. Attlee terminated the correspondence with one minute: 'The Cabinet does not propose: it decides.' And the Cabinet had already decided. As Attlee himself wrote in 1964:

> It is essential for the Cabinet to move on, leaving in its wake a trail of clear, crisp, uncompromising decisions. This is what government is about. And the challenge to democracy is how to get it done quickly.

According to a distinguished civil servant who worked closely with a number of his successors, Attlee was 'orderly, regular, efficient and methodical to a degree that put him in a different class from any of the prime ministers who followed him'. In the first few days of the new administration, his private secretary would take up to the study a supply of papers calculated to occupy the Prime Minister for two hours, but would be telephoned after an hour with, 'I've done that lot', and would have to take up another batch. The speed with which he read would not have made for good administration if it had not been accompanied by the dispatch with which he made decisions. His staff reckoned that in an average day he would dispose of 90 per cent of the paperwork confronting him. Part of his success in dealing with paper came because he was not, as some politicians are, averse to it, and because he appreciated the importance of getting it done quickly. This had a marked effect on the way in which the government of the country was conducted: ministers and their heads of departments soon realized that the quickest way to get action was to send the Prime Minister a paper, rather than wait until they had the opportunity to discuss the matter with him. In turn, he was soon able to gauge which of his ministers were active and which were dilatory, which were positive and which wanted to come and talk. 'Attlee's style and method produced a definite technique of government.'

He was able to conduct his government so well because he read so much. He was able to read so much because he spent as little time as possible listening to people. He had extra time for reading because he spent little time writing. This method of running his government would not have appealed to a more extrovert prime minister; and such concentrated desk work made demands on physical and mental stamina which some prime ministers could not have met. Some prime ministers have enjoyed drafting letters or minutes. Attlee would jot down only a sentence at the bottom of a long memorandum, and if possible he would confine himself to Yes or No. If he subscribed a document with his initials – CRA – it meant that the paper was 'approved'. If he wrote 'Agreed – CRA' it meant that the paper was warmly approved. Except on pet subjects, such as India, he left drafting to his private office and gave them considerable editorial licence, but in early days he occasionally rejected a draft because its language was not the simple prose he personally favoured, or because he thought the communication too long.

'The country was never so well governed, in this technical sense, in living memory as it was under Attlee,' was the conclusion of a distinguished civil servant who served under five prime ministers, working directly to them all. The monument to Attlee's efficiency was the massive, unprecedented amount of legislation enacted between 1945 and 1951, the fact that the whole of the Labour Party's programme was put on the statute book, and the degree to which the body of new law stood the test of time without need for major overhaul.

III

Attlee himself thought that choosing ministers was one of a prime minister's most exacting tasks. In the first days of the administration he made his principal dispositions, of Morrison, Bevin, Cripps and Dalton, to balance personal antagonisms and party strengths for the overall good of the administration. His most controversial appointment was Bevan as minister of health. The interview in which Attlee invited Bevan to join the Cabinet was brief. 'I made it clear he was starting with me with a clean sheet. . . . "You are the youngest member of the Cabinet. Now it's up to you. The more you can learn the better." ' Attlee also took considerable pains with junior members of the administration. Writing in 1949 he reflected that he had been 'determined to give youth its chance wherever possible, especially since the 1945 entry contained many men of high quality'. He did not hesitate to give them jobs in preference to older stalwarts, nor to bring back those, like Strachey and Strauss, whose political careers had been somewhat chequered. He enjoyed appointing three wearers of his old school tie, whose merits had qualified them for their jobs. He wrote to Tom on 30 August 1945:

My young Haileyburians in the House are an able lot. Whiteley selected one for a Whip, and Morrison another for a PPS, while I have another for a like purpose, one de Freitas, President of the Cambridge Union, athletics blue, lecturer in America, manager of Boys Clubs and Labour Committee in Shoreditch, and Squadron Leader in the Air Force; a useful background.

As well as the 'quality' which he attributed to Strauss and Strachey, he also wanted the ballast which came from having 'solid people' in the administration, men who will 'give you the ordinary man's point of view, like little George Tomlinson', who became minister of education.

Attlee thought it was 'generally best' to discuss the choice of under-secretary with the minister concerned, but he did not always do this. When he appointed Harold Wilson president of the board of trade – at thirty-one, the youngest man to become a Cabinet minister – he telephoned him and asked: 'Who would you like as your successor as Secretary at Overseas Trade?' Wilson said he would like Arthur Bottomley. 'Good,' said Attlee, 'because that's who you are getting.' Nor did he always accept the man the minister recommended. The minister might be 'the only one who doesn't usually know his own deficiencies. You may have picked a Minister who is awfully good, but, although he doesn't know it, is rather weak on certain sides, so you must give him an Under-Secretary who fills in the gaps. For instance, if you have a rather obvious member of the intelligentsia it's quite useful to give him a trade unionist, someone who's got a different background.'

The fatal mistake in making appointments was to select 'docile yes-men'. To guard against this Attlee sometimes chose to 'put in people who are likely to be awkward'. These were always to be warned in advance: 'If you don't turn out all right I shall sack you.' To give this warning, he thought, was most important. 'I did it with all my ministers.' And he was as good as his word. He thought it essential for a prime minister to pick his ministers himself. 'My general experience was that when I accepted advice it wasn't very good. I did once or twice have people foisted on me. People don't always understand why a man who seems very clever may not turn out particularly good as a Cabinet Minister.'

Attlee was the undisputed master of a Cabinet which contained a number of the strongest personalities the Labour Movement has produced – 'lions,' said George Strauss. The memories of his colleagues combine to give a clear picture of him as prime minister. He was a good judge of men, objective but with intuition. The emphasis was on a man's trustworthiness. This, says Sir Geoffrey de Freitas, was the origin of his misgivings about Dalton and his suspicions of Morrison – 'Morrison he could not stand.' If he felt he could trust them he was prepared to take risks in appointing young men, though if he made up his mind that somebody had fallen short of what he required, the appointment would be terminated. One junior minister, who is still alive and shall not be named, was summoned precipitately to Number Ten, to be congratulated on the work of his department, he thought. 'What can I do for you, Prime Minister?' he said, as he sat down. 'I want your job,' said Attlee. The minister was staggered. 'But . . . why, Prime Minister?' 'Afraid you're not up to it,' said Attlee. The interview was over.

Once Attlee had appointed a minister, said Lord Robens, he let him get on with the job: 'He did not interfere: he appointed and he sacked.' When it was necessary to remove an unsatisfactory minister Attlee did not beat about the bush. His autobiographical notes include plenty of tributes – 'the outstanding success has been Wilson. . . . McNeil who showed first-class ability has been promoted Minister of State', – also sharp judgements like 'among those of Cabinet rank — failed to come up to expectations and had to go; — was not a success and after a short time at Pensions was dropped'. To the entry 'Ammon has been an efficient Chief Whip', a long-hand note is added: 'Subsequently Ammon made a fool of himself over the Dock Strike and had to go.'

IV

Attlee's staff had ample opportunities for noting his relationships with his colleagues. He was reserved with them all – as he was with his staff – 'like a don, immersed in his subject, shy but not at all cold, and obviously affectionate'. It was relatively easy for him to sack a colleague, since there was little intimacy in any of his political or official relationships; the fact that he was too honest to pretend that there was intimacy where there was not also stood him in good stead. The only minister whose company he seemed positively to enjoy was Bevin. He would often come down to Chequers on a Sunday, talk about foreign affairs, reminisce on bygone strikes and Labour Party crises, tell many egotistical stories, and consume considerable quantities of brandy. He would hold forth sanguinely on project after project, from the Marshall Plan to a new dam in Egypt, outlining the benefits they would confer in time to all the peoples of the world. Attlee, obviously enjoying the talk, always seemed to take the more practical, sometimes less optimistic view, always responsive but sometimes expressing regret that he could not express the same optimism himself.

Though the cause of Bevin's visits to Chequers was official – to bring the PM up to date with foreign affairs – Attlee's staff had the feeling that the meetings had something personal to them. This was not the case with Cripps, who did not have the personality which enabled him to cross the gap produced by Attlee's shyness. Nor did Attlee have the same regard for Cripps's judgement; but knowing that Cripps meant well, Attlee was exceptionally patient with him. He impressed his officials too with his tolerance towards Morrison, at times when his secretaries knew, from listening to officials in other departments, that Cripps and Morrison were expressing criticism of Attlee to other Cabinet colleagues, and, in Morrison's case, to newspapermen. Officials in Number Ten knew that Attlee knew that *they* knew what was going on. But the intrigues were never referred to, and the Prime Minister's words and demeanour were always scrupulously correct.

This of course was part of his strength. 'He was a puritan,' said one of his private secretaries. 'The atmosphere in Number 10 was moral,' said Douglas Jay. 'You felt that policy was not just about what was good judgement and bad judgement, but about what was right and what was wrong.' He never complained about Morrison, and his staff behaved accordingly. He was less ready to be patient with Dalton. Notes to Cripps about Dalton's economic policy suggested that Attlee did not believe in his economic expertise, and relied on Cripps to make this good. Nor did Attlee ever say anything to suggest that he admired Dalton personally. It came as no surprise to one of his officials when, first hearing of the 1947 budget indiscretion, Attlee's guard dropped and he muttered: 'Always was a loud-mouthed fellow.'

No prime minister has been on better terms with his civil servants, and few, if any, as good. This was partly due to his moral rectitude, which led him to respect men whose profession was not to seek power but to serve the state, and partly due to his view that the objective opinion of an official who occupied his job by merit of intelligence, training and experience was at least as worthy of consideration as the aspiration of a leading politician. It was not a matter of weighing the assessments made by civil servants against the proposals made by politicians, as much as considering any view put forward entirely on its merits. Some of his civil servants, looking back on their days with him in Number Ten, recall that he was quite oddly 'apolitical'. His instinct was to find what was a truly national policy. 'I never had the feeling with him that I have had with other prime ministers that while they felt they must do what was good for the country, they must never be expected to shut their eyes to what was good for the party.'

Some prime ministers have introduced political advisers into their establishment at Number Ten, a measure which has frequently caused problems for the civil servants. In his early months Attlee took on Douglas Jay as personal assistant to give him the kind of technical advice about economic affairs which Cherwell had given Churchill about this and other matters. The arrangement worked well, partly for personal reasons – Attlee had known Jay, next door neighbour of Vi's family, for years – but when in 1946 Jay became MP for Battersea, he did not repeat the experiment, preferring to deal only with civil servants. In his first few months he had assumed that technical knowledge of economic affairs was more important than in fact it was, but he had now come to the conclusion that though technical knowledge of economic affairs was important, the civil servants were as able to give it to him as any Labour Party – or non-partisan – economist, and that the ultimate decisions to be taken by the Prime Minister would depend on the exercise of good human judgement and common sense.

V

The main criticism of Attlee made in retrospect by his colleagues was that he was so remote. Though he always worked in the Cabinet Room, in the very central location of power, his ministers thought of him as living his life at a much greater distance away. The flat at the top of the house, in which he spent as much time as he possibly could with Vi, seemed to his colleagues to be psychologically on another planet. He made no effort to appear in touch. Yet, as can be seen from the prime ministerial minutes given in Appendix IV below, no problem was too small to interest him if brought to his notice, and nobody could take the risk of bypassing his authority on the grounds that the matter was not worthy of his attention. John Strachey wished to publish some poems. A colleague pointed out to him that Cabinet ministers could not publish a book without the Prime Minister's prior consent. Strachey wrote to Attlee that he proposed to publish a book, but that he did not think the Prime Minister would wish to see the book since it would consist of poems. Attlee asked to see it. Strachey complied. He heard nothing of the book for three weeks, so made a telephone call to the Prime Minister. Attlee came to the phone. 'You can't possibly publish. The lines don't scan.'

His remoteness was an imperfection in his premiership. He was an excellent listener, but was not good at exchanging views, especially embryonic views. He did not think aloud, and did not encourage the practice in others. Colleagues were expected to have done their thinking before they came to see him, and, as Harold Wilson said, 'You'd think twice before you *asked* to see him.' Some of his junior colleagues complained that he did not encourage them enough, that he behaved less as captain, more as umpire. Some liked his habit of handing out general ideas rather than specific directives, others were worried by this, since they might expect tart comments if their implementation went wrong. 'You felt that there was always a bad-tempered headmaster in the background,' said Strauss.

Yet many letters among Attlee's papers suggest that this was not a universal view – for example a note dated 2 August 1951 from a minister who was by no means close to him, Richard Stokes, then Lord Privy Seal: 'Thanks for your kind words of confidence in my efforts at the Cabinet yesterday. I will do my best.' When he addressed his new junior ministers after he had formed his government in 1945 he made a very good impression on them, especially when he said: 'One more thing: if I pass you in the corridor and don't acknowledge you, remember it's only because I'm shy.' If he was sometimes too shy to make contact, he was always sympathetic. In 1948 he asked Herbert Bowden, later Lord Aylestone, an assistant Whip, to move the Loyal Address. Just before Bowden went into the Chamber he found himself next to Attlee. 'How do you feel?' asked Attlee. 'Very nervous, Prime Minister.' 'Don't worry, I'm *always* nervous.'

By the party as a whole Attlee was personally well liked. Lord Longford spoke of Attlee as 'standing alone in my experience of politicians of both parties for the way in which he was ready to put himself out to assist promising younger men.' Woodrow Wyatt observed:

> In 1945 I was surprised to be with the mighty, and to take part in what appeared to be great events. .... When Clement Attlee spoke kindly to me, I called him Sir. 'Don't call me "Sir"! Call me Clem. We're all in the same party.' I was always nervous of this good man, and the thought that I must address the Prime Minister and the wartime Deputy Prime Minister by his Christian name made me dodge him for some months.

Attlee kept in touch with the rank and file mainly through the veterans, now in the minority, who had been his companions in the thirties. He did so mainly by his visits to the tea-room, but sometimes by summoning them to his room. According to his PPS, Geoffrey de Freitas, he always seemed to know how to get in touch with them at any time of day or night. 'Go and ask Jim Murray to come and see me.' De Freitas had been only a few weeks in the House. 'Yes, Prime Minister, but I don't know him.' 'It's six o'clock. You'll find him in the tea-room, in a dark suit, two kippers and a cup of tea.' And there Jim Murray was.

One of his strengths was that by Cabinet ministers and backbenchers alike he was known to abhor personal gossip. He had no smalltalk, though he was quite happy to join a group in the smoking room, sit and smoke and say nothing. If he said something, it was noncommittal. He would never 'fudge' an issue he did not want to resolve by talking about it. If he fudged, he fudged with silences. He was 'remote', said Harold

Wilson; 'you'd see him often in the tea-room, and he'd sit down somewhere, and in that sense he mingled and was accessible. In the tea-room
he'd listen, and not talk. Whether he was taking anything in, or he
listened because it saved him the trouble of talking, you didn't know.'
Visitors going to see him sometimes became nervous as they entered his
room, said Moyle.

> As they came through his door into the room Attlee would put down his
> pen, raise his head with his nose pointing to the sky and take a long sniff,
> like a fox terrier about to bark. Then he'd stare at the visitor, and say
> nothing. If he wanted to encourage a visitor to leave, which was rarely
> necessary – they were usually ready to go – he'd take his pipe from his
> mouth and put it carefully on his blotter, lift himself out of his chair slightly,
> look across at the clock, and give a little grunt. It never failed.

Making conversation with him was very difficult. One often-quoted but
variously named MP compared smalltalk with Attlee to throwing biscuits
to a dog, who responded with a short, sharp bark, 'Yep.' Another biscuit:
another 'Yep!' 'Very difficult to have a relaxed discussion with him on
any subject except bishops or cricket,' said George Strauss. 'I once went
by car with him to Harwell and I had about the most painful one and a
half hours I ever spent in my life.'

If Attlee did not much endear himself to backbenchers by direct
conversation, they enjoyed his occasional *mots* or the circulated reports of
them: such as a remark he made at a party meeting at the end of a
discussion on the danger of nuclear energy. The last speaker, a Welsh-
man, ended an impassioned speech with a description of the perils which
would be caused by radioactive fish swimming into Western waters.
When he had finished, Attlee rose to his feet, knocked out his pipe, said:
'Yes, we must watch that. Adjourn for lunch.'

In other contexts his dryness could be disconcerting. He once dismayed
Richard Crossman, who was not easily put out of countenance. Attlee
had no use for Crossman: the legend says that his mistrust went back to
the days when he thought that young Dick cheated at tennis, but it was
in fact founded on his view – expressed to the author – that 'Dick is
irresponsible and unstable.' In early 1946 Crossman returned from a visit
to Europe as a member of the Anglo-American committee on Palestine,
anxious to convince the government that Jews in displacement camps
were genuinely determined to go to Palestine. Attlee agreed to see him.
Crossman went to his room in the House, sat down opposite him at his
desk, and waited. 'Go ahead,' said Attlee. Highly nervous – 'it's now or
never, I thought' – Crossman launched into his argument, and spurred
on by his nervousness spoke nonstop for about twenty minutes. There
was a pause, then, 'How's your mother, Dick?' asked Attlee. 'She's very

well,' said Crossman. 'I'm seeing her next week.' 'Good. Give her my regards,' said Attlee. The interview was over.

VI

Attlee's grasp of what was going on in Cabinet, and his remarkable knowledge of the contents of the documents, was purchased at a price: he would frequently stay in the flat with Vi and peruse his papers when he might have made more speeches in the country. Enough has been shown already of his inhibiting shyness to demonstrate that aloofness was a part of his nature that could not be blamed on Vi. But in spite of greatly enjoying many aspects of life as the wife of the PM, Vi was jealous of the office which she felt took her husband away too much from her. She could be miserable and difficult, and needed reassurance. Attlee, to whom her happiness was paramount, did all he could to give it to her.

Vi's first task as prime minister's wife was to move the family into Downing Street, and since Attlee had to go off at once to Potsdam she had to deal with the move herself. Counselled by Mrs Churchill – a real friend – she decided to make no attempt to live in the spacious suite on the first floor but to have the top floor converted into a flat. Attlee reciprocated the Churchills' kindnesses by letting them stay on at Chequers for a few weekends. The new Downing Street flat contained a drawing room, dining room, kitchen, and enough bedrooms to accommodate the children. Attlee had a study on the floor below. While the alterations were being carried out, Attlee lived in a flat in Storey's Gate, on the corner of Parliament Square, and the family lived in Stanmore. They sold the Stanmore house as soon as they could. In view of the housing shortage they asked the Ministry of Health to suggest a fair price, and let the house go at that to the first bidder.

As prime minister, Attlee saw more of his family than he had ever seen before, since he was now 'living on the job'. Janet, working in Bristol, came home frequently. Felicity was teaching in a nursery school in Bermondsey. Martin, now a cadet in the Merchant Navy, came home on leave very often. Alison, still at school, spent her holidays with her parents. The Attlees enjoyed their weekends at Chequers – if they could, they made it a family weekend. They would try to get away between four and seven on the Friday night, and hoped not to leave until after an early breakfast on Monday. They entertained official guests there at weekends, but only when they felt they had to. They came to love the countryside in which it stood, and decided that when the time came to buy another house it should be not far away. In 1948, when he had moved to the West Walthamstow constituency after his old Limehouse seat disappeared under the Representation of the People Act, the Attlees bought Cherry Cottage at Great Missenden. He wrote to Tom:

You will have heard that we are buying a house so as to be ready for all eventualities. It is quite charming standing high near Great Missenden. A well-designed modern cottage has been attached to a three hundred year old low-roofed cottage. The two parts are serviceable but are internally connected; in effect we shall have a very well shaped drawing room, small dining room, a very small kitchen in the new part and a sort of hall, a fair-sized study and a second kitchen in the old part. There is also a small maid's sitting room in the new part. There will also be an adequate number of bedrooms – two bathrooms. There's a garage (wooden) & about an acre of grounds with a number of old cherry trees, much admired, I am told, in blossom time – hence the name of the house, Cherry Cottage. The price is rather steep, but the place has character and charm and we are very fond now of Bucks. We shall try to find a tenant for the next 12 or 14 months as, of course, the General Election is the unknown factor.

If at Chequers the weekend was quiet, on Saturdays they played a great deal of tennis. However hard-pressed he had been in the week, he always had energy for strenuous games of tennis, and some of his private secretaries – these were taken along for the weekend and treated as members of the family – though considerably younger, found that even if they were superior in skill they might not be able to cope with his stamina. He enjoyed being fit, and was proud of the fact that at the age of sixty he could jump over the net. In the evening perhaps a game of bridge, Vi criticizing his play without inhibition in the presence of the private secretaries. They liked to walk, especially on Sunday mornings. Attlee read a great deal: among other works he read the whole of Gibbon at Chequers. When the day's work was done he could switch off. If he had only a few minutes left for reading he would take up a volume of the *Dictionary of National Biography*.

With the exception of three trips, one to Ireland, one to France (they took their own car, and Vi drove) and one to Norway, they spent all their holidays at Chequers. Most of all they enjoyed Christmas there: on Boxing Days they gave a large party for the children of ministers and private secretaries. There was always a conjuror. He wrote to Tom on 29 December:

... just ending a very good ten days Christmas holiday at Chequers. We had quite a considerable party, Edric, Betty, Margaret and Peter and Paul Tomlin besides other young folk coming from time to time. We were lucky to have all the children here also. We had a fine children's party on Boxing Day with games, a Christmas Tree and Cinema. We had some thirty children complete with parents. A large contingent of Pakenhams from Oxford formed a good nucleus with Durbins, Dugdales and Patrick and

Jeremy from that county. . . . We also had a good lot from London, children
of private secs, under secs and solicitor general . . .

When important visitors from abroad had to be entertained at Chequers,
the servant problem was solved by importing a detachment of the ATS,
WRENS or WRAF. When the Attlees did have guests at Chequers the
atmosphere was frequently quite formal. Sir John Colville, when he made
his first visit to Chequers under Attlee's premiership, found a contrast
with the days of Churchill. 'Very much stiff collar and starched shirt. I
remember Attlee introducing me to his new PPS, Geoffrey de Freitas, and
saying "Old Haileyburian, you know." There was never any Old School
Tie talk in Winston's days.'

Even if occasionally formal, Vi's hospitality at Chequers, especially in
those times of austerity, was never lavish, and her belief in the virtues of
fresh air occasionally caused discomfort. Dean Acheson was once taken
to lunch there by Ernest Bevin, and recorded that he had never been so
cold in his life. The house was so cold that Bevin sat inside the massive
chimneypiece to try to get warm. When Acheson asked for a martini, he
was given vermouth, so to get warm when offered the next drink he asked
for undiluted gin. At lunch, all the windows were open and the northeast
wind blew in so strongly that, according to Acheson, the curtains were
parallel to the floor.

Vi was not happy in Downing Street. She enjoyed the sense of sharing
in her husband's life, was not averse to entertaining visitors, and enjoyed
opening house to representatives of women's organizations and national
charities. But she resented that part of life in Downing Street which
excluded her from the company of her husband. What with her temperament, and the occasional traces of her earlier illnesses, which seemed to
his secretaries to be as much mental as physical, she was not cut out for
regular life in Number Ten. When she thought they were putting a
barrier of work and protocol between her and her husband's private life
she could be aggressive towards the civil servants. She would demand to
see what appointments were being made for him, and complain sometimes that she had not been consulted, and, on the other hand, would
sometimes make arrangements for him without telling the civil servants.

Attlee never discussed Vi's incompatibilities with life at Number Ten
with his secretaries, but with an occasional look or word he made it clear
to them all that he knew their problems and counted on their help. It
was another human bond between him and his staff. They were very
aware too of how hard – and successfully – he tried to make Vi feel that
she was as much a part of his daily life as she had ever been – indeed
more. It was understood that unless imperatively necessary he would
stay in the flat with Vi after breakfast, listening to her, and skimming the
newspapers, and not appear in the Cabinet Room, where he nearly

always worked, unless he beat out a speech on his ancient portable typewriter in his study, until 9.30. If he could he would have lunch with her – and spend an hour reading Cabinet Papers – or go up for tea in the afternoon. If there was a lot going on, he could not do this. But the understanding in his office was that the work should be arranged if at all possible so that the Prime Minister could spend the maximum time with his wife.

The result was that Attlee's visible day's work rarely began before 9.30 am. More than one of his private secretaries has said that in the half hour or so after 9.30 he could be 'difficult' – said one: 'snippy, snappy, and sometimes a bit short-tempered, especially if his papers were not in order, but he would soon begin to mellow'. If the Cabinet was not meeting, he would see the Chief Whip at about the same time, and proceed, ten or fifteen minutes later, to a committee, perhaps the Defence Committee at 10 am, or an appointment with the minister, or a visitor from abroad. Francis Williams, his press adviser, came in some mornings at 10.45. Lunch would usually be a formal one in Number Ten, or perhaps an informal one with a minister or two, in Number Ten again, or at some function outside. Whether his presence was required or not, for question time, or to speak in a big debate, he would when he could spend an hour or two in the Chamber listening to the debate, consulting his parliamentary guide when new members rose to speak. If he did not have to go out before dinner with Vi, he would work on his papers in the Cabinet Room, and after go up to the flat at 11 pm, chat a little with Vi, then go to bed. Most nights, however, he worked till midnight, and often until 1.30.

His private secretaries found him quick to make decisions, and though he delegated boldly, nothing was too small to catch his eye; however small, it was to be 'polished off' – a favourite phrase – at once. On one occasion the appointment of a lord-lieutenant came up. It was clear that the name of the candidate had been mis-spelled, so that nobody was sure who it was that was being recommended. Then, one of the private secretaries realized from the biographical detail that this was a man with whom he had served in the North African campaign. 'He was at Oxford, and then he joined the regular army,' he began to tell Attlee, who said, 'Must be the man,' and immediately passed the appointment.

Though in any one week his bed time could vary by anything up to three hours, he could always go straight off to sleep when his head touched the pillow. Not only did he never worry, he never turned matters over in his mind before going to sleep, and he did not know the meaning of the term 'unwind'. Though he preferred not to have to go out to formal dinners, he never gave any sign of minding; he would listen, or appear to listen, to what was said, and generally exuded an air of being complimented at being invited. The only public engagement which distressed him was a night at the opera – he was quite tone-deaf.

In the ordinary run of events, only two things seemed to make Attlee less than courteous and good-natured – not having his papers arranged for him in the right order and at the right time, or if he felt that Vi was not being properly treated. Nothing pleased him so much as a word of praise for Vi, provided he knew it was a reasonable compliment. A fulsome remark about her left him looking stony, but a pleasant remark when she had done something that had obviously gone quite well caused him to beam most generously. He liked very much to hear her chat at lunch with the private secretary, especially if it was one with whom she had earlier had a contretemps. He would sit quietly himself, saying little, but obviously very gratified. The greatest compliment any of the civil servants could be given was to be asked to do things socially with Vi and the rest of the family.

The family, and the children, as well as Vi, were very much included in the public as well as the private life of the Prime Minister. He did not parade his children, and was not in the least concerned about what the public thought about them, but he wanted them to have as good a time as possible. In letters to Tom, for instance, accounts of important public occasions tell more about what the children made of them than about the events themselves, and when he writes of the personages present he does so on a level which equates them with 'the girls':

> We had a very good show up here for the victory celebrations. Janet, Felicity and Alison were all present and had a good view. I gave a large lunch to Winston, the PMs and the Chiefs of Staff etc at which the girls were present. They each had a Field Marshal to sit next to them.
> The fireworks were really very good. We watched them from Bill Jowitt's flat in the House of Lords with the King and Queen and a host of others. The girls were introduced to Al's great pleasure.

He continued to find time for other people's children, who wrote their prime minister letters singularly free from awe or admiration. An exasperated godson, Paul Green, wrote to him in September:

> My dear Godfather,
> It's long past time you started the Hornby factories going again. Shooly they should be started by now.

Attlee wrote back, inquired the gauge and type of the Hornby train required, informed him gravely that it was available, and included a postal order for him to buy it. He wrote frequently to his godchildren, and never omitted to reply to letters from them. He would narrate their accomplishments to his staff with pride. One morning he mentioned to one of his private secretaries that the morrow would be the day of the Trooping of the Colour. 'Your children going?' asked Attlee. 'Alas, no, Prime Minister: I haven't time to take them.' Attlee was quite censorious. 'Well, *I've* got time,' he said. 'Get them here, and I'll take them myself.' He did.

He loved to be in touch with the world of tennis, rugby, football and cricket. It was only partly because he had enjoyed playing these games; it was also because watching them, and reading and learning about them, brought back such happy recollections of his childhood and youth. Few men were less influenced by sentimentality about their early days than he was, but he enjoyed looking back. His interest in games and sport was another bond with Vi. Her passion was tennis. She would tell him about Wimbledon, and he would listen, and grunt, and she would go on talking, and occasionally rap out at him, 'Are you listening, Clem?', to which the answer invariably was, 'Yes, darling – very interesting.'

He made a great deal within the families of his silver wedding anniversary, which fell in January 1947. Vi had found her first sixteen months as wife of the Prime Minister extremely hard going. The anniversary was a most fortunate opportunity for him to put her in the limelight, and make her feel appreciated. To Tom:

> Vi and I thank you all very much for the delightful silver jug, which we both like enormously. We are just coming to the end of our celebrations which have really been great fun. It began on Friday morning with the receipt of many jolly presents. Vi had found for me a pair of branched candlesticks rather like those we have at Chequers. We had a goodly collection of silver and some fine bouquets of flowers. At 12.15 we went to No 11 where almost all the Cabinet and Ministers above the rank of under sec were assembled. Morrison proposed and Bevin supported in very nice speeches the health of us both and presented us with a silver salver whereon were incised the signatures of all the Ministers. Thence we proceeded to the House where Oliver Baldwin had assembled some 54 members of the Party who had been in the House in the 29–31 Parl, had remained faithful and were still in the Commons or the Lords. At the end of lunch a trophy of ice in the form of a great 25 surrounded by 25 lit candles was wheeled in. Then Vi cut an enormous iced cake made by the Chief Chef. Around the sides were latticed doorways wherein were set out the dates of our wedding and the birthdays of every one of the children.

Morrison was host for the silver wedding party, – 'a nice gesture,' say his biographers, 'though perhaps not without an element of political calculation in drawing attention to the party leader's advancing years'. According to the *Daily Herald*:

> a deep chorus of Parliamentary 'hear, hears' greeted Mr and Mrs Attlee when they walked into the Lord President's room in 11 Downing Street at

noon yesterday. Ministerial colleagues and friends were assembled to congratulate them on their silver wedding anniversary. The host, Herbert Morrison, made a short speech about the Prime Minister's 'courage and tolerance, kindliness and comradeship'; and of Mrs Attlee he said: 'She is the perfect Prime Minister's wife.' Ernest Bevin said: 'Clem Attlee was the best man to hold us together and get the team spirit. He does not try to boss us. He co-operates with us.'

Morrison presented the silver salver referred to in Attlee's letter. Maurice Webb spoke about Attlee's technique in his leadership of the Labour Party. It could be summed up, said Webb, in something which happened when he was partnering Attlee in a game of snooker. Webb found himself with a choice between a straight, not very exciting 'pot', and another shot, difficult but enticing, giving promise of much richer gain. Webb thought he should ask his partner's advice. Attlee replied: 'Put the ball into the pocket. We don't want any fancy stuff.' Attlee was interested in results, not in display. The *Herald* quoted Webb as saying: 'We have had more exotic leaders of our Party, more spectacular leaders, more picturesque leaders. But we have never had a better leader than Clem Attlee, never one to whose guidance the Party has responded with greater confidence or greater ease.' Webb, it may be recalled, had been one of the leaders of the movement to substitute Morrison for Attlee in June 1945.

24

Consolidation or Advance?

1948-9

I

Just as 1948 was the year in which the British people had to face a new and unwelcome phase in foreign affairs, marked by the unmasked aggressiveness of the Soviet Union, it was the year in which they had to face the long-term implications of Britain's struggle for economic life. Nationalization, full employment, high wages, welfare state benefits and the certain prospect of Marshall Aid created, in spite of austerity, a widespread sense of security which the British workers had never known before. The new problem was inflation. The *Economic Survey*, published on 8 March, only drove home the lessons which the government had been trying to inculcate in the public mind since the beginning of the year: that even if Britain were to receive the maximum amount of American aid under the Marshall Plan, there would be no hope of maintaining British living standards if the problem of inflation could not be rapidly brought under control. Britain would in any case have to export hard to live; high British prices, full employment in a high-wage economy, and the low level of productivity, dangerously handicapped the all-important export drive.

The first practical step to get inflation under control was a wages policy. On 4 February 1948, Attlee introduced in the House a White Paper on incomes, costs and prices. Two days later he made a broadcast in which he explained what the White Paper was about:

> I know it is very tempting to press for more money when prices are rising and other people have had more. There is no doubt that when a particular group gets an increase it does make matters easier for them for a time. But it is a short-lived advantage, and if no more goods have been produced the shortages will still be there. All that will have happened is that there will be more money about; but this will do them no good because they will be spending it in competition with others who have more money too. This is

bound to drive up prices still farther, and will help to stimulate the black market.

He also warned that wage increases could price British exports – the country's life-blood – out of the international market. Without exports 'there must be mass unemployment and real, desperate hunger. It is only as a great exporting country that Britain can survive, and already some of our best customers are jibbing at our prices.' Attlee also put in the first attack on a trade union prejudice in favour of wage differentials:

> We have long ago got away from the mistaken idea that the man who works in an office should, as a matter of course, always be better paid than the manual worker, and we must also get rid of the idea that the wage of one kind of manual worker must always be 10s. or £1 a week higher than that of another, just because it always has been so, at least since people can remember.

As in his statement in Parliament, he made it clear that all the government sought to do was to outline *a guide* for action: government interference with wages except by taxation was undesirable. The control of incomes was essential, but it should be voluntary:

> The safeguard lies, not in the hands of the Government, which cannot directly control the amount of money people are paid and have no intention of trying to do so, but in the hands of ordinary people. The Government believe that the ordinary people, whether wage-earners or businessmen – that is to say, the mass of the people – are intelligent enough to see and appreciate the nature of the danger and public-spirited enough to join in fighting it.

In retrospect Attlee's appeal for a voluntary wages policy may seem archaic, inconsequential and demure. At the time it created much controversy. Until then, the methods of controlling inflation had consisted mainly of taxation of profits and incomes and relatively heavy indirect taxation. Attlee now announced that this would not solve the problem of inflation if wages continued to rise. This marked the beginning of a tension between Labour governments and the trade union movement which exists to this day. The Minister of Labour, George Isaacs, now sent a letter to wage tribunals and arbitration courts, drawing their attention to the points which had been made publicly by the Prime Minister. Trade union leaders at once went around to Downing Street in a body, and demanded the withdrawal of this 'unacceptable attempt to interfere with free collective bargaining'. Attlee had started the campaign for a national incomes policy, but this first skirmish ended in a hasty retreat by the government. A trade union delegate conference at Central Hall, Westminster, voted by a majority of more than a million to support Attlee's broadcast statement, but a large minority of more than two million voted to reject it. It was clear that to try and deal with the problem of inflation by means of a wages policy would be uphill and dangerous.

The spring weeks presented Attlee with a number of political problems arising out of the countinuing shortages of fuel. From February to May the Conservatives fought the bill to nationalize the gas supply industry. Though the Conservatives had in 1945 accepted the report of the Heyworth Committee, which had recommended public ownership for the industry, they were now determined as a matter of tactics to oppose nationalization of any sort. Gaitskell handled the exhausting operation with great skill and courage, fully vindicating Attlee's decision to promote him to Minister of Fuel and Power the previous autumn.

Then on 3 May, ten days before the Gas Bill cleared the committee stage, Shinwell made a speech in Edinburgh which was represented, not unfairly, as an attack on the shortcomings of nationalization. Shinwell, now Minister of War, and a thoroughly discredited former minister of fuel and power, as chairman of the Labour Party suggested that not enough preparation had been made for public ownership of the coal industry, and not enough provision made for the introduction of indus-trial democracy into the coalfields. The Conservatives took full advan-tage of his public utterances. Colonel Lancaster, the Opposition's expert on the coal industry, wrote a letter to *The Times* and other Conservative MPs raised the matter in the House. An extraordinary meeting of the Parliamentary Labour Party discussed Shinwell's speech, and critical remarks about it included a remarkable attack upon him by a junior minister, James Callaghan. A day later, on 13 May, Sir Charles Reid, a prominent mining engineer, resigned from the Coal Board, adding fuel to the political flames by describing it as a 'cumbersome and uninspiring organisation'.

Gaitskell sent a note to Attlee asking him if he would remonstrate with Shinwell. When Attlee saw him privately, Shinwell claimed that he had been misreported, but promised 'to take care in future'. In fact he made other statements about coal within a week. In his speech, as chairman, at the annual party conference a few days later, Shinwell made some general references to the need for more democracy in the nationalized industries, but had some good things to say about the coal industry. After the conference was over, Attlee saw him again and told him in very clear terms that he would now be expected to give his full attention to his responsibilities at the War Office.

At the conference at Scarborough, Attlee as usual moved the parlia-mentary report:

> I have had twenty-five years in Parliament, and I have never known such good team-work in the Labour Party as we have had in this Parliament....

> Of course we have had a few individualists in our ranks. There is always one who thinks that 'our Johnny is the only one in step' – or should it be 'our Zilly'?

Zilliacus had been one of the signatories of the Nenni telegram. Attlee attacked the rebels not only because they would not play in the team, but because they risked undermining the team by talking as though any government policy was determined by the individual in charge of it:

> We get fine team-work in the Government itself. Our opponents ... try to disrupt our team – and I am sorry to say some of our own supporters are led away by ascribing particular policies to particular members. Thus they talk sometimes of Cripps's 'economic policy' or Dalton's 'financial policy' or Bevan's dealings with the doctors or Bevin's foreign policy, as if there were no co-ordination in the Government.

He made it clear, however, that loyalty to the team did not mean uniformity of opinion. On the Sunday before the conference he had read the Lesson at a service for the delegates – 1 Corinthians 12: 1–12, on the diversity of spiritual gifts – 'Now there are diversities of gifts, but the same Spirit. ... For as the body is one, and hath many members, and all the members of that body, being many, are one body ...' Although he did not choose the Lesson, it accorded well with his own philosophy.

Attlee's reputation stood high in mid-1948. It was just as well; there had been a number of industrial disputes earlier in the year, but none so serious as the London dock strike in June. It began on a small scale in late May, but by 26 June 152 ships were idle. Two days later, after it was clear that the food supply was in danger, Attlee invoked the Emergency Powers Act of 1920 – the first time it had been used since the General Strike of 1926 – and declared a state of national emergency. That night he made a statement on the BBC. The government, he said, could not in any way recognize or deal with those who were leading an unofficial strike. To do so would cut at the whole basis of collective bargaining. If there were grievances they could, and would, be dealt with by the Dock Labour Board. All trade unionists would realize that by striking the dock workers endangered all that had been built up in the years of self-sacrifice.

> I now want to speak to the dockers of the country, and particularly of London. Why have we had to take this action? First, because we must see that the people are fed, and there is not a single docker or his wife who would object to that ... this strike is not a strike against capitalists or employers. It is a strike against your mates; a strike against the housewife; a strike against the ordinary common people who have difficulties enough now to manage on their shilling's worth of meat and the other rationed commodities. And why should you men strike who are well paid compared with the old days, who have a guaranteed minimum wage of £4. 8s. 6d. a week whether you work or not?

In simple man-to-man language he told the dockers of the struggle which had rescued them from the evils of the old days. 'I lived in dockland for many years. I remember the horrible conditions.' Did they? 'Do you remember what it was like to go day after day and, as you arrived home, to be met with "Any work today?" and the answer was "No"? How were you to manage for supper, what were you to do for the children?' He described the efforts of men like Ernie Bevin to secure the guaranteed wage. The strikers thought they had a grievance. 'Why stop a dock over that? Why do you want to endanger the nation and make millions of people miserable over a little thing like this? ... Your clear duty to yourselves, to your fellow citizens, and to your country is to return to work.'

The dockers returned to work within forty-eight hours. 'A brilliant broadcast,' said the Labour member for Rotherhithe, and though he was partial, his views were shared even by members of the Conservative Party. Newspapers, apart from those who could find nothing good to say about him, produced such phrases as 'A wonderful week for Mr Attlee', and praised the broadcast as 'in its simplicity and directness a masterpiece of composition'. Many people would have agreed with Eden who told the author thirty years later: 'I think that broadcast may well have ended the strike.'

II

This peak in Attlee's national prestige came at a most opportune moment. July brought two challenges: at home, the inauguration of the social security system, including the National Health Service; abroad, the Russians' blockade of Berlin. Bevan's large and courageous plans for a National Health Service had attracted extensive criticism, even from some members of the Labour Party, who felt that unnecessary and controversial provisions had been included in the scheme. The National Health Service Bill had received the Royal Assent on 6 November 1946. Throughout 1947 many doctors were fighting a fierce rearguard action against many of its provisions. Bevan secured the Cabinet's approval for a debate in the House on 9 February 1948, the motion solemnly reaffirming the government's determination to introduce the Act on the appointed day, 5 July 1948. The date was kept.

The night before, Attlee delivered a broadcast saying that on the following day the most comprehensive system of social security ever introduced into any country would begin to operate in Britain. The four Acts, he said – National Insurance, Industrial Injuries, National Assistance and National Health Service – represented the main body of the army of social security: 'advance parties, such as increases in old-age pensions and extensions of unemployment benefit, have led the way.' He wished to emphasize a vital point. 'All social services have to be paid for, in one way or another from what is produced by the people of Britain. We cannot create a scheme which gives the nation as a whole more than we put into it. . . . Only higher output can give us more of the things we all need.' The broadcast also included tributes to all political parties for their earlier contributions to the growth of British welfare services.

The same day Bevan addressed a Labour rally at Manchester with a rather different historical perspective: 'The eyes of the world are turning to Great Britain. We now have the moral leadership of the world and before many years we shall have people coming here as to a modern Mecca, learning from us in the twentieth century as they learned from us in the seventeenth century.' He used the occasion to give his views on the progress of the Labour government's programme in general. Bevan was in an embattled mood. In May, at the party conference, Morrison had put the case for 'consolidation' – 'do not ignore the need, not merely for considering further public ownership, but for allowing Ministers to *consolidate*.' This was the first of a number of speeches made by Morrison in the next few weeks, the object of which was to play down further advances in socialization in order to win back the floating voter. Bevan, by contrast, thought that the best defence was attack – it was essential to protect what had been already achieved by pressing on fast 'to further nationalisation, and establish the dominion of the public sector over the whole of the economy' – reach forward and possess the 'commanding heights'. In this mood, he asserted in the Manchester speech that: 'In 1950 we shall face you again with all our programme carried out. And when I say all, I mean all. I mean *steel* is going to be added . . .'

At one point in the speech, contrasting Labour's social programme with the government policies he had suffered from in his youth, when the Means Test was being applied, Bevan said: 'That is why no amount of cajolery can eradicate from my heart a deep burning hatred for the Tory Party that inflicted those experiences on me. So far as I am concerned they are lower than vermin.' The press, which he had recently called 'the most prostituted in the world', seized on the word 'vermin'. Thus began what Bevan's biographer describes as 'that awkward week'.

In the course of that week Attlee sent Bevan a letter in his own hand. The outer envelope was marked 'Strictly Personal'. Inside was another envelope inscribed: 'To be opened by the Minister only. No action till he calls for his secret papers.' The letter read:

My dear Aneurin,

I have received a great deal of criticism of the passage in your speech in which you describe the Conservatives as vermin, including a good deal from our own party.

It was, I think, singularly ill-timed. It had been agreed that we wished to give the new Social Security Scheme as good a send-off as possible and to this end I made a *non*-polemical broadcast. Your speech cut right across this. I have myself done as much as I could to point out the injustice of the attacks made upon you for your handling of the doctors, pointing out the difficulties experienced by your predecessors of various political colours in dealing with the profession. You had won a victory in obtaining their tardy co-operation, but these unfortunate remarks enable the doctors to stage a come-back and have given the general public the impression that there was more in their case than they had supposed.

This is, I think, a great pity because without doing any good it has drawn attention away from the excellent work you have done over the Health Bill. Please, be a bit more careful in your own interest.

Yours ever

Clem

Attlee kept a careful eye on Bevan for the rest of the year. In November Bevan planned to address the Automobile Workers of America. He consulted Attlee about this. Attlee told him that he must not do so. Bevan accepted the decision, but wrote to him as follows:

I would not be more exposed than Cripps, Strachey, Bevin and you in the past or Tom Williams now; so you must think I'm more susceptible to high pressure or attack or less acceptable to some sections of the United States public...

I don't ask you to reverse your decision, as a minister visiting the US could not face attacks in the US press if he knew he had unsympathetic colleagues at home. Still I deplore the tendentious grounds for your decision.

Berlin and Bevan made July a worrying month for Attlee but he was able to go off at the end of the month and enjoy his holiday in Ireland. 'We are having a great time out here ...' he wrote to Tom on 4 August. 'Everyone is extremely friendly and hospitable in this country and seems glad to see us. We had a fine welcome in Dublin where I signed a treaty while the family shopped ...' Soon after his return he entered hospital for three weeks. He went in suffering from eczema, but trouble from a duodenal ulcer was soon diagnosed. This made it necessary for him to shed most of his routine duties for the next three months. It was as if the strain of the past years was catching up with him.

In his diary Dalton (now back in the government as Chancellor of the Duchy of Lancaster) recorded his own good health, which he contrasted enthusiastically with the deteriorating health of his four chief colleagues. According to his account, Attlee was concerned about Bevin and Morrison. Bevin was 'alarmist' about Attlee – 'his mind's gone. It isn't eczema he's got, it's shingles ... his nerves aren't right.' Cripps considered Attlee to be in poor health, unfit in every way to lead the party into the next election; he sounded Bevin again about becoming leader, and met the same refusal, with the addition that Bevin said he would in any case not want to take over since the Parliamentary Party did not like *him*, and he did not like *them*. The Labour government was led by sick and harassed men.

Attlee had certainly 'recovered enough', he told Tom on 17 October, 'to carry on at the [Commonwealth Prime Ministers] Conference', though he did not enjoy the ceremonial dinner, 'which involved a good deal of standing about'. He wrote to Tom on 27 October:

> We had the film *Esther Waters* at Chequers the other day and thought it very good. We also had *Hamlet*, but I did not care for it much. It is suprising how one noticed the cuts. . . . A very successful Commonwealth Conference which meant fairly strenuous work for me, but I did not get over tired. I think I am really progressing. We had a dinner of 75 for the PMs at No. 10 which went off very well. . . . We've just started the Session – quite good pageantry. Old Addison [Lord Privy Seal] held the sword erect for 20 minutes or so, not bad for a man of eighty.

III

There was no major task of legislation or of policy confronting Attlee in the remaining months of 1948, but the political atmosphere was tense and combative. The highly controversial bill for the nationalization of iron and steel was introduced at the beginning of the next parliamentary session. There was little evidence of any great enthusiasm in the public, or even in the party as a whole, for the bill, but the Conservatives were already up in arms about it, and the newspapers and the industrialists were campaigning and giving them generous support.

The bill was published on 29 October, and debated in mid-November. The existing Iron and Steel Board, through which previous governments had controlled development and prices, had been wound up a month before as a result of its members – except the union representatives – refusing to continue to serve on it. Three days before the bill was published, Ivor Thomas, Labour MP for the Wrekin, resigned from the Labour Party, saying that the bill was 'dogma run mad'. It proposed a public corporation which would purchase and control the two thousand firms under the Board, and compensate their stockholders. Vesting day would be 1 May 1950, or within eighteen months from that. When the bill went through its second reading on 17 November, Churchill denounced it as a plot to set up a monopoly by which this industry would be able to 'penetrate and ultimately paralyse every form of free activity'. The Conservative amendment, supported by the Liberals, produced the largest division against the government in the whole of the 1945–50 Parliament (211). The bill then went into the committee stage. Morrison said he would allow no more than thirty-five sittings, since he had no intention of allowing this bill to suffer the 'disgraceful obstruction' encountered by the Gas Bill; it must be back in the House by 17 March. It would be subject to the guillotine. This ultimatum brought more outraged roars from the Opposition. Into this highly charged atmosphere came Attlee's announcement of the Lynskey Tribunal, to examine charges against ministers and officials which had arisen as a result of the Lord Chancellor's investigation into the conduct of the parliamentary secretary to the Board of Trade, John Belcher.

As 1949 opened Attlee's public prestige was high, and his authority over his government widely recognized. On 9 January *The Observer* carried a profile of him, accompanied by a rather grim photograph which made him look like Lenin. The article was well-informed and perceptive; the opening paragraphs reflect the wonderment of many thinking people as they beheld the transformation of a mouselike little man into an outstandingly powerful prime minister.

When Clement Richard Attlee became Prime Minister in 1945, it was commonly assumed that he would prove little more than the nominal head of his Cabinet, a competent and conciliatory chairman; holding office not by reason of positive qualities of his own but as an intermediary between Bevin and Morrison.

Yet he is today the complete master of his Cabinet, and he has quietly carried through changes in Cabinet structure which place in his hand more of the strings of power than have ever before been held by a British Prime Minister in peacetime. Most of his colleagues stand somewhat in awe of him. His prestige with the public has also risen steadily, and stands ahead of that of his Government as a whole . . .

The secret of Attlee's power is often sought in his great integrity. But integrity is not so rare a quality in our political life that its possession, even in a high degree, is sufficient to endow a man with leadership. The secret lies deeper. Mr Attlee's strength comes from a peculiar form of disciplined independence. Even Sir Stafford Cripps, with his monk's pride in his own asceticism, needs the sustenance of a few disciples. Attlee is completely self-sustained. He is not afflicted by unpopularity. He is, in fundamental decisions, even unaffected by the approval or disapproval of intimates, of whom indeed he has few.

Mr Attlee's appearance has been compared to that of Lenin. Wild as the comparison may seem, it is nevertheless true that he has something of that quality of private decision, that ability to follow his own analysis of events to its logical conclusion, unperturbed by the feelings of those around him, unperturbed, also, by his own feelings, fears, or vanities, that Lenin possessed.

But a politician, to manœuvre, also needs tactical skill and a quiet nimbleness. Here, again, Attlee is surprisingly well-equipped. He has successfully ridden every revolt in his party, chiefly by remarkable timing – by knowing when to remain quiescent and when to bring the issue to a climax. Those who have challenged him are never quite sure just how they were defeated. Moreover, he has, to a degree equalled only by Bevin, among the Labour leaders, an almost instinctive awareness of the reactions of the rank and file of his party and of the country at large.

In February Gollancz published (at 7s 6d) a new edition of Attlee's 1937 book, under the title *The Labour Party in Perspective – and Twelve Years Later*. A brief foreword by Attlee made only two points: his unshaken belief in the principles of democratic socialism as he had described them, and the fact that: 'The progress of events since the war has sharpened the distinction which I drew between the socialism of the British Labour Party and the totalitarianism of the Communists.'

Attlee's first major contribution in Parliament in 1949 was to deal with the findings of the Lynskey Tribunal, whose report had been published in January. The Conservatives had hoped to draw some blood. The report, however, found no evidence to support rumours of money paid to ministers or civil servants, and the two men over whom some suspicion hung had resigned. All other charges were dismissed. Attlee made a wise speech in which he showed that the high reputation of the Civil Service, far from having suffered from the inquiry, stood higher than ever as a result of it. The Conservatives responded well. They put away their weapons, and welcomed and endorsed the Prime Minister's statement. Belcher's resignation speech was dignified: the gist of it was that he had been foolish but not dishonest. In a letter to Tom on 7 February, Attlee wrote:

> The Lynskey Tribunal debate passed off all right. On the whole, distressing as the affair has been, it may do some good by stopping the constant campaign of whispering and innuendo that goes on in the constituencies with the active complicity of the Tory party. Winston behaved very well in the Debate.

IV

The spring of 1949 was a good time for Attlee, and the last of the good times for the Labour government. He wrote to Tom: 'We had a pleasant quiet Easter at Chequers.... On Saturday we all went to Bristol ... we lunched in a lovely wood carpeted with anemones, primroses and blue-bells. I've never seen the country more beautiful.... I'm busy seeing PMs today and tomorrow' – a somewhat casual way of referring to the Commonwealth Prime Ministers' Conference of 1949.

428

The beginnings of the government's difficulties could be seen in the budget which Cripps presented on 6 April. He announced that while 1948 had been a year of progress, the country was now faced with a serious and 'baffling' problem – the dollar gap. Somehow this must be bridged by 1952. Internationally there was a pressing need to keep inflation at bay. More investment was required, and this must come from public revenue surpluses and private savings. There had been a considerable redistribution of wealth; now, new wealth must be created, and to this end the provision of more social services must be slowed down. The wage and price stabilization policy would have to be continued for at least another year.

The Labour Party was disappointed, the trade unions bitterly so. There was some truth, as many Labour MPs said, in Oliver Stanley's comment on it, in a budget broadcast on behalf of the Conservative Party, that it was 'the end of an era of socialist policy and socialist propaganda'. Even Attlee admitted that there had been a certain amount of dissatisfaction with this budget. He blamed the press for this – the newspapers had given publicity to 'unwarranted suggestions of further benefits and reliefs of taxation, designed, by raising false hopes, to create alarm and despondency in Labour ranks'.

In the next few days the results of the county council elections came in. In many parts of the country the Labour Party took some punishment, and the Conservatives gained nearly everywhere. The most striking result was in London. The London County Council had been made up of ninety Labour members, twenty-eight Conservatives, two Liberals and two Communists. The new council consisted of sixty-four Conservatives, sixty-four Labour and one Liberal. The London Labour Party complained that: 'London has temporarily been bewitched by the Tories, who dragged national issues into county elections.' Labour's policy statement for the next election, *Labour Believes in Britain*, published on 12 April, could hardly have appeared at a less propitious moment. The municipal council elections were held in May, and again the honours went to the Conservatives.

The shadow of the budget and the local election results hung over the Labour Party conference which opened at Blackpool on 6 June 1949. The delegates would in any event have been in the mood for recrimination. For weeks it had been clear that the conference would be dominated by the argument between Morrison and Bevan, between 'consolidation' and 'advance'; *Labour Believes in Britain* had come down very much on the side of Morrison. The struggle had continued through the winter of 1948/9. Bevan ardently advocated 'advance'. He publicly pressed three points: there must be more nationalization; Tory attacks on the conduct of the nationalized industries by the Labour Party must be countered by denunciations of the inefficiencies and iniquities of private industry; the Labour Party must put forward a list of industries to be nationalized – for instance, chemicals and shipbuilding. If the party would not put its weight behind this three-point programme, said Bevan, it would lose the next election. Morrison, having seen the results of the local government elections, was more than ever convinced that the party's policy must be 'consolidation'. Concerned to woo and maintain the middle-class vote, the last thing he wanted the Labour Party to announce was a 'shopping list' of industries it proposed to bring into public ownership.

Bevan's speech was well conceived. He reduced to the minimum the risk of appearing to attack his colleagues, and declared an optimism about the future of the party which he almost certainly did not feel. At this very moment, according to his biographer, he was considering resigning from the government after the Steel Bill, the last major public ownership measure to which the government was committed, had reached the Statute Book. His speech appealed to the idealism, vision and sense of direction of the Labour Movement. Morrison's speech, presenting the draft of *Labour Believes in Britain*, did not soar into the heights of socialist idealism, but it roused the party for the next election. He too was received with enthusiasm. While describing the need for 'consolidation' – on practical not ideological grounds – he pointed out the passage in the policy document which dealt with the next steps towards a socialist Britain. He adumbrated a notion of what later would be described as 'a mixed economy'. He also introduced, carefully, the idea of retreat from a commitment to nationalization in principle to a pragmatic approach to the extension of public ownership.

The conference was probably the peak of Attlee's success as the leader of his party. The achievements of the government on the domestic front since 1945, the relative stability of foreign affairs marked by the ending of the Berlin blockade, and, above all, Indian independence, combined to give him a prestige he had never had before, and would not have again. Presiding at the conference, Jim Griffiths, listing the merits of the Attlee government to date, chose to regard Attlee's handling of India as its triumph:

> In the Commonwealth Britain has carried through a transformation unprecedented in the history of civilization. I think future generations may well consider our Government's handling of the Indian problem as the greatest of all its many contributions to world progress. Not least of the credit goes to our Prime Minister, Clem Attlee.

Attlee gave all the credit to the team. The following day, in his parliamentary report, he pointed out how unusual it was for a government to produce a clearly defined plan and policy for its work during the lifetime of a Parliament, and for it to carry out that plan:

> In former days governments that I have known, if they introduced just one item of our social programme, would have plumed themselves on being a great reform government. A single effort would have completely exhausted them. But we have in this year completed this great programme. National Insurance and Industrial Injuries Schemes have come into full operation, the National Health Service has been launched...

He went on to refer to the continuous process of raising the standard of the less well-to-do and reducing excessive claims by the wealthy. 'Last year has seen some wonderful advances in productivity.' In foreign affairs Bevin was reaping the reward of his patient diplomacy with Western Union, the Atlantic Pact, the Council of Europe, the OEEC (Organization for European Economic Cooperation), and the lifting of the Berlin blockade. Attlee ended: 'The moral for us is plain: to carry on and preserve our unity.'

The conference ended with a noticeable absence of acrimony. Dalton was surprised by the absence of controversy over foreign affairs or in the debate on the draft manifesto. Indeed, he was worried. After the conference he told Attlee that Morrison's idea of having no new socialization measures in the next Parliament would 'never do'. 'Attlee, as always, appeared to agree.' Dalton should have learned by then that a grunt from Attlee did not mean agreement but, probably, 'your opinion noted'. The results of the local elections and the prospect of a coming general election had combined to sober and quieten potential rebels, who also remembered Attlee's firm handling of the 'Nenni-goats'. His appeal for unity had been delivered from unprecedented strength, and the would-be dissidents were at their weakest. An attempt to allow two expelled MPs, Zilliacus and Solley, to come to the conference and state their case was decisively outvoted. The conference was not in the mood to encourage expostulations on the left, and it broke up on a rare, if unexciting, note of harmony. It was as well for the government's standing with the country, for two strike threats were already looming: on the railways and in the docks. And the devaluation crisis lay ahead.

V

There was a lull before the storm. Attlee took advantage of it. Apart from an almost nonchalant reference to the coming financial crisis, his letters to Tom gave no hint of the impending crises:

> Chequers is looking very lovely just now. Yesterday was the finest June day for years. Vi is a good deal better and is spending a good deal of time

431

just now at Wimbledon. I saw some very good tennis on Saturday besides looking in for an hour at the Test Match...

July looks like being a busy month, especially with this dollar trouble becoming acute again.

I had a good time at Univ with Vio and Flip for the septcentenary Ball. Quite reminiscent of old days. Vio and I returned to town by about 3 am but Flippy danced on till 6.30 staying the night at the Master's lodgings.

To assess the threats of the looming strikes, Attlee called a special meeting of ministers. The breakdown of negotiations over railwaymen's wages led to a complete stoppage on 5 June, followed by intermittent strikes. The Minister of Labour, George Isaacs, refused to intervene until the threat of a national strike was lifted, and the NUR finally accepted the government's offer of a conciliation board. The dock strikes presented even graver problems, not least because the government was convinced that Communists had inspired them. In May British dockers struck, unofficially, in sympathy with the Communist-led Canadian Seamen's Union, which was in rivalry with the Canadian Seafarers' Union. Attlee set up a special Cabinet committee, with himself in the chair, which met first on 23 May. A few days later the government invoked Defence Regulation 1304, and used troops to unload fruit and refrigerated food at Avonmouth. Although the Canadian dispute was settled in late June, the use of troops had caused the British strikes to spread.

Attlee began to prepare public opinion. On 3 July he told a crowd of 12,000 at a Labour rally in Manchester that the only people who gained from unofficial strikes were 'Communist hypocrites who are instruments of an alien dictatorship'. He followed this up with a speech in the House in which he carefully reminded the dockers of what had been done for them by the Labour government, and particularly by Ernest Bevin. Troops went into London docks to move food on 7 July, provoking more strikes. By 8 July, 10,000 men were out and 100 ships idle. That day the government announced that unless work was resumed a state of national emergency would be declared. The King signed the declaration on 11 July 1949. As the Attlee Committee put it to the Cabinet: 'The moral effect of proclaiming an emergency would be considerable, not least in supporting the dockers still at work, and those of the strikers who were out only because of their almost pathological fear of being called "black-leg".' The number of men on strike rose to more than 15,000. Attlee prepared to draft 35,000 men to keep the docks in London moving. But reason was rapidly prevailing. Two weeks later the dockers voted to resume work, and went back three days later. By the end of July the docks were quiet.

Lord Annan, Chief Whip in the House of Lords, and also chairman of the National Dock Board and an old ally of Attlee in early East End days, was a casualty of Attlee's determination to get the strike over quickly, which meant getting it over sensibly. Charlie Annan had said that the government would have 'gone crazy' if it gave in to the dockers' demands – one of which was that he should be made to resign from the Dock Board. The government repudiated his statement, and Attlee asked him to resign. Annan refused. Attlee immediately sacked him from both his posts: 'I sacked him as Chairman of the Dock Board because it was clear he was making irresponsible statements. I sacked him from the Government because he was being disloyal.'

VI

The dock strike marked the beginning of the descent into a trough of troubles. Not only had it struck at exports at the worst possible moment; it had shown that the government had lost its grip on industrial relations. The record of hours lost in stoppages, good in the first few months of the year, now looked very bad. The Conservatives made capital out of the government's failure to communicate with workers and union leaders. The press became extremely critical. The circumstances in which the government had now to confront the financial crisis could not have been less propitious.

Though the shortage of dollars was at the heart of the financial crisis of 1949, and the issue was whether or not to devalue, the basic trouble was the long-term economic problem. Britain's strength, such as it was, depended on Marshall Aid, and Cripps in his April budget warned that the economy must be made self-reliant before American support came to an end in 1952. Meanwhile the welfare state, the rearmament programme and the Berlin Airlift had to be paid for, from resources much diminished by inflation and by the loss of exports due to the strikes. What Attlee described as 'dollar trouble' was discussed by the government's Economic Planning Committee in mid-June. The Chancellor, for the first time, presented his colleagues with a black prospect. Gold and dollar reserves were going down; sterling could shortly be in danger. According to Dalton, Attlee said to him as the meeting broke up, '1931 all over again.'

By the end of the month the government faced another problem. The OEEC, meeting in Brussels, accepted a Belgian suggestion that the drawing rights of Marshall Plan debtors should be freely convertible into dollars, an arrangement which would benefit countries which had a production surplus to export, but not Britain, where exports were low, and where imports were high. Cripps was only able to secure a limitation of convertibility to 25 per cent of the drawing right. Britain could only hope that the Sterling Area would be able to stand the dollar losses.

Events in Brussels made it clear to the British public that they were heading for another economic crisis. A few days later Cripps told the House that the dollar deficit for the second quarter of the year was nearly double that of the first. It was clear that the figure for 1948 had been good because of American expansion; in 1949 the Americans were in recession. Meanwhile newspaper reports indicated that there was a growing feeling in the United States that the Labour government's 'socialist policies' were responsible for Britain's economic problems, and that devaluation of the pound was now essential.

In Britain, the Conservatives, who had entitled their manifesto for the election *The Right Road for Britain*, made their own contribution. Speaking on the day their tract appeared, Churchill claimed: 'Reckless expenditure at home and abroad has been the main cause of our country's difficulties.' The Labour government had hoped to secure more American sympathy and cooperation by attributing some at any rate of Britain's current difficulties to the hard times the British people had experienced in the thirties, to the need for expenditure on reform and rehabilitation, and to the economic demands of the war. Churchill's speech took much of the wind out of these sails. He attacked as 'falsehoods' the claims that before 1945 Britain was 'a backward and miserable country'. The socialist government *after* 1945 had squandered overseas assets. The taxes they demanded were higher than anything required in the war. The 'new cataract of State monopolies' had done nothing but damage to the economy. The Steel Bill was 'a wanton act of party malice'. He ended his speech with a warning about the relation of socialism to communism, along the lines of his egregious broadcast in the election campaign of 1945. Attlee fought back vigorously: 'I am afraid that nowadays the strength of Mr Churchill's language is in inverse proportion to his knowledge of the subjects. It is unfortunate that his words are taken at their face value in other countries. They don't realise that it is just Winnie's way ...' Attlee had no difficulty in refuting these charges, and he demolished some of the alleged facts. But Churchill was widely read and quoted in America, and Attlee was not.

The Cabinet was divided. Cripps and Dalton, backed by advice from the City and the Bank of England, wished to impose a drastically tightened monetary policy, with higher interest rates and cuts in subsidies; they were against devaluing the pound. Morrison opposed Cripps. Possibly because he had his eye on the elections, he was against cuts in food subsidies, and thought that devaluation might perhaps be preferable. Gaitskell assured Cripps and Dalton that devaluation was 'absolutely essential, the only way out', and the sooner the better, early September at latest. During August, Dalton changed his mind in favour of devaluation; Wilson at the Board of Trade had also been converted.

Cripps was now on the sideline; he left for medical treatment in Switzerland on 18 July, and Attlee took charge of economic policy in his absence.

The financial situation precipitated discussion among Cabinet ministers about the timing of a general election. On 19 July Attlee held a meeting with Morrison, Bevin, Bevan, Dalton and the Chief Whip. Cripps, from his Zürich clinic, made his contribution in a letter suggesting an immediate election. Bevan was strongly in favour of an early election: the legislative programme was coming to an end, and after that there was nothing planned which would create a new drive. Bevin and Dalton thought that they must go to the country in February at the latest – certainly before the next budget. Morrison, usually the most incisive of them in such discussions, seemed undecided. Attlee was opposed to an immediate election, and thought that Cripps would not have been so precipitate if he had not been ill. He thought that the election should take place later rather than sooner but before March.

Outside the Cabinet, Labour leaders discussed the pros and cons of an early election. Morgan Phillips, the party secretary, reported that a number of ministers were in favour of an early election. The dollar gap would persist, in spite of cuts in expenditure. The American recession looked like continuing for some time, which would mean further cuts and higher unemployment, a greater shortage of housing, and a general tightening of belts. Meanwhile, polls showed that whereas two months previously the Conservatives had been leading 47 to 42, Labour's position had improved to 45–45, due to derationing of sweets and milk, plenty of fruit and good weather. Against an early election was the fact that Labour's 'best election months' had been in spring and early summer. There was, too, a feeling in the party that there should be no election until 1950, so as to get the Parliament Bill and steel nationalization on to the Statute Book. Attlee also heard from Gaitskell, who favoured a November election, as did his friend Douglas Jay, now Economic Secretary to the Treasury.

Public concern about the financial crisis brought rumours of changes in the leadership. In August the popular weekly *Cavalcade*, in the first of a series of 'Politicameos', prophesied that Attlee would soon go:

> Two qualities took Attlee to the top: loyalty and lack of colour. He couldn't be disloyal if he tried, as all who have worked with him, including Winston Churchill, well know. Ramsay MacDonald, whom Attlee succeeded, killed Labour's trust in colourful personalities for a long time to come.
>
> I believe that Clem Attlee is on the way out. He has discharged his task of keeping the Labour Party's seat warm for a leader a bit broader on the beam all round, a more Falstaffian type who can back-slap and baby the Party along a broader political road than the strait and narrow path prescribed by the London School of Economics.

Such prognostications had no affect upon their subject. Attlee took advantage of the Trades Union Congress at Bridlington to make a major speech. He avoided giving a dissertation on the country's financial situation, for which he was much criticized by the Opposition and the press, and confined himself to warnings and exhortations addressed to the workers. He spoke bluntly of the danger of continuous wage increases, particularly when their object was to maintain differentials:

> A justifiable advance in wages for an underpaid section of the workers results in demands from those who have enjoyed higher wages to have an advance because they desire to maintain the same differential between themselves and the lower paid workers. In my view this is bad economics and bad social morality. I stress the point of social morality because our Labour Movement has an ethical basis. We are trying to get away from the old scramble for competitive advantages. As we move into a juster social order there is need for a higher conception of social obligation.

His address to the TUC was not well received by the press. *The Times* complained that he did not use the occasion 'for the first full-dress pronouncement on the national emergency since Parliament rose a month ago'. But Attlee was not perturbed. A few days later he wrote to Tom:

> Vio and I had a very good visit to the TUC at Bridlington where they gave us a fine reception. The papers all seemed to suggest that I should have made some epoch-making announcement, but this would obviously have been stupid with Stafford and Ernie in the midst of negotiations.
> I am steadily rereading Gibbon and am now in the seventh volume dealing with Justinian to whom, I think, the author does insufficient justice.

In late July 1949 Attlee was receiving a stream of advice about devaluation. In spite of the resistance of Cripps and Bevin, Attlee had decided it was the right course. He had been much influenced by Gaitskell, who, in turn, had been persuaded by Jay. These two carried great weight with Attlee: he had admired Gaitskell's work at the time of the fuel crisis, and he thought highly of Jay, who had been right about the likelihood of a coal shortage in 1947 when Shinwell had been wrong. The advice of Gaitskell and Jay did something to make up for Attlee's lack of economic expertise. Like most of the Cabinet, including Cripps, Attlee was reluctant to devalue sterling and reluctant to undertake the reductions in public expenditure which the Treasury and the Bank of England insisted were an essential accompaniment to devaluation. Attlee's own view, which only Jay was able to modify, was that the external pressure on sterling, leading to the need to devalue, was quite unrelated to domestic policies; he described the alternative view, favoured by the Treasury, the Bank of England and the American government, as 'nineteenth-century economics'. Jay and Gaitskell brought him round. In the last days of July, Attlee decided to inform Cripps that the government should agree to devaluation. Jay, as Economic Secretary to the Treasury, drafted the letter; Attlee signed it, and it was sent to Cripps at the Zürich clinic. 'All of us are now agreed,' said Attlee, 'including the responsible officials, that it is a necessary step.' The Treasury began to plan for immediate devaluation, giving it the codeword 'Operation Rose'.

Cripps returned to London on 18 August. Attlee called a meeting of the full Cabinet ten days later. Cripps resisted devaluation to the last minute, but Attlee made it clear, more by silence than by sound, that the decision was as good as made. 'Opinion,' he said, in opening the discussion, 'has hardened in favour of devaluation.' This would not solve the country's underlying long-term economic problem, but it was an essential step towards so doing. Cripps and Bevin left for the United States at once. The most important discussions with the Americans took place in early September. A key question was whether the new rate should be 3 dollars to the pound or 2.80. The Treasury advisers favoured the lower rate – it would reduce the risk of further devaluation at a future date. The new rate was communicated to London on 12 September. As well as the devaluation agreement the government had obtained a number of concessions, such as the promise of lower US tariffs, simpler customs procedures, more American investment abroad – particularly in undeveloped areas – and, above all, the US Treasury's agreement to an alteration in the terms of Marshall Aid which would enable Britain to buy Canadian wheat with American dollars. In a broadcast on 18 September 1949, Cripps duly announced that the exchange rate with the dollar would be reduced from 4.03 to 2.80.

Parliament was recalled, and asembled on 27 September. Cripps made the best of an uncomfortable situation, and was attacked by Oliver Stanley and Churchill. Churchill's general indictment of the government was answered in a brilliant speech by Aneurin Bevan – 'I welcome this opportunity of pricking the bloated bladder of lies with the poniard of truth. . . . A reason why [Churchill] moves so gracefully across the pages of history is because he carries a light weight of fact.' Attlee wound up the debate for the government. He referred to Aneurin Bevan's 'brilliant reply' to Churchill, then he turned to Churchill's personal criticisms of Cripps. Churchill had accused Cripps of continually misleading the country by repeated denials in August that there would be devaluation. Knowing that Cripps had taken this very badly, Attlee assailed Churchill for his 'very bitter personal attack' on the Chancellor's honesty and integrity. 'I resent this, and I think most people in this country will resent it.' Churchill, he said:

can be a very big man or a very small man. I am always sorry, as one who has seen him in great and generous moods, when he descends to the kind of pettiness and meanness which he displayed yesterday. It did not injure [Cripps], but it will devalue Churchill.

Running through all [Churchill's] excursions into history was just one thread: whenever there was a good government, it was a government of which he was a member. It was rather a complacent recital. . . . His Amendment and his Speech were alike destitute of any constructive policy at all. His only suggestion is, Vote for Me. It is 1945 all over again. It is the same appeal that failed so decisively then. It is the same appeal which has failed at every by-election even when the circus went round.

He ended by castigating the Opposition for damaging Britain's economic prospects, and helping to intensify the crisis, by irresponsible criticism. 'There is confidence in this country abroad and at home ... the right honourable gentleman has found on 32 occasions [by-elections] that there is no confidence in *him*.'

Attlee was not happy about the extent to which he had to defend Cripps, but knew that Cripps had been depressed by the attacks on his integrity. 'Stafford was much too sensitive to that kind of thing.' He knew that Cripps's health was now so weakened that his days in politics might be numbered, and he already had his eye on a replacement – Gaitskell, whose calibre as an economic counsellor had been revealed by the discussions about devaluation.

The Cabinet was now faced by the political problems entailed by devaluation, the solutions of which would be unpopular with Labour as well as Conservative voters. Attlee called another meeting for 12 October to discuss the timing of an election. Bevin, Bevan and Dalton held to the views they had given in July, but this time Morrison firmly opposed an election in the short term because it could create the impression that the government was running away from its responsibilities. Morrison's view was that the government must stand by its policies, however unpopular, fight on through the winter, and go to the country in February. Attlee agreed, and imposed his view with unusual firmness. The following day he called a meeting of the full Cabinet. It was one of those Cabinet meetings at which Attlee put the matter in a manner which did not encourage discussion. The same afternoon Attlee announced publicly that there would be no election in 1949.

The next two weeks were very difficult for Attlee. Alexander threatened to resign if there were cuts in defence, Bevan was threatening to resign if there were cuts in the social services, and Cripps, his nerves frayed by insomnia, seemed, as Attlee said, 'ready to resign about anything'. Even Ernest Bevin spoke of going if defence suffered damage, though Attlee thought later that this was to provide countervailing strength against Bevan. There were some unhappy and enervating discussions before the Cabinet met on 21 October and agreed the programme. Within an hour or two of the programme being agreed in Cabinet, Bevan wrote to protest against the cuts in housing and the leniency to the 'gorged and swollen defence estimates'. Attlee replied tersely the same evening: 'I can't agree with your comparison between cuts in different services.... It is no use talking of "gorged and swollen defence estimates...", these adjectives are not based on knowledge.' Two days later Morrison suggested an inquiry into the health services, such as had 'produced great savings without loss of efficiency' in the information services. Attlee replied: 'I am not sure if Health and Information Services are on all fours. I enclose copy of letter from Aneurin. If you still think an enquiry desirable, we might discuss the best approach.' Morrison replied that he did. 'When I was considering a similar enquiry into the Information Services, I found I was too closely involved to make a detached view. The same applies with the Health Service.' He then sent Morrison's memorandum to Bevan, and had a chat with each of them. That was the end of the matter: Bevan had no intentions of pressing his requests if it meant that other ministers would scrutinize *his* department. Here was Attlee's Cabinet management at its best.

On 26 October Attlee announced the cuts in the House of Commons. There would be cuts in defence; economies in government departments, and various trimmings. Of more concern to Labour backbenchers were increases in some food prices, reduction of agricultural subsidies, a reduction of the housing target by 25,000 dwellings a year and, most important of all because of what it symbolized, a charge of up to a shilling on prescriptions under the Health Service. He concluded his statement with the warning that devaluation might be the last opportunity of restoring the country's position as a trading nation without a drastic lowering of the whole standard of living. The Labour Party sat in silence. The announcement of the cuts received a bad press. That night Attlee made a broadcast. His conclusion was more cheerful than the one which he expressed in the House: 'We have a great opportunity to put things right.' It was not one of his best broadcasts: comment for and against was cool. Attlee's letter to Tom, dated 26 October, has more political content than usual, and consequently shows more than most of these communications how little he was affected by a crisis:

> I am so sorry that I missed writing to you for your birthday. The fact is that I was very full up with work all last week so here are belated good wishes ...
> The Press has been particularly mendacious the last fortnight working up excitement in order to make out that what we were doing would be insufficient. It is purely a political ramp. I am amused to find that the

American press take the line that we have done the right amount. Our Party has taken everything very well. The whole thing is in great contrast to the 1931 business. I think the Party and the electorate have learned a lot since then.

I had not expected Johnny Clynes's death as I had gathered he was fairly well.... He was the last survivor of the 1906 Labour Party and I think after Arthur Henderson the best in his quiet way.

I've now got to get together a few notes for winding up the debate tomorrow.

In the parliamentary debate on the cuts Churchill, well aware of the Cabinet dispute over prescription charges, jeered at Attlee's 'submissive demeanour and docility – unbecoming in one holding such power and responsibility', and contrasted it with Bevan's moral leadership of the socialist cause. Attlee replied with a cut at Sir John Anderson, who had embarrassed many Tories by publicly advocating deflation.:

> I must say I was reminded of an incident in history. [Churchill], who is well versed in history, will remember it. It is the one in which the Carthaginians employed a heavy, sagacious and most honourable animal called the elephant, but unfortunately the elephant ran the wrong way and disordered the ranks.

He denounced the Tories who would attempt to solve the country's economic problem by throwing people on the dole and reducing the standard of living as they had done in the thirties, dividing as well as impoverishing a people whom the Labour government had done much to unite as well as to rehabilitate. What was regarded by all as a critical moment in the country's fortunes required not partisan shouting but a united effort to improve the country's position. Attlee was by now being widely attacked, in the press and in Parliament, for the flatness of his public pronouncements about the crisis. Commenting on his speech at the Guildhall in early November the *Daily Telegraph*, naturally unfavourable, observed that: 'It really is a pity that Mr Attlee so restrained himself last night. To those waiting for understanding and inspiration his speech will be cold comfort.'

Late November brought some cheering news, and welcome support for Attlee's assertion in the debate on cuts that 'the Country's response has been very good'; The TUC General Council announced eight recommendations on a wages policy to meet the crisis. 'An act of genuine courageous leadership,' said Attlee. It was an achievement for which he could claim some credit. Eden spoke of 'sincere respect' for the efforts which had produced the TUC's contribution, referring in particular to Attlee's address to the TUC at Bridlington.

November also saw some settlement of the wearing wrangle over the Steel Bill – and the Parliament Bill, whose provisions for limiting the powers of the House of Lords would be required in order to get the Steel Bill passed. As far back as July the Lords had refused to consider lifting their veto on the bill until after the next general election. There were some angry references to this, especially by Bevan, over the next three months, but in mid-November the Minister of Supply, George Strauss, announced that for practical reasons – recruitment of personnel, for instance – it would be desirable to postpone investiture day – transfer of ownership – until after the next election. This undertaking, he thought, would meet the requirements of their lordships. It did. The Lords had moved their amendment to postpone vesting day from 1 May 1950 until January 1951 in the hope of an election intervening, which might give the Tories a majority in the House, and power to expunge the bill. Attlee therefore agreed that October 1950 would now be the first permitted date for the establishment of the new Steel Corporation, and that the Act would not be put into effect until 1 January 1951. Churchill accepted this arrangement, but made it clear that if the Conservatives won the election, the bill would be removed from the Statute Book. Steel denationalization therefore became an election issue. The Parliament Bill was read in the Commons for the third time on 14 November, and once again was rejected by the Lords. It passed into law under the Parliament Act of 1911.

Attlee called another meeting of senior ministers to discuss the timing of an election. The effective choice was between February and June 1950. Parliament was to be prorogued on 16 December. The Christmas holidays were in sight. Apart from Morrison, who feared the effects of February weather on the Labour turnout, all his colleagues favoured February. Cripps refused to consider another budget until after an election. Bevin was unwell but he sent a message to say he would accept whatever they decided and that anyway he was 'no politician'. Attlee unhesitatingly supported Cripps. The government would go to the country in February.

25

Struggling On, 1950

Nineteen hundred and fifty was the Labour Party's jubilee. Though its fiftieth birthday did not fall until 28 February, from the beginning of the year the party leaders made public speeches citing the list of great achievements – while privately wondering how the party would fare in the imminent general election. On the whole they felt optimistic. The 1949 local elections had inflicted damage, but not one of thirty-five by-elections had been lost since the general election of 1945. The senior men knew that they had called the election not because the Opposition had succeeded in forcing it but because Attlee had accepted Cripps's view that it would be politically irresponsible to attempt another budget before obtaining another mandate. Tired as some of them were, the leaders expected to win the coming election with a small but working majority.

Attlee had time to celebrate his birthday – among his mail was a notice of his election to the Athenaeum – and then he flew to India for a three-day visit as Nehru's guest. He returned to find trade union leaders restive about a speech by Morrison on 7 January which bluntly declared that the country could not afford further improvements in the standard of living. A special conference of trade union executives assembled on 12 January and voted to support the government's wage stabilization policy, but only by 657,000 votes in a total of eight million cast. The election campaign, described by Churchill as 'demure' and 'sedate' – though Cripps complained of Churchill's 'guttersnipe politics' and 'irresponsible vulgarity' – was, in terms of issues, predictable. The Labour Party proclaimed its achievements and warned that the return of the Tories would mean the return of the dole. The Tories complained that the government's incompetence and enslavement to socialist dogma was dragging down the country into bankruptcy and serfdom. There was a degree of division in the Labour's appeal. Morrison tried hard to retain the middle-class vote and also to woo the women's; Bevan frequently sniped at the bourgeois, and called one woman heckler 'a shrill-voiced virago'. The Labour Party election manifesto, *Let Us Win Through Together*, was a condensed version of *Labour Believes in Britain*. It was accompanied by another document which proposed nationalization of sugar, cement, meat distribution and chemical production, and the nationalization of industrial assurance.

The Conservatives complained that the Labour government had ignored the nation's real economic problem, and had boasted about its alleged successes without mentioning the country's dependence on Marshall Aid, which they were squandering on political schemes for which it was never intended. The Tories attacked nationalization, in principle and for its ruinous effect on British industry – 'We shall bring nationalization to a full stop here and now.' The Liberals put 475 candidates into the field – the biggest team they had fielded since 1929 – and as a result the Conservatives stood to lose much more than Labour did. Even so the campaign was relatively quiet, a contest between two sets of party managers and front benchers. News that the turnout broke the existing record – 84 per cent against 74 per cent in 1945 – came as a great surprise. It was the last general election in which the hustings played the dominant part. The age of television politics was in its infancy. On his main tour around the country Attlee spoke to more than 100,000 people from the platform.

He made this 1,300-mile tour in his 14 hp Humber, driven by Vi. Newspapermen reported that he left London looking cheerful – 'rather relieved-looking,' said one – another said he looked 'ten years younger since the election decision had been reached.... Damn it, he's almost jaunty.' He made thirty-four speeches, and was not seen to use a note. He took five-minute cat-naps in the car, and between meetings regaled the accompanying reporters with terse observations about local history and geography. To save his voice he gave up his pipe by day, filling it only for one smoke after the final meeting of the evening. They lunched at convenient hotels: he had a glass of cider, and Vi drank water. Their joint luggage consisted of one suitcase and a cardboard box containing Vi's travelling iron. His meetings, most of them in marginal constituencies, were exceptionally well attended, especially those in the north and midlands. In the market, at Birmingham, there were 15,000 people. He was occasionally greeted with faint cries of 'vermin', but there was little heckling. They averaged seven public meetings a day. Typical was – from his notes:

11 am	West Bromwich
noon	Wolverhampton
1.15	Walsall

3.30   Lichfield
6.30   Stoke
8.15   Burton
9.00   Derby
I then had the rest of the day free to deal with official business with my Secretary...

The picture drawn of him by the press differed in many respects from that of 1945. As prime minister he 'has developed a strong vein of ruthlessness.... He has been a most formidable sacker of men, firing more Ministerial colleagues than almost any other Prime Minister.' As well as strength of character and immense physical stamina, he was reported to have two other strong suits: 'He is free from the trammels of trade union politics in a Government torn between two loyalties' and 'He is a man of conventional education and cultural background in a Government largely lacking in these assets.' It was agreed that he lacked any kind of glamour. 'Mr Attlee's career has been as devoid of colour as the speeches he slowly types with two fingers.' The alleged lack of charisma may have contributed to his success. 'Clement Attlee's very lack of "colourful" personality has been a strength at a time when bombast and prejudice, class arrogance and ignorance, have flooded through the corridors into Whitehall.' Above all, he had displayed the virtue of self-control, particularly when there was heavy pressure on his government. 'He often works 15 hours a day and yet finds time for relaxation, which he gets from attending a children's matinée at a time of crisis, or some other similar inheritance from his social worker days. He is able to keep working and cool in action, if irritable in diction.' Coming from national newspapers committed to support of the Conservative Party, such observations indicated that he had made a kind of mark.

He introduced what was to be a recurrent theme of his campaign at Watford where he started his tour. The British 'are not a down-hearted people – those who talk as if we were make me tired'. Churchill had already opened his campaign at Cardiff, with what Attlee called 'wild whirling words, wild accusations of extravagance and wanton waste'. The Labour Party, he said, would stand by their record. 'I am not going to enter into a slanging match with Mr Churchill, because the issues that face us are too important – they should be settled by solid argument and hard thinking.' At Birmingham he played another Labour card: the remarkable by-election record: '35 matches played, 35 won, no draws, no losses – even Aston Villa can't beat that'. At Sheffield he attacked the Communists: 'Communism denies the dignity of the individual, Conservatism ranges the individuals in classes.... We have set no term for the onward march of the people of this country.' For the people of York he reverted to Churchill, who was 'like a cock that crows and thinks it has

produced the dawn – just words of abuse from a master of words wh
now become a slave of words'. At Falkirk he appealed to the idealis
Labour supporters:

> I get rather tired when I hear that you must only appeal to the incentives
> of profit. What got us through [the war] was unselfishness and an appeal to
> the higher instincts of mankind. What is getting us through in these difficult
> days is a far greater sense of responsibility due to the fact that men and
> women feel they have a far greater stake in the country than they ever had
> before.

Attlee gave the party's last radio broadcast on 17 February 1950. On
Cripps's advice he took the place of Morrison, who had wanted to give
the last broadcast to secure his grip on the party machine. Attlee's appeal
was based on a carefully judged attack on Churchill's irresponsible and
misinformed electioneering, and a bid for the support of all who believed
in social justice and orderly progress, and saw what the 1945 Labour
government had achieved:

> The choice before you is clear. During these difficult years Britain by its
> example has done a great service. We have shown that orderly planning
> and freedom are not incompatible. We have confirmed faith in democracy
> by the example of a Government that has carried out its promises.

Polling day began with blue skies but ended in pouring rain. This does
not seem to have affected the issue greatly, since Labour increased its
total vote by over a million and a quarter, and established a record.
Labour won a majority of all votes cast, nearly 3 per cent more than the
Conservatives, but many of them were 'wasted' in impregnably safe seats.
Over the country as a whole the swing to the Tories was 3.3 per cent.
Attlee, standing at his new constituency at West Walthamstow, had three
opponents – a Conservative, a Liberal, and a fellow-traveller who had
fought the last election as a Labour member, but had been removed from
the party shortly before this election. The two latter lost their deposits.
The figures were:

Attlee	(Lab)	21,095
Paul	(Con)	8,988
Pim	(Lib)	4,102
Hutchinson	(Ind Lab)	704

Some Labour leaders went to bed convinced that they had won a working
majority, and predicted at least a margin of a hundred if the suburban
and rural seats won in 1945 stayed with them. By the next afternoon the
Conservatives had made ground, and the final result was Labour 315,
Conservatives and allies 298; Labour had a majority of only five over all
other parties in the House.

All three parties were disappointed by the result of the election. Only the Labour Party could point to a verifiable factor which had gone against them – their own Representation of the People Act lost them thirty seats, for one of its consequences was to remove the so-called 'Socialist pocket-boroughs', especially those in London. There have been many explanations of how Labour's vast majority of 146 in 1945 was now reduced to 5. Dalton put much of the blame on the 'shopping-list' of industries and services which would be taken into public ownership and 'our controls and rationing and the continuing lack of houses'. Morrison complained about the effect of Bevan's 'vermin' speech and, like Dalton, of the 'shopping-list'. Attlee himself wrote in his autobiography that redistribution was the 'most important' factor. 'Undoubtedly this most honest attempt to give one vote one value hurt Labour very severely.' Asked by the author in 1959 why he had supported the redistribution of seats in London and the great cities which had been 'depopulated' when, as a result of the government's policies it seemed probable that these areas would be repopulated, Attlee said: 'It was the responsible thing to do at the time; and if you do the right thing at the right time you may have to pay a price for it later.'

Late on Friday the Cabinet met, and after discussion decided to carry on in government. King George's biographer wrote:

> There was some talk of an all-party conference to consider the question of carrying on the King's Government, but the idea was rejected by both the Prime Minister, who was determined to meet the new House of Commons, and by Mr Churchill, who, in a letter to Sir Alan Lascelles [the King's Private Secretary], expressed the view that 'the principle that a new House of Commons has a right to live if it can and should not be destroyed until some fresh issue or situation has arisen to place before the electors, is, I believe, sound.'

Attlee was received by the King at 5.30 pm on 27 February, and agreed to form a government. Writing to Tom on 24 March, Attlee said:

> I don't think I have replied to your last letter, but we have been having a pretty busy time.
> The distasteful business of reconstructing the Government is now through. It always means relegating some good friends to the back benches.

As a result of 'the distasteful business' Shinwell became Minister of Defence, succeeding Alexander, who became Chancellor of the Duchy of Lancaster. Dalton was left in his post as Minister of Town and Country Planning, but he was brought back into the Cabinet. Creech Jones – 'one of my mistakes,' recorded Attlee – was replaced as Colonial Secretary by Jim Griffiths, with a seat in the Cabinet. The most significant appointment was that of Gaitskell, who was made Minister of State for Economic

Affairs. This post, given the deterioration of Cripps's health, meant that Gaitskell was the effective chancellor of the exchequer and, without having Cabinet rank, would frequently speak for the Treasury in the Cabinet. The news of Gaitskell's new job greatly disturbed Aneurin Bevan; he remained Minister of Health.

In March 1950 few expected a government with such a tiny majority to last many weeks, and the effort of survival for twenty months put a severe strain, physical as well as psychological, on the Parliamentary Party and on ministers. This increased with the onset of internal discords more serious than any experienced in the previous administration. Cripps was forced by illness to retire in October 1950; Bevin died in office in March 1951 (by this time he had been moved to the post of Lord Privy Seal) after many months of weakness. Attlee, for all the unruffled calm which he continued to display in his letters to Tom, had a recurrence of his duodenal ulcer, and was consequently in hospital, and by no means at his sharpest, during the crisis which led to the resignations of Bevan, Wilson and Freeman in April 1951. Morrison, miscast at the Foreign Office by Attlee by one of the few mistakes which in retrospect he recorded, mishandled the job and destroyed his standing in the party. Dalton never recovered the status he had enjoyed at the time of his resignation in 1947. Bevan, long before his resignation in 1951, was unhappy and frustrated. When Cripps died Attlee would have liked to give the exchequer to Bevan, but knew that if he did so the reaction overseas and in business circles at home would have been disastrous. Gaitskell got the job, ranking fourth in the Cabinet, above Bevan and his former boss Shinwell. His personality clash with Bevan only added to the party's difficulties.

The difficulties were rendered far more acute by the Korean War, which broke out at the end of June 1950. With most of the country Attlee personally gained greatly in prestige both by giving immediate support to the United Nations defensive action in Korea, and by his flight to see Truman that December, when his frank representation of differences in strategy and international policy undoubtedly helped to prevent the hostilities in Korea escalating into a wider conflict, even possibly into a Third World War. But the effects of the Korean War undermined Britain's economic recovery. It involved the Labour government in desperate attempts to budget for a rearmament programme beyond the country's resources, and these put immense strains on a Labour Party whose unity was already cracking. By October 1951, when the next election was held, the scales of public favour were tipped towards a Conservative Party fresh and self-confident, unencumbered by association with tedious controls and wearing austerity. There were few successes for the tired Labour administration in 1951: Attlee himself would have left office standing far higher in reputation if the Conservatives had secured those few extra seats in February 1950.

I

At the opening of Parliament on 6 March the Gracious Speech indicated that the government proposed only minor measures. Churchill interpreted this to mean that: 'My Government will not introduce legislation in the fulfilment of their election programme because the only mandate they have received from the country is not to do it.' Eden followed with an appeal for a strong and imaginative foreign policy and promised no 'fractious opposition', but asked the government to postpone the operation of the Steel Act. The Conservative amendment to the Address sought to delay the operation of the Steel Act until nine months after the next election. Attlee wound up the debate. He made some play with the fact that sometimes Churchill castigated the Liberals – as during the election campaign when they contested many Tory seats – and sometimes wooed them.

> He has been a very ardent lover of this elderly spinster, the Liberal Party. The elder sister – the National Liberals – was married long ago; she is now deceased. This now is the younger sister, but she is getting on. I can never make out whether the right honourable Member for Woodford is going to play Petruchio or Romeo. He gives her a slap in the face, then offers her a bunch of flowers.... [He] has an inescapable belief that sòmehow or other, if it were not for the existence of the Liberal Party, all those who voted Liberal would vote for him. I think that is a matter which is open to doubt. After a considerable experience of the Liberal Party, I am never quite sure how they will vote or, as a matter of fact, whether they will all vote together.

Attlee then went on to try to drive a wedge between the Conservatives who, like Eden and Butler, wanted to be reasonably cooperative, and those who would bring the government down at any cost. Putting down an amendment equivalent to a vote of censure was:

> an irresponsible act, and I think most honourable members of the opposite bench think so too. I watched them very closely when the right honourable Gentleman [Lyttelton] made his speech ... and I have never seen less enthusiasm on those benches.... I am sorry for it, because I have said that in these times we should try to see that the Government of this country is carried on under these very difficult circumstances in such a way as will give confidence to the world, and I think this action will go far to destroy the confidence that people had that the Conservative Party could rise above mere Party manœuvres.

The Liberal MPs thought so too. Attlee had struck the right note when he satirized Churchill's attitude to them. The amendment was defeated by 310 to 296. The debate had shown that, despite acrimony over domestic affairs, government and Opposition were in substantial agreement, in particular over the need to extend the movement for international control of nuclear weapons in the light of President Truman's announcement on 31 January that he had ordered the Atomic Energy Commission to proceed with the development of the hydrogen bomb.

Behind the scenes Attlee had to deal with an altercation in Cabinet between Bevan on one hand and Morrison and Gaitskell on the other hand about the rising costs of the health service. Attlee originally contemplated reorganizing the Ministry of Health so that the health service should have a separate department with a minister outside the Cabinet, while the rest of the ministry's functions – housing, local government and public health – should be added to town and country planning to make a new department. He offered such a department to Dalton, who made it a condition of acceptance that Bevan approved of the arrangement; and when Bevan's disapproval became known, Dalton took over town and country planning alone, with a seat in the Cabinet as fifth in the hierarchy. Bevan later told Dalton that at the beginning of the administration he was urging Attlee:

> to make a drastic reshaping of Ministries, and to announce it with a big splash in Parliament. This would be the right follow-on after our five years of important and far-reaching legislation. With our majority, he said, we could not hope to pass any more important legislation in this Parliament. But Attlee, he said, refused to agree to this.

Attlee's attitude to Bevan at this time was rapidly hardening into what it was to be for the rest of their political lives: he thought Bevan, except for one shortcoming, the ideal leader of the Labour Party. The shortcoming was the lack of self-control: a burst of anger, and Bevan's judgement was momentarily in ruins, and in that moment he could imperil not only his own fate but the fate of the party. Attlee loved Bevan for his colour, his courage, his compassion, and above all for his sense of social justice. He saw little of Marx in Bevan; he saw much of William Morris. He cherished the poet, the artist, the companion, the natural aristocrat in Nye; he had seen enough in his youth of the evils of capitalism to understand why Bevan hated it. But he now had grave doubts about Nye's capacity to qualify as a future leader of the party. As well as a view about Bevan, Attlee had developed a view about what was to become 'Bevanism'. He knew that in the aftermath of the great setback of February 1950 the party would become even more deeply divided between those led by Morrison who wanted 'consolidation' and those led by Bevan who wanted 'advance'. Attlee wanted to prevent an open fight. He had therefore to humour both of them, and risk no recourse to a showdown by letting either of them feel that the leadership of the party was not for him. He had a special worry about Nye: his friends. He believed that what judgement and self-control Nye had was frequently undermined by the advice of his friends, who reported Morrison's and Morgan Phillips's and Attlee's alleged slights and innuendoes in detail. Then there was Jenny Lee. Reminiscing years later about the contribution a politician's wife could make to her husband's career, Attlee said of Nye and Jennie: 'He needed a sedative. He got an irritant.'

The problem of holding the party together was complicated by other factors: Bevin was too ill to give stability; the ailing Cripps was preoccupied with the economy; Dalton had still not re-established his influence; and of the younger generation, Gaitskell and Jay had no political bases in the party, and relied so far on their own ability and the patronage of their elders. On the credit side, however, Attlee could rely on the consolidated strength within the Labour Movement of the trade unions. Full employment, high trade union membership, and the important role they had played in the wartime and postwar economy had made the big three of the union movement, Arthur Deakin of the Transport and General Workers, Tom Williamson of the Municipal Workers, and Will Lawther of the Miners, the predominant power group within the Labour Movement, with great influence over their members; the trio were loyal, stable, and, in party terms, right-wing. Their spokesman on the National Executive was Sam Watson, the leader of the Durham miners. He was intelligent, steady, and extremely tough, and his personal friendship with Attlee – the most intimate relationship which Attlee formed from 1945 on – was a linchpin in holding the movement together in the fifties. Watson had the extra strength of being a personal friend and adviser of Ernest Bevin, and of being a sophisticated student of foreign policy, with special knowledge of the Communist world. Attlee told the author in 1958 that he had wanted Watson to come into Parliament and succeed Bevin at the Foreign Office, but reluctantly had to abandon the idea: 'Sam never wanted to travel south of Durham. Would have been a drawback in a Foreign Secretary.'

In the new Parliament the Conservatives' first attacks were directed against Aneurin Bevan. On 13 March he defended himself successfully against criticism of the housing cuts, but he increasingly felt undermined by Cripps in his struggle to maintain the principle of a free health service. In Cabinet on 13 March, Cripps called for a 'ceiling' on health service expenditure. To cool a hot problem Attlee arranged that Cripps should speak first in the debate on the supplementary estimates the following afternoon, to discuss the 'ceiling', while Bevan should speak later about the health service in general: and Bevan, much of his ground conceded in advance by Cripps, confined himself to defending his department against charges of waste. But he was unhappy about the trend of policy. He wrote to Attlee complaining about the Cabinet minute which noted agreement to resume discussions of health service finance at a later date:

> I do hope that I can have a little peace to get on with my proper work without this continual nibbling, and I must give notice that I intend at the next meeting of the Cabinet to challenge this conclusion.

Bevan believed that the Treasury, led in this respect by Gaitskell and Douglas Jay, was controlling the fate of the health service.

The budget discussion lay only four weeks ahead. Worried by trade union restiveness about wage restraint, the Treasury was fixed on a policy of retrenchment to prevent inflation, and the retrenchment would include cuts in the health service. A meeting of Cabinet ministers was arranged for 3 April. The day before, Cripps wrote a longhand memorandum to Attlee:

> The discussion tomorrow may lead to Bevan resigning.... I agree no cuts if there are *certain* means to stop supplementaries.... It will anyhow take time to work out the best way of making charges. So I would agree to *powers* being taken now but no fresh charges till it's clear the ceiling is being exceeded. This means we would have to decide *before the end of the session* whether charges are needed. It would bring great pressure on those responsible for the Service to make economies quickly. I'm sorry to inflict all this on you, but I want to avoid an awkward political situation arising just now. I couldn't agree to nothing being done; this is the least I can agree to.

Bevan agreed too. Attlee established a weekly Cabinet committee – which he would chair – to keep health service finances under constant supervision. This pleased Cripps, who saw the Prime Minister as an ally, and Morrison who, as we have seen, had wanted for some time to have Bevan's department put under financial scrutiny. But Bevan took it to imply that he was administratively unsound. He may have been, but that was not why Attlee had set the committee up. He had done it to protect Bevan more than to control him. Bevan's ruffled feelings were not soothed by the tone in Cripps's budget speech of 18 April. However, Bevan had succeeded for the time being in preventing the introduction of charges, including prescription charges, and he had 'lived to threaten to resign another day'. Attlee had cleverly obviated a pre-budget crisis within the Cabinet.

During June, Gaitskell in particular continued to raise the question of health service charges at a series of informal dinners which Cripps held for ministers whose departments had close associations with the Treasury. At the end of June Bevan ceased to attend these dinners.

Attlee looked on at these developments, on which he was well briefed by Cripps, with concern and dismay. His sympathies were with Bevan's emotional commitment to the health service. He had no great feeling for Gaitskell – he respected his ability and his integrity, but did not warm to his personality or political stance. But Gaitskell was not rocking the government boat, and Bevan was. Bevan was not facing facts, and Gaitskell was. Policy must face facts, not fly in the face of them.

Cripps's 1950 budget led many, including *The Times*, to believe that the Labour Party's conversion from idealistic theory to common sense had at last taken place, and that the experience of government from 1945 to 1950 had been 'a graveyard of doctrine'. A number of economic controls were jettisoned, and a number of leaders, including the party secretary, Morgan Phillips, Morrison, and John Strachey, the new War Minister, made public statements which seemed to soften the hard edges of Labour's socialism and in particular to put a distance between the Labour Party and Marxism. On 20 May the NEC and senior ministers met at Dorking to conduct a post-mortem on the election. Morrison put forward a memorandum criticizing the party's tendency to press for nationalization, and implying that Bevan's pressure for 'advance' as opposed to 'consolidation' had lost seats in February. Bevan and his supporters resisted, and Morgan Phillips and Sam Watson argued that acceptance of the 'consolidation' thesis by the NEC would disrupt the party at a critical moment. Attlee said very little. There was no need: he knew what Sam Watson was going to say, and this was what he thought himself. He knew that if Sam Watson, Morgan Phillips and Bevan were in his corner, there was no possibility of Morrison getting his way. Attlee referred to the conference in a letter to Tom written just after it. Its main news was of a 'tornado' which, he said, 'must have started very close to Chequers where I had just arrived from the Dorking conference'. He added, parenthetically: 'The latter went very well. The Surrey country-side was lovely.'

In July the NEC met for another attempt to arrive at some kind of restatement of what the Labour Party was about which would be the basis of the manifesto at the next elections – continually seen as around the corner – without provoking a dangerous altercation in the party which would lose the election in advance. A compromise was reached. It was based on acceptance of a key idea: the test of the public good. The next election manifesto would undertake to nationalize any industry if its operations were seen to be against the national interest, but there would be no 'shopping-list', and no list of industries which, as Attlee said, 'had better watch their step'. Apart from this omission, the NEC's proposal was quite vague. The 'consolidators' and the 'advancers' settled for it.

The post-election debate within the party, far from making inroads on Attlee's position, had strengthened it. With Cripps and Bevin ailing, too preoccupied in keeping up enough physical strength to carry out their by now crushing governmental burdens, Morrison and Bevan alone created tension. Attlee had nothing to fear from either because both were locked in mutual conflict. With the country as a whole he stood as well as ever he had. The *Manchester Guardian* remarked on 4 July that an Attlee-must-go movement, conceivable in 1945, was inconceivable in 1950. 'It is hardly too much to say that he is the Party's greatest asset in the popular mind.' From now on to the defeat of his government in 1951, would-be rebels would have to register their dissent by only one method: resignation.

Attlee's popularity remained high. At the end of May a Gallup poll showed that his personal standing had risen since the election, while the government's standing had not shifted at all:

	Today	January
Approve of Attlee as Prime Minister	50	40
Disapprove	39	42
Don't know	11	14

Even in the *Daily Express* a columnist paid Attlee a tribute on 1 July:

Gone is all trace of the sickness that threatened to drive him into retirement two years ago. He has regained a robust health that delights and surprises his doctor. No matter what new responsibility engages him, Mr Attlee has the faculty of shutting it out of his mind at bedtime and dropping instantly into a sound sleep. His new vitality is evident in the Commons. On the front bench with his feet up and his chin tucked into his chest he looks deceptively somnolent. But when his turn comes he is on his feet at once disposing of his critics briskly.

The *Express* reported also, as a sign of his energy, that during weekends at Chequers he played eight sets of tennis (doubles).

That Attlee had time for other concerns is shown by his correspondence with Tom:

Thank you so much for your letter about the vicar of St Keverne and the benefice of Kew. There were a lot of applications but I will see that Brown is fully considered.

I am hoping to see Chris and Bo shortly, as they are coming to the Buckingham Palace Garden Party with us ...

We've just returned from Wimbledon where we saw about the best Men's Doubles that I can remember. Particularly gratifying as Australians beat Americans.

These are rather anxious times with the Korean situation, but I hope that if this is nipped in the bud we shall stop other aggression and armed movements.

II

On 25 June 1950 North Korean forces equipped with Soviet weapons crossed the 38th parallel into South Korea. On 27 June Truman ordered American forces to give cover and support to South Korean troops; a few hours later the UN Security Council, in the absence of the Soviet representative, passed a motion calling for a ceasefire, for the withdrawal of North Korean troops, and for all UN members to assist in executing this resolution. News of the UN resolution was taken to Attlee by a private secretary: 'It'll be all right so long as the bleachers [Americans] don't join in,' he said. Hearing from the same source of Truman's announcement, he said: 'We'll have to support the Yanks.' 'Naked aggression, and it must be checked,' he told the House of Commons the same evening. The following day he announced that British naval forces in Japanese waters would be put at the disposal of the Americans, whose Seventh Fleet had been ordered to prevent any attack being made on Formosa, to which Chiang Kai-shek had withdrawn in 1949 after the Communists had established control of the Chinese mainland. These steps were supported by the Conservatives, as well as by the bulk of the Labour Party. The Korean War, more than any other factor, enabled the Labour government to look in better shape at the end of the session than had seemed possible six months previously. The strains which were shortly to be put on Anglo-American relations, the economy, and the unity of the Labour Party were in the future.

Attlee's main concern was that Russia would be able to use the Korean campaign to tie up large American and British forces, thereby having greater freedom of action elsewhere. He wrote to Truman on 6 July suggesting that steps should be taken to enable Britain and the United States to 'look ahead as far as we can and reach some agreement as to our common policy in these areas in the event of further outbreaks'. He suggested sending British military advisers at once. But military planning should be done in a political context. 'It seems to me that such talks cannot ignore the political implications.' The American State Department should be associated with these talks.

> My colleagues and I attach very great importance to reaching the closest possible understanding with the United States Government so that we can both plan in full confidence that we understand each other's approach to these weighty problems. I therefore deeply hope that you will be able to give me an early and favourable reply to this suggestion.

This letter inaugurated a new Anglo-American partnership which for the next three years, in spite of many strains and tensions, was the closest the two countries have ever achieved in times of peace. Talks began in Washington almost at once – Lord Tedder, Marshal of the Royal Air

454

Force, chairman of the Joint Services in Washington, and the Ambassador, Sir Oliver Franks, were the key British figures in them. Attlee and Truman agreed that it was essential to avoid as far as possible any action that might encourage or allow the Communists to launch an attack at some other point along the line of countries which divided them. Truman acted on this at once. He cancelled orders by the US Air Force for high-flying photographic reconnaissance flights to be made over Darien, Port Arthur, Vladivostok, Karafuto and the Kurile Islands. It was the first of many moves to limit the risk of causing war elsewhere made as a result of Attlee's 'put the brakes on the bleachers' strategy.

The next task was to step up the recruitment programme to meet the emergency. In March the government had introduced a Defence White Paper raising rearmament requirements. At the end of July Shinwell, as Minister of Defence, announced that a further £100 million would be allocated. In winding up, Attlee regretted that 'the more hopeful condition of a few months ago no longer rules'. He warned the House that the new burden of rearmament would put an additional strain on the economy.

> It would not be right to leave the subject of defence without a clear warning to the country that the part we are playing and shall play in defending the free democratic world from aggression is going to face us with difficult economic problems. Not all of the whole new burden of defence can be borne out of increased production.

The government were not at the moment prepared for a further increase in the rearmament programme, but by the time the House rose the United States were asking what extra measures the Western powers were prepared to take. On 8 August the government agreed to the expenditure of £3,400 million in three years for defence. This involved a rise of from 8 to 10 per cent of the national revenue.

The House had now risen. The pressure on MPs had been unprecedented all through the spring and summer – the Whips 'had never worked so hard'. The crisis in the Far East had burst upon ministers already fatigued and overworked. There were extraordinary police precautions for the party rally at Taunton. Attlee gave 5,000 people the message that if the United Nations was not to go the way of the League of Nations, 'it is absolutely and imperatively necessary that a halt should be called to aggression. . . . All honour to the United States who took the appropriate action.' He repeated the message in a broadcast the following night, 31 July, with the warning that sacrifices would be needed and an appeal for increased production and a close watch on the enemy within. The Korean War, he said, was a war against aggression; Britain's security was as much in danger as that of any other country:

The attack by the armed forces of North Korea on South Korea has been denounced as an act of aggression by the United Nations. No excuses, no propaganda by Communists, no introduction of other questions can get over this fact. Here is a case of aggression. If the aggressor gets away with it, aggressors all over the world will be encouraged. The same results which led to the second world war will follow; and another world war may result. This is why what is happening in Korea is of such importance to you.

The fire that has been started in distant Korea may burn down your house.

He outlined the measures which the government had taken to assist the Americans in their military effort, and warned the country once more that production intended for the people at home would now have to be diverted to those away at war. 'There will be few goods available for providing for our standard of life.' The government was making 'a careful survey to see where necessary adjustments can best be made'. He appealed for the qualities which the nation had displayed in the Second World War. 'I know that if, which God forbid, war should break out, every one of you would be ready for any kind of service. It is well worth while to make some sacrifice of leisure now to prevent war.'

The *Daily Worker* commented: 'The colourless prim voice of the Right Honourable Clement Attlee came over the air from Chequers last night in his most viperish anti-Communist utterance yet. It was a Churchill-and-water version of the blood toil tears and sweat oration of 1940.' Attlee wrote to Tom on 8 August: 'Many thanks for your letter. I am glad you liked the broadcast.' He had received an unusually large number of letters, many from friends, and a great number from 'the man in the street'. Many of these were inspired not only by approval of Attlee's broadcast but by fear that another major war was imminent. Attlee so far recognized the danger as to observe to Tom: 'I don't think Stalin wants a major war but there is always the possibility of his chancing his arm too far.'

Although the situation in Korea was grave, Attlee declined to recall Parliament until 12 September, explaining to the King on 18 August that he could not 'find any substantial reason for an earlier recall as it did not seem to me that another debate without definite action to be taken by the House would be useful'. The North Korean invaders attacked across the Naktong River towards the end of August; only one beachhead remained to the UN forces. At Lake Success the Russians had reoccupied their seat at the Security Council, and their delegate, Jacob Malik, exploiting his turn to be chairman, was pumping out anti-American propaganda. At the end of August, as a result of Churchill's representations, there was an exchange of party political broadcasts between the leader of the Opposition and the Prime Minister. Churchill indicted the government for having refused to recall Parliament at an earlier date, castigated it for sending too few troops too late – the first of them arrived at Pusan on 29 August – and denounced it for allowing tank equipment to be sold to Russia.

Attlee used his broadcast to describe the measures the government had already taken about Korea. Then he appealed to the Russian leaders to 'lift the cloud of apprehension which hangs over the world'. He rejected Churchill's charge that national security was endangered by selling machine tools to the Soviet and allied countries: 'We made trade agreements with Russia to our material benefit. They have carried out their side of the bargain, and we are carrying out ours.' He attacked Churchill for seldom attending the House except when he made speeches; the leader of the Opposition was a 'prima donna full of querulous complaint against the people of this country for not having continued him in power'. The *Daily Telegraph* correspondent described Attlee's broadcast as 'ferocious bleating'. The *Manchester Guardian*, in a leader headed 'Mr Attlee', administered a schoolmasterly rebuke to both sides:

> There was much in the Prime Minister's spirited criticism of Mr Churchill that was deserved. Yet, for all the justice of its thrusts, one cannot help feeling that the tone of the broadcast was at this moment a mistake. It was only in the last four of his twenty minutes that the Prime Minister came to deal with the large questions of international policy that really concern this country and on which the voice of the Government has been much too restrained, if not almost silent.

The three-day debate in Parliament began on 12 September. Attlee's speech was one of his longer ones. The main points in the diagnosis were all too familiar, though there were some specific proposals for strengthening the country's defences, and it was announced that the conscription period would be extended from eighteen months to two years; also that agreement had been reached for integrating the Brussels Pact machinery with NATO so as to establish a unified command. The rearmament programme would be increased from £3,400 million to £3,600 million – 'the maximum we can do,' said Attlee, 'by expanding and using to the full our industrial capacity without resorting to the drastic expedients of a war economy'. The Opposition, too, had little to add: everything that had been done, all that was proposed, was much too late. Labour held together sufficiently to win the debate; Attlee told Tom: 'I don't think the Tory attack on us was very effective. I doubt if it will divert people from the strongly held fear that, if Winston got in, he would lead us into war.'

That the government was going to have difficulty in keeping together became clear. Although Attlee went in person to address the annual TUC

Conference at Brighton – 'We are living in anxious days' – the conference, against the advice of the General Council, rejected the policy of wage restraint, narrowly, by 3,949,000 to 3,727,000. Within the Parliamentary Labour Party there was growing resentment at the impact which rearmament would have on the economy, especially on the balance of payments. The press reported rumours that Aneurin Bevan might resign in protest against the cost of the arms programme, though in fact Bevan had come nearer to resignation the previous month.

In mid-September, General MacArthur – in command of the 'United Nations' forces – brought off a brilliant landing behind the enemy lines at Inchon. Twelve days later, he recaptured Seoul, the South Korean capital. The United Nations began a major advance. By the end of the month the North Korean army had been driven back beyond the 38th parallel with heavy losses. MacArthur broadcast a surrender ultimatum. Expectations rose that the Korean fighting was nearly over, and that the danger of it leading to a major war had been much exaggerated.

III

As the party conference approached, domestic rather than international affairs seemed more likely to cause trouble. The Cabinet's fear was that the TUC's rejection of a policy of wage restraint the previous month at Brighton might be carried forward into a similar defeat for the party leadership at Margate. A few days after the TUC conference, Isaacs, the Minister of Labour, had made a statement in the Commons in which he gave some support to reports of systematic attempts to disrupt the economy by union militants who had recently returned from a Cominform meeting in Warsaw. The following day, 16 September, Arthur Deakin, general secretary of the T&GWU, demanded the banning of the Communist Party. Isaacs followed this with a broadcast in which he inveighed against unofficial strikes.

Strong feeling had been generated within the party by another controversy about the nationalization of steel. The government had announced before the general election that vesting day for the nationalization of steel would not be before 1 October. Having been returned to power, the Labour government proceeded with their arrangements. One of the part-time nominees to the board of the new corporation, R.A. Maclean, withdrew his agreement to service, citing as his reason the public unrest about the government's plan to go full steam ahead. This gave new life to the argument for and against the nationalization of the industry. There was another debate in Parliament. Churchill thundered; Morrison countered with allegations of a conspiracy by Tories, Lords, employers and press to sabotage the steel industry in the interests of Conservative propaganda.

The news of the Inchon landing on 14 September came in time to damp things down, and the prospect of dissension diminished. The conference, chaired by the astute Sam Watson, opened on 2 October at Margate. Attlee arrived wearing, according to the *Daily Herald*, 'his gayest suit, a new pepper-and-salt Donegal tweed made for him from a length given him during an Irish holiday by Sean MacBride'. He was in excellent physical condition: 'He's far and away the healthiest man in the Cabinet. His blood pressure is that of a young man...' The *Evening Standard*, in a somewhat jaundiced report on 'the Mr Chips of the Socialist Party', also mentioned his suit, which he must have changed that day:

> This morning as he laid his pipe aside and rose, in a rather baggy blue suit, to deliver his Parliamentary Report ... he seemed positively embarrassed at the enthusiasm with which he was greeted.... It was not a particularly impressive speech. But Mr Attlee is not a particularly impressive figure. Yet for all his deficiencies he completely dominates the Party. His position is quite impregnable. He has no challenger. In this position he displays all the vices of which Sir Stafford Cripps has ever been accused. He remains totally indifferent to public opinion. He referred today with contempt to the views of Liberal voters on the nationalization of steel. He has shown a callous disregard to former colleagues defeated at the polls. There was no kindly remark about them this morning...
>
> It seems he has only to crack the whip, and Mr Morrison and Mr Bevan shake hands in harmony...
>
> Perhaps it's the knowledge that Mr Attlee is so ready to put party before country that accounts for his present overwhelming popularity among the Socialist rank and file.

The main business of the week was to consider the Executive's policy statement, *Labour and the New Society*. Morrison and Bevan both behaved well, and on the face of it the party was united.

A few days after the conference, on 4 October, Cripps wrote to Attlee to say that he wished to resign. This had been expected since shortly after the spring budget, but nevertheless the news put Attlee in a quandary. He could conceivably have appointed one of four men to replace Cripps: Dalton, Morrison, Aneurin Bevan or Gaitskell. Dalton, a former chancellor, had the economic expertise for the job. Morrison had the political weight to be chancellor, but he lacked expertise; indeed, as an economic planner he had already been proved a failure. Shored up by his friend Gaitskell, who had been running the Treasury for several months during Cripps's illness, he might be successful. Aneurin Bevan also had the political weight and seniority; it would be good for him to have to speak for the Treasury instead of against it. But was he stable enough? Would there be more talk of 'vermin'? What would the Americans make of his appointment? Finally, he could appoint Gaitskell, who knew the Treasury well, had formulated much of Cripps's policy, but lacked political weight and was still a junior figure.

Attlee's reasoning was quite simple. Dalton was 'past it'. He would, if Morrison had pressed his claims, reluctantly have given the job to Morrison, trusting that Gaitskell would in fact have determined policy. If he appointed Bevan there would be trouble with Morrison, and a dangerous conflict between left and right in the party. The appointment of Gaitskell, who was in any case the best equipped to do the job, would, in spite of Bevan's animosity towards him, cause least trouble: he was too young, and he did not have enough of a political base within the party to be in the running for the leadership at this stage. Morrison, believing mistakenly that it would prevent conflict within the party, favoured Gaitskell's appointment and thus unwittingly destroyed his own chances for the party leadership. Bevan, who had been preparing his own suggestions about the reconstruction of the government, wrote to Attlee of his 'consternation and astonishment' at the appointment.

For a few weeks there was a lull before the storm. Attlee replied briefly to Bevan on 21 October.

> My dear Nye,
>
> I have your letter, I am sorry you have not let me have the note with regard to the changes of structure, as I do not see that the other matters to which you refer really affect this point.
>
> I should, of course, be glad to have a talk with you, though I do not think that your views are shared by many people.
>
> Yours ever,
>
> Clem.

Attlee offered Bevan the Ministry of Labour, which he declined, telling his friends that he had done so because there would be a new Treasury attack on the health service if he had moved to another department.

Attlee now found time to make a number of public appearances: he opened the William Morris Gallery on 21 October, taking the opportunity to praise his hero, and enjoyed the official opening of the new Commons Chamber. On 7 November he wrote to Tom: 'Acoustics are good, ventilation much criticised. Many cold draughts. The Speaker has a rug. Winston in overcoat. Vi's feather in her hat flutters in the wind. Fairly all right on the Treasury Bench.' In this letter to Tom he had time to indulge himself in discussion of ecclesiastical appointments. In Cornwall, where Tom lived, the Bishop of Truro had died.

> I am sorry to hear of Hunkin's death. I met him several times. Have you any views on his successor? The Abp is away in Australia, but I shall begin

looking round soon. What elevation is desirable now? Something in the middle I should think as you have rather swung from one extreme to another recently.

In the next letter he thanked Tom for his 'useful letter on the Truro vacancy'. He wrote again a few weeks later. 'I've been looking over the runners for the Truro stakes. I can't do anything until the Abp returns, but as at present advised I favour Andrews.' He went down to Limehouse to reopen the town hall and celebrate the fiftieth birthday of the borough council.

IV

All seemed well as Attlee prepared to take part in what was foreseen as a routine foreign affairs debate scheduled for the last days of November. But on 24 November, reacting to General MacArthur's advance into North Korea, Chinese Communist forces launched a great attack across the Yalu River and had driven him back in disarray. Nearly 250,000 Chinese soldiers were in action. A few days later they forced MacArthur's forces back across the 38th parallel. 'We now face a new war,' announced MacArthur, and he demanded the right to retaliate by bombing Chinese territory. At a press conference on 30 November, under some pressure from reporters who knew that MacArthur was in what Dean Acheson later described as a 'blue funk', President Truman made some statements which were widely interpreted to mean that the United States was ready to use the atomic bomb in Korea. Though much qualified and 'clarified' in later announcements, the news caused consternation in Britain. A hundred Labour MPs signed a hastily drafted letter to Attlee. Alarm was not confined to the Labour Party. Churchill, Eden and Butler talked of the need for 'assurance that events in Korea would not propel the world into a major war'. The American embassy in London sent urgent reports to Washington that Parliament had held 'the most serious, anxious, and responsible debate on foreign affairs . . . since the Labour Party came to power in 1945'.

Attlee was less concerned that Truman would use the atomic bomb than that he would be unable to prevent MacArthur undertaking a full-scale war with China. He called a special meeting of the Cabinet in the early evening of 30 November and told his colleagues that since Bevin was not well enough to go to Washington he proposed to go himself.

The Cabinet minutes report him as saying:

It was clear beyond doubt, that at his Press Conference Mr Truman had made a statement which he had later corrected. In spite of this correction, however, the statement had caused great alarm in the House of Commons, and urgent action was necessary in order to allay public anxiety. The critical military situation in Korea and the possibility of an extension of the war made it desirable for [me] to have a meeting in Washington with Mr Truman. The bomb would have to be discussed. The responsibility for deciding on the use of the atomic bomb would have to be defined. A decision of this importance could not be left to the commander in the field or even to the United States government alone. All nations which had contributed to the United Nations forces in Korea should be consulted and there should be unanimity among them before a decision was taken to use the bomb.

After the Cabinet meeting Harold Wilson went across to the House of Commons for dinner and sat at a table with some ministers who were not members of the Cabinet, and knew nothing of the secret visit Attlee was about to make. Attlee suddenly appeared and sat down at the same table. Wilson wondered what kind of conversation to make, but Attlee began it himself. 'Who is the best modern popular historian?' 'Bryant,' said Wilson. 'Quite agree,' said Attlee. They discussed the writing of history throughout dinner. Attlee then returned to Downing Street to await Truman's confirmation that an immediate visit would be welcome. He would make his excuse the raw materials. 'The President of the Board of Trade [Wilson] was talking about Raw Materials this morning, so I'll say I went to discuss them with the President.'

Attlee flew to Washington on Sunday evening, 3 December. He was accompanied by Field-Marshal Sir William Slim, who had succeeded Montgomery as CIGS, and by Far Eastern experts from the Foreign Office. The party arrived in Washington the following morning. Attlee was particularly concerned that the war in Korea must be confined to Korea. For United Nations forces to start fighting across the frontier would, at worst, start a major conflict with China which could develop into a world war. At best it would occupy so much of Western strength in the Far East that the Russians could do as they pleased in Europe. He suspected that Truman might not be able to control MacArthur, for political reasons. A large section of the Republican Party in Congress wanted to re-establish Chiang Kai-shek on the Chinese mainland, and were prepared to risk large-scale war to do so. Many of them, and several Democrats also, were not opposed to 'a preventive war' against Communist China. 'Some people were anxious for a show-down with Russia.' MacArthur was spoken of as a possible Republican candidate for the presidency in the elections of 1952.

Attlee also suspected that the President might not be able to control MacArthur for reasons more related to 'the way they did things over there'. MacArthur, a great proconsul, had not visited the United States since the 1930s. When Truman wanted to talk to him about the Korean War in mid-October, instead of recalling him to Washington the President had obligingly flown to meet the General on Wake Island in the Pacific. 'This appeared to us a curious relationship between Government and a General,' Attlee observed in his autobiography. Another problem requiring urgent settlement was that American stockpiling of raw materials was forcing up commodity prices and playing havoc with Britain's balance of payments. The economic consequences of the war in Korea had already put a pressure on Britain, on the welfare state, on the British standard of living, of a far graver kind than had been imposed by the dollar shortage of 1949.

Attlee knew that as well as asking for reassurances from Truman he had to provide him with some. American public opinion still harboured the view, mainly because of Churchill's speeches, that Marshall Aid had been poured down the drain of the welfare state in the pursuit not of economic health but of doctrinaire socialism. Many Americans identified socialism as but a milder form of communism, and noted that Attlee's government had not only recognized the communist government of China which had just attacked MacArthur, but also were pressing for that government's admission to the Security Council in place of the Chiang Kai-shek government. This was appeasement such as had brought about the Second World War, from which Britain had only been rescued by American intervention. Exploiting a mood of hostility to Attlee's visit, twenty-four Republican senators introduced a resolution requiring that any agreement reached by the President and the Prime Minister must be ratified by the Senate.

In this context Attlee tried to achieve four objectives: to find out what was going on in Korea, to get the United States to end its conflict with China and resume its support for European defence, to set up a joint control of raw materials as in the Second World War, and to establish Britain's right to some participation in any decision to use nuclear weapons. Attlee's visit to Truman in December 1950 was the last great attempt to recreate the kind of special relationship based on equality which had existed in the early days of the war – before Roosevelt had decided that the US–Russian relationship was more important than the Anglo-American relationship and that where necessary to preserve his relationship with Stalin, British judgements must be overridden. As Acheson observed to the author: 'Churchill never asked, or got so much, as Attlee did. He was a very remarkable man.' Acheson further observed:

> Attlee was adroit, extremely adroit, his grasp of the situation was masterly. His method was seduction: he led the President on, step by step, to where he wanted to get him. He would make a statement of what the British wanted as though it was a statement of what the Americans wanted, and pause and say, very quickly, 'I take it we are already agreed about that', and Mr Truman, who was no slouch himself as a negotiator, would answer

'Yes, we are.' I was horrified. That's why I began stepping on the President's foot.... I found that Attlee had been very much underrated. He was a damn good lawyer. All through the talks he was out to get everything he could out of Truman's hands, and into his. The idea that he came over just to expostulate about MacArthur and the Bomb is most misleading; if we hadn't watched him like a hawk, he would have gone back to London leaving American policy hamstrung.

Part of Attlee's strength in Acheson's view was the mutual regard between him and Mr Truman. The President trusted him – he remembered that Attlee had supported him loyally when in 1945/6 the President had let him down over atomic energy. Truman admired Attlee's knowledge of war, Acheson told the author, 'though he was puzzled when Attlee said he had had some experience of evacuating peninsulas – we had to explain that the prime minister was talking about Gallipoli in the First World War. They were both sceptical about leaving policy to the generals. Attlee certainly stiffened our resolve to stand no insubordination from MacArthur.'

Meetings took place over the next four days. Attlee pressed, unsuccessfully, for a ceasefire and the withdrawal of UN troops from Korea. There was agreement to set up study groups on the raw materials question. Attlee asked for continuous consultation on military action in Korea. He raised the 'difficult and delicate question' of MacArthur, and pointed out that the United States' allies had so far had no say in what was being done or planned. On Europe Acheson found Attlee extremely difficult. 'Attlee not only did not want to discuss European defence but positively eluded attempts to draw him into it, leaving discussion to his field and air marshals, Slim and Tedder.' Acheson noted that Attlee never relaxed for a moment his determination to establish a British veto over American strategic action, particularly in the case of the bomb. Acheson told the author:

At the very last moment of the conference Attlee made one more crafty ploy, and nearly got away with it. All business was over, and we were sitting around waiting for the experts to produce the draft of the communiqué. The President and Attlee went off for what I thought was a personal chat to the President's private study. When the drafts were ready we called the President. He came in with Attlee and said blithely something like: 'We've had a good talk about the Bomb. We want to say in the Communiqué that neither of us will use the bomb without prior consultation with each other.' I remember the silence. We were horrified. It seemed that Attlee had raised the matter as soon as they were alone. He asked the President if what he had said at the press conference had after all been intended as a hint that he *had* been giving consideration to the use of the bomb since our forces were in such danger. The President assured him that this had not been the

1950

case – it had been 'an unfortunate' use of words, the subsequent clarifications and denials represented the whole truth and nothing but the truth. Attlee then very suavely said he thought it could do no harm for the President to affirm that he would not use the bomb without consulting his allies. He wanted this for political reasons back home. The President agreed. I passed a note to Franks, and then the President, Attlee, Franks and myself went to the President's office. I had to tell him that he had always said in public that nothing could limit his power to use the bomb if he believed the use of it was necessary – the law did not allow him to limit his powers that way, and if he made that statement, there could be an uproar, and the British would suffer about as much as he would. The other three agreed, but Attlee gave me another of those nasty looks.

The final communiqué did not give Attlee what he wanted on the bomb, and on other matters it said very little, but it certainly did not reveal any disturbing deadlock. Perhaps its main deficiency was the very short first paragraph: 'The military capabilities of the United States and the United Kingdom should be increased as rapidly as possible.' This statement gave no hint of the immense additional pressure which would be put on the British economy as a result of the Americans insisting on a large increase in the UK's rearmament programme; a pressure which was to create a positive crisis for Attlee the following spring. The communiqué recorded differences over the recognition of the Communist government in Peking in a matter-of-fact way. Apart from that, the document emphasized the similarity of the aims and aspirations of the two countries, and the closeness of their views on the threat to freedom in Europe as well as the Far East. That was the official public message.

In private, though, Attlee had got an assurance, which he previously lacked, that the Americans would not – to use his phrase – 'get bogged down in the Far East'; and he was able, largely through an address to the National Press Club, to make it clear to the American people that neither opposition to the extension of the war in Korea nor Britain's recognition of Communist China was a form of 'appeasement'. He told the journalists that: 'As long as the Stars and Stripes flies in Korea the British flag will fly beside it. We have never had any intention of appeasement. . . . There are people, I am told, who believe that is what I have come here to do. That is not true.' Attlee said nothing of his attempts to canvass the idea of both the American and British forces getting out.

Attlee reported to the Cabinet on 12 December. The Minutes read:

The Prime Minister: The President had entirely satisfied him about the use of the bomb. He had assured the Prime Minister that he regarded the atomic bomb as in a sense a joint possession of the United States, the United Kingdom and Canada, and that he would not authorise its use without prior consultation with the other two governments save in an extreme

465

emergency – such as an atomic attack on the United States which called for immediate retaliation.

The communiqué got a good press. Attlee reported to the House on 14 December. On his way into the Chamber through the members' lobby he spotted the Tory Sir John Smyth, for whom he had a high regard as a VC and a former tennis correspondent of the *Sunday Times*. Smyth had been speaking in the House on the night two weeks previously when Attlee had left the House to tell the Cabinet he was going to fly to Washington. 'Oh, Smyth,' he said. 'Awfully sorry I had to go out in the middle of your speech but my wife stayed on to hear it, and she said it was jolly good.' Attlee began his speech saying that he had not expected that his meeting with the President would lead to any 'spectacular action or dramatic announcement'. What he had hoped for, 'and what, I think, we achieved was a closer understanding of the points of view of our two Governments. The attitude of the American Administration could not have been more cordial; they could not have shown themselves more anxious to be helpful. Direct discussion across the table will always do more to clear up misunderstandings than any exchange of formal communications.'

Attlee was very conscious of the fact that what the House most wanted to hear was that he had obtained some guarantee that 'brakes' had been applied to the use of the bomb. He said:

> The close working relationships which grow up in this way [the meeting with Truman] will do far more to harmonise our policies and actions than any written agreements about consultation.... It was in the spirit and against the background of that [wartime partnership] that I was able to raise the vital question of the use of the atomic weapon, and received assurances which I consider to be perfectly satisfactory.

Churchill here interjected: 'We do not know what these assurances were.' Attlee was not to be drawn. Notwithstanding this, Churchill welcomed the Prime Minister's visit to Washington; it had 'done nothing but good. The question we all have to consider this evening is, how much good? Five years is rather a long time between meetings. Why did he not go earlier?' Some Labour left-wingers objected to Attlee's support for even a limited war; but some of them were impressed by his straight talking on China. Morrison in his autobiography bestowed rare praise on Attlee for his handling of the Korean problem:

> The contribution of two men, Truman and Attlee, to saving the peace of the world in 1950 has not been sufficiently recognised. It may well be that if different men, and different parties, had been in control in the United States and Britain at the time of crisis, the third, and possibly final, world war would have broken out.

The last word on Attlee's Washington visit might be left with Michael Foot:

> ... The testimony of Truman's memoirs is there to show that Attlee's was a most formidable performance: a major achievement of his premiership. Confronted with the military and diplomatic chiefs of the greatest power on earth, each smarting from shattering defeats at the hands of the upstart Chinese, and all the more unlikely to tolerate criticism, Attlee nonetheless succeeded in presenting a more sophisticated argument about China and Asia opinion than Truman seemed to be receiving from his own advisers and therefore powerfully reinforced the case for limiting the war. To say that he tipped the scales against MacArthurite adventurism would be excessive and unprovable. But the British weight in the scales counted and the trust established between the two men gave Attlee the chance to argue another day.

In spite of Attlee's widely praised achievement in Washington, however, those who could read between the lines of Britain's commitments to the United States saw that vast problems lay ahead. The burden of additional rearmament to play the role the Americans were expecting would soon lie heavy on the already hard-pressed British economy. The outlook for 1951 was sombre.

26

Downhill,
1951

In the first days of 1951 clouds hung above the government and the
country. Nevertheless, Attlee's New Year's message to the Labour Movement was very positive and revealed few signs of gloom. Socialism was
still the answer to the nation's problems, at any rate so far as the Labour
Party was concerned.

> We have good reason to be proud of [our] fine record, and but for the grave
> events which have darkened the international scene we could certainly
> have looked forward to an even wider extension of the great schemes of
> social betterment which have been enacted since 1945. The demands of
> world security, however, place upon us a heavy responsibility which I know
> is fully appreciated by our Movement. We are seeking to build a free
> democratic society based on social justice. We are firm in our faith that this
> can be done provided that we can inspire the people with our socialist ideals
> and with the realisation that these can only be attained by hard work and
> by bringing the spirit of service into their daily lives.

January had not far advanced before the two grim and related realities
which faced the government began to display themselves – growing
tension between Britain and the United States on the subject of Korea,
and the need for an upscaling of the rearmament programme, which
would require new austerities, and retrenchment on the social services.
'No political leader has yet put before the British people their task for
1951 in all its harshness,' stated *The Times* leader of 5 January. Within a
few days the facts were speaking for themselves. The first revelation was
the strain on Anglo-American relations. At the turn of the year the North
Koreans had accelerated their alarming advance, pushing UN forces
almost a hundred miles below the 38th parallel. The United States,
without British support, unsuccessfully tried to persuade the UN to pass a
resolution 'branding' the Chinese government as an 'aggressor' in Korea;

in January the British delegation supported a resolution calling for a single administration in Korea and a conference of the US, the UK, the Soviet Union and Communist China to discuss Formosa and the representation of China in the UN. The Americans, very embarrassed, decided to support this resolution in the belief that the Chinese would reject it. When the Chinese did reject the proposal, the Americans countered by pressing their 'brand China' resolution, which would commit the UN to 'action' against the aggressor. The Attlee government feared that 'action' would lead to Chinese retaliation against Hong Kong and Malaya; the Americans felt that the UK was too ready to follow the Asian nations in appeasing China, and were well aware that at a recent Commonwealth Conference in London the idea of a four-power conference had been supported. Congressmen complained that Britain was letting down her American allies to keep on good terms with India, and that Britain was dragging her feet over rearmament.

Attlee was now in charge of foreign policy, since Bevin was too ill to act. He told the House on 23 January that a UN resolution proposing further action against China would close the door to negotiations; and two days later Sir Gladwyn Jebb, leading the British delegation to the United Nations, made an influential speech which led to the American 'aggressor' resolution being heavily amended. This was a great achievement for British foreign policy. Attlee decided to support the amended resolution because the economic situation was now so dire that it was important to lose no more American goodwill than was necessary. His first intention had been to oppose the resolution altogether, but he was persuaded otherwise by Gaitskell, who threatened to 'reconsider his position' unless the Cabinet reversed its decision of 25 January against supporting the resolution. By that time the issue was academic: the Americans had agreed that their resolution would be watered down. But the discussions of the matter within the Cabinet intensified the incompatibility of Gaitskell and Bevan, already pronounced as a result of the impact of the rearmament programme on the health services, by adding to it an American ingredient – roughly speaking, Gaitskell figured as pro-American, Bevan as anti-American.

In spite of his misgivings, Bevan decided that after all he would become Minister of Labour – he accepted the job on 17 January. Attlee had been trying to get him out of the Ministry of Health for several weeks: in the Ministry of Health, he thought, Bevan would have too much opportunity to complain about the government's rearmament programme, and to protest that the Labour government's socialist objectives were being frustrated by Gaitskell's economic policies. Attlee thought the Ministry of Labour would put Bevan under the discipline of having to support government economic policy as a whole, to confront, instead of leading, the government's left-wing critics, and of having to come to terms with the powerful right-wing trade union leaders. Aware of all this, Bevan tried to preserve something of his old role as the defender of the socialist faith by agreeing to move from the Ministry of Health, according to Foot, 'on one condition ... that there should be no fresh attack on the social services'. Attlee, according to Foot, 'seemed to agree'.

Later, Bevan spoke as though he had also warned Attlee that the British economy could not stand the strain of the new rearmament programme, and that he resented the pressure which the Americans were putting on Britain to carry it out. If he had communicated these doubts to Attlee at the time – Attlee said later that he did not – Attlee would have agreed with him. The American generals, with backing from their British counterparts, had proposed a £6,000 million programme for the United Kingdom. The Cabinet and the defence departments scaled this down to £4,700 million, an increase of £1,000 million on the total which had been approved in September as the maximum Britain could undertake without putting the economy on a war footing. Even the British figure of £4,700 million meant doubling the pre-Korean level of defence expenditure, and putting it up to 14 per cent of the national income. Harold Wilson had already come to the conclusion that this burden simply could not be shouldered: there is no evidence that Aneurin Bevan had.

Meanwhile, at Lewisham on 28 January, Attlee prepared the country for the new rearmament programme with one of his grimmest speeches; parts of it sounded like a call to arms. Through the socialists of West Lewisham he warned the nation that the defence programme which he would announce in the Commons the following Monday would demand sacrifice and effort from every man and woman in the country. 'Our way of life is in danger, our happiness, and the happiness and future of our children, are in danger; and it is both our privilege and our duty to defend them if they are attacked. War would bring our standards crashing down; defeat would destroy and obliterate them for ever. Make no mistake about that.' He spoke of Russia as though of an enemy. 'One power in the great alliance that overthrew Hitler ... did not turn back to the paths of peace; it went down the roads of conquest and of imperialism.' He described the size of Soviet forces. Russia had a 'vast military machine, yet she is threatened by no one'. Experience had shown that unless the Western powers started from a reasonable basis of strength there would not be much chance of getting agreement. 'We have weighed up all the factors in the situation that faces us today and have decided that it is our duty to increase our armaments.... We would far rather devote our resources to the things of peace and to the creation of a better life for us all. But peace and the better life are in danger today.'

The debate on the armament programme took place two weeks later. The week before it, on 7 February, there was a debate on the government's decision to make 15 February the vesting day for the nationalized steel industry, which Churchill denounced as an act of 'partisan aggression'. Meanwhile Labour members were becoming restive about foreign policy – there was a foreign affairs debate on 13 February – and about the defence debate that was to follow. Attlee was as detached as ever. He wrote to Tom: 'Flippy [Felicity] has returned from Italy speaking quite good Italian and having had a wonderful time. It was pleasant to revive old memories in the light of her recent experiences ... we got through our Foreign Affairs Debate all right yesterday.' The defence debate began on 15 February. From the government's point of view the hero of the day was, of all people, Aneurin Bevan, who defended the rearmament programme and the expenditures it would involve, with immense eloquence and power – and with hardly any reference to the fears he later claimed to have expressed to Cabinet colleagues about the burden it would impose upon the economy. 'Bevan,' recorded Dalton, 'who had often been unsteady on defence, made a notable speech.' A more significant compliment came from Churchill; towards the end of his oration Bevan began to attack the Conservative front bench. 'Don't spoil a good speech now,' Churchill interjected.

Ernest Bevin resigned from the Foreign Office on 9 March 1951 to become Lord Privy Seal. His health had been in decline for months. From time to time he had been in great pain. He had been in hospital or at home so much that the bulk of his routine work had been done by his minister of state, Kenneth Younger. Bravely, but also egotistically, Bevin had insisted on remaining at his post. In this he was sustained partly by his doctors, who for a long time thought that he might be able to carry on, and by Attlee, who was unhappy on political as well as personal grounds at the thought of his old friend resigning – the succession would present problems.

Bevin took his dismissal badly, and Attlee's reputation suffered. According to Morrison, who claimed to have been told by Bevin's wife, Attlee telephoned to ask for the resignation when Bevin was celebrating his seventieth birthday party at the Foreign Office. This story was circulated at the time. Attlee certainly telephoned Bevin one day and said that the time had come to ask him to go, but they had discussed the question of Bevin's fitness to continue on several occasions previously, and in particular they had discussed Mrs Bevin's worry that 'this job is killing Ernie', an anxiety which she had communicated to Attlee. Attlee was also concerned about Bevin's long absences from duty: the Opposition were making much of these in the House. Bevin's own reputation, as well as the government's, was suffering. 'I knew he wouldn't go until I pushed him,' Attlee told the author many years later. 'He knew it too. He would have stayed till he dropped. It was partly because he was stubborn, partly because he thought he could get somewhere with the Russians. I told him he had to go. I thought he might have had some time to live, but he was dead in a few weeks. He was upset, but we both knew I did the right thing.' Within five weeks of the resignation, Bevin was dead. If Attlee is to be criticized, it is for leaving Bevin so long in office.

The choice of a successor raised big problems. The two ministers of state at the Foreign Office, Hector McNeil and Kenneth Younger, lacked standing in the party and the country. The Attorney General, Sir Hartley Shawcross, carried more weight, and had led the British delegation at the United Nations with distinction, but Attlee was averse to having a lawyer as foreign secretary – 'learned that lesson with Simon,' he told Arthur Moyle. His instinct was to appoint Jim Griffiths, then Colonial Secretary. He had a great regard for Griffiths, valued the regard for him in the party, and in principle wanted a trade unionist in the Foreign Office. The job went to Morrison. There was much speculation about why Morrison got it, and whether he wanted it. At the time, Morrison gave friends the impression that he did not want the job. Attlee certainly appointed Morrison with reluctance. He did so because 'Morrison wanted the job: he started spouting on Foreign Affairs everywhere. The Press was saying that the Foreign Office should go to a top-ranking member of the Cabinet. They wanted a big name, and there was nobody else. They were for Morrison. Worst appointment I ever made. Jim Griffiths should have got the job.' What was wrong with Morrison? 'Out of his depth. I hadn't realised he knew so little about it. Not his milieu. He'd spent his life organizing – foreign policy is about negotiating. A trade union leader can do it: a party manager can't. I should have known better.' Dalton recorded his belief that Aneurin Bevan hoped to succeed Ernest Bevin, and that this, his second disappointment about promotion, was responsible for his resignation a month later. Others, including Sam Watson, held the same view. Attlee did not share it. In 1962, on 21 October, he wrote in *The Observer*: 'Among others I asked Bevan whom he thought would make a good Foreign Secretary. I can't remember what he said, but he certainly did not ask for the job himself; and he did not indicate that he wanted it – contrary to what has frequently been said since.'

Exactly a week after the news of Ernest Bevin's resignation, it was announced that Attlee would shortly be going into hospital for a check-up. He had been suffering from intestinal pain, and his doctors had diagnosed duodenal trouble. One of the reasons why he had dealt so swiftly with Bevin's removal from the Foreign Office was that he knew he might have a long spell in hospital himself at a time when problems of foreign policy, particularly in Persia, would put the government under pressure. The *Daily Express*, sending wishes for his recovery, remarked pleasantly: 'Mr Attlee, restored to health, will make an admirable Leader of the Opposition.' He was admitted to hospital on 21 March. Ten days later he emerged briefly to make a party political broadcast in reply to one by Churchill. Churchill had said that Britain was now in even greater danger than in 1940. On grounds of national interest, the Conservative Party would 'do their utmost to bring about an appeal to the nation', and to this end would make full use of their 'parliamentary and constitutional rights'. Attlee accused Churchill of being 'out to get back to power by hook or crook'. His speeches far more partisan than those of any other Conservative leader. 'He lost the cup-tie but demands a replay on his own ground. During the past few months he has been resorting to various political tricks ... to try to defeat or harass the Government. I don't suppose you are much impressed.' *The Times* found the broadcast:

> one of his least happy efforts. ... It was a characteristically moderate retort, but ineffective in that it ignored the real reason why Mr Churchill made his request. This was not that an election now would necessarily restore national unity but that 'a Government without a normal working majority in the House of Commons' have 'all their work cut out in keeping their heads above water from day to day'. Conservative 'tricks' are 'the legitimate Parliamentary devices which any Opposition might use in similar circumstances.'

II

How the political debate between the two major parties would have developed under its own momentum we shall never know. For within a few days of Attlee's removal to St Mary's Hospital the clash between Gaitskell and Bevan, over the proposal to introduce health charges in the coming budget, had taken place. The government was being borne towards the rocks. The conflict between Gaitskell and Bevan can be interpreted in many ways; as a personal struggle for power, as a contest between 'consolidationism' and 'advance', between reformism and socialism, or between the pragmatists and the idealists, as a casualty of the battle between the welfare state and the Treasury, as working-class leadership versus middle-class leadership, or as a symptom of political fatigue.

The crisis, when it came, expressed itself as a difference of opinion about the imposition of charges on the health service spreading to other matters. Waste and abuse in the Ministry of Health's administration of the health service had been criticized in the Cabinet for several months. The need to make the budget economically and politically astringent brought the matter to a head in Cabinet discussions which took place just before Attlee went into hospital.

On 20 March 1951 Gaitskell wrote to Attlee to 'put on record what we agreed this morning' at a meeting between Morrison, Bevan, Attlee and Gaitskell. The net cost to the Exchequer of the National Health Service was to be kept to £400 million, and savings of £10 million made on the hospital service. Gaitskell hoped that prescription charges could be avoided, though there would have to be charges for dental and optical work. In reply, Attlee advised Gaitskell to take care about the presentation of the need for charges: it should be made clear that they 'are being imposed to eliminate waste, not solely to raise revenue'. Attlee's terse advice was crucial. He knew that some of Bevan's friends, like Harold Wilson and John Strachey, had been encouraging him to resign on the rearmament issue, and that if he did so they would follow. He believed that Bevan might decide *not* to resign on the rearmament issue, but would be much more ready to go if he could do so as the working-class defender of the 'free' health service. Unlike most members of the Cabinet, Attlee did not think that Bevan was bluffing to try and get his way.

The Cabinet met on 22 March, the day after Attlee went into hospital, to discuss Gaitskell's proposals. Morrison, presiding, supported Gaitskell's measures, and said they had been approved by the Prime Minister. Bevan and Wilson opposed them. Bevan said that to agree would be to betray the principle of the 'free health service'. Why should the government strain to save £20 million on health charges in a total budget of £3,000 million? Morrison listened to Bevan and Wilson, and then pointed out that apart from them – James Griffiths had some reservations, but did not press them – the Cabinet were in favour of Gaitskell's proposals. Bevan and Gaitskell each offered to retire to the back benches if his view were not accepted. Although knowledge of the disagreement leaked out gradually, there was no public confrontation until 3 April, when Bevan, in an aside at a public meeting, shouted: 'I will never be a member of a government which makes charges on the National Health Service for a patient.' Cabinet ministers, if not the public at large, now realized that the die was cast. Dalton, warning Gaitskell, found him intransigent, willing to see Bevan, Wilson and Strachey leave the Cabinet. Bevan told Dalton that the introduction of charges was a deliberate attempt to drive him from the Cabinet.

On 9 April the Cabinet met for its last discussion of the budget, which was to be announced the following day. Gaitskell stood his ground, making it clear that even if he could cut defence expenditure he would spend the savings not on free spectacles and false teeth but on family allowances and old age pensions. This convinced Bevan that Gaitskell did not believe that 'free health' was a principle at all: he was either selling the socialist pass or trying to get rid of Bevan. Morrison reported Attlee's views, which had been given to the Chief Whip in St Mary's

Hospital that day. The note of the hospital interview survives in Morrison's papers.

PM 1 Must be give and take in budgets. No one can say any particular estimate sacrosanct. Lord Randolph Churchill only one who never recovered.

2 [Bevan] Must think of the Movement – not himself.

3 Crisis at this moment sheer stark folly. Electoral conditions.... Party divided – smashed.

4 Voters would say we can't govern. Tories in for ten years. AB [Aneurin Bevan] would have done it.

5 We must stand by Chancellor of Exchequer – as Cabinet decided with PM in chair.

That evening Bevan and Wilson went to St Mary's to see Attlee, who asked Bevan not to resign when there was the chance of an early election, and said that he would speak to Gaitskell and advise him to 'be more reasonable'. Gaitskell came later in the evening and reported the Cabinet situation as he saw it. Attlee listened, pipe clenched between teeth, spectacles on the end of his nose. Gaitskell was disconcerted when Attlee suggested that to keep Bevan in the Cabinet a ceiling on expenditure could be announced in the budget, and the charges could be imposed at some future date if the ceiling could not be achieved. Gaitskell said he could no longer consider that: he had already committed himself to announcing the health charges. He ended his submission: 'I have done my best to bridge the gap, and I have failed. I am sorry. If you wish it I shall go.' Attlee, his pipe in his mouth, so speaking somewhat indistinctly, said: 'Have to go.' Gaitskell – he told the author some years later – heard this as '*You'll* have to go.' Gaitskell bowed his head and said: 'As you wish, Prime Minister. First thing tomorrow you shall have my resignation ...' Attlee whipped his pipe from his mouth and snapped: 'No! *He'll* have to go!'

Attlee was still hoping that Bevan would stay. Gaitskell's budget was well received by the House; in the economic circumstances it was not particularly stiff, and the raising of the tax-free allowances and old age pensions cushioned the reaction of the Labour back bench to health service charges. Jennie Lee cried: 'Shame', and the Tories shouted: 'Resign, Nye, resign.' That evening Bevan and Wilson once again visited Attlee, who urged them to do nothing until after the PLP meeting which was to take place the following day. The same evening Attlee was visited by John Freeman, the talented under-secretary at the Ministry of Supply, who was also known to be contemplating resignation. Dalton reports that the next day, on Attlee's authority, he offered Freeman promotion if he did not resign. Freeman wrote to Bevan urging him not to resign over the budget, but to wait until he could go out on the issue of the drive towards war and the anti-working-class character of the rearmament economies. At the same time, though, Wilson and Jennie Lee were pressing Bevan to resign at once.

At the party meeting Bevan, who had now been inundated with appeals that he remain in harness, said that he would not resign, but that there were 'others' who had as much responsibility for party unity as he had, and who should do as much for it as he was doing. By 'others' he meant Gaitskell, and what these 'others' should do was to refrain from announcing a date for the introduction of the health charges. Attlee had urged Bevan not to resign before this party meeting because he thought Gaitskell would respond to Bevan's suggestion in a way which would be acceptable to Bevan. But, typically, Gaitskell regarded Bevan's remarks as a criticism of his own behaviour; in any case he seems to have made up his mind, much supported by Morrison, that Bevan must now either come to heel or get out. Attlee, on the other hand, seems to have been impressed by Bevan's conduct at the meeting. He did not write at once. He had been tired by the visits to him in St Mary's before and on Budget Day – on one occasion he had refused to see Morrison – and three days later Bevin died. Attlee wrote to Bevan on 18 April:

> My dear Nye,
>
> I gather that all went off well at the Party meeting and I am grateful to you for the line you took.
>
> The death of Ernie has rather over-shadowed these differences, and I hope that everyone will forget them.
>
> I think that it is particularly essential that we should present a united front to the enemy. The next few weeks will be very tricky.... Hope to be back at work by the end of next week.
>
> All the best,
> Yours ever,
> Clem.

When Attlee wrote this letter he either did not know, or had not grasped, that the time for compromise had passed. The previous day the Cabinet had met and with Morrison and Gaitskell setting the pace had agreed in general that the Health Charges Bill would be introduced at once. The Cabinet met again on the nineteenth. Bevan informed his colleagues that if a date for the second reading of the Health Bill was announced, he would resign, and that he wanted that recorded in the Cabinet minutes. Morrison, Gaitskell, Chuter Ede and Whiteley (the Chief Whip) visited Attlee in hospital that night and persuaded him to send Bevan an ultimatum. Attlee wrote to Bevan the following day:

My dear Nye,

I have a report of yesterday's Cabinet meeting and of subsequent meetings of Ministers on the subject of dental and ophthalmic charges.

I understand that you have stated that, if there were a vote on the Second Reading of the Bill, you would be unable to go into the lobby with the Government. You have also made statements about resignation. You will, I am sure, realize that matters cannot be left like this.

Cabinet ministers must accept collective responsibility for Government measures.

Decisions of the Cabinet taken after full consideration must be supported by all.

I must, therefore, ask you to let me know how you stand in this matter. I have discussed the issues with you very fully.

I shall be glad to know today that you are prepared to carry out loyally the decisions of the Government.

Yours ever,

Clem.

Bevan's letter, dated 2.30 pm 21 April, from the House of Commons, restated his objection to health charges, but so far as Attlee was concerned broke new ground: Bevan now objected to Gaitskell's budget because its provision for expenditure on rearmament was impractical and damaging to the policies which the Labour Party existed to promote:

> In previous conversations with you, and in my statements to the Cabinet, I have explained my objections to many features in the Budget. Having endeavoured, in vain, to secure modifications of these features, I feel I must ask you to accept my resignation.
>
> The Budget, in my view, is wrongly conceived in that it fails to apportion fairly the burdens of expenditure as between different social classes. It is wrong because it is based upon a scale of military expenditure, in the coming year, which is physically unattainable, without grave extravagance in its spending.

Attlee replied that day in his own hand:

> I have your letter of today's date. I note that you have extended the area of disagreement with your colleagues a long way beyond the specific matter to which as I understood you had taken objection.
>
> I had certainly gathered that if the proposal for imposing charges on dentures and spectacles were dropped, you would have been satisfied.
>
> I much regret that you should feel it necessary to offer your resignation, but in these circumstances I have no option but to accept it. I note that you propose to make a statement in the House.
>
> Thank you for the good work that you have done as a Member of the Government during these difficult years.
>
> Thank you also for your good wishes for my health.

Bevan's resignation letter and Attlee's reply were published on Monday 23 April. Wilson's resignation was announced the same day, Freeman's the day after. Wilson's letter to Attlee said that Bevan's letter described his own position:

> The 1950–51 rearmament proposals are impossible, so the programme is bad for the defence effort itself, and bad for the essentials of our economy, eroding the social services further. I am very sorry to have to write you such a letter when you are in hospital recovering from a serious illness. As you know, I thought we could wait until you returned. I am particularly sorry after the privilege of serving under you in a Government with great and solid achievements to its name.

Attlee replied:

> My dear Harold,
>
> I have received your letter in which you ask to be relieved of your office. I regret that you should terminate a useful period of administration for reasons which seem to me to be inadequate to justify such a step.
> I thank you for your good wishes for my restoration to health.

Bevan made his resignation statement in the House the following day. His speech was very much criticized. Even John Freeman told Dalton that: 'Nothing could have done more to influence me the other way than Nye's outburst in the Commons.' Before Bevan rose, it was clear that the great majority of his own party, including many of his personal friends, were against him because his resignation might cause an electoral disaster. Bevan attacked his leaders, their policies, and Gaitskell personally. The £4,700 million arms programme, he said, 'is already dead'. The budget had 'united the City, satisfied the Opposition and disunited the Labour Party – all this because we have allowed ourselves to be dragged too far behind the wheels of American diplomacy'. His attack on the health charges amounted to the implication that Gaitskell wanted to sabotage the welfare state. Many of the fair points he made against the impracticability of the rearmament programme were obscured by his indictment of the Chancellor for betraying the Labour Party's aims and objectives. 'It is in Mr Bevan's personal attack on the Chancellor of the Exchequer,' said *The Times*, 'that the mood and motive of his departure from the Cabinet most clearly show themselves.' At an emergency meeting of the PLP the following morning, Bevan further incensed backbenchers by describing himself as 'martyred'. Why, the word went around, had Bevan supported the rearmament programme so vigorously in January and February, only to oppose it now? Why had he not resigned *then*? The bulk of the Parliamentary Labour Party concluded that he had been carried away into irresponsible behaviour, either by personal ambition or by emotions which he had failed to control.

Immediately after this stormy meeting was over, the PLP walked over
to Westminster Abbey for the memorial service to Ernest Bevin. Bevin
dead, Cripps dying in Switzerland, Bevan storming out of the Cabinet,
Dalton discredited, Morrison insecure, and the leader ill in hospital:
morale in the party was not high. How did Attlee feel? In later years he
expressed the opinion that had he not been ill in hospital he might have
been able to prevent Bevan from resigning. Why did he think so? He told
the author:

> A number of reasons. He would listen to some people, not to others. He'd
> listen if he trusted you. Stafford could talk to him like an uncle. He trusted
> Stafford. Stafford wasn't there – he was ill. I might have been able to talk
> to him myself, but I was ill. We might have got somewhere with deferring
> the dates of the Health charges – dates of introducing them. And how they
> were presented – not to compromise the principle of a free health service by
> making it pay, but to preserve it by preventing abuse; stop abuse, not raise
> money. If it had been put like that to Nye he might have accepted it. After
> all he'd accepted prescription charges in 1950. Accepting prescription
> charges was the same in principle as accepting charges on teeth and glasses.
> It had become clear we couldn't spend all the rearmament money anyway;
> there was a worldwide shortage of raw materials – the stuff wasn't there to
> spend on. There was less need to economise on health than we had foreseen,
> though we were right to try to prevent abuse, yes, different matter. If I had
> been there, I would have had more to say to Gaitskell. I didn't realise he
> was going to present the issue as he did – egged on by Morrison, perhaps.
> Morrison couldn't stand Nye. It was mutual. . . . There was no real issue of
> principle between Nye and the rest of the Cabinet, nothing which couldn't
> have been dealt with if it had been properly handled. Nye should have been
> given more time, Morrison and Gaitskell should not have dug in.

The moment Bevan 'widened the issue' and denounced the rearmament programme, he put an end to any chances Attlee might have had
of effecting a compromise. If Bevan had continued to give nominal, even
silent, public support to the rearmament campaign, Attlee could have
tried at least to use the Cabinet's inability to spend 'all the rearmament
money' as a means of reaching an accommodation with Bevan on the
postponement of a date for health charges. Attlee would have tried to
persuade Gaitskell to stay his hand, and to urge Bevan to wait and see.
But when Bevan widened the issue from health charges to rearmament
the battle was joined; only one outcome was possible. That Attlee was
right when he claimed that Bevan had widened the issue was borne out
by Harold Wilson in an interview with the author in 1963. Wilson
remarked on:

> the mistaken assumption that when I resigned along with him [Bevan] in
> 1951 it was for absolutely the same reason as he did. . . . In fact, he and I

resigned in 1951 for different reasons. Nye was bitterly opposed to what he regarded as an unjust and dangerous undermining of his Health programme. I was opposed to the Government's defence proposals.

Not until the day of their resignation letters, 23 April, nearly a fortnight after the budget, was Wilson able to say in his letter to Attlee that Bevan's resignation letter 'describes my own position. The 1950–51 rearmament proposals are impossible ...' In replying to Bevan's resignation letter of the same date Attlee was correct in observing that he had suddenly extended the area of disagreement with his colleagues.

Very few Labour politicians followed Bevan into the wilderness: the general feeling of the Labour Party in the House of Commons was that his resignation was a betrayal of the party. Shawcross and Robens joined the Cabinet – Dalton telling Attlee that he saw Robens, a young trade-unionist, as the natural successor to Ernest Bevin. Gaitskell had much profited by the crisis; his budget speech had been universally admired for its lucidity and earnest persuasiveness. His courtesy and steadfastness in Cabinet had been appreciated. 'His attitude towards the resignation,' wrote Dalton to Attlee, 'as compared to Nye's, was like a high snow peak with a steaming tropical swamp.'

How did Attlee feel about it all at the time? A week after he had received Bevan's letter of resignation, and just after he had left hospital, he wrote to Tom:

> I think that I owe you a letter. I had three peaceful days at Chequers before starting full work again today. My tummy is pretty well all right though I am much too fat, but I have had a lot of trouble with my teeth. It was found that old Longhurst had failed to see the condition of my gums and I had to have them cut all round.
>
> The Bevan business is a nuisance. The real wonder is that we kept him reasonably straight for so long. But with this and Ernie's death I did not have as restful time as I should have liked.
>
> I see today in *The Times* that John Druce is dead at 93 – a good old age. I saw in the paper the death of Sam Cash, and also of G. B. Wainwright whose son-in-law Wild of Univ I have just had made Dean of Durham. I hope your new Bishop turns out all right. He is well spoken of.
>
> I got through a lot of reading in hospital, but I don't find some of the moderns whom they laud to the skies very much good.
>
> Your loving brother,
> Clem.

III

After his 'three peaceful days at Chequers' Attlee went back into action with an impressive resilience. His personal standing with public opinion was well ahead of the administration's. In May the government's rating was low, only 40 per cent, but 57 per cent approved of Attlee as Prime Minister. Evidently he did not suffer in the public mind from the effect of the recent resignations, while it seemed that the government did. In an article in the *News Chronicle* on 17 May, entitled 'What Makes Attlee Tick?', Francis Williams, describing the government's standing as 'despite the latest upward turn ominously low', pointed out that the Prime Minister continued 'to remain far and away the greatest single political asset the Labour Party possesses'. This was no personal flattery from an old friend and former public relations adviser; on the contrary, Williams went on to say that much as he admired Attlee, 'I confess I see great dangers in the present position', and then embarked upon what could be interpreted as a respectful suggestion that Attlee should cease to be the Labour Party's leader.

On 24 July Attlee wrote in a letter to Tom:

> Vi and I had a very fine visit to Durham staying with the Sam Watsons a most delightful couple. The gala was the biggest and finest ever, over 3000 people and we had a very fine reception. We unveiled a banner on which I am represented nearly life-size, a jolly ceremony with the whole colliery village present ...
>
> On the way home I saw the exterior of Ripon and Southwell Cathedrals, the only ones I had not previously visited, the latter very fine. As it was Sunday we could not go in.
>
> We are in for a good deal of bother with Nye Bevan – too much ego in his cosmos.

The 'bother with Nye Bevan' was expected because of ominous predictions in the Press about the contents of a coming *Tribune* pamphlet, entitled *One Way Only*, to which Bevan had written an introduction. There were rumours that Bevan had written an indictment of his ex-colleagues in the Cabinet, and had forcefully restated his own political position. A false alarm: the pamphlet as a whole was described by Michael Foot as 'an essay in qualified judgements'; one newspaper called it a 'damp squib'. The arguments in *One Way Only* were sincere; its views were held by many who were not 'Bevanites'. There was little in Bevan's introduction to justify Attlee's comment to Tom, 'too much ego in his cosmos', and its economic forecasts proved nearer the mark than the government's. On German rearmament, indeed, Bevan still had an ally in the Cabinet: Dalton. At this time, while Morrison and Shinwell were working on a paper setting out the arguments for rearming the Germans, Dalton, always strongly anti-German, was insisting that German rearmament should not be brought to the Cabinet as a *fait accompli*, and was giving every indication that when it was proposed he would fight it.

Instead of renewed inter-party squabbles, Attlee was brought face to face with serious foreign policy problems in Egypt and Persia, just as Anglo-American relations were on the mend because of the dismissal of General MacArthur. The trouble in Persia, hereafter called Iran, began with a demand made in the Iranian Parliament, the Majlis, for the nationalization of the oil industry, which belonged at that time to the Anglo-Iranian Oil Company. The Prime Minister, Razmara, opposed this when it was put forward in February 1950. Within a few days he had been assassinated, and his successor, Hussain Ala, was forced to resign at the end of April. The new Prime Minister was Mossadeq, who had led demands for nationalization and immediately put through a bill to dispossess the Anglo-Iranian Oil Company.

The crisis in Iran put heavy pressure on Morrison. The United States urged that no force be used, lest Russia intervene and cut off Western oil supplies; the Foreign Office suspected that the United States government wanted to get British oil companies out of Iran in order to get American companies in. Morrison rattled a sabre in the House, but encouraged negotiations and pressed AIOC to compromise. Talks between AIOC and the Iranians broke down, and Morrison responded by sending a para-troop brigade and extra naval forces to the Eastern Mediterranean. Anglo-Iranian was told to begin to withdraw its staff. Morrison, who had recently suffered a blow to his esteem from the defection of Burgess and Maclean to Russia, fumbled. In Parliament he offended his own back-benchers by jingoistic speeches and the Tories by describing them as imperialist. In Cabinet he talked of Britain being 'too United Nationsy'. 'Morrison very petulant. Quite a little Pam,' recorded Dalton. 'I said [to Attlee] Morrison must not try to compensate himself for having been a conscientious objector in World War I and against arms before World War II.'

Morrison's widely criticized conduct of affairs reflected badly on Att-lee, particularly as he had to stand in for the Foreign Secretary in the House during Morrison's frequent absences. Taking advantage of Mor-rison's holiday and a visit to the United States in July, he began to take a greater hand in Iranian policy. The Abadan refinery ceased working on 31 July. In August Attlee sent the new Lord Privy Seal, Richard Stokes, on an emergency mission to Persia; Stokes was recalled on 6 September with no agreement in sight, and reported to Attlee that the best hope was to deal generously with the Iranians and to conduct negotiations with Mossadeq. Morrison was still in favour of 'sharp and forceful action', as he wrote in his autobiography. But according to Dalton, Attlee told him on 16 September, soon after he received the letter from Stokes: 'I am handling Persia. I have made it quite clear that troops are to go in only to save lives.' He later said that he had made up his mind that if Labour won the election he would not send Morrison back to the Foreign Office. On 27 September Attlee led the Cabinet in deciding, against Morrison's advice, to refer the matter to the United Nations; he made it clear that he would not himself support any British military action.

Morrison was almost as isolated – in the Cabinet and in the party – as he was ineffective. In the country his 'jingoism' was more acceptable, and the newspapers with a Tory bias had praise for his stand that Britain 'should not be pushed around'. Could any other foreign secretary, or Attlee acting as such, have done any better? Probably yes; even Stokes's letter to Attlee shows a far more realistic assessment of the situation than Morrison's. Had Attlee received it earlier, Britain might have yielded to the inevitable, and preserved better relations with Iran. As it was, the British oil men evacuated Abadan on 3 October, in an atmosphere one of them described as imposed 'scuttle'. The *Sunday Times* compared Abadan to Munich: 'The worst defeat suffered by Great Britain during the present century in the field of foreign affairs.' *The Observer*, with more understanding of the limits of British power, said it was 'foolish to rattle a sabre one knows one cannot use. Our fault was not excessive meekness but empty bullying. . . . Mr Morrison is rightly blamed for his disastrous mishandling of the Persian oil crisis.'

Even if Attlee could have done much better than Morrison, however, he had to bear his share of responsibility for what Morrison did. It was he who appointed Morrison, and as Prime Minister he was Morrison's chief. The bulk of the Cabinet were against Morrison's handling of Iran from the beginning, and so was the party. On the whole the Opposition behaved reasonably well. The fact that Attlee saw the light in the later stages is the more reason for asking why he did not see it earlier. In his autobiography, though he does not admit to any personal failure of judgement or lack of energy at the time, he certainly admits that Britain's policy left much to be desired, and that Morrison's inclination to resolve the situation by the use of force should never have been tolerated.

Egypt presented the Attlee government with two problems which directly recalled that which was posed by Iran:

> If we cleared out, there would be a vacuum. The Russians would probably move in, and we would lose the Canal, and our oil supplies. The second problem was: we wanted to accommodate Egyptian nationalism, but there was more than one Nationalist party, and none of them was much good: they weren't out for the good of the people, they wanted to feather their own nests. So if we cleared out we would have endangered the security of the Free World, and we wouldn't have helped the Egyptian peasant. As Ernie said, our duty was to the peasants, not the pashas.'

The beginning of the phase of the Egyptian problem which precipitated the crisis which the Labour government had to face was marked by the announcement by the Egyptian government, on 16 November 1950, of its intention to abrogate the Anglo-Egyptian Treaty of 1936. The treaty had affirmed a permanent alliance between the two countries, preserved British rights and interests in Egypt, and in particular had guaranteed the presence of British forces in the Canal Zone for twenty years. From November 1950 on, encouraged and guided by events in Iran, the Egyptians stepped up their campaign to get the British out of Egypt. Pointing out that the treaty could not be abrogated unilaterally, the British government nevertheless worked on the preparation of proposals for the modification of the treaty which might be acceptable to Egyptian nationalism. But on 8 October, 1951, the day Attlee replied to Churchill's attack on the 'scuttle' in Iran, the Egyptian Prime Minister, Nahas Pasha, tabled decrees abrogating the treaty and also the Condominium Agreement concerning the Sudan. All Britain's proposals were absolutely rejected, and Nahas Pasha's bill was passed a week later.

The British government protested, and made it clear that they were not going to be forced out. Alarmed by the possibility of a collapse of Middle East security, the Americans openly supported the British stand. In his autobiography Morrison writes: 'I strongly advocated a stiff line with Egypt and Attlee agreed.' The 'stiff line' was a good deal better justified than in Persia, because of the Egyptian government's declared intention to annex the Sudan; Nahas Pasha's bill had declared Farouk King of Egypt and the Sudan. However, the 'line' was not very 'stiff', and, except for the warning that the Egyptian government must not allow violence against British persons and property, and that Britain would keep a military presence in the Suez Zone until a new treaty was negotiated, it had little substance.

In any case, so far as the Attlee government was concerned, the issue was soon to be academic: it was the Conservatives, by winning the election, who would have the Egyptian problem on their hands.

IV

In the third week of September 1951, after much speculation on possible dates, pre-election fever was growing in intensity. The newspapers began to clamour for an early election. Attlee, one columnist said, was 'lying low, like Brer Rabbit, and saying nuffin'.' At 9.15 pm on 19 September, in a special broadcast after the News, Attlee announced that Parliament would be dissolved on 5 October, and a general election would take place twenty days later. It was the first time such an announcement had been made by radio. He spoke for only two minutes: after eighteen months in office with a very small majority, the time had come for the government to ask the electors 'for a renewal of confidence'. The *New Statesman* commented:

> The Prime Minister's capacity for making everything sound sensible and unimportant was seldom heard to better advantage. If Winston had been speaking, his voice would have conjured up visions of rich robes and pageants; the majestic procession of history would once more have culminated in the great arbitrament of the nation. Mr Attlee's dry and concise voice, devoid of overtones, merely suggested little men and women putting bits of paper into ballot boxes.

The Opposition claimed that Attlee had been driven into calling an election by their denunciation of his mishandling of Iran and Egypt, and by his sudden realization that his government could not handle the problems of rising prices and industrial strife. Morrison's indications of 'surprise' at the announcement lent some colour to their charges. In fact, Attlee had begun to think about the desirability of a general election soon after Bevan's resignation. On 27 May he had written to Morrison informing him that he proposed to hold the election in October. Early in 1952 the King was to make a six-month tour of Australia and New Zealand. Attlee felt strongly that he should call an election in good enough time to enable the country to settle down before the King set out on such a lengthy period of absence. For the King to embark on such a long and important mission without the election having taken place, said Attlee, would be unfair on him, and against the national interest. 'I think,' he wrote to Morrison:

> we ought to go to the country this year [1951]. The real decision is whether to go before or after the Autumn Recess. There are three factors militating against the earlier dates. The Festival of Britain, Wakes Weeks and our own state of readiness and popularity.
>
> I gather that while our position is improving, it is not very good and the local elections confirm this. There is a good prospect of improved meat supplies and a possibility of better weather over the holidays. There may be a change in the Korean and Persian positions. Something may emerge from the Four Power talks. In my view everything points to having an election in the autumn and as early as possible having regard to the late harvest this year.
>
> Late September and early October are best for our campaigning. The Party Conference falls awkwardly. It might be best to make our announcement in time for turning this into a short electoral Conference, and a kick-off to the election campaign, but this will need careful thought. If my reasoning is sound we must consider carefully our tactics in the House and in the country.
>
> I have set out these considerations with a view to an early talk with you. I would like to consider with you what other colleagues to bring into consultation.

According to Dalton Attlee raised the matter privately with other ministers at this time. None of them disagreed with him. When Morrison answered Attlee's letter, he suggested a meeting of a few senior ministers to discuss the timing of the election. Attlee did not act on this. In July Morrison raised the matter with him again, this time raising the possibility of waiting until 1952. 'As you know, I was unhappy about the 1950 date as to which Stafford and Nye were wrong. I don't want us to make another mistake . . .' There is no record of an answer to this second letter: presumably Attlee had been satisfied with the outcome of his other private consultations. Certainly, however, Morrison had several months' advance notice that Attlee thought the election should be held in October, even if the announcement in mid-September, while Morrison and Shinwell were in America, came to them as a surprise.

On 24 June, at a private audience with the King, who was concerned about the government's unstable position, Attlee had said he would ask for a dissolution in the autumn, though he did not at this meeting mention any specific date. In a letter to Attlee on 1 September, the King had asked again about the election date, and:

> . . . it would be very difficult indeed for me to go away for five or six months unless it was reasonably certain that political stability would prevail during my absence.
>
> On the other hand, it would be disastrous if my visits to three of the self-governing countries of the British Commonwealth . . . had to be postponed, or even interrupted, on account of political upheavals at home.
>
> It would be a great relief to me if you could now – or even in the next few weeks – give me some assurance that would set my mind at rest on this score.

Attlee replied on 5 September that Parliament would be dissolved in the first week in October.

> I have been giving much anxious thought to the question of a General Election. Among the factors to which I have given particular attention was the need for avoiding any political crisis while Your Majesty was out of the country. I have come to the conclusion that the right course would be to have a dissolution of Parliament in the first week in October. A later date would, I think, be undesirable, as November is seldom a good month from the point of view of the weather. I should therefore like to make a submission to Your Majesty in about a fortnight's time for the prorogation and dissolution of Parliament in the first week in October.

Two weeks later, three days before Morrison and Shinwell returned from America, Attlee told the Cabinet that he proposed to call a general election and gave them the date. A few days later he learned that the King's health had deteriorated to such an extent that he must undergo

486

a major operation, and that consequently the six-month tour of the Commonwealth might have to be cancelled. It is much to the credit of the King that he was so conscious of how much consideration for his feelings had influenced Attlee's choice of the election date, and the timing of its public announcement, that he asked his private secretary to write the following letter to Attlee immediately he was told he must have an operation:

> So that there is no misinterpretation of recent events by historians in the future, I want to put the following on record in our secret archives here: When the King wrote to you from Balmoral on 1st September urging that a decision should be taken to ensure political stability in this country before he left on his projected Commonwealth tour next January, he had no conception that his physical condition might make it necessary for him to abandon this tour; indeed, he still believes today, on the eve of his serious operation, that he will be able to carry out his tour more or less as planned.

When the election was announced, Morrison, in Ottawa, with Gaitskell and Shinwell for a NATO conference, was questioned about it by journalists. Their queries seemed to take him by surprise – 'his jaw dropped,' said Leonard Miall, the BBC's correspondent who was an eyewitness. Morrison's autobiography gives the date of 8 September for the decision about the timing of the election, which suggests that Attlee had told him the date well before the Cabinet meeting at which he informed the rest of his colleagues. Whether Morrison was happy about the date is another matter. Whatever their source, several newspapers reported that Attlee had announced an election without consulting the Deputy Prime Minister, others saying that Morrison *had* been consulted, but that his advice *not* to hold an election had been ignored. Morrison – who still regarded himself as Labour's expert on election management – recorded that he had cabled Attlee urging him to make no commitment until he and Shinwell had returned to London and could discuss the date with him. 'But Gaitskell wanted it,' said Morrison, 'and Attlee was a willing listener to him.' This was not precisely true: Gaitskell had indeed advocated an autumn election earlier in the year, but by the time he heard the news, which ironically came to him while he was with Morrison in Ottawa, he had changed his mind. 'His jaw dropped too,' said Miall. Most of the government, on the other hand, did not agree with Morrison.

Whatever Morrison thought, for the majority of the voters, Conservative or Labour, an early election was logical and desirable. The general feeling among Labour backbenchers was that since even the modest social programmes drawn up in 1950 could not now be carried out because of the pressure on the economy exerted by the rearmament budget, the longer Labour stayed in office with a majority of only six, the more damage the party was bound to sustain. The polls predicted a Tory victory, though in fact Labour improved its ratings marginally but steadily through the summer months, suggesting that Attlee was right in his view that fear of being involved in foreign wars by Churchill could outweigh concern about the cost of living. In spite of Morrison's view, the balance of arguments seemed to favour an election in 1951 rather than 1952. The main objection was that Labour might go into it with divided ranks.

The state of the economy was already bad from an electioneering point of view. There were a few strikes in the late spring and early summer, but the atmosphere of industrial relations was much improved by the modification in August of Order number 1305, which had first been introduced in 1940 by Ernest Bevin, banning strikes and lockouts and requiring compulsory arbitration of disputes. Under the new Minister of Labour, Alfred Robens, the prosecution of strikes and lockouts under the criminal law was suspended and a new Industrial Disputes Tribunal was established. The main trouble on the industrial front was persistent demands for higher wages without guarantees of higher productivity. The rate of wage increases in the nine months preceding July 1951 rose by more than it had in the previous three years.

The excuse for the barrage of wage claims made in the summer of 1951 was the rise in the cost of living. Attlee, accompanied by Gaitskell, met a hundred trade union representatives who conveyed the rising feeling in the unions. Next day, Gaitskell announced price controls and dividend limitations for a three year period. This did not satisfy the unions, or Harold Wilson, who said that prices would not be affected by anything until the economic programme was revised. In August, the Engineering and Shipbuilding Unions put in a claim on behalf of $2\frac{1}{2}$ million men which would cost £125 million a year. The government's wages policy had failed, and its economic policy seemed rudderless. The country was now facing a new balance of payments crisis, and Gaitskell flew to Washington on 5 September for negotiations with the Treasury. The 'gap' was double what it had been in the most dangerous year of all, 1947. The economy had so far hardly felt the first effects of the rearmament programme and the diversion to export of manufactured goods; an unprecedented inflation was just around the corner.

Although Attlee did not set much store by the results of public opinion polls, he must have been a little disappointed by the Gallup announcement on 24 September that only 44 per cent approved of him as Prime Minister 'today', as opposed to 57 per cent in May. On the other hand, approval of the government had risen from 31 per cent in February to 35 per cent 'today'. Traditional Labour support could be expected to rally as soon as a general election were announced. Attlee was not in the best physical shape for the campaign. In a letter to Tom he mentioned 'trouble with lumbago and sciatica which is rather a nuisance' – it had prevented him from attending a meeting of the National Executive that week. Nevertheless he showed all his old spirit when the campaign began. Addressing the Scottish Labour Party Conference at North Berwick on 23 September, he made digs at Churchill, and went on: 'We are going into this election with good heart. We are proud of our record. We ask the right to continue to apply our principles. I claim that in a world where there are many shadows, Britain has been a beacon of light on the way to peace, freedom and social justice.'

Far fewer Liberal candidates were standing in 1951 than had stood the year before, so it was much more of a straight fight between Conservatives and Labour. The Tories directed their attack to Labour's domestic record – rising prices and continuing shortages, especially housing. In Slaithwaite on 30 September, on the eve of the annual party conference at Scarborough, Attlee claimed that all the evidence showed the Labour government had held prices stable more effectively than any other government in the world. 'I am not promising an easy time,' he said, 'but I am convinced that the more we can put our appeal to the people on the basis of what people can give rather than what they can get, the more successful we shall be. I do not like appealing to cupidity and stupidity.'

Attlee did not benefit much from the three-day party conference at Scarborough which in May he had hoped would be 'a kick-off to the election campaign'; nor did the party. The Iranian situation, the economic crisis and a widespread feeling that Labour had run out of steam more than balanced a feeling of relief that the inevitable election had at last arrived.

It was clear at the conference that Bevanite stock was rising. In the voting for the seven candidates representing the constituencies on the National Executive, who would be prominent in the coming election, the Bevanites made significant gains. Bevan, again at the top of the list, extended his lead. Barbara Castle moved up into second place. In the third and sixth places, Driberg and Mikardo polled larger votes than they had won the previous year. Morrison went down from third place to fifth. Griffiths and Dalton remained on the Executive but lost votes, and Shinwell failed to be re-elected, immediately showing his disgust by leaving the conference. Morrison nevertheless, in the last speech of the conference, scored a great success, and struck a note which, later epitomized by the *Daily Mirror*'s slogan 'Whose finger on the Trigger?', was to become Labour's main theme in the election campaign. The Bevanites did nothing to divide the party, and the conference exhibited an obvious and natural closing of ranks, and a readiness for compromise which, had

Labour won, might have brought its own reward in reduced bitterness between opposing personalities.

Attlee's speech, which opened the debate on the election manifesto, was not a great feat of oratory but it was well adjusted to the mood and state of the Party. 'Let's have a change,' he said, was the only idea which the Tories were putting forward in their election campaign. The Labour Party could campaign on its record. Under Labour the British people had done great work in reconstructing the economy and dealing with the balance of payments problem. In foreign affairs the government had supported the United Nations in Korea and made a full contribution to NATO; in doing so it had balanced the task of rearmament with supporting a viable economy. Attlee concluded by saying that Labour would continue year by year with its policy of redressing the inequalities of wealth, clearing up the mistakes of the past to form a society free from gross inequalities but not regimented and not uniform. He urged the party to go into the election in the spirit of Blake's 'Jerusalem';

> I will not cease from mental fight,
>   Nor shall my sword sleep in my hand,
> Till we have built Jerusalem
>   In England's green and pleasant land.

Several speakers paid tributes to Attlee. One came from Bevan:

> The Tories cannot talk sense about the economic situation. That is why they have chosen as a leader one who is more senseless than anyone else. You are not going to solve these problems by Churchillian perorations. Those difficult, complicated economic operations require economic and mental discipline and not merely perorations. That is why the quiet, moderate, balanced approach of Clem Attlee is more adjusted to the international situation than the romanticism of Churchill.

The conference dispersed in better heart and with a more covincing display of electioneering unity than many delegates had expected.

Attlee opened his campaign on 5 October, in a hall in Walthamstow, 'a thin-skinned place in a park called the Pavilion,' wrote Patrick O'Donovan in *The Observer*:

> Its walls were salmon pink and its roof ribbed with naked girders. A bare trestle table stood on the stage and behind it a row of collapsible chairs. Two red and yellow posters pinned to the wood said, 'Vote for Attlee'. There were no flags, flowers or music. No sign that a Prime Minister of Britain was making his first public speech in a fight to retain power ... the Prime Minister rose to the noise of swift, determined applause, and the lights twinkled on his spectacles. He stood quite still, smiling. The tiredness left his face and he looked affectionately at his loyal electors. He spoke for half an hour, slowly and carefully, never fumbling a sentence. He spoke of

great faraway issues like Persia and he poured a little general mockery over the Conservative manifesto. He held a paper in his left hand, and with his right hand played with a gold chain that shone across his waistcoat. He did not have that air of being more than life-sized that surrounds many British politicians, nor did he display that spurious cheerfulness that suggests that everything is fine, just fine. He looked like a great headmaster, controlled, efficient, and, above all, good.

On 8 October the *Manchester Guardian* leader observed:

Mr Churchill described the campaign of 1950 as 'demure'. That of 1951 is so far no less decorous and restrained. That it is so is due in no small measure to the Prime Minister.... He has never cheapened himself or his argument to gain applause. He has just been his quiet, assured self. What he says may often exasperate but the way he says it is without offence. Even when he appeals to sentiment he makes it hardly distinguishable from an appeal to reason.... He paints too bright a picture, of course. He avoids, for reasons which though plausible are also convenient, the more difficult topics. There is astonishingly little in his speeches about what his Government will do if re-elected. He might even be held to be damping down the natural enthusiasm that rises up at election times. Yet it is an admirable exhibition of one of the supreme arts of politics, the enhancement of personal respect. And, since electioneering in Britain seems to have become so eminently dull and respectable Mr Attlee's technique fits the mood perfectly. Whether political truth is brought any nearer the top of the well than it was in more rumbustious days is matter for doubt.

As in 1950, Churchill made several electioneering sorties in a grand cavalcade. And again Attlee went about the business in his own way, as described by the *Daily Mirror*:

While his wife drives, Mr Attlee puts on his glasses, rests on a brown and green folk-weave cushion, and does newspaper crossword puzzles. Occasionally when they are driving he unwraps a mint from a blue tin marked 'biscuits', and pops one into his wife's mouth. If their car is held up at a level crossing Mrs Attlee gets out her knitting – a pair of grey socks.
 Like a good wife, before they set out every morning, Mrs Attlee puts a crease in her husband's trousers with a portable electric iron.

Attlee's tour was not all cheers and knitting. The day after the *Mirror* article appeared there was an ugly incident at Southampton when he was speaking to a large, chiefly male, audience outside the dock gates at lunchtime. A car appeared and moved round the outside of the crowd, repeating on a loudspeaker several times 'They will never go back.' 'After some people near had started a tentative cheer,' the *Guardian* reported, 'a great growl went up from the body of the crowd.... Mr Attlee was unable to be heard for a moment. It seemed that he had smoothed things over with "It's all right. It's only an example of bad manners", and he was able to finish his speech in comfort.' But after he had left his audience turned on the offending car and nearly overturned it.

Attlee found time to write a letter to Tom on 21 October:

I managed to get down to Eastbourne to do a meeting for Chris [Tom's son, who was standing for Labour in this very safe Conservative constituency]. We had some 3,500 in the audience with a large proportion of Tories. Chris was speaking when I came on the platform and was doing well, making his points clearly and economically. I had some interruptions which were quite useful. I think Chris should increase the vote which is all one can hope for in Eastbourne.

Vi drove me down from Manchester via Chequers doing just under 400 miles for the day without being fatigued.

We had a remarkable tour, immense crowds and great enthusiasm but what it will mean in votes I can't tell. The surprising thing was the big crowds in country towns like Devizes, Westbury and Salisbury.... Vi always gets a great ovation and receives floral tributes everywhere.

The result of the election is anybody's guess depending largely on the way in which the Liberal cat jumps.

At Eastbourne Attlee picked up an accusation of Churchill's about socialist 'levelling down' and said 'it depends on the point of view you started from' – if Churchill had been an agricultural worker or a housewife living on the Means Test, he might have seen it differently; for the majority it was a great levelling up'.

Attlee wound up the Labour Party's national campaign by making the last of the political broadcasts, on 20 October. He ended with 'a few words in conclusion about the danger of last-minute scares and political stunts'. He said that there had been 'a whispering campaign by the other side that after the election I shall resign and be replaced by Mr Bevan, and that Mr Bevan is a Communist'. First: 'I am not going to resign unless the people of the country reject my leadership, and I am in good health, as I think my election tour has shown. Secondly, Mr Bevan is not a Communist. Indeed, he took a leading part in fighting the Communists in South Wales. And, thirdly, the choice of my successor as leader of the Labour Party rests with the members in the House of Commons.' Mr Bevan 'has been a loyal colleague of mine. The fact is that the Tories always want a bogy man. It was the late Mr Laski in 1945 and it is Mr Bevan today.'

The *Daily Herald* for 23 October published a message from Attlee in an interview with the editor, who pointed out to him that: 'You did not deal with international issues in most of your speeches.' Attlee replied:

No, I did not. I knew that those issues were in people's minds. But I did not feel that, as Prime Minister, I should discuss extempore, at hurried meetings, a subject like the Persia dispute when it was being considered by the

Security Council. In any case it was my view from the outset that the Tories had blundered in dragging that issue into the election, and that it would do them no good. I do not think that attacks on Labour's conduct of foreign policy will carry conviction with the electors. Our policy has been based on absolute and vigorous loyalty to the United Nations, as it will continue to be.

But the general theme of 'Whose Finger on the Trigger?' had been hammered and hammered again by Labour throughout the whole campaign. Churchill's reply that if a world war broke out the finger on the trigger would be Russian or American, and that in any case what one did not want was 'a fumbling finger', did not seem an adequate response. At the end of the campaign, 'Abadan, Sudan and Bevan', that trio of socialist failures as Churchill called them, were generally thought to have done the Labour campaign more good than harm. On domestic issues, if Labour seemed only to recite a long list of what they had achieved in the past, the Conservatives seemed over-cautious, critical without being constructive, 'to be campaigning to avoid losing votes rather than riding out to win them', as *The Times* said on the day before the poll.

Attlee spent the closing days of the campaign in his constituency, where he made his last speech of the campaign, the seventy-eighth. At that meeting, he recorded in his autobiography, 'a curious incident was the invasion of one of my school-room meetings by the Fascists. I never saw a more unpleasant-looking collections of "spivs" and "toughs". However they did not effect anything.' He looked back on his constituency campaign with satisfaction. 'I had a straight fight with an able young Conservative and though my vote increased my majority was slightly reduced.' The figures were:

Attlee, C. R. (Lab)	23,021
du Cann, E. D. L. (Con)	11,447
Majority	11,574

He was right about his 'able young opponent'; du Cann became a most successful businessman, an MP, a minister, and chairman of the Conservative Party 1965-7. Attlee was as good at spotting talent in the Conservative Party as in his own.

The result of the general election was a Conservative majority of 17. They had won 321 seats, as against 295 for Labour; besides the six Liberal victories, there were two for the Irish Nationalists and one for Irish Labour. The Labour Party increased its vote, and polled more votes than the Conservatives, 48.8 per cent against 48 per cent, the Liberals dropping dramatically from 9 per cent to 2.5 per cent, from nearly three million votes to less than a million. The issue was decided by the number of Liberals who in straight fights voted Conservative rather than Labour.

Labour had lost no chance of proclaiming themselves the party of peace, and had reiterated the slogan 'You can't trust the Tories.' The Conservatives had put their weight behind scandalized protests at the high cost of living and 'the mess that Labour has made'. Gallup found that on every domestic issue except full employment the Conservatives polled higher than Labour did. Full employment and housing – in spite of the Conservatives' promise to build 300,000 houses – were not major issues, and nationalization figured little at all. The fall of gold and dollar reserves in the third quarter of the year, about 600 million dollars, was a record. But little was said about that in the campaign.

In defeat, Attlee was still considered to be 'the party's greatest asset'. As the *News Chronicle* put it on 6 November, on the occasion of the award to him of the Order of Merit: 'the least controversial figure in the recent election, he commands a general confidence even when his party forfeits it. His is a quiet triumph of character.... His virtues of moderation, dignity and good sense remain as a great national asset in opposition as in government.' The *Manchester Guardian* leader for 27 October had said:

> When Mr Attlee went to the Palace last evening to tender his resignation he must have been consoled by the thought that for eleven years he has held the highest office in the State, first as Deputy Premier, then as Prime Minister, with the respect and regard of his countrymen. The criticism that fell on his government largely spared him.... He goes out knowing that he brought his party almost to the edge of victory. His status in his party will be as strong as ever, and that will matter a good deal in the new Parliament when it will tax statesmanship as much to run a large and keen Opposition as to run a Government.

27
Containing the Storm

Attlee's reputation declined in the four years before his retirement from the party leadership. In the House, especially on foreign affairs, he made speech after speech, of a most statesmanlike character, but he did not capture the public imagination. He was not enthusiastic about moves towards a European Union, but not unhelpful, his attitude being summed up about this time in his instructions to Robens, George Brown and Geoffrey de Freitas: 'I want you to go to this new thing called the Council of Europe. I don't know much about it, but in *your* time, you'll *have* to.' On other major issues of foreign policy he dominated his party. As leader, however, he bore much of the blame for the Labour Party's internal conflicts. His efforts to hold the party together only served, in the eyes of many observers, to prolong dissension. Those of his former admirers who criticized him for remaining leader for a further four years might have moderated their views had they understood his conviction that if he retired earlier Morrison would have succeeded him, and the Bevanites would consequently plunge the party into internecine warfare.

On 14 November 1951 Attlee wrote to Tom, giving family news and adding parenthetically:

> It seems quite odd to be free of heavy responsibility and to look forward to a whole day with nothing particular to do.
>
> I find the train journey rather pleasant giving plenty of time for reading. I've just been reading Arthur Bryant's *Historian's Holiday* which he sent me – pleasantly reminiscent of the turn of the century. I've also read Rowse's last book – very good in parts with curious little strokes of egotism coming in.

A few days later leading citizens of Walthamstow, including Conservative businessmen and Labour Party stalwarts – a non-partisan

495

assembly – presented him with some books. The first signature in the first book was that of Winston S. Churchill, who wrote: 'I am glad that the King has bestowed the high honour of the Order of Merit on Mr Attlee. He was my good and tried comrade and colleague during the War. We have these enduring memories in peace.' In December:

> I dined at Univ last night. A pleasant function. I had some talk with the new President of Corpus. I stayed the night with the Master, Goodhart, in his lovely house on Boar's Hill. He's a very fine person and I was glad they chose him; and an American citizen and a Jew is a new departure for an Oxford college.

The first few months of the new Parliament were comparatively quiet. The Conservatives inherited a balance of payments crisis which was worse than the crisis of 1947, and there was no immediate prospect of breaking the deadlock in Egypt or Iran. The only controversial undertaking in the King's Speech was to denationalize steel. In the debate on the Address on 6 November Attlee congratulated its mover and seconder, 'especially because I suppose no two Hon. Members have ever had to make bricks with so little straw; for this is certainly one of the thinnest Speeches from the Throne that I have ever heard. It exhibits no clear line of policy whatever.' There was a remarkable lack of animosity between the two sides. In the big defence debate on 6 December, Churchill praised the outgoing defence minister, Shinwell, for his patriotism, agreed that the Opposition when in power had been right to slow down the expenditure on rearmament, and gave Bevan 'an honourable mention for having, it appears by accident, perhaps not from the best of motives, happened to be right'.

Churchill's remark served to reactivate the Bevanite controversy in the Labour Party. *Tribune* invited Gaitskell to comment, and he did so in terms which raked up the bitterness between the two men. For the moment, though, Bevan refrained from intra-party controversy, and his supporters, though meeting regularly as a group, did not organize to change party policy. Attlee found himself clashing over foreign policy matters both with Bevan and Churchill. At the end of the year Attlee criticized Churchill in the House for a speech the Prime Minister had made in the United States which appeared to support the blockading of China. In another foreign affairs debate at the end of February 1952 Anglo-American policy towards China again figured prominently. This amounted almost to a vote of censure on Churchill, but he succeeded in turning the tables on Attlee by showing that the Labour Cabinet had 'considered' the possibilities of extending the fighting in Korea to a war against China. In the debate there were references by Labour's left to the danger of using the atomic bomb. Churchill made capital of these in referring to Attlee's decision to manufacture the bomb in the first place. Attlee, he said, was in the position of one who 'did good by stealth and blushed to find it fame'. This caused the left to feel as hostile to Attlee as to Churchill.

The subject came up again ten days later, when Churchill asked Attlee: 'Why didn't you convey the decision [to manufacture the bomb] to Parliament?' Attlee replied that in not doing so he had followed the precedent which had been laid down by Churchill. 'That was in war-time,' answered Churchill, to which Attlee replied: 'Oh no, it was after that.' The exchange was confused and confusing, but since to Labour's left-wingers it suggested that Attlee had been trying to conceal the consensus with the Conservatives over the development of the bomb, they immediately became more restive about the current consensus on defence in general, which was already deeply suspect to a large minority in the Parliamentary Labour Party. Their fear was that the new Secretary of State, John Foster Dulles, intended to use Korea as the base from which Communism in the Far East could be rolled back, and that Churchill had shown himself ready to acquiesce.

A defence debate on 5 March 1952 provoked the first open display in Parliament of the quarrel between the shadow Cabinet and the Bevanites. The shadow Cabinet, believing that another election might not be too far away, was anxious not to make the prewar mistake of voting against defence estimates as a means of protesting against government policy in general. They suggested therefore that the party should table an amendment declaring support for the Defence White Paper, but adding that the Opposition 'has no confidence in the capacity of His Majesty's present advisers to carry it out'. The Bevanites scoffed at this clumsy compromise. When the PLP met to discuss it there was a confused debate after which a Bevanite proposal restating their original objections to the £4,700 million rearmament programme was voted down, and the shadow Cabinet's 'sham amendment' (*Tribune*) adopted. After the meeting Attlee, Morrison and Whiteley, the Chief Whip, sent a joint letter to each MP clearly stating the final decision, which was to support the party's amendment and to abstain on the government's motion. Bevan, followed by fifty-six other Labour MPs, did not vote for the shadow Cabinet's motion, and the government got through by a majority of 95, instead of the usual 20 to 30. On a vote on a subject of prime importance the Labour Whip had been defied.

It was now clear that there were two oppositions, and that the minority had flung down the gauntlet to the majority. Deakin, and other leaders of big trade unions, encouraged by Whiteley, demanded 'recantation' and a promise never to do such a thing again, on pain of expulsion. But the minority in the Parliamentary Party were proportionally by no means as small a minority in the Labour Party in the country, and Attlee was unwilling to risk a fifth of the PLP accepting expulsion rather than recant. When the Parliamentary Party met the following week, therefore – the most crowded meeting since the 'resignation' meeting of April 1951 – Attlee produced a resolution which merely deplored the behaviour of the rebels, brought back Standing Orders (in suspense since 1945), which meant that MPs could not receive the Whip unless they agreed to stand by PLP majority decisions, and required all members to sign an agreement that Standing Orders were accepted. Even this resolution, which stopped far short of what the Chief Whip wanted, was too censorious for some middle-of-the-road members, who, led by Strauss, Strachey and Younger, carried an amendment omitting all references to the past, and calling solely for the introduction of Standing Orders.

The debate which followed showed that the period of comparative live-and-let-live which had characterized the behaviour of the party since the beginning of the election campaign six months earlier had come to an end. The Bevanites argued that Attlee should have withdrawn his own motion, and given his support to the moderate one put by Strauss: the right-wing union leaders complained that Attlee should have demanded recantation and if necessary have forced a split. Attlee, however, had got what he wanted: no precedents were created, no new undertakings were demanded; but Standing Orders were reintroduced.

By the spring of 1952 both the left and some of the right in the Labour Party had shown themselves strongly opposed to German rearmament. Churchill, anxious to rehabilitate himself in American eyes after he had disappointed them by refusing to press ahead with European Union, wanted to accommodate the American wish to bring Germany into the European Defence Force. In the defence debate he spoke of the Labour government's support for such a proposal, evoking a cautious reply from Attlee. In May, just before a debate on the European situation, the NEC issued a statement withdrawing from some of the commitments which Attlee had made as prime minister, stipulating for example that the Germans should not be promised arms until after they had held their next elections. Stung by this, Attlee stated in the House on 14 May that the NEC declaration did not commit a future Labour government, whose policy would be to have strong defence forces in the West and, 'under conditions of safety', a German contribution. This did not please the Bevanites, who planned to make the NEC the basis of their power in the Labour Party. They were not reassured when a Labour foreign policy statement was published in which the NEC resolution on Germany, alone among the policy proposals, was published without a commendatory preface such as 'The Labour Party believes ....' 'It would have been difficult indeed', said a *Manchester Guardian* leader, 'for Mr Attlee and the other responsible leaders to have said more plainly that the Executive's statement on Germany is not their child and they wish to have nothing to do with it, though since it has been fathered by one of the family they cannot ignore it altogether.'

It would have been difficult, too, to indicate more plainly the degree to which the Labour Party was now divided. It was not just a division between left and right, 'advance' and 'consolidation', or, not quite the same thing, Bevanites and the rest, or constituencies versus the trade unions. Across all these divisions cut personalities, and the fact that to the extent that the class factor was being extruded from national political conflict it was intruding into the Labour Party. Part of the trouble in the Labour Party was caused by a protest against the influence of the middle classes, exemplified by Gaitskell. The spring of 1952 marked the beginning of a two-year period in which the tide of Bevanism flowed strongly, reaching its high-water mark at the party conference of 1954 in the debate on German rearmament.

Did Attlee give the party the right leadership in the spring of 1952? Should he have taken the tough, disciplinary 'toe the line or get out' approach which Deakin, Lawther and Williamson wanted him to take? Would that have brought the Bevanites to heel, or would it have smashed the party? Attlee was convinced then, and did not change his mind, that he had gone as far as he could to discipline the party without causing an uproar which might not only paralyse the party for the next election but possibly inflict upon it a trauma comparable to the catastrophe of 1931. He was more than ever sure that he should remain as leader. If he stood down, Morrison, mainly because of his hostility to Bevan, would be heavily backed by the big unions and would almost certainly be elected leader. Relying on trade union support, and in any case anxious to re-establish his reputation, he would set himself up as the Hammer of the Left, and paralyse the party.

If the Labour Party could be held together, Attlee reasoned, there was real prospect of turning out the Conservative government. Their majority was small: a general election might be only just around the corner. During the summer months Attlee said so often. Following a Churchill broadcast predicting three or four more years in office, he said: 'I am convinced that this Government cannot last very long; it is just a short interlude.' After Labour successes in English county council elections, and referring to Churchill's recent promise of three or four years of resolute government, he said: 'I have been in a good many Parliaments and I have never seen a Government side so depressed and the opposition so cheerful as during the last five months. We have seen an amazing example of muddle and incompetence. We have seen Minister after Minister coming forward and having that unappetising meal of eating his own words.' Addressing a vast crowd of miners in Nottingham, he spoke of 'eight months of mess and muddle'.

Soon after this, the United States Air Force bombed power stations on the Yalu River which supplied not only North Korea but parts of Siberia and Manchuria. The Labour Party was able to capitalize on a growing feeling in the country, shared by many Conservative voters, that the Americans were taking dangerous risks, and that the Churchill government was doing little to discourage them. Attlee, though careful to avoid criticizing the Americans directly, observed that the attack was 'a profound mistake in psychology [which] will lessen the chances of an armistice', and held the British government partly responsible. Bevan also attacked the government. Labour's alarm proved less warranted than it looked at the time, but it brought majority and Bevanites together. Attlee was able plausibly to say to the Northumbrian miners in July that there was no real difference of opinion in Labour ranks on rearmament: 'we are resolved not to run away from decisions which we considered necessary when in office just because we are now in opposition.'

A few days later, as the end of the parliamentary session came in sight, rumours mounted that he would resign the leadership at the party conference in the autumn. He decided to make it clear that he had no intention of stepping down. At a lunch in London given for Labour Party organizers from all over the country, he said:

> I have seen in the newspapers that I am supposed to be in bad health. That was news to me. The truth is, I am in excellent health. I only wish I could say the same for the health of the country. The Government is suffering from extremely low blood pressure, and there are symptoms of a general disability to do anything successfully. I have known of Governments which have died of sheer futility. This could be said of the Rosebery and Balfour Administrations. It may well be the same with our present Government. We must be ready. . . . . I have now led the Party in four General Elections. I have been a Member of three Labour Governments. It is my hope that I shall lead the Party when the next time comes along and when we shall see an even more successful Labour Government than the last.

The next blow to Labour unity came, probably inadvertently, from Bevan, still resenting Gaitskell's attack on him in *Tribune* the previous November. In a debate on the economic position at the end of the parliamentary session, just after Attlee had made a good impression on all sections of the party by his attacks on Churchill, Bevan made a speech in which he reverted to his criticism in February 1951 of the rearmament programme. 'Further,' he said, 'when the debate took place, certain precautionary words were put into the Prime Minister's speech. These precautionary words to which the Leader of the Opposition has referred on many occasions and which have become the sheet anchor of some of my hon. friends, were actually inserted in the Prime Minister's speech at my instance.'

Even if no constitutional impropriety had been involved in making this disclosure, it could have been regarded on many grounds as extremely ill-advised. Attlee concentrated solely on its impropriety. The following day he took advantage of the rules of the House and asked the Speaker for permission to make a personal statement – a declaration which by the rules is not subject to debate or comment. Bevan, he said:

> no doubt through inadvertence, made statements purporting to describe actions taken by himself in discussing matters of policy with myself and others during the period when he was a member of the Labour Government. There is, of course, a well-established rule inhibiting members of a Government from revealing what passes either in Cabinet or in confidential discussion. The reason for this is obvious. Unless it is observed, confidence between colleagues is impossible. If I were to affirm or deny the accuracy of my right hon. Friend's statement, I should commit precisely the same error to which I am now drawing attention. This I am not prepared to do. I make this statement lest my silence should be misconstrued.

The next day Bevan in turn asked for permission to make a personal statement. In what *The Times* called 'a dignified performance', he pointed out that collective Cabinet responsibility, which he naturally accepted, clearly ended for a minister when he resigned, otherwise 'a Minister could not say *why* he had resigned'. There were clear precedents for this. 'Therefore,' he concluded his statement, 'I do not plead guilty to constitutional impropriety. On the contrary, what I have done has been strictly in accordance with precedent, and I hope I shall be exempted from any blemish which my right hon. Friend's statement may inadvertently have cast upon my reputation.'

Honours were by and large even. Bevan's speech had certainly suggested that in Cabinet he had told the former prime minister how to conduct his business, which was not very flattering to Attlee; on the other hand, Attlee's personal statement served only to draw attention to the strength of Bevan's 'precautionary words' about rearmament. It was a curious episode, in which Attlee's judgement seems to have been at fault – the exchange received more publicity as a result of correspondence in *The Times*. That the arms programme originated by the Attlee government was now openly admitted on all sides to be economically unviable was thoroughly ventilated; the embarrassment of the shadow Cabinet fanned their animosity towards Bevan. Before the recess began, the stage was set for the ferocious confrontation which was to take place at the party conference to be held at Morecambe at the end of September.

II

During the recess, Attlee made two visits abroad, to Belgium and to Rhodesia. The first was for the Belgian festival of Labour sponsored by the Socialist International at Liège. Attlee made a speech in which he pronounced Stalin's Communism to be 'a miscomprehended Marxism plastered over the despotic heritage of the Tsars'. In the same letter to Tom he talked about the coming visit to Rhodesia:

> Vi has decided to go to Rhodesia with me and we leave by Comet next Sunday afternoon arriving at Livingstone shortly after breakfast on Monday. I have had numerous requests to visit Kenya, Uganda, Nyasaland and the Sudan, but have decided to limit our visit to the Rhodesias as one can't do a Continent in a fortnight. I thought Van der Post's book (*Journey to the Interior*) brilliantly written. I know him well. . . . He is a very fine person, a Boer with a great sense of mission to the negro peoples.
>
> I've not seen the last Webb book. Your criticism is correct. She never uderstood that the new Jerusalem must be built with human beings not institutions. We have Janet and Ann with us for the week end. Mervyn Stockwood has just rung up to say that he is calling for lunch. We lunched this week with Megan Lloyd George. . . . I wish that she would join us, but she thinks it her duty to try to keep the Liberal remnant away from the Tories.
>
> We have masses of cherries . . . . the lawn is covered with the fallen.

The visit to Central Africa was Attlee's first. Plans were going ahead for the federation of Northern Rhodesia (the future Zambia), Southern Rhodesia (Zimbabwe) and Nyasaland (Malawi). This scheme for a Central African Federation had been recommended to the government in June 1951 by officials of the Commonwealth Relations Office, the Colonial Office and the three Central African governments. From the first, African representatives in Northern Rhodesia and Nyasaland had opposed federation, fearing it would be dominated by the whites, and especially the whites of Southern Rhodesia. In December 1951 the plan was rejected by the African Representative Council in Northern Rhodesia. Attlee had supported federation in principle: twenty British Labour MPs had tabled an amendment opposing it. They were 'entitled to their views', he said on arrival at Livingstone Airport; his role was that of an observer who wanted to hear all the pros and cons.

He listened to everybody, but occasionally dissented about matters of fact. In the copper belt he was greeted with an address of welcome by African trade union leaders, which included some criticism of Britain's colonial governors for being reactionary. 'It's a pity you put that in,' Attlee said. 'You see, it isn't true, and makes me doubt other things you say.' However, what he heard made inroads on his previous opinion. Back in Britain after the tour he began to speak about the dilemma in

Rhodesia, and the danger of carrying through federation against the weight of African opinion. The government proceeded with its plans. Over the next few months he moved toward a position in which he counselled delay. The following May, at the second reading of the Federation Bill, he put – very moderately – this view that the Africans had a genuine fear of federation. He was now anxious to give a warning of what might happen if the government pressed ahead too quickly with their plan; but he did not want to add to tensions by demagogic denunciations. He wanted to preserve the rights of the blacks without seeming to impugn the motives of the whites. His compromise was to suggest 'Delay'.

> This experiment, which, if it is to be a success, must be based on good-will and trust and on the conception of partnership, is starting under bad auspices. ... If this becomes the law of the land, it is the duty of all of us to try to make it work to the best of our ability, but even at this eleventh hour I urge that it is worthwhile delaying so that we may get some tangible proof of a new relationship which will bring the Africans into harmony with the scheme.

The government disregarded his advice and imposed a federation which it was necessary to sunder a decade later. Had Attlee's warnings been heeded, events in Rhodesia might have turned out differently. But he can be blamed for not having perceived these dangers when he was prime minister. It was his administration which produced the plan for the Central African Federation. He can also be blamed for not unleashing the full force of the Opposition on it when he realized he had made a big mistake. At the party's annual conference at Margate in the autumn of 1953 Attlee said:

> We opposed the proposal for Central African Federation because it appeared to us that it was not in accordance with the desires of the African people. ... Well, it has been carried through. ... It is not the job of a great movement such as ours to encourage resistance to Acts of Parliament passed at Westminster. [Cries of 'Shame' and shouts of 'Oh'.] No, there is no shame at all, it is a democratic principle. If you want to change it you must change the Government.

To many of his critics – and some of his supporters – this sounded lame.

III

The party conference which opened at Morecambe on 29 September 1952 was as important in the history of the party as it was dramatic. On the eve of the conference Attlee made a speech in which he said that 'the greatest danger to democracy is not the active attacks of its enemies but the apathy of the many'. The Morecambe conference displayed anything but apathy; in Michael Foot's words, it was 'rowdy, convulsive, vulgar, splenetic; threatening at moments to collapse into an irretrievable brawl'. Men and women who had been there spoke of it twenty years later with bated breath. The delegates assembled with anticipation of a battle. Morrison in particular foresaw his fate. The weather was vile – squally rain and high wind. The hall was too small and was badly lighted. Hotel accommodation was inadequate. On the second morning, when the votes for the constituency section of the National Executive were announced, delegates were astonished to hear that the Bevanites had almost swept the board: Bevan, Barbara Castle and Driberg took the first three places; Jim Griffiths was fourth, followed by three more Bevanites, Wilson, Mikardo and Crossman. In the NEC elections Morrison and Dalton lost the seats they had occupied for more than twenty-five years.

That afternoon, winding up the debate on party policy, encouraged by applause on a scale he could not have hoped for, Morrison behaved with a dignity and humility which, his biographers justifiably claim, 'made many in the packed hall feel more than a little ashamed of what they had done to him'. When he sat down many who had voted against him were seen to be cheering him. Taking his defeat as an attack on themselves, some of the big trade union leaders then opened fire on the Bevanites. Arthur Deakin, the leader of the Transport Workers, bringing the customary 'fraternal greetings' from the TUC, made a very un-brotherly attack on the Bevanites, accusing them of a conspiracy to defeat Morrison. This provoked prolonged booing and counter-booing. What was said in public in the conference hall was compounded by the bitter exchanges which took place outside.

Attlee was much criticized, then and later, for not saying a word of sympathy to Morrison in public or in private, and for not taking sides. Deakin in private told colleagues he thought Attlee should be ousted because he would not face the Bevanite challenge. In defence of Attlee it can be said that he did not believe it was his duty to attack the Bevanites, whose views were obviously acceptable to a great many members of the party. To commiserate publicly with Morrison would be to deplore a perfectly legitimate expression of a wish for a change in the membership of the NEC, and to run the risk of damaging Morrison by talking of him as though he had been voted into retirement. His private view of what had happened was expressed in his letter to Tom on 5 October:

> I have just got back from Morecambe. Architecturally it ranks a good second to Blackpool, the former beats it in the atrocious ugliness of its buildings, but Morecambe pulls up on complete absence of planning. Our hotel wing was, however, very comfortable. The Conference was made unhappy by the successful intrigues of Bevan & Co to capture seats on the

Executive. It was also obvious that there had been a considerable infiltration of near communists into the Constituency delegations. I fancy that in weak constituencies the crypto com volunteers to go and pay his expenses. There was quite an organised claque. Morrison made a very fine comeback. He has been under the weather lately, but returned to form, in particular his speech showed generosity, a quality which is generally rather lacking.

Attlee's remark about 'near-communist' infiltration was not a casual one. Many delegates had been struck by the large votes cast for motions which were unusually extreme. A motion calling for strike action organized to bring down the Conservative government, direct industrial action on which the TUC had turned its back at the time of the General Strike, was defeated, but it won 1,728, 000 votes – surprisingly high. Bevanism and the Bevanites was one thing; creeping Communism in the constituency parties was another. But did Communism feed on Bevanism? Deakin certainly claimed that it did; his phrase 'the antics of disruption' was meant to describe what he thought was a symbiosis that could bring about the ruin of the Labour Movement, and in the short term.

Possibly because he believed that it would be unwise to risk anatagonizing the Bevanites by making public speeches, Morrison chose to say little in the period immediately after the conference. Not so Gaitskell, who now set himself up as the spokesman of the Labour right. Four days after the conference he made a speech at Stalybridge in which he attacked both Bevanites and Communists and described the threat of Communist infiltration into constituency parties. Of the Communists, he said, according to *The Times* of 6 October 1952:

> A most disturbing feature of the Conference was the number of resolutions and speeches which were Communist-inspired, based not even on the *Tribune* so much as the *Daily Worker*. I was told by some observers that one-sixth of the constituency party delegates appear to be Communist or Communist influenced. ... It is time to end the attempt at mob rule by a group of frustrated journalists and restore the authority and leadership of the solid, sound, sensible majority of the movement.

The leading Bevanites, and some of the acolytes, wrote for *Tribune* and the *New Statesman*. Driberg's weekly column was carried by *Reynolds News*, Crossman wrote a column for the *Sunday Pictorial*. Many Bevanites, because they were good broadcasters and would speak out, were used by the BBC. 'The group of frustrated journalists' could only have meant the Bevanites. Whether he intended to or not, Gaitskell, by making these remarks, ensured that for years to come there would be two parties within the Labour Movement. If Gaitskell had not created the Bevanites, he perpetuated them.

Attlee decided that feeling was now running so high that he must act to lower the temperature. At a meeting of the PLP at the beginning of the new session he personally moved a resolution which banned all unofficial groups within the party and also forbade all personal attacks. It was approved by 188 votes to 51. The Bevanite group was consequently disbanded – under protest. Bevan probably did more than anybody else to restore some semblance of unity within the ranks when he agreed to accept nomination for one of the twelve shadow Cabinet seats. He was elected – twelfth out of twelve. Attlee's views of these events in the Bevanite campaign were expressed tersely in a letter to Tom on 28 October: 'The Bevanite squabble is a nuisance – very largely a matter of vanity, envy and a dislike of responsibility. I am not unduly worried as I have seen four and twenty leaders of revolt.'

Meanwhile Attlee attended a meeting of the Socialist International in Milan. The *Manchester Guardian* reported:

> Mr Attlee's golden silences, and concise economy of words when he does consent to speak, are accepted in this country as part of his modesty ... Abroad they still come as a shock. The Socialist International has now experienced the same cold douche ... though he delighted the Italian crowds by speaking twice in public in rather literary Italian, his sole intervention at the conference was limited to something under two minutes. It happened in the first morning during the discussion of a proposal to admit a number of refugee socialist parties to membership. Mr Attlee said he would not do that if he were they.

Attlee was as critical of the delegates to the conference as the delegates were puzzled. 'The conference', he told Tom, 'suffered from the interminable prolixity of most of the continental speakers. They thought nothing of speaking for $\frac{3}{4}$ or even an hour. Had I been in the Chair they would have had short shrift.'

IV

At the opening of the new Parliamentary session in November Attlee exchanged some raillery with Churchill on the subject of Europe. When Churchill came to power, the Americans believed that he would lead the way to a united Europe. Their hopes were steadily and not very slowly disappointed. Churchill still talked about Europe but he talked much more about how difficult it was for Britain to enter Europe when she had so many political and economic ties with the Commonwealth. There was consequently a shadow over Anglo-American relations. In his speech Attlee said:

> I note the passage [in the Queen's Speech] on the unity of Europe. I am glad to see that the Government have very largely come to take the same

line as that which the Labour Government took. There was a time when it looked as though the Prime Minister was going to be, so to speak, stroke of the European boat, but he is now only offering a few helpful suggestions from the towpath.

In reply, Churchill hoped that 'the moderation and sobriety of [Attlee's] speech will not expose him to any undue risk from his friends. I am sure I may offer him my congratulations on his being able to address us from those benches as stroke and not, to quote the term he has just used, from the towpath.'

It was clear from the beginning of the session that the action on the political front would be not between the two parties but within the Labour Party. National politics were already moving into the age of 'Butskellism', when for the time being there would be no great battles between the major parties, and when Churchill's desire to establish a settled world order with Russia and the United States led him to do everything to avoid precipitating industrial strife at home. Two men personified the age of Butskellism: Butler, the Chancellor of the Exchequer, pursuing a moderate economic policy, taking a little here, giving a little there; and Sir Walter Monckton, Minister of Labour, always ready in the last moment – under instructions from the Prime Minister – to give the unions what they wanted, rather than risk a strike which might undermine Churchill's position at a summit conference.

This did not mean that political conflict was suspended. The Tories were pledged to denationalize iron and steel and road transport; Labour was determined to resist. On 4 December 1952 Attlee moved a vote of censure, complaining about 'Ministers' efforts to force through measures, unrelated to the needs of the nation, for which they have no adequate support in Parliament or the country'. But even though the issue was nationalization, a debate about procedure was not calculated to generate great excitement in the country. During his speech Attlee remarked: 'The proceedings of this house do not consist merely in counting heads. If that were so we should be beaten every time. The point is that in a debate what is in the heads comes out, and that is where we score.' Nevertheless, he was vulnerable to Churchill's observation that 'the first occasion for 10 months in which the Opposition have moved a formal Motion against the present Government is on terms of a purely technical matter in the conduct of the House, and which has no bearing whatever upon the daily lives of the people or the march of events'. The government went ahead as fast as they could with the plans to denationalize road transport and steel; there was nothing Labour could do to stop them.

Attlee was seventy in January 1953; he had obviously abandoned his much-rumoured intention of retiring when he reached the age of three score and ten: it was more important than ever to stay on to hold the party together. He celebrated his fitness at seventy by flying off directly after his birthday to the Asian Socialist Conference in Rangoon, travelling thence to India.

Nineteen hundred and fifty-three was a quieter year for the Labour Party. There were occasional clashes between right and left, but Attlee began to emerge more as a symbol of unity than as the censor of the Bevanites. In February, the trade union leaders, led by Deakin, and their supporters on the National Executive made an abortive attempt to ban the Bevanite 'Brains Trusts'. This fracas resulted in Attlee reprimanding not the left but the right for disrupting party unity. In February, in an article in the *News Chronicle* headed 'The Doodler Bides His Time', once again Francis Williams questioned whether Attlee was giving the party the right kind of leadership. 'Has the time come for Mr Attlee to stop doodling? ... I suspect that his conception of leadership in opposition differs from his conception of leadership in office. The leader of a party in opposition ought most of all to try to interpret currents of opinion within the Party and wield a suspended judgement until they have had time to work themselves out.' This would explain Attlee's apparent leniency, in the eyes of the trade union leaders, in dealing with the Bevanites, who clearly – by the results of the Executive elections – were popular with the rank and file. In 1953 the doodler's method seemed to be working well.

Attlee wrote to Tom on 28 March 1953 that he had been 'having trouble in the tummy for some time and the doctors think it best to have my appendix out. Vi and I went to HC last night, dined with the Headmaster and saw the boys play *Hamlet*, a very good show. ... We watched the Boat Race from a launch today – Oxford were very disappointing.' He was in St Mary's Hospital for ten days, and convalesced for another fortnight. Morrison, whose political stock was rising again, took charge of the shadow Cabinet.

Returning to the House after his illness, Attlee made two important speeches. They were the calm and wise speeches of an elder statesman, which nobody else on the Opposition benches could have made. One was on the Rhodesia and Nyasaland Federation (quoted earlier), the other on foreign affairs. This was broadly sympathetic to Churchill, who, during Eden's illness, was carrying the burden of being his own foreign minister. Churchill, he said, had:

> made a very remarkable speech, and he will have realised that its general tone and approach were warmly welcomed on this side of the House. ... It is desirable, wherever possible, that in foreign affairs particularly, Government policy should have the support of all. It strengthens us in giving what I believe is a necessary lead in international relations. ... So many critics do not realise that all international relations are a subject for compromise.

... I know that my late colleague Mr Bevin was often quite unfairly criticised because his critics said, 'Why did you not do this?' He could not do it because he had to act with others. We are all united in this House and in this country in our earnest desire for peace, and we all welcome the signs of change in the attitude on the part of Soviet Russia. ... There does seem to be a definite departure from the autocracy of Stalin .... It would be a great thing if we could get personal relations [with the new leaders] which would dissipate some of the Soviet mythology about Britain.

Another point made by the Prime Minister which struck me as wise was that one should not assume that all the troubles of the world are due to Communist initiative. ... It really is an over-simplifying of the problem to put it all down to Soviet intrigue. There is a body of opinion in the United States ... that tends to do just that ....

Having pointed out a few differences between the American and British forms of government, he remarked that 'one sometimes wonders who is the more powerful, the President or Senator McCarthy ....' He went on to warn Churchill against letting the Americans dominate policy in the Far East:

I suggest, therefore, to the Prime Minister that in these negotiations it would be well if there were other advisers from the United Nations States concerned. ... I believe that it would strengthen the hands of the American Administration. ... I am well aware that America has made far the biggest sacrifices in Korea; but I am also well aware that she lays herself open to unjustifiable blame if she keeps everything in her own hands ...

I turn now to China. I do not believe that China is a mere puppet in the hands of Russia. I think that she will wear her Communism with a difference; but I am more certain than ever that, as soon as aggression has been halted, China should take her rightful place on the Security Council. It is really one of the ironies of history that President Roosevelt, against our view, rather pressed that China was a great power. She was not then. She was the rather ramshackle power of Chiang Kai-shek torn with dissension, yet she was put in a position on the Security Council.

Attlee concluded:

We have had a number of remarkable speeches and pronouncements in recent weeks. We have had the speech of President Eisenhower. We had the *Pravda* article, which showed some signs of thaw in the frozen regions of the relationships of Russia with the Western world. I am quite sure that the Prime Minister's speech has made a valuable contribution, and I think this House has, too, because I think the speeches of yesterday were at a high level of debate, and I am quite certain that Great Britain still has the power and the will to give a lead for peace.

The speech, with its criticisms of the United States constitution as 'a document framed for an isolationist State' and other unpalatable remarks, caused something of a furore in America, and McCarthy talked in the *Washington Star* about 'this creature Comrade Attlee – remarks for which Attlee received an apology from the editor of that newspaper.

The Coronation of the young Queen was impending – George VI had died on 6 February 1952. Attlee wrote to Tom on 8 June:

> We had a very good Coronation day despite the rain. We left home at 4.15 with Isobel Cripps and picked up Alison and her babe on the way. Went to the House breakfasted and the ladies put on glad rags. I was already dressed. Flippy joined. She and Al had good seats in New Palace Yard. The babe was parked in my room. At 8 we went across to the Abbey where we had very good seats in the choir alongside Mrs Bevin and the Crown Princesses of Norway and Denmark. The service was most impressive. A friendly Gold Stick came to us at 10 saying there was an interval and we were able to go out for a cigarette and dehydration. We lunched on the Terrace. Vi went to a Ball at the Savoy while I went home. We have had innumerable Parties. Banquets at the Palace and a Reception there. Garden Parties at Lambeth Hatfield and Blenheim. We went to the Derby and from there to Walthamstow where we had four and a half hours going round street parties, a marvellous show of decorations. Walthamstow knows how to do it. We are off to the opera tonight. This week is also full of junketings. Vi is better but had a good deal of trouble last week.
>
> The family was represented at the Coronation in all three services. Martin helped to line the streets. Don marched with the Air Force and Algie Willis drove with the Admirals of the Fleet.
>
> We go to Spithead next Monday.
>
> I am just completing my autobiography, but current events have taken up so much time that I am a bit late with it.
>
> Tito has invited me to Yugoslavia and I expect to go in August.

During July, Churchill and Eden were ill, and Lord Salisbury, the acting foreign minister, attended three-power talks with the United States and France, where it was proposed to hold a new foreign ministers' conference in September with the Russians. Butler reported on this in the foreign affairs debate on 21 July. Attlee, replying, referred to Churchill's speech of 11 May, which had :

> raised great hopes. ... Since then ten weeks have elapsed. ... We are all agreed that the tripartite conference at Washington was inevitably a poor substitute for those high-level talks. We could not expect very much from it, but I must say that I think this White Paper is disappointing. It does not seem to be forward-looking enough or to be really in tune with the Prime Minister's speech. There seems to be too much emphasis on positions already taken up ...
>
> I want to see flowing East and West trade in Europe. I want to see trade with China. Above all, I want to see intercourse between the peoples. I believe there has been some relaxation. If the talks could only get towards

our understanding each other and provide a meeting between peoples, then
the position might be more hopeful. But frankly, I do not think that the
Washington talks have taken us much further on the road of peace.

On 30 July, having asked for the business of the House to be changed
before the summer recess, Attlee expressed the grave disturbance felt by
many people at a unilateral declaration of policy by Dulles at a press
conference:

> because the report seemed to be of a laying down of conditions by the
> United States Government, the taking of a line by the United States
> Government in regard to the political consequence of affairs in Korea,
> without taking into account the views of their colleagues ...
>
> It seems extraordinary to me that a declaration should be made that in
> this conference Korean unity must be achieved and that, failing that, the
> United States representative will walk out of the conference. That seems to
> me to be quite contrary to the whole of the spirit of the working of the
> United Nations. ... There is a further general underlying suggestion that if
> everything does not go exactly as Mr Dulles wants it, then the United States
> may go on its own. I think that is a very dangerous matter ...
>
> We are out to try to get a peaceful settlement throughout the Far East,
> so that this should be the beginning, and the settlement of the Korean
> question is only the beginning. Unless this is taken in a broad and states-
> manlike way, it will not be the beginning of a new era of peace. Therefore,
> I hope the right hon. Gentleman will make it plain that we cannot subscribe
> to these narrow policies, but that we shall put forward our point of view
> and claim that that should have full consideration and, above all, that we
> should insist that this is a United Nations matter and not a matter of purely
> American concern.

It was a short, effective speech, to which Butler, agreeing with most of it,
could only say that representations had already been made to the United
States. Clement Davies, the leader of the Liberal Party, made a very
short speech, observing that there was a general feeling in the House –
and 'indeed, the whole country' – that Attlee had given a national lead
on the line to be taken with an American secretary of state bent on an
anti-Communist crusade. Eden years later told the author that Attlee's
temperate and well-informed warnings to the Americans about the risks
they were taking in the conduct of their foreign policy were of immense
value to the British government at this time. He was able to say things –
and he said them in the right tone – which the British government could
not say in public, but which they could, and did, in private conversation
with the Americans.

On 9 August the *Sunday Express*, no friend of Attlee, commenting that
the Washington Conference was now a proved failure, said: 'Mr Attlee,
having seized the chance offered by Mr Churchill's illness to give the

country a lead, and roll the Tory 2nd Eleven in the mud, has gone off to Yugoslavia with his prestige fully refreshed. This sudden recovery is typical of him. His party were lately assailing him from all sides.' That day Attlee wrote to Tom a letter from Dubrovnik full of enthusiasm about the Yugoslav country and people.

> I am having a wonderful time in this delightful country. After 3 days in Belgrade which was most interesting including a trip out into the country where I lunched in an orchard with peasant co-operators, I came to this fantastically beautiful place. It is really a complete mediaeval city surrounded by great walls . . . . The whole town is paved in stone and is kept scrupulously clean. The buildings are delightful. . . . There is a fine old castle. One evening they played *Hamlet* in the great roofless hall, a wonderful setting with the battlements above for the ghost scene. It was, of course, in Yugoslav, but so admirably done that one could follow it almost word for word. The Hamlet was about the best I've ever seen . . .
>
> We motored up an incredible road cut in the face of Mount Lorelen with many hairpin bends and came in the evening to Cellingen where we stayed the night. My companion is a very charming member of the diplomatic corps who speaks good English. I also converse a good deal in Italian . . .
>
> I find the Yugo Slavs very charming and hospitable. I seem to have something of a name among them as the Labour Prime Minister. They are full of jokes and a really free people. There is nothing of the atmosphere of Russia.
>
> They are running their economy on a basis of free enterprise by co-operation. So far it seems to be working all right. They have a bitter hatred of the Russian communists who tried to do them down and they despise the Italians.

V

On his return, Attlee had to give his attention to preparation for the Labour Party conference at Margate, starting at the end of September. The National Executive had produced a policy document, *Challenge to Britain*, which was an acceptable compromise between the Bevanites and the less radical members of the Executive: it omitted mention of several major items which the Bevanites had wished to be included, but it contained proposals for public ownership of the chemical industry, plans for reshaping the engineering industry, a pledge to renationalize steel and road haulage, and a promise to remove all charges on the National Health Service. Deakin and other trade union leaders felt that too much was being conceded to the Bevanites, and were working behind the scenes to try to redress the balance for the future, mainly by getting Morrison back on to the Executive as party treasurer – with ex-officio membership of the Executive. Greenwood, who had been treasurer for many years, was generally regarded as a spent force, but he refused to resign the treasurership. At the last moment Morrison decided not to run against him. Deakin and his friends began to think twice about Morrison's stomach for a fight.

As it turned out, Morrison did get back on to the Executive, because the National Union of Seamen put forward an amendment which would make the deputy leader of the PLP a member of the Executive ex officio. Morrison, therefore, did not need to fight. But so far as the militant right was concerned he let them down. Deakin spoke of him as 'yellow'. None of this was lost on Gaitskell: to impress the unions you had not only to fight but *show* that you were fighting.

Moving the Executive's resolution on foreign and commonwealth policy, Attlee's speech went down well with all sections of the party. It was a résumé of his speech in the House on foreign policy in which he had warned the Americans that they must face the fact that the Communist government in China was the real government, and that to recognize it as such was 'only common sense'. But once again he tried not to offend the Americans: 'If we think that our friends are following an unwise course, true friendship demands that we should say so.' The following day he wound up in the debate on *Challenge to Britain*:

> We are a responsible Party expecting to have charge of the Government in a very short time. We have to be careful that what is thought to be better should not be the enemy of the good.
>
> The programme represents the views of the majority. We have got to get a majority in the country to put through this programme. We can only do that if we have unity of aim and action. People who want more, unless they are prepared to work with everybody else, will get nothing, because it is no good having a tremendous freight on your train if you have not got an engine strong enough to pull it. We carried our train up a very steep hill and got it a very long way up in 1945 to 1950, because we had a fine engine of 160 or 170 horsepower. By the time 1950–51 came we had about 6 horsepower and some of that was often out of action. The hill was still steep and we could not get very far.
>
> I believe we have an inspiring document here, inspiring because, although its head is looking up at the stars, its feet are on solid ground.

Challenge to Britain was carried almost unanimously. Attlee was photographed chatting amicably to Aneurin Bevan, and exchanging smiles with the rehabilitated Herbert Morrison. The atmosphere at Margate in 1953 was certainly very different from that at Morecambe the year before. He was not exaggerating when he wrote to Tom:

> We had a very good Conference at Margate, an excellent spirit and an absence of personal jars. My speech on Foreign Affairs seems to have pleased all sections.

Though he did not allow his views to mar the appearance of harmony at the conference, Bevan's assessment of the proceedings was very different from Attlee's: 'Margate was indeed a flop, ' he wrote to a friend. 'I am still most unhappy about the situation inside the Labour Party.' At the beginning of the session he again stood against Morrison for the deputy leadership, receiving 76 votes against Morrison's 181, and in the election for the shadow Cabinet he came ninth.

Morrisons's biographers are entitled to argue that for the next two years he and not Attlee was 'the real Opposition leader against the Tories in the sense that he led the partisan attack, and with colour and vigour'. But it was Attlee whom the public thought of as the elder statesman. From time to time he laid himself open to counter-attack from Churchill – as when he demanded control of atomic energy by the House, Churchill riposting: 'We must not forget that when he was in office his Government spent more than £100 million without ever asking the House to be aware of what was going on.' But these lapses were rare. The great majority of his speeches were of a high level. In a debate at the end of October he pointed out that the suspension of the constitution of British Guiana had given the near-Communist People's Liberation Party a rallying cry as champions of democracy against alien rule. 'It seems to me there was no attempt to use any of the reserve powers – there were no light taps until the sledge-hammer was brought in – and it is doubtful whether that was the wisest policy.' Many Conservatives agreed with him. In the foreign affairs debate on 17 December there was a considerable consensus: for instance Attlee could readily support the government's attempts to get a settlement in Egypt – 'Goodness knows, I have reason to know how difficult the Egyptians are in negotiation.'

Contributions like these were good for the image of the party. Only Attlee was high enough above the internal party conflicts to be able to make them. Nobody taking a reasonably objective view could have denied that the Labour Party after their defeat in 1951 had behaved notably more constructively in Parliament than the Tories had after their defeat in 1950. Attlee can claim the main share of the credit for this. He chose to do little to tackle the problem of the internal tensions, but he kept them under a control which held the party together. In the country at large he was still his party's greatest political asset. At seventy-one years of age there was no hint of his retiring. On 7 January 1954 he told Tom about his birthday:

> We had a small dance last Saturday which was a great success. At midnight my birthday was celebrated – a cake with 71 candles was brought in. I extinguished them with one good blow.

28
Bevan or Gaitskell?

I

The 1953 party conference at Margate had gone very well for the leadership, and had thrown up no controversy of serious consequence. But about a month later a cloud rather bigger than a man's hand had appeared above the horizon in the shape of an article in *Tribune* written by J. P. W. Mallalieu, a well-known supporter of Bevan. The article took the form of an interview between the author and an imaginary constituent. Mallalieu asked himself how it was that the constituency parties voted the straight Bevanite ticket at the party conference, while MPs put Bevan three places from the bottom of the shadow Cabinet. He answered that the PLP supported 'consolidation' while the party in the country wanted a more aggressive socialist policy – 'advance'. 'To this,' wrote Mallalieu, 'my constituent objected that he had personally never heard any Labour MP speaking in the country in favour of consolidation. . . . It looks as though some of these chaps say one thing in public in the country and another thing behind closed doors in the party meetings.' Mallalieu suggested that voting lists should be published after PLP meetings. Dalton recorded on 18 November: 'It is clear that the whole bloody Bevanite trouble is being brought up again.'

The NEC reprimanded Mallalieu for attacking a Labour colleague in public; Attlee informed the party that if 'this kind of thing' happened again, the offender would have the Whip withdrawn. He did not make heavy weather of his warning, but it gave the Bevanites occasion to complain that there was one law for the right and another for the left. Within a few weeks the German rearmament issue came up again to widen the rift. The British and American governments had agreed to rearm West Germany, having failed to get Russian agreement to German unification. In the subsequent parliamentary debate Attlee admitted that there were differences of opinion on the issue in the

House and within the Labour Party, though he was 'not ashamed of such differences of opinion'. He personally had reluctantly come to the conclusion that Germany must make a contribution to the defence of Western Europe. 'But of profound importance is the spirit in which this is done. The West Germans should be given arms, but they should also feel that they were contributing to a great effort which would combat Communism not with weapons but with rising living standards. Communism would never be defeated by war, but it could be defeated by getting rid of the conditions which enable this amazing weed to take hold of people.' Churchill praised Attlee for 'a concise, massive, statesmanlike contribution to a subject which has caused much widespread heart-searching among all parties and throughout all parts of the country'. A wholehearted tribute from Churchill to Attlee only exacerbated the rebellious feelings of the Bevanites.

In the early stages the argument about German rearmament was good-tempered, partly because the issue cut across other divisions in the party – many of its prominent members, Dalton, for example, being as opposed to giving guns to Germans as any Bevanite. When the vote was taken at the first meeting of the PLP held to discuss the matter, the rearmers were in a majority of only 113 to 104, four members of the shadow Cabinet abstaining. At the various annual trade union conferences held during the spring and summer, attempts were made to commit the industrial wing of the Labour Movement to one side or the other before the annual party conference in the autumn. As it became clearer and clearer that the division of opinion within the party was narrow, each side strove harder and harder to commit the majority to its view. The good temper disappeared. Gaitskell now revealed himself as a champion of German rearmament, and made it known that he would run for the treasurership of the party in the autumn. His only possible rival could be Bevan.

Fortunately for the public reputation of the Labour Party, the bitterest scenes took place in private, and in any case Churchill and his government were fumbling in the early part of 1954. In March, Churchill failed to allay public anxiety about the effects of the Americans' H-bomb tests. When news arrived that the latest American test had produced unexpectedly high fall-out, which had affected an area far more extensive than had been projected, Attlee pointed out that tests of nuclear weapons in peacetime might cause more damage than conventional weapons did in war. In the subsequent debate Churchill's speech was disappointing. When a Labour resolution called on the British government to press for a summit meeting, there was a feeling that Attlee not Churchill was giving a lead. Derek Marks in the *Daily Express*, no friend of Attlee, in an article on 2 April headed 'Attlee Stops H-Bomb Gamble', pronounced

Attlee's speech to the Parliamentary Party the 'greatest of his 71 years ... he pulled the entire Socialist Party behind him last night on the hydrogen bomb issue. ... He put forward his own solution: Let Churchill, Eisenhower and Malenkov meet at once.' Attlee told the House that 'we are not going to make Party capital out of this issue'. Macmillan, in his memoirs, said that Churchill's speech was a failure while Attlee's had been very effective. Foot says: 'Attlee put the case in what everyone agreed was one of the most impressive speeches of his life.' Attlee told Tom:

> We had a strange scene in the House last Monday. The PM entirely mistook what Jim Thomas would have called the atmosphere. His supporters were utterly dismayed.
> I had given him the opportunity to make a great speech on a high level – to give a lead to the world so to speak. Instead of responding he plunged into the gutter, to everybody's disgust. It would have been an eye-opener to him if he could have seen the faces of his own Party.
> It was a great pity as I had been strictly non-party.

Within a week of a speech in which even Tory papers thought that Attlee had 'pulled the entire Socialist party behind him', Labour's unity was shattered again by an intervention in the House by Bevan. It was interpreted as an open challenge to Attlee's leadership. On 13 April Eden announced to the House that the British and United States governments had agreed to discuss with other countries in South-East Asia the possibilities of establishing 'a collective defence to assure the peace, security and freedom of South-East Asia and the the Western Pacific'. Attlee asked: 'Would the Foreign Secretary realise that, in building up the forces of the free nations of Asia, he must call upon the Asiatic countries as well as those of European descent? Would the new organisation be free for all to enter, thereby avoiding any misrepresentations about the defence of obsolete colonialism?' Eden accepted the question courteously, and gave Attlee the reassurance he had sought. The House was taken aback, therefore, when Aneurin Bevan rose, moved to the dispatch box and – by implication refusing to trust his leader's capacity for obtaining appropriate reassurances from the government – asked a lengthy series of questions:

> Is the Right Hon. Gentleman [Eden] aware that the statement he has made today will be deeply resented by the majority of people in Great Britain? Is he further aware that it will be universally regarded as a surrender to American pressure? Is he further aware that the interpretation that may be placed upon his statement, unless he clarifies it further, is that we shall assist in establishing a NATO in South-East Asia for the purpose of imposing European rule upon certain people in that area, and will he realise that if the course is persisted in, it will estrange the Commonwealth members in that part of the world?'

Bevanites cheered.

At the meeting of the shadow Cabinet next day Attlee rebuked Bevan in carefully chosen terms typical of his touch in dealing with such situations. He did not censure Bevan for insubordination, but complained only that Bevan's intervention suggested that there was a division over policy within the party. This was a mild rebuke indeed, and Bevan could have comfortably accepted it; but he was in a stubborn mood. At a meeting of the PLP next morning, he said he had been deeply shocked by the official leadership's response to Eden's proposals. The setting up of such a collective defence system in South-East Asia must prejudice hopes of a negotiated settlement of the Vietnam War (the peace conference was about to start at Geneva the French having been forced to negotiate with the nationalists by a succession of reverses, to culminate in the great defeat at Dien Bien Phu in May). Such a collective defence system, Bevan said, would assist American policy 'which was tantamount to the diplomatic and military encirclement of China'. This time he did not stop at assailing Attlee: he also announced his resignation from the shadow Cabinet.

Even the 'Bevanites' were dismayed by Bevan's behaviour. Harold Wilson, who had been thirteenth in the last shadow Cabinet elections, showed his disapproval by accepting, against Bevan's expressed wishes, the place in the shadow Cabinet made vacant by Bevan's resignation. Crossman too was critical of Bevan's behaviour. Whereas the Bevanites were shocked, the rest of the party were furious. They believed that a general election was in the offing. Their success in by-elections, the government's weak record, Churchill's personal decline, Attlee's high standing in the country, all suggested that in an imminent poll Labour would do very well. At this very moment Bevan had upset the applecart, not because of some profound and long-term issue but because he could not restrain a splenetic outburst. As Attlee once said to the author, 'Nye seemed to kick through his own goal only when his side was winning.' A few days later, Morrison went some way to matching Nye's performance by publishing an article in the May issue of *Socialist Commentary* in which, against party rules, he attacked Bevan by name. Well might Bevan retort: 'I have always made it a rule never to make personal attacks on any of my colleagues. I do not propose to depart from it on this occasion.' Once again in private he and the Bevanites complained that there was one law for the right, and another for the left.

Within the party Attlee's reputation suffered considerably from the *Socialist Commentary* incident. Morrison had shown him his article before it was published, and Attlee had not objected to it. The excuse he made later was that he did not know that *Socialist Commentary* was sold to the general public; he thought it was circulated privately. A surprising degree of ignorance on Attlee's part, but as he was always truthful, and took very little interest in the media, there is no reason why his explanation should not be accepted. Greenwood died in June. The treasurership, with its valuable ex-officio seat on the Executive, became vacant. Gaitskell immediately announced that he would stand. So did Bevan. A stormy summer and autumn loomed up for Labour.

In his letter to Tom in March in which Attlee wrote about the debate on foreign affairs, he also wrote: 'I have sent you a copy of my autobiography. I am afraid that it is not very good though some people find it interesting.' His modesty was quite appropriate. Some of the reviews were favourable, and several of them were sympathetic, but none of them suggested that the book was of much significance. Tom Hopkinson wrote in *The Observer*:

> The quality of not getting in a flap is admirable in a party leader; in a Prime Minister it may at times be noble. But when it comes to authorship, a rigid self-control, an unfaltering composure, is a handicap.... The furthest Mr Attlee ventures towards an expression of emotion over a personal situation is the use of the word interesting – 'I had an interesting time at the Suvla [Gallipoli] evacuation....' ... It is hard to call *As it Happened* anything but deeply disapppointing. One does not expect to be made a party to a public man's inmost thoughts, but one might perhaps be allowed a look at some of the outmost.... This is not so much the picture of a life as a greatly expanded entry in *Who's Who*.

A few years later, I went to Attlee to discuss a project for a lengthy autobiographical interview with him. I took a copy of *As it Happened* with me for reference to the choice of topics. He looked at it occasionally with a wistful eye, so when I was leaving I asked him if he would 'write something in it'. He could not find a pen so I lent him mine. In a very crabbed hand he wrote 'Attlee'. He gazed at the signature for a few seconds, handed back the book and the pen, and said: 'Not very good.' I didn't know whether he meant the signature, the pen or the book. Some years later, when I got to know him much better, I asked him which he *had* meant. 'The *book*,' he said in a tone of great surprise, as if he could not possibly have meant anything else.

II

Though the Bevanites, with a great deal of support within and outside the party, clamoured for a distinctively 'socialist' foreign policy, Attlee continued to preach and practise bipartisanship. He praised Eden for his part in the Geneva Conference which in June 1954 seemed to promise an end of the Indo-China war. He continued to press for summit talks, preferably in London. 'It would be an enormous advantage if in this country, in the centre of the Commonwealth, fixed between those two great land masses [American and Russia], there should be a meeting of at least the three leaders of their countries . . .' Churchill was grateful to Attlee for his consistent pressure for summit talks. The Americans did not favour a meeting of the Big Three, and on this subject Eden supported the Americans. So long as Attlee continued to call for a summit, Churchill was justified in claiming to the Americans – and Eden – that 'the country wanted one'.

The House recessed at the end of July. In August Attlee led a Labour Party delegation on a visit to China, travelling via Moscow, returning by way of Hong Kong, Sinagpore, Australia, New Zealand and Canada. His companions included the party secretary Morgan Phillips, Wilfred Burke MP, Dr Edith Summerskill MP, Sam Watson and two other trade union leaders, and Aneurin Bevan. The main purpose of the visit, Attlee told the *New York Times* before he left, was to find out what they could in answer to the 'big question'; did the Chinese government wish to establish an 'imperial hegemony' in South-East Asia? Attlee said he was not afraid of being shown only what the Chinese wanted seen: 'I've been exposed to lots of eyewash in my time. I know it when I see it.' He expected to find confirmation of the view he had formed some years previously: that China was 'too proud' to become a satellite of Russia, and that the two regimes, though both Communist, were different from each other and had conflicting interests. This, in 1954, was bold prophecy, but it was to be justified by events.

In a press conference at Hong Kong on 1 September, Attlee said:

> The evidence we have is that this is a Government which is incorruptible, which has been working towards a principle in which it believes and which has done some very remarkable work. We found as we expected that China was being run by the Communists on principles with which we do not agree. We are democratic socialists and we said quite frankly what our views are. 'Eyewash' in China is not excessive. Chinese Communism is more tolerant than Russian, although there are restrictions on freedom of thought, speech and trade unions.

Mao, Attlee said, had urged that the Labour leaders should try to influence the United States to pull out of Formosa and cease to support Chiang Kai-shek. Attlee said he had responded by giving Mao a message for Malenkov. Russia should:

(1) give her people more freedom;

(2) ease restrictions on her satellite states;

(3) stop trying to undermine other governments;

(4) reduce Soviet armaments – if a general reduction was desirable, it

would be a good thing if Russia, the most heavily armed country, set an example.

For this contribution to the dialogue Attlee was immediately attacked by *Pravda* for warmongering: he was 'a tool of the United States aggressive reactionaries'.

Attlee's visit to Australia was not a great success. The Australians were as worried about the Communist government of China as the Americans were, and just as hostile. On arriving in Australia he said in his first speech: 'We have nothing to fear from Communist China; they are far too busy looking after 600 million people.' This remark made him few friends. In New Zealand he again suggested the neutralization of Formosa. 'The sooner we get rid of Chiang Kai-shek and his troops, the better it will be.' *Time* magazine, reviewing Attlee's comments on his experiences in China on 17 September concluded: 'Attlee could walk with Dante through Hell and emerge remarking that different people had different tastes but it did seem rather too hot.' At home the *Daily Mail* for 23 September observed of his visit to China: 'We cannot think that he was wise in leaving Britain while such a dangerous muddle persists in his own party.' The 'muddle' was chiefly on German rearmament, the issue which was to dominate the party conference at Scarborough at the end of the month.

III

By the time Attlee had got back to London the problem of German rearmament had changed. The French Assembly had voted to reject the inclusion of German contingents in the European Defence Force. The Russians had taken advantage of this to urge further talks. There emerged an idea for another four-power conference. The French Prime Minister, Mendès-France, approved, so did Ollenhauer, the leader of the Social Democrats in Germany. Churchill and the American government opposed it, wishing to press on with the rearming of Germany. In the Labour Party, Morrison and Gaitskell stood with Churchill and the Americans. That the question of German rearmament would create dissension between the Bevanites and the rest of the Labour Party had been foreseen, but now it was clear that the Bevanite and German problems were going to be much more closely related.

On the eve of the 1954 party conference, at the end of September, Attlee made his first political speech since his return from China. It was a summary of Labour's foreign policy in a world threatened by the H-bomb. 'A policy of hope in a world in search of peace' said the *Daily Herald*. The next day, opening the conference debate on foreign affairs, he reiterated several of the points he made the day before, and made a report on the visit to China. One sentence was widely remembered later in the conference: 'Foreign affairs lend themselves to emotionalism, which is a bad guide in foreign affairs.' An amendment had been put into the NEC's foreign policy statement in the form of a motion opposing the SEATO pact. It was defeated by 3,669,000 to 2,570,000. The leadership had won, but the vote for the amendment was formidable.

The result of the voting for the treasurership was announced on the second morning of the conference, just before the debate on German rearmament was to begin: Gaitskell 4,338,000 votes, Bevan 2,032,000. The question now was whether the party leadership would be repudiated on the German issue. Several big unions, including the third biggest, the Engineers' Union, were known to be against the leadership. Bevanite hopes ran high. The great debate centred on an emergency resolution submitted by the NEC to deal with 'the situation created by the failure of the French to ratify the European Defence Community Treaty'. The Bevanites submitted an amendment which in effect opposed any move to rearm the Germans. The NEC emergency resolution, which permitted German rearmament, was moved by Attlee. Attlee said: 'I am not in the least likely to underrate the danger of a resurgent military nationalist Germany. But this is a matter in which, as I said yesterday in the debate on foreign affairs, you must not be swayed by emotionalism.... The [Bevanite] amendment condemning all German rearmament will tie the hands of the next Labour Foreign Secretary.' It was a prime minister's speech, rather than a party leader's. During the floor debate there were some angry exchanges. Bevan could not speak in the debate because being a member of the NEC he could speak only on what the NEC deputed to him. His response to attacks from Deakin, therefore, was to shout down from the platform several times: 'Shut up, Arthur, shut up!' Morrison, winding up for the NEC, struck the moderate and conciliatory note which he had adopted so successfully many times in the Commons. The NEC prevailed by a very narrow majority: 3,270,000 against 3,022,000.

The following evening Bevan spoke to the *Tribune* meeting. With Deakin's behaviour in mind he inveighed against the intimidation of the Labour Party by powerful trade union leaders. Taking up Attlee's point that judgements about foreign policy should not be 'swayed by emotionalism' – he did not name Attlee – he said: 'I know I shall be accused of emotionalism. I know now the right kind of leader is a desiccated calculating machine who must not allow himself in any way to be swayed by emotion. If he sees injustice or suffering he must not let it move him.' This remark passed into history as a criticism of Gaitskell. In the context, it applied not to Gaitskell but to Attlee, and Bevan later denied that he was thinking of Gaitskell when he said it.

The following day Attlee gave a special breakfast interview to Percy Cudlipp for the *News Chronicle*. Cudlipp began by noting that on the morning when the national press was debating whether Attlee had won a triumph or had only narrowly escaped political extinction he found Attlee not perusing the editorials and the comments but, as usual, reading the 'Births, Marriages and Deaths' column in *The Times*, no other newspaper being in the room. 'Just as I joined him his eye caught the announcement that one of his acquaintances had passed on. "... no flowers," he murmured.' Attlee then began to eat his breakfast, 'looking as fresh and carefree as a holiday-maker, and his appetite for porridge, bacon and eggs and marmalade was excellent'. He thought the debate had been 'remarkable ... with many fine speeches from both sides. Herbert Morrison did brilliantly in his summing up.' He did not think that German rearmament would be as big an issue at the next year's conference – it would inevitably fade. Cudlipp did not share this view. Nor did Morrison or Sam Watson, who felt the Bevanites had got too close to victory to abandon their efforts now. Attlee, however, was right: the others were wrong.

A few days after the party conference, Attlee made his first major appearance on the television screen in a party political broadcast. Political broadcasting on television was still in its infancy, but even so it was clear that the leader of the Labour Party had much to learn about the use of the medium. Here, giving a fair idea of Attlee's attempt to exploit it to prepare the way for a Labour Party victory in the coming election, are the last few exchanges in a dialogue intended to provide Labour with a platform on which to make resounding propaganda:

Question: I thought the meanest thing on the part of the Prime Minister was to suggest that the pound was of more value today. In fact, I think, since 1951, taken at a pound it's eighteen and tenpence today.

Attlee: That's right. Oh it's come down. Undoubtedly.

Question: That was the subject, of course, of the eulogies of the Chancellor of the Exchequer.

Attlee: Quite.

Question: Have you any comment on the suggestion that our gold and dollar reserves have been rebuilt since the Labour Government, whereas they were dwindling away at an alarming rate at the time when the Conservatives took office?

Attlee: Well, these things go up and down, you know. We had the best reserves of any, and then some event occurs – it's a precarious position either way, and I think is recognized by every responsible statesman.

Question: Wouldn't it be true to say that in fact our dollar and gold reserves at the moment stand rather lower than they did when the Labour Government came out of office?

Attlee: I think so, yes.

Question: It means realistically then – presumably – that the opportunity presented by a fresh Labour Government will recover that position for us?

Attlee: I hope so.

Question: What about the cost of living? We heard a lot about that at the last Election, but it wasn't mentioned at the Tory Party Conference?

Attlee: No, I noticed that omission.

Question: Do you mind if I butt in here – people of my own age tend to be rather cynical of just what to believe, and what to strive for nowadays, what do you think the Labour Party have to offer?

Attlee: Well, you know there's nothing better than the motto that we have in this Borough, by our greatest citizen, William Morris – 'Fellowship is Life' – we believe in the kind of society where we've fellowship for all. You can't get that in a totalitarian society, you can't get that while there's grave inequalities in wealth. That is the hope of the world, and we offer fellowship in our own country and fellowship with all other countries.

Question: Do you find it then apt, Mr Attlee, that we should be meeting tonight in the Borough of Walthamstow, which is the town of William Morris?

Attlee: I think that's absolutely right, yes.

Announcer: Goodnight.

The debate on German rearmament was resumed in the House of Commons in November. The PLP agreed that they should not oppose it. Attlee stated that if a division was called, and a Labour MP did not wish to vote in favour, he was free to abstain. Labour members were then warned – in writing – that to vote in any way contrary to the decision taken by the PLP would be regarded as a serious breach of discipline. In the parliamentary debate on the treaties, Attlee made another of the speeches which drew thoughtful praise from Eden. The Conservative Party listened to him with deep respect. Bevan spoke against, but he obeyed the Whips. Six Labour members of the party ignored Attlee's ruling, forced a division, and voted against rearmament. The Whip was withdrawn from them. Bevan's reputation lost, rather than gained, as a result of this episode. The action taken by the rebels made him look somewhat ineffective, and his speech against the treaties was a poor one. Four days later Deakin and Gaitskell met for lunch, and agreed that Morrison should succeed Attlee as leader of the party.

The parliamentary year ended on a harmonious note. At the gathering of Lords and Commons on Churchill's eightieth birthday, when he was presented with the controversial Graham Sutherland portrait, Attlee made a much-praised speech. He wrote to Tom:

> There's a good deal of criticism of Winston's portrait. I don't like Graham Sutherland's stuff. I tell people that it's lucky that he did not depict the Old Man in plus fours with loud checks with one foot in a grave. That's his usual style.
>
> The Westminster Hall show was very impressive and the night after there was a great party at No. 10. Vio and I were the only Labour guests, but we met a lot of old friends. Characteristically Violet Bonham Carter liked my speech except my allusion to the social reform of the Lloyd George era. She clearly thought that it should have been Asquith. I fear the feud has become an obsession.
>
> I'm just reading Magnus on Gladstone. He really was a frightful old prig. Fancy writing a letter proposing marriage including a sentence of 140 words all about the Almighty.... He was a dreadful person. His guidance by the Almighty was worse than Cromwell's. He seems to have had as little idea of managing a Cabinet as he had of dealing with Queen Victoria. Curious his complete blindness to all social problems except prostitution.

He and Vi celebrated his seventy-second birthday alone. They were not among the guests invited to Morrison's wedding to his second wife three days later.

IV

The year 1955 opened with such tension between the United States and China over Formosa that there was talk of war. At a meeting of the PLP on 27 January, Attlee declared that though Formosa was an integral part of China it was not also an outpost of the American defence system. The PLP gave him unanimous support. He followed this up with an interview in the *Daily Herald*. He was at his most brisk. 'There are three vital steps to end the peril of war over Formosa,' he said. 'Send Chiang Kai-shek and his chief henchmen into exile. Leave Formosa out of America's "island defence ring", for the H-Bomb has made this unnecessary; and neutralise Formosa until its people decide by plebiscite whether or not they want to join Communist China.' The *News Chronicle* commented: 'Mr Attlee's proposals for ending the Formosa deadlock have upset the Chinese Communists, infuriated the Chinese Nationalists, annoyed Washington and outraged the *Daily Mail*.'

The Bevanites, on the other hand, were pleased. Bevan at this time asked Attlee for a private talk. Bevan spoke of the need for the party to reunite so far as possible on what was a considerable basis of agreement on the major issues of foreign policy. Bevan proposed a kind of relaunch of the party's foreign policy, to be signalled by a motion of censure on the government for failing to implement the resolution of April 1954 in which Attlee had called for a summit conference to deal with the threat of the H-bomb. In the shadow Cabinet Gaitskell and Morrison were suspicious; and in view of this resistance Attlee decided not to accept the tactical programme which Bevan had proposed. But strengthened by his knowledge that a new initiative in foreign policy could reunite the Party, he decided to try to concentrate the Opposition's energies on foreign and defence affairs. His first step was to call for discussions within the party, postulating total disarmament by all countries as 'the only ultimate hope of avoiding world destruction from the hydrogen bomb'. He told the PLP that he would pursue his demand for a summit conference, but that short of world disarmament Britain must have the maximum deterrent power in her hands. The 'Attlee Line' was generally approved within the party and well received outside it.

Early in February the Mendès-France government fell. In Russia Malenkov was replaced by Bulganin and Krushchev. Moscow radio was suggesting 'free elections' in Germany, to be followed by reunification. At a meeting of the PLP on 9 February, Bevan proposed that the Opposition should call for immediate four-power talks to discuss the implications of the Russian broadcasts. Attlee and Morrison agreed that the broadcasts should be followed up, but only to the extent of urging the government to inquire through diplomatic channels what their implications were. But Bevan was still determined to exploit every possibility of holding up German rearmament. In mid-February he canvassed the PLP and prepared an unofficial motion which regretted the government's failure to carry out Attlee's motion of the previous April, calling for summit talks on H-bomb tests and the future of Germany. Attlee and the shadow Cabinet refused to countenance this motion, but with one hundred or so signatures in his pocket Bevan went on to claim in *Tribune* that the party leaders had turned their backs on Attlee's call for a summit conference. Within hours of Bevan's article appearing in *Tribune*, the government announced that Britain would begin to manufacture the H-bomb. This news, coming in the wake of Bevan's new revolt against the leadership, caused great turbulence within the party.

Attlee returned to London after visits to the north of England and Holland to find another insurrection inspired by Bevan. Once again he decided to deal with it as a matter of party discipline. At a party meeting on 24 February, he moved a resolution 'regretting' Bevan's action. 'It was reducing party meetings to a farce,' he said tartly, 'if decisions were made at them and unofficial action was then taken in exactly the opposite sense.' Attlee then went on to make a general appeal for party unity. He rattled off the strong positions Labour held on foreign policy, and contrasted that with the fumbling of the Tories. A general election was imminent, and only one obstacle stood between the Labour Movement and victory – unnecessary internal dissension. Before Attlee introduced the resolution rebuking Bevan, Bevan offered to withdraw his motion if the rebuke would be withheld. Attlee, left to himself, would have agreed; but Gaitskell and Morrison insisted on the 'regretting' resolution being put. It was carried 132–72. Attlee's dilemma as leader of the party was now clearly defined. Gaitskell and Bevan each wanted him to force a showdown with the other: this was the last thing he wanted to do, because he believed it would weaken the party.

The debate on the White Paper on the H-bomb began on the first day of March 1955. On the fundamental issue, the decision to manufacture the H-bomb, the government's policy was summed up in Churchill's phrase: 'Safety would be the sturdy child of terror . . .' The Opposition's amendment recognized that for the time being it was 'necessary as a deterrent to aggression to rely on the threat of using thermo-nuclear weapons', and criticized the government only for failing to state what future expenditure on defence would be required, and to account for how defence funds had been expended in the past. It pointedly refrained from censuring the government for its decision to manufacture the H-bomb. Nor did it oppose the government's intention to use the nuclear bomb in retaliation against conventional weapons.

Bevan thought Attlee's amendment 'a monstrous evasion of a cataclysmic issue', and demanded to know from the government whether the West would respond to conventional attack with nuclear weapons; but to the anger of the majority of the party, he also demanded an answer from Attlee: 'I want my hon Friends the leaders of the Opposition to answer me. . . . Do they mean that nuclear weapons will be used with the support of the British Labour movement against *any* sort of aggression?' Bevan continued:

> Let the Prime Minister do deeds to match his great words; not attempt to delude the country by the majesty of his language but inspire it by the dedication of his behaviour. That is what we want from *him*. We want from my right hon Friends the leaders of the opposition an assurance that the language of their amendment, moved on our behalf, does not align the Labour movement behind that recklessness; because if we cannot have the lead from *them*, let *us* give the lead ourselves.

According to Foot, Bevan's words, 'No lead from *them*', were accompanied by a gesture which clearly swept the government front benches.

527

'Them' meant the government; 'us' meant the Labour Party. But within a few minutes there was gossip in the corridors: by 'them' Bevan had meant the leaders of the Labour Party, and by 'us' his supporters. Discussion went on in the lobby and, *sotto voce*, on the benches for more than two hours. Bevan had plenty of time to correct the impression he had made. He did not do so. Instead, he took the first opportunity to confirm that he had said what he meant to say. Attlee rose to wind up the debate for the Labour Party two hours and twenty-one minutes after Bevan had sat down. The White Paper, he said, 'showed evidence of a divided mind', but it was 'not the most terrible we have ever seen ... there is a hope there. It really is more hopeful than those White Papers that contemplated wars with conventional weapons ...' He sat down without having made any reference to Bevan's questions, or to Bevan; he explained later that he did not wish to widen the obvious split in the party.

When Attlee had finished his speech the Speaker called on the Minister of Defence, Harold Macmillan. Macmillan recorded: 'When Attlee sat down the Speaker called on me.... I made a gesture of rising, but as slowly as possible, so as to give time to Bevan to get up, which he did. Peremptory and offensive ... he asked Attlee to reply categorically to his question. Attlee shuffled and hedged: "I was speaking in general terms."' Attlee, records Macmillan, 'did his best, and did not answer the questions raised by Bevan'. But 'Bevan, with a sarcastic gesture, threw up his hands.' Bevan now made it clear that he was questioning his own leaders: 'What we want to know is whether the use of the words to which I have referred in the amendment associates us with the statement that we should use thermo-nuclear weapons, in circumstances of hostilities, although they were not used against *us*.' Attlee's reply was: 'My right hon Friend is asking me that question. I am not referring to anything in the White Paper, but to the general thesis, with which I think my right hon Friend agrees, that deterrents, by the possession of thermo-nuclear weapons, are the best way of preventing war.' Bevan said audibly: 'That's no answer, that's no answer.' This was certainly true, but Attlee's evasiveness was so obviously intended to hold the party together that it bore fruit. Though Bevan was joined by sixty-two Labour MPs in refusing to support the Attlee amendment, several leading Bevanites, including Wilson, Freeman and Crossman, followed Attlee into the voting lobby.

Within hours it was clear that there was a strong feeling in the party that Bevan should be deprived of the Whip or even be expelled, but Attlee, still intent on restoring party unity, decided to placate the Bevanites by modifying the Opposition's position. In the next few days he prepared a statement on foreign policy which would extend pressure on the government, and endorse some of the Bevanites' views. On 7 March

1955, the shadow Cabinet decided to call on the government to seek high-level talks on the H-bomb with the government of the United States and the Soviet Union. It reaffirmed the Attlee resolution of April 1954 calling for a summit and deplored the government's delay in implementing it: that Attlee was now ready to uphold this grievance was a concession to the dissidents within the party. This was a position which Bevan could accept because it represented most of what he had been asking for.

The shadow Cabinet had also to deal with the problem of what to do about Bevan's behaviour in the House in the debate on the White Paper. Attlee made only two contributions to the discussion. At the very beginning, before a word had been uttered by anybody else, he said gruffly: 'I'm against expulsion.' Morrison and Gaitskell argued that the PLP should be asked to withdraw the Whip. 'They made a good case for preserving the authority of the leadership,' Attlee told the author later, 'but what they were really concerned about was their own future. Each of them thought that one day he might succeed me as leader, and he wanted to inherit a disciplined Party. Both wanted Bevan brought to heel well in advance.' It was said afterwards that Attlee could have decided the issue in favour of Bevan. His near-silence, however, was deliberate. He believed that Bevan when he cooled down might well face the fact that there was no division on policy, and would resolve the problem by tendering an apology. He believed that if he tried to protect Bevan he would only aggravate animosity towards Bevan on the part of Gaitskell, Morrison, and the leaders of the big unions. He therefore acted on the principle of 'Least said, soonest mended'. The shadow Cabinet decided by a majority of three to one to recommend to the PLP that the Whip should be withdrawn.

These tactics might have brought about the desired result if the PLP meeting had not been postponed for a week as a result of Bevan succumbing to the flu. In the interval several statements were made by Bevanites which made it harder for Attlee to oppose expulsion. He got no help from Bevan, who went so far as to say publicly: 'What I have said or done is not a challenge to the personal authority of Mr Attlee as leader', but did not do what was required, namely to affirm that there was no real difference between him and Attlee about policy. The Bevanite clamour annoyed the trade union leaders, especially Deakin, and Gaitskell felt encouraged as a result to come out and campaign openly for Bevan's expulsion. 'When Labour MPs meet on Wednesday,' Gaitskell said at Doncaster, 'they will not be concerned with questions of policy, but with standards of loyalty.... I do not see how this sort of thing can possibly be regarded as anything but a direct challenge to the elected leader of our Party and therefore an affront to the Party which elected him.'

During the days before the PLP meeting was to be held several senior members called on Attlee to enlist his support or discover his intentions. He was uncommunicative. Gaitskell also called on Attlee, and complained about the clamour the Bevanites were raising, which threatened the unity of the party when an election was looming. Attlee became annoyed, and rapped out: 'You wanted to expel him; I didn't.' Angry as he was with Gaitskell, Attlee had to face the fact that Bevan had not apologized. He made up his mind, therefore, that unless Bevan made amends at the meeting of the PLP the Whip must be withdrawn. He wanted that to be the end of the affair; he did not want the matter to be referred to the National Executive, which, under the influence of Deakin and the big trade unions, might try to expel Bevan from the Labour Party. He opened the PLP meeting with a matter-of-fact account of Bevan's transgressions. No leader could put up with more of this, he said; he was sure Bevan would not do so if he, not Attlee, were leading the party. Bevan pointed out that he had not broken PLP Standing Orders – technically correct – and said he would never lead a breakaway group, even though he would continue to debate party policy. Attlee's resolution was carried by 141 to 112. The Whip was withdrawn, and the decision was duly notified to the NEC. Some present complained of Attlee's handling of the meeting, but others praised it. To a sympathetic letter from his old friend Jack Lawson, now a peer, Attlee replied:

> Thank you very much for your letter. The meeting was a poor show and there was far too much personal scrapping, malice and uncharitableness. The only speech worthy of the occasion was that of Percy Collick.

Now came the question of whether the NEC would decide to expel Bevan from the party. Despite a huge postbag against expulsion, it looked as if Bevan's opponents on the Executive could muster a majority. Deakin was exerting strong pressure behind the scenes, and in public was making speeches 'hoping that Attlee will give a very, very clear lead'. He told Gaitskell that if Bevan were not expelled the big unions 'would reconsider their relationship with [the party]'. This could mean a threat to withhold funds from the coming election campaign, alarming for Gaitskell as party treasurer. There were now reports that Churchill was about to retire and hand over to Eden, who would take advantage of Labour's disarray and call an early election. Deakin, Morrison and Gaitskell believed that Labour would have a better chance of winning an election with Bevan out of the party, but others recognized that this would offend the constituency parties.

When the NEC met, Morrison and Gaitskell spoke strongly in favour of expulsion; Crossman was vehemently against. When it began to look highly probable that Bevan would be expelled, Attlee broke off his doodling and proposed that Bevan should be asked to prepare a statement for the NEC, and submit to questioning on it by a sub-committee of the Executive, which would report back to the full body. This was accepted by fourteen votes to thirteen. Attlee again made it known that he believed that if Bevan apologized it would be unnecessary to remove the Whip.

This time Bevan responded. He asked Attlee for a personal meeting with him. In Foot's words, 'By now they were almost fellow conspirators against the Deakinites.' Between them, and in private, they worked out a statement which Attlee thought 'would wash'. This was conveyed to the NEC, and Bevan was questioned on it. Gaitskell's interrogation was particularly critical, and in Attlee's view 'unnecessarily hostile – after all, *he* wasn't the Leader of the Party who'd been insulted'. In later years Attlee reminisced with relish about one exchange recorded by Foot: 'Gaitskell, slightly nettled by Bevan's statement, asked simply: "You do agree, don't you, that you *have* made mistakes in the past three years?" "Certainly," said Bevan, "certainly," and then leaning forward, "Have you?" "Naturally," said Gaitskell with some testiness. "In that case," said Bevan, "let's issue a joint statement."'

Bevan's apology read:

> The charge is that in what I have done and also in the way I have done it I have created difficulties for Mr Attlee and caused him embarrassment in his position as the Leader of the Party. This was certainly never my intention. But if my action or speech could lend themselves to the interpretation that such was my motive, then I am sincerely sorry and I apologise to Mr Attlee for any pain I may have caused him.
>
> I ask for nothing more than the opportunity to serve our Party under his leadership. In doing so I claim no more privileges than, and accept all the obligations shared by, other members of the Party.

Attlee seconded a motion accepting Bevan's apology and approving the restoration of the Whip. It was carried by twenty votes to six, but only after the Deakinites had carried an amendment to it warning that the Executive 'will take drastic action against future violations of Party discipline' by fifteen votes to ten (with Attlee in the minority). To the party as a whole the news came as a great relief, especially since it was now certain that Churchill was about to retire and an election was expected within a few weeks. The Whip was restored to Bevan on 21 April, just after a general election had been announced. It had been a near thing, but Attlee had got his way, and he had got it in the nick of time. He had not yielded anything of his bipartisan commitment on foreign and defence policy, he had conceded nothing to the left which militated against the image of Labour as a responsible national party, he had brought Bevan back into the fold and he had reunited the party for the impending election. 'An extremely skilful feat,' said Harold Macmillan to the author in 1976. 'Remarkable feat. But of course, you know, he was an exceptionally gifted Party leader, difficult to name a better one.' In three letters to Tom, dated 15 and 24 March and 4 April 1955, Attlee makes only one reference to the party crisis: 'We are rather full just now with the trouble with Nye Bevan, but it may come out all right.' Meanwhile there were enjoyable relaxations in his private life, like the presentation of his portrait to Haileybury, and a night's stay at Univ, where he found the dons 'very young' – 'There was only Garrett of my time and he is emeritus.' There was Martin's wedding. Later, Felicity's. 'Flip's 'went off very well. First there was the register ceremony. Then with only the immediate family we went to Little Hampden Church which only holds about twenty people. Canon Carpenter of Westminster gave them a full church marriage service.' He told Tom he had just had a letter from his old Indian bearer 'accompanying presents for my grandchildren, remarkable fidelity after 26 years'. There was a pleasant scene of amity in the House of Commons when tributes were paid to Churchill on his retirement. Eden succeeded him. Harold Macmillan became Foreign Secretary; Butler remained Chancellor of the Exchequer. Attlee was the first speaker:

> Today we are parting with a Prime Minister who led this country through some of the most fateful years of its history and who has served in this House for more than fifty years.... He gave a leadership to this country when it needed it most, and in history, as one of the greatest of all Prime Ministers, his place is assured ...

Congratulating Eden, Attlee said he had:

> earned the esteem of hon Members in all parts of the House.... We all wish him health and strength, but we on this side cannot, of course, wish him a long tenure of office. Indeed, it is our duty, as opportunity offers, to try to give him a period of rest. But as a Mr Young said to Lord Melbourne when that statesman was hesitating to accept the Premiership, 'Why, damn it all, such a position was never held by any Greek or Roman, and if it only lasts three months, it will be worth while to have been Prime Minister of England.' So we are glad to congratulate him.

Attlee then left for a short visit to Canada and the United States. On 15 April, while he was away, Eden announced a general election for 26 May.

V

Dalton described the 1955 election as the dullest of all the twelve parliamentary elections he had fought. 'There were no live issues and there was great apathy all over the country except in some marginal constituencies.'

Few disagreed with him. The Conservatives, with a new leader, an efficient party machine, and a humanitarian and reflationary policy associated with R. A. Butler as chancellor of the exchequer, looked more like winners. By contrast, the Labour Party looked what it was, tired, and, in Attlee's words in later years, 'out of steam'. It was led by an old man who had only just managed to rescue his party from the quarrels which had all but torn it apart. Its most colourful figure was Bevan, who did not this time call the Tories 'vermin', but referred to them merely as 'Gadarene swine'. The Labour Party campaigned on a recital of its record – 'in the years from 1945–51 a great and peaceful revolution was carried out'. On the foreign front it advocated 'talks with the leading statesmen of America and Russia . . . with a view to the control of weapons of mass destruction'. Both these points had been heard before. Labour's few promises of further nationalization did not cause excitement one way or the other. The 1955 manifesto, *Forward With Labour*, was essentially a repeat of *Challenge To Britain*, 1952, which Bevan had described as 'cold porridge stirred through a blanket'. Several strikes had turned feeling against the unions, and consequently against the Labour Party; the party machine was in poor condition. For the first time in ninety years, a government after a normal period of power in peacetime was returned to office with an increased majority.

Labour opened the campaign in a hopeful frame of mind. The Gallup poll had given the Conservatives a 3 to 4 per cent lead just before the election had been announced: but when the campaign began the parties were equal. Attlee took the road in high spirits and seemed to be in excellent physical condition. Between 12 and 20 May, chauffeured by Vi, he covered 1,200 miles, and addressed forty meetings. At Glasgow he called on his audience to: 'Wake up this election! The Tories hope to keep it quiet and to sneak back into power before the nation realises what has happened. Labour's job is to bring all these issues into the open – loud and clear.'

Attlee welcomed the livening up of the election campaign by Sir Winston Churchill's attack on himself over the call-up. He rebuked Churchill for misrepresenting his position on nuclear deterrence. Churchill had said that *Tribune* had reported Attlee as declaring that the idea of the H-bomb as a deterrent was a profound illusion, whereas, said Churchill, official Labour policy was in favour of making the H-bomb. 'Where does Mr Attlee really stand?' he demanded to know. It was a slip on Churchill's part. Attlee had said only that: 'Britain must not go around the world threatening to drop an H-bomb whenever trouble broke out.' Attlee took full advantage of Churchill's error. 'My statement was perfectly plain. I replied to him yesterday and quoted again exactly what I said in the House. What more he wants I don't know.' For good measure he answered those Labour dissidents who were opposed to Britain manufacturing the H-bomb. 'I don't quite follow the argument that we shouldn't manufacture it ourselves.' It was no use telling the Russians Britain wouldn't be the first to use it. 'It would be like facing a heavyweight boxer with a revolver and telling him you were not going to be the first to fire.... I have never found that a generous gesture brought any response from the Russian side. They are a tough people. It is no good going to the Kremlin thinking you can read them the Sermon on the Mount.'

Everywhere he spoke, Attlee attacked the new Tory slogan 'Set the People Free'. At Glasgow he gave short shrift to the Conservatives' idea of a property-owning democracy. 'Tory talk about a property-owning democracy is all bunk. One of the best examples of a property-owning democracy is our great Co-operative Movement.' As always he warned the voters to watch out for last-minute Tory stunts. At Walthamstow he held up one of the dummy ration books which the Tories had produced. 'They'll try to tell you that when Labour gets back it will bring back the ration books. This is one of the dirtiest things they have ever put out.'

Sometimes serious, sometimes half-humorous, the long-distance Churchill–Attlee exchanges seemed part of an act. Churchill called Attlee a 'chameleon'. At Edinburgh Attlee replied mildly and said: 'I really don't mind, but the charge comes rather oddly from Sir Winston, who has always been a bit of a chameleon himself.... I can remember when Sir Winston was a Conservative and when for eighteen years he was a Liberal again. I don't know whether that has made him piebald or skewbald.' He dealt with another of Churchill's misrepresentations: 'It is suggested that I said there were no Conservative working men. I never said anything of the sort. I said there were no intelligent Conservative working men. That is quite a different matter, and happens to be perfectly true. The Conservative Government want to keep things as they are. That is why there are no intelligent working men in the Conservative Party.'

When the campaign drew to a close, the Conservatives seemed to be ahead. The result was: Conservatives 324, Labour 277, Liberals 6. The net increase in the electorate since 1951 was 300,000; but the total poll fell by two million, the Conservative vote falling by 412,000, the Labour vote by a significant 1,543,000. In the inquest immediately after the election, Labour's right wing inevitably put much of the blame on Bevan.

Attlee commented on the election result at the Miners' Annual Gala at Durham in early June: the Tories had won because they had taken over as their own policies what Labour had preached and practised from 1945 on. 'They have had to accept what we have done – many things which twenty, thirty or forty years ago they would have denounced as heresies and silly socialism.' In mid-July he wrote in the *Daily Herald*:

'Two things contributed to Labour's defeat at the General Election. The Tories had more money and the bulk of the Press supported them. Lots of people aren't really doing well today, but they think they are because they are told so.' And a week later he told the East Midlands Labour Party: 'I don't want us, when we come in again, to be swept in by some temporary discontent. I want to come in because a larger number of people have accepted the Socialist Creed. The great task facing the Labour Party is to convert more people to a new way of life.... It is for us to study the minds of the younger generation.'

VI

From the day after the election to Attlee's resignation from the leadership in early December, the question of when he would go and who would succeed him dominated discussion within the Labour Party. Attlee wanted to resign the leadership immediately after the election, but he preferred to stay if it was clear that his going would precipitate a struggle for the succession between Morrison and Bevan which would ruin the party. A week after the election, to his bitter regret, the leadership question erupted. The issue was precipitated by a letter from Dalton to Attlee which was intended for immediate distribution to the press. Dalton called for the retirement of all the older members of the shadow Cabinet so that the way was open for the promotion of younger men. He was prepared to retire himself, but he made a point of telling Attlee that: 'your own position is a very special one. It is my strong hope that, in the interests of Party unity, you will continue as leader when Parliament meets.' Realizing what ill feeling this would create, Attlee telephoned Dalton and tried to persuade him not to publish the letter. He failed. The letter was published, and received much comment. The senior members of the shadow Cabinet were most upset at its appearance. 'Seldom has it been such fun to do one's duty,' recorded Dalton.

By encouraging Attlee to remain, Dalton intended to provide time to build up the strength of his protégé, Gaitskell. This conflicted with Attlee's own strategy and personal wish – to go as soon as he felt he could – conveyed quite clearly in a letter to Tom two weeks later, on 21 June 1955:

It's high time the Party found a new leader. I am too old to give a new impetus. I hoped to force their hand by fixing a date for retirement, but they would not have it. Twenty years is quite long enough, I think.

It was with that intention that at the first meeting of the shadow Cabinet after the election Attlee announced that he was ready to go at once or at an agreed date. He was immediately asked to stay, at least to the end of the session. The next day Attlee announced to the PLP meeting that he had told the shadow Cabinet that he wanted to go at once but that he had been asked to stay. Bevan rose, and with great fervour pleaded that he not only carry on but remain indefinitely. Eventually Attlee asked the meeting if this were the general wish. It was. 'Any against?' No. 'Very well,' said Attlee. Dalton noted in his diary that night: 'This is almost certainly the end of Morrison.'

There was a pleasant incident at the opening of the new Parliament. After the new ministers had been sworn in, and it came the turn of the Opposition, instead of taking the Bible, Attlee went over to Churchill, now a backbencher, sitting in the front row immediately below the gangway, shook his hand, and drew him into first place in the Opposition 'queue'. MPs on both sides cheered the gesture. There was another cheer as Churchill, having signed the roll, waited for Mr Attlee to walk out of the Chamber with him. The debate on the Address showed a similar amiable tone. Attlee called the Gracious Speech 'a fairly lengthy document ... paved with good intentions, and we shall have to see how far those good intentions are carried out. ... We shall all welcome the more hopeful signs that there are of peace in the world. We hope especially that the talks at the highest level will proceed as quickly as possible and will deal not merely with procedure but with substance.' Eden could 'only thank him' for his speech. 'It was so kind and so gentle and so generally approving that I feel we can go forward with the execution of this formidable programme under the benevolent aegis of the Hon Members opposite.'

Attlee intervened hardly at all during the short summer parliamentary term. He sat hunched on the front bench, feet on the table, doodling away, though occasionally, and suddenly, rising to make a sharp point or put an awkward question. Morrison took every opportunity of getting to his feet. In Attlee's view he 'tried too hard'; and the harder he tried to shine the more laboured his efforts became. Bevan was on his best behaviour, and the Bevanite group was only a memory. The impression of party unity, at any rate in the House, was enhanced by Attlee's decision to introduce a new shadow Cabinet system whereby shadow ministers were restricted to challenging 'real' ministers only within their 'shadow' briefs – a system both parties are following to this day. The idea was Gaitskell's. Attlee acted on it without enthusiasm.

Attlee had gone off on holiday before Parliament rose. He thereby missed two important debates, one on the summit conference, at Geneva, where Eden had proposed the reunification of Germany; the other on the economic situation, both arranged at the last moment. In a letter to Arthur Moyle from Pembroke it is evident that now that the risk of a

Morrison putsch had been removed he still considered it only fair to give Morrison every chance to stake his claim prior to a fair and open contest for the leadership. 'I felt a bit guilty going away before the House rose, but HM is constantly asking for a place in the sun, so it was quite useful to give him a show.' He had his eye on Gaitskell. 'I read the Hansards with interest and thought Hugh very cogent.' It was a delightful visit. 'A whole week of brilliantly sunny weather. We have spent every day out in one or other of the lovely bays in this beautiful coast.' The holiday helped him overcome his still lingering animosity towards the Germans:

> We took our German maid with us, a very nice girl who has done something to mitigate my prejudice against that people. I read the other day a remarkable little book describing how a few German students in Munich led by a boy and his sister decided that Nazism must be opposed and with great courage indulged in vigorous propaganda. Of course in the end they were all executed but they had demonstrated that there were still Germans with courage to stand out for the freedom of the human spirit.

He also felt more benign about the Russians and the Americans.

> The international situation is distinctly brighter. The Russians have certainly come some way. Also the Yanks are more reasonable. They generally are a year behind us. A year ago they were cussing me for going to China.

Despite this relaxed holiday, the day after he wrote to Tom, on 8 August 1955, Attlee had a stroke. It was slight; ten days later Vi could tell newspaper reporters that he was out of bed and feeling much better. The illness was followed by a new outbreak of eczema, another stress complaint. There were rumours now that he might resign earlier than expected. On 13 September (just after the Attlees returned from Wales) Percy Cudlipp, then writing a weekly column in the *News Chronicle*, visited Cherry Cottage. The resulting column was thought so important that it was splashed on page one, with the headline 'ATTLEE IS READY TO GO'. It was true that Attlee said he was ready to go. After the interview had been published, and had been subjected to expert analysis by the rest of the press for the next few days, Attlee commented about what he had said: 'There's nothing new in that', and a comparison with what he said on several occasions in the past few years revealed that in all respects but two such was the case.

The two differences were, first, that he gave this interview only a few days before the annual Labour Party conference was due to open at Margate; and secondly that in talking of the need for a younger man to lead the party he had specified a qualification:

> Labour has nothing to gain by dwelling in the past. Nor do I think we can impress the nation by adopting a futile left-wingism. . . . The world today is continually presenting new problems. It is no use asking, 'What would

Keir Hardie have done?' We must have at the top men brought up in the present age, not, as I was, in the Victorian Age.

This, as the newspapers pointed out, eliminated Morrison and Griffiths. Bevan was born in Victoria's reign, though not 'brought up' in it. Some of the Bevanites thought the 'futile left-wingism' reference implied that Bevan, also, was out of date. Some newspapers concluded that, as the *News Chronicle* put it: 'Mr Attlee's words will be widely interpreted as advice to look to the generation of which Hugh Gaitskell (born 1906), Mr Alfred Robens (born 1910) and Mr Harold Wilson (1916) are the best-known figures in the Labour Party.' Speculation continued up to, and into, the annual conference at Margate.

The main official business of the Margate conference was to examine the Wilson report on the organization of the party called for as a result of Labour's defeat in the general election, and to discuss ten new policy projects which had been put before the party. The Wilson report was widely described as 'devastating'; he had compared the party machine to a 'rusty penny-farthing'. Morgan Phillips was indirectly subjected to heavy criticism. The opening address, delivered by Jim Griffiths, was on the future Labour policy of which the ten new reports were to be the vehicles. To judge by Griffiths' speech it seemed that Attlee had indeed had Bevan in mind when he spoke of Keir Hardie being out of date and of the necessity for a new approach to new problems. As the correspondent of *The Times* put it: 'All the demands for more socialism and more nationalization and a return to the ideals of the pioneers seemed crude when compared with Mr Griffiths's warm vision of a new society based on the Executive's plan for ten research projects.'

Outside the conference hall it was not the ten research projects or the rusty penny-farthing which people discussed: it was the leadership question. Deakin's death in May had not changed the position of the trade union leaders, who wanted Attlee to make way for Morrison. At a pre-conference demonstration, George Brinham of the Amalgamated Society of Woodworkers had gone so far as to publicly call for Attlee's resignation. The Bevanites made it clear they wanted Attlee to stay; Barbara Castle had opposed Brinham with eloquence and passion. Gaitskell, who retained the treasurership against Bevan's renewed challenge by a larger majority than the previous year, spoke to the conference for the first time as a member of the NEC. His subject was the nationalized industries, and he spoke for several minutes about their role in the national economy in terms which did not excite his audience. But after he had finished his exposition, as though in answer to an unspoken question from Bevan, he launched into a passionate declaration of why he had become a socialist: 'I became a Socialist quite candidly not so much because I was a passionate advocate of public ownership but because at a very early age I came to hate and loathe social unjustice, because I distrusted the class structure of our society, because I could not tolerate the indefensible differences of status and income which disfigure our society.' This was a new Gaitskell. He was given the outstanding ovation of the conference. 'Brilliant speech,' Attlee told newspaper reporters when questioned as he left the hall. Discussing that speech four years later, Attlee told the author: 'Nye didn't learn until it was too late. Gaitskell learned just in time.'

Attlee took little part in the conference. In a debate on the H-bomb and atomic warfare, he made familiar points: 'Some people think it's wicked to produce the H-bomb but all right if you secure it from someone else.' The signs for world disarmament were more hopeful than ever before because governments were facing up to realities. But: 'You can't do these things, you know, just in a moment, and I do not believe you can do it by saying you will set an example and disarming and hope the other fellows will follow suit. It looks a fine gesture, but suppose it doesn't come off, suppose the other fellows don't follow suit.' Apart from the debate, he participated in the proceedings only to present the parliamentary report. He had at first intended to delegate the task to Morrison, but decided not to do so lest he create the impression that Morrison was his favourite for the succession. Attlee's speech won warm support. The day after the conference the *Daily Mail*, with a gibe at 'the leader of the Party without a Policy', said:

> 72-year-old Mr Attlee went from the final session of the Socialist Conference here today a happy man. Anyone less modest could hardly have refrained from proclaiming to his followers, 'If we haven't got a policy, at least we have an outstanding asset, and that's me.' It is true; and it was significant that Mr Attlee displayed a much more animated front to the delegates, who have long been used to his inscrutable doodling expression.

Soon after the party conference, there was more speculation about an early resignation. In a speech at Manchester Robens declared that Attlee expected to announce his retirement on 26 October 1955, the day after Parliament reassembled. The *Daily Herald* was so impressed that it flew its correspondent out to Malta, where Attlee was attending a conference to discuss Malta's integration with Britain. 'I have no intention whatever of resigning at the present time,' he said. 'There is nothing on the agenda of the Parliamentary party meeting about it. I have heard of no one who intends to raise the subject.' This statement had its ambiguities. The phrase 'at the present time' might mean 'not immediately but perhaps quite soon', as the Bevanites feared, or 'for months and months yet', as Morrison's supporters feared. A *Daily Express* correspondent, for instance, suggested that Attlee, well to the left of Morrison and Gaitskell, though now having more cordial relations with Gaitskell, 'carries no flaming torch for him either. So I ask this: does Mr Attlee aim to hold on till Mr Aneurin Bevan is in a position to scoop up the prize?'

Morrison's friends now tried to collect a list of MPs and trade union leaders who would threaten to resign if Attlee did not stand down in favour of Morrison. The effort flopped for lack of support, and Morrison repudiated it. Attlee returned from Malta in high spirits. When a *Sunday Express* reporter put to him his declaration 'that he had no intention of resigning from the leadership of the Labour Party at present, he merely chuckled'. Conservative MPs who had heard how ill he had looked two weeks previously were surprised to see him in such excellent health.

He sailed into action, all guns firing, in the debate on the autumn budget which Butler had been forced to bring in, taking back many of the concessions he had made in the budget presented before the election. 'I must say we have a most temperamental Chancellor of the Exchequer,' said Attlee. 'He was in the depths of gloom in February, he quite brightened up in April and he is down in the dumps again now.... If this was the lot which he had in mind I don't wonder he didn't reveal it to the electors before the election.' It was difficult to find any clear policy in the budget. Many Tories agreed with him. There was no planning in the national interest. 'Anything for the public benefit is to be cut....' All the increased purchasing power 'goes into the hands of the money-lenders.... With absolute hypocrisy, the Government talk about restrictions on spending while they have put up the money for an enormous spending campaign to go into every home in the country. I was forgetting that to keep up with the neighbours, one must have a new looking-in set' (a gibe at the recently introduced 'commercial' television). The net effect, as with all Butler's budgets, he concluded, was 'that it all hits the small man.... Well, they had their time at the last Election, and I am afraid that those electors who voted for the Tories will realize now that they are in for the morning after the night before.'

Attlee's speech made an excellent impression. Morrison's was verbose, confusing and boring. Gaitskell as shadow Chancellor was the leading Opposition spokesman. For some years his duels with Butler had been gentlemanly with rapiers. Now he bludgeoned like a Bevanite. As well as attacking the budget, he cast aspersions on Butler's honour – 'political' not 'personal'. His speech marked the end of Butskellism and the beginning of his rise to the top of the betting in the leadership stakes. Harold Wilson also made an impressive speech, notable for the degree to which he supported Gaitskell. After it, Bowden, the Chief Whip, went to Wilson and said: 'Clem is delighted. Now that you and Hugh are working so well together, he says he's ready to go.' It was at this point that Gaitskell made up his mind to stand for the leadership. He did so, apparently, with great reluctance. In a chat with Wilson he seemed very doubtful of the prospects if he stood against Morrison. 'If you don't stand, I will,' said Wilson. Gaitskell told Morrison that if Attlee resigned he would be a candidate. Morrison encouraged Gaitskell to 'have a go', but he believed that he himself would win on a second ballot by taking Bevan's votes; and he resented the advice of his friends who wanted him to withdraw from the arena.

Meanwhile Attlee showed no sign of resigning. His health was obviously improving. In the first half of November he flew to Ireland and to Austria. On his return from Vienna Attlee found that speculation about his retirement and about a new leader was rife as never before. The excitement had been precipitated by a newspaper article by Leslie Hunter, who had lunched with Attlee just before he had gone abroad, and had then written a column for the *Daily Herald* predicting that Attlee would announce his resignation on or before his next birthday, 3 January, 1956. This was given great prominence. When, back in London, Attlee was questioned about the validity of Hunter's views, he would say only: 'No comment.' The fact that he would say no more and did not contradict what Hunter had reported was generally taken to mean that Hunter's story was substantially correct. Attlee now decided that in view of the restlessness within the party the time had come for him to go. He called in Bowden in late November and said: 'I'm going. Fix a date.' Bowden said: 'We should get it over before Christmas. Let us say December 7.' Attlee nodded. Bowden asked: 'Shall I tell the contenders privately?' Attlee said: 'Tell Gaitskell.'

He wrote to Tom, on 6 December:

> I am tomorrow giving up the leadership of the Party. As you know I wanted to go after the last Election, but stayed on to oblige. There is, however, so much speculation as to the next leader going on that I think it best to retire now. The Party is in good heart.

The last sentence was important. Attlee was ready to go because he believed that there would not now be the fratricidal struggle for the leadership that would have been precipitated if he had resigned immediately after the general election. Morrison's decline had removed that risk.

Attlee told the shadow Cabinet of his intention on the morning of the following day. He did not give advance notice to Morrison. Later that morning he opened a meeting of the Parliamentary Party with these words:

> Before proceeding to the main business for which you have been called, I wish to make a personal statement. After the last general election, I intimated that I would continue as chairman of the Party. It is regrettable, however, that since that date there has scarcely been a week pass without

one prominent member of the Party or another talking about my resignation. That certainly does not help the Party. I desire to intimate that I am resigning from the leadership of the Party and this resignation takes place from now.

He then moved out of the chair. Morrison took his place. He moved a motion accepting Attlee's resignation, and proposed a vote of thanks for Attlee's service to the party. Only about half the Labour MPs were present – they had had no warning. Several speeches were made, some very emotional. According to the *Daily Herald*, 'some MPs were openly weeping. Mr Attlee sat sucking hard at his pipe. But his eyes were moist. The youngest, Mr Anthony Wedgwood Benn, added his tribute. He hoped that if Mr Attlee went to the Lords, he would give that body a new lease of life.' They sang 'For He's a Jolly Good Fellow'. Attlee walked out, leaving Morrison in charge.

On 8 December tributes were paid to Attlee in the House, by Eden, Clement Davies and Morrison. 'There are occasions,' said Eden, 'when personal friendships far transcend political differences, and the Right Hon Gentleman, in the thirty-three years in which he sat in this House, certainly never made a personal enemy ... he was a good House of Commons man, and his translation to another place can never really change that.' The British press were unanimous in their praise of the man who had been leader for twenty years, longer than any other leader of a British party in the century. 'Any man who can hold such a post for so long,' said the *Express* leader, 'is remarkable. But to do it, as Attlee did, in the tumultuous Socialist Party, points to altogether exceptional qualities.'

After the tributes, attention focused on the question of who would succeed him. Morrison's supporters made a clumsy move to get both Bevan and Gaitskell to withdraw in his favour in the interests of party unity. Bevan readily agreed, but was urged by his friends not to give way. Gaitskell had no hesitation about standing, and issued a press statement to say so. The attempt to get Bevan and Gaitskell to stand down harmed both Morrison *and* Bevan, since they were known to have dined together and to have discussed a 'stop Gaitskell' arrangement. The leadership election was held at the next meeting of the PLP, 14 December 1955. There was need for only one ballot: Gaitskell 157, Bevan 70, Morrison 40. Gaitskell had won by an absolute majority. Nobody had expected that Morrison would be so humiliated. Except Attlee: in a congratulatory note to Gaitskell he said: 'I was delighted with your vote which was just about what I had anticipated. It was a pity that Herbert insisted on running. He had, I think, been warned of the probable result. ... I hope that Nye & Co will now go all out to support you.'

Attlee had achieved what he wanted. He had kept Morrison out, and had performed what he thought was a real service to his party. If Morrison had become leader, Attlee believed, the party would have staggered on to another disaster. A year after Attlee chose his time to resign, Bevan was shadow foreign secretary, and two years after it Bevan was a powerful and accepted number two to Gaitskell. The shadow Cabinet was made up of young men far more radical, able and appealing than Morrison would ever have mustered. By keeping Morrison out, Attlee did not create a new, strong and attractive Labour Party, but he saved it from an embittered and destructive wilderness.

What had he really wanted? His secret hope had earlier been that Bevan would mend his ways and become the leader. During the crisis in the party which had been brought on by the attempt to have Bevan expelled, Crossman, as others did, went to see Attlee privately to ask him to intercede. According to Crossman, as quoted by Michael Foot in his biography of Bevan, Attlee said: 'Nye had the leadership on a plate. I always wanted him to have it. But, you know, he wants to be two things simultaneously, a rebel and an official leader, and you can't be both.' In *The Road to Brighton Pier*, Hunter wrote about the conversation between him and Attlee which had provided the material for his article in the *Daily Herald* in November 1955. Attlee, he said, would have liked to see Bevan become leader of the party: 'I'd like to see him get it.... Trouble is he's so unstable, all over the place, you never know where you are with him. Anyway he's cooked his goose for the time being, and the Party would never stand for him'

After the defeat of the Labour Party in the general election of 1959, Gaitskell proposed to a Labour Party conference in Blackpool that Clause IV of its constitution, committing the party to public ownership, should be rescinded. After a debate in which feelings ran very high, Gaitskell's recommendation was rejected. 'He might as well have attacked the 39 Articles,' Attlee told Arthur Moyle. In Attlee's opinion this initiative, he told the author, was 'a great mistake'. The Labour Party had always suffered from 'a passion for over-definition'. A good leader should discourage debates about definitions. Was Gaitskell a good leader? 'Not ideal. Man of character, but lacked experience of the movement, and inclined to be doctrinaire.' What about Nye? 'Nye was the natural leader for the Party, but you can't lead and kick over the traces every time you feel like it, and he wouldn't face this until it was too late.' He said much the same thing publicly in *The Observer*, 21 October 1962: 'I admired much about him, to the extent that I thought he would have been a natural leader of the Labour Party if one was sure he would learn to keep his temper. Far from standing in his way, I tried to bring him on.'

The Chief Whip Bowden summed it up: 'Given time and circumstances there was no doubt that Gaitskell was his man.'

29
The Last Years

In the first letter to Tom after his resignation, the words 'The Rt Hon C. R. Attlee', die-stamped on his notepaper, had been scored out in ink and 'The Rt Hon Earl Attlee' substituted, unmistakably in his own hand. Whenever he had changed houses, he had used all his notepaper, amending the address in ink until he had exhausted his supply. From now on his lifelong habit of economy was reinforced by the conviction – it turned out that he was wrong – that he would die long before Vi, who would have to be provided for, so that what money he had should not be wasted. Some people were surprised that he took a peerage. In fact he had always approved of Honours, and wanted to remain in politics without continuing to sit in the House of Commons, which he thought would be unfair to his successor. He enjoyed discussing his coat of arms with the College of Arms. When they demurred about including the heads of the Welsh terriers, he said: 'They're indispensable – they're my two Welsh PPSS, Arthur Jenkins and Arthur Moyle.' He had already decided on the Haileybury School motto – *Sursum corda* (Lift up your hearts); his other favourite was *Esse quam videri* (Be, rather than seem to be). Tom wrote to say that only in Britain could an Opposition leader resign and receive such tributes from all parties. Attlee agreed: 'You're quite right about the English being unlike any others. Foreign politicians would be horrified to see the letters I've received from political opponents.'

He wrote to Tom again on 30 January 1956, after he had taken his seat in the Lords. He had hoped to have Bertrand Russell as one of his sponsors – an example of how much Attlee could disagree with a man on fundamentals and yet admire his ability and his motives – but 'Bertie' was in the United States and 'could not make it so I fell back on Huntingdon, a Plantagenet, as is also Oliver Baldwin on the distaff side'. Heraldry was fun. 'I am seeing Richmond Herald about arms next week.

544

It's rather a costly business.' Writing of the elder son of Stanley Baldwin reminded him that: 'I've just read young Baldwin's [the younger son] filial defence of his father, quite well done. The poor old boy had no secretary at the end and hence had to see masses of abusive letters from diehard Tories. If I had known about it at the time I should have sent him a line.'

A few days later Vi had a car accident: the side of her head was gashed and two of Attlee's ribs were fractured. From this time on Vi, unfortunately, was receiving publicity as an accident-prone driver. He wrote about his enforced 'rest' to Moyle, ending: 'What an ass Herbert [Morrison] is to sulk.' Morrison was displeased with changes in the Shadow Cabinet which Gaitskell had announced. 'What does he think that he will gain by behaving like a baby? ... Most of the Front Bench arrangements are those which I had already made.'

He soon set the tone for how he would behave in his remaining years. He had no inclination to remain an active politician. He wrote to Tom, three months after he had announced his retirement:

> I find the Lords a very friendly place. I have not yet broken silence, but shall probably to do so on Defence in the near future.... Everyone seems to think that I now have lots of leisure to go to all sorts of functions, but I am trying to get a bit of freedom.... I am doing a good many newspaper articles just now which serve to keep the home fires burning. Payment is in inverse ratio to the character of the paper.

He began the daily routine which lasted over the next ten years. Nearly every morning when the House of Lords was in session Vi drove him to Great Missenden station. He boarded the train, 'well up to the front to try and get a corner seat', and travelled in a third-class compartment to Baker Street, then to Westminster on the Metropolitan Line. In his battered little brown case were usually a few copies of Hansard, two spare pipes, a two-ounce tin of cut Golden Bar – Attlee always filled his pipe from the tin, never from a pouch – and a couple of detective paperbacks. Sometimes he would do *The Times* crossword. Occasionally he was recognized, but very rarely. The next letter to Tom on 8 April runs: 'I have to take part in a ceremony on June 1856 [sic] at Windsor.' (This was to be enrolled as a Knight of the Garter.) 'Roseberry has kindly offered me the loan of his father's robes for the occasion ...' The prospect of the evening inspired him to a limerick:

> Here is a little verse I made for the occasion.
>
> Few thought he was even a starter
> There were many who thought themselves smarter
> But he ended PM
> CH and OM
> An earl and a knight of the garter.

'The Garter Show' (to Tom on 24 June) 'went off very well.' Vi and all the children went:

We drove to Windsor arriving about 11. I chatted with the knights while they robed. We then went along to a room outside the throne room when the Queen and other royalties came along and greeted us. All then went in except the three new boys who waited outside. Our sponsors then came out to us and brought us to our seats. In turn we were called up and the Queen with the assistance of our sponsors put on us the garter, the chain, the star and the mantle, the bishop saying on each occasion appropriate admonitions to fight the good fight etc. We then took an oath on the testament and all left the Hall. We then disrobed and assembled for lunch. . . . I sat between the Queen and the Duchess of Gloucester. . . . After lunch we robed and walked in procession to the Chapel Iveagh and I as juniors leading. He and Winston being both 82 were very rocky on their feet. However all went well. . . . I enclose a copy of the arms. I have the winged hearts for HC and the colouring argent on azure for Univ.

The summer of 1956 was dominated by Suez. In July Gaitskell spoke in support of Eden's outright condemnation of the Egyptian government for nationalizing the Suez Canal in defiance of international agreements – the behaviour of their President, Nasser, said Gaitskell, was 'all very familiar. It is exactly the same as we encountered from Mussolini and Hitler in those years before the war.' Three months later, when the crisis had reached its peak, and in 'collusion' with the French Eden had given instructions for British troops to occupy the Canal area, Gaitskell changed his line and denounced the government's actions as a breach of its responsibility to the United Nations. His July speech was much quoted against him. By contrast Attlee's July speech in the Lords, delivered simultaneously with Gaitskell's, was a model. It placed the Opposition in no risk of being accused of damaging the national interest for the sake of making party capital, but it made many telling points against the government's policy in the Middle East.

When the Suez crisis came to a head at the end of October, Attlee was in India. The news that Eden had sent British troops to reoccupy the Canal zone astounded him. 'Couldn't reconcile it with his whole career – inexplicable.' Attlee believed that, whatever his motives, Eden had jeopardized all the good will Britain had built up in the Middle East and in Asia. In his much-praised speech in July, Attlee had warned the government in particular not to make either of two mistakes: they must not make any move which could incur a charge of aggression; and they must not 'undertake an adventure with France . . . still held throughout Asia to stand for the old colonialism'. Eden had now committed both these errors. Attlee's criticism of Eden went much further. He thought that, having launched the military operation, Eden should have gone through with it and not stopped it until British troops reached the Canal

– 'If you've broken the eggs you should make the omelette'. Given a few hours extra, British troops would have done it.

In September he was among the speakers in a discussion on the role of public opinion at an assembly of the World Federation of United Nations Associations. Attlee said that internationalism required a change in the teaching of history. The history which he had been taught dealt 'exclusively with a people called the English – with a word or two about the Scots and the Welsh – and referred to other countries only in the context of war'. In his day, 'we didn't begin by considering the history of mankind'. There was too much about battles in the teaching of history, and not enough about good works in peace. 'We must be taught that wars were human failure and that peace was success.' He was now well into his role as preacher of world government. He wrote to Tom on 15 September on return from a week's conference in France:

> I had to take part in a function at the Arc de Triomphe laying a wreath on the tomb of the unknown warrior. We had a formal meeting in the Hall of Victories at Versailles where I had to speak. I had a short interview with de Gaulle whom I found very friendly. It was Vi's first visit to Paris and she enjoyed it very much going up the Eiffel Tower etc. . . . We saw the tomb of Napoleon at the Invalides – vulgar I thought, a great contrast to the dignity of the famous Mogul tomb of Humayun at Lahore. From Paris we flew to Royan . . . a town blitzed in error by the Allies in the war and now rebuilt by an energetic and voluble Mayor. Conference mostly distinguished by the inability to be relevant by all save the Anglo Saxons. . . . The town has been rebuilt in very modern style and is a seaside resort superior to Clacton but not quite up to Frinton.

He became a grandfather again, in October, when Anne, Martin's wife, 'was safely delivered of a boy weighing 7 lbs 14 oz much larger than the general run of our family. . . . Martin is full of delight as are we for it was time we had a grandson.' To Moyle, two days later, he wrote: 'We are delighted at the infant's arrival. It had not its grandfather's habit of punctuality.' The visit to India was planned for November. He told Moyle: 'I thought the spirit of the Conference very good and am in hopes that Nye will run straight for a bit now.' This was the first Labour conference for twenty years which Attlee did not attend as leader of the party.

Attlee wrote Tom an exuberant summing up of his Indian visit:

> We had a wonderful time being greeted most warmly, cheering crowds often assembling. India has been making great strides especially in the villages where schools, community centres, etc. are being introduced and even in some instances electric light. . . . We saw Chandrigar the new city capital of Punjab planned by Corbusier, on the whole good. . . . We stayed at Jamnagar with Ranji's son, a good chap, lots of cricketing pictures of

Ranji. Stayed with Maharajah of Jaipur and went up on an elephant into Amber, very fine late Mogul architecture. Got a degree at Madras Univ. Fine time in Kashmir. From hill town had a perfect view of Himalayas 'Nangi Parbat' free from cloud. Saw very fine major hydroelectric and irrigation works under construction in Punjab. Town for 10,000 workers very good with schools hospitals etc. . . . This wretched Suez business spoiled the end of our visit. . . . I'm reviewing Winston's second volume for *The Observer*. It looks to me superficial.

Describing 'a long day in the sun watching the Test Match against Australia' with a very big crowd, he noted that: 'the whole ritual of cricket was carried out in every detail . . . cricket has been taken up in practically every part of the Commonwealth, but nowhere outside. It is certainly one of the bonds that unite us.' He was having trouble with his articles for *The Star* because his typewriter was 'conking out':

I have been doing a good deal of book reviewing lately and also some broadcasting in the Overseas service which is easy money – for three pleasant chats with Francis Williams over tea I netted 75 guineas. . . . We are busy preparing for USA [he was to give a lecture tour]. We shall do a lot of flying as we range from New York to Los Angeles and from Miami to Toronto with many places in between.

In America he 'mostly talked on the evolution of an Empire into a Commonwealth'. This was not only his favourite subject, but the one into which he showed most insight. Typically in his speeches to the Americans in early 1957 he did not claim that the Attlee governments had a monopoly of understanding about what had happened in Asia and was now happening in Africa; on the contrary, he said, Britain's wisdom had been shared by all her political parties.

Attlee's review of the second volume of Churchill's *A History of the English Speaking Peoples* duly appeared in *The Observer* on 25 November 1956.

In the first volume of his history, Sir Winston Churchill brought us in one broad sweep from the earliest times to the end of the Wars of the Roses, the close of the Middle Ages and the accession of the Tudor Dynasty. The pace has now slackened. The story of two centuries fills the 300 pages of this volume. One might, therefore, have hoped for a more comprehensive and balanced survey of the life of the British people, but one is disappointed. Ten pages suffice for a survey of world events including the Renaissance, the Reformation, the Counter-Reformation, and the discovery of the New World, just about as much space as is devoted to King Henry the Eighth's matrimonial adventures. Politics and war, with religion in so far as it affects these paramount interests, are the absorbing topics. Other activities of the people receive slight consideration.

The review is a lengthy one. Attlee had many compliments to pay, including Churchill's 'fine objectivity' in dealing with the Civil War and Cromwell. But he goes on to list topic after topic which Churchill either omitted or skimped, stating succinctly, with aphorisms of his own, why the author should have given them more space. He concludes:

> When we come to the revolution of 1688, interest quickens for the Churchill family which, already noticed in the person of the first Sir Winston Churchill, now reappears in the persons of Arabella and John, preluding the great events of the age of Anne which John will dominate. This is as it should be, for this history is mainly important for the light which it throws on the author's reactions to the past. It might indeed be better called 'Things in history which have interested me'.

In 1957 he reviewed many books. Now, relieved of the cares of office and party leadership, he began to reveal aspects of his personality which previously few people outside the family had known. In an unselfconscious, candid, but objective tone he gave his opinions of books written by men he knew intimately as though he had never met them. 'Hugh Dalton's memoirs have caused some stir in the Party being full of stories about individuals. I pointed out that while I wrote the Acts, Dalton wrote Revelations.' In his review of Dalton he wrote: 'Like most diaries it reveals the author very well. We see his cheerful exuberance and his enjoyment of the political fight with its blows exchanged, mingled with a certain insensitiveness to the feelings of other people.' In various articles he expressed views which would not have been shared by most members of the Labour Party. In April he wrote an article for *The Times* on 'The Future of Parliament'. It was summed up by the headline, 'Fewer Full-time Politicians in a Healthy House'. In his view, 'the ideal House of Commons is one where there is an adequate number of full-time MPs but also a number of part-timers who bring a variety of experience to its deliberations and prevent it from becoming over-professionalised.' In an article for the Labour journal, *Forward*, in November he sounded a call to youth, with the headline, 'Keep fighting, my young friends, for without vision the people perish'. His conclusion was: 'I hope young people realise that we have only gone a few steps towards the kind of society of which we Socialists dream.... The fight may not seem as exciting as when we Socialists were few, but it is just as urgent.'

In his Christmas letter he told Tom he had to write *The Times* an article on Beatrice Webb for the centenary. 'These centenaries of people one knew quite well make one realise one's age. ... We lunched with the Churchills last week. Winston is very deaf and won't use his instrument which made conversation difficult. He recalled with satisfaction that he and I either as allies, or as Government and Opposition leaders, covered fifteen years between us.' He made a speech in the Lords when the Russians launched their first sputnik, which contained a dog. He said it was characteristic of British public opinion that its almost entire interest was 'centred on the welfare of the dog'.

> The dog is no worse off than members of other Russian satellite countries. It is being fed. It even has a possibility of escape. It must be some encouragement to the members of other satellites (laughter).
> One of the lessons was that a great deal of our expenditure on arms was futile. If the money wasted on arms could be used to help less developed nations, that would probably be a greater blow against the Communist danger than anything else.

Early in 1958 Lord Waverley, formerly Sir John Anderson, died. 'The beau ideal of the civil servant,' Attlee told Tom, 'but a bigger man than just a bureaucrat, completely fair and just, and of course the last word in efficiency. Winston had a good word on him one day. Winston and I were both to be out of the country together so I said "who carries on?" Winston said, "It's all right, we hand over to the automatic pilot." ' Waverley died on a Saturday. An obituary notice was required by *The Observer*. Attlee was telephoned by the author. Would he at extremely short notice write a brief appreciation? 'When do you want it?' If possible, for the first edition, in exactly two hours' time. 'How long?' Five hundred words. He telephoned back in an hour and a half. 'I've done it, but it's on the short side.' He dictated 493 words.

Attlee now began a new literary career. He mentioned in a letter to Tom, on 1 November 1958: 'I have a very long article on Montgomery in *The Observer* tomorrow.' In a letter to Moyle on the same date he described *The Observer* piece as 'a whale of an article which I hope will please you'. Moyle read it, and replied: 'Your review of Montgomery's book is regarded as a classic. Not only have you changed your style of writing by throwing all inhibitions to the winds but you have revealed a knowledge of military matters which has surprised people.' The success of *The Observer* review of Montgomery's memoirs – it was not so much a review as an essay on the General in the context of the total conduct of the war – led to many invitations to write and lecture at home and abroad, on subjects which previously he had dealt with on a smaller scale.

Later in November he wrote in the *Fabian Journal* on 'The Role of the Member of Parliament'. Again, but at greater length, he expressed views which might well have found more favour with Tom than with Labour politicians. 'The MP is expected to be guide, philosopher and friend, not to mention poor man's lawyer, to his constituents. ... I think the present practice whereby many MPs spend the bulk of their weekends dealing with constituency cases a very bad one. The MP ought to have leisure for recreation, home life, and home work. Many MPs wear themselves out doing work that ought to be done by others ...' About the alleged deterioration of the quality of MPs, he commented: 'I would say that during my time the quality of the average MP on both sides has steadily improved. They work harder and are better informed than their predecessors.' But he was not satisfied with all contemporary MPs. A few weeks later he wrote an article in the *Political Quarterly* in which he said that while the majority of MPs had entered political life with the incentive of service – 'some wholly so, and they are pure gold' – others were careerists, 'puffed up with self-importance, and putting their own interests first'.

He now made a lecture tour of the United States, much more extensive than before. He drew audiences of several hundred at a time – a thousand people paid to hear him in Milwaukee. 'In both his extemporaneous speech and in fielding questions afterwards,' says a report in the local paper, 'he sparkled with wit and gentle sarcasm, despite the seriousness of his theme.' His subject was world government. The chances were 'quite good', he said, that civilization would go down in utter devastation unless 'big steps are made towards peace'. Calling himself 'not an academic dreamer but an old politician with some experience', he made these recommendations for meeting the dangers of another war, aiming them at American audiences:

Reform the United Nations, so that no one group of nations will run it.
   Set up an international police force, not contingents of various nations but one without individual sovereign interests.
   Halt the stock-piling of dangerous weapons before some trigger-happy fool sets the ball rolling.
   Recognise Red China; this doesn't mean approval.

His American tour was a great success. His unrhetorical, colloquial and dispassionate delivery, his humble yet authoritative bearing, made people listen. They might not have agreed, but they did not bridle. He was very British, but he was British in a style they liked, admired, and enjoyed. He was asked to go again.

On his seventy-sixth birthday Attlee had a large audience for a BBC television interview conducted by Francis Williams. In a letter to Tom (21 January 1959) he writes: 'I am glad you liked the broadcast. We had a set lent us by the BBC and had a party of about 50, mostly neighbours except for the children who viewed. It seems to have caught on quite a lot. Francis Williams and I did it in June or July talking for about two hours.' The programme was originally intended to be shown after Attlee's death, but because of the publicity he had inadvertently created for himself as a result of the Montgomery article, the BBC decided to release excerpts for immediate use. 'I ought to have cut out the part referring to Jinnah which though true annoyed the Pakistanis, but after having heard myself talking for a long time, I did not notice it.' Fortunately Attlee did not say on television what he soon afterwards said in private, that Jinnah 'was the only Indian Fascist I ever met'.

He had not been back a few weeks from the first American lecture tour before he embarked on another – to pay off the mortgage on the new bungalow – another 'Westcott' – which was being built for him up the road. Now that all the children were grown up Cherry Cottage was too big, and too expensive to keep up. He wanted Vi to be settled in there, with all debts paid, before he died, or 'became too decrepit to earn'. He still assumed, reasonably, that he would die first. Apart from the money coming in from the articles and lecture tours, he had only his £2,000 pension, as former prime minister, and his three guineas a day for attendance in the House of Lords when in session. They lived very simply. Vi ran Cherry Cottage helped by a woman from the village who came in for an hour on Fridays and for three hours on Saturday. During the summer vacation they could get a Danish girl. Vi did the garden, drove and cleaned the car, took him to the station, cooked, cleaned, dusted and laundered. He had saved next to nothing in his years in office. So it was off to the States again, to earn some money: fifteen lectures in three weeks.

Soon after Attlee got back from America, Leslie Hunter's book, *The Road to Brighton Pier*, was published. 'Vi was rung up about [it] while I was away,' he told Moyle. 'I have since glanced at it. It's a pretty dirty piece of work. I'm represented as an intriguer inspired by hatred of HM [Morrison]. I rather wonder if HM inspired this book. D[aily] H[erald] wanted me to review it, but for obvious reasons I declined.' Attlee's only public reference to the book was in the course of a relaxed speech he made at a Parliamentary Press Gallery luncheon: 'I notice a certain person has said I hate another Member. I find it awfully difficult to hate anyone. I hated Lloyd George before the first war and when I met him I could not go on doing it. I don't suppose you really hate your political opponents. I don't suppose I hate journalists, though sometimes I am a little impatient with them, especially those in America.' He referred to Morrison again, some months later, after Morrison had gone to the Lords, in a letter to Moyle: 'What price our Herbert in the Lords. I thought that he would come.' (At one time Morrison had strongly advocated the abolition of the second chamber.) 'He can't be Lord Morrison or Lord Lewisham. What about Lord Festival of Battersea?'

Morrison appeared on television in an interview with John Freeman in which he criticized Attlee as well as some of his other colleagues. Attlee asked Moyle: 'Did you see Herbert on television in his mental strip tease act? I fear that it is a pathological case. I was travelling to Durham on the night train when journalists caught me and gave me extracts from the performance. I judged it wise to make no comment. . . . Looking back I think this obsession [about Attlee] dated right from the time when he failed to get the leadership in 1935. . . . Poor little Herbert. What a pity.'

Attlee's standing with the public was indeed very high, as Christopher Hollis confirmed in March 1959 in an article for the *Daily Telegraph*, 'Leader in Retirement'. Hollis wrote: 'Whenever people sit around discussing the coming election, it is these days increasingly common to hear a wiseacre say, "If only Attlee were to come back and lead a party, then, whatever party it was, it would sweep the country." Everyone knows that Earl Attlee will not come back. Nevertheless the British public has in recent months certainly taken [him] to its heart in a remarkable fashion.' One afternoon Hollis and John Betjeman were to go down to Haileybury to sit on a BBC *Brains Trust*. They met in the Oxford and Cambridge Club. Noticing Attlee was sitting reading a paperback detective story, they went over to tell him they were just off to his old school to talk to the sixth forms. 'I'm going down next week,' he said, 'but only for the Upper Fourth.' Hollis concluded: 'In a world in which so many people pretend to be more important than they are, the British people has, I think, shown its wisdom and generosity in taking to its heart a man who spends his time in pretending to be less important than he is.'

On his next tour to the States, one of his audiences was reported to be 4,500. 'Generally we had a question period afterwards. Of course, it's pie to an old parliamentarian.' This time he was able to spend a few days with his daughter Janet and her family, who now lived in the middle west. On this tour Attlee had a great deal to say on a theme which was to become dominant in his mind through the next few years, that money spent on the conquest of space was a complete waste:

It is a matter of complete indifference to me whether the Stars and Stripes or the Hammer and Sickle is hoisted there. The moon may become another Russian satellite or the 50th star in the American flag, for all I care. But one would have thought that, before troubling about other celestial bodies and spending billions of dollars, we might try to make things rather better in the world in which we live.

Asked whether he had met Khrushchev, Attlee answered: 'Oh yes. Rather a noisy fellow.' Asked what he thought he himself would be remembered for, he answered: 'Don't know. If anything India, possibly.' He wrote to Tom in July: 'I was amused after the success of my review of Randolph Churchill's book [in *The Observer*] to receive from the assistant editor of the *Sunday Times* a kind of takeover bid offering me £1,200 for twelve book reviews for the next twelve months. Being wedded to *The*

Observer I declined.' Randolph Churchill's book was *The Rise and Fall of Sir Anthony Eden*. Attlee's review ended: 'Biographies not infrequently reveal more of the character of the author than the subject. Readers of this book will not learn much about Sir Anthony Eden, but they should get a full appreciation of Mr Randolph Churchill.'

Three long *Observer* articles appeared in October and November: on George Marshall, 'an American "Statesman of the Century" '; on Lord Woolton's memoirs, headed 'Uncle Fred Looks Back'; and on the second volume of Alanbrooke's diaries. All three illustrate Moyle's tribute to Attlee's powers of illuminating the subject in the last paragraph. Thus, on Marshall:

> He always struck me as a curiously Roman figure, something of the type of a Roman general who flourished in the days of the Republic: something, perhaps, of a Cincinnatus, always ready to come out and fight, and once the duty was done, anxious to get back to the farm. When Americans are accused of producing 'political' generals, they can always retort with 'Marshall'.

On Woolton:

> Lord Woolton is frank enough to record the opinion of Sir Winston Churchill on business men in politics. After a devastating massacre of the claims of business men to be successful in politics, Winston would end up by saying: 'Surely, my dear Fred, you don't imagine the public look upon you as a business man. On the contrary, the public looks upon you as a great philanthropist.' Precisely: a public uncle.

The last few words of the Alanbrooke review summed up his view on the keeping of diaries: 'If a diary is to enable tense minds to let off steam in private, it cannot be regarded as a safe historical source; and if it is written for use as a future historical document, it is suspect for the opposite reason. One cannot have it both ways.'

Attlee's prostate trouble returned during the summer. Commiserating with Moyle, who suffered similarly, and was about to undergo an operation, Attlee said: 'They do it much better now. In my youth it was a question of to be or not to be, now it is merely to P or not to P.' However, in September Attlee himself 'had to go into the Westminster and had a catheter in for a few days. I shall have to have a push through every few months.' Vi as a car driver was becoming alarmingly accident-prone, but in Attlee's eyes she was always in the right. In May he had written to Tom: 'We had an annoying car accident owing to a BF coming out of a side road right into us – car smashed but no serious hurt to us.' In September he wrote to Moyle:

Vi was coming up to see me there [at the Westminster Hospital] when leaving Amersham driving quietly along a main road [a man] came full speed out of a side road and knocked her right across the road fortunately just not into the ditch. She was very badly bruised and had a broken bone but is getting on all right. The fellow killed his brother-in-law. I hope he gets a sentence. Vi has been overwhelmed with sympathy.

The author was sitting with Attlee in the Westminster Hospital at the time the news of Vi's accident was brought to him. Attlee was expecting Vi to come to the hospital and drive him home the following day. He was sitting in an armchair fully dressed, smoking his pipe, correcting the proofs of his *Observer* article on Alanbrooke, for publication the following Sunday. The ward sister came in and said he was wanted urgently on the telephone in her office. He was away for a few minutes, came back alone, sat down and said, 'Another accident: man been killed. Vi's in hospital,' put his pipe in his mouth and went on correcting the proofs. I collected him the morning after and we drove to Amersham Hospital, met Vi, badly bruised with her arm in a sling, obviously shaken, and took her to Cherry Cottage. Several newspaper reporters and photographers were waiting in the house. They took several photographs and asked for details of the accident. Attlee answered for about five minutes – he kept his hat on all the time – then suddenly rose to his feet, took his pipe from his mouth and in a surprisingly loud and peremptory voice – a sergeant-major's – bellowed: 'That's enough! Clear out!' The house was empty in a few seconds.

The general election came in October 1959. Attlee undertook a heavy list of speaking engagements in the home counties. One evening I attended one of his meetings and drove him home to Great Missenden. He reminisced all the way. 'Was the school librarian once.... Never be lonely if I've got my books, and if I haven't I know quite a bit by heart. Would be all right in gaol.' He thought he might write an essay on the books which had most influenced his thinking, also some essays on individual writers: 'Meredith, now: I'd like to write about *him*.' He moved to the subject of potential political leaders 'who didn't come off ... some of them more interesting than the ones who did' – Halifax, nearly the wartime Prime Minister: 'all hunting and holy communion.' He spoke of some of the leaders who had impressed him: 'F. E. Smith. Rather hear him make a speech in the House than anybody. Brilliant mind. Great judgement. Tories should have had him as leader in the 20s. One of the Tories who understood the working man. Bags of guts.' 'But you've always been against lawyers in politics.' 'FE was an exception – common sense first, law afterwards.'

Immediately after the election he left for Australia on an eight weeks' lecture tour. In Australia he developed what was from now on his main theme: world government – at Melbourne on 25 October he said he planned to spend the rest of his life fighting for it. The progress of invention had rendered national defence entirely obsolete. 'There is no defence today. It is common knowledge that if we could release all the energy, all the power, and all the wealth which we spend on armaments, we could raise the standards of half the world that still lives on the border-line of starvation.' From Australia he went on to the United States on another extremely demanding tour – he was now seventy-seven. His subjects were 'The Future of Europe', 'World Government or World Chaos', 'The Future of Democratic Government', and 'The Two Systems of Democratic Government – Britain and the US Compared'. Whatever his subject, he told Tom, he was always asked many questions about socialism, and 'those are the ones I enjoy answering most.' He told Tom that the most frequent question was: 'How is your Socialist medicine getting on?' To which he always replied: 'First class. How's your Socialist sewage system getting on or do you stick to the old bucket?' He told his questioners: 'It's amusing to see how proud your anti-Socialist Mayors are of their municipal airport and other collectivist enterprises, such as a municipal asphalt plant.' As for American medicine: 'Some light is shown by the case of a young professor. He had piles, had an operation and three days in hospital. He had to pay 2,000 dollars.'

He returned in time to deliver the Chichele Lectures at Oxford – 'Empire into Commonwealth'. 'Quite a good audience with a good sprinkling of non-Europeans. I was a bit nervous as to how they would go off as I used a minimum of notes. However our Master, Lord Somerville, and the Warden of All Souls all said that they were very pleased with them.' They were certainly the shortest Chichele lectures ever given, and when the notes were expanded so that they could be published in book form, the volume they produced was noticeably slim.

In August 1960 he wrote his last letter to Tom. In the June letter Attlee had added a PS: 'We have been thinking of your eightieth birthday in October. We should like to celebrate it by a dinner in the H of L. . . . We are rather a popular resort for dinners. Cholmondeley tells me that we are booked up many weeks ahead.' But at the beginning of October Tom died. Many friends sent Attlee sympathy letters. He kept one which described Tom as 'one of the very few real saints. . . . Tom's moral courage and complete humility and selflessness were inspiring.' From now on Attlee wrote regularly only to Arthur Moyle.

Alas sometimes in these days I find a charming young woman offering her seat to a decrepit old man. . . . I've got to write an introductory essay to a new edition of Fabian Essays which is rather a bore but I could not well refuse. . . . Scarborough [Party Conference] was pretty bad, though I gather Hugh spoke well. [The UN] seems to have a bit of a dog fight.

Khrushchev is not used to democracy. He is like a yard dog brought into the house: he makes pools all over the place.

He had a high regard for Harold Macmillan personally, and never doubted his concern for the 'ordinary man' – 'He demanded proper treatment for the unemployed in the thirties: didn't make him popular with his party' – but he was critical of Macmillan as prime minister. He said little in public, but in some of his letters to Moyle he was more forthcoming. 'A little thought for the new year. A Sunday paper says that 31 members of the Govt are relatives or connections of the PM. Daily prayer to be said by Tory back benchers, "God bless our Mac and his relations, and keep us in our proper stations." ' In another letter, written just after Macmillan had dismissed a third of his Cabinet, Attlee wrote:

What a mess Harold has made of it. Here are some comments off the record:

> Hail to our splendid Mac
> Long live our glorious Mac
> What though we've got the sack
> Enoch and Pete got back
> Why should not we?

> Hail to our fine new look
> Though Selwyn Lloyd's forsook
> Still we've got Henry Brooke
> Surely he'll find a nook
> Somewhere for me.

> Had I but wed his niece
> I might have stayed in peace
> With several other geese
> Is it Too Late?

> Surely some Highland Scot
> Or Yankee girl if not
> Pitying my cruel lot
> Might make a date.

Macmillan's foreign policy was more to his liking – 'colonial policy admirable'. He admired Macmillan's 'Wind of Change' speech, and the effort he had made to modernize the Conservatives' thinking on Africa. 'The problem of a Tory leader is to educate his Party. The problem of a Labour leader is to keep it in order.'

In February 1962 he told the Commonwealth Parliamentary Association that almost all the statesmen he had seen recently were in favour of a step towards a certain degree of world government, but few seemed ready to take the initiative. 'I am going to Moscow on Tuesday to try to

make the same point over there.... In every school in the Commonwealth, the children ought to be taught that the day of the absolute
sovereign state is over and that we are moving on to a world order.' The
visit to Moscow did not produce any significant results. He went on from
there to India and Pakistan, and he developed the same world government theme in the first of the two Azad Memorial Lectures at New Delhi.
Soon after he came back, the Queen made a visit to India. In her speech
at the Guildhall on her return she said: 'There can be no doubt that the
happiness and friendliness which was found throughout India and Pakistan was a triumphant vindication of the vision of the statesmen who
changed the old Empire into a free association of peoples.' Clement
Davies took the occasion to write to Attlee congratulating him as 'the
leader of these statesmen.... It must have been a great moment for you
to have heard those words.' He continued to hammer away in the cause
of world government, making a debate on foreign affairs in the House of
Lords that autumn into another opportunity for pressing the case.

In 1962 Edward Heath was pursuing the negotiations on behalf of the
Macmillan government which it was hoped would result in Britain
entering the European Common Market. Attlee was unreservedly and
vigorously opposed to this:

> I do not believe it would be wise to enter the Common Market on the terms
> which seem to be contemplated by Mr Heath and the present Government.
> We should not be justified in hastily handing over substantial power now
> held by the British Parliament and electorate to untried institutions mainly
> dependent on European countries with unstable political records. Nor
> would it be right to grant tariff preference in favour of foreign countries
> and against countries in the Commonwealth. Any such step would be
> bound to damage the Commonwealth seriously; and in my belief, as
> an association of free countries, the Commonwealth of today, with its
> members in five continents, is a far more hopeful foundation for peace and
> democracy than any narrow European group. I hope the Labour Party
> will stick firmly to the conditions and safeguards they have wisely laid
> down.

In this statement he loyally associated himself with the Labour Party's
official position, which did not oppose membership of the EEC in
principle. The fact was, however, that he was opposed to joining the
EEC in any circumstances. A more realistic representation of his views
appeared in an article he wrote for the *Sunday Express*, inspiring the
headline: 'I SAY HALT – Britain must not become merely a part of
Europe'.

By now he had reached the age of eighty. Moyle asked him what it was
like to be eighty. The answer was: 'Better than the alternative.' Moyle
raised the question of special celebrations. Attlee replied: 'I don't think

the Party should do anything about my 80th, now past and over. The Lords gave me two excellent armchairs.'

Bevan and Gaitskell, both much younger men, were dead. In June 1964 Vi died suddenly, smitten by a cerebral haemorrhage. She collapsed in the kitchen while cooking the Sunday lunch – the first Attlee knew of it was when neighbours came into the bungalow because they could smell the burning cooker. Vi was sixty-eight. For six years, to the author's knowledge, Attlee, in spite of illness, operations, and a good deal of intermittent pain, had only one worry: that he would die, and Vi would be left to live on her own. He took his wife's death stoically. He wrote to Janet on 28 June:

> As you see I am for the time being in an hotel. Martin is with me. I hope to get a flat somewhere near Victoria and yesterday engaged a very nice fellow to look after me. He was formerly in the RAMC and the catering corps which gives him the right background. Just now I am at Flippy's for the weekend. I am still answering the hundreds of kind letters I have had on Vi's death.

He had 'managed to walk in the Garter procession though the Queen tried to persuade me to go in a car. The grandchildren enjoyed a good view. . . . I am hopeful of getting [a flat] which will be quite ideal in Kings Bench Walk, Temple [he had been made an Hon. Bencher of the Inner Temple in 1946]. I shall have a delightful club just across the road and a good many legal friends in the Temple.' The flat had four rooms with kitchen, bathroom and a lift – the only one in the Temple. A fortnight later: 'This has been a great week of functions, a big do at Lancaster House for the Commonwealth PMs. I had a talk over old times with Bob Menzies and met crowds of people. The Queen sent for me for a chat. Everyone is awfully kind to me. I stayed the other day with Arthur Moyle at Sevenoaks, and he drove me over to see Laurence who was very fit. . . . Laker [who looked after him in the flat] is an excellent cook.' In August he wrote to Moyle: 'I do not recall a previous time in my life in which I have nothing that I must do. . . . A young Tory has just called trying to sell some kind of a sweepstake for their funds. Damned impudence. I told Laker to send him off with a flea in his ear.'

In the 1964 general election campaign, 'I had a very good talk with HW [Harold Wilson] yesterday and found him in great form. He says that the reports from the constituencies are most encouraging, a '45 feeling.' To Janet on 6 October: 'I have had a very successful move and the flat really looks very attractive though I still have to get my books in. The Benchers here gave me a very warm welcome. . . . I am busy electioneering. I have had three good meetings and am speaking every night twice until polling day mainly in Kent and Essex.' Norman Shrapnel in *The Guardian* wrote a lively description of Attlee's electioneering, headed: 'Lord Attlee carves them up'. Shrapnel wrote:

In case there are still voters who just cannot see any essential difference between the two sides, Lord Attlee yesterday made it his business to enlighten them. Making his third big speech in 24 hours at the age of 81, he shuffled briskly on to the stage of the St Pancras Town Hall, beamed briefly at the roar of applause and the welcoming cameras, and then – without wasting a word or a second – got down to that essential. The difference was that the Conservatives are all for profit, while Labour exists for serving the community.

It was as simple as that – or Lord Attlee made it seem so. He was giving both sides a lesson in effective electioneering. With never a word out of place, it was a speech with a cutting edge. It did sharp, rather than rough justice. He chipped away with his long accurate memory as if it had been a chisel, carving a swift and derisive memorial to Conservative selfishness.

Labour won the election, with a majority of four. The author interviewed him on television. In view of that hair's breadth majority, for how long did Lord Attlee think the new government could stay in office? 'Not longer than eighteen months.' They lasted for sixteen.

He wrote to Moyle in the first week of 1965: 'Fifty years ago I was training on Salisbury Plain preparatory to going to Gallipoli. It does not feel so long ago.' Sir Winston Churchill was dying: 'We are all waiting here day after day for the death of old Winston but he hangs on amazingly. I am very sorry for poor Clemmie, it must be an awful strain. . . . There is to be a big funeral with a service at St Paul's. I have to be a pall bearer with Anthony but nothing can be fixed until the day.' To Janet on 14 March: 'I felt a bit funny in the House so I went into the Westminster for 4 days. Nothing really wrong. So on Saturday I went to the annual dinner of the Swindon Labour Party.' This meant a journey of about eighty miles from London. He reviewed Violet Bonham-Carter's book for *The Observer*. 'Her picture of Winston, very critical in many respects, is all the more effective for being written in a spirit of love. She gets him right, but she gets him generously. Amazing that her first book, at 78, should be so good. I wonder why she hadn't started before. Too busy talking, perhaps.' On 14 August he wrote to Moyle: 'Herbert Morrison's autobiography . . . a fine work of fiction. All to the glory of Herbert. Did you see he left £28,000!! How did he manage to acquire so much?'

Harold Wilson called a general election for March. Attlee wrote to Janet on 9 March: 'Parliament is up now so I have an idle time ahead. Everyone is in the throes of a general election but I am too old to take part. The pollsters say that we shall have a majority of 75 but I don't see how they make it out. I should be quite content with 20. No one really knows.' (Labour's majority was 97.) In April he had a heavy fall, which injured his back. 'Laid up for a few weeks.' In June he was 'getting a bit stronger'. Good weather came. 'Various people have taken me out.' But the years were going by. 'My old friends die off. In the present House of

Commons there are only three who served before Ramsay MacDonald's desertion and half the Party are since my time.' Later that month: 'I have not been too well lately through having a constant flow of saliva in the mouth, the result, they say, of my last operation. My doctor has consulted numerous eminent docs but apparently they cannot do anything about it so I just have to grin and bear it.'

At the end of 1966 his style was cramped by a slight stroke which temporarily took away his power of speech. As he entered 1967, the last year of his life, his afflictions mounted. But he kept stubbornly on. In March: 'I am doing very little these days. I have not been to the Lords this year.... The Labour Government has been running into difficulties with the Party.' Later that month: 'The government have done very badly in by-elections, losing one and only scraping home in what should have been a safe seat. It's remarkable that in more than 6 years I never lost one, but I had a much better government than the present one.' His dissatisfaction was partly connected with the renewed negotiations for British entry into the Common Market, these being conducted by a Labour government. Shinwell, the 'elder statesman', was mounting a campaign against it, which received a great deal of support from both Conservatives and Labour. The campaign was strengthened by a letter from Attlee published in February 1967: 'My dear Manny, May I express my sympathy with you in your objection to our being hustled into the Common Market. There is a conspiracy in the press and elsewhere to suppress opposition. Yours ever, Clem.'

Attlee's other remaining 'cause', world government, produced his last letters to the press: one in April to *The Times* stressed the need for the British government to continue and increase their efforts 'to promote the development of more effective methods of settling international disputes by peaceful means', and referred to the lead given in developing an informed public opinion by the David Davies Memorial Institute; another, of 5 June, used the latest crisis in the Middle East to point up the urgent need of a world police force.

In April Attlee wrote to Moyle: 'Things have gone on quietly here. I had to go to Toynbee Hall for the opening of the new building by Abp Canterbury. It was 57 years since I was secretary there. I see my old colleague Tom Williams is dead, a grand man.' To Moyle on 12 May: 'I thought Manny's speech on the Common Market very good. Our only hope now is de Gaulle.... We got heavy losses at the local elections.' To Janet on 17 May: 'I spent last weekend at Flippy's' (they now lived in Beaconsfield). '... I am now pretty feeble and am not good at walking upstairs.... Twice last week I sat out for an hour in the Temple gardens, Laker taking me out in a wheeled chair.... I am not feeling awfully well just now.' On 28 June: 'I am not awfully well, but go down for three weeks to Osborn House in the Isle of Wight, Queen Victoria's old home, now a convalescent home for officers.... I went with Flippy to Wimbledon tennis on Monday and saw a very good match but found the strain of sitting rather much for me.'

By now his man, Laker, was nurse as well as cook and valet. Laker had joined Attlee at 'Westcott' after Vi's death – the Attlee's had left Cherry Cottage in 1963 – and had looked after him there for three months before they moved to the Temple. When Laker went to 'Westcott' for his interview, he found Attlee so uncommunicative that he made up his mind not to take the post. Then, after a period of silence, Attlee turned his head and looked at a photograph of Vi. 'That's my dear wife,' he said, and Laker was so touched by his tone that he changed his mind and took the job. On the first day he served lunch, Attlee said: 'Can't we have it together? I hate eating alone.' In the Temple flat he had neither radio nor television. He provided both for Laker, but Attlee ignored them. Once Laker went in and said: 'You're coming up on TV in a minute, sir: would you like to come in and watch?' No, he didn't think so. 'Don't you want to come in and hear what you said?' 'No. I remember.' He read *The Times* thoroughly every day and *The Observer* on Sunday, and the rest of the time he read books and answered correspondence. Of his many visitors, Frank Soskice, Frank Longford and Arthur Moyle were the regulars. Harold Wilson gave him 'a delightful weekend' at Chequers. 'Mr Wilson was a wonderful host,' said Laker. 'He told me that I was to wake him before I woke Lord Attlee so that he would be around when Lord Attlee got up.'

Up to his last day in the flat Attlee was a stickler for punctuality. Sometimes he would send Laker up to Fleet Street for a taxi. If Laker seemed late in returning with one, Attlee would be standing at the door of the flat, with outdoor clothes on, and glowering – 'the only times he got cross'. What else did Laker recall? 'We had lots of discussions about books and poetry. And he couldn't bear bad language. Sometimes I forgot, and said "bloody" or something. He wouldn't say anything, but he'd go very quiet, and I'd remember to try not to say "bloody" again.'

On 8 September 1967 he was admitted to the Westminster Hospital with what was then thought to be a minor condition giving no cause for anxiety. A week later he developed pneumonia, and never recovered, although he lingered on, visited constantly by Felicity, Alison and Martin. On 25 September he was still capable of adding a squiggle of a signature to a note to Moyle:

Dear Lord Moyle,

Lord Attlee sends his very best wishes for a Happy Birthday, and is going to sign this to prove it.

During the last illness Charlie Griffiths, his former batman, who had remained in close touch with him, came in to see him several times. For two days Attlee did not know him, but then suddenly opened his eyes and said: 'Hullo, Griff. How are you getting on?' His son Martin was at his bedside on the night of 8 October when he died peacefully in his sleep.

The funeral service was held in the Temple Church on 11 October. Attlee had arranged these matters well in advance. The lesson was taken from the Book of Revelations, St John's vision of 'The New Jerusalem'. The hymn was 'Jerusalem'. His ashes were buried on 7 November in Westminster Abbey, a few feet from the small diamond-shaped flagstones commemorating Bevin and the Webbs, a few yards from the great green slab inscribed 'Remember Winston Churchill'. The Prime Minister read the lesson, the passage from Ecclesiastes beginning 'Remember now thy Creator in the days of thy youth' and ending 'Let us hear the conclusion of the whole matter: Fear God, and keep his commandments: for this is the whole duty of man. For God shall bring every work into judgment, with every secret thing, whether it be good, or whether it be evil.' For all its positive declaration of belief, apparently out of keeping with his agnosticism, Attlee had chosen it and also the Psalm – 'Lord, who shall dwell in thy tabernacle: or who shall rest upon thy holy hill?' – and the two hymns – 'To be a Pilgrim' and 'I vow to thee, my country'.

In January the terms of Attlee's will were reported in the press: he had left a little more than £6,700. Martin Attlee, who succeeded to the title, was to receive the residue of his father's estate, after bequests, including those to 'Griff' and Laker. Lord Moyle was named as literary executor. The Garter Flag was to go to Haileybury, to be hung above Attlee's portrait in the school dining room.

Two years previously I had asked him about his religious beliefs. The conversation was as follows:

Harris:	*Was it Christianity that took you into politics?*
Attlee:	Social conscience, I would say. Inherited it. My parents were very much that way.
Harris:	But your parents were actually professing Christians, weren't they?
Attlee:	Yes. And my brothers and sisters.
Harris:	But you weren't?
Attlee:	No. I'm one of those people who are incapable of religious experience.
Harris:	Do you mean you have no feeling about Christianity, or that you have no feeling about God, Christ, and life after death?

Attlee: Believe in the ethics of Christianity. Can't believe the mumbo-jumbo.

Harris: Would you say you are an agnostic?

Attlee: I don't know.

Harris: Is there an after-life, do you think?

Attlee: Possibly.

Epilogue

Attlee was a Victorian. In his youth it was the Tory imperialism of that age which appealed to him, but soon after his visit to the Haileybury Club in the East End this was superseded by the influence of the Victorian conscience. Never a Christian, but an admirer of Christian ethics and the courage and good works of true Christians, he was from first to last a man of conscience. A sense of duty and of fellowship were his two main traits. There was no sense of guilt, and no regard for guilt, though he came to feel, and acted, in the spirit of Carlyle's 'divine disgust', not only with those who caused or connived at poverty and injustice but with those who, recognizing them, sought to discharge their responsibility for them merely by charitable works.

Attlee joined the ranks of the socialists because it seemed to him that only they were prepared to tackle causes and not tinker with effects. In so doing, the socialists he knew were activated not by doctrinaire revolutionary principles, but by that vision of society he personally had acquired by studying Carlyle, Ruskin and Morris, and the example of his Christian friends. Aiming for radical change, they were ready meantime to accept reform. This appealed to his practical, empirical cast of mind. His personal vision combined with his everyday experience in the East End; he embraced the political commitment of the Labour Party; and he changed from social worker to politician.

Attlee believed in Clause IV to the end of his days. He hoped that society would become less the product of the profit motive and more the projection 'of the zeal to work for the good of the community'. But he was not in a hurry to see it happen, or ever certain that it would. 'My own view is that where the leadership is good, whether in the private or public sector, the response is satisfactory.' Leadership there had to be: all men were not equal and had not been born equal. But all men had an equal right to try and make themselves equal – or even superior. A society predicated on fellowship did not preclude competition. It was the spirit in which that competition took place which counted. And those gifted enough, or fortunate enough, to achieve superior status or resources must – in the spirit of fellowship – carry out in a moral society the responsibilities which those achievements entailed. A moral society was the end – socialism was only the means. Attlee would have preferred to live in a moral society led by aristocrats rather than live in an immoral society led by collectivists.

Just as the man begot the socialist, the socialist in Attlee begot the politician. Unlike some political leaders, he was singularly free of the certainty that he knew what was right for party and country, and that that knowledge entitled him to impose his will on his followers. He saw enough of the fallibility of generals and the egotism of political leaders to be convinced that a position of authority did not entitle its holder to lay down the law. He believed in authority on the personal level: in his conduct of the Haileybury Club, the Post Office, his wartime committees, and in particular his postwar Cabinet he did not crack the whip, but when necessary he was swift, indeed ruthless, in dealing with rebels or dead wood. But he led the Labour Party on the principle that unless you can carry opinion with you the party, its programme and its principles will perish; and you cannot carry the party with you if it is known that at any time you may decree that part of it should be coerced or perhaps expelled. Since the Labour Party is far from homogeneous, argument must be expected and respected. The leader must be able to live with the party as it is. This is a task for strong men who listen more than they talk, who will probably have to announce more compromises than clarion calls.

One of Attlee's greatest strengths as leader was that he did not represent any of the contending groups in Labour's perennial struggle for dominance. His membership of a trade union was a formality, and his connection with the ILP did not survive that body's decision to leave the Labour Party in 1932. He was not associated closely with the Socialist League, nor with the enduring Fabian tradition in the party. His rise to the leadership demonstrates that the lack of a power base in some section of the party may not be a handicap to an aspiring Labour leader, though a safe seat is an inestimable advantage. He became deputy leader only because nearly all his seniors were defeated in the 1931 election. Only through the inability of rival camps to agree did he become leader in 1935, and the same rivalries sustained his leadership at the next test in 1945. He was thus an 'accidental' prime minister, as his denigrators have been ready to point out. But the serendipity in his rise to power caused him neither embarrassment nor remorse. His occupation of the leadership, as time went on, was justified simply by success and skilled management which commanded the loyalty of many who were potentially his rivals.

When he came to power in 1945 he assembled and managed a team of ministers which carried out a programme of legislation so massive and so radical that, however controversial, it entitles him to be regarded as a great Prime Minister. The nationalization of the basic industries, the foundation of the Welfare State, and the establishment for the first time of the Labour Party as a plausible party of government had an impact on Britain and the world which no British government had made in the twentieth century. To do these things, he had in the first place to bring his party to power. That in itself was a great feat, and one which he thought was his most important achievement: 'to take a party intact into a coalition, keep it intact for five years, bring it out intact, and win an election with it when most people expected defeat. Not many precedents for that.' Moreover, it is inconceivable that any of the Labour Party leaders but Attlee could have controlled the Cabinet, led the party and satisfied the public opinion which was a prerequisite for the success of his legislative programme. Had any of the other possible leaders become prime minister – Bevan, Bevin, Morrison, Cripps, Dalton – there would have been conflicts, more likely than not because of personal clashes, that would have hampered the action and possibly have brought about a débâcle. Attlee's patience, self-control, self-effacement, sense of timing, feeling for what was possible, and his unique knowledge of party and governmental techniques gained in forty years of public work, were his strength – a combination of personal qualities and professional expertise which none of his colleagues could rival.

He was laconic and lacked charisma, yet his personality had a message which reached the people. He was respectable, solid and quiet, a happy family man who wore a business suit, a homburg hat, smoked a pipe and loved cricket. At a time when a socialist programme was being presented in all its might and range to a British middle class whose majority disliked and feared it, the prime minister who presented it could be seen as a symbol of middle-class moderation, decency, respectability and decorum. His very lack of rhetoric and colour was an indispensible contribution to his cause. He was so ordinary that many people accepted – however grudgingly – measures which expressed and executed by a man of passion would have been resisted, or rejected. And for many there was something uplifting about him and his rise to power. He was not 'a great man'; he was not exactly 'the common man'; he was, in fact, an ordinary middle-class figure, and yet he was now the leader of his country. If it could happen to him, it could happen to anybody.

As a statesman, Attlee's record is very good, registering one complete failure, some weaknesses, some successes and one epoch-making achievement. He failed to bring Britain's responsibility in Palestine to an end that satisfied anybody. Perhaps no other prime minister could have done any better; but Attlee failed to perceive in time the strength and determination of the Jews to establish their statehood. Following Bevin and the Foreign Office, he believed that if the Jews were given their own territory, the Arabs would be able to throw them into the sea. If he had changed his mind about Jewish strength and stubbornness as quickly as he came to appreciate that of the Muslims, the Palestine story might have been different. India is another story. If any one man can be said to have given India her independence it was Attlee. The Conservative opposition were against it: within his own Cabinet there was opposition, and even his supporters questioned the nature and the timing of the withdrawal. Only Attlee, while always tactically versatile, was resolute and expeditious in bringing about what he was set on from the start.

He did virtually nothing about Africa: he only got to understand its problems after he left office. The appointment of the man he chose to deal with Africa he afterwards regarded as his second biggest mistake.

He was positive about Europe in principle – 'Europe must federate or perish', but dilatory and inconclusive about Europe in practice. European cooperation for defence he understood, and nourished: he wanted something like NATO long before the war had ended, and got it. As for the Americans, while doubting their judgement on international affairs, he was certain that the peace of the world and the security of the West hung upon the continuation of their presence in Europe indefinitely after the war had ended. He made concessions to get this which caused grave crises within his party; but he got his way. He was enthusiastic about the absolute need for the special Anglo-American relationship; Churchill excelled him on this, but it is possible that the accord between Attlee and Truman – occasionally clouded – was one which Churchill might not have achieved, and it may have been fortunate for both countries that Attlee, not Churchill, was prime minister in the postwar period. When it became necessary to tell the British people that the Soviet Union was a threat to peace the news came more convincingly from a Labour leader than from the man who had inveighed against Russia since the earliest days of the Revolution. Attlee continued to be indicted by some for his decision to provide Britain with the independent deterrent, then represented by the Atomic Bomb: his decision in retrospect looks to have been inescapable.

Attlee was lucky to become prime minister when he did. His reputation has suffered because he did not retire after he lost the General Election in 1951. But he felt he had a fateful task to carry out: to ensure that what the government of 1945-51 had accomplished would not be put in jeopardy by conflict within the party, culminating, possibly, in the election of an unstable leader. He knew he had nothing otherwise to offer; nor could the other giants who were dead, dying or devalued. But if he remained, he could help another leader to emerge who could lead the Labour movement forward 'to the next step'. Not the least of the duties of the leader is to determine and legitimize his successor. Attlee finally managed to engineer the succession of the man best equipped to fill his shoes, but only after the friction he had hoped to prevent had badly shaken the party and after his own reputation had been damaged.

Seen in the context of his time and events, he was a great prime minister. In another context, the assessment might have been different. As it is, the words with which he ended a long appreciation of Churchill might be applied to him:

> He was, of course, above all, a supremely fortunate mortal. Whether he deserved his great fate or not, whether he won it or had it dropped into his lap, history set him the job that he was the ideal man to do. I cannot think of anybody in this country who has been favoured in this way so much. . . . In this he was superbly lucky. And perhaps the most warming thing about him was that he never ceased to say so.

Appendix I
Memorandum on British Industry

[As Chancellor of the Duchy of Lancaster and a member of the Economic Advisory Council (see above, page 87,) Attlee prepared the following memorandum, entitled 'The Problems of British Industry'. It was printed for the Cabinet in July 1930 but never reached the Cabinet for discussion.]

I GENERAL

1 In considering the answer to the question "What is wrong with British Industry?" I have thought it desirable to deal not merely with the specific point, but also with various suggestions which have been made with the intention of improving matters, as a consideration of possible remedies is necessary if the diagnosis of the disease is to be of any use.

In my opinion the general answer to the question is the slowness of adjustment of a highly civilised industrial community to altered circumstances in a period of rapid economic change. The fact that constant change in the direction of economic activity is a normal feature in an advanced industrial society has tended to be obscured by the facts of British industrial history. During the nineteenth century our great staple industries, such as coal, cotton, wool, engineering and shipbuilding, and the great export trade in connection with them, were built up; the importance of their position in the national economy and their long-continued prosperity, gave an impression of stability that was not warranted by the facts of the situation. After the war British industry had to operate in a changed world. New economic forces had evolved. But the facts of the situation were not faced by those responsible for British industry. Masters and men tended to have the delusion that their troubles were only temporary and that some day there would be a return to pre-war conditions. The policy of successive Governments during the post-war period in dealing with unemployment on emergency lines, has on the whole tended to foster this delusion. The individualism of the British industrialist, which in the past had been largely responsible for his success, and his conservatism, have made him slower than his foreign rivals to recognize the need for collective action.

2 There are four main directions in which this attitude has hampered British industry:—

(a) *Failure to Recognise Changed Demand*
    For instance, those responsible for the coal industry failed to recognise that, owing

570

to the rivalry of oil and electricity, the market for coal had contracted and was unlikely to expand, while new sources of supply had developed. The coal owners continued to proclaim that, with longer hours and lower wages, the old markets for raw coal would be recaptured, instead of concentrating on the development of by-products, such as motor fuel. The textile trades failed to recognise the change of demand from cotton and wool to silk, and allowed the new product to be developed in the main in other areas than Lancashire and Yorkshire. The cotton trade tried to meet with old methods the competition encountered in Eastern markets.

(b) *Failure to Rationalise Production*
An examination of the various reports on the coal, cotton, and iron and steel industries, shows how slow has been the progress of rationalization. Proposals for internal reorganization have been refused or delayed. The contrast with the very vigorous post-war reconstruction of the iron and steel industries on the Continent illustrates this point very fully. As the need for rationalization of production is now generally recognized, it is unnecessary to elaborate this point.

(c) *The Failure to Rationalize Distribution*
The most striking defect of British industry has been the failure to organise on up-to-date lines the marketing of British products, especially for export. The report on the iron and steel trade shows German and French industries organised as national units and federated continentally. They have Export Bureaux to deal collectively with external trade. The British iron and steel trade was urged to do the like in 1916, but only made a beginning in 1928. The deficiencies of the cotton trade in this respect are fully exposed in the recent report. The coal trade, apart from the Five Counties Scheme, has shown the same picture of British industrialists by cut-throat competition ruining their own trade. With the exception of the chemical industry, which is closely associated with foreign interests, I am informed that there is no British industry which deals with its export trade collectively. British agriculture shows a similar picture. The British farmer tries to compete as an individual against the standardised products from agricultural countries, such as Denmark. The general impression on a broad review is that, while the importance of marketing is generally recognized, there has been extremely little endeavour to change over from obsolete methods. British industry, in the selling as in the producing process, is hampered by the individualism and lack of co-operation of its direction, which contrast with the mutual helpfulness of American business men.

(d) *Failure to Rationalize Credit*
It is to be noted that on the Continent the banks have taken an important part in stimulating rationalization, whereas in this country, until recently, so far from doing this, the banks have tended by their action or inaction to delay the necessary reform. The closer association of the banks on the Continent with industry has led to their taking a far more active part in assisting the export trades by credits than is the case in this country.

Why Adjustment has been so Slow in this Country
3 There are many reasons for this reluctance to reorganise and for the absence of initiative in British industry, not all of which are attributable to the defects of British business men:—
    (a) Perhaps most important is the steady fall in the price level during the post-war period. Falling prices inevitably damp down enterprise, and this not merely in the rationalization of existing industries but in the development of new projects. At a time when it was necessary that there should be considerable changes in the direction of British economic activity, so that contractions in

571

one trade might be offset by extensions in others, the abrupt return to the gold standard and the steady process of deflation led to depression, lack of confidence and lack of enterprise. It is not intended in this memorandum to discuss the various suggestions that have been made in relation to this point and the one following.

(b) Monetary policy since the war has been favourable to the "rentier" and unfavourable to the "entrepreneur". The actual burden of the indebtedness of industry to capital has increased in this country, whereas on the Continent the period of post-war inflation resulted in virtual extinction of the burden of dead capital.

(c) The lack of confidence caused by falling prices has been enhanced by the uncertainty of markets. The disturbances of the war not only broke up old established economic units, but produced an exaggerated nationalism which found vent in protective policy and high tariffs. This phenomenon is not confined to the Continent of Europe: it is found also in the Dominions and in India.

(d) The new industries, as for instance motor-cars, in the development of which, normally, this country would have taken its full share, were exploited by countries, such as the United States, less affected by the war, with the result that considerable lee-way has to be made up.

(e) Certain psychological factors have made for depression and lack of enterprise. The existence of the heavy national debt and its necessary concomitant, the high rate of taxation, has an effect on the mind greater than the facts warrant. The publication of unemployment figures makes the present depression seem greater than those of the past because it is more correctly known. The existence of a party in the State advocating Protection delays internal reform in industry in favour of agitation for external assistance.

(f) The more elaborate structure of communal provision for social interests makes industry and labour less fluid than formerly. For instance, at the beginning of last century, when there were rapid changes in the location of industry, the factory and a few rows of cheap houses were deemed sufficient, whereas to-day, in areas where industrial extension is occurring, the provision of houses, schools, and other amenities on the modern scale tend to make the change-over slow.

(g) Unemployment insurance probably operates in the direction of retaining in industry business units which should be squeezed out as the burden of keeping in being the necessary labour force during a period of slump has been to a large extent taken over by the community.

(h) Trade Union regulations also to some degree restrict the introduction of new processes.

The Effect of State Action

4 State action to assist industry has for the most part not been of such a nature as to counteract the deficiency noted above. Successive Governments have been so dominated by the urgent need of doing something to meet the immediate situation of the victims of industrial depression, that the possibilities of conscious direction of industrial development have been lost sight of. Conservative Governments, with a protectionist programme suppressed for political reasons, and minority Labour Governments, with Socialist measures in cold storage, have acted in such a way as to foster the delusion that, given time, British industry will recover of its own accord. Such assistance as has been given has tended to be too general and to have lacked specific direction. The coal subsidy is the worst instance of assistance being given to industry unconditionally, and

from the point of view of correcting what was wrong must be regarded as money wasted. Export credits and derating are really of the same nature, being essentially gifts to the industrialist without the exaction of conditions of reform. There have been some instances of Government action to the contrary effect. The Electricity Act is the outstanding example of a broad plan of rationalization by statute, while the beet sugar industry and the motor duties have been effective attempts to foster new and growing industries. The National Mark scheme for Agriculture is an instance of stimulus given to industry to reform itself from within, while the Coal Bill is an attempt to enforce rationalization from without. Despite these instances of control, the general policy adopted has been based on the assumption that what is wrong in British industry will be put right by British industrialists or by the play of natural forces.

2 General Policies

If what is wrong with British industry is a failure in adjustment, it is necessary to consider how far various policies put forward are likely to provide the necessary remedy at the present time. There would appear to be three main policies: The first is that of *laissez faire*, i.e., the belief that industry is not the affair of the State, but that it should be left to those engaged in it; the second is the policy of Protection, with which is often allied the conception of a self-sufficient British Empire; the third is the policy of the conscious direction of industry in the interests of the community.

(A.) *Laissez Faire*

Apart from a few academic publicists, there is little support for a policy of non-interference by the State in industrial affairs. Business men, although theoretically opposed to State intervention and resisting attempts to control their activities, clamour for State assistance for themselves. The idea that without thought or intention the economic affairs of the human race will settle themselves is redolent of mid-nineteenth century optimism, and is unsupported by the facts of the industrial situation to-day. If the diagnosis of the ailments of British industry set out above is correct, and if any lesson is to be learnt from the experience of the past ten years, it would seem that those responsible for British industry have proved incapable of so managing their affairs as to promote the economic welfare of the community.

(B.) *Empire Free Trade*

The argument for Empire Free Trade is generally an extension of the case for Protection, but is based upon the conception of the British Empire as an economic unit. But the accepted principle that the Dominions have an unlimited right to establish their own industries and to dispose of their produce (which in many lines is more than Britain can absorb) in world markets, condemn any "whole-hog" policy of Empire Free Trade. As regards some partial form of Empire Free Trade, it does not appear necessary to state the objections to a tariff on food or raw materials; the arguments are directed against the more plausible case for a duty on manufactured goods.

On this, two general points may be made. First, this country's imports of manufactured goods, which have been rising in recent years, are yet in most cases at about the same level as they were in 1913. The figures have been rising gradually from the low level of the post-war years. Secondly, practically the whole of our imports of manufactures consist of goods on which some further process of manufacture is to be undertaken, such as leather, semi-manufactured steel. No doubt these might be produced in this country, but they must be counted as the raw materials of the industries which consume them, and any rise in price would be a direct hindrance to British industry. Thus this country has a large and growing

573

export trade in tin-plates and galvanized sheets, which are largely manufactured by re-rolling cheap French and Belgian steel bars. Again, any rise in the price of steel would promptly react against the shipbuilding industry.

(C.) *Protection*

The four main grounds on which the case for Protection is usually argued may be met as follows:—

(1) It is suggested that in the interests of national security it is necessary to increase the output of British agriculture, and to a certain extent of other industries; or, in general, lessen our dependence upon export trade in view of the uncertainty of future economic prospects. However, it is fallacious to imagine there is any near prospect of a world food shortage. The price of food relative to industrial produce has been falling heavily during recent years, and there is every sign of a continued world glut of staple foods. The argument that we ought to be less dependent upon our export trade raises more general issues; at the present time we are becoming less dependent upon our export trade, for quite a different reason. That is that every year our receipts from overseas investments pay an increasing proportion of the costs of our imports. Whether or no this is in the long run desirable, there is no sign for years of this country's finding itself in any way put to it to pay for imports unless it encourages overseas investment to an altogether extravagant extent.

(2) It is contended that the abnormal foreign competition to which British industry is at present subjected is neither healthful nor stimulating because of dumping, export bounties, low labour standards abroad, uncertainty of incidence of tariffs, and consequent enhancement of industrial risks. Spasmodic dumping is an evil, though one not without its advantages to consumers: *e.g.*, the west of England stockfarmer was able to buy cheap cereals thanks to the dumping of oats and barley which injured the arable farmers in England and Scotland. Protest by the British Government is rendered difficult by the practice of some of our own industries—*e.g.*, coal—of selling exports below home prices. Uncertainty is a grave drawback; remedy is to be found rather in Import Boards than a Tariff.

While some of our imports are made under lower labour standards than ours, in admitting them we neither endorse such standards nor suffer unfair competition, any more than we do from the high-wage imports of the United States of America. Actual variations in wage rates are due largely to varying geographical or economic conditions and the varying productivity of labour; if Japanese wage rates are $\frac{1}{3}$ of ours, the productivity of labour in Japan (owing to lack of capital, equipment, &c.) is less than $\frac{1}{3}$ of British.

(3) It is claimed that with Protection of the home market British industries with a higher output could spread overhead charges and secure lower costs of production; in general that under the shelter of the tariff we could secure reorganization which would enable British industry to supply the home market more cheaply and to go out and recapture export trade. If, however, it is possible for an industry so to organize and spread its overhead charges under the shelter of a tariff, that it can, as a result of that tariff, sell its produce at a definitely lower price, why is it not possible for industrialists to get together and effect this organization under Free Trade? In so far as they really can produce at lower prices, then prices would by themselves suffice to keep out the foreign products. The iron and steel industry admittedly has high overhead costs due to a low scale of output; but, since 1924, under fierce foreign competition, it has been

574

increasing its efficiency, and output per worker employed has gone up by 20 per cent. No such improvement was observed during the period of prosperity 1922-24, when the industry was virtually protected from foreign competition by the occupation of the Ruhr. Finally, an industry organized as the steel industry claims it could be organized under Protection (so as to reduce overhead costs to a minimum) might produce steel at prices below the present level, but would it sell at these prices except for export? Such a situation is a positive invitation to the industry to form a cartel of the most potent kind, yielding some increase in productive efficiency, but a very considerable increase in the price charged to the consumer. When the complaint is made that Germany is over-rationalized, it is cartelization of this kind which is in view.

(4) It is argued that if this country were protectionist it would have a powerful bargaining weapon with which to secure tariff reductions elsewhere.

This point is illusory. The World Economic Conference at Geneva in 1927 categorically denied that the effect of tariff wars was to bring about any reduction in the general level of tariffs, basing themselves on the experience of recent happenings. (See Final Report of the Balfour Committee.)

Two other points in this connection often escape notice. The first is that if this country became Protectionist we should be deprived in many markets of the most-favoured-nation treatment which we almost invariably enjoy. Secondly, as a result of this most-favoured-nation treatment, if at any time any other country secures any reduction of tariffs through special bargaining, we can automatically participate in it.

While it may be conceded that the conception of the British Empire as a self-contained economic unit has, at any rate, the merit of considering our industrial situation from a broad point of view, and while Protectionist policy involves to some extent a definite conception of the economic structure of the nation, these policies, even if they were possible, fail to deal with the particular deficiencies of British industry in two important respects:—

(1) They disregard the principle which should underlie any policy in regard to British industry, namely, that it must be based on the preservation and enhancement of the standard of life of the workers.

(2) They do not provide for any effective influence being brought to bear on industry whereby it may be rationalized in the interests of efficiency and of the welfare of the community.

(D.) *Deliberate Direction of the Economic Life of the Nation*

The last policy involves the deliberate decision by the Government as to what is the right basis for the economic life of this country and, when the decision has been made, the utilisation by the Government of all forces at its command to implement the decision. It is for the Government itself to decide as to how far in the condition of the modern world it is desirable or possible to depend to as great an extent as formerly on our export trade. If it is decided that the balance should be redressed in favour of a greater production for home consumption, it must be determined what kind of activity should be stimulated. These decisions must be come to with a view of utilising in the best way the economic resources of this country in order that a high standard of life may be maintained. The question of the optimum population that this country can carry is involved. It is clear that these decisions must be made before a definite policy on such matters as the location of industry, the degree of assistance to be given to agriculture and the extent to which migration within the Empire should be stimulated can be decided.

But this is not an advocacy of delaying action until after these underlying problems have been decided. Whether it has a plan or not, the State must of necessity be proceeding

575

continuously with work on rationalisation of industry, on rehousing of slum dwellers, on new roads and on electrification. Is a policy of drift better than an interim policy? Moreover, when the above fundamental points are decided, complete machinery will be required to make the national will effective; and this machinery will have been naturally developed in the handling of the problems discussed below.

3 THE ORGANISATION OF THE EXPORT TRADE

Up to the present efforts to assist the export trade have been too general and have been addressed more to the possibility of a general expansion of trade or the securing of particular overseas orders than to the organisation of the system of marketing. It would seem that one particular side of rationalisation that needs special attention is a change in the method of the selling of British goods abroad. As has already been pointed out, our rivals tend in the direction of collective selling agencies. It should be possible to utilise such devices as export credits and trade facilities to induce a better organisation of export on the part of particular industries. Railway companies might be induced to give special rebates to bulk consignments through selling agencies; in this respect British railways are hopelessly behind Continental practice. Banks might co-operate in the same way by giving easier credit to those industries which were so organized. There is evidence that at present there is far too little co-operation between British sellers abroad and that the sale of goods that are complementary by different agents militates against obtaining orders. There would seem to be no reason why particular industrial groups such as clothing, coal, cotton, wool, heavy iron, steel, machinery, pottery, &c., should not organize collective selling agencies. A corollary of this would seem to be the proper organisation in each country where there is an actual or potential market for our goods of a British selling agency. In each country there should be a trade Commissioner of high standing, whose duty would be not merely to give general reports with regard to British trade and its possibilities, but to act as a focal point for the representatives of the various selling agencies of British industries, the object being to get all sellers of British goods to co-operate and be mutually helpful, so that information of an opportunity in one particular line coming to the notice of a seller in another would be transmitted to the interested party. The Memorandum submitted to the British Consul-General at New York by Mr. Maxwell Magnus is interesting as showing the necessity for this organised system of selling abroad.

4 RATIONALISATION OF INDUSTRY

The policy of rationalisation in industry, which is accepted by all parties, has hitherto been regarded from too narrow a point of view. It is considered as a matter of the organization of the production of British goods and their marketing in the most efficient way, and it seems to be considered that this is, in the main, a matter which concerns those responsible for the particular undertakings. On the other hand, if the repercussions of rationalisation are considered, it is clear that something more than the efficient organis-ation of a particular industry is involved. Rationalisation may result in grave loss to the Nation in both personnel and wealth. The Memorandum of Mr. Bevin brings this out very clearly. Rationalisation means increased unemployment for some persons, for some time, and the length of this period is conditioned by the extent to which the industry is expanding and to the degree of fluidity in the working population. It means very often the concentration of an industry in certain areas and the consequent creation of communities without prospect of employment. It is, for instance, probable that a thorough rationalisation of the cotton industry, with the introduction of modern looms, &c., and the concentration of work in the best equipped units of the industry, would reduce certain Lancashire towns to the position of some of the mining areas.

While it is necessary, if such industries as the cotton trade are to continue to exist, that they should be carried out in the most efficient way, the process of rationalisation might entail an immense economic loss to the community, quite apart from its results on the workers. The social developments of the present day have resulted in sinking a large amount of national capital in the shape of houses, roads, schools, drainage, &c., which may be lost if the industry contracts or changes its location without some other employment coming in to take its place. At the same time, at great expense, new industrial areas elsewhere are being developed, where the entire communal provision for the citizens has to be created, while in general housing and other schemes, being local, are pursued without reference to national planning. This is from the national point of view irrationalisation.

Rationalisation of industry without external stimulus is a slow process, and unless there is some agency to deal with its repercussions much suffering and waste is involved. It is not reasonable to expect the industry which is in process of rationalisation to take up to any great extent the burden of looking after the workers displaced, still less to take steps to introduce new industries into the areas affected by the process; nor, indeed, would it be good policy to try to place such an obligation on particular industries. On the other hand, the instances where communities, through their local authorities or otherwise, have taken the initiative in endeavouring to introduce new industries in place of those declining are few and discouraging.

5 PLANNING OF INDUSTRIAL DEVELOPMENT

It has now become a commonplace that this country is at present going through an industrial revolution, perhaps as extensive as that of the late 18th and early 19th centuries. Its character will doubtless be clearer seen in retrospect than in progress, but already it is possible to indicate its main features. Not only are we losing our position as the world's workshop; to a large extent also this country itself is ceasing to require much of what it used to produce. As the world grows richer and more developed it inevitably requires less of steel rails and coarse cotton goods. In this country the whole tendency of new demand is for services rather than for commodities—for distributive, catering, entertaining, public utility, professional and kindred services. And within the diminishing sphere of manufacture the tendency of demand, at any rate in this country, is for specialities and luxury goods of all kinds, apart from one or two heavy industries, such as shipbuilding and chemicals, in which the geographical compactness of this country gives us peculiar advantages.

This industrial transformation has its geographical counterpart, which is visible to the dullest observer. New industry is streaming into the South of England, to the big cities, like Birmingham and Manchester, and away from the industrialised countrysides of Lancashire and Durham—but *par excellence* the tide is flowing to Greater London.

It seems that we are allowing to go derelict some of the best-equipped industrial areas in the world - the best equipped from the point of view of fuel, power, transport and labour supply. At the same time London and many other areas are being allowed to grow at an unprecedented pace.

This whole development is taking place entirely without plan or control from any outside agency. For the whole of the past century we have been engaged in attempting to patch the appalling defects created by the unplanned career of the last industrial revolution. And we are driven to confess that many of these problems, such as the slums and overcrowding in big cities, are as yet only half-tackled. But at this present moment we are standing by watching a similar industrial development heading straight for chaos.

The social problems created by private enterprise are obvious enough. While it allows some areas to grow derelict, it causes others to grow at an unexampled and uncontrollable pace. Private enterprise, when it sets up its works at the place where considerations of profit or perhaps merely of convenience dictate, is in effect calling upon the community to assist workers to migrate towards it, to provide them with houses, roads, schools and the complete net-work of local government services. And, in addition, in London, and to a less extent elsewhere, we are daily increasing the gigantic cost and complexity of the system of transport required to take the workers to and from their work. Both in cost in money and in cost in leisure any avoidable increase in transportation represents a dead loss to the community.

So far the situation has been viewed from its economic aspect alone, and nothing has been said about the increasing congestion caused by uncontrolled industrial development and the pushing ever further back of the countryside from the dwellers in the centres of cities. This problem in the case of London was bad enough before the recent industrial developments had started, but now it is now being made infinitely worse.

It is necessary to lay down principles on which any social control of industrial development could be expected to act. In the first place, it must be realised that there are certain industries (though only a limited number) whose position is absolutely decided by the nature of their transportation problems. Thus it is elementary that a blast furnace must be near supplies of coal and ore, and a shipyard near to supplies of steel; in general, the location of industry handling heavy and bulky materials must be decided in the light of transport costs. But in the case of the large and increasing body of industries dealing with lighter materials, where transport costs are a very minor consideration, much of the drift to the South of England is quite simply in search of cheap and docile labour, or for convenience in marketing. We are entitled to over-bear these considerations in view of the gigantic difficulties created by the leaving derelict of old-fashioned industrial areas with their population.

As a particular suggestion of an expanding industry which might be planted in a declining area, such as Lancashire, we may take the case of electrical appliances. The Government could well inaugurate a campaign for the more rapid spread in the use of electricity; the Central Electricity Board is in process of completing an elaborate scheme for the supply of electricity, but the present industrial depression is likely to falsify the estimates made of increasing demand. There is, however, considerable opportunity of extended use, especially in an increase of the domestic load. On the general principle that the luxuries of one generation are the necessities of the next one would expect that in a decade or so every family in this country would be using the numerous electrical appliances in the home which are now found only in well-to-do residences. The obstacles in the way of a rapid increase of demand have been the high cost of current and the high cost of electrical appliances. The former has already been taken in hand by the Central Electricity Board. If Government action in co-operation with the trade could introduce the mass production of electrical appliances at a low cost and at the same time could bring about a big campaign by the authorised undertakers for their use, there is little doubt that a very great development would take place. The very heavy fall in the price of copper during this year indicates the presence of a good opportunity for further extension in this direction.

Town and regional plans, at any rate provisionally, have been worked out for the greater part of Great Britain. For Greater London the work is in hand and an interim report has been prepared. The cardinal feature of all these plans is that in each district suitable areas are set aside for industrial sites after thorough consideration of all the factors involved—provision of transport facilities, nearness of labour supply, provision of power, adequacy of housing accommodation and preservation of natural amenities. The whole weight of industrial control should be put behind the guidance of new industries into these sites rather than to elsewhere. For it is at best ingenuous to suppose that a single manufacturer is never shortsighted or that he can hope to make as thorough a survey of the relevant factors as is made by town-planning experts.

It is clear that a very far-reaching co-ordination of governmental activities is required to carry through any such policy. When new functions were attached to the post of Lord Privy Seal 12 months ago, it was stated that it would be his task to co-ordinate the activities of all the departments concerned with industrial problems. But the implications of this declaration of policy have not yet been fully worked out—and they are far-reaching. Thus, it is the function of the Trade Facilities Act machinery to develop new industries—but it falls upon the Ministry of Health to supervise the erection of houses, the Ministry of Transport the planning of roads, the Board of Education the erection of schools. It falls upon the town planning authorities to decide on the best sites for industry, and for housing sites—but they have no power to call upon new industries to occupy the sites chosen. It falls upon municipalities to clear their congested central areas and to re-house in their outer areas. Often, as has been seen, there is a most incredible chaos arising out of the fact that one local authority rehouses in an area subject to the general local administration of another authority. Again, it falls upon the Ministry of Labour to transfer men from decaying industrial areas; but it has no power to give credits for the setting-up of new industries, or to arrange for the building of new houses, in the expanding areas.

Clearly, it is no use suggesting an authority which is to override the departments mentioned, which, through their Ministers, have to bear the responsibilities. But we can attempt to set up an authority which can make recommendations on matters which are at present the functions of existing Government Departments, while it exercises full control over any new powers which may be created.

6 ECONOMIC STABILITY

There is a need for endeavouring to secure a greater stability in the economic life of the nation. The progress of rationalisation would do much to secure this, but active measures are also necessary:

(a) The policy underlying the proposals for a Wheat Import Board and the Quota system is designed to secure the maintenance of a certain minimum amount of cereal cultivation in this country on a profitable basis by securing a firm market. While this policy may be considered from one point of view as only action in an emergency, from another it may be regarded as a considered policy of establishing a certain balance in the economic life of the community. If it can be proved that it is desirable, for broad reasons of social policy, that a certain form of economic activity should be stimulated in this way, there would seem to be no *a priori* objection, although the question of method must be considered.

(b) The invasion of the British market by bounty-fed products from abroad would seem to demand a careful consideration of our treaty and international commitments, more expecially a re-examination of the exact meaning of the phrase "goods of a like nature" by the Law Officers of the Crown.

(c) Every effort should be made to influence demand in such a way as to give a greater stability to industry. If the iron and steel trade were rationalised, it might be possible to make bulk contracts with the selling agency of the trade on behalf of Government, and possibly, also, local authorities, thus securing a sure market for a large bulk of production. Constructional steel work and building materials generally suggest themselves as a possible subject for such agreement. If this were done the trade might be secured that degree of stability in the home market which is plainly necessary for successful operation in the export trade. Regularity of consignments should also secure considerable economies in railway and shipping working.

(*d*) The possibility of bulk contracts with Dominion Governments or organisations in the Dominions, whereby bulk trading between the home country and the Dominions would be effected, might be further explored.

7 THE METHOD OF RECONSTRUCTION: RECOMMENDATIONS

If it be granted that—

(*a*) rationalization of production and of marketing at home and for export is economically necessary;

(*b*) it is not going to take place except slowly, incoherently, and at great social cost, if industry is left to itself;

(*c*) the process of industrial reconstruction involves the deliberate planning of the economic basis of the country, and demands the correlation of various factors;

it would seem to follow that there is needed an organ of the nation's will that can plan on a national scale and translate those plans into action with rapidity and vigour nationally and locally. National action is needed if the nation is to maintain its position in world markets, and, if necessary, changes are to take place with as little friction as possible. Local action is necessary because the problem of declining employment is localized in certain areas. Direct action in particular areas is as much required as is a sound general plan of campaign.

(A.) *Minister of Industry*

What would seem to be required is a Minister and a Department rather than a consultative body or a committee of Ministers. The Economic Advisory Council already exists with the power of suggesting large plans, but the essential thing is the translation of ideas into action. Controlling principles of policy must in the last resort be laid down by the Cabinet, but what is needed is an executive arm, which, assisted by the advice of the Economic Advisory Council, will express policy in action. The country is face to face with an emergency like that of the war. The task of the Minister would be to lay down plans for national reconstruction and set in motion action upon them; he would thus be the organ of conscious direction of national economic life. As such he would of course consult with and co-ordinate the work of other Departments, notably Transport, Health, the Board of Trade and the Ministry of Labour. It would be his business to see that rationalisation—in the widest sense—is in fact carried out, to plan it nationally, and see that it happens regionally. It would be his business to safeguard the standard of life of the workers and to secure that the economic advantages of rationalization accrue to the community and are not monopolised either by individuals or groups.

The extent of the powers with which it would be necessary to arm the Minister is a matter for detailed consideration, but many of them exist but are dispersed and so comparatively ineffective. In particular the power that resides in the credit of the Government should be made use of to induce industry to reform itself. It is remarkable indeed that the immense power of planning rationalisation, which is inherent in the control of the provision of credit for industrial reorganisation, should be in private hands (Bankers' Industrial Development Company). One of the dangers of rationalization is the extent to which private corporations are given power to monopolise certain branches of economic activity and appropriate the whole benefits of reorganisation, and even more, by raising prices against the consumer. One of the most effective means of preventing this form of exploitation is the giving of power to insist on complete publication of accounts.

(B.) *Export Trade*

As suggested above, the main export trade of this country should be transferred as rapidly as possible into the hands of selling agencies, one for each group of industries. These organizations would be closely interlocked with the developments projected below. They would provide organizations capable of taking responsibility on behalf of the industrialists in each trade, for allocating orders and promoting specialisation and rationalization generally.

(C.) *Industrial Development Board*

For the stimulation of rationalization the Minister should set up an Industrial Development Board composed of industrial administrators, representatives of organized labour, and a minority of bankers with himself as Chairman; such Board to have power to—

(*a*) guarantee overdrafts at the Banks for definite or indefinite periods for replacements or extensions;

(*b*) take over and extend the Trade Facilities Act machinery for guaranteeing issues of stock;

(*c*) if found desirable to issue stock on its own responsibility;

(*d*) to take over the existing Bankers' Industrial Development Company;

(*e*) take over the present Public Works Loans Board.

In return for these advantages the Board would have power to demand—

(1) amalgamation or co-operation with any other firm if considered necessary;

(2) the organisation of satisfactory selling agencies;

(3) location of proposed new works where the Minister may require;

(4) the employment of transferred labour;

(5) the return to the Board of full trading accounts, the Board to have power to conduct investigations through its own accountants and to publish information as it sees fit;

(6) the employment by the firms or groups receiving assistance of such means of transport and power supply as may be required.

The Minister may be conceived as acting through particular bodies set up to deal with special tasks. The suggested method of operation might be best explained by taking an example. In the cotton trade, for example, it is generally admitted that nothing will be done until there is superimposed upon the various units of the industry some co-ordinating body which will mobilise the goodwill and the zeal for action of the more alert minds and enable them to coerce the recalcitrant, sleepy-minded or merely despairing others. The Minister, it is conceived, might set up a Regional Board, the duty of which would be, first, to see that the Cotton Report is put into execution, and, secondly, to deal with the problem presented by a county hitherto predominantly dependent on one industry when that industry's market has largely disappeared. The Board would have to see that a joint marketing organization for cotton goods of all kinds was created, a Raw Materials Pool set up and pressure brought to bear on sections of the trade, such as the dyers and finishers, that are at present acting inimically to the interests of the whole. It would also have to deal with the conditions of the workers under the new régime. On the other hand, it would have to survey the possibilities of new industrial developments, the extension of electrification, for instance, the possibilities of large-scale housing and transport development. In this instance the power of the Minister might be largely exercised through finance; the provision of easy credit facilities for the process of reconstruction and for the introduction of new industries into the area would give him considerable powers. In other cases action might only be needed by some body set up to deal with a particular industry.

How far the Minister working through these Boards might find it necessary to have other means than that of credit inducements, and how far he would need to be given coercive powers, would depend on the facts in each particular case.

It would be essential that where schemes of rationalization were undertaken the closest liaison should be kept with the Ministries of Health, Transport and Labour.

8 Effect on Employment

A direct effect of a policy of rationalisation vigorously carried out on the lines suggested would be the expansion of the national outlay on the maintenance and extension of capital, with a consequent demand for the production of capital goods. The underlying economic principles on which we should be working would be the utilisation of a period of slack trade to re-equip ourselves for more efficient production in the future. This policy would have a considerable effect on the unemployment position, and it would do it in the most economical way by employing people in their own trades. The following figures will show the possibilities in this direction.

The country's outlay upon maintenance and extension of its fixed capital in 1929 amounted to some £606,000,000. Perhaps £300,000,000 was required merely to replace obsolescence. It is suggested that a vigorous policy on the part of the Development Board, accompanied by the guaranteeing of credits, might raise by 15 per cent. the outlay under this head. This would immediately provide direct employment for 245,000 men, as shown by the following table: –

	Estimated Outlay in 1929. (£ million.)	Employment directly consequent on a 15 per cent. rise in orders. (Thousands.)
Engineering (including railway engineering and maintenance)	205	71
Electrical equipment	56	23
Ships	35	23
Building	195 ⎱	128
Contracting	115 ⎰	
	606	245

In addition, there would be employed in supplying materials for these industries approximately 170,000 men in all, of whom 50,000 would be in the coal industry and 20,000 in the iron and steel industry; thus providing employment for a total of 415,000 in all. It will be seen that this would at last be really making a substantial impression upon the totals of unemployment.

With regard to the financial aspects of these proposals, it will be seen from the suggested functions of the Development Board that some of the money will be raised by guaranteeing public flotations and some by granting of additional credits from the banks; the extent to which these two policies would be pursued would depend upon the situation at the time. It may be objected that the latter would represent an undesirable expansion of credit leading to a rise in prices, but this criticism carries less weight when it is remembered that this expansion of credit is also accompanied by an increase in the output of goods. Even assuming that the whole £90 millions, which an expansion such as the above would cost, is raised in the form of bank credits, clearly the extreme assumption, only a rise in prices of about 2 per cent. at the end of a year might be expected—a much slower rise than the fall which prices are showing at present. Thus at a time like the present, when prices are being forced catastrophically downwards by shortage of credit and by the unwillingness of private enterprise to make use of existing supplies, the Board, by guaranteeing a big expansion of bank advances, would be helping to stabilise prices and restore general confidence. If, on the other hand, a time came when prices were rising and bank credit expanding the Board would use its powers to restrict industrial capitalisation to within the figure of the proceeds of true investment. In fact, so far from being a disturbing force, the Board would act as a much-needed agent of stabilisation in finance and industry.

SUMMARY

1. The general cause of the difficulties of British industry lies in its slowness of adjustment to economic changes affecting both home and world markets. British industry has suffered worse than that of other countries because of (*a*) our abrupt return to the gold standard and the policy of continued deflation; (*b*) the innate individualistic conservatism of British industrialists; (*c*) our loss of leeway to the United States of America and other countries through the war; (*d*) the failure of this country to learn from the experience of the war; (*e*) the growth of industries, behind tariff shelters, in countries which used to purchase from us; (*f*) the depressing effect of a high national debt and rates of taxation; (*g*) the inevitable reduction of the fluidity of labour consequent upon growth of social services and trade union safeguards, in themselves highly desirable.

2. *Laissez-faire*, the theoretical justification of Governmental inaction, with regard to industries is completely discredited. Effective Government action must take the form either of Protection or of the conscious social control of economic development. State assistance to industry since the war, including derating, export credits, subsidies, safe-guarding, has all been unconditional, and splendid opportunities have been flung away of securing some measure of industrial reorganisation under public control.

3. The case for Protection is thoroughly examined on the four main grounds, (i) national security; (ii) the special arguments against abnormal competition, such as dumping; (iii) the possibility of Protection securing a greater spreading of overhead costs and a general industrial reorganisation; (iv) the use of tariffs as a bargaining weapon. On none of these considerations am I satisfied that the arguments for Protection are adequate.

4. The proposals for closer economic unity with the Empire are valuable only in so far as they recognize the realities of the situation. It must be recognized that the Dominions are not prepared to sacrifice their nascent industries in interests of Great Britain, while we have no right to make the interests of other parts of the Empire subservient to our own. Neither can the importance of the trade done by all parts of the British Empire with the outer world be neglected. The method of proceeding by tariffs seems the least likely to succeed. Other methods, especially projects for bulk trading, should be fully explored.

5. In the whole process of industrial rationalisation and reorganisation, and in the development and proper organisation of export trading, there is ample evidence of the enormous extent to which British industry has lagged behind its continental competitors. Virtually in no sphere is there any effective co-operation for export between British manufacturers.

6. We are now going through a period of economic change so rapid that it may be called a new industrial revolution. The problems of housing, transport, labour migration and town-planning, which are being created, are rapidly becoming overwhelming. The most closely interlocked co-ordination between several Government departments, together with considerable new powers for the State, are required. Every year that these problems are neglected further damage is done and our responsibility to posterity grows greater.

7. My first proposal is that a Minister of Industry, with a staff including experts on labour, industrial management, finance, transport and power, housing and town plan-

ning, shall be appointed not merely to survey but to control the development of the nation's economic life. Its main executive arm will be the Board described below (paragraph 9). On matters, such as housing and transport, affecting other Deparments of State, he will consult with and make recommendations to the Ministers concerned.

8. His first task will be to form a series of export selling agencies for all the main industries, which will eventually handle the whole export trade of the country. Under the guidance of the Minister these bodies should secure export orders and allocate these to the works best fitted to deal with them; and hence function as general agencies for promoting industrial specialisation and reorganisation.

9. A Board of National Development should be set up, taking over the existing Public Works Loans Commission and the Bankers' Industrial Development Company. Its duty should be to make or guarantee loans to industry in return for certain measures of public control, and to stimulate the growth of new industries.

10. A year's vigorous application of the policy of expediting public works has only found employment for a limited number of men, and that spread over a term of years. Even if the world depression had not come upon us last winter, we should only have succeeded in making a small reduction in this summer's unemployment figures below those of 1929. But a vigorous application of the policy outlined above should in a short period find work for some 400,000 men in the vitally necessary work of industrial re-equipment, and permanent work for a larger total based on the secure foundation of better organisation of industry and lower costs of production.

C.R.A.

2, Whitehall Gardens, S.W.1,
July 29, 1930.

Appendix II
Memorandum on British Military Failures

Dominions Office
Downing Street, SW1

6th July 1942

SECRET AND
PERSONAL

My dear Anthony,

I am a good deal disturbed at our failures
in the field.
A few days ago I made the attached
Note of points which I thought require
consideration.
It is very rough being just as I typed it
late one night.
I would like to know whether you think
it would be useful to have a talk about some
of the points raised prior to bringing up the
matter more formally.

Yours ever,

Clem

THE RIGHT HONOURABLE ANTHONY EDEN, M.C., M.P.

SECRET AND PERSONAL

The study of enemy methods and their effect on our own plans.

1 We have suffered a severe set back in Libya due mainly to the shock tactics of a
comparatively small number of highly trained men operating very effective armoured
vehicles. We had an equal or greater number of tanks but mostly of inferior performance. The considerable numbers of infantry which we put in the field have played a
very minor part. It seems to be assumed that this is due to the exceptional conditions
of Libya which is ideal tank country. But substantially Poland, France, Greece were
conquered by the same methods. The Russian retreat was effected by the same means.

In all these instances the land forces received most effective backing from the air not only by reconnaissance but by Dive and other bombers. In this war so far artillery has played a minor part.

2 We suffered very severe defeats at the hands of the Japanese who ran us out of Malaya and Burma and captured Singapore. Japanese methods were adapted to the terrain. The chief cause of their successes seems to have been their mobility. Extremely lightly armed troops with weapons easily to be transported operated in jungles overcoming obstacles thought impassable by our own experts. Their troops were highly trained guerrillas, ours were heavily armed troops encumbered with impedimenta and used to a mass of motor transport. In this campaign also the co-operation of the air and land forces was a notable feature.

3 Another feature of the German campaigns has been their use of air transport for attacking troops, for supplying troops and for maintaining advanced air forces. The Russians have also developed these methods with success.

4 We are now carrying on a campaign in Libya and are planning large scale operations on the Continent and sooner or later we shall try to stage a come-back in the Far East.

To what extent have we learned the lessons of the war? How far have our preparations been affected? The features of the German successes have been the combination of speed, hitting power, mobility and maintenance of forces in the field.

5 To me it appears that we are still very largely bound by conceptions of fighting formed before the present war which express themselves in the establishments and equipment which we maintain.

6 We think in categories. Our unit is the Division, a huge mass of men (40,000) cumbrous to a degree, provided with an immense litter of ancillary services which almost swallow up the fighting men. The provision of a mass of mechanised transport in order to make it mobile has immobilised it. The elaboration of staffs hampers effective staff work.

It has grown on the foundation of the Division of the last war in the tradition of static warfare. Have its establishments ever been overhauled by young fighting soldiers who have experienced modern war?

My impression is that our military minds are establishment-bound. For instance when it was decided to have a mobile force it was at once conceived in terms of an airborne division. Why a division? Because it is the unit to which they are accustomed. I have seen a paper setting out the details of an airborne brigade in India with elaborate calculations for moving a complete force with all the usual ancillaries. Is that the way to think of airborne troops? Has the use of airborne troops by the Germans been studied? Has the use of air transport by the Russians been studied?

7 The use of aircraft with troops is still regarded by the Air Ministry as an illegitimate filching away of their own resources. Their attitude continues to be dominated by the conception that the war can be won by big bombers. If this is right we should not have devoted ourselves to building up land forces beyond the barest minimum to hold this island. We should have put all the rest of our energy into aircraft production. If it is wrong. If the bomber is not going to win the war on its own. If Navies and armies are necessary, then all evidence goes to show that they must be fully provided with air forces and these air forces must be integral parts of the Army and Navy and not mere lendings and scrapings grudgingly subtracted from the Air Force.

8 In fact with the widely dispersed British Empire it is not a politically feasible propo-

sition to say 'We will let India, Egypt, Australia, New Zealand and South Africa go by the Board. We will concentrate on making Britain a secure air base for an immense air bombing force.' In any event that very security entails the provision of aircraft for the Navy as a condition of its maintenance. We are also now deeply committed to an invasion of the Continent some time.

9 Have the tactics and strategy of this invasion been worked out and are the forces we are providing and their organisation right? We talk in terms of putting on the Continent so many divisions, some armoured, some infantry. Have we worked out the role which they are to play? Is our conception of 'Bolero' an allout invasion carried ruthlessly through or the landing of troops and the building up of 'lines' on the Continent? I have a feeling that we still think in terms of lines although linear warfare has been largely stultified by the air and to a lesser degree by the tank. Shall we ever need the masses of guns and shell which we are creating? What has been the expenditure of gun shell in the present war? The Navy is just beginning to realise that the naval gun has for many naval occasions been superseded by the bomb or torpedo carrying plane. Has the army realised the extent to which the bomber can take the place of artillery? I am informed that when we were seeking to reduce rapidly Halfaya, Sollum and Derna, the use of heavy bombers was refused by an air commander on the ground that this was a job for the artillery. This illustrates a mentality.

10 If our air attack on the Continent is to be a Blitz and not a siege, have we not got to sweat down our swollen divisions and attain mobility? Have we not got to consider the use of the air for the carriage of troops and supplies and for nourishing our forward forces? Has this been studied? Have we any staff appreciation of the use of the air in land warfare?

   The German Panzers have shown themselves far ahead of us in maintaining their forces in the field. Has this lesson been studied? Has the maintenance and repair organisation necessary for our air force when on the Continent been studied? By all accounts we have not done too well in the Middle East.

11 Rommel has reverted to an earlier method of command. Like Cromwell and Marlborough he is with the forward troops. With the vastly increased speed of modern war and with the facilities for communication that do exist and ought to be used this is the right place. The general far in the rear is applicable to the days when wars were fought with masses of infantry. Twice in Libya Auchinleck has had to go up to take command. Is not our chain of command over elaborate? I suggest that having regard to its mobility and fire power the Division is too large a unit. The Brigade Group is already superseding it. Is the Corps necessary? I observe from a recent report from Russia that the Russians have cut it out.

12 In Libya close co-operation between Army and Air was sought by putting Auchinleck and Tedder together at GHQ and the former over the latter, but further forward the commands bifurcate. I am told that this caused hesitation. Must not the air be as much at the disposal of the commander in the field as the artillery? In a word must we not for land fighting have a unified force of all arms including the air?

13 I do not think that the questions raised in this paper can be dealt with by the Chiefs of Staff who have their hands full with operations and the pressure of immediate events. They ought to be studied by a combined staff with an officer from one of the services directing and in charge of the study. I do not think that it can be done by a trinity or even by two men.

14 Somewhat similar problems which I have not elaborated need consideration in relation to Naval and Air Co-operation. Without some such study we may well be

making the wrong munitions and when the time comes for the crucial test of the war we may be found wanting.

15 A separate study is required for the war against Japan. The strategy has been dealt with in J.P. (42) 537, but except for suggestions as to certain changes in equipment there is no examination of tactics.

Appendix III
The Reorganization of Government

[Attlee left this memorandum on government, and the covering note of 1948, with his autobiographical notes. It is interesting for the light it throws on how he ran his own government when he became Prime Minister in 1945.]

This memorandum was written by me some time in the 30s before I had had any actual experience of Cabinet.

It is not without interest in view of modern developments. There is a short note on the same subject dating from probably 1932.

C.R.A.   7.6.48

THE MEMORANDUM

One of the most urgent questions requiring decision from the Labour movement is that of constitutional reform, in particular the proper organisation of the executive with a view to effective action when the time comes for Labour to govern. The ineffectiveness of the Labour Government while partly due to its lack of a majority and still more to the defects of its prominent leaders who have now left the movement was still more the result of the failure to adapt the governmental machine to modern needs. The National government is clearly suffering from these unremedied defects.

The Cabinet as we know it has grown up gradually. It is an old piece of machinery ill adapted for modern conditions. It is attempting to perform functions which should be separated.

Differentiation of Function

In the conduct of large scale operations there are two distinct functions that ought not to be confused. They are the thinking out and deciding on a plan of campaign and the detailed application of the plan decided. It is only in small scale operations that these two functions can be performed satisfactorily by the same person or persons.

Two instances will illustrate this. A small business man will direct the policy of his business and at the same time administer it in detail. In a large undertaking the directors will deal only with major decisions while the actual working out of policy is left to the heads of departments who are supreme in their own spheres. In a small military operation the OC troops will make his plan, see to the detailed arrangements and perhaps take part

589

in the action. In large scale operations the General Staff deals with major strategy while the OC's smaller units see to its application.

The Cabinet today is a gathering of some twenty people who with a few exceptions are immersed in detailed administration. It is quite unable to take a broad view on the strategy of the campaign. When it meets it has a crowded agenda which must be got through somehow. The majority of the members have little real knowledge of items not connected with their departments. I do not believe that the Labour Government, except possibly just before its break up, *ever* sat down to discuss the broad situation in which the country, the world, or even the party, found itself. I know that when it called for a comprehensive report on the industrial situation, it never discussed it. All matters of real far-reaching importance were remitted to committees. A confession that the Cabinet itself was not in a position to consider them.

It is true that this was due to some extent to the fact that the Prime Minister was constitutionally averse from taking decisions and entirely incapable of understanding the proper use of committees and experts. No doubt where there has been a strong PM, decisions are come to and a steady course steered, but the fact that similar complaints were made of Baldwin and Asquith indicates that more often than not Cabinets find themselves without the power of taking energetic and rapid decisions. Probably the dominance of Gladstone concealed the essential weakness of Cabinets composed of Departmental heads, while the enlarged scope of the activities of Government make the problem today far more urgent.

The first essential to my mind is to separate the functions of detailed administration of particular departments from that of the decision of broad lines of policy. Heads of departments cannot and do not know sufficient about the work of other departments to be able to discuss usefully their problems. To take a minor instance: at the PO I wished to supersede the autocracy of the Permanent Secretary as sole adviser to the Minister by forming a council of heads. I did not propose to form it of the heads of the Posts, Telephones, Telegraphs, Savings Banks, etc. but of the heads of functions, Staff, Finance, Technical and Administrative. This also was the line taken by Haldane in the reform of the War Office. He did not form a council of a Gunner, a Sapper, a Cavalryman and an Infantryman, but of the heads of the functions of operations, quartering, personnel, supply and finance.

Applying this principle to the Cabinet it seems to me that what is required is a *small* body of Ministers without heavy departmental work, each one in general charge of a particular function of State activity. These Ministers must have leisure to think and a freedom from the pressure of day-to-day business which will enable them to see things in proportion.

I think the following should form the Cabinet: Prime Minister and Ministers representing the functions of Finance, Economic Planning, Social Provision, External Relations, Defence, Law and Order. I will now consider the functions of these Ministers:

The Prime Minister

The functions of a Prime Minister are necessary multifarious. He is expected to be the connecting link between the Government and the Head of the State, the Leader of the House of Commons, the figurehead of the government vis-à-vis the nation, the president of a council of Ministers, a Party Leader, the reconciler of divergent opinions, the ultimate decider of policy, the selector of Ministers, a bestower of rewards and patronage. He has also tended more and more lately to be the representative of his country in its relations with the League of Nations, foreign countries and the rest of the Empire. It is difficult to rid him wholly of any of these functions, but the extent to which he is able to perform them effectively depends in the main on his powers of cooperation and devolution; his sense of proportion and his sense of priorities. A PM who allows himself to be diverted from large matters by petty departmental difficulties cannot do his work. Some PMs have their eyes so closely fixed on the H of C that they see all questions in the light of Parliamentary tactics, some cannot trust their colleagues, and try to do their work for them, others get so obsessed with the figurehead idea that they seek opportunities for strutting before the world, others fail to appreciate the need for keeping themselves in the public eye.

The essential quality in a PM is that he should be a good Chairman able to get others to work. He must be able to decide in the last resort between competing policies. He must have the architectonic sense. He must see the whole building not only the bricks. For most of his functions he needs an alter ego. Someone with whom he is sufficiently in accord so that through him he can be kept in close touch with what is happening in a particular sphere. To take an instance, the PM must be in a position to take decisions on matters of defence. He cannot make himself fully acquainted with the questions at issue. Today he presides over the Committee of Imperial Defence. He goes there as an ignoramus to meet ministers and experts from the fighting services. His position is very weak. If on the other hand there was a minister charged with coordinating defence with a staff drawn from all three services, and some civil departments, he would be the informed assistant of the Prime Minister in relation to this function.

I would sum up the essence of the Premiership by saying that there must be someone to take a decision. The decision that he must take is not that a certain course should be followed but that a decision must be come to. The vice of the modern Cabinet is allowing things to drift because of differences of opinion instead of bringing matters to the decision of a vote.

Economic Planning

The President of the Board of Trade is now an overworked departmental head. He should be Chief of Staff putting into effect the economic plan of the government. He should preside over a Council of Ministers concerned with economic matters. These are the Ministers of internal trade (taking the functions from which the President of the B of T has been freed), the Sec of Overseas Trade, the Minister of Mines, Minister of Transport, Postmaster General, and Minister of Labour. (The allocation of functions among these ministers will be considered later.) The Cabinet Minister in charge of a function is at once the interpreter to the group of Ministers concerned of government policy and decisions, and the interpreter to the Cabinet of the views of the Ministers in the group.

Finance

The position of the Chancellor of the Exchequer is at present too dominating or rather it is dominating in the wrong way. He has tended to become the dictator instead of the colleague. He gives but little account to his colleagues of the financial situation. Finance becomes a mystery beyond the reach of the ordinary minister. The ridiculous system whereby the Budget is the peculiar possession of the Chancellor who does not reveal his proposals to his colleagues until just before presenting them to the House should be ended. The Finance Minister should be in close touch with his Cabinet colleagues and the financial situation should be kept constantly before them. Instead of departments getting a demand for estimated cuts of so much percent, or so many millions, the Cabinet should decide on the allocation of funds on a considered plan.

It is probable that Labour will require the creation of a separate minister to deal with banking, etc. There would be a separation of function between the Minister dealing with State finance and the minister dealing with economic finance. The latter would be in close touch with the economic planning group of which he would form a part. The present dealings of the Treasury with spending departments is most unsatisfactory. I will consider later this problem; the line of advance would seem to be in the creation of regular finance departments in each ministry as at the WO and for regular meetings of the financial officers of the different departments under a treasury chairman.

Social Provision

The planning of the social environment, Housing, Education, Health, Pensions, etc. should be correlated under a Minister of Social Provision. The extent to which these ministries are interdependent needs no stressing. It is clear also that for some purposes the Minister of Transport should belong to this group, e.g. local government. The Minister of Labour may be called in for joint consultation. At the present time, there is no decision as to what services should be provided or paid for by the individual, which communally. The Cabinet Minister in charge would have to consider not only what standard of services the State could afford and the direction in which additional expenditure will be most desirable, e.g. whether a raised school age or cheaper housing is most needed but also the relationship of wages and social services, i.e. how much of a man's wages is the State going to spend for him. A coordinated survey is badly needed. These activities must also be considered with the general economic plan.

External Relations

It is, I think, open to question whether or not the Cabinet should contain one or two ministers dealing with external relations. Probably two would be necessary, one dealing with foreign, the other with imperial matters. The post of Foreign Secretary is so personal that it would probably be impossible for him at the same time to represent in the Cabinet the standpoint of the Dominion and Colonies, although on other grounds there is much to be said for unity.

If the Foreign Minister remains, he must obviously be in the Cabinet. A single Minister should represent in the Cabinet: the Dominions, India, and the Colonies. He would preside over a council of Ministers administering these departments. As occasion served, other Ministers would be present at the group meetings.

Law and Order

At present the Lord Chancellor and the Home Secretary represent these two functions. There are some functions of the Home Secretary which might well be transferred to other departments. The administration of justice and the enforcement of the law might be combined unless it is considered that the Home Secretary represents the power of the State and the Chancellor the rights of the individual citizen. In my view the lawyer qua lawyer is out of place in the Cabinet. He is a technician whose advice on technical matters is required. The A G and S G are the technical legal advisers of the government and I do not think that the Chancellor qua lawyer is wanted in the Cabinet.

Agriculture

The position of agriculture is somewhat difficult. It is essentially an economic function and as such would fall into the economic planning group. It may be, however, that temporarily the Minister of Agriculture may be required in the Cabinet in view of the dominance of the agricultural problem.

Cabinet Minister's Staff

Cabinet Ministers should be housed in a single building as it is essential that they should be in close personal contact. They would have small staffs of officials selected for their wide outlook and range of experience. The relationship of the Minister and his staff to the Ministries within the group will at first be difficult and delicate. The Cabinet Minister's staff will not interfere in the work of subordinate Ministries, but will draw from them the information on which the Cabinet Minister forms his conclusions or rather informs himself so as to be in a position to discuss with Ministers the application of Cabinet policy. The Cabinet Minister and his staff are to the subordinate Ministries as GHQ to Army HQ.

Subordinate Ministers

The position of junior ministers today is not happy. They have responsibility for decisions, the reasons for which they do not know. They seldom have any effective voice in policy. On the other hand most ministries today contain half a dozen Cabinet Ministers who are there for past services or for other reasons unconnected with their present suitability for the positions which they occupy. Some of them are generally too old and out of date.

Among the junior ministers will be found at least half a dozen who are capable of original work, and of giving a lead. They are young and more in touch with the needs of the age.

The generalised undersecretary is often wasted. Some chiefs give their undersecs plenty of chances; others use them merely as convenient reliefs for tedious work. Many have little standing in their offices. Wherever possible undersecs should be replaced by junior ministers in charge of particular functions. For instance the undersec for Health might be specifically in charge of housing.

It is of the essence of this plan that junior ministers should be full members of the ministerial group and should be encouraged to speak their mind even though they disagree with the views of their immediate chiefs.

Advantages of the Group System

The group system should relieve the Cabinet of much detailed discussion on minor points and leave it free to deal with major issues.

Group discussions should lead to closer coordination of the work of the different departments.

It should supersede the system of ad hoc committees of the Cabinet which generally in practice means the relegation of important matters to ministers without special knowledge, selected because the work of their department is not so arduous as others. (This is often the reason why they have been placed there originally.)

The group system should not be worked too rigidly. The group is a permanent nucleus but the attendance of ministers from other groups would often be necessary.

The PM should on occasions attend group meetings to get to know the quality of his ministers.

The 'SHORT NOTE' 1932

The fact that in the August crisis when it was decided to take emergency action, a Cabinet of only ten persons was appointed, showed a realisation of the fact which has become increasingly obvious of recent years that there is something very wrong with our present method of forming the national executive. The main reason for having a Cabinet is due to the impossibility of a large body of persons coming to a number of decisions on policy. The Cabinet is at once the King's Government and a body representative of the dominant party in the House of Commons.

Its essential function is that of decision. Decision on policy requires thought and thought requires a certain degree of detachment from pressing urgency of detailed administration. The functions of detailed administration and the direction of broad policy are entirely distinct and the conjunction of [them] in a single person of qualities suitable for each is rare.

The Cabinet of today consists of a number of persons most of whom are immersed in the very heavy task of administering great departments and at the same time defending themselves in parliament and initiating and piloting through the House legislation. Inevitably the departments in which the strain of administration are greatest such as those of Health, Labour and Transport are precisely those in connection with which new legislation is required. To ask of the holders of these offices that they should at the same time make themselves acquainted with the problems of other governmental activities so as to be able to give a considered view in the Cabinet is to ask the impossible. With the exception of the Prime Minister whose burdens are immense, there are only two members of the Cabinet without departmental responsibilities: the Lord President of the Council and the Lord Privy Seal, for the Chancellor of the Duchy is not infrequently outside it. There are thus only two members who have sufficient leisure to master the mass of documents which descend upon the modern Cabinet Minister. These members are not invariably selected for the quality of decision but because for various reasons their inclusion is desired but their capacity is doubtful.

It follows, therefore, that at any given Cabinet meeting, many decisions are made with but a proportion of the Cabinet being really informed on the subject under decision. This does not necessarily mean that the uninformed leave the decision to those who know, on the contrary there are always a certain number of persons whose strength of conviction is in inverse ratio to their knowledge. Further than this, the great enemy of any government is vis inertiae, the habit of putting off decisions on critical matters from week to week and month to month. The readiest device is to appoint committees or Commissions which suffices to postpone the pain of making a decision for a few months. This vis inertiae derives much of its strength from the existence of the uninformed members. The majority for a positive line of action is difficult to obtain for the uninformed tend to take the safest line by supporting a negative attitude.

The size of the modern Cabinet strongly reinforces the defects of its composition. Discussions tend to be lengthy. The odds in favour of finding some stubborn opponent to any proposal are enhanced. The temptations towards procrastination and weak compromise are made stronger.

I have, therefore, come to the conviction that a radical change in the nature and composition of the Cabinet is required if it is to do the work required of it in the modern state.

The first step on the road to reform is a thorough overhauling of order of precedence and rates of remuneration which offices carry with them. The prescriptive right of a secretary of state to be in the Cabinet in normal times should be abolished. The raising of the number of Secretaryships of State to eight has meant an overburdening of the Cabinet with certain kinds of experience. The function of Defence is represented in the Cabinet by three ministers. Affairs external to the British Isles by four. The provision that only a limited number of Secretaries of State may sit in the Commons House limits unnecessarily the assignment of offices.

Quite apart from the representation in the Cabinet of particular departments, the fact that certain offices carry higher status and remuneration means that persons are promoted to administer certain departments not because they are the best persons available but because their status in the party is considered to entitle them to the higher posts. It appears to me that these distinctions should be abolished and that apart from the Prime Minister, there should be three categories of ministers, the number in each category being equal in status and remuneration.

With these anachronisms removed, it is possible to consider what is the right number of persons to form the Cabinet and what offices should carry with them Cabinet rank. It must be remembered that the present Cabinet being descended from the officers of the Royal Household, there was nothing absurd in former times in officials of minor importance such as the Chancellor of the Duchy of Lancaster, and the Postmaster General, being included. Relatively, owing to the small development of governmental functions, they were high officers of State. It is only the intrusion of new departments which has rightly relegated them to a position of less dignity.

We shall best arrive at the right number for a Cabinet by deciding what we consider to be its functions. For myself I have no doubt but that the most important function of a Cabinet is to take decisions on broad points of principle. I consider that the discussion of the details of a legislative measure in the Cabinet is as out of place as the attempt of the House of Commons to discuss the details of a Bill in Committee of the whole House. Similarly I think that it is not the function of a Cabinet to discuss the details of administration. The Cabinet should decide policy and leave details to ministers charged with administration.

I consider therefore that with few exceptions, the Cabinet should be composed of persons whose departmental duties are extremely light. The Cabinet should be formed of persons, not departments. That is to say the persons selected for Cabinet rank should be there because they represent the experience, position or qualities required. Each member should, however, be charged with the general oversight of a particular function of government. These functions I consider to be Justice, Defence, Finance, Foreign Affairs, Imperial Affairs, Economic Affairs, Social Services, and Home Affairs. These, with the Prime Minister and the Secretary for Scotland, whose presence the composition of our island demands, make up a Cabinet of ten.

For the purpose of securing that the decisions of the Cabinet should be conveyed to Ministers in charge of departments, the Cabinet Ministers concerned with Defence, Economics, Imperial Affairs, should preside over standing committees of departmental ministers. They would interpret the policy of the Cabinet to their Ministers and also be the means whereby the view of non-Cabinet ministers were imposed upon the Cabinet.

To continue them in detail: a minister without portfolio, probably the Lord President of the Council or the Lord Privy Seal, would represent Defence in the Cabinet; he would preside over a committee of the ministers for War, Admiralty and Air. It would be his duty to see that the Defence problem was studied as a whole. He would as a rule preside over the committee of Imperial Defence. I am strongly of the opinion that junior ministers, under-secretaries, should be members of the Defence Committee, not only in order to . . .

[The last two paragraphs are written in Attlee's own hand, and the manuscript breaks off at this point, in mid-sentence.]

Appendix IV
Attlee's Style of Government

[It has been said of Attlee that as Prime Minister he 'chaired' his Cabinet but did not 'run' his government; that he never argued with his foreign secretary, his chancellors or his defence ministers, and had neither the will nor the personal authority to control the members of his government in the conduct of their day-to-day affairs.

In fact, although he did not interfere, he scrutinized, advised, checked, sometimes stopped, and was quick to disagree, correct and rebuke if the occasion required. He also praised. So much is well revealed by the six volumes of 'Prime Minister's Minutes', sample extracts of which are reproduced below.

Readers who might wish to test the validity of the selection can look at the Minutes in the Public Records Office in CAB 21 2277 to 22 81 B inclusive (1945-51). As it happens, the first item, a memorandum to the Cabinet, is not a Prime Minister's Minute but is classed as a Cabinet Paper and will be found under CAB/129/Vol. 1/C.P.(45) 144, dated 1 September 1945.]

To the Cabinet   1.9.1945

FUTURE OF THE ITALIAN COLONIES
Memorandum by the Prime Minister

I am not satisfied with the arguments and conclusions as to the future of the Italian Colonies put forward by the Foreign and Colonial Secretaries.

1 At the back of all the argument is the idea of the defence of the British Empire leading to conclusions as to the importance of our retaining control of strategic areas in the Middle East.

2 Quite apart from the advent of the atomic bomb which should affect all considerations of strategic area, the British Commonwealth and Empire is not a unit that can be defended by itself. It was the creation of sea power. With the advent of air warfare the conditions which made it possible to defend a string of possessions scattered over five continents by means of a Fleet based on island fortresses have gone. In the 19th century the passage of the Mediterranean could be secured by sea power with Gibraltar, Malta and Egypt as its bases. In the air age the neutrality, if not the support, of all countries contiguous to the route are needed. This is only one example.

3 The British Empire can only be defended by its membership of the United Nations

596

Organisation. If we do not accept this, we had better say so. If we do accept this we should seek to make it effective and not at the same time act on outworn conceptions. If the new organisation is a reality, it does not matter who holds Cyrenaica or Somalia or controls the Suez Canal. If it is not a reality we had better be thinking of the defence of England, for unless we can protect the home country no strategic positions elsewhere will avail.

4 Apart from strategic considerations, I can see no possible advantage to us in assuming responsibility for these areas. They involve us in immediate loss. There is no prospect of their paying for themselves. The more we do for them the quicker shall we be faced with premature claims for self-government. We have quite enough of these awkward problems already.

5 After the last war, under the system of mandates, we acquired large territories. The world outside not unnaturally regarded this as a mere expansion of the British Empire. Trusteeship will appear to most people as only old mandates writ large.

6 Cyrenaica will saddle us with an expense that we can ill afford. Why should we have to bear it? Why should it be assumed that only a few great Powers can be entrusted with backward peoples? Why should not one or other of the Scandinavian countries have a try? They are quite as fitted to bear rule as ourselves. Why not the United States?

7 British Somaliland has always been a dead loss and a nuisance to us. We only occupied it as part of the scramble for Africa. If we now add Ogaden and Italian Somaliland we shall have a troublesome ward with an unpleasant neighbour in Ethiopia. The French are on the spot in French Somaliland. Why not let them have it if they like? It will be a sop to their pride, and may help them to put up with the loss of their position in the Levant. There would, of course, be the sentimental objection to giving up a piece of the Empire, but otherwise it would be to our advantage to get rid of this incubus.

8 While condominia elsewhere have been failures because they were at points where there was rivalry between the Powers as at Tangier, I see no objection to trying the experiment of international administration in Somalia. It is out of the way of other countries except Ethiopia, where an example of disinterested rule would be good for the Negus who himself could do with some international tutelage.

[*Author's note:* The Cabinet had met to discuss the difference of opinion between Attlee on the one hand, Bevin and the Chiefs of Staff on the other. Two weeks later (CAB 128, 15 September 1945) Bevin and the Chiefs of Staff reiterated their arguments. Attlee summed up strongly against them. He carried the Cabinet with him. As a result of Attlee's resistance to the original recommendations of the Foreign Office, Colonial Office and Chiefs of Staff, Britain was not lumbered with individual trusteeship for Cyrenaica and conceivably for Greater Somalia.]

Ministers 26.10.45

My attention has been called to several instances in which statements made by Ministers in public meetings have been represented in the Press as statements foreshadowing early legislation on matters on which government decisions have not yet been reached.

Great care must be exercised to avoid making statements of this kind which may create awkward situations in the House.

Ministers should also avoid promising White Papers without consulting the Lord President or myself, as their publication may give grounds for a demand for time for further discussion.

My attention has also been drawn to the excessive length of some replies given to oral questions. Unnecessary information takes up the time of the House . . .

Postmaster General   22.12.1945

I note in your report on Wireless Broadcasting that you have 300,000 on the waiting list for telephones. Please render me a monthly return showing progress in filling this need. You are, I take it, being vigilant in seeing that unwanted equipment does not linger with service and other departments in process of reduction.

Secretary of State for Air   7.1.1946

When travelling on the Staines–Basingstoke road this weekend, I found that the main road running through the Hartford Bridge Flats aerodrome is closed at 5 pm, making a detour of 4 miles. I understand that there is little, if any, night flying at this aerodrome.
    It is time that this block on a main road were removed.
    Please let me know why it is necessary to continue this nuisance.

Secretary of State for India   18.1.46

I do not think you can usefully draft a telegram to the Viceroy until after the Cabinet meeting. Your present draft is much too vague as to the function of the Committe of Ministers.

First Lord of the Admiralty
Secretary of State for War
Secretary of State for Air   1.2.1946
REF: CP (46) 38

This paper shows that this year the tonnage allocated for military purposes is still very large. Please review your requirements and let me have proposals for reduction. You should see that only the really necessary shipments should be met and that stocks drawn are not kept above what is really necessary.

Minister of Labour   7.6.1946

In view of the paramount necessity of increasing coal production in order to build up stocks before the winter, and of the threat to many other kinds of economic activity if this is not done, I hope you will intensify in every way possible your efforts to increase the intake of new manpower into the industry. Great difficulties will have to be overcome if a serious shortage next winter is to be averted and the evidence now available leaves no doubt that a determined and concerted drive is necessary . . .

Secretary of State for War   19.6.1946

Thank you for your letter to me of the 18th June about plans for the accommodation of the wives and children of officers and other ranks who go to Germany.
    This seems satisfactory. You can make an announcement on Thursday.

Secretary of State for War   23.6.1946

Refer my conversation with you on delays in the War Office. Please explain why it took you a week for you to answer my M206/46. The contents of your reply seem to have required no research.

Minister of Labour   28.12.1946

I am obliged to you for your Minute of Dec 24 about the cotton industry's decision to adopt a 45 hour week.

As you know, I have been exchanging Minutes with you for some time about the Evershed Report and urging speed in order to meet the shortage of textile supplies, and clearly the decision to adopt a 45 hour week was very relevant to the whole basis of our exchange of Minutes and the matter should, therefore, have been mentioned to me.

But apart from this, I hope you will ensure that in future important developments of this kind are mentioned to me as soon as they begin to take shape.

President of the Board of Trade 29.12.1946

Bevin has suggested to me that it will be well to see if we are getting enough dollars for our exports to USA. He has been given the impression that whisky is being sold cheap to the United States and retailed at £5 a bottle, the profit going to the middlemen.

He also says we are not sending the right things to the United States. Instead of sending articles of which they are short such as white shirts and chintzes, we are sending goods which compete with USA products. Further we sell mainly in the East, whereas the real market is in the Western States where we have the advantage through carriage by sea instead of overland across the American continent.

I should like your comments.

Secretary of State for War 4.3.1947

I attach an extract from a letter I have received from Lord Harlech, which suggests that the War Office might do well to appoint a civilian architectural adviser. I am sure you will admit that his criticisms of War Office buildings have been lamentably true in the past. I should be glad to have your comments on his suggestions for improving the standards.

Secretary of State for War 19.4.1947

I observe that in the Court Martial proceedings in Hamburg on the case of Lieutenant Tuck it was stated that he had been held in solitary confinement for 150 days.

On the 10th April my Private Secretary wrote to yours with a request for information. After a week an interim reply has been sent which merely states that complicated investigations were required and full time had to be given to the Defence to prepare a case... The fact of this officer being kept under close arrest for nearly five months does not seem to have aroused any interest in your department. I am sure there is something seriously wrong here. I should like a full report as soon as possible ... and for other cases pending where people have been under arrest for more than a month.

Minister of Transport
Minister of Town and Country Planning 19.4.1947

When your Bills come to the House of Lords you should be careful before agreeing to any amendments of substance to consider the effect of such a concession on the Party in the House and, where this may be likely to cause trouble, you should seek authority before accepting them.

Secretary of State for the Colonies 2.6.1947

I have read your memorandum on Ceylon. Its wording is one of the worst examples of turgid jargon that I have ever seen. The draftsman seems afraid to use words of less than five syllables.

There must be a revised draft written in plain and straightforward terms.

Foreign Secretary   10.8.1947

I cannot see how the fact of our needing a Commonwealth base in the Middle East gives us any ground for demanding that that base should be in Egypt, a foreign sovereign state. We have no cause to retain more troops than we are allowed under the Treaty. Our only defence is the difficulty of removal in the time at our disposal. Chiefs of Staff must press on with alternative arrangements.

Minister for Economic Affairs   30.8.1947

When I saw De Valera after the meeting of officials he told me that he had got the impression that our officials looked upon Eire from the point of view of 'what can we get out of them and how little can we give?' He was clearly disappointed.

  While we can do little to help Eire at the moment we should show an interest in Eire's future economic development and encourage them to make plans for the future which will integrate with our own.

To Morrison [Who had sent notes on present situation given by Central Economic Planning Staff with the view to them being used as a basis for a public statement.]
                                                                               20.8.1947

To put out these ill-considered and undigested proposals would be to create panic and unemployment and give the country the impression that the government has lost its nerve. The right announcement will be that a series of actions are being taken to implement the government's decisions which will be announced in the course of the next few weeks, beginning with the agricultural programme, the food cuts, etc.

Minister of Defence   19.11.1947

In course of conversation with Field Marshall Smuts this evening, he mentioned a matter which he would like to discuss.

  The Prince Edward Island group of islands which lie some 800 miles south east of the Cape are unoccupied, but are, he thinks, claimed by us. He would like South Africa to take them over as he thinks that they would be useful as an air station on the route from South Africa to Australia, while if they were in other hands they are in dangerous proximity to South Africa.

  Will you please look into this with a view to meeting the Field Marshall one day next week?

Lord Privy Seal   26.11.1947

Thank you for your Minute about bacon. I have asked the Minister of Food to let me have a note on the question you raise.

Secretary of State for Commonwealth Relations   28.11.1947

I was shocked to be faced yesterday with the draft letter submitted under cover of your Minute serial No. 20/47 of the 26 November. I cannot allow a letter so turgid and illiterate to go out to Chifley over my signature.

  I have recast it; and I should like to see it before dispatch lest, in modifying the manner, I have unconsciously modified the matter.

Minister of Defence   30.11.1947: your Minute of Nov. 28 about the dispositions of the Pacific Fleet.

I should like MacArthur to be informed for his personal information. Perhaps a verbal statement by General Gairdner would do. It is by way of keeping him sweet.

President of Board of Trade [Harold Wilson, on his return from the successful trade mission to Moscow]

10.12.1947

I was very glad to read your telegram to the Chancellor. Well done!

Private and Personal:
Parliamentary Secretary, Minister of Civil Aviation   24.12.1947

Your use of the word 'brats' was most unfortunate. I propose to reply to the letter as follows:

> 'Dear Sir,
>   In reply to your letter. Mr Lindgren has informed me that the word to which you have called my attention was used by him in the heat of the moment and that he regrets its use.'

Foreign Secretary   28.1.1948

By your speech in the House on Thursday you have recovered the initiative in European affairs. But I am sure you will agree that, if this is to be retained, we must soon give evidence of practical action to implement the idea of a closer union of Western Europe.
    I have been considering how Ministers can best be kept in touch with the working out of the practical implications of this policy. I think it would be useful if all this could be guided by a small Ministerial Committee under my chairmanship. That might be composed as follows:

> Prime Minister (In the Chair)
> Lord President
> Foreign Secretary
> Chancellor of the Exchequer
> Minister of Defence
> Secretary of State for Commonwealth Relations

    ... I should be glad if you would consider these suggestions and let me have your views.

Minister of Defence: Foreign Secretary   12.4.1948

I have read telegrams COS (ME) 224 and 220/CCL of April 10. I am disturbed at the general position in the Horn of Africa. I think the position should be reviewed at a Defence Committee, if possible, this week.

Minister of Works   28.4.1948

I have been informed that the statue of General Gordon which used to stand in Trafalgar Square has been sent to Sandhurst. I should like to know by whose orders and on what grounds this has been done.

Home Secretary   23.1.1949

I have your Minute of 21 January in which you submit names of persons to be considered for memberships of the Royal Commission on Capital Punishment.
    I am not much impressed by this list, nor I think, will be public opinion.
    I would like to discuss names with you.

Secretary of State for the Colonies (CAB 21 2280)   15.2.1949

Your Minute P.M. (49) 8 of 12 February. [About a committee to examine constitutional developments in the Colonies.]

I do not know any of these people except Margery Perham and John Maude. Is this John Maud of the Ministry of Education, or John Maude, late of the Ministry of Health? If the latter he is too old. I think that this is overweighted academically. I want some practical administrators, including some Labour men.

Minister of Supply   8.3.1949

I am surprised that a Press announcement about the production of plutonium at Harwell was made on 7 March without previous consultation with me, and I should be glad if you would tell me how this came about.

Minister of Defence   18.3.1949

I am not prepared to take your paper on Demobilisation Clothing for National Servicemen at Cabinet in its present form. I shall be glad if you will revise it to include a statement of the Treasury's view, and also some specific recommendations which we can consider.

Foreign Secretary   8.6.1949

I have no confidence in the existing Kuomintang government to make good even in Formosa. I do not object to the proposed reply, but I should need very strong arguments to allow arms to go to Formosa if there is an effective Chinese government on the mainland even if it is Communist. It would, I think, have severe repercussions on the position of Hong Kong. Both islands would then be regarded as jumping-off points for an attack on China.

Secretary of State for Foreign Affairs   22.10.1949

I have read C.P. (49) 207 [Far East and S.E. Asia].

I agree with the analysis except that I rate the chances of the continuance of French rule and influence in Indo-China very low. I think that France has missed the bus.

Minister of Supply   27.11.1949

Your Minute of 25th November. I am not at all attracted by the proposal to make a film for public exhibition about the non-secret aspects of the atomic energy programme. I doubt whether there is any popular demand, and do not see what good you could hope to achieve by it.

Secretary of State for Foreign Affairs   2.5.1950

I have read with interest your P.U.S.C. (49) 62 which sets out the problem very clearly. The following comments occur to me.

Paragraph 14 starts by stressing the strength of the Western Powers' present position. I am not clear as to the basis of this optimistic statement. It is presumably based on the assumption that Russia is not prepared to embark on a hot war. It also assumes that Russia will not try to force the issue in Berlin banking on the reluctance of the West to take up the challenge. I do not think that either of them can be considered as certain.

I do not think that the military position is sufficiently explored in 15(b). I think it unlikely that Germany will settle down without some armed forces. One must consider the tradition of the German State. Without some armed forces a gendarmerie could be used to create clandestinely the framework of armed forces in the future. Is this not already being done in Eastern Germany by the Communists under Russian guidance?

An alternative which is not considered here is being put forward in some quarters, notably by Churchill. I think also some soldiers are in favour of it.

This is the integration of German Forces in a Western Union Force. As I understand the suggestion it is that German armed forces could be integrated with other Western Union Forces in such a way that while adding substantially to their strength, the German counterpart would not be effective as an independent Force. This proposal should be examined.

I do not know how the French would view such a suggestion, but given the German Military tradition, it is worth considering whether it will be possible to sustain total prohibition indefinitely.

Some such plan as is suggested might at some time give the best change of diverting the German military interest into a channel which would make for peace instead of war.

Secretary of State for Commonwealth Relations   6.6.1950

I think it would be much wiser not to deal with the Schuman proposals in your speech at Blackly.

It would be better to leave it alone until it has been debated in Parliament.

Minister of Labour and National Insurance   21.9.1950

Your letter of the 20 September endorsing the draft of your Broadcast.
I think this is good. You might say somewhere something to this effect:

'Don't let these people kid you that they're out to help you. They don't care a brass farthing for you or your wives and children. They're just out to cripple and destroy this country on the orders of their foreign bosses.'

Minister of State for Colonial Affairs   10.10.1950

I have seen the script of your proposed broadcast in the series 'Commonwealth Survey' and have the following comments.

Page 5–6. There is a non sequitur here. The land has been ruined by too many *cattle*. The remedy is to close it to *cultivation*.

Surely it should be to further pastoralisation.

Page 8, line 13, should read 'hitherto' instead of 'to get before'.

Page 9, line 9. I should prefer 'general' to 'universal'. East Africa's not the Universe.

Minister of Defence   2.1.1951

I have seen your paper on the Increase of Capacity for Production of Tanks (D.O. (50) 106).

I shall want to know at what plants tanks were produced during the last war? Who is the present user of these plants? Cannot they revert to tank production?

Sources

I have used sources of three types in the preparation of this biography: unpublished papers both private and official, interviews with Attlee himself and with those who knew him, and the large body of published matter which is now available about British politics and government in the period of Attlee's life. The book is written for the general reader more than for the scholar, and I have thought it best not to burden the text with an apparatus of footnotes and detailed citations. But for those who wish to know what material has been used, the following notes indicate what I have found most useful.

1 Unpublished material

Attlee's private papers are sparse by comparison with those of other twentieth-century prime ministers. They are distributed in three collections. The forty-one boxes deposited at University College Oxford contain mostly political material covering the period 1939 to 1951, including miscellaneous correspondence 1945-51, official Labour Party correspondence 1939-44, correspondence with party members 1945-50, papers on the 1950 and 1951 elections, and speech notes. This collection is now housed at the Bodleian Library, Oxford. Two files deposited at Churchill College, Cambridge, contain an incomplete draft of Attlee's autobiography, *As It Happened*, with some additional material omitted from the published version, and some autobiographical notes. There is also some correspondence with Churchill, written during the war, and miscellaneous notes on government.

A third collection of documents was handed to me by Lord Attlee when he invited me to write this biography. They include Attlee's own record of his experiences in the First World War, genealogical papers, family correspondence, personal correspondence with friends, constituents and colleagues, his school reports, some press cuttings, and his verses.

The collection of letters from Attlee to his brother Tom, written between 1913 and 1960, is the possession of Tom's daughter-in-law, Mrs Margaret Attlee, who kindly allowed me to make photocopies of them.

Attlee kept little official material from his years in government. I have therefore drawn on the resources of the Public Record Office, in particular the Cabinet papers and the Prime Ministerial papers in the PREM class, for additional material. I was much helped at the Office by R.R. Mellor, and his successor, J.S. Fowler. Transcripts of Crown copyright records in the PRO appear by permission of the Controller of H.M. Stationery Office.

2 Interviews

I have drawn heavily on conversations with Attlee himself which took place over a period of years from 1959 to the year of his death, 1967. Most of them took place in the early 1960s, when Attlee was often invited to comment for *The Observer* on books relating to British politics and politicians. I am also greatly indebted to the following political and personal acquaintances of Attlee, who shared their recollections with me:

Dean Acheson
2nd Earl Attlee
Laurence and Lettie Attlee
Lord Avon
Lord Aylestone
Tom Aylward
Canon Charles Bailey
James Callaghan
Alan Campbell-Johnson
Sir John Colville
Lady Alison Davis (Alison Attlee)
Sir Geoffrey de Freitas
Lord Franks
Richard Girouard
Charles Griffiths
J.A. Green
W. Averell Harriman
Lady Felicity ('Flip' Attlee) Harwood
Mrs Nellie Evans

Christopher Hollis
Douglas Jay
Alfred Laker
Jack Lawder
Lord Listowel
Earl of Longford
Malcolm MacDonald
Harold Macmillan
Leonard Miall
Lord and Lady Moyle
Raymond Postgate
Lord Robens
Mrs Harold Shipton (Janet Attlee)
Sir John Smyth
Lord Strauss
Lord Francis-Williams
Lady Willis (Vi's twin sister)
Sir Harold Wilson
Woodrow Wyatt

I must also record a debt to those who held or are holding official positions, who for that reason cannot be named here, who discussed with me their recollections of Attlee as a minister.

3 Published works

I have used published material both as a secondary source for the history of Attlee's times and for the wide range of primary material about Attlee which is now in print. In particular I must acknowledge a debt to the biographers of Ernest Bevin (Alan Bullock); of Herbert Morrison (Bernard Donoughue and G.W. Jones); and of Aneurin Bevan (Michael Foot) upon whose work I have relied for material in the private papers of those politicians. I owe much also to Professor Margaret Gowing's *Independence and Deterrence*, Trevor Burridge's *British Labour and Hitler's War* and Roy Jenkins's *Mr Attlee*.

The unpublished matter, books and articles recorded chapter by chapter below are those which I have found most useful. In every chapter I have made use of the collection of personal papers in my own possession, and of Attlee's autobiography, *As It Happened*; these sources are not listed separately.

Chapter 1 Youth, 1883-1905

Churchill College papers

Roy Jenkins, *Mr Attlee* (Heinemann, 1948)
Mary Attlee, article in *The Leader*, 29 September 1945

Interviews
Laurence and Lettie Attlee
Canon Charles Bailey

Chapter 2 The making of a Socialist, 1906-18

Churchill College papers

Jenkins, *Mr Attlee*

Interviews
Laurence and Lettie Attlee
Mr J.A. Green (South Lancs Regiment)

Chapter 3 Rising Politician, 1912-22

Churchill College papers

Jenkins, *Mr Attlee*

Interviews
Laurence and Lettie Attlee
Tom Aylward
Charles Griffiths
Jack Lawder
Lady Willis

Chapter 4 The New Member, 1922-4

Churchill College papers

G.D.H. Cole, *A History of the Labour Party from 1914* (Routledge and Kegan Paul, 1948)
Hugh Dalton, *Call Back Yesterday* (Muller, 1953)
W.Golant, 'C.R. Attlee in the First and Second Labour Governments', *Parliamentary Affairs* xxvi (1973)
Richard W. Lyman, *The First Labour Government* (Chapman & Hall, 1957)
David Marquand, *Ramsay MacDonald* (Cape, 1977)
Harold Nicolson, *King George V* (Constable, 1952)
Henry Pelling, *A Short History of the Labour Party* (Macmillan, 1961 and 1968)

Chapter 5 Out of Office, 1925-30

Churchill College papers

Earl of Birkenhead, *Halifax* (Hamish Hamilton, 1965)
Marquand, *MacDonald*

James Cameron, information about Anna Aseervathan

Interview
Mrs Nellie Evans

Chapter 6 Minister of the Crown, 1930-1

Churchill College papers

Dalton, *Call Back Yesterday*
Marquand, *MacDonald*
Nicolson, *King George V*

Chapter 7 Labour Divides, 1931-3

Churchill College papers

R. Bassett, *Nineteen Thirty-One* (Macmillan, 1952)
Alan Bullock, *Life and Times of Ernest Bevin* (Heinemann, 1960)
Lord Citrine, *Men at Work* (Hutchinson, 1964)
Cole, *History of the Labour Party*
Colin Cross, *Philip Snowden* (Barrie & Rockcliff, 1966)
Dalton, *Call Back Yesterday*
Marquand, *MacDonald*
Nicolson, *King George V*
Raymond Postgate, *The Life of George Lansbury* (Longmans Green, 1951)
Robert Skidelsky, *Politicians and the Slump* (Macmillan, 1967)

Interviews
Richard Girouard
Malcolm MacDonald
Raymond Postgate

Chapter 8 To the Leadership, 1933-5

Churchill College papers

Bullock, *Bevin*
Citrine, *Men at Work*
Cole, *History of the Labour Party*
Colin Cooke, *Life of Richard Stafford Cripps* (Hodder & Stoughton, 1957)
Hugh Dalton, *The Fateful Years* (Muller, 1957)
Bernard Donoughue and G.S. Jones, *Herbert Morrison* (Weidenfeld & Nicolson, 1973)
Keith Feiling, *The Life of Neville Chamberlain* (Macmillan, 1946)
W. Golant, 'The Emergence of C.R.Attlee as a Leader of the Labour Party in 1935', *Historical Journal* xiii (1970)
Marquand, *MacDonald*

Arthur Marwick, 'Middle Opinion in the Thirties', *English Historical Review* (April, 1964)

Keith Middlemass and John Barnes, *Baldwin* (Weidenfeld & Nicolson, 1969)

Pelling, *Short History of the Labour Party*

Postgate, *Life of George Lansbury*

Skidelsky, *Politicians and the Slump*

A.J.P. Taylor, *English History 1914–1945* (Oxford, 1965)

Interview
    Raymond Postgate

Chapter 9 Taking Charge: 1935–7

Churchill College papers

C.R. Attlee, *The Labour Party in Perspective* (Gollancz, 1937)

Bullock, *Bevin*

Cooke, *Life of Stafford Cripps*

Maurice Cowling, *The Impact of Hitler* (Cambridge University Press, 1975)

Dalton, *Fateful Years*

Feiling, *Neville Chamberlain*

Golant, 'The Emergence of C.R. Attlee'

Kingsley Martin, *Harold Laski* (Gollancz, 1953)

Nicolson, *King George V*

Ben Pimlott, 'The Socialist League', *Journal of Contemporary History* vi, 3 (1971)

Postgate, *Life of George Lansbury*

Chapter 10 Attlee at Home

Interviews
    2nd Earl Attlee
    Laurence and Lettie Attlee
    Lady Alison Davis
    Mrs Nellie Evans
    Lady Felicity Harwood
    Mrs Harold Shipton

Chapter 11 The Approach of War, 1937–9

Lord Avon, *Facing the Dictators* (Cassell, 1962)

Citrine, *Men at Work*

Cole, *History of the Labour Party*

Dalton, *Fateful Years*

Donoughue and Jones, *Morrison*

Iain Macleod, *Neville Chamberlain* (Muller, 1961)

Interview
    Harold Macmillan

Chapter 12 Patriotic Opposition, 1939–40

L.S. Amery, *The Unforgiving Years* (Hutchinson, 1955)

Lord Avon, *The Reckoning* (Cassell, 1965)

Bullock, *Bevin*

Cole, *History of the Labour Party*

Duff Cooper, *Old Men Forget* (Hart-Davis, 1953)

Donoughue and Jones, *Morrison*

Feiling, *Chamberlain*

Macleod, *Chamberlain*

Taylor, *English History 1914–1945*

Betty Vernon, *Ellen Wilkinson* (Croom Helm, 1982)

Chapter 13 Member of the War Cabinet, 1940–2

Churchill College papers

University College papers

Cabinet papers (CAB 65)

Avon, *The Reckoning*

Bullock, *Bevin*

Lord Citrine, *Two Careers* (Hutchinson, 1972)

Dalton, *Fateful Years*

Donoughue and Jones, *Morrison*

A.J.P. Taylor, *Beaverbrook* (Hamish Hamilton, 1972)

Chapter 14 Deputy Prime Minister, 1942

Churchill College papers

University College papers

Cabinet papers (CAB 66, 87)

Paul Addison, *The Road to 1945* (Cape, 1975)

Avon, *The Reckoning*

Bullock, *Bevin*

Angus Calder, *The People's War* (Cape, 1969)

Dalton, *Fateful Years*

Donoughue and Jones, *Morrison*

Michael Foot, *Aneurin Bevan* (MacGibbon & Kee, 1962)

W. Averell Harriman and Elie Abel, *Special Envoy* (New York: Random House, 1975)

Martin, *Laski*

Emanuel Shinwell, *The Labour Story* (Mac-Donald, 1963)

Chapter 15 Deputy Prime Minister, 1943-4

Churchill College papers
University College papers
Cabinet papers (CAB 66, 87)

Avon, *The Reckoning*
Bullock, *Bevin*
T.D. Burridge, *British Labour and Hitler's War* (Deutsch, 1976)
Lord Butler, *The Art of the Possible* (Hamish Hamilton, 1971)
Dalton, *Fateful Years*
Donoughue and Jones, *Morrison*
Foot, *Bevan*
W.K. Hancock and Margaret Gowing, *The British War Economy* (HMSO, 1949)
Harriman and Abel, *Special Envoy*
Harold Macmillan, *The Blast of War, 1939-1945* (Macmillan, 1967)
Roger Parkinson, *Blood, Toil, Tears and Sweat* (Hart-Davis, 1973)
Roger Parkinson, *A Day's March Nearer Home* (Hart-Davis, 1975)
Henry Pelling, *Britain and the Second World War* (Fontana, 1970)
Sir E.L. Woodward, *British Foreign Policy during the Second World War* (HMSO, vol. I 1970, vol. II 1971)
Kenneth Young, *Churchill and Beaverbrook* (Eyre & Spottiswoode, 1966)
Churchill by his Contemporaries (published for *The Observer* by Hodder & Stoughton, 1965)

Interviews
  Lord Avon
  W. Averell Harriman

Chapter 16 The End of the Coalition, 1944-45

Churchill College papers
University College papers
Cabinet papers (CAB 66, 87)

Addison, *Road to 1945*
Bullock *Bevin*
Lord Chandos, *The Memoirs of Lord Chandos* (Bodley Head, 1962)
Dalton, *Fateful Years*

Donoughue and Jones, *Morrison*
Foot, *Bevan*

Interviews
  Dean Acheson
  Sir John Colville

Chapter 17 Into Power, 1945

Churchill College papers
University College papers

Dean Acheson, *Present at the Creation* (New York: Norton, 1969)
Avon, *The Reckoning*
Bullock, *Bevin*
Butler, *The Art of the Possible*
James Byrnes, *Speaking Frankly* (New York, Harper & Row, 1947)
Diaries of Sir Alexander Cadogan, edited by David Dilks (Cassell 1971)
Hugh Dalton, *High Tide and After* (Muller, 1962)
Donoughue and Jones, *Morrison*
Margaret Gowing and Lorna Arnold, *Independence and Deterrence* (Macmillan, 1974)
Harriman and Abel, *Special Envoy*
R.F. Harrod, *Life of John Maynard Keynes* (Macmillan, 1952)
Memoirs of Lord Ismay (Heinemann, 1960)
R.B. McCallum and A. Readman, *British General Election of 1945* (Macmillan, 1947)
Charles L. Mee, Jr, *Meeting at Potsdam* (Deutsch, 1975)
Harold Nicolson, *Diaries and Letters 1945-62*, edited by Nigel Nicolson (Collins, 1968)
Henry Pelling, 'The 1945 General Election Reconsidered', *Historical Journal* 23, 2 (1980)
Harry Truman, *Year of Decision* (Hodder & Stoughton, 1954)
Harry Truman, *Years of Trial and Hope* (Hodder & Stoughton, 1956)
John Wheeler-Bennett and Anthony Nicholls, *The Semblance of Peace* (Macmillan, 1947)
Francis Williams, *A Prime Minister Remembers* (Heinemann, 1961)
Churchill by his contemporaries

Interviews
    Dean Acheson
    W. Averell Harriman

Chapter 18 Cold Warrior, 1945–9

Churchill College papers
University College papers

Acheson, *Present at the Creation*
Avon, *The Reckoning*
Dalton, *High Tide*
Donoughue and Jones, *Morrison*
Michael Foot, *Bevan*, vol. II (Davis–
    Poynter, 1973)
Harold Macmillan, *Tides of Fortune, 1945–
    1955* (Macmillan, 1969)
John Wheeler-Bennett, *King George VI*
    (Macmillan, 1958)
Wheeler-Bennett and Nicholls, *Semblance
    of Peace*
Cards on the Table (Transport House, 1947)

Interviews
    Dean Acheson
    Lord Avon
    Leonard Miall

Chapter 19 Home Affairs, 1945–6

Churchill College papers
University College papers
Cabinet papers (CAB 128; and Prime Min-
    ister's Minutes, CAB 21, 2277)

Acheson, *Present at the Creation*
Dalton, *High Tide*
Donoughue and Jones, *Morrison*
Anthony Howard, in *The Age of Austerity*,
    edited by Philip French and Michael
    Sissons (Hodder & Stoughton, 1963)
Truman, *Years of Trial and Hope*

Interview
    James Callaghan

Chapter 20 Year of Crisis, 1947

Churchill College papers
University College papers
Cabinet papers (CAB 128; and Prime Min-
    ister's Minutes, CAB 21, 2278)
Attlee interview (Granada Television:
    Panther Record, 1967)

Dalton, *High Tide*

Donoughue and Jones, *Morrison*
Foot, *Bevan*
Wheeler-Bennett, *King George VI*
Wheeler-Bennett and Nicholls, *Semblance
    of Peace*
Philip Williams, *Hugh Gaitskell* (Cape,
    1979)

Interviews
    Lord Francis-Williams
    Lord Moyle

Chapter 21 The End of Empire: India

Churchill College papers
University College papers
Cabinet papers (CAB 128; and India Com-
    mittee papers: CAB 134/341–348)

Alan Campbell-Johnson, *Mission with
    Mountbatten* (Robert Hale, 1951; re-
    printed 1972)
F.S.V. Donnison, *British Military Admin-
    istration in the Far East* (HMSO, 1956)
Lord Listowel, 'The Whitehall Dimension
    of the Transfer of Power', *Indo-British
    Review* (1978)
Lord Listowel, *The British Partner in the
    Transfer of Power* (Nehru Memorial Lec-
    ture, 1980)
Nicholas Mansergh, *Survey of British Com-
    monwealth Affairs, 1939–1952* (OUP, 1958)
Nicholas Mansergh and Penderel Moon,
    The Transfer of Power (HMSO, vol. ix,
    1980; vol. x, 1981)
V.P. Menon, *Transfer of Power in India*
    (Princeton, 1957)
Percival Spear, *Modern India* (OUP, 1978)
Lord Wavell, *The Viceroy's Journal*, edited
    by Penderel Moon (OUP, 1973)

Interviews
    Alan Campbell-Johnson
    Lord Listowel

Chapter 22 The End of Empire: Palestine

Churchill College papers
University College papers
Cabinet papers (CAB 128)

Nicholas Bethell, *The Palestine Triangle:
    Struggle Between the British, the Jews and
    the Arabs, 1935–1948* (Deutsch, 1979)

Martin Gilbert, *Exile and Return* (Weidenfeld & Nicolson, 1978)

Ritchie Overdale, 'The Palestine Policy of the British Labour Government 1945–1946', *International Affairs* (July, 1979)

Ritchie Overdale, 'Britain in Palestine II, 1947', *International Affairs* (January, 1980)

Israel Sieff, *Memoirs* (Weidenfeld & Nicolson, 1970)

Chapter 23 A Man and a Leader, 1945–51

Churchill College papers
University College papers

Dalton, *High Tide*
Donoughue and Jones, *Morrison*
Douglas Jay, *Change and Fortune* (Hutchinson, 1980)
Sir George Mallaby, *From My Level* (Hutchinson, 1965)
Williams, *Gaitskell*
Earl Winterton, *Orders of the Day* (Cassell, 1953)

Interviews
  Dean Acheson
  2nd Earl Attlee
  Lord Avon
  Lord Aylestone
  James Callaghan
  Sir John Colville
  Sir Geoffrey de Freitas
  Lady Felicity Harwood
  Christopher Hollis
  Douglas Jay
  Earl of Longford
  Harold Macmillan
  Lord Moyle
  Lord Robens
  Lord Strauss
  Sir Harold Wilson
  Woodrow Wyatt

Chapter 24 Consolidation or Advance? 1948–9

Churchill College papers
University College papers
Cabinet papers (CAB 128; and Prime Minister's Minutes CAB 21; 2279 and 2280)

Dalton, *High Tide*
Donoughue and Jones, *Morrison*
Foot, *Bevan*
Jay, *Change and Fortune*
Williams, *Gaitskell*

Interview
  Lord Avon

Chapter 25 Struggling On, 1950

Churchill College papers
University College papers
Cabinet papers (CAB 128)

Dalton, *High Tide*
Donoughue and Jones, *Morrison*
Foot, *Bevan*
Wheeler-Bennett, *King George VI*

Interviews
  Dean Acheson
  Sir John Smyth
  Sir Harold Wilson

Chapter 26 Downhill, 1951

Churchill College papers
University College papers
Cabinet papers (CAB 128)

Dalton, *High Tide*
Donoughue and Jones, *Morrison*
Foot, *Bevan*
Wheeler-Bennett, *King George VI*
Williams, *Gaitskell*

Interviews
  Lord Avon
  Sir Geoffrey de Freitas
  Hugh Gaitskell
  Lord Moyle
  Lord Robens
  Sir Harold Wilson

Chapter 27 Containing the Storm

Churchill College papers
University College papers

Dalton, *High Tide*
Donoughue and Jones, *Morrison*
Foot, *Bevan*
Williams, *Gaitskell*

Interview
  Sir Geoffrey de Freitas

Chapter 28 Bevan or Gaitskell?

Churchill College papers
University College papers

Dalton, *High Tide*
Donoughue and Jones, *Morrison*
Foot, *Bevan*
Leslie Hunter, *The Road to Brighton Pier* (Barker, 1959)
Macmillan, *Tides of Fortune, 1945–1955*

Williams, *Gaitskell*

Chapter 29 The Last Years

Interviews
  2nd Earl Attlee
  Lady Alison Davis
  Lady Felicity Harwood
  Christopher Hollis
  Alfred Laker
  Lord and Lady Moyle

Index

A VENETIAN AFFAIR

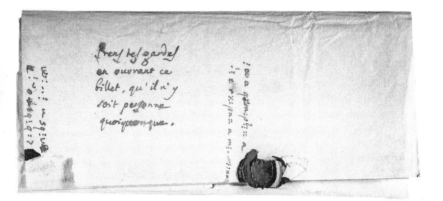

Come hò io vivuto jeri dopo pranzo? Dove ero io a due ore
di notte, cosa facevo alle tre? Cosa sarà di noi oggi dopo pranzo,
questa sera? Questa mattina io vado a buon conto dalla
Contessa Santonini, poi dal Smith. Oggi facilmente non
passerò per casa mia per poter essere a tempo di honorar-
mi *[cipher text]* e *[cipher]* o *[cipher]* o p:o t:u t:e m:u u
s:u pp:a ħ:z: ob:u nn:t+ u :u a s:u ng:i a s:p:t:l:g: u:i q:b:u u:j:u a
ħ:q:l:u a ħ:u *[cipher]* q:i:q:...:..: e :u u o p: w:t:h:u:... Mi dispiace
solamente che in jeri non hò potuto vedere Marieltine
che l'avrei avvisato perché oggi si trovasse da Faustina.
Questo sarà per un altra volta: non vorrei che sospet-
tassi anche questo mio desiderio per uno dei miei soliti
progetti dei quali tu sempre m'incolpi.
Cosa vuoi che ti dica adesso? Avrei assai cose, ma voglio
salvarle per altro tempo. Io son molto contento di te, e
per dir il vero anche di me medesimo che sans aucune
sorte de gêne je peux te sacrifier tous les momens de ma
vie..... Que dis-je sacrifier! oh que ce mot est detestable
a ce propos bien que en bonne langue Françoise, il ne signifie
que simplement dedier.... Io t'amo assai. Ciò che vedrai
adesso non n'è che l'ultimo contrassegno. Mon esprit est toujour
hors de soi même, il est chatouillé de cette aimable coquine......

A Venetian Affair

ANDREA DI ROBILANT

ALFRED A. KNOPF
NEW YORK
2003

Library of Congress Cataloging-in-Publication Data
di Robilant, Andrea, [date]
A Venetian affair / by Andrea di Robilant.
p.   cm.
ISBN 0-375-41181-X
1. Rosenberg-Orsini, Justine Wynne, Grèfin von, 1732–1791.
2. Memmo, Andrea, 1729–1793.   3. Venice (Italy)—Social life
and customs.   I. Title.
DG678.4.D5 2003   2002043438

Endpapers: *Piazza San Marco: Looking East,* by Luca Carlevaris, c. 1722.
Scala/Art Resource, NY. Half title and frontispiece: Courtesy of the author.

In memory of my father,
Alvise di Robilant

A VENETIAN AFFAIR

Prologue

S ome years ago, my father came home with a carton of old letters that time and humidity had compacted into wads of barely legible paper. He announced that he had found them in the attic of the old family *palazzo* on the Grand Canal, where he had lived as a boy in the twenties. Many times, my father had enthralled my brothers and me with stories from his enchanted childhood—there had been gondola rides and children's tea parties and picnics at the Lido, and in the background the grown-ups always seemed to be drinking champagne and giving fancy-dress balls. Equally romantic to us, though much more melancholy, was his account of how my grandparents' lavish and extravagant lifestyle had begun fraying at the edges. By the early thirties, art dealers were dropping by more and more frequently. Large empty patches appeared on the walls. Pieces of antique furniture were carried out of the house. Even the worn banners and rusty swords our fierce ancestors had wrested from the hated Turks were sold at auction. Eventually, my spendthrift grandfather sold off the palace floor by floor, severing the family ties to Venice and leaving my father so bereft that he yearned for his Venetian heritage for the rest of his life. He never lived in Venice again, but even as an older man he continued to make nostalgic pilgrimages to the places of his childhood and especially to that grand old house, which had long ceased to belong to us, but where the family still kept a few old boxes and crates.

The di Robilant family is actually of Piedmontese origin. The Venetian connection was established at the end of the nineteenth century when Edmondo di Robilant, my very tall and rather austere great-grandfather from Turin, married my great-grandmother Valentina Mocenigo, a formidable Venetian *grande dame* with beautiful black eyes and a very sharp tongue. The Mocenigos were one of the old ruling families of Venice—"they gave seven doges to the Republic" my father never tired of repeating to us children. Of course, the glorious days of the Venetian Republic were long gone when my great-grandparents married, but the last Mocenigos still had palaces and money and beautiful paintings. So the impecunious di Robilants moved to Venice after World War I and fairly quickly ran through what remained of the Mocenigo fortune.

My father, having grown up in the fading grandeur of Palazzo Mocenigo, came to revere his Venetian ancestry more than the Piedmontese. To him the box of letters was a small treasure he had miraculously retrieved from his Venetian past. And I remember well the look of cheerful anticipation he had on his face when he arrived at our house in Tuscany and placed it on the dining room table for all the family to see.

The letters were badly frayed and had wax marks and purplish traces of wine on them. They looked intriguing. They were not the usual household inventories that occasionally surfaced, like timeworn family flotsam, in some forgotten recess of the *palazzo* in Venice. We pried them open one by one and soon realized they were intimate love letters that dated back to the 1750s. Some pages were covered with mysterious hieroglyphs that added mystery to my father's discovery. We spent a rainy weekend cracking the strange cipher and trying to make some sense of the first fragments we were able to read. I remember we were wary of delving into secrets buried so long ago. Yet we labored on because the spell was irresistible.

At the end of that long weekend I went back to Rome, where I was then working as a journalist, while my father took on the task of deciphering and transcribing the cache of one hundred or so letters in his possession. What eventually emerged from his painstaking labor was the remarkable love story between our ancestor Andrea Memmo, scion of one of the oldest Venetian families, and Giustiniana Wynne, a bright and beautiful Anglo-Venetian of illegitimate birth. The letters revealed a deep romantic passion that was at odds with the gallant, lighthearted lovemaking one often thinks of as typical of the eighteenth century. It was also, very clearly, a clandestine relationship: the curious-looking dots and circles and tiny geometric figures scribbled across the pages were a graphic testimony to the fear the two lovers must have felt lest their letters fall into the wrong hands.

When my father began to dig around Andrea and Giustiniana's story, he soon found traces of their romance in the public archives in Venice, Padua, and even Paris and London. It turned out that students of eighteenth-century Venice had first become acquainted with the relationship through the writings of Giacomo Casanova, who had been a close friend of both Andrea and Giustiniana. In the first years of the last century Gustav Gugitz, the great Casanova scholar, identified the Mademoiselle XCV who figures prominently in Casanova's memoirs as Giustiniana.[1] Then, in the twenties, Bruno Brunelli, a Venetian historian, found two small volumes of handwritten copies of letters from Giustiniana to Andrea in the archives in Padua. He wrote a book based on those letters and lamented the fact that he had not found Andrea's letters as well. He consoled himself with the notion that they could not possibly have been "as absorbing as Giustiniana's." Judging from her correspondence, he said, it did not appear that Andrea "had the temperament of a great lover."[2]

Other Casanova specialists were drawn to Andrea and Giustiniana. Many combed old bookshops and antique stores hoping to find Andrea's letters, but in vain. The stash my father had stumbled upon as he rummaged in the attic of Palazzo Mocenigo proved to be the missing part of the story—the other voice. Clearly these letters had at some point been returned to Andrea by Giustiniana and preserved by the family; but they were by no means all of Andrea's letters. Many had been burnt, and many more had probably been left to rot and then thrown away. But those we had were rich enough to provide a far more complete picture of the love story—and to disprove Brunelli's contention about Andrea's temperament as a lover.

Once my father finished transcribing the letters, he tried to publish them. Time went by, and I wondered whether he would ever complete his project. My father did not have the natural inclination to put together a book: his real talent was in *telling* a good story. Over the years I heard him talk about Andrea and Giustiniana again and again as he polished their romance into a perfect conversation piece. How vividly he comes back to me now, glass of red wine in hand, charming dinner guests with yet another elegant account of *his* Venetian love story. He revered Andrea, who went on to become one of the last in a long line of Venetian statesmen. And, lady's man that he was, he adored Giustiniana—for her looks, her spirit, and her lively intelligence. My father rooted for them with genuine affection even as he explained to his listeners, who were perhaps not sufficiently well versed in Venetian laws and customs, that it had been *"un amore impossibile"*—an impossible love. It was unthinkable in those days for a prominent member of the ruling elite such as Andrea to marry a girl with Giustiniana's murky lineage. She had been born out of wedlock, her mother's background was checkered at best, and her father was an obscure English baronet and a Protestant to boot. For this reason, my father would explain, they saw each other in secret and often wrote to each other using their strange alphabet. Whereupon he would bring his audience to a peak of excitement by scribbling a few words in the private code of Andrea and Giustiniana.

In the end the treasured letters became, above all else, an excuse for my father to ramble on about his heroes and the city he loved so much. And they probably would have remained just that if events had not taken a sad and completely unexpected turn. In January 1997 an intruder entered my father's apartment in Florence and bludgeoned him to death. It was a senseless, incomprehensible act—a violent end for a gentle, life-loving man. After the funeral my brothers and I stayed in Florence for a week in the hope of being of some assistance to the investigation. During those difficult days the story of Andrea and Giustiniana could not have been further from my mind—until it suddenly appeared in the local newspapers. The carabinieri had found my father's laptop computer open on his worktable, so they had seized it as evidence, together with the floppy disks on which he had transcribed the letters. They went on to leak information about Andrea and Giustiniana to the press.[3] In an even more bizarre twist, the carabinieri sent a few agents up to Venice to check into possible leads.

The murder investigation led nowhere, and two years later it was abandoned. My father's belongings, including Andrea's original letters, the discs with the transcriptions, and the notes on the cipher, were returned to us. By that time I had moved to Washington as the new correspondent for the Italian daily *La Stampa*. But I made a promise to myself that I would do my best to carry out my father's original plan to publish the letters in one form or another once my assignment in the United States was over. My resolve was further strengthened when I found another trove of letters in a library just a short distance away from my new posting as foreign correspondent.

James Rives Childs was an American diplomat and scholar who developed a minor passion for Giustiniana as a result of his studies on Casanova. In the early fifties he was in Venice looking for the unexpected nugget that might enrich his collection of Casanoviana. He came upon a small volume of fifty-four letters from Giustiniana to Andrea, which added another fascinating chapter to their love story. He never got around to publishing them, although a few excerpts appeared in his newsletter, *Casanova Gleanings*. Ambassador Childs died in 1988, having bequeathed his collection—including Giustiniana's letters—to his alma mater, Randolph Macon College, in Ashland, Virginia, a mere two hours away from Washington, D.C. That part of Virginia was already very familiar to me. Childs—the coincidence would have delighted my father—came from Lynchburg, where my mother had grown up (she attended Randolph Macon Women's College). So for me the quest that had begun several years earlier with the letters my father had found in the attic of his childhood home in Venice ended, rather eerily, a few miles up the road from my mother's birthplace in America.

The early 1750s—the period when Andrea and Giustiniana first met—was a particularly poignant moment in Venice's long twilight. The thousand-year-old Republic was less than five decades away from its swift collapse before Napoleon Bonaparte's invading army. Signs of decline had been evident for a long time, and no reasonable Venetian believed the Serenissima, as the Republic had been known for centuries, could reclaim the place it had once occupied among the powerful nations of the world. Yet Venice did not seem like a civilization that was drawing its last breath. On the contrary, it was living a vibrant, even self-confident old age. The economy was growing. The streets were busy, and the stores were filled with spices, jewelry, luxurious fabrics, and household goods. On the mainland, agriculture and stock farming underwent revolutionary changes, and wealthy Venetians built grand villas on their country estates. The population was rising, and Venice, with its 140,000 inhabitants, was still one of the most populous cities in Europe. An experienced and generally conservative government composed of a maze of interlocking councils and commissions (whose members derived from the most powerful families) ran the city in a manner that had altered little for centuries. Venice's ruling class remained an exclusive caste, whose symbol was the Golden Book—the official record of the Venetian patriciate. Its obstinate refusal to let new blood into its ranks, coupled with a deep-seated resistance to change after such a long and glorious history, was weakening its hand. But, as one historian has observed, "the future of this state founded on an intelligent form of paternalism still seemed assured."[4]

The middle years of the eighteenth century also saw an extraordinary flowering of the arts that hardly fits the image of a dying civilization. In fact, it turned out to be the last, glorious burst of Venice's creative genius, and what a feast it was—Tiepolo at work on his celestial frescoes at Ca' Rezzonico, Goldoni writing his greatest comedies, Galuppi filling the air with his joyful music. There had never been more amusements and distractions in Venice. One pictures the endless Carnival, the extravagant balls, and the theaters fairly bursting with boisterous spectators. The stage was flourishing: there were seven major theaters operating in the 1750s and they were filled with rowdy crowds every night. The most popular meeting place of all, however, was the Ridotto, the public gambling house that was famous across Europe. Venetians were in the grip of a massive gambling addiction, and they were especially hooked on faro, a card game similar to baccarat ("faro" stood for "pharaoh," and was the king card). There were several gambling rooms at the Ridotto, with as many as eighty playing tables in all. They opened up on a long, candlelit hall—the *sala lunga*—where an eclectic crowd of masked men and women mingled and gossiped about who was piling up sequins that night and who was piling up debt.

The mask, perhaps more than anything else, was the symbol of those carefree days. It had become, by then, an integral part of the Venetian attire, like wigs and fans and beauty spots. Masks came in two kinds: the more casual black or white *moreta*, that covered only the eyes, and the "cloaked" mask, or *bautta*, which hid the entire head down to the shoulders. Venetians were allowed to wear masks in public from October until Lent, with the exception of the novena—the nine-day period before Christmas—and everyone wore one, from the doge down to the women selling vegetables at the market. The custom added a little mystery and intrigue to everyday life.

The Seven Years' War (1756–1763) between the major European powers would soon come to darken spirits and change the atmosphere in the city. The Venetian Republic, neutral throughout this long conflict, which put an end to French expansionism and marked the rise of Great Britain as the dominant power, was going to feel adrift and ultimately lost after the war. But until then there prevailed a sense that things would go on unchanged as they had for centuries and that life should therefore be enjoyed to the fullest.

In those happier years the house of Consul Joseph Smith, a rich English merchant turned art collector, was one of the busiest and most interesting places on the Venetian scene—a meeting point of fashionable artists, intellectuals, and foreign travelers. It was in Smith's art-filled drawing room at Palazzo Balbi, on the Grand Canal, that Andrea met Giustiniana sometime in late 1753. He was twenty-four; she was not yet seventeen. Andrea was tall and vigorous—handsome in a Venetian sort of way, with the long, aquiline nose that was typical of many patrician profiles. His sharp mind was tuned to the new ideas of the Enlightenment, and he was possessed of the natural self-confidence that came with his class—assured as he was of his place in the Venetian oligarchy. His elders already looked upon him as one of the brightest prospects of his generation. And indeed he must have seemed quite the dashing young man to a girl eight years his junior—wise beyond his age and so much at ease in Consul Smith's rather intimidating *salon*. But Giustiniana too stood out in those assemblies. Behind that innocent, awestruck gaze was a lovely girl brimming with life. She was bright, alert, and possessed of a quick sense of humor. Andrea was instantly taken with her. She was so different from the other young women of his set—familiar, in a way, for after all she was a Venetian born and raised, yet at the same time very distinctive, even a little exotic, not only on account of her English blood but also because of her unique character.

Andrea and Giustiniana met again and again at Consul Smith's. The physical attraction between them was plain to see: soon they could not bear to be apart. But something deeper was going on, too, more magical and mysterious: it was the blending of two souls that were very different and nevertheless yearned for each other. "My passion for him swallowed everything else in my life,"[5] Giustiniana recalled many years later. Andrea too was overwhelmed by his feelings in a way he had never been before.

Alas, the earliest part of their love story has remained blurred. If they wrote letters to each other during that time—as is probable— those letters have never surfaced. But in the later correspondence there are echoes of their first enchanted days together, as they chased each other in the rooms of Palazzo Balbi searching for a darkened corner where they could hold each other and kiss in the full rapture of new love.

From the very beginning the love story of Andrea and Giustiniana bore a note of defiance toward the outside world. Carried along by the sheer power of their feelings, they pursued a relationship in the face of social conventions that were clearly stacked against them. It is true that by the mid–eighteenth century, as pre-Romantic stirrings spread through Venetian society, young men and women who loved each other were beginning to challenge the rigid customs of the aging Republic. The number of clandestine marriages, secretly sanctioned by the Church, saw a considerable increase in those years. But the costs of breaking the rules were still very high. As one historian has put it, "Any patrician who attempted a secret marriage put himself quite inevitably in direct conflict with his family and institutions. By bringing dishonor on himself he renounced any political career and lost the privilege of seeing his own children recognized as members of the patriciate. He might lose all economic assistance from the family and be disinherited."[6]

The clandestine marriages that did take place mostly involved impoverished patricians or members of the lesser nobility, who did not have much to lose by defying their elders. To Andrea, with his family history, his education, his strong sense of duty toward the Republic, the idea of secretly marrying Giustiniana seemed completely irrational. Apart from the shame it would have brought on his family, it was hard to see how the marriage would have survived from a practical point of view. Where would they have lived? What would they have lived on? Despite her youth and her intense emotions, even Giustiniana was realistic enough to see that if they fought the time-honored customs of the Republic they would be crushed.

A few months into their affair, Giustiniana's mother stepped in. Mrs. Anna had one pressing task, which was to find a suitable husband for her eldest daughter. This meant she had to keep Giustiniana at a safe distance from hot-blooded young Venetian patricians—who might try to seduce her for the sake of intrigue and entertainment but would never marry her—while she looked out for a sensible if less glamorous match. She could not allow Giustiniana to wreck her plans with a relationship that in her eyes had no future and would only bring dishonor upon the family. So in the winter of 1754 she told Andrea never to call on Giustiniana at their house again and forbade the two lovers from seeing each other.

Mrs. Anna's ban seemed to spell the end of their forbidden love. But their timeworn letters have continued to surface over the years—in the archives in Padua, in the attic at Palazzo Mocenigo, at Randolph Macon College—to reveal that in fact this was only the beginning of a remarkable love story.

CHAPTER *One*

E arly in the evening Andrea caught up with Giustiniana at the theater. She was radiant in her brocaded evening cape, and the anxious way she was looking around for him made her seem lovelier than ever. She smiled as she saw him, and they exchanged a few signals from a safe distance, apparently without raising Mrs. Anna's suspicions. After the play, Andrea followed mother and daughter to the Ridotto, keeping close to the walls of the narrow streets and casting nervous glances ahead. In the gambling halls, among the late-night crowd of masked men and women hovering around the faro tables, he had a much harder time avoiding Mrs. Anna as she flitted in and out of the shadows in the candlelit rooms. He was terrified she might suddenly come upon him and make a horrible scene. Unnerved by all the difficulties, he finally gave up and went home without having had his cherished moment alone with Giustiniana.

That night he hardly slept, shifting restlessly in his bed, wondering if he had abandoned the Ridotto too abruptly and not made it sufficiently clear to Giustiniana why he was leaving the scene. The next morning he rose early and wrote to her at once:

My beloved,
I am very anxious to know whether your mother noticed any-
thing last night—any act of imprudence on my part—and if you
yourself were satisfied or had reason to be cross. Everything is so
uncertain. At the theater things didn't go badly, but at the
Ridotto—I don't know how it all ended at the Ridotto. As long as
I was in your mother's range I tried to conceal myself—as you
probably saw. And rest assured that when I did not show myself to
you it was because Mrs. Anna was looking in my direction. Once

you left the rooms I no longer saw our tyrant and imagined we had lost her for good—your own gestures seemed to suggest as much.... But I asked around and was told she was still there.... I waited a while to see for myself, and sure enough there she was again. So I resolved to put myself out of her sight. *

Mrs. Anna clearly hoped that, thanks to her intervention, the passion so perilously ignited in the house of Consul Smith would subside before any irreparable damage was done to her daughter. But she had wrenched them apart just as they were falling deeply in love. Their need to be together was stronger than any obstacle she could put in their way; the thrill of their forbidden relationship only drew them closer. As Andrea pointed out to Giustiniana, her mother's relentless watch and the atmosphere of general disapproval she helped to foster around them made their desire to be together "even more obstinate." In fact, there had been no separation to speak of in the wake of Mrs. Anna's pronouncement. The two lovers continued to look for each other ever more frantically, playing a highly charged game of hide-and-seek in the streets of Venice, at the theater, among the crowd at the Ridotto.

It is easy to see Mrs. Anna in the role of the insensitive and overly censorious mother—a tyrant, as the two lovers called her. But she had good reason to be firm. She was a woman of experience who had worked hard to gain respectability, and she well understood the intricate workings of Venetian society, in which the interests of the ruling families were supreme. She was also very much aware of Andrea's special place in that society—and what a formidable opponent he was in her struggle to protect her daughter.

. . .

*In order to avoid burdening the general reader with repetitive notes I have not sourced each quotation drawn from the correspondence between Andrea and Giustiniana (unless otherwise specified), hoping that a short note on the various sets of letters, to be found after the text on page 293, will make it easy enough for readers with a bibliographical interest to know where the quotation comes from. The reader may also wish to know that in translating the letters from Italian into English I did my best to preserve their original eighteenth-century flavor, though I eliminated excessive capitalization and made changes in the punctuation in order to facilitate the reader's ease and comprehension.

The Memmos were among the founding fathers of Venice in the eighth century—historians have even traced the lineage of Andrea's family as far back as the *gens Memmia* of Roman times. There was a Memmo doge as early as the year 979, and over the next eight centuries the family contributed a steady flow of statesmen and high-ranking public servants to the Republic. By Andrea's day they were still very influential in Venetian politics—an elite within the elite, at a time when many other patrician families living in the city had become politically irrelevant.* But they were not among the richest families; by the 1750s, their income had dwindled to about 6,000 ducats a year, and they would have needed at least double that amount to face comfortably the expenditures required of a family of such elevated rank (the wealthiest families had incomes ten times as large). They earned barely enough from their estates on the mainland to live with the necessary decorum at Ca' Memmo, the large family *palazzo* at the western end of the Grand Canal.[1]

Andrea's father, Pietro Memmo, was a gentle, virtuous man long weakened by ill health. His mother, Lucia Pisani, came from a wealthy family that had given the Republic its greatest and most popular admiral—the fierce Vettor Pisani, who had saved Venice from the Genoese in the fourteenth century. Pietro was always a rather remote figure—he and Andrea could find little to say to each other—and Lucia was not especially warm with her children either; her stiff manner was fairly common among the more old-fashioned patrician ladies of that time. Nevertheless, she was by far the more forceful of the two parents, and Andrea felt closer to her than he did to his father. The one person in the family he truly adored was Marina, his older sister by six years: a sensitive, kind-hearted young woman whom he could always confide in. Andrea had two brothers: Bernardo, who was one year younger than him, and Lorenzo, who was four years younger. The three boys, being fairly close in age, spent much of their time together when they were growing up. There was also a younger sister, Contarina.

The family patriarch was Andrea Memmo, Andrea's venerable uncle, known for his courage and strength of character; he had

*Regardless of political influence, twenty-four families were considered founding families of Venice, and of these, twelve traced their roots to early Christianity and called themselves "apostolic." The Memmos were among these twelve.

been imprisoned and tortured by the Turks while he was ambassador to Constantinople in 1713. The senior Andrea served the Republic with great distinction and ended his political career as procuratore di San Marco, the second most prestigious position in government after the supreme office of doge. He went on to become a respected elder statesman whom his peers considered "possibly the greatest expert in Venetian matters."[2] He died at the age of eighty-six in 1754—the same year Andrea and Giustiniana's secret love affair began.

Andrea's uncle ruled over the family with a steady hand for decades, overseeing everything from political alliances to business decisions, from household expenses to the education of the younger Memmos. During his long stewardship, Ca' Memmo was known for its strong attachment to tradition. But it was also considered a progressive house where writers, artists, and composers were always welcome. The new ideas from Paris, especially the political writings of Montesquieu (Venetians had a predilection for anything involved with the machinery of government), were discussed spiritedly at the dinner table.* Their friend Goldoni, the great playwright, was a frequent lunch guest. So was the German composer Johann Adolph Hasse, the "divine Saxon" who had married the diva Faustina Bordoni and ran the music conservatory at the Incurabili, one of the hospices where young orphans were trained as musicians and singers.

Very early on, Andrea senior had chosen his favorite nephew and namesake as his successor. Over the years he instilled in him a sense of duty toward family and nation that would remain with him all his life. And he prepared him for a career in the service of "our wise Venetian Republic, which has seen the largest and wealthiest kingdoms fall over the past ten centuries and more, and yet has managed to stand firm amid everyone else's misfortune."[3]

Andrea received his first formal education from Eugenio Mecenati, a Carmelite monk who worked as preceptor in several patri-

---

*Montesquieu's *Esprit des lois* was published in Venice in 1749. Montesquieu himself had come to Venice to study its laws and system of government. He was run out of town by the inquisitors and legend has it that he threw all his notes into the lagoon as he made his escape toward the mainland. Jean-Jacques Rousseau was also a familiar figure, having been secretary to the French ambassador in Venice in 1743–1744.

cian families. But his mind wasn't really turned on until he met Carlo Lodoli, a fiery and charismatic Franciscan monk. During the 1740s Lodoli established himself as Venice's controversial resident philosopher. He was a brilliant scholar and teacher, equally at ease talking to his students about astronomy, philosophy, or economics. Lodoli's great passion was architecture, a field in which he applied the principles of utilitarianism to develop his own visionary theories about function and form. Wrapped in his coarse habit, the monk had a rugged, unkempt look about him that could be quite intimidating: "The red spots on his face, his wild hair, his unshorn beard, and those eyes like burning coals—he very nearly scared off the weaker spirits,"[4] Andrea wrote many years later. Lodoli's disciples came from the more enlightened families in Venice. He never wrote books but kept students under his spell through the force of his personality and the probing power of his Socratic "conversations." His mission, as he saw it, was to open the mind of young patricians. The Venetian authorities were wary of the strong influence the monk had on his disciples. But Lodoli was not interested in subverting the established political order, as his conservative critics suggested: he wanted to improve it—by improving the men who would soon be called upon to serve the Republic.

Andrea remained devoted to Lodoli all his life, but the moral rigor of the Franciscan, his ascetic lifestyle, could be a little hard going. It is easy to see why Andrea's sensual side was somewhat starved in his company, and why he spent more and more of his time in the splendid house-museum of Consul Smith on the Grand Canal, just a short walk down the street from Ca' Memmo. He spent hours studying the vast collection of paintings and sculptures the consul had assembled over the previous thirty years and happily buried himself in the library—an exceptional treasure trove of classics and moderns in beautifully bound volumes.

Smith had arrived in Venice in the early years of the century, when the city still attracted a good number of foreign merchants and businessmen. He had gone to work for the firm of his fellow Englishman Thomas Williams and had been successful enough to take over the company when Williams retired a few years later and returned to England. Smith went on to build a considerable fortune trading in the East, buying goods from Venetian merchants and selling them on the British market. In 1717 he married Catherine Tofts, a popular singer who had made a name for herself in the London theaters before coming to Venice. Wealthy and well connected, Catherine was certainly the major drawing card of the Smith ménage in the early years of their marriage. But over time she gradually withdrew from society, perhaps never recovering from the loss of their son, John, who died in 1727 at the age of six.

As his business flourished, Smith purchased Palazzo Balbi, which he had rented ever since his arrival in Venice, and commissioned the architect Antonio Visentini, a friend and protégé, to renovate the façade. After some plotting within the English community in Venice and a great deal of pleading with the government in London, he eventually obtained the consular title in 1740. Much to his chagrin, he never became the British Resident (ambassador).

Consul Smith would probably have long faded into history had he not branched out into art and become one of the greatest dealers of his time. He made a habit of visiting artists, many of whom had studios a short walk away from his home. Smith had a good eye, and he delighted in friendly haggling. His collection included beautiful allegorical paintings from Sebastiano Ricci and Giovan Battista Tiepolo, grand vistas by Francesco Guardi, intimate scenes of Venetian life by Pietro Longhi, and several exquisite portraits by Rosalba Carriera. But his special admiration was reserved for Canaletto's clean and detailed views of the city, and over the years he developed a close professional relationship with the great Venetian *vedutista*.

Smith combined the eye of an art lover with the mind of a merchant. He realized he was living at the heart of an extraordinary artistic flowering and was in a unique position to turn his patronage into a profitable business. He commissioned works from his favorite artists and sold them to wealthy English aristocrats just as the fashion of collecting art was spreading. (He was so successful in marketing his beloved Canaletto that the artist eventually moved to London to paint views of the Thames for his growing clientèle.) In the process, Smith built up his own collection, enriching it with important paintings by old masters. Works by Bellini, Vermeer, Rembrandt, Van Dyck, and Rubens adorned the walls of his *palazzo*. Books, perhaps even more than paintings, were his true passion. He purchased valuable editions of the great classics as well as original manuscripts and drawings, and he participated directly in the publishing boom that was taking place in Venice. Smith invested in Giovan Battista Pasquali's printing shop and bookstore, and together they published the works of Locke, Montesquieu, Helvetius, Voltaire, Rousseau, and Diderot and his fellow Encyclopédistes (the first volumes of the revolutionary *Encyclopédie* appeared in 1751). Pasquali's shop soon became a favorite gathering place for the growing Venetian book crowd. "After having enjoyed the fresh air and shared the pleasures of Saint Mark's Square," wrote the French traveler Pierre Jean Grosley, "we would go to Pasquali's shop or to some other bookseller. These shops serve as the usual meeting point for foreigners and noblemen. Conversations are often seasoned with that Venetian salt which borrows a great deal from Greek atticism and French gaiety without being either."[5]

Smith's drawing room was, in a way, an extension of Pasquali's shop in more elegant surroundings. It was the center of the small English community (and it somehow never lost its touch of English quaintness). But more important, it was a place where artists, intellectuals, and Venetian patricians could congregate in an atmosphere of enlightened conviviality. Carlo Goldoni dedicated one of his plays—*Il filosofo inglese*—to Smith. In his flattering introduction, he wrote: "All those who enter your house find the most perfect union of all the sciences and all the arts. You are not a lover who merely gazes with admiration but a true connoisseur who is keen to share the meaning and beauty of the art around him. Your good taste, your perfect knowledge have inspired you to choose the most beautiful things, and the courage of your generous spirit has moved you to purchase them."[6] Andrea spent many happy days at Palazzo Balbi. It was in the consul's library that he learned his Vitruvius, studied Palladian drawings, and pored over the latest volume of the *Encyclopédie* (he got into the habit of copying out long passages to better absorb the spirit of French Enlightenment). Smith, his only child having died so many years earlier, developed a genuine affection for Andrea and as he grew older came to depend on him as a confidant and assistant. By 1750 he was already in his seventies. He had lost his sure touch in business transactions, and his weakened finances would only get worse. Having no heir and less and less money, he conjured up the deal of his lifetime—an ambitious plan to sell his huge art collection and his library to the British Crown.[7] He enlisted Andrea to help him catalogue all his paintings and books.

Under the influence of Goldoni, Andrea also developed a strong interest in the theater. During the season, which ran from October through May, he went to the theater practically every night. He threw himself with enthusiasm into the raucous debate that was raging between conservative and progressive critics. Though Goldoni was twenty years older than Andrea, he enjoyed the young man's company, regarding him not just as a promising member of the ruling class but also as a possible ally in his crusade in favor of plays that were closer to the everyday life of Venetians. In 1750 he dedicated his *Momolo cortesan* to Andrea, telling him he hoped that together they would "rid the stage of the obscene and ill-conceived plays"[8] produced by his conservative rivals. With Goldoni's encouragement, Andrea started to work in earnest on the idea of opening a new theater entirely dedicated to French plays, from Molière's classics to the light comedies of Marivaux. The goal, he said, was "to improve our own theater . . . and lift the common spirit in an honest way."[9]

While Andrea waited patiently for his turn to serve as a junior official in the Venetian government, his days were filled with his work for Smith, his new theater project, and the increasing load of family responsibilities being thrust upon his shoulders by his aging uncle. There was still plenty of time for evening strolls and gallantries in Campo Santo Stefano and Piazza San Marco, late-night discussions in the coffeehouses and *malvasìe* (wine shops that specialized in the sale of malmsey) and even the occasional trip to the Ridotto—though Andrea was never much of a gambler and went there mostly to meet friends and survey the scene.

Among his new friends was Giacomo Casanova, who returned to Venice in 1752 after his first trip to Paris. He and the three Memmo brothers were often seen together at one of the popular *malvasìe,* where they drank until late, played cards, and boisterously panned the latest play by the Abbé Pietro Chiari, Goldoni's chief conservative rival. Andrea's mother was not happy about her sons' friendship with Casanova. She saw him as a dangerous atheist with low morals who was bound to corrupt her children, and she alerted the authorities through her political connections. It turned out that the Inquisitori di Stato—the secretive three-member committee that oversaw internal security—viewed Casanova much in the same light and were already compiling a hefty dossier on him. Indeed, the band of merry revelers was being watched by the few shopworn informers still on the government payroll, one of whom confidently explained in his report that what bound Casanova and his friends was the fact that "they are philosophers of the same ilk . . . Epicureans all."[10]

In spite of his busy life and his many distractions, Andrea's sense of duty to the Republic was so ingrained in his mind that he saw his passion for architecture, his love of the theater, and his knowledge of painting and drawing not as ends unto themselves but as additional endowments that he would put to practical use during his public service. It did not occur to him to seek a different road from the one his uncle Andrea had set for him. He clearly considered marriage from the same perspective. Before meeting Giustiniana, Andrea had enjoyed a number of affairs. He loved the company of women and from a young age was much in demand among his female friends—he was also quite a dancer, which helped. But he had had no great romance or lasting relationship. He knew and accepted the fact that he was bound to marry a young woman from his own social class and that the families would seal the marriage after long negotiations that would have little to do with the feelings of the bride and the groom. Everything young men like Andrea had been taught at home "underscored the irrationality of choices made solely on the basis of sentimental feelings."[11]

Andrea's world—rich and varied and challenging but also largely predictable—was suddenly shaken up when Giustiniana stepped into it in late 1753. She came from another sphere entirely, having just returned with her mother and siblings from London, where they had traveled to collect the family inheritance after the death of Sir Richard, her beloved father. During her yearlong absence, she had blossomed into a lively and very attractive young woman. The Wynnes had a two-year, renewable residency permit; they were not Venetian citizens and therefore, like all other foreigners, had to obtain a special authorization to stay in the city. They settled in a rented house in the neighborhood of Sant'Aponal and at first led a quiet life, mostly within the small English community.

Sir Richard Wynne had left his native Lincolnshire distraught after the death of his first wife, Susanna. He journeyed across Europe and arrived in Venice in 1735 "to dissipate his affliction for the loss of his lady,"[12] as Lady Mary Wortley Montagu, famed and restless English traveler disapprovingly put it during one of her many stays in Venice. He was soon introduced "by his gondolier" to Anna Gazzini, a striking twenty-two-year-old Venetian with a less-than-immaculate past. Anna had actually been born on Lefkos, a Greek island in the Ionian Sea, where her father, Filippo Gazzini, had once settled to trade, but the family returned to Venice when she was still a little girl.

Anna became Sir Richard's lover soon after they met. Two years later, she gave birth to a baby girl who was baptized Giustiniana Francesca Antonia Wynne on January 26, 1737, in the Church of San Marcuola. Sir Richard doted on his daughter. He did not return to England, married Anna in 1739, and legalized Giustiniana's status six years later. (The legalization papers refer to Anna's father as "Ser Filippo Gazzini, nobleman from Lefkos,"[13] but this belated claim to nobility had a dubious ring to it even back then.) Anna gave birth to two more daughters: Mary Elizabeth in 1741 and Teresa Susanna in 1742, known as Bettina and Tonnina. Their first son, Richard, was born in 1744, followed by William in 1745. A fourth daughter, Anna Amelia, was born in 1748 and died two years later.

Mrs. Anna must not have been much fun to be around. Perhaps to atone for sins of her youth, she became a fierce Catholic who dragged her children to church and pestered her Anglican husband endlessly to convert. She was a strict disciplinarian, bent on giving as traditional an education as possible to Giustiniana and her younger brothers and sisters: music, dance, French, and little else. Sir Richard was quite content to leave the upbringing of the children to his wife and retreat to his well-stocked library. As his gout worsened, he withdrew from family life even more. Many years later, Giustiniana remembered him sitting with a book in his favorite armchair "the six months of the year he didn't spend in bed."[14]

Despite his poor physical condition, Sir Richard developed a close bond with Giustiniana. They shared a love of literature, and he gave her the keys to his library. From a young age she read eagerly but with no guidance or method, moving randomly from travel books to La Fontaine's fables to heavy-going tomes such as Paolo Sarpi's history of the Council of Trent—a book the Inquisition had banned for its sympathetic view of the Reformation. Giustiniana was caught reading it secretly. From the little we know of Sir Richard, he must have chuckled at his daughter's temerity. Anna, on the other hand, had a fit and threatened to lock Giustiniana up in a convent.

Sir Richard died in 1751, and the following year Mrs. Anna dragged her five children to London to claim their inheritance. It was a long, tedious journey. Many years later, Giustiniana would remember only the dirty hotels, the bad food, and "all those churches [in Germany] so heavy with ornaments." But she loved London—"the parks, the noise in the streets, the pretty hats . . . and the general air of opulence"—and she would have gladly stayed on. "I had learned English well enough, was rather good at handling a fork, and was expecting to put my new skills to good use."[15] Mrs. Anna, however, was there for the money. When she finally got her hands on some of it, thanks to the intercession of the children's guardian, Robert d'Arcy, Earl of Holderness, a former British Resident in Venice, the family packed up once more and headed home—this time taking the more pleasant route, via Paris.

Giustiniana was not yet sixteen when she arrived in Paris with her mother and her brothers and sisters. But she did not go unnoticed during her brief stay. Casanova met her in the house of

Alvise Mocenigo, the Venetian ambassador. Forty years later, he still had a vivid memory of that first encounter. "Her character," he wrote in his memoirs, "was already delineated to perfection in her beautiful face."[16] Giustiniana loved Parisian life—"the theater, the elegance of men, the rouge on women's cheeks"[17]—but Mrs. Anna was anxious to get back to Venice, so they made their way home, taking with them a French governess, Toinon, who was much loved for her skill in combing the girls' hair.

The return of the Wynne sisters—*"le inglesine di Sant'Aponal,"*[18] as they quickly became known—generated a certain amount of excitement among the young men in town. Sure enough, Casanova—who had also returned to Venice in the meantime— came knocking at their door shortly after they had settled in, claiming that he had fallen in love with Giustiniana. Mrs. Anna, aware of his reputation and keen to keep her daughter out of trouble, turned him firmly away. (In his *History of My Life*, Casanova claimed that Giustiniana then wrote him a charming letter "which made it possible for me to bear the affront calmly."[19]) Mrs. Anna had every intention of keeping her daughters on a very short leash, and Giustiniana, who was just beginning to enjoy the pleasures of society, discovered, to her dismay, that their life in Venice "had been reduced to a small circle indeed." Much of their time was spent at home, "where we went on about Paris and London."[20] It was all rather glum.

The house of Consul Smith, one of the few Mrs. Anna allowed her daughters to frequent, was their link to the world. The consul, who had known Sir Richard well, was one of the most prominent foreign residents in town. He had seen the Wynne children grow up and had promised his old friend he would watch over his family and help Mrs. Anna sort out her finances. Palazzo Balbi became a second home to the young Wynnes, a place removed from their dreary house at Sant'Aponal, filled with beautiful objects, where the conversation had a cosmopolitan quality that reminded them of Paris and London. The consul, for his part, looked upon the Wynne children with avuncular affection. He was especially pleased with Giustiniana, who always brought a breath of fresh air to his house. "Mister Smith shared with me his love for his paintings, his antiquities, his library in order to enrich my passion for learning,"21 she later reminisced. One suspects he also rather enjoyed parading through his magnificent rooms with such a lovely young girl on his arm.

During one of her visits to Palazzo Balbi the consul introduced Giustiniana to his dashing young assistant. As soon as Mrs. Anna heard about her daughter's infatuation, she became very anxious.

Since the death of Sir Richard, she had lived in the fear that the respectability she had so stubbornly built up over the years might abate, leaving her and her family exposed to insidious and materially damaging forms of social discrimination. Her fear was well founded. Even in the relatively tolerant atmosphere of eighteenth-century Venice, many people still made a point of remembering that Lady Wynne was in fact the daughter of a "Greek" merchant. And there were lingering rumors about the amorous adventures of her youth: some even murmured that she had given birth to a child before taking up with *il vedovo inglese*—the English widower. Now she was a widow herself, living in a rented house with five children and with past sins to hide, and it is easy to see why she felt her position in society was so precarious—all the more so since she was in Venice at the pleasure of the authorities. Her residency permit might not be renewed or might even be revoked. So she had to act judiciously to maintain the standing Sir Richard had bequeathed to her.

However detestable her unyielding attitude must have seemed to the two lovers, it was certainly justified in the eyes of the English community. Consul Smith was fond of both Andrea and Giustiniana, but he was a practical man. When Andrea confided in him he sympathized with the lovers to a point. Nonetheless, he was very much on Mrs. Anna's side. The few Venetian families with whom the Wynnes socialized also supported her—especially the powerful Morosinis, with whom the Memmos had a long-running political feud and whom Andrea detested. But her chief ally, as opposed as they were in character and inclination, was Andrea's mother. Lucia saw, perhaps more clearly than the rest of the Memmos, the material disadvantages that a union with Giustiniana would bring to an old house which needed to reinvigorate its weak finances. And she feared the political damage the Memmos would suffer if her eldest and most promising son ever betrayed the family and crossed the inquisitors by marrying a woman beneath his rank.

The difference between the two mothers was that Lucia simply wanted to make sure Andrea did not get it into his head to marry Giustiniana. If in the meantime he dallied with her, as young men often did before settling down, it was no great worry to her and would not damage his future prospects. Mrs. Anna, on the other hand, was fighting a daily battle to prevent any contact between the lovers that might taint the family's reputation and jeopardize her daughter's chances of a respectable marriage.

Mrs. Anna was losing the battle. Andrea's courtship was assiduous, visible to everyone, and highly compromising. He saw Giustiniana every day at the Listone in Piazza San Marco, where Venetians gathered for their evening stroll, and often later on as well, at one of the theaters. He frequently moored his gondola to the narrow dock below the Wynnes' house and called on Giustiniana in full view of the family. In the winter of 1754 Mrs. Anna finally confronted him. She caused a terrible scene, declaring Andrea persona non grata in their house and making it clear she never wanted to see them together again. All communication was forbidden: letters, messages, the merest glance. It had to finish, she yelled—and sent him on his way.

News of Mrs. Anna's dramatic stand traveled quickly around town. Andrea referred to the scene as his *cacciata funesta*[22]—his fateful banishment, and the starting point of all their misery.

Mrs. Anna was a fierce watchdog, always on the alert and obsessively suspicious. She kept a close eye on her eldest daughter and did not let her go out without a chaperon—usually herself. Her spies were planted wherever the lovers might seek to escape her gaze, both within the English set and among Venetian families, and she kept her ears constantly pricked for gossip about the lovers. Venice was a small world. Everyone knew who was losing his fortune at the Ridotto on a particular night and who was having an affair with whom. Andrea and Giustiniana were aware of the risk they were taking in defying Mrs. Anna's ban; they had to be extremely careful about whom they spoke to and what they said. At a deeper level, they knew the future offered little promise of an end to their difficulties. But it was too soon, and they were too young, to worry about the future. For all the trouble their love had already caused, only one thing mattered to them in the winter and spring of that year: exploiting every opportunity to be together. Just as Mrs. Anna resorted to the Venetian arts of intelligence, Andrea set up a small network of informers to obtain daily information about Giustiniana's movements. His chief spy was Alvisetto, a young servant in the Wynne household, who was not always dependable because his fear of Mrs. Anna was sometimes stronger than his loyalty to his secret paymaster. He had the unfortunate habit of disappearing during his missions, leaving Andrea flustered and clueless on a street corner or at the side of a bridge. "Alvisetto did not make it to our appointment and I went looking for him all morning in vain," he complained. "Poor us, Giustiniana. Sometimes I lose all hope when I think in whose hands we have put ourselves."

Alvisetto was also the chief messenger, and he shuttled back and forth between Andrea and Giustiniana with letters and love notes. Occasionally, the gondoliers of Ca' Memmo would moor at a dock near the Wynnes' to drop off or pick up an envelope. If Mrs. Anna was at home, the two lovers would fall back on "the usual *bottega* for deliveries," a general store around the corner from Giustiniana's home, run by a friendly shopkeeper. When Andrea's message could not wait—or if the urge to see her was irrepressible—he would appear at the window of Ca' Tiepolo, the imposing *palazzo* across a narrow waterway from the Wynnes' more modest house.

Ca' Tiepolo belonged to one of the oldest and grandest Venetian families. Its wide neoclassical façade stood majestically on the Grand Canal. From the side window of the mezzanine it was possible to look directly across to the Wynnes' balcony. The ties between the Tiepolos and the Memmos went back many centuries. Andrea was a good friend of the young Tiepolos and especially close to Domenico, better known by his nickname Meneghetto, who was among the few to know from the start that Andrea's love affair with Giustiniana was continuing in secret. Meneghetto was happy to help, and Andrea often dropped by after sending Giustiniana precise instructions. "After lunch," he advised her in one note, "find an excuse to come out on the balcony. But for heaven's sake be careful about your mother. And don't force me to edge out as far as the windowsill because she will certainly see me."

Andrea's portable telescope was very useful. He would point it in the direction of Giustiniana's balcony from a *campiello*, a little square, across the Grand Canal, to check whether she was at home or to find out whether she might be getting ready to go out or, best of all, to watch her as she leaned lazily over the balcony, her hair wrapped in a bonnet, watching the boats go by. When he observed her from such a distance—about a hundred yards—Giustiniana was not always aware Andrea was spying on her. "Today I admired you with my *canocchiale* [telescope]," he announced to her mischievously. "I don't really care if your mother saw me. . . . After all, the rules merely state that I cannot come into your house and that I cannot write to you."

From a purely technical point of view he was also within bounds when, thanks again to the benevolence—and the sweat—of his gondoliers, he came down the Grand Canal and signaled to Giustiniana from the water. On days when she was confined to the house and they had no other way of seeing each other, Andrea's sudden appearance at her neighbor's window or the familiar plashing of the Memmo gondola down below was a welcome consolation. "Come by the canal as my mother doesn't want me to go out," she would plead. "And make an appearance at Ca' Tiepolo as well, if you can."

They developed their own sign language so they could communicate from a distance during the evening walk at the Listone or at the theater or, later in the night, at the gambling house. "Touch your hair if you're going to the Ridotto," he instructed her. "Nod or shake your head to tell me whether you plan to go to the piazza." These little signals sometimes caused confusion if they were not worked out in advance. They also had to be given very discreetly, lest they set off Mrs. Anna's alarm bells. "When you left the theater," Andrea wrote anxiously, "you signaled something to me just as your mother turned around, and I think she might have noticed that. If this were the case it could damage us, since she might also have noticed all the other gestures we had made to each other from our boxes." Despite his occasional burst of bravado, Andrea remained deeply worried not just by what Mrs. Anna might have seen but also by what she *thought* she might have seen. He went to such extremes to avoid creating false impressions that he sometimes sounded like an obstinate stage manager. "You must realize that if your mother catches you laughing with someone she can't see, she will assume that you are laughing with me," he once said to her in a huff. "So try to be careful next time."

Andrea fretted constantly about how dangerous it was to write to each other. If their correspondence ever fell into the wrong hands, there would be an explosion "that would reduce everything to a pile of rubble." Still he deluged Giustiniana with letters and notes, often filling them with practical advice and detailed descriptions of his frantic chases around town. "We are completely mad. . . . If only you knew how afraid I am that your mother might find out we are seeing each other again."

It was a glorious adventure. There were times when they managed to get close enough to steal a quick embrace in an alcove at the Ridotto or in the dark streets near the theaters at San Moisè, and the thrill was always powerful. "Last night, I swear," Andrea wrote to his beloved the morning after one of these rare encounters, "you were so heated up, oh so heated up, such a beautiful girl, and I was on fire." But in the beginning they tended to hold back. They made their moves with deliberation. They kept each other at a safe distance: lovemaking was mostly limited to what their eyes could see and what their eyes could say.

It is easy to imagine how, in a city where both men and women wore masks during a good portion of the year, the language of the eyes would become all-important. And what was true in general was especially true for Andrea and Giustiniana on account of the rigid restrictions that had been imposed on them. Andrea was being very literal when he asked anxiously, "Today my lips will not be able to tell you how much I love you. . . . But there will be other ways. . . . Will you understand what my eyes will be saying to you?" What their eyes said was not always sweet and not always clear. With such strong emotions at play, it could take days to clear up a misunderstanding precipitated by a wrong look or an averted gaze. One night, Andrea returned to Ca' Memmo after a particularly frustrating attempt to make contact with Giustiniana. It had taken him all evening and a great deal of effort and ingenuity to find her at one of the theaters. Yet in the end she had displayed none of the usual complicity that made even the briefest encounter a moment of joy. In fact, she had been so annoying as to make him wish he had not seen her at all:

> *Yesterday I tried desperately to see you. Before lunch the gondoliers could not serve me. After lunch I went looking for you in Campo Santo Stefano. Nothing. So I walked toward Piazza San Marco, and when I arrived at the bridge of San Moisè I ran into Lucrezia Pisani!* I gave her my hand on the bridge, and then I saw you. I left her immediately and went looking for you everywhere. Finally I found you in the piazza. I sent Alvisetto ahead to find out whether you were on your way to the opera or to the new play at the Teatro Sant'Angelo, so that I could rush over to get a box in time. Then I forged ahead and waited for you, filled with desire. Finally you arrived and I went up to my box so that I could contemplate you—not only for the sheer pleasure I take in admiring you but also in the hope of receiving a sign of acknowledgment as a form of consolation. But you did nothing of the sort. Instead you laughed continuously, made loud noises until the end of the show, for which I was both sorry and angry— as you can well imagine.*

A few days later Andrea tracked her down after yet another chase along crowded streets and across canals. This time the reward was well worth the pursuit:

> *I caught sight of your mother and hoped you would be with her. I looked for you left and right. Nothing. Your mother left, I followed. She went to San Moisè, I went to San Moisè. In fact, I got so close to her that we would have bumped into each other at the entrance of a* bottega *if I had not been so quick. . . . [Later] I waited in vain for Alvisetto, whom I had instructed to follow your mother. . . . Then I got your letter telling me that you would be going to San Benetto, so I rushed over only to realize with regret*

*Andrea's cousin by marriage and a close friend.

that you had already arrived and that the opera had begun. . . . Oh Lord, what will Giustiniana say. . . . Let's see how she will treat me. . . . Goodness, there she is, that naughty girl [who wouldn't look at me] the other evening. . . . Will she look at me this time or won't she. . . . Come, look this way my girl! . . . And little by little I began to feel better. And then much better when I moved into that other box because I could see you and you could see me so well and with no great danger that your mother might notice every little gesture between us.

As an overall strategy, Andrea felt it was important to convince Mrs. Anna that the love between him and Giustiniana had indeed subsided and that she could finally let her guard down. It would be easier for them to find ways to see each other. So whenever Mrs. Anna took her daughter to a place where there was a good chance they might see him, Giustiniana was to feign complete disinterest:

Sometimes, in taking risks, one must be willing to be la dupe de soi-même. *So arrange things in such a way that she will feel she is forcing you to go to all the places where she knows you might run into me, such as San Benetto or the Ridotto. . . . And when the weather is nice, show little interest, even some resistance, to taking a walk to the square. . . . Believe me, our good fortune depends on the success of our deception. . . . To avoid coming to San Benetto, all you have to do is tell her you don't feel well. As for the Ridotto, you can say, "In truth, Mother, it bores me too much. Besides, we have no one to speak to and I don't feel like playing [cards]. And we don't make a good impression anyway, walking around with no other company. So let me go to bed." And if she refuses and takes you out with her, you will see me and she will say, "Giustiniana doesn't fret about Memmo anymore."*

In public Andrea and Giustiniana behaved like two strangers. Yet if their relationship was ever to develop, if they were to make arrangements in order to meet somewhere safely and actually spend time together, they were going to need more reliable allies than Alvisetto—friends willing to take the risk of giving them cover and providing them with rooms where they could see each other in private. Andrea worked hard to identify those who might be most useful to them. He gave precise instructions to Giustiniana as to how she should behave to bring this or that friend over to their side. But his instructions were not always clear. When Giustiniana innocently told a potential ally that she no longer loved Andrea when in fact Andrea had asked her to say the opposite, he gave her a sharp rebuke: "As soon as I do a good piece of work, you ruin it for me. The truth is . . . and I am very sorry to have to say this, you have not been up to my expectations."

Andrea could be equally hard when he thought Giustiniana was not keeping enough distance from possible enemies. He was wary of the young Venetian nobles who hung around the Ridotto and who delighted in gossip and intrigue. It was important not to give them a reason to unleash their malicious tongues. As a rule, he explained to Giustiniana, "it is good for us to have the greatest number of friends and the least number of enemies." But there was no need to be closer to that crowd than was strictly necessary. And he criticized her when he saw her displaying too much friendliness to acquaintances he did not consider trustworthy.

He was especially suspicious of the Morosinis, who had always sided with Mrs. Anna in her battle against the two lovers—merely to spite him, Andrea thought. The Wynnes were often lunch guests at Ca' Morosini on Campo Santo Stefano, and Giustiniana's persistent socializing with the enemy infuriated Andrea. She had to choose, he finally said to her, between him and "those Morosini asses":

> *I know it is a lot to ask, but I can ask no less. . . . I must put you through this test, and I shall measure your love for me by it. . . . Giustiniana, I shall be very disappointed if you disregard my wish. I have never met anyone so impertinent and so false toward both of us. . . . They like you merely because you amuse them. . . . By God, you will not be worthy of me if you lower yourself to the point of flattering these . . . stupid enemies of mine . . . these rigid custodians of Giustiniana who spy for your mother. . . . They are evil people with no human qualities and no respect for friend-*

*ship. . . . Forgive me for speaking this way to you, but I am so
angry that I cannot stand it anymore.*

In the early stages, Andrea had a patronizing tone toward Giustiniana and a tendency to take control of every aspect of their relationship. He was, of course, several years older than she, and it was fairly natural that he should take the lead while she deferred to his judgment. But over the months she grew more confident in her ability to conceal and deceive. And in spite of Andrea's occasional hectoring, she began to enjoy plotting behind her mother's back. She took a more active role in planning their meetings and often marveled at her own audacity: "Truly, Memmo, I do not recognize myself. I do things I never would have done. I think in ways so different that I do not seem to be myself anymore."

It was Giustiniana who eagerly informed Andrea that N., a friend on whom they had worked hard to bring over to their side, had finally agreed to let them meet at his *casino,* one of the little pleasure houses that were all the rage in those years and were Venice's very practical answer to a diffuse desire for comfort and pleasure. (There were as many as 150 such *casini* in the city, which were used as boudoirs, as seditious salons, and—quite often—as discreet love nests.) "I've made arrangements for Friday," she wrote self-confidently. "We can't see each other before. I didn't feel I could press him and so I let him choose the date. He has become my friend entirely and confides his worries to me and even vents his domestic frustrations."

Their excitement grew every day in anticipation of the moments they would spend together. It was not enough anymore to exchange loving glances and signals from afar. If Giustiniana had become much bolder in just a few weeks, it was because her yearning was now so powerful. She longed to be kissed by Andrea, to be held in his arms. And their scheming was finally producing results. Here is Giustiniana, three days before their secret appointment at N.'s *casino:*

*Friday we shall meet—at least we know as much. But my
God, how the time in between will seem interminable! And afterward what? Afterward I shall think about our next meeting so*

*that I shall always be having sweet thoughts about you. . . . Tell
me, Memmo, are you entirely happy with me? Is there any way I
can give you more? Is there something in my behavior, in my way
of life that I might change to suit you better? Speak, for I shall do
anything you want. I cannot think of anything more precious than
to see you happy and ever closer to me. I never thought it was possible to love with such violence.*

The following evening Alvisetto appeared in Giustiniana's
room bearing a reply from her lover. "My soul," Andrea wrote,
"what a complete delight it will be. Love me, adore me. . . . I
deserve it because I know your heart so well. Oh Lord, I am so
dying to see you that I am jumping out of my skin." Alvisetto
also handed to Giustiniana a small, delicately embroidered fan—
a gift to make the waiting more bearable. In order to avoid raising Mrs. Anna's suspicions, Andrea suggested that Giustiniana ask
her aunt Fiorina to pretend the fan was for her. In the past Mrs.
Anna's sister had shown a certain amount of sympathy for her
niece's predicament. Andrea, always in search of reliable allies,
felt this subterfuge would not only allay whatever doubts Mrs.
Anna might have about his gift but also give them a sense of how
much Aunt Fiorina was prepared to help them in the future.

On Thursday, the day before their meeting, Alvisetto delivered
a long, tender letter to Andrea:

*And so, my dear Memmo, tomorrow we shall be together. And
what, in the whole world, could be more natural between two people who love each other than to be together? I could go on forever,
my sweet. I am in heaven. I love you. I love you, Memmo, more
than I can say. Do you love me as much? Do you know I have this
constant urge to do well, to look beautiful, to cultivate the greatest possible number of qualities for the mere sake of pleasing you,
of earning your respect, of holding on to my Memmo. . . . Be
warned, however, that your love for me has made me extremely
proud and vain. . . . Where does one find a man so pleasant, so at
ease in society, yet at the same time so firm, so deeply understanding of the important things in life? Where does one find a*

*young man with such a rich imagination who is also precise and
clearheaded in his thinking, so graceful and convincing in expressing his ideas? My Memmo, so knowledgeable in the humanities,
so intelligent about the arts, is also a man who knows how to dress
and always cuts quite a figure and knows how to carry himself
with grace . . . he is a man who possesses the gift of being at once
considerate and bold. And even if at times he goes out of bounds,
he does it to satisfy the natural urges of his youth and his character. And therein lies the path to happiness. You are wild as a
matter of principle, as a result of hard reasoning. Aren't you the
rarest of philosophers? . . . And what have you done, what do you
do to women? Just the other day N. said to me: How did you
manage to catch that fickle young man? And I was so proud,
Memmo.*

As for the fan, she added, "I will ask Fiorina to accept it in my
place. I don't know whether she is on our side or not, but at least
she seems willing to fake it."

The morning after their meeting at N.'s, Giustiniana, enthralled
by the sweetest memories of the previous evening, wrote to
Andrea entirely in French—not the language she knew best but
the one she evidently felt was most appropriate in the lingering
afterglow of their reunion:

*Ah, Memmo, so much happiness! I was with you for close to
two hours; I listened to your voice; you held my hand, and our
friends, touched by our love, seem willing to help us more often.
After you had left, N. told me how much you love me. Yes, you do
love me, Memmo, you love me so deeply. Tell me once more; I
never tire of hearing you say it. And the more direct you are, the
more charmed I shall be. The heart doesn't really care much for
detours. Simplicity is worth so much more than the most ornate
embellishments. You are the most charming philosopher I have
ever listened to. . . . If only I could be free . . . and tell the world
about my love! Ah, let us not even speak of such a happy state.
Farewell, I take leave of you now. When shall I see you? Tell me,
are you as impatient as I am?*

She added teasingly:

Oh, by the way, I have news. My mother received a marriage proposal for me from a very rich Roman gentleman. . . . Isn't it terrible, Memmo? Aren't you at least a little bit jealous? And what if he is as nice as they say . . . and what if my mother wanted him. . . . I can't go on. Not even in jest. . . . I am all yours, my love. Farewell.

CHAPTER Two

A ndrea and Giustiniana were so secretive during the first
months of their clandestine relationship that only a handful
of trusted friends knew what they were up to. As Andrea had predicted, Mrs. Anna eventually began to lower her guard and focus
on possible new suitors for her eldest daughter. By the fall of 1754
the two lovers were seeing each other with great frequency and
daring. They now had several locations at their disposal. N.'s
casino was often available. Meneghetto Tiepolo had given them
access to an apartment on the mezzanine of his *palazzo*. They also
went to a woman named Rosa, who lived in a small and very
simple house near the Wynnes and often let them have a room. Setting up a secret encounter was often the work of several days. It
took reliable intelligence and good planning. Alvisetto shuttled
furtively between the Wynnes' house and Ca' Memmo, delivering
letters with the latest arrangements or news of an unexpected
change of plan. Much was written about the dropping off and
picking up of keys.

The feverish preparatory work, coupled with the constant fear
of being caught, made their encounters all the more passionate.
"How could they be so stupid," Giustiniana noted with delight,
"not to realize what refinement they bring to our pleasure by
imposing all these prohibitions? [At the beginning of our relation-
ship] I was always very happy to see you, of course, but the emotions I feel now, the sheer agitation, the overwhelming feeling of
sweetness, were certainly not as intense."

As their love deepened and their relationship became more
sexual, jealousy too began to creep into their little world. Despite
Mrs. Anna's more relaxed attitude, Giustiniana was still not as free

to move around town as Andrea was. This put her at a psychological disadvantage. Who was Andrea seeing when he wasn't with her? She had his letters, of course, filled with detailed accounts of his daily activities. But how reliable were they? In her relative confinement in the house at Sant'Aponal she had plenty of time to work herself into a state of anxiety. A hint of unpleasant gossip was enough to send her into a rage.

One of Andrea's best friends was his cousin Lucrezia Pisani, the young lady he had bumped into on the bridge as he was chasing Giustiniana. She was lively and attractive and popular among Andrea's set. She often had interesting company at her house, and Andrea liked to drop by. His breezy reports on his visits there, however, made Giustiniana feel excluded. When she heard he was seeing Lucrezia more and more frequently on the days when they could not be together, she protested angrily. Andrea was taken aback by her attitude. Lucrezia was an old friend, he argued, an ally; she was one of the few who knew about their love affair. He reacted to Giustiniana's indignation with even greater indignation:

What have I done to you? What sort of creature are you? What on earth are you thinking? And what doggedness! What cruelty! So now it would appear that I have been courting Lucrezia for the past ten days. . . . Well, first of all, the timing is wrong: she's been in the countryside for the past several days. I would have gone with her. I chose not to. Meanwhile, I've been at home most of the time, evenings included. I've had lunch with her once. True, every time I have met her at the theater I have sat in her box. . . . But could I have sat alone or even with a single friend throughout an entire show? . . . I am mad to even defend myself. Yes, I like her company and I admit it. First of all because she is one of the easiest women to be around. . . . She is also witty, knowledgeable, clever. You can talk to her freely, and she often has good company. . . . Besides, she is your friend, she often asks about you with interest. . . . You are crazy, crazy, crazy. You will drive me mad with your endless suspicions. Still, I guess I must try to appease you in any case. So rest assured: I won't be seen with her anymore. But where may I go? Anywhere I went there would be new gossip and new scenes. . . . By God, I will have to lock myself up in my room, under permanent surveillance, otherwise you still won't believe me. But of course when no one sees me around people will start thinking that I'm enjoying myself even more secretively. What a life.

Giustiniana's suspicions, however, were not entirely unjustified: there was talk around town that Lucrezia did indeed have a liking for Andrea that went beyond their old friendship. When Giustiniana's mood did not improve, Andrea realized he would have to do something more drastic to placate her. He went about it in a manner that revealed his own penchant for intrigue:

This is a difficult thing to ask, but you are so easy, so free from prejudice, you have such a good spirit and are always so obliging with me that it is possible you might grant me this favor. Lucrezia torments me by always asking if she can see some of your letters to me—which I have never permitted her to do. Therefore I would like for you to write me a letter in French in which you praise her. You might add in passing that, while not jealous of her, you do think she is too intelligent not to realize that it would be preferable if I were not seen so often with her. She already knows all the love I have for you and your commitment to me. I assure you that the only reason I am asking you to do this is so that she will convince herself that I am in love with a woman more special than her. . . . If you're not up to it, it doesn't really matter. It's enough that you love me.

Giustiniana was uncomfortable with this sort of game playing. A little deception to avoid Mrs. Anna's controls and to meet Andrea on the sly was one thing. But she found his recourse to artifice for the sake of artifice a little unsettling. The ease with which he could transform himself from the most tender and loving companion to the craftiest manipulator was a trait that seemed embedded in his character. And whereas Lucrezia, an experienced operator herself, would probably not have given Andrea's behavior great significance, Giustiniana found it much harder to understand. She too had a seductive side, a propensity to flirt with men both young and old. But excessive ambiguity made her ill at ease. She held fast to a rule of love that was not very common among other young Venetians: the exclusivity of romantic feelings. So she was stunned to hear, when she went over to the Morosinis' for lunch shortly after the Lucrezia episode, that Andrea was also flirting with Mariettina Corner, another well-known seductress. Mariettina's love life was complicated enough as it was: she was married to Lucrezia's brother, had an official lover and was having an affair with yet a third man, Piero Marcello—a gambler and philanderer who happened to be a neighbor of the Wynnes'. Giustiniana was told that though Mariettina was carrying on the relationship with Piero, it was really Andrea she had her eyes on.

Again she confronted him, and again he blamed her for believing every scrap of gossip floating around the Morosinis': "What are they telling you, these people with whom you seem to enjoy yourself so much? And why do you believe them if you know they hate me? You accuse me of making love to Mariettina. . . . But why is it you always fear I'm causing you offense with all the women I see?"

The story of Andrea's presumed affair with Mariettina had all the ingredients of a Goldoni farce. It turned out that Andrea, at Mariettina's request, had acted as a go-between in her secret romance with Piero. And Giustiniana—as Andrea was quick to remind her—had even encouraged him to take on that role because she felt that as long as Mariettina was busy with other men she would not present a threat to her. But Andrea's comings and goings between the two lovers had provided the gossipmongers with plenty to talk about. In the ensuing confusion Giustiniana didn't know whom to believe. Andrea acknowledged that "some people might well have thought Mariettina had developed an interest in me. . . . After all, I was constantly whispering in her ear and she was whispering in mine. . . . She talked to me, gestured to me, sat next to me while apparently not caring a hoot about [her lover], her husband—indeed the world." He insisted it was all a terrible misunderstanding: he was innocent and Giustiniana was "stupid" if she bothered "to spend a moment on all this talk the Morosinis fill your head with."

It wasn't easy for her to dismiss the things she heard about Andrea, because so much of his life was invisible to her, out of reach. The rumors were all the more hurtful because they reverberated in circles to which she was admitted but to which she did not truly belong. Giustiniana knew or was acquainted with most of Andrea's friends and was a welcome guest in the houses of many patrician families. But even though the veil of social discrimination was perhaps not as visible as elsewhere in Europe, it was very real; it governed Venetian society in subtle and less subtle ways—as in the case of marriage. When Giustiniana wrote to Andrea about his woman friends, there was often an undercurrent of anxiety that went quite beyond a natural romantic jealousy.

Still, she had her own little ways of getting back at him.

As Andrea and Giustiniana struggled to clear up the misunderstanding about his role in their friends' affair, Mariettina threw one of her celebrated balls on the Giudecca—an island separated from the southern side of Venice by a wide canal, where patricians had pleasure houses with gardens and vineyards. This was one of the major social events of the season. Preparations went on for days. Young Venetian ladies had a notorious taste for luxury. They liked to wear rich and elaborate but relatively comfortable outfits, so they could move with greater ease during the minuets and *furlane*, a popular dance that originated from the Friuli region. They spent hours having their hair coiffed into tall beehives, which they decorated with gems and golden pins. Their long fingernails were polished in bright colors. They drenched themselves with exotic perfume and chose their beauty spots with special care (the *appassionata* was worn in the corner of the eye, the *coquette* above the lip, the *galante* on the chin, and the *assassina*—the killer—in the corner of the mouth).[1] They carried large, exquisitely embroidered fans and wore strings of pearls and diamonds. High heels had long been out of fashion: Venetian ladies preferred more sensible low evening shoes, often decorated with a diamond buckle. These were fabulously expensive but very comfortable, especially for dancing. Men wore the traditional French costume: silk long jacket, knee-length culottes, and white stockings. Elaborate cuffs and jabots of lace from the island of Burano gave a Venetian touch to their attire. Their elegant evening wigs were combed and groomed for the occasion.

Mariettina's ball offered a chance for Andrea and Giustiniana to see each other and clarify things once and for all. But Giustiniana, still feeling vexed by the whole imbroglio, was not in the mood for such a demanding social event. She sent this note to Andrea just as he was dressing for the evening:

If the bad weather continues I will certainly not come to Marietta Corner's festa. *You know my mother and how she fears the wind. She has warned that she will not cross the canal if there is the slightest bit of wind. In the end it is probably better that such a reasonable pretext should excuse me from coming as I believe you and I would both have a terrible time. . . . Still I will try to convince my mother to get over her fear—I hope you will acknowledge my goodwill. I have already opted for a new course: henceforth you will be able to do as you please; I will neither complain nor bother you with accusations. When you will cause me displeasure I will try to convince myself that you won't have done so out of ill will but because you do not believe I am sensitive to those things. . . . By the way, all those pleas for forgiveness and that habit you have of carrying on exactly in the same manner even though you know you offend me—I really cannot stand it. The truth is, I will continue to give you proof of my real affection while you will hurt me more and more. And who knows if all my suffering will change you one day. . . . Good-bye now, Memmo. I would not want to keep you from your toilette.*

In the end Giustiniana did not prevail over her mother—if she ever tried—and she did not go to Marietta's ball. The next day she sent Andrea this bittersweet note: "I did not write to you this morning because I felt you might be tired after last night and needed your sleep. The bad weather prevented me from coming, but as I told you I believe in the end it was for the better. Today I was half hoping I would see you at the window at Ca' Tiepolo, but I guess I fooled myself. This evening we are going to Smith's. I will write to you tomorrow. I have nothing else to ask you except to love me much—if you can. Farewell."

Andrea always reacted defensively, even impatiently, to Giustiniana's outbursts of jealousy. He was not immune to similar feelings, but in the abstract he espoused what he considered a "philosophical" approach. "It is practically impossible for me to be jealous," he explained:

> *Not because I have such high esteem for myself that I do not recognize others might be worthy [of your attentions]. No, the reason is that I don't want to believe you are flighty or coquettish or fickle or careless or mean. If ever there came a point in which I really did nurture doubts about you . . . then I would simply think of you as a different woman. The pain I would feel on account of your transformation would certainly be intense, but to me you would no longer be the lovable, the rarest Giustiniana. And by losing what ignited my deepest love and continues to nourish it, I would lose all feeling for you and return to the Memmo I was before meeting you.*

This was the theory. In reality Andrea was fairly quick to lose his cool when other young men prowled around Giustiniana. He was particularly wary of Momolo Mocenigo, better known as Il Gobbo—the Hunchback—on account of a slight curvature of his spine, but in fact rather good-looking and quite the ladykiller. "He was the handsomest of all the patrician gamesters at the Ridotto," Casanova wrote in his memoirs.[2] When he was not taking bets at his faro table, Il Gobbo hung around the theaters, where he bothered the ladies and tried to make mischief. He especially enjoyed gallivanting with Giustiniana, and her willingness to indulge him annoyed Andrea to no end. Once, after catching her yet again in "a very long conversation" with him, he let her have it: "Everyone knows Il Gobbo for the first-class whoremonger that he is. You should know he once [told me] in front of other people that I should be thankful to him because he chose not to seduce you even though you showed a certain kindness to him. . . . I refused to give in to such abuse, and I dare say my reaction did not make him very happy. . . . But why did you have to go talk to him without your mother? Why speak to him practically in the ear? Why whisper to him that you were going to San

Moisè so he could then come and tell me with a tone that so displeased me?"

Another evening, Andrea was at home nursing a fever and a terrible sore throat when he suddenly learned that the "first-class whoremonger" was on his way to meet Giustiniana. He became so upset that he dashed out of the house, ran across town, and burst into the busy gambling rooms of the Ridotto. "I looked for you everywhere, and I finally found you in the same room where [Il Gobbo] had just been," he wrote to her angrily and with a good deal of self-pity. The incident, he assured Giustiniana, had "redoubled the flames that were already engulfing my throat."

Still, Il Gobbo was a lesser irritant than Piero Marcello, the handsome *coureur de femmes* who was courting Mariettina Corner but also had eyes for Giustiniana. Andrea considered Piero to be frivolous and vain, the sort of young man who would buy a new coat and then "make a ruckus just to attract attention to it." Piero's gondola was often moored at the same dock as the Wynnes'. "How appearances can trick one," Andrea noted, for he was worried people might wrongly assume that Piero was visiting Giustiniana and her sisters, when in fact Piero simply lived nearby. Indeed, some already referred to them as "Piero Marcello's girls." Piero not only flirted with Giustiniana, he also needled Andrea in public, wondering aloud whether he and Giustiniana were secretly still seeing each other. The two nearly came to blows over her, as Andrea reported to Giustiniana with more than a hint of braggadocio in this account of their confrontation:

> PIERO: *Are you jealous of me? Oh . . . but I have no designs on her. True, when women call me it is hard for me to resist. . . . But I am your friend, I would not betray you. I stay away from my friends' women. And if you have the slightest suspicion, I will never see her again.*
>
> ANDREA: *Who do you think you are, the Terror of the World? Do you really think I'm afraid of losing Giustiniana to you? If she were crazy, like all your previous lovers were, if she wanted your money, . . . if she had all the weaknesses, all the silliness, all the prejudices of the average woman, if she could not tell the true value of better men, if she were a coquette or worse, then, yes, I*

probably wouldn't trust her. But my dear Piero, who do you think you're dealing with?

Andrea concluded, "I told him these things with my usual straightforwardness, so that after affecting surprise he turned the whole thing into a joke."

Things did not end there. Days later Andrea saw Piero and Giustiniana talking to each other again. He gave her a stern warning: "Now I speak to you as a husband: I absolutely do not want you to show in public that you know Piero Marcello. I was very sorry that Mariettina, noticing that I was trying to see with whom you were laughing, came over and whispered into my ear: 'She's laughing with Piero down there.' "

Even after such a reprimand Andrea would not admit to being the slightest bit jealous:

> *I've told you a hundred times: I don't forbid you to see Piero out of jealousy. . . . But I absolutely do not want you to look at him in public or even say hello, all the more so because he affects an equivocal manner that I simply don't like and that I find insolent in the extreme. . . . Piero and Momolo are not for you. . . . Piero frets while Momolo affects his usual mannerisms, both with the same end: to make people believe that there has been at least a little bit of intimacy with all the women they are barely acquainted with. And for this reason the two of them are a real nuisance to young lovers.*

Despite the misunderstandings and squabbles that ensued, Andrea and Giustiniana's relationship deepened through the spring and summer of 1755 to the point that very little else seemed to matter to them anymore. All their energies were devoted to making time for themselves and finding places to meet. They had become experts at escaping the restrictions imposed on them and moved stealthily from alcove to alcove. Their love affair consumed their life, and it gradually transformed them.

Giustiniana had been known as a lively and gregarious young woman. The affectionate nickname *inglesina di Sant'Aponal* conjured up a refreshing image of youth and grace. Soon after returning to Venice, Giustiniana, being the eldest, had begun to share with her mother the duties of a good hostess while Bettina, Tonnina, Richard, and William were still under the care of Toinon. This role had come naturally to her. She had felt at ease in their drawing room or over at the consul's, delighting everyone with her charm. But by 1755 she was tired of all that, tired of performing onstage. She hardly recognized herself. "Coquetry was all I really cared for once," she told Andrea in a moment of introspection. "Now I can barely manage to be polite. Everything bores me. Everything annoys me. People say I have become stupid, silly; that I am hopeless at entertaining guests. I realize they're right, but I don't much care." She spent her days writing letters to Andrea, worrying about whom he was seeing, planning their next meeting—where, at what time, and, always, what to do with the keys. When she did go out with her mother—to lunch at the consul's, or to church, the theater, the Ridotto—the people she chose to talk to, what she said, how she said it: everything she did, in one way or another, related to Andrea.

The affair had become all-consuming for Andrea as well. "My love, you govern my every action," he confessed to her. "I do not think, I do not feel, I do not see anything but my Giustiniana. Everything else is meaningless to me. . . . I simply cannot hide my love for you from others anymore." He still made the usual rounds—a family errand, a trip to the printer Pasquali on behalf of the consul, a lunch at Ca' Tiepolo, and in the evening a visit to the theater. But his life outside the secret world he shared with Giustiniana no longer seemed very stimulating or even much fun. After the death of his uncle Andrea the year before, Ca' Memmo had received fewer visitors and had ceased to be the scintillating intellectual haven of years past. At this time, too, Andrea's mother, obsessed about Casanova's influence on her three boys, finally had her way and convinced the inquisitors to have him arrested.* The

*It is probable that a combination of factors determined Casanova's arrest on July 25, 1755—his openly proclaimed atheism, his dabbling with numerology, his reputation as an able swindler of a rather gullible trio of old patricians. Lucia Memmo's pressure on the inquisitors also played a role. Certainly Casanova was convinced of this. "His [Andrea's] mother had been a party to the plot that sent me to prison,"[3] he later wrote in his *History of My Life.* But he never bore a grudge toward the sons.

heated, late-night conversations at the crowded *malvasìe* on the latest book from Paris or the new play by Goldoni had lost their most entertaining participant.

Andrea's personal project for establishing a French theater in Venice was going nowhere, and Giustiniana worried that she might be the main cause of his lack of progress: "Are you not working on it because of me? Dear Memmo, please don't give up. If only you knew how much I care about your affairs when your honor is at stake. Especially this project, which, given its scale, the detailed manner in which you planned it, and the excellence with which you carried out every phase, was meant to establish your reputation. And to think that my feelings for you—true as they are—might have caused you so much damage. I am mortified." Andrea admitted that he had made little progress and "all the people involved" in the project were furious with him. "They say I have been taking them for a ride all along. The talk of the town is that the theater project has fallen through because of my excessive passion for you. By God, I couldn't care less. I only wish to tell you that I love you, my heart." Sweetly, he added that he would now start working on it again "because it will feel I will be doing something for you. [After I received your letter] I dashed off to the lawyers to get them started again. They weren't in the office, but I shall find them soon enough." In the end, despite fitful efforts, the project never got off the ground.

Andrea kept up with his mentor Carlo Lodoli, the Franciscan monk who continued to hold sway among the more open-minded members of the Venetian nobility. Now that he was no longer Lodoli's student, Andrea saw him less often, but he was anxious that Giustiniana should also benefit from the mind that had influenced him so profoundly. He encouraged his old teacher to visit her as much as possible and draw her into his circle of followers. Giustiniana always welcomed these visits, starved as she was of new books and new ideas in the restricted intellectual environment her mother fostered at home. Most of all she delighted in the chance to spend time with a person who knew the man she loved so well. When Lodoli came to visit, it was as if he brought Andrea with him—at least in spirit. "He just left," Giustiniana reported to her lover. "He kept me company for a long time, and we spoke very freely. I appreciated our conversation today immensely—more than usual. He is the most useful man to society. . . . But beyond that, he talked a lot about you and he praised you for the virtues men should want to be praised for—the goodness of your soul and the truthfulness of your spirit."

For several years Consul Smith's library had been a second home for Andrea. He continued to visit the consul regularly during his secret affair with Giustiniana, helping him catalogue his art and book collections. Nearly two years had gone by since the two lovers first met in that house. As Andrea worked, he luxuriated in tender memories of those earlier days, when they had been falling in love among the beautiful pictures and the rare books. "Everything there [reminds] me of you. . . . Oh God, Giustiniana, my idol, do you remember our happiness there?"

In reality, Andrea stopped at the consul's more out of a sense of duty and gratitude than for pleasure. The old man could be demanding. "When he starts talking after his evening tea, he never stops," Andrea reported with a sense of fatigue. "He generally asks me to stay on even while he has himself undressed." These man-to-man ramblings often touched on the Wynnes, and on several occasions Andrea could not help but notice with amusement the vaguely lustful tone Smith had begun to use when he talked about Giustiniana.

Inevitably, as Andrea and Giustiniana's lives became more entwined and inextricable, so the hopelessness of their situation gradually sank in, bringing with it more tension and crises. Andrea filled his letters with declarations of love and devotion, but he never offered much to look forward to—there was no long-term plan that, however vague, might allow Giustiniana to dream about a future together. Instead, he made offhand remarks about how much simpler it would be if she were married to someone else or, better still, if she were a young widow "so that we wouldn't have to take all these precautions and I could show the world how much I adore you."

Giustiniana was having a harder time than Andrea. Her letters, always more impulsive and emotional than his, grew wilder as she swung between bliss and despair. Venice could seem such a hostile place—a watery labyrinth of mirrors and shadows and whispers. She could not get a grip on Andrea's life or, as a consequence, on her own. The more time passed, the more she felt she was losing her way. Again and again she was overcome by waves of jealousy that brought her to breaking point.

Caterina (Cattina) Barbarigo was a great beauty and a notorious *femme fatale*. She held court in a *casino* that was much in vogue among progressive patricians and viewed with suspicion by the inquisitors. Though older than Andrea—she was married and the mother of two beautiful daughters—she liked surrounding herself with promising young men. He, in turn, was delighted to be drawn into her circle of friends—even at the cost of hurting Giustiniana's feelings. "All day you've been at Cattina Barbarigo's, haven't you?" she asked accusingly. "Enough, I shan't complain about it. But why have I not seen you? Why have I not received a line from you? Now that I think of it, it is perhaps better not to have received a note from you because you probably would have written late at night, in haste, and maybe only out of a sense of duty. Tomorrow, perhaps, you will write to me with greater ease." But there was no letter on the following day, or the next, or the one after that. On the fourth day of silence her anxiety turned into rage:

You should be ashamed of yourself, Memmo. Could one possibly behave worse toward a lover one claims to be desperately in love with? I write to you on Saturday, and you don't answer because you are at Barbarigo's house. Sunday I never see you even though I spend the entire day at my window. And no letter—even though you know very well that on Mondays I go out and you should want to find out what the plan is in order to see me. Or perhaps you did write to me but your friend could not deliver? Do you suppose I will believe that you could not find another way of getting a letter to me, considering I had been two days without any news about you? . . . My mother has been ill for many days, and we could have been seeing each other with fewer precautions. But no—Memmo is having fun elsewhere. He does not even think about Giustiniana except when a compelling urge forces him to.

What must I think? I hear from all sides about your new games and your oh-so-beloved old friendships.

Naturally, Andrea pleaded complete innocence: "For heaven's sake, don't be so mean. What rendezvous are you talking about? What have I done to merit such scorn? My dear sweet one, you must quiet down. Trust me or else you'll kill me." He explained, rather obliquely, that tactical considerations and nothing else occasionally forced him to be silent for a few days or to interrupt the flow of letters. But she should never forget that if he sometimes made himself scarce, it was for *her* sake and certainly not because he was chasing young ladies around: "You know I love you, and for that very reason, instead of complaining about your perpetual diffidence, I only worry about your position. I would have written to you every day to tell you what I was up to, but you know how afraid I am about writing to you—your mother is capable of all sorts of beastliness. All I care about is making sure the members of your household and our enemies and the crowd of people that follow every step we take do not discover our relationship by some act of imprudence on our part."

Giustiniana was not reassured by Andrea's words. In fact, his shifty attitude was making her more upset and more defiant:

How could you swear to me that all you cared about was my position, when in fact you were merely trying to get away from me using prudence as a pretext to rush over to see N. *? Don't be so sure of the power you have over me, for I shall break this bond of ours. I have opened my eyes at last. My God! Who is this man to whom I have given my deepest love! Leave me, please leave me alone. I'm just a nuisance to you. Before long you will hate me. You villain! Why did you betray me? . . . Everyone now speaks of your friendship with N. At first you explained yourself, and so I was at peace again and I even allowed you to be seen with her in public . . . and after our reconciliation you rushed off to see her again. What greater proof of your infidelity? Damn you! I am

---

*Clearly a different N. from the one who was lending them the *casino.*

so angry I cannot even begin to say all I want. . . . Don't even come near me, I don't want to see you. . . . Now I see why you told me to pretend that our friendship was over; now I plainly see how fake your sincerity was, your infamous caution. . . . Now I know you. Did you think you could make fun of me forever? Enough. I cease to be your plaything.

Were the rumors true? Was Andrea pursuing N., or was Giustiniana working herself into a spiral of groundless jealousy? Whatever was going on, Andrea had clearly underestimated the depth of Giustiniana's desperation. He suddenly found himself on the defensive, struggling to contain her rage: "How can I describe to you the state I am in, you cruel woman? My mind is busy with a thousand thoughts. I'm agitated and worried about a thousand questions. And you, for heaven's sake, find nothing better to do than to treat me in the most inhuman way. Where does it all come from? What have I done to deserve all this? . . . Can it be that you still don't know my heart? . . . Come here, my sweet Giustiniana, speak freely to your Memmo."

Andrea understood more plainly now that as long as Giustiniana felt locked into a relationship with no future she would only become more anguished and more intractable and their life would become hell. But he remained ambivalent: "Tell me if you want to get yourself out of this situation you're in. Tell me the various possibilities, and however much they might be harmful to me, if they will make you happy. . . . Speak out, and you will see how I love you." Was he conjuring up the idea of an elopement? Was he beginning to consider a secret marriage, with all the negative consequences it would have entailed? If so, he was going about it in a very circuitous and tentative way, as if this were merely a short-term device to placate Giustiniana's wrath. In fact, already in his next letter he retreated to his older, more traditional position: their happiness, as far as Andrea was concerned, hinged on finding Giustiniana a husband. "Alas, until you are married and I am able to see you more freely, there won't be much to gain. Meanwhile let us try to hurt each other as little as possible."

Giustiniana, however, had not exhausted her rage. Andrea's letters suddenly seemed so petty and predictable. Where was the strong, willful young man she had fallen so desperately in love with? In the increasingly frequent isolation of her room at Sant'Aponal, she decided to put an end to their love story. Better to make a clean break, as painful as it would be, than to endure the torture Andrea was inflicting upon her.

This is the last time I bother you, Memmo. Your conduct has been such that I now feel free to write you this letter. I do not blame you for your betrayal, your lack of gratitude, the scarcity of your love, your scorn. No, Memmo. I was very hurt by all this, but I've decided not to complain or to wallow in vindictive feelings. You know how much I have loved you; you know what a perfect friend I have been to you. God knows that I had staked my entire happiness on our love. You knew it. Yet you allowed me to believe that you loved me with the same intensity. . . . And now that I know you, that I see how you tricked me, I give you an even greater token of my passion by breaking this tenacious bond. After all your abuse, your disloyalty, I was already on the verge of abandoning you. But your scorn of the last few days, the lack of any effort on your part to explain yourself, your continuous indulgence in the things you know make me unhappy, your complete estrangement have finally made me see that you could not hope for a better development. I have opened my eyes, I have learned to know you and to know me, and I have become adamant in my resolution never to think again about a man capable of such cruelty, such contempt, such utter disloyalty to me.

So everything between us is over. I know I cannot give you a greater pleasure than this. . . . And I also know that my peace of mind, my well-being, maybe even my life will depend on this break. I shall never hate you (see how much I can promise), but I will feel both pleasure and displeasure in your happiness as well as in your misfortunes. I will say more: I will never again love anyone the way I have loved you, ungrateful Memmo. You will oblige me by handing over all my letters . . . as they serve no other purpose than to remind me of my weakness and your wickedness. So please give them back so that I may burn them and remove *from my sight everything that might remind me of all I have done for such an undeserving man. Here is your portrait, once my delight and comfort, which I don't want anywhere near me. Ask the artist* to bring me the one you had commissioned of me—I will pay for it in installments and keep it. Your vanity has already been sufficiently satisfied as it is. Everyone knows how much I have loved you. Please don't let me see you for another few days. I know how good our several days' separation has been for me, and I have reason to believe that I will benefit by extending it. I forgive you everything. I have deserved this treatment because I was foolish enough to believe that you were capable of a sincere and enduring commitment; and I guess you are not really to blame if you can't get over your own fickleness, which is so much a part of your nature. I ask neither your friendship nor a place in your memory. I want nothing more from you. Since I can no longer be the most passionate lover, I don't want to be anything else to you. Adieu, Memmo, count me dead. Adieu forever.*

Giustiniana's dramatic break cleared the air. Within days the poisonous atmosphere that had overwhelmed them dissolved and they were in each other's arms again, filled with love and desire. Giustiniana even laughed at her own foibles:

Oh God, my Memmo, how can I express these overflowing emotions? How can I tell you that . . . you are my true happiness, my only treasure? Lord, I am crazy. Crazy in the extreme. And what about all that happened to me in the last few days? Do you feel for me? . . . With my suspicions, my jealousy, my love. . . . Only you can understand me because you know my heart and the power you have over it. . . . I don't know how my mood has changed so quickly, and why I even run the risk of telling you this! No, I really don't know what's happening to me. . . . Anyway, we'll see each other tomorrow. Meanwhile I think I'll just go

*Andrea had commissioned a portrait from "Nazari," possibly Bartolomeo Nazzari (1699–1758), a fashionable artist in Venice at the time and a protégé of Consul Smith. Alas, the portrait has never been found.

straight to bed. After having been wrapped up in sweet thoughts about my Memmo and so full of him, I couldn't possibly spend the rest of the evening with the silly company downstairs!

Andrea was so eager to hold Giustiniana in his arms again that even the twenty-four-hour wait now seemed unendurable to him. Alone in his room at Ca' Memmo he let himself drift into erotic fantasies, which he promptly relayed to his lover:

> *Oh, my little one, my little one, may I entertain you with my follies? Do you have a heart to listen? I am so full of dreams about you that the slightest thing is enough to put me into a cosmic mood. For example, I read one of your letters . . . and I focus on a few characters in your handwriting and I begin to stare at them and I tell myself: here my adorable Giustiniana wrote . . . and sure enough I see your hand, your very own hand, oh Lord, I kiss your letter not finding anything else to kiss, and I press it against me as if it were you, oh, and I hug you in my mind, and it's really too much; what to do? I cannot resist any longer. Oh my Lord, oh my Lord, now another hand of yours is relieving me, oh, but I can't go on. . . . I cannot say more, my love, but you can imagine the rest. . . . Oh Lord, oh Lord. . . . I speak no more, I speak no more.*

In such moments of playful abandon Andrea felt he was capable of doing "even the most irresponsible thing . . . yes . . . I feel this urge to take you away and marry you." And when he opened up that way, Giustiniana always gave herself completely: "My Memmo, I shall always be yours. You enchant me. You overwhelm me. I will never find another Memmo with all the qualities and all the defects that I love about you. We are made for each other so absolutely. All that needs to happen is for me to become less suspicious and for you to moderate that slight flightiness, and then we'll be happy."

After these moments of ecstasy, however, the gloominess of their situation would steal over their hearts once more. Andrea wondered how their relationship could possibly survive. "We will never have a moment of peace and quiet. Meanwhile, you, believing as you do in everything you hear. Good Lord, I don't know what to do anymore! You will never change as long as I have to be away from you. I see that it is impossible for you to believe that I am all yours, as I am, and it is impossible to change your mother, or your situation, so what am I to do?" he asked Giustiniana with quiet desperation. "I don't know how to hold on to you."

CHAPTER Three

I n early December 1755, news quickly spread that Catherine
Tofts, the elusive wife of Consul Smith, had died after a long
illness. She had once been an active and resourceful hostess, often
giving private recitals in her drawing room. There is a lovely
painting by Marco Ricci, one of Smith's favorite artists, of Catherine singing happily with a chamber orchestra. But the picture was
painted shortly after her marriage to Smith and before the death of
her son. As the years went by, she was seen less and less (Andrea
never mentions her in his letters). Toward the end of her life it was
rumored that she had lost her mind and her husband had locked
her up in a madhouse.

Smith organized a grand funeral ceremony, which was attended by a large contingent of Venice's foreign community (the
Italians were absent because the Catholic Church forbade the
public mourning of Protestants). A Lutheran merchant from
Germany, a friend of the consul, recorded the occasion in his
diary: "Signor Smith received condolences and offered everyone
sweets, coffee, chocolate, Cypriot wine and many other things; to
each one he gave a pair of white calfskin gloves in the English
manner." Twenty-five gondolas, each with four torches, formed
the procession of mourners. The floating cortege went down the
Grand Canal, past the Dogana di Mare, across Saint Mark's
Basin, and out to the Lido, where Catherine's body was laid
to rest in the Protestant cemetery: "The English ships moored
at Saint Mark's saluted the procession with a storm of cannon
shots."[1]

The consul was eighty years old but still remarkably fit and
energetic. He had no desire to slow down. By early spring gossips
were whispering that his period of mourning was already over and

he was eager to find a new wife—a turn of events that caused quite a commotion in the English community.

John Murray, the British Resident, had had a prickly relationship with Smith ever since he had arrived in Venice in 1751. Smith had vied for the position himself, hoping to crown his career by becoming the king's ambassador in the city where he had spent the better part of his life. But his London connections had not been strong enough to secure it, and Murray, a bon vivant with a keener interest in women and a good table than in the art of diplomacy, had been chosen instead. "He is a scandalous fellow in every sense of the word," complained Lady Mary Wortley Montagu, who, rather snobbishly, preferred the company of local patricians to that of her less aristocratic compatriots. "He is not to be trusted to change a sequin, despised by this government for his smuggling, which was his original profession, and always surrounded with pimps and brokers, who are his privy councillors."[2] Casanova, predictably, had a different view of Murray: "A handsome man, full of wit, learned, and a prodigious lover of the fair sex, Bacchus and good eating. I was never unwelcome at his amorous encounters, at which, to tell the truth, he acquitted himself well."[3]

Smith did not hide his disappointment. In fact he went out of his way to make Murray feel unwelcome, and the new Resident was soon fussing about the consul with Lord Holderness, the secretary of state, himself an old Venice hand and a friend to the Wynnes: "As soon as I got here I tried to follow your advice to be nice to Consul Smith. But he has played so many unpleasant tricks on me that I finally had to confront him openly. He promised me to be nice in the future—then he started again, forcing me to break all relations."[4]

Catherine's death and, more important, Smith's intention to marry again brought a sudden thaw in the relations between the Resident and the consul. Murray conceived the notion that his former enemy would be the perfect husband for his aging sister Elizabeth, whom he had brought over from London (perhaps Murray also calculated that their marriage would eventually bring the consul's prized art collection into his hands). Smith was actually quite fond of Betty Murray. He enjoyed her frequent visits at Palazzo Balbi. She was kind to him, and on closer inspection he found she was not unattractive. Quite soon he began to think seriously about marrying "that beauteous virgin of forty," as Lady Montagu called her.[5]

Murray and his sister were not alone in seeing the consul in a new light after Catherine's death. Mrs. Anna too had her eye on him, because she felt he would be the perfect husband for Giustiniana: Smith could provide her daughter a respectable position in society as well as financial security. Furthermore, he had been a friend of the family for twenty years, and he would surely watch over the rest of the young Wynnes—at least for the short time that was left to him. After all, wasn't such a solution the best possible way to fulfill the promise he had made to look after Sir Richard's family? Mrs. Anna began to lure the consul very delicately, asking him over to their house more frequently, showing Giustiniana off, and dropping a hint here and there. She set out to quash the competition from Betty Murray while attempting to preserve the best possible relations with her and her brother. Inevitably, though, tensions in their little group rose, and Betty Murray reciprocated by drawing the consul's attention to the fact that, as far as she could tell, Giustiniana still seemed very much taken with Andrea.

At first Giustiniana was stunned by her mother's plan, but she knew that the matter was out of her hands. And although she was only eighteen, she did not express disgust at the idea of marrying an octogenarian. She was fond of Smith, and she also recognized the material advantages of such a marriage. But all she really cared about was how the scheme would affect her relationship with Andrea. Would it protect their love affair, or would it spell the end? Would it be easier for them to see each other or more difficult? The consul was so old that the marriage was bound to be short-lived. What would happen after he died?

Andrea had often said, sometimes laughing and sometimes not, that their life would be so much happier if only Giustiniana were married or, even better, widowed. It had been fanciful talk. Now, quite unexpectedly, they contemplated the very real possibility that Giustiniana might be married soon and widowed not long after. Andrea became quite serious. He set out his argument with care:

> *I want you to understand that I want such a marriage for love of you. As long as he lives, you will be in the happiest situation. . . .*

You will not have sisters-in-law and brothers-in-law and God knows who else with whom to argue. You will have only one man to deal with. He is not easy, but if you approach him the right way from the beginning, he will eagerly become your slave. He will love you and have the highest possible regard for you. . . . He is full of riches and luxuries. He likes to show off his fortune and his taste. He is vain, so vain, that he will want you to entertain many ladies. This will also open up the possibility for you to see gentlemen and be seen in their company. We will have to behave with great care so that he does not discover our feelings for each other ahead of time.

Andrea began to support Mrs. Anna's effort by dropping his own hints to Smith about what a sensible match it would be. Giustiniana stepped into line, though warily, for she continued to harbor misgivings. As for the consul, the mere prospect of marrying the lovely girl he had seen blossom in his drawing room put him into a state of excitement he was not always able to contain. Andrea immediately noticed the change in him. "[The other evening] he said to me, 'Last night I couldn't sleep. I usually fall asleep as soon as I go to bed. I guess I was all worked up. I couldn't close my eyes until seven, and at nine I got up, went to Mogliano,* ate three slices of bread and some good butter, and now I feel very well.' And to show me how good he felt he made a couple of jumps that revealed how energetic he really is."

Word about a possible wedding between the old consul and Giustiniana began to circulate outside the English community and became the subject of gossip in the highest Venetian circles. Smith did little to silence the talk. "He is constantly flattering my mother," Giustiniana wrote to Andrea. "And he lets rumors about our wedding run rampant." Andrea told Giustiniana he had just returned from Smith's, where a most allusive exchange had taken place in front of General Graeme,† the feisty new commander in chief of Venice's run-down army, and several other guests:

*The consul had a villa at Mogliano Veneto, on the mainland.
†General William Graeme, a Scotsman, had succeeded Marshal Johann Matthias Shulenburg that very same year (1756). Throughout its history the Republic hired non-Venetians to lead its land forces.

[The consul] introduced the topic of married women and after counting how many there were in the room he turned to me:
"Another friend of yours will soon marry," he said.
"I wonder who this friend might be that he did not trust me enough to tell me," I replied.
"Myself. . . . Isn't that the talk of the town? Why, the General here told me that even at the doge's . . ."
". . . Absolutely, I was there too. And Graeme's main point was that having mentioned the rumor to you, you did nothing to deny it."
"Why should I deny something which at my old age can only go to my credit?"

Andrea had come away from the consul's rather flustered, not quite knowing whether Smith had spoken to him "truthfully or in jest." He asked Giustiniana to keep him informed about what she was hearing on her side. "I am greatly curious to know whether there are any new developments." No one really knew what the consul's intentions were—whether he was going to propose to Giustiniana or whether he had decided in Betty's favor. It was not even clear whether he was really interested in marriage or whether he was having fun at everyone's expense. Giustiniana too found it hard to read Smith's mind. "He was here until after four," she reported to her lover. "No news except that he renewed his invitation to visit him at his house in Mogliano and that he took my hand as he left us."

Andrea feared Smith might be disturbed by the rumors, ably fueled by the Murray clan, that his affair with Giustiniana was secretly continuing, so he remained cautious in his encouragement: perhaps the consul felt he needed more time; his wife, after all, had only recently been buried. Mrs. Anna, however, was determined not to lose the opportunity to further her daughter's suit, and she eagerly stepped up the pressure.

In the summer months wealthy Venetians moved to their estates in the countryside. As its maritime power had started to decline in the sixteenth century, the Venetian Republic had gradually turned to the mainland, extending its territories and developing agriculture and manufacture to sustain its economy. The nobility had accumulated vast tracts of land and built elegant villas whose grandeur sometimes rivaled that of great English country houses or French châteaux. By the eighteenth century the villa had become an important mark of social status, and the *villeggiatura*—the leisurely time spent at the villa in the summer—became increasingly fashionable. Those who owned a villa would open it to family and guests for the season, which started in early July and lasted well into September. Those who did not would scramble to rent a property. And those who could not afford to rent frantically sought invitations. A rather stressful bustle always surrounded the comings and goings of the summer season.

Venetians were not drawn to the country by a romantic desire to feel closer to nature. Their rather contrived summer exodus, which Goldoni had ridiculed in a much-applauded comedy earlier that year at the Teatro San Luca,* was a whimsical and ostentatious way of transporting to the countryside the idle lifestyle they indulged in during the winter in the city. In the main, the country provided, quite literally, a change of scenery, as if the *burchielli,* the comfortable boats that made their way up the Brenta Canal transporting the summer residents to their villas, were also laden with the elaborate sets of the season's upcoming theatrical production.

Consul Smith had been an adept of the *villeggiatura* since the early twenties, but it was not until the thirties that he had finally bought a house at Mogliano, north of Venice on the road to Treviso, and had it renovated by his friend Visentini. The house was in typical neo-Palladian style—clear lines and simple, elegant spaces. It faced a small formal garden with classical statues and potted lemon trees arranged symmetrically on the stone parterre. A narrow, well-groomed alley, enclosed by low, decorative gates, ran parallel to the house, immediately beyond the garden, and provided a secure route for the morning or evening walk. The consul had moved part of his collection to adorn the walls at his house in

---

*Goldoni wrote his *Villeggiatura* trilogy for the Carnival season of 1756.

Mogliano, including works by some of his star contemporaries—
Marco and Sebastiano Ricci, Francesco Zuccarelli, Giovan Battista
Piazzetta, Rosalba Carriera—as well as old masters such as Bellini,
Vermeer, Van Dyck, Rembrandt, and Rubens. "As pretty a collec-
tion of pictures as I have ever seen,"[6] the architect Robert Adam
commented when he visited Smith in the country.

The consul had often invited the Wynnes to see his beautiful
house at Mogliano. Now, in the late spring of 1756, he renewed his
invitation with a more urgent purpose: to pay his court to Giustiniana with greater vigor so that he could come to a decision about
proposing to her, possibly by the end of the summer. Mrs. Anna,
usually rather reluctant to make the visit on account of the logisti-
cal complications even a short trip to the mainland entailed for a
large family like hers, decided she could not refuse.

The prospect of spending several days in the clutches of the
consul did not particularly thrill Giustiniana. She told Andrea she
wished the old man "would just leave us in peace" and cursed "that
wretched Mogliano a hundred times." But Andrea explained to her
that Smith's invitation was a good thing because it meant he was
serious about marrying her and was hopefully giving up on the
spinsterish Betty Murray. Giustiniana continued to dread the visit—
and the role that, for once, both Andrea and her mother expected
her to play. Her anguish only increased during the daylong trip
across the lagoon and up to Mogliano. But once she was out in the
country and had settled into Smith's splendid house, she rather
began to enjoy her part and to appreciate the humorous side of her
forced seduction of *il vecchio*—the old man. The time she spent
with Smith became good material with which to entertain her real
lover:

> *I've never seen Smith so sprightly. He made me walk with him
> all morning and climbed the stairs, skipping the steps to show his
> agility and strength. [The children] were playing in the garden
> at who could throw stones the furthest. And Memmo, would you
> believe it? Smith turned to me and said, "Do you want to see me
> throw a stone further than anyone else?" I thought he was kid-
> ding, but no: he asked [the children] to hand him two rocks and
> threw them toward the target. He didn't even reach it, so he*

blamed the stones, saying they were too light. He then threw more stones. By that time I was bursting with laughter and kept biting my lip.

The visit to Mogliano left everyone satisfied, and even Giustiniana returned in a good mood. Smith was by now apparently quite smitten and intended to continue his courtship during the course of the summer. As this would have been impossible if the Wynnes stayed in Venice, he suggested to Mrs. Anna that she rent from the Mocenigo family a pleasant villa called Le Scalette in the fashionable village of Dolo on the banks of the Brenta, a couple of hours down the road from Mogliano. Smith himself handled all the financial transactions, and since the rental cost would have been high for Mrs. Anna it is possible that he also covered part of the expenses.

Needless to say, Giustiniana was not happy about the arrangement. It was one thing to spend a few days at Mogliano, quite another to have Smith hovering around her throughout the summer. Meanwhile, where would Andrea be? When would they be able to see each other? She could not stand the idea of being separated from her lover for so long. Andrea again tried to reassure her. There was nothing to worry about: it would probably be simpler to arrange clandestine meetings in the country than it was in town. He would come out as often as possible and stay with trusted friends—the Tiepolos had a villa nearby. He would visit her often. It would be easy.

In the meantime Andrea decided he needed to spend as much time as possible with the consul in order to humor him, allay his suspicions, and steer him ever closer toward a decision about Giustiniana. It soon became apparent that the consul, too, wished to keep his young friend close to him. He said he wanted Andrea at his side to deal with his legal and financial affairs but he was probably putting him to the test, observing him closely to see if he still loved Giustiniana. Never before had he seemed so dependent on him. The two of them became inseparable—an unusual couple traveling back and forth between Venice and Mogliano, where Smith's staff was preparing the house for the summer season, and making frequent business trips to Padua.

Giustiniana was left to brood over her future alone. She complained about Andrea's absences from Venice and dreaded the uncertainty of her situation. She did not understand his need to spend so much time with that "damned old man." She felt they were "wasting precious time" that they could be spending together. Yet her reproaches always gave way to words of great tenderness. During one of Andrea's overnight trips to the mainland with the consul, she wrote:

You are far away, dear Memmo, and I am not well at all. I am happier when you are here in town even when I know we won't be speaking because I always bear in mind that if by happy accident I am suddenly free to see you, I can always find a way to tell you. You might run over to see me; I might see you at the window. . . . And so the time I spend away from you passes less painfully. . . . But days like this one are very long indeed and seem never to end. . . . Though I must say there have been some happy moments too, as when I woke up this morning and found two letters from you that I read over and over all day. They gave me so much pleasure. . . . I still have other letters from you, which I fortunately have not yet returned to you—those too were brought out and given a "tour" today. And your portrait—oh, how sweetly it occupied me! I spoke to it, I told it all the things that I feel when I see you and I am unable to express to you when I am near you. . . . My mother took me out with her to take some fresh air, and we went for a ride ever so lazily down the canal. And as by chance she was as quiet as I was, I let myself go entirely to my thoughts. Then, emerging from those thoughts, I looked around eagerly, as if I were about to run into you. Every time I saw a boat that seemed to me not unlike yours, I couldn't stop believing that you might be in it. The same thing happened when we got back home—a sudden movement outside brought me several times to the window where I always sit when I hope to see you. . . . The evening hours were very uncomfortable. We had several visitors, and I could not leave the company. But in the end they did not bother my heart and thoughts so much because I went to sit in a corner of the room. Now, thank God, I have retired and

I am with you with all my heart and spirit. This is always the happiest moment of the evening for me. And you, my soul, what are you doing in the country? Are you always with me? Tonnina now torments me because she wants to sleep and is calling me to bed. Oh, the fussy girl! But I guess I must please her. I will write to you tomorrow. Wouldn't it be sweet if I could dream I was with you? Farewell, my Memmo, farewell. I adore you. . . . Memmo, I always, always think of you, always, my soul, yes, always.

As the *villeggiatura* approached, Giustiniana's anxiety increased. Andrea still spent most of his time with the consul, working for their future happiness, as he put it. But there was no sign that the consul was any closer to a decision. Furthermore, the idea of spending the summer in the countryside deceiving the old man disconcerted her. She grew pessimistic and began to fear that nothing good would ever come of their cockamamie scheme. Andrea was being unrealistic, she felt, and it was madness to press on: "Believe me, we have nothing to gain and much to lose. . . . We are bound to commit many imprudent acts. He will surely become aware of them and will be disgusted with both you and me. You will have a very dangerous enemy instead of a friend. As for my mother, she will blame us as never before for having disrupted what she believes to be the best plan she ever conceived." The two of them carried on regardless, Giustiniana complained—she by ingratiating herself to the consul every time she saw him "as if I were really keen to marry him," thereby pleasing her mother to no end, and Andrea by "lecturing me all day that I should take him as a husband." But even if she did, even if the consul, at the end of their machinations, asked her to marry him and she consented, did Andrea really think things would suddenly become easier for them or that the consul would come to accept their relationship? "For heaven's sake, don't even contemplate such a crazy idea. Do you believe he would even stand to have you in his house or see you next to me? God only knows the scenes that would take place and how miserable my life would become, and his and yours too."

In June, as Giustiniana waited for the dreaded departure to the countryside, Andrea's trips out of town increased. There was more to attend to than the consul's demands: his own family expected him to pay closer attention to the Memmo estates on the mainland now that his uncle was dead. As soon as he was back in Venice, though, he immediately tried to comfort Giustiniana by reiterating the logic behind their undertaking. He insisted that there was no alternative: the consul was their only chance. He argued for patience and was usually persuasive enough that Giustiniana, by her own admission and despite all her reservations, would melt "into a state of complete contentment" just listening to him speak.

Little by little she was beginning to accept the notion that deception was a necessary tool in the pursuit of her own happiness. But the art of deceit did not come naturally to her. When she was not in Andrea's arms, enthralled by his reassuring words, her own, more innocent way of thinking quickly took over again, and she would panic: "Oh God, Memmo, you paint a picture of my present and my future that makes me tremble. You say Smith is my only chance. Yet if he doesn't take me, I lose you, and if he does take me, I can't see you. And you wish me to be wise. . . . Memmo, what should I do? I cannot go on like this."

"Ah, Memmo, I am here now and there is no turning back."

In early July, after weeks of preparations, the Wynnes had finally traveled across the lagoon and up the Brenta Canal and had arrived at Le Scalette, the villa the consul had arranged for them to rent. The memory of her tearful separation from Andrea in Venice that very morning—the Wynnes and their small retinue piling onto their boat on the Grand Canal while Andrea waved to her from his gondola, apparently unseen by Mrs. Anna—had filled Giustiniana's mind during the entire boat ride. She had lain on the couch inside the cabin, pretending to sleep so as not to interrupt even for an instant the flow of images that kept her enraptured by sweet thoughts of Andrea. Once they arrived at the villa and had settled in, she cast a glance around her new surroundings and had discovered that the house and the garden were actually very nice and the setting on the Brenta could not have been more pleasant. "Oh, if only you were here, how delightful this place would be. How sweetly we could spend our time," she wrote to him before going to bed the first night.

The daily rituals of the *villeggiatura* began every morning with a cup of hot chocolate that sweetened the palate after a long night's sleep and provided a quick boost of energy. It was usually served in an intimate setting—breakfast in the boudoir. The host and hostess and their guests would exchange greetings and the first few tidbits of gossip before the morning mail was brought in. Plans for the day would be laid out. After the toilette, much of which was taken up by elaborate hairdressing in the case of the ladies, the members of the household would reassemble outdoors for a brief walk around the perimeter of the garden. Upon their return they might gather in the drawing room to play cards until it was time for lunch, a rather elaborate meal that in the grander houses was usually prepared under the supervision of a French cook. After-noons were taken up by social visits or a more formal promenade along the banks of the Brenta, an exercise the Venetians had dubbed *la trottata*. Often the final destination of this afternoon stroll was the *bottega*, the village coffeehouse where summer resi-dents caught up with the latest news from Venice. After dinner, the evening was taken up by conversation and society games. Blind-man's bluff was a favorite. In the larger villas there were also small concerts and recitals and the occasional dancing party.

Giustiniana did not really look forward to any of this. As soon as she arrived at Le Scalette she was seized by worries of a logisti-cal nature, wondering whether it would really be easier for her to meet Andrea secretly in the country than it had been in Venice. She looked around the premises for a suitable place where they could see each other and immediately reported to her lover that there was an empty guest room next to her bedroom. More important: "There is a door not far from the bed that opens onto a secret, nar-row staircase that leads to the garden. Thus we are free to go in and out without being seen." She promised Andrea to explore the sur-roundings more thoroughly: "I will play the spy and check every corner of the house, and look closely at the garden as well as the caretaker's quarters—everywhere. And I will give you a detailed report."

The villa next door belonged to Andrea Tron, a shrewd politician who never became doge but was known to be the most powerful man in Venice (he would play an important role in launching Andrea's career). Tron took a keen interest in his new neighbors. As an old friend of Consul Smith, he was aware that the death of Smith's wife had created quite an upheaval among the English residents. Like all well-informed Venetians, he also knew about Andrea and Giustiniana's past relationship and was curious to know whether it might still be simmering under the surface. He came for lunch and invited the Wynnes over to his villa. Mrs. Anna was pleased; it was good policy to be on friendly terms with such an influential man as Tron. She encouraged Giustiniana to be sociable and ingratiating toward their important neighbor. In the afternoon, Giustiniana took to sitting at the end of the garden, near the little gate that opened onto the main thoroughfare, enjoying the coolness and gazing dreamily at the passersby. Tron would often stroll past and stop for a little conversation with her.

Initially Giustiniana thought his large estate might prove useful for her nightly escapades. She had noticed that there were several *casini* on his property where she and Andrea could meet under cover of darkness. But thanks to her frequent trips to the servants' quarters, where she was already forming useful alliances, she had found out that Tron's *casini* were "always full of people and even if there should be an empty one, the crowds next door might make it too dangerous" for them to plan a tryst there.

In the end it seemed to her more convenient and prudent to make arrangements with their trusted friends, the Tiepolos: their villa was a little further down the road, but Andrea could certainly stay there and a secret rendezvous might be engineered more safely. Giustiniana even went so far as to express the hope that they might be able to replicate in the countryside "another Ca' Tiepolo," which had served them so well back in Venice. She added—her mind was racing ahead—that when Andrea came out to visit it would be best "if we meet in the morning because it is easy for me to get up before everyone else while in the evening the house is always full of people and I am constantly observed."

As Giustiniana diligently prepared the ground for a summer of lovemaking, she did wonder whether "all this information might ever be of any use to us." Andrea was still constantly on the move, a fleeting presence along the Brenta. When he was not with the consul at Mogliano, he was traveling to Padua on business, visiting the Memmo estate, or rushing back to Venice, where his sister, Marina, who had not been well for some time, had suddenly been taken very ill. Giustiniana might hear that Andrea was in a neighboring village, on his way to see her. Then she would hear nothing more. Every time she started to dream of him stealing into her bedroom in the dead of night or surprising her at the village *bottega*, a letter would reach her announcing a delay or a change of plans. So she waited and wrote to him, and waited and wrote:

I took a long walk in the garden, alone for the most part. I had your little portrait with me. How often I looked at it! How many things I said to it! How many prayers and how many protestations I made! Ah, Memmo, if only you knew how excessively I adore you! I defy any woman to love you as I love you. And we know each other.so deeply and we cannot enjoy our perfect friendship or take advantage of our common interests. God, what madness! Though in these cruel circumstances it is good to know that you love me in the extreme and that I have no doubts about you: otherwise what miserable hell my life would be.

A few days later she was still on tenterhooks:

I received your letter just as we got up from the table and I flew to a small room, locked myself in, and gave myself away to the pleasure of listening to my Memmo talk to me and profess all his tenderness for me and tell me about all the things that have kept him so busy. Oh, if only you had seen me then, how gratified you would have been. I lay nonchalantly on the couch and held your letter in one hand and your portrait in the other. I read and reread [the letter] avidly, and for a moment I abandoned that pleasure to indulge in the other pleasure of looking at you. I pressed one and the other against my bosom and was overcome by waves of tenderness. Little by little I fell asleep. An hour and a half later I awoke, and now I am with you again and writing to you.

Andrea was finally on his way to see Giustiniana one evening when he was reached by a note from his brother Bernardo, telling him that their sister, Marina, was dying. Distraught, he returned to Venice and wrote to Giustiniana en route to explain his change of plans. She immediately wrote back, sending all her love and sympathy:

> *Your sister is dying, Memmo? And you have to rush back to Venice? . . . You do well to go, and I would have advised you to do the same. . . . But I am hopeful that she will live. . . . Maybe your mother and your family have written to you so pressingly only to hasten your return. . . . If your sister recovers, I pray you will come to see me right away. . . . And if she should pass away, you will need consolation, and after the time that decency requires you will come to seek it from your Giustiniana.*

In this manner, days and then weeks went by. Eventually, Giustiniana stopped making plans for secret encounters. There were moments during her lonely wait when she even worried about the intensity of her feelings. What was going on in *his* mind, in *his* heart? She had his letters, of course. He was usually very good about writing to her. But his prolonged absence disoriented her. She needed so much to see him—to see him in the flesh and not simply to conjure his image in a world of fantasy. "I tremble, Memmo, at the thought that my excessive love might become a burden on you," she wrote to him touchingly. ". . . I have no one else but you. . . . Where are you now, my soul? Why can't I be with you?"

While she longed for Andrea to appear in the country, Giustiniana also forced herself to be graceful with the consul. He called on the Wynnes regularly, coming by for lunch and sometimes staying overnight at Le Scalette, throwing the household into a tizzy because of his surprise arrivals and the late hours he kept. He took Giustiniana out on walks in the garden and spent time with the family, lavishing his attention on everyone. There was no question in anybody's mind that the old man was completely taken with Giustiniana and that he was courting her with the intention of marriage. Even the younger children had come to assume that the consul had been "tagged" and already "belonged" to their older sister, as Giustiniana put it in her letters to Andrea.

As she waited for her lover, Giustiniana watched with mild bewilderment the restrained embraces between her sister Tonnina and her young fiancé, Alvise Renier, who was summering in a villa nearby. "Poor fellow!" she wrote to Andrea. "He takes her in his arms, holds her close to him, and still she remains indolent and moves no more than a statue. Even when she does caress him she is so cold that merely looking at her makes one angry. I don't understand that kind of love, my soul, because you set me on fire if you so much as touch me." She was being a little hard on her youngest sister. After all, Tonnina was only thirteen and Alvise little older than that; it was a fairly innocent first love. But of course every time Giustiniana saw them together she longed to be in the arms of her impetuous lover.

Mrs. Anna, unaware of the heavy flow of letters between Le Scalette and Ca' Memmo, could not have been more pleased at how things were developing. With Andrea out of the way, the consul seemed increasingly comfortable with the idea of marrying Giustiniana. It was not unrealistic to expect a formal proposal by the end of the season. The other summer residents followed with relish the comings and goings at the Wynnes'. The consul's visits were regularly commented upon at the *bottega* in Dolo, as was Andrea's conspicuous absence. Were they still seeing each other behind the consul's back, or had their love affair finally succumbed to family pressures? Giustiniana's young Venetian friends often put her on the spot when she appeared to fetch her mail. However circumspect she had to be, she could not give up the secret pleasure of letting people know, in her own allusive way, that she still loved Andrea deeply. "Today we were talking about how the English run away from passions whilst the Italians seem to embrace them," she reported. "I was asked somewhat maliciously what I thought of the matter. I replied that life is quite short and that a well-grounded passion for a sweet and lovable person can give one a thousand pleasures. In such cases, I said, why run away from it? The same person pressed on: 'What if that passion is strongly opposed or if it is hurtful?' I answered that once a passion is developed it must always be sustained. . . . Must I really care about what these silly people think? I have too much vanity to disown in public a choice that I have made."

The consul's repeated visits—and Andrea's continued absence—created an air of inevitability about her future marriage that took its toll on Giustiniana. In public, she did her best to put on a brave front. But as soon as she was alone the gloomiest premonitions took hold of her. The hope that when it was all over—when the marriage had taken place—she would be free to give herself completely to the man she loved sustained her through the performance she was putting on day after day. But she could not rid herself of the fear that for all their clever scheming, once the consul married her she would not be able to see Andrea at all. As an English friend summering by the Brenta whispered to her one day, "I know my country well, and I am quite sure the first person Smith will ban from his house will be Memmo." She wrote to Andrea:

Alas, I know my country too! So what is to be done? Wait until he dies to be free? And in the meantime? And afterward? He might live with me for years, while I cannot live without you for a month. . . . True, any other husband would stop me from seeing you without having the advantages Smith has to offer, including his old age. . . . But everything is so uncertain, and it seems to me that the future can only be worse than the present. Of course it would be wrong for the two of us to get married. I wouldn't want your ruin even if it gave me all the happiness I would feel living with you. No, my Memmo! I love you in the most disinterested and sincerest way possible, exactly as you should be loved. I do not believe we shall ever be entirely happy, but all the same I will always be yours, I will adore you, and I will depend on you all my life. . . . So I will do what pleases you, [but remember] that if Smith were to ask for my hand and my Memmo were not entirely happy about it I would instantly abandon Smith and everything else with him, for my true good fortune is to belong to you and you alone.

In August Marina's health briefly improved and Andrea was finally free to go to the country to see Giustiniana. He was not well—still recovering from a bad fever that had forced him to bed. But he decided to make the trip out to Dolo anyway and take advantage of the Tiepolos' open invitation. Giustiniana was in a frenzy of excitement. "Come quickly, my heart, now that your sister's condition allows you to. . . . I would do anything, anything for the pleasure of seeing you." It was too risky for Andrea to visit her house, so she had arranged to see him in the modest home of the mother of one of the servants, thanks to the intercession of a local priest in whom she had immediately confided. "I went to see it, and I must tell you it's nothing more than a hovel," she warned, "but it should suffice us." Alternatively, they could meet in the caretaker's apartment, which was reached "by taking a little staircase next to the stables."

These preparations were unnecessary. Andrea arrived by carriage late in the night, exhausted after a long detour to Padua he had made on behalf of the ever-demanding consul. He left his luggage at the Tiepolos' and immediately went off to surprise Giustiniana by sneaking up to her room from the garden.

The following morning, after lingering in bed in a joyful haze, she scribbled a note and sent it to Andrea care of the Tiepolos: "My darling, lovable Memmo, how grateful I feel! Can a heart be more giving? Anyone can pay a visit to his lover. But the circumstances in which you came to see me last night, and the manner and grace you showed me—nobody, nobody else could have done it! I am so happy and you are wonderful to me. When will I be allowed to show you all my tenderness?"

Giustiniana fretted about Andrea's health. He had not looked well, and she feared a relapse: "You have lost some weight, and you looked paler than usual. . . . I didn't want to tell you, my precious, but you left me worried. For the love of me, please take care of yourself. How much you must have suffered riding all night in the stagecoach, and possibly still with a fever. . . . My soul, the pleasure of seeing you is simply too, too costly." Yet she was so hungry for him after his long absence that she could hardly bear not to see him now that he was so close: "Maybe you will come again this evening. . . . Do not expose yourself to danger, for I would die if I were the cause of any ailment. . . . If you have fully recovered, do come, for I shall be waiting for you with the greatest impatience, but if you are still not well then take care of yourself, my soul. I will come to see you; I will . . . ah, but I cannot. What cruelty!"

Andrea settled in at the Tiepolos' for the rest of summer. His health fully regained and his sister apparently out of immediate danger, he was anxious to catch up on the time not spent with Giustiniana. They were soon back to their old routine, working their messengers to exhaustion and conniving with trusted allies to set up secret meetings. Giustiniana's muslins were swishing again as she rushed off on the sly for quick visits to the "hovel"—which she now called "our pleasure house"—or to the caretaker's, to the Tiepolos', or even to the village *bottega* if they were feeling especially daring. When they were not together, they sent notes planning their next escapade. Giustiniana was in heaven. There were no worries in her mind, no dark clouds in the sky: "Am I really entirely in your heart? My Memmo, how deeply I feel my happiness! What delightful pleasure I feel in possessing you. There were times, I confess, in which I doubted my own happiness. Now, Memmo, I believe in you completely, and I am the happiest woman in the world. What greater proof of tenderness, of friendship, of true affection can I possibly want from you, my precious one? My heart and soul, you are inimitable. And it will be a miracle if so much pleasure and joy do not drive me entirely mad."

In the tranquil atmosphere of the Venetian summer, when the days were held together by card games, a little gossip, and an evening *trottata*, the sudden burst of activity between the Tiepolos' villa and Le Scalette did not go unnoticed. There was much new talk about Andrea and Giustiniana among the summer crowd. Even certain members in the Wynne household grew worried. Aunt Fiorina, always sympathetic to their cause, had been aware of the intense correspondence between the two lovers over the course of the summer but had refrained from making an issue of it. When she learned that Andrea and Giustiniana were actually seeing each other, however, she put her foot down and subjected her niece to "a long rebuke." The stakes with the consul were too high for them to be playing such a dangerous game, she explained.

Fiorina's alarm presaged worse things to come. Andrea went back to Venice on family business for a few days. Giustiniana wrote to him several times, but the letters never reached him; her messenger had been intercepted. Someone in the Wynne household—perhaps in the servants' quarters—had betrayed Giustiniana and handed the letters over to Mrs. Anna. The last lines of a frantic message to Andrea are the only fragment that has survived to give us a sense of the panic and chaos that ensued:

> . . . the most violent remedies. It is known that I have written to Venice, but not to whom! Everyone, my Memmo, is spying on me. . . . Don't abandon me now, and don't take any chances by writing to me. I won't lose you, but if something violent were to happen, I feel capable of anything. If you leave me I shall die, my soul!

Alas, Mrs. Anna knew very well to whom Giustiniana had written in Venice because she was also in possession of some of Andrea's letters—letters she had intercepted before they could be delivered to her daughter. She confronted Giustiniana, shaking with anger. "All day was an absolute hell—if Hell can really be that horrible," Giustiniana wrote to Andrea a few days later, when she was finally able to seclude herself ("I must write to you where and when I can"). At the height of her fury Mrs. Anna threatened to sue Andrea and "expose him as a seducer who upsets peaceful families," she raged, "for the letters I have in my hands prove that he is just that." Giustiniana pleaded for mercy with such force and conviction that eventually she managed to calm her mother down. In tears, Mrs. Anna withdrew her threat but warned her daughter there would not be another reprieve: "I will have you watched all the time, I will keep my eyes wide open, I will know everything. And remember that I have enough in my hands to ruin Signor Memmo."

The worst was avoided—what could have been more nightmarish than seeing their love story torn to shreds in a courtroom? But the betrayal had suddenly exposed the secret life of the two lovers. The places they met, their secret arrangements, their promises of lifelong love and devotion—everything was now known to Mrs. Anna. She had a list of the names of their messengers and accomplices. There was not much she could do about the Tiepolos except prohibit her daughter from setting foot in their house. But within the Wynne household, retribution was swift. The servants who had abetted the lovers were given a scolding and punished harshly. Alvisetto, who had been in on the whole thing from the start, was sent away.

There is something deeply sad about Alvisetto's dismissal, which reminds us to what degree a servant's life was in the hands of his *padrone*—his master. In general the master of the house and his wife had a formal, even distant relationship with the servants. But the younger members of the household had a closer rapport with the house staff. They would often appear in the servants' quarters to trade gossip or ask a favor. And it was not uncommon for a daughter of the house to confide some of her secrets to a maid (or for a son to seek sexual favors). But it was always an imbalanced and ultimately ambiguous relationship. And there was often as much room for treachery as there was for connivance—on both sides. After all, Giustiniana found her allies in the kitchen at Le Scalette, but she had probably found her betrayer there as well. Goldoni made fun of the complicated relations between masters and servants in one of his most popular plays. But poor Alvisetto was nothing like "the wily and dumb" Truffaldino, the main character in *A Servant for Two Masters*. One has the feeling that, all along, he had been forced by Giustiniana and Andrea to cooperate with them against his better judgment. Now he was being made to pay, very dearly, for a mess that was not of his making. And they could do nothing to save him.

The two lovers managed to resume communications within a

few days. Giustiniana barricaded herself in a kindly peasant's home on the property, where she hastily scribbled her notes to Andrea. But seeing each other was out of the question, given the circumstances. "Ah, Memmo, what must I do? . . . Will I ever see you again? I love you more than ever, but I am losing you! . . . Help me, tell me what to do." It was not long before they found a solution. Andrea suggested he write a letter to Mrs. Anna, professing his undying love for Giustiniana and offering to marry her in a couple of years if Consul Smith did not make an offer. It was a bluff: Andrea and Giustiniana both knew he was not planning to make good on the promise. But he thought it would convince Mrs. Anna that his intentions were honorable and she might therefore allow them to see each other. It was a risky strategy for a short-term gain. Nevertheless, Giustiniana agreed to the plan and decided to bring her aunt Fiorina in on it to a point—telling her about the letter Andrea wished to write to Mrs. Anna but without explaining to her that it was a deception. Aunt Fiorina responded with mixed feelings. "There is no denying that Memmo loves you and that he is a gentleman," she said to her niece. His proposal was "very reasonable." The problem, as she saw it, was getting Mrs. Anna to consider listening to him. But she was willing to help.

Even with Aunt Fiorina on their side, Giustiniana felt that, in the end, success or failure hinged on Andrea finding the right tone and words with which to address her mother. Her instructions to him were very precise—and they showed a considerable determination to take charge of the situation.

You will begin your letter by complaining that I have not written to you. You will tell me that you know in your heart that I love you deeply. You will assure me that you love me in the extreme and that to prove it you had written to my mother because you wanted her to hear an important suggestion you had to make—at which point you will copy the letter you have prepared for her. The most important thing (and here, my dear, you need to be artful and I want you to trust me) is to show yourself resolute in offering to write up a document in which, as you have said, you will promise to marry me in two years if Smith or some better party does not come along and propose to me. Give several reasons why it would be advantageous for me to marry you and add that it is your deep love for me that brings you to make this proposition, which you already know will be embraced by me with all my heart. And say you will have to wait because your present circumstances do not allow you to go through with the proposal at this time but in two years things should happen that could make us happy and comfortable for the rest of our lives. . . . [Add] that we would be very careful to keep this promise a secret.

It is hard to imagine that deep in her heart Giustiniana, though fully aware it was all a scheme, did not hope it would all actually come true, and that in two years' time she would be married to Andrea. If she did, she kept it to herself.

Andrea struggled over a first draft. Giustiniana showed it to Fiorina, who was "satisfied with [Andrea's] sentiments" but a little daunted by the resentment he expressed toward Mrs. Anna. "She told me to tell you that to seduce that woman one must flatter her—not be aggressive." She asked Andrea to try again. "My love," she added to encourage him, "what happiness will come our way if we manage to deceive her! Either Smith will marry me, in which case we won't need [the subterfuge], or he won't marry me, in which case she certainly won't take away from the man whom she thinks will one day marry me the freedom to be with me from time to time."

Andrea's second draft, however, was even more disappointing.

My Memmo, this is not the sort of letter that will get us what we want. . . . It is weak and useless, so you will understand why I haven't shown it to my mother and not even to my aunt. The other one was stronger and would have served our purpose wonderfully if you had simply deleted the few lines in which you insulted my mother. . . . In this one I see only the lover. . . . So write a new letter or rewrite the first one the way I told you to. . . . Send it immediately. . . . My aunt has already asked me if it had arrived, and it would be a pity if she saw us so unhurried in a matter of such importance.

Part of the problem was that Andrea was holding back in case their plan backfired. In his drafts, he committed himself to marrying Giustiniana only in the vaguest terms, because he feared the letter might get him into trouble with his own family if Mrs. Anna misused it. Giustiniana guessed what was bothering him and came to his rescue, suggesting that he tell the truth to *his* mother, even let her read a few of Giustiniana's letters to convince her that they had no intention of following through, that it was only a scheme to deceive Mrs. Anna, and that she—Giustiniana—would "never accept your hand" because she was well aware of the damage she would cause to the Memmos. There is no evidence, however, that he followed her advice.

In none of their letters to each other did either Andrea or Giustiniana suggest that they might actually marry one day. They stubbornly kept the thought at bay. This is somewhat ironic: Mrs. Anna was growing increasingly fearful that the two lovers were going to marry whether she liked it or not. Indeed, she came to suspect, in the paranoid state she had slipped into after intercepting the latest batch of letters, that the two lovers had already wed in secret.

In this sense Andrea's concocted letter, once it was finally approved by its exacting editor and delivered, must have provided some relief to Mrs. Anna. But there was little else in it to mollify her, and the deceit ultimately made matters worse. At first she thought the letter was a hoax. When her sister Fiorina finally convinced her in good faith that it was authentic, Mrs. Anna explained to Giustiniana in very sobering terms why she could not accept Andrea's proposition. This is Giustiniana's account of her mother's reaction:

I have read Memmo's letter and I believe he honestly wishes to marry you. You like Memmo, Memmo loves you, and your union would certainly be desirable. But, my dear Giustiniana, you cannot be his wife. I will now tell you something you might not have known the rest of your life. My dear daughter, the marriage contract would never be approved. Anyone but a Venetian nobleman would be good for you. Think about it and decide for yourself. Do you want to be shunned by all and barred from entering any nobleman's home, quite apart from being hated by the Memmo family . . . and doing so much harm to that poor man? And what about the harm you would inflict on the children you two would have? Come, my child, take courage. I can feel your pain in losing the man you adore just at the time you felt so close to possessing him. But if you love him, surely you will not want to ruin him or his sons. Marry, and then you may carry on a friendship that is so dear to you.

Her savvy line of reasoning was, in fact, surprisingly similar to Andrea and Giustiniana's own way of thinking. It was also the first time she showed any degree of empathy toward her daughter. Despite her severity and her terrible scenes, she apparently understood what Giustiniana was going through (did it perhaps remind her of some painful separation in her own youth?). Of course, it is impossible to be certain how faithful a transcription of Mrs. Anna's reaction this really was. Certainly, according to the version Giustiniana supplied to Andrea, her mother even seemed to be sanctioning the possibility that their love affair continue once she was safely married.

In any case, Mrs. Anna was not finished. She told Giustiniana that as soon as they returned to Venice (the season was now over, and the Wynnes were getting ready to leave Le Scalette), she wanted to discuss things directly with Andrea. Meanwhile, she instructed her daughter to write a letter making a formal request for the return of all her correspondence, in which she was also to refuse Andrea's hand: for his own good and that of his family, and for the good of her brothers, whose future in England might be put in jeopardy if she married a Catholic.

Shortly after the Wynnes returned to Venice, Mrs. Anna and Andrea met face to face. This was their first encounter since Andrea's *cacciata funesta*, his fateful banishment two years earlier, and it was not easy for either of them. Still, they managed to be polite, and Mrs. Anna even showed a little compassion, assuring Andrea that she did not harbor ill feelings toward him. She understood how much they loved each other, she told him, and was convinced that in the future they could be together, but for the time being it was out of the question. This was a very sensitive moment, she explained: as he well knew, the consul was interested in marrying Giustiniana and the future of her family was at stake. Again she demanded that Andrea cease all communication with her daughter.

Subtly, Mrs. Anna was, in effect, entering into a secret pact with her archenemy. If he agreed to step back and allow her to bring her delicate transactions with the consul to a successful conclusion, she, in turn, would not obstruct their relationship in the future. Andrea agreed to her demands—after all, he had had the same objective all along. He promised he would not write and would not see Giustiniana until her marriage with the consul was sealed. Upon Mrs. Anna's insistence, he also wrote a letter to Fiorina renouncing his intention to marry Giustiniana in two years' time—a request he found easy to satisfy. Separately, Andrea wrote to Giustiniana that, given the circumstances, it would indeed be prudent to cease all contact. Mrs. Anna had scored a complete victory.

Giustiniana was stunned by Andrea's betrayal. She could not believe he had acquiesced to her mother's demands so meekly. "Do you believe I can live without writing or seeing you? . . . You ask too much. . . . I would rather die." Andrea tried to placate her, but he remained adamant: "We are made for each other, and everyone will see it in the future, but believe me, this is not the time. . . . We have no choice. . . . If you need something, send someone for me . . . [but] for heaven's sake do not write to me. . . . The best answer you can give to this letter is not to answer it. . . . Love me, Giustiniana. . . . Have faith in me. . . . I leave you now."

Giustiniana could not stop the rage growing within her:

If you are willing to feel content, I am not. You do not know me yet. I feel the most violent passion and am capable of anything. You have reduced me to a horrible state. Do you think I will simply wait peacefully as you amuse yourself with the best company and the fairest women in the country? Put yourself in my position, and tell me if you would feel at ease. Of course you

*probably would because you don't understand these things. . . .
Meanwhile, I am left to wait with indifference for an uncertain
marriage. What kind of love is this? . . . Your letter made me
shed so many tears that I had to hide my face all morning. . . .
How did you have the heart to ask me to break off our relationship? How could you not take pity on me, on my heart, on my
love? Memmo, I have no one else in the world but you, and now
you tell me you will no longer be mine?*

Andrea was exasperated by her reaction. Even though he was
"afraid to break the agreement" with Mrs. Anna, he sent Giustiniana an angry note: "You have managed to turn my pain into wrath.
What must I do for you? Pray tell me, you beast. What kind of
love is this that you are never happy with what I do? I adore you
and the desire to live with you kills me a little more every day. . . .
My one sin is that I do not write to you, but how can I write to you?
You know very well all the risks involved."

The only reasonable thing to do, he insisted, was to fix their
attention on the consul and help Mrs. Anna achieve her goal as
quickly as possible. It was still the surest path to their happiness.
Although Giustiniana never ceased to be skeptical, Andrea's hope
that things would work out to their advantage increased every day.
"The time will soon come," he declared, "when I shall be able to
enjoy your happiness and the pleasure of showing the world how
much I love you." Once again he broke the embargo he had
solemnly accepted in order to explain to Giustiniana that, in fact,
things could not be going any better:

*By God, Giustiniana, we are lucky . . . because the only way
to bring this comedy to a happy conclusion is through Smith. . . .
And we are luckier still because he is old, because he is rich, because
he is my friend, because he stands in awe of society, because he
stands in awe of me . . . because he is vain, because he is crazy,
and because he has everything we can possibly need. Must I say
more? Listen, the truth is that our present misfortune—having to
bear with it for so long—is really our greatest fortune, provided it
comes to an end. . . . I ask: if Smith had married you when he*

knew my love for you was still too hot . . . would it really have been possible for me to come to you? Believe me, it takes time to seduce an old cat and then play him for a sucker. But now I know that I have prepared everything well, that I have brought him closer to me, that he loves us all the more and that he trusts us. I have made a great deal of progress, and I hope at least we shall be happy.

The old cat wasn't napping, though. Back in Venice after his *villeggiatura* in Mogliano, it did not take long for Smith to learn about Mrs. Anna's confrontation with Andrea and, even more infuriating for him, about Giustiniana's prostration at the thought of not seeing her lover anymore. Andrea and Giustiniana did not make things easier for themselves: they were incapable of observing the ban on their correspondence, and messengers were once again shuttling between them. Soon they began to see each other, sometimes even in Piazza San Marco or Campo Santo Stefano during the evening stroll. It was only a matter of time before someone told Smith, and there was no shortage of people in Venice willing to trade on the misfortune of others.

One such person was the Abbé Testagrossa, a shady character who eked out a living in Venice by means of flattery and gossip. He had found employment as a secretary in the French Embassy but was still in the habit of crying poverty to cadge his lunches and dinners, for which he would sing whatever tune was required. For anyone with a secret, he was a man to be kept at a distance. One evening Andrea and Giustiniana were talking in a secluded corner near Campo Santo Stefano when the Abbé Testagrossa appeared from nowhere and passed by them, smiling. Andrea became so worried that the abbé might create a scandal that he went out of his way to be nice to him, and next time he saw him he even invited him to lunch at Ca' Memmo. "What could I do?" he sheepishly explained to an even more anxious Giustiniana. "I ran into him on the water near my house, and he said to me, 'I no longer have a kitchen, and I am forced to go out begging for a meal here and there.'" Andrea reassured her that he had "no intention" of being nice to Testagrossa again and would "treat him with so much formality it will be plain to him that this [lunch] does not represent the resumption of a friendship. But you wouldn't have wanted me to get on the wrong side of this indiscreet chatterer, would you?"

Still, he agreed with Giustiniana that the abbé would probably try to "hurt" them anyway because of "the sheer weirdness of his character." Given what we know of Testagrossa, it is certainly plausible that he casually told the consul—perhaps over a meal at Palazzo Balbi—that he had seen the two lovers alone near Campo Santo Stefano.

August turned into September, and still the consul made no official proposal. Andrea grew desperate to know what might have been said to Smith. Was it enough to undo all the work he had accomplished over the summer? Somehow the whole enterprise seemed to be more difficult to manage in the city, with its malicious whispers and knowing conversations. Andrea sought the consul's company to keep a close eye on him. But he could not read him as well as in the past. At times Smith seemed his usual old self. At others, his voice would take on a tone of sarcasm that worried Andrea. Here is a fragment of a conversation he had with Smith, which he transcribed for Giustiniana:

> *"What is the matter, dear Memmo, that you should sigh so heavily?"*
>
> *"I don't know. I'm not feeling very well. Maybe the sirocco . . ."*
>
> *"Ah, but it must be something else. These are not sirocco sighs . . ."*

Had he discovered their plot? "And yet the man treats me kindly, in his islander's sort of way," Andrea mused.

There was increasing pressure at home as well. The Bentivoglios, a rich family from the mainland, had spoken to Pietro and Lucia Memmo, offering the hand of one of their daughters for Andrea. The Memmos had agreed to initiate a preliminary round of negotiations through the offices of an intermediary. At first

Andrea went along with it, hoping the talks would bog down on their own, as was so often the case in these complicated matrimonial deals. He told Giustiniana not to worry, assuring her that in the end nothing would come of it.

Far more worrisome to him was the growing distance of the consul. He stopped talking about marrying Giustiniana, and his bantering tone vanished entirely. And he was cold not just toward Andrea but toward Mrs. Anna as well. The sudden change in his attitude threw her into a state of near panic. One night she took a gondola to Ca' Memmo and demanded to see Andrea. His servant woke him, and Andrea straggled downstairs: "I get in the gondola, she tells the gondolier to get out of the boat, and then she blurts out, 'You're killing me, you're murdering me. . . . Are you a gentleman or a traitor, Memmo?' " Andrea tried to placate her fury and claimed that in spite of his feelings he was not seeing Giustiniana anymore. He agreed to talk directly to Smith and tell him their affair was finished. As a further reassurance, he let her in on the secret marriage negotiations with the Bentivoglios. Neither she nor the consul had anything to worry about, he said.

But that was only a delaying tactic. Discussions with the Bentivoglios were going nowhere, the principal reason being that Andrea was now refusing to cooperate. He realized it was a very advantageous match—as he put it, "it contains all the elements I would not have found separately in other offers." But he belonged "entirely" to Giustiniana. As long as their situation was not settled one way or another, he was not going to marry anyone else. The Memmos were concerned that other prominent Venetian families might step in and make a deal with the Bentivoglios. Andrea's dillydallying irked them, and they pressed him for a straight yes or no. When he refused to give his consent, his mother, Lucia, exploded.

For months she had been under the impression that relations had cooled between Andrea and Giustiniana and that the consul was indeed going to marry her son's lover. Suddenly confronted with Andrea's recalcitrance, she was seized by a horrifying vision—as Mrs. Anna had been before her. All her son's talk about the consul marrying Giustiniana was really just a front to cover an unspeakable truth: Andrea and Giustiniana were already secretly married. "So all I heard about Smith was not true!" she yelled at him. "Oh, my God, Andrea, you've done it. Tell me the truth: you've married Giustiniana. Or you've given your word that you will. One of the two, I'm sure."

His mother's onslaught hurt Andrea. How could she believe him capable of dishonoring the family name? But it was the spectacle of his old and feeble father "with tears in his eyes" that really broke his heart.

The plan Andrea and Giustiniana had worked on since the spring finally spun out of control. Talks with the Bentivoglios collapsed at the end of September. Andrea's family put the blame entirely on him, and his life at Ca' Memmo became intolerable. When Smith learned that Andrea would not be marrying the Bentivoglio girl after all, he felt that all his suspicions about the two young lovers had been indirectly confirmed. In a dramatic and painful confrontation, he accused Andrea of plotting against him behind his back. He dismissed any further talk of marrying Giustiniana and abruptly sent him away.

It was a terrible blow for Andrea. As he expected, Mrs. Anna railed against him for scuttling what had seemed to her a done deal. But he was stunned by the amount of criticism he received from all sides for his embarrassing failure. "I have lost much more than my friendship with Smith," he wrote self-pityingly to Giustiniana. "Everyone accuses me of being imprudent, disloyal, not enough of a friend to you. If Smith has decided to renounce the project of marrying you—they say—it is on account of my lack of honesty and wisdom." Giustiniana's worst fears had come true. She was so crushed, so disoriented by all the mayhem that she did not know what to say to Andrea anymore and withdrew into silence.

Within days Smith proposed to Betty Murray, who had been waiting in the wings all along. "Old Consul Smith, who buried his wife nine months ago, has thrown himself at my sister's feet but has not yet bent her to his will,"[7] the Resident wrote at the beginning of October, savoring the moment with mischievous pride. Her resistance, if ever there was any, did not last long. They were married by the end of the month.

The winter of 1756–1757 was the coldest in living memory. By late October, autumn's golden light turned to a chilly gray. The *bora* blew in from the north. Snow fell early, swirling over the dark, brackish water. Some days the temperature dropped so low that the lagoon was frozen solid. A thick silence enveloped the city, pierced only by the mournful toll of church bells and the isolated cries of gondoliers. Inside the crowded *botteghe* and *malvasìe*, the talk among Venetians was mostly about the war that had broken out in the summer.

Ever since Austria had lost the rich eastern province of Silesia to Prussia in the War of the Austrian Succession of 1740–1748, it had schemed to reclaim it for the vast Habsburg Empire. With that objective in mind, Vienna had worked successfully to bring France, Prussia's traditional ally, to its side. Russia and the Electorate of Saxony also joined the new coalition. Suddenly surrounded by this powerful array of forces, Frederick the Great of Prussia, the restless "philosopher-king," struck an alliance with Great Britain and its German appendage, the Hanoverian state. In late August 1756 he staged a surprise attack against Saxony, the weakest link in the enemy camp, and marched all the way to Dresden.

Frederick's assault was the opening shot of the Seven Years' War, the last great conflict between the European powers before the French Revolution and one that would redraw the balance of power in favor of Great Britain and Prussia. The Venetian Republic never took part in that drawn-out war fought on three continents. Her neutrality, however, owed more to her growing irrelevance on the European stage than to her once proverbial diplomacy. The city remained at peace but still suffered the indirect consequences of the conflict. Trade plummeted, and the economy entered a period of decline. Venice would feel more and more isolated as the war dragged on, and a numbing fear of the future would creep into the population.

At Ca' Memmo the atmosphere was particularly gloomy that winter. Andrea's beloved sister, Marina, after a short reprieve, had died in terrible pain at the end of the summer. His father, Pietro, old and weak, was devastated by the loss of his daughter. Andrea found him "sitting alone by the fire" on a cold day. "He didn't know whether he wanted to eat or sleep." All his life Andrea had looked up to his uncle in a way he never had to his father, whom he considered excessively ingenuous and impractical. But he knew the tired old man hunched in the armchair by the fire loved him dearly, and there were times when he felt that his father understood, perhaps better than others, the depth of his feelings for Giustiniana. Andrea did not expect their relationship to change in any fundamental way at this stage in their lives, but now his filial devotion stirred in him more strongly than it had in the past. "His stomach convulsions do not let him sleep all night," he worried, "not to mention the gout and the fever. Poor old man! If only he were as sensible as he is generous, how much more I would love him."

Andrea had always been on more intimate terms with his mother, Lucia, but he saw little of her during that winter. The halls of Ca' Memmo were so cold that she hardly ever left her apartment. It wasn't just the chill in the air that kept her so withdrawn. The Smith imbroglio had offended her deeply, and for months she continued to brood over Andrea's embarrassing actions in the frosty confinement of her rooms.

Giustiniana herself remained so distant Andrea feared he would lose her as well. "Our love has not vanished no matter how much it has been threatened," he reminded her, gently suggesting new approaches to deal with her furious mother. But Giustiniana was still too dejected to give him anything more than passive, perfunctory replies. He felt her slipping away. "Why don't you defend me?" he complained. "Your mother hates me. . . . She slanders me. . . . Why don't you show her how wrong she is? . . . Because you don't love me anymore. . . . Oh God, I am lost. My soul, my sweetest soul, think hard before you ruin me."

Despite the biting temperatures, Andrea came by the house at Sant'Aponal regularly. He stood shivering under Giustiniana's window while his gondola sloshed about in the freezing water. Sometimes she did not even come to the window. She left Andrea's letters unanswered for days and seldom went out, usually only walking the short distance to church with her mother when she did. Andrea's pleading became increasingly desperate: "Oh God, if you want me to cease tormenting you, let me at least believe that we part as good friends and that you would still consider me worthy of you if circumstances were different."

Winter seemed to drag on endlessly, but in early spring Venice gradually regained her scintillating colors. The narrow streets again bustled with activity. The canals filled with boats of every size. After months of hibernation, the chattering crowds returned to the Listone for their daily stroll. Giustiniana was not immune to the changes around her. She responded a little more warmly to Andrea's letters. Warily, she agreed to see him again in secret. Andrea was grateful and extremely solicitous. He fretted over her health and her diet and was full of practical attentions as well. "I must look for some reed matting so that room of Rosa's will be less uncomfortable," he wrote in a touching display of domesticity. "My heart, how much I love you. I'm so full of you and so happy you will be mine forever."

On the surface, things gradually went back to the way they had been before. Of course, Alvisetto was no longer on the scene, but a replacement had been found: Martino, the bellboy at the Regina d'Inghilterra, the fashionable inn in the Frezzeria where Andrea sometimes stopped for a quick bite at lunchtime, now handled most of their secret correspondence.

Yet their relationship was not as it once had been. At the time of the conspiracy against Consul Smith, Giustiniana had given herself to Andrea with abandon because, in the end, she had allowed herself to believe in the success of their preposterous scheme.

Now, as they met like thieves in Rosa's unadorned little room, what prospect did their love have? "You will be mine forever," Andrea kept assuring her. But how was this to be? Again Giustiniana had nothing to look forward to: only uncertainty and more pain seemed to lie ahead. She gave in to Andrea's entreaties, spurred by her own physical desire to be in his arms, yet she remained emotionally aloof. Moreover, on the practical side she felt her mother was right: her marriage prospects *had* been seriously damaged. So there were a number of reasons why she was wary of following her lover along another tortuous path of deception. She preferred to live her passion day by day, avoiding her own thoughts about the future.

Andrea, however, had changed. It had been a painful winter for him, and the possibility of losing Giustiniana in the aftermath of the Smith debacle had made him even more aware of the depth of his feelings for her. As their clandestine relationship entered its fourth year with no hope of finding a practical arrangement that would allow them to be lovers in a less secretive manner, he began to contemplate what until now had been unthinkable. He loved her deeply. He wanted to be with her, to have children with her. If marriage was the only way they could be together, perhaps the time had come to take that bold step while trying to minimize the negative consequences as much as possible.

Without telling Giustiniana, Andrea had approached Clemente Sibiliato, a prominent lawyer, and the Abbé Jacopo Facciolati, a legal scholar and close friend of the family, to discuss the idea of submitting a marriage contract to the Avogarìa di Comun, the powerful three-member panel that had jurisdiction over such matters. The conversations were less discouraging than Andrea had feared, and he had come away with new hope. In the past, he had not even considered this possibility on the assumption that such a contract would never have been approved and the effort would only have discredited the two families. The same line of reasoning had led Mrs. Anna to banish Andrea in the first place. But circumstances had changed rather dramatically in the meantime, and with no serious alternative in sight, marriage did not seem such an unreasonable solution anymore. In many ways, it had become the only possible one.

Andrea grew increasingly convinced that the Venetian authorities would accept the petition, provided the two families preempted the veto of the Avogarìa di Comun by agreeing to endorse the marriage contract before it was presented. After all, he reasoned, the role of the Avogarìa was to protect Venetian customs and institutions and therefore, by extension, the interests of the ruling oligarchy. Where would the three *avogadori* find the legal authority to reject a marriage contract endorsed by one of the founding families of the Republic? All he had to do was persuade the two families. The rest would take care of itself.

Andrea figured he could bring his father over to his side. To convince his uncle—the old Procurator Andrea Memmo, hero of Constantinople and stern guardian of Venetian tradition—would have been an entirely different proposition, but the gentle Pietro Memmo, ailing and deeply loving, would not disappoint him, and his mother, despite their frosty relations, would follow in the end. The great obstacle, Andrea realized immediately, was Mrs. Anna. Giustiniana would have to work hard on her mother to bring her to agree, after all that had happened, to negotiate a marriage contract with the Memmos.

Despite his growing optimism, Andrea never lost sight of the fact that such a course of action was very risky for everyone involved. If in the end the Avogarìa rejected the contract, the Memmos' reputation would be tarnished for years to come. As for Giustiniana, her prospects of finding a husband would be so badly damaged that the Wynnes would probably have to leave the city. But a lucid assessment of the situation, combined with a good dose of wishful thinking, brought Andrea to rely on the ultimate wisdom of the *avogadori*. "I am sure," he told Giustiniana when he finally suggested to her this new course of action, "that if your mother gives in even only an inch, the path ahead will clear."

Giustiniana balked at Andrea's bold new plan. She feared confronting her mother, and furthermore she had little faith in the success of the petition. All through the spring and summer of 1757, as Andrea continued his talks with the lawyers, he cajoled and tried to reassure her. "I understand how mortifying it must be for a young girl to reveal her passion to her own mother—and a mother with such a temperament, who has already forbidden that passion," he told her. "But you are not like other girls, and this is the reason I speak to you the way I do." She resisted for months, and for a brief moment in the summer of 1757 they seriously contemplated going behind the back of his parents and Mrs. Anna and marrying in secret.* But in the end Andrea always went back to the idea of giving their best effort to a proper marriage, and Giustiniana's refusal even to broach the subject with Mrs. Anna started to wear him down. He complained gently at first: "My imagination and my heart grow warmer every day, and I think about you all the time, but alas you are so distant in every way. My precious life, give me the comfort of seeing you do as I say in such an important matter." Then, in the face of her obduracy, he grew more impatient: "All this time you've wanted to do things your own way, but what have we gained?" He could not understand why Giustiniana was so fearful. Did her resistance reflect a woman's congenital incapacity to plan ahead? he wondered, attempting to apply a philosophical veneer to his exasperation. "For [a woman] never thinks about the future. And not because of any fault of hers but because of her internal organization, which does not allow her to bear for very long the effort needed to work out a complicated scheme."

Giustiniana's letters from that period are missing, so we do not know how she reacted to these misogynistic thoughts. But it is easy to imagine her eyes glazing over as she read Andrea's pompous reflections on the character of women. Their secret encounters became tense again and were often the scene of more arguments.

However, Andrea was relentless, and in the fall of 1757, more than six months after he had first suggested the plan, Giustiniana finally mustered the courage to tell her mother that she and Andrea were still in love and wanted to get married with her consent. Andrea was euphoric, and he became even more so when Giustiniana reported to him that Mrs. Annà, after initially stiffening, had been surprisingly receptive to the idea. "How much effort and pain

*In July 1757 Andrea and Giustiniana contacted the religious authorities at the Patriarchal Chancery in order to begin the process leading to a clandestine union (choosing witnesses, gathering sworn statements), but it is unclear how far they went before giving up on the idea. In the archives of the Patriarchal Chancery there is a folder with their names in the register of secret marriages, but the contents have been removed.[1]

it has cost me to bring you back on the right track!" he exclaimed at his victory.

Mrs. Anna's volte-face was not without reason. After all, she had opposed the relationship with Andrea because she was convinced the Memmos would block a marriage contract by any means possible; if this was not the case, the matter would be worth pursuing. Prudently, she decided to wait for the Memmos to make the first move.

At Ca' Memmo, Andrea's optimistic prediction was borne out. Relations between him and his parents had improved, thanks to his deliberate efforts to be accommodating and helpful in the daily running of the house and their estate on the mainland. His diplomatic maneuvering led to an emotional family summit at which Pietro and Lucia Memmo agreed to a preliminary negotiation for the submission of a marriage contract to the authorities. Now it really looked as if Andrea's gamble might pay off. News trickled out and became grist for Venice's inexhaustible rumor mill. "Everyone in town speaks of our marriage as a done thing," he reported happily to Giustiniana.

The two sides had to agree to the terms of the contract, which usually consisted of lengthy and very detailed documents, filled with financial statements and numerous clauses and conditions. Once the contract was drawn up, it was presented to the *primario*, a sort of general secretary, of the Avogarìa di Comun for a preliminary review. If the review was successful, the contract was submitted to the three-member panel for final approval.

Mrs. Anna insisted that Andrea and Giustiniana should not see each other or be in communication during the negotiation. She decided to accompany Giustiniana to Padua, where they were to be the guests of Bernardino Renier, the prominent patrician whose son Alvise was still wooing the lackadaisical Tonnina. The rest of the children stayed in Venice with Toinon. Before leaving, Mrs. Anna hired a lawyer, Signor Faccini, to handle the negotiations with the Memmos while she and her daughter were away. Discreetly, she also turned to Consul Smith for financial advice. A full year had gone by since he had married Betty Murray, and Mrs. Anna felt it was time to renew a precious friendship.

It was hard on Andrea and Giustiniana to be separated now that things were looking so hopeful. But it was harder still to have to cease their correspondence at such a critical juncture. Andrea had felt very much in charge, directing the course of events. He needed to remain in touch with Giustiniana, if only to know what decisions were being made on the other side. At the same time he realized that if a compromising letter were found the entire plan would be instantly derailed. A strategist to the core, he concluded that the only solution was to develop a secret cipher. He spent several sleepless nights rearranging dots and lines and circles and triangles to create a coherent alphabet and sent it to Giustiniana so she too could master their secret language. This was the final combination they agreed on:

a	b	c	d	e	f	g	h	i	j	k	l	m	n	o	p
-θ-	....	?	!	:	,	.	z	:			ω	υ	t	::	s
q	r	s	t	u	v	w	x	y	z	,					
r	q	p	n	∴	m			h	˜o						

At first they used their cipher only to dissimulate the most sensitive information: names, places, details of their plan or their own intimate messages. But eventually they became so fluent they could shift back and forth between the standard alphabet and the secret one with ease. Sometimes they would slip in one or two words in cipher and then carry on in Italian; other times they would cover an entire page with their tiny hieroglyphs, giving a rich and mysterious texture to the letter.

When she was in Padua, however, Giustiniana was still trying to learn the symbols Andrea had submitted to her, and she did not really have the strength for daily practice. Soon after arriving at the Reniers' with her mother, she took to her bed complaining of fevers and stomach pains and general weakness. The doctors tormented her with a succession of bleedings that sapped what little energy she had while her mother forced her to follow a punitive diet that consisted mostly of garlic. Andrea was "devastated" by the news of her ill health and weighed in with some medical advice of his own: "More bloodletting will surely do you good, but at

least wait until you are not so weak and are feeling a little better."
He also reproached her for not standing up to her mother: "Garlic
is very bad for you, and yet you keep eating it."

Away from home, bedridden and feverish, Giustiniana struggled to find some peace of mind. Was her mother sincere about
wanting to go ahead with the marriage contract? Despite Andrea's
frequent coded messages, she felt isolated from him and lonely.
Once more, she was overcome by waves of jealousy and mistrust.
Was he seeing his old girlfriends Marietta and Lucrezia in Venice
while she was stuck in Padua, half a day's journey away from her
loved one? Even more troubling to her was talk that the Memmos
were contemplating yet another marriage offer.

This time there was none of Andrea's old defensiveness in his
attempt to reassure Giustiniana: "My dearest one, . . . how do you
think I spend my days so far away from you? I spend them thinking about our tender passion. And still you think I am lost in
thoughts about Mariettas and Lucrezias! One is so precious, the
other so flighty. . . . One day I will paint a true picture of their
character for you so that you will be able to judge for yourself
if there ever was any reason to harbor doubts about me." As for
what she was hearing about another marriage proposal, Andrea
explained that a relative of the Memmos had indeed approached
his parents with an offer from a wealthy family, the Baglionis,
which included a handsome dowry of 12,000 ducats. "But rest
assured," he told Giustiniana, "I paid no attention, and neither did
anyone else in my family."

Andrea was being truthful. Once his parents had agreed to
go ahead with the marriage, they had embraced the idea wholeheartedly and were now working hard to ensure the contract was
approved: their prestige, as well as their son's future, was at stake.
Lucia Memmo, who had looked down on the Wynnes ever since
Giustiniana had come into their lives, now became one of her most
ardent supporters. "She's crazy about your portrait!" Andrea
exclaimed, hardly recognizing his mother but delighted at how
sentiments were changing all around. Even more important, from
a practical point of view, was the change in his father. In an
extraordinary gesture of goodwill toward his eldest son, Pietro
Memmo had secretly lifted the *contraddizione*—the power of veto a

patrician family had over a marriage contract until it was signed—before the negotiations had even begun in earnest. This move was very generous but also imprudent; Andrea's uncle would never have approved it had he still been alive. Although Andrea was grateful to his father for removing a major obstacle before the talks had started, the future statesman in him must have winced. Using their code, he told Giustiniana about the new development and asked her to keep the secret. It would be humiliating for the Memmos if the news became public. Worried about a possible leak, Andrea's mother and brothers went to the Patriarchal Chancery and told the officials in charge of the case to inform anyone who asked that the *contraddizione* was still in place and to refuse to show the official ledger containing Pietro Memmo's declaration. Andrea explained to Giustiniana that this was "the only way to protect us as well as my parents, who have already been condemned by all of Venice for not having prevented our union so far." He was moved by Pietro and Lucia's flouting of convention for their sake and lost no opportunity in his letters to Giustiniana to remind her how grateful they should be to them.

The mood was now upbeat. Pietro's decision was bound to speed up the process. Andrea told Giustiniana not to worry: "The contract will be approved, and once it is, all the rest will fall into place." He ran into Signor Faccini, Mrs. Anna's lawyer, who assured him that their side of the contract would soon be completed and taken over to the designated *primario*, Signor Bonzio, a man apparently well disposed toward the two lovers. Andrea was also getting inside information from a well-placed source: Signor Bonzio's secret lover, Donada. "There will be important news in a few days," he informed Giustiniana. "And then who will dare keep me separated from my spouse?" He added a short note in cipher: "Tuesday or Wednesday you will return to Venice by order of the inquisitors."

Giustiniana's brief exile in Padua thus came to an end. The lovers were still not allowed to see each other, but it was impossible for them to remain apart now that they were both in Venice. The sense that negotiations were moving swiftly to a conclusion increased their desire to be together at whatever cost, and their physical love blossomed again as another frigid winter set in. "I am writing to you from home," Andrea told Giustiniana before he left the house for Rosa's. "But when you receive this envelope I shall already be where you know. . . . Run, for I am there already, waiting for you with open arms." Now Giustiniana gave herself to her lover more freely than ever before. Andrea was overwhelmed. He confessed to being *"ingiustinianatissimo"*—completely enthralled by her.

They made love in Rosa's dank little room, swaddled beneath layers of woolen clothes to keep out the cold. These encounters were necessarily hurried—there was always the fear of being found out, and, anyway, it was too icy to linger among the hardened sheets. They left their alcove still filled with desire for each other, and their lovemaking continued in their compulsive letters and notes—protected by the shield of their secret language:

When I left you, I came home and went straight to bed. As soon as I was under the covers my little nightingale felt an urge to fly back to you. I wanted to keep him here. I wanted him to stay quiet until the morning. But as much as I tried to distract him with fantasies about the nice legs of Cattina Barbarigo, the soft little tummy of Countess Romilii, and the pretty cheeks of Cattina Loredan, he would have none of it. He wanted satisfaction. Would you believe he even convinced me you had ordered him not to let me sleep if I did not satisfy his every desire? Thankful at last, and generous toward me, he wished to produce on this piece of paper the evidence of his satisfaction so that I in turn could prove to you, at the first opportunity, my blind obedience to all your wishes.

Such playful but rather extreme displays of affection were not always to Giustiniana's taste. Yet he developed a habit of sending small samples of his semen to her as a tangible sign of his love. He would spread them on a piece of paper, which he then folded into what he referred to as his special *"involtini"*—borrowing a common Italian culinary term. At first, Giustiniana reacted with disgust to those sticky little envelopes that had traveled across town in the hands of their messenger. But she grew accustomed to them, even indifferent, and eventually Andrea gave up sending them while lamenting the fact that he had never received similar tokens of her love. "They would have caused such transport," he sighed. There were changes at Rosa's. The two lovers were saddened to learn that "their" room was now being let out to other clandestine couples. The traffic around the house also made it more likely that they would be recognized. It was imperative that they both keep their mask on whenever they visited. But even that precaution was not always enough. For Andrea certainly had his mask on when he stepped out of Rosa's house alone one day (they were always careful to leave separately), wearing a bright red cloak over many layers of warm clothes and the typical Venetian three-cornered felt hat. It should have been very difficult for anyone to know who he was, especially since his face was entirely hidden. Yet when he suddenly found himself face to face with Giacomo Zandiri, a friend of Mrs. Anna's, he had the sinking feeling he had been found out by just the wrong person.

Zandiri, like Mrs. Anna, had emigrated as a child from one of the Greek islands. His brother worked as a butler for the Bragadins, a well-known Venetian family. Giacomo, on the other hand, had no fixed employment. He had managed to weasel his way into Mrs. Anna's home by being on hand to help out with the daily chores necessary to running a large household. A nosy fellow by nature, he also kept an eye on Giustiniana's comings and goings, and on several occasions he had provided Mrs. Anna with secret intelligence about her oldest daughter. "Stay away from him," Andrea had warned her many times, "and never forget how much he has hurt you in the past."

After his chance encounter with Zandiri, Andrea dashed off a note to Giustiniana in cipher: "Giacomo found me at Rosa's doorstep just as I was leaving. I am convinced he recognized me because he acted surprised and stopped to look at me for a while. I pretended not to know him and hid from him as best I could. But I feel it is nearly impossible that he won't tell your mother, even on the strength of a mere suspicion."

What to do? Andrea needed a convincing alibi in case Zandiri mentioned having seen him coming out of Rosa's. Giustiniana, meanwhile, should deny very firmly that she had been with him there and suggest that the man Zandiri had seen at the door might have been Lucatello Loredan, a friend of Andrea who also met his lover at Rosa's and "who wears a hat similar to mine and white stockings and has thin legs like I do." Andrea then remembered an important detail: upon leaving Rosa's he'd realized he had left his *manizza*, the fur hand warmer Venetians wore in winter, in their room, but he hadn't gone back to fetch it "because I didn't want [Rosa] to know we had been together for so long." Since the man Zandiri saw on Rosa's doorstep was obviously not wearing a *manizza*, Giustiniana should convince her sister Bettina to say she had seen Andrea pass in his gondola on the Grand Canal wearing his red coat *and his manizza*. "What I fear the most are the stupid answers Rosa and her servants might give if they are asked. So tomorrow morning you must make sure [they] deny I was ever there."

The following morning Andrea waited in vain for a letter to reach him at Ca' Memmo. Then he checked at the various *botteghe* he and Giustiniana used as mailboxes. Nothing. Finally, in the evening, his gondolier brought him the news: no one had dared deliver Giustiniana's letters to Andrea because of the "the terrible uproar" that had taken place at the Wynnes' after Mrs. Anna had discovered that the two had seen each other. So he'd been right about the wretched Zandiri, and none of his efforts to cover his tracks had made the slightest difference.

They stopped seeing each other at Rosa's. It was too risky. Meanwhile, the negotiations had stalled. The times called for maximum prudence. Yet Andrea continued to write, mostly in cipher now, to keep Giustiniana abreast of developments.

Even before the Zandiri incident, Mrs. Anna had made a series of demands that were clearly at odds with the goodwill displayed by the Memmo family. Andrea was especially incensed by her insistence on the inclusion of a clause stating that if the contract were not approved, all correspondence between Andrea and Giustiniana would have to cease by order of the court. Mrs. Anna was trying to protect her daughter's chances of marrying someone else, and Faccini told the Memmos she insisted on having her way on that point. Andrea protested vehemently: "What a foolish request! If I agreed to it, my family would immediately think: Ah, then Andrea is not so attached to Giustiniana after all."

It was not so much the specific clause that worried Andrea. He felt that Mrs. Anna's attitude was self-defeating: by negotiating as if the contract would never be approved, she would inevitably undermine the whole effort. He sent Giustiniana a message explaining that the Memmos would not respond to Mrs. Anna's requests until she had made clear the names of all her counsels. "Then I will reason with them. . . . Don't worry, my beloved wife. . . . I have thought of everything." Andrea had in fact lost all confidence in Faccini, who kept him out of the loop and came to Ca' Memmo "his belly sticking out, asking to speak to my mother alone without having talked things over with me first." Not only was he hurt, he thought his exclusion unwise: he, more than anyone else, could help finesse the agreement since he knew what both families wanted.

The difficulties raised by Mrs. Anna made the Memmo camp nervous because they had already put their reputation on the line. "My mother is now desperately worried that the news that she has lifted the *contraddizione* will become public too soon," Andrea complained, twisting the facts a little. His father, of course, had lifted it—he was the titular head of the Memmo clan and was the only person entitled to do so. To tell Giustiniana that his *mother* had done it was technically incorrect but rather revealing about who was really in charge of the negotiation. Lucia Memmo, however, was no longer as optimistic as she had been. She feared her family would be dragged into quicksand. Why was Mrs. Anna not pressing for the contract to go forward? Andrea's mother feared "very much" that she was stalling simply because she was afraid it would not be approved—which Mrs. Anna had in fact already said to several people outside the negotiating circle.

To make matters worse, the dreaded Morosinis were once again poking around, advising Mrs. Anna on what course to take. Encouraged by her mother, Giustiniana had continued to visit their *palazzo* despite Andrea's old plea that she never be seen with his "enemies" again. For a long time he had turned a blind eye, but now the negotiations were so precarious that he insisted the Morosinis stay out of the picture. "I absolutely do not want [them] to meddle in our affairs." And why was Mrs. Anna consorting with them anyway? Was she having second thoughts? Despite the persistent optimism he displayed to Giustiniana, Andrea, like his mother, became wary of Mrs. Anna's true intentions.

While she privately continued to pursue a deal with the Memmos, in public Mrs. Anna became so negative about the chances of success that she even began to question the benefit of going forward. "She tells everyone that we are crazy, that I am a rogue, a liar, and a cheat, that it is not true that my parents are happy, and that I made it up in order to deceive you and your mother," Andrea wrote in bafflement. "Luckily my parents could not be any sweeter. . . . By God, they are true heroes."

Yet more mischief on the part of Mrs. Anna was on its way. A young Frenchman who went by the name of Comte de Chavannes arrived from Paris intending to spend part of the long Carnival season in Venice. He was charming and good-looking and had an air of sophistication about him that thrilled young Venetian ladies. He was immediately taken with Giustiniana when he was introduced to her. He plied her with gallantries, escorted her to the theater, danced with her, and took her to the Ridotto for some cardplaying. Mrs. Anna was delighted to see such a fine young man lavish her daughter with attention. Behind the scenes she did her best to facilitate Chavannes's courtship even as she continued to be engaged—formally at least—in marriage negotiations with the Memmos.

The worst part for Andrea was that Giustiniana was not insensitive to the charm of the *soi-disant* Comte de Chavannes.

The Carnival of 1758 offered Giustiniana a pleasant break from the drama and the draining intensity of her relationship with Andrea. By the mid-eighteenth century the Carnival had become "a less raucous, more polite affair than its Rabelaisian antecedent."[2] Plebian celebrations like human pyramids and the war of fists, bullfights and regattas had been suppressed. Still, the streets and bridges were packed with jesters, fire-eaters, and prodigies of all kinds. Music and dances and drinking went on late into the night. The throngs were so thick that it was always a struggle to move from one place to another, but it was also easier to move anonymously through that crowd of dominoes.

Chavannes, who had decided to stay on through the festivities, was thrilled by the excitement and the licentiousness that filled the air, and Giustiniana could finally indulge the more coquettish side that she had repressed for so long. She enjoyed her time with the young Frenchman—the air of Paris always went to her head, even when she breathed it in Venice. And she did not shy away when he kissed her at the end of a happy evening—not just a French kiss on the lips, as Andrea later reminded her, shocked by her slovenliness, but a deep, long kiss "in the much more fervent Italian manner," according to witnesses who had been quick to tell him. Didn't she know people talked? Didn't she realize her behavior risked jeopardizing all their plans for the future? What was she *thinking* "as she chatted continuously" with Chavannes in public? They were the talk of the town, Andrea reported reproachfully. Many people were already saying that Giustiniana was risking "losing her husband just to gallivant with a silly Frenchman who will soon be leaving Venice anyway." And what about the pain she was inflicting on him? The last time he had seen them together, at the theater, he had had to run away in order not to see Chavannes "offer you his arm and you getting into his gondola and maybe even going to the Ridotto with him." Not to mention those awful Italian kisses Andrea felt he would "never have the heart to erase" from his memory.

Andrea's nightmare ended at Lent, when the Frenchman returned to Paris, apparently still pining for Giustiniana. The tireless Mrs. Anna pressed her daughter to keep up a correspondence with Chavannes and sit for a portrait to be sent on to him in Paris. But after the initial thrill Giustiniana had lost interest in her French suitor, wrote lazily to him, and looked for excuses every time the portraitist came by the house. His courtship had been a distraction for her, and now that all the craziness of Carnival was over she was ready to throw herself back into the arms of her true love. Andrea was relieved, but he could not resist carving out his pound of flesh in a long and rambling letter he wrote late into the night:

> *Listen to me: we all saw your mother rise from an unhappy and miserable station to become the wife of an English chevalier. Your mother does not have the best reputation. You have nasty relations and little dowry. You are a Catholic, and therefore one*

assumes nobody will want you back in England or in any case you will choose not to go. Your education does not please. The liberties you take are viewed with suspicion. You are a bright girl. How easy it would be for anyone—a man, or better still, a woman— to believe that all this time you have cultivated me out of self-interest when they see a nice young Frenchman . . . make love to you and be gallant and draw sighs from you at a time when you should appear particularly respectful of me. For heaven's sake, it would have cost you nothing to tell that silly young fellow off— your reputation would have gained so much. Of course a scene with your mother would have been costlier, but that too would have been manageable. And you would have earned so many points with me, my blessed Giustiniana. . . . Oh, never mind, but let this be the last "distraction" before our wedding. This time I will consider you innocent—I will not infer from this episode an easy yearning to please on your part or an overconfident attitude toward your Memmo in love, always good to you, full of respect for you, and blindly faithful. But if it happens again I promise nothing. . . . I still don't know whether I will be a victim of the weakness husbands in love often fall prey to—jealousy. So far, my respect for you and the low opinion I have had of my rivals have spared me this curse, but who can tell what will happen in the future. . . . Remember that I marry you out of boundless love and deep esteem, and for this very reason I am convinced that my eternal happiness can come only from you. And that the only dowry you bring to me is your love, so perfectly sincere, and a character worthy of all my admiration. Remember that I give to you the love of my father, my mother, my brothers, my parents, my friends, the esteem . . . of the rest of my world, the advantages that come with me and my house, and maybe even more.

Giustiniana must have shown some regret for the forwardness she had displayed with Chavannes, for in his next letter Andrea was glad to declare the hostilities between them officially over. "*Trêve donc des inutiles querelles,*" he joked, using French to communicate the truce in their pointless quarrels. "I couldn't be happier about it; stick to your resolutions, and everything will be fine." He snickered at the portrait being shipped to Chavannes in

Paris. Such poor quality, so few sittings . . . should he worry about the bad impression it might make among Parisians?

His truce with Giustiniana, however, did little to improve their overall prospects. Six months had gone by since the first contact between the Memmos and Mrs. Anna, and after initial encouraging signs, very little movement had occurred. The draft of the wedding contract had not even been presented to Signor Bonzio at the Avogarìa. Mrs. Anna was still dragging her feet and looking out for other options. The Memmos could not allow the negotiation to languish any longer: their prestige was in danger. Andrea felt it was time for another bold move: he decided to call on Consul Smith, who was again exerting a great deal of influence over Mrs. Anna.

Relations between Andrea and the consul had not improved since the previous year's embarrassments. Though civil to each other in public, they had maintained their distance. Now Andrea realized he needed to have the consul on his side. Besides, he was happily married to Betty, and Andrea was no longer a threat. There was no reason why they should not be friends again. Except pride, of course; but in his dealings with the consul, Andrea had learnt that his pride could be overcome with the right amount of flattery. "We must work on the consul until he does our bidding," he wrote to Giustiniana. "We must help him rid himself of that special dourness he harbors toward us."

Andrea knew that the consul was facing serious financial and legal difficulties and could use some help from a well-connected patrician like himself. In his old age Smith had lost his keen commercial touch. A series of business deals had gone sour. Quite apart from the loss of money, these setbacks had tarnished his reputation. It was said in Venice and London that he had resorted to dishonest practices to patch up his damaged finances. While it was certainly true that his affairs were in disarray, Consul Smith seems to have been the victim of his own ingenuousness more than the avid perpetrator of shady schemes, as some of his enemies claimed. The consequences of one particular deal, in which he had been brazenly duped by a professional swindler, had been worrying him for many months.

The previous year a man who went by the name of Captain

John Wilford had taken over a merchant ship belonging to an English trading firm, changed her name from *Nevis Planter* to *Fuller*, and crisscrossed the Mediterranean buying and selling goods. Wilford had arrived in Venice to unload merchandise and, needing a large sum of money to finance his next expedition, had asked the consul to advance it. The unsuspecting consul had obliged him with a maritime loan drawn against the value of the ship. Wilford, however, had had no intention of paying him back. Upon his return to Venice he had secretly registered the *Fuller*—which wasn't his to begin with—in the name of his fictitious children. The consul had sued Wilford, as had the legitimate owners of the ship, but to no avail. Wilford had taken advantage of a loophole in the Venetian maritime law to keep the boat. His "children" had materialized out of nowhere to produce a tearful performance at the trial, and the consul had never recovered his money. Wilford had added insult to injury by bragging all over town about how he had tricked the old man. It had been a trying experience for Smith.[3]

Andrea approached the consul in the aftermath of the Wilford incident, at a time when the old man felt distraught and vulnerable. He was glad to make peace with his young friend and promised to help sway Mrs. Anna. Andrea informed Giustiniana that the consul would soon be calling on her mother. He added that, in order to test his goodwill, he would ask him to give Giustiniana a small enameled snuffbox as a gift from him "so that your mother won't realize it is from me. . . . Consider it my present to you on the day of my *festa*, which is tomorrow." A few days later the consul called on Mrs. Anna as promised but failed to speak in defense of the two lovers. Andrea backed up his new ally, explaining to Giustiniana that "even though he came by your house expressly to speak to [your mother], in the end he decided not to push the point because he felt it was inopportune. But he did ask her how the contract was going . . . and she told him things were as good as they could possibly be at this time." Andrea continued to press him. A few days later, he informed Giustiniana that the consul had finally "sworn" to him that he had had "a very long conversation with Mrs. Anna and that he had gained quite a lot already and was now confident he could bring her completely to our side, having shown the care and the zeal with which he continues to protect your house and you in particular."

Andrea himself was not quite as sanguine as Consul Smith. Mrs. Anna's attitude toward the lovers remained cold, and he was irritated by the way she spoke about his family in public and felt strongly that her behavior was not helping their cause. "You do remember, don't you, how your mother went about saying that my close relations were horribly critical about us and how they were slandering her behind my back. Smith asked her what those accusations were based on since he knows the Memmos to be upright and wise and he is very much aware of our thinking on this whole matter. She was quite embarrassed and admitted she had no proof. She had heard . . . she had thought . . . so there. It turns out we Memmos are gentlemen after all, we have not dishonored her, we have not caused her family's ruin, its collapse, its violent death."

As Andrea drew the consul into the picture, he also edged himself back into the consul's life, offering advice on how to disentangle himself from new legal disputes. Once again Andrea was at his most Machiavellian. He instructed Giustiniana "to cultivate Mr. Smith and his wife," bearing in mind that "they probably believe we are already married one way or another, for I have done my best to excite their suspicion without ever stating things clearly." Soon Andrea was able to report that he was once more "at the very center" of the consul's activity. "Here I am, necessary to him, willing and helpful."

There was a cruel edge to Andrea's treatment of the consul. It was not just the arrogance of the young dealing with the old. There was a lingering hint of resentment, a suggestion that all was not entirely forgotten. Their rapprochement was borne of mutual convenience, and the two did not really recover their close relationship. Here is how Andrea described him to Giustiniana in a particularly mean-spirited letter: "I tell you: Smith is bound to do all he can for us unless he is the most ungrateful man on earth. For he surely would have lost at least fifteen thousand sequins, not to mention his peace of mind and his honor, if it had not been for my advice, which was the opposite of what he and his counselors had argued. So I will not ease the pressure on him. The worst part of it is that he really is an ass, that he doesn't know how to handle a deal, that he's English and old."

The consul may have lost his ability to handle a deal, but his word still carried weight with Mrs. Anna, who was mindful that the young Chavannes had been sucked back into the Parisian whirlwind and no longer seemed seriously interested in Giustiniana. Besides, she had found out that, contrary to his claim, he was not really a count. After a long winter lull, negotiations suddenly began to move forward again. In the early spring of 1758 Mrs. Anna, under pressure from the Memmos, finally instructed Signor Faccini to present a draft of the marriage contract to Signor Bonzio, the *primario*, for preliminary scrutiny. Andrea was thrilled: "How happy we shall be. Yes, I am sure of it now, my little one."

Anticipating a wedding agreement, the lovers' temptation to see each other became irresistible. Andrea paraded up and down the Grand Canal in his gondola two or three times a day. He was delighted to see her at her balcony again: ". . . and with that night-cap of yours, oh dearest, oh my rarest Giustiniana, my desire for you. . . . I feel I cannot resist it." Yet a treacherous winter chill was still in the air, and he warned her to be careful. " For heaven's sake, don't come to the window," he pleaded one morning. "It is still too cold." A few days later he sent another worried note: "Ask one of the maids or a houseboy to watch for me in your place. They can call you as soon as they see me from afar. Otherwise I will worry too much."

It started with a splitting headache. Then a fever set in and Giustiniana's temperature rose, and then came the dreaded stomach pains. Andrea followed the progress of the illness from the window at the Tiepolos' with increasing agitation: "You seemed to be burning last night, and the way you repeatedly put your hand to your forehead gave me so much grief." Andrea was in a state of great agitation. It was the second time Giustiniana had fallen seriously ill in the space of six months. She was again subjected to a debilitating cycle of leech-induced bloodletting by Dr. Trivellati, one of Venice's leading physicians. Her mother force-fed her the usual supplement of garlic, which Andrea insisted was "really very bad" for her. It was hard for him to communicate with her and to get credible news on her health. His sister Marina's death was recent enough that a creeping fear reinforced Andrea's anxiety about Giustiniana's health. Most nights he returned home late after wandering aimlessly around town, stopping at friends' "and talking about you while the others played cards." In his room he would battle the cold and his sleeplessness by pacing back and forth in front of the fire. Or he would wrap himself in blankets and stay up writing by the stove until the chiming of the first call to mass. Images of Giustiniana kept him awake: "You cannot imagine how my heart is filled with worries and endless pangs of anxiety and how my mind is full of thoughts of terrible things that surely will not happen. . . . Now I see my Giustiniana in a bed, her head so hot, her body wracked by fluxions and fever and pains and debilities of all sorts . . . without her Memmo, without a hope of having him near even for a moment."

A chance encounter with Dr. Trivellati in the street provided the first relief: "He told me your pulse had slackened after the last bout of fever. He said he had decided to go ahead and draw more blood now that your headache has subsided somewhat and you have had a copious clearing out. How his words, so precise and truthful, have consoled me."

In spite of all the bloodletting, which probably weakened Giustiniana more than the actual ailment, her health gradually improved. As the weather warmed, she returned to the balcony. She looked pale and thin under her beribboned nightcap, but she smiled in the bright sunshine and squinted and waved to her lover down below. As she recovered, deeper stirrings came back to her as well, and with them the usual logistical problems. Ever since Andrea was spotted leaving her house, Rosa had been reluctant to help the two lovers. She claimed to be ill and made herself generally unavailable. Andrea pleaded with her so forcefully she finally agreed to let them use their room "one more time," with the understanding that it would be the last.

Other friends now willingly stepped in. Johann Adolph Hasse, the German composer, and his wife, Faustina, the celebrated diva, had always had a tender spot for Andrea since the days when Uncle Andrea, the old patriarch, had still been alive and they had been frequent guests at Ca' Memmo. Their daughters, Beppina and Cattina, had grown, and now they too had become friends of Andrea and Giustiniana. The Hasses were a joyous, fun-loving family, and they were more than happy to connive with the two young lovers. On the appointed day, Giustiniana would tell her mother she was going to pay a visit "to the Hasse girls." Andrea would arrive there shortly before her, to be whisked up to the girls' room on the second floor. This way Giustiniana could go upstairs and meet Andrea even if she had the misfortune of being accompanied by her mother.

More surprisingly, the consul himself agreed to give Andrea the keys to his box at the Teatro San Giovanni Grisostomo, a rather traditional establishment with an uninspiring program—which suited Andrea and Giustiniana just fine. They met there at their leisure and made sure the little curtain was drawn. They were seldom tempted to watch the play. "Of course it has become my favorite theater," Andrea now said after having criticized the San Giovanni Grisostomo for years. "That box is very comfortable indeed. Oh, I hope we shall go there often. . . . There is such peace and quiet. . . . And of course the privilege of not having to listen to the performances, which are usually so bad."

Now that the marriage cavalcade was moving again, Andrea was "immersed in the pleasure of our present condition." He could not get enough, even when they were not together:

> As I lay in bed alone for so long I thought of the days when we will be together, comforting each other at night. This idea led to another and then to another and soon I was so fired up I could see you in bed with me. You wore that nightcap of yours I like so much, and a certain ribbon I gave you adorned your face so sweetly. You were so near to me and so seductive I took in your tender fragrance and felt your breath. You were in a deep sleep— you even snored at times. You had kept me company all evening long with such grace that I really didn't have the heart to wake you up . . . but then a most fortunate little accident occurred just as my discretion was exhausting itself. You turned to me at the very moment in which you dreamed of being in my arms. Nature,

perhaps encouraged by habit, led you to embrace me. So there we were, next to each other, face to face and mouth to mouth! Your right leg was leaning on my left leg. Little by little the beak of the baby dove began to prick you so forcefully that in your sleep you moved your hand in such a way the thirsty little creature found the door wide open. Trembling from both fear and delight, it entered oh so gently into that little cage and after quenching its thirst it began to have some fun, flying about those spaces and trying to penetrate them as far as it could. It was so eager and made such a fuss that in the end you woke up.

The greatest intimacy came naturally to them. The playful tone softened the raw sexual desire. And the writing too, one feels, prolonged and completed their pleasure. Andrea returned to his room at Ca' Memmo one evening, his head filled with sexual thoughts about Giustiniana. He considered masturbating but then thought better of it: "I felt terribly in love with you. . . . But I didn't want to force nature for a third time, having it forced with such profit in the morning."

During the spring of 1758 Andrea's letters were filled with a mixture of sexual exuberance and serious talk about their future life as husband and wife. When the lighthearted side of his personality took over, Andrea reveled in the pursuit of pleasure. But his serious side, which carried the weight of tradition and family responsibility, was never far behind. He begged Giustiniana, for the sake of his reputation as well as her own, to be more circumspect in her public demeanor and always wary of that "malicious world" out there, which preyed on the smallest glimmer of gossip. Sometimes this sanctimonious carping irritated Giustiniana's rebellious spirit, but Andrea pressed on regardless, teaching her the ways "of this Venetian world of ours, as a good friend would." When he did not write to her as a playful lover, he took the approach of a philosopher-husband whose passion should always remain firmly fastened to reason: "Believe me, my little one, a simple rapture would not have led me to risk everything I have in order to marry you. What led me to do it was the clear and perfect picture I have of my Giustiniana, the deep and well-founded respect I have for her, and a sentiment far stronger than the most virtuous and sincerest of friendships. And all of this has led me to pursue my goal with as much prudence and patience and industry and foresight as I could muster." Had he been more fickle, had his love been "not as deep as it is," he might have tempted her "to run away" with him during one of their many moments of despair. Or he could have found "an honorable way" out of their relationship: "Yet these thoughts never even entered my mind. I have remained constant. I feel as strong and resolute as I did on the very first day—before which I had already reflected on our fate far more than you could possibly imagine."

In early summer Venetian society prepared itself once again for the yearly ritual of the *villeggiatura*. But it was hard for the Memmos and especially the Wynnes, who did not own an estate in the country, to firm up their plans at a time when the negotiations on the marriage seemed to be reaching a critical stage. Mrs. Anna discarded the idea of renting a place, instead accepting another invitation from the Reniers to spend some time at their house in Padua. Andrea decided he would stay in Venice, where Signor Bonzio would be examining the marriage contract, and made plans to ensure he and Giustiniana could be in constant communication while they were apart. After four and a half years of subterfuge, Andrea had become a master at handling the intricacies of maintaining the flow of their correspondence: "I will draw two small lines under the name of the county. That will tell the postmen in Venice [the letters are from me]. . . . They will deliver them in the morning. . . . If anyone should check at the Padua post office or the Venice post office, they will find nothing—it will not be your writing, the letter will be addressed to a Venetian gentleman, there will be no *poste restante*, hence no reason to suspect anything."

The rest of the Memmo family left town to seek respite from the heat. Pietro was so frail that Andrea wondered if he'd make it through the summer. He gave Giustiniana a touching description of their leave-taking: "I think he will stay out at our villa for a long time because it is good for his health. . . . After lunch I kissed his hand, which is not something we Memmos usually do. After that blessed moment we were unable to speak because our eyes filled with tears."*

Life in the city slowed down considerably. Except for the great Festa del Redentore on the third Sunday of July, there were no major festivities. The theaters were closed. The palaces on the Grand Canal were empty. The *botteghe* and the *malvasìe* were less crowded than usual. Andrea did not have much to do except run a few errands, browse among the picture dealers, and make sure Signor Bonzio had everything he needed. "Early this morning I went by Tonnin Zanetti's shop† to see some drawings by Titian and cultivate a priest who might prove useful to us one day. As I savored those magnificent drawings I thought, 'If only I could have Giustiniana, who is so far away from me.' That's the way it always is. You're always in my heart, and I would feel so undeserving of you if I did not think about you constantly." Alone in the stifling heat of the city, he marveled at how things were turning their way: "Do you know that it is nearly impossible to be blessed by that good fortune that God is preparing to bestow upon us after all our grief? To discover such kinship between us, to see reason and virtue guide our love and give true and everlasting pleasure . . . these are things that don't often come along. Oh, when will we be together, my dearest little one? And what delight I shall feel in pleasing you, in making you happy, in loving you! How sweet your company will be."

His happy thoughts soured, though, when he was told about a sudden change of plans: the Reniers had invited Giustiniana and a few other guests to leave Padua and travel to their villa at Mirano, another little town by the Brenta. Mrs. Anna would have to remain in Padua with Tonnina, who was convalescing after a brief illness, and it was a little odd that Giustiniana should have been asked to go without a chaperon. Andrea was miffed. After all, the Reniers knew very well that he and Giustiniana would soon be married. Even more irritating to him was the fact that Giustiniana herself felt inclined to go. "Do as you please," he wrote to her peevishly,

*Though frail, Pietro went on to live until the age of 93. He died on February 14, 1772.[4]
†Antonio Maria Zanetti was an important collector and dealer of Venetian artists. He was a friend and at times a rival of Consul Smith.[5]

"but I want you to know that I don't like this idea at all. . . . It is never a good thing to generate suspicions, and it would be utterly foolish to do so given our circumstances. . . . [Renier] should respect the fact that I don't like you to go around without your mother." He then took his complaint directly to Alvise Renier, listing "all the reasons why I dislike the idea of this little trip" and lamenting the indifference with which he felt Alvise could abuse him. Andrea expected to be treated with greater respect by Alvise, who was quite a bit younger than he. To treat his wife-to-be in such a fashion, he concluded bitterly, was nothing less than "the act of an uncivilized lout."

Giustiniana was in a difficult spot. She wanted to please Andrea but felt he was being excessively protective of her and making things difficult. The Reniers had been kind to her family, and she didn't see the point of making such a fuss. Andrea sensed that Giustiniana had neither the strength nor the inclination to say no to the trip to Mirano. He made some mild threats: "You will not have any news from me until you return to Padua. . . . And you will not see me until you come back to Venice." In a final taunt he asked her to please tell him quickly whether she was going to Mirano or not so that he could make arrangements "to spend the next fifteen days or so in some other place and get some exercise, which I really need." He added a postscript that was typical of Andrea. If there was no way out, if she really *had* to go to Mirano, "then I hope you will at least make the effort of staying close to Bonzio's lover, that woman Donada, and to Bonzio himself if he should also come out there. Cultivate them as much as you can, and remember to always call him 'Your Excellency.' "

In the end Giustiniana went to Mirano. Andrea swallowed his pride and informed her that he had little choice but to join her there as soon as possible: "I've explained to my young friend Renier that he cannot treat me like a radish. . . . I am sorry for everything I said to you. . . . It was all on account of the pain I felt. . . . To calm you down, and to bring you completely onto my side . . . I see no other solution but to come straight to Mirano." Before leaving Venice, he made arrangements to take a room above the haberdashery in the main square of the little town and sent new instructions to Giustiniana: "As soon as you get [to

Mirano], go to the *bottega* in the square and ask the owner for a letter addressed to a certain Battista. . . . I love you, my soul, I love you to excess. For this reason I will come to Mirano. . . . I must run now, hopefully to hear good news about our papers. . . . Everyone says we are already married. . . . Our wedding is all people are talking about."

As soon as he reached his destination, he dashed off a note to Giustiniana, who had only just arrived at the Villa Renier herself: "I love you so much that I had to come despite all the objections. I am writing to you from Mirano, my soul, I am here, at the *bottega*, on the right-hand side of the arcade, near Signora Laura Angeloni's haberdashery, just as I had said to you. I will not move from here. I don't want to cause a scene that might make people talk about us. . . . I cannot wait to see you. Forgive my sloppy writing, my love, but I sleep as I write."

The following morning Giustiniana arranged to walk by the arcade during the promenade. Andrea could hardly contain the joy of seeing her after so many weeks: "My God, what consolation. . . . I am out of my wits now that I am near you again, that I have seen you. I actually felt I was holding your hand tightly and talking to you and kissing you. . . . You can imagine the state I'm in right now! What shall we do, my little one? . . . Tomorrow is market day. If possible, I would like to see you at the very least. How are you? My God, this is killing me. . . . My mind, my soul, my entire body are in such turmoil now. . . . Oh Christ, I have this huge desire to press you against my chest! By God, I cannot stand it anymore. . . . I wish we could be alone for half an hour and live out our love's apotheosis."

That night Andrea let himself into Villa Renier. At last he felt Giustiniana in his arms again, shivering with happiness and desire. This was how it was going to be—a life together, filled with their love for each other.

News from Venice suddenly shattered Andrea and Giustiniana's dreamy world in Mirano. The examination of the marriage contract had come to a halt. This time it had nothing to do with Mrs. Anna's demands or hesitations: her own past had surfaced to cast a disreputable shadow over her daughter's future. Sifting through old records, Bonzio had discovered that in the early 1730s, before Sir Richard had arrived in Venice, Mrs. Anna had been "deflowered by a Greek"—these were the actual words the *primario* later used with Andrea. She had become pregnant, and nine months later a baby boy had been handed over to an orphanage. Mrs. Anna's family had apparently taken the Greek man to court, but it was unclear whether the trial had ever taken place because Bonzio's office had been unable to locate all the documents.

Andrea was stunned. Now it was clear to him why Mrs. Anna had been so shifty and difficult. All the while, as she had badmouthed Andrea and his family and made up excuses to slow the process, she had in fact been hiding this secret. Andrea was furious with her. He rushed back to Venice to see the *primario*. "The meeting lasted for two hours," he reported back to Giustiniana, who was, if possible, even more distraught about the revelation than he was. "Bonzio had an extremely serious expression on his face. He seemed disgusted . . . and very well informed about everything that can be prejudicial to us: the year of the trial, the name of the Greek, the place where the suit was filed, the intervention of the *avogadore*, the boy sent to the orphanage, and, especially, every detail about your mother's life."

It is possible that the unctuous Bonzio had his own reasons for being upset. At the start of such negotiations it was expected—and certainly the Memmos had assumed the same in this case—that at some point it would be necessary to oil the bureaucratic machine a little by passing a few sequins to the *primario* under the table. Indeed, the general feeling among those who knew about the Memmo-Wynne negotiations was that with a bribe of one hundred sequins "the contract will surely be approved." Over the previous months, however, Mrs. Anna's delaying tactics had disheartened Bonzio and his colleagues to such an extent that, according to Andrea, "they did not expect to receive a single coin from her." She had added insult to injury by telling people such as Zandiri, who had spread the word, that the Memmos would get the contract approved only by "drowning" Bonzio in gold. According to Andrea, the *primario*'s conclusions, while delivered to him in the most obsequious manner, could not have been more discouraging:

"Your Excellency," Bonzio had said to him, "if we were to find a document in which Mrs. Anna herself publicly declares to have been deflowered by that Greek, what could Your Excellency possibly want us to do? These are not matters for arbitration. We depend on the laws absolutely, and they are very strict, and if it turns out there was a public dispute at the Quarantìe* a mere twenty-five years ago—for it seems there was an appeal at the Quarantìe even if the case was never actually examined there—well . . . what would Your Excellency expect us to do in that case? Our honor is publicly committed, and we would find ourselves publicly exposed, and people would be right to assume that Your Excellency 'is drowning the *primario* in gold,' as they say."

The message was clear, and the concluding allusion to Mrs. Anna's comment made Bonzio's little speech even more devastating. Once again, all their painstaking work had been torn apart. But unlike the Smith imbroglio, this storm would never blow over. Everyone knew that. The damaging court papers Bonzio referred to in his talk with Andrea were never actually produced. It is possible the *primario* did not even look for them. It was not worth his trouble anymore; enough of Mrs. Anna's story had been resurrected from the dusty Venetian archives to seal the fate of the marriage petition, which never even reached the final stage.

"This is our situation," Andrea summed up sadly. "Could our misfortunes be any worse?"

*The Republic's judicial council. It was made up of forty patricians.

On the morning of October 2, 1758, Mrs. Anna and her five children, accompanied by Signor Zandiri and Toinon, left the familiar city of Padua in two hired carriages—one for luggage, one for passengers—and took the road to Vicenza, their first stop on the long, uncomfortable journey across Europe. It would take them three to four days just to reach the end of Venetian territory, which extended westward all the way to the city of Brescia and a little beyond. Then they would travel through the Duchy of Milan and the Kingdom of Piedmont, make the arduous crossing of the Alps, descend toward Lyon, and finally head straight north for Paris. It was a daunting prospect, and not just because of the length of the journey (three to four weeks) and the size of the party. The cramped circumstances and the loud clatter of the carriage as it sped along the uneven dirt track made travel by coach an exhausting experience. The posts along the road, where horses were changed and the passengers could stretch and take a breath of fresh air and have a meal, were often rather seedy places. There were bound to be delays as well—a wounded horse, a broken wheel, a sudden rainstorm. And then there was the tedious everyday paperwork: rooms had to be booked and horses hired, and the right documents—passports, entry permits, exit permits—had to be in order every time one crossed a border. Zandiri was there for that; Mrs. Anna, believing it was more prudent and practical to travel with an adult male, had asked him to come along and manage the trip as far as Paris.

Huddled inside the crowded coach, Giustiniana was oblivious to her physical discomfort. As the city walls of Padua gradually disappeared from view, she drifted into melancholy thoughts. She was leaving the world she had lived in all her life. And she was leaving the man who for so long had been at the center of that world as her lover, her best friend, her guiding hand. As the carriage barreled down the road, she fixed her mind on Andrea to keep herself from feeling lost.

When the negotiations on the marriage contract had collapsed, Mrs. Anna had decided to leave Venice at once and seek a new life for herself and her children in London. What would be the point of staying on in the wake of the scandal? Giustiniana's prospects of finding a husband in the Republic were ruined. And Mrs. Anna's past, which she had fought so hard to bury and forget, had suddenly resurfaced to humiliate the whole family. So she had packed her belongings and uprooted her children with the same determination she had shown in the past, as she had struggled to preserve the respectability Sir Richard had bequeathed to her upon his death.

She was in a hurry now to cross the Alps before winter set in. The onset of the war would make their journey even more uncertain than it might otherwise have been, since they would be traveling through France as British subjects—and France and Great Britain were enemies. But Mrs. Anna counted on the good auspices of the Abbé de Bernis, the former French ambassador to Venice who was now foreign minister. Once they were safely in London, Lord Holderness, the children's guardian, would introduce them to their English relatives and help them settle down. He might possibly arrange a presentation to Court. Seven years after Sir Richard's death, his family was going home.

During their final days in Venice, Andrea and Giustiniana had been inseparable. Mrs. Anna's hostility toward Andrea had mellowed as the separation neared, and she had allowed him to take the boat trip from Venice to Padua with the family. In Padua, where the Memmos owned a large property, he had escorted Giustiniana around town as last-minute preparations were made for the trip. Andrea had even taken his meals with the Wynnes in an atmosphere of general reconciliation. After his final, wrenching farewell with Giustiniana, he had galloped ahead of the carriage to wave one last time from the bridge at the Gate of Santa Sofia. But Giustiniana had already withdrawn into her shell.

The Wynnes arrived at their inn in Vicenza very late that night. Giustiniana felt drained and completely disoriented. After a light dinner she went to her room and wrote to Andrea about the confusion in her heart:

> *Mon cher frère,*
>
> *Where am I, sweet Memmo? How awful is my pain! What desperation! Oh I do love you, alas; and I cannot cease telling you even in the first moments of our separation! How I have penetrated your being. . . . How I have felt! Ah, there is no point in telling you. I am desperate. . . . I did not have the strength to call you back when you drew away from me, so I followed you with my soul. I heard you stopped at the Bridge of Santa Sofia, but I did not see you.*

From the very beginning of their new life apart, Giustiniana addressed her letters to "Mon cher frère," my dear brother—a semantic device designed to put some distance between them and somehow ease the disentanglement of their feelings. She was quick to admit it was a weak subterfuge: "I will call you mon cher frère, but you will still be everything to me."

In reality this new form of address masked a deeper change in their relationship, which had actually occurred a few weeks before her departure from Venice. Giustiniana never spoke very openly or clearly about the matter in her letters to Andrea; she never mentioned a name or a place or a specific date. But she said enough to leave us in no possible doubt. At some point in 1758, either shortly before the revelations about Mrs. Anna or, more probably, in their aftermath, she had tired of the endless waiting game. She had tired of being isolated, tired of being shuttled back and forth between Venice and Padua, tired of being forcefully kept away from the man she loved. For a moment she had even tired of Andrea and his seemingly futile machinations. She had felt the utter hopelessness of her situation just as she had two years before, after their dramatic failure with Consul Smith. And for a short period of time—

she called it her "moment of weakness"—she had given in to the gallantry of another man.

For all we know it was a brief affair, probably a matter of a few weeks. Her feelings for Andrea had not died, however, and when her fling was over she had gone back to him more in love than she had been in a long time. Andrea himself had learned of the deception only later that summer. After Mrs. Anna's sudden decision to drag the family to London, Giustiniana had confessed her betrayal to Andrea, believing, in a contorted sort of way, that by painting herself as fickle and weak she would somehow diminish "the terrible pain" he would feel at their separation.

Andrea had forgiven Giustiniana—he was never a resentful man. But their relationship was not the same after her "cruel and spontaneous confession." Giustiniana had allowed someone else to come between them, and this shadow had lingered on. There had been lies, and then there had been remorse. But even after Andrea had forgiven her, even after their tearful farewell in Padua, Giustiniana continued to damn herself. "I despise my life and I despise myself even more," she wrote to him that first night in Vicenza, contemplating "the unhappy combination of events that has ruined me in your eyes."

Despite the changes in their relationship, Andrea and Giustiniana were still very much together when the Wynnes left Venice in the autumn. They saw themselves as a couple and intended to meet soon. They still talked about spending their life together—one way or another. In fact, they were already working on a new scheme.

Their most urgent goal was to thwart Mrs. Anna's plan to settle in London. Giustiniana had agreed with Andrea to try to extend their stay in Paris for as long as possible and hopefully to avoid reaching London at all. In Paris, Giustiniana was to aim her powers of seduction at Alexandre Le Riche de La Pouplinière, an aging widower, great music lover, and one of the richest *fermiers généraux,* the famously wealthy French tax collectors. It looked very much like a variation on the plan they had tried unsuccessfully on Consul Smith two years earlier.

Monsieur de La Pouplinière had been Andrea's idea. Exactly a decade before, the old tax collector had been at the center of the notorious *scandale de la cheminée*. The Duc de Richelieu, a powerful figure at the court of King Louis XV and a flamboyant womanizer, had seduced Monsieur de La Pouplinière's beautiful and much younger wife. The duke and the tax collector happened to be neighbors in Paris. To facilitate the secret encounters with his new lover, the duke had had a secret passageway built in a huge fireplace that led directly into Madame de La Pouplinière's music room. The tax collector eventually discovered the ploy and banished his wife from his household. The episode had caused a huge scandal at the time—as much because of the affair itself as because of what was perceived as La Pouplinière's unnecessarily cruel treatment of his wife. The *fermier général* had never remarried while his wife was alive, but she had recently died and Andrea had heard from his Venetian friends in Paris that the old man, now well into his sixties, was looking for a new young wife.

Monsieur de La Pouplinière was probably not uppermost in Giustiniana's mind the day she left Padua. But she had gone along with the idea when Andrea had discussed it before her departure. As at the beginning of their relationship, perhaps on account of the guilt she still felt for her "moment of weakness," she was again deferring to his judgment. She promised absolute transparency: "Let God separate us forever if I do not tell you everything that happens to me. And you must do the same with me even at the cost of hurting me." She yearned to please him in the hope of possessing him again completely. "You will know everything, and I shall win back your tenderness—you will see . . ."

Yet for all her resolutions, for all her valiant efforts to harness her feelings for Andrea, Giustiniana had little control over the sheer sadness that kept assailing her. If only she could give in to her emotions from time to time . . . "Your *tenderness*, Memmo! Oh God, may I speak to you this way? Do you allow me to do so? I have not shed a tear after those I shed with you in Padua, but I am immersed in desperation. Oh God! What will happen to me, and to you, Memmo? . . . I can only speak to you of love. Allow me to surrender for a few moments to my excessive feelings."

After a sleepless first night away from Andrea, she added this rambling postscript to her letter as she waited for their little convoy to get started again:

> *I wept a great deal [all during the night] and was inconsolable. I made a thousand plans to go back to you if you do not find a way to your Giustiniana. What misery is mine! You are always on my mind, and at this very moment I am kissing your little portrait. Let me speak to you about my passion. I shall be wiser when I will have persuaded myself that I am far from you; but will I ever be able not to talk to you about my passion? You allowed me to talk about it again, and now I feel it with such power that it is impossible for me to bury it. May I hope, mon cher frère, to find the words 'I love you' in the letter I will receive from you in Turin or Lyon? Write long letters to me, be my friend always, love me as much as you can. I owe you so much. I feel close to you in all those things to which my soul will always be sensitive. May God give me a fortune so that I can run off to live wherever you may be. . . . Farewell, my love. Take care of yourself for me, take care of yourself for Giustiniana, who is so unhappy now but will soon be near you and happy again.*

Andrea and Giustiniana found themselves in each other's arms much sooner than they could possibly have expected. A short distance outside Vicenza the axle of the carriage in which the Wynnes were traveling cracked and the vehicle crashed to the ground, damaging the luggage carriage as well. All the passengers came out of the wreckage unscathed, if a little shaky. Back at the inn, a dejected Zandiri informed the Wynnes that fixing the carriages could take as much as four days.

Giustiniana seized her chance: she summoned a messenger and dashed off a note to Andrea, who was still in Padua on business, telling him to join her in Vicenza immediately. "My mother thanks the Virgin for having saved us," she quipped. "I thank her because I am not moving from here." He could justify his sudden appearance in Vicenza, she added, by telling Mrs. Anna that having heard of the accident he wished to make sure Giustiniana and the rest of the family were all right. "If I get to see you again, I will certainly believe in miracles. Let me say no more. I want the lackey to fly to you immediately."

Andrea arrived at the inn the next day, wearing an appropriately worried expression, and inquired about the Wynnes. Mrs. Anna was resting, and she exploded when she heard that Andrea was downstairs, cursing him and even accusing him of having somehow orchestrated the entire incident. Zandiri, who was already beside himself because of the delay, slammed the door of his room in Andrea's face and refused to speak to him. Not to be outdone by Mrs. Anna, Zandiri then threatened to kill Andrea, who had already prudently retreated to a nearby inn. Giustiniana sent her lover a dramatic report of what had happened after he had quit the scene:

> *A firestorm, my dear Memmo, a terrible firestorm. My mother is so furious she says she wants to notify the authorities. . . . She treated me abominably and I suffered in a thousand different ways, but when all the composure I had in me was finally exhausted I gave in to my anger. . . . [Zandiri] said loudly that he wanted to knife you. . . . I told him you would have him caned very soon, and he answered he would have you caned first. Everyone in the next room heard each word, as there were no other noises in the house. We cannot see each other here anymore. Go to Venice, take legal action, and, if you can, try to arrange things in such a way that [Zandiri] will be arrested tomorrow. He did threaten to kill you.*

Andrea was utterly unprepared for the violent reaction his appearance had provoked—after all, Mrs. Anna and he had parted amicably in Padua only two days before. Then again, she had always been a difficult woman. But Zandiri's behavior really incensed him. Andrea would teach him a lesson, give him a scare he would not forget. The law was on his side: threatening the life of a prominent Venetian patrician was a serious offense, and for once Andrea had every intention of using the prerogatives of his rank. Besides, the bewildered clientele of the inn had overheard everything. Zandiri had sealed his own fate.

However, rather than taking legal action in Venice, as Giustiniana had pressed him to do, Andrea decided to seek justice on the mainland, away from the city gossips. He asked Giustiniana to provide him with signed statements from three patricians who had been present at the scene in the inn and had heard Zandiri's curses against Andrea, as well as sworn depositions by several servants attesting to the fact that Andrea had not provoked Zandiri—had not even been given the chance to speak to him. Once Giustiniana supplied the evidence, Andrea contacted the all-powerful Venetian *rappresentante* in Verona, who in turn ordered the chief of police to follow Andrea's instructions to the letter. In effect, the *rappresentante*, himself a member of the ruling oligarchy and a friend of the Memmo family, allowed Andrea to take justice into his own hands.

Mrs. Anna spent most of the following day in church. In her absence, the two lovers had ample opportunity to plan their legal offensive together. Brazenly, they even visited some of the architectural marvels of Vicenza, including Andrea Palladio's famous Teatro Olimpico. It was a good day, one of their best in a long time:

> *Seldom have we had a chance to be together as long and as sweetly as today. Alas, this good fortune comes to me now, ensuring that the pain of separation will be stronger still! It is my fate. . . . But oh my God, I cannot tell you more because my mother is calling me now. Tomorrow I shall be at the Due Torri [in Verona]. You will spy on us, I am sure, and I will be told everything. . . . I hope our time together will not be bad there either. Meanwhile, give the go-ahead to our great coup, and have a good trip. God! We are rushing simultaneously toward new bliss and new danger! If you love me, be passionate about everything, and fear nothing.*

It felt as if their conspiratorial days were back. Secret messengers shuttled between them as they prepared the "great coup": Zandiri would be arrested and thrown into jail. Giustiniana egged Andrea on, encouraged him to use all the powers in his hands to finally rid them of the "scoundrel."

As soon as Andrea left for Verona that evening, however, doubts began to creep into Giustiniana's mind, for she and her family now faced the prospect of a long and difficult journey without the protection of a man. Suddenly she wasn't so sure: "If [Zandiri] comes with us it will be hell, and if he stays we will have to deal with a thousand dangers."

That night a messenger sent by Giustiniana went looking for Andrea "all over Verona," shaking guards out of their slumber and even forcing the deputy mayor from his bed to deliver an express letter to him. On the envelope, Giustiniana had used their old cipher to write:

Don't be amazed, just laugh.

Sleepily, Andrea read on:

I cannot be entirely evil. I have worries and fears. My wish for revenge is giving in to my good heart, and I am about to ask you that yours give in as well for love of me. I foresee a thousand troubles if you have [Zandiri] detained. My mother would be so furious she would be capable of abandoning the family and ruining us all. Memmo, give in to me, give up your resentment to your Giustiniana, who beseeches you. Let me leave with a renewed admiration for your soul.

Andrea did not want to leave Zandiri rotting indefinitely in some godforsaken prison of the Venetian Republic. He only wanted to give the man a scare. A public apology, he reassured Giustiniana, was all that was needed to grant Zandiri's release. Meanwhile, the carriages in Vicenza had been repaired, and the next day, October 7, the Wynne party arrived in Verona and took up lodgings at the Due Torri, not far from where Andrea was staying.

The lovers managed to steal another full day together, roaming the streets and squares of the town while Mrs. Anna attended a succession of church services and Zandiri took care of travel arrangements. Before curling into bed, Giustiniana wished Andrea a good night:

*Sleep well, my heart, for you will need it after all the walking
we did. I could learn so much traveling with you! You've seen
everything, you know everything, and you are so good at pointing
out things and drawing distinctions. . . . I love you, yes, I do love
you. Oh God! How much there is to say—more than I even dare
to wish or say. . . . Good night. . . . Dream of me. . . . Love me
much. Will you always let me ask you to love me?*

The Wynne party started early the next morning on the road to
Brescia, most of them unaware of the trap that Andrea and Giustiniana had laid for Zandiri in what was then the last major city
of the Venetian State before entering the Duchy of Milan. They
spent the night in the small town of Desenzano and arrived in
Brescia the following afternoon. The two lovers kept in regular
contact during the trip through brief express notes sent from the
stations along the road; it was important to synchronize the steps
that were to lead to what Giustiniana, perhaps not fully anticipating the seriousness of the matter, was now calling "the great
prank."

The Wynnes had barely settled into their lodgings in Brescia
and were still unpacking when loud noises were heard in the foyer:
police officers had arrived at the inn, shouting orders and creating
great alarm among the guests. They summoned Zandiri downstairs and, after questioning him briefly, dragged him away.

For all her conniving, Giustiniana was suddenly frightened.

*God only knows what is going on. I tremble for my own sake as
well. My mother is spewing fire at this moment. . . . If you love
me, Memmo, try to be as prudent as you can. I never thought
things would take such a turn. They tell me [Zandiri] is in jail!*

That afternoon word came back to the Wynnes confirming that
Zandiri had been roughly interrogated by the police and locked up
in the Castello, Brescia's intimidating fortress in the Old City. Mrs.
Anna became incandescent when she realized that her traveling
companion would not be returning to the inn that night. She
accused Andrea of acting out of spite and vowed to expose him in
Venice. Then she turned on her daughter.

I warn you: my mother is in a fury, and she blames me for everything. She also says she will take her vengeance on me and plans to send all the letters she has—mine and yours—tomorrow morning by courier either to the [British Resident in Venice] or to someone else—I don't quite know; right now she swears she will ruin me. If she continues to insult me the way she has, I might have to make a decision. . . . I cannot stand it any longer.

Giustiniana hoped things could still be resolved the following morning with a simple apology by Zandiri, but she feared that his own pride and her mother's anger might conspire to make matters worse for everyone: "If he asks your forgiveness and if you grant it immediately, as you intend to," she wrote to Andrea before retiring that evening, "things will settle themselves. But if he behaves crazily, God only knows what we must fear!"

The next day Giustiniana awoke to find her mother's fury unabated. She had taken the affront personally, and she seemed determined to wage war on them even if it meant keeping Zandiri locked up a while longer. "My mother has sworn to ruin us," she told Andrea. "She doesn't want [Zandiri] to say he's sorry. . . . I'm desperate." It was pure theater: Mrs. Anna was in one corner of the room writing a letter to Murray, the British Resident, while Giustiniana was sitting across the room writing frantically to Andrea about Mrs. Anna writing to Murray. ". . . She makes it appear as if [Zandiri's] arrest were the result of some violent action on your part designed to keep us here. God only knows what else she will make up."

In open revolt against Mrs. Anna, Giustiniana decided to send her own version of events to the Resident in order to preempt her mother's letter to him.

Sir,

I will be in serious danger if you do not help me and grant me your protection in a case so clearly ruled by vengeance alone—not by justice. Hear me, sir, and save me.

When we arrived in Vicenza our carriages broke down, and we were told the repairs would take four days. I immediately informed Memmo with the sole purpose of bidding him farewell just one more time; and he, hoping for the same, rushed to Vicenza. My mother was asleep when he arrived at the inn. He waited for her to wake up in order to congratulate her on the fact that nothing distressing had happened to the family on account of the crash. Having observed that was the case with his own eyes, he was about to go back—as he had promised my mother and as she herself seemed convinced he would do, since he was without coffer and manservant.

*Meanwhile, I called in Zandiri—the very stern and knowledgeable manager of our trip—to explain to him all that was going on. But he simply walked from one room to the next without greeting [Memmo] and even slammed the door in his face. That wasn't enough: when I went down, I was upbraided by my mother in the usual manner while Signor Zandiri hurled insults at Memmo and threatened to kill him even though he was by then far away. His insults were heard by three gentlemen and by many servants. Once Memmo was informed of all this he thought he would simply remind Signor Zandiri that such a rodomontade was very much to his own disadvantage, and in lieu of availing himself of the harsh instruments he had at his disposal, the use of which might have offended our family, he asked the three noblemen for their honest testimony and gathered more evidence of the fact that he had not even spoken to Zandiri; then he turned to the [Venetian] *rappresentante *to obtain justice. The *rappresentante *happened to be out of town, and [Memmo], who, despite his gentle manner, was determined to make [Zandiri] feel his superior status and mortify him, went ahead of us to Verona, whence the *rappresentante *had in fact just left for Vicenza. This unexpected turn of events forced [Memmo] to go on to Brescia, where he was finally able to present his case and where Zandiri was reprimanded by the Tribunal in presence of the authorities as well as many gentlemen and then transferred to the Castello and put at [Memmo's] disposal.*

My mother went into a fury when she heard of the arrest and blamed me for everything and swore to ruin Memmo and me— again. She doesn't want [Zandiri] to tell Memmo he's sorry, even though that would put an end to everything. . . . We could resume our journey as early as tomorrow and Memmo could return to Venice. But no, she wants to move ahead and take her revenge on us for no fault of our own. As she is now writing to you, I have decided to inform you as quickly as possible of the facts, all of which can be proven by eye-witness noblemen.

I know, Mr. Murray, your sense of justice as well as your prudence. And I know that, once well apprised of all the facts, you will not encourage her unfair wrath. I have left Memmo to go to London in accordance with the orders my mother has received [from Lord Holderness]—though under the laws of my country no one could have forced me to had I decided to do otherwise.

Truth reigns in all I have said to you, and all I ask is that you consider it well. I have reason to be fearful, and I put myself in your hands for whatever future violence I might suffer. Whatever you have heard about me, I am sure you will do right. . . . My character is not tainted. You have had occasion to know me. Meanwhile I am fearful of everything, and the only prudent course of action I can take is to ask for your useful and experienced assistance. Use your best judgment in reading my letter written in the greatest haste. . . . I also beg for the protection of Lady [Murray], your wife, to whom I have the honor of being . . .

It was a remarkable letter, scribbled at top speed with one eye on the page and the other on Mrs. Anna sitting across the room. Her tone was respectful, even obsequious, but with just enough familiarity to give her appeal a personal touch, enhanced by her prudent inclusion of the Resident's wife in her plea.

The last thing Murray could have wished was to become embroiled in a dispute in a remote provincial town between an angry Anglo-Venetian lady with a rather stained reputation and a well-known member of a prominent Venetian family. Luckily, the confrontation was defused before it could escalate into a full-blown diplomatic incident.

Giustiniana told Andrea about the two letters that were due to leave for Venice, and he informed the *rappresentante*. The following morning, the police intercepted Mrs. Anna's messenger, who had been instructed to slip out of town unnoticed. Her letter to Murray and the accompanying documents—a selection from the two lovers' correspondence—were handed over to Andrea, who, in a magnanimous gesture, returned them to Mrs. Anna unopened. But the *rappresentante* stepped in to remind Mrs. Anna of a basic fact of life in the Venetian Republic: Andrea's word carried more weight than hers. There was really no point, he added, in pursuing the matter further. She would only damage herself and her family.

In the end, Murray did not receive either of the letters (Giustiniana's was held back after Mrs. Anna's had been intercepted), though he was probably informed about the incident in detail. Meanwhile, the *rappresentante* sent his military aide to the prison at the Castello to work on Zandiri, who finally caved in and wrote a submissive letter of apology to his sworn enemy. Andrea promptly pardoned Zandiri. Giustiniana was delighted and sent Andrea a short adulatory note: "You are a great man in every respect, my Memmo! And such cold blood, such dexterity, such quick and firm decisions in moments of great pressure! Oh, I shall never find another man like you if I live a thousand years."

The next day a grumbling Zandiri returned to the inn. "No one spoke," Giustiniana noted. "He and my mother appear to be fairly calm. . . . No secret meetings so far and no new letters." Victory made her bold again, even reckless. "I am dying to see you. . . . If per chance this evening you should feel inclined to come visit me in the same room as last night, be sure that I would feel infinite comfort in seeing you."

The lovers spent the night together—the last before they parted ways.

On October 12 the Wynnes headed for Milan. Ten days had passed since the carriage had broken down. Andrea and Giustiniana had to go through a painful separation all over again. "Everything that has happened in between has made me feel that I belong to you even more," Giustiniana wrote. "I feel this separation very deeply. . . . I've never felt such pain, my Memmo—not even in Padua." There, at least, they had had more time to take leave from each other. Their parting in Brescia was a rushed and brutal affair. After a long day on the road that left her exhausted and "completely battered," she began to take stock. As in her first letter from Vicenza, she reverted to addressing her lover as her dear brother:

> *Mon cher frère,*
> *I am far from you, my dear Memmo, I will not see you again, and I am so sure of it now that all I feel is pain and desperation. It was so difficult to leave [this morning]! They had to call for me ten times because I had locked myself in a room and had spread out your letters and was crying and feeling completely desolate. But what's the point? In the end I had to leave, and now you are so far away that I have finally come to realize I will not see you for a very long time. But I had to tear myself away without even a farewell, an embrace, a few shared tears! Oh God! . . . Oh, my Memmo, why do I love you so? Your friendship is such a rare thing that I would have felt bound to you forever even without having any other feelings for you. Oh, wretched circumstances! And you, Memmo, will you still love me? Yes, you will; but do not tell me, or else just tell me with the coldest words. I feel I could become extravagant: so far away that I cannot lay a claim on you nor give in to my feelings. Ah, if only you knew how torn I am! The past, your kindness, your friendship. All this love I have for you, it startles me, it fills me completely. I love you more and more, and more and more I see the miserable difficulties ahead. . . . Oh God! Memmo, my Memmo, still forever mine, oh God, pity me. And you, my heart, how will you remember me? Forget the past; be generous to me the way only you can be, and promise to think of me only the way I will be from now on. I will tell you everything, do not doubt that; I will keep you informed of my conduct, my opportunities, my feelings, my prudence. Yes, I shall be prudent—you mustn't doubt that any longer. If only you knew how I feel now about caprice and weakness, I think you would be satisfied; but do not worry: my prudence will not be excessive; it is wise, well founded; and it will not vanish. Think well of me, if you still can, and expect to think even better of me yet. Tell me everything; continue to lend me your tender assistance. I will depend on it: I am yours. My dearest Memmo,* mon aimable frère, *you are such a rare being. Where else to find you if not in*

you? And will I not look for you and find you again? Wait for me,
wherever you want.

It was typical of Giustiniana to address her letter to her *cher frère* and ramble on for pages, as if the actual scribbling of all those words dulled the pain and provided a small measure of relief. Invariably, however, the indulgent musing stopped as she reminded Andrea—and herself—that circumstances called for more disciplined behavior. After all, there were things to be done in Paris, urgent matters to attend to:

> *I will also take a keen interest in La Pouplinière and my future state, which will depend entirely upon myself and my reputation. . . . With my good manners, my cleverness, and my talent in eliciting the sympathy of others, I will make the catch; and then, Memmo, others will depend on me as I now depend on others, for, believe me, I will have a name and all the rest. . . . Trust me; I will tell you everything; I have given you my sacred word, and I intend to keep it. Look over me, my heart, and help me, but above all love me always.*

The Wynnes arrived in Milan on the evening of October 13 and took rooms at Il Pozzo, a fashionable inn not far from the Duomo. It was the first time Giustiniana had left Venetian territory since her trip to London after her father's death, when she had been fifteen. Once she was outside the Republic, her distance from Andrea seemed even greater. In her thoughts she traveled back to him constantly in order "to penetrate his being," as she was fond of writing. She conjured, as a lover will against all odds, Andrea's magical appearance in the most unlikely places: at street corners, in shops, even in the foyer of the inn where she was staying. To free herself from the suffocating presence of Mrs. Anna, Zandiri, Toinon, and her four younger siblings, she went out to explore the city in Andrea's imaginary company.

Squeezed between the Venetian Republic and the rising Kingdom of Piedmont and Sardinia, the Duchy of Milan was a shadow of its former self—little more than a city-state on the southern rim of the Austrian Empire, which had extended its authority over the duchy after the War of the Spanish Succession. The city was fairly prosperous, yet its morale had long been sapped by the rule of the invaders. "There seems to be a provincial atmosphere everywhere here," Giustiniana wrote, complaining that people stared at her "as if they had never seen a foreigner."

She visited the Duomo, watched charlatans sell their miraculous balsams and unguents in the square, wandered around the streets, peered into fancy stores, observed the clothes people wore. She was struck by the great number of elegant carriages congregating in the main square for the evening stroll, and she also noticed the poverty and filth and the high number of beggars in the streets. As for the ladies, always the object of her special attention, her verdict was rather damning: "Mostly ugly, mostly clumsy."

One way or another, the Milanese always came up short in her running conversation with Andrea. "I had a different idea of Milan," she concluded petulantly. ". . . I make comparisons, and at present I like Venice in the extreme."

Giustiniana went to the theater with Mrs. Anna and thought the show so boring that she stared blankly at the stage until she was overwhelmed by a wave of nostalgia: "It occurred to me I was in a *theater,* and so I was taken over by the strongest melancholy. I remembered . . . Oh, what I remembered. . . . Do you remember all that I remember? If you can, then surely you will pity my state."

The Venetian Resident, Giuseppe Imberti, offered the Wynnes a seat in his box at the Opera. On her first night there, Giustiniana loudly complained that the singing was "dreadful." The Resident agreed, and since he knew Andrea well, he showed himself more eager to catch up on the latest twist of their love saga than to listen to the music. Mrs. Anna, still recovering from the jolting trip from Brescia, arrived late at the opera, so Imberti had plenty of time to tease Giustiniana.

I confessed to him that I love you, but I also told him we are now bound only by friendship. He asked me if I had your portrait. I showed it to him and kissed it in his presence. . . . Then he wanted to know how much I was willing to pay in order to see you and I said: Everything. And I said it with all my heart! He asked how much I would give him if he produced you in less than twenty-four hours. . . . In the end he only promised to show me a letter of yours tomorrow. Still, I hope to God he will. He then tried to make me believe that you were hidden somewhere inside the hall. At that point, I must confess, I began to fantasize that you might actually be there, and much to my embarrassment I started looking for you in every box. You can imagine my state when I couldn't find you! How terrible I felt until the opera was over! I feel miserable, Memmo. . . . If you love me, if you are my friend, arrange things in such a way that you can visit me soon, and I will not fail to come looking for you.

The Wynnes stayed three full days in Milan while their carriages were refitted for the next leg of the trip—straight west toward Piedmont and its capital, Turin. Giustiniana was incapable of reviving her initial curiosity about the city and grew more miserable with each day. She got up late, went to mass with Mrs. Anna before lunch, and took uninspired walks around the neighborhood. She had little interest in the people she met. "Everything bores me . . ."

For lack of anything better to do, she went to the "dreadful" opera again, figuring Imberti would be there—as indeed he was—and they could talk about Andrea: "I came home in the Resident's carriage, and I talked about you along the way, telling him, as always, part of our story. I had talked to him about you at the Opera as well—during the first act and the dancing part."

The solicitous Resident enjoyed Giustiniana's company, not to mention the whiff of Venetian intrigue she had brought with her. He gave a dinner party for the Wynnes on their last evening in town (since he knew they had not unpacked their trunks entirely and did not have their evening gowns available, he downgraded the formal dinner to a more casual affair—but still "with many guests"). Despite her melancholy mood, Giustiniana was a breath of fresh air in that musty Milanese crowd of retired generals and diplomats and crumbling aristocrats. She was the object of everyone's curiosity: even strangers came up to her and asked shamelessly about her "well-known passion." And when her mother was not within earshot, Giustiniana indulged in Andrea-talk, which invariably brought on a familiar mixture of pleasure and pain: "The few I choose to speak to all know I adore you."

Imberti was sorry to see Giustiniana leave. The night before the Wynnes' scheduled departure, he begged her to stay on a few days and even offered to hide Andrea in his house. Andrea was in fact on his way to Milan on business, but he was waiting for the Wynnes to leave Italy before making an appearance there. It was unthinkable that the two lovers should find themselves again in the same city so soon after the Zandiri incident—and with Mrs. Anna still in a rage. "I explained to him your justified worries, as well as the dangers for me." Still, Giustiniana now had a useful ally in the Resident, who agreed to handle their secret correspondence in the days ahead.

It was a gray, dreary afternoon on October 17 when the Wynnes drove away from Milan. Before leaving the inn, Giustiniana scribbled one more note to Andrea and pressed it into the hands of Imberti, who had come to say farewell:

If you do come to Milan and you don't stay at the Resident's, come here and take the room I was in. . . . Come to [Il Pozzo] and ask for the San Carlo room. There are two beds, and you must sleep in the one next to the wall. . . . Remember that from that bed I sent you a million sighs, and in that bed I shed a few tears as well. . . . Tell me everything about your life. . . . Be mine forever. . . . Love me as much as you can and as long as you can.

And off they clattered toward the Alps. It took them three days and three nights to reach Turin, where they planned to rest a few days and make the inevitable repairs to the carriages. The journey was especially tiring and uncomfortable. "Always rain and always this awful cold," Giustiniana complained. They were knocked about against the hard wood of the coach till the bruising became "unbearable." Their feet were damp, their clothes splattered with mud:

And with all that, my mother still insisted on keeping a window open all the time. I pretended to sleep in order not to have to talk or pray with the others, but I was always in the blackest mood. I can only think about how to be near you again.

Her mood did not improve. They spent one night in the "dreadful" village of Bussalova. The following day they stopped for an "awful meal" in Novara. They left the plains of Lombardy and drove through the soggy rice fields of eastern Piedmont. Giustiniana scarcely looked out the window. She had only one thing on her mind: Andrea's letter waiting for her in Turin.

You will have received mine from Milan. When will I have one from you? Can I hope to receive one the day after tomorrow? Where are you? How many questions I have for you. Do you love me now? Will you always love me? . . . Come to me, please. I make myself crazy; I want my Memmo absolutely. The ambassador told me the other evening that we really are made for each other. And it would be so true if only I had been a better person. How much I have lost! But will I have your love again? I tell everyone we have established a simple friendship between us; but then I immediately add that I adore you . . . Yes, I adore you, and with greater strength than I want to.

In Vercelli, the Wynnes arrived haggard and exhausted in the middle of the night and left before dawn the next morning. They stopped for lunch and changed horses in the "wretched" hamlet of Livorno Ferraris and spent the last night in the old border town of Chivasso before making the straight run over the undulating plain of the Po valley, all the way to the bustling capital of Piedmont.

Turin was the center of a growing young state ably ruled by King Charles Emmanuel III. Giustiniana had visited it once already, on her return journey from London six years earlier. She loved this sturdy little city at the feet of the Alps. The avenues were neat and clean, the squares were pretty, the symmetry of the city's layout softened by the curves of the late baroque palaces and churches:

"The city has a beautiful appearance, and, though small, it is organized in the most graceful way possible. Beautiful streets, beautiful houses, beautiful setting, and charming surroundings."

Unlike the Venetians, Charles Emmanuel III had taken advantage of his kingdom's neutrality in the war to turn his attention to domestic improvements and reform. Political debate was lively. Intellectual and scientific associations were multiplying. True, social life was a little stiff, certainly by Venetian standards. But there was nothing provincial about the city. Giustiniana could not help but notice that, unlike Venice, Turin was a busy place with a growing sense of its own importance.

When she arrived there in the early afternoon of October 20, however, she had little desire for sight-seeing. She wanted to know whether Andrea's letter was waiting for her at the Venetian Embassy and what was the quickest way of getting her hands on it. The Wynnes were held up for several hours at customs outside the city gates because Mrs. Anna fussed and argued with the officers. Giustiniana grew so impatient that she convinced Zandiri to go on ahead and announce their arrival to the Resident, Giannantonio Gabriel. Zandiri returned clutching Andrea's letter. The irony was not lost on the poor man. "I was never your go-between in Venice," he hissed. "Now I am reduced to being one here."

Giustiniana stifled a laugh and ran off "trembling" to read the letter.

It was not what she had expected; certainly not what she had hoped for, and she replied heatedly:

Every sentence of that letter produced its share of tears! Oh yes, I am truly and completely unhappy. I have adored you, I have betrayed you for weakness, I have consequently deceived you, I have at times hated you, I have admired you, and I have fallen in love with you again and I love you now—and I am honest with you and I always will be. Do you doubt my friendship now? Come, Memmo, don't offend me; don't make me lose heart. I would like to be just a friend to you; I would like to harbor nothing but fraternal feelings; but I love you—even though I now understand I will never have a hold on your heart. What do you want me to do with your admiration *for me if I love you? Hear it one more time: I am jealous, and I still expect from you what you will not give to me—out of deliberation as well as necessity.*

Andrea's letters from this period are lost, so it is impossible to know what, exactly, he was writing to her, but Giustiniana's reaction to his words certainly gives us a sense of what they felt like to her. Clearly he did not respond to her outpourings with enough enthusiasm. He seemed evasive, perhaps even a little ambiguous. All she could think of was how to get her letters to him and stay in touch. He, on the other hand, was not nearly as meticulous. She did not even know where to send her next letter. Why was there no forwarding address? How could he be so forgetful? And then the needless cruelty of telling her he had met a young nun who would certainly have "reawakened his senses" if his heart had not been Giustiniana's: "The Nun! Why do you imagine she might awaken your senses? . . . You add: If Giustiniana were not so much in your heart. Oh believe me, Memmo, he who imagines feelings already has those feelings. The portrait you sketch for me is much too seductive."

Giustiniana was struggling to stay calm. She felt the need to declare her love loudly and incessantly and claimed the right to tell Andrea—her *cher frère* now, but still the man she loved more than anyone in the world—how afraid she was of losing him entirely:

Forgive me, but you must understand all my weakness even as I thank you for your sincerity—which I continue to beseech of you for a thousand reasons. I am always looking for tokens of your love; and I might still need to do so. Your character, your words, your noble actions are always such that whatever will happen to us you will always have the strongest, truest interest in me; but I fear that eventually your heart will be possessed by a much stronger feeling—and that I will not be the object of that feeling. I am crazy; I go looking for my own misery. Yes, but can anyone say it will not be that way? That is the only certainty. . . . Ah, Memmo, pity me. I really need your counsel.

Giustiniana went to bed exhausted, lay awake all night, and the next morning continued to write:

I have not been able to stop thinking about our whole history together. I have lost a great deal, my Memmo . . . and nothing can possibly bring any consolation to me now except the knowledge that my confession (which probably no other woman would have been able to make) has at least eliminated the extreme pain you would have felt at the moment of our separation had you believed you were losing a faithful Giustiniana. . . . Yet I am sure that if they hadn't kept me away from you for so long I would never have given you an opportunity to accuse me of infidelity. . . . But let us not talk about this anymore.

Bad weather forced the Wynnes to stay in Turin a full week. The heavy autumn rains had swelled the Dora River outside the city, and there was the added risk of flooding. The high mountains west of the city were covered with snow, and Giustiniana feared a "difficult journey" over the Alps. She tried to make the best of the situation, though, and with the help of the Venetian Resident, Mr. Gabriel, she and her sisters blended effortlessly into Turin life. They received guests at the embassy, members of the small English community for the most part. They visited palaces and churches. Occasionally the skies cleared and they rode a carriage out to the Valentino Royal Park—"which is really more of a grand alley with a view of the Po and the hills in the background." In the evening, Mr. Gabriel took them to the opera.

Giustiniana found the Turinese to be "very sociable, though they adhere to the most rigid etiquette, and extremely reserved." She was struck by the fact that "ladies may not go out in their carriage in the company of a male escort." And gallantry, she added, perhaps with her old Venetian friends in mind, was "conducted terribly." The formality of Turinese society she ascribed to the influence of the court of Charles Emmanuel III, "which is most serious-minded."

Luckily the king and his family were at their country estate in Venaria, so Giustiniana could look around the Palazzo Reale at leisure. She wandered for hours in the grand halls, taking her time to inspect "every apartment," and although she did not particularly like the sumptuous rococo style of the furniture, she loved the openness of the space, the sweeping perspective, "the long enfilade of rooms that offers such a pleasant view"—an effect that was more difficult to achieve in the smaller Venetian *palazzi*. As royal palaces went, the Palazzo Reale was modest in size, in keeping with the sobriety of the House of Savoy, "yet it is certainly more beautiful than [Versailles]. Everyone says so."

Over the years the king had assembled an impressive collection of drawings and paintings by Italian and other European masters. He was very proud of his recent acquisition *The Woman with Dropsy*, a masterpiece by Flemish artist Gerrit Dou, which had received a great deal of publicity. Now that she was suddenly face to face with the famous painting, Giustiniana could compare it to a similar work of Dou's, *A Sick Woman Being Visited by the Doctor*, which belonged to Consul Smith.[1] She thought the latter far superior, perhaps out of loyalty to her old friend. "Next time you see Smith," she wrote to Andrea, "please tell him I defended his painting in front of many people who wanted to stone me to death."

Far away from Venice, Giustiniana looked for connections with the more familiar world she had shared with Andrea. And she sometimes found them in the most unexpected places. Shortly after arriving in Turin, she met Filiberto Ortolani, a young scholar and collector and a dear friend of Andrea's who had studied in Venice with Lodoli and had fallen under his spell. They connected immediately. "I told him I knew him well [through you], and he said he knew me well through the same channel, and we quickly became best friends in the world. I went to see his apartment, his rooms. . . . He gave me a few things to read, he talked about Lodoli, he talked about you a great deal. . . . He is a very good man." She could speak to Ortolani about Andrea "with great liberty," so she sought his company as much as possible. When they were together, deep in conversation and reminiscence, she easily lost track of the time.

Giustiniana had been spending the afternoon with her new friend one day when she suddenly realized she was late for the opera. She picked up Bettina and Tonnina and rushed to the performance wearing a large, frilly bonnet *à la française* (she wore her traveling dress under her cloak, as most of their trunks were still packed). The house was full when the three girls made their entrance (Mrs. Anna had stayed home), and the show was well under way. Not that the Turinese were paying much attention to the singing: "The three of us—my sisters and I—were the real show in the theater," Giustiniana bragged. "Everyone was staring at us." Not because they were more beautiful—she conceded that there were many beautiful women in Turin, "if horribly done up"—but simply because they were from out of town. "The mere fact of being foreigners here is enough to earn us praise."

Chevalier B., captain of the Royal Guards, stared at Giustiniana with such intensity he made her blush. He took a seat right in front of her, in the box that belonged to the Marquise de Prié, a lover of music and a prominent member of Turinese society, whom Giustiniana had briefly encountered in Venice some years before.

"Mademoiselle, do not move," the captain cried out. "You look exactly like the woman who was my very first passion."

Giustiniana curtsied and turned further away.

"Yes, I can see the very same features to which I am so sensitive," the captain insisted, calling on the marquise to take a look for herself.

Again Giustiniana curtsied, but the man wouldn't give up. So she finally blurted out in her uncertain French, "Sir, if what you say is true you put me in the odd position of having to either consider your taste to be poor or feel flattered by a vanity I don't believe to be justified."

Delighted by Giustiniana's reply, the marquise stepped in at her side: "Ah, *mon Dieu*, she is charming! How well she has answered! I was right to say that by the sheer look of her one could guess she had spirit."

The captain continued relentlessly to compare Giustiniana to his first love: "I can assure you, Countess Castelli was a beautiful dame. And here I see the same eyes, the same significant features, those eyelashes, that silhouette, that same serious yet seductive look . . ."

"She might well have been very beautiful," Giustiniana interrupted, by now rather enjoying this impromptu duet, "and I might indeed have some slight resemblance to her without of course having her charms, Monsieur. But I am surprised you should find the resemblance so perfect. I am of the opinion that one never encounters such resemblances to the people one loves."

"Well, Mademoiselle, you can therefore appreciate your own power over me if it is God's will that what I see in you is only an illusion."

By this time a small crowd had gathered under their boxes and clapped at Giustiniana's repartees while she feigned annoyance and made endless curtsies. The marquise laughed and applauded her new young friend. Nobody was paying much attention to the singers on stage.

"I know you, Mademoiselle," the marquise whispered to Giustiniana. "I had the privilege of seeing you in Venice, and people spoke well of you."

"And I, Madame, had the privilege of admiring you more than anyone else, even though everyone who sees you admires you." Turning to the besotted captain, she said, "Here is the most beautiful dame I have ever seen, and the most agreeable; so I question your good taste: How can you talk about an old passion in such gorgeous company?"

The captain was not to be daunted, and turned again to Giustiniana: "Mademoiselle, this particular triumph of yours is but a measure of your charm. Though I stand next to the most beautiful lady of the land, I only have eyes for you. If only God willed that you be my last passion just as your look-alike was my first! I am certain it would be so if you stayed on [in Turin]."

Giustiniana dismissed the hopeless suitor and turned again to the marquise, who wanted to know if she and her family were on their way back to Venice.

"No, no, we have left. We are going to London."

"I understand," the captain interrupted. "You are engaged to someone in Venice."

"It could well be, Monsieur."

"I knew it. . . . Those eyes are not meant to be useless; there is a fire in them that needs to be tended. Ah, who is the happy man? I must meet him, I must at least make myself useful to him. . . . Mademoiselle, please appoint me your personal secretary. . . ."

Giustiniana laughed off his histrionics, but the marquise, too, now wanted to know the name of the mysterious man in Venice.

"Madame, you know him very well, for he often had the honor of dining with you and Countess Romilii."*

"Ah yes, now I remember. It must be Monsieur Memmo, the eldest . . ."

How well the marquise spoke of Andrea! How good it was to hear such words! But the opera, alas, reached its conclusion "and we had to put an end to a conversation that had become so sweet for me."

The war had entered its third year when the Wynnes were in Turin on their way to Paris. The political atmosphere was less tense there than elsewhere in Europe, since the kingdom was not directly involved in the conflict. Still, the English in town did not speak to the French, as the two countries were at war. The French ambassador, Monsieur de Chevelin, on the other hand, was full of attention for the Wynnes and was often seen in their company, together with his young secretary, who had a weak spot for the eldest of the *demoiselles anglaises.*

One afternoon the British chargé d'affaires, Ralph Woodford,[2] and his party went out to the Valentino Park to join the Wynnes for a stroll. Giustiniana and her sisters were already in the company of a small French crowd, so the English simply greeted them from a distance and continued along. No matter: Giustiniana preferred to spend her time with the French anyway. On several occasions she complained to Andrea that the English in Turin "are really not much"—except for Woodford, who was in her view "the most relaxed Englishman" she had ever known.

Woodford felt at home on the Continent, having spent a happy time in Madrid, and he was now enjoying his post in northern Italy. He did not miss England and rather dreaded the day when he would be recalled to London, where, he told Giustiniana, he did not expect much happiness. "In fact, he says I shall not be able to stand it." Especially young English men. "As long as you stay in London," he assured her, "you will certainly remain faithful to your worthy lover because you are not likely to meet anyone

*See p. 98.

among our young men who can show such tenderness in affairs of the heart."

The young chargé d'affaires had a refreshing spontaneity that set him apart from the rest of his countrymen in Turin. When Mr. Gabriel gave a farewell dinner for the Wynnes at his home, he did not invite the stuffy English contingent. They all took offense, except for Woodford, who happily "invited himself over."

During her week in Turin, Giustiniana took advantage of the French ambassador's interest in her to practice a little diplomacy. The Wynnes' travel papers allowed them to spend only a few days in Paris, but Giustiniana's long talk with Woodford had made her even more determined to stay in the French capital for as long as possible. The first order of business in Paris would be to make a formal request for an extension of their permits, which would not be easy to obtain; they were, after all, subjects of Britain, at war with France. But Monsieur de Chevelin had assured Giustiniana he would inform the French authorities of their arrival in Paris and write a personal letter of recommendation to the Abbé de Bernis, the French foreign minister, whose help in this matter Giustiniana was already counting on.

The Abbé de Bernis had first met the Wynnes during his tenure as ambassador to Venice from 1753 to 1756. In those years he had also befriended Casanova and the two had shared a lover, a very intriguing and beautiful nun who used to escape under cover of darkness from the nunnery on the island of Murano to meet the two men in a *casino* rented by Bernis. (Casanova later claimed that the abbé had not always been an active participant in their sexual escapades, preferring to indulge in his taste for voyeurism.) Upon his return to Paris, Bernis had quickly risen to power under the sponsorship of Louis XV's mistress Mme de Pompadour and had played a key role in the sudden redrawing of European alliances, which had led to war in the summer of 1756. But the vivid memories of his Venetian days had stayed with him even during his meteoric ascent at Versailles, and he had kept in touch with his old friends in Venice. So he had probably heard through the grapevine that the Wynnes were on their way to Paris. Given his interest in gossip and intrigue, he was also likely to know quite a bit about the ill-fated love story of Andrea and Giustiniana. There was no real need for an introduction from the French ambassador in Turin—Giustiniana was certainly aware of that. But she must also have felt that a letter of recommendation would be a useful reminder of their imminent arrival at a time when Bernis was surely distracted by grave affairs of state. In any case, she expressed her deep gratitude to the solicitous M. de Chevelin when she saw him at the theater on the eve of their departure. "He came to visit us in our box, and despite the presence of the English chargé d'affaires, he praised me very much and assured me he had written to Bernis."

At last the Wynnes departed. The traveling plan decided upon by Zandiri was to head northwest for the town of Susa, then veer sharply to the west and upward over the pass of Mont Cenis, at seven thousand feet. The party would then travel down the steep road that led to the valley of the Are, along the river to Modane, and west to where the Are meets the Isère, a few miles north of Chambéry. From there it would be a fairly easy ride to Lyon.

Giustiniana did not feel well the day they left—bouts of nausea, mostly, as well as an incipient cold. The weather was not promising, and she was apprehensive about the passage over the Alps, even a little fearful. "I will write to you from Lyon," she scribbled to Andrea as the carriage was being fitted out. "Remember to tell me everything with the same precision I use with you. . . . Dear Memmo, am I still your little one?"

Giustiniana's cold got progressively worse as they climbed toward Mont Cenis, and by the time they reached the rocky pass it had settled in her chest. The ride downhill into France was even more miserable. The wind kept blowing snow into the post chaise through cracks and openings, and as they made their uncomfortable descent she was wracked by a violent cough.

The cold was so extreme I could no longer use my legs and feet and hands. I spent a whole day in that state, and by the time we got to [Lanslebourg] I couldn't stand up anymore. I was sat down near the fire with other travelers, and soon I felt a fever coming on. We had to stay there for two whole days, as our luggage had not yet arrived, and I was in a most pathetic state the entire time. My nose bled profusely. I lost my voice. And I felt a terrible pain in my chest, together with the coughing and the fever. Still, I did not want to linger in that place, for the Savoyard doctors scared me even more than their unbearable mountains.

At the height of her delirium, as the snow fell on the tiny mountain village, she dreamed of Venice and Andrea:

> *I waited for you at the dock [at Ca' Memmo], and after a long time you came into my boat. I reproached you for your scarce love, and full of passion I told you a thousand things. You apologized, my Memmo, by shedding many tears and holding me tightly in your arms without a word but with that rare expression on your face that I noticed when you arrived in Vicenza. What a moment! My tears joined yours, and I woke up. If this were the price to pay, I would want to be ill all the time. . . . You would be so tender with me, so loving. Oh Memmo, Memmo.*

The carriage with their luggage finally caught up with them at Lanslebourg, and the Wynnes continued their journey through Modane and Chambéry and on to Lyon. The skies gradually cleared. Giustiniana's health improved every day, and as she regained her color, the daunting mountains behind her receded until they were little more than an unpleasant memory. "Mountains and more mountains. Terrible beds and awful food. . . . What a life!" she exclaimed. But at last she was in France. Lyon, where they planned to stay a few days, was known for its theater, its shops, and especially its beautiful silks. And beyond Lyon was Paris, a mere ten to twelve days away by regular coach.

Giustiniana missed Andrea terribly, and she was disappointed to discover that the letter she was hoping to find in Lyon was still stuck in Geneva because he had not put enough stamps on it. (She had money sent to Geneva to have it forwarded to Paris.) "You can imagine the pain. . . . I reached Lyon longing for a letter from you, longing to hear whether poor Giustiniana still reigns in your heart as you reign in hers. . . . Ah, my Memmo, what are you up to?

Where are you? . . . If only I had a compass that could tell me where you are."

Yet there was a lightheartedness in her tone that hadn't been there in a long time. She sounded less frantic, her feelings less jumbled. It was as if the physical barrier, concrete and inexorable, that had come between them after the passage of the Alps allowed her to focus more easily on the road ahead.

"Here all people talk about is fabrics," she quipped after her first tour of the city. She bought two dresses, a formal one with an autumnal motif of yellow leaves and green velvet ribbons and a simpler one of striped satin with flowers, "which will do just fine for a *déshabillé*."

She was already in Paris.

"I had my hair done," Giustiniana proudly announced in her first letter from the French capital. She had not even finished unpacking, and already she had summoned the coiffeur and his little army of stylists. "Don't laugh: the hairdresser kept me in his clutches from ten in the morning until six in the evening, with no interruption for lunch." He had snipped and trimmed and shaped her hair until about noon. Then his three assistants had planted "at least four hundred curling papers" about her head. In the afternoon, when the curls had set, the hairdresser had removed the papers, combing and puffing Giustiniana's hair carefully while his wife prepared her unguents for an extra-large chignon: "She mixed eight ounces of cream with as many ounces of powder. I'm not teasing you. It's absolutely true. They rub the mix into the hair, and thanks to the powder it grows into an enormous mass." Giustiniana was thrilled with the result: "In truth no hairdo has ever suited me so well." In Venice she had let her dark curls fall naturally around her face. Now she wanted to experiment with new styles, "and my hairdresser told me he will try a new one every time he combs me."

Alas, Parisian society was still officially in mourning for the death of the Duc de Luynes,[1] the former governor of Paris and a distinguished member of the Court at Versailles, and she was not allowed to parade her new coiffure beyond the confines of their hotel.

Upon arriving in Paris, Mrs. Anna had rented furnished rooms at the Hôtel d'Anjou, a comfortable house on the rue Dauphine, in the heart of the Faubourg Saint-Germain. To the right, their street led to the Seine, and then to the Tuileries Palace on the other side of the river. To the left, rue Dauphine wound its way past the bustling market and toward the old Church of Saint-Germain-des-Prés. The Wynnes occupied a large apartment on the ground floor. They had their own living room and dining room and were attended on by servants "with liveries, braids, and silver buttons."

During the journey to Paris, Giustiniana had always shared a room with Bettina or Tonnina, and sometimes with both. Now she fought hard—and successfully—to have one of her own. She was given a small "cabinet" with just enough space for a bed and a writing table. It had the disadvantage of being next to Mrs. Anna's boudoir but came with a nice view of the inner court and garden. Besides, it was somewhere she could finally have a little privacy after living in such close quarters with the rest of the family ever since they had left Venice.

The innkeeper lived on the first floor with her three daughters, who were "rather coquettish and not all that ugly," according to Giustiniana's preliminary reckoning. They often invited their guests for a meal or some musical entertainment. Among the other lodgers, Prince Dolgorouki and another Russian aristocrat, whom Giustiniana rather mysteriously referred to as "the Muscovite," immediately stood out: they dressed with flair, talked loudly in their native tongue, and brought a touch of cosmopolitan panache to the atmosphere of the hotel. Giustiniana also noticed a French officer, a royal *mousquetaire.* She thought him rather intriguing and not a bad-looking fellow, either. Unlike the noisy Russians, he spoke little and kept mostly to himself.

The arrival of the Wynne girls at the Hôtel d'Anjou did not go unnoticed, of course. But they behaved discreetly during their first days in Paris, as much on account of their own uncertain status in France as of the official mourning. Their loyalty to Britain was not very deeply felt—certainly Giustiniana never took sides in her letters to Andrea. Nevertheless, they were strangers in the land of the enemy and anxious to obtain an extension of their residency papers before venturing out into society. The Venetian ambassador, Niccolò Erizzo, was supposed to speed up matters, but he received the Wynnes with no great enthusiasm. He vaguely promised he would soon have them over for dinner and would talk to Bernis, the minister of foreign affairs on whom they had pinned their hopes, about obtaining permission for them to stay through the winter. But Giustiniana had the clear impression that Erizzo was not about to make a major effort on their behalf. "So far he has given me no reason to be satisfied with him," she complained to Andrea, trading haughtiness for haughtiness. "His superficial and patronizing tone does not suit my character at all." Erizzo's behavior so piqued her, she added, that she was tempted to tell him not to bother with the papers at all. Bernis had always been courteous to them in Venice, and he would surely grant them the "small favor" they were asking, even without Erizzo's intercession. She checked herself in the end, believing, like all proud Venetians, that an official step by their ambassador "means something after all."

Despite the "curfew," Giustiniana wasted little time in preparing for her first sortie onto the Parisian scene. After the hairdresser's visit, it was the dressmaker's turn. She bought winter capes and shawls, equipped herself with many "ornaments," and had a new morning *déshabillé* made of batavia, a delicate fabric she had purchased in Lyon. To keep herself warm, she added a muff and a stole in matching leather, with a fashionable motif of "birds from Lake Geneva." In the privacy of her small room, Giustiniana tried on her new clothes.

She also applied rouge to her cheeks for the first time.

The late fall of 1758 was one of Paris's strangest seasons. The war, now well into its third year, was not going well for France. The Grande Armée had suffered defeat after defeat at the hands of the Prussians. In America, the French were losing their colonies to the British. In India, too, they were retreating before the Union Jack. These endless military campaigns had defeated the Treasury. France was on the verge of bankruptcy, and the government was squeezing the people with intolerable taxes. Louis XV had benefited from a brief surge of sympathy in the wake of the assassination attempt against him the year before, when a deranged man by the name of Robert François Damiens had walked out of the crowd and stabbed him. The reprieve was over now, and his popularity was falling again. Mme de Pompadour, still the most influential force at court, was increasingly the object of public scorn. Posters denouncing her and the king appeared mysteriously around the city. The police cracked down ruthlessly on the populace. A person could be hanged for speaking the wrong word.

At Versailles, the crusty aristocracy lived on a diet of whispers and murmurs about who was in favor at Court and clung to the tired daily rituals dictated by royal etiquette. But in the city, society life carried on more splendidly than it had in a long time, as if the gloom spreading from the battlefields needed to be exorcized with special éclat. Every night there were lavish dinners, the theaters were full, and the public *bals de l'Opéra* were such crowded affairs they often turned into glittering stampedes.

Giustiniana could not resist the call for very long. When the period of mourning ended a week after her arrival in Paris, she was already dressed and coiffed *à la française* and eager to take a quick peek around and do a little showing off. After attending Sunday mass at the Church of Saint-Sulpice, she went for a spin in the Tuileries Gardens with Bettina and Tonnina. A crowd of carriages was out parading on the grounds despite the bitter cold. Later, when Giustiniana returned to the hotel, the flush of excitement still lingered. "We went around only twice in our *déshabillé,* and yet we were much looked at, and heard we were the most beautiful and best-looking women there," she reported proudly. She thought her rivals unimpressive: "Not a single beauty, many average-looking women, and an infinite number of ugly ones." But she was startled by the audacity of their *décolletés:* "All of them are naked . . . with nothing but a *petit collier* around their neck, covered by a *tour de gorge.*"

She had been out only a couple of hours, but she had surveyed the scene with a reporter's eye, noticing how the delicate silk scarves always matched the dresses. There were fewer hoops than when she had been in Paris six years earlier, and they were not as wide. "And all the ladies wear muffs that are covered with capon feathers that also match the color of their dress." She was certainly relieved that she had made her purchases in Lyon and did not have to go out in her old and rather passé Venetian dresses.

If she indulged in these descriptions, it was because, apart from her own love of beautiful fabrics and clothes, she knew of Andrea's keen interest in the latest Parisian fashions. "The men are magnificent," she assured him. "Their velvet suits are adorned with rich embroidery. Most wear black velvet with a gold or silver waistcoat and no frills. But the really fashionable men wear a *pensée* suit lined with the soft black wool of baby lambs taken straight from the mother's womb. Muffs are lined with Siberian wolf's hair, which is very long and white and bristly." She also kept Andrea up to speed on the latest in men's hairstyles: a large toupee, combed *à la cabriolet*—"wavy, without many curls, ending with a *frisé* and firmed up with a small metal bar in the back." And if he really wanted to impress his friends at the Listone, Andrea should consider having the heels of his black buckled shoes painted bright red—a little touch she found especially chic.

The gorgeous clothes, the stylish hairdos, the sheer luxury and flamboyance of the spectacle she had glimpsed outside the hotel dazzled Giustiniana. Even the carriages she found "truly beautiful," so finely lacquered in black and gold, with "painted bouquets of flowers that seem embroidered onto them." If only she could share that splendid stage with Andrea. Together they would charm Parisian society with their youthful good looks and clever conversation. "Why are you not with me?" she asked from the quiet of her room in Paris.

In moments of greater lucidity—and greater melancholy—Giustiniana saw clearly how the great distance that now separated them made "my longing for your love all the more ridiculous." From her new vantage point she was also able to appreciate more fully all that Andrea had meant to her: "You revealed all the mysteries of life to me. You gave thunder to my soul. You made my spirit delicate and noble. . . . You were my guide in everything, my Memmo, a huge presence in me always." Her own "foolhardiness" in once deceiving him haunted her still. There were times when she longed to regain "the innocence of when you first met me." Yet despite her "despicable" behavior of the previous summer, she still dared "to claim those feelings you had for me in another time." She was not about to give up on him, no matter how irrational her enduring love seemed to her at times. And so she was left to contend with the confusion in her heart: "I love you; I am afraid; I am angry with myself; I call upon Philosophy to help me, yet I also despise her; and so my soul is torn."

Initially Giustiniana's letters from Paris took time to reach Andrea because he had not yet returned to Venice and she was never quite sure where she should mail them. After their final separation in Brescia, he had lingered on the mainland, visiting friends and building up his contacts. In recent years he had neglected his political career to the point that his younger brother Bernardo had already entered government service while Andrea still had no official occupation. Now Andrea's first appointment by the government appeared to be imminent—word had it he would be named *savio agli ordini,* a junior commissioner with responsibility for maritime affairs (the position was also used to train promising young patricians in the art of administration). He needed to redirect his energies toward the duties and responsibilities that befitted a young member of the ruling class. True to his character, he also indulged in what Giustiniana teasingly called his "amusements and distractions" during his tour of the Venetian mainland territories. As the rising hope of an old and prestigious family, he was fêted everywhere he went, and he was also, inevitably, introduced to young women looking to be married—though he dutifully assured Giustiniana that none of them could replace her in his heart.

Curled up in her cabinet at the Hôtel d'Anjou, Giustiniana read Andrea's reports on his "little travels" with a mixture of delight and apprehension. All those young ladies he glibly mentioned in his letters . . . was it true she had not been replaced in his heart? And what about the beautiful and mysterious "nun" he wrote about? Giustiniana was having nightmares about her: "You were in her arms. . . . Yes, I even heard you shout your happiness. . . . You had penetrated the convent, you had struggled to get through the iron bars. . . . And finally there was the beautiful nun. . . . Ah, I can see you now with her. . . . I only wanted to put an end to your delight, to upset your pleasure; instead I suddenly fainted and went completely numb. Then I woke up, and I was soaked with tears and sweat."

In general, she did her best to strike a lighthearted tone when she touched on Andrea's relationships with other women. Nagging would do no good. She knew from experience how much she had to lose by appearing excessively jealous. Yet even her bravest attempts at dissimulation were marked by the fear of dispossession:

What is keeping you in the provinces? At times I do not read through you, and the words you tell me are not enough to calm my wary soul. . . . I know that on the mainland, perhaps even more than in Venice, you are bound to stand out. You will set the tone, you will set the fashion, and so inevitably you will be master of all the ladies. You tell me all of this does not touch you. But is it really possible for a young man so good-natured and lively and open to new possibilities as you are to resist temptation for very long . . . ? Do not speak to me of what is impossible. Speak to me with sincerity. I can see you now en petit Sultan, *bothering all the ladies, expertly casting your glances around and negotiating with skill the favors you must surely bestow. Nothing could be more amusing, and I honestly hope that this will in fact be your behavior. It is in my interest that you act like a* petit-maître *[dandy]. . . . I much prefer to see you wasteful than moody and even melancholy. I allow your head to play as much as you wish; but your heart . . . Oh God! Your heart . . . I know it is uncorrupted still; and you are keeping it for me even though you might not even realize it. I notice you are happy with all women and therefore undecided. . . . I believe you have more than one woman by now, and I will not take seriously any declarations to the contrary. . . . You say you like the lively one with the beautiful eyes and that she is willing but you hold back? Ah, Memmo! She does not stir you? How can that be since you admit to liking her? In the end, I do not wish to second-guess you, and even less do I wish to quarrel. Will you be my friend? Alas, it may well be the only thing you will ever be to me. . . . Ah, it would be so much better if you remained fickle and seductive and vain and crazy.*

Giustiniana's own future seemed so uncertain that the notion of returning to Venice just to be close to Andrea was never far from her thoughts. Once her brothers had settled in England could she not make her way back, unmarried and unmarriageable perhaps, and therefore free of the burden that had forced her to abandon Venice? "I will come to live there in whatever circumstances," she wrote. "In the end I need little and much prefer peace and a quiet life to all the efforts I would have to undertake to change my situation; anyway, what good would I ever be capable of away from you?"

The fantasies faded as quickly as they formed. It was enough to look up from the paper she was writing on to remind herself that she was in Paris with a mission. Although her heart was not really in that far-fetched plan to seduce La Pouplinière, the old *fermier général*, Andrea need not worry: she had not forgotten it. "I will attend to it because I promised you I would. I will set my thoughts on him as soon as I am allowed out. But returning to be with you—forgive me—will always be my primary aim."

However, their *démarche* with Bernis to obtain residency papers did not look promising: "We are anxiously awaiting a reply, but it might be difficult to get permission to stay." There was even talk of "a new edict against the English." (In September ten thousand British troops had landed in Brittany, and they had frayed French nerves considerably before being pushed back to sea.) Cooped up at the Hôtel d'Anjou, Giustiniana and her family lived in fear of a sudden expulsion from the country. There was a great deal of tension, and as usual Mrs. Anna was taking it out on everyone, including the faithful Zandiri: "She's become unbearable. . . . Even Giacomo she cannot stand anymore. She torments him to the point that I have come to pity him."

Each day the sense of isolation increased. The Wynnes had no life outside the hotel. Ambassador Erizzo's invitation to dinner had failed to materialize even though they had been in Paris nearly a month. To make matters worse, Giustiniana had lost a batch of letters of recommendation Andrea had written for her before her departure from Venice—and she suspected her mother had taken them. Even the one person she had been confident would rush over to see her—young Chavannes, her former suitor—did not come to visit. "Perhaps he is still upset that we stopped writing to him when he revealed to us that he was not a count," she ventured. "I don't much care about that really . . ."

In December Bernis finally sent word to the Wynnes. He begged their forgiveness for the tardiness of his reply "with very graceful expressions." Unfortunately, he could grant them permission to stay in Paris for only another fifteen days, twenty at the most. It was depressing news. What the Wynnes did not immediately realize was that Bernis himself would remain in Paris for even less time.

As Ambassador Erizzo explained to the Wynnes, Bernis was a "creature" of Mme de Pompadour. He had risen to power in large measure because he had agreed to become the instrument of her new policy of friendship with Austria at the expense of Prussia, France's traditional ally. That momentous switch in alliances had set the stage for the bloody conflict that was now raging in Europe, North America, and the Indian subcontinent. Bernis, however, had never been an enthusiastic supporter of the war against Prussia and England, which was proving very costly. He agonized over French losses and looked for ways to reach an honorable peace. Mme de Pompadour, backed by Louis XV, felt it was impossible to come to terms from a position of weakness. The war effort had to go on—at least until France's negotiating position improved. The mere sight of Bernis's glum round face at Versailles had become intolerable to the king and his mistress. He had to go. Louis XV arranged for him to be raised to the purple by Pope Clement XIII and then dismissed him from his post. "Cardinal de Bernis's health, which has not been good for some time, makes it impossible for him to keep the position of minister of foreign affairs," it was announced in the authorities' official *Gazette de France*.[2] A few days later, on December 13, the king exiled the new cardinal to his estate at Vic-sur-Aisne, near Soissons, a full day's trip north of Paris. His demise had been even swifter than his rapid climb to power three years earlier.

"Now, here is a lost cause," Giustiniana noted wistfully. "What is the use of having memorized all his works to learn to think like him and say the right things when we met?" Overnight, people ceased talking of Bernis except in the most derisive manner. "The *bon mot* currently making the rounds," she told Andrea, "says he was given a cardinal's cap so as better to take his bow."

The Wynnes' petition was passed on to the new minister of foreign affairs, the Duc de Choiseul. There was little else Giustiniana could do during that cold December except bide her time and avail herself of the distractions offered by the house. "I have a whole crowd of the most unbearable worshipers here," she wrote to Andrea, hoping perhaps to make him jealous. "I laugh with them, but I never give them any hope. I make them despair over me. This is my amusement."

The main protagonists in this amorous siege were the two Russian aristocrats, Prince Dolgorouki and the Muscovite. They were distant cousins and quarreled constantly, bad-mouthing each other at every opportunity. The two of them were friends of Princess Galitzine, the wealthy wife of the Russian ambassador, who lived not far from rue Dauphine, surrounded by a circle of expatriates who frequently dropped by the Hôtel d'Anjou, bringing with them an air of Russian exuberance. The French *mousquetaire* still lurked in the background, though Giustiniana had managed to draw him out a little. "He's not a bad type," she wrote Andrea. "He speaks to me often, but when the Muscovite approaches he moves away." Lesser characters "tormented" her as well, including "a rather grand individual" whose "endless sighs" she really could not stand, and "a foreigner who is here with his wife. Imagine . . ."

Among this eclectic band of *innamorati* Giustiniana had a marked preference for the Muscovite, a tall, handsome twenty-seven-year-old, "magnificently dressed and quite a gentleman." He said he was related to Princess Galitzine but explained, perhaps taking a swipe at his less prepossessing rival Dolgorouki, "that he does not wish to use his own title because he considers it a ridiculous affectation some Russian aristocrats tend to indulge in, especially here in Paris." Giustiniana knew little about him except that he had arrived in Paris ten months earlier, had already spent a fortune, and had conquered the hearts of many French ladies. Her frequent updates from the Hôtel d'Anjou made it clear to Andrea that she herself was not insensitive to his charms:

> *Last night the innkeeper's daughters asked us to stop by their apartment because a woman was going to sing* chansons poissardes, *songs about the Pont Neuf that I enjoy very much. So we*

went and found ourselves among a large company. The Muscovite came over to me and showered me with expressions of love.
I was in a good mood and I made fun of the things he said to me,
insisting that his little speech was very old style and his bleeding
heart and all the rest were quite unfashionable. I must say, he
does *have a sense of humor, and he handles himself well.*

A few days later she was still on the lookout for the handsome
Russian:

*I was lying in bed this morning when I heard a few shots in the
garden. The Muscovite was target shooting with a Frenchman. I
went down with the innkeeper's daughters. I took a few shots
myself and won the round. I then recalled that day in Padua
when I was trying my hand with a pistol and nearly killed you by
mistake. Do you remember?*

After a couple of weeks the Muscovite was clearly enlivening
her confinement:

*He spends most of the day here at the hotel, he leaves the shows
early to come back as soon as possible. He is happy when he can be
with me. . . . Every morning when I wake up I see him either in the
garden or at his window, across the garden; he waits until my windows are opened, and he comes to me as soon as I get up.*

Then he spoiled things by losing control of himself:

*The other evening, after I left the innkeeper's apartment, the
Muscovite took my hand in a small passageway and started to hug
me tightly. He used his strength, his prayers, and all his weapons of
seduction to take liberties with me; he touched my breast, and he
pressed me; but I held him back despite his insistence—and the
natural temptation I might have felt for a man who was quite
beside himself over me—until I saw that he was in quite a state,
trembling and loving at the same time. I managed to run away
from him, not without first having torn his sleeve and scratched
his hands.*

The following day Giustiniana avoided the Muscovite as much as possible. "I just gave him the opportunity to make a thousand apologies and blame everything on love, as you men are wont to do." But the Hôtel d'Anjou was a small establishment, and unless she locked herself up in her room it was unlikely she could keep the Muscovite at a safe distance for long, especially since he gave every indication that he was eager to go back on the offensive. Indeed it appeared his Russian heart pounded faster than ever after his clumsy assault outside the innkeeper's apartment. He sought Giustiniana out in the hallways of the hotel and whispered "a thousand things" to her.

As he read her reports, Andrea must have wondered how much longer she could possibly resist the *avances* of the handsome Russian. Hadn't she just mentioned in passing the temptation she had felt during her scuffle with the Muscovite? But then he knew her well enough to appreciate the way in which she was trying to get even with him for the anxiety he had caused her with his careless talk about the beautiful nun.

One night Giustiniana had been sleeping for several hours when she was suddenly awakened by the sound of scratching at the end of the bed. In the darkness she did not immediately realize that she was lying in her nightdress completely uncovered, her blankets bunched up by her feet. "I did not move," she later wrote to Andrea. "I did not breathe. After a short while I heard the sound of footsteps—someone walking away and lowering himself into the garden. I was shaken. I pulled my blankets up, got under the covers, and thought: the Muscovite must have come to my window from the garden and, seeing that a pane of the window near the end of the bed was broken, he had grabbed the blankets from outside and pulled them toward him, uncovering me."

Giustiniana went back to sleep thinking she would let him have it the next morning. Fifteen minutes later she felt her blankets slip away again and the bed begin to shake.

"Who's there?" she cried out.

"Not a peep, Mademoiselle; just come to the window and hear

me." To her complete surprise, she recognized the voice of the *mousquetaire.*

"How do you expect me to listen to you at this late hour? Leave at once."

"I have come to tell you I adore you, and I intend to prove it to you."

"You are mad, Monsieur. Your brain has gone soft. So leave the window at once and don't bother me anymore, or else I shall look upon you as the last of the scoundrels."

The *mousquetaire* insisted she come to the window until he realized the key to the glass-paned door next to the window had been left in the outside lock. He let himself in "and threw himself on the bed in an instant."

"You villain, what do you want to gain with this violence?" Giustiniana lashed out. "I detest you. Leave at once!"

He took off his dressing gown and forced himself into her bed.

"I felt only anger and contempt," she told Andrea. "I defended myself with all my strength, using my nails and my cape, which luckily I had used as a cover. He gradually relented and began to use kind words to seduce me. He whimpered and begged. Contemptible man! . . . I hate violence and I hated him, but how could I get rid of him?" If she yelled, her mother, who was sleeping next door, would have come rushing in "and God knows what would have happened if she had found me with that man." She struggled and prayed and covered him with so many insults that after a while the *mousquetaire* saw "the impossibility of success." He got up, begged her not to say a word about his failed incursion, and sheepishly left the room.

Giustiniana ran to the door, locked herself in, went back to bed, and lay awake until morning wondering how best to handle the episode. What if the *mousquetaire* spread "his own version of the story" among other guests in the hotel, distorting the facts to make it sound as if his pathetic assault had been a success? Upon returning from mass the next day she found the Muscovite waiting for her at the hotel with the hairdresser, who had come to prepare a new chignon for her. On impulse, she took the Muscovite aside and told him what had happened "in order to have a witness on my side." He was only mildly surprised, for it turned out that the *mousquetaire* had informed him in advance that he was planning a nocturnal visit. Suspecting it was just talk, the Muscovite had not bothered to warn Giustiniana. Now he advised her to "vent all her resentment" by giving the *mousquetaire* a serious dressing-down and then let the matter rest.

As soon as she took her leave to join the hairdresser, the Muscovite raced off to tell everyone the story. The *mousquetaire* was so embarrassed he did not show his face for nearly a week. Giustiniana claimed to be annoyed by the Muscovite's indiscretion but decided it was punishment enough for her aggressor and forgot all about it.

The Muscovite lost interest in her. "He is too much a man of the world to be wasting his time with me after what happened," Giustiniana noted with sarcasm. But then how could these comedy characters, these good-for-nothing half-men, possibly be compared to her Memmo? Her feelings for him were undiminished, and though they caused her sadness they also brought her comfort when she felt low: "I love you, my Memmo. Yes, I love you so much. Too much for my own sake and perhaps even for yours, because if you know your feelings for me are not as strong as mine are for you, my love will surely be a heavy burden." But if he still loved her, he needn't worry: "I am as well behaved as you may possibly desire. . . . And I have not forgotten my financier. If perchance we are allowed to stay [in Paris], I will arrange to meet him, and, with enough time to do the job, I will do with him what you want."

The week before Christmas, when hope for a favorable word from the French authorities had faded and the time left on their permit was running out, Choiseul informed the Wynnes that they would be allowed to stay through the winter and possibly even beyond. Giustiniana was greatly relieved. She had Prince Dolgorouki to thank for the permits: he had brought the case to the attention of a powerful general in the Grande Armée, Prince de Clairmont, under whom he had fought at the beginning of the Seven Years' War. All her friends at the Hôtel d'Anjou received the news with delight, especially Prince Dolgorouki, whose courtship of Giustiniana had become more pressing since the Muscovite had withdrawn from the field.

The nod from Choiseul instantly gave the Wynnes a more respectable status, and the elusive invitation to dine at the Venetian ambassador's residence duly materialized. True, it was not the fanciest occasion—the only other guests were Tommaso Farsetti, a dour Venetian poet then living in Paris, and Signor Pizzoni, first secretary to the embassy. But Giustiniana managed to make the most of the small Venetian soirée by lavishing her attention on Farsetti, who claimed to know Monsieur de La Pouplinière very well. "Deftly, I hinted that I would be happy to meet [the old man]," she boasted to Andrea.

While she waited for Farsetti to come through, she renewed her old love of the theater, though the first thing she discovered, to her embarrassment, was that in Paris, unlike in Venice, it was "not considered *bon ton* to arrive late at the show." On the whole, Parisians were just as obsessed with the stage as Venetians were. The Comédie Française and the Comédie Italienne, the two most popular theaters, were full to capacity every night. Many spectators had a genuine interest in the performance, but many more went to see and be seen. In their flamboyant suits and with their elegant coiffures, they put on such colorful and lively displays that it was sometimes hard to distinguish the stage from the floor.

The hit of the 1758–59 season was a tragedy in verse called *Hypermnestre*, by a young author, M. Lemierre, who was sponsored by the *Mercure de France*, the widely read monthly on culture and current affairs. Giustiniana made her Russian friends take her to the opening night. "All Paris was there," she wrote to Andrea, who was keen to hear the latest on French theater even though his own project had never seen the light. "The tragedy was divine, and the applause went on forever. I was very moved and cried. The entire theater was moved. How well the French act!" The star of the evening was Mlle Clairon, the most celebrated, ambitious, talented, and spoiled prima donna of her day. Giustiniana had heard about her back in Venice, and she was glad to report that the great actress was indeed "a true prodigy."

Giustiniana was eager to explore the city in earnest. Two months after she had arrived in Paris, her world had still not expanded far beyond the Hôtel d'Anjou. Mrs. Anna did not encourage her daughters to broaden their circle of friends and was constantly reining them in. So when Giustiniana did go out with her sisters, it was usually in the company of their Russian friends.

Princess Galitzine was the main organizer of their evenings at the theater. It was an open secret that she was smitten with Mlle Clairon. "People say she loves her with a tender passion," Giustiniana wrote. "She trembles when she sees her, she becomes pale, she is beside herself. . . . She always has her over for dinner. . . . People say she has spent more than a thousand francs on this *comédienne.*" The princess commissioned Charles Van Loo, first painter of the king, to do a portrait of Mlle Clairon. He painted her as Medea standing atop a chariot, a dripping dagger in her hand, her two dead children at her feet, and Jason's expression filled with terrible wrath. The unveiling of the painting at the artist's studio at the Louvre became an event in itself. "A crowd of admirers has seen Van Loo's masterpiece, and never has a painting been praised so unanimously," glowed the art critic of the *Mercure de France,* quite mesmerized by Jason's "fiery eyes" and the slain bodies of the two infants "that still tremble before us."[3] Giustiniana went to see the painting with the princess and her large train of squabbling Russians, and she was not quite so impressed. "It cost six thousand francs," she remarked. "The colors are pretty, the characters meaningful; still, there *are* defects."

Yet despite her criticism, indeed despite the affected annoyance that often filled her descriptions of her friends, the pleasure of feeling more and more connected to the Parisian scene began to come through her weekly reports to Andrea. True, she occasionally tired of running around town with the Russians. She wanted to shine in the famous literary *salons* and at the elegant dinners she kept hearing about. "I would like to meet ladies, I would like to meet men of intelligence, literary people as well as members of the Court. I would like to be received in the good houses of Paris. But with my mother here, and two sisters in tow, it's impossible. . . . Ah, if only we were traveling together, you and I, what a difference it would make! But who knows? That day may yet come." Waiting for the day when she and Andrea might converse with Diderot and the Encyclopédistes in the drawing room of a Mme du Deffand or show themselves off among the *crème de la crème* of French aristocracy, Giustiniana could nevertheless console herself with the fact that she saw plays everyone talked about, read the new books, and was up to date with the latest gossip at Versailles. The trusty *Mercure de France* kept her abreast of the great debates of the day, whether they touched on the celebrated polemic between Rousseau and d'Alembert about the corrupting influence of the theater, the controversial vaccine against small-pox, or even the imminent appearance of Mr. Halley's comet in the eastern sky. As for pure distraction, she could always count on the latest installment of the unending comedy unfolding at the Hôtel d'Anjou.

Around Christmas, Prince Dolgorouki and the Muscovite quar-reled badly over Giustiniana, and events took a grave turn. She was frantic—and perhaps a little thrilled as well—"at the thought that very shortly I will be the topic of every conversation in Paris."

The row blew up shortly after the *mousquetaire* episode. Dol-gorouki was ten years older than the Muscovite and had neither his grace nor his good looks. He was making little progress in his pursuit of Giustiniana. She found him charmless, meddlesome, and excessively irascible—a real nuisance at times. Dolgorouki was under the impression—not an entirely false one—that he was making little headway because Giustiniana was still attracted to the Muscovite. So he told her that he had heard the Muscovite slight her in public and that he had been compelled to come to her defense. Giustiniana quickly informed the Muscovite, "and he had a fit, protesting his innocence and insisting [Dolgorouki] was only acting out of jealousy. . . . He stormed off in a fury."

After dinner that night a doleful Dolgorouki told her that he and the Muscovite were to fight a duel. He added, in a rather macabre voice, that he was "happy about it." Giustiniana begged him to give up such a crazy idea. He and the Muscovite had been the closest friends; they were even related. Besides, had he not considered how it would affect her reputation? She enlisted the help of the innkeeper and the other guests in the hotel, but Dolgo-rouki remained deaf to their pleas. So she went to the Muscovite and "with tears in my eyes" implored him not to fight. After much pleading and cajoling on her part, he agreed to avoid Dolgorouki for four or five days to see if his rival would calm down and the episode could be forgotten. This did not work. On Christmas Day, Giustiniana wrote to Andrea in a state of great agitation. The Muscovite had tried to stay away from Dolgorouki, but the latter had become a "beast." He had provoked and attacked the Muscovite at every opportunity. He had accused him in front of the other guests of being "fickle and thoughtless" and "unworthy" of courting her—this at a time when the Muscovite had already put an end to his clawing ambushes in dark corners of the hotel.

One evening the two Russians came to blows in the common room, up in the innkeeper's apartment. Guards had to be called in, and both men were put under surveillance. Under pressure from the Russian Embassy, Dolgorouki and the Muscovite agreed to sign a document renouncing their intention to duel. But the matter did not end there. Though dueling was illegal in France, many people still felt it was the only honourable way of resolving a conflict of that nature. "They will either fight or face infamy," Giustiniana worried. "Surely they will lose the respect of their regiment if they don't." The Russians kept quiet, but word had it that the duel had simply been postponed. They would travel secretly to Flanders to fight, and if that became impossible they would wait until spring and duel after they returned to Russia. Thus the dramatic *dénouement* was postponed just in time for the New Year's visit to Versailles.

The Court had announced that on the first of January the king would bestow the prestigious Cordon Bleu on eight new members of the Order of the Holy Spirit. The Wynnes planned to attend the ceremony with Ambassador Erizzo and remain in Versailles until evening to witness the *dîner du Roi*. On the appointed day, Mrs. Anna and her three daughters (the boys stayed in Paris with Toinon) left the Hôtel d'Anjou dressed in their very best gowns and beautifully coiffed. The ride took about an hour. Once in Versailles, they stopped at an inn to refresh themselves and pick up Ambassador Erizzo before going to the palace. He was running late, so they arrived halfway through the mass. The crowd was so thick that they couldn't reach the inner chapel. But even from afar the youthful, forty-eight-year-old king looked magnificent. "He is a very handsome man . . . very grand and majestic," wrote Giustiniana. Despite the distance between them, she was sure he had cast "the most graceful and unaffected glance" upon her and her sisters.

The Wynnes and the ambassador went back to the inn in the town of Versailles to wait for the next ceremony. There they were joined by the Russian contingent minus the Muscovite, who was still avoiding Dolgorouki. A Galitzine prince, cousin of the princess, had come in his place but fell asleep upon arriving and snored through the meal, which Giustiniana predictably found "bad, long and very boring. . . . Nobody had anything amusing to say. Everyone yawned or slept." At last they returned to the palace and filed into the Antichambre du Grand Couvert, where the king and queen, their backs to the fireplace, dined with their immediate family as a crowd of visitors slowly rustled by. "The room is rather small, not very well lit, and rather unremarkable," she later wrote to Andrea. "There were so many people we were not directly in the king's view; yet he saw us and observed us attentively. . . . He has very beautiful eyes, and he fixes them on one so intently that one cannot sustain his gaze for long."

At around eleven, while the crowd still milled about in the palace, Giustiniana went to rest in the carriage. It had been a long day, and she was tired. While she waited for the others in the dark, her thoughts drifted back to the handsome king and the way he had looked at her. "Then I closed my eyes and slept until Paris."

Shortly after the New Year, Giustiniana was with her mother at the Comédie Italienne when she heard loud cheers coming from a box near theirs. It was her old friend Casanova, "making a magnificent appearance." She pointed him out to Mrs. Anna, who smiled and beckoned to him with her fan. Mrs. Anna had not seen him since he had preyed on her sixteen-year-old daughter. Five years later and so far away from Venice, she was not unhappy to see him again. Besides, he was now a celebrity. Everyone wanted to meet him.

Back in November 1756, sixteen months after he had been thrown into jail thanks to Andrea's mother, Casanova had staged a spectacular escape from the prison of the Leads. With the aid of a rudimentary pike he broke a hole in the ceiling of his cell, clambered onto the roof of the Ducal Palace, worked his way down to an adjacent canal, and left Venice under cover of darkness. He walked for days across the Venetian mainland territories, steering clear of the police patrols sent to hunt him down. Famished and exhausted after covering more than two hundred miles, he eventually reached the northern city of Bolzano, where he rested for a week. He then crossed the Alps at the Brenner Pass, traveled to Munich, and from there went on to Paris—this last leg in comfort, having found a means of transport and pleasant company. He arrived in Paris on January 5, 1757—the very day of the assassination attempt on the king.

The first person he went to see was his old "comrade in arms," the Abbé de Bernis, then at the height of his power. The foreign minister gave him a warm welcome and filled his pocket with a roll of louis d'or, and later that year he sent him on an intelligence-gathering mission to Dunkirk. Upon his return, Casanova convinced the cash-starved French government to launch a national lottery, which he had devised with Giovanni Calzabigi, a financial wizard working for the ambassador of the Kingdom of the Two Sicilies. The project was a success, and Casanova's cut of the ticket sales brought him a steady income.

The following year the government, desperate to revive the sagging price of French bonds and stave off financial collapse, entrusted him with a highly sensitive mission. The idea was to sell twenty million francs' worth of those rapidly depreciating bonds on the Amsterdam market at a limited loss and use the cash to purchase securities from a country with better credit. After several weeks of negotiations with Dutch brokers and frantic exchanges with the French government, Casanova pulled it off by convincing his counterparts that a peace treaty between the Great Powers was imminent and it therefore made sense to buy French bonds at a discount. He raised a huge amount of cash for France and in the process helped to revive the French securities market.

He returned from Holland a hero. During his absence, however, Bernis had been removed from power. Casanova went to see him the day he returned to Paris. "You have performed miracles," his old friend told him. "Now go and be adored."[4] It was that night, when Casanova went to bask in acclaim at the Comédie Italienne, that he saw Mrs. Anna and Giustiniana waving at him. Surprised by the warmth of their greeting, he went over to their box "at once" and promised to visit them the next day at their hotel. The sight of Giustiniana, fully grown and beaming in the lights of the theater, stirred his old yearning. "She looked like a goddess," he wrote decades later, an old man hunched over his desk in the castle of Dux. "After a sleep of five years my love [awoke] again with an increase in power equal to that which the object before my eyes had gained in the same period."[5]

In early January the Wynnes left the Hôtel d'Anjou. Mrs. Anna felt it had become "too noisy and crowded," and she didn't like the way the innkeeper tried to meddle in their family affairs, with her indiscreet queries and her unsolicited advice. They moved to the Hôtel de Hollande, just around the corner, in rue Saint-André-des-Arts. Casanova was among the first to visit them in their new lodgings, and he quickly made a habit of stopping by. "He is with us every day even though his company does not please me, and I don't think these visits are in our interest," Giustiniana complained to Andrea. "He has a carriage and lackeys and is attired resplendently. He has two beautiful diamond rings, two tasteful pocket watches, snuffboxes set in gold, and always plenty of lace. He has gained admittance, I don't know how, to the best Parisian society. He says he has a stake in a lottery in Paris and brags that this gives him a large income. . . . He is quite full of himself and stupidly pompous. In a word, he is unbearable. Except when he speaks of his escape, which he recounts admirably."

Ambassador Erizzo strongly disapproved of these visits—Casanova was a Venetian fugitive, after all. Quite apart from the requirements of his office, the ambassador felt a deep aversion for the man and an even deeper distrust. He warned Mrs. Anna about the corrupting influence Casanova would have on her daughters and sons. She listened to Erizzo, and her old wariness gradually resurfaced, but Casanova was so persistent it was hard to keep him at a distance. The other Venetian in their circle, the poet Farsetti, had a strong dislike for Casanova as well. His feelings for Giustiniana, however, were even stronger, so he took his *merenda* (afternoon meal) every day at the Hôtel de Hollande with the Wynnes, even if it meant he had to sit through Casanova's performances.

The two men irritated each other to no end. Casanova flirted incessantly and played to the gallery with elaborate accounts of his adventures that kept everyone spellbound—especially the two boys, Richard and William, who stared at him with envy and growing admiration.* Farsetti meanwhile sipped his chocolate and looked on in disapproval. "I think Farsetti is a little in love with me," Giustiniana confessed to Andrea, begging him not to gossip about it with their friends in Venice. "He grows pale when he sees me, he shakes when we are alone, but he has yet to make me laugh." Farsetti held her attention by bringing daily assurances that the invitation to the house of Monsieur de La Pouplinière, which he had promised, was imminent. He also brought his "little poems and plays" in the hope of softening Giustiniana's heart. "But I don't tell him whether I find them good or bad . . . and if he doesn't deliver on his promise, I shall treat him harshly."

A few days later her patience with Farsetti was rewarded. "It is arranged at last," she wrote to her lover and accomplice. "I am going to La Pouplinière's this evening with the rest of the family."

The old *fermier général* was indeed, as Andrea had assured Giustiniana, one of the richest men in Paris, having raked in millions of francs by collecting taxes for the king. He lived in a splendid house on the rue de Richelieu and owned a country estate at Passy, just outside Paris. Chamber music had become his passion, and the exquisite concerts he hosted every Saturday were favorite rendezvous of Parisian society. The playwright Jean-François Marmontel, a frequent guest, later wrote that the house was always

---

*Richard and William, fourteen and thirteen, often sneaked out of the hotel to get their own taste of Paris. Richard in particular was having his first sexual experiences and often relied on Casanova to get him out of trouble. "He showed me a chancre," Casanova recounts, "of a very ugly kind, which he had acquired by going all by himself to a place of ill fame. He asked me to speak to his mother and persuade her to have him treated, complaining that Signor Farsetti, after refusing him four louis, had washed his hands of the matter. I did as he asked, but when I told his mother what the trouble was she said it was better to leave him with the chancre he had, which was his third, for she was sure that after he was cured of it he would simply go and get another. I had him cured at my expense, but his mother was right. At the age of fourteen his profligacy knew no bounds."[6]

filled with the sound of music: "The players lived there. During the day they prepared in beautiful harmony the symphonies they executed in the evening. And the best actors and singers and dancers of the Opera were there to embellish the dinner parties."[7]

Now sixty-six years old, semiretired, and still recovering from an illness that had nearly killed him two years earlier, La Pouplinière had lost much of his joie de vivre. Ten years had passed since he had banished his beautiful wife in the wake of the infamous *scandale de la cheminée.* Yet he had never forgotten her, and obviously she had not forgotten him. When he had fallen ill she had returned to Paris to nurse him, even though she herself was already ravaged by cancer. In the end he survived and she did not. A year after her death he still carried the burden of her loss.

During the years of his wife's banishment, La Pouplinière had had a succession of mistresses. When he was finished with them he would either pay them off, take them in, marry them off, or a combination of all three. It was the job of M. de Maisonneuve, who was half secretary, half pimp, to take care of the arrangements. In the meantime, this peculiar mix of promiscuity and generosity had caused the large house at rue de Richelieu to evolve into the strangest ménage, where musicians, mistresses past and present, and members of the family all lived together in a rather poisonous atmosphere.

The doyenne of La Pouplinière's mistresses was Mme de Saint Aubin, a former singer and musician who ruled over the household "like an old sultana," as Giustiniana put it. La Pouplinière had long since ceased to love her, but he did not have the strength to send this crafty and rather domineering woman away. She had become an accomplished hostess, having taught herself how to organize a good concert and an elegant dinner, and the old man depended on her to run his crowded house. When she raised hell—which she often did—he simply raised her income.

Mme de Saint Aubin's major enemies in the house were M. and Mme de Courcelles, La Pouplinière's brother-in-law and his pretty young wife, who occupied a large apartment in the house with their daughter, Alexandrine. The Courcelles were allied with the Zimmermans—he a retired Swiss Guard, she the former Sophie Mocet, La Pouplinière's most recent mistress—and had the backing of La Pouplinière's scheming nephews. M. de Maisonneuve, on the other hand, was in the camp of Mme de Saint Aubin, together with the latest entry in the household, Emmanuel-Jean de La Coste, a seedy-looking former Celestine monk who had escaped from his monastery some years earlier and run off to Holland with a girl and a bag of stolen diamonds. He had returned to France and lived by doing small spying jobs for the government. In Paris he had crossed paths with Casanova and tried to swindle him for a thousand écus worth of lottery tickets. When that had failed, he had managed to worm his way into La Pouplinière's household and, through flattery and favors, had become his close adviser.

The challenge of seducing a rich old man who stubbornly refused to remarry and over whom so many Parisian women were fighting appealed to Giustiniana's vanity. She had done her homework, and she knew she was stepping onto a treacherous stage. But she also knew her strengths—her charm, her vivacity, her youth—and a part of her was eager to test them outside her usual circle of Russian and Venetian friends. "Who knows?" she gamely wrote to Andrea. "In the end, for the sake of doing you a favor, I might succeed in moving him more than all these other women have."

The long-sought-after invitation also made her deeply apprehensive. This was not entirely a game; it was a scheme that could change her life forever. She knew herself well enough to foresee that once she started, she would probably play her hand to the end. The seduction of Consul Smith had been a similar proposition, but then she had had Andrea to back her up. Now she was alone, on unfamiliar terrain, facing a cast of complete strangers.

She was also three years older—wiser, perhaps, but also a little more oppressed by the sense of time passing quickly by:

Ah, Memmo, tell me where those happy hours have gone? Where are you, my true heart? . . . When will your head and your heart be joined to mine? If only you knew how much I love you and how unhappy I am! Nothing moves in my heart anymore unless I think of you. I shall soon be twenty-two years old, and you know what it means for a woman to be twenty-two. . . . Half my life, or in any case half of the better part of life, has gone by.

How have I lived it? . . . *Only you know everything about my life, and I would be so happy if it could end with you. Farewell, my Memmo. I shall never be happy if I cannot join you somewhere, somehow. Love me as hard as you can, and remember your truest and most unhappy friend. Farewell, I embrace you a thousand times.*

It took Giustiniana less than a month to ensnare La Pouplinière. These are the accounts she gave Andrea of her success:

Paris, January 22

Mon cher frère,

. . . *I went to La Pouplinière's on Monday.* . . . *There was quite a crowd, and the master of the house was very sweet with us. The concert he gave was in our honor, and I must say it was the best orchestra in the world. I have never heard a better cello or a better oboe. The* hautbois des forêts *and the clarinets—wind instruments that are not much used in our parts—are admirable. I praised with honesty, I hope I praised with grace. I looked at him with great composure, and I never spoke excessively, though I could have spoken more. He in turn praised the precision with which I judged what I heard and what I saw; I am told he never pays this kind of compliment. With great courtesy he invited us to the regular Saturday concert. What do you say of my beginning? But enough of this.* . . . *It is too early to justify your hopes.* . . . *Farsetti came to see us on Tuesday and stayed all day. He brought me a book of French ariettas.* . . . *I spent a good deal of time learning a few of them well: if I want to please the old man, I will have to have him ask me to hum a few French songs.*

Paris, January 29

Mon cher frère,

. . . *Saturday I went to the great concert at La Pouplinière's and there were lots of people. He was rude to everyone but very sweet with me and invited me for dinner on Wednesday. Let me handle this, but you must be patient.* . . . *Would you believe how many compliments I received at La Pouplinière's on Saturday? Two ladies sent the ambassador of Naples here to tell*

*me a thousand things. . . . I will wait for you here: we shall
live together whatever way we may. Do you have the courage for
that? . . . Come laugh with me about all these crazy people. . . .
And don't stop loving me, my heart.*

Paris, February 12

Mon cher frère,

    *Listen: I have many things to tell you. I see my luck approach-
ing; but since your insistence has brought me to where I am, I
want your advice to count. My dearest friend, my heart and my
soul are always with you. . . . I stayed home until Wednesday,
when I had dinner at La Pouplinière's. There I noticed that my
innocent efforts had touched his heart because his attentions
toward me were considerable. . . . Friday he paid us a visit, a
favor he never bestows, and Saturday we went out to Passy with a
huge crowd. It is a large house, beautiful and full of those com-
forts that are so scarce in Italy and that you are so fond of. It is
divided into small apartments, with a splendid salon. We walked
in the garden, which is even more beautiful than the house but not
very green. We left Passy, and we had lunch at his house in Paris
around one o'clock. So many attentions! . . . In short: he told me
he did not want me to go to London under any circumstances,
saying he would die at the thought that I should leave him; he
asked me to stay in his house, provided I was willing to live with
his sister-in-law here in Paris, and promised he would make me
happy. You can imagine how little I liked his proposition; but we
must see where it leads. . . . One must raise the stakes and then be
willing to take half. So I mentioned a few problems, but I did not
say no. . . . He is an extremely generous man. . . . What I fear,
though, is his passion for arranging marriages. He has a nephew
who looks like a chaise porter. . . . I'd rather marry the old man.
What do you think? Would I be fulfilling your project with
honor? Enough: you can trust me. . . . The next day his secretary
came to see me, and after lengthy preambles he said he was sure
his master would offer me a life annuity of between eight and ten
thousand francs and his house to live in if I stayed in Paris. You
can imagine my surprise! And my answer! I pretended I did not
believe the proposition came from his master, whose sensitive way*

of thinking I went on to praise, even though I knew perfectly well that it did. I pointed out to him in the most delicate manner that perhaps he did not realize the kind of person I was or my station in life, and at that I let the matter drop, though I did mention, in passing, that if I wished to marry the way an honest girl like myself should, I hoped that good and noble proposals would not be lacking in my father's country. We'll see what effect these words will have. . . . Meanwhile, I'm rather happy with myself, and I hope you are as well. . . . I hope I'm being clear despite the rush with which I'm writing you; but since you know my heart I'm sure you understand me perfectly. . . . Farewell, love me. All the handsome men I see are not worth your little finger.

Paris, February 26

Mon cher frère,

I didn't write to you last week, my dearest friend . . . but it wasn't my fault. Last Monday I was about to sit down to write my letter when Mr. de La Pouplinière came to see me—for the third time. After we had exchanged the greatest courtesies and I had said a few words I thought would be to his liking, he asked me to go with him to the new Opéra Comique. How could I refuse? But you'll be surprised to hear the rest. . . . Not only has La Pouplinière fallen in love with me: he will marry me. That's what he said, and he promised he would give me an income worth his reputation. Who would ever have thought a man in his sixties could even think of marrying a foreigner whose character and station, so to speak, he hardly knows? Yet that is the way it is, my Memmo. Your prayers, your advice, my own wisdom . . . and above all the wish to see your project, about which we laughed so much, succeed—all of these have made my good fortune.

Everything was falling neatly into place, it seemed, but the deal was not yet sealed. In the weeks ahead, indeed right up to the wedding ceremony itself, Giustiniana used all her charm and her manipulative skills to make the marriage happen, even as a sharp anxiety began to gnaw at her. Her first move had been to seek the support of Mme de Saint Aubin. She had "worked on her" until she had her "completely" on her side, she told Andrea rather naively. The truth was that the old mistress was playing her own game: she saw Giustiniana as a useful if temporary ally in the drawn-out struggle against the other ladies of the house and gladly instructed her on how best "to please the sultan." More coaching came from the duplicitous runaway monk La Coste, who became Giustiniana's friend "by dint of his clever ways." Meanwhile, the Courcelles and the Zimmermans remained highly suspicious and treated her with deliberate coldness. Quietly, they started a denigration campaign against her. Anonymous letters began to circulate, accusing her of "the most infamous behavior." She received threats and was followed around by shady characters.

Well aware that members of his own household were trying to discredit Giustiniana, La Pouplinière nevertheless continued his assiduous courtship. He took her to the theater almost every night and had her over for dinner at his house after the shows. This was usually a relatively intimate affair—fifteen to twenty people, mostly members of the household. Mme de Saint Aubin made sure that even such small "family gatherings" were tastefully organized and the musical entertainment was of a superior standard. "When it's time for dessert," Giustiniana wrote to Andrea, "the horns and clarinets blend with other, gentler wind instruments and produce the sweetest symphony." Those celestial sounds helped her bear the strain of those evenings, during which she was "treated like a queen" but openly despised. It was a truly joyless home. "The sadness that lines the old man's face makes the gaiety of the younger members of the household look so affected. Everyone laughs to make *him* laugh. The place reminds me of the backstage at the Opera, with all the springs and the ropes of the set in full view."

Yet the more her own mood blackened, the more La Pouplinière was drawn to her. He saw the two of them as kindred spirits. "What interesting melancholy dwells in your soul?" he asked her one evening when she was particularly downcast. "For it stirs my own, it pokes at it. . . . All my happiness depends on whether I can make *you* happy. You'll find honesty and candor in my character. You'll see: I'll succeed in earning your respect, and that's really all I hope for." Giustiniana was touched by the sweetness of the old man's words, and she admitted as much to Andrea: "His eyes were veiled with tears as he said these things to me; he cried and was not afraid to show me all his tenderness. . . . He really moved me. I told him I was filled with feelings of gratitude toward him. He could see it was true, and he looked happy. . . . He gave me his hand and told me to swear I will be his."

Mme de Saint Aubin planned a surprise party for La Pouplinière's Saint's Day. She alerted Giustiniana, so she would not forget to bring a present, and purposely left Mme de Courcelles and Mme Zimmerman in the dark. The "old sultana" choreographed the event with exquisite taste. When all the guests had arrived, two singers who had pretended to be playing chess at one of the little tables in the first salon rose and sang a beautiful duet in praise of La Pouplinière. As soon as they finished, "the most heavenly" music started in the next salon and the guests moved along. In the middle of the room Mme de Saint Aubin herself was giving a virtuoso performance at the harpsichord of a piece she had written for the occasion. When the last notes of her composition had died, the guests were drawn by lively sounds further down the suite of glittering rooms, where a group of singers acted out scenes with a La Pouplinière theme—his wealth, his generosity, his love of the arts. The program ended with Mme de Saint Aubin reciting a musical poem in honor of the master of the house while she plucked skillfully at the strings of her harp.

"La Pouplinière was so moved he wept the whole evening," Giustiniana reported. "And in the end I did too, though I don't quite know why." The success of the soirée was also a reminder of the importance and the power of Mme de Saint Aubin's role in the house. "Everything was this woman's creation, and she was praised by all but the other ladies of the house, who had not been told a thing." When the musical entertainment was over, Giustiniana gave La Pouplinière his present, embellishing the moment with a bit of stagecraft of her own. Playfully, she drew the old man aside. "Come, now," she said. "I must give you something too." She was wearing a black braided string around her neck from which hung a little heart of gold "gently resting on my breast." She took out a pair of tiny scissors, and with one clean clip she cut the little heart loose. "This is for you, it will remind you of mine," she said to the old man, while to Andrea she wrote: "How happy he was! He adores me . . ."

La Pouplinière was now in a hurry. He realized that the embittered members of his extended family would go to any length to sabotage his marriage to Giustiniana—including Mme de Saint Aubin, who had never seriously thought he would actually take her young protégée for a wife. He acted with speed and secrecy. Before the end of February he instructed his lawyer, M. Brunet, to work on Giustiniana's naturalization papers. He made her sit in front of the portraitist "every morning until two hours past midday." He pressed the Wynnes to send immediately for the wedding authorization from the Venice Archdiocese (an official document signed by the archbishop stating that Giustiniana had no other ties and was free to marry). Finally, he presented Giustiniana with an engagement ring—two hearts elegantly entwined—and the promise of a generous income. "I think he has in mind something on the order of forty thousand francs," she told Andrea. "That would be ten thousand silver ducats a year. What do you say?"

It was nearly twice as large as the income of the entire Memmo family.

Andrea had finally returned to Venice, and from what we can infer from Giustiniana's letters he was following the developments very closely. Without his letters, it is impossible to know how he really felt about the situation. Still, the plan had been his idea from the beginning, and as far as one can tell, he seems to have been very interested in the details of the arrangements. He certainly said little to dissuade her from going ahead with the marriage. Indeed, when the Wynnes' request for an authorization from the archdiocese arrived in Venice, Andrea was quick to offer his assistance and even pulled a few strings to accelerate the matter.

By early March, on the other hand, Giustiniana was facing a serious crisis: the prospect of spending the rest of her life in that extravagant and poisonous household was making her very anxious. There was no way of telling how Andrea could ever fit into such an arrangement as long as the old man was alive. And after La Pouplinière's death, then what? The likeliest outcome would be total war between her and the mistresses, the relatives, and the various hangers-on. It was easy enough to see the material advantages the marriage would bring her. It was not so easy to imagine how she could live happily as the *maîtresse de maison* at rue de

Richelieu. "How important can those advantages be when they are measured against one's happiness?" she asked Andrea. "As rich as he is about to make me, it will never be worth what I am giving him. My happiness for money! But does my happiness have a price? It is all so different from the way we once thought we could live, always free, always together in boundless happiness. . . . I speak to you of things that truly sadden me, and I wonder if you feel what I say with the same power I feel in saying it."

Giustiniana still had time to stop the plan from being rushed through. As hard as it was, and as pressing as La Pouplinière could be, she could still say no and keep her reputation—and her future—intact. She often felt "the strongest desire to refuse the greatest fortune ever offered me." Yet despite her wavering she continued to let events unfold, reminding herself of the logic behind this improbable marriage: it would bring her and Andrea close again. "You will come to Paris shortly, won't you?" she asked Andrea uneasily. "Whatever I will be able to give you is yours, and I would resent you as much as I have admired you if you were moved [to refuse it] by a form of false sensitivity. . . . I want you to be my husband's best friend, and I want him to satisfy all your needs. Leave it to me."

On March 6, she wrote, "My good fortune is still moving forward steadily. The old man wishes to marry me in a month's time." The pace of events accelerated. The following week she wrote, "I don't have a minute to myself. . . . The man can be brutal. . . . He evicted a niece of his from the house by doing all sorts of impertinences because she occupied the best apartment—which as of today is being readied for me."

Inevitably, word about the impending marriage began to leak out. By the end of March the story about how the young and beautiful Venetian had hooked one of the wealthiest men in Paris was on everyone's lips. Mme de Pompadour herself, perhaps longing for distractions from the gloomy war bulletins, was said to be following the story with amusement from her chambers at Versailles. At the Hôtel de Hollande there was an atmosphere of celebration. The Wynnes were thrilled at Giustiniana's catch. Mrs. Anna in particular could not believe her daughter's luck and was furiously corresponding with the religious authorities in Venice. All the

Russians came to congratulate their friend. Prince Dolgorouki and the Muscovite were so caught up in the general excitement that they even stopped talking about their duel.

The wedding was to take place in mid-April, on the first Sunday after Easter. The Venetians felt especially proud. On April 1, Ambassador Erizzo informed his friends in Venice about Giustiniana's "spectacular good fortune."[8] Farsetti, the spurned suitor, now filled his days running errands and acting as Giustiniana's secretary at the Hôtel de Hollande. He consoled himself with the notion that he had been instrumental in arranging the excellent match. "Your Excellency must surely know," he wrote to Andrea, "that Signora Giustiniana Wynne is close to making a very advantageous matrimony, even though her husband-to-be is not young. What gives me pleasure is that I brought her into that house and introduced her to that person."[9]

He added, at the request of Giustiniana, that it would be nice if Andrea could make the journey to Paris on this "splendid occasion."

CHAPTER *Seven*

Early on April 4, as a new day was breaking over Paris, Giustiniana sneaked out of the Hôtel de Hollande wrapped in a
cloak, the hood pulled over her head. She took a horse-drawn cab
to a nearby church, paid the coachman, got into a second cab, and
had herself driven to yet another church. From there she took a
third cab and exited the city from the eastern Porte Saint-Antoine,
leaving an erratic trail behind her to confound any pursuer. At full
gallop, the coachman drove her out to a Benedictine convent in
the small village of Conflans, some two leagues beyond the city
limits.[1]

The abbess, Henriette de Mérinville, was expecting Giustiniana. She took her in under the pseudonym of Mlle de la Marne and
assigned her to a small room in her own private apartment. The
past few weeks had been especially hard, and Giustiniana immediately felt relieved in the company of this warm, generous woman
who went by the religious name of Mother Eustachia. It was so
peaceful. From her window Giustiniana looked down to the valley
where the Marne flowed gently into the Seine. Angelic chants rose
from the chapel and drifted to her quarters. Everything around
her, even the crisp cleanliness of her simple room, had a soothing
effect on her frayed nerves. At last she felt safe behind the thick
convent walls.

The strain had started long before the marriage preparations.
When Giustiniana had left Venice in September 1758, she had been
keeping a secret she had not shared with anyone—not even
Andrea. She continued to hide it day after day, in solitude, conceal-
ing her growing despair behind her infectious charm. She coped in

silence with violent bouts of nausea during the long trip to France. In Paris, frequent spells of drowsiness forced her to seek refuge in the privacy of her small room. Yet she threw herself into the social mêlée with as much energy as she could muster, and she made her way into La Pouplinière's heart with the kind of recklessness that comes from sheer desperation. But she could not hide her condition indefinitely: by the end of January she was already five months pregnant. She decided to confide her secret to the one person who might spare her the sermonizing and help her find a practical way out of her trouble.

After his triumphant return from Holland, Casanova had moved out to Petite Pologne, a small community northwest of Paris, just beyond the city walls. He lived in style: he rented a large house called Cracovie en Bel Air, with two gardens, stables, several baths, a good cellar, and an excellent cook, Mme de Saint Jean, who went by the name of "La Perle." He kept two carriages and five very fast *enragés,* the mettlesome horses bred in the king's stables and known for their furious speed—one of Casanova's greatest pleasures, he tells us in his memoirs, was "driving fast"[2] through the streets of Paris.

Initially Giustiniana was somewhat dismissive of Casanova. She invited him over to the Hôtel de Hollande, but she did not encourage his advances. In fact, when she wrote to Andrea she was quite biting in her description of his general demeanor. Very quickly, though, she began to warm to him—and she stopped mentioning him in her letters. One night in late January she went to the Opera Ball wearing a black domino that covered her face completely. She cut herself loose from the rest of the company—Ambassador Erizzo, Farsetti, the Russians, her sisters—and sought out Casanova. He was thrilled by her attention, of course, and when they finally managed to be alone in a box, he smothered her with declarations of undying love. The next day he showed up for dinner at the Hôtel de Hollande, covered with snowflakes. Giustiniana was in bed writing a letter and received him in her small room. The two of them talked until dinner was called. Not feeling hungry, she stayed in bed. Casanova, smiling at the pleasant intimacy growing between them, bade her farewell, and went downstairs to sup with the rest of the family.

Two days later, a young footman came out to Cracovie en Bel Air and handed Casanova an envelope from Giustiniana. It contained a stunning letter, written in great haste, that was rambling, confused, and filled with desperation. In the interest of secrecy it was unsigned and bore no date:

> *You wish me to speak, to tell you the reason for my sadness. Well, then, I am ready to do so. I am putting my life, my reputation, my whole being in your hands and through you I hope to find my salvation. I beg you to assist an unhappy soul who will have no other recourse but to seek her own death if she cannot remedy her situation. Here it is, dear Casanova: I am pregnant, and I shall kill myself if I am found out. It is now five months since my weakness and someone else's deception caused me to hide in my breast the unhappy evidence of my ignorance and carelessness. No one knows about this, and the very author of my misery has been kept in the dark. I have managed to hide my secret so far, but I will not be able to deceive the world much longer. . . . My belly will begin to show. . . . And my mother, so proud and unreasonable, what will she do with me if she learns the truth? You think like a philosopher, you are an honest man. . . . Save me if it is still possible and if you know how. My whole being, and everything I possess, will be yours if you help me. I will be so grateful. . . . If I go back to my original state my fortune is assured. I will tell you everything: La Popinière [sic] is offering me his house, he loves me and will provide for me in one way or another if only I can keep the whole thing from collapsing. Farsetti too is offering me his hand, but I am sure I can get all I want from the former provided I free myself of the burden that dishonors me. Casanova dearest, please do your best to help me find a surgeon, a doctor . . . who will lift me out of my misery by delivering me with whatever remedy and if necessary by force. . . . I do not fear pain, and as for payment, promise [the surgeon] anything you like. I will sell diamonds; he will be amply rewarded. I trust you: I have only you in the whole world. You will be my*

*Redeemer. Ah Casanova, if only you knew how much I have
wept! . . . I have never had anyone to confide in, and you are now
my guardian angel. Go see some of the theater girls, ask them if
they've ever found themselves in the need to deliver themselves
the way I wish to do. . . . I didn't have the courage to speak to you
in person about this. Oh God, if only you knew what I am going
through! Let's do all we can to make me live. . . . Farewell. . . .
Save me. I trust you.* *

Stunned by Giustiniana's revelation, Casanova rushed over
to the Hotel de Hollande. He was surprised that she was already
five months pregnant because she was "slim" and her figure was
"beyond suspicion."³ She said she wanted to go ahead with the
abortion as soon as possible. He warned her that it could endanger
her life; besides, it was a crime. Giustiniana repeated that she
would rather die than tell her mother the truth. "I have the poison
ready,"⁴ she blurted out. Casanova took pity on her and agreed,
against his better judgment, to take her to a midwife who might
suggest a remedy. They planned to meet again at the following
Opera Ball and sneak out together.

The next ball was held in mid-February, at the height of Carnival. Giustiniana and Casanova arrived separately. Both wore
a black domino, but Giustiniana could easily identify Casanova
because he wore a white Venetian mask with a small rose painted
under his left eye. After midnight, when the crowd was at its thickest, the two slipped away, found a hackney cab, and drove back
across the Seine to the Left Bank, to meet the midwife in a run-
down little apartment in rue des Cordeliers, near the Church of
Saint-Sulpice.

Reine Demay, a louche, unkempt woman in her thirties, let them
in. Her late-night visitors in their full Carnival attire impressed her.
Giustiniana in particular struck her as "a young and pretty woman,

---

*This remarkable letter from Giustiniana to Casanova was sold at auction in Paris at
Maison Drouot on October 12, 1999. The sale was brought to my attention by the
dean of Casanova specialists, Helmut Watzlawick. The present owner of the letter,
who has asked to remain anonymous, has kindly allowed me to print its contents.

magnificently dressed, wrapped in a pelisse of grey silk lined with sable; the skin of her face was very white, her hair and eyebrows dark brown; she was neither tall nor small . . . spoke French with difficulty."[5] She too noticed how Giustiniana was "very thin," considering the fact that she was by then into her sixth month.

According to Casanova, Reine Demay said she would prepare a potion that was certain to induce an abortion, adding that it would cost them the considerable sum of fifty louis—half the yearly rent he paid for Cracovie en Bel Air. And if perchance it did not work, she would teach them a surefire way to kill the fetus. The conversation turned uncomfortable. Abortion was a serious crime, punishable by death. It occurred to Casanova that he should have been more circumspect in the matter. It was certainly not prudent to bring Giustiniana to this shady midwife in the dead of night. Suddenly he was in a hurry to leave. He left two louis on the mantelpiece. Awkwardly, he pulled out two loaded pistols he had brought with him. Was he threatening the midwife? Was he trying to reassure Giustiniana? Whatever his intention—it may be he simply pulled them out in order to get dressed—the sight of the pistols sent a shiver down Giustiniana's spine. "Put those weapons away," she said. "They frighten me."[6]

It was after three in the morning when they stepped outside. Giustiniana complained that she was cold. They decided to drive out to Petite Pologne, warm up by the fire, and have a quick bite to eat before returning to the Opera Ball. The streets were empty. A cab took them flying across Paris. It did not take more than fifteen minutes to reach Cracovie en Bel Air. Casanova lit a fire, opened a bottle of champagne, and asked La Perle, grumpy and sleepy-eyed, to fix an omelette. The nasty aftertaste of their visit to rue des Cordeliers quickly faded, and the host was now in his most gallant mood. As they sat by the fire, talking and sipping champagne, Giustiniana's reticence also seemed to fade, as if she wished to forget for a while the reason that had brought them together. Casanova was quick to seize the moment. "And now we have finished the bottle"—this is how he describes the scene in his memoirs—"and we rise, and half-pleadingly half-using feeble force, I drop onto the bed, holding her in my arms; but she opposes my intention, first with honey-coated words, then by firm resistance, and finally by defending herself. That ends it. The mere idea of violence revolts me."[7]

Casanova drove Giustiniana back to the Opera Ball and soon lost her in the crowd. She found her friends, who asked her where she had been for so long. She waved to them mysteriously and headed for the dance floor. She danced hard until six in the morning while a thousand candles slowly burnt themselves out in the hall. The crowd gradually thinned. In the smoky predawn haze she wondered whether her movements had been sharp enough to damage the child growing inside her.

In her letter to Casanova, Giustiniana had not revealed who the father of the child was. It may have been Andrea: if she was into her sixth month when she went to visit Reine Demay, it meant the child had been conceived in the last days of August or the first days of September—in other words, during the month or so before the Wynnes' departure from Venice. And if Andrea was the father, one must presume she decided to keep him in the dark in order to protect him. But it is just as plausible that her pregnancy was the fruit of her brief and much-regretted affair with her nameless lover. The picture of what exactly transpired during Giustiniana's last few months in Venice is too blurred to provide a definitive answer. So blurred, in fact, that yet another possibility comes to mind: the day the child was conceived might have been so close to Giustiniana's reconciliation with Andrea that it could well be that she herself was not entirely sure whose child it was. Whatever the truth, Giustiniana, mindful of the price her mother had had to pay for secretly having her child, was determined not to keep the baby.

Casanova had been right to think he had made a mistake in taking Giustiniana to Reine Demay. Word of their visit quickly spread in the shady underworld around the *foire* in Saint-Germain-des-Prés. On February 26, less than two weeks after their unpleasant meeting with the midwife, a man appeared on Monsieur de La Pouplinière's doorstep claiming to have very damaging information on the young Englishwoman who frequented his house.

Louis de Castelbajac was an impoverished marquis and a well-known crook. Tall, gaunt, and somewhat sinister-looking, with devilish eyes and a pockmarked face, he had migrated to Paris from his estate near Toulouse and lived by extortion and larceny. Working the streets at the *foire,* he had picked up information about the nocturnal visit to the midwife and decided to profit by it. He teamed up with Reine Demay and called on La Pouplinière—possibly with the connivance of some of the *fermier général'*s embittered relatives. He told him that a young woman whom he identified as Giustiniana had gone to see Reine Demay two weeks earlier. The midwife had examined her, he said, and had found her to be in an advanced state of pregnancy. The young woman had asked for an abortion, and the midwife had refused. La Pouplinière showed Castelbajac the door, insisting that the person in question could not have been Giustiniana. On his way out, Castelbajac said he would send the midwife over to confirm the story. Sure enough, later that day, Reine Demay appeared at La Pouplinière's and repeated what Castelbajac had said. She too was promptly dismissed.

A few days later, La Pouplinière instructed his trusted secretary Maisonneuve to pay Giustiniana a visit, just to be on the safe side. Rumors about her pregnancy had been whirling around ever since La Pouplinière had begun to court her. Several anonymous letters had surfaced, one of which—apparently penned by the duplicitous Abbé de La Coste—accused Giustiniana of having already given birth to two children in Venice, besides being pregnant with a third. La Pouplinière had expected his family to undermine Giustiniana any way they could. For that very reason he was pressing ahead with the marriage as fast as possible. But he was not about to abandon all prudence.

The day after the strange visit by Castelbajac and Reine Demay, Maisonneuve called on Giustiniana at the Hôtel de Hollande. There was nothing unusual about his appearance, as he often came by on behalf of La Pouplinière, whether on business related to the marriage or simply to drop off a gift: theater tickets, a piece of jewelry, a basket of fruit for the family, a fresh catch of fish on a Friday. This time, however, he cut the civilities to a minimum and went straight to Giustiniana's room. "He told me of the slander being thrown at me," she wrote to Andrea. "Laughing a little, and using as much grace as he possibly could, he asked me if I would allow him to put his hand on my belly. I was happy to oblige him, and he begged to be forgiven a thousand times even as he cursed the slanderers."

Giustiniana said very little in her letters to Andrea about what was actually going on behind the scenes. She told him about the threats, the slanderous attacks, but she was never very specific; as she explained it, it was all part of a vague and mysterious plot set up against her by La Pouplinière's relatives. But she did tell Andrea about the bizarre Maisonneuve episode—indeed, she told other people as well, as if she had a particular interest in advertising both the motive and the outcome of his visit. How could she possibly have been in a state of advanced pregnancy, she seemed to be implying, if La Pouplinière's own secretary had put his hand to her belly and had pronounced it to be flat? But then it was probably a more cursory inspection than she was letting on, for even if her pregnancy was not very visible it is hard to imagine Maisonneuve taking a close look and still walking away convinced that everything was normal.

Whatever Castelbajac's objective was—a straightforward pay-off from La Pouplinière's relations, hush money from La Pouplinière himself, extortion money from Casanova, or perhaps all three—his nefarious scheme quickly backfired. After he and Reine Demay brought formal charges against Casanova and Giustiniana for demanding an abortion, La Pouplinière had Castelbajac followed and soon found out that he was indeed plotting with his relatives. The *fermier général* immediately brought a countercharge against the marquis and the midwife. Castelbajac, Demay, La Pouplinière, Casanova—all but Giustiniana—gave sworn testimony to the police during the legal proceedings in March, even as the wedding preparations moved rapidly forward. The three inquiring officers were inclined to believe that extortion was indeed the prime motive behind the initial charges brought by Castelbajac and Demay. "Threats, anonymous letters, paid agents: nothing was spared to give [La Pouplinière] the sorriest impression of me. Thank God they have failed and all their plots were uncovered,"

Giustiniana assured Andrea, who was finding the situation more and more confusing.

The case against Casanova and Giustiniana, however, was not closed. As a precautionary measure, La Pouplinière instructed his new confidant, the Abbé de La Coste, to write up a memorandum "on the whole Miss Wynne affair,"[8] a copy of which was sent to Choiseul, the increasingly powerful minister of foreign affairs who had granted the Wynnes an extension of their stay. Gossip about Giustiniana's pregnancy was still rife, and La Pouplinière evidently wanted to set the record straight so as not to jeopardize her application for naturalization.

The immediate threat of a trial had receded but there was little relief in sight for Giustiniana. By the end of March she was nearing the eighth month of her pregnancy. The quack brews Casanova was secretly administering to her were having no effect. And though she was still unusually thin, the daily task of hiding her condition was becoming more and more involved. She had to be alone when she dressed and undressed. She had to be careful not to raise suspicions with her secretive behavior. She had to choose with care the clothes best suited to camouflage her growing silhouette. Hardest of all was the constant, searing anxiety that her mother, who apparently was not aware of the rumor, might find out. Giustiniana became so desperate to dislodge the child inside her that she did not balk when Casanova came to her with a most outlandish proposition.

Casanova's principal benefactress at the time was the Marquise d'Urfé, a rich Parisian lady obsessed with the occult. He had managed to convince her he had special divining powers—he could read numbers, he was in touch with fundamental forces, he knew the secrets of the cabbala. He often dined alone with the marquise and cultivated her credulousness to his material advantage. It was said that she was at least partly responsible for his lavish lifestyle in Petite Pologne. One evening, in the penumbra of Mme d'Urfé's drawing room, he asked her whether she knew the alchemistical formula to induce an abortion. She answered that Paracelsus's *aroma philosophorum,* better known to his adepts by the contraction "aroph," was an infallible remedy.

Aroph was indeed a well-known medicament among alchemists

of the sixteenth and seventeenth century, and one finds several formulas for the potion in their writings. The basic ingredient was powdered saffron, which was believed to induce menstruation, and it was usually mixed with a paste of honey and myrrh. Casanova read all he could find on aroph in Paracelsus and in the *Elementa Chemiae* of the Dutch physician Herman Boerhaave. The special brew, he learned, was not only supposed to bring on menstruation but also to loosen the outer rim of the womb, thereby facilitating the discharge of the fetus. It was to be applied at the top end of a cylinder and inserted "into [the] vagina in such a way as to stimulate the round piece of flesh at the top of her such-and-such."[9] This was to be done three or four times a day for a week. Casanova burst out laughing when he read these careful instructions.

He went over to the Hôtel de Hollande and told Giustiniana of his latest discovery. In a typically Casanovian gesture, he supplied an addition of his own to the list of instructions: in order to make the potion more effective, it was necessary to mix it with freshly ejaculated semen. Giustiniana gave him a slanted look and asked if he was joking. Not at all: he would show her the manuscripts. She told him not to bother—she was hardly in the mood for reading the arcane theories of some alchemist she had never heard of.

Casanova writes that Giustiniana "was very intelligent [but] the candour of her soul prevented her from suspecting a fraud."[10] It seems more likely that she was simply at the end of her tether. They agreed to meet secretly in the garret of the Hôtel de Hollande when the rest of the lodgers had retired. In the meantime Casanova enlisted the help of the kitchen boy and Giustiniana's chambermaid, Magdeleine (he had discovered they had been using the garret for their private amusement and blackmailed them into becoming his accomplices). A mattress was taken upstairs as well as blankets and pillows. On the appointed night, Casanova let himself into the hotel through a back door and made his way up to the rudimentary bedchamber carrying his alchemist's paraphernalia. Shortly after eleven Giustiniana joined him upstairs. There were no preliminaries. The mood was very businesslike: "In our utter seriousness we appeared to be a surgeon getting ready to perform an operation and the patient who submits to it. [Giustiniana] was the operating surgeon. She sets the open box at her right then lies down on her back, and, spreading her thighs and raising her knees, arches her body; at the same time, by the light of the candle, which I am holding in my left hand, she puts a little crown of *aroph* on the head of the being who is to convey it to the orifice where the amalgamation is to be accomplished. . . . We neither laughed nor felt any desire to laugh, so engrossed were we in our roles. After the insertion was completed, the timid [Giustiniana] blew out the candle."[11]

Needless to say, the magic potion did not work, on that night or the few others in which they met in the garret. In fact, Casanova never even experimented with aroph: unbeknown to Giustiniana, he brought along whatever homemade concoction he could put together at Cracovie en Bel Air before coming into town for his nocturnal exercises—usually just plain honey. Faced with yet another failure, Giustiniana finally gave up the idea of ridding herself of the fetus and instead turned her attention to finding a suitable place where she could deliver the baby clandestinely. It was a common enough practice. She had heard there were convents where young pregnant women could go. It was a matter of finding a friendly place where she could feel comfortable and where her secret would be kept safe.

By the end of March the search had become frantic. The pressure from La Pouplinière was becoming unbearable. Giustiniana's naturalization papers, signed by Louis XV, had arrived from Versailles.[12] The Venetian documents were also ready and on their way to Paris. There was nothing to prevent the marriage from going ahead as planned in mid-April. Even the official portrait was near completion. And the impatient *fermier général* kept asking Giustiniana to set up an appointment with his dressmakers—which gave her a nightmarish vision of a busy band of seamstresses laying their searching hands all over her.

This time Casanova came through for her. He turned for advice to the Countess du Rumain, a well-connected Parisian *grande dame* "who was more beautiful than pretty . . . and was loved for the sweetness of her character."[13] The countess was intrigued by Casanova's divinatory powers (later on she too became an adept of the "abstruse sciences"), but she was also a practical woman and enjoyed using her influence to help others.

Casanova told the Countess du Rumain the whole story. At the end, he asked if she knew of a safe refuge where Giustiniana could deliver the baby. The countess wasted no time. She contacted another friend, Madame de Mérinville, who was evidently quite experienced in such matters, and begged her to receive Giustiniana as soon as possible as her pregnancy was already so advanced. The financial and logistical arrangements were worked out by the countess, Madame de Mérinville, and Casanova, who claimed he gave Giustiniana fifty louis to pay for transportation and expenses during her stay at the convent. Within a few days everything was ready. La Pouplinière's dressmakers visited Giustiniana at the Hôtel de Hollande on April 3 and discussed various ideas for her wedding trousseau. It was a brief, preliminary meeting—no searching hands. Early the following morning she made her escape to the convent in Conflans.

Giustiniana left two letters behind—one for her mother and one for La Pouplinière. To both she wrote that she had been forced into hiding because of the constant threats she kept receiving by those who opposed the marriage. It was not just her reputation that was being sullied; she feared for her life. Under such circumstances she could not possibly go ahead with the marriage, and she would not reveal her hiding place until it had been called off. To mislead the police, she said she was staying within the city of Paris.

As Giustiniana settled into her spare room at the convent, fear and confusion took over at the Hôtel de Hollande. When Mrs. Anna finished reading Giustiniana's letter, she immediately suspected Casanova of kidnapping her daughter. Ambassador Erizzo, who had admonished the Wynnes against having anything to do with him, was also convinced of Casanova's involvement. Casanova, of course, feigned complete ignorance about Giustiniana's whereabouts. In fact, he even appeared for dinner at the Hôtel de Hollande the very day of her disappearance, asking with a perfectly straight face why everyone was wearing such a sullen expression and whether Giustiniana was upstairs in her room. The next day Mrs. Anna drove out to Petite Pologne with Farsetti and begged Casanova to tell her where her daughter was. Again he assured her he didn't have a clue and promised he would do all he could to help find her. A few days later Mrs. Anna, with the full blessing of Ambassador Erizzo, sued Casanova for conspiring to kidnap her daughter.

Soon Giustiniana was able to reassure her family. She befriended the uncle of Mother Eustachia's chambermaid, who worked at the convent, and paid him to take her letters into town and deliver them to another intermediary, a man she referred to as "the Savoyard," who posted the sealed envelopes at different mailboxes around Paris. Giustiniana assured Mrs. Anna and her siblings that she was well but insisted she would not reveal her hideout until she was sure she would not have to marry La Pouplinière. Communicating with Casanova was easier: she sent her letters for him directly to Countess du Rumain via Mother Eustachia. She was deeply grateful to him and to his lady friend, she wrote. She had found peace at the convent and the abbess was very kind. There were books to read and plenty of time to rest, though she complained that the absolute confinement imposed by Mother Eustachia weighed on her spirits at times.

In Paris, meanwhile, the inquiry into the ill-fated trip to Reine Demay's was slowly moving forward. Antoine Raymond de Sartine—a rising star in the city's judiciary, whom Louis XV would soon name chief of police—summoned Casanova for an informal talk at his private home. He told him he was going to have to answer the very serious charge of having solicited Demay to perform an abortion on Giustiniana. But if he was innocent, he should tell him the whole truth—tell him why Giustiniana had disappeared and where—and the entire matter would be quickly settled. Casanova assured Sartine that the charges were false. "Alas, Monsieur, there is no question of abortion; other reasons prevent her from returning to her family. But I cannot tell you more without a certain person's consent, which I shall try to obtain."[14]

Casanova realized that his vague explanations had not convinced the magistrate and he would soon find himself in very serious trouble unless he told him the truth about why Giustiniana had run away. But he needed to have Countess du Rumain's permission. He went to her the next day, and, pragmatist that she was, she called on Sartine and told him the whole story herself. Giustiniana was indeed pregnant, she explained, but no abortion had been performed; she was now waiting to deliver in a convent near Paris and would go back to her mother after the baby was born.

Sartine was an understanding man; he knew the ways of the world. He listened carefully to what the countess said. It was all he needed to know; they could count on his discretion. A few days later Casanova was summoned for a formal deposition before the presiding judge, who was none other than Sartine himself. He admitted going to the Opera Ball wearing a black domino on the night that was mentioned in the suit but denied ever paying a visit to Reine Demay. As for Giustiniana, he said, "neither I nor any member of her family ever thought she was pregnant."[15]

Sartine spared Casanova an arrest warrant but advised him not to leave Paris until the case was closed. For good measure, Casanova dropped a handsome bribe of three hundred louis into the lap of the court clerk. Shortly after his testimony, Castelbajac sidled up to Casanova with an offer: Demay was ready to retract her accusation—claiming she had mistaken his identity—in exchange for a hundred louis. The midwife appeared at his house in Petite Pologne a few days later in the company of a conniving witness and, after taking a look at Casanova, said loudly that he was not the man she was looking for: "I have made a mistake."[16] She was not the only one trying to make some quick money from the sordid episode. Mrs. Anna's lawyer, M. Vauversin, also stepped into the fray, secretly offering Casanova advice on how to counter his client's suit against him.

Delighted at the opportunity his enemies were handing him, Casanova sent a detailed report to Sartine on all the financial shenanigans. In short order, Demay was arrested and imprisoned at the Grand Châtelet for attempted extortion; Castelbajac was sent to the Bicêtre, a prison just south of Paris, for his complicity in the affair; and M. Vauversin was temporarily disbarred, much to Mrs. Anna's discomfiture.

Casanova could breathe again, but despite the arrest of two of the claimants he was still not cleared and the two cases that had been brought against him remained pending. Giustiniana's disappearance continued to be a topic of gossip in Paris throughout the spring of 1759. "You would not believe, sir, the noise this affair has made here," one of Andrea's correspondents wrote. Several weeks after her escape "she still remains the news of the day in a country that usually thrives only on novelty. If poor Miss Wynne had wanted people to know she was in town, I can assure you she would have been very satisfied, for I can't remember anyone being talked about so much."[17]

Inside the court, Casanova had testified that pregnancy was not the cause of Giustiniana's disappearance. But of course the talk outside the court was that she was indeed expecting a child. How else could one explain her sudden bolting and, even more so, her refusal to emerge from hiding? Her own explanation—that she was running away from threats and a marriage she couldn't face— simply did not make sense. The substance of Castelbajac and Reine Demay's depositions soon became general knowledge. An anonymous and very derogatory pamphlet on Giustiniana made the rounds. Andrea's name cropped up frequently in conversations around town as the presumed father. And La Pouplinière, of course, was made to look like a fool.

Inevitably, rumors about the causes of Giustiniana's disappearance reached Venice as well. Andrea did not quite know what to believe. He had stopped receiving letters from her after she had gone into hiding. His friends were asking whether what they heard was true. He did not know what to say. Her mysterious behavior had left him defenseless in the face of the most insidious attacks. Utterly confused, he resorted to reading excerpts of some of Giustiniana's earlier letters out loud to prove to others that she had harbored misgivings about the marriage and might well have fled out of sheer panic. But beyond defending Giustiniana's honor, what was he to believe? Could it be that she was really pregnant? If so, who was the father?

Andrea's attempts to get credible information from his friends in Paris were frustrated. "You must let me know once and for all precisely what has occurred," he urged Casanova, to no avail. Farsetti was not much help either. He wrote to Andrea about Giustiniana's "enemies" but never provided a convincing picture of what was actually going on, probably being in the dark himself.

Farsetti seemed more interested in denigrating Casanova at every opportunity: "If she had never met that man or if she had sent him away as I told her to do, she would be married by now."[18]

Even more disquieting than Casanova's prevarications and Farsetti's petulant letters was the short note Ambassador Erizzo sent Andrea in reply to his frantic queries. Erizzo was a respected statesman, a senior member of the Venetian ruling class. Even though Andrea belonged to a younger generation, the ambassador always addressed him as one of his own. His harsh words must have weighed heavily on Andrea's heart.

> *Esteemed Friend,*
>
> *I had the honor of receiving two letters in which you urge me to tell you what has happened to your beautiful Miss Wynne, who has not written to you for many days, and who, to your surprise, is beginning to be talked about in the most equivocal manner; and so you would like me to give you an accurate report on what has occurred. I very much wish I were in a position to oblige you; but the anecdotes are numerous and of such a nature that I would be compelled to write for two hours—and this after I have just finished writing a long dispatch. Suffice it to say that her conduct was ridiculous and imprudent in the extreme, and if she had sought advice from sensible people everything would have been settled. I believe it is entirely superfluous to say more since it would appear, if what I have been told is correct, that you are in a better position to inform me than I am to inform you. It is believed, among other things, that she has rushed to Venice or wherever you might have told her to go. Please forgive me.*[19]

April turned into May. The days grew longer and warmer. The countryside around Conflans teemed with new life. Spring showers washed over the lush green hills and the air was sweet with the scent of lilac. Inside the convent, Giustiniana waited peacefully for the birth of her child. She had grown close to Mother Eustachia despite their difference in age; the abbess was nearly thirty years her senior. During their long conversations, she had talked to her as if to an older sister about her love for Andrea, the hardships they had faced together, her uncertainty about the future. Little by little the spiritual quality of the place had affected Giustiniana. She was more at ease with herself despite a natural trepidation as her labor approached. Many hours passed in prayer, and the amiable Father Jollivet often took her confession. It was a difficult time, but Mother Eustachia and Father Jollivet made her feel a little less alone.

At the end of May, Mother Eustachia informed Countess du Rumain and Casanova that Giustiniana had given birth to a baby boy. The delivery had not presented special problems, and the mother was in good health. No official record of the birth has survived. The boy's destiny remains a mystery. Even his name is unknown. Mother Eustachia arranged for the child to be sent "to a place where he would be properly cared for"[20]—perhaps a local peasant family or else an orphan's home, as was the custom in such cases. Giustiniana never mentioned him in her correspondence. She certainly never spoke of him to Andrea. Only a handful of people knew what had happened at Conflans, and the secret would have died with them had Casanova not betrayed it in his memoirs some thirty years later.

Giustiniana could now reveal her whereabouts and go back to her family after a short period of recovery. But her return had to be negotiated with as much skill and diligence as had been used to organize her disappearance. As soon as she was fit to be seen in public again—albeit only behind the grille of the convent parlor— she wrote to her mother and told her where she was. Mother Eustachia also contacted Mrs. Anna, explaining that she had just discovered Giustiniana's real identity. The letter, dated May 27, is a little triumph in the art of deception:

Mlle Justiniana Wynne finally opened up to me yesterday evening. She told me, Madame, that you are presently living at the Hôtel de Hollande, rue Saint-André-des-Arts. Had I known this before, I could have spared you so many worries. She has been with us ever since coming here on April 4. You mustn't begrudge me my taking her in. I did not dare expose a young woman of her age and station to the dangers of wandering alone in search of other communities, certain as I was that someone would soon come to claim her. Yet nobody came to ask for her. . . . She has seen no one in the parlor and has received no letters. She has conducted herself with great piety here. She has a charming character. I love her with all my heart, and I would be handing her back with the greatest regret if I didn't know it was for her greater happiness. I would be delighted, Madame, to give you a token of my respect at any time, and I have the honor of being your very humble and very obedient servant.

Sister de Mérinville, abbess of Conflans[21]

The letters drew a stream of people to Conflans. Mrs. Anna arrived at the convent the very next day. She was accompanied by M. de La Pouplinière, who had his personal train of followers: M. de Maisonneuve; his confidant, the Abbé de La Coste; and his notary, Maître Fortier, who had come to take a sworn deposition from Mother Eustachia in order to establish the exact date of Giustiniana's arrival at the convent and the length of her stay. Father Jollivet also gave testimony that he had "taken confession many times" from Giustiniana.[22] Amidst the general confusion, La Pouplinière advised Mrs. Anna to have notarized copies made of Mother Eustachia's letter to her and Father Jollivet's deposition as soon as she got back to Paris. It was important, he explained, to protect Giustiniana's reputation with official documents.

Once the formalities were out of the way, the little crowd gathered by the grille, behind which Giustiniana was smiling coyly. There was a very emotional exchange. Giustiniana feigned surprise at what had been said about her in Paris during her absence. She acted bewildered when she was told that criminal charges had been brought against Casanova on her account. La Pouplinière led the conversation, and Giustiniana was struck by "the expressions and tears of the old man, who loves me to the extreme." Her miraculous reappearance—the actual sight of her as she sat behind the grille, looking "even more beautiful than before"[23]—so galvanized the *fermier général* that he saw no reason why the marriage could not go forward after all. Mrs. Anna announced that she was withdrawing her charges against Casanova now that her daughter had reappeared and the matter had been cleared up (that wasn't enough for Casanova, who requested a written apology that he then had notarized). The other, more serious charge of attempted abortion was still in place, and the pending trial was a problem, of course. But La Pouplinière felt it was much simpler to clear Giustiniana's position now that the truth was out. The wedding, he proclaimed as he took leave and headed back to Paris, would take place "as soon as the trial is done away with."[24]

When her visitors had left, Giustiniana withdrew to her chamber to review the situation with Mother Eustachia. It had been a turbulent and confusing day. She was baffled by La Pouplinière's plan to go ahead with the wedding. Even though she was no longer pregnant and there was no practical obstacle to the marriage, she had had plenty of time during her long seclusion to reflect on the wisdom of that enterprise. The idea of being thrown back into the clutches of La Pouplinière's avaricious relations terrified her. Perhaps more important, her stay at Conflans had changed her: the extravagant notion of marrying the old *fermier général* seemed to belong to another life.

Giustiniana and Mother Eustachia agreed that there was no need to rush back to Paris. Besides, if she left the convent she might well be called to testify in the proceedings that were continuing against Casanova. Even worse was the possibility that Reine Demay—who had been released after spending three weeks in jail—might be asked to identify Giustiniana as the woman who had visited her in rue des Cordeliers on the infamous night of the Opera Ball in the company of Casanova. Better to allow La Pouplinière time to sort things out with the court officials and return once the proceedings were over.

In the following weeks Giustiniana gradually recovered her spirits as well as her slender silhouette. She was allowed out of the convent for short walks in the gardens, and she received regular visits at the grille from a doting La Pouplinière, as well as all the clamoring members of her family and her many friends. Toward the end of June her visitors planned a *fête* outside the convent to honor Mother Eustachia and the Benedictine nuns for looking after Giustiniana so well.

Andrea, meanwhile, was still very confused. Giustiniana was in a hurry to renew her correspondence with him in order to reassure him. As a gesture of goodwill, Mrs. Anna handed over to Giustiniana those of Andrea's letters that she had intercepted during the previous weeks—most of which she had opened and read anyway. But she forbade her daughter to write to Andrea because she still suspected him of having had a hand in Giustiniana's disappearance. Farsetti, terrified of incurring Mrs. Anna's wrath, at first resisted Giustiniana's pleas to act as her secret postman. Only at the end of June, during her final days at Conflans, did he finally agree to mail her first letter to Andrea since she had sneaked out of the Hôtel de Hollande nearly three months earlier.

Mon cher frère,
My dear Memmo, forgive me. I know you will forgive me in the end. But still I begin by asking you to forgive me; to make it easier for you to read my letter with a favorable attitude, I shall first accept some blame. But the only crime I have committed is not having written to you for so long; and if I prove to you, my dear friend, that it was impossible for me to do so before, I think you will want to forgive me. I love you, I am your friend; my Memmo will always mean the same to me; and your letter, which Farsetti showed me yesterday, which made me feel that despite my enemies' craftiness, despite all that was said about me, you always held me innocent, even though my silence with you suggested I might be guilty, would have convinced me more than ever of the excellence of your character—if I had needed any more convincing. You are well worth my breaking the prohibition to write to you. Let me rise to this renewed expression of respect and friendship I receive from my Memmo, even if it means that everything might go to hell. I begged Farsetti with so much fervor that he promised he would send you my letter; and so I write to you stealthily, even as I am being watched, and I want to tell all my story.

Here at last was the letter Andrea had been waiting for. Of course Giustiniana's narrative was skillfully edited. She told him that the warnings and threats she had received from anonymous writers had compelled her to go into hiding. "All the necessary preparations have been made for your downfall," she quoted from memory. "Go into hiding as soon as you can. This is a serious affair." It had reached the point where she was seeing "poison everywhere." La Pouplinière himself had told her their enemies were "capable of anything." She had had no option but to escape somewhere. "The day before I left," she added, recasting events in such a way as to make her tale more credible, "the old man's dressmakers came by to take my measurements, and it was a good thing they came because it eased the suspicions instilled in him after my flight." She described her trip to Conflans and her meeting with the "excellent and very amiable" Mother Eustachia—who, she added, was related to some of the best houses of France. At first the abbess had not wanted to take her in, Giustiniana told Andrea, contradicting Casanova's version of the facts, but the sight of such "a nicely dressed young woman with jewels" had moved her. Mother Eustachia had questioned her intensely during the first few days, and eventually she had relented. "She could see I was still frightened, and since she cared for me, she stopped questioning me so as not to agitate me further." Her identity would have remained a secret, Giustiniana claimed, if on May 23 she had not heard Father Jollivet speak in such a way as to force her to reveal who she was:

> *That day the confessor came to the abbess's parlor and unwittingly started to tell her what I recognized was my own story—by chance I was there keeping the abbess company—as if telling the latest gossip from Paris. He talked about the girl's flight just before her wedding to a rich financier, he mentioned all the equivocal things being said about her, including the fact that she had run away to give birth and that Monsieur de La Pouplinière was convinced about it. Such were my surprise and my confusion that without even realizing what I was saying I blurted out, "It is not true. Miss Wynne is a lady who belongs to one of the oldest and noblest families. Miss Wynne is an honorable young woman. I am that young woman . . ." You can well imagine their surprise. Both tried to explain to me how imprudent I had been in not hav-*

ing identified myself before, and they persuaded me to write to my mother. Which I did.

La Pouplinière now came regularly to the convent, the letter went on. He was working hard to close down the Casanova trial. "God only knows what happened . . . because I know nothing about what Casanova is up to," she assured him. In any case things looked promising on that front. "I believe I shall be cleared very shortly." Of course there was again all this talk about the marriage, she wrote in conclusion. "The old man is waiting for everything to be over to marry me; but I am still unsure (and please leave me free to decide for myself). I am not counting on it as much as others are, even though it does appear to be so close."

In fact, it was not nearly as close as she thought.

Giustiniana left the convent sometime between the end of June and the beginning of July. Her return to Paris came on the heels of several weeks of behind-the-scenes negotiations involving La Pouplinière, members of his family, and the office of Choiseul at Versailles. The Wynne Affair, as it was known, had caused such a commotion in Parisian society that the government was no longer well disposed toward Giustiniana, and her position was not improved by the fact that the British were pounding the French at Le Havre. Louis XV had signed her naturalization papers only three months before. But they had been intended to open the way for her marriage to La Pouplinière before the scandal. In the wake of her disappearance and the drama that had ensued, not to mention the fact that she still might be summoned as a codefendant in the trial of Casanova, her position was quite different. La Pouplinière's relatives took advantage of this new mood of impatience at Court. They used their strong connections with the Choiseul camp to obtain nothing less than Giustiniana's banishment from the country. There was no need for a dramatic announcement; the Wynnes were simply informed that their papers, which were expiring anyway, would not be renewed. Technically, of course, Giustiniana was now a naturalized citizen. But there was little point in challenging the powerful Choiseul. The time had clearly come to continue their journey to England.

Choiseul's office convinced a reluctant La Pouplinière to go along with the decision by suggesting that Giustiniana might go abroad for a while, possibly no further than Brussels, and return to Paris once the situation had cooled down. To many it was clear that the old man had been fooled. "Monsieur de La Pouplinière flatters himself that the noise will die down as soon as she is out of the kingdom and that he will then manage to settle things more easily," one observer wrote to Andrea. "I wouldn't want him to be taken by surprise and led to rid himself, unwittingly, of Miss Wynne."[25]

Giustiniana was confined to the Hôtel de Hollande from the day she left the convent until her departure to Brussels, initially set for July 14. "It is my mother's idea, and you know one has to do things her way," she told Andrea. Mrs. Anna hardly spoke to her daughter. She had been on the brink of an exceptional marriage only four months earlier; now the family had to suffer the humiliation of being kicked out of the country on Giustiniana's account. The atmosphere in their apartment was tense. And the summer heat made packing their trunks all the more uncomfortable.

Mon cher frère,

We leave for Brussels having been dismissed by the minister, probably thanks to the work of the old man's relatives, who will have had no trouble in convincing the authorities that it was wrong for such a fortune to end up in the hands of an Englishwoman— especially in these times. As an excuse, we were told that our papers had expired and winter had been over for a long time. . . . I cannot tell you how disgusted I am with this country and with [La Pouplinière's] household. . . . Oh, why are you not here to advise me? Dear Memmo, how many woes I have suffered, how many scares, how many slanders! My story is so unlike me. Never mind . . . you will know all. . . . You have always been my best friend and always will be. I still love you, Memmo. You know that. I always wonder whether I shall ever find my Memmo again. Shush, I know I shall one day. . . . I'll write to you every week. . . . . While I appreciate your intention in reading my early letters to many of your friends so they might see that what was being said about me was very unlikely, I must confess that I feel bad about the fact that what I wrote to you in private for only you to read should be judged by others. Farewell, my Memmo; love me and write me long letters.

The pressure on Giustiniana to testify at Casanova's trial evaporated once it became clear she would be leaving town. La Pouplinière insisted that it would be "indecent" to summon her before the judge, offensive to her *and* to him, since after all he still intended to marry her. His embittered relatives saw that there was no point in dragging out the fight. Choiseul himself probably let it be known that he would be happy to see the Wynne Affair come to a swift conclusion. In the end, Giustiniana was spared a humiliating trip to court and her name was officially cleared. "The sentence that establishes my innocence is all I really [wanted]," she wrote to Andrea, greatly relieved.

There was one last, pathetic scene at the Hôtel de Hollande. A few days before her departure for Brussels, Giustiniana sent a note over to La Pouplinière thanking him for all he had done to get her out of her legal troubles. She also told him with a clarity she had never used before that it was foolish to continue talking about marriage even as she was packing her trunks. But since he persisted in holding on to that illusion, she felt compelled to refuse his hand. It was a strong letter and unambiguous for once. "Imagine a well-thought-out, well-crafted piece of work," she proudly told Andrea.

The effect of her letter was not what she had expected: "The old man rushed over to see me, and his tears were the only answer I got from him." Not at all resigned, La Pouplinière sent the Abbé de La Coste and Mme de Saint Aubin to talk things over with Giustiniana and her mother. But it was much too late in the game. Even Mrs. Anna, who had been such a keen supporter of her daughter's marriage to the *fermier général*, could see through that shady, calculating couple. She gave them "a very rough dressing down" and accused them of giving the old man the runaround for their personal benefit. "She so treated them as scoundrels that they rushed off, saying 'Madame hears no reason. . . . It is impossible to come to terms with her.' "

The Wynnes left Paris for Brussels around mid-July. They had certainly made their mark since arriving from Lyon nine months earlier, and Giustiniana, of course, had been the talk of the town during much of their stay. Now they were the enemy on the run— a disgraced English family fleeing through the back door in the stifling midsummer heat. Giustiniana was glad to escape, to leave it all behind her—the deception, the intrigue, the lying, the sheer awfulness of what she had lived through. As far as she was concerned, it was already part of the past. "I look upon this story with such indifference I feel it never happened," she wrote to Andrea, who was apparently still somewhat "distressed" over the lost opportunity of a great marriage. She, on the other hand, was already looking ahead to their short stay in Brussels and their new life in London. After all she'd been through, she added with a bit of sarcasm, it shouldn't be too hard for her "to ensnare an English duke."

In her letters there was, of course, no mention of the baby she was leaving behind. Did she ever visit him before departing? Did she stay in touch with the people he had been entrusted to? One searches in vain for an answer in her correspondence: there is not even a hint as to what she was going through because of this separation. However intense her maternal feelings toward the child might have been, she forced herself to keep them secret. With Andrea so far away, she had no outlet for her pain. Casanova, to whom she had become so close in a short period of time, had already drifted out of her life by the time she left Paris. In his memoirs there is no mention of a final farewell between the two. He had simply moved on to his next adventure.

Meanwhile, the original traveling party had lost two of its members. Zandiri had returned to Venice, and Toinon, who had seemed destined for spinsterhood, announced to everyone's surprise that she was staying in Paris because she was about to become engaged. So there was going to be a marriage after all. "Plain as she is, she has nonetheless managed to find a lover who will marry her as long as she has a virginity to lose," a well-informed friend of the family wrote to Andrea. "She claims to be intact from that point of view, and so this happy wedding will take place shortly."[26]

The Wynnes ended up staying in Brussels more than a month. They took rooms at the elegant Hôtel de l'Impératrice and waited for instructions from Lord Holderness. Giustiniana was determined to make the most of their stay. "I have decided to enjoy myself . . . and to humor my temperament," she wrote, flaunting her brittle new gaiety. "I spend my time as best I can; I laugh at everything and often at myself." Brussels was the ideal place to have some fun. It had the insouciance of a provincial capital governed by a wise and popular ruler, Prince Charles of Lorraine. Giustiniana, Bettina, and Tonnina were soon regulars at the theater and the opera. They dressed up, they danced, they flirted. "We are the beauties of the land," she reported with a cheerfulness Andrea had not heard for months.

The dreary Farsetti quickly arrived to spoil the fun. Still obsessed with Giustiniana, he followed the Wynnes to Brussels convinced that the moment was finally his. He had stood by her during difficult times, he had lent her money, he had posted her love letters, he had tried to protect her from other suitors—as well as from her own imprudence. The time had come to claim Giustiniana for himself. But Giustiniana was tired of Farsetti's nosy, self-righteous manner. Her resentment toward him, long stifled out of self-interest, was ready to burst.

"Farsetti joined me here shortly after my arrival and immediately started to show off," she complained to Andrea. "He was full of claims, full of jealousy. . . . I dismissed him a thousand times so that he would return to Paris, and a few times I was rather sharp. . . . I owe him a lot because he was full of attention for me [in the past]; but I cannot forgive his doggedness in loving me." The poor man did not know what had hit him. Utterly stunned, he left Brussels the day after his arrival. As for Giustiniana, she continued to have fits of rancor even after his departure: "Ah, Memmo, that Signor Farsetti was deadly. . . . His envy, his designs. . . . No man has ever hurt me more. . . . The whole of Paris knew that he wanted to marry me and that I constantly had to refuse him. . . . [Ambassador Erizzo] always claimed it was Farsetti who messed up the deal with the old man. All I know is that he must have cried often for having taken me to him in the first place."

After Farsetti left town, Giustiniana threw herself into Brussels' festivities with a greater vengeance. Prince Charles, the attractive and amiable governor, was quick to notice her. "He looks at me, he laughs with me, he pays me a thousand compliments," she reported. She was flattered by the prince's attentions, but she knew a man of such lineage would always be beyond her reach. It was Charles's closest friend, the Count de Lanoy—"handsome, broad-shouldered and full of spirit"—who caught her fancy instead. The attraction was mutual. Soon the young count was openly court-ing her. She did not discourage him. Her coquettish self was back, and she savored anew the pleasure of being wooed by a dashing young man.

"There is someone here whom I believe I would rather come to like if I were staying in Brussels longer," she confessed to Andrea. "He's always with the prince, but he does his best to see me as much as he can. And I must say I find him very lovable." The count followed her everywhere. At the theater he always sat in a box next to hers, from which "he never ceases to look at me." She had enticed him with her new liveliness and the "attitude of *petite-maîtresse*" she had adopted "to amuse myself." Giustiniana's attrac-tion to him was easy to explain: "I found in him something which reminded me of my Memmo, and I liked him."

After much chasing around, she and the count met in the merry confusion of a *bal masqué:* "I went, and, holding my mask up as I approached him, I pretended not to know him, took his hand, called him some English name, and asked him to take off his mask. He laughed at what he thought was my mistake, followed me around, and teased me a thousand times. He told me he loved me all the while he pretended to be the Englishman. Prince Charles then came toward me, and the three of us started a conversation that turned out to be very lively because, pretending not to recog-nize the prince behind his mask, I said a thousand crazy things."

That night the count wore a cocked hat with a white feather, and a mask in the Venetian style. His resemblance to Andrea sent shivers down Giustiniana's spine: "Oh God, Memmo. . . . He is your size, and he moves his head exactly the way you do. . . . He makes a thousand movements similar to yours. . . . And, if I may say so, even his wit is similar in tone to yours." Despite the count's insistence, though, Giustiniana never asked him to visit her at the hotel. "What say you about my success? It cost me something, 'tis true; but I wanted to put myself to the test, and I now find one can manage anything."

As their stay in Brussels came to an end, the pleasant but somewhat futile flirtation with Count de Lanoy gave way to reveries of a deeper kind about Andrea. She was, she now realized, the victim of a well-known conundrum of the heart: drawn to men because they reminded her of her true love, she inevitably discarded them because they were not him. "Ah, dearest Memmo, where are you? In truth, I have little to thank you for: you have robbed me of any chance I might have had of loving someone else. . . . I love no one, and, by God, I have loved no one after my Memmo. And what is better still—and worse for them—is that I tell all my admirers: No, I shall never love anyone after my Memmo. One can love but once in a lifetime."

Strangely, there is no deep sadness in these letters to Andrea. It is as if Giustiniana were beginning to draw strength from the very notion that she would never love anyone again the way she had loved and still loved him. The endurance of her feelings gave her a sense of security, even of well-being. It was not entirely paradoxical, for the dream of a life together was always with her, seemingly irrepressible. "Oh, dear Memmo, will you be able to make the long trip to London one day? In that case, good-bye to all our lovers, good-bye to our friends, good-bye to the whole world. . . . Don't you think? I know: you don't have money. But don't worry, the day will come when we will both have some."

Giustiniana's spirits were up when the Wynnes left for London in mid-September. Apart from crossing the choppy Channel, the family was looking forward to the end of a very long and tumultuous journey. Lord Holderness had secured a temporary house for them in a pleasant part of London. He had also sent a French tutor, M. Verdun, over to Brussels to get acquainted with Giustiniana's young brothers. Lord Holderness intended to send Richard and William, who were now fifteen and fourteen, up to Cambridge to get a proper education. Mrs. Anna was of a different mind, but this was no time to quibble. As for the "three Graces"—Giustiniana, Bettina, and Tonnina—Lord Holderness was already looking around for suitable matches. "A viceroy for me, or maybe a governor in America," Giustiniana bantered. "Don't laugh, and be patient. Giustiniana was born to be someone, you'll see."

Nearly two months in Brussels had indeed invigorated her. Only a few days before she and her family left Brussels, however, the Parisian nightmare was suddenly brought back to her by the shocking news that La Pouplinière had married a young and pretty woman, Thérèse de Mondran, in a rushed ceremony in Paris. Giustiniana had never met her, but it turned out that the Abbé de La Coste and Mme Saint Aubin had been plotting in favor of this marriage even as they had been pleading with Giustiniana at the Hôtel de Hollande. Undoubtedly bruised, Giustiniana nevertheless maintained her sense of humor: "I heard, to my surprise, I must confess, about the marriage that was arranged for him in a flash. . . . I then remembered that the other old man, Smith, had done the same. . . . I haven't any luck with these old men."

CHAPTER *Eight*

The crossing from Calais to Dover took no more than a few hours, but the sea was rough and the passage seemed interminable. Giustiniana was hugely relieved when she stepped ashore and felt the firmness of the ground beneath her feet. She had sat belowdecks with the rest of the family and had been "sick to death" as the boat had pitched and crashed in the murky Channel waters. Now, as she stood safely on the windswept pier, in full view of the chalky white cliffs, the dizziness and nausea abated and her natural color returned. It felt strange to be back in England—the Wynnes' "other" home. But it felt good, too. Seven years had gone by since she had last come to her father's country. She had been a young girl then, and Sir Richard had died only a few months before. This time it was different: she was coming to find a husband. She was coming to stay.

A government coach sent by Lord Holderness met them at Canterbury. The family traveled to London in great comfort. They were dropped off at "one of the prettiest houses" near Saint James's Park, which was to serve as their temporary home. The Wynnes were not accustomed to such luxury. "We could not have come to London through a better door," Giustiniana exclaimed, beaming. Holderness at once sent his personal secretary to see them settle in, and in the evening he appeared at the house himself.

He was not a very handsome man. He had a large nose, a sagging jaw, and a skin condition over much of his face that made his appearance somewhat "offensive" to the more squeamish.[1] He carried himself with an air of such gravity that he came off as slightly pompous. Nevertheless, he welcomed Giustiniana and her siblings "like a father" (he was cooler toward Mrs. Anna) and announced that his wife, Lady Mary, would be back from the country the following month and would introduce them to society. He would personally make sure they were soon presented to Court as well. Until then, it would be good form if Giustiniana, Bettina, and Tonnina stayed mostly around the house.

Holderness's directive must have sounded excessively rigid to these cosmopolitan girls who had danced till dawn in Paris and Brussels, but it was no time to show resistance: they were entirely in his hands. Besides, he had explained that he was imposing this temporary confinement for their benefit. That first night Giustiniana went to bed exhausted but reassured—even flattered—by the solicitude of this important man.

Robert d'Arcy, Fourth Earl of Holderness, had indeed reached a position of considerable power and influence, much to the surprise of some of his contemporaries. In the mid-forties, after he returned to London from his diplomatic posting in Venice, he joined the Society of Dilettanti and became a busy bachelor on the London social and artistic scene—he cultivated a passion for opera and masquerades that he had picked up in Venice. In 1749 he was named ambassador to The Hague. There he married Mary Doublet de Groeneveldt, the daughter of a prominent Dutch businessman. He seemed destined for an honorable if not particularly brilliant diplomatic career in His Majesty's service. But the Duke of Newcastle, then prime minister, "fetched"[2] him from his post at The Hague in 1751, and, at the age of thirty-one, Holderness was appointed secretary of state alongside William Pitt the Elder.

His meteoric rise caused many to shake their heads in disbelief. Pitt himself considered Holderness a "futile"[3] young man. Horace Walpole described him as a lightweight and a "blabberer"—though he acidly acknowledged that the young secretary of state at least "did justice to himself and his patrons, for he seemed ashamed of being made so considerable for no reason but because he was so inconsiderable."[4]

Holderness had enough ability to hold on to what was given to him, and he remained a loyal protégé of the Duke of Newcastle for most of the decade. But by the end of 1759, after three years of war, he was looking over his mentor's shoulder to the growing "peace party" that was gathering at Leicester House around the Earl of Bute, the rising star in Parliament (and future prime minister under George III).

Bute knew all about the Wynnes through his mother-in-law, Lady Mary Wortley Montagu, who was still living in Venice. She had sent her daughter a warning about Mrs. Anna and her children just as they had set off on their journey across Europe the previous October:

> *My dear child,*
> *I am under a sort of necessity of troubling you with an impertinent letter. Three fine ladies (I should say four including the Signora Madre) set out for London a few days ago. . . . As they have no acquaintance there, I think it very possible (knowing their assurance) that some of them may try to make some by visiting you, perhaps in my name. Upon my word I never saw them except in public and at the Resident's, who, being one of their numerous passionate admirers, obliged his wife to receive them. . . . I have said enough to hinder your being deceived by them, but should have said much more if you had been in full leisure to read novels. The story deserves the pen of my dear Smollett.*[5]

By the time the Wynnes finally arrived in London, long preceded by this unflattering introduction, Holderness was in the thick of his political maneuvers aimed at endearing himself with the Bute camp. Clearly he did not want his guardianship to get in the way of his more important pursuits. Since leaving Venice the Wynnes had acquired a reputation as something of a traveling circus, and the recent gossip coming from Paris about Giustiniana's adventures there had done nothing to improve their reputation. While Holderness felt compelled to sponsor their presentation to Court, if only to honor Richard Wynne's memory, it was important to him that it be done judiciously. The last thing he wanted was for his Venetian charges to be running around London out of control.

Initially, the Wynne children took Holderness's orders in stride.

After all, their momentary seclusion gave them a little extra time to prepare for their appearance in the best houses of London. Giustiniana looked forward to reading "new English books in order to take my bearings in my country and not appear too much the foreigner." The picaresque tales of Lady Montagu's "dear" Tobias Smollett were probably a little old-fashioned for her. But after the dryness of the French *philosophes*, she was eager to immerse herself in the English novels she had heard so much about. Henry Fielding and Samuel Richardson had already produced their great works the previous decade. Now Laurence Sterne was the new author everyone in London was talking about—he had published the first two volumes of *Tristram Shandy* only a few months before the Wynnes arrived.

However, reading books was not enough to keep the family quietly occupied. After just a few weeks of Holderness's strict regime, a grumpy mood took over the household. "We're all bored in the extreme with London since we cannot go out or see anyone," Giustiniana complained. "We cannot even go to the park. . . . His lordship keeps us in perpetual servitude."

Holderness did make one concession: the Wynnes were allowed to visit the Venetian ambassador and his wife, over on Soho Square. This privilege hardly enlivened their social life. Count and Countess Colombo were a "charming couple," but they were not much fun. The Countess was "always amiable [but] practically always ill . . . and always alone." Giustiniana went to the embassy mostly to collect her mail and talk about Andrea with the ambassador, who, like other diplomats before him, was so titillated by their story that he offered to become their secret go-between.

The Wynnes were also allowed to receive a select list of visitors at home, but Giustiniana found the guests who crowded their small drawing room even duller than the ambassador and his wife. They were either old acquaintances of her mother's from their previous trip to London or part of the steady trickle of nondescript Wynne relations who came over out of curiosity about their Italian cousins. None of them earned an individual mention in Giustiniana's letters. "I do not enjoy myself with these people," she complained. "We are always onstage. And everyone stares at us and talks as if we were the most beautiful women in the whole kingdom."

The mood in London was very different from the one in Paris. England was winning the war; the Wynnes arrived in town as His Majesty's soldiers were taking Quebec and routing the French in Canada. Confidence was high, and a growing sense of predestination gave a purpose to the conflict that the French increasingly seemed to lack. Newspapers and periodicals led the patriotic fanfare:

> *Come on ye brave Britons, let no one complain*
> *Britannia, Britannia, once more rules the main.*[6]

It was turning out to be "the glorious fifty-nine," to use the expression in vogue that season.

After three long years, however, a feeling of lassitude was taking hold of the country, even as dispatches continued to bring good news from the battlefields. Whereas Parisians went from deep gloom to wild celebration depending on the latest war bulletin, the British seemed far more subdued in their reactions. "You must not imagine that victories are received here with loud cheers," Giustiniana explained to Andrea, who was eager to learn all he could about the war. "At the most, a few burning candles appear on the windowsills. . . . One hardly talks about the war. . . . There is more interest in it in Venice than here, where it truly matters. Maybe the English talk about it between themselves. Maybe they're just tired."

Admittedly, Giustiniana was catching only glimpses of London, but the little she saw was uninspiring. The ladies did not dress well. Their hairstyles were out of fashion. Conversations rarely went beyond polite formalities. There was no exciting intellectual dispute to follow—nothing like Rousseau and d'Alembert battling each other's ideas in the press or the polemics surrounding the publication of a new volume of the *Encyclopédie*. Indeed, aside from lengthy reports on the war and rousing calls to victory, the periodicals seemed mostly preoccupied with such mundane topics as the latest development of the ribbon loom or the newest method of collecting taxes. There were few public festivities and no *bals masqués* whatsoever, the Anglican bishops having recently managed to have them outlawed.

It is not surprising that Giustiniana thought the most interesting figure parading through this gray landscape was the flamboyant Kitty Fisher, courtesan extraordinaire, who had managed to set herself up quite extravagantly: "She lives in the greatest possible splendor, spends twelve thousand pounds a year, and she is the first of her social class to employ liveried servants—she even has liveried chaise porters. There are prints of her everywhere. She is small and I don't find her beautiful, but the English do and that is what matters."

The notorious rivalry between Kitty Fisher and Lady Coventry, the former Mary Gunning, was a favorite source of social chitchat. "The other day they ran into each other in the park," Giustiniana wrote to Andrea, trying to entertain him with some local color, "and Lady Coventry asked Kitty the name of the dressmaker who had made her dress. [Kitty Fisher] answered she had better ask Lord Coventry as he had given her that dress as a gift. Lady Coventry called her an impertinent woman; the other one answered that her marrying a nutty lord had put enough social difference between them that she would have to withstand the insult. But she was going to marry one herself just to be able to answer back to her."

Giustiniana had arrived in London in early autumn determined to charm her way into the best houses of London. By November her enthusiasm was already flagging. There was so little going on in her life that she had to spice her letters to Andrea with secondhand anecdotes. As she waited for Lady Holderness to return from the country and rescue her, a feeling of futility took hold of her. She became more introspective. Her life was so unsettled now, so uncertain; that she missed Andrea was one of the few certainties. She felt the emptiness every day. Brief trips to pick up his letters at the Venetian Embassy were her only joy. But each one of those journeys also brought more confusion. "You are still more precious to me than anything else in the world, and you always will be," she wrote tenderly. ". . . But I am so unsure about everything. And do you know why this is? Because I still love you horribly."

The prospect of another round of husband hunting was suddenly very dispiriting. During those long, rainy autumn days, she wondered for the first time whether a husband was necessary at all. How "convenient" could a marriage of convenience really be? Could she not find a better way to live? Perhaps it had to do with her character, she mused, perhaps with the way she had lived her life so far—but it occurred to her that she had come to value her independence more than the security that might come with a good marriage. Surely an income of her own, even a small one, would give her the freedom she needed to shape her life. "You want me to find a duke or an earl," she complained to Andrea. ". . . I believe I want none of that. . . . A husband is a nasty thing."

Holed up in Holderness's guest house, Giustiniana explored alternatives to marriage. One solution was to invest the small inheritance she had received from her father—fifteen hundred pounds—in order to generate an income she could live on instead of using that sum as a dowry. She admitted that such an arrangement might force her to live more modestly than was her taste: "I hate mediocrity . . . and I am not virtuous enough to live well in a lesser rank." But at least she would no longer feel hostage to the imperative of a "good" marriage. There was no doubt in her mind that her future would feel less uncertain. In that sense, she would certainly "improve her condition."

She pictured Andrea raising his eyebrows as he read her letter in the privacy of his room at Ca' Memmo. His protestations, she warned him, were not going to stop her: "You will scold me, of course, but I have already written to Paris to gather information. I understand that interest rates are much higher there. I will live here for the time being, and I shall have my seat at Court if I choose to wait long enough. And if I get bored I'll move back to France, unless of course you should ask me to rush back to Venice."

Perhaps she was getting a little ahead of herself, she admitted. These were still little more than "barely sketched and rather confused ideas." Andrea needn't worry: she wasn't giving up the plan "to ensnare" that English duke. Not yet, at least. But she was "disenchanted" with people of high rank and their society, and serious about wanting to take charge of her own life. She needed to keep her head clear, to weigh her options more realistically. Even though Mrs. Anna's friends downstairs kept blabbing away about what an excellent husband she would find, she knew that the more time passed the harder it would be to find a match that would suit her. And the more she thought about cutting herself loose from the obsession with marriage, the more she liked the feeling: "If I keep on thinking in this manner, maybe these ideas will take shape after all."

There were also physical changes that needed to be taken into account. Giustiniana was still a very pretty young woman—"the belle of the belles," as she said to Andrea with a lingering sense of entitlement. Now that her Parisian experiments in hairdressing were over her black curls again fell freely over her sweet, lively face, and her dark, beautiful eyes were as penetrating as ever. Yet the youthful glint that had warmed so many hearts in Venice and Paris and Brussels had lost some of its sparkle. Motherhood had left her a little rounder, too. "I'm becoming womanish," she observed with a touch of sadness as her birthday approached. "I'm nearly twenty-three. The best part of my youth is behind me. . . . What beauty I had is probably fading."

Her sister Bettina was four years younger and bursting into full bloom. It was her turn now. She would be the one attracting all the attention when the Wynne sisters were launched into society. "She's a beauty now, and she is kind and spirited without ever being affected," Giustiniana remarked proudly. "We'll see how she is received when we go out in public this winter. Her figure would certainly not be considered slight in Italy or France, but it is very much appreciated here." Right behind Bettina was Tonnina, who would soon turn eighteen. The youngest of the three sisters had much matured since the days when she had stood passively in the arms of Alvise Renier. Giustiniana assured Andrea that he would scarcely recognize her: "She's never been more beautiful or more charming. . . . If she doesn't put on more weight, she will please very much. If you could see her bosom now, her arms, her hands, her natural whiteness, and the self-assurance she has gained with the help of some graceful manners she acquired in France."

As for the unmarried older sister, she was apparently quite

ready to cede center stage: "I'm no longer tempted to please, and I really no longer wish to work hard to bring a man where I want him to be. I'm so tired of whimsical love, yet I feel I have lost the kind of sensibility one needs for a great passion. . . . Ah, you know me well enough. You know I'm meant for an unhappy life. The idea of marriage scares me more and more. I would never marry a man I admired so as not to make him unhappy. And I would never marry one I despised so as not to make us both unhappy."

This was Giustiniana's life in London as she depicted it—a solitary life of reading and writing, a life into which "not a single man" ever strayed. And what of Andrea? He went to the theater. He attended amusing dinners at their friends' palaces on the Grand Canal. And by his own admission he was enjoying a new season of gallantries. While she lived the life of a recluse, she complained, "you happily make love to the ladies." Her tone was often self-mocking, and one feels that despite the complaining, she derived real pleasure from writing to Andrea. Her letters to him were more and more an outlet for her powers of observation, her sense of irony, and her humor.

Andrea teased Giustiniana about his flirtations in Venice—had they not renewed their vow "to tell each other everything" after the Paris scandal? Yet he now confessed that there was one young woman in particular who was vying to become his *favorita*. The problem, he explained, was that the lady in question was very jealous of Giustiniana and could not stand to see her picture still hanging so prominently among Andrea's collection of portraits and miniatures. In fact, she had demanded its prompt removal. He sheepishly admitted that he had given in to her request. Giustiniana skewered him for this act of betrayal with a comic description that was all the more admirable given the circumstances:

Imagine making such a demand! And worse, having it fulfilled! I'm furious about this. It is too awful! Too horrendous! My heart is filled with rage. . . . What now? My portrait is no longer in the middle of all those pictures of gorgeous sultanas that enlivened that extraordinary cabinet? . . . My glory hath been crushed, and now I have been thrown into the chaotic throng of your old mistresses! . . . Oh, you unfortunate portrait! Your reign is over. . . . And so you are left to dangle from the victorious chariot of a rival. . . . My dear Memmo, as you can see. . . . I hold the destiny of my exiled portrait close to my heart. And the consequences of this shameful removal make me tremble, for I can gauge the power of the person who now occupies you by the quality of the sacrifice you have made (you will forgive my vanity).

Giustiniana took a guess. "Quick: tell me her name," she quizzed him nervously. "Admit the *belle coquette* is M.C." And indeed it turned out that it was Marietta Corner, the same young woman who had caused her so much grief in the early days of her relationship with Andrea. This time Giustiniana was not going to let her heart be torn apart by pangs of jealousy. She tried to laugh about it, to treat Andrea's dalliance with Marietta as lighthearted comedy: she wanted to show herself in command of her emotions. "I take pity on you, my dear Memmo," she went on, "for you are dealing with someone who has only her beauty to offer, and surely she will bore you very soon. I know you well. . . . I bet she'll use gentle violence on you by asking to read my letters so as to calm her anxiety, real or fake as it may be. . . . Well, if that's so I'll turn very mean and tell you that I love you with the greatest intensity. . . . I will also tell you freely that I'm sure I shall never be forgotten by my Memmo."

Her jocular tone did not entirely mask her sadness. A whole year had passed since she had last seen Andrea. So much had happened in both their lives, yet he was still at the center of hers. She loved him—"horribly" was the word she had used—and she was not ready to be pushed into the background by another woman. Did she seriously feel threatened by Marietta? Probably not. She knew Andrea too well to fear that he might attach himself to a woman who had, as she put it, "only her beauty to offer." But all his light talk about portraits being shifted around was hurtful. Even though she hid the pain so artfully, it still showed through her persiflage in the most touching ways. She could go on at length poking fun at her rival, making sarcastic remarks, ridiculing the whole affair; then, practically in the same breath, she would start writing about the two of them again. She would soon be presented to Court. What would he like her to wear? What colors did he have in mind? "I thought I might wear *pensée* or yellow, the color dark-haired women use in France. I could wear a satin dress lined with marten furs—I have some beautiful ones. . . . But tell me what you'd like. . . . See, I fret over these little things as if I were still there with you."

The distance between them, however, was real, and news traveled even more erratically than usual on account of the war. There were plenty of opportunities for delayed information to play havoc with their lives. It was autumn—Giustiniana had left Paris three months before—when Andrea first heard of a nasty anonymous pamphlet about her that had apparently made the rounds in the French capital at the time of the Castelbajac-Demay affair. Andrea never actually read the incriminating "brochure," but, from what he was told, he understood that it contained a description of Giustiniana's behavior that was very much at odds with the one she had given to him back in June. It was only hearsay, of course, but Andrea was assailed by unpleasant doubts all over again. He confronted Giustiniana with the rumors he was hearing. Coldly, he asked if he should be writing to her at all.

Giustiniana's heart sank. Why was Andrea needlessly digging up the past, throwing at her the sad debris of her Paris debacle? His cruelty wounded her: "Your friendship is so unpredictable, you give credence to the most horrible things so easily. . . . I shall only tell you this: no such brochure against me exists and the ill-informed people who are spreading this around with the object of hurting me are misleading you. Believe in your Giustiniana, who has never debased herself to the point of hiding the truth from you. She tells you she is innocent of all the accusations that have been made against her. . . . I will force you to be my friend in spite of yourself and your mistresses. . . . I have lost your heart, but I have not deserved all the rest."

There was no reply for nearly a month, and this silence broke her even more than the accusations. Then one day she found a clutch of three letters from Andrea waiting for her at the Venetian Embassy. She was overwhelmed with happiness:

So many riches to bring me joy! You remember me and I find you are still my friend, and maybe something more? My poor Memmo, you are still mine, then! How much we have lost, both of us, in robbing ourselves of our hopes and dreams! You seem to have lost your aptitude for refined pleasures; I have no true enjoyment left and cannot find a man I like as much as you, nor will I ever. In the passion I used to feel for you there were a thousand combinations that kept my mind and my soul perpetually excited. Oh, I loved you so! And by God, I do not feel my heart has yet been emptied of all that passion. I make this wager: that if I should ever come close to you again I will love you madly, if only you will allow me to.

In mid-November the Wynnes moved to a smaller house on Dean Street, near Soho Square. It had been "elegantly furnished" by the previous occupant, the paramour of "one of the richest men in England." But they felt a little cramped in their new home— something that was not likely to improve the atmosphere in the house very much. Dean Street itself was a busy commercial lane. The neighborhood was respectable but no longer as fashionable as it had once been—occasionally one even caught a whiff of the crowded taverns and seedy bathhouses of Drury Lane, just a couple of streets away. For some time, what was known as the "polite end of town" had been moving to the west of Soho, toward Grosvenor Square and Cavendish Square.

The two boys, Richard and William, were still living with the family in the house on Dean Street. Holderness had arranged for them to go up to Cambridge shortly after their arrival in London, but Mrs. Anna had resisted in the hope of providing them with a Catholic education (in this she was abetted by an Irish priest she had known during her first stay in London, who had now reappeared in their life). Holderness, of course, would hear nothing of it. Mrs. Anna made hysterical scenes and even threatened to follow the boys to Cambridge. Tensions in the house were always high.

Increasingly wrapped up in his political schemes, Holderness visited less and less often. "I fear his lordship will soon be disgusted with my mother," Giustiniana worried. "She is inconceivably mad."

The bad feelings between Holderness and Mrs. Anna were exacerbated by the difficulties he was facing in getting the papers for the Wynnes' formal presentation at Court. Mrs. Anna's ancestry was again an issue; her title of nobility seemed as dubious in London as it had in Venice. More paperwork was needed; dispatches had to travel to and from Venice across war-torn Europe. It was all terribly time-consuming. Again Giustiniana enlisted Andrea to help speed things up. "Imagine this to be one of your many projects," she said to encourage him, adding that her mother was especially "grateful" to him. "She sends her regards and begs you to continue to assist us. . . . How different from what she once was like! If only she had known you then the way she knows you now, she could have spared herself, and us, so much pain."

The Venetian authorities might also have been somewhat hesitant to vouch for Mrs. Anna's title of nobility lest Andrea and Giustiniana take advantage of their seal of approval and resuscitate their marriage plan. Giustiniana felt it was crucial to disabuse them on this point: "They must be absolutely certain that not only are we not planning to return to Venice . . . but we could not possibly be thinking of getting married because we have come to understand the permanent damage we would be inflicting upon ourselves. . . . We will never marry, not even if you came to London. Besides, I hate the idea of marriage too much even to think about it."

Their subtle diplomacy did not produce results. There was, briefly, some talk about a possible presentation in the future. "Presently all seats at Court are occupied, and not until the Prince of Wales's wedding might there be room for me."* But those vague hopes soon flagged. The Wynnes "could not have come to London through a better door," as Giustiniana had put it so enthusiastically, but a month and a half after their arrival, they still languished on the fringe of London society.

It was partly to relieve the tension in the house that Mrs. Anna

---

*The Prince of Wales did not marry Charlotte Sophia of Mecklenburg until September 8, 1761. By that time he had already succeeded his grandfather as George III.

accepted an invitation from a friend of the family to spend a few days in the country. It was hardly the sort of adventure to lift Giustiniana's spirits: she had no particular longing to be in the countryside, and she was tired of making polite conversation with Mrs. Anna's dreary little set. "They are of course very good people, with the best possible hearts, and so enchanted by us they would do for us anything we pleased. . . . But unlike what you might think, they are not to my taste." No doubt Giustiniana would have preferred to stay home rather than trundle out to the country with the rest of the family. In the end she went "to make Mother happy" and hoped "to alleviate the boredom" by reading more of those "new English books" she had told Andrea about.

The five-day visit to the country turned out to be even more dreadful than Giustiniana had anticipated: "I was bored to death. Imagine a crowd of pompous councillors and self-important English barristers. The horror!" The food was lousy and the company unspeakably dull. She was forced to escape to the garden so many times that she caught her first English cold.

In late November Lady Holderness finally came to town, to the immense relief of the three Wynne sisters. She immediately invited them over to take a good look at the young Venetian girls her busy husband had entrusted to her care. There followed a more formal invitation to her first "assembly" of the season.

Lady Holderness was an attractive woman of about forty, with a pleasant manner and a warm smile. Giustiniana was touched "by her ladyship's goodness." She found her "still beautiful and very charming"—the sort of woman only "a truly fickle man or else a husband could ever tire of." There was an advantage, she explained to Andrea, to being shown in society by such a fine lady: "I hear there is great impatience to see Bettina; and we are expected to make a charming impression." They had waited around the house for too long, but there was some compensation in hearing that "the country is curious in the extreme to see us, including the princesses, who have been asking about us."

There was a good deal of wishful thinking in all this. London society was terribly stuffy and exclusive—far more than Paris society—and it was not about to swing its doors wide open to the Wynne girls. True, there was some curiosity about them, especially Giustiniana. "There is a Miss Wynne coming forth, that is to be handsomer than my Lady Coventry," Horace Walpole wrote to a friend with anticipation. But it was the sort of curiosity reserved for the amusing and the vaguely exotic. Even Walpole was mindful that a different young beauty threatened Lady Coventry at the end of every summer "and they are always addled by winter."[7]

A year had passed since Lady Montagu had sent her acidulous missive to her daughter, Lady Bute, whose influence in society was rising in tandem with that of her husband in politics. Now it was Lady Bute's turn to regale her mother with unflattering reports on the Wynnes in action. And Lady Montagu, sitting in her rented *palazzo* in Venice, made it sound as if she could not wait for the next installment of her favorite saga: "I am very much diverted with the adventures of the Three Graces lately arrived in London. . . . I am heartily sorry their mother has not learning enough to write memoirs."[8]

Giustiniana's initial burst of excitement at the prospect of going out in the world soon exhausted itself as she attended a string of "boring dinners" and "unbearable assemblies." She spared Andrea the details of these tedious evenings for fear of "passing my distaste on to you." With one partial exception: her evening at the home of Lady Northumberland, the most celebrated London hostess. Thanks to Lady Holderness, the Wynne sisters had received the coveted invitation. This time Giustiniana was suitably impressed by the grandeur of the scene. "The house is very large, magnificent, richly lit up and one can see the most beautiful paintings," she conceded. But she went on to describe herself wandering among a tired and aimless crowd. There were at least a thousand people at Northumberland House that night: "Some of them played cards out of sheer duty, others ambled distractedly, and everyone was bored. I was certainly in that number. . . . What was the use of hearing people say how pretty we were or clap their hands at a curtsey only less clumsy than those one ordinarily sees here?"

The only episode worth mentioning at all occurred in the picture gallery, where she suddenly came face to face with a celebrated Titian painting depicting an illustrious Venetian family.* It produced something of a shock. The contrast between the vague familiarity of the scene on the large canvas and those unfriendly surroundings unleashed a rush of nostalgia for the world she had left behind. Still, even a very good painting was not enough to fill an evening. "By misfortune I was unable to have a carriage until midnight."

Giustiniana began to turn down invitations, something she had rarely done before, whether in London, Paris, or Venice. "I go out very little in public so as to preserve the applause for my sisters," she joked. As she had predicted, the "applause" was going mostly to Bettina, now the most admired of the three sisters. Lady Montagu, hardly a fan of the Wynnes, had conceded even before they had left Venice that Bettina was likely to blossom into a paragon of Hanoverian beauty. She was tall, she said, "and as red and white as any German alive. If she has sense enough to follow good instructions she will be irresistible."[9]

Occasionally, Giustiniana attended a *conversazione*—a rather large assembly where there was, in fact, very little conversation. As many as a hundred ladies would gather in one of the better houses of London, with the odd gentleman in attendance, invariably "old or blind or loud." Giustiniana was freer to move around than she had been in other more formal occasions, but even these events she found tedious and suffocating. Few ladies were interested in speaking to her, and those who deigned to address her were not particularly friendly. "One ends up speaking only to people one knows, and the people one knows tend to spend their time at the gambling tables like almost everyone else." Giustiniana felt more and more alienated: "One is made to feel so isolated in this grand society. What a life!" She was especially disappointed by the lack of warmth and solidarity between women: "You cannot imagine the degree to which [they] are malicious. Friendship does

---

*Giustiniana wrote to Andrea that she saw at Northumberland House "a famous painting by Titian of a Cornaro family." That is indeed how the family in the painting was identified at the time. Recent scholarship has revealed that it is actually a portrait of the Vendramin family.

not exist among them. . . . I could never become a friend of any of them, and so I treat everyone well and pay many compliments."

In her letters she went out of her way to make her London life sound dreary and wasteful: "I don't go to the park so as not to die of cold . . . I read . . . I eat . . . I sleep a lot." There was no point in fretting about what dress to wear at Court, she groused, because Holderness confirmed that there were still no seats available for them. The damp London weather did not help raise her spirits: she spent half her time in bed nursing head colds that never seemed to end: "I am so congested I cannot stand it anymore. . . . This damned climate is damaging my health. . . . It is more unpredictable than Giustiniana herself." But there was no use blaming the rain, she added wistfully. The ennui that was sapping her energy "has more to do with my nature than with the climate."

In fact, Giustiniana was not being entirely truthful when she depicted herself as a depressed stay-at-home who spent her time curled up in bed, writing to her long-lost lover in Venice and pining for his replies. She had met, through the Holdernesses, a handsome young man who came calling on her at Dean Street and found, to her own surprise, that his pleasing manner and his sensitive nature were beginning to warm her heart.

Giustiniana's new admirer was Baron Dodo Knyphausen, a brilliant Prussian diplomat who was thirty years old—the same age as Andrea.* George Townshend drew a couple of sketches of him that are now at the National Gallery; in them he appears as a smartly dressed young man with thin legs, a pointed nose, a broad forehead, and strands of curly hair combed straight back.

Knyphausen had been in London little more than a year but had immediately been very much at the center of things, with easy access to the highest reaches of government as well as the most elegant houses in London. Frederick the Great held him in very high regard: he had named him Prussian ambassador to Paris when he was only twenty-four. In France, Knyphausen had demonstrated his considerable skills in the complicated diplomatic game that had

---

*Giustiniana wrote that Knyphausen was twenty-eight when she met him, but according to the *Allgemeine Deutsche Biografie* he was born on August 3, 1729, and was therefore two years older.

preceded the outbreak of the Seven Years' War, and his dispatches had been instrumental in paving the way for the alliance between Prussia and Great Britain. When war broke out, Frederick saw him as the ideal man to nurture the relationship with the British ally. The baron arrived in London as Frederick's special envoy in 1758 and developed a close working relationship with William Pitt, the principal advocate of the war. By the time he met the Wynnes, he had already negotiated three contracts for British war subsidies to Prussia.

Giustiniana was flattered by the visits of such a coveted young man. "All the ladies want him," she assured Andrea when she told him about Knyphausen. "He is the only fashionable man in England." It was not just the sudden gratification of male attention that drew her to him. She was intrigued by this thoughtful, introspective man with whom she could carry on a conversation that ranged beyond the niceties of social chitchat. As the weeks passed she caught herself thinking about him more and more; waiting for him to appear and brighten up the day. He too reminded her of Andrea, though in a deeper way than had the frivolous Count de Lanoy in Brussels at the end of the summer: "I find myself busy thinking about a man who not only resembles you physically but also has a similar character. . . . That is why I find him so special and why I like him so. . . . Will you forgive me this new friendship? Oh, if only you knew how much he is worthy of it."

Giustiniana grappled with these new feelings without quite knowing what to make of them. This was very different from willfully seducing an old man; different, too, from flirting gaily behind a Carnival mask. There was no room for coquetry here. Part of her wanted to give in to the new stirrings she felt inside her, yet after all that she had been through in Venice, and then in Paris, she was wary of more emotional strain. She was also confused: "I don't even know if what I feel for him is love or respect. . . . I tremble at the idea of giving myself over to a passion. I fear passion. I try to convince myself that I should always preserve the will of reason. I already worry about the future, and I am fragile and I am anxious."

As she ventured out cautiously on this new journey, she realized she wanted to have Andrea by her side. She would describe her feelings to him. She would take him along step by step. "Do not reproach me for this new folly," she pleaded. "For heaven's sake, be indulgent and charitable in the face of a weakness that in the beginning came about because of you."

Soon Knyphausen was stopping by the Wynnes' "every evening at the hour of the *conversazione*." He showed Giustiniana "a thousand concerns, a thousand attentions," but he was careful not to raise suspicions in the house by expressing "too evident a preference" for her. His assiduity kept her enthralled, to the point that she once forgot to post her weekly letter to Andrea. "I know my Memmo will forgive me," she wrote apologetically the following week, "for an involuntary sin. The mail day was taken up with my new Memmo, whom I believe I love with a good heart and who gives me no reason to complain or wish for anything better. . . . If what keeps me so occupied is but a passing fancy, I would to heaven that all my previous ones had been grounded in such respectable foundations. Each day I find this man to be worthier of my esteem. I have for him the same kind of respect I have felt only for you in all my life."

Soon Giustiniana and Knyphausen were also seeing each other "in secret, one, two, three times a week." They talked for hours, confiding in each other, testing each other, stretching the bounds of their new friendship. They were drawn together by the ease, the subdued joy they felt in each other's company, more than by physical attraction. "Respect and compassion are what our friendship is built upon," she told Andrea.

Knyphausen had only recently recovered from his own painful love affair. For many years he had been secretly in love with a young and beautiful lady whose reputation had been sullied by "a thousand weaknesses"—most especially a severe gambling addiction. A young baronet had then come along and offered his hand, and she had accepted without telling him about her debts. Though not rich, Knyphausen had stepped in to pay them and thus save her reputation. He had also paid for the wedding, as the baronet had not yet come into his inheritance, and kept his grief to himself. "He wept, he was in great despair, but he no longer saw this woman."

Giustiniana felt that Knyphausen was a kindred spirit. He was curious about her life without being censorious. He showed understanding, he was sensitive, and above all, he listened. And she was grateful to have someone she could count on to talk to without fear of exposure. At last she had found a refuge in the frosty landscape of London society. Knyphausen gave her comfort and made her smile. She told him what she could about her life in Venice, her great journey across Europe, her adventures in Paris. Andrea loomed large over their long conversations. He had been the love of her life, she told Knyphausen. Now, she reassured him, he was a very close friend—her *cher ami*.

They continued their clandestine meetings. The only other person who was certain of their relationship was Andrea himself, the silent partner who, for all we can guess, seems to have been more curious than jealous. "Nobody knows anything about my involvement," Giustiniana assured him. "... There is barely a suspicion in my own house." She and Knyphausen had no compelling reason to behave so secretively. Neither was married, neither was officially involved with anyone else. Yet for all their intimacy they still circled around each other with a lingering hesitancy, still unsure of themselves as much as each other. Secrecy, one feels, suited both of them.

Giustiniana reverted quite naturally to some of her old Venetian ways in order to deceive her mother and meet Knyphausen on the sly. She told Andrea about her frequent escapades so she could, in a sense, share the thrill with her old accomplice. She boasted, for example, of the time she wangled an invitation to lunch at some friends' house a couple of miles outside London. As soon as she arrived at the house she promptly took leave of her hosts, explaining that pressing business called her back to town. But instead of going home to Dean Street, she went directly to see Knyphausen, who lived just a few streets away: "He was busy with a government minister, from whom he took his leave. He put on a coat and left the house on foot. I followed him from a distance until we reached a little house he had at his disposal, and we walked in. We lunched, and a bottle of champagne put us in such an intimate mood that we shared our secrets and commiserated with each other until we were both crying. What a happy state it would have been if that mutual trust, that familiarity, had lasted longer! But he doesn't trust me entirely, nor do I trust him."

Over the course of the winter Giustiniana's doubts about Knyphausen gradually dissolved. "I am still enchanted by my man," she wrote in mid-February. "He's the most charming and the most decent one there is. We see each other; we tell each other all sorts of tender things. But are we quite sure of ourselves?" In March she was already more hopeful: "I could be happy with this man, dear Memmo, if my anxious soul would only let me enjoy the moment without all the inner turmoil. . . . He believes in me; I'm very close to believing in him. He sympathizes with me; and I do respect him. His soul is so pure! Oh, do let me tell you: he's just like you, and God knows it's the truth. And you do look very much alike, though I promise you are more handsome." By early spring Giustiniana felt more confident about her feelings for Knyphausen than she ever had, and Andrea must have assumed by then that they were lovers: "My love life goes on, and it looks as if we really love each other. I have nothing much to say beyond that, except to mention that we do have our moments of scorn, our bouts of jealousy, our tantrums, our peacemaking; usual things, and of no great importance. . . . Do you think I love the Baron? I firmly believe I do."

How far should she go? How far did Andrea want her to go? "Give me your advice, help me keep a little mistrust alive; tell me his heart is not as good as it appears to be. You are my only friend, and you will be as long as you live. . . . Oh, if only I could see you now!"

To Andrea, this longing Giustiniana had to see him, so emphatically stated even as she was meeting secretly with her new lover, sounded disingenuous. He chided her, surmising that if he were to appear suddenly in London she would receive him with much less affection than her letters suggested. Giustiniana was hurt by his sarcasm: "Oh God, you can be so unfair. Come here and see for yourself what my feelings are for you. Then you will judge me. I have hardened out of necessity, but I have remained your loving friend."

In this Giustiniana was truthful. She could not let go of Andrea—did not want to let go of him. And her letters, while mostly about her new lover, were still filled with ambiguous references to their own relationship. Yes, she loved Knyphausen, "but not in the way I once loved you. Oh, what a difference! Oh, happy rapture! How many times I have wept over you!" And again: "You know you can always expect the most tender transport on my part."

In a world of fantasy, she said, she would have loved both men. Had Andrea come to London to see her, had money not been an obstacle, "I would have introduced you at once to the man I respect more than anyone else after you, and who is so dear to me." They would have been together, the three of them, in a strange and happy harmony. "I would no longer have made distinctions between my lovers, and you would have both been my friends. What happiness! What joy I would have felt to be between these two dear persons! I would have held no preference, for I would have omitted everything that might have caused it. Oh God! Why are you not here now to make me revel in this pure and perfect happiness?"

In the real world, however, Andrea was far away and not at all likely to make the journey to London. Giustiniana could tell from his letters, affectionate as they were, that he was busy building his own life in Venice, courting other women, working on his political career. In London, it was Knyphausen who kept her heart warm and her mind occupied. She noticed how her daily life seemed less tedious now. He gave her new zest. "I go out nearly every evening," she noted to her own surprise.

By the end of the winter Knyphausen was often by her side, even in public. Officially, their liaison was still a "secret." But rumors, as ever, had spread, thanks largely to the indiscretion of the Venetian ambassador. Giustiniana discovered with horror that "charming" Count Colombo had been reading her letters to Andrea. Including, she fumed, "the one in which I gave you a detailed summary of my love life." In revenge, she immediately sent off "a short but strong" letter to Andrea, blasting Colombo for "his shameful behavior." She knew it would circulate in Venice and dishonor the ambassador. "By God, he will get what he deserves," she quipped.

One outcome of Colombo's "shameful curiosity" was that it no longer made much sense to go to extremes in order to conceal her friendship with Knyphausen. So they went to the Opera together to hear the Italian singers, and they visited the London gambling houses—always rife with crazed addicts—to watch and comment on the crowd. Giustiniana was still untouched by the disease: "All my pleasure is in making remarks, in criticizing, in amusing myself . . . with the Baron always with me," she wrote to Andrea, recalling their own thrilling nights at the Ridotto in Venice. The dinners and assemblies were as "insufferable" as ever, but now she had someone to laugh with during those stuffy affairs. They whispered clever remarks to each other, smiled in wry amusement. Their favorite little game consisted of "discovering a caricature in all the people we run into."

Giustiniana was having a fine time with Knyphausen, but she was not growing any more comfortable with the English aristocracy. Quite to the contrary, she felt increasingly at odds with the people she had come to dazzle. She had lost her natural gaiety, she complained. She began to strike a pose and suffer from ennui. Her occasional pleasure in going out endured only because Knyphausen, an outsider like her, played along. Giustiniana was genuinely fond of him. She treasured his company and his camaraderie, although she never spoke of their relationship in hopeful terms, at least not in her letters to Andrea. Marriage, apparently, was never seriously discussed. If Knyphausen ever considered the possibility, he did not make a decisive move in that direction. There were the usual obstacles: the difference in religion (he was a Protestant), the difference in social standing. He also had pressing issues on his mind: he was in the middle of intense negotiations with Pitt in a frustrating and ultimately unsuccessful attempt to persuade him to send a British fleet to the Baltic Sea to protect the coast of Prussia. As for Giustiniana, her letters to Andrea consistently maintain that marriage was something she no longer wanted. In fact, her hostility to the idea of marrying anyone at all hardened during that winter despite her feelings for Knyphausen. If she talked about the subject at all, it was in the frivolous context of finding Knyphausen the best possible wife: "I've got it into my head to set him up, and I've already made my choice; but it'll be hard because this little person I have in mind is very sly. . . . If she won't fall in love with him it'll be my fault; and the amount of effort I put into making him agreeable to her is the most ridiculous thing in the world."

Even as she felt her bloom was fading, Giustiniana was determined to keep her independence, and she willfully relegated the issue of marriage to the background.

In early March Andrea sent word to Giustiniana that their old friend General Graeme was on his way to London and would call on her as soon as he got there. The news filled her with joy. It felt as though a warm, familiar breeze had suddenly blown into town, bringing back memories and stirring old yearnings.

Graeme, a prominent member of the English community in Venice, had been a good friend of the Wynnes before their departure, particularly Giustiniana. As commander in chief of the army he was also in close contact with all the ruling families of the Republic and was a coveted lunch and dinner guest at all the best Venetian houses. He had grown very fond of Andrea, and their friendship had deepened during Giustiniana's absence despite the considerable difference in their ages. Graeme had had to sit out the war due to Venice's neutrality. But at seventy, the energetic general still hankered for some action. He even hoped his visit to London might help him obtain a command in North America.

In any circumstances, the arrival of this old Venetian friend would have been cause for celebration. But Giustiniana still felt so unsettled in her London surroundings that the news jolted her into a state of feverish excitement. She waited for him like a sentinel standing guard. At the end of March, she heard that Graeme was at last in town. Just as she was getting ready to pay him a visit, the old soldier suddenly appeared at the Wynnes' and she rushed into his arms: "I truly felt as if I saw a part of myself in him as I knew he was coming from where you are. . . . I ran to embrace him and then I kissed him for you, and now it seems I cannot see enough of him. . . . I speak about you all the time. . . . I assailed him with so many questions all at once! So my Memmo still remembers me, and I hear this from someone who sees him and is with him nearly every day. . . . Graeme made me laugh by assuring me that you still love all the ladies; which means you don't love any one of them. Gius-tiniana may still hope to be dear to you."

She and the general saw each other again the following evening at Knyphausen's and spent all their time together, catching up on Venetian gossip. They were not really free to talk there, particu-larly not about Andrea. Next morning, Easter Sunday, the general came by the Wynnes' again. Giustiniana became so engrossed in their conversation that she forgot to join her mother at Easter mass. "He stayed with me from eleven until after two. . . . What a good soul! Right now he is the only man I love. . . . I would be so happy if I could have him with me at the theater tonight. And all this rapture is because I talk about you. Because all I do is think about you. I am beside myself, by God, I still love you too much."

Her agitated ramblings with Graeme had brought Andrea back to her in such vivid colors that Knyphausen, by contrast, appeared bland. "I am afraid I shall grow bored with the baron," she con-fided to Andrea. "I love him and he loves me. We see each other quietly. Our pleasures are always quiet. But though I make up wor-ries and cause little quarrels and disputes and bring up suspicions to give us a little vivacity, I fear we are deluding ourselves."

The general stayed only a few weeks, enough to take care of some family business and to realize that, much to his disappoint-ment, he was unlikely ever to see any more action in the field. But the impact of his short visit on Giustiniana was considerable. It unleashed a torrent of emotions that was bound to crash into the still waters of her placid romance with Knyphausen.

Their "quiet pleasure" lasted through the spring. They shared more dinners, more assemblies, and more *conversazioni*. "I am certainly not lacking invitations," Giustiniana said with more than a hint of disaffection. They still met discreetly at Knyphausen's little annex around the corner from his house "on account of his many ser-vants." The weather improved and brought new distractions. A boxing match between the Irish and English champions kept tongues wagging for days. Military operations on the European front and in North America had resumed after the winter lull, bringing another string of victories for the Anglo-Prussian coalition and more calls for peace. Lord Bute, backed by the Prince of Wales, continued to strengthen his hand at the expense of Pitt. Holderness, though still secretary of state, had thrown in his lot with the rising new leader, prompting Pitt to comment with sarcasm that he was likely to become "the vortex"[10] of a future Bute government. Knyphausen, on the other hand, probably realized that his own star was already dimming with that of the Great Commoner.

Giustiniana no doubt followed these developments simply by virtue of the fact that she knew so many of the participants. Yet she seldom described the political scene for Andrea even though he would surely have been very interested in it. She did not have a taste for politics. Her taste was more for observing society. In the spring of 1760 nothing captured her imagination as much as the trial of Laurence Shirley, Fourth Earl of Ferrers.

Back in January, Lord Ferrers, an eccentric old man who lived in seclusion on his vast estate in Leicestershire, had summoned his faithful steward, Mr. Johnson, ostensibly to complain about certain accounts. When the steward had entered the parlor, Lord Ferrers had locked the door behind him, ordered the poor man to his knees at gunpoint, and told him "to make his peace with God, for he never should rise again till he rose at the Resurrection." Mr. Johnson protested that all the accounts were in order. Lord Ferrers replied that "he did not doubt his accounts, but he'd been a tyrant and he was determined to punish him" and discharged his pistol at close range.[11]

Lord Ferrers was brought down to London, imprisoned in the Tower, and tried for murder by his peers in the House of Lords. Giustiniana was riveted by the case. All the major newspapers and periodicals printed detailed accounts of the inquiry and long features on the streak of madness than ran through this illustrious family. Lord Ferrers begged for mercy on the grounds of insanity, not an unreasonable plea on the part of a man who, according to *Gentleman's Magazine*, "was subject to causeless passions, . . . walked hastily about the room clenching his fists, grinning, biting his lips and talking to himself, . . . [was] frequently absent when spoken to, [and made] mouths in the looking glass."[12]

He was nevertheless found guilty in the course of a three-day trial that attracted "all of London," as Giustiniana put it to Andrea. She managed to get into two of the crowded sessions and came away with the sickening impression of having been to another of those elegant assemblies rather than to a murder trial. "The ladies were dressed for a gala, and the trial room, very large, was entirely draped in red and crammed with people. I have never seen such a grandiose spectacle. His lordship's predicament was terrible, but the sheer magnificence and diversity of the scene were such that the death of that poor man was the last thing people thought about."

Lord Ferrers, the last member of the House of Lords to be tried by his peers, was executed on the morning of May 5. It is said a silk noose was used in deference to his rank.

Now that summer was near, the evenings were warmer and Giustiniana was often invited to dine at Vauxhall, the fancy pleasure garden built on the other side of the Thames. The excursion always made her apprehensive. She did not like crossing the river on the unsteady little ferryboats. The Thames was not particularly wide at the crossing point—"no wider than the Giudecca Canal," she explained to Andrea, referring to the waterway separating Venice proper from the Giudecca. It scared her nonetheless: "Yesterday evening . . . the tiny size of the little boat, the fact the boatman only had one arm and was accompanied by his ten-year-old son, I think all of those things together increased my fear. Anyway, whatever the reason, everyone had a good laugh at my expense."

Knyphausen was a reassuring presence in such circumstances. He was always tender with her, always considerate. But there was no real spark between them, no strong physical attraction. There never had been. And no matter how much Giustiniana kept telling herself what a likable man he was, how really fond she was of him, she could not bury her feelings for Andrea. They kept coming to the surface, sapping the energy she needed to stop her relationship with Knyphausen from running out of steam.

On a hot morning in early June, Giustiniana was at home, still in her nightgown, writing her weekly letter to Andrea. It was a perfectly innocent letter. She mentioned a dinner at Vauxhall, said she was glad a rumor about Voltaire having died had turned out to be false, and, with evident annoyance, promised she would send the petulant Marietta Corner an English cloak if she insisted. "But I must warn her that the cloaks here are nothing special. In fact, everyone seems to like Italian ones very much." Only toward the end did her tone become more personal as she again touched on the vexing subject of marriage. Oh, she would find a husband, no doubt, if only she set her mind to the task: "Everyone predicts I will get myself one if I stay here." But she did not want to remain in London much longer, not with her social position still so uncertain. What was the point? She had not come all the way to England to marry a dreary solicitor. Marriage, she insisted, was no longer a necessary part of her plans. "I mostly wish to choose a place to live in that I will like and where I will feel free. If I manage to get an income of six to eight hundred pounds sterling a year, as I hear I may get, then I can live well anywhere. As soon as I have secured that sum I will share my plan with you and ask for your advice. You know I love you and that I have always looked up to you."

Just as she was finishing up her letter, Knyphausen was announced. Giustiniana rushed into the next-door room to put some clothes on "and in my usual absentmindedness I left the letter on the table." Knyphausen walked into the room and saw it lying there. The temptation was too strong: he picked it up and read it, and when Giustiniana returned to the drawing room he made a "horrible" scene. She was a "wicked" woman, he shouted at her, and "thoughtless" and "duplicitous." He could not contain himself. "For two hours I had to withstand the assault of a man who rarely gets angry at all." She had never seen him explode like that before.

Later in the day the tempest finally subsided, and Giustiniana and Knyphausen made peace. She held her ground, insisting she would not give up writing letters to Andrea. "You are my true friend, as he himself has accepted." The baron, in turn, laid down his conditions: henceforth Giustiniana was to show him all their correspondence—her letters to Andrea as well as Andrea's to her. "What can I do, dear Memmo? Will you forgive me for this too? He is such an upright man, and I owe him so much I had to give in. So please refrain from writing about him. Do not show him you know about us. . . . He would never forgive me if he knew that I had divulged this secret to you. . . . Keep our friendship alive since that is all we may count on; and forgive my weakness for a man who is really quite worthy of respect."

She could feel her relationship with Knyphausen growing hollow even as she wrote these words.

G iustiniana spent much of the summer in bed. The air was hot and sticky. The marshes around the city seethed with malevolent insects, and fevers spread easily. Bouts of high temperature kept her confined to her room. Outside her window, the bustle in Dean Street had quieted. The "polite end" of London was mostly empty, its inhabitants having migrated to their country homes after the King's birthday in June. Lady Holderness had left town as well. Word was that only poor Lady Coventry was still at home, slowly dying of lead poisoning from using too much whitening powder on her delicate skin.

It was a strange time. In late winter the end of the war had seemed so near. Then, in early spring, news had come that preliminary peace talks at The Hague had collapsed. William Pitt, still in charge of government policy, was bent on crushing France's fleet and dismantling its overseas possessions. So the war had to go on: at sea, in North America, and on the Continental battlefields, where the exhausted Prussian Army, supported by the English Treasury, fought strenuously against France, Austria, and Russia. In London pro-German sentiment continued to be high. A poetry collection by Frederick the Great was the season's best-seller. "Mostly odes and a poem on the art of war," Giustiniana wrote wearily. "They read it here as if it were a reliquary."

Some days she was worn out by fever and shifted uncomfortably under piles of damp, crumpled sheets; others she was suddenly better and enjoyed the long hours she had to herself. Propped up by a pile of cushions, she read, she wrote, she slept. During those long, sweltering days she felt her tenuous ties to London dissolve as her mind wandered dreamily back to Venice. She imagined Andrea's life from what he told her in his letters. She saw herself floating back into his arms. The thought of returning to Italy was often in her mind, and she did not resist it.

Knyphausen hovered around her, ever solicitous. "He certainly loves me," she told Andrea, as if registering a self-evident fact; but she added little about her own feelings. She was annoyed by his insistence that he read her correspondence and was not beyond writing a few fake letters in order to mislead him. Nor did she hand over to him everything she wrote. In a letter clearly intended to elude Knyphausen's eye, she confessed to Andrea, "I might as well tell you, for your own glory, that I love less and less the man I should be loving more and more."

In mid-July she was shaken out of her feverish reverie. For weeks Andrea had continued to write with the detached tone he had been asked to use in order to avoid exciting Knyphausen's suspiciousness. In fact, he had become so adept at playing the part of the old friend—never allowing himself the slightest slip—that his coolness often made Giustiniana uneasy. The letter she now received was far more disturbing than anything he had written to her before.

Andrea confessed that he was tired of "easy, everyday gallantries." His brief affair with Marietta was over. He wanted to organize his love life more efficiently and possibly settle down with a lover who would also be good company "during the intervals." A woman he could talk to. A woman he could enjoy and respect at the same time. He went on and on, filling the page with justifications of every kind.

Giustiniana understood what this unpleasant letter was all about. She knew Venetian society well enough to see that Andrea was adapting to the local custom. He needed to focus on his political career, and his distracting love life would not do anymore. It was fairly common practice for a young Venetian patrician to seek a stable relationship with a married lady. Andrea had just turned thirty-one and was still a bachelor. He felt that at this point in his life it made sense to find himself an "official" lover.

Giustiniana must have half expected that this would happen one day, but the abruptness of Andrea's announcement was the real shock—not to mention his manipulative desire to involve her in the whole process. At the end of the letter he informed her that he had already whittled down the list of candidates to three names: M., C., and B. All of them were married, he added, and all of them were more or less available. Giustiniana was overcome by a feeling of dread when she realized the preposterous nature of Andrea's request: he wanted her to help him decide which of the three ladies was best suited for him. In her reply she accused him of using all his "accursed skill" to avoid responsibility for her "eternal downfall."

Knyphausen laughed loudly when she explained Andrea's predicament to him. He laughed out of relief as much as amusement. "Most of all," she noted bitterly, "he was glad to learn from your letter that there are no more ties between us that might give him reason to be jealous." There were moments when she thought she recognized, behind the screen of Andrea's outrageous proposition, the smirk of the inveterate prankster. But after reading his letter several times she became "quite certain" that his intention "to seduce those three dames was not a practical joke at all."

She was hurt, and the insidious way in which he made it sound "as if I should be thankful to you for this great token of your friendship" made it even more painful. "I still don't understand you," she confessed in yet another letter clearly written behind Knyphausen's back. "Are you seeking revenge? Are you putting me to the test? . . . Why is it you can upset me so much even from so far away? Even when I am willing to love someone else? Alas, you are the only one in my heart now. And I feel you want me to renounce all my claims forever."

Something in Andrea had changed. He was looking beyond her, looking for an attachment that would suit his life in Venice. Giustiniana understood all that, yet she also felt she had not entirely lost her place in his heart. She was going to fight for it, knowing well that if she had any chance at all of succeeding she would have to match his "accursed skill" with her own. "Besides," she concluded dryly, "if I leave the choice to you, I run the risk that you will pick one not to my liking."

With gritted teeth, she delineated her recommendation:

So you want to live your life openly, you want to be able to visit their house, you want to be able to be seen in their company because you are tired of all the discomforts of secret lovemaking, and you wish to see your heart involved to some extent as well as satisfy your mind. In that case I'm afraid that C. will not give you what you want. She is pretty, possibly the prettiest of the three; but if my memory is correct you were not so sure about her spirit. She also happens to have an unbearable husband who actually lives with her, and the company she keeps is not the most suitable for someone with your intelligence. B., who cannot be said to be pretty but is worth more than a few pretty ones together and who probably would flatter your vanity and excite your spirit more than the other one, lives too much of a sheltered existence to fit into your new lifestyle. Besides, I don't know whether she keeps any company at all; whether she is free to live as she wants within the family; whether she may come and go at her pleasure; I happen to know that her parents would curse you; that her husband is not at all accommodating and would never leave you alone. As you can see, I am inclined to believe that both C. and B. would be better suited to your old lifestyle rather than the one you wish to adopt. As for M., I have other reservations. It seems to me you wish to love with a cold heart; but I can assure you that if you ever did make love to her you would fall prey to a most powerful and most inconvenient passion. She is too beautiful, has too much heart, too much grace, . . . too many devilish tricks not to get you involved little by little. The trust she has so blindly put in you for so long is another obstacle. . . . Still, I do not have the heart to criticize her and am inclined to favor her. Of these three pieces of advice, take the one that most satisfies you. If you choose the first or second, I think I will flatter myself into believing that I will not lose you forever. If you choose the last, I will pin my hopes on the strong objections you would find blocking the way. . . . I have good reason to believe that M. does not hold the best impression of you. You, however, become twice as strong when you stick obstinately to an idea. And if indeed you manage to make her succumb, you will win twice. I also happen to believe, from the portrait you draw of her and the circumstances she finds herself in, that you were inclined in her direction before asking me for my

*choice. . . . But do as you please, for I confess that I do not have it
in me to say more.*

Giustiniana felt so close to Andrea and knew him so well that
she could not stifle a generous impulse toward him even in a matter
so obviously painful for her. Besides, she knew she had no right to
ask Andrea to remain faithful to her—certainly not as long as she
lived in London and Knyphausen was lurking in the background.
In a way she was conceding this to him by stoically supplying the
advice on the three young ladies that he had requested. Yet she also
thought that circumstances might conceivably change and that,
from a purely rational perspective, it was a mistake to give Andrea
the impression that she actively approved his plan. London had
turned into quite a disappointment, and it was beginning to look as
if they might not stay on for long after all. Was he not thinking at
all of the possibility that they might be together again soon? "It's
true that for some time now I have stopped expecting tenderness
from you, but if I should come back to Venice one day—which is
not impossible—I will be coming to you as a new person, changed
in my ways as well as my physical appearance, and in that case I
might well expect some of that tenderness again. Who knows?"

This was the first time Giustiniana had mentioned to Andrea the
possibility she might soon return to Venice. In the past two years
she had often entreated him to join her—in Paris, in Brussels, and
lately even in London—but it had been little more than wishful
banter. She knew he didn't have the money for the journey and
was too proud to accept it from others. In any case, she had always
imagined Andrea traveling to her—wherever she happened to be
at that time. Now she said she might be coming back to him. This
was not just a ploy to distract him from pursuing M., C., and B.;
she was speaking in earnest.

In late spring, when Holderness's disaffection for the Wynnes
had reached a critical point and hopes for a presentation to Court
had all but vanished, Mrs. Anna had quietly contacted the Venetian
authorities through Ambassador Colombo, seeking permission to
return to Venice with her children. She did not feel at home in
London and was increasingly nostalgic for her familiar Venetian
life. Once financial arrangements related to the children's estate

were worked out (the matter was apparently settled, though Giustiniana does not spell out the details), there was no compelling reason for the family to stay in London as far as she was concerned. On the whole, the children did not disagree. The girls were growing bored of living in a social limbo, and the boys, having returned to Dean Street for the summer holidays after a short trial period at Cambridge, were knocking around the house in the heat with little to do. The truth was that all of them missed Italy.

If Giustiniana had not raised the possibility of her return with Andrea before, it was partly because she had been less than certain that her mother's petition to the Venetian authorities would be accepted. The Wynne imbroglio had not been forgotten in Venice, and, furthermore, unflattering news about Giustiniana's antics in Paris had continued to reach the authorities there long after she had left the city. Yet the Wynnes were not seeking to return so that Giustiniana could marry Andrea—that much was clear. So it was not unreasonable to hope the Republic might prove lenient toward a family that had always considered Venice its home and whose connections there still counted for something. Giustiniana would probably have preferred to remain silent on the topic while the papers went back and forth between London and Venice, but Andrea's letter had upset her enough that she broached the subject of her return to test his reaction and possibly to delay his plan to seduce a new lover.

As the summer advanced, Giustiniana's health did not improve. She was under strict orders not to tire herself excessively by writing letters, but this was not the time for a lull in their correspondence. "Despite having been told not to, I cannot resist sending you a tender farewell from my bed. I continue to sweat profusely, which is a good sign. My God! If you were here at my side, keeping me company, I would not feel my illness at all. In fact, your presence would make me fond of it. But it is best I leave you now in the hope that I will be able to give you better news of my health."

A week later she gave Andrea a more detailed description of her condition:

I write to you from my bed, where I have been confined for the past six weeks. My illness started with a violent fever for which I was bled several times. It then turned into scarlet fever, and my skin was covered with red spots and pustules. When that was over I developed tertian fever, with such seizures that for the first time I feared for my life. Imagine: I felt my heart freezing over, and then the same sensation moving to my bones. I was increasingly short of breath, my limbs were hot as coals, and my trembling body was covered with big drops of sweat. These fits happen in the evening and often last more than two hours. While they last, I imagine I am dying, for surely this must be what one feels when it happens. . . . If I get up from bed I am immediately seized by the illness, which doctors look upon with great fear. As for me, I can say that it is the worst ailment that has ever befallen me, and whenever I have an attack I feel like calling the confessor as well as the surgeon. Yesterday evening I had a seizure that lasted all night. I have not recovered even as I write, and the deep chill inside me has not subsided. I don't know what will happen.

As Giustiniana battled her fever, the worst possible news arrived from Venice—it was extraordinary how untimely the mail could be. Evidently, the possibility of her return was not going to deter Andrea from carrying out his plan. He had already made his choice: he was going to pay court to M., the very one Giustiniana had been partial to despite her misgivings. Now she was sorry she had played along. Andrea did not make things any easier by pressing the point that he was merely following her suggestion. "I am, as you say, the principal cause of your current commitment, and I cannot complain," Giustiniana accepted grudgingly. "But I would much rather think of you making love to all the ladies, as things were before. . . . I would much prefer you were unattached, even if it meant you would not be attached to me either. . . . Oh, how I wish that letter in which I chose your lover had gone astray."

In mid-August the Venetian Embassy informed the Wynnes that they had been granted permission to return to Venice. The permit was valid for only eighteen months, but Mrs. Anna hoped it might be extended once they had settled there. The plan was to start the trip in September in order to avoid the worst of the summer heat.

They would travel by the same route they had used on their outward journey to England: Calais, Brussels, Paris, Lyon, then eastward into Savoy, hoping to cross the Alps before the cold and arrive in northern Italy sometime in October. They would stop for eight to ten days in Padua while Mrs. Anna went on to Venice alone to find a suitable house for the family. In fact, Giustiniana added, marveling at how Andrea continued to be very much in Mrs. Anna's good graces, her mother wished to know whether he could possibly secure them a temporary lodging in Padua through his family connections there.

After months of lethargy, the Wynne household came alive again. Mrs. Anna took command of operations, issuing orders to children and servants. A boat passage to France was secured. Clothes and linens were packed. Relatives and friends were notified of the imminent departure. Last-minute arrangements were worked out with Holderness, who did not appear especially sad to see them leave. While the rest of the city dozed off in the August heat, the house on Dean Street buzzed with activity.

The boys too were going back to Venice. Richard and William had spent but a few weeks at Cambridge in the spring, and Holderness would have liked them to return in the autumn, but Mrs. Anna managed to prevail. A tutor would travel with them to Italy to ensure their continued education, receiving a stipend of two hundred pounds a year plus room and board, all taken care of by the Wynne estate. "I can't begin to tell you," Giustiniana commented admiringly, "how Mother pulled it off."

While the rest of the house was busy with preparations, Giustiniana remained under observation lest her poor health jeopardize the travel plans. "They've reached the point that they very nearly prescribe the exact number of words I may set down on paper," she griped. After the drenching sweats, the worst seemed to be over. On August 19 she got out of bed for the first time in nearly two months. She felt very weak and was short of breath: "There is nothing worse than not being able to breathe: you can feel the most minute gradations of dying." Still, she was confident she would recover in time for the journey. "Exercise and a breath of fresh air will bring relief," she predicted. The prospect of returning to Italy was already improving her spirits.

Andrea was taken aback by the swiftness with which plans in London were changing. During the two years he and Giustiniana had been apart, their relationship had lived on through their letters. Knyphausen had been jealous because he had rightly sensed that things were not entirely over between them. Even as they had carried on their separate lives, they had continued to write to each other more as lovers than as friends. Yet, like all long-distance relationships, a large part of it had become imaginary—a dream world disconnected from reality. Giustiniana's sudden return seemed disruptive to Andrea. It was not clear to him what she expected of him, and he was worried about how Giustiniana's presence in Venice would affect his new relationship with M. Did she not realize they would be the talk of the town again? How should they behave in public?

Andrea's fretting startled Giustiniana. She tried to reassure him. He need not worry so much about the two of them being in Venice together again: it was not her intention to settle there. The dazzling city of her youth—the Venice she had known with him— was part of her past. The memories were still there, of course; they were the best she had. But she wanted to put all that behind her. The gossip, the intrigue, the small-town pettiness: it was all too tiresome, too suffocating, too upsetting. As far as she was concerned, the fact that Mrs. Anna was going to rent a house there was merely incidental. "I am returning to Venice, but Venice is not for me. . . . If I thought I would have to live in Venice, I would not come. . . . Let it suffice for now, and don't speak of this to any other living soul."

What did she have in mind? "I have a project, and I will tell you everything," she said. "But I cannot speak now. . . . Allow me to remain silent for a while more. . . . I will tell you in person." She never spelled out what her mysterious project was. From what she had told Andrea in the previous months about her desire for independence and a large enough income to get by on, it is plausible that she wanted to set up house on her own, cultivate the people she liked, and continue to travel at leisure. Where would she eventually live? Not in Venice, if she could avoid it. There were many small cities on the mainland territories of the Venetian Republic where it was possible to lead a pleasant life in the company of interesting, lively friends: Padua, of course, and Vicenza, Treviso and many others.

Part of the difficulty in imagining such a future was due to the fact that she was exploring a little-tested terrain. Other women in her social class were pioneering a similar lifestyle in the Venetian Republic, but they were either wealthy or divorced or both. It would be substantially harder for Giustiniana to manage on her small income. One also gets the feeling that she deliberately kept her project vague because she wanted Andrea to fit into it in some way. As a lover? As a friend? As her *cher frère*? Those questions she left unanswered.

Giustiniana was equally vague about her relationship with Knyphausen, which she had successfully kept hidden from Mrs. Anna. Andrea asked how his "rival" was taking the news of her sudden departure from London—an unsubtle way of shifting some of the burden of guilt onto Giustiniana by reminding her that she too had her own relationship to tend. She gave him little satisfaction on that count. "He loves me," she wrote hurriedly, "of that I am certain. You will know everything upon my arrival." Not a word about her own feelings.

The date of departure was fixed for the second week in September. Soon the rush was on: "I don't have a free moment because we have so many visits and my duties take up all my time during these last days here." Her letters became increasingly hasty and confused. Last-minute instructions were mixed with bursts of anxiety. She asked Andrea to call on Consul Smith to tell him they were arriving—she had never forgotten that "he was always a friend to me"—and also on her dear aunt Fiorina, whom she promised to buy a dress when they stopped in Paris; and on "all those whom you believe to be my friends." The passage across the Channel was constantly on her mind: "You cannot imagine how scared I am of it and how ill it makes me feel." Could he also remember to make arrangements for the house in Padua? "One must try to please [my mother], for after all she is still the same woman she once was. But now I believe she cannot get in the way of a pure and decent friendship [between us], nor does she plan to. Not after all the tokens of friendship you have given me."

Giustiniana knew that the difficulties in her relationship with Andrea would not come from her mother anymore but from what she called, with evident annoyance, his own new "lifestyle." "I regret more and more the advice I gave you to attach yourself to Signora M.," she confessed, "because I respect her too much and because she is the only one who is capable of kidnapping a friend away from me. . . . But we'll talk about all that." Andrea had never been very clear about his feelings for M. Did he love her? Giustiniana made a show of backing off, assuring Andrea she felt she had no claim on him anymore: "I want only friendship and sound advice from you, and I believe I deserve these." But her hope ran much deeper than that, and Andrea's lukewarm response to the news of her return made her departure all the more unsettling: "Will you be glad to see me after all? Will you still look fondly upon the woman you have been treating as a sister and a friend?" In her last letter to Andrea from London, dated September 5, she wrote, "You will see how much weight I have put on. But even if I had grown more beautiful, would it have made a difference? . . . I long to know whether you'll be happy to see me arrive. I am your friend, you know, and I would be so disappointed if, given such faint expectations on my part, I were to find you cold or little satisfied. . . . In the meantime, you may reassure your lady friends that I am not in a position to be feared. Farewell."

The Wynne caravan set off from Dean Street in mid-September. Mrs. Anna squeezed into the coach with her five children. The tutor hired by Lord Holderness would join them later on in Italy. But they had a new traveling companion, Miss Tabitha Mendez, an unmarried lady they had met shortly after arriving in London who had become a friend of the family. She intended to spend a year traveling in Italy and was happy to hitch a ride with the Wynnes. "She is thirty-two years old, ugly, comes from a Christian family, has assets worth twenty thousand lire," Giustiniana noted rather unkindly. She could be a little clinging "but is well read and rather witty," and it would be nice if Andrea could "pay her some attention" as she planned to stay in Venice for a month.

The passage to France was delayed for several days due to a mix-up in the booking arrangements. A vessel was eventually found, and this time the crossing went smoothly despite Giustiniana's fear of the sea. They arrived in Calais on September 22. *"Le plus dangereux est achevé,"* she wrote to Andrea, switching to French as soon as she was on French soil. "The worst is over." She also shifted to the formal mode of address, *vous,* as if a strange new reserve impelled her to put some distance between them at the start of the journey that would reunite them.

The original plan had entailed traveling to Brussels first, but the Wynnes changed their itinerary to make up for lost time and headed straight for Paris instead. Giustiniana feared the change might cause her to lose some precious letters from Andrea: "I have written to Brussels to request they be forwarded to me in Paris—in case you have sent me a few, as I asked you to."

A year had gone by since the Wynnes had left Paris under a cloud. On the surface not much had changed. France was still losing the war. The king was increasingly unpopular. Mme de Pompadour was losing her power and her health. There was growing disarray in Versailles, but the sprawling city was as restless and vibrant as ever. After four years of war, it was still the world capital of entertainment and fashion.

To Giustiniana, however, Paris seemed very different. She felt disconnected—an intruder in familiar surroundings. Ambassador Erizzo had returned to Venice. Casanova was in Genoa after having spent most of the year in Germany. Farsetti was still in town, but Giustiniana had no desire to see him. She knew, of course, that La Pouplinière had married. Now she learned that the new young wife, Thérèse de Mondran, had ousted the "old sultana," Mme de Saint Aubin, as well as most of her husband's extended family, from the house. The Abbé de La Coste had been paid off and sent packing too. In fact, of all the actors embroiled in the sordid Wynne affair, he was probably the one who had suffered the worst ending. In January of that year he had been jailed at the Bastille for forging lottery tickets and had been sentenced to "imprisonment in perpetuity." One of La Pouplinière's nephews saw La Coste "chained in public squares, an iron collar around his neck, and a sign over his stomach exposing him as a counterfeiter, his hat on the ground in front of him so that passersby might throw in a coin."[1]

The Wynnes were in Paris for a week. It gave them just enough time to organize the long trip to Italy and make a few purchases. Giustiniana was not in good shape. She had not fully recovered from her summer illnesses. Also, she was disturbed by the ghosts of her recent past, which still lingered in the city. She tried to distract herself by taking short walks and doing some shopping. She bought the dress for Fiorina and also looked, in vain, for a special pair of long muffs Andrea had asked her to buy him, which were still fashionable in Venice but had already gone out of style in Paris. "You can blame [the French]," she wrote irritably. "They have decreed that such muffs are no longer *à la mode* and have made them impossible to find."

Shortly before leaving Paris, Giustiniana received a letter that caused a pang of anxiety to rip through her. Andrea declared he could not wait to see her. He offered to come out to meet her, possibly somewhere in northern Italy. This was so unexpected. And what did it really mean? She was tempted to send him a detailed itinerary of their trip. "I will trace the road we will follow and the time it will take before I will see you again," she wrote, suddenly overcome with excitement. By the time the Wynnes left Paris, though, she had given up on the idea. She was afraid of building up her expectations. She never sent him the details.

Nevertheless, the fantasy of Andrea appearing along the road smiling sweetly and beckoning her into his arms stayed with Giustiniana throughout the several-day trip to Lyon. Her heart was full of him when she arrived in the city. She went looking for his muffs during their brief stopover, and this time she found them. She packed them in her trunk with the idea of buying a nice gift box when she got to Italy. As she put them away, she felt the strangeness of holding in her hands something that would soon belong to him. "I hope you will be happy with them," she wrote.

Her desire for Andrea now became overwhelming. During the long, difficult passage over the Alps, she dreamed he would be waiting for her in Turin. They would take walks together in the

Valentino Park. They would look at the pictures in the Palazzo Reale. They would go to the theater together. The theater! Did he remember the sweet hours they had spent together in their favorite Venetian theaters?

Andrea was not in Turin; how could he have known when she would be there? Giustiniana hoped he would be in Milan, where they arrived at the end of October. Instead, she found two letters waiting at the house of the Resident. In one letter Andrea told her he had found a house for them in Padua. It belonged to the family of Niccolò Erizzo, the former Venetian ambassador to Paris. They would be able to stay there while her mother sought a house in Venice. He offered to help Mrs. Anna look for one as soon as she arrived. In the second letter he apologized for not being in Milan. But she had not written him the details of the trip as she had promised. He could not understand why she had been so mysterious. Did she imagine he would have gone looking for her, clueless, in the taverns of Piedmont and Lombardy? Besides, the gossipmongers were already feasting on the news of her return.

Giustiniana did not hide her disappointment. She wrote to him in Italian now, but she still used the formal *voi:*

> *I did not write to you from either Paris or Turin because, without my realizing it, a fantasy took hold of me that you would come to me. Forgive me for thinking it; I have since come to appreciate your not having acted so foolishly. . . . I thank you for your nice thoughts and for your friendship; but I fear you, and I do not wish to appear so very weak. Let people say what they want about me in Venice; it is not in Venice I must or even want to live. I have entirely lost the pleasure I once felt in being there, and I know I will not regain it. During the time I spend there, it is likely that I shall live a withdrawn life. I am only trying to find some peace of mind, and I am sure you will not make my life difficult. I want you to know that while I shall always be grateful for your company I am determined not to see you too often, even if you should insist. I respect your new ties. You have made me believe that I am responsible because I was the one to recommend them. Now I say you may even strengthen those ties since I must*

live happily with them. In fact, I beseech you to do just that, for without them God only knows what the two of us would be vulnerable to. I leave tomorrow morning. I will be in Padua within six days at the most, and I don't expect to see you there either. . . . Farewell. . . . Do not meet me there; I forbid you to. We shall see each other eventually, I will embrace you, and I will always be your friend. Will this not satisfy you? Have you ever expected anything different—or will you ever? Leave me to my peace and quiet; and let this be my biggest debt to you. . . . . Farewell again.

Giustiniana had arrived in Italy with her dream of a life with Andrea still alive, but the signals coming from Venice were not what she had hoped for. She sensed the danger ahead, and she was looking to protect herself. If the end of their love story were indeed nearing, she would need "peace and quiet" to manage her emotions with dignity. But even as she prepared herself to let go, she could not extinguish all hope.

The following morning the Wynnes left Milan headed for Padua. They stopped in Brescia. They spent two days in Verona, where they visited the Venetian *rappresentante*, Alvise Contarini, "who treated us with the greatest kindness." Giustiniana took advantage of their stay in that city to buy an elegant box for Andrea's French muffs. They continued on to Vicenza, and the landscape became more and more familiar. The Wynnes had traveled the same road two years earlier at exactly the same time of year. As they coasted along the same fields, passed through the same villages, stopped at the same taverns, it felt to Giustiniana as if her life were winding back in time. Memories came flooding back as the coach sped along the road. Her longing for Andrea grew sharper.

Giustiniana had specifically asked him not to come to Padua. *"Ve'l proibisco,"* she had commanded. "I forbid you." Yet she must have hoped he would not listen to her and would read her words for what they really meant.

The dusty carriage splattered its way into the courtyard of Ca' Erizzo around lunchtime on November 5. The servants came out looking surprised. It appeared they had not been informed about the Wynnes' arrival after all. Giustiniana showed the letter in which Andrea told her that Chevalier Erizzo would let them stay in the house. The housekeeper grudgingly allowed them in upon the promise that a notice from the master of the house was on its way. The six Wynnes plus Miss Mendez stepped out of the carriage one by one, horses were led to drink, trunks were unloaded, servants raced about getting the house ready. In the general confusion, Giustiniana tried to keep at bay the sadness she knew would otherwise engulf her completely.

There was a letter from Andrea waiting for her inside. She tore it open. He sent his greetings. He hoped the trip had gone well and that the house was adequate. He also complained about Giustiniana's "style" of writing. Why was she sending such confusing messages to him? Why did she forbid him to come to Padua?

The pain was searing. She wrote back that same night:

Why, dearest Memmo, why humiliate me so the very first moment of my arrival? Why not see me before passing judgment on me? Do you know why I forbade you to come meet me? Because I'm still fearful of my mother; because one day she says one thing and the next day she says another. . . . You deplore my "style"? But my dear Memmo, would you have obeyed me if I had written to you more tenderly? Forgive me. Come see me anytime you want. But be easy on me. My only wish is to be your friend. Help me keep my resolution. . . . Farewell, dear Memmo. Forgive me for my brevity. I long to see you. You are and always will be my best friend. I will be here for a few days: take your bearings calmly. Try to understand what I'm saying to you. Know my heart. Do you really think I can be any different from what I am? Oh God, I have so many things to tell you! . . . Please tell Signora M. I send my most respectful greetings. . . . Farewell.

She hoped Andrea would show up the following day or the day after that—it was only a half-day trip up from Venice. But he didn't. Nor did he send a word of explanation. Meanwhile, Mrs. Anna had slipped into one of her foul moods. She was tired, she said, and the family was such a burden. She threatened to stay in Padua instead of going on to Venice to secure a house. At the end of a difficult day Giustiniana sent off a bitter note to Andrea—in French again:

Mon cher frère,
I hoped to receive news from you today, but you have not written to me. I am delighted to find you at fault! I hope you will now agree we are even. . . . I shan't write to you. . . . I will pay a little price for it, no doubt, but I also hope to profit by your indifference.

In the morning she received a surprisingly tender letter. There was little in it to justify new hope: Andrea did not put into question his relationship with M. But he admitted that he had not come to Padua yet because he was unsure how he might react when he saw her. His words suggested that he too was confused, a vulnerability that touched her. She seized this chance to regain some emotional balance of her own.

Mon cher frère,
I take comfort in the fact that you seem calmer and more certain about my friendship. I have always treasured your sincerity, and, believe me, I treasure it even more when it springs from such delicate feelings. And to hear that you still fear me is no small glory. What is more, I am your true friend. I have proved it to you so far, I believe. I swear I will remain so until I die. . . . Should this friendship please you, rest assured it will be yours forever.
When you say you want to protect me, I feel the power of your gentleness. I'm also grateful for the effort you are making in not coming out to see me. It's your decision, and I respect it. However, I can't but laugh when I hear that so many people are closely watching every move you make, and it will be wonderful to tell them all at last how wrong they were to think that you would leave Signora M. and attach yourself to me again. I know the country too; but I swear I never intended to defy its customs upon my return or to expose you to slander, disapproval, or embarrassment. I will stay but a short while, and during that time I will only seek peace and quiet. So I don't really care if people know me for who I am now—an enemy of falseness, of seduction, of

*things contrived, and above all of things that can cause damage
by hurting the souls of delicate people. . . . How you wrong me,
dear Memmo, in not treating me as a true friend! . . . I praise, I
admire your gratitude, your friendship, your commitment to the
gracious M., and I must be the first to applaud them. You needn't
fear I will come looking for you or force you to deceive her. She
can be at ease and trustful—and who, more than she, deserves to
be so? . . . Of course the sacrifice you made for her in not coming
out to see me displeased me. But now I swear I feel my soul is
large enough to make her a gift of my own displeasure. You are
worthy of her, she of you, and the more so for your mutual commitment. . . . But more to the point, Memmo, . . . give yourself
some credit for my feelings for you. Make sure she understands
the full value of your sacrifice. She is safe; of this you can be sure.
. . . Farewell now. And be glad I treat you as a friend.*

Giustiniana made it clear, however, that being his friend did
not mean she would assist him in his amorous intrigues. "If I
can help you in any way, I shall, with all my soul. But I'll be truthful: I'm simply not up to attracting [M.'s] husband's attention
for your sake." Had Andrea actually made such an indelicate proposal, or was she merely trying to forestall a request she saw coming? Whatever the case, she really didn't have the heart for that
sort of thing anymore. "I'm afraid that since leaving Italy I no
longer see the point of these games. . . . I will do whatever else
you ask."

Andrea expressed the hope that Giustiniana and M. could be
"good friends." She replied without a shred of irony, "It goes
without saying that I'm with you. You can imagine my strong
desire for such a thing to happen. [M.] is a lovely person." Giustiniana's offer of friendship showed remarkable self-control. It
also gave her the moral high ground. Andrea again brought up the
subject of Knyphausen to add some ballast to his side of this difficult correspondence. She replied with less ambiguity than in the
past. Marriage was not a likely outcome, she explained, on account
of her own disinclination: "I do not believe I will make a commitment so easily. Whatever my feelings are for the baron, I will work
to arrange my life in such a way that he will always be pleased to

regard me as his good friend. As for me, I value that man's friendship immensely."

Mrs. Anna traveled to Venice on November 8, leaving Giustiniana in charge of the family. "May God protect you," she quipped in a note of encouragement to Andrea. "My mother is very wicked." But time and circumstances had blunted the old animosity. When he went to pay his respects and offer his help in finding a house, his erstwhile enemy appeared genuinely glad to see him; she certainly was grateful for his practical assistance. Giustiniana was happy to learn that the two were getting along so well: "Do continue in the same way. To make her less wild if nothing else."

Encouraged by so much cordiality, Andrea wondered whether he might ask Mrs. Anna's permission to visit her daughter secretly in Padua, conjuring up an excuse for the sake of M.'s peace of mind. Giustiniana put her foot down. A visit by Andrea would have put her in an awkward position vis-à-vis M., when she wanted to make as smooth a return to city life as possible. "I absolutely insist that you remain in Venice. No matter what excuse you might contrive in order to come here, your friend will not approve of it . . . ; and you would risk losing moments of happiness I would not be able to pay back. . . . You can easily see how the danger would be far greater than the gain. . . . What difference does it make if we see each other in Venice or Noventa*? The distance between us is always the same, whether we are separated by a mile or by the thickest wall."

M. was indeed growing wary of Andrea's solicitude toward Mrs. Anna and the Wynne family. She suspected him, quite rightly, of being in touch with Giustiniana. The messages traveling between Venice and Padua became increasingly garbled: "Mon cher frère, I . . . believe we don't understand each other much; but since I am willing to believe anything I can assure you that you will have little trouble in persuading me of anything. I do not doubt your sincerity. In fact, I sometimes feel you are too sincere. It's consoling to hear that the mere mention of my name creates such an impression on your friend, not to mention the glory gained by my self-esteem."

*A small town in the Veneto.

M.'s flare-ups reminded Giustiniana of her own "agitation" when she had first fallen in love with Andrea nearly seven years before and the pain and the pleasure she had felt at the time. "Do you remember, Memmo, the old, fleeting jealousies in the early days of our love? Oh, the sweet and blessed moments we enjoyed when peace would break out again! . . . Rejoice in what you have."

It was Miss Mendez's turn to make the half-day trip to Venice. Giustiniana reminded Andrea to take care of her: "Be so generous as to give her all the enlightenment a newcomer to the country will need in order to see all the major points of interest, get some learning, and have fun at the same time. . . . I shall be as grateful to you as if the kindnesses I ask of you were addressed to me." She tried to press Andrea's large muffs into the box she had purchased in Verona, but they wouldn't fit. So she asked Miss Mendez to pack them with her own clothes and give them to him in Venice. "Don't ask me what the price was," she wrote to him in an accompanying note. "I had money in Lyon, and I always meant for them to be a gift."

Each day Giustiniana felt lonelier. She was tired of being stranded in the dank and inhospitable house of the Erizzos. The late autumn cold chilled her bones. The wet weather sapped her spirit. She was saddened to learn about the death of King George II (he had died October 25). The rumors about Frederick of Prussia's health affected her even more. But it was not the news from abroad that depressed her so much as the ambiguous, hopeless notes she kept receiving from Andrea. He seemed so defensive—always asking forgiveness, always making excuses: M. forbade him to see her . . . M. forbade him to write to her. . . . How was she supposed to react? How was she supposed to feel?

A deep sadness was taking over. Nearly two weeks had gone by since she had arrived in Padua exhausted but also exhilarated at the thought of finally setting eyes on Andrea. The fantasy she had fed during the long trip home dissolved little by little. The remaining ambiguity in Andrea's letters only hurt her more. She could not bear the confusion anymore. She yearned for some final clarity—even as she dreaded it.

Mon cher frère,

   . . . I haven't written to you. Why I haven't written to you I don't really know, and I hardly know what I should be writing now. There are times I understand you, and there are times I don't. There are times I think you despise me, and there are times I think you are my friend. Now you treat me as your confidante, now it looks as if you are in love with me. I know the circumstances you find yourself in, and you know mine. Why all the intrigue? If your good friend forbids you to write to me, give her satisfaction. . . . A friend must be sympathetic, and I would be quite an ungrateful one if I expected you to sacrifice the slightest pleasure for my sake. I was so struck by this idea yesterday that I didn't want to write to you anymore. Believe me: let us speak the truth. If we meet, I will behave with the grace that my immutable friendship as well as the memory of my gratitude will inspire. But you have to live in Venice, and I don't. You have to cultivate the Venetian spirit, its genius, its weaknesses, and I don't—though I can accept all these attitudes and prejudices in you. So write to me about the king of England, write to me about the war or other news. I shall be happy. But don't write to me about other things, I beg you. And let us stop deceiving or hurting each other. Farewell.

During the next several days Giustiniana did her best to contain her anger for fear of making things worse between them. "I read and I keep myself busy trying not to get too bored," she wrote with a heavy dose of sarcasm. "Nothing much happens here, but I find that if I keep my expectations low time goes by just the same." On November 17 she received another rambling letter from Andrea. As usual, he was full of tenderness but also vague, evasive, inconclusive. This time she let him have it:

Mon cher frère,

   Such a long letter! So many justifications! And such sweet expressions! But Memmo, shouldn't I find it offensive that you should think such a letter necessary? Do you doubt my friendship to such a degree? Do you really think I would fail you? You force me to speak! You want me to explain the situation of my heart?

Well, then, I should adore the baron, yet I love him less than he deserves. But I am his friend and I will remain so for eternity. You want me to speak about you? All right, I'll give myself away. Your words, the letters I received from you during the last period in London and during the journey back, led me to believe that your commitment to me only involved your head. So I nourished the sweet illusion that I would find you again, not as my lover—for that was no longer suitable for either of us—but as my friend. . . . To do you a favor, I forbade you to come meet me as you had promised; but still I flattered myself that at least in Padua the first man I set eyes on would have been Memmo. It seemed to me I had a thousand things to tell you and a thousand things to hear from you. I thought about it a lot. I liked the idea. It often troubled me as well. I arrive; and I do not find you. Instead I hear a lot of talk about responsibilities, affections, feelings apparently stronger than those I thought you harbored. I must fight my first impressions. You force me to do so every day. I humiliate my vanity. I destroy my expectations. I vanquish my self-esteem. I even sympathize with you when you do not fly here to see me because love is apparently stronger than our very tender friendship. I make an effort and I gain control over myself. But I remain in a terrible mood, and my courage fails me. This is why I have been so erratic. This is the reason for my slights, for my nonsensical letters. But I'll put an end to it, I swear. You have sympathized with me a thousand times, and I sympathize with you and I forgive you. Perhaps I should even thank you since God only knows where all that excitement I felt when I arrived in Padua might have led if it had been encouraged in any way; whereas you know we must love each other only as friends. I have done a thousand crazy things. You had to take on a new commitment, for which you asked my advice and my approval. I too have a commitment, and I would be desperate if I could not keep it. Venice is not the country for me. I cannot live there with the freedom to which I am now accustomed; and then I cannot see myself living in a place where people affect superior airs with me or feel they have to extend their protection to me. I'm not sure yet where I'll go, but I have plans and I won't tell you about them because there is nothing more ridiculous than plans that are divulged too soon. A passion between us would be a real curse, and I know it might be rekindled in me. So again I thank you for having put me in a position to renounce such a passion forever.

I'll stop writing now because I don't feel at all well. . . . Farewell, and forgive me for not matching all your kind words.

Today I have been sincere with you, and my sincerity cannot but tell you things which prove my fondest affection and friendship for you.

Giustiniana felt her strength failing after sending off her letter, and she retired to her room. "I've become melancholic, and this malady is affecting my mood and my spirits. I am not the same person anymore, and every pleasure has become dull and burdensome." The next day she felt worse, and after another difficult night she called for help. "I'm really not well," she wrote, switching back to French. "My health is very weak, and last night I really thought it was the end. I was forced to call Dr. Berci in at four o'clock in the morning. I've decided to put myself in his hands to cure what he calls my 'attacks of melancholic hysteria.'" She asked Andrea not to mention any of this to her mother in Venice. There was no point: "Apart from the fact that my suffering is great and my anxiety even greater, these illnesses are not dangerous."

Andrea wrote several times a day now—affectionate letters in which he wished her well. But Giustiniana no longer had the energy to write much at all. She asked him to forgive her "for not replying to all your letters." Andrea thanked her for the muffs. He and Miss Mendez had not taken to each other, he was sorry to report. Giustiniana asked him to make an effort despite what she now realized was a "silly" idea to get them together: "Try to appease her; she can be mean, and it is an advantage to have such people on one's side. You will tell me you don't much care. But my vanity is sensitive to compliments paid to you, and so I beg you to do this for me—even if it is but a whim on my part. . . . I'll stop now. I'm weak and this evening I'll take a cure. Again, I forbid you to say anything about this to my mother."

She spent the next few days drifting about the house, awaiting news from Mrs. Anna. Her tone with Andrea became more distant. On November 23: "I haven't written in two days. I really haven't had time. . . . A thousand necessary chores have robbed me of all my time. I have not had an hour to myself." And later: "Mon cher frèrc, forgive me, I have written little or nothing. I'm not well. I'm melancholic. The saddest curse has fallen upon me, and everything has become unbearable. I have received your letters regularly, and if I were sensitive to anything it would be to your kindness. . . . I'm sorry to hear about the difficulties you're facing in your love life. But Memmo, if you're sure of her, does anything else matter?"

The Wynnes had meant to stay no more than ten days in Padua. Three weeks had now gone by, and they were still camping out at Ca' Erizzo. There was apparently a bureaucratic hitch. Mrs. Anna had found a house, but she was hesitating because it was available for only six months. The city authorities, meanwhile, were waiting for Mrs. Anna to sign the lease before issuing an entry permit for the family, which was needed in addition to the residency permit they had already received when they were still in London. The delay was making Giustiniana irritable: "Why doesn't my mother take the house? And why haven't you persuaded her yet? Meanwhile, I'm stuck here; I'm not well, and I'm bored. . . . Since my mother can take the house for only six months, why all the fuss about the entry permits? We'll be there such a short period of time. . . . Come, Memmo, free us from this hindrance."

Giustiniana would think about the future later on. Right now she just wanted to rest; she wanted her room and fresh linen and a little peace. "Allow me to come to Venice and trust me, as you should, for I have forsaken all claims."

Finally, on November 26, word came that Mrs. Anna had secured the house and the entry permits had been granted. It would be another couple of days before their trunks were ready, and there were still a few errands to do before the trip to Venice. But the news cleared the air, and Giustiniana's spirits lifted for the first time since arriving in Padua. "It seems I am happy today, or at least not as sad as I usually feel. . . . I am much obliged for your sweet words in your last letter. But Memmo, you know we must not believe in them. And poor us if we should still listen to our hearts. I don't know what mine tells me about you; but even if it spoke out it would gain nothing, for I have sworn to be deaf. For pity's sake, let us remain friends.

"So I'll see you at Mira? I feel pleasure in imagining this reunion. . . . I don't drive the idea away from me. . . . *Basta.* Enough now. . . . Farewell, Memmo."

Did Giustiniana and Andrea ever meet at Mira? This is the last fragment of their correspondence to have come down to us, so we are left without an answer. One day, perhaps, other letters will reveal to us what happened that morning. But it is hard to escape the feeling that the little river town ten miles up the road from Padua was indeed where the final act of their love affair took place—whether or not Andrea ever made it to their appointment. Giustiniana's last letters are filled with so much foreboding that we, the prying readers, understand it is over perhaps even before she does. Yet in the tone of those letters we recognize a new resoluteness as well. It is the clearheaded determination of someone who has weathered a storm and is leaving it behind. Giustiniana was now ready to complete her journey, even as she made it clear that Venice was not her final destination and she was going to live her life beyond its stifling confines. And so we picture her boarding the *burchiello* at Mira with a steady foot and traveling confidently down the gentle waters of the Brenta, past fishing villages and elegant villas, then out into the lagoon, toward the shimmering city across the horizon.

Epilogue

G iustiniana's return to Venice after more than two years abroad was not a festive homecoming. Amid all the fuss over the Wynnes' staggered arrival in the city, with Mrs. Anna's fastidious search for an apartment and the bureaucratic difficulties over the entry permit, not to mention Andrea's panicky state and M.'s suspiciousness, one can easily imagine the chattering men at the Listone indulging in snide little jokes about the return of the *inglesine* while the ladies chuckled behind their embroidered fans.

Even the small English community, which had always been a haven for Mrs. Anna and her children, received them with a certain reserve. Joseph Smith, now well into his eighties, was in the process of resigning his consulship. He had settled into his new marriage and was obsessively taken up with the sale of his large art and book collection to the new English monarch, George III. The aging Lady Montagu was her usual mordant self; according to a shocked young English visitor by the name of Thomas Robinson, she had also become "scurrilous in the highest degree."[1] Ambassador Murray, who had been quite happy in the company of the Wynnes in the past, casting his interested gaze on the girls, now plainly made fun of them in his dispatches to London. Mrs. Anna and her daughters were contributing "not a little" to the city's "amusements," he wrote to Lord Holderness. "Their manner of going on has been so very outré that I have no thoughts at present of visiting them, as I don't care to be an eye-witness to the ruin of a family when there is no possibility of saving them."[2]

It was not just the atmosphere in the English community that felt different. The city as a whole had changed while the Wynnes had been away. The long war combined with Venice's isolation had dampened spirits and accentuated a general feeling of stagnation. The more enlightened Venetians had lost their earlier enthusiasm for modernizing the state. Father Lodoli, the charismatic Franciscan monk, had left Venice in semiexile and was living out his last days in a state of destitution on the mainland. Little if anything remained of the hopeful band of reformists whom he had nurtured in the years before the war. The Tribunal of the Inquisitors had strengthened its oppressive presence in everyday life, and the secretive Council of Ten—the executive branch of government—ruled with a growing disregard for the Maggior Consiglio, the assembly of patricians that for centuries had been the very heart of the Republic.

A few months after her return, Giustiniana witnessed at first hand a turning point in the drift of the Venetian Republic toward an increasingly authoritarian government in the hands of the Council of Ten. Her friend Angelo Querini, a decent, civic-minded young senator who had been (with Andrea) among Lodoli's most ardent followers, was charged with conspiring against the Republic and thrown into jail. Querini was hardly a revolutionary: his ambition was to give back to the Maggior Consiglio some of the authority that had been usurped by the Council of Ten. His arrest came as a stern warning to the reformers of his circle, and it helps to explain the more prudent approach Andrea would adopt in his political career.

In her letters from Padua, Giustiniana had told Andrea she intended to live as quietly as possible while she stayed in Venice. But as Murray's disobliging remarks remind us, it was not long before she was causing a certain commotion in town. Thomas Robinson, the twenty-two-year-old son of Lord Grantham who had been so surprised by Lady Montagu's loose tongue, was quite taken with Giustiniana when he met her in the fall of 1760—to the point that he apparently wanted to marry her. From the very beginning, however, the fact that he was a Protestant and Giustiniana a Catholic was seen as an insurmountable obstacle. The young Englishman was soon out of the picture: in early spring he left Venice—the last stop on his Italian tour—and made his way back to London.

Shortly after Robinson's departure, however, Giustiniana startled everyone by accepting the hand of Count Philip Orsini-Rosenberg, the imperial ambassador of Austria to the Venetian Republic. It was a remarkable coup; certainly that is how everyone around her perceived it. The count, a seventy-year-old widower, came from a very aristocratic Austrian family that claimed to descend from the Roman clan of the Ursini. He was ending his long diplomatic career with a luxurious posting, housed in the magnificent embassy on the Grand Canal.

His wife, Maria von Kaunitz, had died in 1755, a year after their arrival in Venice. After a brief period of mourning, the count had given himself over to a fairly dissolute life and was to be found gambling with his friends at the Ridotto when he was not chasing young actresses at the theater or visiting his favorite courtesans. Giustiniana's reappearance on the scene changed all that. The count must have known her from the old days—he had probably met her at Consul Smith's early on, when her love affair with Andrea had been the talk of the town. But now he saw her in a new light: She was a mature young lady of twenty-four, with experience quite beyond her age. Her lively spirit enchanted him, and those "womanish" features she had complained so much about undoubtedly did as well. He fell in love with her, as other older men had before him.

Giustiniana must have been a little stunned to receive a proposal from a man of such exalted station. Of course, she had said that marriage "was not for her," that she prized her independence more than the security provided by a husband. But she had expressed those thoughts when she was still trying to make room in her life for Andrea, groping for an unconventional solution to an unconventional situation. Now her long affair was over, and she was doing her best to put it behind her. She needed to be practical, and she might well have concluded that her quest for independence required a detour through a few years of married life.

Ambassador Murray, so quick to dismiss the Wynnes when they had returned to Venice, deemed the news of such importance as to warrant a diplomatic notice to William Pitt himself. "The conversation of the town is taken up about a marriage which is shortly expected between Count Rosenberg and the eldest Miss Wynne,"[3] he wrote to the Great Commoner, treating the information as a matter of official significance, as indeed it was: Giustiniana, after all, was marrying an important minister of a Great Power with which Britain was still at war.

Andrea, still entangled in his complicated affair with M., must have appreciated the logic behind Giustiniana's snap decision: after all, he had always encouraged her to marry an old man and the *cher frère* in him surely saw the practical benefits of her situation. But it is hard to imagine that the news did not set off a certain amount of inner turmoil in the old lover.

The count and Giustiniana were married on November 4, 1761. The ceremony probably took place at the embassy. There was no fanfare, not even a public notice: it was a rushed, hushed affair in the presence of a priest, a few intimate friends, and her family (one imagines Mrs. Anna smiling, happy at last). Still, everyone in town knew about it. Lady Montagu was no longer on hand to deliver a pointed remark on the event, having finally returned home to England upon her husband's death, but her Venetian friend Chiara Michiel made sure she was kept informed: "Monsieur de Rosenberg married Giustiniana without declaring her either wife or ambassadress. . . . Such a marriage is well below his rank . . . but is worthy of his heart."[4] Lady Montagu replied rather philosophically, "Your words are subtle and just and noble, and I understand all that."[5]

Giustiniana, now Countess Rosenberg, settled into the elegant *palazzo* the Austrian government had leased from the Loredan family. As long as her husband was alive, she was guaranteed a very comfortable life. After his death, she would not inherit his possessions, which were already destined to her stepson, but the count set up a small trust that would give her an income of 2,000 Austrian florins a year for as long as she kept his name. That would be enough for her to live decorously, though not in luxury.

Her social rank, however, remained ambiguous. She was Countess Rosenberg in the eyes of her husband, but she was not—as Chiara Michiel had been quick to underline—the "ambassadress." Nor had the marriage put an end to all the talk about her questionable titles of nobility. The snobbery and condescension were depressing and terribly familiar to Giustiniana.

The Court in Vienna, not officially informed of the marriage, expressed deep misgivings. Prime Minister Anthon von Kaunitz, a cousin of Rosenberg's deceased first wife, involved himself personally in the matter and begged the ambassador to tell him exactly how things stood. Here is the count's reply—an extraordinary "confession," at once poignant and pathetic, by an old libertine in love with a much younger woman:

> *Sir, the trust and very special esteem I have always had for your Excellency make me seize with joy the opportunity I am offered to open my heart to you and make the disclosure you ask of me. It is true that I have married Miss Giustiniana Wynne in secret,* and the marriage will remain such as long as I shall be ambassador. But it is not true that she is the daughter of an English merchant. Chevalier Wynne, who died a Catholic some ten years ago in Venice, was a gentleman and belonged to one of the oldest houses of Wales. He was traveling in Italy when he married the daughter of Count Gazzini. After his death Lord Holderness was appointed governor of the family—just fifteen days ago the two Wynne [brothers], who are still minors, received written orders to return to England, where the eldest has an income of 6,000 pounds sterling from his estate. I say all this so Your Excellency may see that the family is very noble and I hold indisputable proof.*[6]

The count added that if this were still deemed insufficient, the Austrian Court should consider the following information as final proof of Giustiniana's aristocratic lineage: "Andrea Memmo, a Venetian nobleman belonging to one of the oldest families, was ready to marry her with the full consent of his entire family, but Mme Wynne did not grant her consent because he was a very disturbed young man. Similarly, Lord Grantham's son wished to

---

*In the register of secret marriages at the Patriarchal Chancery there is indeed a dusty old folder with the names of Giustiniana and Count Rosenberg scribbled on it. Unfortunately, as in the case of the folder related to Giustiniana and Andrea, the papers are missing.

marry her last year, but the young lady refused him as he was a Protestant."

The count "implored" the prime minister to grant his "protection" to Giustiniana, but Kaunitz was not impressed by the clarifications he received—he probably had less biased information to rely on than the one his old ambassador provided him. He left Count and Countess Orsini-Rosenberg hanging.

It cannot have been an easy period for Giustiniana, no matter how used she had become to this type of social ostracism. Was her disappointment lessened by the joys of marriage? It is difficult to imagine Giustiniana falling deeply in love with the count, but she might well have felt a growing affection and respect for this distinguished old man who was willing to put himself on the line for love of her. Despite the difference in age, people certainly assumed that the marriage was consummated and the relationship was physical, not only because of Rosenberg's reputation as a sexually active septuagenarian but because his young wife quickly became pregnant. "One hears the beautiful Giustiniana will soon give a new fruit to the world,"[7] Lady Montagu chuckled from London, eager to stay abreast of things in Venice. If it is true she became pregnant after marrying Count Rosenberg, then she must have lost the child—presumably to Vienna's great relief.

As the new Countess Rosenberg, Giustiniana was isolated on all sides. Not only was she not accepted by her husband's government, she was also cut off from Venetian society, for if Vienna did not recognize her as the wife of the Austrian ambassador, the Venetian authorities certainly did. As a foreign dignitary she was not allowed to come into direct contact with local patricians. The law was a residue of a past age. Yet it had lived on, much to the distress and irritation of the ambassadorial corps, and was being enforced with even greater severity than usual since the beginning of the war. If she and Andrea communicated at all at this point, it had to be in secret, as so often in the past.

In early 1763, however, they did see each other publicly at the house of a mutual friend, and the inquisitors deemed the episode "very serious in all its circumstances."[8] Andrea had just been elected to the position of savio di terraferma, with administrative duties on the mainland territory. One of his first and most delicate assignments was the resolution of a dispute with the Austrian government over the postal system. Giustiniana suggested she might be able to help, using her husband's connections, and they discussed the issue in front of other guests that evening. She then sent him a note on the matter. He was imprudent enough to reply.

Andrea realized his mistake, or perhaps he was tipped off that a government informer was about to denounce him for having communicated with the wife of a foreign ambassador. In any event, he went directly to the Tribunal of the Inquisitors and confessed his crime. The Tribunal stated that his action deserved "the sternest and most solemn punishment" but spared him in the end on account of his "spontaneous confession." There was a final warning, however: "In the future you will refrain from any contact whatsoever with the wife of [the] ambassador and with the family of that wife as well . . . and you are prohibited from going near her at public functions and celebrations. . . . You are hereby also informed that an attentive eye will always be watching you."[9]

The reprimand was so severe—and so reminiscent of his "fateful banishment" a decade earlier—that one has to wonder whether Andrea and Giustiniana were again seeing each other on the quiet and the information had reached the inquisitors. Alternatively, it is possible that the count himself tipped off the authorities preemptively, to make sure that Andrea would stay away from his young wife. Whatever the case, Andrea must have taken the rebuke seriously. His career was on track by then—he was moving ahead under the aegis of Andrea Tron, the powerful procuratore di San Marco who had been the Wynnes' neighbor back in the summer of 1756—and he certainly wouldn't have wanted to tarnish his reputation by breaking a law of the Republic, no matter how obsolete he may have considered it.

So after all that had passed between them, this is how matters stood between Andrea and Giustiniana in 1763, the year the war ended with the treaties of Paris and Hubertusburg and peace finally returned to Europe.

In 1764 the Austrian Court recalled its ambassador to Venice and sent him into retirement. Count Rosenberg had made no headway in his painful dealings with his government over his new spouse. He and Giustiniana left Palazzo Loredan and moved to Klagenfurt in the Austrian province of Carinthia, where the Orsini-Rosenbergs had their family seat. Despite his declining health, the count continued to press Prime Minister Kaunitz to grant protection to his wife. Once they were back in Austria, the possibility that they would not be received at Court in Vienna loomed as the worst possible nightmare. Giustiniana decided to take matters into her own hands. She enlisted the help of Lord Stormont, the British ambassador to Vienna, who asked the secretary of state, Lord Sandwich, to sign a declaration reaffirming that the Wynnes were indeed from a "very noble and very ancient Family."[10]

The statement was signed and sealed within a matter of days. Surely the irony was not lost on Giustiniana that the British, so maddeningly rigid when she had wanted to be presented to Court in London, were now so ready to help. Nonetheless, the Austrian government remained unimpressed. That summer Giustiniana wrote directly to Kaunitz:

> *Sir, it is with the greatest pain that I have learned of the deadly grief my husband has had to suffer on my account. I thought that such an authentic and honorable statement by the King of England*about my family as the one you received would have sufficed as proof of its antiquity. . . . I have no fear that once Her Majesty the Empress is informed of the truth she will not want to take away from me what I have been given by God, who wished me born a lady in a great nation and in a very old family. Your Highness, you know the ways of the world so well—could you not explain to Her Majesty the righteousness of my cause and the fatal consequences that might otherwise occur? Sir, your sense of justice is too well known for me to think that you might refuse your powerful help to a Lady who implores it.*[11]

The letter was sent at the end of July 1764 and was signed "Your humble and very obedient servant Countess de Rosenberg née Wynne." Kaunitz, well aware that her husband was not well,

---

*She is referring to the document signed by Lord Sandwich.

was clearly buying time. His tactic was soon rewarded. Count Rosenberg died the following winter, and the vexing issue of their presentation to the Court disappeared.

Her husband now dead, Giustiniana was free to leave Austria. But where should she go? There was no compelling reason for her to rush back to Venice. She had no house to return to. She was not particularly eager to live with her mother and her sisters again, and her brothers were studying in England. So she remained in Klagenfurt, staying on for another five years. Little is known about her Austrian period. It seems she overcame the initial hostility of the local nobility and managed to establish cordial relations with the Rosenberg family. Her character would have led her to make the best of her stay and to gather as many interesting people around her as she could. Still, she must have remained an outsider in the eyes of the provincial Klagenfurt society: it is hard to imagine Giustiniana turning into a German-speaking Austrian countess. In the end, one suspects she stayed in Austria in no small part because she wanted to set her financial affairs in order and ensure for herself an income from her former husband's estate that would give her the independence and the security she needed before she went back to Italy.

She returned to Venice around 1770. She was still only in her early thirties, and after six quiet years in Austria she was eager to lead a more engaging existence. However, she found that life in Venice had deteriorated greatly. Society had become stale. Cultural life was dead. Corruption was rife. Prostitution and gambling were out of control. These were all symptoms of a much deeper crisis. The Venetian ruling class seemed incapable of providing a sense of direction, of lifting its eyes beyond the lagoon that surrounded it. To Giustiniana, who had spent so much time abroad, the Republic must have appeared very old and tired—a wrinkled *grande dame* gazing out over the backwaters of Europe.

She took a house near Piazza San Marco and tried to build herself a new life as the widowed Countess Rosenberg. She called on old friends, and now that she was no longer the wife of the Austrian ambassador she was free to see Andrea again. She gathered a small *salon* around her and did what she could to interest herself in the life of the city. But her heart was not in it; the city no longer felt like home. Again one hears the echo of that earlier cry: "Venice is not for me!" She escaped when she could, often traveling to Paris and London. Each trip meant a tiring journey across Europe, but it gave her the oxygen she lacked in the stagnant atmosphere of the lagoon.

This was more than mere estrangement. Giustiniana felt increasingly vulnerable in Venice's vice-ridden atmosphere. She started to gamble and, like many of her friends, soon lost control over her habit. By 1774 gaming was ravaging so many lives that the government decided to close down the Ridotto, where she and Andrea had spent so many memorable nights stealing kisses and watching others play cards. Illegal gambling houses sprang up overnight in private homes and the streets around Piazza San Marco. Giustiniana dragged herself from one seedy hovel to another in the worst company, spending her limited money and amassing enormous debts. In a single night of madness she lost more than three thousand florins—one and a half times her yearly income. Her life was rapidly falling apart.

To extricate herself from this downward spiral, she decided to spend more time in Padua, where life was not as decadent and had a gentler rhythm. Although it was a provincial town, it was strangely more cosmopolitan than Venice. Perhaps it had to do with the old university, which was going through one of its better moments, or maybe it was due to the proximity of the countryside and the pleasant life that revolved around some of the elegant villas nearby. The environment was certainly more stimulating for Giustiniana. She rented an apartment in a *palazzo* by the Duomo. With the help of loyal friends and her own determination, she gradually pulled herself together—and out of debt.

She retained the house in Venice and followed closely what went on in the city, even though it was increasingly with the eye of an observer one step removed from the action. Her connections abroad and her knowledge of languages made her the ideal chaperon for foreign travelers, especially the English. The writer William Beckford, who became a close friend, describes how happy he was to have been recommended to "the fascinating" Giustiniana.[12]

When Archduke Paul and Archduchess Maria of Russia made a "private" visit to Venice in 1782 to honor the new commercial ties between the two states, she wrote a vivid account of what was possibly the last big extravaganza staged by the Republic. She wrote it in French, in the form of a long letter to her brother Richard, and it was published as a short book first in London and then in Venice. It was very well received in literary circles, and it remains immensely enjoyable to read today. Her old friend Casanova, who was back in Venice—now, ironically, working as a government informer and living in reduced circumstances—wrote her a fan letter praising her "easy and unpretentious style."[13] She replied with a very formal thank-you note. Neither made the slightest reference to the past, nor did they renew their close friendship.

Writing was Giustiniana's true calling. Her letters to Andrea bear testimony to her growing talent, of course, but now she devoted herself to the craft with more discipline and method. Her second book, also in French and published in London in 1785, was a collection of essays and reminiscences on a variety of topics, from education to the devastating effects of gambling. In one delightful chapter on the art of smiling there is a revealing passage that has its share of sorrow for the passing of time—she was then approaching fifty—but ends on a note of good-natured resignation:

Laugh heartily, charming and innocent youth! The age of smiling will soon be upon you. That will be followed in turn by the years of the expertly contrived smile: an air of peace and serenity will often hide the truly agitated state of your soul. And in your old age, when the book of passions is over, it will be too late even to smile. Your face will have lost all of that soft elasticity that allowed your expressions to change with so much ease. The Scissor of Time will have deepened those furrows drawn by the passions of your life: they will have become wrinkles that will never be erased. So what purpose could an awkward smile possibly have? It would only suggest ridiculous claims. An air of thoughtfulness and kindness will be all you really need. That is the natural order of things in the revolution that takes place on the face of a woman.[14]

Giustiniana established a pleasant, productive routine for herself. She wintered in Padua, making frequent forays into Venice.

In the summer she moved to Alticchiero, a delightful villa on the southern bank of the Brenta, just a couple of miles from Padua, that belonged to her old friend Senator Angelo Querini. After his release from jail in 1763, the senator, disillusioned with Venetian politics, had retired to this "rustic house with no view."[15] Over the years, he had transformed it into an elegant country retreat devoted to classicism and the art of the "philosophical garden."

Giustiniana's friendship with Querini went back to the 1750s, but in those days her heart had belonged entirely to Andrea. She had kept in touch with Querini over the years—they shared many of the same friends, Andrea certainly being the first among them—but their paths had seldom crossed again until she left Venice for Padua. When finally they had the opportunity to spend time in each other's company it was perhaps too late for a full-blown romance between them. Yet their friendship acquired a romantic tinge it never lost. At Alticchiero, Giustiniana was always more than a guest: she was the lady of the house.

In homage to her beloved senator she composed a lovely guidebook to the villa and the garden—an enlightened and highly entertaining tour of the Querini estate. It was published in Padua in 1787 with excellent prints of the sculptures that adorned the property.

There was another man in Giustiniana's life at that time, very different from the senator. Count Bartolomeo Benincasa was an impoverished adventurer running away from a failed marriage in his native Modena when he arrived in the Venetian Republic sometime around 1780 and found his way into Giustiniana's circle of friends. He was a restless soul with literary ambitions, which she admired, and he was also ten years younger than she. In little time he joined her household and became her secretary and administrator, and perhaps her lover as well.

Benincasa was the opposite of Querini: verbose, affected, and shady, he made pocket money passing information to the inquisitors about the senator and his guests at Alticchiero. Yet despite his duplicity, he remained devoted to Giustiniana until the end. In 1788, with his help, she published her only novel, *Les Morlacques*, a romantic tale of love and death set in the rugged mountains of Dalmatia. The book is imbued with social commentary inspired by Rousseau on the evils of the city and the essential goodness of man in nature, but the pathos she brought to the story—not to mention the vampires and fairies that populate its pages—are the product of an imagination that in many ways already belonged to the nineteenth century.

Les Morlacques was her greatest literary success. By 1790, at the age of fifty-three, Giustiniana was at the top of her game: beloved hostess, respected intellectual, accomplished writer. She had not remarried but seemed content with the affection of Querini and the devotion of Benincasa and her many friends. Describing her small salon in Padua, where men of sciences, writers, and artists mingled with foreign travelers, Casanova, who had moved on to Dux, in Bohemia, and was at last scribbling away at his memoirs, wrote that Giustiniana, though sadly not rich, nevertheless "shines for her wisdom and all the social virtues she possesses."[16]

She would not enjoy her triumph for long. The illness that took her to her grave the following year—most likely cancer of the uterus—was already spreading inside her. She battled with it for nine months and suffered excruciating pain. An anguished Benincasa dutifully related the progress of the illness in letters to family and friends. Giustiniana's twelve-year-old niece, Betsey, who was summering in the countryside north of Padua with her family, the Richard Wynnes, wrote in her diary: "The poor Countess is to die. There is no remedy for her. Papa says they are all in a very great distress about it."[17]

As death neared Andrea too arrived in Padua—an old friend drawn to his first love. He was "distraught" by the sight of her ravaged body and the pain she was suffering, and he grieved quietly at her bedside. During the night "she started hemorrhaging again"; a priest was called in and "she was given extreme unction."[18] In the diaphanous early morning light Andrea bid her his final farewell.

Giustiniana died on August 22, 1791, in the house she had rented for the summer: a small, elegant *palazzo* with a pretty garden. Benincasa wrote a long, tearful report on her death for the inquisitors. Querini nursed "the bitter wound"[19] in his heart and placed a marble bust of Giustiniana in the garden at Alticchiero. She was buried in the Church of San Benedetto in Padua. Her brother Richard, who was with her at the time of her death, had a small memorial tablet placed in the church, high above the entrance portal.

Giustiniana was greatly mourned. Her virtues were praised in every form available, from the elaborate Latin inscription on the memorial's marble plaque to a long panegyric printed by her friends. But to my mind the simple words of an obscure Paduan chronicler by the name of Abbé Gennari evoke her best. "She was very beautiful in her youth," he wrote in his diary on the day of her death. "And always lively and full of spirit."[20]

I like to think this is how Andrea remembered Giustiniana in the darkening rooms at Ca' Memmo, where his own death was now casting its shadow. As he grew older, he revisited more frequently those hopeful days of his youth, when his heart had been filled with love and the end of the Republic had not loomed so near. No doubt he sometimes traveled as far back as the day he had first seen Giustiniana, so starkly beautiful, in the house of Consul Smith. Were those memories ever tinged with regret? Andrea was never one to dwell morosely on the past, but surely the irony was not lost on him that he had sacrificed the great love of his life for the sake of a dying Republic. He had served with great distinction. He had traveled widely. He had become a statesman, respected at home and admired abroad. He had accomplished what had been expected of him—and more. Yet each year he had grown more disgusted with the lethargic ruling class to which he belonged and more disillusioned about the future of Venice. Like so many patricians of his generation, he had become a deeply cynical man. And he had tempered the bitterness in his soul by giving himself over to the earthly pleasures life still had to offer a man with appetite and, as he put it, "good teeth."[21]

Andrea's political beginnings had coincided with the end of the Seven Years' War in 1763. Europe was at peace again, and he still believed that the strength and prestige of the Republic could be restored to a degree with the right mix of policies. He also felt that any radical approach to change would be counterproductive; in this he was far more pragmatic than his friend Querini, who spent two years in jail for openly challenging the status quo. Instead, Andrea focused his considerable intellectual energies on learning the inner workings of Venice's venerable but outdated machinery of government. He learned fast and got himself elected to a succession of important administrative posts, blending into the bureaucracy as he waited for the most propitious moment to step forward and effect some real change.

On the personal side, his dalliance with M. failed to produce the stable relationship he had been looking for. But in 1763, at the age of thirty-four, he met a stunning girl some fifteen years younger than he with whom he began an affair that was to last, on and off, for more than two decades. Contarina Barbarigo was the beautiful daughter of her famously beautiful mother, Caterina Sagredo Barbarigo.* She had wit, flair, and glamour. Eighteenth-century miniatures depict her with sharp, striking features, her hair piled up in a very tall beehive. Like her mother, she grew up to become the most celebrated Venetian beauty of her generation.

Did Giustiniana unwittingly plant the idea of seducing Contarina in Andrea's head? In a letter she wrote to him during her depressing stay in Padua, back in the fall of 1760, Giustiniana mentioned paying a courtesy visit to Contarina's famous mother, Caterina: "Mon cher frère . . . I can assure you that I was impressed by how cultivated and pleasant a lady she was. Her daughters are absolute wonders, and the one called Contarina is so gracious and well mannered—as well as being a real beauty and therefore very similar to her mother—that she is seen as a true marvel here. . . . In fact, she would be considered a sheer delight anywhere."

Contarina, however, was destined for another member of the patriciate. In 1765 she married Marino Zorzi, but the marriage was soon dissolved because he was impotent. Her affair with Andrea resumed—if it had ever stopped. But the politics of marriage among the ruling class were inexorable. In 1769, the year before Giustiniana's return to Venice from Austria, it was Andrea's turn

*See p. 49.

to marry. His bride was Elisabetta Piovene, a pretty girl of twenty who came from a good family in Vicenza. He does not appear to have been deeply in love with her, but there was no reason to believe they could not have a decent marriage and raise a good family. They had two daughters, Lucietta and Paolina, upon whom Andrea doted.

Andrea's career, meanwhile, had reached an important crossroads. In 1771, after a decade-long apprenticeship, he made his first important political move: a bold attempt to free Venetian industry and commerce from the suffocating control of the guilds. The reforms he advocated were intelligent and well thought out, but he found himself face to face with the "obtuse indolence"[22] of the Senate. Ultimately defeated by the conservatives, he was nevertheless rewarded with the powerful post of governor of Padua.

He ran the city during much of the 1770s and became a popular governor. He devoted a great deal of his energies to an ambitious and somewhat extravagant architectural project—the creation of a vast oval plaza on the eastern rim of the city, known as Prato della Valle—in which he tried to put into practice some of the principles of rational architecture advocated by his teacher Father Lodoli. His stewardship of one of the largest cities in the Venetian State was deemed a success. In 1778 he was appointed ambassador to Constantinople, a prestigious post and, for Andrea, a highly symbolic one: his uncle Andrea Memmo, his role model and mentor, had been ambassador there half a century earlier.

From the point of view of his career, the 1770s were productive and rewarding. "Four men like Senator Memmo would be enough to govern Europe without difficulty,"[23] Emperor Joseph II of Austria is said to have declared after meeting Andrea. The statement might be apocryphal, but the currency it gained over the years reflected Andrea's growing reputation as a wise and effective statesman.

His marriage to Elisabetta, on the other hand, was not a success despite a fairly hopeful start. Andrea's continuous affair with Contarina cannot have helped. But family and friends mostly blamed Elisabetta's "bilious" character and poor health—not to mention her habit of drinking vinegar in the morning to stay thin. With time she grew weaker and became more withdrawn. When she died of "gastro-rheumatic fever"* in Venice in 1780, Andrea was not by her side but away in Constantinople, still serving as ambassador to the Porte.

During his five-year stint there—his first real time abroad—he began to see Venice's decline in sharper, more dramatic terms. Still, he did not give up looking for new opportunities that might give the Republic another lease on life. Like Giustiniana, he was an admirer of Empress Catherine the Great of Russia, and he worked tirelessly while in Constantinople to establish official relations with Moscow and build a powerful new commercial alliance with the emerging European power.

Upon his return to Venice in 1782, however, Andrea's confidence collapsed. The passivity and resignation of his peers depressed him profoundly. He accepted the ambassadorship to Rome, once an important post but by then little more than a sinecure. "I decided not to stay in Venice for a while," he explained to a friend, "because I knew it would have saddened me. I needed to distract myself for the sake of my health."24

He was fifty-four and a single parent with two daughters in tow when he arrived in the lazy and decadent Rome of Pope Pius VI. He had come to "distract" himself, as he had put it, and that is what he did. He cultivated the pleasures of a good table and threw himself into a whirlwind of sexual intrigue, becoming a favorite with Roman women—aging princesses as well as their shapely young maids. "Anything pleases these lovable sluts," he confided to a

---

*It was Giuseppe Perlasca, a well-known physician in Venice, who wrote that Elisabetta had "a bilious temperament" and was "frail on account of her abuse of vinegar, which she had taken in large quantities for a very long time early in the morning and on an empty stomach for fear of growing fat." She had developed "a yellowish mucus, itchy patches all over her body, insomnia, yellow blemishes." In addition, "her uterus was severely damaged, she had splitting headaches and gastro-rheumatic fevers." Perlasca ordered her to drink lemon juice and linseed oil, but she apparently drank only wine. Much to his frustration, she refused to be bled. A chronicler of those times, the Abbé Carlo Zilli, claims (see his manuscript memoirs quoted in Brunelli, *Un'amica del Casanova*, p. 260) that Perlasca attributed the actual cause of death "to the excessive amounts of mercury" his chief rival, the physician Fantuzzi, had prescribed to Elisabetta to remedy the consequences of a sexual indiscretion. Needless to say, this bit of information did not find its way into Perlasca's ten-page report to Andrea on Elisabetta's death, though it was apparently on everyone's lips in Venice.25

Florentine friend, "as long as they can possess a man who was never possessed by any woman for more than a few minutes." Tenderly, he added, "apart from la Rosenberg."[26]

Andrea took his job as a father very seriously—possibly more so than his position as ambassador. Despite his numerous gallant affairs, he made a point of spending time every day with Lucietta and Paolina, "my only true loves." He planned their education with the help of an able tutor and a French governess. "My girls will be beautiful and well educated. They're still a little rough around the edges, but far less than they would be if they had stayed in Venice."[27]

During his Roman days Andrea decided to rescue the memory of Father Lodoli from oblivion. The inquisitors had seized Lodoli's papers after his death in 1761, leaving them to rot in a damp cell in the prisons at the Ducal Palace. Two decades later, during one of his regular trips up to Venice, Andrea went rummaging there. All he found were piles of sodden and illegible paper. The discovery filled him with sadness. It also encouraged him to press on. He plumbed his own memory and used every scrap of information he could find—notes, letters, and above all the recollections of the monk's many devoted former students—to put together an extraordinary tribute to his teacher.

The first book of his two-volume work was published in 1786; the complete edition came out posthumously some fifty years later. *Elementi dell'architettura Lodoliana* was more than a book on Lodoli. The spirit of the 1740s and 1750s, when so many of the most promising sons of the Republic had "shaped their minds and improved their souls" at the school of the Franciscan monk, came to life again in its pages. In Andrea's eyes, Giustiniana had been an important part of that bygone world, so that the memories of the period became entwined with memories of "the one to whom I was entirely dedicated." In a whimsical, affectionate digression, he praised "her original mind" and those "rare qualities that made her soul sublime."[28]

Andrea's book was so rich in autobiographical references to his own youth that one has to wonder if the daily exercise of writing it, during those otherwise dissolute Roman days, was not also an attempt to redeem himself from the failure to live up to his own expectations.

His career, however, was not yet over. Just as he was distancing himself from the depressing political scene in Venice, the Maggior Consiglio, the supreme assembly of the Republic, elected him to succeed Andrea Tron, his political mentor, in the prestigious office of procuratore di San Marco. All at once he was catapulted back into the fray. His initial displeasure at having to leave behind his leisurely if somewhat futile Roman life quickly vanished. This unexpected tribute on the part of his peers renewed his vigor. He returned to Venice in 1787 and took up his new position amid great pomp, decking out the palace on the Grand Canal with banners and family crests and hosting the customary balls and receptions.

That same year, at the end of a long and difficult negotiation, Andrea married off his daughter Lucietta to Alvise Mocenigo, a member of one of the richest and most powerful Venetian families. (It was thanks to this marriage that Andrea's letters ended up at Palazzo Mocenigo, where my father found them two centuries later.) Andrea was doubly pleased: the match made sense from a practical point of view, and he was overjoyed because Lucietta and Alvise were genuinely in love with each other: "My Lucietta makes her husband happy, and he makes her happy. They are in love for their essential qualities, and they respect each other as much as they adore each other. They have become the paradigm of the enviable marriage. There are no displays of jealousy on either part nor the slightest appearance of infidelity."[29]

As was the custom, a stream of celebratory poems and miscellanies was printed at the time of the wedding. One slim publication, beautifully bound and illustrated, stood out among them. Giustiniana, by then living mostly in Padua, had come into town for the occasion and presented the bride and groom with a sweet allegorical composition in which Curiosity and Love conspired to join two lovers and then left the field to Perseverance—the only one who could make their happiness endure. She had written it in honor of Alvise and Lucietta, but it was, in fact, dedicated, in large, bold letters, to her own first great love—the father of the bride. She added these few lines, adapted from Lucretius, in which she invoked the aid of "nurturing Venus":

> *Thee I crave as partner in writing these verses*
> *I essay to fashion for my good Memmo,*
> *whom thou, goddess, hast willed at all times*
> *to excel, endowed with all gifts.*[30]

Andrea entered new negotiations to marry his second daughter, Paolina, to Luigi Martinengo, heir to another big fortune. The talks proceeded laboriously and then stalled altogether when the inquisitors put the future groom under house arrest for his licentious behavior (Andrea complained that Luigi had "taken on a Roman slut" while declaring his love for Paolina). They eventually resumed, and the wedding took place in 1789. The price, however, was high: Andrea's financial resources were so depleted that he was forced to cede Ca' Memmo to the Martinengos as part of Paolina's dowry.

Now that he faced the prospect of living out his old age in solitude, Andrea seriously considered marrying again. He broached the idea with his old flame, Contarina, who was not against it. But the conversation apparently soured over practical arrangements and led, unexpectedly, to the end of their long affair. "After twenty-five years of gallantry, love, and friendship," he wrote to Casanova bitterly, ". . . my relationship with Signora Contarina has suddenly ended on account of a trifling matter—and will not resume ever again."[31] He did not say what the trifling matter was.

Casanova frowned at the lost opportunity. He reminded his old friend that Contarina was rich and could have helped finance Andrea's renascent political career. Andrea was piqued: "You are wrong if you think she could have assisted me. . . . She is not as rich as she was. . . . I was going to marry her out of friendship, not out of material interest. . . . Naturally she would not have been a burden on me in any way, not even in bed—she would have had a separate apartment. I was not very keen on all that flabby flesh. . . . Good company, mutual assistance in our approaching old age, and nothing more. With time, the assurance of a comfortable life and good . . . food on the table—since you ask, I will tell you I am still a glutton, and though I eat less I still eat a lot since all my teeth are still healthy."[32]

Like an aging Don Juan, Andrea enjoyed gabbing about his active sex life with Casanova. "You cannot imagine what I have had to go through to cut off a useless correspondence with twenty ladies from different countries, all of whom wish me to believe they are endlessly in love with me," he bragged. Venice, he added, offered more than enough distractions: "I spend my time with my lovable old lady friends, and with even more lovable young ones. They are beautiful and crazy, and they might not give me everything I ask, but they still give me plenty."[33]

When he turned sixty he explained the logic of his frantic womanizing to his old companion: "I need the release, and since I do not gamble and there is nothing I want to buy for myself and I cannot stand trying to reason with our politicians and having nothing more to read . . . I spend my time with the ladies. Oh, you should see, Casanova, how many gorgeous girls have suddenly appeared in our little world here since you left! Surely you understand me if I tell you I try with every one in the hope of succeeding with a few. Without ever losing my sleep or my appetite over them."[34] In truth, he was not always up to par. To a less promiscuous friend than Casanova he once admitted offering a lady friend "a cock that was not as hard as she deserved."[35]

As the powerful procuratore di San Marco, Andrea seemed a strong candidate for the supreme office of doge. The old reformers—the friends of his youth—rallied around him in a futile burst of political activism. Andrea's vanity was certainly flattered by this belated support, but he quickly saw the drawbacks of a candidacy. They were financial, to begin with: it would be a very costly political campaign, and he simply didn't have the money to run. Furthermore, the Memmo family was on the way to extinction—neither Andrea nor his brothers had a male heir. Why bother to enter the race, he asked, if there would be no more Memmo descendents "to enjoy the glory" a *corno*, or ducal cap, would bring to the house? Finally, and perhaps most important, why give up the good life to spend his last years sequestered in the Ducal Palace? "Once elected doge," he explained to Casanova, "if I should chance to see a countess or a marchionness with beautiful eyes and pretty tits, light-hearted and lively, how do you suppose I could have her without being able to seduce her with the tools that I, as procuratore, am still allowed to use? For pity's sake, don't take the pleasure of women away from me, for it will lighten my spirit when I am a hundred years old. . . . Doges cannot indulge in such divine treatment."[36]

For all his genuine misgivings, Andrea's political ambition won the day. When the old doge, Paolo Renier, died in February 1789, he entered the race. For a moment, it looked as if he had a real chance of being elected by a reformist alliance. But it was much too late in the game. The dominant conservative forces in the old Venetian oligarchy coalesced to neutralize his candidacy. Andrea was outsmarted. On March 9, 1789—four months before the storming of the Bastille—the Maggior Consiglio elected a man so timorous of the weight that had been thrust onto his shoulders that he tearfully begged to be spared the honor. His name was Ludovico Manin, and he made history as Venice's last doge.

After his electoral defeat, Andrea threw himself back into work. Interestingly, he focused his efforts on Dalmatia—the very same region that had inspired Giustiniana to publish her novel, *Les Morlacques*, only the year before. The backwardness of this Venetian territory just across the Adriatic had become a vexing problem for the Republic and a real embarrassment. Andrea worked tirelessly on a plan to improve living conditions in those poor, disease-ridden provinces. After much prodding and cajoling, he was finally able to get a package of agricultural and administrative reforms approved by the Senate in 1791, around the time Giustiniana died.

Andrea's own health had already started to deteriorate. Gangrene was slowly spreading in one of his legs, and before the year was out he was confined to his rooms at Ca' Memmo. It was not just the atrocious pain that made the ensuing months so hard to bear; he was dying a poor man. There was very little left of the Memmo possessions; many of them had been wasted on an expensive political career. Even the family *palazzo* in which he was dying was no longer his. "Memmo is destitute," wrote a friend sadly. "He has had to give up his gondola too."[37]

It took Andrea another year to die. An endless stream of friends and former lovers came to see him as he lay slowly rotting in his bed, surrounded by medicines and surgical instruments and confabulating doctors. Among the well-wishers was a French artist and traveler by the name of Dominique-Vivant Denon, who later went to Egypt with Napoleon Bonaparte and became the founding director of the new Musée du Louvre. The man who would one day be known as "the Eye of Napoleon" kept a detailed record of Andrea's last days. "I went over to see poor Memmo this evening," he wrote to a friend on October 15, 1792. "It looks quite bad, and he knows it." Two days later: "His old lovers insist his blood is excellent. . . . But the disease keeps gaining ground." On October 26 Denon ran into Memmo's doctor, who said nothing "but lifted his eyes to the sky." He went back to see Andrea on November 1: "They amputated his big toe. . . . It is what I call uselessly tormenting the victim. At this point one must either amputate the leg or let him die as peacefully as possible."[38]

Andrea's ordeal lasted another two months. He died on January 27, 1793.

Four years later Bonaparte invaded northern Italy. With the French Army fast approaching, the Venetian Senate voted hurriedly for surrender and the Republic died a swift and inglorious death.

Postscript

"At least Andrea and Giustiniana did not live to see the end of their beloved Republic!" my father scribbled wistfully at the end of his notes to the letters. It was a typical thing for him to say: two centuries after Bonaparte's victorious invasion, the old Venetian in him still ached at the Republic's ignominious end. As I read those words I was also reminded of how much he had identified with Andrea, not to mention the terrible crush he had developed on Giustiniana and his disappointment at how things had turned out between his two lovers.

In September 2001, nearly five years after my father's death, I went to Venice with my family to write the book he had wanted to write. We found a small house on the Campiello agli Incurabili, just off the Zattere. It was right on the water and had a small enclosed garden filled with oleanders and laurels and roving wisteria. In daytime the reflections of the sun danced on the walls and created a sense of perpetual movement. At night, when the city was silent, the rhythmic sloshing in the canal signaled the ebb and flow of the tide.

I had never lived in Venice before. To me it had always been the city of my father's childhood. I saw it as I imagine most people do: as a museum full of tourists, a dead city. But as Venetians well know, it is much more than that. In Venice the past has remained alive in a vivid, disorienting way. It is with you all the time. It blends with the present. And sometimes, walking around the city, my head filled with Andrea and Giustiniana, I found myself slipping back in time so effortlessly that I didn't know what century I was living in anymore.

I passed by Ca' Memmo every week on my way to my youngest son's music class. It stands imposingly to the east of the vaporetto stop of San Marcuola, on the north shore of the Grand Canal. Consul Smith's *palazzo* is a little further along, on the same side of the Grand Canal, before the bend of the Rialto Bridge. It was recently converted into a luxury condominium for wealthy foreigners, yet the outward appearance of the building is the same as when Andrea and Giustiniana exchanged their first furtive kisses there two and a half centuries ago. Whenever I went by the very grand Palazzo Tiepolo, now Palazzo Papadopoli, I scratched my head trying to figure out which was the window on the mezzanine floor from which Andrea used to woo Giustiniana when the Wynnes lived next door.

The buildings are the same. The streets haven't changed. Even the names on the doorbells are familiar. Gradually, I came to see how much the love story my father had dug up in the dusty attic of Palazzo Mocenigo had taken him back not just to the city of his childhood, but to a place of the imagination where the great Venetian Republic lived on. And how the unraveling of Andrea and Giustiniana's long affair had evoked in him—in a way that was still somewhat mysterious to me but that I was beginning to understand—the much vaster demise that was taking place all around them.

On the other hand, I am sure my father took comfort in learning, as he progressed in his research, that his two heroes went on to have full and fascinating lives. Each went his own way: Giustiniana became an accomplished author; Andrea became Venice's last great statesman. But over the years they remained very close. Their world—the vanishing world of the Venetian Republic—was small enough that they were never very far apart. And when their paths did cross, they always met with that tenderness a first great love can create to last a lifetime.

Would Andrea and Giustiniana have been as distraught by the passing of the Venetian Republic as my father assumed? Probably not. Andrea always knew his life was tied to the fate of the city. But as much as he revered the Venice of the past, one has to wonder whether he would have shed a single tear for the passing of the inglorious Republic he had known in his lifetime. True, he was spared the final demise because his own death came sooner, but he was too intelligent a man not to see that Venice could not continue to survive by small concessions to change. By the time the gangrene began to spread in his own body, he knew the Republic was also doomed. As for Giustiniana, she died at a time when her life was no longer rooted in Venice. She lived mostly on the mainland. Her horizon had widened considerably. She traveled often. She wrote in French. She published her books in London. She was self-sufficient, independent, and worldly. In many ways she had become the woman she had tentatively begun to sketch in her letters to Andrea many years before, when she had so accurately predicted their separate fates: "You have to live in Venice, I don't."

NOTES

A Note on Sources

The letters on which I have based *A Venetian Affair* do not make a complete set. In Chapters 1 to 4 I have relied on Andrea's original letters to Giustiniana, which are still in my family's possession. Those letters are undated, and their exact chronological order is unknown. I have used them in the order that seemed to me most logical, but it is quite possible that certain events—minor ones, I hope—occurred either before or after the time in which I have set them. This section also contains several letters from Giustiniana to Andrea from the period 1756–1757. Chapters 5 to 9, on the other hand, are based entirely on Giustiniana's letters to Andrea. These are not the original manuscripts but handwritten copies that I suspect date back to the end of the eighteenth century. Of these, two incomplete and overlapping sets are available to the public. One is in the Biblioteca Civica di Padova (Bruno Brunelli used this set to write *Un'amica del Casanova*, his book about Giustiniana, published in 1924). The other was purchased in Venice by James Rives Childs in the early fifties and is now at Mr. Childs's alma mater, Randolph Macon College, in Ashland, Virginia. There exists at least one other set, identical to the one in Ashland, which is the property of Giuseppe Bignami, a Genoese collector.

It is unclear who transcribed the original letters from Giustiniana to Andrea and why he or she did so. I am inclined to believe that Andrea returned the letters to Giustiniana and someone in her entourage—possibly Bartolomeo Benincasa—transcribed them later on, perhaps with the idea of publishing them as an epistolary novel when the two protagonists were no longer alive. But until the original letters by Giustiniana surface, we will not know how faithful the copies really are. Of course, historians have by now corroborated most of the events in this extraordinary tale. But it is quite possible that the mysterious transcriber of the original letters indulged in a little editing for the sake of convenience.

Prologue

1. Gustav Gugitz, "Eine Geliebte Casanovas," *Zeitschrift für Bucherfreunde* (1910), 151–171; and *Giacomo Casanova und sein Lebensroman* (Vienna: Strache, 1921), pp. 228–261. Gugitz does not explain why Casanova chose to call Giustiniana's mother Madame XCV and Giustiniana Miss XCV. James Rives Childs suggests that the initials stood for "Xè'l Cavalier Vinne," Venetian for "It is Chevalier Wynne"; see Francis L. Mars, "Pour le dossier de Miss XCV," *Casanova Gleanings* 5 (1962): 21. More simply, the X could stand for the Latin

Notes

preposition "ex"; in this case the initials could mean "formerly of Chevalier Wynne." The letter "w" does not exist in the Italian alphabet and in the eighteenth century was often transcribed as "v."

2. Bruno Brunelli, *Un'amica del Casanova* (Naples: Remo Sandron, 1924), 21.

3. "L'epistolario, ultimo giallo," *La Nazione*, January 22, 1997, iii.

4. Jean Georgelin, *Venise au siècle des lumières* (Paris: Ecole des Hautes Etudes en Sciences Sociales, 1978), 18.

5. Giustiniana Wynne, *Pièces morales et sentimentales* (London: J. Robson, 1785), 36.

6. Luca De Biase, "Vincoli nuziali ed extramatrimoniali nel patriziato veneto in epoca goldoniana: i sentimenti, gli interessi," *Studi Trentini di Scienze Storiche*, vol. LXI, no. 4 (1982): 363. On the topic of clandestine marriages, see Gaetano Cozzi, "Padri, figli e matrimoni clandestini," *La Cultura*, no. 2–3 (1976): 169–213; and "Causarum matrimoniorum clandestinorum," Archivio di Stato di Venezia, Inquisitori di Stato, envelopes 528–534.

Chapter One

1. Gianfranco Torcellan, *Una figura della Venezia settecentesca: Andrea Memmo* (Venice: 1963), 23 and n. 2. In 1740 the Memmos' income had been 10,000 ducats a year, according to the official census of that year. See Georgelin, *Venise au siècle des lumières*, 521.

2. Marco Foscarini, *Della letteratura veneziana,* vol. 1 (Padua: 1752), 258, n. 99.

3. *Elogio di Andrea Memmo Cavalier Procuratore di S. Marco* (Venice: 1793), 5–6.

4. Andrea Memmo, *Elementi dell'architettura Lodoliana* (Zara: Battara, 1833), 77–78.

5. Pierre Jean Grosley, *Nouveaux Mémoires ou observations sur l'Italie et sur les italiens*, vol. 2 (London: Jean Nourse, 1764), 10.

6. Carlo Goldoni, *Il filosofo inglese*, in *Opere*, vol. 5 (Milan: Mondadori, 1959), 261.

7. Smith entered into negotiations with the Crown during the last years of King George II's reign. But it was not until after King George III's accession to the throne in 1760 that the talks accelerated. The deal was finally sealed in 1763. Smith's paintings and drawings became the cornerstone of the Windsor collection, and the Bibliotheca Smithiana is part of the Royal Library at the British Museum. On the sale of Consul Smith's collection to George III, see in particular Frances Vivian, *Il Console Smith, mercante e collezionista* (Vicenza: Neri Pozza, 1971), 69–93; Francis Haskell, *Patrons and Painters, Art and Society in Baroque Italy* (New Haven, Conn.: Yale University Press, 1980), 310; Anthony Blunt and Edward Croft-Murray, *Venetian Drawings of the XVII and XVIII Centuries in the Collection of Her Majesty the Queen at Windsor Castle* (London: Phaidon Press, 1957).

8. Quoted in Torcellan, *Una figura*, p. 42. For a more detailed description of Andrea's ideas about the theater and his admiration for French culture and language, see his report "Storia della Deputazione Straordinaria alle Arti" in the

Archivio di Stato di Venezia, "Inquisitorato alle arti," envelope 2, bundle 4, 33–36.

9. From Goldoni's dedication to Andrea in *L'Uomo di mondo*, previously published in *Opere*, vol. 1, 777–778.

10. "Appunti sul Giovan Battista Mannuzzi (1750–59)," in Archivio di Stato di Venezia, Inquisitori di Stato, referta del 22 marzo 1755. On the general topic of secret informers see Giovanni Comisso, *Agenti segreti veneziani nel '700* (Milan: Bompiani, 1945). Giovan Battista Mannuzzi was the best-known spy operating in Venice at the time, and he kept a close eye on Casanova. In an earlier report he described him as "a man with a tendency to hyperbole who manages to live at the expense of this or that person on the strength of his lies and his ability to cheat." Another insightful report by a lesser-known informer stated that Andrea's brother Bernardo was somewhat torn by his relationship with Casanova: "he is often with him, and he alternatively loves him and thrashes him." In general the government's once formidable system of informers suffered a steady decline in the eighteenth century. By 1760 the budget had dwindled to 4,000 ducats and only three spies were receiving full pay. One official deplored the fact that they were "so few and so mediocre."

11. De Biase, *"Vincoli nunziali,"* 319–367.

12. Lady Mary Wortley Montagu to her daughter, Lady Bute, October 3, 1758, *The Complete Letters of Lady Mary Wortley Montagu*, vol. 3, ed. Robert Halsband (Oxford: Clarendon Press, 1967), 179.

13. Quoted in Brunelli, *Un'amica del Casanova*, 4.

14. Wynne, *Pièces morales*, 195.

15. Ibid., 34.

16. Giacomo Casanova, *History of My Life*, vol. 3 (Baltimore: Johns Hopkins University Press, 1997), 172.

17. Wynne, *Pièces morales*, 35.

18. Letters of Andrea Memmo to Giustiniana Wynne (author's collection).

19. Casanova, *History of My Life*, vol. 5 (Baltimore: Johns Hopkins University Press, 1997), 171–172.

20. Wynne, *Pièces morales*, 35–36.

21. Ibid., 36.

22. Letters of Andrea Memmo to Giustiniana Wynne (author's collection).

Chapter Two

1. Pompeo Molmenti, *La storia di Venezia nella vita privata*, vol. 3 (Bergamo: Istituto italiano di artigrafiche, 1908), 175.

2. Giacoma Casanova, *History of My Life*, vol. 4 (Baltimore: Johns Hopkins University Press, 1997), 75.

3. Ibid., 191, 249.

Notes

Chapter Three

1. From the diary of Johannes Heinzelmann (December 10, 1755), quoted in Vivian, *Il console Smith*, 52.
2. Lady Montagu to Lady Bute, *Complete Letters*, vol. 3, 127.
3. Casanova, *History of My Life*, vol. 4, 136.
4. Murray to Holderness, August 15, 1755, British Museum, Egerton Papers, 3464, f. 272.
5. Lady Montagu to Lady Bute, May 13, 1758, *Complete Letters*, vol. 3, 145.
6. John Fleming, *Robert Adam and His Circle* (London: John Murray, 1962), 171.
7. Murray to Holderness, October 1, 1756, British Museum, Egerton Papers, 3464, f. 274.

Chapter Four

1. "Matrimoni Segreti," Anno 1757, n. 47, Archivio della Curia Patriarcale di Venezia.
2. John Eglin, *Venice Transfigured: The Myth of Venice in British Culture 1660–1797* (New York: Palgrave, 2001), 57.
3. Vivian, *Il console Smith*, 55.
4. "Atti di morte," Archivio di San Marcuola, Curia Patriarcale. Curiously, Andrea Memmo's biographer, Gianfranco Torcellan, states that Pietro "died prematurely" and was therefore unable to exert on his son an influence comparable to that of his older brother Andrea, the family patriarch. Torcellan, *Una figura della Venezia settecentesca*, 27. In reality Pietro died long after his older brother, so it appears his lesser influence on young Andrea was related more to character than to age.
5. For Antonio Maria Zanetti's dealings with Smith, see in particular Vivian, *Il console Smith*, and Haskell, *Patrons and Painters*.

Chapter Five

1. Vivian, *Il console Smith*, 210. The painting was eventually sold to George III. As for *The Woman with Dropsy*, it was taken to Paris by French troops in 1798 after Napoleon's invasion of northern Italy. Today it hangs in the Musée du Louvre, where it is registered as "the first gift to the Louvre."
2. Ralph Woodford was secretary to the British delegation in Turin. When Giustiniana met him, he was acting chargé d'affaires as Lord Bristol, the outgoing ambassador, had left in August, and the new ambassador, John Stuart MacKenzie, would not arrive until November 14, 1758. See John Ingamells, *A Dictionary of English and Irish Travellers in Italy 1701–1800* (New Haven, Conn.: Yale University Press, 1997), 1017.

Chapter Six

1. The Duc de Luynes died on November 2, 1758; *Gazette de France*, November 1758.
2. *Gazette de France*, December 1758.

3. *Mercure de France*, February 1759.
4. Casanova, *History of My Life*, vol. 5, 170.
5. Ibid., 172.
6. Ibid., 196.
7. Jean-François Marmontel, *Mémoires*, ed. John Renwick (Paris: Clermont-Ferrand, G. de Bussac, 1972), 104.
8. Niccolò Erizzo to Antonio Grimani, April 1, 1759, James Rives Childs Collection, Randolph Macon College, Ashland, Va.
9. Tommaso Farsetti to Andrea Memmo, March 26, 1759, James Rives Childs Collection.

Chapter Seven

1. In describing Giustiniana's escape from Paris I have used the information contained in her letter to Andrea dated June 24, 1759. The facts coincide roughly with those provided by Casanova in his *History of My Life* (see vol. 5, p. 212). Giustiniana wrote to Andrea that she had left Paris for Conflans on the morning of April 5. However, Mother Eustachia declared in a notarized statement that Giustiniana arrived at the convent on April 4 (see Francis L. Mars, "Pour le dossier de Miss XCV," *Casanova Gleanings* 5 [1962]: 25), and I have used that date.
2. Casanova, *History of My Life*, vol. 5, 182.
3. Casanova, *History of My Life*, vol. 5, 188.
4. Ibid., 187.
5. *Déposition de Reine Demay au commissaire Thiéron*. Archives Nationales (Châtelet), 10873, liasse 154. First quoted in Charles Henry, "Jacques Casanove de Seingalt et la critique historique," *Revue Historique* 41 (novembre–décembre 1889), 314.
6. Ibid., 315.
7. Casanova, *History of My Life*, vol. 5, 192.
8. "Mémoire de Emmanuel Jean de la Coste à Monsieur de Sartine, maître des requêtes et lieutenant général de la police de la Ville de Paris," May 2, 1760, Archives de la Bastille, Ravaisson-Mollien, 12099.
9. Casanova, *History of My Life*, vol. 5, 196.
10. Ibid., vol. 5, 198.
11. Ibid., 206.
12. "Naturalité à Justine Françoise Antoine Wynne . . . , Par le Roy, Versailles, 13 mars, 1759." The document, which also spells out in detail all of Giustiniana's rights as a French citizen, was published in its entirety in Mars, "Pour le dossier de Miss XCV," 27.
13. Casanova, *History of My Life*, vol. 5, 185.
14. Ibid., 238.
15. Ibid., 240.
16. Ibid., 242.
17. Anonymous letter to Andrea Memmo, July 10, 1759, James Rives Childs Collection.
18. Tommaso Farsetti to Andrea Memmo, September 3, 1759, James Rives Childs Collection.

Notes

19. Niccolò Erizzo to Andrea Memmo, May 27, 1759, James Rives Childs Collection.
20. Casanova, *History of My Life*, vol. 5, 242.
21. "Alexandre Fortier, notaire au coin de la rue de Richelieu et de la rue Neuve des Petits Champs," Archives Nationales, Minutier Central, Etude XXXI. Quoted in Mars, *"Pour le dossier de Miss XCV,"* 24.
22. Mars, *"Pour le dossier de Miss XCV,"* 25.
23. Anonymous letter to Andrea Memmo, July 10, 1759, James Rives Childs Collection.
24. Giustiniana Wynne to Andrea Memmo, Conflans, June 24, 1759, James Rives Childs Collection.
25. Anonymous letter to Andrea Memmo, July 10, 1759, James Rives Childs Collection.
26. Ibid.

Chapter Eight

1. Horace Walpole, *Memoirs of the Reign of King George II*, vol. 1, ed. John Brooke, (New Haven, Conn.: Yale University Press, 1985) 132.
2. Ibid.
3. Lord Newcastle to the Earl of Hardwick, January 2, 1760, British Library, Manuscripts, Additionals 35406.
4. Walpole, *Memoirs*, vol. 1, 132.
5. Lady Montagu to Lady Bute, October 3, 1758, *Complete Letters*, vol. 3, 179.
6. "The Year Fifty-Nine. A New Song," *The Gentleman's Magazine* XXIX (December 1759), 595.
7. Horace Walpole, *The Letters of Horace Walpole*, vol. 3, ed. Peter Cunningham (London: Richard Bentley, 1857), 263.
8. Lady Montagu to Lady Bute, November 9, 1759, *Complete Letters*, vol. 3, 227.
9. Ibid.
10. Lord Newcastle to the Earl of Hardwick, January 2, 1760, British Library, Manuscripts, Additionals 35406.
11. *The Gentleman's Magazine* XXX (February 1760), 44.
12. "Account of Lord Ferrers," *The Gentleman's Magazine* XXX (May 1760), 230–236.

Chapter Nine

1. Georges Cucuel, *La Pouplinière et la musique de chambre au XVIIIème siècle* (Paris: Fishbacher, 1913), 242.

Epilogue

1. Ingamells, *A Dictionary of English and Irish Travellers*, 672.
2. John Murray to Lord Holderness, December 1760, British Library, Manuscripts, Egremont 3464, ff. 272–286.

3. John Murray to William Pitt, July 10, 1761, British Library, Manuscripts, SP 99/68, ff., 184–185.

4. Chiara Michiel to Lady Montagu, March 10, 1762, *Complete Letters*, vol. 3, 288, n. 2.

5. Lady Montagu to Chiara Michiel, April 1762, *Complete Letters*, vol. 3, 288.

6. Count de Rosenberg to Prince von Kaunitz, Venice, March 21, 1762, quoted in Gugitz, *Giacomo Casanova*, 250.

7. Lady Montagu to Chiara Michiel, London, May 8, 1762, *Complete Letters*, vol. 3, 292.

8. Annotazioni n. 537, January 9, 1763, Inquisitori di Stato, Archivio di Stato di Venezia.

9. Ibid.

10. Statement by Lord Sandwich, London, May 21, 1764; quoted in Gugitz, *Giacomo Casanova*, 252.

11. Giustiniana Wynne to Prince Von Kaunitz, Klagenfurt, July 30, 1764; quoted in Gugitz, *Giacomo Casanova*, 254.

12. William Beckford, *Dreams, Waking Thoughts and Incidents*, ed. Robert Gemmett (Rutherford, 1971), 118.

13. Casanova's letter and Giustiniana's reply, dated March 18, 1782, appear in Aldo Ravà, *Lettere di donne a Casanova* (Milan: Treves, 1912), 227–228.

14. Wynne, *Pièces morales et sentimentales*, pp. 112–113.

15. Giustiniana Wynne, *Alticchiero* (Padua: 1787), 2.

16. Casanova, *History of My Life*, vol. 3, 172.

17. Elizabeth Wynne, diary entry June 23, 1791, *The Wynne Diaries*, ed. Anne Fremantle, vol. 1 (Oxford: Oxford University Press, 1935), 67.

18. The description of Andrea at Giustiniana's deathbed is in a letter by his daughter Lucietta to her husband, Alvise Mocenigo, dated June 17, 1791. The author's private collection.

19. Angelo Querini to Clemente Sibiliato, August 24, 1791, in *Alcune lettere inedite di illustri veneziani a Clemente Sibiliato* (Padua: 1839).

20. Abate Gennari, "Notizie giornaliere," ms. in the Biblioteca del Seminario, Padua, cod. 551.

21. Andrea Memmo to Giacomo Casanova, July 9, 1788, *Epistolari veneziani del secolo XVIII*, ed. Pompeo Molmenti (Milan: Remo Sandron, 1914).

22. Gianfranco Torcellan, "Andrea Memmo," in *Illuministi italiani*, vol. 7. (Milan: Ricciardi, 1965).

23. Brunelli, *Un'amica del Casanova*, 277.

24. Andrea Memmo to Giulio Perini, September 17, 1783, Archivio di Stato di Firenze, Acquisti e Doni, 94, bundle 146.

25. Biblioteca civica, Correr Manuscripts, Misc. IX, 1138.

26. Andrea Memmo to Giulio Perini, November 2, 1784, Archivio di Stato di Firenze, Acquisti e Doni 94, bundle 146.

27. Andrea Memmo to Giulio Perini, April 30, 1785, Archivio di Stato di Firenze, Acquisti e Doni 94, bundle 146.

28. Andrea Memmo, *Elementi dell' architettura Lodoliana*, 166.

Notes

29. Andrea Memmo to Giacomo Casanova, July 26, 1788, *Carteggi casanoviani* (Florence: Archivio Storico Italiano, 1911), 330.

30. Giustiniana Wynne, Countess Rosenberg, *À André Memmo Chevalier de l'Étiole d'Or et procurateur de Saint Marc, à l'occasion du mariage de sa fille ainée avec Louis Mocenigo* (Venice: Rosa, 1787).

31. Andrea Memmo to Giacomo Casanova, July 9, 1788, *Epistolari veneziani del secolo XVIII*, ed. Pompeo Molmenti, 192.

32. Ibid.

33. Ibid.

34. Ibid.

35. Andrea Memmo to Giulio Perini, Archivio di Stato di Firenze, Acquisti e Doni, 94, bundle 146.

36. Andrea Memmo to Giacomo Casanova, March 29, 1787, *Epistolari veneziani del secolo XVIII*, 185.

37. Pietro Zaguri to Giacomo Casanova, January 15, 1791, *Epistolari veneziani del secolo XVIII*, 119.

38. Dominique-Vivant Denon, *Lettres à Bettine*, ed. Piergiorgio Brigliadori et al., (Arles: Actes Sud, 1999), 126, 129, 137, 142.

SELECT BIBLIOGRAPHY

Archives

Archives de la Bastille, Paris
Archives Nationales (Châtelet), Paris
Archivio della Curia Patriarcale di Venezia
Archivio di Stato di Firenze
Archivio di Stato di Venezia
Biblioteca Civica Correr, Venice
Biblioteca Civica di Padova
British Library (Manuscripts), London
Biblioteca Marciana, Venice (Ulrich Middeldorf Collection)
Library, Randolph Macon College, Ashland,
Virginia (James Rives Childs Collection)

Secondary sources

Anderson, Fred. *Crucible of War: The Seven Years' War and the Fate of Empire in British North America, 1754–1766.* New York: Knopf, 2000.

Barbier, Edmond Jean François. *Journal historique et anecdotique du règne de Louis XV.* Paris: Renouard, 1847–56 (4 vols.).

Beckford, William. *Dreams, Waking Thoughts and Incidents.* Edited by Robert Gemmett. Rutherford, 1971.

Bernis, François-Joaquin de. *Mémoires du cardinal de Bernis.* Paris: Mercure de France, 2000.

Bignami, Giuseppe. "Costantina dalle Fusine: un incontro," *Intermédiaire des Casanovistes* 13 (1996): 23.

———. *Mademoiselle X.C.V.* Genoa: Pirella, 1985 (an introduction to Giustiniana's work).

Blunt, Anthony, and Croft-Murray Edward. *Venetian Drawings of the XVII & XVIII Centuries in the Collection of Her Majesty the Queen of Windsor Castle.* London: Phaidon Press, 1957.

Brooke, John. *King George III.* London: Constable, 1972.

Brosses, Charles de. *Lettres d' Italie du président de Brosses.* Paris: Mercure de France, 1986.

Brunelli, Bruno. *Un'amica del Casanova.* Naples: Remo Sandron, 1924. In English, *Casanova Loved Her.* New York: Liveright, 1929.

Select Bibliography

Brusatin, Manlio. "Qualche donna e l'architettura funzionale a Venezia nel XVIII secolo," *Scritti di Amici per Maria Cionini*. Turin: 1977.

———. *Venezia nel Settecento: stato, architettura, territorio*. Turin: Einaudi, 1980.

Capon, Gaston. *Casanova à Paris*. Paris: Schemit, 1913.

Casanova, Giacomo. *Fuga dai Piombi*. Milan: Rizzoli, 1950.

———. *History of My Life* (12 vols.). Translated by Willard Trask. Baltimore: Johns Hopkins University Press, 1997.

Childs, J. Rives. *Casanova*. London: Allen & Unwin, 1961.

Comisso, Giovanni. *Agenti segreti veneziani nel '700*. Milan: Bompiani, 1945.

Craveri, Benedetta. *La civiltà della conversazione*. Milan: Adelphi, 2001.

———. *Madame du Deffand e il suo mondo*. Milan: Adelphi, 1982.

Cucuel, Georges. *La Pouplinière et la musique de chambre au XVIIIème siècle*. Paris: Fishbacher, 1913.

Damerini, Gino. *Settecento veneziano*. Milano: Mondadori, 1939.

Da Ponte, Lorenzo. *Memorie*. Milano: Garzanti, 1976.

Darnton, Robert. *The Business of Enlightenment*. Cambridge: Belknap Press, 1979.

Davis, James C. *The Decline of the Venetian Nobility as a Ruling Class*. Baltimore: Johns Hopkins University Press, 1962.

Denon, Dominique-Vivant. *Lettres à Bettine*. Edited by Piergiorgio Brigliadori et al. Arles: Actes Sud, 1999.

Desprat, Jean-Paul. *Le cardinal de Bernis (1715–1794): la belle ambition*. Paris: Perrin, 2000.

Eglin, John. *Venice Transfigured: The Myth of Venice in British Culture 1660–1797*. New York: Palgrave, 2001.

Einaudi, Luigi. "L'economia pubblica veneziana dal 1736 al 1755." *La Riforma Sociale* 14 (1904).

Fleming, John. *Robert Adam and His Circle*. London: John Murray, 1962.

Freemantle, Anne, ed. *The Wynne Diaries*. Oxford: Oxford University Press, 1935.

Fumaroli, Marc. *L'Age de l'éloquence*. Paris: Champion, 1980.

George, M. D. *London Life in the 18th Century*. London: Penguin, 1966.

Georgelin, Jean. *Venise au siècle des Lumières*. Paris: École des Hautes Etudes de Sciences Sociales, 1978.

Goldoni, Carlo. *Memorie*. Torino: Einaudi, 1967.

———. *Opere*. Milan: Mondadori, 1959.

Gozzi, Carlo. *Memorie inutili (1722–1806)*. Turin: Unione tipografica edtrice torinese, 1923.

Grosley, Pierre-Jean. *Nouveaux mémoires, ou observations sur l'Italie et les italiens*. London: Jean Nourse, 1764.

———. *A Tour to London* (2 vols.). London: Lockyer Davis, 1772.

Gugitz, Gustav. "Eine Geliebte Casanovas." In *Zeitschrift für Bucherfreunde*, 1910, 151–171.

———. *Giacomo Casanova und sein Lebensroman*. Vienna: Strache, 1921.

Haskell, Francis. *Patrons and Painters, Art and Society in Baroque Italy*. New Haven, Conn.: Yale University Press, 1980.

Havelock, Ellis. "An Anglo-Italian friend of Casanova's," *Anglo-Italian Review* 2, no. 12, 206–220.

Henry, Charles. "Jacques Casanova de Seingalt et la critique historique." *Revue Historique* 41 (novembre–décembre 1889), 311–316.

Infelise, Mario, ed. *Carlo Lodoli: Della censura dei libri*. Venice: Marsilio, 2001.

Ingamells, John. *A Dictionary of English and Irish Travellers in Italy 1701–1800*. New Haven, Conn.: Yale University Press, 1997.

Isenberg, Nancy. "Mon cher frère: Eros mascherato nell'epistolario di Giustiniana Wynne a Andrea Memmo (1758–1760)." In *Trame parentali/trame letterarie*, ed. M. Del Sapio. Naples: Liguori, 2000, 251–265.

Lane, Frederic C. *Venice, a Maritime Republic*. Baltimore: Johns Hopkins University Press, 1973.

Lever, Evelyne. *Madame de Pompadour*. Paris: Perrin, 2000.

Marmontel, Jean-François. *Mémoires*. Edited by John Renwick, Clermont-Ferrand, G. de Bussac, 1972.

Mars, Francis L. "Pour le dossier de Miss XCV." *Casanova Gleanings* 5 (1962): 21–29.

————. "Une grande épistolière méconnue: Giustiniana Wynne." In *Problemi di lingua e letteratura italiana del '700*. Wiesbaden: F. Steiner Verlag, 1965. pp. 318–322.

McClellan, G. B. *Venice and Bonaparte*. Princeton: Princeton Univeristy Press, 1931.

Memmo, Andrea. *Elementi dell'architettura Lodoliana*. Rome: Pagliarius, 1786.

————. *Elementi dell'architettura Lodoliana. Edizione corretta e accresciuta dall'autore*, (2 vols.). Zara: 1833–1834.

Mitford, Nancy. *Madame de Pompadour*. London: Hamish Hamilton, 1954.

Molmenti, Pompeo. *Carteggi casanoviani*. Milan: Remo Sandron, 1920.

————. *Epistolari veneziani del secolo XVIII*. Milan: Remo Sandron, 1914.

————. *La storia di Venezia nella vita privata* (3 vols.). Bergamo: Istituto italiano di arti grafiche, 1908.

Monnier, Philippe. *Venice in the Eighteenth Century*. London: Chatto & Windus, 1906.

Montagu, Mary Wortley. *The Complete Letters of Lady Mary Wortley Montagu* (3 vols.). Edited by Robert Halsband. Oxford: Clarendon Press, 1967.

Morris, Jan. *Venice*. London: Faber & Faber, 1960.

Norwich, John Julius. *A History of Venice*. New York: Knopf, 1982.

Ortolani, Giuseppe. *Voci e visioni del Settecento veneziano*. Bologna: Zanichelli, 1926.

Parreaux, André. *Daily Life in England in the Reign of George III*. London: Allen & Unwin, 1969.

Picard, Liza. *Dr. Johnson's London*. London: Phoenix Press, 2000.

Pupillo, Marco. "Contarina Barbarigo: primi appunti sui disegni di architettura e le collezioni d'arte." In *Gentildonne artiste intellettuali al tramonto della Serenissima*. Milan: 1998.

Ravà, Aldo. *Lettere di donne a Casanova*. Milan: Treves, 1912.

Rudé, George. *Hanoverian London, 1714–1808*. London: Secker and Warburg, 1971.

Rykwert, Joseph. *The First Moderns*. Cambridge: MIT Press, 1980.

Samaran, Charles. *Jacques Casanova, vénitien*. Paris: Calmann-Levy, 1914.

Tabacco, Giovanni. *Andrea Tron (1712–1785) e la crisi dell'aristocrazia senatoria*. Trieste: Tip. Smolars, 1957.

Tassini, Giuseppe. *Curiosità veneziane*. Venice: Filippi, 1990.

Torcellan, Gianfranco. "Andrea Memmo." In *Illuministi italiani,* vol. 7, Milan: Ricciardi, 1965.

———. "Contarina Barbarigo." In *Settecento Veneto e altri scritti storici.* Turin: 1969.

———. *Una figura della Venezia settecentesca: Andrea Memmo.* Venice: 1963.

Vivian, Frances. *Il console Smith, mercante e collezionista.* Vicenza: Neri Pozza, 1971.

Walpole, Horace. *The Letters of Horace Walpole* (8 vols.). Edited by Peter Cunningham. London: Richard Bentley, 1857.

———. *Memoirs of the Reign of King George II.* New Haven, Conn.: Yale University Press, 1985.

Watzlawick, Helmut. "Clarification of Dossier Wynne." *Casanova Gleanings* 16 (1973): 31–32.

———. "Note on Giustiniana Wynne's Marriage." *Casanova Gleanings* 16 (1973): 14.

Williamson, Rebecca. "Giustiniana's Garden: An Eighteenth Century Woman's Construction." In *Gendered Landscapes, An Interdisciplinary Exploration of Past Place and Space.* Edited by B. Szczgiel, J. Carubia, and L. Dowler. University Park, Penn State University Press, 2000.

Wolff, Larry. *Venice and the Slavs.* Stanford, Ca.: Stanford University Press, 2001.

Wynne, Giustiniana. *À André Memmo Chevalier de l'Etoile d'Or et procurateur de Saint Marc à l'occasion du mariage de sa fille ainée avec Louis Mocenigo.* Venice: Rosa, 1787.

———. *Alticchiero.* Padua: 1787.

———. *Du séjour des comtes du Nord à Venise.* London: 1782.

———. *Il trionfo dei gondolieri.* Venice: Stamperia Graziosi, 1786.

——— with Bartolomeo Benincasa. *Les Morlacques.* Modena: 1788.

———. *Pièces morales et sentimentales.* London: J. Robson, 1785.

Zorzi, Alvise. *La repubblica del leone, storia di Venezia.* Milan: Rusconi, 1979.

ACKNOWLEDGMENTS

This book would not have seen the light if my father, Alvise di Robilant, had not discovered the letters of Andrea Memmo to Giustiniana Wynne. By the time of his death in 1997, he had spent many hours decoding and transcribing the letters and had done considerable research on the main characters of this story. The material he collected, his notes, and, above all, the many conversations we had about his discovery have inspired me throughout the writing of *A Venetian Affair*. It is his book, too, in more ways than I can say.

I first mentioned the story of Andrea and Giustiniana to Michael Carlisle, an old friend from Columbia University, in a long and rather rambling e-mail I sent to him in the winter of 2000. His enthusiastic response was crucial in getting me started on this project. Within a matter of days he became my agent, sold the book proposal, and set me to work. His encouragement and support have been unstinting.

My publisher, Sonny Mehta, took a gamble on a first-time author. I am deeply grateful to him for taking it. From day one it has been a privilege and a pleasure to work with all the people involved in the making of this book at Knopf. Deborah Garrison has been a devoted editor, stepping in nimbly to egg me on or to help me out. Her assistant, Ilana Kurshan, has been an effective and cheerful coordinator of our busy transatlantic correspondence.

I spent a year in Venice with my family to write *A Venetian Affair*. Claudio Saracco let us stay in his lovely little house at Campiello agli Incurabili and turned out to be a delightful and undemanding landlord. Most of the book was written at the Fondazione Querini Stampalia, off Campo Santa Maria in Formosa. I could not have dreamed of finding a more pleasant atmosphere in which to work. My sincerest thanks go to Giorgio Busetto, the indefatigable director of the foundation, and to his wonderful staff.

The first person to ever write extensively about Andrea and Giustiniana was the Venetian historian Bruno Brunelli. His book, *Casanova Loved Her*, published in 1924, was based in large part on Giustiniana's letters to Andrea. A lot of rich material has surfaced since then, apart from the letters discovered by my father, so it was possible for me to write a more complete and possibly more accurate account of their love story. Yet I always felt I was working in Brunelli's shadow, and *A Venetian Affair*, perhaps inevitably, owes much to the lingering appeal of his book.

Rebecca Williamson, of the University of Illinois at Urbana-Champaign, who has written perceptively about Giustiniana, gave me helpful guidance and advice. The architectural historian Susanna Pasquali, of the University of Ferrara, shared with me her knowledge about Andrea's later correspondence. I also benefited from

Acknowledgments

the suggestions of a happy band of *casanovisti:* Helmut Watzlawick, Giuseppe Bignami, and Furio Luccichenti. My greatest thanks go to Nancy Isenberg, of the University of Rome. Nancy has developed quite a passion for Andrea and Giustiniana's story over the years. She has shared her considerable knowledge with me generously and enthusiastically, and has made important contributions to the final shape of my work.

A Venetian Affair has been at the center of my family's life for three years. My young sons Tommaso and Sebastiano have been devoted supporters of the book even as they knew it was taking much of my time away from them. To my wife, Alessandra, I owe the most: for joining me in a project that has meant so much to me, and sharing in the many joys and the occasional miseries that have accompanied the writing of this book.

INDEX

Index

A Note About the Author

Andrea di Robilant was born in Italy and educated at Le Rosey and Columbia University, where he specialized in international affairs. He currently lives in Rome with his wife and two children and works as a correspondent for the Italian newspaper *La Stampa*. This is his first book.

A Note on the Type

Pierre Simon Fournier (1712–1768), who designed the type used in this book, was both an originator and a collector of types. His services to the art of printing were his design of letters, his creation of ornaments and initials, and his standardization of type sizes. His types are old style in character and sharply cut. In 1764 and 1766 he published his *Manuel typographique*, a treatise on the history of French types and printing, on typefounding in all its details, and on what many consider his most important contribution to typography—the measurement of type by the point system.

Composed by Creative Graphics,
Allentown, Pennsylvania
Printed and bound by R. R. Donnelley & Sons,
Harrisonburg, Virginia
Designed by Anthea Lingeman